The African Studies Companion:
A Guide to Information Sources

4th revised and expanded edition

Some other books by Hans Zell

The African Publishing Companion: A Resource Guide
(Hans Zell Publishing, 2002)

Book Marketing and Promotion: A Handbook of Good Practice
(International Network for the Availability of Scientific
Publications/INASP, 2001)

The Electronic African Bookworm: A Web Navigator
Print version   2nd revised edition
(African Books Collective Ltd, 2000)

A Handbook of Good Practice in Journal Publishing
2nd revised edition
(International African Institute & African Books Collective Ltd, 1998)

*Publishing and Book Development in Sub-Saharan Africa:
An Annotated Bibliography*
(with Cécile Lomer)
(Hans Zell Publishers, an imprint of Bowker-Saur, 1996)

The African Studies Companion:

A Guide to Information Sources

4th revised and expanded edition

Editor:
Hans M. Zell

Hans Zell Publishing
Lochcarron ✦ Ross-shire ✦ Scotland

First edition 1989
(published as *The African Studies Companion. A Resource Guide and Directory*)
Second edition 1997
Third edition 2003
(published as *The African Studies Companion: A Guide to Information Sources*)
Fourth edition 2006

British Library Cataloguing in Publication Data

The African studies companion : a guide to information sources.
  4th rev. and expanded ed.
  1. Africa – Study and teaching 2. Africa – Bibliography
  I. Zell, Hans M.
  960′ .07
  ISBN - 10: 0954102924

ISBN 0-9541029-2-4   (ISBN-13: 978-0-9541029-2-0)
Published by Hans Zell Publishing (T/A Hans Zell Publishing Consultants)
Glais Bheinn ◆ Lochcarron ◆ Ross-shire IV54 8YB ◆ Scotland ◆ UK

Telephone: +44-(0)1520-722951 Fax: +44-(0)1520-722953

Email: hanszell@hanszell.co.uk or hzell@btopenworld.com
Web site: www.hanszell.co.uk and at www.africanstudiescompanion.com

Online access is bundled with print. Purchase of this print edition of *The African Studies Companion* entitles purchasers to free access to the electronic version, and online updates for a limited period. To access the online version please see the instructions on page xxix. Registration, access and delivery is at www.africanstudiescompanion.com.

Cover design by Michael Stuart Green, Lochcarron, Scotland.

Printed on acid-free paper.

Printed and bound in the United Kingdom by Antony Rowe Ltd., Chippenham, Wiltshire.

Contents

Preface to the 4th edition

This information source builds on three previous editions of the *African Studies Companion* and the new fourth edition, like its predecessor, is again published both in print and in electronic formats.

The new edition has been thoroughly revised and updated, and once again substantially expanded. Although over 170 entries have been dropped, the page extent has almost doubled to that of the third edition, and the total number of entries has grown to more than 2,900.

While fully updated and including a large number of new entries, the aim of this fourth edition remains essentially the same as that of previous editions: to provide a compact, timesaving, and annotated guide to print and electronic information sources, and to facilitate easy access to a wide range of information in the African studies field. The fully searchable electronic edition is regularly updated online to provide maximum currency.

Content is arranged in an expanded format of 25 main sections, many with several sub-sections, offering a wide array of specifics for most entries. As for previous editions, the majority of listings identify *general* (multidisciplinary) and *current* sources of information, primarily those in English, but organized from a wide international perspective.

Updating and verifying existing entries, particularly for online resources, journals, organizations, publishers, and libraries in Africa, has been a time-consuming task. Quite apart from changes in personnel and contact information, URLs and email addresses do change frequently, for example in the section relating to journals and magazines over 40 per cent of all Web sites had changed since publication of the last edition. There have also been a very large number of URL changes in the section on academic libraries in Africa, as many institutions moved from various host servers to their own new domains.

Critical evaluation of sources
As in many other disciplines, there is now growing information overload on Africa and African studies in today's cyber world. This makes the need for critical evaluation evermore important, and annotations in the *African Studies Companion* are now more evaluative rather than purely descriptive.

As in the previous edition, attention is drawn to particularly outstanding online resources – in terms of depth of information, currency, utility and functionality, and good navigation features – by highlighting them with a ⓘ symbol.

Some of the annotations of recently published print reference works draw on a series of book reviews published by the Editor in the section "New reference sources of note" in the quarterly ➔ **African Book Publishing Record (384)**.

Prices and subscription rates/Publishers' online catalogues

Prices of all book titles in print format have been updated if they are still available from the publishers. However, Web links to specific title information on publishers' Web sites and online catalogues are no longer included as the URLs change far too frequently.

Subscription prices for African studies journals, some of which continue to escalate at an alarming rate, have also been fully updated with current (2005) rates.

Online vs. print

There are obvious advantages in maintaining a fully searchable electronic edition of the *African Studies Companion,* with hundreds of click-through Web links to external links and email addresses, extensive cross-referencing with hyperlinks, and regular online updating. Moreover, providing information as an online resource allows multiple users to access the contents concurrently, and from a place of their own choosing. However, we will continue to publish in both print and online formats. A well-organized, compact, and portable print reference work that pulls together a broad range of information otherwise available only through consultation of many separate sources, is still the best reference tool for many users. As Jill Young-Coelho, Librarian for sub-Saharan Africa at Harvard University, has stated in her essay ➔ **"Once, Present (and Always?) Africana Acquisitions Strategies" (1900)** "…print has its advantages. It sits quietly on a table, can be consulted backward and forward by merely flipping pages, does not crash, and does not require a connection of any sort." She goes on to say, bearing in mind libraries in Africa, "this last advantage is an important one for libraries without reliable Internet access. The original browsing can be done in the book, and online time can be focused on a few sources."

What is new in this edition?
There are 475 entirely new entries in existing sections, of which over 180 are new online resources, 48 new print reference works (and a small number of microfiche or CD-ROM products), 86 new (or newly included) African studies journals, plus over 70 new entries for publishers with African studies and African literature lists, of which 47 are African publishers. Additionally, there are a substantial number of new entries in most other sections – including those listing libraries, dealers and distributors of African studies material, vendors of African films and videos, international organizations, NGOs, networks, societies, associations, and more. The editorial closing date for inclusion of new entries was the end of October 2005.

Among the over 80 new entries for journals there are 46 new entries for African-published serials. African journals seem to be enjoying a period of resurgence, with a number of exciting new literary and cultural magazines such as *Kwani?* (Kenya), *Chirumenga* magazine (South Africa), or the print and online *Farafina Magazine* (Nigeria) launched in 2005. Additionally, several high-quality scholarly journals have started publication in Kenya, Nigeria, Senegal, and in Uganda. A significant and much welcome new initiative was the launch of the CODESRIA-published *Africa Review of Books*, the first issue of which appeared in early 2005.

Additionally, some other African scholarly serials have been given a new lease of life: for example, an important journal, *Quest. An African Journal of Philosophy*, originally published in Zambia over several years (albeit irregularly), has been resuscitated and is now re-appearing from the Netherlands. The annual *Lagos Notes & Records* is another of the long-established journals which have been restarted. These are all welcome developments, and it is to be hoped that the journals will receive the necessary support – by way of library orders or subscription renewals – to help them to survive instead of becoming dormant yet again.

New sections
This fourth edition contains two entirely new sections, which we hope will further enhance the utility of the *African Studies Companion:*

(1) ➔ **11 The African press** provides essential information for over 250 of the continent's leading newspapers and news weeklies, as well listing African news and press agencies; (2) ➔ **14 Centres of African studies and African studies programmes and courses worldwide**, a directory of over 300 entries, which also lists the leading African American/Black Studies programmes in the USA, which include African studies and/or African arts, literatures and cultures as a component of their Master's, Bachelor's or certificate degrees programmes.

While there are many Web pages with links to electronic African newspapers – albeit some rather patchy in coverage, or lacking currency – as well as Web links to African studies teaching and research, courses and programmes, there are currently no up-to-date resources in print format. There have been no further editions of the ➜ **African Studies Association's (2755)** *Directory of African & Afro-American Studies in the United States*, last published in an eight edition in 1993, but now so dated that it has been dropped from this edition of the *African Studies Companion*. Likewise, there have not unfortunately been new editions of the ➜ **International African Institute's (1622)** excellent resource the ➜ **International Directory of African Studies Research (274)**, last published in a third edition in 1994.

We therefore hope that these two new sections, accessible both online and in print format, will help to fill a gap.

Other new features

- A number of existing sections, for example online resources in Section 1, have been expanded and now include additional sub-sections.

- Extra contact names and email addresses have been added for some sections, for example for libraries and many organizations.

- While content and scope is still principally restricted to multi-disciplinary sources, there are now also a small number of entries of more subject specific (but broad-based) online databases in some fields, for example in African arts, anthropology and ethnology, education, history, and religion. This is however restricted to online resources listed in Section 1.

- Section 6, covering statistical, economic and financial data, now also includes resources for African population statistics and social indicators.

- In Section 9, Journals and magazines, links (the specific URLs) to African serials covered by ➜ **AJOL (554)** and ➜ **SABINET Online (560)** Web sites are now included.

- In Section 10, and in some other sections, there are links to RSS News feeds. Many news services and other information providers, as well as book and journal publishers and book review media, now offer delivery options by RSS/XML feeds, as do a small number of African journals and research institutions. Where available, a small

RSS button is included with the entry to indicate that RSS feeds are offered, together with the URL that links to it. Although the number of RSS feeds is still relatively small at this time, this will no doubt grow substantially in the years ahead.

- Section 23, the annotated guide to Web sites and Internet documents on information and communication development in Africa, has been completely revised and updated. It is an area that is crucially important for the dissemination of African scholarship, but ICT in Africa is a quickly evolving landscape. Many articles and other documents published before 2002 are now dated and have been dropped, while details of a substantial number of important more recent studies, reports, and articles have been added, as has a new sub-section on digital libraries.

- **Using Google for African studies research: a guide to effective Web searching**
The new edition of the *African Studies Companion* includes an updated and condensed version of this popular guide, previously published in a pilot edition at http://www.hanszell.co.uk/google/. Liberally interspersed with examples of searches and search strategies, the guide is designed to help the user get the most out of Google's Web searching techniques and at the same time providing a critical evaluation of Google's many Web search features, services and tools. The updated version now also devotes some space to new Google services launched since publication of the pilot edition, e.g. Google Scholar and Google Earth. The much longer pilot edition, which also includes a detailed analysis of Google Answers on African studies topics, will remain freely accessible, but will not be updated any longer.

Additional information regarding updates and revisions can be found in the explanatory notes on scope and content under individual sections.

Deletions

A total of 171 entries have been dropped for a variety of reasons: for example, because Web sites have either disappeared, have not been updated and lack currency, or current content no longer justifies inclusion.

Some entries for which it has not been possible to verify information, or current availability status, have been deleted. A number of reference tools published in print format have been dropped because they are now too dated and no new editions have appeared. However, a number of print reference resources of lasting value, although not re-issued in new editions, have been retained.

A few entries in the section on major African studies library collections have been dropped as online catalogue searches of these libraries revealed that the library no longer holds significant and current African studies resources. Sadly, there have also been a small number of deletions of specialist African studies libraries that have been closed, or whose collections have been integrated into larger institutional libraries.

Future editions
New and fully updated editions of the *African Studies Companion* are now scheduled to appear every three years, and will continue to be published in print and online formats, with a new 5th edition provisionally scheduled for publication sometime in 2009.

Acknowledgements
In the preparation of both the print edition, as well as development of the database for the new electronic version, I wish to acknowledge the help and expertise provided by Sue Martin of Smart Internet Services, Helston, Cornwall.

Hans M. Zell
Lochcarron, Wester Ross, Scotland
December 2005

Introduction

The African Studies Companion seeks to bring together a wide range of sources of information in the African studies field covering both print and electronic resources. It is published in a print edition and is also available as an electronic version at http://www.africanstudiescompanion.com. Access to the regularly updated electronic edition is bundled with the print edition.

Scope and definitions
The majority of listings identify primarily general, multidisciplinary sources of information, for the most part those in English and relating to sub-Saharan Africa. Purpose, scope, limitations and exclusions are further identified in the introduction to individual sections.

Subject- or country-specific resources are *not* covered, with the exception of a small number of fairly broad-based online databases that are good first-step sources for research. For more specialist reference works, for example those in the field of African art and African literature, or those in agriculture, economics, environment, politics, sociology, women's studies, etc., readers will need to consult sources that support more focused research, and elsewhere in this volume we draw attention to a number of guides to more specialist bibliographies and reference tools.

As in previous editions, sources for African American and Black studies (also frequently termed Africana studies) are not covered here, although we do now include entries of African American studies programmes in North America in the new section on African studies teaching and research worldwide, in as far as all of them include courses relating to the study of Africa and its people and cultures.

While this new edition includes an even more substantial number of online resources, many Africana reference works of enduring value are still not available – and are unlikely to become available – in electronic formats. The electronic databases that are now accessible have greatly facilitated African studies research, but the online resources that are available at this time still do not fill the gaps, and for many print reference tools there are no electronic equivalents as yet. Therefore, and for the foreseeable future at least, the point of departure for many Africa-related questions, or research on specific topics, will continue to have to include print and archival resources.

The African Studies Companion contains details of many Africa-specific databases, but more general databases, or the indexing and abstracting services that are likely to be consulted as part of most research topics in African studies, are not included. Among these are *Anthropological Index Online, Anthropology Plus, Arts and Humanities Citation Index, British Humanities Index, Columbia International Affairs Online, Devline, Dissertation Abstracts Online, Historical Abstracts, Humanities Abstracts*; FRANCIS, ELDIS, ➔ **JSTOR (558)**, *Lexis-Nexis*, the *MLA Bibliography, Pro-Cite, Social Sciences Citation Index, Sociological Abstracts*; various ISI databases and indexing services in the sciences, and UnCoverWeb/CARL UnCover, the major database of current periodical articles from some 25,000 publications, which is now available through the Web at Ingenta. Sometimes major biographical reference works, for example the *Oxford Dictionary of National Biography (ODNB)*, can also be a rich source for Africa related material.

Entries, annotations, reviews, and honours
Most of the entries are extensively annotated, both for print and online resources. Attention is drawn to particularly outstanding online resources, and the very best starting points on the Web, by flagging them with a ⓘ symbol (more about this in the introductory notes preceding Section 1).

Many of the annotations for databases and other online resources also include guidance how to make the most effective use of each source, with tips about navigation, use of search facilities, and how to find and access documents.

For Section 2, as well as some other sections, there are references to reviews from *Choice/Choice Online* and ➔ **African Research & Documentation (748)**, and, where available, there are also links to online reviews if freely accessible (others can be accessed through subscription-based databases of book reviews). Additionally, for print resources, titles that were awarded *Choice* "Outstanding Academic Title" honours are identified with details of the year when awarded; and the winners, or joint winners, of the ➔ **Africana Librarians Council's (1885)** biennial ➔ **Conover Porter Award (2828)** are similarly identified.

All of the online resources, and most of the titles in print format, have been personally examined by the compiler; for new print resources primarily based on the supply of review or examination copies provided by publishers, or via demo access to databases. Sources that have not been examined are indicated accordingly, and for such entries annotations are based on listings in publishers' catalogues and/or reviews.

Prices/Subscription rates

In Sections 2 to 8 prices are indicated for print resources, and journal subscription rates are given in Section 9. Prices are current as at mid-2005 and are based on information provided in publishers' catalogues and on Web sites. However, all prices are of course subject to change. Older print titles that do not show a price are likely to be out-of-print, but most will be found on the shelves of the major African studies library collections.

Data gathering and verification

All information has been verified and fully updated, primarily from the Web. However, where necessary and appropriate, information has been verified individually, for example for some African studies journals, libraries, publishers, and organizations, and when information pulled from Web sites was either not adequate, incomplete, or apparently dated. For online resources, as well as Web sites listed in all other sections, every site was re-visited and updated as appropriate, or deleted (see also Preface). Material for new entries, and the two entirely new sections, was collected during the course of 2004 and the first half of 2005, but with all Web sites thereafter re-visited and verified during the period July to October 2005. The date last accessed/verified is indicated for each entry, in square brackets.

Web sites and email addresses/Online updates

The *African Studies Companion* contains a massive number of email addresses and links to Web sites and Internet documents. While every effort has been made to verify information as far as is possible, email addresses and Web sites do tend to change frequently, and we would be grateful if any changes, inaccurate information, or dead links could be brought to our attention. Please email these to hanszell@hanszell.co.uk. Changes and updates will then be made in the online version.

Alphabetization style

Alphabetization, including listings in the various directory-type sections, is letter-by-letter style, with the exception of North American entries in Section 14, where African and African American/Black studies programmes are listed in alphabetical order by name of main institution. For purposes of alphabetization, the definite article in titles, 'The' (including book titles, journals, newspapers, etc.), or indefinite articles 'A' or 'An', are ignored.

Cross-references

The print edition of the book is extensively cross-referenced, as is the electronic version. A ➔ cross-reference symbol followed by an entry number indicates that further (or related) information on the particular organization, institution, publication, or source, etc. can be found as a separate entry in other sections of the *African Studies Companion*. In the electronic version the cross-references lead directly to the entry as a hyperlink.

Abbreviations/Telephone and fax numbers

Where applicable, keys to abbreviations used are indicated at the beginning of some sections; "n/a" indicates information is either not available or could not be verified.

Telephone and fax numbers are given in a standardized format, and are listed with their full international dialling codes. However, the '0' figure following the country code and preceding the area code has been omitted, except for UK telephone and fax numbers. In many countries international network access is obtained by dialling '00' (or '011' in the US), followed by the country code, the area code and the number, although some countries, including several in Africa, require no area code.

Index/Search facilities

An index is included in the print edition, and the online version is fully searchable using a search facility and database.

Access to the electronic edition

Online access to *The African Studies Companion* is bundled with print. Purchase of the print edition entitles purchasers access to the regularly updated electronic version at no extra charge. Providing the online resource as an integral part of the printed guide allows multiple users to access its contents concurrently, and from a place of their own choosing.

1. Registration, access and delivery is at
http://www.africanstudiescompanion.com

2. Access can be via Username and Password for individuals or organizations that connect to the Internet through a dial-up service, or via IP Address Recognition for libraries and institutions requiring their own authentication methods. For libraries and other institutional purchasers who have arranged electronic access via IP Address Recognition, access is restricted to authorized users of these institutions' secure library networks (on campus connected to the network directly, or off campus using the institution's proxy server and dial-in services).

3. Authorized users at academic institutions shall be identified by authorized Internet Protocol (IP) addresses. Customers must limit on-site access to current students, faculty, and staff who are primarily affiliated with the licensed campus, as well as walk-in users who are permitted access to the secure network from computer terminals within the library premises and who are making inconsequential use of the resources for their scholarly, research, educational, or personal use only. Remote access is limited to current students, faculty, and staff.

4. Electronic access will require registration at the above URL, following purchase of the print edition. Applicable IP ranges can be indicated when registering for online access. As part of the registration process customers will also be asked to indicate an approximate date of purchase of the print edition, and whether the book was purchased direct from the publisher, through a vendor (vendor name is required), or acquired through other means (e.g. donation).

5. There is no need for a formal exchange of a licensing agreement. The terms and conditions for online access are set out as part of the registration

pages at http://www.africanstudiescompanion.com/terms.shtml, and in registering for electronic access to the *African Studies Companion* customers agree to be bound by the terms and conditions by clicking the "I accept" button.

6. Access to the electronic version will expire upon publication of a new 5th edition of the *African Studies Companion*, provisionally scheduled for publication in 2009.

7. If you encounter any problems in accessing the electronic version please get in touch with the publisher at hanszell@hanszell.co.uk.

1

General online resources on Africa and African studies, and the best starting points on the Web

This is a guide to general, for the most part *multidisciplinary*, online resources on Africa and African studies. With the exception of some broad-based online databases in a number of fields (e.g. on African arts and culture, anthropology, the environment, history, natural history, and politics), subject-specific resources are not included, nor are those that are country-specific.

Entries are grouped under three principal sections: (i) African search engines, Web directories, and portals; (ii) General Web resources on Africa; and, (iii) Academic and scholarly Web resources on African studies, grouped under a number of sub-sections. Four further sections list online directories of African studies scholars, online teaching guides and overviews of current African studies research, guides to funding sources, and sources for e-theses and dissertations.

Each resource is described and evaluated. Every Web site listed was visited at least twice during the course of 2004 and early 2005, and re-visited during the period June to October 2005. The most recent date the site was accessed is indicated in square brackets following the description of the site.

The editor's choice – The best starting points on the Web ⓘ
Resources flagged with a ⓘ symbol are sites which, arguably, are considered to be the very best points of departure on the Web; and which, in the editor's view, are the most outstanding information resources in terms of *content and scope* (substance and depth), *authority* (institutional or organizational affiliation and developer/compiler credentials), *currency* (frequency of updates or revisions), *organization/structure* (including ease of navigation, and search facilities), and *functionality*. However, the absence of an ⓘ icon is not to suggest that other Web sites listed here are not also useful resources, and as indeed is reflected in the descriptions. It also has to be recognized that the value of any Web resource will inevitably vary for different audiences, and/or in different types of subject domains.

ⓘ This symbol indicates "The editor's choice" of a particularly outstanding online information resource.

African search engines, Web directories, and portals

The Web sites listed below are confined to African search engines, directories, and portals (African-based or otherwise) that cover the whole of Africa, although some may be especially strong on a particular country or region. For more African search engines, directories, and national portals check out *Search Engine Colossus*, the international directory of search engines at http://www.searchenginecolossus.com/, which offers links to search engines and directories from 232 countries around the world, including many in Africa; or check out some of the major African studies gateway sites listed in the sub-section ➔ **Academic and scholarly resources on African studies**.

1 AfricaResource.com
http://www.africaresource.com
Founded by Nkiru Nzegwu, this gateway provides access to a wide variety of resources, databases, and information about Africa, both of a scholarly and a more general nature, as well as giving free access to five electronic journals. The site offers sections on African art, galleries and exhibitions, books, poetry, narratives and stories, by both established and aspiring writers keen to break into print (or publish their work online), together with a collection of online essays, some by distinguished African writers and scholars such as Chinua Achebe, Ali Mazrui, Kole Omotoso, and Peter Ekeh. There are data resources on Africa and the diaspora, and particularly valuable is a Bibliolist, an extensive database containing (select) bibliographies of the published works of a large number of African and Africanist scholars, including a number of articles available online. These can be accessed either by name of author, or by twelve broad subject groups. [19/06/05]

➔ **allAfrica.com** *see* **10 News sources for Africa** entry 851

2 Ananzi
http://www.ananzi.co.za/
This South African portal and search tool is primarily devoted to South African business, entertainment, industry, motoring, property, sports, travel, and online shopping etc., but there are also some extensive listings under, for example, Reference & Publications, which has links (each with a short description) to publishers and other book-related sites, magazines, newspapers and other media information, videos, as well as city guides and maps. Search or browse 24 broad subject categories, which include a good range of links in the area of the arts and culture, including literature and poetry sites, museums and galleries, performing

arts, and the visual arts. There are also strong sections on education, with links to training institutions and schools (primary, secondary, and higher education), educational organizations, distance learning, etc. [19/06/05]

3   Blog Africa
http://allafrica.com/afdb/blogs/
On open listing and catalogue of Africa-related Web logs. New blogs can be added, or existing blogs can be edited from here, but this requires first setting up an account with AllAfrica.com (although there are no charges for this.) Blog Africa is a loose collaboration between a number of individuals at Geekcorps, ➔ **AllAfrica.com, (851)**, and the Berkman Center for Internet and Society. There is a search facility to search for people or blogs, or alternatively all blogs in the catalogue can be browsed, although they are listed in completely random order. For each listing there is a direct link to the blog, and for some of them there are links to user pages. The content of some blogs can be guessed from the name of some of the blogs, but others such as "Stuck in the Duck", "Mindbleed", "Froboy" "360 Degrees of Sky", "The Lensbox Soapbox" etc. give no indication of the nature of the discussions—which range from serious discussions about social and political issues of Africa on some blogs, while others are pure trivia, and there are also some "adult" and pornographic sites with no relevance to Africa whatever, and it is surprising that they are included here. [13/08/05]

4   Country Based Search Engines [Africa]
http://www.philb.com/countryse.htm
Phil Bradley's regularly updated guide to country and regional search engines, currently (July 2005) a total of 2,609 search engines and 216 countries, territories and regions. Listings for Africa include directories and portals, and sub-sections from major African search engines such as ➔ **WoYaa! (9)** ➔ **Africa.no (74)**. Listings for African countries, include, for example for Algeria (10), Angola (3), Botswana (2), Burkina Faso (3), Cameroon (5), Cape Verde (2), Congo (4), Eritrea (2), Kenya (5), Gambia (2), Ghana (4), Lesotho (1), Nigeria (7), Mauritius (3), Senegal (3) Sierra Leone (3), Somalia (4), South Africa (15), Tanzania (3), Zambia (3), or Zimbabwe (5). [02/07/05]

5   Funnel
http://www.funnel.co.za/funnel.php
Funnel indexes and searches South African sites only. It currently searches almost 3.3 million South African Web pages and is quite useful if your search is exclusively concerned with South Africa-related topics, or searching for Web pages about individual writers, artists, or scholars in South Africa, or resident in South Africa. Advanced search facilities include search on a site or domain only, or finding pages linked with the page. [18/06/05]

6   Mbendi ⓘ
http://www.mbendi.co.za/
Another South African-based portal, primarily business-orientated, and offering a massive amount of information on countries and industry sectors, especially oil and gas, electrical power, chemicals, mining and telecommunications, together with

guides to importing and exporting, news releases and commentary, and information about business opportunities. While the bulk of the information relates to South African business, finance and industry, there is good coverage of countries elsewhere on the continent. Particularly valuable are the extensive databases of companies, organizations, projects, and publications, backed up by a sophisticated search facility. Search for any type, sector or sub-sector, of industries or professions (or government organization), by location (country/region) or continent-wide. Search results matching selection criteria are summarized on an intermediate page, and a series of coding symbols indicate whether the profile/link will lead to basic information, additional information, or a Web site. For each country section there are links to additional information and databases (if available), together with short summaries of the political and the economic outlook for each nation. An MBendi Travel section was added in 2004, and is an impressive Internet source of information on travel in Africa (and other parts of the world). [19/06/05]

7   Mbolo.com
http://www.mbolo.com
A portal in French that aims to promote, and provide more visibility for African-hosted Web sites, and encourage the use of the Internet in Africa. Offers links to almost 7,500 sites covering news and media, current affairs, business, trade, organizations, telecommunications, tourism, education, health, leisure and culture, as well as a calendar of Africa-related events in seven European countries. Browse by broad category, or search by African country. Each main category has various sub-sections, and most links have a short description and an indication of the country in which it is hosted. There are quite a few links under Leisure and Culture – for example Web sites of African writers, artists, musicians, and scholars, especially those in francophone Africa – not readily found on similar portals. However, some other sections, e.g. Education and Sciences, are less successful and tend to be too much of a mixed bag—and not helped by the fact that, irritatingly, links in all sub-sections are listed in random rather than alphabetical order. [19/06/05]

8   Warmafrica.com
http://www.warmafrica.com/
An African community portal that provides local information on variety of topics, including news, travel, sports, politics, business, the economy, weather information etc., as well as offering a practical means for communication for members of the community. Also features an Africa E-Village section, a discussion forum, and a directory with some 17,000 links. [29/06/05]

9   WoYaa! The African Internet Portal
http://www.woyaa.com/index.html
This African search engine and Web portal, sadly, has been in decline in recent years and is now highly commercialized. It claims to offer links to almost 1.5m Web sites, but your pop-up blocker will be working overtime as you search or browse by broad 16 subject categories, or by individual African countries. It has a good arts and crafts section, with a very substantial number of links to individual artists, illustrators, performers, and photographers; a large number of links to galleries, museums and links to current exhibitions, and there are good media links to magazines, newspapers, radio and TV, and news providers. There is, however, a totally

bewildering sub-section for Arts-Literature-Writers, which indicates that there are an astonishing 24,654 entries (June 2005), but which includes a vast number of links (many duplicated) which by no stretch of the imagination could possibly be called to be "writers"-related. And there are hundreds of links to writers such as e.g. Mongo Beti, but which in fact are simply search results containing the words "Mongo Beti", and which would appear to be a copy-and-paste job picked up from search engine results rather than individually compiled. [19/06/05]

General Web resources on Africa

This section brings together a broad selection of online resources and Web sites on Africa of a more general nature. They are resources for anyone interested in Africa – its people, arts and cultures, and current African affairs – although many will be of equal interest to scholars and students of African studies, and will be useful as online resources for education in the arts and humanities, and for classroom use. Also included are a number of Web sites and databases that, while not Africa-specific, contain a substantial amount of information or resources that are Africa-related.

For more academic resources *see* ➜ **Academic and scholarly resources on African studies**.

See also ➜ **African search engines, Web directories, and portals**

10   Africa Focus: The Sights and Sounds of a Continent (i)
http://africafocus.library.wisc.edu/
This impressive online collection is a joint project of the African Studies Program and the General Library System at the ➜ **University of Wisconsin-Madison (1345)**. It contains digitized visual images and sounds of Africa stored in a freely accessible database and containing more than 3,000 slides, 500 photographs and 50 hours of sound from 45 African countries. Browse by collection, subject, or country; through an interactive search atlas, or search by collection, subject, country, by keyword or by multiple fields. Visual images are stored, and can be displayed, in three different sizes: brief records with thumbnails, full records as quarter size images, or full screen. The digitized sound recordings are available in two formats related to connection method, one best suited to network connections and the other to modem, and these choices are presented as icons in both the brief and full record displays. There are also instructions for citing the records. This is an excellent resource for visual images and audio records on African art and life. [19/06/05]

11   The Africa Guide (i)
http://www.africaguide.com/
This is not a site for academic resources, but the Africa Guide is an excellent and very attractively presented resource for more general information on Africa, and especially travel information and conservation projects. There is a wealth of

information on climate, currency, travel health advice, accommodation, getting around, places to visit, national parks and game reserves, over-landing, working in Africa, and a discussion forum. Additionally there are maps of African countries, African flags, audio files of African national anthems, African cooking and recipes, a photo library, and more. There is also fairly detailed information on each country, its people and culture, together with good sections on travel guides, books, maps and atlases for individual African countries (with links to Amazon.com/amazon.co.uk), and there is an extensive catalogue of videos and DVDs. An online shopping service is also offered (not supplied by the Africa Guide but through a number of affiliates.) [19/06/05]

12   Africinfo. Réseau d'Information Culturelle en Afrique et en Europe (RICAFE)/ Cultural Information Network in Africa and Europe
http://www.africinfo.org/index.asp [in French and English versions]
Africinfo.org is the Web site for the RICAE cultural information network in Africa and Europe, which aims to provide more effective dissemination of African cultural information. The home page offers a diary of African cultural events and various news items, and the site can be browsed either by a number of headings (music, theatre, cinema, fine arts, photography, literature, dance, fashion, media, and interdisciplinary), or by country. Particularly useful is a database of artists, writers, actors, musicians, photographers, etc. which can be searched by type of cultural activity or by an A-Z of artists (including groups, bands, etc.). The database contains a substantial number of entries and is constantly growing, although at this time it is still very heavily dominated by artists from francophone Africa. Most entries offer a short biographical profile, with photographs for some; helpfully it also includes links to artists' and writers' Web sites where they exist. [13/08/05]

13   Africa Information Centre (AIC)
http://www.africainformation.net/
The Birmingham UK-based Africa Information Centre consists of a small team of development analysts and consultants specializing in sub-Saharan Africa, providing information and research to the development community, governments, academic and commercial organizations. Its Web site offers links to African higher education institutions and to African studies teaching institutions elsewhere, some links to online journals and Internet resources, African government Web sites, and numerous Africa-based organizations whose activities and concerns are devoted to African issues either partly or wholly. There are also links to some African university libraries (mostly southern African), a few map resources, and a "Country files" section provides basic "Vital statistics" for each African country, with links to media and newspapers, some academic and government Web sites, and a number of other relevant resources. [13/08/05]

14   Africa Meets Africa
http://www.africameetsafrica.com/index.php
Hosted by Angelique Shofar, this is the Web site of an hour long, weekly radio magazine (as at August 2005, at 9:00 pm Eastern Standard Time, Pacific Radio 89.3 FM WPFW, or via live web stream at http://www.wpfw.org) that showcases the diversity and resources of the continent of Africa and its diasporas. It features African people, culture, and the arts, and examines political, social, economic,

environmental, women and other issues that shape and change the continent and its people. The site also offers news about and from Africa (from ➜ **allAfrica.com (851)** feeds), articles, a forum, and an events calendar. [13/08/05]

15   Africancolours.com
http://www.africancolours.net/
Nairobi-based, Africancolours.com offers a virtual showcase for the promotion of African arts, and a platform and online resource for African artists to promote contacts within African countries and facilitate communication in the rest of the world. The main part of the site consists of a constantly expanded database of a large number of African artists, providing profiles, each with a photograph and contact information (email addresses and telephone numbers for most of them), details of exhibits held, and examples of their work. Browse by artist name or by countries. Additionally, there is regular news about African arts events and exhibits, new projects, together with articles and links to art books, art book reviews, magazines, art archives, art training, and more. [19/06/05]

16   The African Commune
http://www.theafricancommune.com/
An information-rich Web resource created and hosted as a personal project by Oumani de Songhai. It aims to facilitate review of and access to information and articles on African studies, and "to document, add value, and re-brand information and perspectives about African culture and history." There is an online library offering a variety of articles and "TAC readings"; a short abstract leads to the full text of the article, which have been contributed by authors both from within Africa and African studies scholars elsewhere. There are also news items and notices, a gallery of photographs, biographical profiles (with photographs) of African leaders, personalities, artists, musicians, and writers; and a discussion forum. However, the home page, and other pages, was very slow in loading when visited on the last two occasions. [30/09/05]

17   African Crafts Online
http://www.africancraft.com/
Dedicated to bring the arts and the artisans of Africa online, and to provide a venue for African artisans to showcase their work. The site offers links and pages devoted to craftspeople, artists, designers, and "shops" offering African arts and crafts where several retailers offer their product catalogues under a unified ordering mechanism. The site also provides access to online articles about crafts and craftspeople, and there are links to related Web sites arranged by broad topics, e.g. artists sites, museums, online exhibits, photography sites, shops selling African crafts, etc. [19/06/05]

18   African Digital Library
http://www.AfricaEducation.org/adl/
Established by Technikon South Africa's Centre for Lifelong Learning, in collaboration with the ➜ **Association of African Universities (2580)**, this is a free public library but *is restricted to users in Africa*. (Those in Africa who wish to use the service will need to complete an application form to open a free account, and which will include a username and password.) A variety of publishers and organizations

provide access to full-text books, and at this point the library contains over 8,400 titles, plus access to a number of resources that are publicly available. Encryption ensures that only one user will access a book at any one time, and loan periods are restricted to a few hours as users work with the books. [20/06/05]

19 African Governments ⓘ

http://www.columbia.edu/cu/lweb/indiv/africa/cuvl/Chiefs.html
Based on information provided by the US Central Intelligence Agency, this site provides details of current African heads of state and cabinet ministers of African governments since 2000. For each country it gives the name of the head of state, deputy/Vice President, ministers for all government ministries, the attorney general, solicitor general, governor of the Central Bank, as well as the names of the current Ambassador to the US and Permanent Representative to the United Nations. The date the information was last updated is also indicated for each country. Currency is excellent, and when last checked in June 2005 there was evidence that many countries were updated during the early part of 2005. [20/06/05]

20 African Governments on the Internet

http://www.uneca.org/aisi/nici/africagovinternet.htm
Part of the UN ECA's NICI (National Information and Communication Infrastructure Strategies) Web site (*see also* **2869**) this is a useful (albeit slow loading) directory to African governments on the Web. For each African country it provides links to Web sites of the main government bodies, Web sites of ministries, other government agencies, media/broadcasting organizations and corporations, and diplomatic missions abroad. The number of links varies considerably for each country, but for some, e.g. South Africa, listings are remarkably full, although for several countries there are also quite a few dead links, and the individual country profiles provide no indication when the information was last updated. Another resource on this site, African Local Governments on the Internet can be found at http://www.uneca.org/aisi/nici/africalocalgov.htm. [20/06/05]

21 African Governments on the WWW

http://www.gksoft.com/govt/en/africa.html
Compiled by Gunnar Anzinger, this is part of the global Governments on the WWW, which contains some 17,000 entries from more than 220 countries and territories. For Africa choose from the menu by countries, which indicates the number of entries provided for each, the file size, and the dated when last updated. For each entry there are links to parliaments, ministries and other national institutions and offices, local embassies and diplomatic representation overseas, political parties (for some), together with further links to sources providing general background on each country or political information. A useful source, although, when last visited in June 2005, most of the African countries had a "date of last change" going back to 2001 or 2002, and some information is therefore bound to be dated. [20/06/05]

→ **African Internet Radio and Online News Radio** [links collection] *see* **Multilingual Books** in section 17, entry **2363**

22   African Odyssey Interactive
http://artsedge.kennedy-center.org/aoi/
The purpose of African Odyssey Interactive (AOI) is to promote an ongoing exchange of ideas, information, and resources between artists, teachers, and students of African arts and culture. It is based on an adjunct initiative of the Kennedy Centre in New York and its African Odyssey Festival program (held during the course of 1997), and the Kennedy Center Education Department 'Artsedge' programme. Contents is arranged under seven main sections: Dance, Literary, Visual, Music, Theatre, History (including Country/Art form profiles), and Lessons (with related links). A series of follow-up activities to the Kennedy Centre initiatives will be organized by the ➜ **The Africa Society of the National Summit on Africa** (*see also* **26, 2570**). [20/06/05]

23   African Timelines: History, Orature, Literature, and Film
http://www.cocc.edu/cagatucci/classes/hum211/timelines/htimelinetoc.htm
Compiled by Cora Agatucci, and part of an online course of the Humanities Department at Central Oregon Community College, this is a chronology of Africa, in five parts: Ancient Africa, African Empires, African Slave Trade & European Imperialism, Anti-Colonialism, and Post-Independence Africa. Includes a list of works cited in the compilation of the site, and an extensive bibliography for further study. The site is regularly updated. [20/06/05]

➜ **Africultures** *see* **9 Journals and magazines** entry **673**

24   Africa. One Continent. Many Worlds ⓘ
http://www.nhm.org/africa/index.htm
A collaborative project of The Field Museum, the Natural History Museum of Los Angeles Country, the California African American Museum, and the Armory Center of the Arts, this Web site is "designed to provide the museum-goer with a rich experience and to provide the educator with the knowledge and tools to bring the experience to the classroom." This virtual exhibit includes over 60 minutes of video, hundreds of photographs of cultural objects from the African collections of the above museums, together with presentations on the accomplishments and stories of Americans of African descent. The menu offers a range of "African stories" and "American stories"; "The Community's Choice" (a selection of 150 pieces chosen by Los Angeles community leaders from among the 5,000 objects in the collections); Natural History of the African Continent, a presentation designed to introduce teachers and students to the natural history of Africa; an Atlas section which shows each African country on a map of the continent and provides basic details about each country; and a fascinating Object Database for each African country, showing photographs of everyday household tools used in Africa, clothing and footwear items, baskets, gourds, cooking utensils, bracelets, necklaces, masks, musical instruments, and more. A rich resource, for hours of pleasurable browsing. [20/06/05]

25   Africa Server/Het leuke van Afrika (English and Dutch versions)
http://www.africaserver.nl/front_uk.htm
Although this site primarily provides information on Africa-related activities in the
Netherlands, it also serves as a portal for a wider audience, with good sections
arranged by broad topics – and each link with a short description – including guides
to news sources on Africa, sections (or 'modules') on arts and culture, and virtual
exhibitions. There is also a directory, *Africans in Holland,* compiled in co-operation
with the ➔ **African Studies Centre in Leiden (1594)**, which lists over 800 African
organizations and businesses and is designed to help to locate African expertise and
African entrepreneurs in the Netherlands. (Current as at February 2002). [19/05/06]

26   The Africa Society of the National Summit on Africa
http://www.africasummit.org/index.html
Launched in January 2002, the mission of the non-profit, non-partisan Africa Society
– a direct outgrowth of the National Summit on Africa – is "to educate all Americans
about Africa and its people, to build bridges of understanding and partnership, and
to facilitate the Continent's social development and political transition to more open,
democratic societies." It aims to advocate on behalf of Africa and provide a forum for
building knowledge about the fifty-four countries of the continent. The Society's
links pages, categorized under five themes, are designed to be a clearinghouse for
information on a wide range of topics within US-Africa relations, including links to
partner organizations. [20/06/05]

27   AfricaTime.com
http://www.africatime.com/
Promises rather a lot ("All African Web sites", "All national and African news", etc.)
but primarily covers the francophone countries of Africa. Browse or search. Poor on
academic resources, but there are some quite good sections on arts and culture, news
and media sites, and business and financial information, each with a short
description (in English or French). Clicking on to individual countries offers a good
range of fairly up-to-date news stories from francophone African newspapers and
other media. [19/06/05]

28   Afrique francophone
http://www.lehman.cuny.edu/depts/langlit/french/afrique.html
Hosted by the Department of Languages at Literatures Lehman College, CUNY, this
is a useful compilation of a substantial number of links focusing on, but not limited
to, francophone Africa. It covers general resources, including press and media,
journals, culture/music, literature, museums, discussion forums, and links to
country-specific Web sites on/in francophone and North Africa, which include links
to African radio stations. Most links include a very short description of content.
[20/06/05]

29   Art and Life in Africa Online
http://www.uiowa.edu/~africart/toc/index.html
Contains a wealth of information about various aspects of African art and culture,
part of it adapted from the ➔**Art and Life in Africa CD-ROM (356)**, but some
materials included here cannot be found on the CD. The site offers the abbreviated
online version of Key Moments in Life, a range of essays on African history, and

"Snapshots of Daily Life in Mali and Burkina Faso", and images and essays about art by contemporary artists in Mali. A Countries Resources section provides information for 27 sub-Saharan African countries, while Peoples Resources presents information for 107 African cultures (both last revised November 1998), adapted from the CD-ROM. [20/06/05]

30 ArtSiteAfrica.com
http://www.artsiteafrica.com/
Compiled and hosted by two individuals, Kerry Joyce and Dominique Delapointe, this portal to African art resources provides a guide to over 800 African art sites. The site is supported by a search facility and resources are grouped into 42 categories and include topics such as African art history, architecture, baskets, beads, fashion, masks, musical instruments, photography, pottery, rock art, sculpture, textiles, etc. Additionally there are links to freely accessible articles and papers on various aspects on African arts and crafts, links – each with a short description – to almost a hundred African art galleries worldwide, 40 museums of African art (or with collections on African art), lesson plans, information about and links to current and forthcoming exhibitions with dates and descriptions, reviews of exhibits, news items, links to blogs on African art, and more. An impressive resource with a nice, clean interface. [13/08/05]

→ **Awards for Books about Africa** *see* **21 Awards and prizes in African studies** entry **2824**

→ **BBC News – Africa** *see* **10 News sources for Africa** entry **852**

31 BBC News World Edition: Country Profiles/Timelines – Africa
http://news.bbc.co.uk/2/hi/africa/country_profiles/
The BBC News's Country Profiles and Timeline pages are a good general resource for up-to-date and reliable broad overview information on each African nation. The Country Profiles give basic information about each country, including details of the current government, the press, TV and radio (all with links where available), while the Timelines provide a chronology of key events in each country's history. Additionally there are profiles of the →**African Union (2504)**, ECOMOG (set up by → **ECOWAS (2512)**), and the Non-Aligned Movement. [12/08/05]

32 Birdlife Africa Programme Database ⓘ
http://www.birdlife.org/worldwide/regional/africa/index.html
This is part of Bird Life International's constantly expanding World Bird Database (WBDB). There are over 2,300 bird species in Africa and almost 10 per cent are globally threatened. BirdLife International works to secure a future for birds and people across Africa in partnership with 18 national conservation organizations and the BirdLife Africa Division office located in Kenya. The database is supported by sophisticated search facilities. For a basic search select Data Zone and then click Search Species (or you can choose Endemic Bird Areas of the World /EBAs, or Case Studies) and then select Africa as the Region and/or specific Africa countries. The results will be displayed as a list of all species that match the search criteria. To see the account for a particular species, click on the name of the species in the table, and

which will then open a fact sheet giving information about family/sub-family, species name, author, taxonomic source/s, recommended citation, and a summary. You can also choose to view additional data tables by clicking the 'show additional data' link at the top right of the fact sheet. [26/06/05]

33   Commission for Africa
http://www.commissionforafrica.org/
34   Learning Africa
http://www.learningafrica.org.uk/
Available in English or French versions this is the Web site (now serving as an archive only) of the → **Commission for Africa (2590)**, an important new initiative launched by British Prime Minister Tony Blair in February 2004. The aim of the Commission was to take a fresh look at Africa's past and present and the international community's role in its development path. There are 17 members of the Commission, most of them from Africa, and all are active and influential in the differing spheres of work and expertise. From this site you can download (pdf) the Commission for Africa's report, published on 11 March 2005. It is available to download either as one large file of the full report (3,585kb) or as individual chapters and sections. The Commission welcomed written submissions from a wide range of individuals and organisations throughout its work. Most substantive submissions were received in response to the Commission's Consultation Document (see link to Consultation Document on Consultation Intro page). All these can be viewed and are grouped by those received from organizations and individuals. The website was updated for the last time on 29 July 2005. The companion **Learning Africa**, is a useful Web site that offers support for teachers wishing to explore Africa in the classroom, and which provides a series of classroom activities and learning resources which draw on and help to address the issues raised by the Commission for Africa, and can be found at the separate URL listed above. [22/08/05]

35   Contemporary Music and Arts Archive (CAMA)
http://www.cama.org.za/index.htm
36   Culture Africa Network (CAN)
http://www.africa-can.org/
The CAMA Archive is a multi-media documentary initiative for African arts and culture, based in the Faculty of Science and Montebello Design Centre at the University of Cape Town, South Africa. It seeks to develop a pan-African, freely accessible arts and culture archive and, through this, the means to acknowledge creativity in the arts in Africa on a continental scale. The project focuses on documenting and disseminating audio-visual materials about the lives and work of artists, musicians and others who create culture in Africa. The site can be searched by countries, art (with fairly detailed profiles of artists, some with examples of their work), music (profiles of artists, orchestras/bands, musical styles and genre etc., and cultures (select by African ethnic group). With assistance of the → **Ford Foundation (2733)**, CAMA is also hosting the pilot *Culture Africa Network (CAN)* project and has helped to establish documentary centres in seven countries in Africa: Mali, Ghana, Sudan, Ethiopia, Kenya, Mozambique and South Africa. The project aim is to facilitate the local gathering and sharing of high-quality digital documentary resources for education, research and the promotion of Africa's artistic heritage and its culture. The resources include a variety of multi-media cultural materials,

documentation of living artists, musicians and their work, as well as art, music and ethnographic materials from existing holdings within several participating African museums and universities. The Web site contains excerpts from the output of Phase 1 of the CAN project. [21/06/05]

→ **Culture Africa Network (CAN)** *see* **Contemporary Music and Arts Archive (35)**

37   Cycles: African Life through Art ⓘ
http://www.ima-art.org/cycles/
As is stated in the introduction to this marvellously interactive site and online exhibit hosted by the Indianapolis Museum of Art, many cultures in Africa "see the stages of life bound together in a continuous cycle—a circle of birth, growth, maturity, transition and rebirth." The site offers a glimpse into this life through a selection of art and rituals, grouped under four cycles (as four quadrants that open up in the browser window): ancestors, youth, adulthood, and leadership. Graphic elements and images are combined with helpful text, and supported by voice audio clips and audio-playing music and songs. You can, for example, select by region to view zoomable images of artefacts with descriptions and "context" links. The zoom/magnification features allows viewing objects in extraordinary amount of detail. This is an innovative, rich and visually appealing Web resource, which also includes a glossary and a section on teachers' materials. [07/06/05]

38   Earthwire Africa
http://www.earthwire.org/africa/
Supported by NORAD and UNEP/GRIP, Earthwire Africa is an environmental portal providing daily environmental news from 14 countries in southern Africa and covering environment-related news stories from 40 newspapers. Stories can be viewed by country, topic, time period, or by keywords. An archive of articles and news stories can be accessed by a number of environmental topics headings, each with various sub-categories. A good source for students and researchers looking for current information on the state of the environment in Africa. [20/06/05].

39   Foreign Governments – Sub-Saharan Africa
http://www.lib.umich.edu/govdocs/forafr.html
From the University of Michigan Documents Center, this is a central reference and referral point for government information, whether local, state, federal, foreign or international. Its Web pages are designed to provide a reference and instructional tool for government, political science, statistical data, and news. The pages devoted to sub-Saharan Africa provide links to government and official Web sites, US diplomatic missions in each African country, information about African governments, together with economic, business and tourist information, as well as election, census, and statistical data. However, although the site is apparently updated regularly, information provided for the countries of Africa remains rather patchy. [20/06/05]

40   Frank's Compulsive Guide to Postal Addresses [Africa pages]
http://www.columbia.edu/kermit/postal.html#africa
Hosted by Frank da Cruz and part of the Kermit Project at Columbia University
http://www.columbia.edu/kermit/index.html, this useful Web site describes
conventions for addressing postal mail from within the USA to other countries. It is
designed to ensure that the address complies with the addressing guidelines of the
originating country (USA in this case) and is dispatched to the correct destination
country without any delay caused by the address itself; and that the address
complies with the addressing requirements of the destination country and is
dispatched to the target address without address-related delay. The Africa section
provides a table of countries of continental Africa and nearby island nations,
showing the USPS name for each country, the ISO (International Organization for
Standardization) and UN Car Codes (or the ISO 3166 Alpha-2 Code for some other
countries) the city line format, and a sample city line. Individual country links lead
to the sites of national postal services, where more details can be found about postal
regulations. [02/06/05]

41   Freedom in the World 2005: Civic Power and Electoral Politics [Africa]
http://www.freedomhouse.org/research/survey2005.htm (Main page)
http://www.freedomhouse.org/research/freeworld/2004/countries.htm#dropdow
n (Country and territories drop down menu)
The non-partisan and broad-based Freedom House has championed the rights of
democratic activists, religious believers, trade unionists, journalists, and proponents
of free markets since 1978, and publishes this annual comparative survey of the state
of political rights and civil liberties in 192 countries and 14 related and disputed
territories, including all the countries of Africa. It provides an evaluation of the state
of global freedom as experienced by *individuals*. (The survey does not rate
governments or government performance per se, but rather the real-world rights and
freedoms enjoyed by individuals.) The methodology of the survey established basic
standards that are derived in large measure from the Universal Declaration of
Human Rights. Each country is assigned a rating for political rights and a rating for
civil liberties based on a scale of 1 to 7, with 1 representing the highest degree of
freedom present and seven the lowest level of freedom. Each country report begins
with an overview of basic political, economic, and social data and thereafter reviews
the current state of political rights and civil liberties, showing scores and a ten year
ratings timeline. [12/06/05]

42   Global Mappings: A Political Atlas of the African Diaspora ⓘ
http://diaspora.northwestern.edu/
A fascinating interactive Web site that gives scholars, students and the public an
opportunity to explore the political linkages between African-descended
organizations and individuals across national and regional boundaries through the
twentieth century. The site is the culmination of a partnership between the ➔
Program for African Studies (1719) and the ➔ **Department of African-American
Studies (1718)** at Northwestern University to create a virtual archive housing
scholarly entries that demonstrate the linkages between transnational Black politics,
social movements and world historical events of the twentieth century, thus enabling
students and scholars to comprehend the spread of ideologies, political aspirations,

and social movements of people of African descent. It includes maps that trace and chart the cultural transmission and dissemination of African religious practices and cosmologies to the New World and beyond, as well as the circulation of specific African populations within the New World through the Middle Passage. Currently (as at June 2005) there are 56 entries in the Atlas covering two separate time periods. [20/06/05]

43   The Harriet Tubman Resource Centre on the African Diaspora
http://www.yorku.ca/nhp
Opened in September 2002, the Harriet Tubman Resource Centre on the African Diaspora is a digitalized research facility that focuses on the history of the African diaspora and the movement of Africans to various parts of the world, particularly the Americas and the Islamic lands of North Africa and the Middle East. The Tubman Centre is part of the Department of History at York University in Canada, and includes a digital library and repository as well as facilities for the digitization of materials. Projects/areas of research include the York/UNESCO Nigerian Hinterland Project, a Biographical Database of Enslaved Africans, a Historical Atlas of Slavery, and an archival inventory of primary sources designed to facilitate accessibility to and preservation of the vast archival holdings that are relevant to the study of the diaspora. There is also a good links collection drawing attention to Web sites and resources of related interest on the diaspora, the slave trade, African-Canadian links, etc. [20/06/05]

→ **Keeping up with Africa: A Selective Annotated Bibliography**, by Mason-Middleton, Cheryl J. (print and online) *see* **2 The major general reference tools: Bibliographies and guides to sources** entry **226**

44   KWETU African Resource Service (subscription based)
http://www.kwetu.net/first.asp
This Kenyan database service – owned by Kwetu Media LLC, Delaware,USA and Verve K.O Ltd, Nairobi – aims to offer "an exhaustive resource of African content" on a subscription basis. (Individual subscription $50 annually; rates for institutions/organizations, subject to a user license agreement, $800-$1,200 annually depending on size of institutions; reduced rates apply for institutional subscribers in Africa). Subject areas include agriculture, aids, animal rights, arid lands/pastoralism/wildlife, children/youth, communication and journalism, education, environmental conservation and energy, development, commerce and industry, peace and conflict resolution, politics and elections, population issues, transport, urban development, women and gender issues, etc. A listing of African partner organizations can be found at http://www.kwetu.net/partners.asp. Types of documents covered include annual reports, audio clips, project reports, publicity materials, speeches, thesis and dissertations, videos, and more. Access is offered in trial/demo mode. However, a range of test searches conducted proved to be rather unsatisfactory, and it would appear that the search facilities still require a lot of tweaking. There is also a need for better guidelines about search strategies, especially as the FAQs don't provide a great deal of guidance. There is a puzzling statement in the FAQ pages stating that around 80 per cent of the documents available are *unpublished* material, but in tests virtually all the search results generated documents of published material, with year of publication. There is also inadequate information

about the data gathering process, what its core elements are, and how the database is being expanded and kept up-to-date by the collaborating institutions and organizations that feed KWETU with data. This is an interesting Africa-based initiative, but KWETU's claim that it is "the most comprehensive resource on Africa available anywhere" is not supported by what is currently available here. [05/06/05]

→ **Learning Africa** *see* **Commission for Africa (33)**

45   Links to Africa Gateway
http://us-africa.tripod.com/link.html
This is part of an Internet portal of the US-Africa.org, which provides a freely accessible "Window" to Africa for business, travel and education. In addition to country files, it offers an excellent and attractively presented A-Z links collection compiled by Willem Tijssen, with generally good, informative descriptions, and covering a very large number of Africa and African studies-related sites. This includes Web sites of organizations and NGOs of all descriptions concerned with Africa, foundations, publications, associations, societies, biographical profiles, sites on African arts and culture, African travel, photo galleries, and a variety of other Web-based resources. [04/08/05]

46   Living Encyclopedia for East Africa -- Teaching and Learning about East Africa Project (TLEAP)
http://www.sas.upenn.edu/African_Studies/NEH/neh.html
A collaborative project between the → **African Studies Center (1799)** at the University of Pennsylvania and the School District of Philadelphia's Department of African and American Studies, this ongoing project offers a "living library" of resources for teaching and learning about East Africa and about Swahili. It covers Kenya, Tanzania and Uganda, and also Burundi and Rwanda. For each country it provides access to a variety of basic information, e.g. on agriculture, archaeology, communication, education, ethnic groups, geography, government, history, languages, material culture, trade and transport, etc. This is not intended to be an academic resource, but it primarily for use by K-12 students and by teachers. [20/06/05]

47   Multi F contact
http://www.refer.org/
This somewhat obscurely named site (formerly called REFER), sub-titled "L'information scientifique et technique en français our les universitaires Nord-Sud" was formerly called, more appropriately, "Des sites sur l'Afrique faits par des africains". Hosted by the → **Agence Universitaire de la Francophonie (1662)**, it provides access to a "Bibliothèque en ligne", an online resource that offers a substantial collection of links to Web sites in francophone Africa (as a well as some in Europe and Vietnam), as well as access to e-books and online articles. (To access the menu of subject categories you need to click the "Advanced search" search box.) Although the sub-title of the site would seem to imply an emphasis on science and technology, there is also much here on the arts and humanities and the social sciences.[20/06/05]

48   Notícias Lusófonas
http://www.noticiaslusofonas.com/
A useful Web site for information relating to the lusophone world, drawing on a variety of sources. Has news stories, opinions, and interviews, together with a large number of news items about the lusophone countries in Africa: Angola, Cape Verde, Guinea-Bissau, Mozambique, and São Tomé e Principe. Also offers business-related information. [09/06/05]

49   Open Directory Project – Regional: Africa
http://dmoz.org/Regional/Africa/
The Open Directory Project (ODP) is also known as DMOZ, an acronym for Directory Mozilla, which reflects its loose association with Netscape's Mozilla project, an Open Source browser initiative. The ODP was developed in the spirit of Open Source, where development and maintenance are done by net-citizens, and results are made freely available for all net-citizens. The Google search engine updates its own *Google Directory* entries based on DMOZ entries. The project attempts to provide the largest, most comprehensive human-edited directory of the Web, constructed and is maintained by a global community of volunteer editors. The content for Regional: Africa currently (June 2005) contains almost 15,000 entries, which can be accessed by a country menu (this includes one or two puzzling entries, e.g. five links to Heard Island, which in fact are part of Australian territory, or links to the sub-antarctic Bouvetøya/Bouvet Island, which is Norwegian territory), or by 17 broad categories, all of which have further sub-menus. Clicking on to any country menu also leads to a sub-menu of 16 or more sub-categories, some further sub-divided, e.g. News and Media is further sub-divided by magazines, newspapers, online news, radio and television. Short descriptions are offered for most links. There is also a further category Science: Social Sciences: Area Studies: African Studies (85 links). [20/06/05]
Note: for a fuller discussion of this directory, and the *Google Directory* see → **Using Google for African studies research: a guide to effective Web searching. Google's other search services: Google Directory.**

50   OPIC Information Gateway – Africa/Middle East ⓘ
http://www.opic.gov/links/links-afr.htm
The core mission of the Overseas Private Investment Corporation (OPIC) is to support economic development by promoting US private investment in developing countries and transition economies. OPIC's Investor's Information Gateway Country Link Database offers access to more than 20,000 documents and other sources of economic, business, political and social data for all of the countries and areas in which OPIC can currently do business. The links are grouped into some 20 major broad categories, and, typically, about 140 or more links are available for each country and region. Information sources include various federal agencies such as the Department of Commerce, the CIA and the State Department, multilateral organizations such as the World Bank, foreign government agencies and embassies, non-governmental organizations such as chambers of commerce and various trade and investment promotional organizations, travel information Web sites, and many others. For example, for Ghana the OPIC database provides links to a total of 214 resources, including a wide variety of overview information, together with sources

for agricultural and food industries, banking, business information (including directories) and business promotion, as well as sources in these sectors: culture, demographics, development, diplomatic, government, education, environment, health, human rights, labour, legal, military, natural resources, press, trade and investment, travel and tourism, and more. This is an impressive resource. [13/08/05]

51 Places Online [Africa]
http://www.placesonline.org/sitelists/africa/africa.asp
Hosted by the Association of American Geographers, this Web resource aims to provide access to the World's very best place-based Web sites that provide original quality content about place(s). The criteria for selection are that they must contain substantive, geographic content with a focus on specific places (town, city, region, route, field site, field trip, etc.), and map-based sites are especially favoured. They must "provide the viewer with a good place experience, as if she or he is actually present observing the human and/or physical environment." Effective use of images, including maps, is also considered important. At this time (August 2005) there are links to recommended resources for 25 African countries. A short description is provided for each site. [13/08/05]

52 The Pulse of Africa. How Africans View their Lives, their Countries, their Continent, their Future, the World
http://news.bbc.co.uk/nol/shared/bsp/hi/pdfs/18_10_04_pulse.pdf
The Pulse of Africa is the result of a survey conducted by the ➔ **BBC World Service (853)** (and coordinated by the South African research agency, Markinor, http://www.markinor.co.za/) in April and May 2004, during which time more than 7,500 people in 10 African countries were interviewed. The interviews were primarily conducted in urban areas, with samples randomly collected. The report (275k pdf, 27 pp., August 2004) – supported by graphs, charts and tables – groups interview responses into broad areas of the "African Landscape" (Global Contribution, Being an African, Big Problems, Muslim/Non-Muslim, Information Sources, and Government Competence); "African Outlook" (What Worries Africans?, Personal Situation, Role Models); "Passions & Aspirations" (Fashion & Music, Leisure, Country to Live), as well as "Family Roles" and "World Players-African Views". The analysis makes for interesting reading and the survey shows that Africans see themselves at odds with how the rest of the world sees Africa: while a large number of people outside Africa see the continent as plagued by war and poverty, many Africans are far more positive about their lives. [02/06/05]

53 Smithsonian Institution--National Museum of African Art ⓘ
http://www.nmafa.si.edu/index2.html
This superb Web resource from the Smithsonian Institution invites you to discover Africa's rich cultural diversity. The collections of the Smithsonian's National Museum of African Art embrace the diverse artistic expressions found throughout Africa, from ancient to contemporary times. Collection objects range from ceramics, textiles, furniture and tools to masks, figures and musical instruments. The arts of painting, printmaking, sculpture and other media are well represented by living artists whose works highlight individual creativity. From this site you can access virtual exhibitions, view and listen to African musical instruments, check out events

and forthcoming exhibitions, listen to Radio Africa streams from the collections of Smithsonian Global Sound, and there is also a Playtime! section for children, with "seek-and-find", drawing, and designing activities. Additionally the site offers access to the Eliot Elisofon Photographic Archives, a research and reference centre devoted to the collection, preservation and dissemination of visual materials that encourage and support the study of the arts, cultures and history of Africa. There are a variety of free downloads, and the Museum's Store http://africa.si.edu/about/store.html offers a wide selection of merchandise inspired by the collections and the arts and cultures of Africa. A wonderful resource. [20/10/05]

54   Smithsonian Natural History Web: African Voices ⓘ
http://www.mnh.si.edu/africanvoices/
Another marvellously interactive site from the Smithsonian, presenting a virtual exhibition "that examines the diversity, dynamism, and global influences of Africa's peoples and cultures over time in the realms of family, work, community, and the natural environment." Included are historical and contemporary objects from the Museum's collections, as well as commissioned sculptures, textiles, and pottery. The site also offers video inter-actives and sound stations that provide selections from contemporary interviews, literature, proverbs, prayers, folk tales, songs, and oral epics. [20/10/05]

55   Spartacus Internet Encyclopaedia: British History 1700-1930 – The Slave Trade
http://www.spartacus.schoolnet.co.uk/slavery.htm
This is part of the excellent, interactive Spartacus Internet Encyclopaedia (freely accessible), and these pages are devoted to the horrors of the slave trade and Britain's role in it. It includes slave accounts by people such as Frederick Douglass, Olaudah Equiano, Harriet Tubman, Nat Turner and Phillis Wheatley; descriptions of the slave systems, accounts of slave lives, important events and issues in the history of the slave trade, together with entries about anti-slavery movements and the groups that fought for the abolition of the slave trade including profiles of, for example, Thomas Clarkson, Granville Sharp, and William Wilberforce. There are also sections on legislation about the abolition of the slave trade (e.g. the 1833 Abolition of Slavery Act), as well as a large number of portraits of US campaigners against slavery. Each section has very extensive cross-referencing of links leading to other sections within the encyclopaedia. [05/06/05]

56   Telephone Directories on the Web - Africa
http://www.infobel.com/teldir/teldir.asp?page=/eng/afri
Infobel.com (formerly TelDir) is possibly the most complete index to online phone books worldwide, although the number of African sources are still fairly limited, e.g. Ghana (1), Kenya (3) Nigeria (2), Senegal (4), South Africa (5), or Zimbabwe (3). Each source is briefly described. The name of the site is a bit of a misnomer, as most of the sources are not in fact national telephone directories issued by the various national telecom organizations, but Yellow Pages, White Pages, and trade and business directories. [21/06/05]

57   Visual Arts Data Service (VADS) – African and Asian Visual Artists
       Archive (AAVAA)/Diversity Art Forum
http://vads.ahds.ac.uk/collections/AAVAA.html
Hosted by the Surrey Institute of Art & Design, University of East London, this is a
freely accessible collection of visual arts digital resources, allowing access to nearly
12,000 cross-searchable visual arts images for use in research, learning, and teaching.
It includes the *African and Asian Visual Artists Archive* (AAVAA, recently re-launched
as the Diversity Art Forum), containing nearly 2,000 digital images, and which is the
most comprehensive slide archive of contemporary visual art by artists of African
and Asian descent working in the UK since the post-war period. [21/06/05]

58   Voices from Africa: A Letter to World Leaders
http://www.royalafricansociety.org/voices_africa
During the course of 2004 the ➔ **Royal African Society (2780)** invited some African
leaders and scholars who are not politicians to write a short personal letter to the ➔
Commission for Africa (33, 2590), defining what Africa can do for itself and what the
rest of the world can do for Africa. It asked them "to do the impossible", to address
these difficult issues in one thousand words, and on the basis of these three
questions: 1. Where do you think Africa will be in 2015? 2. How can it get there? 3.
Why has it not got there already? Sixteen African scholars and writers, economists,
journalists, ICT specialists, activists, and others present their views here, in a very
interesting contribution to the debate, among them John Adeyemi-Adeleke,
Emmanel Akyeampong, George Ayittey, Peter Egom, Stephen Karangizi, Greg Mills,
Célestin Monga, Charles Onyango-Obbo, Ato Quayson, and Veronique Tadjo.
[26/06/05].

59   Wikipedia – Africa pages
http://en.wikipedia.org/wiki/Africa
Wikipedia is a searchable free-content encyclopedia that anyone can edit. It was
started in 2001, and currently (August 2005) contains almost 700,000 articles. Articles
are written collaboratively by many of its readers and users. "Free content" is
considered to be "any kind of functional work, artwork, or other creative content
upon which no legal restriction has been placed that significantly interferes with
people's freedom to use, understand, redistribute, improve, and share the content."
Anyone can edit or "improve" entries in the encyclopedia, and there are hundreds of
hourly changes all of which are recorded on the page history for each entry,
including the pages relating to Africa and African topics. Click on to "Discussion" for
any entry to follow comments and debates about the evolving content on any page.
From the main Africa pages you can access quite substantial articles, a well as
summaries about geography, history, politics, demographics, languages, culture,
religion, and other topics, for example entries on colonialism, the slave trade, human
rights, AIDS, ethnic groups, language groups, etc. as well as a fairly substantial
number of entries for African authors, with extensively cross-linked biographical
profiles. However, irritatingly, some of these are in fact blind entries indicating, for
example, "Wikipedia does not yet have a page called Ayi Kwei Armah." There are
also pages for each country in Africa, which on the whole seem to be well compiled,
fairly accurate, and up-to-date. However, the external links section for both the main
Africa and individual country pages are poor for the most part. Wikipedia is an
innovative and exciting concept, a kind of global memory bank, contributed by

people from all over the world, but the information it offers for some entries can be simplistic, uninformed, inadequately documented, or highly contentious. So it goes without saying that information contained in the Wikipedia should not be regarded as sacrosant. [13/08/05]

60   Wonders of the African World
http://www.pbs.org/wonders/
This attractive site was created to accompany the television programme of the same name created by Henry Louis Gates jr., originally aired on US TV in October 1999. It aims to take you on a journey to discover a wealth of African history and culture in "Wonders of the African World." Explore the site by selecting a topic from six themes: Black Kingdoms of the Nile, The Swahili Coast, The Slave Kingdoms, The Holy Land, Road to Timbuktu, and Lost Cities of the South. Additionally, a section entitled "Retelling the Story" provides access to a number of articles on, for example, Black identity in Africa, slaves and the slave trade, African daily life, or Western stereotypes. [21/06/05]

61   The World Factbook 2005 [Africa]
http://www.cia.gov/cia/publications/factbook/index.html
Published annually by the US Central Intelligence Agency and updated periodically throughout the year, the pages of the *World Factbook* devoted to African countries provide basic background and factual information about each African nation, under eight broad subject headings: Introduction, Geography, People, Government, Economy, Communications, Transportation, Military, and Transnational Issues, each with a menu of sub-topics. The opening page for each country shows a map and indicates when the pages were last updated. Useful for quick access to basic facts and figures, the economy, growth rates, political parties and leaders, etc. *See also* ➜ **African Governments (19)**. [21/06/05]

Academic and scholarly resources on African studies

see also ➜ **22 Information and communication development in Africa: a guide to Web sites and resources**

This section offers listings of the major African studies portals and mega sites, together with a number of other multidisciplinary online resources, such as databases, indexes, and directories. Biographical sources, guides to African language resources, guides to statistical sources, economic and financial data, cartographic sources, and guides to film and video resources are listed in sections 4-8, while news sources for Africa are listed in sections 10 and 11.

Note: Resources that are available in dual electronic and print formats are listed under section ➔ **2 The major general reference tools** but are cross-referenced here.

ⓘ **This symbol indicates "The editor's choice" of a particularly outstanding online information resource.**

Beginners' guides and Web tutorials

➔ **Africana Resources for Undergraduates: A Bibliographic Essay** *see* **236**

62   Guide to Resources for the Study of Africa
http://library.albany.edu/subject/guides/AfricaGuide.htm
Compiled by Deborah LaFond, the primary purpose of this guide is to introduce students to the library collections at the ➔ **University at Albany (1331)**, State University of New York, but it will be useful for students elsewhere starting off in African studies. It offers helpful tips for locating books and journals, searching for journal articles by topic, and then describes the principal reference sources for the study of Africa and the African diaspora, with informative annotations for most of them. An extensive list of African studies Internet resources can be found in a separate section at http://library.albany.edu/subject/africana.htm. [29/08/05]

63   Ohio University Libraries, Research Guides: African Studies
http://www.library.ohiou.edu/subjects/africa/asubmain.htm
While primarily intended for researchers exploring library resources at ➔**Ohio University Alden Library (1324)**, this is a helpful concise introduction to African studies Internet resources. Compiled by Loyd Mbabu, Africana Bibliographer at the Alden Library and its Center for International Collections, the guide provides a beginner's guide to locating books on Africa and African topics, including Africa-related journals, African newspapers, indexes and bibliographies, government documents, maps collections, vendors and booksellers, descriptions of other major Africana collections, and other resources. Some sections would benefit from updating. [21/06/05]

64   Research Tools for African Studies
http://www.lib.berkeley.edu/doemoff/africana/sources.html
Compiled by Phyllis Bischof, this is another good introduction to the most appropriate research tools to find information related to African studies, covering sources such as archival collections, atlases, maps and gazetteers, biographic sources, country data sources, dictionaries and thesauri, encyclopaedias, government information sources, image and sound databases, library and book catalogues, organizations, as well as sources for statistical and numeric data. All materials can be found in the collections at the → **University of California-Berkeley (1333),** but most will also be available in major African studies collections elsewhere. [20/09/05]

→ **Using Google for African studies research: A guide to effective Web searching** *see* Section **25.**

65   Web Resources for the Study of Africa
http://www.bu.edu/library/instruction/africa.html
Prepared by Gretchen Walsh, Head of → **Boston University's African Studies Library (1300),** this is a good basic tutorial for tracking down Web resources for the study of Africa, albeit now in need of some updating. While it is principally intended for those who use the resources at Boston, there is some good sensible advice here for all novices in African studies research, including guidance on the use of library guides and principal resources, browsing the table of contents of African studies journals, surfing the Web, using search engines, evaluating the results of what search engines find, and citing Web resources. Boston University Libraries also offer a range of library guides and tutorials in several more specific areas, for example, Women's Issues in Africa: Finding Information on the Web, or Web Resources for the Peoples and Cultures of Africa, all available online. [21/06/05]

Gateways, portals and mega sites

66   Africa Action
http://www.africaaction.org/index.php
Africa Action is an organization that works for political, economic and social justice in Africa – and aims to widen the policy debate in the USA around African issues and the US role in Africa – through the provision of accessible information, up-to-date analysis, and resources. It incorporates the American Committee on Africa, the Africa Fund, and the Africa Policy Information Center. The site provides access to a number of useful resources, policy and action documents, reports, campaign documents, discussion groups and roundtables, and a very substantial number of links to data and meta sites. There is also a forum for activists who work on issues related to U.S. Africa policy to share information and experience. [21/06/05]

67   Africa Focus Bulletin. News-Analysis-Advocacy
http://www.africafocus.org/
Launched by William Minter in November 2003, this Web site features analysis and progressive advocacy on African issues, with particular attention to priority issues affecting the entire continent. It is designed to highlight particularly important policy statements and background information on policy issues. It is not a news service, and

is not intended to substitute for news coverage on specific topics or countries. The heart of the site consists of issues of the *Africa Focus Bulletin*, produced and distributed one to three times a week to subscribers, including individuals, organizations, and list servers. Current issues are featured on the home page, while a full archive is also available on the site, and can be searched by date, by place, or by topic. The *Bulletin* does not publish original articles, but only material that has previously been published, in electronic or print format, and that is available for reposting. Access is free but readers are encouraged to send in a voluntary subscription payment. [18/06/05]

68   Africana Reference Sources: A Selected Guide with Annotations
http://www.lib.ku.edu/~biblio/african/AfricanaStudiesResources.shtml
Compiled by Ken Lohrentz, African Studies Bibliographer at the ➔ **University of Kansas Library (1340)**, this is an excellent annotated guide to print and online African studies resources, both general and specialist. It focuses primarily on reference works that have been published since 1995, although some earlier material is also included. Content is arranged under three principal sections: (1) Reference Sources by Continent, sub-divided by 14 groups (archives and manuscripts, atlases and maps, bibliographies, conference papers, dictionaries and encyclopaedias, directories and handbooks, dissertations and theses, Internet gateways, media resources, photographic archives and collections, etc.); (2) Reference Sources by Region, sub-divided into eight regions of the continent; (3) Reference Sources by Country. It should be noted that print sources are only included if they are available in the University of Kansas collections. Each entry gives the call number as catalogued by the Watson Library of the University of Kansas, together with an informative annotation, many of them drawn from the annual listings ➔ **"Africana Reference Works: An Annotated List of ......Titles" (383)** published in ➔ **The African Book Publishing Record (384)**. However, some sections lack currency (especially of online resources) as the site has not apparently been updated since March 2003. [14/08/05]

69   Africa South of the Sahara – Selected Internet Resources ⓘ
http://www-sul.stanford.edu./depts/ssrg/africa/guide.html
Created and developed by Karen Fung at ➔ **Stanford University Libraries (1327)** for the Information and Communication Technology Group (ICTG) of the (US) ➔ **African Studies Association (2755)** and launched in 1994, this was the first, pioneering online resource for African studies material. It has grown very substantially over the years and – very frequently updated – it is now widely recognized to be one of the very best sites for Internet resources on Africa. It is an ideal gateway and starting point for Africa-related Web searches. Access is offered through two main menus, by topics, or by countries/regions. The topics menu currently consists of 50 headings, from African studies (programs, organizations), art, birds, book dealers, book donations, business through to science, sports, statistics, student organizations, travel, weather, and women, including not only academic but also more general topics, for example cookery and recipes. There are also excellent sections on discussions groups, grants and fellowships, libraries/archives, media, publishers, journals and magazines, radio stations, and

much more. Each resource listed includes a short informative description, and there is a search facility. Highly recommended. [21/06/05]

➔ **African Digital Library** *see* entry 18

70   African Cultural Policy Resources (i)
http://www.imo.hr/ocpa/resources/index.html
This site is part of the Observatory of Cultural Policies in Africa (OCPA), created in 2002 with the support of the ➔ **African Union (2504)**, ➔ **UNESCO (2533)** and a number of donor organizations and foundations. OCPA was set up as an independent pan-African professional organization designed to enhance the development of national cultural policies in the region, and their integration in human development strategies through advocacy and promoting information exchange, research, capacity building and cooperation at the regional and international level. The rich resources pages list African regional and local cultural policies – with links to other relevant documentation, including reports and working papers – as well as providing access to a wide variety of information on projects, events, publications, and more. There is also a very substantial link collection to foundations, African regional and sub-regional organizations, African cultural institutions, government ministries involved in cultural polices, networks and research centres, NGOs, and museums. Additionally, OCPA offers a useful ➔ **OCPA Newsletter (581)**. [14/08/05]

➔ **African Online Digital Library** *see* entry 2905

71   African Political Resources
http://www.politicalresources.net/africa.htm
Similar to ➔ **African Governments on the WWW (21)**, this is part of the global Politicalresources.net hosted from Italy, edited by Roberto Cicciomessere, and containing over 24,000 links worldwide. It is a good starting point for basic political resources on Africa which can be selected from a country menu (with flags in colour of all African nations), and leading to government sites, political parties, political forums, trade union sites, Web pages of activist organizations, analysis of recent election results, as well as many links to media. "Last updated" dates are indicated for each country, and updates would appear to fairly frequent. [21/06/05]

72   African Studies Centre, Leiden University. Library, Documentation &
       Information Department (i)
http://www.ascleiden.nl/Library/Catalogue/
http://opc4-ascl.pica.nl/DB=3/LNG=EN/ (OPAC English version)
The Online Public Access Catalogue of the ➔ **African Studies Centre Library (1246)** in Leiden is an excellent source not only for book searches, but also for finding African studies periodicals and tracking down periodical literature. The catalogue links up with the ASC's ➔ **African Studies Abstracts/African Studies Abstracts Online (396)**. The African Studies Centre library currently holds over 60,000 books and brochures, receives about 450 journal subscriptions and about 240 of these are regularly scanned and abstracted, together with abstracts of select literature of papers appearing in edited collections. Over 65,000 journal articles are available at

this time. The search facilities are very sophisticated and searches can be conducted by author, full title, words in title, country/subject code, words contained in the abstracts, all words (excluding abstracts), person or subject, organization, series, publisher, words in conference name, ISBN, ISSN, and call number. Search results bring up the full bibliographic citation, a country/subject code, plus an abstract for most. The search facilities also cover the library's extensive collections of books, reports, microfiche, etc., although these do not include abstracts. Additionally, the ASC pages provide a useful listing of free online journals and newsletters, ➔ *see* entry **549**. [21/06/05]

73   **African Studies WWW – University of Pennsylvania African Studies Programme**
http://www.sas.upenn.edu/African_Studies/AS.html or
http://www.sas.upenn.edu/African_Studies/Home_Page/WWW_Links.html
Together with the Stanford ➔**Africa South of the Sahara – Selected Internet Resources (69)** this site, maintained by Ali B. Ali-Dinar, was until recently one of the premier Web resources for African studies. However, it would not appear to have been significantly updated, or new resources added, since February 2000. Nonetheless, it is probably still useful, primarily for its section Africa Web Links: An Annotated Resource List, grouped by 29 broad subject groups, although coverage is nowhere near as comprehensive as the Stanford site. Much more up-to-date are the "What's New" pages on the African Studies Center's Web pages, at http://www.africa.upenn.edu/Home_Page/Whats_New.html, containing a variety of documents, including updates and analysis of African political developments, conference news, call for papers, scholarship information, etc. with access to the complete news archive. [21/06/05]

74   **Afrika.no. The Index on Africa** ⓘ
http://www.afrika.no/
Hosted and created by the Norwegian Council for Africa, Index on Africa is a gateway to information on Africa on the Internet, currently (June 2005) with over 3,800 links. It is managed in collaboration with a team of African editors, and enjoys the financial support of the Norwegian Ministry of Foreign Affairs and ➔ **NORAD (2683)**. Search or browse by countries, by 17 broad subject categories, or by news links. The country links are offered under the same topics categories. Every link is accompanied by a short descriptive annotation, the date when the site was added, together with an indication of the number of hits each link has enjoyed since it was added. Afrika.no also offers an interactive discussion forum for debates and for information exchange, together with an "Africa News Update" email notification service with daily news briefings from African news sources. Although not all that strong on academic resources for African studies, this is a good general starting point for Internet resources on Africa. [21/06/05]

75   **Afrol .documents – Center for African Documentation**
http://www.afrol.com/archive/documents/documents.htm
From the news agency ➔ **Afrol.com/Afro News (850)** this is a valuable collection of key historical documents as well as updated reports and treaties of contemporary importance, including election, mission and observer groups' reports, declarations,

statements, accords, UN documents, etc. and covering areas such as human rights, elections, labour, law, politics, and refugees. Select documents by topic or by country, and retrieve the full text of these documents, with a summary of author/instigator, date, title, nature of document, subject matter, and source. [21/06/05]

76   Att studera Afrika. Vägar till källorna (in Swedish only)
http://www.nai.uu.se/webbshop/epubl/others/rylander2.pdf
Compiled by Kristina Rylander, with the assistance of several of her colleagues at the library of the ➔ **Nordic Africa Institute (1260)** in Uppsala, this is a comprehensive 130-page online guide (in pdf format) providing a critical introduction to the major handbooks and reference works on Africa and African studies, covering both print and online resources. Part 1 deals with bibliographies, guides to sources, databases, yearbooks, journals, Internet resources (including helpful tips and guidance about searching and evaluating Internet resources), statistical and map resources, as well as government and official publications. Part 2 covers subject-specific resources, with chapters on History, Politics and Economics, Geography, African Culture and Anthropology, and Education and Training. This is a very useful resource (also published in a print version), albeit only available in Swedish at this time. [19/06/05]

77   A-Z of African Studies on the Internet ⓘ
http://www.lib.msu.edu/limb/a-z/az.html
This was one of the very first guides to African studies online resources, first issued as a print edition in 1995, and with an updated version first posted electronically on H-Africa in August of the same year. Jointly edited by Peter Limb, Africana Librarian at ➔ **Michigan State University Library (1317)** and Ibra Sene of MSU's history department, it is high quality annotated guide, very frequently updated and constantly expanded, to a very large number of Africa-related Web sites, online discussion groups and mailing lists, and other sources of relevance to African studies. Access is by an A-Z menu – grouped by 32 sub-sections e.g. B3 Com-Dic, N1 Na-Nig, or T5 Zell-Zulu – which includes African countries with sub-sections (the main heading for Zimbabwe, for example, has 35 topic specific sub-sections), subjects/topics, titles, authors of Internet documents, names of groups, institutions, names of African writers, names of journals and newspapers, African language resources, and much more. Many of the entries include a short one or two line description. If you can't find what you want, or are not keen to scroll through sections of the alphabet, there is a Google search facility to assist with topic specific searches. However, one minor flaw with the search facility is the fact that search terms entered will search the entire Michigan State University Libraries Web site rather than just this A-Z. [21/06/05].

**78   Center for African Studies. University of Illinois at Urbana-Champaign -
        UIUC Library Africana Reading Room**
http://www.afrst.uiuc.edu
and http://www.afrst.uiuc.edu/lib.html (Africana Reading Room)
This site presents the combined resources of the UIUC African Studies Centre and the ➔ **University of Illinois Library's (1338)** Africana collections, which are among the finest in the world. Africa information sources are presented under a range of

broad topic headings, including arts and culture, governments and IGOs, libraries and publishing, research links, news sources, outreach centres, Web guides and portals, and there is a particularly strong collection of links (each with a short description) on human rights in Africa, including African human rights organizations. Additionally, there is a menu for information by countries, with links to a number of Web sites offering basic factual information on each country. The Africana Reading Room pages present information on the African studies collections, acquisitions lists, links to research guides, and guides to major indexes and reference sources. [21/06/05]

79   Center for Electronic Resources in African Studies (CERAS)
http://sdrc.lib.uiowa.edu/ceras/
Launched in 1998, the ➔ **University of Iowa's (1339)** Center for Electronic Resources in African Studies is a "virtual space for creating, disseminating and accessing scholarly electronic resources in text, multimedia, and interactive format to support students and faculty, as well as other scholars nationally and internationally." Among its projects are the ➔ **Electronic Journal of Africana Bibliography (806)**, an online Dogon dictionary, the University of Iowa ➔ **Art and Life in Africa (29, 356)** project, the African Peace Information Locator, the journal *Baobab* (dedicated to the study of African expressive culture, last issue March 16, 1997), and the Arts of Central Africa course Web site. Future projects identified include the development of interactive journals on African studies and on African art and cultural topics, digitizing of African literary works, and digitizing a selection of important (non-copyrighted) international documents pertaining to Africa. However, none of these projects seem to have materialized thus far (and as at June 2005); the original mission statement has not been updated since December 2000, and the Resources sections were last updated in April 2001. [21/06/05]

80   Columbia University Libraries – African Studies Internet Resources ⓘ
http://www.columbia.edu/cu/lweb/indiv/africa/cuvl/
Columbia's extensive site, together with the Stanford ➔ **Africa South of the Sahara – Selected Internet Resources (69)**, are arguably the two very best freely accessible starting points for searching the Web for African studies Internet resources. Since the beginning of 1999 the Columbia site has also been the "official" Web site for the World Wide Virtual Library http://vlib.org/. Compiled and maintained by Joseph Caruso, Africana Librarian at ➔ **Columbia University Lehman Library (1303)**, material can be accessed from a main menu covering resources by region or by country, by organization or associations, and by topic, each main group broken down into several sub-menus. The topics menu offers 22 categories, including African biography, African diaspora sources, African language resources, art and archaeology, climate and environment, health information, history and culture, literature, films and videos, news and information services, etc., as well as more general topics such as cooking recipes, flags, maps, and information about embassies and UN missions of African countries. There is also an extensive section on the Internet in Africa. Additionally, there are guides to African studies programmes, research centres, universities, and links to the online catalogues of the world's top libraries with African studies collections; together with sections on electronic journals and newspapers on Africa, libraries, book dealers and publishers, and an

International Directory of African Studies Scholars (*see* separate entry in this section, entry **181**). In addition to a search facility, many sections offer access through different options, e.g. African Studies programmes, research centres, and universities, and can be accessed alphabetically or by geographic region. Very regularly updated, the site has a crisp and clean interface, and virtually every resource includes a short description, and/or excerpts about aims and objectives quoted from mission statements of the resources listed. This is an enormously rich resource and is highly recommended. [21/06/05]

81   Development Gateway ⓘ
http://home.developmentgateway.org/
A Web portal incubated by the ➔ **World Bank (2548)**, and now a part of a non-profit organization, the Development Gateway Foundation. It is an interactive site that brings together people, resources, and information on development and poverty reduction, providing a space for communities to share experiences and resources on development efforts. Access is free, but requires registration. Information is grouped under four principal sections: (1) Topic Pages: online communities where development professionals come together to exchange specialized information. (2) dgMarket: a global online service that provides access to government contract tenders from around the world; you can view more than 40,000 tender notices for a huge variety of projects. (3) Country Gateways: locally-owned information service providers that promote national development and build enterprise. (4) AiDA (Accessible Information on Development Activities): a consolidated directory of information on development activities found on the Web sites or internal information systems of major bilateral donors, multilateral development banks and UN agencies. Participating organizations share information on planned, current and completed projects and programmes that they fund, execute or implement. Currently AiDA contains over 400,000 records of development activities, and enables you to access historical and current records on planned, current, and completed activities and programs from international organizations. View programs and projects by country, region, sector, or thematic area. A most impressive resource. [22/06/05]

82   ELDIS Regional Profile: Africa South of the Sahara ⓘ
http://www.eldis.org/africa/index.htm
RSS RSS feed, regional Africa
http://www.eldis.org/newsfeeds/rss/2/abafrica.xml
This is part of the ELDIS Gateway to Development Information, edited and hosted by the Institute of Development Studies at the University of Sussex, a portal to information on development issues, providing free and easy access to very wide range of high quality online resources. It is an enormously content-rich site, offering access to some 15,000 online documents, 4,500 organizations, 15,000 email messages, 32 email bulletins and over 30 news feeds. It is fully searchable. From the Regional-Africa main page you can access country profiles for each African nation, with a selection of documents on each country, including all the latest online documents from ELDIS and all the latest print documents from the ➔ **British Library for Development Studies (1272)** collections. Alternatively, use the Sectoral Profiles options to limit the documents displayed to a more specific topic, covering Health, Education, Gender, Agriculture, Trade and Finance, Governance, Environment,

Poverty, Food Security & Emergencies, and Aid and Debt. ELDIS is also available as an RSS news feed, on 25 topics. [14/08/05]

83   A Guide to Africa on the Internet. Selected Information Sources and Databases ⓘ

http://www.nai.uu.se/links/linkseng.html

Compiled and edited by Håkan Gidlöf and hosted by the ➔ **Nordiska Africainstitutet/The Nordic Africa Institute (1611)**, this collection of information sources is primarily research-oriented, but it also provides links to Web sites with a broader or more general content. There are menus for regional and country-specific information resources and those relating to subjects/topics, together with sections on libraries and databases, journals and magazines, news agencies, broadcasting and African radio stations, research institutes and universities (including a separate section on Nordic research institutes and university centres), and more. Each link is accompanied by a concise description. Not as comprehensive as some of the other mega sites on African studies, but this is a good point of departure for African studies research. [22/06/05]

84   Habari

http://www.africa.u-bordeaux.fr/links.asp

Compiled by staff at the ➔ **Centre d'Etude d'Afrique Noire (CEAN), Université de Bordeaux IV (1565)**, this is a directory of Internet resources on African studies primarily in the social sciences and the humanities. At this time (June 2005) it provides 2,344 links (in the francophone world and elsewhere) with short descriptions, grouped under 36 broad subject groups, including sections on the press and publishing, African studies centres, university institutions, and much more. Each link indicates when last verified, and the number of visitors it has attracted to date. A search facility is provided. At the foot of the page is a panel with links to the six most recently added new sites, plus a panel showing the "Les 6 liens les plus visités". However, this seems to lack credibility as the two Web sites listed in second and third place, a University of Bordeaux *Rapport sur le développement en Afrique* http://www.africa.u-bordeaux.fr/links_id.asp?id=2436, and a site called *Collection d'object d'Art sur l'Afrique* at http://site.voila.fr/public/divers/404.html, both turn out to be dead links (as at June 2005). Nonetheless, this is a good starting point on the whole, especially for francophone sources. [22/06/05]

85   H-Africa Network ⓘ

http://www2.h-net.msu.edu/~africa/

Based at Michigan State University, H-Africa is a member of H-Net's consortium of scholarly lists, and the H-Africa list encourages discussion of Africa's history, culture and African studies generally. There are also links here to all related lists (arts, cinema, literature, politics, etc.) which are part of the H-Africa Network; *see also* ➔ **21 Online forums and mailing lists**, entries **2810-2821**. The site provides access to all the discussion logs and discussion threads, and the entire H-Africa network logs can be searched from this page. The complete H-Africa book review archive can also be found here, as can be a useful index to selected discussion threads. Additionally, the site offers a wide variety of other resources of interest to Africanists, including a range of essays, reports, and briefing papers, links to African studies programmes worldwide, and more. The site also offers an "Ask a Librarian" email service, provided by Gretchen Walsh, Head of the ➔ **Boston University African Studies Library (1300)**. [22/06/05]

➔ **Index on Africa** *see* **Afrika.no. The Index on Africa (74)**

➔ **International Documentation Network on the Great African Lakes Region** *see* **Résau Documentaire sur la Région lacs Africains (95)**

86   Internet African History Sourcebook
http://www.fordham.edu/halsall/africa/africasbook.html
The Internet African History Source books are a component and sub-set of the Internet History Sourcebooks Project developed at the History Department at Fordham University in New York. It was developed and is edited by Paul Halsall with the assistance of numerous other contributors. The project is designed to provide easy access to "classroom usable" primary sources and other "copy-permitted" (for personal and educational use) teaching materials which are in the public domain. Each sub-set provides links to documents and Web resources, including secondary articles, reviews, ongoing discussions on a given topic, as well as links to mega sites and Web sites focussing on specific topics. Contents for the African sourcebook is arranged under twelve headings, e.g. Africa-Origins, Egypt, Ancient African Societies, Greek and Roman Africa, Africa and Islam, European Imperialism, Modern Africa, etc. The site was last updated in February 2001. [27/11/03]

87   Islam in Sub-Saharan Africa
http://www.ascleiden.nl/Library/Webdossiers/IslamInAfrica.aspx
A Web dossier compiled by the staff at the ➔ **African Studies Centre Library (1246)** in Leiden to coincide with a conference on 'Islam, Disengagement of the State, and Globalization in sub-Saharan Africa' held at UNESCO in May 2005. The conference was jointly organized by the Leiden ➔ **African Studies Centre (1594)** and the ➔ **Centre d'étude d'Afrique noire (1565)** in Bordeaux, who have been running a collaborative project to study Islam in sub-Saharan Africa. The listing of books and articles are based on the ASC library's collection and cover material published over the last two decades. Each title links directly to the corresponding record in the Library's online catalogue, which provides full details about the title as well as abstracts of articles and edited works. A small a number of Web resources on Islam in Africa are also included. [19/06/05]

88   Library of Congress. Country Studies/Area Handbook series [Africa]
http://lcweb2.loc.gov/frd/cs/continent_africa.html
This Web site contains the on-line versions of books previously published in hard copy by the Federal Research Division of the ➔ **Library of Congress (1316)** under the Country Studies/Area Handbook Program sponsored by the US Department of Army. At present, 101 countries and regions are covered, and, for Africa, 20 nations are covered at this time. The date of information for each country appears on the title page of each country and at the end of each section of text. Each study presents a description and analysis of the historical setting of the country and its social, economic, political, and national security systems and structures, and examines the

interrelationships of those systems and the ways they are shaped by cultural factors. [22/07/05]
Note: hard copy editions of all books in the series can be ordered from the US Government Printing Office's online bookstore at http://bookstore.gpo.gov/index.html. Sixteen of the African country studies are also available as a CD-ROM, *see* ➔ **Africa on CD ROM (323)**.

89   Library of Congress: Portals to the World--Africa
http://www.loc.gov/rr/international/portals.html
As part of a project called 'Portals to the World', the African and Middle Eastern Division of the ➔ **Library of Congress (1316)** has created a range of country portal pages citing selected Internet resources for African countries. Each country portal provides some general background information, a map, plus a menu of links grouped under 17 categories such as business/economy, culture, education, government, history, language and literature, media and communications, etc. as well as sections for listservs/newsgroups and country-specific search engines. With each link a short descriptive annotation is provided. While the range of links under some categories are still rather patchy for a number of countries, this is a helpful starting point for more general Africa-related information. [22/06/05]

90   Mutations Africaines dans la longue durée
http://mald.univ-paris1.fr/index.htm
This is the joint portal of three research institutions at the Université Paris 1 Panthéon Sorbonne/CNRS, brought together under the name Mutations africaines dans la longue durée (MALD): the ➔ **Centre de recherches africaines (1563)**, the ➔ **Laboratoire d'anthropologie juridique de Paris (1573)**, and the ➔ **Centre d'etudes juridiques et politiques des mondes Africains (1568)**. It provides access to a variety of resources (primarily in French) in the field of African history, politics, anthropology and law, including news about seminars and conferences, current teaching and research at these institutions, new publications, pages devoted to theses and dissertation, new acquisitions by the ➔ **Bibliothèque de recherches africaines (1191)**, and more. [30/06/05]

91   OneWorld – Africa ⓘ
http://www.oneworld.net/africa/
➔ **OneWorld (2614)** is a networking community of over 1,600 organizations working for social justice, promoting human rights awareness, and fighting poverty worldwide. The extensive number of pages devoted to the African continent provide news, opinion, perspectives, and special reports, and can be browsed or searched by topic or by country/region. There are particularly good news sections – each news story with a succinct summary – updated daily. They feature stories from a whole array of Africa-based NGOs on human rights and sustainable development, providing an African perspective on issues frequently dominated by powerful Western voices. OneWorld's global partners database provide links to a very large number organizations, networks, alliances, government agencies, projects, donors, etc. based in Africa or working in Africa, each with a short description, and linked to almost 2,000 relevant documents. An excellent search facility in the OneWorld

Partner Directory lets you search for partners' sites by name, country, type of organisation, field of interest, or languages. [22/06/05]

92   Political Communications Web Archive Project
http://www.crl.edu/content/PolitWeb.htm
A project of the ➔ **Center for Research Libraries (1302)** in association with a number of university institutions, this is a new initiative to develop effective methodologies for the systematic, sustainable preservation of Web-based political communications. The project will focus on Web materials produced by political groups and NGOs in Latin America, sub-Saharan Africa, Southeast Asia, and Western Europe. Materials will include reports, manifestos, constitutions and declarations, official statements, and other documents dissemination via the Web by individual political activists, political parties, and popular front and radical organizations. [28/07/05]

93   Opportunities in African Studies Worldwide ⓘ
http://africa.wisc.edu/opportunities/index.htm
This is an excellent resource from the ➔ **African Studies Program, University of Wisconsin-Madison (1810)**. It provides up-to-date information and alerts on a variety of "opportunities" in the field of African studies covering ten different categories: Awards/Prizes, Calls for Papers-Conferences, Calls for Papers-Publications, Conference Listing, Employment Opportunities, Fellowships-Graduate, Fellowships-Post-Graduate & Faculty Development, Institutes and Center Opportunities, Study Abroad & Internship Opportunities, and Volunteer Programs. The pages are updated every Monday morning, with the main page showing the most recent posting, and clicking on to the different categories will bring up the complete listing for each heading. Click on to any listing and it will open a new window giving full information and contact details, etc. For each section the site also provides links to additional sources of interest. The African studies community is invited to submit opportunities for posting by contacting the Webmaster of the site. [14/08/05]

94   Reconciliation Processes in Africa
http://www.loc.gov/rr/amed/africanreconciliation.html
Created and maintained by the ➔ **Library of Congress African & Middle Eastern Division (1316)**, and part of the LC's Portals to the World, this guide provides a selected sampling of online information resources dealing with reconciliation processes in African nations. The annotated set of resources listed includes information on country-specific case examples of current reconciliation initiatives; primary documents from truth and reconciliation commissions; conference proceedings, scholarly articles, and reports issued by major government, international, and civil society organizations (particularly interfaith, community, and women's organizations). Also included are references to electronic bibliographies and research tools, electronic journals, and electronic discussion groups addressing issues central to the subject of reconciliation. Browse by countries or by category. [08/07/05]

95   Résau Documentaire sur la Région lacs Africains/International
        Documentation Network on the Great African Lakes Region (i)
http://www.grandslacs.net/index.html (accessible in French or English versions)
A collaborative project of a number of academic institutions in Belgium, France,
Switzerland, and institutions in Burundi, the Democratic Republic of the Congo,
Rwanda, and Tanzania. It offers a vast number of original documents on a variety of
topics, freely accessible in pdf format. Each month the site provides a listing of new
documents added. Special emphasis is put on elusive and grey literature, including
unpublished documents. There are also a substantial number of maps (from the UN
Cartographic Section). A sophisticated search engine enables searches by full-text,
types of sources, keywords, and more. For those unable to access the documents on
the Internet a CD-ROM is offered of the contents of the entire site (at a charge). This
is an outstanding information resource. [22/06/05]

96   Resources on African Health & Disease
http://www.africa.upenn.edu/health/
While specialist medical or scientific resources are not covered in the *African Studies
Companion*, this new Web site is included here because it is of interest to the broader
Africanist community. Hosted by the ➔ **University of Pennsylvania African
Studies Center (1799)** and financially support by a grant from Merck & Co Inc, the
site is intended "to counter sensational and often inaccurate reporting of the health
situation in Africa, and to provide the public with information on a wide array of
health-related initiatives, facilities, and opportunities on the continent." The site
offers information on common diseases in Africa (e.g. Ebola, HIV/AIDS,
Leishmaniasis, Malaria, Sicklecell disease, Yellow Fewer, etc.); links to African health
organizations (multilateral, NGOs and community organizations) each with a short
description; health ministries and hospitals in Africa (the latter still somewhat patchy
as only a relatively small number of hospitals in Africa have their own Web sites at
this time); as well as links to discussion groups and mailing list relating to heath
issues in Africa, and jobs and grants information. [11/06/05]

97   SARDC Democracy Factfiles/Country Insights
http://www.sardc.net/sd/factfiles/
Developed by the Sustainable Democracy in Southern Africa Programme of the
Harare-based ➔ **Southern African Research and Documentation Centre/SARDC
(1497)**, this is a regional project designed to improve the flow of information on
democracy and governance in the 14 member countries of the ➔ **Southern African
Development Community/SADC (2518).** Although now a little bit dated here and
there, it provides a helpful resource for quick factual information about the state of
democracy and the current political situation in every SADC member country. For
each country it offers a 4-8 pp. document (in pdf format) providing essential
historical background, recent political developments, governance, gender equality,
human rights, and civil society, together with listings of the major media in each
country (newspapers, radio and TV). Most information is current as at 1999/2000.
[18/06/05]

98   Striving for Good Governance in Africa. Synopsis of the 2005 AGR
http://www.uneca.org/agr/
A synopsis (in 7 parts, and also available in a French version) of the *African Governance Report* (AGR), a major continent-wide study to measure and monitor "Progress towards good governance in Africa", undertaken by the ➔ **UN Economic Commission for Africa/ECA (2523)**. The study conducted surveys and desk research in 28 project countries. ECA initiated this work to gauge citizens' feelings about the state of governance in Africa, to gather information on best practices, and to identify the main requirements for capacity development in the region. "The project identified four positive trends on the road to creating capable states in Africa: democratic transitions, political inclusiveness, voice and accountability, and economic management." The synopsis contains the Executive Summary, Part 1: *The State of Government in 28 African Countries*; Part 2: *Building the Capable and Accountable African State*, together with notes and references, and annexes. The full report can also be downloaded from this site. [17/07/05]

99   Teach Africa
http://www.teachafrica.net/
Maintained by Carmela Garritano at the University of St. Thomas, St. Paul, Minnesota, TeachAfrica is dedicated to the teaching of Africa and the African diaspora across the disciplines. It is a moderated, community-maintained digital repository of electronic resources related to African studies, available free-of-charge to registered users. Resources include books and teaching guides, online resources (each with a short description), downloads, photo and audio galleries, as well as information about conferences, symposia, festivals, fellowships, grants, and jobs. While nowhere near as comprehensive as some of the major African studies portals and mega sites listed elsewhere in this section, this is a useful and attractively presented resource. [02/06/05]

100   Yale Africa Guide Interactive
http://research.yale.edu/swahili/serve_pages/africa.php
From the ➔ **Yale Council of African Studies (1827)** and the Kamusi Project (*see also* ➔ entry **462**) this site offers almost 1,200 links, country or topic-specific and grouped under a range of broad subject headings such as business and industry, development and social action, education, African languages, nature and wildlife, news, arts, travel. Most links have a short description, together with an indication when first included, number of hits received, rating and votes, although a very large number of sites, despite many hits, have no "votes". An interesting feature is a kind of "league table", listing details of the top 10 rated sites (the Kenyan site Mwambao.com at http://www.mwambao.com/index.htm comes out streets ahead of anyone else.) Some sections of this resource are a bit patchy, but there is a good and quite extensive section on African languages and linguistics, including dictionaries and other language learning resources. [23/06/05]

ⓘ **This symbol indicates "The editor's choice" of a particularly outstanding online information resource.**

Databases, indexes, and thesauri

see also ➔ **Directories** (in this section)
- ➔ **4 Major biographical resources: Online**
- ➔ **6 Guides to statistical sources, economic and financial data**
- ➔ **23 Information and communication development in Africa: a guide to Web sites and resources: Digital libraries and digitization projects**

101   Aequatoria Book Bank Online (ABBOL)
http://www.abbol.com/
A project from the ➔ **Centre Aequatoria (1378)** in the Congo Democratic Republic that offers an electronic library from which Africanists, students, and scholars in sub-saharan Africa (and elsewhere) will be able to access full-text of important scholarly publications free of charge, and with an emphasis on materials in the human and social sciences. The Centre Aequatoria collection is especially rich in monographs and periodicals that have appeared during the 19th century and in the first half of the 20th century (up to 1960), some of which are becoming more and more difficulty to find in libraries across the world. The site currently offers full-text access to over 100 such monographs – and some published earlier, such as Leo Africanus's *Description of Timbuktu* (published in 1526) – together with full-text of a number of documents on colonial history, and some other resources. [23/06/05]

➔ **ASC Thesaurus for African Studies: Thesaurus of African Peoples** and ➔ **ASC Thesaurus for African Studies: Thesaurus of African Polities** *see* **14 Africanist documentation and African studies bibliography** entries **1894-1896**

102   Africabib
http://www.africabib.org/
Maintained by Davis Bullwinkle, Director of the Research Library at the Institute for Economic Advancement, University of Arkansas at Little Rock, this site provides free access to three African studies databases: (1) Africana Periodical Literature Bibliographic Database http://www.africabib.org/africa.html indexing over 50,000 articles from over 450 periodical titles; (2) African Women's Bibliographic Database, http://www.africabib.org/women.html, which contains over 30,000 citations from 1986 to the present, and (3) a bibliography on women travellers, explorers and missionaries to Africa http://www.africabib.org/book/title.htm, covering the period 1763 to 2004. There also links to a number of other databases. The Africana Periodical Literature Database is frequently updated and new journals are added regularly; a complete list of periodicals indexed is available on the site. Journal articles that are freely accessible online are accompanied by a note/link "See this Document". The database can be searched by geographical location, name of periodical (from a pre-set pull-down menu), broad subject groups, author, title, key word and year/year range, with sorting options by author, title, or year. However, the 'Subjects' search/browse facility is limited to choosing from 25 fairly broad based subject groups, and for some searches they tend to bring up far too many hits to be of much use. Moreover, "Literature" is strangely lumped together with "Mass Media and the Press" in the subject pull down menu, while "Bibliography/Research" seems

rather ambiguous, and "Miscellaneous (i.e. Demography, Refugees, Sports)" is a very odd heading. Searching (in free-text searching mode) by key word produces better results, although limited to a single search word. For example, a search with the two key words "refugees migration" will generate zero results, but entered on their own will result in a substantial number of hits for either regional or country-specific searches. There is no provision for Boolean searching at this time, but there are some helpful tips and FAQs for effective search strategies. Overall, Africabib is an impressive resource, but the search facilities and subject thesaurus would benefit from some further fine-tuning. [23/06/05]

103   Africa Collection for Transition (ACT)
http://www.certi.org/act/index.htm
Developed by the Payson Center for International Development and Technology Transfer at Tulane University, this digital library offers access to over 300 publications in English and French that relate to natural disasters and emergency management in sub-Saharan Africa, including areas such as conflicts and conflict resolution, migration and refugees, recovery and reconstruction, training, and communication. The overall goal of the project is to provide those active in the areas of international development and humanitarian assistance with access to information containing multidisciplinary insights and solutions. The materials can be browsed or searched by broad topic, title, publisher, organization, or keyword. [14/06/05]

104   African Feminist Studies: 1980-2002 ⓘ
http://www.gwsafrica.org/knowledge/index.html
Compiled by Desiree Lewis and edited by Barbara Boswell, this review essay is part of the African Gender Institute's (AGI, based at the University of Cape Town) "Strengthening Gender and Women's Studies for Africa's Transformation" project, an ongoing regional movement devoted to enhancing the intellectual quality and practical relevance of research and teaching on women and gender. The review essay is a sequel to Amina Mama's *Women's Studies and Studies of Women in Africa During the 1990s* (Dakar: CODESRIA, Working Paper series, 1996, 96 pp., out-of-print), which was the most comprehensive survey of African feminist scholarship at that time. This more recent essay presents a comprehensive overview of the rapidly expanding and now voluminous work on women and gender studies published in Africa and elsewhere. It is arranged by broad topics (each with further sub-divisions) covering Feminist Theory and Women's Movements in Africa; History and Social Transformation; Women, Politics and the State; Labour, Economy and Development; Women's Health, Religion and Education; Life History, Oral Narratives and Biographies; and Literary and Cultural Studies. This is followed by the Bibliography with full citations, including links to a small number of online articles. [25/07/05]

→ **African Online Digital Library** *see* **23 Information and communication development in Africa: a guide to Web sites and resources: Digital libraries and digitization projects** entry **2905**

→ **African Women's Bibliographic Database** *see* **Africabib (102)**

→ **Africa-Wide: NiPAD** [database] *see* **2 The major general reference tools: Bibliographies and guides to sources** entry **217**

105   The Anthropological Index of the Royal Anthropological Institute ⓘ
http://lucy.ukc.ac.uk/AIO.html
This index – freely accessible for educational and non-commercial purposes (including private study) – is based on the journal holdings of the Library of the Department of Ethnography at the Museum of Mankind, now → **British Museum Anthropology Library (1273)**. The library receives periodicals from around the world in all areas of cultural and social anthropology, ethnography, and material culture. The fully searchable index covers articles in all languages and provides English translations of citations from non-Roman scripts. Results of index searches can either be displayed online, or sent as an email message to the searcher's email address. Online help lines and lists of journals indexed are also available. New data is being added on a regular basis. During 2000 and early 2001 a retrospective conversion was undertaken which has added some 100,000 records going back to 1957. These were originally published on paper as vols. 1-22 of the *Anthropological Index*. [23/06/05]

106   Caribbean Studies, Black and Asian History (CASBAH)
http://www.casbah.ac.uk/
Developed by the → **Institute of Commonwealth Studies (1279)** and the → **National Archives (1282)** this is a pilot Web site for research resources relating to Caribbean studies and the history of Black and Asian peoples in the United Kingdom. The database contains information from a UK-wide sample of relevant archive, printed and audio-visual resources held in academic, public and special libraries and repositories. At this time (September 2005) the CASBAH database contains a demonstrator sample of about 400 records, including a substantial amount of data and resources relating to peoples of African origin. There are good search facilities, including subject and free-text search. [15/09/05]

107   Contemporary African Artists Database
http://arts-lib.library.cornell.edu:8080/aafweb/index.htm (site not currently available)
Financially supported by the → **Rockefeller Foundation (2743)** and directed by Salah Hassan at the History of Art Department at Cornell University, the aim of this ambitious project is to create a computerized database of contemporary African artists and generate a series of bio-bibliographic dictionaries (both online and in print format), all fully illustrated. It seeks to promote networking among African artists throughout the world and to encourage new initiatives in the collection, documentation and dissemination of contemporary African art. The database is classified by country and includes artists who have been working since the 1920's, in addition to important artists from earlier dates. Both database and printed volumes will also include sections on public and private art museums, galleries, archives, collections, art schools, and other resources relevant to each country. Artists who wish to be considered for inclusion in the database can submit a completed questionnaire (with a personal information and copyright release form) accessible at the site. At this time 462 records/images can be browsed/viewed or searched, but

the database would not appear to have been updated beyond May 2001. [site not available 25/11/05]

→ **Database of African Theses and Dissertations (DATAD)** *see* **203**

108   Deutscher Kolonialismus in Afrika/German Colonialism in Africa
DOK-line Afrika: Annotierte Online-Bibliographie 2004, no. 3 (15 August, 2004))
http://www.duei.de/dok/de/content/bibliographien/pdf/dok-line_afrika_2004_3.pdf [26/08/05]
A short online bibliography compiled by Anne Jansen (11 pp. pdf) of some 70 annotated entries, arranged geographically, and thereafter by date of publication. For each title library holdings in German libraries are indicated. The material is drawn from the database *Internationale Beziehungen und Länderkunde"* (IBLK)/*Specialized Information Network International Relations and Area Studies* (FIV-IBLK) freely accessible at http://www.ubka.uni-karlsruhe.de/hylib/iblk/.
Note: more online bibliographies in the → **Deutsches Übersee-Institut (1224)** DOK-line Afrika series are accessible at
http://www.duei.de/dok/show.php/de/content/bibliographien/bibliographien.html

109   Digital Africana Repositories Community (DARC) ⓘ
http://www.ascleiden.nl/Projects/Darc/ (DARC home page)
http://www.connecting-africa.net/ (Connecting Africa)
The DARC project is an innovative initiative of the → **African Studies Centre/ASC (1594, 1246)** in Leiden designed to make all Africanist research material and information in the Netherlands accessible through a community portal on the Internet. It aims to provide an integrated information service to answer all questions relating to Africanist research in the Netherlands, and takes over from the former Nuffic/Prism *Database of Africanists in the Netherlands,* discontinued in January 2003. The pilot service of the project (DARC-1), **Connecting-Africa,** was launched in April 2004, and provides access to African research information and materials produced in the Netherlands. The service offers information and full contact details about researchers on Africa at universities and research institutes in the Netherlands; details of organizational units of Dutch universities and research institutes where research on Africa is being undertaken; titles of published research on Africa in the Netherlands, with abstracts (where available) and links to the full-text of publications (where accessible). ASC researchers will submit digital materials to the repository of Leiden University Library in stages, and this new portal for African studies will eventually provide easy access to university repositories and other resources, including library catalogues and publishers' services. The DARC-2 project will run from September 2004 to March 2006. During this period, the pilot service will be extended with more functionality, full participation by four universities (Amsterdam, Groningen, Leiden and Wageningen), to provide a learning environment for the proposed Research Masters Programme in African Studies that is due to start in September 2005.
Note: For a PowerPoint demonstration of the project see
http://www.ascleiden.nl/Pdf/Darc/DARC-AEGIS-2005.ppt. [14/08/05]

110   Diplomacy Monitor [Africa] ⓘ
http://diplomacymonitor.com/stu/dm.nsf/regiond?openform&cat=Africa (Africa regional menu)
Diplomacy Monitor, hosted by the St. Thomas University School of Law in Miami, deploys specially developed proprietary software to monitor the document output of official government Web sites in near real-time. The system tracks hundreds of diplomacy-related Web sites around the clock. Covered sites include those of heads of state, foreign ministries, embassies, missions and consulates. Newly issued communiqués, official statements, press briefings, position papers and news releases related to diplomacy or international trade are identified and channelled into a synthesized information stream for scholars, diplomats, journalists, researchers, and students. Fully searchable, the database can be browsed by regions, issues, or other topics (e.g. human rights, commerce and trade), by nation (source) or nation (affected), including most African countries. Each result provides a link to the document on the originating server, and shows the date of document and date indexed, a link to the cached version, and computerized translation for documents in languages other than English. An outstanding resource. [14/08/05]

111   EVIVA. Virtuelle Fachbibliothek Ethnologie/Virtual Library of Social Anthropology ⓘ
http://www.evifa.de/cms/en/ (English version)
Hosted by the → **University Library, Humboldt University (1221)** in Berlin (and available in German and English versions) this virtual library of social anthropology offers a wide variety of anthropological and folkloristic information from a single source, including a substantial amount of Africa-related material. Supported by excellent search facilities, resource include inventories of special library/subject collections in Berlin and in Frankfurt/Main, a data bases of articles, access to e-journals (a substantial number with free access), and Ethno Guide, a catalogue of ethnological Web sites and resources, accessible, first, under a broad thematic groups and thereafter by numerous sub-sections as part a complex classification tree (*see* http://www.evifa.de/cms/uploads/media/Ethno-Guide-Systematik_01.pdf).   It currently (September 2005) contains almost 1,200 entries, and each link leads to a short description of the site or the resource, or the full record (in German). For articles a document delivery service is available (at a charge) via SUBITO. Aptly described by the hosts as "a kind of Ethno-Yahoo", this is an outstanding resource. [16/09/05]

112   Food Security and Food Policy Information Portal for Africa
http://www.aec.msu.edu/agecon/fs2/test/index.cfm
Hosted by the → **United Nations Economic Commission for Africa (2523)** Sustainable Development Division, in cooperation with African food security and policy networks and Michigan State University's Department of Agricultural Economics, this is the demo version (available in English, French and Portuguese) of what promises to become a major portal and directory for resources on food and agricultural security in Africa, and which aims to assist country/region-specific African food security and food policy researchers to find high quality Internet resources of data and information. Browse or search by topic, or by individual

African country. The site also has sections on building professional skills and developing IT know-how. [25/09/05]

113   Gallica. Voyages Afrique
http://gallica.bnf.fr/VoyagesEnAfrique/
A massive, attractively presented database from the ➔ **Bibliothèque nationale de France (1194)** relating to the history, exploration, slave trade, evangelization, and colonialization of Africa up to 1914. It draws on 900 volumes of text (most of it in French), including catalogues and bibliographies, historical studies, geographical accounts, books on the church and missionary activities, ethnology and anthropology, literature, and more, together with material from 20 periodicals. Also accessible are 80 maps, 6,500 photographs from the Société de Géographie, and 20 hours of audio. The database can be searched by authors, titles of books and other documents, key words, types of documents (books, periodicals, maps, photographs), by geographical regions, or by century/date of publication. [23/06/05]

114   Getty Thesaurus of Geographic Names
http://www.getty.edu/research/tools/vocabulary/tgn/index.html
Part of three vocabulary databases – the others are the *Art & Architecture Thesaurus* and the *Union List of Artist Names* – the Getty *Thesaurus of Geographic Names* is a structured vocabulary of about 1.3 million geographic names, including vernacular and historical names. Search search result brings up the place record with its geographical latitude and longitude, short notes for some, its hierarchical position, variant name spelling, and sources. A useful resource for finding African place names. [23/06/05]

➔ **H-Net Reviews/H-Africa Reviews** *see* **3 Current bibliographies, indexing and abstracting services, and review media** entry **409**

115   L'Institut du Monde Arabe/Arab World Institute [Database]
http://www.imarabe.org/perm/mondearabe/pays/index.html (Main home page)
http://www.imarabe.org/index-ang.html (English version)
The Arab World Institute is a foundation in France that seeks to raise the profile of Arab culture, and encourage cultural exchanges, communication and co-operation with the countries of the Arab world. In addition to links to IMA's Library (*see* **1205**), there is a calendar of events including cinema, music and theatre events, and a database offering links to individual country sections of the Arab world including those in Africa: Algeria, Djibouti, Egypt, Libya, Morocco, Mauritania, Somalia, Sudan, and Tunisia. Information provided for each country (last updated in January 2003) includes general overviews of the history, geography, economic development, and the educational sector in each country. A search facility is also available. [14/08/05]

116   International Network for Higher Education in Africa (INHEA)
http://www.bc.edu/bc_org/avp/soe/cihe/inhea/index.htm
Based at Boston College, the INHEA Network aims to strengthen and foster interest in African higher education through information sharing and to become a central forum for keeping track of information, up-to-date data, and relevant discussions in higher education in Africa. These pages, although still a little bit uneven in places,

provide a rich resource for the study of the current state of African higher education. It consists of: (1) An A-Z listing of links to organizations and institutions dedicated to higher education in Africa. Access can be alphabetically by name of organization or by country. (2) Details of upcoming conferences and workshops related to higher education in Africa. (3) A directory of experts and researchers active in scholarship and development work in the field of higher education in Africa, giving full name and email address, institutional affiliation, and geographical or thematic expertise. (4) Profiles and short overview essays on the state of higher education in countries across Africa, each providing a brief history of higher education in the country, with information on enrolment in universities, academic staff, governance and administration, private higher education, funding and resources, publishing and research, and gender issues. (5) A bibliography (no annotations) of works published on African higher education, including dissertations, published primarily in English since 1980. Access is by countries, regions, or themes and covers books, papers in collections, periodical articles, and doctoral dissertations. [14/08/05]

117   Literature and Culture of Francophone Africa and the Diaspora
http://dl.lib.brown.edu/francophone/
Compiled by library staff at the → **Rockefeller Library, Brown University (1301)**, this bilingual site features selected Internet resources on (primarily) francophone African and diasporic cultural expression. Select from a broad main menu divided into Cinema, Dance, Literature, Music, Theatre, Visual Arts, plus a section for socio-cultural context for journals and other resources whose focus "is the socio-cultural context in which such artistic creation occurs." Structured as a database each link/record is neatly presented indicating name, site type, language(s), region(s), together with a brief description of contents. Sophisticated search facilities are offered enabling users to conduct searches by region of interest, the type of Web site, the language used, as well as the specific features sought, such as audio clips, bibliographies, lyrics, photographs or scholarly articles. Last updated in March 2004. [23/10/05]

118   Partnership for African Higher Education
http://www.foundation-partnership.org/
Supported by four major US foundations, the Partnership for Higher Education in Africa is an initiative launched in May 2000, representing both a belief in the importance and viability of higher education in Africa and a mechanism to provide meaningful assistance to its renaissance. The Web site contains information about the Partnership, the full text of publications sponsored by the Partnership, as well as links to and resources to other sites. The resources section African Research Online, is a listing of Web sites with African content arranged in six categories: Biomedical and Health Sciences, Building Blocks for Online Teaching, Food Security, Multidisciplinary Resources, Resource Management and the Environment, and Social Sciences and Humanities. Each entry offers a short description. A further section, African Educational Resources, provides a variety of information on higher education in Africa, primarily in six countries — Ghana, Mozambique, Nigeria, South Africa, Tanzania, and Uganda. It includes African organizations, non-African international organizations with interests in African higher education, the home pages of ministries of education in Africa, as well as sites with information on relevant conferences and/or the full-text of papers that are hard to locate. [14/08/05]

119   Social Capital in African Studies
http://www.socialcapitalgateway.org/NV-eng-africa.htm
Edited by Fabio Sabatini of the Department of Public Economics at the University of
Rome "La Sapienza", this Web resource brings together a collection of some 80
papers, all available online, which have a common a focus on topics related to social
capital and development in Africa. Suggested readings are listed grouped under the
particular country they refer to. An initial section is devoted to "Essential readings",
followed by 23 country-by-country sections. Most papers are freely accessible, but a
few are subscription based and/or require login via Ingenta or Athens. [03/07/05]

→ **Source OECD** *see* **12 Major African studies library collections in Europe, North
America, and elsewhere outside Africa** entry **1210**

120   United Nations Cyber School Bus – InfoNation ⓘ
http://cyberschoolbus.un.org/
InfoNation, part of the → **United Nations (2529)** global teaching and learning project
(available in several languages), is an interactive database that allows you to view
and compare the most up-to-date statistical data for all the member states of the
United Nations. It was recently re-launched in a new version that introduced several
new features. First, you can now choose between a basic or advanced version of the
database. In the basic InfoNation you can choose up to six countries from an
alphabetical list of all countries. In the advanced version you can choose up to six
countries from 57 different country groupings arranged by geographic region,
membership in intergovernmental organizations, or socio-economic status. (First
time users should read the FAQ s for guidance on use of the database.) To conduct a
search, first you select country groupings from a pull-down menu, thereafter a
country (or countries), and then the data category. The InfoNation database is very
useful for quick factual information and statistics, whether it is area, languages
spoken, population figures, GDP, life expectancy, illiteracy rate, spending on
education, parliamentary seats (women/men), school enrolment, telephones,
television receivers, and much more. And you can compare the statistics from several
different countries at a time. Some pages contain dynamically-generated bar graphs
to illustrate the numeric data. This is one of the very best and most reliable resources
for accurate, up-to-date information, and the latest statistics regarding the countries
of Africa, and other nations of the world. [24/06/05]

121   United Nations Official Document System (ODS) ⓘ
http://documents.un.org/
The United Nations Official Document System (ODS) became open to the public on
31 December 2004, and contains a huge number of UN documents relating to Africa
and African countries. It covers all types of official UN documentation originating
from UN duty stations worldwide, including selective documents of UN regional
commissions. Comprehensive coverage starts in 1993. Older United Nations
documents are added to the system on a daily basis. Selective coverage of General
Assembly and Security Council documentation currently reaches back to 1985. The
ODS also provides access to the resolutions of the General Assembly, Security
Council, Economic and Social Council and the Trusteeship Council from 1946
onwards. It does not however contain press releases, UN sales publications, or

information brochures issued by the Department of Public Information. At this time (June 2005) there are approximately 800,000 files, and the UN intends to add about 100,000 year. The format is primarily PDF, but many can also be downloaded as Word files. A welcome screen currently offers you access in English, Arabic, Chinese, French, Russian, Spanish and German. Choose simple search or advanced search to search the database. The advanced search features a drop-down menu that offers various search options, including words in title of the document, subject, full-text search; search by release date, searching specific UN databases, and more. For example, a simple keyword search "Sierra Leone women" produced the maximum of 1,000 results, sorted by publication date. (Searches that generate over 1,000 results are limited to the first 1,000.) Result listings include publication date, document symbol, and title. Clicking on the document symbol will take you to a page where you can download the PDF or a Word file (in one of several languages) and get further information on the document, including full title, subject terms, and agenda items. A further search facility, "Global Search", was recently added; it is a new full-text search option that uses a different type of search engine than that used for simple or advanced search described above. This is an immensely rich database. [21/06/05] *Note:* a PowerPoint presentation, *Introduction to the ODS*, can be found at http://www.un.org/Depts/dhl/resguide/odsweb.ppt. It describes the types of material found in the database, demonstrates effective search methods for retrieving documents, explains the functionality of the "Advanced Search" screen, and shares essential search tips.

➔ **Virtual Library of Social Anthropology** *see* **EVIVA. Virtuelle Fachbibliothek Ethnologie (111)**

122   World Bank: Countries and Regions – Africa
Sub-Saharan Africa:
http://www.worldbank.org/afr
Middle East and North Africa:
http://web.worldbank.org/WBSITE/EXTERNAL/COUNTRIES/MENAEXT/
Presents a variety of resources on Africa, including links to ➔ **World Bank (2548)** special programs, projects, partnerships and regional initiatives in sub-Saharan Africa, World Bank documents, publications and databases, as well as news items. Browse or search by topics or sector, and/or by country. There is, for example, a useful sub-Saharan Africa Data Profile drawn from the **African Development Indicators 2005 (467)** database giving indicators (with definitions) for People, the Environment, Economy, Technology and Infrastructure, and Trade and Finance, for 1999, 2002 and 2003. There are also extensive sections on individual African countries. Separate pages are available for the Middle East and North Africa. [17/09/05].

123   World Bank Africa Region Database
http://www4.worldbank.org/afr/pubs/index.cfm
A database of publications written by Africa Region staff of the ➔ **World Bank (2548)**, designed to make the more informal publications of the region accessible to the public. Search the database by country or region, by World Bank sector topics, or enter a key word to search. This will search on the title and summary fields of the database for the key word or phrase entered. Work published by staff that receives a

Library of Congress number and a copyright is available through the World Bank bookstore or its international publications networks. [14/08/05]
Note: the complete list of WB publications on sub-Saharan Africa (in title order) and be found at http://publications.worldbank.org/ecommerce/catalog/category_3911.

ⓘ **This symbol indicates "The editor's choice" of a particularly outstanding online information resource.**

Guides to library, archival and manuscript collections, and sound archives

→ **Africa Focus: The Sights and Sounds of a Continent** [visual images and sounds database] *see* entry **10** in this section

124   Africana Microform Collections. University of California at Berkeley
http://www.lib.berkeley.edu/Collections/Africana/microform.html#ucb
The → **University of California-Berkeley Library (1333)** and the nearby Graduate Theological Union maintain sizable collections of important microfilm and microfiche editions of research materials in several fields of African studies, including missionary archives and US Department of State records relating to individual African countries. Descriptive information about the holdings includes a short summary for most items, details of size of collection, location and call number. [23/06/05]

125   African Activist Archives
http://www.africanactivist.msu.edu/directory.php
This is part of the →**Michigan State University African Studies Center's (1710)** African Activist Archive Project that seeks to preserve the record of activities of US organizations and individuals that supported African struggles for freedom, and which had a significant collective impact on US policy during the period 1960-1994. It focuses mainly on smaller local and regional organizations that supported the struggle against colonialism and white minority rule in Africa, especially in Angola, Guinea Bissau, Mozambique, Namibia, South Africa and Zimbabwe. The project aims to locate material produced by these organizations (including newsletters, pamphlets, leaflets, policy papers, meeting minutes, strategy papers, correspondence and visual material such as posters, buttons, photos, slideshows and videos) and preserve it by placing it in archives at depository institutions. A by-product is this database, the *Directory of African Activist Archives*, which aims to list all collections of individuals and organizations involved in the solidarity movement that are already in a depository institution or held by an individual. Each record in the directory gives location, time span covered, a summary of the records, type of media, catalogue/finding aids available, precise location of the material with full address details including email address, and Web sites where available. [26/07/05]

126   African Archives: Guides and Resources on the Web and in Print
http://www.bu.edu/library/instruction/africanarchives.html
One in a series of guides and tutorials from the → **Boston University African
Studies Library (1300)**. Describes guides and links to archives on the Web, archival
material in library collections, print guides and finding aids, and offers advice how to
use search engines to find archival material. [23/06/05]

127   African Presidential Archives and Research Center (APARC)
http://www.bu.edu/aparc/
The African Presidential Archives and Research Center at Boston University is a
unique approach to studying democratization and free market reform in Africa.
Through a residency program for former democratically elected African leaders and
access to their papers, and through access to present democratically elected leaders,
the Center provides a forum for them to share – and a venue for others to benefit
from – their insights and expertise. APARC focuses on thirteen African countries and
the past and present leaders of those countries, and a "Public Papers/Private
Conversations Project" will be the first step in the development of the archival work
of the Center. The intent of the project is to digitize the materials collected and
develop ways to make the information available to collaborating institutions and the
broader community. Access to archival material will become possible from this site
in due course, although (as at August 2005) none is available as yet. Meantime
resources currently available include a small links collection of information sources
on the thirteen African countries covered, and access to a number of addresses and
speeches by President Karl Auguste Offmann, former President of the Republic of
Mauritius; President Ruth Sando Perry, former interim President of the Republic of
Liberia; and President Kenneth Kaunda, first President of the Republic of Zambia.
[14/08/05]

→ **Africa Research Central** *see* **13 Major academic libraries and national archives in
Africa: Online guides and directories of African libraries** entry **1358**

→ **Afrique, une histoire sonore 1960-2000** *see* **2 The major general reference tools:
Guides to library collections and archival sources** entry **316**

**128   Der Bildbestand der Deutschen Kolonialgesellschaft in der Stadt- und
        Universitätsbibliothek Frankfurt am Main** ⓘ
http://www.stub.bildarchiv-dkg.uni-frankfurt.de/
A massive archive of some 57,000 pictures and photographs of the Deutsche
Kolonialgesellschaft (German Colonial Society) Library, which are now archived at
→ **Frankfurt University Library (1232)**. It covers material from countries (and
former German colonial territories) such as Burundi, Cameroon, Namibia, Rwanda,
Tanzania, and Togo. The database, currently still in a test phase, provides access to
about 50,000 photographs at this tine. Click on to small photos to view a larger
version. Search the database by keyword, region, subject areas, or people,
photographers, etc. Search results will then show a small image of each photograph,
together with a short description. An impressive database. *See also* entry **131**.
[23/06/05]

Note: An article about the project, "Preservation of the Photographic Archive of the German Colonial Society and Making it Accessible at the Stadt- und Universitätsbibliothek Frankfurt a.M.", by Irmtraud Wolcke-Renk, can be found at http://www.stub.bildarchiv-dkg.uni-frankfurt.de/dfg-projekt/bildprojekt/DFG-Projekt/aufsatz1e.htm.

129   British Library Sound Archives [Africa]
http://www.bl.uk/collections/sound-archive/nsa.html (Main home page and catalogue)
http://www.bl.uk/collections/sound-archive/archsoundrec.html (Archival Sound Recordings Project)
http://www.bl.uk/collections/sound-archive/asrtencollections.html (Initial collections)
The British Library Sound Archives catalogue includes entries for three-and-a-half million recordings held in the Sound Archive and is updated daily. It is one of the largest catalogues of its kind anywhere in the world, covering both published and unpublished recordings in all genres from pop, jazz, classical and world music, to oral history, drama and literature, dialect, language and wildlife sounds. Funded by the UK's Joint Information Systems Committee (JISC), its Archival Sound Recordings Project will make 4,000 hours of digitized audio freely available, and this will include unique, previously unpublished African field recordings and oral history material for the first time. Among nine audio collections which are currently (August 2005) being digitized are: (1) *D. Rycroft South Africa Recordings 1960s-70.* David Rycroft was a linguist and musicologist who worked in the 1960s and 1970s in South African towns documenting and recording daily life. (2) *Klaus Wachsmann Uganda Recordings 1949-54.* As curator of the Uganda Museum in Kampala, Klaus Wachsmann made many field recordings of traditional music in Uganda. (3) *African Writers Club.* This was a regular and popular programme on Africa broadcast by the ➜ **BBC World Service (853)** during the 1960s and 1970s. It covered current affairs, the arts and literature, as well as heritage programmes, and included writers and others reading from their own work and panel discussions. [21/08/05]

Guides, Collections and Ancillary Materials to African Archival Resources in the United States *see* ➜ **1 The major general reference tools: Guides to library collections and archival sources** entry **204**

130   The Henry M. Stanley Archives Inventory
http://www.africamuseum.be/publications/publications/StanleyArchives
From the ➜ **Musée Royal de l'Afrique Centrale/Royal Museum for Central Africa in Belgium (1183),** and supported by financial assistance from the King Baoudouin Foundation, this is an archival inventory devoted to exploratory expeditions in central Africa and the journeys and commissions of Henry Morton Stanley (1841-1904). Most of the material was originally held at Stanley's country estate in "Furze Hill" in Pirbright, Surrey, before being acquired by the Museum, which has also acquired related material from other sources over a period of years. The archival material was classified and inventorized by Peter Daerden and Maurits Wynants, and it is freely accessible as a 1.9MB pdf file of 426 pages. The main part of the archive, Part 1, cover Journals and Notebooks, Correspondence, Manuscripts, and Miscellanea, while Part 2 is devoted to the Welsh artist Dorothy Tennant –

Stanley's wife and biographer – including diaries and correspondence. Content is easily accessed through a detailed contents menu with links leading to various sub-sections. Brief annotations are included, and there is also an index of named persons, which can be keyword searched with the Adobe software. [16/07/05]

131   Katalog der Bibliothek der deutschen Kolonialgesellschaft in der Stadt-und Universitätsbibliothek Frankfurt a.M.
http://publikationen.ub.uni-frankfurt.de/volltexte/2005/507/pdf/band1.pdf
(vol. 1, 5,272KB)
http://publikationen.ub.uni-frankfurt.de/volltexte/2005/507/pdf/band2.pdf
(vol. 2, 5,599KB)
The massive catalogue of the Library of the German Colonial Society, here accessible as two large pdf files. Geographically, the area covered by the collection is Africa south of the Sahara; the subject matter covers all fields, with the exception of modern economics, law, medicine and the natural sciences. The present holdings are constantly being enlarged and form part of ➔ **Frankfurt University Library's (1232)** Sondersammelgebiet Afrika südlich der Sahara. The library now attempts to acquire as completely as possible all available research literature from Europe and North America, as well as material directly from Africa, and the Africa collection has grown to over 120,000 volumes. *See also* entry **128**. [23/06/05]

132   MUNDUS Gateway to Missionary Collections in the United Kingdom
http://www.mundus.ac.uk/
Missionary materials – for example archives, personal papers, books and pamphlets, published annual reports, missionary magazines, photographs, films, sound recordings and artefacts – are being increasingly used and appreciated by scholars from a variety of disciplines. Compiled by project staff at the ➔ **School of Oriental and African Studies (765)**, University of London, the Mundus Gateway is a Web-based guide to more than four hundred collections of overseas missionary materials held in over 40 institutions the United Kingdom. These materials document from an early date, in both written and visual form, the encounter between Western missionaries and the peoples and terrain of Africa, Asia, the Pacific Islands and the Americas. Each description provides content and contextual information, and details of finding aids and access conditions. [23/06/05]

133   National Union Catalogue of Manuscript Collections ⓘ
http://lcweb.loc.gov/coll/nucmc/
The NUCMC, or the National Union Catalog of Manuscript Collections, is a free-of-charge cooperative cataloguing programme operated by the ➔ **Library of Congress (1316)**. It can be an excellent starting off point for tracking down and locating archival holdings on Africa in US repositories. There are currently (June 2005) almost 1.4m bibliographic records available in the online database of the Research Libraries Group (RLG) Union Catalog, describing archival and manuscript collections and items in research libraries, museums, state archives, and historical societies located throughout North America and around the world. To start a search select Search the RLG Union Catalog and thereafter choose Easy Search Form (Wordlist). Access is via the LC WWW/Z39.50 Gateway http://www.loc.gov/z3950/gateway.html. Results are displayed with brief details, but a link "More on this record" leads to fuller

information, including title, description, subjects, and frequently quite extensive notes about the material, together with location details, and (where available) links to online access to collections of papers, archives, that can now be accessed on the Web. A splendid resource. [23/06/05]

Note: repositories of primary sources in Africa and the Near East can be found at http://www.uidaho.edu/special-collections/africa.html.

134   Répertoire de bibliothèques à Paris et en régions dont les fonds présentent un intérêt pour la recherche sur l'Afrique
Index des bibliothèques:
http://www.ehess.fr/centres/ceaf/pages/bibliotheque/index-bibl-alpha.html
Directory (pdf):
http://www.ehess.fr/centres/ceaf/pages/bibliotheque/repertoire-biblio.pdf
Compiled by library staff at the ➔ **Centre d'etudes africaines (1198)** in Paris, this is a directory of 64 libraries in Paris and elsewhere in France – large and small – that have some form of collections on Africa. It includes academic, institutional, public and special libraries, and those of a number of international organizations. Each entry gives full name and address, telephone and fax numbers, Web sites for some, information about access, opening hours, focus and size of collections (books, journals, maps, and other material), type of catalogue maintained, and availability of databases. [23/06/05]

135   South African Research and Archival Project (SARAP)
http://sarap.howard.edu/
The South African Research and Archival Project (SARAP), located on the campus of Howard University in Washington, DC, works closely with the ➔ **Moorland Spingarn Research Center (1312)**, also at Howard University, and has established relationships with other archives in the United States and in South Africa. It is a documentation project that identifies, inventorizes, and facilitates access to archival collections that demonstrate linkages between Americans and South Africans, principally African Americans, during the anti-apartheid movement. (The concept includes black South Africans in southern Africa generally). To date, SARAP has inventorized the following seven collections, which are now accessible at the Web site: (1) African National Congress United Nations Mission Records, (2) African National Congress Washington, DC Mission Records, (3) National Archives & Records Administration Records, (4) Pan Africanist Congress United Nations Mission Records, (5) Records of the House sub-Committee on Africa in the Charles C. Diggs papers; (6) materials in the southern Africa Support Project Collection, and (7) southern African References in the American Society of African Culture Collection. The table of contents for each collection has a link to scope and content notes specific to each collection, with an indication of their locations. [09/06/05]

136   West African Arabic Manuscript Database
http://www.arabic.uiuc.edu
Edited and maintained by editors at the College of Liberal Arts and Sciences University of Illinois at Urbana-Champaign, the West African Arabic Manuscript Database (formerly known as Arabic Manuscript Microfilm Project/AMMS, *see* http://test.atlas.uiuc.edu/amms/) is a bi-lingual finding aid for over 20,000 Arabic manuscripts from West Africa. The six collections in the database map across the

breadth of the West African Sahel and thus provide a representative cross-section of nineteenth-century literary activity in that region. The database provides easily searchable access to records of the literary activity of Muslim literati in the Sahel region during the approximately 150 years prior to colonial conquest. Records in the database and the search engine are available in both Latin and Arabic characters. Any computer that can view Arabic Web pages can use the Arabic search engine and view the Arabic version of the bi-lingual records. [14/08/05]

Guides to media and the press

See also → **10 News sources for Africa**
→ **11 The African press**

137   Africa South of the Sahara – African Newspapers/News (country)
http://www-sul.stanford.edu/depts/ssrg/africa/current2.html
Arranged by country and part of the Stanford → **Africa South of the Sahara – Selected Internet Resources (69)**, this is probably one of the most comprehensive collection of links to African newspapers, news sources, portals, directories and other reference resources on African media and the press, as well as subscription-based news services, each with a brief description. There is also a separate section, African Newspapers Holdings in the US, with information on African newspapers in print and microform held by US libraries [04/07/05]

→ **AFRINUL** *see* **The Cooperative African Newspapers Project/African Newspapers Union List (139)**

138   African Economics Journalism (AEJ) Online-African Media Directory
http://journ.ru.ac.za/economics/aej/media-a.htm
The African Economics Journalists Forum is a network of economics, business and financial journalists in Africa based at Rhodes University in Grahamstown, South Africa. Its Web pages include a good and generally fairly up-to-date directory of media in all the countries of Africa, including newspapers, radio and TV stations, and major magazines, each with basic address and contact details. The site also provides a directory of African chambers of commerce, stock markets, central banks, as well as links to other financial and economic sector information and resources. [08/08/05]

139   The Cooperative African Newspapers Project/African Newspapers Union List (AFRINUL)
http://www.crl.edu/areastudies/CAMP/afrinul.htm
A project to create an electronic database of holdings information for newspapers (all formats and all languages) published in sub-Saharan Africa. Initially this database, the African Newspapers Union List (AFRINUL), will consolidate holdings information for collections in North America, but will later expand to include holdings of libraries in Africa, Europe, and elsewhere. The project is sponsored by the → **Africana Librarians Council (1885)** of the → **African Studies Association (2755)**, and the → **Cooperative Africana Microform Project (1889)** of the → **Center**

for Research Libraries/CRL (1302). The complete Union List database will be accessible from this site in the near future. [04/07/05]
See also ➔ Electronic Newspapers of Africa — African Newspapers Union List Project (140)

140 Electronic Newspapers of Africa — African Newspapers Union List Project
http://www.columbia.edu/cu/lweb/indiv/africa/cuvl/newspapers.html
This list of online newspapers, maintained by Joseph Caruso at ➔ Columbia University's (1303) African Studies Library is part of a larger, on-going project – *see* ➔ The Cooperative African Newspapers Project/African Newspapers Union List/AFRINUL (139) – whose ultimate goal is the publication on the Internet of a union list of African newspapers held by research libraries in North America, Europe, and Africa. It presents, in alphabetical order, links to a large number of full electronic text newspapers published in sub-Saharan Africa that are available online without a subscription. For each entry it provides name of newspaper, place of publication, year first published online, together with notes about frequency and availability of back-issues/archives. The site is very frequently updated. [04/07/05]

141 International Journalists' Network (IJNet)
North Africa & Middle East:
http://www.ijnet.org/FE_Article/Region.asp?REgionID=788&UILang=1
Sub-Saharan Africa:
http://www.ijnet.org/FE_Article/Region.asp?REgionID=1&UILang=1
The International Journalists' Network (IJNet) is an online service for journalists, media managers, media assistance professionals, journalism trainers and educators, and anyone else with an interest in the state of the media around the world. The IJNet is hosted by the International Center for Journalists (ICFJ) in Washington, DC. Available in English, Spanish and Portuguese versions there are extensive regional sections devoted to North Africa and the Middle East, and sub-Saharan Africa, with sub-menus for individual countries. It is a rich source of information and for each country it offers media assistance news, a news archive of items of interest relating to media in the country, information about training for journalists, listings of media organizations and networks, media outlets (although coverage of newspapers is rather patchy and not always current), and a "Press overview" with links to information on the current media situation, the state of press freedom, and media laws prevalent in each country. [04/07/05]

142 The Kenya Indexing Project ⓘ
http://www.indexkenya.org
Financially supported by the ➔ Ford Foundation (2733), this is an online index of articles published in (at this time, August 2005) ten Nairobi-based Kenyan newspapers, providing full publication details for each item. As at August 18, 2005, the database contained 19,982 articles indexed from 1993 to 2002, but it will ultimately include details of all newspaper articles published since 1980. Full-text access to the articles is not provided, but hard copy versions of any article indexed can be ordered directly from the Kenya Indexing Project at modest cost (Email Info@IndexKenya.org for details of charges). The database is organized by broad subject categories that can be browsed, or searched by specific subject terms, title of

article, or author. Additionally, an extensive online thesaurus lists alphabetically all the terms that can be used to search the database. This is an excellent resource, and hopefully will be replicated for other African countries in the near future. [18/08/05]

143   Media Institute of Southern Africa
http://www.misa.org/ (Home page)
http://www.misa.org/africannews/sadcnewspapers.html (Links to SADC newspapers)
Based in Windhoek, Namibia, the ➔ **Media Institute of Southern Africa/MISA (2612)** is an NGO with members in 11 of the ➔ **Southern Africa Development Community/SADC (2518)** countries. Established in September 1992, MISA focuses primarily on the need to promote free, independent and pluralistic media, as envisaged in the 1991 Windhoek Declaration. Its Web pages offer media alerts, news items about the press and press freedom in southern Africa – including reports about arbitrary imprisonment, violence, and threats against journalists – together with a links section (with short descriptions) of major newspapers, radio and TV stations in the SADC region. There are also individual sections with information about MISA activities of member organizations. Additionally, the site offers free downloads of annuals reports, newsletters published by country offices, and the 5th edition of the very useful *Southern African Media Directory 2004/5*, which can be downloaded as a pdf file and which is also available in a print version (139 pp., 2004). [18/08/05]

144   Presse, Radio et Télévision en Afrique de l'Ouest
http://www.panos-ao.org/rubrique.php3?id_rubrique=46#
Developed and hosted by the ➔ **Institut Panos Afrique de l'Ouest /The Panos Institute West Africa (2601),** this is a valuable resource to track down media organizations in West Africa. Each entry provides basic contact information, email address, Web site (where available), and date founded. Browse or search by name of organization, type of media, nature of organization, country, or frequency of publication. Although a good number of entries consist of nothing more than a name, postal address, and telephone number, coverage is remarkably comprehensive, and even for small countries like, e.g. Sierra Leone, there are a very substantial number of links. In addition to daily newspapers, and radio and TV stations, this also includes weekly, monthly, and bi-monthly publications. A separate section on the Panos Web site is devoted to press agencies, media and journalist's organizations, which can be found at http://www.panos-ao.org/rubrique.php3?id_rubrique=103. [26/08/05]
Note: a print edition, **Répertoire des médias en Afrique de l'Ouest,** edited by Codou Bop (591 pp. 2004) is available from the ➔ **Institut Panos Afrique de l'Ouest /The Panos Institute West Africa (2601)**

145   Shayne, Mette African Newspapers Currently Received by American Libraries. Revised ed. Summer 1999. Evanston: Melville J. Herskovits Library of African Studies, Northwestern University, rev. ed. Summer 1999. 51 pp. print and online gratis
Online at http://www.crl.edu/areastudies/CAMP/newscurrent99.htm
A union list that aims to help researchers to locate African newspapers in US libraries. The list surveys the holdings of 19 libraries, and contains over 200 titles. Arrangement is by country of publication, with library location symbols indicated with each newspaper. Starting dates of holdings are indicated, as is frequency if

known. North African newspapers are not included. The list is current as at Summer 1999. It has not been updated since that time, but current listings of African newspaper holdings in the US will eventually become available through → **The Cooperative African Newspapers Project/African Newspapers Union List /AFRINUL (139)** [18/08/05]

146   WorldPress.org – Newspapers and Magazines, Africa
http://www.worldpress.org/newspapers/AFRICA/
Founded in 1997, Worldpress.org is a non-partisan magazine whose mission is to foster the international exchange of perspectives and information. It contains articles reprinted from the press outside the United States, as well as original material. The pages on Africa offers news stories, country profiles, factual information and maps for each African nation, as well as links to African newspapers and monthly or weekly magazines, with brief details about political orientation, etc. [07/07/05]

Guides to museums

147   Directory of Museum Professionals in Africa
http://www.africom.museum/directory.html [site not available 24/11/05]
Compiled by the → **International Council of African Museums/Conseil International des Musées Africains (2604)** this is an updated version and second edition of a directory first published (in print format only) in 1993. However, the online version was not accessible when last visited in November 2005.
Note: also available in a print version as *Directory of Museum Professionals in Africa*, edited by Lorna Abungu; Nairobi: AFRICOM [PO Box 38706 Ngara, Nairobi 00600], 2003. 206 pp. [Not examined]

148   West African Museums Programme (WAMP)
http://www.wamponline.org/ (home page, English and French versions)
http://www.wamponline.org/partners/newpart/partners.htm (Online directory)
Since its inception under the auspices of the International African Institute in 1982, the West African Museums Programme has actively worked towards promoting and strengthening museums in all parts of West Africa. WAMP works in association with 146 museums in the region, has an active publishing programme, and also maintains a documentation and information centre for museums and African cultural heritage. Its online directory of partner organizations is a good source for information about the activities of museums in West Africa. Click on to a country selection and then select "Choose a museum" in the pull-down menu in the left hand panel. The directory is regularly updated, and while information is incomplete for several museums, a full entry includes postal address, telephone and fax number, email address, type and status of the museum, dated founded, governing body, together with details of the museum's collections, publications, opening days and hours, admission fees, facilities and services, and contact information. [18/08/05]

Photographic images and objects databases and archives

➔ **Africa Focus: The Sights and Sounds of a Continent** [visual images and sounds database] *see* entry **10** in this section

149   Africa-Photo.com
http://www.africa-photo.com/
Hosted by the Essen-based Das Fotoarchiv GmbH, this site claims to be "the world's most comprehensive Africa photo file on the Web." Browse by 24 broad categories, each with a sub-menu of more specific topics. A basic search – resulting in thumbnail images – is free, but downloading and supply of high-resolution pictures is subject to registration and payment of a fee. [26/09/05]

150   Africa South of the Sahara: Contemporary/Historical Photographs
http://www-sul.stanford.edu/depts/ssrg/africa/photographs.html
Part of ➔ **Africa South of the Sahara – Selected Internet Resources (69)** this is a 22-page annotated listing of a wide variety of Web sites and resources for both contemporary and historical photographs on Africa, including collections of photographs on individual African countries, photo albums, Web sites of photographers, library collections and archival material, commercial vendors of photographs, photo libraries, and more. [26/09/05]

151   The Atlantic Slave Trade and Slave Life in the Americas: A Visual Record
http://hitchcock.itc.virginia.edu/Slavery/
A joint project of the Virginia Foundation of the Humanities and the Digital Media Lab at the ➔ **University of Virginia Library (1344)** and assembled by Jerome S. Handler and Michael L. Tuite Jr., this Web site tries to give a diasporic perspective on the life of enslaved Africans and their descendants in the New World. The thousand images in the collection, arranged under eighteen categories, have been selected from a wide range of sources, most of them dating from the period of slavery. The collection "is envisioned as a tool and a resource that can be used by teachers, researchers, students, and the general public–in brief, anyone interested in the experiences of Africans who were enslaved and transported to the Americas and the lives of their descendants in the slave societies of the New World." Select a category and then click on to the image, which brings up a larger image accompanied by information about the source together with a short description. Click on the image again to open a larger, full screen version in a new window. [05/08/05]

152   British Library Images Online [Africa]
http://www.imagesonline.bl.uk/britishlibrary/
This searchable database provides access to thousands of images from the ➔ **British Library's (1271)** collections, although, at this time at least (September 2005), it contains a relatively small number (about 200) of images relating to Africa. Content is primarily from the 19th century or earlier, and includes water colours and early maps. Browse with the assistance of a subject and title index, or search for specific topics. Search results lead to a thumbnail and larger images with a description, including record and shelfmark ID. A printable record is available for free, while

Low Resolution JPEG (5MB uncompressed) files can be ordered for downloading at a modest charge. [02/09/05]

→ **Eliot Elisofon Photographic Archives** *see* **Smithsonian Institution--National Museum of African Art (53)**

→ **Google Image Search** *see* **Using Google for African studies research: a guide to effective Web searching. Google's other search services: Google Image Search**

153   Images of Africa Photo Library
http://www.imagesofafrica.co.za/
This database is maintained by an associate company of the → **New Holland/Struik (2099)** publishing group, the leading illustrated book publisher in southern Africa, and offers over 40,000 unique African images, all available to view on this Web site. Categories include concepts, flora, food, people and culture, travel and locations, ethnic, marine and wildlife. You can browse and search the images database, but to view the detail and larger version of each image you must be registered and logged in. Registration is free. [20/07/05]

154   Internet Mission Photography Archive
http://www.usc.edu/isd/archives/arc/digarchives/mission/
The photographs in this searchable digital archive come from Protestant and Catholic missionary collections held at a number of centres in Europe and North America. The pictures record missionary endeavours and document indigenous peoples' responses to Christian missions and the history of indigenous churches, as well as offering views of landscape, cites and towns, for the period between the mid-19th to mid-20th centuries. The photographs relating to Africa (at this time from Ghana, Madagascar, Nigeria, Sierra Leone, Tanzania, Zambia and Zimbabwe) come from the archives of the Moravian Church (Die Herrnhuter Brüdergemeine), the Leipzig Mission (Evangelisch-Lutherisches Missionswerk), and the Norwegian Missionary Society, as well as from holdings deposited at the → **School of Oriental and African Studies, University of London (1289)**. A search facility provides two methods for searching, which can be used independently or in combination. Drop-down menus are provided for searching or limiting by a specific repository or geographic region. A customized image viewer is provided to enable readers to adjust the size of the viewing window, zoom in on the image, navigate within an image, or jump anywhere on a page. [26/06/05]

→ Pinfold, J., Barringer, T., and C. Holden (eds). **Images of Africa: The Pictorial Record. Papers presented at the SCOLMA Conference, London, 9-10 June 1994** *see* **15 Africanist documentation and African studies bibliography** entry **1913**.

155   Posters from the Melville J. Herskovits Library of African Studies
http://www.library.northwestern.edu/africana/collections/posters/index.html
The → **Melville J. Herskovits Library of African Studies (1322)** at Northwestern University is the largest separate Africana collection in the world, and among its rich resources are over 4,000 posters reflecting contemporary African history and culture. A total of 365 of these posters have been digitized to date to be viewed on this site. The posters generally represent three themes: the 1970's liberation movements in the

former Portuguese colonies; the Anti-Apartheid groups flourishing outside of South Africa in the 1970's and 1980's; and political campaign posters from the historic South African election of 1994. You can search by key words or wildcard character, or browse posters by date, by title, or by topic/theme. [22/07/05]

156   James J.R. Ross Library-African Objects Database
http://www.whirl-i-gig.com/vogel/format_samples.html (format samples only as at August 2005)
Intended to become a comprehensive database of the illustrations of figurative African objects published between 1800 and 1920 contained in the James J. Ross Library. Over 2,500 images have been catalogued thus far and, when completed, the database will include a total of about 4,500 individual records. Each record will provide information on the object images and/or its context (ethnic/style name and short description), publication and illustration details, style and location, original caption and text, original or later collections, location (if not in the Ross collection), and more, and the database will be supported by a powerful search function. The Web site is expected to go live late in 2005. [18/08/05]

157   Royal Commonwealth Society Photograph Project
http://www.lib.cam.ac.uk/rcs_photo_project/homepage.html
Maintained at ➔ **Cambridge University Library (1287)**, the Royal Commonwealth Society Photograph Project contains over 70,000 images from throughout the world, including all the countries of Africa that are part of the Commonwealth. Dating from the mid-1850s to the mid-1980s, the photographs provide insight into the history of the Commonwealth, documenting developments in a wide variety of fields, including trade, industry, agriculture, mining, immigration, education, health, and family life and recreation. The online part of the collection, which is supported by links to related Web sites and publications, will eventually contain almost 700 digitized images. A photographer's index is also provided, intended to record the majority of professional and amateur photographers whose work is represented in the collection. Permission to download single copies of images and photographs from this rich collection is given free of charge, without agreement and without license or royalty fee, provided it is strictly for private study and research, and provided due acknowledgement is made to the copyright holders of the materials. [18/08/05]

158   USAID in Africa: Photo Gallery
http://www.dec.org/partners/afr/photogallery/
This is a growing collection of photos taken by ➔ **USAID (2623)** staff and development partners consisting of African "daily life scenes" and photographs reflecting some of USAID's work and activities in Africa. There are currently some 500 images available, which may be downloaded for non-commercial and educational purposes only and must include proper attribution to USAID and the photographer's name. Some pictures are also available in high resolutions suitable for print publications. The gallery can be searched by keywords, country, or sector, and the home page provides links to the most recently added photos. [18/09/05]

159   The Winterton Collection of East African Photographs: 1860-1960 ⓘ
http://www.library.northwestern.edu/africana/winterton/index.html
The ➔ **Melville J. Herskovits Library of African Studies (1322)** at Northwestern
University acquired the Humphrey Winterton Collection of East African
photographs in December 2002. It comprises about 6,500 photographs organized in
75 separate albums, scrapbooks or loose collections and taken primarily in East
Africa between about 1860 and 1960. Assembled by the British collector Humphrey
Winterton over about 30 years, the collection depicts and documents African life,
European life in Africa in all its manifestations, and the African landscape, in
particular as it changed over time. The Web site provides access to the collection's
inventory (in pdf format), together with a sample of (currently) 101 images from the
collection. Plans for the future include digitization of many of the images and
making them available in addition to what is already here. To view albums, click one
of the thumbnail images in the frame to the left; the image will open in this frame for
viewing (as zoomable images). Photographs of this nature have always been an
integral part for the study of Africa, and this is a valuable and fascinating resource.
[18/08/05/]

Directories

See also ➔ **Directories of African studies scholars**

160   African and International Women Organisations
http://www.wougnet.org/Links/africa_int.html
Compiled by the Women of Uganda Network (WOUGNET), this is a useful and
constantly expanding collection of links to African (and some international) women's
organizations and networks, each with a short description of the organization's
objectives, nature of activities, etc. [19/06/05]

161   African Higher Education Resource Directory ⓘ
http://africa.msu.edu/AUP/
This Web resource is a collaborative project of the ➔ **African Studies Center at
Michigan State University (1710)**, the ➔**Association of African Universities (2580)**,
and the ➔ **African Studies Association (2755)**. The site is designed to support higher
education in Africa and all the faculty, administrators, and foreign partners working
to sustain and renew it. It seeks to make African tertiary institutions more readily
accessible to their African partners and others seeking to link or partner with
them. Its main component is a Directory of African Higher Education Institutions,
which can be searched by country or region, institution name, and field of study.
While information provided is fairly basic for some small institutions such as
colleges of education, it can be very full for universities, including not only full
address details, telephone and fax numbers, email address, and Web site (where
available), but also information on staff size, student population, library size, and
more. The site also has links to many African organizations and associations, relevant
non-governmental organizations, projects and programmes, conferences and

seminars, databases, and Web directories. This directory is an excellent starting off point to track down contact information on tertiary institutions in Africa. [19/08/05]

→ **The African Publishing Companion. A Resource Guide** *see* **2 The major general reference tools: Directories of publishers and the media** entry **259**

162 African Scientific Societies and Associations
http://www.aaas.org/international/africa/soclist.shtml
This 18-page directory was compiled primarily by means of a survey conducted in 1997 and 1998 by the → **American Association for the Advancement of Science Africa Program (2575)**, and supplemented by information drawn from the 6th edition of the *World Guide to Scientific Associations and Learned Societies* (1994, Michael Zils, ed.). It is not claimed to be comprehensive "although efforts are being made to update the list as new information becomes available." However there is no indication on the site when it was last updated. Societies are listed in country order, giving full postal address details, telephone and fax numbers for the majority of them, and contacts and email addresses for some of them. The directory can also be browsed by discipline, and there is a section on regional and Pan-African societies. [24/06/05]

163 Directory of Book Donation Programs
http://www.albany.edu/~dlafonde/Global/bookdonation.htm
Based on a 1992 directory compiled by Gretchen Walsh and the Book Famine Task Force of the → **African Studies Association (2755)**, and recently updated and revised by Deborah M. LaFond for the → **Africana Librarians Council's (1885)** Book Donation Committee (*see also* http://www.loc.gov/rr/amed/afs/alc/bkdncte.html), this is an annotated listing of book donation programs active in Africa, primarily those in the US. It provides a brief description of each organization's range of activities, full address details including Web site, and contact personnel. An introductory section sets out guidelines for good practice in book donation projects and offers some suggestions for both recipients and donors. The directory is regularly updated, most recently in September 2004. [24/06/05]

164 Directory of Development Organizations: Africa - Afrique - África ⓘ
http://www.devdir.org/index.html (Main site)
http://www.devdir.org/africa.htm (Africa pages)
Created and maintained by Bert Wesselink and currently in its 5th edition 2005, this freely downloadable and searchable directory of 43,500 development organizations has been prepared to facilitate international cooperation and knowledge sharing in development work, both among civil society organizations, research institutions, governments and the private sector. It covers (1) international organizations; (2) government ministries, government institutions, planning agencies; (3) private sector support organizations; (4) finance institutions; (5) training and research organizations; (6) civil society organization, including development foundations and associations, membership development organizations, development programmes and projects, etc.; (7) development consulting firms, (8) information providers (such as development newsletters/journals, development publishers, Web resources, databases); and (9) grant makers, including fundraising, charity and philanthropic

organizations. Browse by individual countries or download the complete regional database in two pdf files: Africa I.A (A-L 5.6MB,385 pp.), Africa I.B (M-Z, 7.7MB, 521 pp.). Alternatively access or download individual country files. Within country files each entry gives full postal and physical address, telephone and fax numbers, email address and Web site (where available), and a classification in one of nine categories above. Frequently updated and also accessible in French and Spanish versions, this is a most impressive resource, containing over 13,500 entries for the countries in Africa, and providing Web links to over 8,000 of them.. [24/07/05]

165   Directory of Peace Studies in Africa 2004
http://www.africa.upeace.org/documents/dpsa2004.pdf
Compiled by the UPEACE Africa Programme and the African Centre for the Constructive Resolution of Disputes (ACCORD), this valuable directory (60 pp. in pdf format) and database is the result of a continent-wide survey – conducted during 2002 and 2003 – targeting established institutions in Africa, and intended to solicit feedback from participating institutions on existing programmes in the field of peace studies in terms of teaching, research and community service. The database offers information on 121 departments in 109 institutions, in 34 African countries. Many entries are very full: in addition to complete address details, telephone/fax numbers, email, and Web site (where available), details include information about peace-related themes in general courses, or specific peace-related modules offered as part of training programmes, certificates/diplomas awarded, and current research and community service activities. [24/07/05].

→ **INASP Directory** (print/online) *see* **2 The major general reference tools: Directories of organizations and institutions** entry **264**

166   PACA Directory. A Directory of African Artists, Africanist Scholars, Some
         Art Enthusiasts and Institutions
http://www.panafricanartists.org/directory/
Compiled by the Pan-African Circle of Artists – currently based in Enugu, Nigeria – this is a useful directory of artists living and working in Africa, although it lacks adequate introductory matter setting out how the database was compiled (most entries are apparently based on self-submissions), the scope and criteria for inclusion, and currency of the information that is provided here. It consists of two principal sections, the African Artists Directory, browsable in an A-Z format by name, with each entry giving date of birth of the artist, area of activity/specialization (i.e. painting, sculpture, textile design, ceramics, graphic design, etc.), full address (including email addresses for a substantial number of entries), details of exhibitions held, and membership of professional associations. The second section is an extensive A-Z listing entitled Useful Contacts, giving name, postal address and email addresses for some. It is something of a mixed bag and includes African art collectors, art scholars, cultural and fine art institutions and centres, museums, associations, and more. There is also a search facility. [14/08/05]

167   Programme for Development Research -- PRODDER Directory ⓘ
http://www.prodder.org.za/index.php
Originally published in print format by the ➔ **Human Sciences Research Council
(1858)** between 1987 and 2001, PRODDER is a well-established reference tool on
southern African development. This new online version, now hosted by ➔ **Sangonet
(2879)**, includes all the original entries from the last published *PRODDER Directory*
plus a considerable number of new organizations. Although the majority of
organizations listed are NGOs (and, at this time at least, primarily in South Africa),
the directory is not exclusively for such organizations. Other development
organizations included are parastatals, community based organizations, bilateral and
multilateral agencies, embassies, government bodies, as well as foundations and
trusts. Browse alphabetically, or search by name, type of organization, or programme
areas and nature of activities. Each entry provides full address details, email, Web
site (where available), date founded, key personnel and other contact details, type of
organization, geographical areas served, programme areas, together with a mission
statement. Organizations can update their details online, while thus far unlisted
organizations are given the opportunity to add their details. A superb resource.
[01/09/05]

Sources for e-books

168   ACLS History E-Book project (HEB) – Africa (Subscription based)
http://www.historyebook.org/
For details about pricing, licenses, and subscriptions see
http://www.historyebook.org/pricingsubscriptions.html
A project of the American Council of Learned Societies, with the collaboration of
working groups from several ACLS learned societies and generously funded by the
➔**Andrew W. Mellon Foundation (2739)**, the History E-book project was launched
in September 2002 and currently (August 2005) brings together 1,000 books of high
quality in the field of history, accessible through institutional and individual
subscription. Titles for this ever-expanding and fully searchable collection of out-of-
print and in-print books were selected for their continued importance to historical
studies, both for research and teaching purposes. The project plans to add about 250
books annually to the collection, and a range of completely electronic titles will also
be added shortly. Two ACLS constituent learned societies, the Association for Asian
Studies and the ➔ **African Studies Association (2755)** have joined the History E-
Book Project and plan to add 200 significant titles during the course of 2005-2006. At
this time (August 2005), 37 African history titles are available and include works by,
among others, J.F.Ade Ajayi, Kartin Barber, Edna Bay, Basil Davidson, Kwame Yeboa
Daaku, Kenneth Dike, Thomas Hodgkin, John O. Hunwick, John Iliffe, Martin Klein,
Robin Law, Phyllis Martin, Valentin Y. Mudimbe, Bethwell Ogot, J.D.Y. Peel, George
Shepperson, and Charles van Onselen. Currently e-books are accessible to students
and scholars through subscribing libraries and through their learned societies, but
individual subscriptions are now available (or will shortly become available) for a
small additional fee through membership to the American Historical Association and
other participating learned societies of the ACLS History E-Book Project. Institutional
subscription rates range from $350 to $2,000 annually, depending on size of

institution, or size of population served by subscribing public libraries and public library systems. MARC records with 856 fields are available free to subscribers. [19/08/05]

169   Africana Digitization Project
http://libtext.library.wisc.edu/Africana/
Developed by the Digital Content Group at the ➔ **University of Wisconsin-Madison Libraries (1345)**, this is a project that aims to digitize rare, elusive, and out-of-print Africana materials and make them available in electronic format. At this time (June 2005) the project offers access to four titles translated, privately produced and circulated in very small quantities by the late Paul Hair, namely two titles by Andre Alvares de Almada, *Brief Treatise on the Rivers of Guinea*, (c. 1594), and *Ethiopia Minor and a Geographical Account of the Province of Sierra Leone; Jesuit Documents on the Guinea of Cape Verde and the Cape Verde Islands, 1585-1617*; and Barbot's West *African Vocabularies of c. 1680*. The other titles are J.D. Fage's ➔**A Guide to Original Sources for Precolonial Western Africa Published in European Languages (222)** (1994), Adam Jones's *Raw, Medium, Well done: a critical review of editorial and quasi-editorial work on pre-1885 European sources for sub-Saharan Africa, 1960-1986* (1987), and *Africans in Bondage: studies in slavery and the slave trade: essays in honor of Philip D. Curtin on the occasion of the twenty-fifth anniversary of African Studies at the University of Wisconsin*, edited by Paul E. Lovejoy (1986). Browse individual titles, or search text of an entire work, section titles, or search within a specific title. [25/06/05]

➔ **African Language Materials Archive (ALMA)** *see* **5 Guides and resources for African languages** entry **452**

170   Digital Book Index
http://www.digitalbookindex.com/index.htm
There are several general resources that can help you track down availability of digital books. The Digital Book Index is one of the best databases and provides access to more than 105,000 English language title records of e-books in various formats, commercial and non-commercial, from more than 1,800 publishers and public archives. Roughly a third of the titles are available in full-text format at no charge, while the rest are fee-based. The database includes a growing number of titles on African studies (e.g. African history, travel, and exploration) and a very large number of African-American titles. Use of the site is free, but requires registration. Search by author, title or title keywords, or browse by a detailed list of subjects, or by publishers' list. [25/06/05]

171   Ebooks.com
http://www.ebooks.com/ (Main site)
http://usa2.ebooks.com/subjects/browse.asp?SID=581 (History: Africa pages)
Ebooks.com offers a small selection of titles on African studies and almost 100 on African history, *at a charge*. This covers both titles by contemporary authors (including some out-of-print titles from Indiana University Press, Routledge, Cambridge University Press, and Frank Cass now available again in electronic formats), and those no longer living (e.g. early travel books by David Livingstone and Henry Stanley). There are also a small number of titles of African literary

criticism. Search by broad subjects, author or title. Results displayed show a cover image of the book, publisher, price, and a short description. [25/06/05]

172   Project Gutenberg

http://promo.net/pg/

First conceived in 1971 and the brainchild of Michael Hart, Project Gutenberg's mission and philosophy is to make freely available electronic texts of classic books after they have entered the public domain. (This is currently 50 years after the death of the author, and which at this time roughly means books published before 1940, although public domain copyright conventions can vary from country to county, and some Project Gutenberg e-texts have some restrictions about distribution.) It now offers access to some 16,000 books in the Project Gutenberg Electronic Public Library, covering both fiction and non-fiction, and which can be downloaded as compressed files at no charge. An average of one new e-text is published every day. The e-text files are not actually kept at the Gutenberg Web site, but at many FTP sites throughout the world that hold the whole Project Gutenberg archive of texts, and more details about these can be found on the Web site. Titles of interest to Africanists currently available include early travel accounts such as John Hanning Speke's *Discovery of the Source of the Nile*, Sir Samuel White Baker's *The Albert N'Yanza. Great Basin of the Nile*, David Livingstone's *Missionary Travels and Researches in South Africa*, and classics of African writing such as Sol Plaatje's *Native Life in South Africa* or Olive Schreiner's *The Story of an African Farm*. Browse or search by author, title key words, subject, language, or Library of Congress class, with the support of some advanced search facilities. [25/06/05]

173   University of California Press e-Scholarship Editions [African Studies]

http://escholarship.cdlib.org/ucpress/

The University of California Press e-Scholarship Editions are made available through a California Digital Library purchase from NetLibrary of 1,400 electronic book files on behalf of the UC community. Over 350 of the titles, many of which are out of print, are freely available to the public; the rest are for University of California faculty, staff, and students only. Titles are being released in stages and about a third of them are University of California Press books, covering a wide range of topics in the humanities, social sciences, and sciences. In the African studies field, e-Scholarship Editions currently (June 2005) offers 47 titles, plus 17 on African history, and titles in some other disciplines are also likely to be of interest, for example 120 titles on cultural anthropology, or 35 in postcolonial studies. Search, or browse by subject, author or title, and then access full-text contents, on a chapter-by-chapter basis and also including prelim matter and the documentary apparatus for each book. An added valuable feature is the fact that each title can be individually searched. [25/06/05]

174   University of Virginia Electronic Text Center

http://etext.lib.virginia.edu/

A very substantial number of publicly available e-books can be accessed from the ➜ **University of Virginia Library (1344)** Etext Center, including classic British and American fiction, major authors, American history, and more. While there are no African studies titles here at this time, there are a substantial number of e-books by or about African Americans, including classic books by Frederick Douglass, W.E. du Bois, Harriet Beecher Stowe, and Booker T. Washington, and which can be found at http://etext.lib.virginia.edu/subjects/African-American.html. Browse by author or by subject. Many of the titles in the Modern English Collection are now also available as e-books for the Microsoft Reader. [27/06/05]

Directories of African studies scholars

See also (for print resources) ➔ **2 The major general reference tools: Directories of research and teaching, and of Africanist scholars**

175   Africanists in the Nordic Countries ⓘ
http://www.nai.uu.se/africanists/africanistseng.html
Maintained by the ➔ **Nordic Africa Institute (1611)** in Uppsala, this is a register and database containing details about 270 researchers in the Nordic countries with an advanced university degree in the social sciences or humanities engaged in research on Africa and "whose work is clearly, although not exclusively focused on Africa or relevant to Africa." Browse or search by name, institution, thematic or geographical key word(s). In addition to postal and email address details – and with hyperlinks to universities or university departments – information provided is very full and includes a profile of research activity, research interests, fieldwork, and publications. This is well organized database of the highest quality. [27/06/05]

176   African Studies Association of Australasia and the Pacific–Membership list
http://www.ssn.flinders.edu.au/global/afsaap/
A partial listing of members of the ➔**African Studies Association of Australasia and the Pacific (2754)** providing details of institutional affiliations (but no postal addresses), email address, and research interests. [27/06/05]
Note: the online *Directory of Africanists in Australia and the Pacific*, listed as entry 94 in the previous edition of the *African Studies* Companion, has been reissued in a 6th edition, but would not appear to be available online any longer; *see* ➔ entry **269**)

**177   Afrika-studies in België, Sociale en Humane Wetenschappen/
          Etudes africaines en Belgique, Sciences Sociales et Humaines**
http://home.scarlet.be/~hv980630/afrika-studies_in_Belgie.htm or
http://home.scarlet.be/~hv980630/etudes_africaines_en_belgique.htm
Hosted by the ➔ **Belgische Vereniging van Afrikanisten (2768)** these pages provide links to the principal institutions and university departments involved in research and teaching in African studies in Belgium. [15/08/05]

178   Canadian Association of African Studies – List of members
http://caas.concordia.ca/htm/list.htm
An 23-page A-Z listing of current (2005-2006) members of the ➔ **Canadian Association for African Studies/Association Candienne des Etudes Africaines (2769)**, each entry giving full name and address, telephone, email, and areas of expertise and research interests. [25/08/05]

179   Canadian Council of Area Studies Learned Societies/Conseil canadien
       des sociétés savantes d'études régionales--Specialist Directory: Africa
http://ccasls.concordia.ca/sd/contactsByArea.htm#Africa
A recently launched initiative taken by the Canadian Council of Area Studies
Learned Societies (CCASLS) to compile an electronic list of scholars from across
Canada with an expertise in one of its affiliated areas of study. The directory can be
viewed by area of interest, covering Africa, Asia, Latin American and the Middle
East. Alternatively names can be found listed by province in Canada. The amount of
information provided for each entry is a little bit patchy at this time, but a full entry
gives name, institutional affiliation, telephone/fax numbers, email, an indication of
research interests, and select recent publications. For Africa it currently (October
2005) lists 78 entries. [28/10/05]

→ Connecting-Africa [Database of Africanist research in the Netherlands]
see Digital Africana Repositories Community (109)

180   Directório de Investigadores Pesquisando sobre os Palop/
       Lusophone Africa Researchers Directory
http://www.cea.iscte.pt/Directorio_PALOP.htm
Compiled by → Centro de Estudos Africanos (1600) in Lisbon, this is a useful, albeit
agonizingly slow loading directory of African studies scholars with special interests
in lusophone Africa. Search the directory by researcher's nationalities and continents
(Africa, North and South America, and Europe), or by special geography/country
interests in Angola, Cabo Verde, Guinea-Bissau, Mozambique, or São Tomé e
Principe. For each scholar listed it provides, name, academic degree, areas of research
and country focus, and email addresses for most. [02/06/05]

181   International Directory of African Studies Scholars (IDASS) ⓘ
http://www.columbia.edu/cu/lweb/indiv/africa/cuvl/directory.html
Maintained by Joe Caruso at → Columbia University Lehman Library (1303), this is
an online, regularly updated and constantly expanded international directory of
individuals involved in African studies. Entries are submitted by the persons listed
(and can be in English or French), and give details of name and address, title,
affiliation, telephone and fax numbers, email, Web pages for some, and a submission
date. Most entries also include a short statement of current activities of each scholar,
teaching and/or research interests, and a list of publications. The Directory is fully
indexed allowing searches by name or keywords (for example subject/research
interests, city or country, university affiliation, etc.). Alternatively, it can be browsed
in its entirety, alphabetically by name. A fine resource, although entries in this
database are still fairly heavily US-dominated. [25/06/05]

182   Mande Studies Association-Membership Directory 2004
http://uweb.txstate.edu/anthropology/mansa/mansa_membership_directory.htm
Covers members of the → Mande Studies Association (2774) worldwide – with
academic or professional interest in the Mande region of West Africa – giving full
address details, and email addresses for most. [19/11/05]

183   Scotland Africa. Directory of Expertise on Africa in Scottish Universities
http://www.ed.ac.uk/~direct/menu.htm
Compiled by the → Centre of African Studies, University of Edinburgh (1617), this
directory contains entries for over 230 people in universities across Scotland with
African expertise; it is searchable by name, university, country of expertise, or field of
expertise. An introductory overview of institutional activity on Africa at nine Scottish
universities sets the scene for the main alphabetical listing. However, the directory
was apparently last updated in June 1997, and some entries may no longer be
current. [25/06/05]

Online teaching guides and overviews of current African studies research

See also → 2 The major general reference tools: Directories and guides to
research and teaching, and of Africanist scholars (in print format)

184   Africa Forum
http://www.h-net.org/~africa/africaforum/index.html
Africa Forum is a regular → H-Africa (2810) column that features essays by, and
interviews with, notable Africanists around the world. It encourages contributions
both from veteran and younger Africanist scholars in any field of African studies. It
also includes useful (albeit a number of them now somewhat dated) overview essays
on the state of African studies research and teaching in different parts of the world,
including *African Studies in Africa: Quo Vadis?* (1998), *African Studies in Australasia*
(1998), *African Studies in Russia* (2001), *African Studies in the West Indies* (2001), *African
Studies in the Netherlands: a Brief Survey* (2001), *African Studies in Japan* (2001), and
African Studies in France (2001, in English and French). [19/08/05]

185   Forum: Teaching Africa in History: Issues and Approaches
http://worldhistoryconnected.press.uiuc.edu/2.1/
Published by *World History Connected* http://www.worldhistoryconnected.org this is
a special issue (vol. 2, no. 1, November 2004, freely accessible), containing several
articles on various issues as they relate to teaching African history, e.g. "Reading
Africa: An Interdisciplinary Approach to Teaching World History" by Dixie Grupe
and Jill Taylor Varns, "Connecting African History to the Major Themes of World
History" by Candice Goucher, and "Teaching about the African Past in the Context
of World History" by R. Hunt Davies. Additionally there are a couple of resource
listings "Suggested Readings in African History for Non-Specialists: An Annotated
List" by David Northrup, and →"Creating Africa: A Brief Tour of European
Cartography of Africa" by Jonathan T. Reynolds (*see* separate entry, 502) [30/ 09/05]

186   "Perspectives of African Studies." Special issue of *Afrika Spectrum*, vol. 40,
2005, issue 3
http://www.duei.de/iak/shop/afrika_spectrum.php
This special issue of → Afrika Spectrum (699) focuses on current issues relating to
the study of Africa, both from a German and an international perspective. Contents
includes Henning Melber "African Studies: Why, What for and by Whom?"; John

Lonsdale "African Studies, Europe & Africa"; Peter Probst "Betwixt and Between. An Anthropologist's Perspective on the History of African Studies in Germany"; Dieter Neubert, "Researching Africa south of the Sahara. A Sociologist's Perspective"; Peter Nunnenkamp "Mehr Entwicklungshilfe ist nicht genug" ("More aid is not sufficient"); Patrick Chabal "Area Studies and Comparative Politics: Africa in Context"; Jean-Pierre Olivier de Sardan "Classic Ethnology and the Socio-anthropology of Public Spaces in Africa"; Toyin Falola "Writing and Teaching National History in Africa in an Era of Global History", and Julie Parle and Thembisa Waetjen "Teaching African History in South Africa". [forthcoming at press time, not examined].

187   PhD Programs in Africa: Current Status and Future Prospects
http://ias.berkeley.edu/africa/Research/AfricanPhDCover_Report_Ref.pdf
A working paper (April 2002, 61 pp., pdf format) by David L. Szanton and Sarah Manyika, published by the Institute of International Studies and the ➜ **Center for African Studies, University of California at Berkeley (1761)**. Originally written as a report to the ➜ **Rockefeller Foundation (2743)**, it examines current PhD programmes in the social science and humanities in African universities, and suggests possible means to strengthen them. The paper is divided into four parts: Section 1 surveys the production of PhDs in sub-Saharan African universities; Section 2 deals with the experience of "sandwich" programmes as elements of a PhD; Section 3 describes some current or planned innovative PhD programmes, while the final Section 4 narrows to the social sciences, arts, and humanities, and sets out a number of recommendations to develop PhD programmes in African universities in these particular fields. {19/08/05]

188   Robinson, Pearl T. **"Area Studies in Search of Africa."** In *The Politics of Knowledge: Area Studies and the Disciplines*, edited by David L. Szanton. University of California Press/University of California International and Area Studies Digital Collection, vol. 3, 2003. 42 pp.
http://repositories.cdlib.org/uciaspubs/editedvolumes/3/6 (pdf)
A wide-ranging article that examines the development of African studies in the USA from its introduction in the historically Black colleges and universities (HBCUs) toward the end of the 19th century through its move into the academic mainstream. The author shows that the current landscape of African studies is both constrained and propelled by discourses of knowledge and power on and about Africa, and that "the rationale for African studies has shifted over time, while efforts to combat notions of hierarchy and the reality of marginalization have profoundly influenced its intellectual agenda." [19/08/05]

189   The Survey of African Studies Faculty in the United States, 2002. Inter-university Consortium for Political and Social Research (ICPSR). Study no. 3887, released 2004-03-22. Principal Investigator: Larry W. Bowman.
http://webapp.icpsr.umich.edu/cocoon/ICPSR-STUDY/03887.xml
Undertaken during the period October-November 2002, this survey (*see also* print article ➜ **"Identifying New Directions for African Studies"**, entry **273**) examines faculty attitudes about a range of issues facing African studies programmes at colleges and universities in the United States. Questions focused on teaching African

studies, study abroad programs, African language study, and attitudes toward Africa. Faculty were also asked to give their views and opinions on African Studies programmes at their own institutions. Data from the survey were entered in SPSS (Statistical Package for the Social Sciences) data format to provide maximum statistical analysis of variables with the data set. The complete study consists of five files: a PDF-format codebook (2,785KB), an ASCII data file (148KB), SPSS and SAS data definition statements (75KB/73KB), and an SPSS-portable version of the data file (132KB). [22/08/05]

190   "Zur Lage der Afrika-Forschung in Deutschland. Verlauf einer engagierten Debatte"
http://www.duei.de/iak/de/content/publikationen/forschungsdebatte.html
In the first issue for 2003 the journal →Afrika Spectrum (699)
http://www.duei.de/iak/de/content/publikationen/pdf/asengel.pdf published a somewhat controversial paper by Ulf Engel, "Gedanken zur Afrikanistik – Zustand und Zukunft einer Regional Wissenschaft in Deutschland" ("Reflections on African Studies. The status and future of an area study in Germany"), which provoked some partially sharp reactions from members of the Africanist community. This Web page provides full-text access to 8 articles on the debate (all in German, except for one which is available both in German and in English). [28/10/05]

Guides to funding sources and study abroad programmes

See also → **19 Major foundations, donors, government and aid agencies**
→ **22 Awards and prizes in African studies**

Note: For an interesting recent article on the topic of study abroad programmes, *see* "African Studies and Study Abroad" by David T. Lloyd (St. Lawrence University) *Frontiers: The Interdisciplinary Journal of Study Abroad* 6 (Winter 2000):99-11; online at http://www.frontiersjournal.com/issues/vol6/vol6-07_Lloyd.pdf.

191   Africa Grantmakers' Affinity Group (AGAG)
http://www.africagrantmakers.org/
The → **Africa Grantmakers' Affinity Group (2554)** is a membership network of foundations that are currently funding in Africa or are interested in funding in Africa. AGAG was established as a forum for foundations to exchange information and work together in an effort to amplify current foundation funding and promote increased and more effective grant making in Africa to better address Africa's development challenges. Its Search for Funding database provides search facilities by countries and/or categories, but access is *restricted to AGAG Member Foundations only*. However, the Web site has a useful list of links (freely accessible) to resources offering information to both funders and grantee partners in Africa, and there is also a complete listing of AGAG members with links to their Web sites. [26/06/05]

192   Africa South of the Sahara: Grants & Fellowships
http://www-sul.stanford.edu/depts/ssrg/africa/grants.html
Part of the Stanford ➔ **Africa South of the Sahara – Selected Internet Resources (69)**, this is a seven page listing of some 40 organizations, associations, foundations, programs, etc. that provide fellowships, grants, and scholarships for African studies. [27/06/05]

193   CODESRIA – Training and grants
http://www.codesria.org/training_grants.htm
➔ **CODESRIA's (1851)** Training and Grants Programmes include The Small Grants for Thesis Writing, the ➔ **CODESRIA Prize for Doctoral Theses (2827)**, the Advanced Research Fellowships Programme, and several other programmes. [27/06/05]

194   Council of American Overseas Research Centers (CAORC)
http://www.caorc.org/
The members of the Council of American Overseas Research Centers have centres in many parts of the world, including several countries in Africa. They serve as a base for American scholars undertaking research in the host countries. COARCs Multi-Country Research Fellowship Program for Advanced Multi-Country Research is open to US doctoral candidates and scholars who have already earned their PhD in fields in the humanities, social sciences, or allied natural sciences and wish to conduct research of regional or trans-regional significance. [26/06/05]

195   ExcelAfrica. Excellence for Africa
http://www.excelafrica.com
A site (in French) primarily designed to assist African students to study in North America and Europe (and in Africa as well), with guides to colleges and schools, grants and fellowships, and practical information on application procedures, visa requirements etc. Additionally, there are regular announcements that provide details of current bursaries, employment opportunities, and more. [27/06/05]

**196   Finding Funding Resources: Guide to Funding Resources for African
        Students Studying Abroad**
http://www.rockfound.org/Documents/519/ADIA_fundingsources.doc
Part of the Web site of the ➔ **Rockefeller Foundation (2743)**, this annotated ten page guide provides African students interested in studying abroad – most particularly in North America – or in conducting research in Africa, with a sampling of the organizations that provide awards or financial support for Africans or nationals from developing countries. As this document was issued in 2002 it may now be marginally dated. [27/06/05]

197   Five College African Scholars Program, Amherst, Massachusetts, USA
http://www.fivecolleges.edu/sites/asp/
A competitive residency fellowship program for junior and mid-level scholars employed full-time in African universities. Eight fellowships are awarded each year to African scholars for four-month residencies at one of the five colleges. *See also* ➔ **16 Centres of African studies and African studies programmes worldwide,** entry **1681**. [25/06/05]

198   The Ford Foundation – Guidelines for Grant Seekers
http://www.fordfound.org/about/guideline.cfm
Provides helpful guidelines for submitting a grant application to the ➔ Ford
Foundation (2733), and sets out the Foundations policies in deciding what to
support, how a grant is selected and made, and how it monitors grants. It also
provides access to a ten page pdf document with more information about the
Foundations current (2005) interests and programmes, together with contact points
of Ford Foundation offices worldwide, including its four offices in Africa. [27/06/05]

➔ Ford Foundation International Fellowship Programs *see* 18 Major foundations,
donors, government and aid agencies entries 2733, 2736

➔ Fulbright Scholarships *see* 18 Major foundations, donors, government and aid
agencies entry 2732

199   Grants Web
http://www.srainternational.org/newweb/grantsweb/index.cfm
Maintained by the Society of Research Administrators International (SRA), this is a
general (*not* African-studies-specific) Web resource for grants information and
funding opportunities available from (US) local, state, federal governments and
agencies, as well as foundations, international governments, and private funding
information. [27/06/05]

200   Information on Fellowships for African Students
http://ias.berkeley.edu/africa/fellowships/4Afstudents.htm
From the ➔ Center for African Studies, University of California at Berkeley (1761)
these pages offer some information and resources that might be useful to students
from African countries interested in finding fellowships to study in the United States.
Last updated in February 2003. [27/06/05]

201   Kubatana.net: 2002-2003 Resource Guide: a Selected List of Fellowships,
        Scholarships, Grants and other training opportunities for African Women
        Students/Scholars
http://www.kubatana.net/html/archive/women/021216iewad.asp?sector=RESOU
R
Compiled by the staff of the Institute for Education of Women in Africa and the
Diaspora (IEWAD), and released in December 16, 2002, this is a substantial 138-page
guide, downloadable either as a pdf file (685KB) or in Word 97 (699KB). For each
entry it gives a fairly full description, together with application details and deadlines,
contact points, and Web sites. [27/06/05]

➔ National Endowment for the Humanities *see* 18 Major foundations, donors,
government and aid agencies entry 2740

➔ Robert S. McNamara Fellowship Program *see* 18 Major foundations, donors,
government and aid agencies entry 2741

202   SIT Study Abroad: African Studies
http://sit.edu/studyabroad/themes/Africa.html
SIT Study Abroad programmes in Africa offer students an opportunity to gain international and local perspectives as they interact with members of urban and rural African communities; and experiences with individuals, families, organizations, and educational institutions will help to immerse them in the diverse points of view concerning critical issues facing Africa today. 20 programmes in 12 African countries are currently available, and these pages provide more information about the nature of each programme and its different components, the educational excursions that form part of the programme, profiles of the academic directors for each of them, how to apply, scholarships that are available, and health and safety issues. [21/07/05]

Theses/e-theses and dissertations

See also ➔ 2 The major general reference tools: Theses and dissertations

Note: Several South African university libraries now offer electronic thesis and dissertations databases (ETD-db), which can be browsed or searched – with most allowing free access to recent full-text e-dissertations (in pdf format) – while the University of Namibia Library has a *Register of Theses*. Details and access points are as follows:
Rhodes University Electronic Theses and Dissertations Initiative
http://www.ru.ac.za/library/theses/rutheses.html
University of Johannesburg [formerly Rand Afrikaans University and Wits Technikon]
Electronic Thesis and Dissertation Database (ETD-db)
http://etd.rau.ac.za/
University of Namibia: Register of Namibian Theses
http://greenstone.unam.na/gsdl/cgi-bin/library?site=localhost&a=p&p=about&c=theses&ct=0&l=enhttp://greenstone.unam.na/gsdl/cgi-bin/library?site=localhost&a=p&p=about&c=theses&ct=0&l=en&w=utf-8
University of the Orange Free State ETD Collection
http://etd.uovs.ac.za/cgi-bin/ETD-browse/browse
University of Pretoria Electronic Theses and Dissertations http://upetd.up.ac.za/UPeTD.htm
(*see also* entry ➔ 207 below)
University of South Africa Unisa ETD: Electronic Theses and Dissertations
http://www.unisa.ac.za/Default.asp?Cmd=ViewContent&ContentID=16097
University of the Witwatersrand EDT collection (*see also* entry ➔ 208 below)
http://www.witsetd.wits.ac.za/ETD-db/other_etds.htm

203   Database of African Theses and Dissertations (DATAD) (Subscription
        based)
http://www.aau.org/datad/ (Home page)
http://www.aau.org/datad/database/ (Data base)
Annual subscription rates (US Dollars): within Africa—AAU members $100, non-AAU members $250, individuals $100; outside Africa—institutions $400, individuals $250 (The current database is also offered on a CD-ROM, for prices see Web site)

Free trial access is offered to African institutions by the ➔ **International Network for the Availability of Scientific Publications (2608)** through its PERI programme. For more details see http://www.inasp.info/peri/resources/datad.shtml
DATAD is a programme to improve management and access to African scholarly research, of which theses and dissertations represent a significant proportion of research activity. Working in collaboration with 11 African member institutions in (at this time) 10 African countries, the programme was launched by the ➔ **Association of African Universities (2580)** in April 2003. The aim is to build a regional database of theses and dissertations and thus contribute towards the creation of an environment conducive for research and publication in African universities, and to provide more visibility for, and facilitate the access to, the work of African scholars both within and outside the continent. The DATAD database contains citations and abstracts for theses and dissertations completed in African universities. At this time (August 2005) this includes about 15,000 records and covers works from all subject areas in the ten participating universities, and includes abstracts written by the authors. Limited demo access is available free-of-charge, but users must register and then log in to access 20 sample records in the database. To search and access the entire database users will need to register and then subscribe (see rates above), or connect from a subscribing institution. There is no access to full-text dissertations at this time, nor provision of document delivery, but such services may be offered in the future, and once matters regarding copyright issues have been resolved. More information, including a DATAD Methodology Manual, and details about future expansion plans, are available from the Web site. [13/08/05]

➔ Easterbrook, David L. **"African Theses and Dissertations in Academic Libraries in the United States: Background and Current Practices."** *see* **15 Africanist documentation and African studies bibliography** entry **1902**

204   **Theses Canada** [for theses on African topics] ⓘ
http://www.nlc-bnc.ca/thesescanada/
Hosted by the National Library of Canada (NLC) this is a central access point for Canadian theses in print and electronic formats. It is a superb database, and a marvellous resource for tracking down Canadian theses on African topics. The NLC's theses collection was established in 1965, but full-text electronic versions of Canadian theses and dissertations are available in pdf format for those theses published from the beginning of 1998 to August 31, 2002. You can locate a specific thesis by clicking either on Search or Advanced Search. Select by "All theses" or "Electronic theses", by title of thesis, author, or by keyword(s). For example, a search by the very broad keyword "African" bring up 854 records, and all search results can be sorted by title or name in descending or ascending order. "Zimbabwe" shows 128 theses, or a slightly more specific search, "Women Zimbabwe", generates 15 records of theses on the status of women in Zimbabwe, women's rights, gender studies, etc. "Sierra Leone" shows 41 results, and it works very well, for example, to track down theses on African ethnic groups or on individual African writers. For example "Chinua Achebe" displays 12 theses, two of them available in pdf format. Within the search results, clicking on to any thesis brings up the full title record, with available formats, type of thesis, a short abstract and reference number. The next click provides

a fuller abstract, and the URL for the e-location of the theses, if available in pdf format, where the full text can be downloaded. [18/08/05]

205   Theses in Progress in Commonwealth Studies
http://www.sas.ac.uk/commonwealthstudies/tip.htm (Home page)
Theses in Progress in Commonwealth Studies: A List of Research in UK Universities 2005 (Print and online)
http://www.sas.ac.uk/commonwealthstudies/resource/tip2005.pdf (2005 volume)
An annual listing of MPhil and PhD research being carried out at UK universities, derived from the *Register of Commonwealth Research*, a database of theses completed or in progress, currently (August 2005) containing over 11,000 records, with coverage extending back to the 1920s. The geographical range encompasses the former British Empire, the Commonwealth of Nations, and all their member countries, together with countries formerly under British Protection. The Register is maintained at the →**Library of the Institute of Commonwealth Studies (1279).** The latest edition, *Theses in Progress in Commonwealth Studies: A List of Research in UK Universities 2005,* edited by Patricia M. Larby, contains titles believed to be in progress at the end of 2004, and supersedes all previous edition. It includes (pp. 4-39) a substantial number of theses on Africa. (A print version, 117 pp. can be purchased for £25.) [23/08/05]

206   UNESCO. African Universities Project for the Electronic Production and Publication of Theses and Dissertations [no project title as at August 2005]
http://portal.unesco.org/ci/ev.php?URL_ID=12450&URL_DO=DO_TOPIC&URL_S
ECTION=201&reload=1071228982   [first announcement, 25/08/03]
A new project funded by UNESCO and jointly hosted (initially as a pilot project) by the University of the Witwatersrand and Addis Ababa University, and in collaboration with the → **Association of African Universities (2580)** It will be based on the principles, guidelines, workflow models and best practices described in the *UNESCO Electronic Theses and Dissertations (ETD) Guide,* Paris: UNESCO, 2002) .
No further information available as at August 2005. [23/09/05]

207   UPeTD. University of Pretoria Electronic Theses and Dissertations
http://upetd.up.ac.za/ETD-db/
208   Wits ETD. University of the Witwatersrand Electronic Theses and Dissertations
http://www.witsetd.wits.ac.za/ETD-db/
Forms part of the Network Digital Library of Theses and Dissertations (NDLTD) http://www.ndltd.org/ to facilitate open access to graduate research information by making it available on the Internet and, to provide more international visibility for participating institutions. These two databases cover theses and dissertations submitted to the University of Pretoria and Witwatersrand University Browse the collections by author or by department, or search by author and/or keywords and phrases. For each thesis or dissertation it provides the following information: document type, author, email of author, URN (location reference), document title, type of degree, department, name of supervisor, keywords, date presented, availability (i.e. restrictions, if any), and a fairly extensive abstract. Additionally it indicates (pdf) file names and sizes on a chapter-by-chapter basis, and likely download times using a 56k modem, or downloaded via ISDN lines. [18/08/05]

2
The major general reference tools
(print or print/online, CD-ROM, and microform)

This section provides details of the major general reference tools in the African studies field, primarily those written in English, and with an emphasis on material published over the last decade or so. Most of them are published in print format, but there also listings of some titles that are available in dual print and electronic formats, on CD-ROM, and in microform.

For this new edition information provided has been revised and updated, and entries for 48 new print reference works have been added. Some titles listed in the previous edition have been deleted. However, a number of other older titles – mostly bibliographies, guides to archival sources, and some classic Africana reference works of enduring value – have been retained. Price details have been updated for titles still in print, or, alternatively, details of new editions are indicated. All entries without price information are likely to be out-of-print.

Listings are confined, for the most part, to *general*, multidisciplinary reference works, bibliographies, and guides to sources. There are entries for a few regional resources and area bibliographies, but country-specific reference works are not included, nor are subject-specific sources, with the exception of a small number of reference tools that, although focussing on a particular area such as the arts, provide descriptions and contact details for organizations across several cultural sectors, for example those including information on libraries and museums.

Reference works on Africa primarily aimed for middle- and high-school students are not included, unless they are also considered to be of interest for possible purchase by college and public libraries.

A number of print titles and CD-ROMs covering African American and Black history and culture are included, but only if content includes substantial information on Africa and African studies.

Other reference sources
For subject and country-specific bibliographies, specialist resources, directories, etc. readers should consult other well-established reference

works, notably Yvette Scheven's award-winning ➜ **Bibliographies for African Studies 1970-1986 (234)** and its supplement ➜ **Bibliographies for African Studies 1987-1993 (235)**, and John McIlwaine's classic ➜ **Africa: A Guide to Reference Material (227)**, a new second revised edition of which is scheduled for publication in late 2006. Alfred Kagan's ➜ **Reference Guide to Africa. A Bibliography of Sources (225)** is another benchmark Africana reference tool, and the new second edition published in 2005 covers material published up to 2004. Together these three sources remain the first port of call for the researcher, librarian, or bibliographer interested in Africa. They contain a vast number of specialist references resources, most of which will never become available electronically, or which are patchily indexed in major databases and may not be picked up in online searches.

The best source for tracking down new subject- and country-specific reference sources are the annotated listings of new Africana reference works that have appeared annually in ➜ **The African Book Publishing Record (384)** since 1986. The lists are currently edited by Jill Young-Coelho, Librarian for sub-Saharan Africa at ➜ **Harvard College Library (1309)**, with the active collaboration of a number of Africana specialist librarians at major US institutions. They cover reference works published in all parts of the world, primarily in English, but there are also frequent listings of new titles in French, German, Portuguese, and in some other languages.

Links and references to reviews
Some entries include references to book reviews which have appeared in *Choice/Choice Reviews Online* at http://www.choicereviews.org (the *Choice* database offers online reviews from September 1988 onwards), but online access to these reviews requires a subscription/license. Names of reviewers are included, and titles singled out by *Choice* as 'Outstanding Academic Title' (OAT) are also indicated. *Choice* OAT's (formerly 'Outstanding Academic Book') are selected for "being of permanent value or of such topical importance that they belong in every academic library." We have also flagged winners, or joint winners, of the ➜ **Africana Librarian's Council's (1885)** ➜ **Conover-Porter Award (2828)**, awarded biennially for "outstanding achievement in Africana bibliography and reference works".

Additionally, there are references to reviews that have appeared (since issue no. 55, 1991; published in print format only) in ➜ **African Research & Documentation/ARD (748)**, which is the journal of the ➜ **Standing Conference on Library Materials on Africa/SCOLMA (1892)**. Apart from *Choice, ARD* is probably the only other journal that publishes reviews of new Africana reference works on a regular and systematic basis. Librarians at major African studies collections in the UK write most of its reviews.

Annuals and yearbooks

209 **Africa Contemporary Record. Annual Survey and Documents.** New York: Holmes & Meier, London: Rex Collings [1970-76] vol. I, 1968-69-, published annually (later bi-annual), latest volume vol. XXV, 1994-1996. publ. 2000, 1,068 pp. $495.00 vol. XXVI, 1996-98, 1,130 pp. $495.00, vol. XXVII, 1999-2000, 1,200 pp. $495.00 [not examined]. Ed. by Colin Legum & John Drysdale [to 1988]; ed. by Marion Duro [1989-1991]; 1992-1994- edited by Colin Legum

Originally an annual, later bi-annual publication, the publication schedule of this title has been falling further and further into arrears. The most recent volume, published in 2003, covered the three-year period 1999-2000. Past volumes have provided extensive analysis of political, economic, social, and constitutional developments covering all the countries on the African continent, with detailed articles and reviews on each African country. Also records the year's key documents from organizations such as the OAU, the UN, and the US House Committee on Foreign Affairs, and provides summaries and statistics regarding population growth, per capita GNP, oil and gas production, foreign aid, etc.

210 **Africa Review. The Economic and Business Report, 2003/4.** London: Kogan Page Business Books/Stylus Publishing, 2003. 25th ed. 288 pp. £50.00/$120.00 [previous eds. published by World of Information, Saffron Walden] Annual economic and business survey of 55 African countries. Includes introductory articles on economic and political developments and a general analytical overview, together with chapters on each African country, each with analysis of the year's events, a country profile, key indicators, important facts, and a business directory with listings of useful addresses of organizations, etc. Outline map for each country.

211 **Africa South of the Sahara.** 35th ed. [2005 edition] London: Europa Publications, 2005. 1,488 pp. £365.00/$638.00 print

212 **Africa South of the Sahara Online** ⓘ £300.00/$525.00 online only £465.00/$813.00 print and online bundle Part of Europa World Plus. Access and delivery of the online edition is at http:// www.europaworld.com, and from where free trial access can also be requested.

Published since 1971, this annual survey and directory covers the main political events, and social and economic developments during the preceding year in the 52 African countries that comprise Africa South of the Sahara. Each country section includes background essays, economic, demographic and statistical survey/data, plus a wide-ranging directory of essential names and addresses most with telephone and fax numbers, email addresses, and many with Web sites. Part 1 of the book, the General Survey, provides a history of the continent and includes a series of essays by acknowledged experts on African affairs, covering topics such as recent political events, current economic trends, evaluations of industrial and agricultural development prospects for sub-Saharan Africa, and of production, marketing and price movements in the principal African commodities. Part 2, preceding the individual Country Surveys, provides details about the activities of African regional organizations. Each annual edition is fairly substantially revised and updated to encompass the latest available facts, statistics and directory information, providing quick access to a wide range of data. However, the list of African studies journals "Select Bibliography (periodicals)" is flawed and contains entries that are dated, or covers journals that have not been published for some time now.

The online edition is impressive, easily navigated, and with good advanced search facilities. Search options include (1) full text by content type (i.e. type of entry, country statistics, government and politics, society and media, business and commerce) region or country; (2) searches by organizations and people (individual names, organization type, job title, location or country); or (3) by publications. Alternatively, browse the General Survey, regional countries, or regional organizations.

Note: from 2005 *Africa South of the Sahara* and ➜ **The Middle East and North Africa (215)** are also available online as part of Europa's *Regional Surveys of the World 2005*, as a complete set of 9 volumes, £2,045/$3,578 online only, £3,530/$6,177 print and online bundle. More information at http://www.online.taylorandfrancis.com/.

➜ **Africa Survey 2005** see **9 Journals and magazines, The Africa Report** entry **672**

213 **Africa Yearbook 2004. Politics, Economy and Society South of the Sahara.** Edited by Andreas Mehler, Henning Melber, and Klaas van Walraven. Leiden and Boston: Brill Academic Publishers, 2005. 512 pp. €40.00/$54.00
A new English-language publication that will be published annually as from 2005, with the first volume covering the year 2004. It forms a continuation of the German-language *Afrika Jahrbuch* published by the ➜ **Institut für Afrika-Kunde (1580)** in Hamburg, which published its last yearbook in 2004 (on the year 2003, *see* http://www.duei.de/iak/shop/en/csc_article_details.php?nPos=0&saArticle[ID]=1 82). The new *Africa Yearbook* (in English) will provide annual overviews of the major developments in each sub-Saharan African country, and is the result of a collaborative undertaking by the ➜**African Studies Centre (1594)** in Leiden, the ➜ **Institut für Afrika-Kunde (1580)** and the ➜ **Nordic Africa Institute (1611)**, emerging from their collaboration within the ➜**Africa-Europe Group for Interdisciplinary Studies/AEGIS (2749)**. A total of 49 Africanist scholars from a variety of disciplines contribute articles, which cover domestic political developments, the foreign policy of sub-Saharan states, and socio-economic trends – all related to developments in one calendar year – and there are also overview articles on each of the four sub-regions (West, central, eastern, southern Africa), focusing on major cross-border developments and sub-regional organizations. While this new annual publication is a scholarly work of reference, it is targeted at a wider readership, including students, politicians, diplomats, teachers, journalists, as well as business people. Modestly priced, this is a useful new reference resource to keep up-to-date with political and socio-economic developments in sub-Saharan Africa.

214 **The Middle East and North Africa.** 51st ed. [2005 edition] London: Europa Publications, 2004. 1,370 pp. £350.00/$612.00 print
215 **The Middle East and North Africa Online** ⓘ
£300.00/$525.00 online only £465.00/$813.00 print and online bundle

Part of Europa World Plus. Access and delivery of the online edition is at http://www.europaworld.com, and from where free trial access can also be requested.

The companion volume to ➔ **Africa South of the Sahara (211)** covering the Middle Eastern world and North Africa (Algeria, Egypt, Libya, Morocco, Spanish North Africa, and Tunisia). Like the volume on Africa South of the Sahara, it includes a range of background essays on topics relating to the region as a whole, and individual country surveys with articles on its recent history, economy and geography, and a wide array of statistical data on each country. For each there is also a directory of essential names and addresses covering government, the judiciary, political organizations, diplomatic representation, religious groups, the media, finance, trade and industry and tourism, plus details of major international organizations active in the region, and bibliographies of books and journals. The online edition is structured along the same lines, and has the same advanced search facilities as ➔ **Africa South of the Sahara Online (212)** described in the above entry. *Note:* from 2005 *The Middle East and North Africa* and ➔ **Africa South of the Sahara (212)** are also available online as part of Europa's *Regional Surveys of the World 2005*, as a complete set of 9 volumes, £2,045/$3,578 online only, £3,530/$6,177 print and online bundle. More information at http://www.online.taylorandfrancis.com/.

216   **The State of Africa 2003/4: A Thematic and Factual Review**. Edited by Pierre Hugo and Eddy Maloka. Pretoria: Africa Institute of South Africa, 2004. 175 pp. £17.95/$24.95 (distributed by African Books Collective Ltd, Oxford)

This book represents the first of what is intended to become an annual publication from the ➔ **Africa Institute of South Africa (1854)** on the "state of Africa". It is an attempt to assess the condition of the African continent without judging or coming to a "definitive" diagnosis. Intended primarily for general reader, the volume offers wide-ranging coverage of the contemporary African condition, and aims to provide an informative contemporary overview on a range of important topics. The book is organized in four major sections: Politics and Governance; Meeting the Millennium Development Goals; Peace and Conflict; and Regional Developments. Over 30 African scholars and researchers (mostly South African) contribute to the volume. An extensive number of maps, diagrams, basic demographic information and country-by-country fact sheets are included.

Bibliographies and guides to sources

See also ➔ **3 Current bibliographies, indexing and abstracting services, and review media**

Africa (General)

➔ **African Books in Print/Livres Africains Disponibles** *see* entry 385

➔ **African Studies Database** *see* **Africa-Wide: NiPAD** entry 217

217   Africa-Wide: NiPAD
Baltimore & Grahamstown, South Africa: National Information Services Corporation
(NISC), 1994- (in progress)
http://www.nisc.com (US company)
http://www.nisc.co.za/databases?id=1
Total records: 1,757,125+ Dates of coverage: 19th century to current
Formats: BiblioLine and CD-ROM   Update frequency: Quarterly
Database content: *see* details below.
Subscription pricing: (as at 01/08/05) Single Concurrent User: US$2,585;
2-5 Concurrent Users: US$3,877; 6-10 Concurrent Users: US$5,170; Unlimited
Concurrent Users: US$6,462 (A 15% discount applies to current subscribers of NISC's
South African Studies)
The somewhat obscurely named *Africa-Wide: NiPAD* is a combination of (i) *African
Studies;* (no longer offered as a separate database subscription; *see* entry 114 in the
3rd, 2003 ed. of *The African Studies Companion*), which includes almost a million
records from databases from Africa, Europe and the United States, providing access
to multidisciplinary information on Africa; and (ii) *South African Studies,* which
includes over a million records providing access to the great majority of documents
published in and about South Africa. Sources include books, periodical and
magazine articles, radio and TV broadcasts, newspapers, pamphlets, maps, reports,
theses, music recordings, and more.

→ **The National Information Services Corporation/NISC (2097)** compiles database
aggregations and has developed software to integrate large and small databases into
single information sources, eliminating duplications, and adding keywords to
enhance the information value of the composite records. NISC bibliographic
databases with African content are of two types: (i) either subject specific databases
where African information is incorporated with major European and/or American
databases, or (ii) they consist of multi-topic databases, all of whose references are
African or of particular African relevance. NISC says "each database is unique and
special in its own way, but it is only by combining a multitude of sources that we can
begin to attempt comprehensive coverage of African output."
See also "Online Access to the Research Output from and about Africa through
Database Aggregation and Full Text Linking" by Margaret Crampton and Frances
Hulley, http://www.codesria.org/Links/conferences/el_publ/crampton.pdf

Africa-Wide: NiPAD is a very substantial database, and NISC expects to add further
databases as they become available. It can be accessed for a 30-day free trial period.
The publisher's product fact sheet indicates "access 2 million records with full-text
links", but access to full text is in fact only available for a relatively small proportion
of all records. Usefully, some database records have abstracts, for example all the
records retrieved from past issues of the former print version of →**African Studies
Abstracts (396)**. Some database providers whose products are included offer a
document delivery service. The BiblioLine search facilities are extensive and
sophisticated, with Boolean search operators, wildcards, and more, and there are
good help pages to assist with searching. Names of authors can be searched in exact
word order, using any words, or in other combinations. Searching works well if you
are searching for authors of books and articles, names of journals or specific

documents. For example it can be searched by names of individual African writers, and it is especially strong on southern African writers.

However, browsing is less successful, and can be very time-consuming. The search facility invites users "To browse, type a term and click Find Term", but many are not proper index terms conventionally used in libraries, and there are also numerous styles for bibliographic citations. The fact that there are different styles of citing author surnames (full names spelt out or just with initial/s, with or without punctuation after initials, first name followed by surname or v.v., etc.) is less distracting than the different styles for subject descriptors. The access point for subject browsing is a "Subject/Topic Search Fields Index". There are a total of over 2.2 million "Index entries", but a huge proportion of these contain just one or two records, and the choice of the word "index" is somewhat misleading. It is partly an index of subject headings, and partly an index of words and phrases as cited in database records. When subject headings (e.g. those using *Sears List of Subject Headings*) were provided by the suppliers/publishers of the many databases included here, then these duly appear when database records are displayed, together with various other information provided for each record. However, for the most part the rest of the "index" entries or terms are simply words or phrases picked up from the records, including words that are misspelt. For example, browsing for records on publishing and the book industries in Africa leads to a very large very number of index entries; some are helpful and a sizeable number use Sears subject headings e.g. "Publishers and publishing–Zimbabwe–Directories", "Publishers and publishing–South Africa–Directories", or "Publishers and publishing–South Africa–History" etc. If all database records would show such Sears (or Dewey, LC etc.) headings, that would be ideal. But unfortunately they do not, and about 300 index entries in this test search, many with just one or two records, simply contain the word "Publishing" plus a second term, for example "Publishing Contracts", "Publishing Law", "Publishing Costs", together with some totally meaningless terms such as "Publishes" (76 records), "Publishin [sic]", or "Publishing Process", for which plural form entries, "Publishing Processes", shows two records. Others retrieved were "Publishing Areas", "Publishers Blue", "Publishers' Introduction", or "Publishers Press". There is a general index entry for "Publishing", with 4,223 records, but this large number of records makes it completely unmanageable; there are 3 entries for "Publishing–Africa" and 2 entries "Publishing in Africa", but which then in fact retrieve 242 records when activated in search mode. Another index entry "Publishing, Namibia" shows only one index entry although the database does in fact contain a great deal more. Similarly, browsing under an alternative range of subject headings, "Book industries and trade", and its various sub-sections is equally awkward for the most part, and again contains completely meaningless terms, e.g. "Book Evaluations", "Book Extracts", "Book.html", "Book-Entry", "Book Wurms [sic]", "Book Back", or "Book Announcements" etc. The same pattern was repeated for some other subject terms that were put to the test.

This is a valuable combination of databases, albeit assembled in slightly hotchpotch fashion, and some resources included are more valuable than others. The wide scope – in terms of range of languages covered, formats, and the wide variety of material included that is included – is impressive, and some content is very rich. However

Africa-Wide: NiPAD is still flawed in certain respects as set out above and requires much more rigorous quality control, as well as easier navigation. While it can be a good point of departure for many searches in the African studies field, the publisher's claim in their product overview that "all you need to know about Africa is now on one database" is totally unsupported.

Africa-Wide: NiPAD database content (all details of records and coverage as provided by the publisher, and current as at March 2005):

1. Databases also included in *African Studies*

Africa Institute Database
Records: 78,193 Coverage: 1981 to current
Database of over 78,000 references, many with abstracts, based on the ➔ **Africa Institute of South Africa (1454)** collection of over 67,000 volumes and 500 periodical titles as well as thematic maps

African Periodicals Exhibit (APEX)
Records: 135
Lists details of 135 scholarly African serial publications displayed at the Zimbabwe International Book Fair in 1997.

African Studies Abstracts
Records: 62,157 Coverage: 19th century to current
Compiled by the ➔ **African Studies Centre Library (1246)** in Leiden, Netherlands, and also includes six volumes of its predecessor, *Documentatieblad,* which was published from 1988 to 1993. This database has been combined with the African Studies Centre's library catalogue of books and periodicals. *See also* ➔ **African Studies Abstracts (396).**

Afro-Tropical Bird Information Retrieval Database
Records: 73,202 Coverage: 20th century to current
Compiled in collaboration with the Percy FitzPatrick Institute of African Ornithology at the University of Cape Town, this database offers comprehensive current and historical coverage of all publications on Afro-Tropical birds.

Bibliography on Contemporary African Politics and Development
Records: 21,583 Coverage: 1981-1992
Compiled by Vijitha Mahadevan and Michael F. Lofchie (originally published by Lynne Rienner, 1994).

Business & Industry: Africa
Records: 11,036 Coverage: 1994 to current
Indexes the facts, figures and key events of companies, industries and markets based in Africa; more than 500 business-related publications from around the world are reviewed. Records are provided from Responsive Database Services, Inc Business & Industry database, as well as the new African Subset of NTIS (National Technical Information Service). Covering 1990 to present, the African Subset of the NTIS database consists of records with a relevance to Africa and provides full descriptive summaries of documents and other materials NTIS has received from government agencies since 1990.

The Campbell Collections of the University of Natal, Killie Campbell Africana Library
Records: 29,291 Coverage: 19th century to current

This collection of the ➔ **Killie Campbell Africana Library (1465)** includes a wide range of published works and an extensive manuscript collection dealing with southern Africa in general and with the KwaZulu Natal region in particular.

Database of Swiss Theses and Dissertation
Records: 570 Coverage: 1897 to current
Compiled by Roger Pfister; lists 519 Swiss doctoral dissertations on sub-Saharan Africa.

Don Africana Collection
Records: 47,281 Coverage: 16th century to current
David Don's original collection of documents donated in 1916 and updated constantly since then (*see also* ➔ entry **1456**). Subjects covered include African religion, archaeology, art, economics, education, exploration, flora and fauna, geography, history, law, literature, missionary accounts and politics.

IBISCUS
Records: 156,808 Coverage: 1970-2002
This database is built by a group of compilers in 19 countries, with 54 input centres in Africa, Europe and Canada. It contains development-related information on francophone Africa. Subjects covered include agriculture, health, economics, transport, environment and society.

International Library of African Music (ILAM)
Records: 8,021
Contains recordings and publications from the early 20th century to current. The database includes annotated records pertaining to indigenous African music in the ILAM collection. The regions covered are central, eastern and southern Africa. Soon to be added is the database of musical instruments and photographs. (Note: to obtain musical recordings contact: International Library of African Music, Rhodes University, Grahamstown, 6140, South Africa, Email: ilam@ru.ac.za)

NAMLIT
Records: 51,500 Coverage: 19th century to current
Initiated in Germany in 1978, NAMLIT is now compiled by the National Library of Namibia and offers a comprehensive bibliography of Namibia-related literature.

Natural and Cultural Heritage of Africa (NATCHA)
Records: 29,005 Coverage: 1960 to current
Compiled by the Naturalist Niche in Port Elizabeth, offering current and historical coverage of articles from natural history, zoology, botany and museum journals published in Africa and relating to the continent.

NOAK (Nordic Africa Institute Online Catalogue)
Records: 49,496
The ➔ **Nordic Africa Institute (1260)** database contains literature on modern Africa and covers the entire continent with an emphasis on contemporary history, politics, education, economics and other social sciences as well as African fiction. Language coverage is English, French, German, Portuguese and the Nordic languages.

School of Oriental & African Studies (SOAS) Library Catalogue: Africa
Records: 190,318 Coverage: 1989 to current
The catalogue records of the ➔ **School of Oriental & African Studies (1289)** at the University of London, one of the largest and most important library collections of Africana materials in the world.

The Southern African Database (Sardius)
Records: 32,312 Coverage: 1961-1997
Compiled by the staff of Jan Smuts House Library (Johannesburg) and includes the
bibliographic series of the ➔ **South African Institute of International Affairs (1862)** at the ➔
University of the Witwatersrand (1475). Coverage includes political, economic and social
research in the SADC region with information on leaders, conflict and conflict resolution,
reform, development and foreign relations.

2. New to Africa-wide NiPAD (including databases from *South African Studies*)

The Africa Book Centre (London)
Records: 268
Extracts from the online catalogue database of the ➔ **Africa Book Centre Ltd (2331)**, a UK
specialist bookseller and distributor.

African Books Collective (Oxford)
Records: 1,050
Extracts from the online catalogue database of the Oxford-based ➔ **African Books Collective
Ltd (2332)**, the distributor of a very large number of African publishers.

The Centre for Rural Legal Studies Database
Records: 5,172 Coverage: 1987 and earlier to current
Subject coverage includes issues relating to agriculture and farm workers in South Africa and
elsewhere, specifically labour law and relations, working conditions, housing/tenure and socio-
economic conditions. Issues such as land reform, rural local government and gender are also
covered.

Index to South African Periodicals
Records: 432,061 Coverage: 1987 to current
A database is compiled by the State Library in Pretoria, now part of the National Library of
South Africa. Topics covered include scientific and technical articles, law, education, agriculture
and municipal affairs.

KnipKat
Records: 68,131
From the Nasionale Afrikaanse Letterkunde Museum en Navorsingsentrum (NALN), this is an
indexed database of press cuttings from newspapers and magazines relating to Afrikaans
language, literature and culture with information about writers of the Afrikaans language.

National English Literary Museum
Coverage: 1990 to current
Includes six databases from the ➔ **National English Literary Museum (1457)** in Grahamstown.
   Select Index to South African Literature in English, Critical Writings (27,072 records)
   Select Index to South African Literature in English, Creative Writings (139,199 records)
   NELM – Main Catalogue (18,116 records)
   Manuscripts (34,464 records)
   Literary Awards (1,721 records)
   A Bibliography of Anglophone Literature and Literary Criticism by Black South Africans
   (7,898 records)

NEXUS
Records: 135,375
This database on current and completed research in South Africa is compiled by the National
Research Foundation (NRF) in Pretoria. It provides information on South African current and
completed research projects, including theses and dissertations. The records of the Union

Catalogue of Theses and Dissertations (UCTD) formerly maintained by the Library of ➔ **Potchefstroom University (1458)** are now included. This source provides information on all fields of science since 1900. It also includes abstracts.

Political Information and Monitoring Service Database (PIMS)
Records: 575
This database is compiled by the ➔ **Institute for Democracy in South Africa (2086)** and offers comprehensive, plain language summaries and key details to the bills, acts and amendments of South African Parliament

South African Legal Abbreviations
Records: 1,624
A database of legal abbreviations compiled by law librarians at the University of South Africa Law Library.

South African National Bibliography
Records: 74,884 Coverage: 1988 to current
This is a comprehensive record of South African publishing output compiled by the National Library of South Africa.

Witwatersrand University Management Research Reports
Records: 1,782 Coverage: 1970 to current
The Witwatersrand Library of Management database contains records on management in South Africa

to be included shortly:

The Bibliographic Database of the Dictionary Unit for South African English
The Unit was established in 1969 to collect and record English as it is used in South Africa. Examples of South African English have been identified in publications and the references collected were first recorded on index cards and then in electronic format. New records from a variety of sources are being added and, over time, the thousands of index cards will be scanned or keyed into the database. This material provides the reference collection used by the Unit when writing dictionaries, but it can also used as a general research tool.

Other recent additions (August 2005) include the ➔ **African Journals Online/AJOL (554)** database; the Netherlands Institute for Southern Africa (NiZA)-BIDOC current catalogue; a Media Africa Database, and an African Development Database, which is currently still in its infancy with some 1,000 records. For more details see the NISC Web site above.

218 Barringer, Terry **Administering Empire: An Annotated Checklist of Personal Memoirs and Related Studies**. London: Institute of Commonwealth Studies, School of Advanced Study, University of London [28 Russell Square, London WC1B 5DS], 2004. 139 pp. £15.00
Note: a second revised edition is in preparation for publication in 2006.
This is a valuable annotated bibliography of almost 500 items on the Colonial Service in the 20th century. It focuses on memoirs, biographies and autobiographies, but also includes some general and comparative studies. Following an introduction providing a survey of the literature, material is listed alphabetically by author, each entry giving full bibliographic details, an informative short annotation, and key words. There are indexes of Colonies, Territories and Areas, and of Professional Services and Other Special Groups. As a useful additional feature many items in the bibliography also include details of reviews that have appeared in African studies periodicals and

in some other journals such as the *Overseas Pensioner*. This, the author points out, "allows the reader to trace changing attitudes to the memoir genre and to the British Colonial Service itself." She goes on to say that academic historians have been slow to recognise the value of this material, although the picture is now gradually changing. Anthony Kirk-Greene, in an introductory essay, "Why Memoirs of Colonial Service are Important", echoes the same point and states that the importance of Colonial Service memoirs – not just as secondary sources but as primary documentation – is only now beginning to be recognized by post-colonial scholars.

219   Besterman, Theodore **A World Bibliography of African Bibliographies.**
Revised and updated by J.D. Pearson. Oxford: Blackwell (Totowa, NJ: Rowman and Littlefield), 1975. 241 columns
An extract of 1,136 titles from Besterman's *A World Bibliography of Bibliographies* (4th ed. 1963), together with a further 498 items added by J.D. Pearson, and published between 1963 and 1973. Entries are arranged under geographical divisions and thereafter in regional or subject division; plus an author and title index.

220   **Black Studies on Disc.** New York: G.K. Hall, 1995- Annual CD-ROM 1 disc
$1,175.00 Latest release 2004
A single CD-ROM providing access to a very large number of sources for African American and African studies, and the diaspora, with full bibliographic data. The database covers books, periodical articles, as well as other types of material such as microforms, films, sound recordings, manuscript collections, and artworks. Contents is made up of two components: (1) the ➜ **Schomburg Center for Research in Black Culture (1319)** catalogue of almost 198,000 records, and (2) the ➜ **Index to Black Periodicals (400),** published since 1988, which covers a wide range of scholarly and popular journals. Keyword searching or browsing by various indexes. Search results can be tagged, sorted and/or printed/saved. [Not examined]
Choice review:
Choice March 1996 (reviewed by E.C. Burt)

221   Duignan, Peter, and Helen F. Conover **Guide to Research and Reference Works on Sub-Saharan Africa.** Stanford: Hoover Institution Press, 1971. 1,102 pp. (Hoover Institution on War, Revolution and Peace, Bibliographical Series, 46)
A major and pioneering reference source for material published to 1969/70. 3,127 fully annotated entries arranged in topical and geographical sections, each with extensive details about bibliographies and other reference works, as well as serials. Indexes by author name, title, subject, and geographical location.

222   Fage, J.D. **A Guide to Original Sources for Precolonial Western Africa Published in European Languages: For the Most Part in Book Form**. Rev. ed.
Madison, WI: African Studies Program, University of Wisconsin, 1994. 200 pp.
Provides critical annotations of a large number of published sources from ca. 800 to 1871. This guide is now available electronically as part of the University of Wisconsin-Madison ➜ **Africana Digitization Project,** *see* entry **169.**

223 International African Bibliography 1973-1978: Books, Articles and Papers in African Studies. Edited by J.D. Pearson. London: Mansell, 1982. 374 pp.
Cumulates 24 consecutive issues (vols. 3-8) of the ➔ International African Bibliography (387), and adds some 3,000 further entries. Arrangement is by subject and regions, and thereafter sub-divided by country/subject.

224 International African Institute **Cumulative Bibliography of African Studies.** Boston: G.K. Hall, 1973. Microfilm. Author catalogue, 4 reels Classified catalogue, 6 reels
Contains all the titles of books and articles listed in the quarterly bibliography published in the journal ➔Africa (734), from 1929 to 1970, and in the ➔ International African Bibliography (387)), during 1971 and 1972.
(*Note: see also* Hall, D. **"Cumulative Bibliography of African Studies: A Guide"** In *Africa Bibliography. Works on Africa published during 1997*, edited by Christopher Allen. Edinburgh: Edinburgh University Press; London: International African Institute, 1999, vii-cvii.)

225 Kagan, Alfred **Reference Guide to Africa. A Bibliography of Sources.**
2nd rev. ed. Lanham, MD, and Oxford: Scarecrow Press, 2005. 231 pp. $55.00/ £36.00/€61.76
Note: 1st ed. Scarecrow Press, 1998, edited by Alfred Kagan and Yvette Scheven
A new 2nd edition of this benchmark African studies reference tool was published in late 2005. The second edition includes many more works for the study of North Africa and Islam in Africa, as well as more sources in electronic format, although the emphasis is still very much on print reference works. More than half the entries are either new or have been modified in some way. A fairly substantial number of older titles have been dropped. Details of ➔ **Conover-Porter Award (2828)** winners, and those singled out for honourable mention, are now identified with entries. The basic concept has not changed, and arrangement is the same as for the previous edition. The guide lists and annotates the most important resources for the study of Africa, primarily in the humanities and the social sciences. The second edition contains 793 entries, but resources useful for more than one topic are entered as often as appropriate. Most titles are in English, but there are also a small number of entries of material in French. Annotations are descriptive for the most part, rather than critical. The guide is divided into two major sections: General Sources and Subject Sources, followed by author/title and subject indexes. Both sections include reference resources such as bibliographies and indexes, handbooks and directories, encyclopaedias, surveys, biographical works, government publications and statistical sources, electronic databases, and online resources. Most listings refer to book titles, but there are also citations of serials, chapters in books, articles in periodicals, CD-ROMs and other electronic products. The subject sections comprise seventeen chapters, covering specific academic disciplines. Each chapter suggests Library of Congress subject headings, and is preceded by helpful introductory notes and guidance.
Online reviews: (of 1st ed.)
African Studies Quarterly, vol. 3, no. 1, 1999 (reviewed by Gregory A. Finnegan)
http://web.africa.ufl.edu/asq/v3/v3i1a8.htm
Africana Libraries Newsletter, no. 100, Fall 1999 (reviewed by Patricia S. Kuntz)

http://www.indiana.edu/~libsalc/african/aln/fall99.html
ARD review:
African Research & Documentation, no. 81 (1999): 81-82 (reviewed by Sheila Allcock)
Choice review:
Choice June 1999 (reviewed by David Westley)
CHOICE OUTSTANDING ACADEMIC TITLE 1999

→ **L'Afrique en Livres** *see* **388**

226　　Mason-Middleton, Cheryl J. **Keeping up with Africa: A Selective Annotated Bibliography.** *Reference Services Review* 31, no. 22 (February 2003): 185-202. Online at
http://www.emeraldinsight.com/Insight/viewContentItem.do?contentType=Articl e&contentId=861734 (Subscription based) or
http://www.geocities.com/cjmasonm/CJMM/p185.pdf
Written principally for reference librarians who may find themselves faced with more and varied questions concerning African affairs and current events, this article presents resources for developing an understanding of African affairs, and keeping up-to-date with African economic, governance, and development issues on a day-to-day basis. It lists over 70 recent resources – all with fairly detailed evaluative annotations – grouped by topics such as history and background, foreign aid, conflict resolution, politics and governance, democracy, corruption, development and human rights. It also offers a section on select news resources for Africa, in both print and online formats. A good starting point for the non-specialist, and for public libraries.

227　　McIlwaine, John **Africa: A Guide to Reference Material.** 2nd rev. and expanded ed. Locharron, Scotland: Hans Zell Publishing, 2006/07 (forthcoming late 2006/early 2007) ca. 600 pp. ca. £120.00/€180.00/$240.00
First published in 1993, this is a new revised and substantially expanded edition of a classic African studies reference work that evaluates the leading sources of information on Africa South of the Sahara (other than bibliographies, for which consult items → **225, 234, 235,** and **383).** The second edition will contain some 2,000 annotated entries, covering encyclopaedias, dictionaries, directories, handbooks, atlases and gazetteers, almanacs, yearbooks, topographic reference sources, directories of organizations, as well as biographical and statistical sources. Each title – most of them personally examined by the compiler – is described and analysed for content. Bibliographies on Africa, and inter-lingual dictionaries, are not included, as they are already well covered in a number of other sources, both retrospective and current. Following a general section on Africa as a whole (with sub-divisions by special subjects), material is arranged under broad regions of Africa, and then by individual countries. In addition to including new reference material that has appeared in print format since 1992, this new edition now also lists a substantial number of electronic resources, which are critically reviewed and evaluated. The second edition will focus on reference material published since 1938, and will not repeat the entries for 19th and early 20th century publications contained in the first edition. (London: Hans Zell Publishers, 1993). Entirely new sections will include a selection of the principal reference sources in the biological sciences, especially on flora and fauna, and the earth sciences, including habitat and geology. With a combined author, title and topics index.

ARD review: (of 1st ed.)
African Research & Documentation, no. 62 (1993): 50-51 (reviewed by Barbara Turfan)
Choice review:
Choice October 1993 (reviewed by Gretchen Walsh)

228   Mohan, P.C. **Bibliography of Publications, Technical Department, Africa Region, July 1987 to April 1996**. Washington, DC: The World Bank, 1996. 52 pp. (World Bank Technical Paper, 329)
A complete annotated listing of all formal and informal publications produced by the staff and consultants of the Africa Technical Department of the World Bank, from July 1987 through April 1996, covering the Technical Department's work in Africa in all sectors. Arranged by departmental and divisional publications, and chronologically within each section. Information is also given how to acquire these publications. *See also* ➔ entry **229** below.

229   Mohan, P.C. **Bibliography of Publications: Africa Region, 1993-98.**
Washington, DC: World Bank, 1999. 59 pp. (World Bank Technical Paper, 425)
A list of formal and informal publications produced by the staff and consultants of the ➔ **World Bank's (2548)** Africa Region from 1993 through April 1998. It covers the region's work in Africa in all sectors. Publications listed in the bibliography include World Bank Technical Papers, Discussion Papers and monographs, regional monographs, and publications from the regional studies program. *See also* ➔ preceding entry **228**.

230   Northwestern University. Melville Herskovits Library of African Studies.
Africana File Listing as of April 1988. Evanston, IL: Melville J. Herskovits Library of African Studies, Northwestern University Library, 1988. 61 microfiche
An index of all major publications in ➔ **Northwestern University Library's (1322)** extensive Africana vertical files, containing African government publications, political party and trade union materials, and company reports. 16,000 records are accessible by 37,000 index entries. Volume holdings of serials are included. There is a combined index by author, title, and added entry, in a single alphabetical sequence. [Not examined]

231   Phillips, Joan T. **Africa.** Maxwell Air Force Base: Air University Library [600 Chennault Circle, Building 1405, Maxwell Air Force Base, Alabama 36112-6424], 2001. 235 pp. (Special Bibliography, 159, suppl. no. 32) print and online
online at http://www.au.af.mil/au/aul/bibs/africa/aftoc.htm [29/06/05]
Further supplements:
July 2002, http://www.au.af.mil/au/aul/bibs/africa02/aftoc02.htm [29/06/05]
July 2003, Special Bibliography, 159, suppl. no. 36
http://www.au.af.mil/au/aul/bibs/africa03/aftoc03.htm [29/06/05]
December 2004, Special Bibliography, 159, suppl. no. 37
http://www.au.af.mil/au/aul/bibs/africa04/afr4toc.htm [29/06/05]
A series of regular bibliographies (and supplements thereon) on topics and regions currently being studied at Air University. Provides annotated listings of some general Internet resources, followed by topic-specific sections on economic conditions, foreign relations, health, history, the military, natural resources, politics

and governments, social aspects, and the African Union, plus sections on regions and individual countries. Each section lists recent book titles, periodical articles, and some other documents. Useful for tracking down recent literature in the above areas, and especially for its numerous links to articles that are available online.

232   Porges, Laurence **Sources d'information sur l'Afrique noire francophone et Madagascar. Institutions, répertoires, bibliographies.** Paris: La Documentation française/Ministère de la coopération, 1988. 389 pp

A comprehensive guide to sources of information on francophone Africa and Madagascar, containing 1,498 mostly annotated entries, and several indexes. Part 1 lists sources for research institutions, associations and societies, libraries and documentation centres, official publications, magazines and periodicals, theses, and general and specialist bibliographies. Part 2 provides an inventory of bibliographies, directories and other sources of information on a country-by-country basis, with each country section also including information about institutes, research centres and universities, as well as museums, archival collections, and more. Unfortunately no further editions would appear to have been published of this valuable reference resource.

233   Porter, Andrew, ed. **Bibliography of Imperial and Commonwealth History since 1600.** Oxford and New York: Oxford University Press, 2002. 1,080 pp. £95.00/ $275.00

This volume is part of the Royal Historical Society bibliography *The History of Britain, Ireland and the British Overseas* project containing almost 24,000 items and arranged under 14 sections, e.g. Population and Environment, Social Structure and Organization, Gender, Economic Activity and Organization, Slavery, the Arts, Religion and Belief, etc, further divided in geographical/chronological sub-sections. The volume contains a substantial number of entries relating to African countries that are part of the Commonwealth, but coverage is rather patchy, and there are no annotations.

ARD review:
African Research & Documentation, no. 92 (2003): 75-77 (reviewed by John McIlwaine)
Choice review:
Choice May 2003 (reviewed by C.E. King)
CHOICE OUTSTANDING ACADEMIC TITLE 2003

234   Scheven, Yvette **Bibliographies for African Studies, 1970-1986.** Oxford: Hans Zell Publishers, 1988. 637 pp.
235   Scheven, Yvette **Bibliographies for African Studies, 1987-1993.** London: Hans Zell Publishers, 1994. 198 pp.

The definitive resource for bibliographies published in the African studies field up to 1993. The volume covering the period 1970-1986 provides 3,245 annotated references, with each entry giving information about the scope and number of items in each bibliography, whether it is annotated, how it is arranged, and the type of index(es) included. The continuation volume for 1987-1993 gives details of a further 834 titles. Arrangement in the 1970-1986 volume is by some 100 subject and geographical sections; the supplementary volume lists titles under Library of Congress subject headings. Author and subject indexes facilitate access. Continued by "Africana

Reference Works: An Annotated List of ....Titles" appearing annually in ➔ **The African Book Publishing Record** (*see* separate entry **383**).
WINNER (1987-1993 volume) CONOVER-PORTER AWARD 1990
ARD review: (review of 1987-1993 volume)
African Research & Documentation, no. 69 (1995): 55-56 (reviewed by John McIlwaine)
Choice review: (review of 1987-1993 volume)
Choice May 1995 (reviewed by Gretchen Walsh)
CHOICE OUTSTANDING ACADEMIC TITLE 1995

236 Schmidt, Nancy J. **"Africana Resources for Undergraduates: A Bibliographic Essay."** In *Africa* ed. by Phyllis M. Martin and Patrick O'Meara, 3rd ed. Bloomington, IN: Indiana University Press; London: James Currey, 1995, 411-434.
online at http://www.indiana.edu/~libsalc/african/schmidt.html [21/06/05]
A bibliographic essay – now a rather dated, but still helpful both for undergraduates, and librarians who select materials for undergraduate collections – that forms a chapter in a popular introductory text for African studies courses. It describes general, easily accessible, resources for students starting off in African studies, with a focus on resources in English, published or reissued since 1980. It includes details of a number of audiovisual and computer resources, as well as journals and reference materials. Arranged under broad subject sections.

237 Scott, Rebecca J., Thomas C. Holt, Frederick Cooper, and Aims McGuinness **Societies after Slavery. A Select Annotated Bibliography of Printed Sources on Cuba, Brazil, British Colonial Africa, South Africa, and the British West Indies.**
Pittsburgh, PA: University of Pittsburgh Press, 2002. 432 pp. $65.00 cased $39.95 pap.
Aims to identify primary and secondary sources on all aspects of slavery and the emancipation of slaves, including parliamentary and congressional hearings and enquiries, reports of governmental and international agencies, missionary records and documents, census reports, personal memoirs, surveys, autobiographical accounts, sociological and ethnographic studies, and transcripts of oral interviews. There are more than 1,600 entries, in many languages, most of them annotated and arranged geographically and sub-divided by type of resources. For Africa the work provides 279 references relating to British Colonial Africa and 139 for South Africa. Lacks an index.
Choice review:
Choice December 2002 (reviewed by B.D. Singleton)

238 Thomas, Norman E. **International Mission Bibliography: 1960-2000.**
Lanham, MD and Oxford: Scarecrow Press 2003. 888 pp. $130.00/£99.00/€169.83
(ATLA Bibliography Series, 48)
Contains 15,850 entries listing the most important works in all areas of mission-related disciplines published from 1960 to 2000, providing full bibliographic data for each entry, together with a short annotation describing content of each item. An international team of 37 sub-editors assisted the editor in the compilation of this massive reference resource, which covers books only and periodical articles are not included. It is arranged under a series of subject headings based on those of the Library of Congress and the Religion One Index, and further developed building on subject headings used by a number of missiological institutes and documentation centres. Major headings (each with extensive sub-sections) include Missions: History,

Theology, Methods, Social Aspects, Economic Life; Communication and Missions, Education and Missions, Evangelism and Missions, Missionaries, Spirituality, and more, together with sections on Africa, the Americas, Asia, Europe, and Oceania. Each main section is preceded by a short introduction by the editor. The section on Africa, for which Walter Cason and the late Adrian Hastings (former editor of the ➔ **Journal of Religion in Africa (768)**) acted as the sub-editors, has 1,375 annotated entries grouped under a number of sub-headings such as Bibliographies, Serials, Documentation and Archives, General Works, History, Conferences and Congresses, Church and Society, African Biography (of both missionaries and national Christian leaders), African Theologies, etc. together with regional and country sub-sections. While the bulk of the entries relate to books published in English, there are a good number of listings of literature in French, German, Italian, and Portuguese. There is an extensive index of personal names. The culmination of eighteen years of work, this is a key resource for research on all aspects of missiology.
Choice review:
Choice May 2004 (reviewed by D.R. Stewart)

239   Travis, Carole, and Miriam Alman **Periodicals from Africa: A Bibliography and Union List of Periodicals Published in Africa.** Boston: G.K. Hall, 1977. 619 pp.
Lists 17,000 titles with locations in 60 British libraries, covering all countries except Egypt. *First Supplement* by D.S. Blake and C. Travis (Boston: G.K. Hall, 1984, 217pp.) gives a further 7,000 titles published through August 1979. (A *Second Supplement,* by D.S. Blake, is reportedly in preparation, but has not been examined.) Published for the ➔ **Standing Conference of Library Materials on Africa (1892)**.

240   **USAID Publications on Africa**
USAID Publications on Africa 1999 to the Present. Washington, DC: USAID-Sub Saharan Africa, 1999. 12 pp.
online as a pdf document
http://www.usaid.gov/regions/afr/pubs/docs/2001pubslist.pdf [01/07/05]
USAID Publications on Africa 2002 to the Present. Washington, DC: USAID-Sub Saharan Africa, 2004. 21 pp. [covers mainly titles published between 2001 and 2003]
online as a pdf document http://www.usaid.gov/locations/sub-saharan_africa/publications/docs/pubslist05.pdf [01/07/05]
Lists a selection of publications produced by the ➔ **USAID's Bureau for Africa (2623)** and its partners from 1999 onwards, and is periodically updated. Most titles are available electronically (or, at a charge, in paper or diskette format) from Development Experience Clearinghouse 8403 Colesville Road, Suite 210 Silver Spring, MD 20910, Email: docorder@dec.cdie.org, and can be downloaded at http://www.dec.org. Earlier (biennial) compilations were published in print format by the USAID Center for Development Information and Evaluation, Arlington, VA.

241   **World Bibliographical Series** Santa Barbara, CA, and Oxford: ABC-Clio, 1979-2002. [discontinued]
The *African Studies Companion* does not include country-specific bibliographies, but it is appropriate to offer a comment here about this series, although now *discontinued* by ABC Clio:

The **World Bibliographical Series** consists of a number of selective annotated bibliographies that aim to cover every country in the world. Each multidisciplinary volume has been prepared by a recognized country specialist, and the series includes more than 200 titles, of which 47 are on the countries of Africa. Each volume consists of annotated entries of selected literature on the country's history, ethnic groups, politics, arts and cultures, religion, education, geography, etc. Most volumes in the series aim to focus on materials in English that are accessible to general readers and available in most public libraries, with an emphasis on current publications and monographs, although journal articles are also covered, albeit selectively. Each volume starts off with an introductory essay and the annotated entries that follow – for the most part descriptive rather than critical annotations - are organized under 30 or so subject divisions, and they also offer listings of references works and periodicals which help the reader to locate other finding tools for the study of any country. The number of entries varies from country to country, from around 300-400 citations (for a small country like The Gambia) to 1,000 or more for larger countries. The main bibliographic sections are followed by author, title, and subject indexes. Several of the more recently published volumes also include listings of theses and dissertations, most include chronologies and charts, and some include map listings.

Some regional bibliographies and resources

242   Blackhurst, Hector **East and Northeast Africa Bibliography.** Lanham, MD, and Oxford: Scarecrow Press, 1996. 301 pp. $68.00/£52.00/€89.21 (Scarecrow Area Bibliographies, 7)
List 3,838 entries arranged by subject headings and covering Djibouti, Eritrea, Ethiopia, Kenya, Somalia, Sudan, Tanzania and Uganda. The bibliography covers titles published between 1960 and 1994, but is limited to books and monographs, without any details of periodical articles, nor are there any annotations. With an author index.
ARD review:
African Research & Documentation, no. 75 (1997): 58-59 (reviewed by Barbara Turfan)
Choice review:
Choice March 1997 (reviewed by Alfred Kagan)

243   Harris, Gordon **Central and Equatorial Area Bibliography.** Lanham, MD, and Oxford: Scarecrow Press, 1999. 256 pp. $68.00/£52.00/€89.21 (Scarecrow Area Bibliographies, 18)
Lists 1,764 items, arranged geographically and by topics, covering Chad, Central African Republic, Saõ Tomé e Principe, Equatorial Guinea, Gabon, People's Republic of the Congo, Democratic Republic of the Congo, Rwanda, Burundi, Zambia and Malawi.
Choice review:
Choice February 2000 (reviewed by Gretchen Walsh)

244   Musiker, Reuben, and Naomi Musiker **Southern Africa Bibliography.**
Lanham, MD, and Oxford: Scarecrow Press, 1996. 287 pp. $58.00/£44.00/€75.48
(Scarecrow Area Bibliographies, 11)
Aims to bring together all books published during the past half century (i.e. since
1945) dealing with southern Africa: Angola, Botswana, Lesotho, Malawi,
Mozambique, Namibia, South Africa, Swaziland, Zambia, and Zimbabwe.
Arrangement is alphabetical by country, sub-arranged by fairly broad subject fields,
some of which have further sub-divisions. Author index.
ARD review:
African Research & Documentation, no. 76 (1998): 56-58 (reviewed by John McIlwaine)

245   Nuñez, Benjamin **Dictionary of Portuguese-African Civilization.** 2 vols.
Volume 1: **From Discovery to Independence.** Volume 2: **From Ancient Kings to
Presidents.** London: Hans Zell Publishers, vol. 1, 1995 560 pp.; vol. 2, 1996, 502 pp.
Volume 1 includes some 3,000 terms and phrases as they relate to the Portuguese
presence in Africa, covering historical and political events, social life and customs,
religion, geographical names, flora, fauna, artefacts, organizations, literature, culture,
and more. Volume 2 provides over 2,000 biographical sketches of Europeans,
Africans, Arabs and others who played an important role in the making of the five
Portuguese-speaking countries of Africa.
ARD review:
African Research & Documentation, no 70 (1996): 75 (reviewed by Patrick Chabal;
review of vol. 1 only)
Choice review:
Choice November 1995 (vol. 1) October 1996 (vol. 2) (reviewed by M.L. Grover)

246   Skreslet, Paula Youngman **Northern Africa. A Guide to Reference and
Information Sources.** Greenwood Village, CO: Libraries Unlimited, 2000. 405 pp.
$93.95
Containing nearly 1,500 entries (including some 400 Web sites), this impressive and
well-organized annotated bibliography describes a broad range of print and
electronic resources published over the past decade or so on Northern Africa and the
Maghreb, the Sahel region, and the Horn of Africa. The book is organized under
three sections: part 1 covers general works, part 2 lists area studies references by
subject, and part 3 gives sources by regions and by country. The annotations are
quite substantial, drawing attention to special features and merits of each work cited.
An excellent index covers ethnographic, geographic, language names, and topics;
and by authors, title of work, and subject. An outstanding reference tool.
ARD review:
African Research & Documentation, no. 87 (2001): 102-103 (reviewed by John
McIlwaine)
Choice review:
Choice March 2001 (reviewed by Gretchen Walsh)
Online review:
H-Africa, February 2003 (reviewed by Daniel A. Reboussin)
http://www.h-net.org/reviews/showrev.cgi?path=116171047793336

Dictionaries and glossaries

247   **Historical Dictionaries of Africa** Lanham, MD, and Oxford: Scarecrow
Press, 1974- (in progress)
For complete list of titles in the series visit the publisher's Web site at
http://www.scarecrowpress.com/ and search for "Historical Dictionaries of Africa"
Country or subject-specific references sources are not included in the *African Studies
Companion,* but we offer this general note about the series:

This well established series of reference resources on Africa from Scarecrow Press,
begun in the mid-seventies, now covers more than 50 African titles, with many of
them reissued in second, third, or fourth editions. Each casebound volume costs
between $80-$120 depending on length and date published. In addition to the series
devoted to countries, there are also sub-series devoted to cities of the world,
organizations, and dictionaries of war, revolution and civil unrest. Books in the
country series provide, in dictionary format, contemporary information about each
country, and its history, economic and social aspects, geography, ethnic groups, etc.
together with factual information on events, institutions, and biographical profiles.
The biographical entries cover past and present political leaders, statesmen and
women, diplomats, military leaders, educators, labour leaders, religious leaders,
entrepreneurs, business leaders, and more. Most volumes include a chronology,
statistical tables, a few maps, lists of ethnic groups, lists of acronyms and
abbreviations, and a selective but frequently quite extensive bibliography, albeit
without annotations. The series is edited by Jon Woronoff.

248   Arnold, Guy **Historical Dictionary of Civil Wars in Africa.** Lanham, MD,
and Oxford: Scarecrow Press (Historical Dictionaries of War, Revolution, and Civil
Unrest, 11), 1999. 480 pp. $78.00/£59.00/€101.21
Provides information about civil wars that have taken place in Africa during the
years of the independence area since 1945 (and up to 1998). Following an
introduction and a chronology of events at the beginning of the book, the entries
cover civil wars and conflict, individual leaders, liberation movements, political,
military, and guerrilla groups involved in these conflicts, and the external countries
and agencies that have attempted to mediate. The book includes a fairly extensive
bibliography, but lacks an index.
ARD review:
African Research & Documentation, no. 84 (2000): 77-78 (reviewed by Sheila Allcock)
Choice review:
Choice February 2002 (reviewed by R.B.M. Ridinger)

249   Collins, Robert O. **Historical Dictionary of Pre-Colonial Africa.** Lanham,
MD, and Oxford: Scarecrow Press (Historical Dictionaries of Ancient Civilizations
and Historical Areas, 3), 2001. 688 pp. $107.00/£82.00/€140.67
Seeks to familiarize the reader with pre-colonial Africa (with some emphasis on
northern Africa, Egypt and the Arab countries), from 500 BC through to the period
just before European colonization in the 19th century. A general introduction is
followed by a chronology of the rise and fall of the dynasties that ruled the great
kingdoms of Africa. The dictionary part consists of about 2,000 short entries covering

individuals, ethnic groups, languages, places, and events, etc. There is an extensive bibliography, arranged by regions and sub-topics, and the book also includes an introductory essay in which the author reviews the literature and seminal texts of note.
Choice review:
Choice December 2002 (reviewed by E.B. Lindsay)

→ **Historical Dictionary of Women in Sub-Saharan Africa**, edited by Kathleen Sheldon *see* **4 Major biographical sources** entry **430**

250 **International Dictionary of Historic Places**, vol. 4: **Middle East and Africa.** Edited by K.A. Berney and Trudy Ring. Chicago: Fitzroy Dearborn Publishers, 1996. 766 pp.
Contains 94 entries on African historic places. Each article, with information on location, description, and site office details, is several pages long and has a short bibliography. Includes a list of places by country and an extensive index. Illustrated in black and white with photographs and maps. [Not examined]

251 Majumdar, Margaret A. (ed.) **Francophone Studies: The Essential Glossary.** London: Hodder Arnold; New York: Oxford University Press 2002. 320 pp. £16.99/ $35.00
Designed as an introduction to francophone culture and society and as a roadmap to further study, this glossary-cum-dictionary contains around 400 short explanations of the key words, events, figures, and concepts in francophone studies since 1945. It covers politics, popular culture, private life, cultural institutions, and biographical information, including a substantial number of entries relating to francophone Africa.

252 Olson, James S. **The Peoples of Africa: an Ethnohistorical Dictionary**. Westport, CT: Greenwood Press, 1996. 681 pp. $151.95/£87.00
Provides descriptions (and population estimates for many) of some 1,800 African ethnic groups, some of which are discussed in terms of their geographical settings, religion, population, and economy. Most entries – some rather eclectic, or very brief – cite sources of information (albeit not always complete and some lack imprint information), a description of the locale of the group, population estimates, and brief ethnographic descriptions for many. The volume is extensively cross-referenced. Also contains a chronology of African history and a select bibliography, but which is somewhat flawed.
Choice review:
Choice December 1996 (reviewed by D.S. Azzolina)

253 **A Political and Economic Dictionary of Africa.** Edited by David Seddon and Leo Zeilig. London: Europa Publications, 2005. 400 pp. £100.00/$195.00
A guide to the politics and economics of the African continent, with detailed and cross-referenced entries covering regions, ethnic groups, religions, political parties, prime ministers, presidents and other politicians, as well as business organizations, geographical features, and border disputes. Each country, and their economies, are also dealt with in separate essays. Organizations listed include contact details wherever possible. [Not examined]

254   Scheub, Harold **A Dictionary of African Mythology. The Mythmaker as Storyteller.** Oxford and New York: Oxford University Press, 2002. 384 pp. $16.95
Online: http://www.oxfordreference.com/pages/Subjects_and_Titles__2E_MF01
(part of Oxford Reference Online premium collection, available by annual subscription for institutions and individuals. For subscription rates see URL above.)
A collection of 400 entries, arranged alphabetically in dictionary format, of African myths and folk tales that touch on virtually every aspect of religious belief, and capturing the diversity of African mythology. Scheub not only retells each story, but provides information about the respective belief system, the cultural contexts of the stories, the main characters, related stories or variants, and emphasizes the role of mythmaker as storyteller, as a performer for an audience. Entries cover the entire continent, including North African as well as sub-Saharan cultures. [Online version not examined]
Choice review:
Choice June 2000 (reviewed by David Westley)
CHOICE OUTSTANDING ACADEMIC TITLE 2000

Directories of libraries and museums

See also ➔ **Guides to library, archival and manuscript collections**

255   **Africana Librarians Council Directory.**
Comp. by Greg Finnegan. Cambridge, MA: Africana Librarians Council. [c/o Greg Finnegan, Tozzer Library, Harvard University], 1999.
Superseded by online edition, compiled by Miki Goral and Joanne M. Zellers, published as **Africana Librarians Council (ALC), ALC Directory as of October 20, 2004** [latest version, freely accessible]
http://www.loc.gov/rr/amed/afs/alc/alcdir10202004.html   (
Compiled for the use of members of the ➔**Africana Librarians Council (1025)** of the (US) ➔**African Studies Association (1773),** this directory lists the names of Africana librarians at the major institutions in the USA, as well as listing a small number of Africana book dealers, and some other people associated with African studies librarianship. The latest online edition gives 85 names and addresses, with telephone, fax numbers and email addresses.

256   Bannerman, Valentia, comp. **Directory of University Libraries and Professional Librarians in the West African Sub-Region.** Winneba, Ghana: Standing Conference of African University Libraries - Western Area (SCAULWA), c/o UCEW Library, University College of Education of Winneba [PO Box 25, Winneba, Ghana; Email: ucewlib@libr.ug.edu.gh or valnin@yahoo.com], 2002.
411 pp. $40.00/£26.00 (includes airmail postage)
This is an information resource on academic libraries and the library professions in anglophone and francophone West Africa. It is both a directory of university libraries, as well as a kind of who's who in academic librarianship in the region. Data was collected through questionnaire mailings and, when duly completed and returned to the compiler, information provided can be very full, although there are also a substantial number of entries where the information is scant because

respondents failed to complete all sections of the questionnaire. For each country/institution information includes: (1) details about each library with full address and contact details, telephone/fax number, email, Web sites for a small number, names and positions of senior staff, number of professional and para-professional staff, opening hours, type of library users served, major subject coverage, special collections, classification system used, type of library catalogue, services provided, size of book collections, size of serial collections, and publications. This is followed by, (2) listings of professional staff at each library, with details of position held, date of birth, nationality, professional qualifications and degrees, personal email address (where available), publications over the past five years and papers presented at conferences and workshops, areas of special interest, and more.

➜ **The Book Chain in Anglophone Africa. A Survey and Directory**, edited by Roger Stringer, *see* **Directories of publishers and the media** entry **260**

➜ **Directory of Museum Professionals in Africa** *see* **1 General online resources on Africa and African Studies and the best starting points on the Web: Guides to Museums** entry **147**

257   **Directory of Museums in West Africa/Répertoire des musées de l'afrique de l'ouest.** Dakar: West African Museums Programme [BP 357, 11 route du Front de Terre, Dakar, Senegal], 2002. 222 pp.
A bi-lingual directory containing extensive information on 145 museums in West Africa, including full address details, status, governing body, size of collections, opening hours, admission fees, and name of director or curator.

258   Visiting Arts **"Visiting Arts Southern Africa Regional Arts Profile" series**
Researched and written by Tim Doling
Angola Arts Directory 60 pp.; **Botswana Arts Directory** 60 pp.; **Lesotho Arts Directory** 56 pp.; **Namibia Arts Directory** 76 pp.; **Malawi Arts Directory** 48 pp.; **Mozambique Arts Directory** 63 pp.; **South Africa Arts Directory** 252 pp.; **Swaziland Arts Directory** 48 pp.; **Tanzania Arts Directory** 72 pp.; **Zambia Arts Directory** 64 pp.; **Zimbabwe Arts Directory** 96 pp. £10.00 each (£11.00 for the South Africa Arts Directory), or £75.00 per complete set, plus postage and packing
London: Visiting Arts, Publications Department [11 Portland Place, London W1N 4EJ], 1999. [Orders to: Cornerhouse Publications, 70 Oxford Street, Manchester M1 5NH, Email: publications@cornerhouse.org]
This impressive series of arts directories covering 11 countries in southern Africa is designed to promote each country's arts and culture at a practical level, and to stimulate international arts and cultural activity. Many African scholars and specialists in the arts have contributed to the project, and which also enjoyed the active collaboration of British Council offices throughout the region. Each directory is preceded by an introduction that gives essential historical and other background information about the country. The directory sections follow a standard format and provide descriptions and contact details for organizations across the various cultural sectors: cultural agencies and institutions in each country (government ministries, national institutions, NGOs, etc.); performing arts venues, visual arts galleries, studios, craft shops and workshops; museums and heritage sites; arts festivals, arts training and research institutions; cultural information centres (archives, libraries,

and resource centres), and sources for arts funding. Entries are very full, providing not only complete name and address, telephone, fax, email addresses (plus Web sites where available) and contact personnel, but also a brief description of the activities of each organization or institution, opening hours (where appropriate), and more.
ARD review: (of *South Africa Arts Directory*)
African Research & Documentation, no 87 (2001): 110-111 (reviewed by Terry Barringer)

Directories of publishers and the media

See also → **1 General online resources on Africa and African studies, and the best starting points on the Web: Guides to media and the press**

259   The African Publishing Companion. A Resource Guide. Compiled and edited by Hans M. Zell. Lochcarron, Scotland: Hans Zell Publishing, 2002. 356 pp. wire-bound print edition and online £80.00/€158.00/$130 (online version no longer available)
Containing over, 1,600 entries and extensively cross-referenced, this is probably the most complete and up-to-date documentation and information resource on African publishing and the book trade currently available. Content includes (1) a directory of almost 700 African publishers' email addresses and Web sites (where available), including those of NGOs and research institutions with publishing activities. (2) Over 500 annotated directory listings of organizations, associations, book development councils, networks and donors supporting African publishing, bibliographic tools, journals and magazines, book review outlets, dealers and distributors of African books, booksellers and library suppliers in Africa, African book fairs and book promotional events, book and literary awards, book industry training courses, and more; full address and contact information is provided for each entry, including email addresses and Web sites, where available. (3) A separate section describing schemes, book series, and other projects promoting African book and journal publishing. (4) Information and resources on African publishing statistics and publishing capacity, and a chronology of key dates in the development of indigenous African publishing. (5) The final section is an extensive bibliographic guide to current literature about African publishing and book development – in print format and available online – arranged by topics, and containing almost 500 entries, most with abstracts. No new editions are planned at this time.
Choice review:
Choice November 2002 (reviewed by Alfred Kagan)
Online review:
H-Africa, June 2003 (reviewed by Gretchen Walsh)
http://www.h-net.org/reviews/showrev.cgi?path=247181058802294

260   The Book Chain in Anglophone Africa. A Survey and Directory. Edited by Roger Stringer. Oxford: International Network for the Availability of Scientific Publications (INASP), 2002. 274 pp. print ed. £30.00,
online, accessible free, http://www.inasp.info/pubs/bookchain/index.html [07/07/05]
CD-ROM version (in English and French) available early in 2003.

This valuable information resource provides a country-by-country analysis of the "book chain" in 18 English-speaking Africa countries, together with an annotated directory of the major players that make up the book chain within those countries. Four introductory articles provide overviews of book and library development in anglophone Africa from different perspectives. These are followed by country surveys, each prepared by a book professional from the country concerned, most of them librarians. The final section, a 170-page Directory of Selected Organizations in the Book Chain in Anglophone Africa, provides listings of the major players in the book chain in each of the countries covered, including professional associations, major publishers, printers, booksellers and libraries; regional and international bodies supporting book development, and training institutions for librarianship and the book industries. Each entry gives full address, telephone and fax numbers, email addresses (and Web sites for some), and many entries include a short description. The extensive listings of libraries – national libraries, public libraries/national library services, national archives, academic/higher education, and special libraries – and in the absence of other recently published directories of libraries in Africa, makes this volume probably the most up-to-date and most comprehensive source to the library world in English-speaking Africa currently available in print format, although there are a few curious omissions, e.g. no listings of Nigerian academic libraries.

261   **Directory of African Media**. Edited by Adewale Maja-Pearce. Brussels: International Federation of Journalists/Féderation internationale des journalistes [rue Royale 266, 1210 Brussels, Belgium], 1996. 384 pp.
(Also available in a French edition, *Annuaire de la presse africaine*)
Compiled with the active collaboration of African journalists who assisted with data gathering for individual African countries, this is a comprehensive source to the press in sub-Saharan Africa, although it covers only independent newspapers and is now inevitably very dated; and the title is slightly misleading as no other media such as broadcasting and TV stations, are included. It lists not only large-circulation newspapers for each country, but also a substantial number of news weeklies and current affairs magazines. Information for each entry is very full, and country listings are preceded by insightful short essays providing an overview of the state of the media in each Africa country (as at 1995), "identifying the ups and downs in the fight for press freedom." No new editions have been published to date.

➜ **Répertoire des médias en Afrique de l'Ouest** [print version] *see* **1 General online resources on Africa and African studies, and the best starting points on the Web: Guides to media and the press** entry **144**

➜ **Southern African Media Directory 2004/05** *see* **1 General online resources on Africa and African studies, and the best starting points on the Web: Guides to media and the press** entry **143**

Directories of organizations and institutions

262 DeLancey, Mark W., and Terry M. Mays **Historical Dictionary of International Organizations in Sub-Saharan Africa.** 2nd ed. Lanham, MD, and Oxford: Scarecrow Press (International Organizations series, 21), 2002. 408 pp. $125.00/£95.00/€162.97

An extensive research guide, in dictionary format, to international and inter-governmental organizations and NGOs active in sub-Saharan Africa: regional, pan-African, sub-regional, African-European and African-Arab. Entries cover not only organizations – with descriptions of their roles and activities – but also include short entries and profiles of individuals who have played a significant part in the history of African international organizations. Additionally, the volume contains a very substantial bibliography of some 2,500 items by theme, a detailed chronology of organizations, a list of acronyms and abbreviations, and three appendixes: African organizations classified by field of activity; the charter of the Organisation of African Unity; and a listing of the past Secretary Generals of the OAU and the Executive Secretaries of the UN Economic Commission for Africa. The new 2nd edition provides entries for the many new African international organizations that have been chartered since 1995. It also includes updates to previously listed African international organizations, updates of the international events and agreements related to these bodies, and an update of the chronology.
Choice review:
Choice January 1995 (reviewed by P.W. Wilkins, review of first edition)

263 **Guide to Higher Education in Africa.** 2nd ed. London: Palgrave-Macmillan, 2002. 560 pp. £60.00

The second edition of a co-publication of the International Association of Universities and the ➔ **Association of African Universities (1608)**, this guide provides information on higher education throughout Africa, covering over 800 institutions in 46 African countries, as well as containing quite extensive background information on each country's national education system (structure, national bodies, admission to higher education, etc). Arranged alphabetically by country, most of the information provided is based on the academic year 2000-2001, and includes not only universities but also other public and private institutions of higher learning. Each entry gives full name and address, telephone/fax numbers, email addresses and Web sites (where available), and the names of the principal academic and administration officers. This is followed by details of faculties, colleges, schools, institutes, and departments for each institution, with the names of deans of faculties or directors of institutes; additional information includes a brief historical background about the institution, admission requirements, academic year, degrees and diplomas offered, student enrolment, number of academic staff, publications (for some), as well as information about links and cooperation arrangements with university institutions in other countries. There is also information about of the size of library collections at each institution.
ARD review:
African Research & Documentation, no. 96 (2004): 87 (reviewed by Terry Barringer)

264   International Network for the Availability of Scientific Publications (INASP) comp. **INASP Directory 2002/2003.** Oxford: International Network for the Availability of Scientific Publications, 2002. 350 pp. £30.00 (£10.00 as CD- ROM) Full-text online at http://www.inasp.info/pubs/directory/index.html [07/07/05] While not specifically focusing on Africa, this directory from the ➔**International Network for the Availability of Scientific Publications (2608)** is a useful resource as it provides detailed information on 348 agencies, organizations, institutions, learned societies, professional associations, donors, and foundations involved in activities that support the production, access and/or dissemination of information and knowledge in or between developing countries. It covers both subject-specific organizations in particular areas of the sciences, as well as organizations that specialise in library and book development, and for both groups this includes details of book and journal assistance schemes operated, or other type of support provided. Information is very full, and for most entries includes name and address, telephone/fax numbers, email address and Web site, contact personnel, aims and objectives and/or a mission statement, target audience, countries of operation, current activities, publications (if applicable), and future plans. A new edition is currently in preparation. Meantime many entries in the 2002/2003 edition have been updated to May/June 2004, and several entirely new entries have also been added.

265   Olsen, Kim **Contact Africa: Africa 2001. A Directory of US Organizations Working on Africa.** Washington, DC: The Africa-America Institute, 2001. 4th ed. 400 pp. $65.00
This is a handy resource from the Washington office of the ➔**Africa-America Institute (2727)**. The volume is arranged in six *separately* numbered sections, as Sections A to F, plus four indexes as Sections G to J. Section A contains quite full details on over 500 non-government organizations from US 42 states, with full postal address, email address, Web site, points of contact, dated founded, number of staff, mission statement, programme areas, countries of focus, offices in Africa (where applicable) and more. Sections B-F provide details and contact information for 40 executive branch federal agencies; congressional policymakers and committees including key US Senate and US House members; top officials at the World Bank, the IMF, the UN, and some other major international organizations; and Sections E and F are directories of African diplomatic representation in the US, and US diplomatic representation in Africa (both with full contact information and names of ambassadors). Sections G-I are Project Country Index: Non-Governmental Organizations, State Index: Non-Governmental Organizations, and Sector Index: Non-Governmental Organizations. A good starting point for anyone who wants to connect with the many US-based NGOs who have an interest and/or are active in Africa, or for use as a tool to contact government agencies and multilateral institutions working on Africa. However, no new editions have apparently appeared since the 4th edition was published in 2001 and therefore some information may now be dated.

Directories and guides to research and teaching, and of Africanist scholars (in print format)

See also ➔ 1 General online resources on Africa and African studies, and the best starting points on the Web: Online guides to African studies programmes and research centres

266   Aldridge, Delores, P. **Out of the Revolution: the Development of Africana Studies.** Lanham, MD: Lexington Books, 2000. 583 pp. $32.00 pap. $100.00 cased
A collection on 31 essays on the development and teaching of "Africana studies", but primarily related to African American and Black Studies in the USA. Contributions are presented in ten parts, and topics addressed include epistemological considerations, the role of bureaucracy and the academic institutions; social, political and economic dimensions; the position of black women in the field, and the future of Africana studies.
Choice review:
Choice October 2001 (reviewed by W.K. McNeil)

267   Bastian, Misty L., and Jane L. Parpart **Great Ideas for Teaching about Africa**. Boulder: Lynne Rienner, 1999. 244 pp. $29.95 pap. $55.00 cased
Designed for university undergraduate curricula and classroom instruction. Contains nineteen essays by scholars and teaching practitioners, divided into four parts: The Arts as Resources for Teaching, Controversial Subjects and Current Issues, New Technology in the Classroom, and Broader Approaches to Teaching about Africa. Each essay is followed by a bibliography and supplementary readings that were assigned. Although now a bit dated, there are lots of ideas here for the teaching of African studies, and how to enliven classroom instruction.
Choice review:
Choice November 1999 (reviewed by R.O. Ulin)
CHOICE OUTSTANDING ACADEMIC TITLE 1999

268   Conyers, James L. **Africana Studies. A Disciplinary Quest for Both Theory and Method**. Jefferson, NC: McFarland, 1997. 147 pp. $45.00
Explores the development of theory and methodology in establishing African and African diaspora studies as an academic discipline. Fifteen leaders in the field of Africana studies provide the conceptual framework for establishing the field as a mature discipline. The focus is on four basic areas: administration and organizational structure; disciplinary matrix; Africana womanism; and cultural aesthetics. The work examines both the theory and the method of scholars in African and African-diaspora studies.

269   **Directory of Africanists in Australia and the Pacific.** 6th ed. Compiled by Graeme Counsel and Wayne Pelling. Melbourne: African Studies Association of Australasia and the Pacific, 2005. AUD$10.00 (plus local or international postage) [Order from: Graeme Counsel, AFSAAP Secretary, c/o UMPA, Graduate Centre, University of Melbourne, Parkville, 3010, Victoria, Australia, Email: g.counsel@umpa.unimelb.edu.au]

The 6th edition of this directory published by →**African Studies Association of Australasia and the Pacific (2754)** contains over 300 entries with current contact information on African studies specialists and community organizations in Australasia and the Pacific regions. Each entry identifies the individual's research interests, disciplinary field, and geographic region(s) of specialization, in addition to listing their publications.

270 **A Directory of Africanists in Britain.** Compiled by Anne Merriman and Richard Hodder-Williams. 3rd ed. Bristol: University of Bristol on behalf of the Royal African Society [order from Professor Hodder-Williams, Department of Politics, University of Bristol, Bristol BS8 1TH, UK], 1996. 165 pp. £12.50
A who's who of Africanists in Britain, giving full names and address and institutional affiliations of 488 UK or UK-based African studies scholars, including telephone/fax numbers and email addresses. Other information given includes subject/regional interests, primary research areas, research in progress, and major publications. Indexes by discipline and by country of research. Unfortunately no further editions have been published to date.
ARD review:
African Research & Documentation, no. 70 (1996): 74-75 (reviewed by John McIlwaine)

271 Gordon, Jacob U., ed. **African Studies for the 21st Century.** Hauppauge, NY: Nova Science Publishers, 2004. 187 pp. $49.50 print/hardcover $39.00 e-book
Preceded by a foreword by Molefi Kete Asante, this volume brings together 15 essays on various topics relating to the field of African studies. Chapters include "African Studies: An Historical Perspective" (Augustine Konneh), "African Studies at Historically Black Colleges and Universities" (Alton Hornsby, Jr.), "African Studies in the Caribbean" (Patrick A. Grant and Pauline B. Grant), "African Studies in Special Education Programming: Problems and Prospects" (Festus E. Obiakor and Gathogo Mukuria), "Where Do We Go From Here?: Literature and African Studies" (Tara T. Green), "African Studies at the Undergraduate Level: A Perspective (I. Peter Ukpokodu), "African Languages: A Proven Pedagogy into the Window of the African Mind" (Michael O. Afolayan), and "African Studies and Black Women Studies" (Eunice Matthews). [Not examined]

272 Guyer, Jane I. **African Studies in the United States. A Perspective.** Atlanta, GA: African Studies Association Press, 1996. 106 pp.
Full-text available online at
http://www.africanstudies.org/guyer_index.html [07/07/05]
An overview of the status of African studies in the USA in the mid-1990s. Examines orientations in the scholarship on Africa in the US, linkages with Africa, patterns of advanced training in African studies, institutions involved in African studies and their future, and current debates and challenges. Also includes a variety of statistical analysis (e.g. on annual dissertation output), and a bibliography.

273 **"Identifying New Directions for African Studies."** *African Issues*, 15, no. 2 (2002) [publ. 2003], 88 pp. Editors: Cyril K. Daddieh and Jo Ellen Fair; Guest Editor: Larry W. Bowman
An informative and timely special number of → **African Issues (797)**, containing a collection of provocative papers that examine the challenges facing African studies in

an era of globalization, of African marginalization in the world's political economy, "and of contentious debate within American colleges and universities about how to best preserve and protect the field of African studies." It is based on a study – available online, *see* ➔ **The Survey of African Studies Faculty in the United States, 2002 (189)** – which surveyed African studies scholars on a range of issues facing the field, and is supported here by additional papers especially commissioned to complement the survey data, and to provide more detailed analysis of key issues and problems in African studies research.

274   International Directory of African Studies Research/Répertoire international des études africaines. Edited by the International African Institute and Compiled by Philip Baker. 3rd ed. London: Hans Zell Publishers, 1994. 344 pp.
Probably still the most comprehensive, but now inevitably very dated reference resource to African studies research and teaching worldwide. Provides information on over 1,800 academic institutions, research bodies, associations, and international organizations involved in African studies research in all parts of the world. Entries are set out in alphabetical order by name of institution, and include the following information: full name and address, telephone and fax numbers, and email address where available; name of head/director and details of staff, including their fields of specialization; principal areas of current African studies research; courses offered and degrees awarded; library holdings; publications issued; and various other information such as sources of funding, and links with other institutions and organizations. Five indexes: thematic index by area/country; index of international organizations; index of ethnonyms and language names; index of serial publications; and index of personnel. Regrettably no new editions have been published to date.
ARD review:
African Research & Documentation, no. 70 (1996): 75-76 (reviewed by Tom French)
Choice review:
Choice June 1995 (reviewed by Nancy Schmidt)

275   Register of Social Scientists in Eastern and Southern Africa. Compiled by Taye Assefa, 2nd ed. Addis Ababa: Organization for Social Science Research in Eastern and Southern Africa (OSSREA), 2001. 326 pp. £16.95/$29.95 (distributed by African Books Collective Ltd, Oxford)
Online, index of subject areas
http://www.ossrea.net/publications/registers/subject/a.htm [16/06/05]
Online, index by scholars
http://www.ossrea.net/publications/registers/name/a-c.htm [16/06/05]
This register aims to facilitate networking and collaboration between social scientists in the countries of the South as well as between them and peers in the North. The minimum requirement for inclusion is at least a master's degree and one research publication. Information for each profile is very full for the most part, and includes current address, date of birth, education and degrees, research interests and projects, current institutional affiliation, number and type of publications, and membership in professional associations. There are indexes by name and by subject areas, which are also available online (last updated in March 2002). However, one minor drawback with the online indexes is that they only provide names and nationalities, but not institutional affiliations and addresses, and for which you will still need to consult the print edition. Nonetheless, this is a very useful resource.

General interest reference resources

276   Asante, Molefi Kete **The Book of African Names**. Trenton, NJ: Africa World Press, 1991. 64 pp.
Lists some 1,200 male and female names in two separate sections, under five African regions, and gives interpretations of their English meaning.
Choice review:
Choice September 1992 (reviewed by E.D. Lawson)

277   Kirchherr, Eugene C. **Place Names of Africa, 1935-1986. A Political Gazeteer.** Lanham, MD, and Oxford: Scarecrow Press, 1987. 144 pp. $43.00/£33.00/€56.61
An alphabetical guide to current and past names of African states, with supplementary notes (supported by 23 line maps) on name and boundary changes, former colonies mandates and trusteeships, former Italian colonies and British territories, secessionist states, etc. A useful reference resource for tracking down changes in African place names over a period of time.
Choice review:
Choice September 1988 (reviewed by Gretchen Walsh)

278   Madubuike, Ihechukwu **A Handbook of African Names**. 2nd ed. Colorado Springs, CO: Three Continents Press, 1994. 158 pp.
A guide to African male and female names, together with short essays on a number of African languages.

279   Musere, Jonathan **Traditional African Names.** Lanham, MD, and Oxford: Scarecrow Press, 1999. 416 pp. $70.50/£53.50/€91.78
This compilation is something of a tour de force, but the title could be a bit misleading as the volume covers primarily personal names used in ten countries of eastern, central, and southern Africa, but not in West Africa. The book provides an alphabetical listing of some 6,000 African names (complete with pronunciation guidelines). Each entry discusses the origins of the name, its meaning, and the cultural and social connotations of its use.
ARD review:
African Research & Documentation, no. 85 (2001): 73-74 (reviewed by Sheila Allcock)

280   Nussbaum, Stan **The Wisdom of African Proverbs: Collections, Studies, Bibliographies.** Colorado Springs, CO: Global Mapping International [15435 Gleneagle Drive, Suite 100, Colorado Springs, CO 80921 USA, Email: info@gmi.org] Version 1.2. 1998. 1 CD $99.95 ($49.95 for purchasers in Africa)
Windows 3.1, DOS 6.2, 386DX, 2X CD-ROM drive, 4MB RAM, 7.5MB hard disk space.
The culmination of a three-year international research project funded by The Pew Charitable Trusts – and previously published as *African Proverbs: Collections, Studies, Bibliographies* (1996) – this CD contains the information equivalent of over 30 printed volumes including: over 27,000 proverbs from dozens of African languages; 23 complete books, including 9 previously unpublished works; an annotated bibliography of over 800 African proverb collections; an annotated bibliography of

279 research articles on African proverbs; 35 previously unpublished essays on the study and use of proverbs, 42 maps showing the status of African proverbs in over 1,200 languages; a directory of over 1,500 African languages, variant names, dialects, and locations; and more. [Not examined]

281 Room, Adrian **African Placenames: Origins and Meanings of the Names for over 2000 Natural Features, Towns, Cities, Provinces, and Countries**. Jefferson, NC: McFarland, 1994. 234 pp. $49.95
Etymologies of over 2,000 place names (i.e. countries, capitals, rivers, lakes, mountains, deserts, islands, etc.), with an emphasis on southern and northern Africa. Includes a bibliography, plus an appendix providing a chronology of explorations of Africa, and a section giving basic demographic, linguistic and religious information. No index. This is more in the nature of a semi-popular work for the general reader rather than for serious scholarly study and research.
ARD review:
African Research & Documentation, no. 70 (1996): 74-75 (reviewed by John McIlwaine)
Choice review:
Choice September 1994 (reviewed by Nancy Schmidt)

282 Stewart, Julia **1,001 African Names: First and Last Names from the African Continent**. New York: Carol Publishing Group, 1996. 214 pp.
Lists African first and surnames alphabetically and by gender. Includes an index to African peoples and languages, and an index to African names. [Not examined]

Guides to government, official, and UN publications

This section contains a number of general reference works listing government and official publications worldwide that include extensive coverage of Africa.

For listings of additional sources, including US government and archival publications, or sources for international and African national documents, consult the section on Government Publications in Alfred Kagan's ➜ **Reference Guide to Africa. A Bibliography of Sources (225)**

283 **Bibliographic Guide to Government Publications – Foreign 2003** (latest ed.) Boston: G.K. Hall [now part of Gale Group], 1975- annual 1,750 pp. [2003 volume, published September 2004] $880.00
Based on materials (with imprint dates of 1994 to the present) catalogued by the Library of Congress, this is probably the best source for tracking down African government publications and public documents at the various national, provincial, and regional levels. Includes official gazettes, parliamentary debates and papers, session laws, treaties, departmental reports, censuses, statistical annuals and reports, and more, together with publications from international and regional agencies.

➔ **Index to African Official Publications/Index des Publications Officielles Africaines** *see* **3 Current bibliographies, indexing and abstracting services, and review media** entry 399

284 **PAIS International/PAIS Archive** New York: OCLC Public Affairs Information Service, 1972- monthly (with cumulative subject and author indexes), now published by Cambridge Scientific Abstracts, Bethesda, Maryland
In addition to print format, *PAIS International* is available on a number of different platforms and media.
More details and subscription rates at
http://www.csa.com/factsheets/pais-set-c.php
PAIS International is a major index to political, economic, social issues, and current debate – with more than 553,300 records in its database (as at July 2005) – containing journal articles, books, government documents statistical directories, conference proceedings, grey literature, research reports, and Internet documents from all over the world. Each record has a mini-abstract describing the content of the item, together with very full bibliographic information, LC catalogue card number, ordering information and up to nine subject headings are assigned for each record. PAIS is one of the most comprehensive sources for international affairs materials, and for tracking down national government/official publications, as well as those from intergovernmental organizations, including those relating to Africa. **The PAIS Archive** database comprises a retrospective conversion of the *PAIS Annual Cumulated Bulletin*, Volumes 1-62, published 1915-1976. Currently available on the CSA Illumina platform is Part I of this conversion project, containing over 850,000 records covering the years 1937-1976. Part II of the Archive will be available in the autumn of 2005 and will include records covering the years 1915-1936. When complete, the PAIS Archive will contain over one million records. The PAIS Archive is available as part of an enhanced subscription to PAIS International on CSA Illumina.

285 **Selected Papers of the IFLA Anglophone Africa Seminar on Government Information and Official Publications held at the University of Zimbabwe in Harare 15-18 December 1994**. Edited by M.M. Moshoeshoe-Chadzingwa. Boston Spa, Wetherby, West Yorkshire [LS23 7BQ, UK]: IFLA Offices for UAP and International Lending, c/o British Library, 1998. 182 pp. £5.00
Contains a variety of papers on government and official publications from Africa, starting with a review, by Dupe Irele, of the publication output of the OAU – now ➔ **African Union (2504)** – and ➔ **ECOWAS (2511)** and their dissemination of these publications, or rather the lack of it. Other papers cover aspects such as collection development strategies, acquisitions problems, education and training needs of government information and official publications librarians, access to electronic documents from the UN system, etc.

286 Westfall, Gloria **French Colonial Africa: A Guide to Official Sources**.
London: Hans Zell Publishers, 1992. 224 pp.
Provides access to information on political, economic, social and cultural conditions in the former French colonial territories in Africa. Covers the basic reference tools, research guides and bibliographies, archival sources in France and in Africa, official and semi-official publications, and publications of colonial governments. Many entries are annotated. With an index of authors, subjects, and titles.

Choice review:
Choice April 1993 (reviewed by R. Dyson)

287   Westfall, Gloria **Guide to Official Publications of Foreign Countries** 2nd
ed. Bethesda, MD: Congressional Information Service (now part of LexisNexis
Academic and Library Solutions), 1997. 494 pp. $250.00
Prepared under the auspices of the International Documents Task Force of the
Government Documents Round Table (GODORT), a unit of the American Library
Association, this guide provides access to major documents published by foreign
governments including those in Africa, with a brief description of contents for each,
acquisitions information, and a title index. Arranged by continent, then by country
(with a separate chapter on UN publications), it lists documents in a total of 19
categories, including laws and regulations, economic affairs, legislative reports and
judicial proceedings, development plans, central bank publications, budgets,
censuses, health, labour, education, court reports, environment, and human rights
and status of women. There are also helpful listings of the principal repositories of
government information.
Choice review:
Choice March 1998 (reviewed by E.F. Kondering)

288   Witherell, Julian **The United States and Sub-Saharan Africa: Guide to US
Official Documents and Government-Sponsored Publications, 1785-1975.**
Washington, DC: Library of Congress, 1978. 949 pp.
Over 8,800 annotated entries, in five chronological sections that are sub-divided by
region or country (and 1952-75 further sub-divided by subjects). Covers largely
holdings at the Library of Congress, plus some at 45 other libraries; very extensively
indexed. Continued by Witherell's *The United States and Sub-Saharan Africa: Guide to
Official Documents and Government-Sponsored Publications, 1976-1980,* listing a further
5,074 entries. (1984. 721 pp.)

Guides to library collections and archival sources

See also ➔ **Directories of libraries and museums**
         ➔ **1 General online resource on Africa and African studies, and
         the best starting points on the Web. Academic and scholarly
         resources on Africa: Guides to library, archival and manuscript
         collections**

289   **British Documents on Foreign Affairs – Series G: Africa. Reports and
Papers from the Foreign Office Confidential Print**
General Editors: Parts I & II – Kenneth Bourne and D. Cameron Watt
Parts III, IV and V – Paul Preston and Michael Partridge
Part I: Africa from the Mid-19th Century to the First World War
25 volumes. (*Note:* Part I is limited to coverage of the sub-Saharan regions and
draws heavily on sources in the Colonial Office Confidential Print)
Part II: Africa from the First to the Second World War 30 volumes
Part III: Africa, 1940–1945 5 volumes

Part IV: Africa, 1946–1950 5 volumes
Part V: Africa, 1951-1956 6 volumes
Part I $5,310, Part II $6,360, Part III $1,060, Part IV $1,060, Part V $1,280
Bethesda, MD: LexisNexis.
For further information (and other Africa-related titles), pricing and discounts *see*
http://www.lexisnexis.com/academic/2upa/Issas/bdfaSeriesG.asp and
http://www.lexisnexis.com/academic/catalog/2004pdfs/Sub-
SaharanAfricanStudies.pdf
The Confidential Print comprises diplomatic reports, dispatches and other papers
that, with dates varying from country to country but in general beginning in the
1850s, were printed for limited circulation within the British government. It offers
contemporaneous records of observations of domestic and international affairs
throughout the world. Part 4, covering 1946–1950, comprises seven geographic series,
like Part 1 through Part 3, plus one topical series. All the series in Part 4 are being
published in segments by year. Each volume contains the general editor's
introduction, a series introduction by the series editor, a chronology of events
important to the series, a table of contents, and a subject index. [Not examined]

290   Brown, Clare **Manuscript Collections in the Rhodes House Library,
Oxford.** Oxford: The Bodleian Library, 1996. 171 pp. £5.00
One in a series of guides to the ➔**Rhodes House Library (1269)** very substantial
collections of archives and private papers relating to the colonial empire (other than
India and Sudan). The guide contains almost 900 entries (of which over 600 are on
Africa), covering accessions from 1978 to 1994. Material is divided into British
Empire, non-African colonial regions, and some 20 individual African territories.
Each entry provides a short description on the nature of the deposit, together with its
shelf number. With an index to people, organizations and institutions, and an index
of countries.
ARD review:
African Research & Documentation, no. 72 (1996): 72 (reviewed by Donald Simpson)

291   Burg, Barbara; Richard E. Newman, and Elizabeth Sandager **Guide to
African American and African Primary Sources at Harvard University.** Westport,
CT: Oryx Press/Greenwood Publishing Group, 2000. 304 pp. $151.95/£87.00
An inventory of the vast and rich interdisciplinary African and African American
primary holdings residing in twenty-two ➔ **Harvard (1309, 1310)** libraries and
museums, intended to make these sources more visible and easier to locate by
providing detailed information about the sources in a single printed guide. Arranged
alphabetically, it identifies 845 primary source materials, giving a description, the
subject heading, call number or other identifying information, location, a summary,
as well as historical notes for each item. Several collections that it identifies are not
yet available via the Harvard (HOLLIS) online library catalogue. A detailed index
provides access to subjects and formats, including materials such as photographs.
Choice review:
Choice May 2001 (reviewed by A. Salter)
CHOICE OUTSTANDING ACADEMIC TITLE 2001

292   Conseil International des Archives. **Sources de l'histoire de l'Afrique du Sud du Sahara dans les archives et bibliothèques françaises.** Volume 1: **Archives** Volume 2: **Bibliothèques** Volume 3: **Index.** Zug, Switzerland: Inter Documentation Co., 1976. 3 vols. 959 pp., 932 pp., 178 pp. (Guides des sources de l'histoire des nations, 3 & 4)
Descriptions of archival holdings relating to Africa in libraries (public, government, private) in France. Extensively indexed. (For other volumes in the series *see* entries ➔ 298-307).

293   Cook, Chris **The Making of Modern Africa. A Guide to Archives.** New York: Facts on File, 1995. 218 pp.
Brings together, from many geographically diverse locations, archival information available in over 1,000 collections of personal papers and private archives "of value to the historian of modern Africa" (excluding governmental and official archives however, which are well documented in other sources). The period covered is 1878 to the early 1990s. The guide is arranged by personal name, with each entry giving brief career details, followed by concise notes on the location and contents of the archive, describing size and contents of the collections. With archive and subject indexes.
Choice review:
Choice November 1995 (reviewed by Gretchen Walsh)

294   **Directory of Photographic Archives in West Africa/Répertoire des archives photographiques en Afrique de l'Ouest**
Dakar: West African Museums Programme [BP 357, 11 route du Front de Terre, Dakar, Senegal], 2001. 132 pp.
Guide to 146 photographic archives in the countries of West Africa, with information on the type of archive, status, date of creation, nature and size of collections, period covered and geographical areas covered, publications (where published), access and facility, opening hours, and name of officer in charge.

295   Filesi, Cesira **L'Archivio del Museo Africana di Roma: presentazione dei documenti.** 2nd ed. Rome: Istituto Italiano per l'Africa e l'Oriente, 2001. 190 pp. (Collana di studi africani, 13)
Published by the ➔ **Istituto Italiano per l'Africa e l'Oriente (1591)** this is an update of the previous edition published in 1980, providing an inventory of the collections (including personal papers and correspondence) in the archives of the Museo Africana di Roma, with personal name and geographic indexes.

296   Geber, Jill **"Southern African Sources in the Oriental and India Office Collections (OIOC) of the British Library."** *African Research and Documentation,* no. 70 (1996): 1-35.
An extensive bibliographic essay that focuses on the range of sources to be found in the British Library's Oriental and India Office collections for the study of southern Africa. Draws attention to almost 200 sources, including archival sources, manuscripts, official publications, those in the map collections, as well as illustrated material, paintings, prints, and printed books and serials.

297   Gosebrink, Jean E. Meeh **African Studies Information Resources Directory.**
Oxford: Hans Zell Publishers (New York: K.G. Saur), 1986. 585 pp.
Provides a comprehensive reference and research tool for identifying sources of
information and documentation on sub-Saharan Africa located in the United States.
Conceived as a partial revision of Peter Duignan's *Handbook of American Resources for
African Studies* (1966) it covers material in 346 collections. Now very dated, but still
useful because of the amount of detail provided in the descriptions of manuscript
and archival material to be found in the collections.
JOINT WINNER CONOVER-PORTER AWARD 1988

**298 "Guides to the Sources for the History of the Nations/Guides des sources de
l'histoire des nations/Quellenführer zur Geschichte der Nationen"**
Ed. by the International Council on Archives/Conseil international des archives.
The aim of this vast project is to provide easy access to the rich source materials
preserved in European libraries and archives relating to the history of countries
formerly under colonial rule. In addition to entry **292** above the following titles also
cover archival holdings on Africa. (The complete 3rd series is available at €1,278).

299   *2nd series* vol. 9: **Sources of the History of Africa South of the Sahara in the
Netherlands.** Compiled. by M.P. Roessingh & W. Visser. Munich: K.G. Saur Verlag
[for International Council on Archives], 1978. 241 pp.

300   vol. 10: **Indian Sources for African History: Guides to the Sources of the
History of Africa and of the Indian Diaspora in the Basin of the Indian Ocean in
the National Archives of India.** Compiled by S.A.I. Tirmizi. Delhi: International
Writers' Emporium, in association with UNESCO. 1988/89. 2 vols. 382 pp.

301   *3rd series* vol. 3, pt. 1: **Sources of the History of North Africa, Asia and
Oceania in Denmark.** Compiled by C. Rise Hansen. Munich: K.G. Saur Verlag, 1980.
842 pp. €158.00

302   vol. 3, pt. 2: **Sources of the History of North Africa, Asia and Oceania in
Finland, Norway, Sweden.** Compiled by Berndt Federley *et al.* Munich: K.G. Saur
Verlag, 1981. 233 pp. €88.00

303   vol. 5: **Sources de l'histoire du Proche Orient et de l'Afrique du Nord dans
les archives et bibliothèques françaises.** Edited. by the Commission française du
guide des sources des nations. Part 1: **Archives** Part 2: **Bibliothèque Nationale**
Munich: K.G. Saur Verlag, pt 1, 3 vols., 1996. 1,365 pp. €428 (set 3 vols.); pt. 2, 1984.
480 pp. €120.00

304   vol. 6: **Quellen zur Geschichte Nordafrikas, Asiens und Ozeaniens in der
Bundesrepublik Deutschland bis 1945.** Edited by Ernst Ritter. Munich: K.G. Saur
Verlag, 1984. 386 pp. €88.00

305   vol. 8: **Quellen zur Geschichte Nordafrikas, Asiens und Ozeaniens im
Oestereichischen Staatsarchiv bis 1918.** Edited by the Generaldirektion des
Oestereichischen Staatsarchiv. Munich: K.G. Saur Verlag, 1986. 272 pp. €110.00

306 vol. 9: **Sources of the History of Africa, Asia, Australia and Oceania in Hungary. With a Supplement: Latin America.** Munich: K.G. Saur Verlag, 1991. 451 pp. €158.00

307 vol. 10: **Sources of the History of Africa, Asia, and Oceania in Yugoslavia.** Edited by the Union of Societies of Archivists in Yugoslavia. Munich: K.G. Saur Verlag, 1991. 164 pp. €88.00

308 Howell, John Bruce, and Yvette Scheven **"Guides, Collections and Ancillary Materials to African Archival Resources in the United States."** African Studies Program, University of Wisconsin [1454 Van Hise Hall, 1220 Linden Drive], 1996. 108 pp. $18.00 print and online
Online published in *Electronic Journal of Africana Bibliography (see* ➔ **806**) no. 1 (1996): http://sdrc.lib.uiowa.edu/ejab/1/index.html [08/07/05]
Primarily based on the holdings of the University of Iowa and the University of Illinois at Urbana-Champaign – but also including the collections at some other US research libraries – this is a list of published guides to the archives of Africa, especially those in microform. It includes inventories, records, catalogues, finding tools, indexes, annual reports, etc. arranged by regions and countries (excluding Egypt). Material covered includes titles in English, French, and Portuguese.

309 **Library of Congress. African and Middle Eastern Division. Africana Collections: An Illustrated Guide.** Edited by Joanne Zellers. Washington, DC: Library of Congress, 2001. print 64 pp. $37.00 [sold as one of three guides to the collections, in slip-cover, and sold as a set only]
online (freely accessible) http://www.loc.gov/rr/amed/guide/afrillguide.html [08/07/05]
This attractive guide provides an overview and introduction to one of the three major collections of the ➔ **Library of Congress African and Middle Eastern Division (1316)** – the other two are the Near East and Hebraic collections – and narrates the collection's growth. The book contains over 50 illustrations, many in colour, covering different materials that make up the collections, including books, manuscripts, maps, posters and photographs. Additionally it includes a select list of Library of Congress publications on Africa (which can be found at http://www.loc.gov/rr/amed/guide/afr-publications.html), and a bibliography of writings about the collections.

310 McIlwaine, John **Writings on African Archives**. London: Hans Zell Publishers (for Standing Conference on Library Materials on Africa/SCOLMA), 1996. 297 pp. £55.00/$95.00 [now stocked/distributed by James Currey Publishers]
Provides an inventory of materials – monographs, articles, reports, conference papers and academic exercises – written about archives and manuscript collections within Africa, as well as about African-related archives located outside Africa. Contains 2,355 entries, many with brief annotations, and the volume is indexed by authors, editors, series titles, and names of individuals and institutions. The book was joint winner of the Africana Librarian Council's ➔ **Conover-Porter Award (2828)** for 1998, and described by the jury as "the most comprehensive work of its kind" on Africana archives and archival management, "including every conceivable print format,

ranging from monographs to conference papers to archival finding aids." The book has been kept up-to-date by a series of supplementary listings published in ➜ **African Research & Documentation (748)** (*see* entry **311** below).

ARD review:
African Research & Documentation no. 74 (1997): 86-87 (reviewed by Rosemary Seton)
Choice review:
Choice November 1996 (reviewed by R.B.M Ridinger)
JOINT WINNER CONOVER-PORTER AWARD 1998

Supplementary listings to entry **310** above:
311   McIlwaine, John **"Writings on African Archives (London, Zell, 1996)"** –
Supplements:
Supplement 1. *African Research & Documentation* 73 (1997): 30-38.
Identifies further material not included in the original compilation, most published in the 1990s, but also some earlier references.
Supplement 2. *African Research & Documentation* no. 76 (1999): 34-42.
A further 90 entries.
Supplement 3. *African Research & Documentation* no. 79 (1999): 39-61.
Includes all entries in, and therefore *supersedes* Supplements 1 & 2 above, listing a total of 239 references.
Supplement 3, Part 2. *African Research & Documentation* no. 80 (1999): 39-42.
Five further entries, together with the index to the 239 entries listed in Supplement 3.
Supplement 4. *African Research & Documentation* no. 84 (2000): 9-25.
Continues the series of supplements to the original volume. This supplement is concerned principally with material published since 1995, but also includes some earlier publications.
Supplement 5. *African Research & Documentation* no. 87 (2001): 75-89.
Further citations of mainly post-1995 published material.
Supplement 6. *African Research & Documentation* no. 91 (2003): 11-58.
Continues the practice whereby every third supplement to the main work is a cumulation of new entries together with those in the immediately preceding two supplements, and includes an index. Thus Supplement 6 cumulates and supersedes Supplement 4, and should be used in conjunction with Supplement 3, and with the original work.
Supplement 7. *African Research & Documentation* no. 94 (2004): 21-37.
A further supplement, listing primarily material published since 1995. Should be used in conjunction with Supplement 3 and Supplement 6 above.

312   Miescher, Giorgio, and Dag Henrichsen, eds. **African Posters. A Catalogue of the Poster Collection in the Basler Afrika Bibliographien.** Basel: Basler Afrika Bibliographien, 2004. 301 pp. CHFr.85.00
This is a splendid book that makes an important contribution to the documentation of African mass media and visual communication. It demonstrates vividly the importance of posters in everyday African life, as well as their significance for historical and social research. Drawing on the rich collection of several thousand African posters held by the library of the ➜ **Basler Afrika Bibliographien (1262)** the catalogue shows some 900 posters – most of them in full colour – from and on southern Africa (with a very large number from Namibia), together with a range of posters from West and northeastern Africa. The catalogue is preceded by an

informative introduction on posters as part of a visual history of Africa. This is followed by eight chapters grouping posters by themes and providing an introductory text for each chapter, setting out the historical context. The themes are (each with a number of sub-topics): Liberation Movements and Exile; Solidarity and Anti-apartheid; Elections; Nation Building; Awareness and Health; Economy; Knowledge, Information, Belief; and Leisure and Pleasure. While most of the posters catalogued here are those produced within Africa, the book also includes material from outside the continent, for example posters produced by the anti-apartheid movement and African solidarity groups, as well as posters used to publicize Africa-related exhibitions in museums and art galleries, and some promoting travel and tourism in Africa. Most of them date from the period of the early 1970s through to the late 1990s, but there are also several more recent posters from the years 2000 and 2001. For each item full bibliographic data is provided, including title/theme, artist, photographer or designer (where available), publisher or printer, date published, dimensions, and printing method. Each entry also indicates the BAB collection number and is accompanied by descriptive keywords that are used to form an index at the end of the book, covering both topics/themes and countries.
ARD review:
African Research & Documentation, no. 96 (2004): 87-88 (reviewed by Terry Barringer)

313   The New York Public Library. Schomburg Center for Research in Black Culture **Schomburg Clipping File.** Cambridge: Chadwyck-Healey (Alexandria, VA: Chadwyck-Healey), 1986. [now distributed by ProQuest]
Part I, 1924-1975: 9,673 microfiche with printed names and subject index
Africa: 1,362 microfiche with printed names and subject index
Index: Index to the Schomburg Clipping File, 1986 176 pp. (print)
Part II, 1975-1988: 3,861 microfiche
More details and pricing information at http://www.il.proquest.com/research/pt-product-Schomburg-Clipping-File-214.shtml
A collection of newspaper and magazine clippings, pamphlets and ephemera on all aspects of the Black experience held by the → **Schomburg Center for Research in Black Culture (1319)**. It includes typescripts, pamphlets, programmes, book reviews, and various other short publications dealing with black history and culture. The "Africa" part is a selection from the complete file, covering material devoted to the various countries of Africa. A printed index to the microfiche edition lists almost 7,000 subjects, of which 650 are on Africa and which are listed separately. [Not examined]

314   Pearson, J.D. **A Guide to Manuscripts and Documents in the British Isles Relating to Africa**. 2 vols. London: Mansell Publishing [now part of Pro-Quest], Volume 1, 1993. 320 pp. , Volume 2, 1994. 576 pp.
This monumental and indispensable two volume guide is a much expanded and revised edition of Noel Matthews and Doreen Wainright's *Guides to Manuscripts and Documents in the British Isles Relating to Africa* (1991). It lists and describes manuscripts (both in African and Western languages) relating to Africa South of the Sahara held in public and private collections in Britain. Volume 1 covers institutions in London – including the extensive collections of the British Library – and volume 2 lists collections in the British Isles outside London, geographically grouped under

England, Wales, Scotland, and Northern Ireland: under each of these, repositories are arranged alphabetically by cities of their location (including, for example, the large collections at Rhodes House Library in Oxford). A single combined index covers names, titles, and subjects.

ARD review:
vol. 1:*African Research & Documentation* no. 65 (1994): 42-43 (reviewed by John McIlwaine)
vol. 2: *African Research & Documentation* no. 67 (1995): 30-31 (reviewed by John McIlwaine)

➜ Pinfold, J., Barringer, T., and C. Holden, eds. **Images of Africa: The Pictorial Record. Papers presented at the SCOLMA Conference, London, 9-10 June 1994** *see* **15 Africanist documentation and African studies bibliography** entry **1913**

➜ **Répertoire de bibliothèques à Paris et en régions dont les fonds présentent un intérêt pour la recherche sur l'Afrique** *see* ➜ **General online resources on Africa and African studies, and the best starting points on the Web: Academic and scholarly resources on African studies** entry **134**

315 Rhodes House Library **Rhodes House Library Subject Catalogue**.
Cambridge: Chadwyck-Healey/Pro-Quest, 1990. 477 microfiche with printed guide
More product information and pricing at
http://www.proquest.com/research/pt-product-Rhodes-House-Library-Subject-Catalogue-160.shtml
A reproduction, in microfiche format, of the original subject index cards at ➜ **Rhodes House Library (1269)** in Oxford, which has one of the most extensive collections on Africa, the Commonwealth, and the former British empire, including archival collections acquired through the Oxford Colonial Records project. There are entries for some 175,000 printed works from 1760 to 1988. Detailed subject classifications within each of the 92 countries and regions facilitates access to any subject within any country or region. Includes a *Guide and Listing to the Microfiche Edition*, compiled by Peter Wilkinson. [Not examined]

316 Sainteny, Philippe, and Elikia M'Bokolo **Afrique, une histoire sonore 1960-2000**. Paris: Radio-France internationale, Institut national de l'audiovisuel, 2000, distributed by Frémeaux et Associés [20 rue Robert Giraudineau, 94300 Vincennes, France, Tel: +33-1-43 74 90 24 Fax: +33-1-43 65 24 22]
7 CDs and booklet €59.00
From the archives of Radio International France, this is collection of radio broadcasts concerning the history of francophone Africa, with commentary and some music. It covers 40 years of the political history of French-speaking Africa – originally broadcast between January 30, 1944 and July 12, 2000 – featuring the voices of the principal statesmen, leaders, and politicians of the time. It includes historical recordings of Léopold Sédar Senghor, Felix Houphouët-Boigny, Ahmed Bella, Hassan II, Kofi Annan, Nelson Mandela, Muammar Kadhafi, Mobutu Sese Seko, Habib Bourguiba, Bokassa Ier, Omar Bongo, Desired Kabila, Abdelaziz Bouteflika, Bachir Ben Barka, General de Gaulle, George Pompidou, Valéry Giscard d' Estaing, François Mitterrand, Jacques Chirac, and Lionel Jospin, among others.

317 **The SCOLMA Directory of Libraries and Special Collections on Africa in the United Kingdom and in Europe**. Edited by Tom French. 5th ed. London: Hans Zell Publishers (for Standing Conference on Library Materials on Africa/SCOLMA), 1993. 366 pp.

Note: Publication of a new 6th edition, online and print, has been announced by SCOLMA for some time now, but no further information is available as at December 2005. However, more details will be become available shortly at this page: http://www.lse.ac.uk/library/scolma/directory.htm

Published on behalf of the → **Standing Conference on Library Materials in Africa/SCOLMA (1892)**, this is a valuable guide for all those who need to locate research material on Africa available in the libraries of the UK and in Europe. Contains 392 entries; each entry includes full name and address, name of chief librarian and/or person in charge of Africana collections, telephone/fax numbers, email addresses for some, and (if information was duly supplied) details of opening hours, conditions of access for external readers, size of library/collection, loan and reference facilities, the scope and depth of each collection, CD-ROM and on-line databases, audio-visual materials available, and publications issued. With an index covering institutions, organizations, subjects, and countries. A new 6th edition is currently in preparation by SCOLMA.

ARD review:
African Research & Documentation no. 65 (1994): 38-39 (reviewed by Anne Thurston)
Choice review:
Choice June 1994 (reviewed by Nancy Schmidt)

318 South, Aloha **Guide to Federal Archives Relating to Africa.** Waltham, MA: Crossroads Press, 1977. 556 pp.

Guide to federal archive holdings in the USA; lists over 800 record groups. Information for each entry includes details of footage of Africa-related material, geographic areas covered, etc. Extensively indexed.

319 South, Aloha **Guide to Non-Federal Archives and Manuscripts in the United States Relating to Africa.** Oxford: Hans Zell Publishers (New York: K.G. Saur, Inc), 1989. 2 vols. 1,266 pp.

This massive two-volume guide, published for the National Archives, Washington DC, describes textual and non-textual materials, relating to the African continent and offshore islands and which are located in public and private manuscript and archival depositories in the United States. Entries in the *Guide* indicate the scope and content of each collection, as well as the subject of documents contained in a collection or series. Documents include correspondence, letterbooks, journals, logbooks, photographs and slides, sound recordings and films. Includes an extensive 127-page index.

Choice review:
Choice March 1990 (reviewed by Alfred Kagan)

320   Thurston, Anne **Guide to Archives and Manuscripts Relating to Kenya and East Africa in the United Kingdom.** 2 vols. Volume 1: **Official Records**. Volume 2: **Non-Official Archives and Manuscripts**. London: Hans Zell Publishers, 1991. Vol. 1, 634 pp., vol. 2, 576 pp.

This two-volume guide surveys official and non-official records in over 150 repositories in the United Kingdom. The earliest located sources are from the 17th century, although the bulk of the records described date from the end of the Second World War. Collections covered include the extensive holdings of the ➔ **Public Record Office (1282)** (now The National Archives), the large number of manuscript holdings at the ➔ **Rhodes House Library (1269)** in Oxford, as well as holdings of local record offices, university libraries, museums, Royal societies, and other special repositories.

ARD review:
African Research & Documentation no. 58 (1992): 32-34 (reviewed by John McIlwaine)

321   Thurston, Ann **Sources for Colonial Studies in the Public Record Office: Records of the Colonial Office, Dominions Office, Commonwealth Relations Office and Commonwealth Office.** London: Institute of Commonwealth Studies/HMSO, 1995. 479 pp. £60.00 (British Documents on the End of the Empire. Series C: Sources for Colonial Studies in the Public Record Office, vol. 1)

322   Thurston, Ann **Sources for Colonial Studies in the Public Record Office: Records of the Cabinet, Foreign Office, Treasury and Other Records.** London: Institute of Commonwealth Studies/HMSO, 1998. 564 pp. £80.00 (British Documents on the End of the Empire. Series C: Sources for Colonial Studies in the Public Record Office, vol. 2)

Part of the British Documents on the End of the Empire (BDEEP) scheme, of which Series C covers sources, and which at the same time constitutes a revised and updated version of *The Records of the Colonial and Dominions Offices*, by R.B. Pugh, which was first published in 1964. The first volume in Series C is a companion to the records of the Colonial Office, and the second volume provides coverage of the records of the Cabinet and its committees, the Prime Minister's Office, the Foreign Office, and the Treasury. Volume 1 includes several historical overview chapters on the organization of the records, as well as information on how to use the records, and deals with questions of access, finding aids, registry codes, etc. There is a who-was-who of office holders in Colonial and Dominions Offices over two centuries, an extensive listing of PRO records, followed by an account of the records of the CO's Subject Departments. A highly detailed index completes this exemplary archival guide and working tool. [Vol. 2 not examined]

ARD review: (of vol. 1)
African Research & Documentation no. 75 (1997): 62-64 (reviewed by Harry Hanam)

Handbooks and encyclopaedias

323   **Africa on CD ROM**. Compiled by Richard Selzer. 1 CD $29.00
Order online from http://www.samizdat.com/africancd.html or
http://store.yahoo.com/samizdat Email: seltzer@samizdat.com
Contains the full text of 16 African country studies published in the Library of
Congress Country Studies/Area Handbook series: Algeria, Angola, Chad, Egypt,
Ethiopia, Ghana, Ivory Coast, Libya, Madagascar, Mauritania, Nigeria, Somalia,
South Africa, Sudan, Uganda, and Zaire. Each country study is presented as a single
document, in plain text format, easy to read, to print, and to search, rather than as a
collection of over 100 separate documents for each book that is available on the Web,
see ➔ **Library of Congress. Country Studies/Area Handbook series** [Africa] **(88).**
The tables in the appendix of each book are presented as html documents. In
addition the CD also includes the 2003 edition of the *CIA World Factbook*, and some
other materials.

324   **Africana: The Encyclopedia of the African and African American
Experience.** 2nd rev. and expanded ed. Edited by Henry Louis Gates, jr. and Kwame
Anthony Appiah. New York: Oxford University Press 2005. 5 vols. 3,968 pp. $525.00
set
Note: First edition: New York: Basic Civitas Books, 1999. 2,095 pp. Also available as a
CD-ROM product *see* **347**. A condensed version of the first edition is still available
from the Perseus Group/ Running Press. This was published in 2003 and costs
$29.95/£20.00
A new, substantially expanded edition (now published in five casebound volumes)
of an outstanding reference resource first published in 1999, and inspired by the
dream of the late African American scholar W.E.B. du Bois for a comprehensive
Encyclopaedia Africana. The second edition, thoroughly updated and revised and with
a comprehensive new index, contains some 4,500 entries contributed by over 200
African, British, and African American contributors. Some entries, e.g. some
biographical entries, are relatively short and between 400-1,000 words, but there are
also many extended essays of longer length and on the principal themes. The
encyclopaedia includes over a thousand illustrations (most in full colour) including
many maps. Its scope is the entire history of Africa and the African diaspora.
Attractively designed and arranged in A-Z format, with colour-coded major subject
areas to facilitate easy cross-referencing, the encyclopaedia contains clear contextual
information with numerous cross-references accompanying entries. Roughly half the
encyclopaedia is about African American themes, and conveys the history and scope
of cultural expression people of African descent; a further 10% or so is Caribbean
orientated. Supported by a substantial bibliography arranged by topic, this is a
superb reference work, depicting the cultures of the African continent and her
peoples in great depth and in all their variety.
Online reviews: (reviews of the 1st ed.)
Booklist, February 2000
http://www.ala.org/booklist/v96/rbb/fe2/44africa.html
Whole Earth, Summer 2000
http://www.wholeearthmag.com/ArticleBin/382.html
H-Africa, February 1999

http://h-net.msu.edu/cgi-bin/logbrowse.pl?trx=vx&list=h-
africa&month=9902&week=a&msg=3Fd1qg9Nz8uoGsxJJMbTxQ
(reviewed by Molefi Asante)

➔ **Africa on File** *see* **7 Cartographic sources/Maps sales and map vendors** entry 491

325   **Africa Today**. Publisher and editor-in-chief: Raph Uwechue. Senior
Research Editor: Jonathan Derrick. 3rd ed. London: Africa Books Ltd, 1996. 1,684pp.
A comprehensive, although now partially dated source on the history, geography,
economics, politics and current affairs, culture, language, and religions of Africa,
with black and white maps for each African country, and 14 pages of 'Peters
Projection' maps in full colour. The country surveys provide basic factual
information for every African nation, each with extensive introductory material on
geography, history and politics, the economy, and with details of government (as at
April 1996), addresses of African and non-African diplomatic missions in each
country and diplomatic missions abroad; plus many statistical tables, covering
balance of payments, agricultural production and livestock, trade and industry,
employment, education, health, environment and natural resources, and more.
Additionally, the volume includes 25 essays contributed by prominent
African/Africanist scholars.

326   Asante, Molefi Kete, and Abu S. Abarry **African Intellectual Heritage. A
Book of Sources.** Philadelphia: Temple University Press, 1996. 828 pp. $37.95 pap.
(cased edition no longer available)
A rich collection of primary sources and more contemporary writings that have
shaped the intellectual history of Africa and the diaspora. Grouped under six major
themes – The Creation of the Universe, Religious Ideas, Culture and Identity,
Philosophy and Mortality, Society and Politics, and Resistance and Renewal – the
book brings together a wide range of materials, and documents from many societies.
There are a total 129 sections. This includes, for example, creation myths and
narratives, prayers, hymns, praise poems, invocations, oral epics, proverbs,
spirituals; addresses and orations, declarations, charters and statements; through to
classic texts by Mary LcLeod Bethune, Edward Wilmot Blyden, W.E.B duBois,
Amilcar Cabral, Cheikh Anta Diop, Frantz Fanon, Marcus Garvey, J. Caseley
Hayford, Africanus Horton, Martin Luther King, Mazisi Kunene, Ali Mazrui, Kwame
Nkrumah, Julius Nyerere, Olaudah Equiano, Paul Robeson, Walter Rodney, Léopold
Sédar Senghor, Wole Soyinka, Nat Turner, Booker T. Washington, Malcolm X, and
many more.

327   Biebuyck, Daniel; Susan Kelliher, and Linda McRae **African Ethnonyms:
Index to Art-Producing Peoples of Africa.** New York: G.K. Hall; London: Prentice-
Hall International, 1996. 378 pp.
A valuable, meticulously compiled reference source of ethnonyms of African
traditional cultures and ethnic groups in their alternate spellings, i.e. the
names/spellings by which African people identify themselves, or spellings used, or
assigned, by Europeans and other outsiders. Arranged alphabetically in dictionary
format – clustering alternate spellings and variant name forms under a single entry,
and with an indication where the groups are located – it contains more than 4,500

names for over 2,000 ethnic groups, drawing on numerous sources, including linguistic and ethnographic surveys of Africa, as well as from a very large number of books and catalogues of African art. A secondary index lists ethnic groups by country, with notes on history and language, and there is an extensive bibliography of over 1,000 items. The sub-title, "art-producing people" could be a bit misleading and "art" is in fact very broadly interpreted, and virtually all known African peoples would appear to be included. This therefore makes this a good tool for verifying variant names of African ethnic groups, and for which it is one of the most comprehensive sources.
Choice review:
Choice June 1997 (reviewed by E.C. Burt)
CHOICE OUTSTANDING ACADEMIC TITLE 1997

328 de Villiers, Les **Africa 2005.** Washington, DC: Corporate Council on Africa/Business Books International, 5th ed. 2005. 400 pp. $28.95 CD-ROM available separately at $38.95, or $50.40 in combination with the book.
Sample chapters freely accessible at
http://www.businessbooksusa.com/images/AFRICA2005Sample.pdf
Published in conjunction with the Washington-based ➔ **Corporate Council on Africa (2591)**, this book describes itself as a "comprehensive guide for American individuals and businesses seeking to learn more about doing business with the nations of Africa." It includes overview chapters – with colour illustrations, and with some excellent maps, charts and tables – on the geography, population and economy of the continent, trade and investment, and other key sectors and topical issues, followed by sections on each of the 53 independent countries of Africa. Modestly priced, this is a good and well-organized reference resource for quick facts, although it is primarily for the general reader and for public libraries, or those who want to do business in Africa.
Choice review: (of 2002 edition)
Choice April 2002 (reviewed by P.W. Wilkin)

329 The Diagram Group, eds. **The Encyclopedia of African Peoples.** New York: Facts on File; London: Fitzroy Dearborn Publishers, 2000. 400 pp.
Profusely illustrated (about 1,500 two-colour illustrations and 200 maps), this encyclopaedia and ethnological survey divides Africa into five major sections: Africa Today, Peoples of Africa, Culture and History, Nations, and Biographies. Following an introductory essay, each ethnic group – about 200 of which are discussed in some depth, while smaller groups have more concise entries – is analysed by its history, language, social life and customs, culture and religion, and each includes a time line. The section on "Nations" provides basic factual data on all 53 countries of Africa, including demographic statistics, recent historical facts and events, governments, geographical and economic information, as well as other basic information such as currencies, climate, national flags and anthems, etc. The biographical section contains over 300 thumbnail biographies of the men and women who have shaped the course of African history, as well as including biographical profiles of the major African writers. An impressive and handsomely produced resource, but primarily for general readers, school and public libraries.
Choice review:
Choice September 2000 (reviewed by C.S. McGowan)

330   The Diagram Group, eds. **Nations of Africa** New York: Facts on File, 1997. 112 pp. $28.00 (Library price $25.20)
A separate edition of the sixth volume of ➔ **Peoples of Africa** (*see* **331** below), providing key data and profiles of the 52 nations of Africa, together with about 300 biographical sketches of prominent Africans, including statesmen, ancient kings, artists, sports personalities, etc. [Not examined]

331   The Diagram Group, eds. **Peoples of Africa.** New York: Facts on File, 1997. 6 vols. 672 pp. $180.00 (Library price $153.00) set 6 vols., or available individually at $30.00/$27.00
Aimed primarily at middle and high school students [in the US grades 6 through 12] these six volumes – all extensively illustrated and with a very large number of maps – provide a broad introduction to the history, culture, customs and traditions of the major African ethnic groups, together with basic access facts and information. Volumes 1-5 are regional volumes covering North, East, West, central and southern Africa. The sixth and final volume presents vital statistics of the continent itself and profiles each of the 52 African nations, from Algeria to Zimbabwe. [Not examined]

332   **The Encyclopedia of Africa and the Americas.** Edited by Noelle Morrissette Searcy and Richard M. Juang. Santa Barbara, CA: ABC-Clio, forthcoming 2006. 3 vols. (An Encyclopedia in the Transatlantic Relations Series).
Will provide an overview of the cultural, political, and historical relations between Africa and the Americas, from the fifteenth century to the present day. It will offer entries on specific topics, people, groups, events, institutions, and countries. The encyclopedia will be appropriate for a general readership and for students from the secondary school level to advanced undergraduates and individuals conducting research. The entries have been written by contributors from North America, Latin America, Europe, and Africa. [Not examined, provisional information supplied by editors]

333   **Encyclopedia of the Modern Middle East and North Africa.** 2nd ed. Edited by Philip Mattar (Editor-in-chief) New York: Macmillan Reference, 2004. 4 vols. 2,000 pp. $475.00
A new edition, with expanded title and coverage, of the *Encyclopedia of the Modern Middle East* (1996) with nearly 600 new entries and over 1,000 updates, for a total of over 3,000 entries. It covers the modern history of the Middle East and North Africa (generally from 1800 to the present), with major sections on colonialism and imperialism, the World Wars, the Arab-Israeli conflict and the United Nations involvement in the region. Each country in the region is reviewed in depth, detailing its history and politics, population, geography, economy, culture and society, as well as covering gender, languages, the arts, and religion. Articles have been contributed by almost 400 scholars in the field of anthropology, history, political science, religion and social sciences, and most include a bibliography. Approximately a third of the entries consist of informative biographical profiles, including some 200 new entries for women and women organizations. With many black and white illustrations and maps, together with genealogical charts, a glossary, and a full index.
Choice review:
Choice December 2004 (reviewed by F.H. Dagher)
CHOICE OUTSTANDING ACADEMIC TITLE 2004

334   Esterhuysen, Pieter, and Elizabeth le Roux, eds. **Africa at a Glance. Facts and Figures 2001/2002.** 11th ed. Pretoria: Africa Institute of South Africa, 2002. 104 pp. £29.95 /$46.95 (distributed by African Books Collective, Oxford)
The 11th edition of a useful, modestly priced, and accessible general reference resource from the → **Africa Institute of South Africa (1853)** drawing on some 40 major sources – and illustrated with graphs, pie-charts and maps in colour – the statistical data is presented as a series of tables and figures under four major sections: 1. Introductory Data (country checklist, dependencies and islands, languages, geographical data); 2. Social Data (population, urbanization/urban population growth, human development, education, literacy and written media, life expectancy, etc.); 3. Economic Data (currencies/exchange rates, GNP, economic growth, external debt and trade, principal exports, physical infrastructure etc.); and 4. Political Data (present African leaders as at 1 January 2002, leadership changes since independence, elections, conflict zones, military expenditure, and more). Explanatory notes set out the context and scale to the data presented. No new editions have been published since 2002.

335   Falola, Toyin **Key Events in African History. A Reference Guide.**
Westport, CT: Greenwood Press/Oryx Books; Oxford: Harcourt Education, 2002. 376 pp. $70.95/£48.00
Primarily intended as a reference source for high school and college libraries, this guide contains chapters on thirty-six significant events that have shaped the history of the African continent from the earliest times to the present, analysing these singular events in some depth, including their historical, social, and geographical ramifications, and drawing connections between the past and the present. The guide opens with a timeline of key events and an overview of African history, followed by the individual chapters arranged in chronological order, and which include, for example, The Civilization of Ancient Egypt, 3100 BC+; Kingdoms of West Africa: Ghana, Mali, and Songhay, AD 1000-1600; The Spread of Christianity, 1804 Onward; The Colonial Experience, 1900-1939; The End of European Rule, 1951-90; *Ujamaa* and Policy Choices, 1967 Onward; A Continent in Deep Crisis, 1980 Onward; and the final chapter is on The Fall of Apartheid and the Advent of Nelson Mandela's Government, 1994-99. Suggestions for further reading are offered at the end of each chapter, which are further enhanced through a range of maps and black and white halftones, and there is an index.
Choice review:
Choice June 2003 (reviewed by R.R. Atkinson)

336   Finkelman, Paul, and Joseph C. Miller, eds. **Macmillan Encyclopedia of World Slavery.** New York: Macmillan Reference [now part of Gale Group]/Simon & Schuster and Prentice Hall International; London: Simon & Schuster and Prentice Hall International, 1998. 1,065 pp. $290.00
Spanning all historical eras and continents, this encyclopaedia provides detailed information about all forms of human bondage, and all the people and civilizations affected by slavery. Contains signed essays by prominent scholars with bibliographical references, and the work concludes with a longer bibliography. Includes statistical tables, black and white illustrations, and maps. [Not examined]
Choice review:
Choice July 1999 (reviewed by C.S. McGowan)

337   The Greenwood Encyclopedia of Women's Issues Worldwide. Lynn
Walter, Editor-in-chief. Westport, CO: Greenwood Press, 2003. 6 vols. 3,340 pp.
$550.00/£310.00 set
Vol. 6: Sub-Saharan Africa, edited by Aili Mari Tripp (not available separately)
Part of a multi-volume reference work that documents the achievements and current
challenges for women in more than 130 countries of the world (another volume is
devoted to women in North Africa and the Middle East). Each volume is edited by
an expert in the area, supported by a host of contributing specialists. Following an
informative general overview essay on women's issues in the sub-Saharan Africa
region, entries are arranged alphabetically by country, with narrative descriptions
examining African women's status in matters of education, employment and
economics, legal standing, family and sexuality, health, politics, religion and
spirituality, violence, together with an "Outlook for 21st Century". Illustrated with
maps, tables and photographs, each country entry is subdivided into uniform
categories, thus allowing cross-country comparison of historical and current issues.
This is a useful feature. The volume also includes a resource guide with suggested
reading, audio-visual materials, Web sites, and a list of organizations. This is a well-
structured and informative reference tool.
Choice review: (review of six volume set)
Choice May 2004 (reviewed by P. Palmer)

338   Hall, David E. **African Acronyms and Abbreviations. A Handbook.**
London: Cassell Academic/Mansell, 1996. 364 pp.
This remarkable compilation lists an astonishing 12,000 or so acronyms and
abbreviations relating to Africa and African studies. Most relate to entities in Africa,
i.e. official and unofficial bodies, political parties, educational establishments,
institutions, business and trade organizations, etc., and also includes entries for other
acronyms, which do not specifically relate to Africa but constantly recur in Africanist
publications, for example those of international donor organizations, missions, and
other bodies. The primary sources for the dictionary were the authority files which
the compiler has maintained over many years of work on the ➜ **International
African Bibliography (387)**. For each entry the country of origin is cited, as the same
abbreviation frequently relates to different organizations (as many as 16 on the
evidence of this dictionary). Both current and lapsed organizations are listed – albeit
neither with any descriptive details about the organizations – and there are cross-
references to changes of name or acronyms and alternative terms.
ARD review:
African Research & Documentation, no. 72 (1996): 69-70 (reviewed by William Noblett)
Choice review:
Choice October 1996 (reviewed by Alfred Kagan)

339   Hawley, John C. **Encyclopedia of Postcolonial Studies.** Westport, CT:
Greenwood, 2001. 510 pp. $115.95/£66.00
Provides an overview of the present state of post-colonial studies. Arranged
alphabetically, it contains more than 150 fairly detailed entries on individual writers
and scholars, together with entries on the major theoretical schools and concepts, and
on national literatures. Usefully, each entry has suggestions for further reading, and
there is also a general bibliography. Entries on individual writers – which include a
sizeable number of African writers and theorists – provide some basic biographical

details, but are primarily concerned with examining each author's handling of postcolonial themes.
Choice review:
Choice March 2002 (reviewed by E.B. Lindsay)

340   Irele, Abiola, and Biodun Jefiyo, eds. **The Encyclopedia of African Thought**. London: Routledge, forthcoming January 2007. 792 pp. £110.00
The Encyclopedia of African Thought will contain almost 500 entries, with individual entries   on African writers and scholars and those from the diaspora, African philosophers, nationalists, theologians and religious leaders, statesmen and women, together with wide-ranging entries about terms, concepts and topics in African thought, ideologies, main trends in political thought, religious ideas and cosmologies, and much more. [Not examined, information drawn from publisher's advance information]

341   Jenkins, Everett, jr. **Pan-African Chronology I. A Comprehensive Reference to the Black Quest for Freedom in Africa, the Americas, Europe and Asia, 1400-1865.** Jefferson, NC: McFarland, 1996. 448 pp. $75.00
342   Jenkins, Everett, jr. **Pan-African Chronology II. A Comprehensive Reference to the Black Quest for Freedom in Africa, the Americas, Europe and Asia, 1865-1915.** Jefferson, NC; London: McFarland, 1998. 572 pp. $75.00
343   Jenkins, Everett, jr. **Pan-African Chronology III. A Comprehensive Reference to the Black Quest for Freedom in Africa, the Americas, Europe and Asia, 1914-1929** Jefferson, NC; London: McFarland, 2000. 628 pp. $75.00
A massive chronology of historical events among Black peoples, taking place concurrently in various parts of the world. The first volume covered the period 1400 through the end of the Civil War in the United States, and in the second volume the author chronicles the most significant events in the African diaspora from the end of the Civil War through to the pre-World War I years, a period during which the eradication of slavery as a legalized institution was finally realized in the Americas. In the most recent third volume the story of the African diaspora continues during some of its most challenging times, and during this period people of African descent experienced two seminal events: World War I, and what the author describes as "the Black Awakening" (or also termed as the Harlem Renaissance). Much of the information has been compiled using secondary sources, such as other chronologies, histories, and biographical dictionaries, and each volume is divided into years. Events in each year are grouped by regions – The United States, The Americas, Europe, Australia, Asia and Africa, the latter further sub-divided by regions – or presented as "Related Historical Events." For the United States there are additional divisions pertaining to particular categories such as the Socialist Movement, the Labour Movement, the Civil Rights Movement, Notable Births, Notable Deaths, Notable Cases, Scholastic Achievements, the Black Church, the Arts, the Performing Arts, Music, Scientific Achievements, Technological Innovations, Black Enterprise, Sports, and other topics. Contains an excellent and very detailed index that facilitates easy access to contents: people, places, events, institutions, organizations, movements, publications, African ethnic groups, and more.
ARD review: (of vol. 2)
African Research & Documentation no. 77 (1998): 54 (reviewed by David Killingray)

Choice review: (of vol. 3)
Choice December 2001 (reviewed by Gretchen Walsh)

344   Lea, David *et al* **A Political Chronology of Africa.** London: Europa
Publications, 2001. 508 pp. £100.00
This is the fourth title in a six volume series of 'Political Chronologies of the World'.
It aims to provide an impartial record of the political events that have shaped the
social, cultural, geographical and economic history of each country of Africa.
Arranged in country order, each chronology "begins at least as early as the
emergence of an entity resembling the modern nation, and in many cases
considerably earlier." For sub-Saharan Africa the editors have attempted to include
some pre-European history in each country's chronology, although greater emphasis
is given to more contemporary events, including elections, recent conflict and wars,
treaties, political upheavals etc. For Egypt, for example, it begins with an entry for ca.
3500 BC followed by about 500 short entries and ending with an item for August
2001; Benin begins with c. AD 1000-1500, followed by 90 concise entries, the last one
an item for 11 August 2001, on the death of the Army Chief of Staff in a helicopter
crash; or for Zimbabwe it starts off with c. 400 BC, followed by 140 entries, ending
with various items for September 2001 relating to the land crisis. Some entries border
on the trivial, but the series concept of providing a first point of reference for concise
information on the history of each nation works quite well on the whole, although a
serious shortcoming is the absence of a bibliography or listing of sources.

➔ **Library of Congress. Country Studies/Area Handbook series** [Africa] *see* **1
General online resources on Africa and African studies, and the best starting
points on the Web** entry **88**

345   Lugan, Bernard **Atlas historique de l'Afrique des origines à nos jours**.
Monaco: Éd. du Rocher, 2001. 268 pp. €37.90
This remarkably detailed historical atlas of Africa deals with the entire continent, and
covering all periods, from ancient Africa through to the year 2000. The 150 maps deal
with an abundance of themes – each a high-quality black and white map, with text
and commentary on the opposite page – and diverse topics such as the exploration of
Africa, mountains and vegetation, wars, ethnic conflict, migration, displaced peoples,
and recent conflicts in countries such as Liberia, Sierra Leone, Chad, Rwanda, etc.
Includes bibliographical references and an index.

346   Lye, Keith and The Diagram Group, eds. **Encyclopedia of African Nations
and Civilizations.** New York: Facts on File, 2002. 400 pp. $75.00/£45.00 (Library
price $67.50)
Extensively illustrated, this encyclopaedia presents broad historical overviews of the
major civilizations and the 52 nations of Africa in an A-Z format. Each nation's entry
narrates the history of the region from the early developments of its peoples to the
political, cultural and economic circumstances that characterize the area today. There
are also biographical profiles on major political and cultural personalities, past and
present, and there are a range of feature articles on topics such as Bantu migrations,
the spread of Christianity, the spread of Islam, European exploration, trade routes,
slavery, and colonization. A bibliography, a glossary, and a series of chronologies, is
also included. For undergraduate levels, schools, and general interest.

Online reviews:
H-AfrTeach 29 October 2003 (reviewed by Paul Thomas)
http://h-net.msu.edu/cgi-bin/logbrowse.pl?trx=vx&list=h-
africa&month=0310&week=e&msg=jBPDXzxkaybfxdnWs4USlQ&user=&pw=

347 **Microsoft Encarta Africana, version 3.0** 3rd edition. Edited by Kwame
Anthony Appiah and Henry Louis Gates, jr., CD-ROM, 2 disks, Windows 95,
Windows 98, Windows NT 4. Redmond, WA: Microsoft Corp, 2001. $59.95
Note: not currently listed as available in Microsoft products catalogue, but still
available from various vendors. For ➔ print version *see* entry **324**
An interactive exploration of the historical and cultural achievements of Africa and
people of African descent, from early man's appearance 4 million years ago on the
African continent to the present. Prepared under the guidance of a 36 member
advisory panel, the latest version includes over 3,600 articles, almost 3,000 photos,
audio clips, video clips and interactive maps of ethnicity, art, architecture,
geopolitics, topography, flora, fauna, and the African diaspora featuring the
dispersion of Africans to the Americas. There are also hundreds of Web links and 200
sidebars. Other features include a virtual tour section with 360-degree panoramic
views of historically important sites and locations, a civil rights chronology, a library
of black literature (the complete texts of 160 poems, essays and novels about the
experience of being of African descent in America), and 'Topic Treks' a feature that
allows users to explore various topics in greater depth. The search facilities are
impressive, and easy to use. This is an excellent product.
Choice review: (1st ed.)
Choice September 1999 (reviewed by R.B.M. Ridinger)
CHOICE OUTSTANDING ACADEMIC TITLE 1999

348 Middleton, John, Editor-in-chief **Encyclopedia of Africa South of the
Sahara.** New York: Charles Scribner's Sons/Gale Group, [distr. in the UK by
Prentice-Hall], 1997. 4 vols. 2,466 pp. $525.00/£318.00
Note: A separate edition aimed at college and graduate students, **Africa. An
Encyclopedia for Students,** containing some updates and expanded information on
North Africa, was published by the Gale Group in 2002. 900 pp. 4 vols. $415.00 set
Conceived in 1991 "to be the standard four-volume encyclopaedia on Africa south of
the Sahara; earlier works were either too short, too limited in content, outdated or
out-of-print." Members of the main editorial board include J.F. Ade Ajayi, Goran
Hyden, Joseph C. Miller, William A. Shack, and Michael Watts; plus an advisory
board and consultants, which includes several African scholars. Contains 896 signed
articles/entries, including many by African contributors. Entries are arranged
alphabetically, most are self-contained, while others take the form of composite
entries comprising several individual articles on a particular topic. There is extensive
coverage of the arts of Africa, both traditional and modern, including architecture,
art, clothing and body adornment, dance, film masks and masquerades, music and
song, literature, popular culture, rock art, and weaving. About 400 (black and white)
illustrations and 90 maps. Liberally cross-referenced, and with a detailed subject and
keyword index in volume 4. Winner of the Africana Librarian Council's ➔ **Conover
Porter Award (2828)** for 2000, it was described by the jury as "an impressive work,
unique it its coverage of its target region through a wide range of topics, and in its

inclusion of diverse perspectives on contemporary knowledge about Africa and its peoples, their histories, and their cultures...the appeal of the encyclopaedia reaches beyond the scholarly community to schools, public libraries, and people in the general public with an interest in learning about Africa and Africans."
Choice review:
Choice September 1998 (reviewed by P.W. Wilkin)
CHOICE OUTSTANDING ACADEMIC TITLE 1998
WINNER CONOVER-PORTER AWARD 2000

349 Murray, Jocelyn **Cultural Atlas of Africa.** 2nd rev. ed. New York: Facts on File, 1998. 240 pp. $50.00 (Library price $45.00)
A richly illustrated update of the 1981 edition, depicting the culture, history and geography of the African continent, and combining text with captioned colour photographs and many maps. Arranged in three parts: Physical Background, Cultural Background, and Nations of Africa. Includes cultural overview essays for each African region and country, and 84 maps in colour show physical features and climate, agricultural and mineral resources (but not language areas or ethnic groups). Includes an index, gazetteer and a country/region bibliography. Also contains flags of African countries and other special features such as housing types, masks and dance, Nigerian bronzes and woodcarvings. A most attractively produced reference resource, with great photography and excellent maps, although some users may object to somewhat pejorative terminology in a few chapters.
Choice review:
Choice April 1999 (reviewed by Alfred Kagan)

350 Nantet, Bernard **Dictionnaire d'histoire et civilisations africaines.** Paris: Larousse, 1999. 228 pp €16.00
A pocket dictionary of African history and civilizations, extensively cross-referenced, and with a range of maps. Primarily for the general public.

351 Nohlen, Dieter; Thibaut, Bernard, and Michael Krennerich **Elections in Africa – A Data Handbook.** Oxford: Oxford University Press, 1999. 1,000 pp. £107.50
Based on a research project funded by the German Research Council and conducted at the Institute of Political Science of the University of Heidelberg, this impressive volume contains exhaustive electoral data and statistics for all the countries of Africa, from the colonial era through to Africa's "second independence" beginning in 1989. It is presented in a comparative manner, thus allowing for both historical and cross-national comparisons. Each country chapter also examines the history of the institutional and electoral arrangements, the evolution of suffrage, and current electoral provisions. Tables in the country sections are organized in ten parts: Dates of national elections, referendums and coups d'état, electoral body, abbreviations; electoral participation of parties and alliances; distribution of votes in national referendums, elections to constitutional assembly, parliamentary and presidential elections, composition of parliament, and loss of power holders.
Choice review:
Choice July 2000 (reviewed by M.E. Doro)
CHOICE OUTSTANDING ACADEMIC TITLE 1999

352   Page, Melvin E., General ed. **Colonialism.An International Social, Cultural, and Political Encyclopedia.** Santa Barbara, CA: ABC-Clio, 2003. 3 vols. 1,208 pp. (vols. 1-3) $285.00 (print) $310.00 e-book $450.00 (print and e-book)
An exhaustive reference resource on the subject of imperialism and colonialism over the last 500 years, focusing on the politics, economy, culture, and society of both colonizers and colonized. More than 600 essays contributed by leading scholars — historians, political scientists, economists, and sociologists — analyse the origins of imperialism, the many forms it took, its impact worldwide, as well as examining imperialism's bitter legacy, and the gross inequities of global wealth and power that divide   the   former   conquerors   from   the   people   they   conquered. The entries cover ideologies, religions, theory, geography, imperial nations, colonies, colonized regions, ethnic groups, individuals, and treaties. Includes bibliographical references and an index. [Not examined]
Choice review:
Choice March 2004 (reviewed by C.V. Stanley)
CHOICE OUTSTANDING ACADEMIC TITLE 2004

353   Page, Willie F., and R. Hunt Davis, jr. eds. **Encyclopedia of African History and Culture.** 2nd rev. ed. New York: Facts on File, 2005. 5 vols. (General Editor of the 2nd ed. R. Hunt Davis, Jr.) 2,176 pp. $425.00 (Library price: $382.00)
A new second edition, now published in five volumes, of an encyclopaedia on African history with a broad cultural and geographic sweep. Volume 1 is devoted to Ancient Africa (Prehistory to 500), volume 2 covers the period from approximately 500 through 1500, encompassing the African kingdoms of Ghana, Mali and Songhai, while the third volume, From Conquest to Colonization, covers the period from approximately 1500 to 1850, taking in the slave trade, European exploration, colonization and the partitioning of West Africa, the spread of Christianity, etc. and the traditional governments, religions and social structures of the period. Volumes 4 and 5 are devoted to The Colonial Era and Independent Africa respectively. There are a large number of black and white photographs and illustrations and maps, and entries in the volumes are fairly extensively cross-referenced. Probably more suitable for high school and public libraries, rather than academic collections. [2nd ed. not examined]
Choice reviews: (of 1st ed.)
Choice April 2002 (reviewed by Gretchen Walsh)
Online reviews:
H-Africa 18 October 2003 (reviewed by Inge Brinkman)
http://h-net.msu.edu/cgi-bin/logbrowse.pl?trx=vx&list=h-africa&month=0310&week=c&msg=NHHHP5Lyk19rGkLkj5Y1pQ&user=&pw

354   Peek, Philip, and Kwesi Yankah, eds. **African Folklore. An Encyclopedia**. London and New York: Routledge, 2004. 625 pp. £120.00/$170.00
Published in a large size format, this attractively-produced encyclopaedia contains over 300 entries, contributed by an impressive panel of more than 160 subject experts from many parts of the world. It offers extensive survey essays, as well as shorter entries, on folklore in individual African countries, on ethnic groups, hunters and pastoralists, farmers and fisherfolk, orality and oral traditions, praise poetry, epics, proverbs, religious practices, ceremonies and festivals, artistic genres, performing arts, visual arts, popular culture, traditional drama and folk theatre, tricksters, griots

and griottes, masks and masquerades, myths, music, songs, and numerous other concepts related to written and oral folklore. There are also regional surveys on the major folklore forms of these areas, together with maps highlighting major ethnic groups for each region. Black and white photographs accompany some of the entries, and the book is liberally cross-referenced, with a good index. A number of indexes include a listing of African studies centres and libraries in the USA and in Africa with special collection interests in African folklore, a filmography of documentary films on African folklore, and a catalogue of the complete holdings of field and broadcast collections of African music and oral data at the Indiana University Archives of Traditional Music (ATM). This can serve as a useful print format adjunct to finding collections of interest at the ATM's electronic catalogue at http://www.indiana.edu/~libarchm/index.html. The editors acknowledge that the volume cannot be considered absolutely all-inclusive, covering all forms of folklore among all of Africa's ethnic groups, but this is probably the first work of its kind to offer something close to comprehensive coverage of folklore throughout the African continent in a single source, as well as covering the African diaspora.
Choice review:
Choice June 2004 (reviewed by David Westley)

355 Peregrine, Peter N., and Melvin Ember **Encyclopedia of Prehistory,** Volume 1: **Africa.** Dordrecht and New York: Kluwer Academic/Plenum Publishers [now part of Springer Group). 2001. 336 pp. €220.00/$230.00/£142.50
Prepared under the auspices and with the support of the Human Relations Area Files, this encyclopaedia presents an overview of all of human history from two million years ago to the historic period. The encyclopaedia is organized regionally with entries on each major archaeological tradition written by experts in the field. The entries follow a standard format and employ comparable units of description and analysis, making them easy to use and compare. [Not examined]

356 Roy, Christopher **Art and Life in Africa**. Iowa City IA: Art and Life in Africa Project, Oberman Center for Advances Studies, University of Iowa, IA, 1998. CD-ROM, 1 disk, with teachers guide. $60.00. Re-issued commercially by Kendall/Hunt Publishing Company [4050 Westmark Drive, PO Box 1840, Dubuque, IA 52004-1840; Email: orders@kendallhunt.com], 2002. $36.76 Windows 95/98, Windows XP, Mac OSX
UK edition published by Macmillan Online, 2000. CD-ROM, 1 disk £30.00
Based on the Stanley Collection at the University of Iowa Museum of Art, supplemented by additional images from collections across the US, and through a set of 37 essays by African art scholars (primarily US scholars), this exciting interactive CD-ROM charts the evolution and purpose of the African artistic tradition and describes the themes, functionality and diversity of African art. Using text, objects, field photos, video and music, it explores how Africans make and use art - in its various forms, sculpture, masquerading, textiles, body arts, etc. – at important events throughout their lives to solve problems, overcome adversity, and meet the challenges of life in an African environment. Grouped under 11 chapters, discussions include topics such as Key Moments in Life (which is also accessible for free at the Web site), Ancient Africa, Arts of Healing, Cultural Exchange, Art and Education, Divination, The Arts of Governance and Social Order, and Sacred Spaces, among

others. The CD includes over 10,000 images of 600 objects and 750 field photographs, 107 ethnographies, 27 ethnographic maps, a bibliographic database of some 1,400 entries, together with 15 short video clips and 6 music recordings. The essays by subject specialists include chapters on some broader topics, other than African art and culture. Features include search facilities, and a slide show maker for creating custom presentations. The CD is linked with the University of Iowa → **Art and Life in Africa project (29)** which is continually updated with new information and images, providing a world-wide resource on African art and culture.
Choice review:
Choice June 1999 (reviewed by E.L. Cameron)
Online reviews:
H-AfrTeach, January 2002 (reviewed by George Ulrich; review of ALA CD)
http://www2.h-net.msu.edu/reviews/exhibit/showrev.cgi?path=179

357 Shillington, Kevin **Encyclopedia of African History**. Chicago and London: Fitzroy Dearborn Publishers [now part of Routledge/Taylor & Francis Group], 2004. 3 vols. 1,912 pp. $495.00 set
Note: for more information, including a complete A-Z entries list, a complete list of thematic entries, contributors, and board of advisors *see*
http://www.routledge-ny.com/ref/africanhist/index.html
Compiled in collaboration with 330 international scholars and historians (with over one third from Africa), this massive encyclopaedia consists of almost 1,100 entries, covering the widest practicable range of topics in African history, and the whole continent of Africa, from the earliest times to the present. It aims to provide "a new reference resource on the history of the African continent and an up-to-date survey of the current state of scholarship at the turn of the new millennium." The selection of entries includes not only well-established topics, but also looks at the social, economic, linguistic, anthropological, and political subjects that are currently being re-evaluated or newly opened up for historical analysis by recent research and publication. Essays (in A-Z format) are organized into composite entries on the major regions, states, themes, societies, and individuals of African history. Within these multiple-entry composites, the essays are organized in a broadly chronological order: Entries range from factual narrative entries of at least 1,000 words, to full length essays of 3,000-5,000 words in length that analyze broader topics: regional general surveys, historiographical essays, and wide historical themes, such as the African diaspora, African political systems, and Africa in world history. The encyclopaedia contains a substantial number of black and white illustrations and 95 maps, one for each of the 55 modern states and 45 specially designed historical maps. A full index is included.

358 Stewart, John **African States and Rulers.** 2nd ed. Jefferson, NC: McFarland & Co., 1999. 415 pp. $95.00/£56.25
This is a considerably expanded and fully updated edition of a reference resource first published in 1989, now containing over 11,000 entries, not only entries for countries and rulers, but also ethnic groups, empires, cities and towns, political systems and federations, names of former colonies, territories, and regions. Each entry gives the official name of the country or region, etc., the dates during which it went by that name, location, capital, alternative names, its history and administration, and a list of rulers (i.e. administrators, governors, presidents, prime

ministers, etc.) with dates of power where known. A new feature in the second edition is a very detailed chronology that enables the reader to see at a glance the events that were happening all over Africa at any given time. There is an index of places and persons, together with an index of rulers of almost 100 pages. This is a remarkable compilation although it lacks an adequate explanation or statement about the sources relied upon to provide, for example, the very precise dates of years of reign of ancient rulers. One has to assume that information and sources of facts have been culled from the books listed in the bibliography (of some 150 items) but this is not specifically stated anywhere; and statements referring to "available data (mostly oral tradition)" without citing of the sources are not very helpful.
Choice review:
Choice October 1989 (reviewed by Gretchen Walsh)

359 Vogel, Joseph O., and Jean Vogel, General eds. **Encyclopedia of Precolonial Africa.** Walnut Creek, CA: Altamira Press. A Division of Sage Publications Inc., 1997. 606 pp. $129.95
An encyclopaedia of pre-colonial Africa (primarily sub-Saharan), surveying its history, archaeology, linguistics, and socio-cultural anthropology. It contains ninety-four summary essays contributed by 81 Africanist scholars, providing a synthesis of developments in different subject areas, with each essay accompanied by a bibliography to guide readers to further research and sources. The book includes a large number of rock art reproductions, as well as maps, photographs, and charts. The articles are arranged under five major thematic groups: African Environments, Histories of Research (including historical archaeology and historiography), Technology (stone working, metallurgy), People and Culture (languages and modes of production, rock art etc.), and Prehistory of Africa (human development, social complexity, trade and commerce, etc.). There is a good index.
Choice review:
Choice February 1998 (reviewed by P.W. Wilkin)
Online reviews:
African Studies Quarterly, vol. 2, no. 1, 1998 (reviewed by Jon Unruh)
http://web.africa.ufl.edu/asq/v2/v2i1a7.htm
CHOICE OUTSTANDING ACADEMIC TITLE 1998

360 Yakan, Mohamad Z. **Almanac of African Peoples & Nations.** New Brunswick, NJ and London: Transaction Publishers, 1999. 847 pp. $125.00/£94.95
In his introduction the author of this somewhat quirky reference source claims this to be "a first interdisciplinary attempt at understanding African pluralism, past and present", and that he "tries to forecast possible inter-ethnic conflicts in the future" (on the evidence of the last six years, not too successfully). The bulk of the volume consists of a listing of African peoples and ethnic groups presented in an A-Z arrangement, with descriptions for each entry of various lengths. Other sections list (1) African languages by country, noting the official language of each country and other languages spoken, and (2) African peoples by country, with descriptive text on each, including 1998 population estimates and listings of ethnic groups, together with maps showing the location of the many ethnic groups in each African country. There is a select bibliography, but which has some notable gaps.
ARD review:

African Research & Documentation, no. 82 (2000): 86-87 (reviewed by Terry Barringer)
Choice review:
Choice February 2002 (reviewed by Gretchen Walsh)

361   Zeleza, Paul Tiyambe, and Dickson Eyoh, eds. **Encyclopedia of Twentieth Century African History.** London and New York: Routledge, 2003. 672 pp. £125.00/$225.00
Containing nearly 250 signed entries, this encyclopaedia explores the ways in which the peoples of Africa and their polities, states, societies, economies, environments, cultures and arts were transformed during the course of the 20th century. Aided by a large international team of consultant editors and contributors (many of them African scholars), the encyclopaedia aims to capture the intellectual ferment in African historical studies of the 20th century by offering entries "that present critical interpretation which is placed in the context of the pertinent historiographical debates." It seeks to survey "the constellation of global and local forces that interacted to shape political, economic, social, cultural, artistic, and environmental developments and relationships within Africa and between Africa and the rest of the world." Within this framework the entries examine patterns across the continent and within particular regions and countries, and provide a detailed examination of the forces that shaped the changes that the continent underwent, combining essential factual description with evaluation and critical interpretation. There are three types of entries: (1) article-length interpretative essays of about 4,000 words each, which explore key topics; (2) shorter entries, also covering specific topics, themes or events, consisting of about 2,000 words, and (3) a further group of entries consist of "area surveys" (geographical, environmental, linguistic, etc., and including entries for countries and cities), of between 600 to 1,500 words. Each entry offers suggestions for further reading; the book is extensively cross-referenced, and includes an index. An outstanding reference resource.
Choice review:
Choice April 2003 (reviewed by Alfred Kagan)
CHOICE OUTSTANDING ACADEMIC TITLE 2003

Research materials in microform

For additional Africana microform resources *see also* ➜ **Cooperative Africana Microform Project (1889)**

➜ **Africana Microform Collections. University of California at Berkeley** *see*
1 General online resources on Africa and African studies, and the best starting points on the Web: Guides to library, archival and manuscript collections entry **124**

➜ **African Biographical Archive** *see* **Major biographical sources** entries **415, 416**

362   **CIA Research Reports – Africa, 1946–1976** 35mm microfilm (3 reels) with printed guide Bethesda, MD: University Publications of America/LexisNexis. $480.00

Filmed from documents released to UPA by the Central Intelligence Agency, this series, covering the three eventful decades starting in 1946, comprises 206 titles. Roughly a third deal with international questions; of those focusing on individual countries, the Congo is given most attention (85 titles), having been the subject of weekly reports for six months starting in November 1964. A good proportion (47) of the total are designated biographical reports, offering profiles of relatively unknown leaders of the time. [Not examined]

363   **Confidential US State Department Central Files. Africa: Internal Affairs and Foreign Affairs, 1945–1959**
British Africa: Internal Affairs and Foreign Affairs, 1945–1949
35mm microfilm (14 reels) with printed guide
British Africa: Internal Affairs and Foreign Affairs, 1950–1954
35mm microfilm (29 reels) with printed guide
British Africa: Internal Affairs and Foreign Affairs, 1955–1959
35mm microfilm (39 reels) with printed guide
Bethesda, MD: LexisNexis. Complete collection $15,730 (also available separately)
For further pricing information, current availability status, and information on discounts apply to publisher or *see* publisher's Web site.
http://www.lexisnexis.com/academic/2upa/Issas/CIArrAfrica.asp

Documents the post-war period during which passions and demands for independence grew in British Africa. The Central Files collections for 1945–1949, 1950–1954, and 1955–1959 cover Gambia, Sierra Leone, Gold Coast (Ghana), Togoland and Cameroons (mandates), Nigeria, Anglo-Egyptian Sudan, British Somaliland, Uganda, Kenya, Tanganyika, Nyasaland, Northern Rhodesia, Southern Rhodesia, Bechuanaland, and Swaziland and Basutoland (protectorates). [Not examined]

364   **Foreign Nations: Special Studies — Africa, 1962–1997**
Africa, 1962–1980
35mm microfilm (7 reels) with printed guide
Africa, 1980–1985 Supplement
35mm microfilm (11 reels) with printed guide
Africa, 1985–1988 Supplement
35mm microfilm (10 reels) with printed guide
Africa, 1989–1991 Supplement
35mm microfilm (10 reels) with printed guide.
Africa, 1992–1994 Supplement
35mm microfilm (10 reels) with printed guide.
Africa, 1995–1997 Supplement
35mm microfilm (8 reels) with printed guide.
Bethesda, MD: University Publications of America/LexisNexis. Complete collection to date $10,750 (also available separately)
For further pricing information, current availability status, and information on discounts apply to publisher or *see* publisher's Web site.
http://www.lexisnexis.com/academic/2upa/Issas/SpecialStudiesAfrica.asp

The UPA *Special Studies* series offers federally commissioned, in-depth research on topics of the highest priority from leading public and private research facilities. The authors of these studies are associated with such institutions as the Army War College's Strategic Studies Institute, the National Defence University, the Institute for Defence Analysis, the Army Command and General Staff College, the Naval Postgraduate School, the Central Intelligence Agency, Department of Energy, Center for Disease Control and Prevention, Economic Research Service, Industry and Trade Administration, International Trade Commission, the American Institutes for Research, and major international institutes at Harvard, Columbia, Stanford, Georgetown, Ohio, MIT, and Yale. [Not examined]

365   IDC Publishers [Africa-related titles in microform]
http://www.idc.nl/ [select Africa Studies from menu)
➔ **IDC Publishers (2195)** offer various collections of research materials on Africa, including newspapers, serials/periodicals, social and economic development plans and statistical reports, census reports, missionary archives, as well as the library catalogues of the Royal Commonwealth Society and the ➔ **School of Oriental and African Studies (1289)**, University of London, approximately 690,000 catalogue cards of approximately 175,000 items on Oriental and African studies added between 1978 and 1989 to the holdings of the SOAS Library, price € 8,340 [11/07/05]

366   Microform Academic Publishers [Africa-related titles in microform]
http://www.microform.co.uk/academic/index.php (enter "Africa" and/or "African studies" in search box)
http://www.microform.co.uk/html/body_african.html
➔ **Microform Academic Publishers (2225)** offer a substantial number of Africa-related titles on microfilm and microfiche, covering African studies journals and magazines, archival papers and collections, catalogues, reports, military accounts, government publications, and parliamentary papers, etc. [16/02/03]

➔ **Norman Ross Publishing** [African studies microform products] *see* ➔**University Microfilm International/ProQuest - African American and Africana Catalog of Microform (367)**

367   University Microfilm International/ProQuest - African American and Africana Catalog of Microform (Research Collections, Serials, Books on Demand and Dissertations)
http://www.umi.com/umi/subjectcatalogs/Africana_Catalog.pdf
This 101-page catalogue provides full details of relevant products available through ProQuest, including microfilm sets published by UMI, Chadwyck-Healey, the former Norman Ross Publishing, and also a number of other firms distributed by UMI. It contains approximately 170 research collections and over 530 serials, including a substantial number of products of interest to Africanists and African studies libraries, covering titles on anthropology and sociology, geography, government and economics, history, mission papers and archives, anti-slavery materials and collections, etc. The catalogue also offers information about how to obtain dissertations on African American & Africana Studies, as well as out of print books, through UMI's Books on Demand service.

368 **World Microfilms** [Anti-slavery materials]
http://www.microworld.ndirect.co.uk/wmcats.htm
Offers various microfilm resources on anti-slavery studies, including the collection of
anti-slavery material at ➔ **John Rylands Library, University of Manchester (1293)**
the collection at ➔ **Rhodes House, Oxford (1269)** – a major non-researched source
for the history of the anti-slavery movement in the 19th century – and the digitized
Heartman Manuscript Collection on Slavery at Xavier University in New Orleans, a
substantial collection of manuscripts relating to the North American slave trade
during the period 1724-1897. It can be supplied on CD-ROM, DVD, or as a download
from the Web. [30/07/05]

Theses and dissertations

See also ➔ **1 General online resources on Africa and African studies, and
the best starting points on the Web: Theses/e-theses and dissertations**

369 Afulezi, Ujo Nkwocha, and Ijeoma Ogwogo Afulezi **African (IGBO)
Scholarship: A Bibliography of Doctoral Dissertations and Some Masters Degree
Theses at American, Canadian, Australian, and European Universities, 1945-1999,**
vol. 1 Lanham, MD: University Press of America, 2000. 336 pp. $47.00
Collates studies conducted by African American scholars at universities in America,
Canada, Australia and Europe, between 1945 and 1999. [Not examined]

370 Curto, Jose C., and Raymond R. Gervais **Bibliography of Master's Theses
and Doctoral Dissertations on Africa, 1905-1993**. Montréal: Canadian Association of
African Studies, 1994. 311 pp.
Lists 3,112 references, arranged alphabetically by author with sections for individual
African countries, regions, and the continent in general. Each entry provides details
of author, title, degree, institution, and year. There are indexes by author, subject and
degree-granting institutions. Also includes some data and analysis on African studies
research in Canada, with tables showing the number of dissertations done by year,
by discipline, region or country, and by institution.
Online reviews:
H-Africa, July 1995 (reviewed by Gretchen Walsh)
http://www2.h-net.msu.edu/reviews/showrev.cgi?path=8949851378714

➔ **Database of African Theses and Dissertations (DATAD)** *see* **1 General online
resources on Africa and African studies, and the best starting points on the Web:
Thesis/e-theses and dissertations,** entry **203**

➔ Easterbrook, David L. **"African Theses and Dissertations in Academic Libraries
in the United States: Background and Current Practices"**, *see* **15 Africanist
documentation and African studies bibliography** entry **1902**

371   Larby, Patricia M. **"Theses on Africa Completed 1992-1993."** *African Research & Documentation*, no. 62 (1993): 68-71.

372   Larby, Patricia M. **"Some Completed Theses on Africa 1993-1994."** *African Research & Documentation*, no. 69 (1995): 69-82.

373   Larby, Patricia M. **"Theses on Africa Completed at UK Universities 1994-1996. Part 1. Africa in general, West Africa, Central Africa."** *African Research & Documentation*, no. 77 (1998): 71-90.

374   Larby, Patricia M. **"Theses on Africa Completed at UK Universities 1994-1996. Part 2. Eastern Africa, Southern Africa."** *African Research & Documentation*, no. 78 (1998): 82-103.

The above four entries are supplements to continue ➔ **SCOLMA's (1892)** guides on **Theses on Africa** (*see* **376, 377**). The titles listed are derived from those recorded in the *Register of Research on Commonwealth Studies* maintained at the ➔ **Institute of Commonwealth Studies (1279)**, University of London, and from where the annual listings of *Theses in Progress in Commonwealth Studies* can be downloaded free-of-charge at http://www.sas.ac.uk/commonwealthstudies/tip.htm.

375   Lauer, Joseph J., Gregory V. Larkin, and Alfred Kagan **American and Canadian Doctoral Dissertations and Master's Theses on Africa, 1974-1987**. Atlanta, GA: African Studies Association/Crossroads Press, 1989. 377 pp.

A continuation of entry **379**, providing details for more than 8,500 dissertations and theses. Arranged by country and region, with author, institution, and subject indexes. Kept up-to-date by the quarterly listings ➔ **Recent Doctoral Dissertations** (*see* **378**), which appear in ➔ **ASA News (803)**.

376   McIlwaine, J.H. St. J. **Theses on Africa, 1963-1975. Accepted by Universities in the United Kingdom and Ireland**. London: Mansell Publishing, 1978. 140 pp.

Originally published as an annual publication between 1966-1970 (published by Frank Cass, London, on behalf of ➔ **SCOLMA (1892)**; six volumes published to the volume covering 1967-68), this volume covers theses presented at British academic institutions between 1963 and 1975. Contains 2,335 entries, arranged geographically and by broad subject headings, with an author index. Continued by entry **377**.

377   Price, Helen C., Colin Hewson, and David Blake **Theses on Africa 1976-1988. Accepted by the Universities in the United Kingdom and Ireland**. London: Hans Zell Publishers (for Standing Conference on Library Materials on Africa/SCOLMA), 1993. 350 pp.

Continues entry **376** and earlier (annual) listings published by ➔ **SCOLMA (1892)** and provides details of 3,654 theses covering all regions of Africa and all subjects. Arranged by region, subdivided by country and subject, and with extensive subject and author indexes. Continued by entries **371-374**.

ARD review:
African Research & Documentation no. 65 (1994): 40-42 (reviewed Donald Simpson)
Choice review:
Choice September 1994 (reviewed by Donald Altschiller)

378   "Recent Doctoral Dissertations." [in African studies]. Compiled by Joseph J. Lauer and Daniel Britz, *ASA News*, 1990- Atlanta, GA [now New Brunswick, NJ]: African Studies Association. Currently compiled by Joseph J. Lauer
A supplementary and updating service to → **American and Canadian Doctoral Dissertations and Master's Theses on Africa, 1974-1987 (375)**, which lists theses as reported in *Dissertation Abstracts International* and *Index to Theses with Abstracts Accepted for Higher Degrees by the Universities of Great Britain and Ireland*. Arranged by broad subject groups; includes the order number for each citation, and guidance on how to order copies. In recent years listings have appeared somewhat sporadically. As at July 2005, 66 quarterly supplements had been published. US and Canadian theses are usually available from ProQuest; for more details see http://wwwlib.umi.com/dissertations/gateway.

379   Sims, Michael, and Alfred Kagan **American and Canadian Doctoral Dissertations and Master's Theses on Africa, 1886-1974.** Waltham, MA: African Studies Association, Brandeis University, 1976. 365 pp.
Lists 6,070 theses classified by geographical area and thereafter by discipline; indexed by subject and author. Continued by entry **375**.

→ **Theses Canada** [for theses on African topics] *see* **1 General online resources on Africa and African studies, and the best starting points on the Web: Thesis/e-theses and dissertations,** entry **204**

→ **Theses in Progress in Commonwealth Studies/Theses in Progress in Commonwealth Studies: A List of Research in UK Universities 2005** (Print and online) *see* **1 General online resources on Africa and African studies, and the best starting points on the Web: Theses/e-theses and dissertations,** entry **205**

380   **Union List of Theses and Dissertations Held by Universities and Research Institutions in Kenya** CD-ROM, issue no. 1, March 2003. Kenya Information Preservation Society, c/o Rev Fr Maurice Kisenyi, Catholic University of Eastern Africa [PO Box 24205, Karen, Nairobi, Kenya Email: kenyadocuments@yahoo.com] $17.00
Contains citations of approximately 3,000 theses and dissertations, including theses which reflect research undertaken in Kenya by which are held by institutions outside Kenya. No abstracts at this time, but may be included in future releases, and there is also a possibility that the database may be mounted on the Web site of the → **Kenya National Archives (1523)** in the near future. [Not examined]

3

Current bibliographies, indexing and abstracting services, and review media
(print and online)

Only the major *general* current bibliographies, continuing sources, and abstracting and indexing services are listed here. For more specialist continuing sources consult ➜ **Bibliographies for African Studies 1970-1986 (234)** and its supplement ➜ **Bibliographies for African Studies 1987-1993 (235)**; ➜ **Africa: A Guide to Reference Material (227)** (new edition due 2006); and ➜ **Reference Guide to Africa. A Bibliography of Sources (225)**.

ⓘ **This symbol indicates "The editor's choice" of a particularly outstanding online information resource.**

Current bibliographies and continuing sources

See also ➜ **Collective online databases**

381   Accessions List of the Library of Congress Office, Nairobi, Kenya. [formerly *Accessions List: East and Southern Africa*] Nairobi: Library of Congress Office, 1968-
ISSN 1527-5396 six times yearly gratis on request
[In the US use the following ordering address: Field Director-LOC, Unit 64110, APO AE 09831-4110, Email: nairobi@libcon-kenya.org]
The Library of Congress Office in Nairobi is one of six overseas offices administered by the African/Asian Acquisitions and Overseas Operations Division of the ➜ **Library of Congress (1316)**. The office acquires and catalogues publications from 25 countries primarily in eastern and southern Africa, but as from 1998 is also started acquiring material from West Africa. Acquisitions include publications from many sources: commercial publishers, international, governmental and non-governmental organizations, and also includes a great deal of ephemera and grey literature. As a record of the publications it acquires the office publishes this bi-monthly accessions list, with a biennial Serials Supplement (available on CD-ROM only) and a useful *Annual Publishers Directory*. Additionally the office publishes the ➜ **Quarterly Index to African Periodical Literature (404)**. All these publications are freely available to libraries and other institutions on request.

382   **Africa Bibliography.** Edinburgh: Edinburgh University Press (in association with the International African Institute), 1985- [in North America order from St. Martin's Press] annual ISSN 0266-6731 £75.00/$137.00 (also available as part of a subscription to *Africa*, see below) Edited by T.A. Barringer

Published annually as a supplement to ➔**Africa. Journal of the International African Institute (734)**, this bibliography records books, articles, pamphlets, and essays in edited volumes, principally in the social sciences, environmental sciences, humanities and the arts, but some items from the medical, biological and natural sciences are also included. Covers the whole of Africa, primarily works in English, but also including some literature in French, Portuguese, and German. Arrangement is by region and country (with a preliminary section for the continent as a whole), and each region or country is sub-divided into subject fields/topics. With author and subject indexes. The latest annual volume published in 2005 – covering works published on Africa during 2003 – contains 5,078 items entries, with an author and subject index. Each volume also includes an informative guest essay on topics such as Africana bibliography, African publishing, librarianship in Africa, or African studies research.

383   **"Africana Reference Works: An Annotated List of [1984/85-] Titles."** *The African Book Publishing Record*, 12, no. 2 (1986)- Edited by Joe Lauer *et al* [to 1988]; edited by Yvette Scheven *et al* [1989-1992]; edited by Phyllis B. Bischof *et al* [1993-1996]; edited by Mette Shayne *et al.* [1997-1998]; edited by Jill Young-Coelho *et al* [1999-]

Published in the third issue of each volume of ➔ **The African Book Publishing Record (384)** (in the second issue up to vol. 26, 2000), this is a valuable annual listing which records, classifies and annotates new reference works on Africa published worldwide during the preceding year. Each list is compiled by a number of librarians from leading Africana libraries in the USA. It is generally limited to titles in European languages that have been examined by the compilers. Titles are arranged under LC subject headings. Full postal and email contact information is provided for many of the smaller or non-commercial publishers that are not usually included in the major book trade directories. In addition to citations of print reference works, it is now also including a growing number of new sources available in electronic formats.

384   **The African Book Publishing Record.** Oxford: Hans Zell Publishers, 1975-1979; Munich & London: Hans Zell Publishers, an imprint of K.G. Saur Ltd., 1980-1988; Sevenoaks, later East Grinstead: Hans Zell Publishers, an imprint of Bowker-Saur Ltd., 1988-2000; Munich: K.G. Saur, 2001- quarterly ISSN 0306-0322 €348.00 annually. Edited by Hans M. Zell & Cécile Lomer; from vol. 28, no. 3, 2002- edited by Cécile Lomer

Editorial address: Cécile Lomer, Editor, The African Book Publishing Record, Petit Bersac, 24600 Ribérac, France, Tel/Fax: +33-553-905576, Email: CecileLomer@cs.com

Currently (2006) in its 32nd year of publication, the quarterly *African Book Publishing Record* (ABPR) is probably the single most comprehensive source of current African book publishing output. Since ABPR first started publication in 1975 it has listed over 55,000 new African-published books, from some 1,600 African publishers, research institutions with publishing programmes, as well as NGOs, professional associations and learned societies, and others. Moreover, it has published over 3,500 book reviews, contributed by reviewers from all over the world, including many in Africa. ABPR provides bibliographic coverage of new and forthcoming titles in English and French, as well as those in African languages. Its bibliographic sections provide triple access to new books: by subject, by author, and by country of publication, and in each issue there is directory of publishers whose titles are listed in that issue. Complete bibliographic and acquisitions data is provided for each title. ABPR also includes news items, and occasional articles, relating to various aspects of publishing and book development in Africa, as well as news and reports about book promotional activities and events. All titles published in ABPR are cumulated in ➜ **African Books in Print/Livres Africains Disponibles (385).**

385   African Books in Print/Livres Africains Disponibles. 6th edition. Edited by Cécile Lomer. Munich: K. G. Saur, forthcoming, 2006. 2 vols. ca. 2,304 pp. two volume set ca. €898.00 set (Distributed in the US by Gale)
A major source of reference and selection tool for African book publishing output. *African Books in Print* (ABIP) cumulates and updates titles listed in ➜ **The African Book Publishing Record/ABPR (384).** Volume 1 includes the introductory and prelim matter, the directory of publishers, and the subject index – listing titles under some 7,500 subject headings/sub-headings, country and regional headings, language headings, etc., and extensively cross-referenced – with the author and title indexes making up volume 2. ABIP aims to provide a systematic, reliable and functional reference tool and buying guide to African-published material currently in print. The latest (6th) edition provides full bibliographic details of more than 35,000 titles in print as at the end of 2005, from 1,600 publishers and research institutions with publishing programmes, in 55 African countries. This includes a cumulation of all titles listed in volume XXVI, no. 1, 2000 through volume XXXI, no. 4, 2005, of the quarterly ABPR; plus more than 4,000 additional records not previously listed in either ABIP or ABPR. The directory of publishers in each edition of ABIP provides full name and address details of all publishers included, with telephone and fax numbers, email addresses and Web sites where available, and the names and addresses of European and US distributors (where applicable). [6th ed. not examined]
JOINT WINNER (4th ed.) CONOVER-PORTER AWARD 1994

386   A Current Bibliography on African Affairs. Farmingdale, NY: Baywood Publishing Co 1963- [New series 1968-] quarterly ISSN 0011-3255 $287.00 annually. Edited by Roger W. Moeller
Each issue features articles and commentary, a number of book reviews or review articles and bibliographic essays, plus a topical and geographical list of books, documents, and periodical articles. Typically, each issue includes around 400-500 entries, and all entries include a brief annotation. An author index is included in each issue, and a subject/regional index appears in the fourth issue of each volume. While this is a useful resource, coverage – especially of periodical articles – is nowhere near as comprehensive as the ➜ **International African Bibliography (387).**

387   International African Bibliography. Current Books, Articles and Papers in African Studies. London: Mansell Publishing, 1971-1992; London: Hans Zell Publishers and imprint of Bowker-Saur, 1993-2000. Munich: K.G. Saur, 2001- quarterly ISSN 0020-5877 €310.00 annually. Edited by David Hall, in association with the Centre of African Studies at the Library, School of Oriental and African Studies, University of London

This fine quarterly bibliography – probably the most comprehensive index to Africana materials – lists books, articles and papers in all fields of African studies, primarily in the social sciences and the humanities, but also includes scientific articles, especially those relating to geography, natural resources and the environment. Includes over 4,000 entries annually, drawn from about 1,150 periodicals (about 250 of which are African serials), as well as a substantial number of other publications such as conference proceedings and chapters in edited volumes, reports, dissertations, official publications, etc. Entries are grouped under (1) Articles, and (2) Books/Monographs, arranged geographically (for articles a full subject classification is indicated), with a subject index of articles. It covers articles in English, French, Italian, Dutch, Portuguese, and occasionally other European languages. An extensive cumulative index to each volume appears in the last issue of each volume, and consists of indexes by subject, authors and personalities, ethnic groups, languages, and other names and special terms.

388   L'Afrique en Livres. Paris: France Edition [115 boulevard Saint Germain, 75006 Paris, France], 1998. 333 pp.

Something of a mini books-in-print for African material in French, this useful catalogue lists some 4,000 books in French on Africa, from 600 publishers, including many published in francophone Africa. Titles (with full bibliographic details and prices) are arranged under six major headings and a range of sub-headings. Part 1 provides an extensive listing of African literature titles, part 2 is devoted to books for children, part 3 covers the humanities and social sciences under a number of subject groups, and which is followed by sections on the sciences, 'Vie Pratique' (cookery, travel, etc.), and a final section devoted to the arts, cinema, music and photography. No further editions have been published to date.

389   Recent Publications about Eastern Africa and the Indian Ocean Region. Washington, DC: African Section, African and Middle Eastern Division, Library of Congress. July 2003- monthly by email free on request

To subscribe to this service apply to: Joanne M. Zellers, Area Specialist for Eastern Africa and the Western Indian Ocean, Islands, Email: jzellers@loc.gov

A free bibliographic service by email from the African and Middle Eastern Division of the →**Library of Congress (1316)**, designed to assist scholars in the identification of, and increase access to, recently published materials in this area of study. The service offers bibliographic updates for a total of 16 lists, consisting of a Regional Focus category (Eastern Africa, Indian Ocean region, Horn of Africa, and the Red Sea) and 15 country lists that cover materials published both in as well as about each country. The period of coverage varies from country to country, and documents are distributed as Word or WordPerfect documents only. Participants in the service also receive information about Library of Congress events, collections, services, and noteworthy new acquisitions of interest to scholars of Eastern Africa and the Indian Ocean region. This is a very useful service.

Collective online catalogue databases

390   The Africa Book Centre Ltd
http://www.africabookcentre.com
This specialist UK dealer and library supplier of books on Africa, maintains a database of about 35,000 titles and stocks of some 5,000 books are carried, including an extensive range of African-published material. The company does not, at this time, maintain a complete integrated online catalogue as such, but you can access the complete archive of weekly listings going back for a few months, plus an archive of select backlist titles. There are special sections devoted to new titles, book of the month, African languages and linguistics, award winners, signed copies, African music and CDs, children's books, African food and drink, or browse by country/region or by subject. *See also* ➔ **2331** [12/11/05]
Note: for the complete list of African publishers distributed by the Africa Book Centre's associate company, Global Book Marketing, *see* ➔ **16 Dealers and distributors of African studies materials** entry **2338**.

391   African Books Collective Ltd
http://www.africanbookscollective.com
The Oxford-based African Books Collective (ABC) provides a single source of supply for the books from over a hundred African publishers, from 18 African countries, with a current stock inventory of some 1,600 titles. The complete stock list can be accessed at the ABC Web site, which provides a secure ordering environment. Browse by new titles, by broad subject groups, or search for specific titles. Under subject groups titles are listed by year of publication, with the most recent titles on top. The site also offers author profiles, news about exhibits, and information about award-winning books. The online catalogue of African Books Collective's North American distributor ➔ **Michigan State University Press (2271)** can be found at http://www.msupress.msu.edu/series.php?seriesID=22, while an attractive showcase for ABC-distributed titles, "The African Books Collective Reading Room", at http://www.msupress.msu.edu/Reading%20Room_abc_page.php, offers an opportunity to preview books, browse catalogues, view sample chapters, illustrations, or other extracts from a very wide range of ABC-distributed African titles. From this page you can also download the *Kitabu, Iwe, Buku* catalogue of select titles stocked by MSUP – including many titles that will be of interest to public and school libraries – or download sections of it (all in pdf format). *See also* ➔ **2332**. [12/11/05]
Note: for the complete list of African publishers distributed by African Books Collective Ltd *see* ➔ **16 Dealers and distributors of African studies materials** entry **2332** , or (for North American customers) view the full list at http://www.msupress.msu.edu/abc_order_form.pdf

392   Afrilivres. Livres d'Afrique et des Disasporas
http://www.afrilivres.com/
An important new initiative launched in November 2002 by the journal ➔ **Africultures (673)**, in partnership with the organization Culture et Développement, the ➔ **French Foreign Ministry (2651)**, and financially supported by the ➔ **Charles Léopold Mayer Foundation (2650)**. It is a collaborative Web portal for a group of francophone African publishers, currently (July 2005) comprising 54 publishers from 15 African nations, and offering over 1,300 titles online. The full publisher list can be found at http://www.afrilivres.com/index.asp?navig=annuaire. The site offers access to new books – with cover images, full bibliographic data, and ordering information – and profiles about participating publishers, as well as details of their various book series. It incorporates an online catalogue of select backlist titles, which can be browsed by broad subject groups or by publisher, and which also includes children's books. A large proportion of the books can be ordered online in a secure environment via the distributor Servédit (prices are quoted in Euro); others can only be ordered direct from the publishers. The site also offers a facility to search by title, by subject groups or key words, or by name of author, publisher, ISBN, country; or the database can be searched for titles which are immediately available via Servédit. There are also some pages devoted to book trade events and book fairs, and literary and cultural events on Africa. [12/07/05]

393   L'Alliance des éditeurs indépendants pour une autre mondalisation [Online catalogue]
http://www.alliance-editeurs.org/catalogues/accueil.php?l=1
Set up in 2002 and supported by the ➔ **Fondation Charles Lépold Mayer (2650)** and the ➔ **Ford Foundation (2733)**, L'Alliance des éditeurs independents pour une autre mondalisation is a not-for-profit alliance and network of independent, progressive publishers, at this time primarily those in the French-speaking areas of the world, including many in Africa. Members of the group meet regularly, develop and facilitate co-publishing projects and, as part of collaborative marketing schemes, this also includes joint exhibits at major international book fairs. On the occasion of the Salon du livre de Genève in 2005, it published a collective catalogue of select titles from 28 of its member publishers, with full ordering and contact information. It is published both in print format and available online. Access is by publisher and for each title complete bibliographic and price information is provided, together with a short description of content and a small cover image. It includes both scholarly and general publishers (and those publishing children's books) from Benin, Burkina Faso, Cameroon, Côte d'Ivoire, Gabon, Guinea, Madagascar, Mali, Morocco, and Tunisia. For each publisher the Web site also offers informative company profiles. [01/07/05]

Abstracting and indexing services

394   Africana Conference Paper Index
http://www.library.northwestern.edu/africana/resources/index.html
(then click on to the database required) or
or http://nucat.library.northwestern.edu/cgi-bin/Pwebrecon.cgi

An index to the individual papers (in Western European languages) of conference proceedings – mostly in the African studies field – held by ➔ **Northwestern University's Melville J. Herskovits Library of African Studies (1322)**. The file is updated daily, and currently (November 2005) contains 109,817 individual papers in 6,118 conference proceedings. Search for authors of individual conference papers, conference titles/papers from a particular conference, or search using keywords. [22/11/05]

395   Africana Vertical File Index
http://www.library.northwestern.edu/africana/resources/index.html
(then click on to the database required) or
http://nucat.library.northwestern.edu/cgi-bin/Pwebrecon.cgi
Covers an extensive collection (over 20,000 items) of uncatalogued ephemera, including government documents, official publications, pamphlets, annual reports, laws, commission reports, material from trade unions, political parties, etc. held in vertical file cabinets by ➔ **Northwestern University's Melville J. Herskovits Library of African Studies (1322)**. The file is updated daily and is searchable by title, author, or keyword. [13/07/05]

396   African Studies Abstracts/African Studies Abstracts Online ⓘ [succeeds *Documentatieblad. The Abstracts Journal of the African Studies Centre*, Leiden, 1967-1993] London: Hans Zell Publishers, an imprint of Bowker-Saur (for the African Studies Centre, Leiden, Netherlands) volume 25, 1994-volume 31, 2000; Munich: K.G. Saur, volume 32-33, 2001-2002, quarterly, ISSN 1352-2175; print version ceased with volume 33, no. 4, 2002; as from volume 34, no. 1, 2003- published as *African Studies Abstracts Online*, ISSN 1570-937X, available free at
http://www.ascleiden.nl/Library/Abstracts/Asa-online/ (pdf format).
Abstracts produced by Michèle Boin, Elvire Eijkman, Katrien Polman, Tineke Sommeling, and Marlene C.A. van Doorn
Provides access to abstracts of articles that have appeared in some 230 periodicals and edited works on Africa in the social sciences and the humanities, and available at the ➔ **African Studies Centre Library (1246)** in Leiden. This includes all the leading journals in the field of African studies, as well as a number of other journals dealing with Third World countries and development studies in general. A selection of edited works is also accessed and abstracted on a chapter-by-chapter basis. Each issue contains up to 425 abstracts, arranged geographically, with author, subject and geographical indexes, and a listing of the journals and edited works abstracted in each issue. While the print version is no longer published, *African Studies Abstracts* is now freely available online in pdf format. The master list of the 232 periodicals currently   abstracted   and   indexed   can   be   found   at http://www.ascleiden.nl/Library/Abstracts/, with links to the full catalogue record for each periodical. [13/07/05]

397   Index Islamicus. Current Books and Articles on Islam and the Muslim World. Cambridge: Cambridge University Library, 1958-1985. London: Mansell Publishing [as *Quarterly Index Islamicus*], 1986-1991. London: Bowker-Saur, 1992-2001. Leiden & Herndon, VA: Brill Academic Publishers, 2002- quarterly ISSN 1360-0982 [previously 0309-7395]

Edited by C.H. Bleaney and C.J. Roper
Print €887/$1,098 annually [vol. 27, 2005], Online €3,350/$4,200; CD-ROM, Edition 6,
Network edition (1-4 users, including Yearbooks with titles 2001 and 2002)
€2,750/$3,500
Related product:
*Concise Biographical Companion to Index Islamicus. An International Who's Who in Islamic
Studies from its beginnings down to the Twentieth Century. Bio-bibliographical Supplement
to Index Islamicus, 1665-1980, 3 vols. 2004.* Compiled by Wolfgang Behn. €186/$266
per vol.
For more information about *Index Islamicus* related products *see* publisher Web site at
http://www.brill.nl/m_catalogue.asp?sub=4
Originally published in book form, this is a comprehensive continuing source on the
literature of Islam and Middle Eastern studies, which also includes a substantial
number of citations for African countries, with sections for North and West Africa,
Sudan and East Africa. Over 3,000 periodicals are surveyed, including general
history, social science, history of science and arts titles, as well as area-specific
journals. Arranged by subjects and geographically. The fourth issue of each year is a
hard-bound cumulation containing cumulated indexes for the year. Now also
available in electronic formats.

**398   Index of African Social Science Periodical Articles/Index des articles de
périodiques africains de sciences socials.** Dakar: CODESRIA [distributed by African
Books Collective Ltd, Oxford], 1989- annually (ceased, two volumes only published)
ISSN 0850-9379 Volume 1: 1989, 112 pp. Volume 2: 1993, 248 pp.. Compiled and
edited by the CODESRIA Documentation and Information Center (CODICE)
This source from ➔ **CODESRIA (1851)** promised to become an important indexing
and abstracting service of African social science journals, but unfortunately only two
volumes were ever published: volume 1, 1989, which covered material published
between 1985-1987, with 216 records from 24 African-published journals; and volume
2/3, 1990-1991 (published in 1993) which covered material for 1988-1989 and
included 548 records from 49 journals. Abstracts are provided in the original
language of publication, together with subject descriptors in English and French. Five
indexes are included: authors, English subject descriptors, French subject descriptors,
names of periodicals, and titles.

**399   Index to African Official Publications/Index des Publications Officielles
Africaines.** Addis Ababa: Library of the United Nations Economic Commission for
Africa [PO Box 3001], 1997- no ISSN [ECA reference: E/ECA/LIB/SER.G/1/97]
Twice yearly   Print and online
Online formerly at http://www.un.org/Depts/eca/info/iaop.htm but not currently
(September 2005) available
Indexes materials deposited by government offices and ministries of ECA member
states. Listings are arranged under two major groups: (1) material from African
government offices, ministries and institutions, classified as official publications, and
which are listed alphabetically organized by country and by the issuing government
office; (2) material produced by African inter-governmental organizations, for
example the Organization of African Unity, now ➔ **African Union (2504),** and which
are also grouped alphabetically by the issuing body. Descriptor terms selected from
the thesaurus of the UN Bibliographic Information System (UNBIS) are used to

describe the principal content of each publication. Subject, author/publisher, and geographic indexes facilitate access, and there is also a directory of publishers and other issuing bodies with full addresses.

400   Index to Black Periodicals. Edition 2003. Boston: G.K. Hall/Gale, 2004. $250.00
Indexes 35 journals, both popular and scholarly, combining authors and subjects in a single alphabetical arrangement. Includes a small number of journals on African studies and African literature and culture, but most are journals on the African American experience and Black studies. [Not examined]

401   International Development Abstracts. Norwich, UK: GeoAbstracts for the Centre for Development Studies, University College Swansea, 1982- six times yearly ISSN 0262-0855 Now published by Elsevier Science €1,098/$1,227 annually
Also available as part of GEOBASE through DIALOG. A CD-ROM version is available through Silver Platter either on GEOBASE or on the subset disc: Geography disc
Edited by F.K. Cooper *et al*
A major source for literature on topics and issues relating to all aspects of development and developing countries, including very substantial coverage of Africa. Arranged under 40 main topics headings, with a subject and regional index in each issue, plus an annual subject, regional, and author index. Some 600 core journals are abstracted on a regular basis, together with additional material from books, monographs, edited collections and conference proceedings, theses, reports and newsletters. Coverage includes all areas of the social sciences, as well as agriculture, environment and development, industrial policy, health, gender and culture, and more. Includes a significant number of entries of material published in languages other than English, and English title translations are provided for non-English papers.

402   International Index to Black Periodicals Full Text. Cambridge: Chadwyck-Healey [now part of ProQuest], 1998- available as an annual subscription with monthly updates on the Web. For subscription options *see*
http://www.chadwyck.com/chadwyck/tr-trial.shtml or visit
http://www.chadwyck.com/products/pt-product-IIBPFT.shtml
The current (July 2005) release of *IIBP Full Text* contains 190,151 records, and offers access to abstracts and current and retrospective bibliographic citations to some 150 scholarly and popular journals, newspapers and newsletters from the US, Africa, and the Caribbean pertaining to African and African American studies. Full-text access is provided for 40 key scholarly journals from 1998 onwards, and there are bibliographic citations for retrospective records (about 120,000 citations) from 1902 onwards. Coverage is both international and multidisciplinary (cultural, economic, historical, social, political and religious issues), A search interface provides 12 search fields where users, besides key word searches, you can search any combination of categories, including title keyword, author, subject, document type, language and date.   The   complete   title   list   can   be   found   at
http://iibp.chadwyck.com/morehome/htxview?template=basic.htx&content=mi_fr
am.htx.

403 **Middle East: Abstracts and Index.** Pittsburgh: Northumberland Press, 1978-1985. Seattle: Aristarchus Knowledge Industries/Northumberland Press, 1986-1995. Seattle: Reference Corporation Aristarchus Knowledge Industries, 1996- irregular between 1978-1991, annually after 1992
Volume D, Maghreb-Sahel-Horn covers fourteen African countries from the region: Algeria, Chad, Djibouti, Eritrea, Ethiopia, Libya, Mali, Mauritania, Morocco, Niger, Somalia, Sudan, Tunisia, and Western Sahara. Includes a broad range of materials in various disciplines, including anthropology, art, economics and economic development, history, language, and religion. Entries are arranged by country, then by title. [Not examined; not verified]

404 **Quarterly Index to African Periodical Literature.** ⓘ [formerly *Quarterly Index to Periodical Literature, Eastern and Southern Africa*] Nairobi: Library of Congress Office [PO Box 30598] Nairobi, 1991- ISSN 1527-5388 quarterly gratis on request Subscribers in the US should use the following ordering address: Library of Congress Office, Unit 64110, APO AE 09831-4110, Email: nairobi@libcon-kenya.org] online database freely accessible at http://lcweb2.loc.gov/misc/qsihtml/ [13/07/05]
This is another outstanding resource from the Library of Congress Office in Nairobi (*see also* ➔ **381**), which provides an index to over 300 selected periodicals that are acquired regularly from 29 African countries, most of them of a scholarly nature. Each issue includes a register of citations listing articles under some 30 broad subject groups, and, additionally, each number also contains an author index, geographical index, subject term index, and a title of article and title of journal index. The freely accessible online database is supported by excellent search facilities: search by title, author, subject, date, country or journal; or browse by index term, article title, author, journal, broad subject area, or geographic area.

Book review media and book review indexes

Many of the African studies journals listed in section ➔ **9 Journals and magazines** carry book review columns, usually reviewing a handful of new titles in each issue. In addition to those listed below, multidisciplinary African studies periodicals that have fairly extensive book review columns include ➔ **Africa. Journal of the International African Institute (734)**, ➔ **Africa Today (793)**, ➔ **African Affairs (741)**, ➔ **African Studies Review (800)**, ➔ **The Australasian Review of African Studies (663)**, ➔ **Canadian Journal of African Studies (784)**, ➔ **Journal of African History (761)**, ➔ **Journal of Modern African Studies (766)**, and ➔ **Politique Africaine (694)**. However, access to these reviews is not available free, and requires either a subscription to the print edition, or purchase of combined print and online editions of these journals (where electronic formats are available). One freely accessible online journal, and which now publishes an average of more than a dozen reviews in each issue, is ➔ **African Studies Quarterly (799)**; the complete reviews archive is available at the journal's Web site. The ➔ **H-**

Africa Network/H-Africa Review (409) reviews African studies scholarly titles regularly, although the number of reviews published annually seems to be on the decline. The book review pages of the African news provider ➜ AllAfrica.com's (851) are excellent, and are particularly valuable for the wide number of book reviews they pull together from African online newspapers (and *see also* section ➜ 11 The African press).

For African-published material the ➜ African Book Publishing Record (384) is the major review outlet and publishes some 40 reviews in each quarterly issue. CODRESIA's recently launched ➜Africa Review of Books (406) pledges to give prominent attention to publishing reviews of African-published scholarly titles (although this was not in fact reflected in the first two issues), while the online - with an almost identical title - ➜ African Review of Books (407) publishes primarily reviews of new fiction, drama, poetry, biography, and new general interest books on Africa rather than academic titles.

For reviews of new reference works on Africa, the three main sources are ➜ African Research & Documentation (748), ➜ The African Book Publishing Record (384) (in its column "New reference sources of note", which reviews new Africana reference works published worldwide), together with the major library journal and review media *Choice*, available in print or online formats, which also carries many reviews of new monographs in the African studies field. There are also occasional reviews of new reference works in ➜ Africana Libraries Newsletter (801).

Book review media (print and online)

> ⓘ This symbol indicates "The editor's choice" of a particularly outstanding online information resource.

405   The Africa Book Centre Book Review. London: The Africa Book Centre, 1995- print and online three times yearly ISSN 1363-2477 print £20.00 annually in the UK, £25.00 overseas. Edited by Adrian Howe & Saara Marchadour
Email: info@africabookcentre.com
online free at http://www.africabookcentre.com/abc/Review%2028.pdf [20/09/05, latest issue, URL changes with each issue]
The *Africa Book Centre Book Review* "aims to be the best source of timely and current information on the African book industry." Contains occasional book reviews or review essays, together with news items, but the most substantive part of the journal consists of two separate listings 'New Books from Africa' and 'New Books on Africa'. These are arranged under broad subject groups with a brief annotation on each title,

together with prices and full bibliographic and ordering data. All books listed can be ordered from the → **Africa Book Centre (2331)** and entries are marked indicating availability status. While this is not strictly speaking a review media, it is a good source for keeping up-to-date about new African studies titles from publishers in all parts of the world.

→ **The African Book Publishing Record** *see* **384**

406   The Africa Review of Books (ARB)
www.codesria.org/Links/Publications/review_books/current_issue.htm [13/08/05; this URL changes for each issue]
Dakar: Council for the Development of Social Science Research in Africa (CODESRIA), 2004- twice yearly (in English and French) ISSN 0851–7592
Subscription rates: print: n/a (US$1.50 cover price per issue) online: free
Editors: Bahru Zewde & Hassan Remaoun (French Editor)
Managing Editor: Zenebeworke Tadesse
Editorial address: Forum for Social Studies, PO Box 25864 Code 1000, Addis Ababa, Ethiopia, Email: arb.fss@telecom.net.et
Editorial address for contributions in French: CRASC, Cité Bahi Ammar, Bloc A, N° 01 Es Sénia, Oran, Algeria, Email: crasc@crasc.org
The maiden issue of the long-awaited *Africa Review of Books* (ARB) – not to be confused with the very similarly named → **The African Review of Books** (*see* entry **407** below) – appeared in late 2004, in a somewhat awkward oversize format. It covers works on Africa in the social sciences, humanities, and the creative arts, and, additionally, the journal intends to serve as forum for critical analysis, reflections, and debates about Africa. According to an inaugural mission statement in the first issue, the new review journal will also seek to "bring interesting work published in Africa, but which are not sufficiently well disseminated, to the attention of a wider reading audience both within and outside the continent." Reviews are published in English and French; most are in-depth critical reviews or review essays, and there are also general articles. In addition to the print version, all reviews and articles are also freely accessible online. Despite the sentiments expressed in the inaugural statements that promised that special attention would be given to books actually published on the continent, there is not much evidence of this as yet – on the basis of the first two issues – and it is to be hoped that more space will be devoted to African-published scholarly books in future numbers. The second issue, published in September 2005, included a series of articles dedicated to an assessment of events and developments that have been unfolding in three African countries (Algeria, Rwanda, and South Africa) in the last decade or so, together with a small number of book reviews. At this time at least, *ARB* lacks currency, which is an essential requirement for a book review media: three of the nine books reviewed in the first issue were published in 1999 and 2001 respectively, and another three each published in 2000 and 2002, while the second number included reviews of books published as long ago as 1997 and 1998. However, these flaws apart, this is an important and much needed new review outlet for books in the African studies field.
ARD review:
African Research & Documentation, no. 98 (2005): 91-93 (reviewed by Hans Zell)
Online review:

Africana Libraries Newsletter, no. 115 (April 2005): 12-13 (reviewed by Hans Zell)
http://www.indiana.edu/~libsalc/african/aln/no116.pdf

407   The African Review of Books (AroB)
http://www.africanreviewofbooks.com [16/08/05]
2003- online free Salisbury, UK: African Review of Books, [Kelsey Cottage
2 The Green, Laverstock SP1 1QS, UK] and Johannesburg: African Review of Books
[PO Box 10024, Johannesburg 2000, South Africa]. Edited by Richard Bartlett and
Raks Seakhoa. Email: mail@africanreviewofbooks.com
The online, freely accessible, *African Review of Books* (easily confused with the ➜
Africa Review of Books, see preceding entry **406**) aims to provide "a space in which
the books, literature and scholarship of Africa can be discussed and debated", and "a
step towards bringing together, in one place, news, reviews and information relating
to Africa's publishing industry and African scholarship." Features reviews of books
published both within and outside Africa, together with essays, news, and
announcements about new books, book fairs and book promotional events, book
prizes, and obituaries. The emphasis is primarily on fiction, drama and poetry, and
biography rather than academic titles. Also offers a free email newsletter. This is a
very useful resource.

408   AllAfrica.com – Book reviews
http://allafrica.com/bookreviews/
➜ **AllAfrica.com (851)**, the major African news provider, started publication of
online book reviews in 2003, drawing on their own commissioned reviews, as well as
providing access to book reviews published in many African newspapers. To quickly
retrieve the latest reviews published in online African newspapers click on to
http://allafrica.com/books/, and which also includes book industry news and links
to news stories about book launches, book promotional or literary events, and book
awards and prizes.

409   H-Net Reviews/H-Africa Reviews
http://www.h-net.org/reviews/ (Main H-Net reviews page)
http://www.h-net.org/~africa/reviews/ (H-Africa Reviews)
RSS RSS feed: http://www.h-net.org/reviews/rss/H-Africa.rss
H-Net Reviews in the Humanities and Social Sciences is an online scholarly review
resource, and each H-Net discussion network has its own review editor(s). An
interesting aspect of H-Net Reviews is that it seeks to facilitate discussion of new
works and, to this end, H-Net is endeavouring to develop new professional norms
that encourage dialogue between authors and their reviewers. The group of **H-Net
Africa** lists (*see* ➜ **2810-2821**) represent some of the major African studies online
forums, and which have also generated a sizeable number of book (and multimedia)
reviews over the years. Reviews are primarily of material in the humanities and the
social sciences. H-Africa Reviews is currently edited by Amin Alhassan
(Communication Studies, York University, Toronto) and Mark L Lilleleht
(Department of African Languages and Literature, University of Wisconsin-
Madison). Access to the complete H-Africa reviews archive from 27 March 1995
through 31 July 2004 (at as July 2005) can be found at the above Web site, and
includes reviews of a small number of CDs, Web sites, exhibits, films and videos. The

complete archive of reviews can be accessed and searched by author, title, year of publication, publisher, ISBN, name of reviewer, H-Net Africa list, date of review, and Library of Congress call number or subject classification. A very useful resource. [13/07/05]

410   Notre Librairie: Revue des littératures du Sud. Paris: Association pour la Diffusion de la Pensée Française (ADPF), [Ministère des Affaires Etrangères 6 rue Ferrus, 75683 Paris Cedex 14], 1969- Print and online quarterly ISSN 0755-3854 Print subscription: in Europe €39.50, outside Europe €44.00, Africa/Caribbean €35.00, Ed: Nathalie Carré Email: notrelibrairie@adpf.asso.fr
Online: articles, news items, and book reviews, etc. are freely downloadable in pdf format (text only, without illustrations) at http://www.adpf.asso.fr/librairie/
A very attractively produced journal that covers various aspects of African literature, sometimes reviewing literary output by country and sometimes choosing special subject areas such as theatre, poetry, lusophone and Hispanic literature. Other recent numbers have included issues focussing on the African cinema, African music, bookselling in Africa, literature and development, emerging new African writers, and language and linguistics. Includes articles, interviews, profiles of African writers, and an extensive number of book reviews in each issue, covering titles on Africa or African literature published in France as well as in francophone Africa, and providing full bibliographic and acquisitions data.
Note: An "Index général des articles 1969/2005" (offering various search modes) can be found at http://www.adpf.asso.fr/librairie/index-articles00.html

➔**Takam Tikou. Le bulletin de la joie par les livres** *see* **697**

Book review indexes (multidisciplinary)

411   African and African American Studies Middletown, CT: Choice, 1992. 146 pp. (Choice Ethnic Studies Reviews)
A cumulative volume of 754 book reviews which appeared in volumes 27-29 (September 1989-July 1992) of *Choice*, the publication of the Association of College and Research Libraries, a division of the American Library Association. Arranged by subject, with indexes by author and title.

412   Easterbrook, David L. Africana Book Reviews, 1885-1945. An Index to Books Reviewed in Selected English-Language Publications. Boston: G.K. Hall, 1979. 247 pp.
1,725 items from 44 English-language journals; with a title index.

413   Howell, J.B., with Steven James Browne and Barbara M. Howell. Index to the African Studies Review/Bulletin and the ASA Review of Books, 1958-1990. Atlanta, GA: African Studies Association, 1991. 227 pp.
An index to articles in the *ASA Bulletin* (later ➔ **African Studies Review** *see* **603**) to 1990; also provides indexes to book reviews in the latter and the *ASA Review of Books*, and the names of reviewers in these two sources.

4
Major biographical resources
(print, microfiche, and online)

Print resources listed here include only *general* biographical resources, and do not include, for example, biographical reference works or who's who of African literary figures available in print formats. There are, however, listings of a small number of *online* biographical resources devoted to African writers.

For biographical information and profiles of African studies scholars worldwide *see* → **1 General online resources on Africa and African studies, and the best starting points on the Web: Directories of African studies scholars,** and → **2 The major general reference tools: Directories of research and teaching, and of Africanist scholars**

Print and microfiche

414 Adi, Hakim, and Marika Sherwood **Pan-African History. Political Figures from Africa and the Diaspora since 1787.** London: Routledge, 2003. 194 pp. £65.00/$114.95
A collection of short biographical accounts on some of the key Pan-Africanist thinkers and activists from the Anglophone and Francophone worlds of the past two-hundred years. It provides basic insights into the lives of forty political figures and other players, "women and men of African descent whose lives and work have been concerned, in some way, with the social and political emancipation of African peoples and those of the African diaspora." It includes well-known figures such as Malcolm X, W.E.B. Du Bois, Kwame Nkrumah, Frantz Fanon, George Padmore, Walter Rodney, or C.L.R. James, but also lesser-known figures such as Sierra Leone's Constance Cummings-John or South African anti-apartheid activist Alpheus Hunton. Each entry sets out the significance, activities, and the larger political context of each biographical subject, and is accompanied by a bibliography of further reading.
Choice review:
Choice December 2003 (reviewed by L. Lampert)
Online reviews:
African Studies Quarterly, vol. 2, no. 2, 2005 (reviewed by Mark Christian)
http://www.africa.ufl.edu/asq/v8/v8i2a10.htm
H-SAfrica, H-Net Reviews, April, 2005 (reviewed by Robert Trent Vinson)
http://www.h-net.msu.edu/reviews/showrev.cgi?path=7701119383442

415   African Biographical Archive/Archives Biographiques Africaines
Microfiche edition. Compiled by Victor Herrero Mediavilla. Munich: K.G. Saur
Verlag, 1994-1997. [In US Thomson/Gale] 457 fiches 3 index volumes €9,800.00
(diazo) €10,800.00 (silver)
Note: for → **African Biographical Index**, published separately in 3 volumes as a
print product, *see* entry **416** below
This very expensive reference source on microfiche contains 121,800 biographical
entries for 87,800 individuals from the age of the Pharaohs to the present day,
drawing on 314 sources published between 1807-1993, in several Western languages.
The sources used comprise a variety of biographical reference works and works of
collective biography. Unpublished and archival sources are not included. The
Archive covers eminent African personalities from all walks of life, including
political and religious leaders, scholars, artists and writers, as well as including non-
African persons such as explorers, immigrants, settlers, colonial rulers,
administrators, and missionaries, etc. For titles published before 1960 there is a heavy
emphasis on non-African peoples who travelled or lived in Africa, or colonized
Africa.

416   African Biographical Index/Index Biographique Africain. Compiled by
Victor Herrero Mediavilla. Munich: K.G. Saur Verlag, 1998. 3 vols. 1,134 pp. €678.00
(€620.00 for purchasers of African Biographical Archive)
http://www.saur.de/bioarch/africin.htm (title information)
Print format index to the → **African Biographical Archive (416)**, that can be
purchased separately. It provides access, and condensed information, to the 87,000
individuals and some 121,800 biographical articles that are listed in the Archive. Each
entry lists every individual's name, with short biographical and
historical/geographical data, together with references where the entries can be found
in the microfiche Archive, and the abbreviated titles of the biographical sources used.

417   African Biography. New York: UXL Publishing [now part of Gale Group],
1998. 3 vols. 602 pp. $165.00 set
Provides profiles of 75 current (as at 1997) and historical African leaders, as well as
major writers, artists, religious leaders, and others that have helped to shape Sub-
Saharan Africa. Includes portraits and maps. Primarily for middle and high-school
libraries and students.

→ **Historical Dictionaries of Africa** series *see* **247**

418   Africa Who's Who. Publisher and editor-in-chief: Raph Uwechue. Senior
Research Editor: Pramila Bennett. 3rd ed. London: Africa Books Ltd, 1996. 1,507 pp.
Biographical profiles of about 14,000 eminent Africans. Each entry includes full name
and address (and telephone/fax numbers for many), date and place of birth and
nationality, marital status, occupation, education, degrees awarded, education, career
details and appointments held, current position/affiliation, major publications, and
hobbies. The introduction does not provide details of the data gathering and
verification process (or whether all entrants in fact verified or updated their entries).
However, for the most part information seems to be current as at the end of 1995,
although some entries are dated. This impressive who's who includes not only
politicians, diplomats, and statesmen/women, but also broadcasters, writers,

journalists, artists, academics, librarians, civil servants, military personnel, trade unionists, lawyers and jurists, scientists, physicians, engineers, clergymen, sportsmen and women, as well as prominent figures from business and industry. Although no new editions have appeared to date, and now inevitably very dated, *Africa Who's Who* remains one of the best resources for biographical information on eminent Africans of the 20th century.

419   Brockman, Norbert C. **An African Biographical Dictionary.** Santa Barbara, CA & Oxford, England: ABC-Clio Ltd, 1994. 440 pp.
Contains 549 concise biographical sketches (some accompanied by photographs) of prominent Africans, as well as foreigners, who have affected the continent's history, with an emphasis on the 20th century. They cover political leaders, writers, artists, religious figures, scientists, as well as entertainers and sports personalities. Each entry gives date of birth, country, a chronological sketch, and biographical references. A number of appendices list individuals by country and by field of accomplishment, and there is also a listing of heads of state since independence, and a short bibliography.
ARD review:
African Research & Documentation, no. 75 (1997): 56-57 (reviewed by Terry Barringer)
Choice review:
Choice May 1995 (reviewed by Donald Altschiller)

420   **Dictionary of African Biography/Encyclopaedia Africana.**
Accra: Encyclopaedia Africana Project; Algonac, MI: Reference Publications Inc, 1977- 20 vols. [planned]
Volume 1: **Ethiopia-Ghana.** 1977. 370 pp. $84.00
Volume 2: **Sierra Leone-Zaire.** 1979. 374 pp. $84.00
Volume 3: **South Africa-Botswana-Lesotho-Swaziland.** 1995. 304 pp. $84.00
An ambitious project that had its roots in an idea for a comprehensive 'Encyclopaedia Africana' first proposed as far back as 1909 by W.E.B. du Bois, and revived by Kwame Nkrumah in the early 1960s. Unfortunately, the project has been plagued by numerous problems, political upheavals, and funding difficulties. To date only three volumes have appeared. Written by Africanist scholars, each volume contains a series of full biographies (preceded by an historical introduction). Volume 1 contains 152 biographies on Ethiopia and 138 on Ghana; volume 2, 137 biographies on Sierra Leone, and 103 on Zaire (now Congo Democratic Republic). And the latest volume on southern Africa published in 1995 contains 228 biographies, together with photographs, maps, a concise guide to names and terms, bibliographies, many cross-references, and an extensive subject index.
Note: According to the Web site of Encyclopaedia Africana Secretariat in Accra, Ghana (*see* http://www.endarkenment.com/eap/index.html) further volumes are planned: "Presently, articles covering biographies from Nigeria (EA Volume 18) and Egypt (EA Volume 15) are being compiled and organized in preparation for review and publication. In addition, articles from Libya (EA Volume 11), originally written in Arabic, are being organized for translation into English." However, no precise publication schedule is available at this time (September 2005).
Choice review:
Choice March 1996 (reviewed by Alfred Kagan)

421 Glickman, Harvey **Political Leaders of Contemporary Africa South of the Sahara: A Biographical Dictionary**. Westport, CT: Greenwood Press, 1992. 364 pp. $96.95/£55.00
Contains detailed and generally well-informed profiles (albeit it now somewhat dated) of 54 major, politically influential personalities in Sub-Saharan Africa since 1945. Entries – contributed by African studies scholars in the field of political science – provide basic information on each leader's life, their education, schooling, training, leadership skills, political goals (and the extent to which these goals were achieved), an assessment of each leader's impact on his country, within Africa and internationally, together with a short bibliography. An appendix provides a listing of leaders by country and a chronology from 1892 to 1991.
Choice review:
Choice February 1993 (reviewed by Nancy Schmidt)
CHOICE OUTSTANDING ACADEMIC BOOK 1993

422 Kirk-Greene, A.H.M. **A Biographical Dictionary of the British Colonial Service, 1939-1966**. London: Hans Zell Publishers, 1991. 420 pp.
A massive who's who of the British Colonial Service during the final quarter-century of Britain's imperial history. The dictionary consists of nearly 15,000 entries, listing every member of the British Colonial Service whose name appeared in the official Colonial Office Lists. It covers the professional as well as the administrative services, and includes teachers, judges, doctors, etc.. Although now long out-of-print, it will continue to be a valuable source for biographical data on all those who collectively made up the Colonial Service.
ARD review:
African Research & Documentation, no. 57 (1991): 31-33 (reviewed by Terry Barringer)
Choice review:
Choice December 1991 (reviewed by E. Patterson)

423 Lipschutz, Mark R., and R. Kent Rasmussen **Dictionary of African Historical Biography** 2nd ed., Berkeley: University of California Press, 1986. 328 pp.
Arranged in dictionary format and containing some 900 biographical sketches of African historical figures, living and dead, in Sub-Saharan Africa before 1960. The second edition has a supplement that also covers 57 post-1960 political leaders, and there is a detailed bibliography. Although published 20 years ago, this work remains a biographical reference resource of enduring value.

424 **Makers of Modern Africa. Profiles in History**. Publisher and editor-in-chief: Raph Uwechue. Senior Research Editor: Appiah Sackey. 3rd ed. London: Africa Books Ltd, 1996. 733 pp.
Illustrated throughout with halftones and drawings, this volume sets out the life histories of some 600 distinguished Africans, both past and present (and both those living and dead) who have played a significant part – in a social, political, economic, or cultural sense – in shaping the continent that is Africa today. Each entry provides a fairly full biographical sketch. For those still alive, information is up-to-date to the end of 1995. This is a companion volume to ➔ **Africa Who's Who (418)**, and ➔ **Africa Today (325)**.

425   **Profiles of African Scientists**. 3rd. ed Nairobi: African Academy of Sciences, 1996. Kshs.200.00/$25.00 284 pp.
Some 350 biographical profiles of African scientists and their work. Arranged by country, information for each entry includes biographical data and full contact address, professional/academic career, professional qualifications, achievements, major publications, and current research interests. With an index by name and scientific disciplines. Most entries include a small photograph. Unfortunately no new editions have appeared to date.

426   Rake, Alan **100 Great Africans.** Lanham, MD: Scarecrow Press, 1994. 441 pp.
Contains fairly extensive biographies of about 3-6 pages each, from ancient Egypt to the present time. A series of accompanying maps show how empires rose and fell, conquests, exploration of Africa, and the emergence of independent African nations. Primarily for the general reader.

427   Rake, Alan **African Leaders. Guiding the New Millenium.** Lanham, MD, and Oxford: Scarecrow Press, 2001. 261 pp. $51.95/£40.00/€68.62
This volume provides profiles of sixty leading African political leaders and military rulers currently (late 2000) in power, and their main political rivals "most likely to replace them" in 48 countries, although it is only for five countries for which there is more than one profile. Each profile, which is grouped alphabetically by country, assesses the character and career of the specific leader, followed by a fairly full chronological life history. The book does not attempt to be as comprehensive as the author's previous *Who's Who in Africa: Leaders for the 1990s (1992);* it concentrates on the top leaders only, but treats them in greater depth, assessing the parts they have played in the history of their nations. The author, who was formerly editor of ➔ **New African (770)** magazine in London states, disarmingly, that this is essentially a journalistic undertaking, "not based on profound academic research". While lacking depth, the profiles are very readable, generally informative and are interspersed with anecdotes and commentary on the leaders' personalities. However, some people might well have a gripe about the lack of any indication of sources, other than one or two journals, Patrick Smith's ➔ **Africa Confidential Who's Who in Southern Africa (430)**, and "frequent references" to Scarecrow's ➔ **Historical Dictionary of Africa** series **(247)**.
ARD review:
African Research & Documentation, no. 88 (2002): 90-91 (reviewed by Terry Barringer)

428   Reich, Bernard **Political Leaders of the Contemporary Middle East and North Africa: A Biographical Dictionary.** Westport, CT: Greenwood Press, 1990. 557 pp. $132.95/£76.00
Biographical profiles on 70 prominent Middle East and North African political leaders (of which 18 are from North Africa) who have had a significant impact on the political development of the Arabic-speaking countries of the Middle East and North Africa since World War II. It includes short bibliographies of works by and about the entrants, and there is also a detailed chronology of events from 1869 to 1989. This volume covers an area where there is still relatively scant biographical information available in English, and it is a valuable resource.
CHOICE OUSTSTANDING ACADEMIC TITLE 1990

429   Schwarz-Bart, Simone, with André Schwarz-Bart **In Praise of Black Women.**
(Translated. from the French by Rose-Myriam Réjouis, Stephanie K. Turner , and Val
Vinokurov) Madison, WI: University of Wisconsin Press, in association with Modus
Vivendi Publications, 2001-2004. 4 vols. (*see also*
http://www.inpraiseofblackwomen.com/)
Vol. 1: **Ancient African Queens.** 2001 456 pp. $60.00
Vol. 2: **Heroines of the Slavery Era.** 2002 250 pp. $49.95
Vol. 3: **Modern African Women.** 2003 250 pp. $49.95
Vol. 4: **Modern Women of the Diaspora**. forthcoming in 2006
Note: this series originally appeared in French as a six-volume work entitled
Hommage à la Femme Noire, published in 1988 by Editions Consulaires. Volume 1 in
English combines the French volumes 1 & 2. Volume 2 in English is a translation of
volume 3 in French. Volume 3 in English is a translation of volume 4 in French, but
also includes new material. The forthcoming volume 4 in English will combine the
French volumes 5 and 6, but will also include new material.
Published under the auspices of UNESCO, *In Praise of Black Women* is a visually
stunning, richly illustrated tribute to women in Africa and the African diaspora from
the ancient past to the present, with text written and selected by the Guadeloupean
novelist Simone Schwarz-Bart. The four-volume series pays homage to the
remarkable women who distinguished themselves in their time and shaped the
course of culture and history. The volumes include illustrations of many rare
photographs and archival documents. Volume 1, Ancient African Queens, portrays
women rulers, warriors, prophets, heroines and folk legends. Volume 2, Heroines of
the Slavery Era, narrates the life of women in the slavery area from the fifteenth to
the nineteenth century. The latest volume 3, Modern African Women, covers the
period from the nineteenth century to the present, and covers African queens, rulers,
and contemporary visionaries; women involved in the liberation struggle and civil
rights leaders, as well as women writers. It contains 14 biographical portraits and life
histories, which are interspersed with narrative text written in accessible style,
extracts from books and scholarly works on Africa, autobiographical accounts, prose
and poetry. Among those featured are Madam Yoko, national heroine of Sierra
Leone; Queen Nana Ya Asantewa the Great of the Gold Coast, now Ghana; Empress
Zauditu, the daughter of Menelik II, King of Ethiopia; through to more contemporary
figures such as Princess Kesso, a Fulani Muslim princess from Guinea (who became
one of the world's first black models); Ellen Kuzwayo, member of the African
National Congress who fought for civil and women's rights in South Africa; Miriam
Makeba, the celebrated South African singer; and three African women writers: the
late Mariama Bâ from Senegal, first winner of the ➔ **Noma Award for Publishing in
Africa (2833),** Buchi Emecheta who led an impoverished life in London with her five
children before she achieved international acclaim as the author of 15 books; and the
South African writer Bessie Head who died in 1986. Volumes are lavishly illustrated
with some fine colour photographs and a wide range of monochrome illustrations of
early photographs and archival material. At the modest price of only $49.95-$60.00
the large-size, splendidly produced volumes are an absolute bargain.

430 Sheldon, Kathleen, ed. **Historical Dictionary of Women in Sub-Saharan Africa.** Lanham, MD, and Oxford: Scarecrow Press 2005. 448 pp.
$80.00/£61.00/€104.64 (Historical Dictionaries of Women in the World, 1)
Published as the first title in a new Scarecrow series, "Historical Dictionaries of Women in the World", this valuable new resource guide includes almost 1,000 entries. Preceded by an informative introductory essay by the editor, it offers short biographical profiles on notable African women in the field of history, politics, religion, social movements, and the arts, including political leaders and activists, spiritual leaders, journalists, writers and poets, filmmakers, musicians, painters and sculptors, and more. These are interspersed with entries on women's organizations and entries on a range of topics important to women in general, as well as issues and events of significance to African women in particular, and which have helped to bring about dramatic and positive changes to the lives of many African women. Some of these events are charted in a chronology, from the earliest times through to 2004, culminating in Getrude Mongella's election as president of the parliament of the ➔ **African Union (2504)**, and Kenyan environmentalist Wangari Maathai being awarded the 2004 Nobel Peace Prize. Entries are extensively cross-referenced throughout. An appendix lists dictionary entries by country. This is followed by a very substantial and well-structured bibliography of over a hundred pages – including books, articles, and papers in edited collections – listing key general monographs and collections, sources that serve as guides to major historiographical and methodological issues, together with a section grouped by topics and important historical events. A list of bibliographies, periodicals, films, and Web sites complete the bibliography. No index.
Choice review:
Choice September 2005 (reviewed by N. Taylor)

431 Smith, Patrick **Africa Confidential Who's Who of Southern Africa**. Oxford and Malden, MA: Blackwell Publishers, 1998. 256 pp.
Based on ➔ **Africa Confidential's (736)** network of correspondents and contacts, this volume contains some 400 insightful biographies and political commentaries on the people who are shaping Southern Africa today (as at 1998). It includes politicians and statesmen and women, business people and entrepreneurs, the military, writers, and social and religious leaders. Each entry gives basic biographical and career information together with analysis, as well as providing a fairly detailed political context. The book is divided into five sections, covering Angola, Mozambique, South Africa, Zambia and Zimbabwe, and in addition to biographical entries each section is accompanied by political and economic analysis for every country, plus maps, economic data, and some other essential information.

432 **Who's Who of Southern Africa.** Johannesburg: Combined Publishers/Ken Donaldson, 1908 [published as *South African Who's Who* 1908-1958; expanded coverage 1959-]. Annual. Latest volume 2004, 97th ed. Johannesburg: Who's Who of Southern Africa [PO Box 411697, Craighall 2024, South Africa], 2005. R495
Fully searchable online edition, subscription/membership based, at
http://www.whoswhosa.info/SouthAfrica.asp
For price/membership terms apply to publisher at whoswho@media24.com

Biographies in this who's who are categorized according to sphere of influence in the following sections: Politics & Government; Business & Finance; Professionals & Academics; Personalities in Media, Arts and Entertainment; Sport; and Community. Each entry contains the full name and current position, followed by additional information such as date of birth, education, degrees, career history, major publications (where applicable), recreational activities, and contact details. According to the publisher, "each entry is compiled using details provided by the biographees and supplemented with additional research." Although a regional who's who, coverage is still strongest for South Africa, but there are also entries for Botswana, Lesotho, Mauritius, Namibia, and Swaziland. Includes cabinet members, members of the national assembly/members of parliament, government ministers and deputy ministers, leading politicians, the judiciary, diplomats, trade union leaders, business executives, as well as heads of religious, professional and scientific bodies, artists and musicians, and sportsmen and women.

Online

(i) **This symbol indicates "The editor's choice" of a particularly outstanding online information resource.**

---

433   African Biography on the Internet
http://www.columbia.edu/cu/lweb/indiv/africa/cuvl/afrbio.html
Part of the Columbia University Libraries → **African Studies Internet Resources (80)**, this is an annotated listing of a number more specialist online biographical resources, for example on individual African statesmen, prominent writers, and musicians. [14/07/05]

→ **Africancolours.com** [Database of African artists] *see* **1 General online resources on Africa and African studies, and the best starting points on the Web: General Web resources on Africa entry 15**

434   African Postcolonial Literature in English
http://www.scholars.nus.edu.sg/landow/post/misc/africov.html
The Postcolonial Web is a project funded by University Scholars Programme of National University of Singapore. The pages devoted to African writers provide a general introduction to the work of 34 African writers, including discussions (with links to articles) of genre, politics, literary themes and subjects, narrative structure, setting, etc. and most (but not all) include a biographical profile and/or a chronology, and a bibliography. Most of the material has been compiled by students under the direction of George P. Landow, at Brown University, Providence, Rhode Island. [14/07/05]

435   African Writers. Voices of Change/Francophone African Poets in English Translation

http://web.uflib.ufl.edu/cm/africana/writers.htm (Writers)

http://web.uflib.ufl.edu/cm/africana/poets.htm (Poets)

Compiled by Daniel A. Reboussin, African studies specialist at the ➔ University of Florida George A. Smathers Libraries (1337) these two online resources offer a range of concise but informative portraits of 17 major African writers and their work, together with biographical profiles of 11 poets from francophone Africa whose work has appeared in English translation, with examples/extracts of their poetry. [14/07/05]

436   Black People Directory

http://www.bpdir.net/

The first edition of this new bi-lingual who's who – a "biographical dictionary of personalities of African origin or inspiration in the world" – is promised for publication in December 2005. It will be offered (at a charge) as a Web-based online resource, on CD-ROM, or in print-on-demand format. However, at this time (August 2005) very limited details about content, complier credentials, and prices, etc. are available at the Web site. [03/08/05; not examined]

437   Contemporary African Database (i)

http://africadatabase.org/

Hosted by the ➔ Africa Centre (2551) in central London, this database is a continuously growing, participatory online project designed to provide easily accessible and current information concerning prominent Africans and African institutions and organizations. At this time (July 2005) you can browse or search for 11,231 people in the *CAD People/Les Personnes* database, a who's who of prominent Africans currently living or who have died since 1950, covering all disciplines and all fields of endeavour. You can also browse the database by almost 40 categories, or by countries. *CAD Institutions* (2,325 entries as at July 2005), a directory of African institutions, including governments, pan-African bodies, educational institutions, NGOs, and significant businesses, has recently been added as a further database; and *CAD Chronology Africa*, a chronology of important events and dates in the contemporary African calendar, is promised for sometime in 2006. A final objective is for *CAD People Africa* to eventually become a skills database of Africans inside and outside the continent. Biographical, bibliographical, and other information on some entrants is still rather patchy at this time, and a substantial number of records do not offer a great deal more than name, date of birth, sex, and nationality. However, a good number also include details of current or past institutional position or affiliation, selected publications, some links to online newspaper articles, online interviews, or links to entries in the ➔ Wikipedia (59); while "Internet Resources" leads to searches for individuals in Google Web Search or in Google News (*see also* ➔ **25 Using Google for African studies research: a guide to effective Web searching**). For writers there are links to informative and very full profiles appearing in an online version of *The Companion to African Literature* by Douglas Killam and Ruth Rowe (James Currey Publishers, 2000). Some browsing by institution categories can bring up disappointing results: for example "Publishing companies by countries" displays just 17 entries, "Literature organisations by country" 15 results, "Media companies" less than ten, while "Museums and libraries by country" is a mixture of small museums and a few national libraries, but contains virtually no listings of academic libraries. Much better is "Universities and Colleges by country", which offers fairly comprehensive listings, for example 22 higher education institutions for Nigeria, most leading to full address details and names of current Vice-Chancellors and leading members of faculty (if they are included in the *People* database). It should be noted that in the *People* database – and probably for good reasons – none of the entries indicate personal or institutional contact details, although there are links to a number of personal Web pages. However, address details, telephone/fax numbers, and Web sites for some, are given in results displayed in the *Institution* database. An interesting feature is a listing of "most visited" people, based on visitor counts of the preceding day or the preceding month(s), and the complete archive, going back to March 2002, is at http://people.africadatabase.org/en/n/top/toppeople.html. Additionally, you can also search by past winners of major book or cultural prizes, for example the Booker, the Caine Prize, Commonwealth Writers Prize, FESPACO, Nobel, etc. While some aspects of this massive database are still a little bit flawed, this is an outstanding, freely accessible information resource. [15/07/05]

438   Dictionary of African Christian Biography

http://www.gospelcom.net/dacb/index.html

Developed by the Overseas Ministries Study Center in New Haven, Connecticut, under the directorship of Jonathan J. Bonk, this impressive project aims to produce an electronic database containing the essential biographical facts of African Christian leaders, evangelists, and lay workers chiefly responsible for laying the foundations and advancing the growth of Christian communities in Africa. An international team of scholars and church leaders – primarily of African citizenship – is facilitating the project. Contributors are drawn from academic, church, and mission communities in Africa and elsewhere. Work began in 1997 and is expected to continue through 2010. The dictionary covers the whole field of African Christianity from earliest times to the present and over the entire continent. Broadly inter-confessional, historically descriptive, and exploiting the full range of oral and written records, the dictionary is being produced electronically, initially in English and ultimately in French, Portuguese, and Kiswahili. Search by subject or by country. Biographical profiles provided are very full for the most part, and most entries include a bibliography. [15/07/05]

5
Guides and resources for African languages
(print and online)

Print (or print/online, and microfilm)

➔ **Agence de la francophonie et la Communauté française de Belgique.** Cahiers du Rifal, **no. 23, November 2003. Special issue on** "Le traitement informatique des langues africaines" *see* **23 Information and communication development in Africa: a guide to Web sites and resources: Some recent studies, reports and articles** entry **2888**

439   African Language and Literature Collection, Indiana University Libraries, Bloomington. Bloomington, IN: African Studies Program [221 Woodburn Hall, Indiana University, Bloomington, IN 47405], 1994. 515 pp.
Indiana University has one of the largest collections of materials on African linguistics and texts in African languages in the USA. It includes published materials housed in the Main Library in both catalogued and uncatalogued collections, and field recordings housed in the Archives of Traditional Music. It covers material received through early 1993, providing details of over 8,000 works in over 700 languages from 36 countries. It is arranged by language and indexed by author.
See also ➔ **African Language Collection. Indiana University Libraries, Bloomington** entry **450**

440   Bade, David W. Books in African Languages in the Melville J. Herskovits Library of African Studies, Northwestern University. A Catalog. Evanston, IL: Program of African Studies, Northwestern University [620 Library Place, Evanston IL 60208-4110] (PAS Working paper, 8, vols. 1 & 2), 2000. 1,045 pp. $65.00 set 2 vols. online http://www.northwestern.edu/african-studies/working%20papers/wp8bade.pdf [17/06/05]
Vol. 3 published (as a supplement, and with an addenda to the above) as **Books in African Languages: Recent Acquisitions 1999-2000.** Evanston, IL: Program of African Studies, Northwestern University (PAS Working paper, 8, vol. 3), 2004. $15.00 (print only)
A massive inventory of the rich collections at ➔ **Northwestern University Library (1322)**, which lists 10,600 publications in over 300 languages (Afrikaans and Arabic are excluded), and includes short title, name, language, and country indexes. Material is listed in order of language, and thereafter by title. It includes information on the variant names used by the library catalogues of the ➔ **Library of Congress 1316)**, the ➔ **School of Oriental and African Studies (1289)** and those in the Mann and Dalby ➔ **Thesaurus of African Languages (445)**. A vital source for African language material, this amazing labour of love can also be accessed online as a large pdf file, at the URL indicated above.

ARD review:
African Research & Documentation, no. 88 (2002): 93 (reviewed by Terry Barringer)
JOINT WINNER CONOVER-PORTER AWARD 2002

441   Gordon, Raymond G., Jr (ed.) **Ethnologue. Languages of the World.** 15th edition. Print version. Dallas, TX: SIL International [7500 West Camp Wisdom Road Dallas, TX 75236-5699, USA, Email: academic_books@sil.org], 2005. 1,272 pp $80.00

Web version (free access) ⓘ
http://www.ethnologue.com/web.asp (Main page)
http://www.ethnologue.com/country_index.asp?place=Africa (Africa, country index)

This latest edition of *Ethnologue* includes more than 50,000 updates of the 14th edition published in 2000, and contains 6,912 language descriptions organized by continent and country, 39,491 primary names, alternate names and dialect names, 208 colour maps showing location and distribution of languages, together with statistical summaries with numerical tabulations of living languages and number of speakers by continent, by language size, by language. African languages are very strongly represented with 2,092 entries (representing 30.3% of the total number of languages). The electronic version of *Ethnologue* presents the data used to prepare the printed volumes, along with links to the SIL Bibliography and the International Academic Bookstore. To get started, using the *Ethnologue* Web version, it is advisable to first read the Introduction, Thereafter browse the page which displays the primary table of contents for *Ethnologue*, organized by geographical areas and countries, or use the search function. A country page contains descriptions of all the languages spoken in that country, each entry with a short description of the language, language code, the areas where it is primarily spoken, an estimate of the approximate number of speakers, alternate names, language classification, as well as a link leading to more or related information, including a number of online articles drawn from the SIL bibliography. A quite superb reference resource. [15/07/05]

442   Hendrix, Melvin K. **An International Bibliography of African Lexicons.**
Metuchen, NJ: Scarecrow Press, 1982. 370 pp $48.00/£37.00/€63.47
Published more than twenty years ago, but still useful and still in print. Spanning over 400 years of African lexicographical writing and research, the book includes some 2,700 entries, representing almost 700 African languages and over 200 dialects, accompanied by very brief annotations. Arranged by language, together with additional sections on polyglot, special and classified, conversation and phrase books, and serial publications. Includes a language and dialect index, and an author and name index. A useful update to this work was recently published by David Westley, *see* entry ➔ **448.**

443   Kagan, Alfred **"Sources for African Language Materials from the Countries of Anglophone Africa."** *IFLA Journal* 22, no. 1 (1996): 42-45.
online at http://www.ifla.org/IV/ifla61/61-kaga.htm [15/07/05]
[Also published in *Collection Building* 15, no. 2 (1996): 17-21]
This article, now somewhat dated, provides guidance on how to acquire materials in African languages outside their countries of origin, and sets out the mechanisms in collecting this material. Notes the standard current reference sources, blanket and

approval plan dealers, bookshops and publishers, printed and online catalogues, and two microform collections.

444 Mann, Michael, and Valerie Sanders. **A Bibliography of African Language Texts in the Collection of the School of Oriental and African Studies, University of London, to 1963**. London: Hans Zell Publishers, 1994. 448 pp. (Documentary Research in African Literatures, 3)
A massive inventory of over 7,000 African language titles in over 300 different languages. It covers the combined collections and archival holdings of African language texts at the ➜ **School of Oriental and African Studies (765)**, the International Institute of African Languages and Culture (later International African Institute), and the Christian Literature Bureau for Africa (later International Committee on Christian Literature for Africa).
ARD review:
African Research & Documentation, no. 65 (1994): 39-40 (reviewed by John McIlwaine)
Choice review:
Choice July 1994 (reviewed by David Westley)

445 Mann, Michael, and David Dalby **A Thesaurus of African Languages: A Classified and Annotated Inventory of the Spoken Languages of Africa. With an Appendix on their Written Representation**. London: Hans Zell Publishers, 1987. 325 pp.
Published for the ➜ **International African Institute (1622)** this is probably the most complete inventory of African languages yet compiled. It includes a methodological introduction, an annotated inventory of 2,550 African languages classified into 315 sets and sub-sets, a country-by-country survey of languages, an extensive bibliography, together with a language index of some 12,000 entries.

446 Moseley, Christopher, and R. E Asher **Atlas of the World's Languages**. London and New York: Routledge, 1993 £600/$1,050 384 pp.
This impressive global atlas aims to provide a definitive analysis of the known languages of the world, including those on the point of extinction, and accurately map the location of every living language. It contains 130 full-colour maps, detailed bibliographies, and there is a comprehensive index. The atlas is divided into eight sections, each of which has been edited by a leading authority in their field. There are two sections for Africa: Middle East and North Africa (5 maps) by A. Irvine (SOAS, University of London); Sub-Saharan Africa (35 maps), by Benji Wald, a US African language policy consultant. Each has an introduction, a list of major languages, language charts, and explanatory text for the maps, thus providing a good synopsis of African languages.

➜ **National African Language Resource Center** *see* **458**

447 **Swahili Manuscripts from the School of Oriental and African Studies**
Part 1: ca. 21 reels of 35mm silver-halide positive microfilm £1,900/$3,200 2004
Part 2: ca. 24 reels of 35mm silver-halide positive microfilm £2,200/$3,600 2005
Marlborough, Wiltshire, UK: Adam Matthew Publications Ltd.

Coninciding with the launch of the ➔Swahili Manuscripts Database (460), Adam Matthew Publications are offering this microfilm copy of nearly a hundred of the manuscripts. [Not examined]

448   Westley, David **"WorldCat and African Lexiography Since 1980."** In *Africanist Librarianship in an Era of Change*, edited by Victoria K. Evalds and David Henige. Lanham, MD: Scarecrow Press, 2005, 167-197. (*see* ➔ entry **1904**)
A useful update to Melvin Hendrix's ➔ **An International Bibliography of African Lexicons (442)**, covering works of African lexicography published since 1980 with more than 150 pages in length, and for languages with over one million speakers. At the same time the author demonstrates that OCLC's WorldCat can be a good tool in identifying North American library holdings of dictionaries on African languages. Lists a substantial number of dictionaries grouped into monolingual, bilingual, trilingual, non-African-to-African, African-to-non-African, as well as online dictionaries.

Online

ⓘ **This symbol indicates "The editor's choice" of a particularly outstanding online information resource.**

---

449   AfLangDirectory
http://www.humnet.ucla.edu/humnet/aflang/
The University of California system has a number of African languages specialists on its faculty and several campuses offer African language instruction in scheduled classes or as directed studies tutorials. This is a directory of resources on these languages. At this time there are pages for information on the Chadic language family and sources relating to the Yobe Languages Research Project for the five languages spoken in Yobe State, Northeastern Nigeria: Bade, Bole, Karekare, Ngamo, and Ngizim. Additionally there are resources on Chichewa, Ewe, Hausa (including information about a Hausar Baka video course), Kiswahili, Wolof, and Zulu, each contributed by a language specialist. Resources include bibliographies and reference works, courses, exercises, lessons, and various background information. [25/10/05]

450   African Language Collection. Indiana University Libraries, Bloomington
http://www.indiana.edu/~librcsd/afrlg/ [site down 25/10/05]
This catalogue – arranged by language, using primarily the Library of Congress classification schedule – has been compiled to draw attention to Indiana University Libraries' rich collection of materials in African languages. Among the largest in the US, the entire collection is accessible to the public. The focus of this catalogue is material in African languages and literatures materials in the Library of Congress 'P' classification, although some materials in other LC classifications are also included, Search or browse the catalogue by a vast number of African languages. To provide more information about the languages represented in the catalogue, the language

names have been linked to the 13th edition of ➜ **Ethnologue. Languages of the World (441)**. There is also a listing of serials on African languages and linguistics, and a listing of films in African languages in the Media Center, Undergraduate library. *See also* entry ➜ **439**. [site down 25/10/05]

451   African Language Expert Directory
http://www.lib.msu.edu/lauer/alc-catcom/ALEdirectory.htm
Compiled by Gretchen Walsh at Boston University, this directory is primarily intended for librarians cataloguing materials in African languages. It provides details of some 30 experts in Africa and the US who have volunteered to provide language expertise for library cataloguers. Each entry gives full contact information, and details of the particular language expertise. There have been no updates since 2000 and therefore some information may not be current any longer. [15/07/05]

452   African Language Materials Archive (ALMA)
http://www.aiys.org/aodl/public/access/alma_ebooks/index.php
This is s a project of the ➜ **West African Research Center (1849)** and the American Overseas Digital Library (AODL) – a joint venture of fifteen American Overseas Research Center libraries - supported in part by UNESCO and Columbia University. It offers, as a publicly accessible online catalogue and database, a number of e-books in several West African languages, at this time 14 in Wolof, 10 in Mandinka, and 10 Pulaar language books. From an index to catalogue records you can either click on to a full record about each title or read the book, which are in pdf format. File sizes are indicated on the index pages. A "MyList" function allows you to save a list of items you can e-mail. [15/07/05]

453   African Language Resources on the Internet
http://www.columbia.edu/cu/lweb/indiv/africa/cuvl/langs.html#NALRC
Part of ➜ **Columbia's African Studies Internet Resources (80),** these pages provide links to various African language resources accessible online, including resources and dictionaries, etc. devoted to individual African languages, at this time including resources for Bemba, Hausa, Kiswahili, Luganda, Maasai, Mandinka/Wolof, Pular, Sesotho, Shona, Soomaali, and Yoruba. [15/07/05]

454   African Languages – Göteborg University, Department of Oriental and African Languages
http://www.african.gu.se/index-eng.html (Main department page
http://goto.glocalnet.net/maho/webresources/index.html (Web resources for African languages)
Provides access to a number of resources on African languages, and offers a mailing list and discussion forum for African languages. The site also has a useful *The Languages of Tanzania: A Weblinks collection*, a constantly updated Web appendix to *The Languages of Tanzania: a bibliography*, compiled and edited by Jouni F. Maho and Bonny Sands (*Orientalia et Africana gothoburgensia*, v. 17, 2003), and which can be found at http://www.african.gu.se/tanzania/weblinks.html. [15/07/05]

➜ **ASC Thesaurus of African Studies: Thesaurus of African Languages** *see* **15 Africanist documentation and African studies bibliography** entry **1894**

455   Bisharat! ⓘ

http://www.bisharat.net

Bisharat (Arabic for "good news") is a language, technology, and development initiative designed to promote the use of African languages in sustainable development, combining this with research, advocacy, and networking relating to the use of African languages in software and Web content. The site provides over 200 annotated links to other sites on African languages and language resources, research projects, initiatives on languages and ICT, online dictionaries for African languages, as well as software and fonts for African languages, including automatic translation software. There are also two special sections: (1) an A12N Gateway on African language encoding (Unicode Afrique), including discussion forums, reference and demo pages, and resources on characters and encoding; (2) Machine translation (MT) for Africa-Computer translators and African languages. The site is in English and French throughout and, frequently updated, this is an excellent resource. [16/07/05]

456   Comparative Bantu Online Dictionary Project

http://www.cbold.ddl.ish-lyon.cnrs.fr/

Started in 1994 under the direction Larry Hyman and John Lowe at the University of California at Berkeley – working with linguists in the United States, France, Belgium, the Netherlands, Cameroon, Tanzania and other countries – this project aims to develop a collaborative and freely-accessible lexicographic database to support and enhance the theoretical, descriptive, and historical linguistic study of the languages in the important Bantu family. The database includes a substantial list of reconstructed Proto-Bantu roots, several thousand additional reconstructed regional roots, and reflexes of these roots for a substantial subset of the 500+ daughter languages. Published and unpublished dictionaries of selected Bantu languages have been scanned, converted to text, and entered into the database. In addition to searchable dictionaries and bibliographic resources, the site also offers Bantu maps, computational tools, and links to other African language resources. [16/07/05]

457   Helsinki Corpus of Swahili (HCS) ⓘ

http://www.csc.fi/kielipankki/aineistot/hcs/index.phtml.en

http://www.aakkl.helsinki.fi/cameel/corpus/intro.htm (for instructions about access and retrieval tools)

This is a massive annotated corpus of standard Swahili text. It contains news excerpts from several current Swahili newspapers, as well as from the news site of Deutsche Welle. Additionally, it offers extracts from a number of books, containing prose text, including fiction, educational material, and material relating to the sciences. The total size of the corpus is 12.5 million words. The Helsinki Corpus of Swahili is hosted by the Helsinki University Language Corpus Server. Access to the server is granted to university researchers on application and is subject to a signed agreement. (These precautions have been taken because the corpus contains material that is subject to copyright restrictions.) The Helsinki Corpus of Swahili now also offers now a possibility to use the SALAMA (Swahili Language Manager) in corpus work, a multi-purpose language management environment, developed at the University of Helsinki by Arvi Hurskainen, Professor of African languages. SALAMA makes use of language analysis and thus offers more accurate and wider ranging possibilities for work with corpus texts than traditional string searches. This facility is currently (November 2005) in a test phase. [22/11/05]

➔ **H-Hausa** *see* **21 Online forums and mailing lists,** entry **2817**

➔ **H-Swahili – Network on Swahili Language and Culture** *see* **21 Online forums and mailing lists,** entry **2820**

➔ **Multilingual Books** [supplier of courses, tapes, videos on African languages] *see* **17 Dealers and distributors of African studies materials,** entry **2363**

458   National African Language Resource Center
http://african.lss.wisc.edu/nalrc/home.html
The National African Language Resource Center at the University of Wisconsin-Madison is non-profit national foreign language centre dedicated to the advancement of African language teaching and learning in the United States. The Center's mission is to serve the entire community of African language educators and learners in the United States by sponsoring a wide range of educational and professional activities designed to improve the accessibility and quality of African language instruction in the US. It also offers a range of (print) publications on African languages, including dictionaries, grammars, language primers, and an "African Language Vocabulary Flash Cards Series". [16/07/05]

459   The Rosetta Project ⓘ
http://www.rosettaproject.org/live
The Rosetta Project at ➔ **Stanford University Libraries (1327)** is a global collaboration of language specialists and native speakers working to build a publicly accessible online archive of all documented human languages. Its goal is to create the broadest and most complete reference work on the languages of the world to date. As at October 2005 there is a documents database containing details of almost 2,400 languages, and over 78,000 individual text pages. Additionally, Rosetta has started a new initiative to curate word lists for all the languages documented thus far, a total of 1,384 to date, with over 400,000 distinct words. You can select from the currently available languages to create a custom word list chart. Browse or search by name of language, country, language family, or countries where spoken. Search the archive by the same criteria and which also includes a search facility by ➔ **Ethnologue (441)** code. For example, browse by country for Ghana generates search results for 58 languages spoken in Ghana (and some neighbouring territories), for which the Rosetta database currently contains information. Eventually the Rosetta archive will be publicly available in three different media: a free and continually growing online archive, a single volume monumental reference book, and as an extreme longevity micro-etched disk, a new high density analogue storage device. The 1.0 version of the Rosetta disk is now available (the disk requires a microscope, either optical or electron). Rosetta plans to globally distribute significant numbers of these disks with protective containers to thousands of interested individuals, organizations and native communities. Disks will available through purchase or donation. [25/10/05]

→ Kagan, Alfred **"Sources for African Language Materials from the Countries of Anglophone Africa"** *see* entry **443**

460   Swahili Manuscripts Database
http://www.swahilimanuscripts.soas.ac.uk
The library of the School of Oriental and African Studies holds the largest public collection of Swahili manuscripts in Britain. It includes more than 250 manuscripts dating from the 1790s to the 1970s, contained in the papers of William Taylor, Alice Werner, William Hichens, Wilfred Whiteley, Jan Knappert and Yahya Ali Omar. The library also holds microfilms of the manuscripts that were deposited by J.W.T Allen at the University of Dar es Salaam. The manuscripts are a rich resource for the study of cultural and literary history, and for research on East Africa. Many were scribed in Arabic script, and many contain poetry composed in northern Swahili dialects. Letters, stories, notes, essays on history and culture, and drafts of published and unpublished books, number among the collection's rich offerings. The Swahili Manuscripts Project aims to create a comprehensive catalogue of the SOAS manuscripts, thus enabling researchers and more general readers to make focused and, it is hoped, greater use of an illuminating collection. A search facility assists finding files, or to conduct searches for particular items by keywords. [23/08/05]

→ **Unicode-Afrique** *see* **21 Online forums and mailing lists**, entry **2823**

461   The Webbook of African Language Resources ⓘ
http://www.isp.msu.edu/AfrLang/hiermenu.html
Hosted by the → **African Studies Center, Michigan State University (1710)** and the → **African Languages Teachers Association (2752)** – and compiled in collaboration with numerous individuals around the world who have contributed to various aspects of the project – this very impressive site provides extensive information about the human, institutional and material resources that are currently available for the teaching and study of African languages. The Webbook and directory is intended to serve as a guide to the 82 "high priority" African languages for the purpose of teaching and learning priorities (in the US), and as determined by 32 African language specialists that met at a conference at Michigan State University in March 1979. Each language is profiled according to language classification and (where spoken) number of speakers, usage, dialect survey, orthography status, sets of learning materials required (textbooks, dictionaries, readers, etc.), resources (both human and institutional), and materials bibliography. The organization and structure of the directory is very clearly set out, together with explanatory notes, and resources for individual languages can be accessed through an A-Z menu. A search facility allows searching by languages/people, by institutions, or by language materials. An outstanding resource. [16/07/05]

462   Yale Guide to Resources in African Languages and Literature
http://www.yale.edu/ycias/african/ygrall/index.htm
Conceived by Sandra Sanneh, Director, Program in African Languages at Yale University, this site offers a wide variety of resources on (at this time) three African languages: IsiZulu, Kiswahili, and Yoruba. Categories in a sidebar for each language let you access university programmes, study abroad opportunities, instructor online

resources, newspapers, Web sites devoted African languages projects, documents, and more. A useful resource, although there were rather a lot of dead links when last visited. [28/07/05]

463   yourDictionary.com – Language Dictionaries
http://www.yourdictionary.com/languages.html (Dictionaries)
http://www.yourdictionary.com/grammars.html (Grammars and language courses)
One of the most comprehensive directories to over 300 online dictionaries, word lists, grammars, glossaries, and other data on languages, together with links to profiles about the languages and language families, and to others sources. The site includes a substantial number of links to African language dictionaries and wordlists available online, grouped by their principal African language groups and their branches, for example Amharic, Basa, Bemba, Bukusu, Fang, Hausa, Ibgo, Kiswahili, Koromfé, Lingala, Lozi, Mandika, Ndebele, Shona, Wolof, Venda, Zulu, and more. A separate section is devoted to grammars and language courses. [16/07/05]

6

Guides to statistical sources, economic, financial, and population data (print, microfiche and online)

For general sources, guides, and directories containing substantial African statistical data, including social indicators and demographic data, see also chapter 6 in Alfred Kagan's ➔ **Reference Guide to Africa: A Bibliography of Sources**, 2nd ed. **(225)**. There is also extensive coverage in John McIlwaine's ➔ **Africa: A Guide to Reference Material (227)**, a new second edition of which is forthcoming in late 2006.

Print

➔ **Africa South of the Sahara 2002** *see* entry **211**

464   African Development Bank. **African Development Report 2005.**
Oxford and New York: Oxford University Press, 2005. 360 pp. £16.99/$29.95 [earlier annual volumes also still available]
The African Development Report is a comprehensive yet concise annual survey of economic and social progress in Africa, presenting analysis and statistical data on the state of the African economy, and examining development policy issues that affect the economic prospects of the continent. Each report has a special theme, e.g. in 2005 it was "Public Sector Management in Africa", and in the previous year it was "Africa in the World Economy. Africa in the Global Trading System: Economic and Social Statistics on Africa". Contents is grouped under three parts, the first covers Africa in the world economy (including regional economic profiles), the second has contributions on the annual theme, and the third part presents economic and social statistics on Africa.

465   Batiste, Angel D. **"African Business and Economic Resource Index: Selected Internet Resources"** In *Research, Reference Service, and Resources for the Study of Africa*, edited by Deborah M. La Fond and Gretchen Walsh. Special issue of *The Reference Librarian*, edited by Bill Katz, volume 42, issue 87/88, pp. 109 – 149. Binghamton, NY: The Haworth Press, 2004. (*see* entry ➔ **1905**)
online at http://www.haworthpress.com/store/ArticleAbstract.asp?ID=39247
Note: online access requires purchase of the article, or subscription/purchase of this issue of *Reference Librarian*.
While principally devoted to African business, commerce, investment, and trade, this useful survey of resources also provides access to more general economic information available via the Internet and, additionally, includes an appended

selection of information sources available in print format. The compilation draws on a multiplicity of Internet-based sources, including African commercial and government agencies, US commercial and government agencies, and international organizations engaging in economic, business, and trade issues in sub-Saharan African countries. Coverage includes general business directories; financial, legal, and marketing information; industry analysis; basic country economic and statistical data; business and industry news; stock and currency exchanges; and electronic journals. [25/08/05]

466   Blake, David **"From Paper to PDF? The Publications of Africa-Related International Organisations, Past, Present and Future."** *African Research & Documentation,* 89 (2002): 57-67.
An insightful article that examines the publishing activities of a number of major African organizations – the **→ United Nations Economic Commission for Africa (2523)**, the former Organization of African Unity and now the **→ African Union (2504)**, the **→ African Development Bank (2501)**, and two regional organizations, the **→ Economic Community of West African States (2511)** and the **→ Southern African Development Community (2518)** – and the extent of library holdings of publications from these bodies by libraries in the UK and by the **→ Library of Congress (1316)** in the USA. The paper also evaluates the organizations' Web sites, their currency, ease of navigation, the online availability of major documents, reports, and statistical data, and the archiving of these digital documents. The author poses some questions about the value of these Web sites both for users in Africa and elsewhere, and discusses some of the problems that they raise for librarians.

→ The Middle East and North Africa 2002 *see* entry **214**

467   The World Bank **African Development Indicators 2005: Drawn from the World Bank Africa Database.** Washington, DC: The World Bank, 2005. 436 pp. $ 50.00/£31.50 (distributed in the UK and Europe by Eurospan). [earlier volumes also still available]
Online: Overview booklet, including the introduction, table of contents in English and French, and Chapter One: Basic indicators and Technical notes, freely accessible at http://www4.worldbank.org/afr/stats/adi2005/adi05_booklet_rev_061505.pdf
Still available online: Selected Chapters from the Africa Development Indicators 2004 http://www4.worldbank.org/afr/stats/adi2004/default.cfm
This World Bank source, derived from the (CD-ROM) **→ World Bank Africa Database 2005 (490)**, offers a very detailed collection of development data and statistics on Africa in a compact single volume, presenting data from 53 African countries, and arranged in separate tables or matrices for more than 500 indicators of development. For most indicators the volume provides data from 1980-2003 with indicators grouped into 15 chapters: background data, national accounts, prices and exchange rates, money and banking, external sector, balance of payments, external debt and related flows, government finance, agriculture, power, communications, and transportation; public enterprises, labour force and employment, aid flows, social indicators, environmental indicators; and HIPC debt initiative. Each chapter begins with a brief introduction describing the nature of the data and their

limitations, followed by a set of statistical tables, charts, and technical notes that define the indicators and identify their specific source.
Choice review: (of earlier edition)
Choice December 2002 (reviewed by Gretchen Walsh)

Microfiche

468   **African Official Statistical Serials, 1867-1982.** Cambridge: Chadwyck-Healey (Alexandria, VA: Chadwyck-Healey), 1985 [?]. [now distributed by ProQuest]
For more details, and number of fiche for each country, see product Web site below.
http://www.umi.com/research/pd-product-African-Official-Statistical-Serials-170.shtml
This microfiche collection consists of general statistical compendia – economic, financial, social and demographic statistics – issued by National Statistical offices and bureaux, Censuses and Statistical Departments, or Ministries of Economic Planning, etc. of nearly every African country. [Not examined]

Online (or print/online)

ⓘ **This symbol indicates "The editor's choice" of a particularly outstanding online information resource.**

---

469   **Administrative Divisions of Countries ("Statoids")** ⓘ
http://www.statoids.com/statoids.html
This remarkable resource, compiled by Gwillim Law, presents an immensely detailed guide to the "statoids" – the primary administrative divisions (states, provinces, regions, and other units – of each country in the world. While the Web resource can be used independently, it is principally designed to be an extension and a constantly updated supplement to the author's *Administrative Subdivisions of Countries* (Jefferson, NC: McFarland & Company, 1999). The international standard ISO 3166 is the source for the list of countries, a total of 240, including all countries of Africa. The book, and the supplementary Web site, attempts to satisfy two types of enquirer: "those who simply want a quick answer to a specific question about present-day subdivisions, and those who want to solve a problem involving conflicting data from different sources." The Web site is also designed to provide corrections and updates to the original print resource, and the author frequently draws attention to discrepancies of information provided in various sources and, sometimes, their unreliability. The list of country codes shows selected standard codes for each of them, and the alphabetical links by country presents links to (mostly) online primary and secondary resources (regional, state, county, district, departmental, provincial, municipal, local authority, etc.), as well as providing links to a variety of available statistical resources, links to online maps, and, usefully, sources for country post codes (albeit with quite a few dead links). For each country

it also indicates international telephone dialling codes and time zone data. For several African countries, for example for Botswana and Namibia, there are updates to take into account new administrative divisions, recent census reports, new population figures etc., and for many there are also interesting discussions about the matter of conflicting sources, and their reliability, or unreliability rather, cited in the original print edition. While the Web site is freely accessible Statoids data of 4,0000 primary administrative sub-divisions of countries can also be purchased as spreadsheets at $160, which can be delivered by email or CD-ROM (format can be flat file, Excel or others on request). This is an extraordinary resource and is highly recommended. [25/08/05]

470   African Development Bank **African Development Report 2004. A summary**
http://www.afdb.org/pls/portal/docs/PAGE/ADB_ADMIN_PG/DOCUMENTS/
ECONOMICSANDRESEARCH/ADR%20SUMMARY-2004.PDF
This freely accessible 33-page pdf document summarizes the annual **African Development Report** (*see* **464** above, summary is for 2004 report). [16/07/05]

471   African Development Bank **ADB Statistics Pocket Book/Livre de poche des Statistiques de la BAD, 2005.**
Abidjan: African Development Bank, 2005. 164 pp.
Note: current ordering address for print version: Statistics Division, Development Research Department, African Development Bank, Temporary Relocation Agency (TRA), BP 323, 1002 Tunis Belvédère, Tunis, Tunisia, Email: statistics@afdb.org.
Online:
http://www.afdb.org/pls/portal/docs/PAGE/ADB_ADMIN_PG/DOCUMENTS/
STATISTICS/POCKETBOOK%202005_WEB.PDF
The *ADB Statistics Pocketbook* (in English and French) presents summary economic and social data on regional member countries and on the operational activities of the
➔ **African Development Bank Group (2501)**. Most of the indicators shown are selected from the other Bank publications: *Compendium of Statistics on Bank Group Operations, Gender, Poverty and Environmental Indicators on African Countries*, and *Selected Statistics on African Countries*. [16/07/05]

472   African Development Bank **Selected Statistics on African Countries/ Statistiques choisies sur les pays africains, vol. 24, 2005.** Abidjan: African Development Bank, 2005. 300 pp. (ISSN 1561-2805)
Note: current ordering address for print version: Statistics Division, Development Research Department, African Development Bank, Temporary Relocation Agency (TRA), BP 323, 1002 Tunis Belvédère, Tunis, Tunisia, Email: statistics@afdb.org.
Online:
http://www.afdb.org/pls/portal/docs/PAGE/ADB_ADMIN_PG/DOCUMENTS/
STATISTICS/SELECTED%202005_WEB.PDF
Prepared by the African Development Bank (ADB) this is an annual publication (in English and French) presenting data on major development indicators of African economies. Part one gives cross-country statistics on selected indicators (human development, macroeconomic, and external sector economic indicators), while part two provides country-specific time series. [16/07/05]
Note: other ADB publications include the annual ➔ **African Development Report (464)**, and the three-times yearly ➔ **African Development Review (743)**.

473   African Population Database Documentation
http://grid2.cr.usgs.gov/globalpop/africa/
Compiled by Andy Nelson at the University of Leeds, UK (based on previous documentation and methods by Uwe Deichmann at the National Center for Geographic Information and Analysis/NCGIA at the University of California, Santa Barbara) and supported by the → **United Nations Environment Programme (2534)**/Global Resource Information Database (UNEP/GRID), this the fourth version of a very substantial database of administrative units, or boundaries, with associated population figures for Africa. It provides details of more than 109,000 administrative units, 83,000 of which are in South Africa. In addition, for each of these units a population estimate was compiled for 1960, 70, 80, 90 and 2000, thus providing an indication of past population dynamics in Africa. Part 1 consists of boundary and population data, while part 2 is the Raster data. [25/08/05]

474   AFRISTAT
http://www.afristat.org (Main home page)
http://www.afristat.org/Afristat/Presentation/accueil_presentation-english.htm (Summary in English of activities)
AFRISTAT (L'Observatoire Economique et Statistique d'Afrique Subsaharienne) is an international organization created by a treaty and signed in September 1993; its headquarters are in Bamako, Mali, and it currently comprises 18 members states of francophone Africa. AFRISTAT's objective is to strengthen the development of economic, social and environmental statistics in member states and to improve their expertise in these areas. The site offers access to (1) a directory of national institutes of statistics in Africa, with full address information including email address, structure, hours, personnel contact information (Director or heads of divisions), as well as some other information, with most details provided current as at 1998 or 1999. (2) A database of a wide variety of statistical information selectable by country. For each country there is a menu covering general data, and data for climatology, demography, education/health education, the economy, foreign trade, consumer price index, national accounts, currency and finance, transport and telecommunications, and tourism and the environment. Within each group there are further sub-divisions. Most statistics cover the period from around 1990 to 1999, but for some countries there is more recent (2000-2002) data. All data can be freely downloaded as Excel files. (3) Supplementing the statistical data by country, a separate section, updated weekly, offers more recent statistical data covering principal indicators, and which can also be downloaded. [25/08/05]

475   Afrobarometer ⓘ
http://www.afrobarometer.org
Afrobarometer seeks to build a body of scientifically reliable data on comparative public opinion on democracy, economic conditions and economic reform, socio-cultural values and civil society in African countries, thus measuring the social, political and economic atmosphere, and public attitudes, on the continent. A collaborative project between Michigan State University, the Institute of Democracy in South Africa, and the Centre for Democratic Development in Ghana, and working with national partners in participating countries, Afrobarometer surveys are currently (August 2005) conducted in 15 African nations. Round 1 surveys were

conducted from July 1999 through June 2001 in 12 countries. Round 2 surveys were conducted from May 2002 through October 2003, in 15 countries. Round 3 surveys in at least 18 countries are planned for 2005-6. Each survey data contains questionnaire responses from between 1,000 to 3,000 people, depending on the sample size. In addition to Afrobarometer data sets accessible through the Web site, information also appears in two finding series, Afrobarometer Briefing Papers and Afrobarometer Working Papers. This is a very impressive resource for statistical data and analysis. [25/08/05]

476   Bayerische Landesbank – Country Analyses [Africa]
http://www.bayernlb.de/p/_en/idx/maerkte/laender/laender.jsp
This substantial database from the Bayerische Landesbank in Germany, provides quick factual data about the economic outlook of most countries of the world, including those in Africa. A few are available in German only, but most are in English and are all freely accessible. Select from an A-Z menu to choose a country, for each of which it then offers two pdf files, a three page country report on economic outlook, and a single page of facts and figures and economic indicators. The country reports provide basic structural data and short overviews of foreign policy, macroeconomic development, foreign trade, the budget situation, financial status and an assessment of the economic outlook, while the facts and figures page show economic indicators over the past four years, including domestic, external economic, and financial indicators. Reports are prepared by individual experts, and each report indicates the sources used and shows the date when completed. [28/08/05]

→ **Development Gateway (World Bank)** *see* **1 General online resources on Africa and African studies, and the best starting points on the Web** entry 81

477   Economist Intelligence Unit – Africa titles, country forecasts, profiles, etc.
(subscription based)
http://www.store.eiu.com/index.asp?layout=region_home_page&eiu_region_id=12 10000321
These pages provide details of a suite of business and economic intelligence sources on Africa from the Economist Intelligence Unit, including Country Commerce, Country Finance, Country Forecast, Country Profile, Country Risk Service, Country Data, etc. and the journal *Business Africa*. Services are offered on a fairly high priced subscription basis; or purchase the most recent issue via Web delivery or in print format, and you can also purchase archival issues or specific articles. [28/08/05]

478   Index of Economic Freedom [Africa]
http://www.heritage.org/research/features/index/countries.cfm?sortby=country
(Country menu, alphabetical)
http://www.heritage.org/research/features/index/countries.cfm (by score)
Co-hosted by the Heritage Foundation and the *Wall Street Journal*, this is a practical annual reference guide to the world's economies, including all those in Africa. It measures economic freedom in each country on the basis of a set of economic criteria to present a theoretical analysis of the factors that most influence the institutional setting of economic growth. The latest volume of the index measures 161 countries against a list of 50 independent variables divided into 10 broad factors of economic

freedom, which include trade policy, fiscal burden of government, government intervention in the economy, monetary policy, capital flows and foreign investment, banking and finance, wages and prices, property rights, and more. For each country there is a summary report, including a chart showing past and present scores. You can also download individual chapters, charts, maps, or the entire book in English or Spanish. In the 2005 Index the two African countries with the best scores were Botswana and Madagascar, the two worst Zimbabwe and Libya. [15/06/05]

479   Organization of Economic Cooperation and Development, OECD Development Centre, and African Development Bank. **African Economic Outlook 2004/2005.** Paris: OECD Development Centre, 2005. Print/Paperback ed. [OECD Code 412005011P1] 540 pp. €76.00/$99.00/£51.00; e-book (pdf format) [OECD Code 412005011E1] 1,088 pp. €53.00/$69.00/£35.00 [also available in French]
More details about e-book version at
http://www.oecdbookshop.org/oecd/display.asp?TAG=X77YK8XX59889X763TL1
QX&CID=&LANG=EN&SF1=DI&ST1=5LGXS13NFJF1#OtherLanguages
Based on data for the 22 most significant African economies, this is the third edition of an annual assessment of economic and social development in African states prepared by the OECD Development Centre and the ➜ **African Development Bank (2501)**, with contributions by leading African economists. Like its predecessors, it aims "to provide a tool for understanding current economic and social conditions, and for highlighting the development prospects for the African continent." Part One offers an overview of the international economic environment, current (2003/2004) macroeconomic performance and economic growth in Africa, a progress report on millennium development goals, together with sections on current governance and political issues, energy supply and poverty, and electricity sector reforms. Part Two consists of 22 country reviews with in-depth analysis of key macroeconomic and structural variables and short-term projections, employing a single, unique model. A substantial Statistical Annex completes the volume. The Web online version offers freely accessible extracts from the book, including an overview "Growth Trends and Outlook for Africa", access (in pdf formats) to the 22 country surveys, as well as selected sample statistics from the Statistical Annex: Average Growth Performance by Region; Income Poverty Target in sub-Saharan Africa (in % of population), and Energy Consumption in Africa and the world. [17/07/05]

480   **Population Index on the Web** [Africa] ⓘ
http://popindex.princeton.edu/
Hosted by the Office of Population Research at Princeton University, *Population Index* is the primary reference tool to the world's population literature, and this Web site provides a good starting point for searches of recent population studies and statistics on Africa. The print version of *Population Index* (subscription-based) is a quarterly annotated bibliography covering books and other monographs, serial publications, journal articles, working papers, doctoral dissertations, and machine-readable data files. The Web site offers a freely accessible, searchable, and browsable database containing 46,035 citations and abstracts of demographic literature published in *Population Index* in the period 1986-2000. You can browse all issues published between the Spring of 1986 (Volume 52, Number 1) and (at this time, August 2005) the Spring of 2000 (Volume 66, Number 1), including the table of contents for each

number and the very useful cumulative geographical indexes, which can be browsed by regions or by individual African countries. There is an excellent search interface to the entire database, which can be searched by author, subject, region or free-text appearing anywhere in a citation. An outstanding resource. [25/08/05]

481   Regional and National Population Information – Africa
http://www.un.org/popin/regional/africa/
Part of the United Nations Population Information Network, which provides guides to population information on UN system web sites, this site offers access to a range of demographic and other databases for regional or national population information for the countries of Africa. There are also links to the Population Information Network for Africa (POPIN-Africa) and to a number of POPIN-Africa Web sites. [25/08/05]

482   Statistical Resources on the Web [Africa]
http://www.lib.umich.edu/govdocs/statsnew.html
This collection of resources from the University of Michigan Documents Center contains quite a substantial number on Africa and African countries. The pages are clustered by broad subject areas, such as Agriculture, Business and Industry, Consumers, Demographics, Foreign Governments, Foreign Trade, Government Finances, Health, Housing, Labour, etc. Alternatively, browse the Web site directory for more specific topics, and/or for African regions or countries leading to, for example, census data, development indicators, Web sites of African governments and African embassies in the US; or resources providing background information, news reports, conference documents, protocols, policy papers, press releases, human rights documents, documents on US foreign policy, and more. A useful feature is a "What's new" section, offering monthly updates of new resources. [25/08/05]

483   Status of Women in Africa
http://www.uneca.org/eca_resources/cdroms/status_of_african_women/default0.htm
A Web site hosted by the UN's ➔ **Economic Commission for Africa's (2523)** African Centre for Women that offers data in some of the key areas of the UNECA 'Platform for Action', and which best illustrate the status of women in Africa, namely: Economic Activity of Women, Education, Gender Gaps and Disparities, Health, The Human Rights of Women and the Girl-Child, and Women in Power and Decision Making. "These areas were chosen because it was felt that they best illustrate what the governments and women themselves have achieved, or otherwise, in the last twenty years or so. Secondly, these indicators deal with the issues of access to the very basic resources without which human life loses its dignity." This is a useful resource, but the site is not very well sign-posted, and to access the actual data you will need to scroll to the foot of the home page and then select either general data or country data. (The link to "Data" in the left-hand panel on top of the page was not html active when accessed on a number of occasions). For each country you can then access information based on the above key indicators identified, and there are also graphs relating to national literacy rates, school enrolment rates, mortality and infant mortality rates. [25/08/05]

484   United Nations. Conference on Trade and Development (UNCTAD). Least Developed Countries Report [print and online]
http://www.unctad.org/Templates/Page.asp?intItemID=3073&lang=1 (access to all 1995-2004 reports)
485   The Least Developed Countries Report, 2004. Linking International Trade with Poverty Reduction Geneva: UNCTAD, (UNCTAD/LDC/2004) 2004 389 pp.
Sales no. E.04.II.D.27 $40.00 (developed countries) $18.00 (developing countries)
online http://www.unctad.org/Templates/WebFlyer.asp?intItemID=3074&lang=1
(2004 report)
The UNCTAD Least Developed Countries Reports provide a comprehensive and authoritative source of socio-economic analysis and data on the world's most impoverished countries. The Reports are intended for a broad readership of governments, policy makers, researchers and all those involved with least developed countries in particular and development policy in general. Each Report contains a statistical annex, which provides basic data on the LDCs. The *2004 Least Developed Countries Report Report*, assesses the relationship between international trade and poverty within the LDCs, and identifies national and international policies that can make trade a more effective mechanism for poverty reduction in these countries. You can download the full report (also available in French and Spanish versions) as one file (5,010kb), download pdf files of individual chapters, or download just the Statistical Annex: Basic Data on the Least Developed Countries (49 pp. 392kb) at http://www.unctad.org/en/docs/ldc2004annex_en.pdf. [11/07/05]

→ **United Nations Cyber School Bus – InfoNation** *see* **1 General online resources on Africa and African studies, and the best starting points on the Web: Databases, indexes, and thesauri** entry 120

486   United Nations Economic Commission for Africa. African Statistical Yearbook. Addis Ababa: United Nations Economic Commission for Africa, 1970- [latest available volumes, published in 2004, is the *African Statistical Yearbook* 2002]. 2 vols. Vol. 1: Part 1-North Africa, Part 2-West Africa; vol. 2: Parts 3-Central Africa, Part 4-East Africa, Part 5-Southern Africa. var. pp/$40-$40 per part [orders from the US to United Nations Publications, 2 United Nations Plaza, Room DC2-853, New York, NY 10017, Email: publications@un.org; those from Europe and elsewhere order from the United Nations Publications, Sales and Marketing Section Bureau E-4, CH-1211 Geneva 10, Switzerland, Email: unpubli@unog.ch]
Full list of available titles https://unp.un.org/catalogue.aspx
http://www.un.org/Depts/eca/stats/intro.htm (online version; 16/07/05; however although it states "Please click on the hot link on tables to go the country tables", the tables are not in fact accessible online)
Presents summary tables in Section A, covering population, national accounts, agriculture, forestry, and fishing, industry, transport and communications, foreign trade, prices, finance, and social statistics, and Country Tables in Section B. Usually covers the last 8-10 years for which data are available.

487   United Nations Economic Commission for Africa. Economic Report on Africa. Addis Ababa: United Nations Economic Commission for Africa, 1997 [?]- 96 pp. $32.00

A series of annual reports, supported by a large number of country tables, that review the performance of Africa's economy during the preceding year and considers the prospects for the short and medium term. Each report focuses on a special theme, and/or a range of individual African countries.

Online reports: (freely accessible)

Economic Report on Africa 2004 - Unlocking Africa's Trade Potential
http://www.uneca.org/era2004/ [16/07/05]

Economic Report on Africa 2003 - Accelerating the Pace of Development
http://www.uneca.org/era2003/ [16/07/05]

Economic Report on Africa 2002 – Tracking Performance and Progress
http://www.uneca.org/era2002/ [16/07/05]

Economic Report on Africa 2001 [not published? not available online]

Economic Report on Africa 2000 – Transforming Africa's Economies
http://www.uneca.org/eca_resources/Publications/books/ERA2000/ERA2000.htm [16/07/05]

Economic Report on Africa 1999 – The Challenges of Poverty Reduction and Sustainability
http://www.uneca.org/eca_resources/Publications/ESPD/economic_report_1999.htm [16/07/05]

32 pages of appendices and country tables are available as a pdf document at http://www.uneca.org/eca_resources/Publications/ESPD/annex.pdf (or available as a Word document). [16/07/05]

also available:

African Women's Report 1998
http://www.uneca.org/eca_resources/Publications/ACW/fulltext/report_98/report98.pdf [16/07/05]

488   United Nations Educational, Scientific, and Cultural Organization. UNESCO Education Statistics

http://www.uis.unesco.org/ev.php?URL_ID=5187&URL_DO=DO_TOPIC&URL_SECTION=201   (Education statistics)

http://www.uis.unesco.org/countryprofiles/html/selectCountryProfile_en.aspx (Country profiles)

Provides a set of statistical tables of core education indicators which are divided into five categories: AP - Access and Participation (participation rates, intake rates); EF – Efficiency (repetition and survival rates); RE - Resources (teaching force, financial information); LA - Literacy and Attainment (literacy rates, educational attainment); MD - Meta-data (characteristics of the education system). Click on to interactive tables and then select Africa as a continent or individual African countries. Or select Country profiles from the menu panel to view key statistics and indicators – albeit some of it not very up-to-date – on education, science and technology, and culture and communication on a country-by-country basis. [16/07/05]

489   **United Nations Educational, Scientific, and Cultural Organization.**
UNESCO Statistical Yearbook. (Annual, to 1999)
Print: Paris: UNESCO, 1963-1999. 1999 ed. 840 pp. €73.22 (distr. in the US by Bernan
Press, 4611-F Assembly Drive, Lanham MD 20706-4391)
http://www.uis.unesco.org/en/stats/statistics/yearbook/YBIndexNew.htm
The latest volume of UNESCO's flagship publication is that for 1999, but →
UNESCO (2533) announced sometime ago that there will be no further volumes after
the 1999 volume. The Yearbooks, revised annually, have provided key statistical
information on education, science, technology and communication in more than 200
countries. They are arranged under three major sections: Education (illiteracy,
enrolment, graduates, teaching staff, expenditures); Science and Technology
(manpower and expenditure in R & D), and Culture and Communication (libraries,
books/publishing, films and cinemas, newspapers and broadcasting).
1999 volume online: (no further volumes published in print format or online)
Education and Literacy
http://www.uis.unesco.org/en/stats/statistics/yearbook/tables/ed.htm
[16/07/05]
Science and Technology
http://www.uis.unesco.org/en/stats/statistics/yearbook/tables/ed.htm
Culture and Communication [16/07/05]
http://www.uis.unesco.org/en/stats/statistics/yearbook/cult.htm [16/07/05]

490   **The World Bank Africa Database 2005.** Washington, DC: The World Bank,
2005. CD-ROM, 1 disk Single-User CD-ROM $100.00/£61.50 Multiple-User CD-
ROM $200.00/£125.00 (distr. in the UK and Europe by Eurospan).
This CD-ROM contains over 1,200 indicators of macro-economic, sectoral, and social
data for 53 African countries and 20 regional country groups. The CD-ROM is the
electronic version of the World Bank's →**African Development Indicators 2005** (*see*
entry **467** above) and contains Country at-a-Glance tables for all African countries,
Excel-based Executive Summary Briefings, and an electronic copy of the publication
tables. It also offers a year-by-year time series of most indicators going back to 1970,
and thus assists in the tracking down of data and analysis to help place the most
recent years in a historical context. Data is pre-formatted with instructions on how to
transfer them to other programs for further manipulation, such as mapping, charting,
or benchmarking.

7

Cartographic and geographic information sources/ Map sales and vendors
(print and online)

Print

491   Africa on File. Compiled by Mapping Specialists Ltd. 2 vols. Volume 1: **East, Southern, and North Africa**; Volume 2: **West and Central Africa**: Regional issues. New York: Facts on File, 1995. 384 pp. [loose-leaf] $185.00/£140.00
A visual survey and inter-disciplinary portrait of the physical and human geography of 52 sub-Saharan African countries. Includes over 300 maps, charts, fact-sheets and timelines. The Contemporary Regional Issues section illustrates 20 topics, including ethnic groups, internal migration, language groups, population distribution, economic growth, migration, famine, civil wars, deforestation, daily calorie intake, interstate conflicts, religions, urbanization, and other topics. With a geographical and subject index.
Choice review:
Choice May 1996 (reviewed by K.Y. Stabler)

492   Bassett, Thomas J., and Yvette Scheven Maps of Africa to 1900. A Checklist of Maps in Atlases and Geographical Journals in the Collections of the University of Illinois, Urbana-Champaign. Urbana-Champaign: University of Illinois Library, Graduate School of Library and Information Science, 2000. 317 pp. $35.00
A checklist, arranged geographically by region, of 2,416 maps, compiled from atlases and geographical journals held in the collections of the ➔ **University of Illinois at Urbana-Champaign (1338)**. The maps listed date from the early sixteenth century to the end of the nineteenth century. Each entry is annotated (showing the UIUC library location code) and indexes of map authorities, titles, and inset maps facilitate map identification. An extensive introductory essay on the historical significance of maps of Africa prior to the 20th century provides summary information on the total number of maps by date, region, and country of origin, showing the relationship between the regional focus of journal maps and the colonial interests of the country in which the maps were published. Also includes a bibliography of atlases and journals referred to in the entries. The Joint Winner for 2002 of the Conover-Porter Award, this checklist was cited to be a "groundbreaking" work by the Award's jury.
Choice review:
Choice September 2001 (reviewed by S. Jent)
JOINT WINNER CONOVER-PORTER AWARD 2002

493   Jacobson, William R. **The Rediscovery of Africa 1400-1900: Antique Maps & Rare Images.** Stanford, CA: Stanford University Libraries, Department of Special Collections, 2004. 96 pp. $25.00

The collections of antique African maps at → **Stanford University Libraries (1327)** are one of the largest in the world, with almost 600 maps from the 15th to the 19th century, as well as some from the early 20th century. The entire Stanford African map collection has recently been digitally photographed and the digital images are now freely available for viewing on the Web. It includes the Oscar I. Norwich (1910–1994) collection of Maps of Africa and Its Islands, 1486–ca.1900, acquired by Stanford in 2001 (*see also* → **Norwich's Maps of Africa: An Illustrated and Annotated Carto-Bibliography** entry **495**). As part of the Stanford Department of Special Collections exhibits program, an exhibition, "The Rediscovery of Africa 1400-1900: Antique Maps & Rare Images", was on view at Stanford's Peterson Gallery from April to June 2004, and this volume presents a permanent record and catalogue of the exhibit as well as providing a narrative history. The narrative part includes sections on the origins of cartography, and the views of Africa by the Greek and Roman worlds, while other sections examine Chinese, Muslim, and Byzantine influences from the 5th to the 15th centuries cartographers and their craft, European visions of Africa from 1300 to 1900, the "discovery" of West African kingdoms by European explorers, and the scramble for Africa, 1800–1914. The maps reveal the sometime extraordinary European perceptions of Africa – and European ignorance about Africa – over five centuries, as well as the myths and legends that fuelled the quest to circumnavigate and explore the continent. The volume, attractively produced and copiously illustrated with colour plates, photographs, and other illustrative material, also includes a bibliography and an index.

494   McIlwaine, John **Maps and Mapping of Africa. A Resource Guide.** London: Hans Zell Publishers, 1997. 419 pp. £60.00/$100.00 [now stocked/distributed by James Currey Publishers, Oxford]

A comprehensive guide to maps and map making across the whole of the African continents and its Atlantic and Indian Ocean island groups. It covers cartographic activity in Africa from the earliest times to the present. Arranged in three parts – Africa in General, Africa Mapped by Colonial and Overseas Agencies, and Africa by Region and Country – it provides (1) a guide to bibliographies and catalogues of maps of all periods and types, (2) a list of significant works of cartographic references such as atlases and gazetteers, and related topographical reference works, and (3) a bibliography of writings on maps and survey material, place names, map collections and other cartographical subjects and reference sources. Contains a total of 3,231 entries, together with a name index and subject index. An outstanding reference tool.

ARD review:

African Research & Documentation, no. 81 (1999): 82-83 (reviewed by Ann Taylor)

Choice review:

Choice April 1998 (reviewed by Donald Altschiller)

495   Norwich, I. **Norwich's Maps of Africa: An Illustrated and Annotated Carto-Bibliography.** 2nd ed., revised and edited by Jeffrey C. Stone. Norwich, VT: Terra Nova Press, 1997. 443 pp. $145.00 (distributed by University Press of New England) Based on "what is probably the finest private collection of early maps on Africa...[which] elevates the record of a private collection into a work of reference." This valuable inventory is a revision of Norwich's classic *Maps of Africa* published in 1983, and includes reproductions of maps from Norwich's collection, plus additional maps selected by editor from his own collection. It covers maps of Africa from the 15th to the 20th century. Each map is accompanied by its bibliographic description, scale, title, as well as historical context. It includes over 350 black and white and colour illustrations. Also contains a bibliography and an introductory essay, "Maps of Africa: A Summary History."

CD-ROM

496   **AFIM Africa Interactive Maps.** Version 1.0 Designed and produced by W. Bediako Lamouse-Smith and Joseph School. 1 CD-ROM Windows 3.1, 95, 98, and NT. $30.00 single user $200.00 institutional users Odenton, MD: AFIM [PO Box 188, Odenton MD 21113], Email: africamaps@mindspring.com
More information on publisher's Web site http://www.africamaps.com/index.html Designed at the Department of Africana Studies, and Department of Geography and Environmental Systems, University of Maryland, Baltimore, this is a learning and teaching tool that aims to communicate basic geographic information about Africa. It combines a large number of colour maps with graphics, statistical tables, photographs and short texts. The program is designed to be used as a self-paced study aid or in conjunction with textbooks and lectures on Africa. 700 maps provide visual and textual facts on many topics, including physical geography, political boundaries, population, climate, vegetation, cash crops, minerals and natural resources, ethnic groups, languages, religions, etc. [Not examined]

497   **Africa Data Sampler: A Geo-Referenced Database for All African Countries.** Washington, DC: World Resources Institute [10 G Street NE, Suite 800, Washington DC 20002], 1995. 1 CD-ROM, plus 148 pp. User's Guide $179.00 (list price) $100.00 sale price
Contains a set of internationally comparable digital maps at a scale of 1:1 million for every country in Africa, in PC ARC/INFO format in Robinson Projection. Based on the *Digital Chart of the World*, the Africa Data Sampler includes data on protected areas, forests, mangroves, and wetlands, as well as drainage, topography, infrastructure, and sub-national administrative boundaries with corresponding population estimates for the entire continent. The digital format allows users with the appropriate software (ArcView 1 for Windows) to view, query, print, and distribute maps. [Not examined]

Online

498   Africa Data Dissemination Service (ADDS)
http://igskmncnwb015.cr.usgs.gov/adds/
The US Agency for International Development Famine Early Warning System Network (FEWS NET) is an information system designed to identify problems in the food supply system that potentially lead to famine, flood, or other food-insecure conditions, in sub-Saharan Africa. Maintained by the US Geological Survey, the ADDS data holdings provide access to a variety of data on Africa, which can be accessed by geographic area, region/country, and/or data theme. This includes satellite/image data, tabular data (e.g. for agricultural statistics), digital map data covering administrative boundaries, agro-climatic zones, cropland use intensity, elevation hydrology, railroads, train stations, roads, and vegetation. Although data is still fairly uneven for some countries, this is an excellent resource. [18/07/05]

499   Africa South of the Sahara. Topics: Maps
http://www-sul.stanford.edu./depts/ssrg/africa/map.html
Part of the excellent Stanford ➔ Africa South of the Sahara (69) site, this is a 12-page descriptive listing of online resources for African maps and atlases and other cartographic materials, including some more specialist resources on individual African countries. [17/07/05]

500   AfriTerra
http://www.afriterra.org/
The AfriTerra Foundation and Free Library in Boston is a not-for-profit archive of mostly antique maps and books that aims to provide an educational resource for students, academics, and the general public to study and preserve original rare maps of Africa, and to serve as a medium linking art and science and history. The AfriTerra Library is the most complete collection in North America for original rare maps focused on early Africa. It includes 5,000 original rare maps, engravings, archive papers and rare book text and references, covering seven languages (English, Latin, Dutch, French, German, Portuguese, and Italian), and dating from 1480 to 1900. Work has now started to digitize the collection to create a new online searchable database of the maps in the AfriTerra collection for browsing or searching. Along with raw data about the maps, a new set of high-resolution scans will begin. AfriTerra's goal is to have several hundred new images catalogued and available at this Web site by the beginning of 2006. At this time (July 2005) about 30 maps can be accessed, with zoomable images that enables you to examine minute details of the maps. [18/07/05]

501   Boston University Library. African Map Collection
http://www.bu.edu/library/asl/maps/index.html
The ➔ Boston University African Studies Library (1300) has an extensive collection of over 1,500 maps on Africa and its countries. They range from those published in the seventeenth century to recent years and focus on entire countries, subsections of Africa, as well as small towns and city environs. The collection includes maps that cover a wide variety of subjects from topography and geology to cattle distribution

and rainfall. Browse the collection by date of publication, by country, or by title. [17/07/05]

502   Creating Africa: A Brief Tour of European Cartography of Africa
http://worldhistoryconnected.press.uiuc.edu/2.1/resources.html
This is one of the resources listed in a special issue on teaching African history online published in *World History Connected* (*see* entry ➔ **185**). Compiled by Jonathan T. Reynolds it is a useful annotated listing – in chronological sequence, covering the period from the 15th through the 20th centuries – of online historical maps. They are "presented with the goal of getting students to investigate and critically access the cartographic 'creation' of the continent of Africa as we have come to understand it. " The maps can either be presented by an instructor as a "guided tour," or, if time and computer resources allow, the students can be allowed to examine them on their own. Many offer "zoom" functions that allow them to be examined in remarkable detail. [26/08/05]

503   Earth Sciences and Map Library. University of California, Berkeley
http://www.lib.berkeley.edu/EART/MapCollections.html
The Earth Sciences and Map Library at the University of California-Berkeley has the largest collection of maps in northern California and is one of the largest university map collections in the United States. There are over 450,000 maps and aerial photographs in its collection, issued by local, federal, commercial agencies, foreign governments, and international organizations. Original maps for the 20th century and later, and facsimile maps for pre-1900 maps, cover all countries of the world at various scales. The collection contains general maps as well as thematic maps showing a wide variety of cultural, economic, and physical subjects. It is also useful for tracking down maps of African cities. To search/retrieve maps or atlases there are links to Pathfinder (the University of California-Berkeley Web catalogue) or MELVYL (the catalogue of the University of California Libraries), where you can search by subject or title keyword, and limit the search by publication format to "Maps." Each search result provides details/locations and author, title, publisher, year of publication, series, and format. The site also includes links to Internet resources in cartography. This is an excellent source for African maps. [25/06/05]

504   Geo e-Links Africa
http://67.95.153.93/DevecolAfrica/GeoElinks/Intro_GeoElinks/Africa_intro.htm
A rich online information resource for sustainable rural development in Africa, which employs maps to display locations where experiences or research about sustainable development have been documented. From the map the user can link to the documents in the Alexandria, VA-based Development Ecology Information Service (DEVECOL) digital library. The resources comprise base maps, thematic maps, and a growing, geo-referenced database of case studies that can be accessed from the site's digital library or via hyperlinks from other Web sites, for example those from the ➔ **Food and Agriculture Organization of the United Nations (2526).** To find and access documents, click Map search, which leads to an index and base map displaying areas that can be viewed in greater detail, and the locations of sites for which documentation exists about development or research experiences in agriculture, natural resources management, and drought mitigation or prevention. [18/07/05]

505   GEONet Names Server [for African countries]
http://earth-info.nga.mil/gns/html/cntry_files.html
This huge online searchable database consists of nearly 4 million world place names
and foreign geographic features with over 5 million feature names. It is developed
and maintained by the National Geospatial-Intelligence Agency (NGA) and the US
Board on Geographic Names (BGN) and is updated biweekly. The digit-description
of names files for countries and territories formats are set out on the site. Country
files, including all those for Africa, are accessed and downloaded by clicking on to an
A-Z index, which also indicates the country code, the date generated, most recent
modification date, most recent source date, and number of records. Data is in tab-
delimited text, UTF-8 ISO/IEC 10646 (UNICODE) compliant format. Files are in
compressed zip format, and downloading can take a little while depending on the
number of records for each country. The country files are also available on the FTP
site, ftp://ftp.nga.mil/pub/gns_data/. [26/08/05]

→ Getty Thesaurus of Geographic Names *see* 1 General online resources on Africa
and African studies, and the best starting points on the Web: Databases, indexes
and thesauri entry 114

→ Google Earth *see* Using Google for African studies research: a guide to effective
Web searching. Some other Google offerings: Google Earth

506   Maps of Africa: A Guide to Uncataloged African Maps in the Geography-
       Map Library at Indiana University, Bloomington
http://www.indiana.edu/~librcsd/mapafr/ (site down 15/11/05, moving to new
server)
Compiled by Naomi Fisher, this site provides access to a collection of uncatalogued
African maps available in Indiana University's Geography Map Library. It consists of
a text-only index of over 1,300 maps and map series produced by governments and
agencies of Europe, Africa and North America, searchable by country, region and
keyword. The database provides access to records through a search menu (by region
or individual countries) providing basic publishing information – map title,
producer, edition, publisher, series, and scale – and call numbers for locating the
maps. While map images *cannot* be viewed at this site, they are available for use in
the Geography Map Library, Student Building 015, on the Bloomington campus of
Indiana University. [Site down 15/11/05 and earlier, information not verified]

507   Map Libraries and Map Archives/Kartensammlungen und Kartenarchive
http://www.maps.ethz.ch/maplibraries.html
While not Africa-specific, this is a very comprehensive collection of links to map
libraries in all parts of the world, including a large number in Canada and the USA,
the UK, France, Germany, Italy, the Netherlands, Portugal, and those in other parts
of Europe. Compiled by staff at the Map Library at the ETH-Bibliothek in Zurich.
[26/08/05]

508   Mapping Asia in UK Libraries [for North African map collections]
http://www.asiamap.ac.uk/index.php
The title of this excellent Web resource could be a bit misleading as, in addition to
collection descriptions in all subject areas of the humanities and the social sciences

relating to Asia and the Middle East (and supported by a searchable database), it also covers North and northeastern Africa: Algeria, Djibouti, Egypt, Eritrea, Ethiopia, Libya, Morocco, Somalia, Sudan, and Tunisia. The collection descriptions give details of resources housed in university, public or specialized libraries in the United Kingdom, including information on the content of collections, history and development, strengths, subjects, languages and countries covered, collection material and size, catalogue and collection management information. Additionally the site provides access to holdings information about newspapers published in the regions and held in UK libraries. The database offers bibliographic records of newspaper titles and holdings information and is searchable by title, city, country, and language. [22/06/05]

509   National Geographic Map Machine [Africa]
http://www.nationalgeographic.com/maps/
The Africa pages of this attractive site offer some general, physical, and regional maps, as well as satellite maps and aerial imagery. Browse by region (Africa, Continent), or search by country or region. Alternatively, click on to Country profiles and then select specific African countries and view a dynamic map with zooming/enlargement features, or print an outline map. Also provides some basic factual information about each country. [19/07/05]

510   Perry-Castañeda Library Map Collection. African maps
http://www.lib.utexas.edu/maps/africa.html
One of the most comprehensive collections of African maps, hosted by the Perry-Castañeda Library at the ➜ **University of Texas at Austin (1343)**. It provides links to a very large number of maps, (general, country, city maps, etc.), most produced by the US Central Intelligence Agency. Each link indicates file size of map, and format. For each country there are also links to maps and map collections on other Web sites. [18/07/05]

Places Online [Africa] *see* **1 General online resources on Africa and African studies, and the best starting points on the Web: General Web resources on Africa,** entry 51

➜ Room, Adrian **African Placenames: Origins and Meanings of the Names for over 2000 Natural Features, Towns, Cities, Provinces, and Countries** *see*
2 The major general reference tools: General interest reference resources entry 281

511   United Nations. Cartographic Section. Maps and Geographic Information Resources
http://www.un.org/Depts/Cartographic/english/index.htm
This UN resource (also accessible in a French version) includes country profile maps and general maps on Africa, as well as very up-to-date maps of UN peacekeeping operations, e.g. UNAMSIL in Sierra Leone, MINURSO in the Western Sahara, UNMIL in Liberia, or ONUB in Burundi, etc. Select maps from a country pull-down menu. The maps are of a high quality, and most are very current. There is a link to the map collection ➜ **UN Dag Hammarskjöld Library (1330)**, which houses over 80,000 maps, some 3,000 atlases, gazetteers, travel guides, reference works and digital products. [18/07/05]

512   United Nations. Relief Web – Africa Maps   ⓘ
http://www.reliefweb.int/rw/dbc.nsf/doc100?OpenForm (Home page)
http://www.reliefweb.int/rw/dbc.nsf/doc103?OpenForm&rc=1#show (Africa pages)
ReliefWeb, administered by the UN ➜ **Office for the Coordination of Humanitarian Affairs/OCHA (2528)**, is an electronic clearinghouse for those needing timely information on humanitarian emergencies and natural disasters. The site offers a very large selection of African maps. From the menu select an item under Current Complex Emergencies or Current National Disasters, which then displays the very latest updates and bulletins, a choice of relief sectors (e.g. security, food, shelter, health, water and sanitation, etc.), and maps. Alternatively select by country, for example Sudan, which offers a further list of sub-topics and maps that are available (e.g., in July 2005, maps for Sudan-Darfur: Affected Population by Locality; OCHA Darfur Humanitarian Needs and Gaps by Sector; or Sudan-Darfur: Chad Border Region: Confirmed Damaged and Destroyed Villages.) While some of these are specialist maps relating to drought, civil war situations, food emergency situations, satellite maps, etc. there are also some very good and fairly up-to-date general administrative and country maps. You can preview maps in a small size, or view full size, and for each map it indicates the source, date, and file size. Save documents, maps, and other content to read, print or email later. There are excellent advanced document search/map search and filtering facilities to combat information overload. [18/07/05]

Map sales and vendors

This listing is restricted to some of the major outlets for purchase of African maps, and includes some of the principal vendors and distributors, but does not include individual map publishers.

France

513   **Institut Géographique National**
        IGN Sologne
        Administration des ventes
        41200 Romorantin-Lanthenay
Tel: +33-2-54 94 13 40 Fax: +33-2-54 88 14 66 Email: ign-sologne@ign.fr
Web: http://www.ign.fr/affiche_rubrique.asp?rbr_id=1122&lng_id=FR
Agents in the UK:
Navigator Maps Ltd, PO Box 6242, 41a Kilbourne Road, Belper, DE56 1HA
http://www.navimaps.co.uk/ and ➜ **Mapworld/Footprint Maps Ltd (517)**
Agent in the US: ➜ **Map Link Inc (521)**
Offers Africa-related all-purpose maps, tourist guides and plans, city and country maps, and large-scale topographical sheets. Strong on maps of former French colonial territories, and present-day francophone Africa, some of which were produced in collaboration with national mapping agencies and surveys. Also sells photographs and aerial maps. From the Cartes d'Afrique pages select the country of your choice, which then displays available maps, their scale, and prices.

Germany

514 GeoCenter (ILH-Internationales Landkartenhaus)
GeoCenter Scientific Cartography
Schockenriedstrasse 44
70565 Stuttgart
Tel: +49-711-490 72210 Fax: +49-711-490 72211 Email: info@ilh-stuttgart.de
Web: http://www.geokatalog.de/
Customers in the US may also order through:
East View Cartographic
3020 Harbor Lane North
Minneapolis MN 55447
Tel: +1-763-550 0961 Fax: +1-763-559 2931
Email: maps@eastview.com
Founded in 1971, GeoCenter is the leading German map house, distributing a vast
number of German and international topographic and thematic maps, travel guides,
atlases, and geo-scientific maps. It claims to stock more than 100,000 titles, and this
includes a substantial amount of general and specialist material on the African
continent. Its GeoKatalog 1 covers general, tourism-related maps and guides, while
GeoKatalog 2-Geosciences covers more specialist/scientific cartographic materials--
from aeromagnetism to zoogeography. One drawback, though, is the fact that while
the site offers a monthly list of selected new titles, there is no online catalogue to
view products for sale, and before you can order you will need to purchase the
GeoKatalog 2, published in three volumes and costing €255 (and an annual updating
service is offered at €82). For availability of new maps recently added to the stock
inventory check out http://www.geokatalog.de/intsel.htm.

South Africa

515 Carte Afrique (Pty) Ltd
PO Box 1943
Houghton 2041
Tel: +27-11-487 2680 Fax: +27-11- 648 6935 Email: info@carte.co.za (General
enquiries) sales@carte.co.za (Sales)
Web: http://www.carte.co.za/
Johannesburg-based dealer and distributor of maps of the African continent. Holds
stocks of maps at multiple scales of all areas of Africa and the surrounding islands.
Additionally, the company will endeavour to source maps and related products on
request. Will ship maps to anywhere in the world and can assist in procuring maps
that are not normally available by mail order.

516 Map Studio
7 Wessel Road
PO Box 277
Rivonia 2128
Tel: +27-11 807-2292 Fax: +27-11 807-0409 Email: sales@mapstudio.co.za
Web: http://www.mapstudio.co.za/

Part of the ➜ **New Holland/Struik (2099)** publishing group, Map Studio is South Africa's leading cartographic publisher, offering a wide range of street and city maps and plans, atlases and globes, tourist maps, educational maps, wall maps, and digital maps. The emphasis is on South Africa and, to a lesser extent, southern Africa and other parts of the continent. In the online catalogue each product is described with a short summary of content, publication date, scale, size, ISBN and price,

United Kingdom

517   MapWorld/Footprints Maps Ltd
Footprint Maps Ltd
25 Saltersford Lane
Alton ST10 4AU
Tel: +44-(0)1538-703842 Fax: +44-(0)1538-702019 Email: info@footprintmaps.com
Web: http://www.lynx.net.uk/aspidistra/
Holds stocks of a sizeable number of African maps, although primarily general country maps, maps for travel and tourism, and some city maps. Product details include a brief description, publisher, scale, and price.

518   Ordnance Survey International
Romsey Road
Southampton SO16 4GU
Tel: +44-(0)23-8079 2912 Fax: +44(0)23-8079 2230 Email: osi@ordsvy.gov.uk
Web: http://www.ordnancesurvey.co.uk/oswebsite/aboutus/international/
The Ordnance Survey International Library holds an extensive collection of 50,000 maps, 1.5 million aerial photographs, and survey data and map production records from Africa, the Caribbean and South Atlantic, Pacific and Indian Ocean regions. However, following a strategic business review, which focussed on providing improved access to and use of the Ordnance Survey International Library, a decision was taken to close the contents of the Library to the public from 28 March 2003, and seek a new home for these public records. The list of institutions that will in future hold the records is available at the above Web site. The records will now be known as 'The Ordnance Survey International Collection'. Ordnance Survey also announced that as soon as practical it "will establish and subsequently maintain a Web site to provide background information to the collection and to act as a 'signpost' to the various components of the original collection; thus enabling the establishment of a virtual collection." For a limited period at least, DOS/OS International printed maps will continue to be available through Ordnance Survey trade outlets, but Ordnance Survey will no longer revise, print or stock such maps. Remaining stocks of Ordnance Survey International maps were purchased by ➜ **Omni Resources (522)**, which can now process orders for select stocks that are still available.

519   Stanfords
       Edward Stanford Ltd
       12-14 Long Acre
       London WC2E 9LP
Tel: +44-(0)20-7836 1321 Fax: +44-(0)20-7836 0189 Email: sales@stanfords.co.uk
Web: http://www.stanfords.co.uk/ (Home page)
http://www.stanfords.co.uk/navigation/navig?action=top_category&loc_id=9
(Africa pages menu)
Stanfords was established in 1852 by Edward Stanford, map seller. Today, over 150 years on, Stanfords is the UK's leading specialist retailer of maps and travel books. Stanfords flagship store in London's Covent Garden first opened its doors in January 1901 and today it carries under one roof a very broad range of maps, travel guides, and other travel-related materials. Search the online catalogue by destination, by special interest drop-down menus, or browse listings by continent, countries or major cities, and local regions. The main menu for Africa offers wall maps, continent maps and atlases, regional maps, road maps, energy and mineral resources maps, navigational charts, satellite images and aerial photos, CD-ROM mapping, a pull down menu for African city maps, together with a very wide range of books and travel guides on Africa. Sub-menus cover countries, local regions and local cities, and which for many African countries include topographical maps, thematic maps, as well as maps for hiking and trekking. Title, publisher price, scale, stock availability, brief description, catalogue number, format, size, and ISBN are indicated for each product.

520   Maps Worldwide Ltd
       Datum House
       Lancaster Road
       Melksham SN12 6TL
Tel: +44-(0)1225-707 004 Fax: +44-(0)1225-707 062
Email: customers@mapsworldwide.co.uk.
Web: http://www.mapsworldwide.com/mwwlive/dir.asp?secid=23 (Africa pages)
UK-based vendor and distributor of world maps and travel guides of all kinds. Will ship to anywhere in the world. The main menu on Africa offers general maps of Africa, along with guidebooks, wall maps, and satellite images of Africa. For more specific maps and books on Africa, e.g. on individual African countries, use the search facility to track down available products. There are over 40 pages of African maps (in English and French), each providing details of scale, publisher, price and most with a short description.

United States

521   Map Link Inc
       30 South La Patera Lane Unit #5
       Santa Barbara CA 93117
Tel: +1-805-692 6777 Toll-free (US/Canada only): 800-962 1394
Fax: +1-805- 692 6787 Toll-free fax (US/Canada only): 800-627 7768
Email: custserv@maplink.com

Web: http://www.maplink.com/
Note: A comprehensive list of retailers and map dealers stocking Maplink products can be found at http://catalog.maplink.com/scripts/cgi-bin/cgiip.exe/retailpartnerslist.r

Founded by Bill Hunt and Laura Ericson in 1984, Map Link is now probably the largest map wholesaler and distributor in the world, carrying stocks of more than 100,000 titles from over 500 different publishers. Its inventory includes an extensive selection of all types of maps: city plans, regional, touring, recreation, state, country, continent, world and specialty maps and atlases, guides, globes, CD-ROMs and many international topographic maps. To search Maplink's impressive online catalogue choose Keywords/Description or Geographic search to find available maps for Africa, including general maps, wall maps, scientific maps, national and city maps, and much more. Its online ordering facilities are a model of clarity, providing, first, a short description of each item, and with a pull-down menu giving more precise details, including size, format/theme, a short description, publisher and publication date, ISBN, stock availability, product code and price. For a good number of maps the pull-down menu also offers two images, one a cover illustration of the map, and the other an extract from the map.

522   Omni Resources
1004 South Mebane Street
PO Box 2096
Burlington NC 27216-2096
Tel: +1-336-227 8300 Fax: +1-336-227 3748
Email: inquiries@omnimap.com or custserv@omnimap.com
Web: http://www.omnimap.com/maps.htm (Home page)
http://www.omnimap.com/catalog/int/africa.htm (Africa pages)

Omni Resources is one of the major US distributors of maps, globes, and teaching materials. Its specialty is international mapping, and it offers maps for nearly all countries and regions of the world. The main menu for the continent of Africa offers topographic maps, geologic and thematic maps, travel maps, and physical and political maps. There is good selection of general and thematic maps for the continent of Africa, and fairly extensive stocks of thematic, topographic (at various scales), and travel and specialist maps for individual countries, for example African railways maps. It also offers a large number of nautical charts for the Western Africa and the Mediterranean region, and that of eastern/southern Africa and the Indian Ocean. Omni Resources points out that the former British colonies tend to be better mapped than the ex-French, ex-Portuguese, or ex-Belgian colonies. For each product there is a brief description, details of format, publication date and price. For a number of the African physical and political maps there are thumbnails of the maps and, usefully, for some maps you can view samples. Omni Resources has also recently acquired remaining stocks of the ➔ Ordnance Survey International (518) maps.

8
Guides to film and video/DVD resources
(print and online)

Print

523   **A Directory of Audio-Visual Archives in Eastern and Southern Africa.** Comp. by the Eastern and Southern African Regional Branch of the International Council on Archives (ESARBICA). Pretoria: National Archives of South Africa, 1997. 44 pp.
Describes audio-visual archives in Botswana, Kenya, Malawi, Namibia, South Africa, Zanzibar and Zimbabwe with information on holdings, facilities and accessibility.

524   Ballantyne, James and Andrew Roberts. **Africa: A Handbook of Film and Video Resources**. London: British Universities Film & Video Council [77 Wells St., London W1T 3QJ], 1986. 120 pp. (with Supplementary List, May 1987, 23 pp.)
Describes major archival collections of non-fiction films on Africa in Great Britain, together with a separate section with details of films on Africa which can be hired or borrowed, covering mostly history, politics and ethnography, the latter part arranged by subject with country subdivisions, and country, title and distributor indexes. The subject sections give details of distributor, year released, production company, length and other technical details, together with a brief annotation. Also includes a list of distributors' addresses and a bibliography. Unfortunately the 1986 edition is out-of-print and no new editions have been published to date.

525   Lems-Dworkin, Carol. **Videos of African and African-related Performance: An Annotated Bibliography**. Evanston, IL: Carol Lems-Dworkin Publishers [POB 1646, Evanston, IL 60204-1646], 1996. 353 pp. $57.00
Somewhat oddly sub-titled "an annotated bibliography" this is in fact a videography, whose primary purpose is to help people locate videos showing aspects of African or African-related performance. This covers African music, dance, drama, rituals, oral tradition, storytelling, carnivals, folklore, ethnographic studies, women's studies, children's videos, and more. Also includes select videos from the African diaspora showing significant links to Africa (e.g. jazz, blues, gospel, steel pan, calypso, reggae). There are 1,390 entries, most quite extensively annotated. Each entry gives details of video formats and standards, duration, year released, names of directors/producers, etc., country of origin, and information about purchase/rental and distributor. A Distributors Index gives full names, addresses, and telephone and fax numbers (Email address and Web sites for some). A 37-page subject index, and a names index, add to the value of this remarkable compilation.
ARD review:
African Research & Documentation, no. 74 (1997): 89 (reviewed by Keith Hart)
Choice review: *Choice* October 1992 (reviewed by Kazadi wa Mukuna)

526   Wiley, David S. **Africa on Film and Videotape: A Compendium of Reviews**.
East Lansing, MI: African Media Program, African Studies Center, 1982.
Lists over 750 reviews of films and videotapes on Africa released between 1960 and
1981 which are available in the US. Includes critical annotations, and full details of
length, date released, director/producer, distributor, etc. Indexed by topic, country,
and by language. An updated version is now also available online as part of the ➔
Africa Media Program (528) database.

Online

527   **African Films (in COCC Collections) and Resources**
http://web.cocc.edu/cagatucci/classes/hum211/afrfilms.htm
A useful set of summaries of 26 major African films used a part of a course, Culture
& Literature of Africa, including African Orature & Film, as offered by Cora Agatucci
at Central Oregon Community College, with links to reviews and external movie
databases. There is also a short bibliography to online articles on African cinema.
[21/07/05]

528   **African Media Program (AMP)** ⓘ
http://ngsw.org/~afrmedia/
A project of ➔ **Michigan State University's African Studies Center (1710)**, the
African Media Program offers a comprehensive online reference guide to
approximately 10,000 films, videos, and other audiovisual materials concerning
Africa (both Sub-Saharan and North Africa). The searchable database, continuously
updated, includes film and video productions made in Africa and around the world,
on many aspects of the peoples, geography, and societies of the African continent.
The database incorporates and updates material contained in the previous print
publication ➔ **Africa on Film and Videotape: A Compendium of Reviews (526)**,
and adds many new reviews. As far as is possible full details are provided on each
film or video, including title, alternate title, series title, year of release, producer,
production company, director, length in minutes, and distributor information. For
many of them it also offers ratings by reviewers in terms of each product's accuracy,
organization, photographic quality, audio graphic quality, and editing, and for some
productions, it provides synopses, minute-by-minute inventories of the content,
critical evaluations, and viewing recommendations. The evaluation criteria guiding
reviews and evaluations focuses on their utility in introducing Africa to US
audiences. Additional resources available on the Web site include recommended
curriculum resources, as well as access to a separate database The South Africa Film
and Video Project (SAFVP). There is also a *Bibliography of African Cinema, Film, and
Video Studies*, a fairly substantial bibliography, albeit rather unsatisfactorily
organized (partly by year of publication, and partly by author), and missing out on
some important earlier bibliographies on the topic. Overall though, AMP is a
marvellous resource. [22/07/05]

529   Film, Media and Video Resources for African Studies
http://www.ias.emory.edu/catalog.cfm?new=yes
This online catalogue and searchable database lists some 450 African films and videos held by ➜ **the Institute of African Studies, Emory University (1679)**, dealing with topics ranging from literature, politics, art and religion to wildlife. The holdings include over 60 feature films. Entries are arranged alphabetically by title, each entry giving length, date released, an abstract of contents, keywords and topic descriptors, and the catalogue reference. Searching can be by year, title, or key words. [22/07/05]

530   Films and Videos on Africa
http://www.columbia.edu/cu/lweb/indiv/africa/cuvl/video.html
Part of Columbia University Library's ➜ **African Studies Internet Resources (80)** this is a guide to a substantial number of resources for films and videos on Africa, including video collections and Web sites at other major American universities, production companies, film libraries, film festivals, documentary resources, TV series, film suppliers, and more. [22/07/05]

531   John Henrik Clarke Africana Library. Video/DVD collection
http://www.library.cornell.edu/africana/visual/
Cornell's ➜ **John Henrik Clarke Africana Library (1304)** has a large collection of over 400 video tapes, covering both locally produced videos (documenting on-campus lectures and conference panel sessions), and commercially produced video cassettes. It focuses primarily on the Black experience in America and the diaspora. There is a short description for each video, with details of producers, date, length etc., and the video collection catalogue reference number. [22/07/05]

532   Media Resources Center. Moffitt Library, University of California at Berkeley – African Studies
http://www.lib.berkeley.edu/MRC/AfricanVid.html
533   African Cinema and African Cinematic Representation: A Selected Bibliography/Videography of Materials at UC Berkeley
http://www.lib.berkeley.edu/MRC/AfricanBib.html
The Media Resources Center (MRC) is the ➜ **University of California Berkeley Library's (1333)** primary collection of materials in electronic and non-print formats. The collection is particularly strong in holdings of humanities and social sciences materials, as well as a broad range of general interest materials in the fields of science and technology. It includes dramatic performances, literary adaptations, speeches, lectures and events, and primary source recordings such as historic TV commercials and newsreels and documentaries. Apart from general videos on Africa, access to the collection is by country, and each video has a short description of contents. Also on this site is a useful *African Cinema and African Cinematic Representation: A Selected Bibliography/Videography of Materials at UC Berkeley*, arranged by book titles, journal articles (some accessible as full-text, for but UC users only), as well as reviews and articles about individual films that can be found in the MCR collections. [25/07/05]

534   Melville J. Herskovits Library of African Studies. Africana Video
        Collection
http://www.library.northwestern.edu/media/docs/africana.pdf
A 175-page guide in pdf format to the Africana video collection available in →
Northwestern University Library's (797) Marjorie Iglow Mitchell Multimedia
Center. Arranged in three parts, Africana Documentaries, Africana Feature Films,
and Africana Television, and under each group alphabetically by name of film title.
Each entry gives the call number, date produced, name(s) of producer/director, US
distributor for some, rights holder, length/number of video cassettes, a summary of
content, and other relevant information. [22/07/05]

535   Web Dossier: African Cinema
http://www.ascleiden.nl/Library/Webdossiers/CinemaAfrica.aspx
Compiled by staff at the Documentation and Information Department of the Leiden
→ African Studies Centre Library/ASC (1246), this useful Web dossier on African
cinema lists books, journals, and periodical articles on African film and video
published in the last ten years. Includes titles in English, French, and German. Each
title links directly to the corresponding record in the ASC online catalogue, which
provides more details and cataloguing data about each title, and abstracts for articles
and edited works. Also contains a list of African videos from the ASC collection, and
a selection of Web resources. [26/08/05]

Vendors and distributors

This section includes a small number of both commercial and non-
commercial vendors and distributors of African films and videos, but it is
not a comprehensive listing. For details of other distributors consult the
films and videos topic pages at the Stanford → Africa South of the Sahara
Web (69) site http://www-sul.stanford.edu./depts/ssrg/africa/film.html.

For those interested in purchasing Nigerian video films, there is an
informative article, "Pursuing Nigerian Video Films" by Lauris Olson
(University of Pennsylvania Library) in issue 177, July 2005 (pp. 12-13) of the
→Africana Libraries Newsletter (801), also accessible online at
http://www.indiana.edu/~libsalc/african/aln/no117.pdf.

536   AfricaMovies.com
http://africamovies.com/
The Nigerian film industry – Nollywood, as the flourishing industry has christened
itself – is the now one of the biggest in the world, and there are numerous suppliers
of these low budget movies, as well as several Web sites devoted to the genre.
AfricaMovies.com is one such supplier, including romance, comedy, thrillers, etc and
popular Nigerian videos/DVDs in Yoruba and Ibo. It also offers titles such as the
film of Chinua Achebe's *Things Fall Apart*. An artist and title index is provided on the
Web site. [28/08/05]

537   AllAfricanMovies.com
http://www.allafricanmovies.com/index.php
Another vendor of Nigerian home-grown films. Offers a huge inventory of popular
DVDs, including comedy, drama, romance, and family entertainment, primarily
from Nigeria, but also movies from Ghana, Mali, and Senegal. Each item for sale has
a short plot summary, together with names of director and actors, manufacturer,
format, price, and stock availability, and some have online reviews contributed by
AllAfricanMovies customers. [12/07/05]

538   Bullfrog Films
http://www.bullfrogfilms.com/subjects/africanstudies.html
Bullfrog Films is a leading US publisher of independently-produced, environmental
videos and films, and its producers include the National Film Board of Canada, CBC,
Television Trust for the Environment, BBC-TV, the World Wildlife Fund, and the
Australian Broadcasting Corporation. It offers a sizeable number of videos on Africa,
not only on environmental issues, but also on social development, human rights,
children's education and health, globalization, cultural values, women in Africa, and
other topics. [22/07/05]

539   California Newsreel. Library of African Cinema
http://www.newsreel.org/nav/topics.asp?cat=4
The Library of African Cinema is probably North America's most extensive primary
source for African videos/VHS, DVDs and 35mm film, covering both feature films,
as well as documentaires and educational films and videos. The site provides access
to the collection, with a complete A-Z listing of all titles, and can also be browsed by
broad topics, or by films in French or Portuguese. There are currentlly (July 2005) 82
titles available in the Library of African Cinema. The Web site offers a full summary
of each film, extracts from critical reviews, details of available formats, and pricing
information. All material can be ordered online. The site also has some helpful
background resources for viewing African cinema, and a series of "Facilitator
Guides." [21/07/05]

540   Cine3Mondes – La Médiathèque des Trois Mondes
http://www.cine3mondes.com/index.cfm (Main home page)
http://www.cine3mondes.com/index.cfm?CFID=2052450&CFTOKEN=63039091&
MRq=384 (Catalogue vidéo – Afrique)
Cine3Mondes is a major French distributor of films and videos in French on Africa,
Asia, and Latin America. The online catalogue offers a large number of titles, on
many topics and subject areas. Each film or video has a description, title/producer,
length, date of release, formats, and price. [22/07/05]

541   The Cinema Guild – African Studies
http://www.cinemaguild.com/catalog/catalog_african_studies.htm
The Cinema Guild's catalogue of videos includes documentaries, narrative features,
short fiction, animation, 'how-to' videos, and children's and young adult
programmes. While they are primarily intended for classroom instruction and
curriculum enrichment, many have broad general interest and entertainment appeal.
In the African studies field it offers films on historical, social and religious topics;

African traditions and traditional healing, national liberation in Africa, the social and political struggle of life under Apartheid, and videos on the political history of several African countries. Each title listing has a synopsis, and details of year of release, director, format, duration, and price for purchase or for rental. [22/07/05]

542   Concord Video Council
http://www.btinternet.com/~concordvideo/cp1home.html
A major distributor in the UK of films and videos, available for hire or for purchase. Includes a substantial number of videos on Africa; select International in the menu and thereafter click the Development Education and/or other categories in the online catalogue. For each product the catalogue details give a description, running time, formats, publisher, year of release, and hire or purchase prices. [22/07/05]

543   Films for the Humanities & Sciences
http://www.films.com/
Offers more than 7,000 video, DVD-R, and digital-on-demand programmes covering a broad range of subject areas appropriate for schools, colleges, and public libraries, and the prices of all titles include public performance rights. An editorial board chooses each programme on the basis of the importance of its subject, the quality of its production, and its relevance as an instructional aid. There are a substantial number items on Africa-related related topics, and good advanced search facilities help you to find the product that most closely fits your needs. Each catalogue entry gives a description of the product, copyright date, formats available, and prices. [26/08/05]

544   MDFI African Films and Videos (formerly African Social Message Films and Videos)
http://www.mfdi.org/
MFDI is an American non-profit agency that works closely with the Zimbabwean charity → **Media for Development Trust** (*see* entry **545** below). They work together in film productions as well as distributing African social message films and videos. MFDI stocks about 1,000 VHS videos, and a small collection of 35mm prints. All titles are available in English and many titles are available in several other languages. All are available in the VHS PAL and NTSC formats, and the French products are also available in SECAM. The online catalogue can be searched, or browsed by topics such as agriculture/ecology, AIDS, conflicts, education and training, feature films, health, teenage pregnancy/family planning, or women's issues. Each title lists the synopsis, length of video, production information, formats and languages they are available in, and price. Prices are generally modest. [22/07/05]

545   Media for Development Trust
http://www.mfd.co.zw/index.cfm (Home page)
http://www.mfd.co.zw/viewinfo.cfm?linkcategoryid=9&siteid=1 (Film catalogue)
The Media for Development Trust is a not-for-profit, Harare-based NGO that seeks to promote development through communication, in particular through the production and distribution of high quality, socially conscious films and videos. It works in collaboration with organizations in South Africa, the UK and North America. It offers feature films, drama, animation, and training videos. Over 250

African films are currently (July 2005) available, most on Video or CD, and a number in DVD. Browse the catalogue by broad topics such as agriculture, children/children at risk, culture, environment, gender, history, health, HIV/AIDS, etc. Most of the films are available not only in English, but also in numerous African languages. [22/07/05]

546   Off the Fence
http://www.offthefence.com/
An independent Dutch TV production and distribution company, specializing in non-fiction programmes for the international marketplace, with an emphasis on wildlife, anthropological and adventure programmes, including films on Africa, (primarily on nature and wildlife). [22/07/05]

547   Villon Films
http://villonfilms.com/
Villon Films was founded by Peter Davis, who has written, produced, and directed more than thirty documentaries to wide acclaim, and which have been shown on major television networks (*see also* The Black Film Center/Archive, the Peter Davis Collection http://www.indiana.edu/~bfca/collection/special/peterd.html). Villon Films has a strong focus on socio-political documentaries, and the collection spans such issues as government, history, ecology, culture, health and science, women's issues, biography, and the apartheid period of South African history. Use the search facility to find details and descriptions of films on Africa, with names of producers, directors, date of release, and length, etc. Villon Films offers a "Preview" facility prior to ordering. [22/07/05]

9

Journals and magazines
(print and online)

Guides to journals and journals online

(i) This symbol indicates "The editor's choice" of a particularly
outstanding online information resource.

---

548   Africa South of the Sahara – Topics: Journals
http://www-sul.stanford.edu./depts/ssrg/africa/journal.html
Stanford's ➔ **Africa South of the Sahara (69)** is probably the most comprehensive,
and most frequently updated guide to journals on Africa and African studies, the
majority of which now have a presence on the Web in one form or another. The
Stanford pages provide (1) an alphabetical listing (in two parts, A-I and J-Z) of
African/African studies journals and newsletters including many subject-specific
and specialist serials – including scientific, medical and technical journals - most
with a brief description of content; (2) a separate listing of South African journals, all
with short annotations; (3) two topic-specific listings of journals, in the field of
education, and history. (4) a guide to journal indexes and databases, including
databases for more specialist research, not specifically focusing on Africa but offering
substantial coverage of Africa, such as *Agricola, Anthropological Index Online, Columbia
International Affairs Online, Current Geographical Publications, ELDIS, IBISCuS,
MEDLINE, New York Times Book Reviews, Population Index*, etc. (the majority of which
are subscription/license based, but to which most major academic libraries
subscribe.) Interestingly, the pages include some fairly obscure, radical, or
"alternative" journals, but, perhaps for reasons of their obscurity and/or precarious
existence, there are also a fairly large number of dead links. [03/08/05]

549   African Studies Centre, Leiden University. List of Free Online Journals [on
Africa]
http://www.ascleiden.nl/Library/FreeOnlinePeriodicals.aspx
From the Library, Documentation and Information Department of the ➔ **African
Studies Centre Leiden University (1246)**, this a useful 12-page listing of over 100
online journals, bulletins, and newsletters on Africa/African studies which can be
accessed for free. *See also* entry **72**. [03/08/05]

550   Black Studies Library Periodicals: An Annotated List
http://www.lib.ohio-state.edu/OSU_profile/bslweb/serials.html
Hosted by ➔ **Ohio State University's Black Studies Library (1323)** and compiled by
Bassey Irele, this is a useful annotated listing of a large number of African and Black

studies journals, with links to the Web sites of the journals (where they exist), and/or to full text databases (access to full text is only available to patrons of the OSU Columbus campus at this time). The list was most recently updated in May 2004. [03/08/05]

551   Centre d'Etude d'Afrique Noire. Université de Bordeaux. Périodiques reçus actuellement par la bibliothèque du CEAN
http://www.cean.u-bordeaux.fr/appel%20perio.html
The online catalogue of African studies serials received by the library at ➔ **CEAN (1197)**. Arranged in A-Z order, it provides basic details for each serial including year first published, ISSN, frequency, CEAN catalogue codes, and journal Web sites for a good number of them. It also includes journals that ceased publication or are currently dormant, and this makes it a useful source to track down basic details of elusive African studies periodicals, especially those published in French. [03/08/05]

➔ **Quarterly Index to Africana Periodical Literature** see **3 Current bibliographies, indexing and abstracting services, and review media** entry 404

552   South/Southern African Online Scholarly and Professional Journals
http://www.nrf.ac.za/yenza/research/sajourn.htm#Journal
Part of the Yenza! 'Start your Research' pages, this is a fairly comprehensive (albeit not entirely up-to-date) list of some 80 South African scholarly and professional journals currently online in some form or another (i.e. some full-text, others with table of contents listings and/or abstracts only), with details of formats, an indication of what can be accessed online, and links to their URLs. [03/08/05]

Table of contents alerting services and other journal resources

Note: for indexing and abstracting services of African/Africanist journals *see* ➔ **3 Current bibliographies, indexing and abstracting services, and review media**

553   African e-Journals Project (AEJP)
http://www.isp.msu.edu/africanstudies/aejp/
This ambitious project seeks to provide better access to African academic journal scholarship in the US and globally. It "aims to design an economically sustainable cost-recovery system that provides fair recompense to African publishers and greatly heightened access to US scholars." The project is a collaboration of the ➔**Association of African Universities (2580)**, the (US) ➔ **African Studies Association (2755)**, the ➔ **Council for the Development of Social Science Research in Africa (1851)** and Michigan State University (MSU). At MSU, the project has been organized by the ➔ **African Studies Center (1710)** in cooperation with MSU Libraries, MSU Press, and MSU Matrix: The Center for Humane Arts, Letters, and Social Studies Online. The journals included in the project are being made available electronically through Project MUSE and online at this site. At this time (August 2005) back issues for 11 African journals have been digitized, mainly those in the social sciences, humanities, and international development fields. According to the Web site "the AEJP is

pledged to create a database of the full corpus of African journals, providing content, subscription and other information. In its initial phase, the database will include more than 700 journals from and about Africa." [05/08/05]

554 African Journals Online (AJOL) ⓘ
http://www.ajol.info
Conceived and until recently hosted by the ➔ **International Network for the Availability of Scientific Publications/INASP (2608),** the African Journals Online (AJOL) project is a free service that provides online access to the tables of contents and abstracts of scholarly journals published in Africa, backed by a document delivery service (there are some restrictions to this, see Article Ordering Information on the Web site) The project, funded by several donors, is designed to create increased awareness of and promote the greater use of scholarly journals published in Africa. AJOL currently (as at August 2005) offers access to the tables of contents and abstracts of articles of 218 African-published journals from 21 countries. It covers journals in the agricultural sciences and resource management; arts, culture, language and literature; health; science and technology; the social sciences; as well as multidisciplinary journals. Currently more than 13,000 article abstracts are available on the Web site. View or browse journals alphabetically, by subject, or by country. Sophisticated search features include a facility to key word search the AJOL pages by subject, and there are links to full text (where available). AJOL also includes information and cover images for each participating journal, a description of focus and scope, name(s) of editor(s) and details of editorial boards, author guidelines and submission requirements, subscription rates, and full ordering information. The service has now become a major showcase for African journal publishing, and this is an outstanding resource.
See also "African Journals OnLine (AJOL). An Internal Evaluation, 2000-2002", by Diana Rosenberg, Oxford: INASP, 2003. 15 pp. (print on demand), online at http://www.inasp.info/ajol/evaluation2002/report.pdf [25/09/05]; and "African Journals OnLine (AJOL)", by Sioux Cumming, http://www.inasp.info/newslet/jul05.shtml. [22/08/05]
Note: in July 2005 it was announced that the AJOL project would be relocated to Africa and moving it to African management. The South African branch of the ➔ **National Inquiry Services Centre/NISC Pty Ltd (2097)** http://www.nisc.co.za/ was selected to manage AJOL in future, and to spearhead further development and collaboration within the continent. NISC has formed a not-for-profit company that will manage the affairs of AJOL.
See also "An African Vision for African Journals OnLine (AJOL)", by Margaret Crampton, http://www.inasp.info/newslet/jul05.shtml#2.

555 Bioline International
http://www.bioline.org.br/
Bioline International is a not-for-profit electronic publishing service committed to providing open access to quality research journals published in developing countries, primarily in the fields (*not* covered by the *African Studies Companion*) of tropical medicine, infectious diseases, epidemiology, emerging new diseases, biodiversity, the environment, conservation and international development. It includes journals from 14 countries, including these journals from Egypt, Kenya, Nigeria, Senegal, and Uganda, and for which free access to full-text articles is

offered: *African Crop Science Journal, African Journal of Biomedical Research, African Journal of Biomedical Research, African Journal of Biotechnology, African Journal of Food and Nutritional Safety, African Journal of Reproductive Health, African Journal of Traditional, Complementary and Alternative Medicines, Annals of African Medicine, Biokemistri,* ➔ **Journal of Applied Science and Environmental Management (591),** *The Journal of Food Technology in Africa, Journal of Community Medicine & Primary Health Care, Middle East Fertility Society Journal, Nigerian Journal of Physiological Sciences, Nigerian Journal of Surgical Research,* and the *Tropical Journal of Pharmaceutical Research.* [04/09/05]

556   Digital Imaging Project Africa (DISA)
http://disa.nu.ac.za/
The aim of the DISA project is to make accessible to scholars and researchers worldwide, South African material of high socio-political interest that would otherwise be difficult to locate and use. In addition, the project aims to provide experience and develop knowledge and expertise in digital imaging amongst archivists and librarians in Africa.   The title of the first project chosen (DISA 1) is *South Africa's Struggle for Democracy: Anti-Apartheid Periodicals, 1950-1994.* It covers the three key decades in the growth of opposition to Apartheid rule, a period when the African National Congress, black consciousness, and other resistance movements were very active. 43 periodical titles have been selected for inclusion, have been digitized, and complete or near-complete back runs are now freely accessible on line as full-text (a total of approximately 55,000 pages of fully searchable text.) For each journal an abstract is provided, and indication of dates covered, number of issues available online, and for some journals, for example *Sash,* the file size (in pdf), is also indicated. With the assistance of a further grant from the ➔ **Andrew W. Mellon Foundation (2739),** work has recently begun on DISA 2, entitled *Southern African Freedom Struggles, c.1950 – 1994.* This is an excellent resource, but it should be noted that some pdf file sizes are very substantial and will take some time to download; and even for access to relatively small journal issues the download process is rather laborious and can be time-consuming. [08/08/05]

557   H-Africa: African Studies Journals – Table of Contents
http://www.h-net.org/~africa/toc/index.html
This service from the H-Africa Network, provides access to the table of contents to the current issues, as well as back numbers, of almost 180 Africanist journals, covering both general African studies journals, as well as those devoted to African art, archaeology, economics, literature, politics, religion, sociology, etc. Access is by two options: for tables of contents posted to H-Africa click on to a TOC icon, or, alternatively and if available, click on to the journal's Web site for basic editorial and subscription information and (sometimes) also tables of contents. Unfortunately, at this time (August 2005) the service lacks currency and seems to be seriously in arrears, and for most journals, including several major UK- or US-published African studies journals, the last TOCs posted are those for issues published in 2000, 2001, or earlier. There are also numerous dead links, and the service is in need of a major facelift. [08/08/05]

558   JSTOR
http://www.jstor.org/
JSTOR (Journal STORage) is a unique digital archive of the back runs of a large number of core scholarly journals, starting with the very first issues. JSTOR started as a pilot project in the United States, funded by the ➔ **Andrew W. Mellon Foundation (2739)**. Now operating as an independent, non-profit making organization, JSTOR's aim is to provide a solution to the increasing costs to libraries of storing back runs of journals. It covers about 30 disciplines at present, covering material from the 1800s up to a "moving wall", representing the time period between the last issue available in JSTOR and the most recently published issue of a journal before current publication (generally ranging from 3 to 5 years). JSTOR is made available to academic institutions around the world on a site-licence basis. Users at participating institutions can view, search, browse, print and save any article from the collection from any networked location. New journals are added all the time, and recently this has included several of the leading African studies periodicals, as well as a small number of Africa-related cultural and literary magazines. [08/08/05]
Note: in the directory of African studies journals that follows this section, an indication is provided at the foot of journal entries whether back runs can be accessed via JSTOR, with details of JSTOR coverage (current as at September 2005), and a link to the relevant JSTOR URL. At this time this primarily covers journals published in North America and the UK.

➔ **Periodicals from Africa: A Bibliography and Union List of Periodicals Published in Africa** *see* **2 The Major general reference tools: Bibliographies and guides to sources,** entry **239**

559   Peuples Noires – Peuples Africains, online ⓘ
http://www.arts.uwa.edu.au/mongobeti/
From 1978 to 1991 the distinguished Cameroonian writer Mongo Beti (1932-2001) - living in exile in France for much of his life – and his wife Odile Tobner published an important bi-monthly radical, social and political magazine entitled *Peuples Noires – Peuples Africains*. In addition to papers of a political and militant nature it contained frequent scholarly contributions on African writing, articles on literature, culture and society, and the committed African theatre. Thanks to an initiative of the Faculty of Arts at the University of Western Australia and the journal ➔ **Mot Pluriels (664)** the first 35 issues, up to September/October 1983, of the journal are now freely accessible online in their full-text versions, and subsequent issues (up to the final print issue of no. 90) are being added to the site at the rate of about one per month. The site also includes a search facility. [04/09/05]

560   SABINET Online – E-Journal Project (Subscription based; trial access available)
http://www.journals.co.za/collections/
http://www.sabinet.co.za/journals/journals_publist.html (complete list of journals)
For subscription/pricing information see the SABINET Web site.
Complete list of journals http://www.journals.co.za/
A comprehensive electronic collection of South African scientific and scholarly journals, most of them peer reviewed. The service brings together, soon after publication, the tables of contents, abstracted records, and full-text documents of a

large number of journals published in South Africa. A total of 192 titles are covered at this time (September 2005), with new journal titles being added on an ongoing basis. Subscription options are available for all titles in the service, or selections bundled by broad subject areas: Business & Finance, Law, Medical & Health, Religion, Science, Technology & Agriculture, and Social Sciences & Humanities. Subscriptions to individual journals are *not* available through SABINET. Subscribers to the full SA ePublications Service will also get access to a comprehensive database of indexed and abstracted South African journals articles, extracted from more than 500 journals and containing approximately 440,000 articles. [04/09/05]

561   SARA – Scholarly Articles Research Alerting
http://www.tandf.co.uk/sara/
The Taylor & Francis group (now incorporating the Carfax and Routledge imprints) publishes over 1,050 academic peer-reviewed journals across a variety of disciplines, including several African studies and development journals. SARA is a service designed to deliver by email the tables of contents of forthcoming journal issues from the group. The service is completely free of charge, but requires registration. You can select to receive alerts by keyword, title, sub-category or main category. [05/08/05]

African studies periodicals – a directory

Scope
This directory has again been considerably expanded for the 4th edition of *The African Studies Companion*, now listing almost 300, for the most part *multidisciplinary*, African studies periodicals. They are primarily those in the social sciences and the humanities, and African law, but there are also entries for a number of the leading, more specialist African studies journals of long standing (especially if they are inter-disciplinary in scope), as well as some general interest and current affairs magazines on Africa, and a selection of African literary, cultural, and arts magazines with a fairly broad scope. Additionally there are listings of a small number of the major development journals that have strong Africa interests, but African American/Black studies journals are not covered.

Medical, scientific, and technical journals, and those in the field of agriculture and natural history, are *not* included, although there are entries for a small number of applied science and environmental journals and those covering agricultural extension and rural development. To access the table of contents, abstracts, subscription and other information of a very substantial number of African-published journals in the agricultural sciences, medicine/life sciences, and science and technology, visit ➔ **African Journals Online/AJOL (554).**

Also not included are journals that focus entirely on a single African country, e.g. *Journal of Eritrean Studies, Religion in Malawi, The Uganda Journal,* etc.

Updates and verification
All information previously contained in the third edition has been systematically verified and updated, including subscription rates, email addresses, Web sites, editorial contact information, etc. A total of 22 journals listed in the previous edition, that are no longer published, currently dormant, or for which we have been unable to ascertain that they are still active, have been dropped for this new edition. A small number of other journals for which we have been unable to verify current availability status have been retained for the time being, but a note regarding availability, or details of the latest volume or issue available (as at September 2005), appears at the foot of such unverified entries.

While African-published journals have always lived a somewhat precarious existence, it should perhaps be added that there are also a good number of African studies journals published elsewhere, for example several in the US, which are seriously in arrears in their publication schedules, or would appear to be currently dormant.

Arrangement

Journals are listed alphabetically by region and then by country. Please note that they are listed under the country *from which they originate editorially*, for example the *Journal of Religion in Africa*, published out of Leeds University, appears under the United Kingdom, although published by Brill in the Netherlands.

Information provided for each entry

The following details are provided: full name and publisher address including telephone and fax numbers (omitting the '0' prefix except for UK numbers), email address, and Web site (where available), year first published, formats, ISSN/E-ISSN, frequency, and subscription rates (if, for online journals, access is free this is indicated in lieu of subscription rates); name of editor/s and editorial address, email, etc. (please note that academic titles such as Dr. or Prof. are *not* included); name of book review editor/s and address if different from editorial address. Subscription rates are for volumes published in 2005 for the most part. If print and online formats are indicated, both ISSN and online/E-ISSNs are given, if available. If available in both print and electronic formats, the subscription rates are normally the combined rates for print issues and online access, unless otherwise indicated.

Each entry includes a brief outline of contents and scope or a mission statement, in *italic type,* and for the most part as quoted by the journals' editors or publishers (albeit edited to eliminate undue hype). Broad submission guidelines provide an indication in which particular areas contributions are welcomed (unless it is the same as the mission statement), or drawing attention to any special focus of the journal. Information as it relates to style guidelines, recommended length for articles, nature of illustrative material used, submission and format requirements etc., is not included, as most of this submission information is easily available from journal publishers' Web sites.

Please note that the Web sites of some African-published journals suffer from frequent down time, and a "not found" error message is not necessarily an indication that the Web site has moved or is no longer available.

There are cross-references to professional associations and societies, or other organizations, for all those serials that are the official journals, or published on behalf of, African studies associations and societies.

Peer review
Most of the journals listed here – other than more general interest current affairs or African cultural and literary magazines – are peer-reviewed, and therefore we do *not* indicate whether or not a journal is peer-reviewed as part of the entry.

Online access/Document delivery
Most publishers allow online access at no extra charge as part of the institutional subscription rate quoted (but not always as part of the individual rate), with access either from the journal's Web site and/or via Catchword/Ingenta, Swets Navigator, EBSCO Online, or other services. Publishers' "bundled" print/online subscriptions usually also include access to all the electronic back files available through the journal's Web site.

The Taylor & Francis Group, Oxford University Press, Blackwell's and a number of other publishers offer special rates for subscriptions from countries defined by the latest UNDP Human Development Report as a "developing country".

Most journal Web sites nowadays allow free online access to table of contents of recent issues and/or abstracts, and many provide details of the abstracting and indexing services in which the journal is covered. Many publishers also offer a content alerting service by email. For journals published by commercial publishers, document delivery service for articles is usually available on the basis of single article purchase.

A welcome development since publication of the previous edition of the *African Studies Companion* is the fact that more and more African studies journals published by institutions, NGOs, or associations, although essentially subscription based, now offer free full-text access to all or most back issues published, usually in pdf format.

Table of contents services
Journals covered in the ➜ H-Africa: African Studies Journals – Table of Contents (557) service, which includes archives of TOCs of past issues going back several years, are indicated by "H-Africa TOC" at the foot of the entry. Similarly, African-published journals included in the ➜ African Journals Online/AJOL (554) table of contents service are flagged accordingly. It should be added however that the H-Africa TOC service – which is driven by volunteer labour, and depends on publishers submitting regular TOC information – is currently not as up-to-date as it used to be, and for several journals, including some of the major African studies periodicals, the latest table of contents posted relate to issues/volumes published several years ago.

JSTOR

We also flag journals that can be accessed via ➔ **JSTOR (558)**, a unique digital archive of large number of core scholarly journals. At the foot of journal entries covered by JSTOR we provide details of JSTOR coverage (volumes/years, as at August 2005), together with JSTOR's journal URL. At this time this includes only a dozen or so African studies serials, but new journals are being added to the JSTOR database all the time. For a complete list of journals visit http://www.jstor.org/about/alpha.content.html. Please note that in order to access JSTOR you must be part of a US, UK/European, or participating institution in other countries.

Project Muse

Several of the US-published journals listed here are available for electronic campus-wide access and combined print/electronic subscriptions via Project Muse, including access to archives, either as single title subscriptions or a basic subscription license to all journal packages from participating publishers. The complete Project Muse list of journals can be found at http://muse.jhu.edu/journals/index.html; for subscription plans and pricing see http://muse.jhu.edu/about/subscriptions/subscriptions.html.

RSS feeds

As an entirely new feature in this edition, we indicate with an RSS icon whether the journals provide RSS/XML feeds, together with the URL giving more information of the RSS feeds service, or the actual URL of the feed pages. (You will need an RSS reader for this; for more information about RSS feeds and RSS readers see also the introductory comments in section **10** ➔ **News sources for Africa**.) At this time only a small number of African studies journals offer this service, but the number is likely to grow in the years ahead. In most cases RSS feeds are available for the latest or recent issues, providing table of contents and abstract information. If you wish to view the full text of any article listed in the RSS feed, simply click on the article's link, which will lead to the online journal site.

An important note about submissions

Information provided in the *African Studies Companion* relating to "Submissions" covers the principal areas in which original contributions are invited, intended to provide guidelines for potential contributors relating to special interests or a special focus of a journal. More detailed submission information is available on most journals' Web sites under sections such as "Notes for contributors", "Instructions for authors" or "How to submit your article", usually covering manuscript preparation, length, presentation, text format and style, acceptable delivery formats/preferred file formats, abstracts, notes and references, tables and figures, copyright, supply of offprints, etc.

It is important to read these instructions carefully before submitting articles.

Most journals do not accept unsolicited manuscripts by email, and it should also be noted that the majority of journals will not accept papers which are submitted to several journals at once, and/or are already under consideration elsewhere.

Abbreviations and symbols used:

[?]	Indicates queried information which we have been unable to verify and which may not be accurate or current
Affil	affiliation (affiliation with association/society or other professional body/institution; and/or the journal of that association)
AJOL	Table of contents service offered by ➔ **African Journals Online (554)**, including abstracts for many
Ann	annually
Biwk	bi-weekly
Book rev	journal carries book reviews
Book rev ed	Book review editor
corp	corporate (business) subscription rate
Dept	department
Ed/s	Editor/s

€	Euro (Currency, approx £/$ equivalent, as at November 2005, €1.46 to £1.00, €0.84 to US$1.00)
ext	extension (for telephone numbers)
Found ed	Founding editor
H-Africa TOC	journal covered in the ➜ **H-Africa Table of Contents (557)** service
indiv	individual subscription rate
inst	institutional subscription rate
ISSN/E-ISSN	International Standard Serial Number (and/or E-ISSNs for electronic journals)
Managing ed	Managing editor
Mon	monthly
2Mon	twice monthly/fortnightly
n/a	no details provided/available, and/or unable to verify
Online	journal published online/in electronic format
Print	journal published in print format
Publ	Publisher
Qtly	quarterly
stud	student subscription rate
Submissions	submissions/contributions [welcomed in ...]
Subs	subscription rates [annually, non-members rate, surface post unless otherwise indicated]
Wk	weekly
2Yr	twice yearly
3Yr	three times yearly
6Yr	six times yearly/bi-monthly

AFRICA

A note about journals published in Africa:
Many African-published journals lead a somewhat precarious existence, and several lag behind in their publication schedules, sometimes by a year or more. All the journals listed here have been ascertained to be still active, although in some cases the most recent issues published go back to 2003 or 2004. Where the current availability status is uncertain, this is indicated in a note with the entry.

The following African journals have been *dropped* from this edition, as we have been unable to verify information on current publication status:

Acta Academia (Bloemfontein)
The African Communist (Johannesburg)
African Social Research (Lusaka)
Alternation (Durban)
Current Viewpoint (Ibadan)
Journal of Black and African Arts and Civilization (Lagos)
Muntu (Libreville)
Okike. An African Journal of New Writing (Nsukka)
Pretexts: Literary and Cultural Studies (Rondebosch, ceased, with vol. 12, no. 3, November 2003?)
Revue Culturelle Tapama (Bamako)

Benin

562 **Répliques. Le journal de l'Académie africaine**
La Médiathèque des Diaspora
04 BP 792
Cotonou
Tel: +229-947 57 00
Email: camouro@yahoo.fr
Web:
http://www.mediaspora.net/repliques.htm
2004- Print ISSN n/a Mon
Subs: in Africa CFA 12,000, outside Africa €36/$36
Ed: Camille Amouro
The monthly journal of the Académie africaine, which aims to provide a platform for serious intra-African debate about important current issues affecting the continent.
Submissions: as above

Botswana

563 **Pula. Botswana Journal of African Studies**
The Educational Book Service
(Attn. Ms Ivy Molokwane)
Private Bag BR-42
Gaborone
Email: ivy@ebs.info.bw
Tel: +267-393 0354 Fax: +267-393 0358
Web: http://www.thuto.org/pula/html/
1984- Print ISSN 0256-2316 2Yr
Subs: in Africa $50 inst $25 indiv, elsewhere $90 inst $45 indiv
Ed: Isaac Mazonde, Office of Research & Development, University of Botswana
Private Bag UB00708, Gaborone
Tel: +267-355 2900 Fax: +267-357573 Email: mazondei@mopipi.ub.bw
An interdisciplinary journal (humanities, education, social sciences mainly) of African studies, with a focus on southern Africa in particular.
Submissions: welcomes contributions that cross disciplinary boundaries from scholars anywhere in the world.
Note: irregularly published, last issue was vol. 18, no. 1, 2004.

Cameroon

564   The African Anthropologist. Journal of the Pan African Anthropological Association
BP 1862
Yaoundé
Tel: +237-234227 Fax: +237-221873
Email: icassrt@camnet.cm
Web: http://www.upe.ac.za/paaa/
1998- Print ISSN 1024-0969 2Yr
Subs: in Africa $60 inst $25 indiv $15 stud, elsewhere $70 inst $40 indiv $20 stud
Ed: Paul Nchoji Nkwi,
Email: nkwi@lom.camnet.com
A forum for intellectual and scholarly debate on specific problematical and theoretical issues in the social sciences, and the development of methods and theory.
Submissions: as above

565   Polis
Groupe de Recherches Administratives, Politiques et Sociales (GRAPS)
BP 7759
Yaoundé
Fax: +237-223859
Email: cpsr@hotmail.com
Web: http://www.cean.u-bordeaux.fr/polis/index_eng.html
1996- [No ISSN] 2Yr
Subs: on application
Ed: Luc Sindjoun, Université de Yaoundé II, Yaoundé
A political science review covering national and international political life.
Submissions: articles in French and English.
H-Africa TOC

Congo Democratic Republic

566   Annales Aequatoria
Centre Aequatoria
Maison MSC
BP 779
3ième Rue
Limete
Kinshasa 1
Outside Africa:
Te Boelaerlei 11
2140 Borgerhout
Belgium
Tel: +32-16-464484 Fax: +32-3-32101
Email: vinck.aequatoria@skynet.be
Web: http://www.aequatoria.be/English/HomeEnglishFrameSet.html
1980- Print ISSN 0254-4296 Ann
Subs: in Africa $35, Europe €24, North America $35
Ed: Honoré Vinck (Address in Belgium: Stationsstraat 48, 3360 Lovenjoel)
Book rev
Covers a wide range of subjects: African linguistics, cultural anthropology, literature and languages, history, archaeology, religion and missiology.
Submissions: as above; contributions in French or English
H-Africa TOC, AJOL

Ethiopia

567   Eastern Africa Social Science Research Review
Organization for Social Science Research in Eastern and Southern Africa (OSSREA)
PO Box 31971
Addis Ababa
Tel: +251-1-239484 Fax: +251-1-223921
Email: pub.ossrea@ethionet.et
Web: http://www.ossrea.net/publications/eassrr/
or:
Michigan State University Press
1405 South Harrison Road
25 Manly Miles Building
East Lansing MI 48823-5245
USA
Tel: +1-517-355 9543 Fax: +1-517-432-2611
Email: msupress@msu.edu
Web: http://muse.jhu.edu/journals/eas/
available online, free-of-charge (for project MUSE subscribers, as part of the ➔ **African e-Journals Project (553)** or also at
http://muse.jhu.edu/journals/eastern_africa_social_science_research_review/toc/eas19.1.html
1985- Print and online (January 2002-) ISSN 1027-1775 (E-ISSN 1684-4173) 2Yr
Subs: print, in Africa $23, elsewhere $35; online: free
Ed: Alfred G. Nhema, Executive Secretary, OSSREA,
Email: executive.secretary@ossrea.net

Book rev
Serves as a regional forum for critical reflection and discourse on the economic, political, and social aspects as well as development concerns of the countries in eastern and southern Africa. Includes critical analysis on contemporary and regional policies and issues of interest to researchers, development planners, decision-makers, and academics.
Submissions: scholarly articles, book reviews, and short communications, in the area of anthropology and sociology, political science, economics, education, gender, environment and demography.
H-Africa TOC, AJOL

Ghana

568   **African Agenda**
Third World Network - Africa
9 Ollenu Street East Legon
PO Box AN19452
Accra-North
Tel: +233-21-503669/500419
Fax: +233-21-511188
Email: communications@twnafrica.org
Web:
http://www.twnafrica.org/africanagenda.as
p
1994- Print (and partially online) [No ISSN]
6Yr
Subs: print, in Africa $45 inst $35 indiv,
UK/Europe £45/€70 inst £35/€55 indiv,
North America and elsewhere
$70 inst $55 indiv; online free
Eds: Yao Graham, Tetteh Hormeku
African Agenda reflects the Third World Network's concerns and campaigns around issues of economic policy, sustainable development, trade and investment, gender, environment, politics, culture and civil society, and aims to provide cutting-edge analysis on economic and social issues.
Submissions: as above, in English or French
H-Africa TOC

569   **African Journal of Environmental Assessment and Management**
c/o Osman A. Sankoh
INDEPTH Network
PO Box KD 213 Kanda
Accra
Tel/Fax: n/a

Email: oasankoh@ajeam-ragee.org
Web: http://www.ajeam-ragee.org/
1999- Print and online (2002-) ISSN 1438-7890
2Yr
Subs: in Africa $30 inst $14 indiv, elsewhere
$50 inst $24 indiv
Eds: Osman A. Sankoh (at address above),
Pierre Andre; contributions in English may
also be sent also to Aiah A. Gbakima,
Department of Biology, School of Arts and
Science, Morgan State University Spencer Hill
G12
Coldspring Lane and Hillen Road, Baltimore
MD 21239 USA, Email:
agbakima@jewel.morgan.edu; contributions
in French to Pierre Andre, Département de
Geographie
Universite de Montréal
CP 6128, Succursale Centre-ville, Montreal,
Quebec H3C 3J7, Canada
Email: andrep@ajeam-ragee.org
An academic journal and "best practice" forum focusing exclusively on environmental issues in Africa. Publishes articles of interest to natural and social scientists, policy makers, and professional practitioners.
Submissions: in English or French; articles on the development of environmental assessment and management in Africa, methodologies applied, environmental modelling and policies.

570   **IEA Policy Analysis**
Institute of Economic Affairs
PO Box OS 1936
Christiansborg
Accra
Tel: +233-21-244716/244717
Fax: +231-3-222313
Email: iea@iaeghana.org or iea@ncs.com.gh
Web: http://www.ieaghana.com
2004- Print ISSN 0855-2460 Mon
Ed: George A. Apenteng
Ed contact: Jean Mensa, Administrator
Monthly publication of the Institute of Economic Affairs, a policy research and advocacy organization. Each issue is devoted to a particular topic in the areas of monetary policy, econometrics, banking and financial markets, and sustainable development in Africa.

**571   Institute of African Studies
       Research Review**
Institute of African Studies
PO Box 73
Legon
Accra
Tel: +233-21-502397 Fax: +233-21-513389
Email: iaspubs@ug.edu.gh
1965- Print ISSN 0855-4412 2Yr
Subs: in Ghana Cedi20,000 per issue,
elsewhere $35 annually
Ed: Mary Esther Kropp Dakubu
Book rev
*An interdisciplinary scholarly journal of the
humanities and the social sciences in Africa.*
AJOL
Note: abstracts available on line at Fort Valley
State University-State University of Georgia,
as part of the DCTAW project at
http://www.dctaw.org/Review.html

**572   Transactions of the Historical
       Society of Ghana**
Sankofa Educational Publishers
PO Box C 1234 Cantonments
Accra
Tel: +233-21-777866 Fax: +233-21-778839
Web: n/a
1957-1975, new series 1995- Print
ISSN 0855-191X Ann
Subs: not known/unable to verify
Ed: R. Addo-Fening, Department of History,
University of Ghana
PO Box 12 Legon, Accra,
Tel/Fax: + 233-21-502397,
Email: asafo@ghana.com
or per.hernaes@hf.ntnu.no
*An open forum for historical and interdisciplinary
academic debate.*
Submissions: contributions are welcomed
from writers who take an interest in African
studies, not only historians.
Note: irregularly published, last issue was
New Series, vol. 4/5 (2002).

Kenya

573   Africa Woman
Hurlingham   Medicare Plaza
3rd floor Room 324
Argwings Kodhek Road
PO Box 6064
Nairobi 00200
Tel: +254-20-272 1429

Fax: +254-20-272 1439
Email: info@africawoman.net
or africawoman@swiftkenya.com
Web: http://www.africawoman.net/
2001- Primarily online, print editions
published on the occasion of special events
[No ISSN] Mon
Subs: n/a
Ed: Lucy Oriang, Email: loriang@nation.co.ke
or lucyoriang@yahoo.com
*Africa Woman connects 80 female journalists
from Ghana, Kenya, Zimbabwe, Uganda, Malawi,
Tanzania, Zambia and Nigeria, who meet in a
monthly virtual newsroom (VNR) to create the
magazine.*

574   Azania
The British Institute in Eastern Africa
PO Box 30710
Nairobi
Tel: +254-2-434 3190/434 3330
Fax: +254-2-434 3365
Email: bieanairobi@africaonline.co.ke
Web:
http://www.britac.ac.uk/institutes/eafrica/
1966- Print ISSN 0067-270X Ann
Subs: £22 (£44 for double vols.
Ed: Innocent Mwangi Gathungu
Book rev
*Covers the history, archaeology, and related
studies of eastern Africa broadly defined. Through
original articles, notes, and reviews, it documents
new research and the advancement of knowledge
in this field.*
Submissions: as above

**575   The East African Journal of Human
       Rights and Democracy**
Millimani Suite A6
PO Box 11391-0100
00100 Nairobi
Tel: +254-20-2730158
Fax: +254-20-2730159
Email: eajournal@email.com
Web:
http://www.eahumanrights.org/journal.php
2003- Print ISSN 1686-900X Qtly
Subs: in North America $412 inst $240 indiv,
Europe and Australia $308 inst $240 indiv, in
Kenya and East Africa $80 inst $54 indiv,
elsewhere in Africa $120 inst $100 indiv
Ed: Atunga Atuti
*Published by the East African Human Rights
Institute, the journal intends to provide a
professional forum for highlighting perspectives
and issues relevant to the promotion and*

entrenchment of human rights and democratic ethos by facilitating people to people and organizational contacts and synergy as a medium for consolidating democracy and development. Submissions: focusing on eastern Africa, the journal publishes articles on a broad spectrum of issues relating to human rights, democracy, social justice and human security issues, including crime and corruption, small arms control, peace building initiatives; as well as articles dealing with the interplay between economics, politics, society and culture, and human security and stability.

576   **The Eastern Africa Journal of Humanities & Sciences**
Department of Research
Missio Hall
PO Box 62157
Nairobi
Tel: +254-2-891601-6 Fax: +254-2-891084
Email: research@cuea.edu
Web:
http://www.fiuc.org/iaup/esap/publications/cuea/cueapub.php
2003 [?]- Online ISSN 1681-0007 2Yr
Subs: free
Ed: P. A. Ogula Book rev
An international refereed journal devoted to theory development and empirical research in the humanities and sciences.
Submissions: carries critical essays, articles, and research that deal with matters of importance to the church and society; publishes and reports major advances and current trends in the theory and practice in the humanities, social sciences and natural science.

577   **Kwani?**
PO Box 75240
00200 Nairobi
Tel: + 254-2-892165 Fax: +254-2-316719
Email: admin@kwani.org
(Sales/Subscriptions)
editors@kwani.org (Editorial)
Web: http://www.kwani.org/
2003- Online ISSN n/a Qtly [three issues published through August 2005]
Subs: print: issues individually priced, approx. ca. Kshs.650/$6 per copy, see Web site; online (extracts): free
Ed: Binyavanga Wainaina; submissions to submissions@kwani.org

A literary journal founded by some of Kenya's new writers to provide the Kenyan reading public with writing of the highest quality, to create innovative ways of encouraging a new generation of writing talent, and to get people reading again by providing them with a forum that helps them answer questions about themselves. Kwani? seeks to entertain, provoke, and create.
Submissions: the journal includes fiction, short stories, discussion and debate, and "is open to all Kenyans, wherever they may be, who have something new to say". While the content of the journal is generally reflective of the Kenyan cultural scene it accepts, at the discretion of the editors, stories from non-Kenyan writers that fit its profile.

→ **Quarterly Index to Africana Periodical Literature** *see* **3 Current bibliographies, indexing and abstracting services, and review media** entry **404**

578   **Wajibu. A Journal of Social and Religious Concern**
Likoni Lane
PO Box 32440
Nairobi
Tel: +254-2-712632/311674
Email: wakuraya@alphanet.co.ke
Web:
http://www.peacelink.it/wajibu/index.html
1985- Print and online (recent issues)
ISSN 1016-9717 Qtly
Subs: in Kenya Kshs.480 inst Kshs.400 indiv, in Africa $42 inst $30 indiv, elsewhere $54 inst $42 indiv
Ed: Gerald J. Wanjohi
Intended for everyone who is concerned about keeping the African traditions alive and adapting them to the modern way of life. Offers a dialogue between people of different backgrounds, traditions and religions for the promotion of peace and understanding.
Submissions: as above
Note: irregularly published, last issue was vol. 18, nos. 1-2 (2003).

Lesotho

579   Review of Southern African Studies
Institute of Southern African
Studies
National University of Lesotho
Roma 180
Tel: +266-340601 Fax: +266 340000
Email: t.khalanyane@nul.ls
Web:
http://www.nul.ls/institutes/isas.htm
1995- Print ISSN 1024-4190 2Yr
Subs: in Africa R60 inst, elsewhere $50
Ed: editorial board, editorial correspondence
to t.khalanyane@nul.ls
Book rev
*A multidisciplinary journal of the arts, social, and
behavioural sciences.*
Submissions: southern African studies;
research and original papers in the arts,
social, and behavioural sciences, with a
preference for articles which cut across
disciplinary boundaries.
AJOL
Note: irregularly published, last issue was
vol. 4, no. 1 (2000).

Malawi

580   Journal of Humanities
Chancellor College Publications
University of Malawi
POB 280 Zomba
Tel: +265-522222
Email: publications@chanco.unima.mw
1987- Print 1016-0728 Ann
Subs: in Africa $15/£9 inst $5/£2 indiv,
elsewhere $15/£9 inst, $8/£4 indiv
Ed: Daveson Nyabani Book rev
*A theoretical journal that aims to challenge,
provoke and excite thinking in the areas of the
classics, fine and performing arts, literature and
orature, linguistics, theology and philosophy.*
Submissions: priority is given to articles
focusing on east, central and southern Africa.
The journal takes a pluralistic and non-
partisan approach.
AJOL
Note: irregularly published, last issue was
vol. 17 (2003).

Mozambique

**581   OCPA Newsletter. Observatory of
African Cultural Policies**
Observatory of Cultural Policies in
Africa (OCPA)
11 rua Comandante Augusto Cardoso
Maputo, Mozambique
PO Box 1207
Maputo
Mozambique
Tel: +258-1-301015 Fax +258+1-312272
Email: secretariat@ocpanet.org
Web:
http://www.imo.hr/ocpa/news/index.html
2003- Online [No ISSN] 2Mon
Subs: free
Ed: Máté Kovács,
Email: ocpanews@ocpanet.org
The newsletter of the ➜ **Observatory of
Cultural Policies in Africa (2613),** *created in
2003 as an independent pan-African professional
organisation that aims to support and strengthen
the development of national cultural policies in the
region and their integration in human
development strategies through advocacy, and
promoting information exchange, research,
capacity building and cooperation at the regional
and international level.*
See also ➜ **70**

Nigeria

**582   African Journal of Economic
Policy**
Trade Policy Research and Training
Programme
Department of Economics
University of Ibadan
Ibadan Oyo State
Tel/Fax: n/a Email: asbanky@yahoo.com
Web: http://www.ajol.info/journals/ajep
(AJOL)
1993- Print ISSN 1116-4875 2Yr
Subs: in Africa $30 inst $20 indiv, elsewhere
$60 inst $40 indiv
Ed: Abiodun Bankole
*Provides a forum for development and equity on
the African continent, focusing on the efficacy of
the various economic policies for the welfare of
African peoples.*
Submissions: welcomes papers on the
implications of a specific economic policy, or
a set of economic policies, for growth,

development and equity within individual African countries, a group of African countries, or the continent as a whole. AJOL

583   African Journal of International Affairs and International Development
College Press Ltd
42 UI Secretariat Road
PO Box 30678
Secretariat
Ibadan Oyo State
Tel: +234-2-810 4165 Fax: +234-2-810 1963
Email: jowoeye@skannet.com or collegepresspublishers@yahoo.com
1995- Print ISSN 0117-272X 2Yr
Subs: $50 (airmail)
Ed: Jide Owoeye Book rev
Articles, commentary, research notes and book reviews on the legal political-diplomatic, economic, socio-cultural, and military-security issues at the core of Africa's foreign relations and world affairs.
Submissions: articles on legal, political, diplomatic, economic, socio-cultural issues, as well as papers on the environment, development, conflict and cooperation. AJOL
Note: irregularly published, last issue was vol. 7, no. 1 (2002).

584   Gender and Behaviour
Ife Center for Psychological Studies/Services
PO Box 1548
Ile-Ife Osun State
Tel/Fax: n/a
Email: ifepsy@yahoo.com
Web: http://www.ajol.info/journals/gab (AJOL)
2003- Print and online ISSN 0117-7322 Ann
Subs: $80 inst $40 indiv, online version available via → SABINET Online (560)
Eds: Editorial Board; correspondence and submissions to Okinsola Olowu, Project Coordinator, Department of Psychology, Obafemi Awolowo University, Ile-Ife, Nigeria, Email: ifepsy@yahoo.com or wanawake2002@yahoo.com
Book rev
An interdisciplinary journal offering articles that reflect psychological and behavioural aspects of gender in general.

Submissions: welcomes scholarly manuscripts from authors all over the world on a wide array of subjects concerning psychological and behavioural aspects of gender in general. AJOL

585   Farafina Magazine
25 Military Street Onikan
Lagos
PO Box 73940
Victoria Island
Lagos
Tel+ 234-1-263 7895/264 7527
Email info@farafina-online.com (General enquiries) subscriptions@farafina-online.com (Subscriptions) submissions@farafina-online.com (Submissions)
Web: http://www.farafina-online.com/ or http://farafina.dbweb.ee/
2005- Print and online [No ISSN] Mon
Subs: in Nigeria Naira 6, 000, elsewhere $79.99 (includes airmail postage)
Ed: Muhtar Bakare
Book rev
Farafina Magazine showcases the best in contemporary African ideas."Our goal is to tell our own stories".
Submissions: stories, poems, essays, cartoons, memoirs, photos are welcome. Submissions can be on any topic relating to any part of Africa or to peoples of African ancestry living in any part of the world.
Note: also publishes issues focussing on special themes. See Web sit for details of forthcoming issues.

586   Glendora Review. African Quarterly on the Arts
Glendora International (Nigeria) Ltd
168 Awolowo Road
POB 50914 Ikoyi
Lagos
Tel: +234-1-480 5222
Fax: +234-1-269 2762/269 2762
In the UK:
16 Skelley Road
London E15 4BA
Email: editor@glendora-eculture.com
Web: http://www.glendorabooks.net/GR/default.htm
1995- Print and (partly) online ISSN 1118-146X Qtly [irregular]

Subs: in Africa $82 inst $70 indiv, Europe £70 inst £58 indiv, North America $112 inst $92 indiv;
Ed: Olakunle Tejuoso, Editorial director;
Managing ed: Ololade Bamidele
Book rev
Covers all fields of the arts: film, music, theatre, visual arts, architecture, photography etc. Has a special interest in topical issues and discourse to benefit researchers and general cultural workers. Mode of presentation aims to be intellectual yet accessible.
Submissions: as above
Note: irregularly published since 2000; latest issue was vol. 3, no. 3; unable to verify current availability status.

587   Global Journal of Humanities
c/o Prof Barth N. Ekueme, Editor-in-Chief
Global Journal Series
University of Calabar
PO Box 3651 Unical Post Office
Calabar Cross River State
Tel/Fax: n/a
Email: bachudo@yahoo.com
Web:
http://www.ajol.info/journals/gjh
(AJOL)
2002- Print ISSN 1596-6232 2Yr
Subs: in Nigeria N3,000, elsewhere $80
Ed: Innocent I, Asouzu, Department of Philosophy, University of Calabar, Calabar , Cross River State, Nigeria
Aims to promote research in all areas of the humanities including philosophy, languages, linguistics, literature, history, fine/applied arts, theatre arts, architecture, etc.
Submissions: as above
AJOL

588   Humanities Review Journal
Humanities Publishers
University of Ibadan
PO Box 14177
Ibadan Oyo State
Tel/Fax:: n/a
Email: infohumpub@yahoo.co.uk or infohumanities@yahoo.com
2001- Print ISSN 1596-0749 2Yr
Subs: in Nigeria N600 inst, N700 indiv, elsewhere £21/$39 inst £16/$26 indiv
Ed: (Mrs) Foluke Ogunleye, PO Box 1904, Department of Dramatic Arts, Obafemi Awolowo University, Ile-Ife, Osun State,

Email: sefoleye@yahoo.com or foluleye@oauife.edu.ng
Book rev
Publishes papers, review essays, interviews and commentaries that offer new insights into the various disciplines in the humanities. Covers the fields of the theatre arts, music, philosophy, English language, literature in English, history, music, communication arts, and anthropology.
Submissions: as above; the focus is on issues about Africa, but comparative works from Western and other cultures designed to enhance the vitality of humanistic studies in Africa will also be considered.
AJOL

589   Ife Psychologia
Department of Psychology
Obafemi Awolowo University
PO Box 1548
Ile-Ife Osun State
Tel: +234-803-711 6382/+234-805-6343255
Email: contact@ifepsychologia.info
Web: http://www.ifepsychologia.info/
http://www.ajol.info/journals/ifep
(AJOL)
1992- Print and online ISSN 1117-1421 2Yr
Subs: in Africa $20, elsewhere $40; online version available via → **SABINET Online (560)**
Ed: Akinsola A. Olowu,
Email: sola@ifepsychologia.info or solowu@ouaife.edu.ng
Book rev
The journal has a multidisciplinary focus and is not intended for psychologists alone, but for anyone with an interest in the current state of psychology in Africa.
Submissions: welcomes articles on all aspects of human behaviour and experiences.
AJOL

590   Journal of Cultural Studies
PO Box 909
Marina
Lagos Lagos State
Tel/Fax: n/a
Email: yakubj@yahoo.com or makwemoisa@yahoo.com
1999- Print ISSN 1595-0956 2Yr
Subs: in Nigeria N3,000 inst N2,000 indiv, in Africa (airmail) $60 inst $35 indiv, elsewhere $80 inst $50 indiv
Eds: Uduopegeme Joseph Yakubu, Anthonia Makwemoisa

Book rev
Published by the Nigerian Group for the Study of African Cultures (NIGSAC), a non-profit organization that focuses on cultural and development issues in Africa. The journal aims to explore the varied socio-cultural experiences of the African peoples through various academic disciplines.
Submissions: welcomes contributions in all fields as long as they are within the scope of the journal's focus on African cultures.
AJOL

591   Journal of Applied Science & Environmental Management
Department of Pure and Industrial Chemistry
Faculty of Science
University of Port Harcourt
PMB 5323
Port Harcourt   Rivers State
Tel/Fax: n/a
Email: horsfalljnr@yahoo.com
Web: http://www.ajol.info/journals/jasem (AJOL)
1996 – Print and online   ISSN 1119-8362 2Yr
Subs: print: in Nigeria N3,600 inst N2,500 indiv N1,200 stud, elsewhere $150 inst $80 indiv $50 stud; online: full text freely accessible at http://www.bioline.org.br/ja
Ed: F.D. Sikoki Managing ed: M. Horsfall, jnr. Book rev
Publishes original research findings and occasional interpretative reviews on the toxic effects in plants, animals or humans of natural or synthetic chemical occurring in the human environment. In addition, studies relating to food, water, and other consumer products, papers on industrial and agricultural chemical and pharmaceuticals are published.
Submissions: welcomes original research papers, review articles, case studies, and short communications; papers from the areas of health, science, engineering, as well as the social sciences will also be considered.
AJOL

592   Journal of Environmental Extension
Department of Agricultural Extension and Rural Development
Faculty of Agriculture & Forestry
University of Ibadan
Ibadan Oyo State
Tel/Fax: n/a
Email: vichenfel@yahoo.com

Web: http://www.ajol.info/journals/jext (AJOL)
2000- Print ISSN 1595-5125 Ann
Subs: n/a
Ed: A.E. Adekoya
Aims to generate ideas on the formulation, packaging, dissemination and consequential impacts of ideas and policies relating to the quality and sustainability of the environment.
Submissions: the focus is on environmental impacts of practices, policies and technologies; the development of indigenous environmental practices, ideas and management; and enhancing participatory approaches to technology development for sustainability, biodiversity conservation and environmentally friendly practices.
AJOL

593   Lagos Historical Review
Department of History & Strategic Studies
University of Lagos
Arts Block Room 401,
Akoka
Yaba Lagos State
Tel: +234-1-5454891 ext 1345
Email: sarlek@yahoo.com
Web: http://www.ajol.info/journals/lhr (AJOL)
2002- Print ISSN 1596-5031 Ann
Subs: $45 inst $30 indiv
Ed: Ademola Adeleke,
Email: sarlek@yahoo.com
Book rev
An international and interdisciplinary journal publishing papers with a historical focus. The journal generates and participates in debates to advance the discipline of history and promote its relevance to development.
Submissions: welcomes scholarly submissions on any aspect of history, and policy formation.
AJOL

594   Lagos Notes and Records
Department of English
Faculty of Arts
University of Lagos
Akoka
Yaba Lagos State
Tel: +234-1-7940754
+234-080-2322 0393 (Mobile)
Email: lagosnotes@yahoo.co.uk

1967- Print (online as from 2006)
ISSN 0075-7640 Ann
Subs: $45 inst $35 indiv
Ed: Hope Eghagha
Book rev
An interdisciplinary journal of the humanities published by the Arts Faculty of the University of Lagos. It is devoted to the publication of well-researched articles in all subjects in the arts, social sciences, and law.
Submissions: as above

595 Position. International Arts Review
13 Modupe Street, Off Alhaja
Kofoworola Crescent
Balogun Bus stop
PO Box 604
Yaba Lagos State
Tel: +234-1-472 9048/8959036
+234-1-8033052279 (Mobile)
Email: positionngr@yahoo.com
Web:
http://www.positionmagazin.com/index.ht
ml
In the US:
989 Sanford Avenue
Irvington NJ 07111
2000- Print ISSN 1595-6512 Qtly
Subs: in Nigeria N5,000 inst N3,000 indiv, in Africa (airmail) $85 inst $70 indiv, elsewhere $135/£75 inst $95/£68 indiv (2003 rates, later rates n/a)
Ed: Dapo Adeniyi Book rev
Publishes views, reviews and interviews focusing on African arts in its various spheres – music, literature, and the visual arts, including photography and architecture.
Submissions: as above
Note: irregularly published, unable to verify current availability status.

Senegal

**596 Africa Development/
Afrique et Développement**
CODESRIA Avenue Cheikh Anta
Diop x Canal IV
BP 3304
Dakar
Tel: +221-825 9822/23 Fax: +221-824 1289
Email: codesria@codesria.sn
http://www.codesria.org/Links/Publication
s/Journals/africa_development.htm
1976- Print ISSN 0850-3907 Qtly Subs: in

Africa $32 inst $30 indiv, outside Africa
$45 inst $30 indiv
Ed: Francis B. Nyamnjoh, Managing ed:
Sulaiman Adebowale
Book rev
A social science journal whose major focus is on issues that are central to the development of society. Its principal objective is to provide a forum for the exchange of ideas among African scholars from a variety of intellectual persuasions and various disciplines. The journal also encourages other contributors working on Africa, or those undertaking comparative analysis of developing world issues.
Submissions: contributions, in English or French, which cut across disciplinary boundaries.
AJOL

**597 Africa Media Review/Revue
Africaine des Médias**
CODESRIA
Avenue Cheikh Anta Diop x
Canal IV
BP 3304
Dakar
Tel: +221-825 9822/23 Fax: +221-824 1289
Email: codesria@sentoo.sn
Web:
http://www.codesria.org/Links/Publication
s/Journals/africa_media_review.htm
1992- Print ISSN 0258-4913 3Yr
Subs: n/a
Eds: Peter Nwosu and Kwasi Ansu-
Kyeremeh,*et al*
All submissions to (Ms) Chifaou I. Josiane
Amzat, Departmental Secretary, Publications
and Communication
CODESRIA, Fax: +221-864 0143,
Email: Chifoau.amzat@codesria.sn
A collaborative publication between CODESRIA and the → **African Council for
Communication Education (2560)**, *the journal provides a forum for research and debate on communication theory, practice and policy in Africa. It seeks to raise awareness about the interconnections between media, communication and social processes in Africa, and how these shape and are affected by policies and practices at global, regional and local levels.*
Submissions: welcomes contributions, in English and French, on all aspects of communication informed by or relevant to the predicaments of Africa.

598 **African Journal of International Affairs/Revue africaine des affaires internationales**
CODESRIA
Avenue Cheikh Anta Diop x
Canal IV
BP 3304
Dakar
Tel: +221-825 9822/23 Fax: +221-824 1289
Email: codesria@codesria.sn
Web:
http://www.codesria.org/Links/Publication
s/Journals/ajia.htm
1998- Print ISSN 0850-7902 2Yr
Subs: in Africa $32 inst $20 indiv, elsewhere
$45 inst $30 indiv
Ed: Adebayo Olukoshi Book rev
Offers a platform for analyses on contemporary issues in African international affairs in relation to global developments as they affect Africa.
AJOL
Submissions: contributions, in English and in French, from both African scholars and scholars elsewhere working on Africa.

599 **African Population Studies/Etudes de la Population Africaine**
Union for African Population Studies
(UAPS)
BP 21007
Dakar Ponty
Dakar
Tel: +221-825 5951/+221-824 3528
Fax: +22- 825 5955
Email: uaps@sentoo.sn or uapas@uaps.org
Web: http://www.uaps.org/ (click on to
Publications)
1985- Print and online ISSN 0850-5780 2Yr
Subs: print: in Africa $20 inst $15 indiv,
elsewhere $30 inst $20 indiv; online: full text
freely accessible at
http://www.bioline.org.br/ep
Eds: Uche C. Isiugo-Abanihe , (Ed-in-chief,
and submissions in English), Department of
Sociology, University of Ibadan, Ibadan,
Nigeria, Fax: +234-2-810 3451, Email:
ucheia@uaps.org or abanihe@operamail.com;
Akoto Eliwo Mandjale (Rédacteur en Chef
Adjoint and submissions in French) IFORD,
Yaoundé Cameroun, Tel: +237-22 24 71 Fax: +
237-22 67 93, Email: eliwoa@uaps.org ;
akoto_zr@yahoo.fr
A bilingual journal (French and English) published by the Union for African Population Studies offering dependable and timely
information emanating from original research on African population, development, and related fields.
Submissions: papers are invited from researchers and others working in the population field discussing original research within any area of population.

600 **African Sociological Review/ Revue Africaine de Sociologie**
CODESRIA
Avenue Cheikh Anta Diop x
Canal IV
BP 3304
Dakar
Tel: +221-825 9822/23 Fax: +221-824 1289
Email: codesria@codesria.sn
Web:
http://www.codesria.org/Links/Publication
s/Journals/african_sociological_review.htm
1997- Print ISSN 1027-4332 2Yr
Subs. in Africa R80 inst R50 indiv, elsewhere
$80 inst $50 indiv
Eds: Fred T. Hendricks *et al*
All contributions to Managing Editor, African
Sociological Review, Department of
Sociology, Rhodes University, PO Box
94, Grahamstown 6140, South Africa, Email:
F.Hendricks@ru.ac.za or CODESRIA, Avenue
Cheikh Anta Diop x Canal IV, BP 3304 Dakar,
Senegal, Email: codesria@sentoo.sn
Book rev
Book rev ed: Alcinda Honwana
Social Sciences Research Council New York,
USA, Email: honwana@ssrc.org
Aims to stimulate and publish vigorous theoretical debate, and seeks to encourage scholarly work in social analysis broadly conceived, without an undue concern with narrow disciplinary and institutional boundaries.
Submissions: articles and other academic communications from scholars in Africa and elsewhere regarding issues of African and general social analysis. The Review exists in the first instance to promote the extension of sociological and anthropological thought among scholars working in Africa. Relevant work from elsewhere will however also be considered.
H-Africa TOC, AJOL

→ **The Africa Review of Books** *see* **3 Current bibliographies, indexing and abstracting services, and review media**
entry **406**

601 Afrika Zamani. An Annual Journal
of African History/
Revue annuelle d' histoire africaine
CODESRIA
Avenue Cheikh Anta Diop x
Canal IV
BP 3304
Dakar
Tel: +221-825 9822/23 Fax: +221-824 1289
Email: codesria@codesria.sn
Web:
http://www.codesria.org/Links/Publication
s/Journals/afrika_zamani.htm
Eds: Doulaye Konaté, Ibrahima Thioub
1993- Print ISSN 0850-3079
Subs: in Africa $15, elsewhere $25
*Devoted to the history of Africa, covering all
periods.*
Submissions: solicits articles, in English,
Arabic, French and Portuguese, that analyse
historical processes, reflect critically on
methodological approaches and
historiography.

602 Afro-Arab Selections for Social
Sciences [in Arabic]
CODESRIA
Avenue Cheikh Anta Diop x
Canal IV
BP 3304
Dakar
Tel: +221-825 9822/23 Fax: +221-824 1289
Email: codesria@codesria.sn
Web:
http://www.codesria.org/Links/Publication
s/Journals/afro_arab_selection.htm
2000- Print ISSN n/a Ann
Subs: n/a
Ed: Helmi Sharawy, Arab Research Centre,
8/10 Mathaf El Manial, Cairo, Egypt,
Email: arc@ie-eg.com
*An annual publication of the Arab Research
Centre in Cairo, Egypt and CODESRIA. It
contains a selection of articles published in
CODESRIA journals during the year, and
selections from other publications in the Arab
World. The journal is published in Arabic.*

603 **CODESRIA Bulletin**
CODESRIA Avenue Cheikh Anta
Diop x Canal IV BP 3304
Dakar
Tel: +221-825 9822/23 Fax: +221-824 1289
Email: codesria@codesria.sn
Web:
http://www.codesria.org/Links/Publication
s/Journals/codesria_bulletin.htm 1996- Print
and online ISSN 0850-0712 Qtly Subs: free
within Africa, elsewhere $25
Ed: Francis B. Nyamnjoh, Managing ed:
Sulaiman Adebowale; all contributions to (Ms)
Chifaou I. Josiane Amzat,
Departmental Secretary, Publications and
Communication, CODESRIA,
Fax: +221-864 0143,
Email: Chifoau.amzat@codesria.sn
*Contains brief research reports, policy-oriented
debates and discussions, offering both new
insights and theoretical perspectives on current
themes and topical issues; also includes conference
reports and announcements.*

604 Identity, Culture and Politics. An
Afro-Asian Dialogue/
Identité, Culture et Politique: un
dialogue afro-asiatique
CODESRIA
Avenue Cheikh Anta Diop x
Canal IV
BP 3304
Dakar
Tel: +221-825 9822/23 Fax: +221-824 1289
Email: codesria@sentoo.sn
Web:
http://www.codesria.org/Links/Publication
s/Journals/Identity,%20Culture%20and%20P
olitics.htm
2000- Print ISSN 0851-2914 2Yr
Subs: in Africa and South Asia $16 esewhere
$50
Eds: Imtiaz Ahmed, Ousmane Kane;
contributions to Prof. Imtiaz Ahmed, Co-
Editor, Identity, Culture and Politics. An
Afro-Asian Dialogue, Dept of
International Relations, University of
Dhaka, Dhaka 1000, Bangladesh, Email:
imtiaz@bangla.net; or Ousmane
Kane, Co-Editor, Identity, Culture and
Politics. An Afro-Asian Dialogue, School
of International and Public Affairs,
Columbia University, 420 West, 118th
Street, MC3331, NY 100027, USA,
Email: ok2009@columbia.edu
*A biannual publication of the International Centre
for Ethnic Studies, Colombo, Sri Lanka and the
Council for the Development of Social Science
Research in Africa. It aims to disseminate
knowledge and promote the exchange of ideas and
projections amongst African and Asian scholars
and activists.*
Submissions: in English and French

→ **Journal of Higher Education in Africa** *see* under United States, entry **821**

605   SudLangues. Revue électronique
internationale
Faculté des Lettres et Sciences
Humaines
Université Cheikh Anta Diop
BP 5005
Dakar-Fann
Tel/Fax: n/a
Email: sudlang@refer.sn
Web:
http://www.refer.sn/spip/sudlangues/
2002- Online ISSN 0851-7215 2Yr
Subs: free
Ed: Modou Ndiaye, Faculté des lettres et
sciences humaines, Université Cheikh Anta
Diop de Dakar, Senégal
Tel: +221-548 8799/825 2625 ext 257,
Email: mondiaye@ucad.sn
A pluridisciplinary online journal covering the
science of language in all its dimensions: syntax,
morphology, semantics, phonology, socio- and
psycholinguistics, linguistic diversity, multi-
lingualism, the relationship of the French
language to other languages, and other socio-
cultural realities.
Submissions: as above, open to researchers in
all parts of the world but contributions by
scholars in Africa and other developing
countries are especially welcome.

606   WAMP [West African Museums]
Bulletin
11 Route du Front de Terre
BP 357 - CP18524
Dakar
Tel: +221-827 3389 Fax: +221-827 3369
Email: wamp@wamponline.org or
wamp@sentoo.sn
Web:
http://www.wamponline.org/publications/
newpubli/publications.htm
1990- Print [no ISSN] Ann
Subs: in Africa CFA 10,000 inst CFA6,000
stud, Europe €30 inst €20 stud, North
America $40 inst $30 stud
Ed: Boureïma Tiékoroni Diamitani,
Email: bdiamitani-wamp@sentoo.sn
The annual WAMP Bulletin is designed to
strengthen the exchange of information between
museums, cultural heritage professionals and
specialized international institutions in Africa and
outside of Africa.

South Africa

Note: a large number of South African
journals are now available online via the
(subscription-based) → **SABINET Online**
(560). However, in some cases online access is
only available for current and/or recent
volumes. For precise details of availability of
online volumes click on to the SABINET
Online URL indicated for each journal.

607   Africa Insight
Africa Institute of South Africa
POB 630
Pretoria 0001
Tel: +27-12-328 6970 Fax: +27-12-323 8153
Email: ai@ai.org.za
Web:
http://www.ai.org.za/africa_insight.asp
1970- Print ISSN 0256-2804 Qtly
Subs: R180/$120 (airmail)
Ed: Elizabeth le Roux
Email: beth@ai.org.za
Book rev
An independent publication promoting insight
into the process of change in Africa. Publishes
scholarly articles in the social sciences aimed at
the interested layperson and serious student.
Submissions: publishes interdisciplinary
research and writing in the social sciences,
covering trends and developments in Africa
in a wide variety of subjects.
AJOL

608   African Finance Journal
African Finance Association
Africa Centre for Investment Analysis
(ACIA)
University of Stellenbosch Business
School
PO Box 610
Bellville 7535
Tel: +27-21-918 4347 Fax: +27-21-918 4262
Email: chantelp@acia.sun.ac.za (General
enquiries and subscriptions)
Web: http://www.ajol.info/journals/afj
(AJOL)
http://www.acia.sun.ac.za/projects/afa/afj.
htm
1999- Print and online ISSN 1065-9786 2Yr
Subs: in Africa $90 inst $35 indiv, elsewhere
$150 inst $50 indiv (reduced rates for
students); online version available via →
SABINET Online (560)

http://www.journals.co.za/ej/ejour_finj.htm
l
Ed: Nicholas Biekpe, Email:
afa@acia.sun.ac.za; electronic submissions to
Dina Potgieter, Assistant Editor,
Email: dinap@acia.sun.ac.za
*Published jointly by the African Finance
Association (AFA) and the University of
Stellenbosch, the journal is primarily devoted to
the study and promotion of knowledge about
finance relevant to development in Africa. It also
aims to promote investment and economic
integration within the continent.*
Submissions: the journal publishes significant
new research in finance and strives to
establish a balance between theoretical and
empirical studies. Papers written in any areas
of finance, accounting and economics will be
considered for publication. The journal also
publishes one Finance Letter per issue. This
does not have to contain original research and
can be a literature review on a specific topic
of relevance to the broader finance
community.
AJOL

609   African Identities
        Taylor & Francis Journals
        4 Park Square
        Milton Park
        Abingdon OX14 4RN
        UK
Tel: +44-(0)20-7017 6000
Fax: +44-(0)20-7017 6336
Email: tf.processing@tfinforma.com
Web:
http://www.tandf.co.uk/journals/titles/147
25843.html
In the US:
Taylor & Francis Journals (US)
325 Chestnut Street Suite 800
Philadelphia PA 19106
Tel: +1-215-625 8900 Fax: +1-215-625 8914
2003- Print and online ISSN 1472-5843
(E-ISSN 1472-5851) 2Yr
Subscription rates: £127/$210 inst £25/$42
indiv
Eds: Abebe Zegeye, University of South
Africa, PO Box 392, Unisa 0003
Tel: +27-12-429 6475 Fax: +27-12-429 3221,
Email: zegeye@unisa.ac.za;
Pal Ahluwalia, Department of Politics,
University of Adelaide, Adelaide 5005,
Australia, Tel: +61-8-8303 5570

Fax: +61-8-8303 3446, Email:
pal.ahluwalia@adelaide.edu.au or
african.identities@adelaide.edu.au;
Managing ed: Beth Le Roux, University of
South Africa, Email: beth@ai.org.za
Book rev Book rev ed: Pietro Toggia
University of California at Los Angeles
*Provides a critical forum for the examination of
African and diasporic expressions, representations
and identities. The aim of the journal is to open up
various horizons in the field: to encourage the
development of theory and practice in a wider
spread of disciplinary approaches; to promote
conceptual innovation and to provide a venue for
the entry of new perspectives.*
Submissions: as above

**610   African Journal in Conflict
        Resolution**
        ACCORD
        Private Bag X018
        Umhlanga Rocks 4320
Tel: +27-31-502 3908
Fax +27-31-502 4160
Email: info@accord.org.za
Web:
http://www.accord.org.za/ajcr/intro.htm
2000- Online ISSN 1562-6997 Ann
Subs: free
Eds: Jannie Malan, Jakes Gerwel
*Published by the African Centre for the
Constructive Resolution of Disputes (ACCORD),
an international civil-society organization
working throughout Africa to bring appropriate
African solutions to the challenges posed by
conflict on the continent. The journal aims to
promote African ideas, thought patterns, and
writing in the field of conflict resolution.*
Submissions: articles are in-depth and
academic in nature, while remaining
accessible to a wider audience.

**611   African Journal of Political
        Science**
        African Association of Political
        Science/Association africaine de
        science politique
        PO Box 13995
        The Tramshed 0126
        Pretoria
Tel: +27-12-343 0409 Fax: +27-12-344 3622
Email: program@aaps.org.za
Web: http://www.aaps.org.za/
1986- Print and online ISSN 1027-0353 2Yr
Subs: in Africa $30, elsewhere $40 inst $30
indiv (Full text access to articles which have

appeared in Volume 1, no. 2 December 1996 - onwards is available for those who become members of the Association)
Ed (Acting): Musa Abutudu,
Email: program@aaps.org.za
Book rev
Aims to provide a platform for African perspectives on issues of politics, the economy and society in Africa.
Submissions: contributions, in English or French, on political, social and economic developments in Africa yesterday, today and tomorrow.
AJOL
Afffil: → **African Association of Political Science (2750)**
Note: formerly published in Zimbabwe, now published from South Africa.

612   **African Security Review**
         Institute for Security Studies
         Bronkhorst Street
         Block C Brooklyn Court
         New Muckleneuk
         PO Box 1787 Brooklyn Square
         Pretoria 0075
Tel: +27-12-346 9500/2 Fax: +27-12-460 0998
Email: *iss@iss.co.za*
http://www.iss.co.za/Publications/Asrindex.html
1992- [previously published as the African Defence Review (1994) and the Southern African Defence Review (1992-1993)]Print and online ISSN n/a Qtly
Subs: in South Africa R140, elsewhere in Africa $32, rest of the world $48
Ed: Jakkie Cilliers et al
Email: JKC@iss.co.za
Book rev
Aims to provide a regular high-quality forum for the dissemination of research findings and information through the publication of research reports, policy papers and articles on security and related issues in sub-Saharan Africa.
H-Africa

613   **African Studies**
         Taylor & Francis Journals
         4 Park Square
         Milton Park
         Abingdon OX14 4RN
Tel: +44-(0)20-7017 6000
Fax: +44-(0)20-7017 6336
Email: tf.processing@tfinforma.com

Web:
http://www.tandf.co.uk/journals/carfax/00020184.html
In the US:
Taylor & Francis Journals (US)
325 Chestnut Street Suite 800
Philadelphia PA 19106
Tel: +1-215-625 8900 Fax: +1-215-625 8914
1921- Print and online ISSN 0002-0184
(E-ISSN 1469-2872) 2Yr
Subs: £172/$282 inst £42/$71 indiv
Ed: Editorial Committee, Clive Glaser *et al* (Editorial Committee), Department of History, University of the Witwatersrand, PO Wits 2050, Tel: +27-11-717 4313
Email: glaserc@social.wits.ac.za
With the transformations underway in southern African society and universities, African Studies *provides a forum for writing in which metropolitan concerns are transformed and recast in the light of indigenously generated ideas and debates. It also encourages dialogue between scholars writing in, and about, different countries in the South.*
Submissions: as above

614   **Africanus. Journal of Development Studies**
         Unisa Press
         University of South Africa
         PO Box 392
         Muckleneuk
         Pretoria 0003
Tel: +27-12-429 3081/429 2953
Fax: +27-12-426 4449
Email: unisa-press@unisa.ac.za or delpoa@unisa.ac.za (Subscriptions)
Web:
http://www.unisa.ac.za/default.asp?Cmd=ViewContent&ContentID=932
1970- Print and online (2000-)
ISSN 0304-615X 2Yr
Subs: in South Africa R30, elsewhere $10 available via → **SABINET Online (560)**
Ed: Linda Cornwell,
Email: CornwL@unisa.ac.za
An annual journal published for the Department of Development Studies of the University of South Africa. Publishes articles on development problems with special reference to the Third World and southern Africa, as well as politics and policy concerning intergroup relations.
Submissions: contributions should reflect practice (e.g. case studies dealing with practical aspects of development), and the application and interpretation of theory in the

Third World, particularly in the southern African context.

615   Agenda
PO Box 61163
Bishopsgate 4008
Tel: +27-31-304 7001 Fax: +27-31- 304 7018
Email: info@agenda.org.za or
subs@agenda.org.za (Subscriptions)
Web: http://www.agenda.org.za/
1987- Print and online ISSN 1013-0950 Qtly
Subs: various according to status, *see*
http://www.agenda.org.za/index.php?optio
n=com_wrapper&Itemid=110 (Online
subscribers receive the electronic version of
the journal, plus four print copies)
Ed: Gill Harper
Email: editor@agenda.org.za
A feminist project committed to giving women a forum, a voice and skills to articulate their needs and interests towards transforming unequal gender relations in South Africa.
Submissions: welcomes articles, interviews, biographical stories, briefings, poetry, cartoons, artwork or photographs that will enhance an understanding of gender issues.
H-Africa TOC
Note: for an online index to all articles published in Agenda to date *see*
http://www.agenda.org.za/images/stories/
index-upload.htm

616   Botsotso
Postnet Suite 136
Private Bag X2600
Houghton 2044
Tel: +27-11-487 2112 Fax: +27-11-648 7666
Email: artstudio@artslink.co.za
Web: http://www.111.co.za/botsotso.htm
1994- [?] Print and online ISSN n/a Ann
Subs: print: n/a online: free
Eds: Allan Kolski Horwitz, Isabella
Motadinyane *et al*
Botsotso is a grouping of poets, writers and artists who wish to both create art as well as to generate the means for its public exposure and appreciation. Botsotso Magazine is an independent cultural magazine that publishes poetry, cultural features, short stories, and artwork.
Submissions: as above

617   Chimurenga Magazine
PO Box 15117
Vlaeberg 8018
Tel/Fax: +27-21-426 4478
Email: chimurenga@panafrican.co.za
Web: http://www.chimurenga.co.za/
April 2002- Print and online (free online sample copy) [No ISSN] Qtly ["now appears whenever"]
Subs: in South Africa R300 inst R150 indiv, rest of Africa $70 inst $35 indiv, elsewhere $120 inst $70 indiv
Eds: Ntone Edjabe
A review of the arts, culture and politics from and about Africa and its diaspora, including poetry, interviews, reviews and visuals by writers, artists and photographers at the frontlines. Chimurenga has strong Pan African ambitions and reflects the pluri-lingual fabric of the continent. It orients itself not only to radical people that form its immediate target group, but also to the lay reader. Also offers an online forum.
Submissions: seeks unconventional essays, memoirs, reviews, interviews, poetry, short/long stories, photography, and art.

618   Conflict Trends
ACCORD
Private Bag X018
Umhlanga Rocks 4320
Tel: +27-31-502 3908 Fax +27-31-502 4160
Email: info@accord.org.za
Web:
http://www.accord.org.za/ct/intro.htm
1998- Online ISSN 1561-9818 Qtly
Subs: free
Ed: Vasu Gounden *et al* (Editorial collective)
Published by the African Centre for the Constructive Resolution of Disputes (ACCORD) an international civil-society organization working throughout Africa to bring appropriate African solutions to the challenges posed by conflict on the African continent. Offers at-a-glance overviews of both developments in conflicts, and positive steps towards renaissance on the continent of Africa. Submissions: in-depth articles focusing on conflict analysis.
AJOL

619   Critical Arts. A Journal of South-North Cultural and Media Studies
Centre for Culture, Communication
and Media Studies
University of KwaZulu-Natal
Durban 4041
Tel: +27-31-260 2505 Fax: +27-31-260 1519
Email: govends@ukzn.ac.za
Web:
http://www.ukzn.ac.za/ccms/publications/
criticalarts/criticalarts_default.asp

In Europe:
Intervention Press
Castenschioldsvej 7
8270 Højbjerg
Denmark
Fax: +45-86-275133
Email: interven@inet.uni-c.dk
1980- Print and online ISSN 0256-0046 2Yr
Subs: in southern Africa R70 inst R50 indiv,
elsewhere $80 inst $45 indiv
available online via ➔ SABINET Online
(560), EBSCO, and Gale
Ed: Keyan G. Tomaselli, Email:
tomasell@nu.ac.za, Managing ed:
Miranda Youg-Jahangeer, Email
Govends@nu.ac.za
Examines the relationship between texts and
contexts of media in the Third World, cultural
formations and popular forms of expressions. It
aims to create a space for an African and Third
World perspective of media (both formal and
informal) in culture and social theory.
Submissions: original and theoretically
cutting edge articles. Publishes the work of
established scholars but it also offers space for
new, young, and dynamic authors whose
emerging work is conceptually innovative
and critically challenging.
AJOL

620   **Current Writing**
       Programme of English Studies
       University of KwaZulu Natal
       Memorial Tower Building (MTB
       E106)
       Durban 4041
Tel: +27-31-260 2334 Fax: +27-31-260 1243
Email: cwriting@nu.ac.za
Web:
http://www.nu.ac.za/currentwriting/index.
html or
http://www.und.ac.za/und/english/curwrit
1989- Print and (partly) online
ISSN 1013-929X 2Yr
Subs: in southern Africa R75 inst R65 indiv,
UK and Europe £30 inst £24 indiv, North
America $57 inst $47 indiv
Eds: Duncan Brown, Michael Chapman,
Margaret Daymond, Johan Jacobs
Book rev
Focuses on literary and cultural debate around
contemporary and re-published texts from
southern Africa, and on the interpretation of
world texts from a southern African perspective.
Submissions: as above

621   **Development Southern Africa**
       Taylor & Francis Journals
       4 Park Square
       Milton Park
       Abingdon OX14 4RN
Tel: +44-(0)20-7017 6000
Fax: +44-(0)20-7017 6336
Email: tf.processing@tfinforma.com
Web:
http://www.tandf.co.uk/journals/titles/037
6835x.asp
In the US:
Taylor & Francis Journals (US)
325 Chestnut Street Suite 800
Philadelphia PA 19106
Tel: +1-215-625 8900 Fax: +1-215-625 8914
1983- Print 0376-835X 2Mon
Subs: £211/$349 inst, £82/$135 indiv
Ed: Caroline Kihato, Development Bank of
Southern Africa, South Africa
Submissions should be sent to: Rina
Roothman, Publications Co-ordinator,
Development Southern Africa, PO Box 1234,
Midrand, Halfway House 1685, South Africa,
Tel: +27-11 313 3972, Fax: +27-11-313 3533
The aim of the journal is to interrogate current
notions of development discourse, which are often
narrowly conceptualised, both locally and in
international academic writing. Through raising
difficult questions around who is included and
excluded in development discourse, it seeks to play
a role in ensuring that the voices of marginalized
populations are heard in ways that begin to inform
both the practice and theory of development.
Submissions: invites submissions that address
inter alia the following issues: gender, the
state, infrastructure, rural, urban, citizenship,
poverty, aid, governance, human rights,
culture, environment, NEPAD, globalisation,
conflict, social movements, democracy, and
how these intersect with development.
H-Africa TOC

622   **Ecquid Novi. Suid-Afrikaanse**
       Tydskrif vir Navorsing in die
       Joernalistie/South African
       Journal for Journalism Research
       School for Communication
       Studies
       Potchefstroom University
       Private Bag X6001
       Potchefstroom 2520
Tel: +27-18-299 1640 Fax: +27-18-299 1651
Email: ecquid-novi@puk.ac.za

Web:
http://journals.sabinet.co.za/ej/ejour_novi.h
tml (SABINET Online)
1980- Print and online ISSN 0256-0054 2Yr
Subs: in Africa R60 inst R30 indiv, elsewhere
$60 inst $30 indiv
online version available via ➔ SABINET
Online (560)
Ed: Arnold S de Beer,
Email: a.debeer@mweb.co.za
Book rev Book rev ed: Book Review Editor,
Ecquid Novi, PO Box 20603, Noordbrug 2522,
South Africa.
*A journal for journalism research on the African
continent. The journal's focus is on southern
Africa and Africa, but its academic interest and
scope is international. It aims to foster a better
understanding of journalism, media studies and
mass communication as research disciplines, and
to build links between these academic fields and
media professions.*
Submissions: as above; are published in
English, and occasionally in Afrikaans, Dutch
and German.
AJOL

623   **English in Africa**
        Institute for the Study of English in
        Africa
        Rhodes University
        6140 Grahamstown
Tel: +27-46-622 6093/+27-46-603 8565
Fax: +27-46-603 8566
Email: J.King@ru.ac.za
Web:
http://www.ru.ac.za/institutes/isea/eia/in
dex.htm or
http://www.journals.co.za/ej/ejour_iseaeng.
html (SABINET Online)
1974- Print and online ISSN 0376-8902 2Yr
Subs: print: in South Africa R70 inst R60
indiv, elsewhere in Southern Africa R95 inst
R85 indiv, outside Africa £21/$32
online version available via ➔ SABINET
Online (560)
Ed: Craig MacKenzie
Book rev Book rev ed: Greg Hacksley
*Provides a forum for the study of African
literature in English, publishing previously
unpublished or out-of-print primary material,
including articles and letters by writers of Africa.
The journal also publishes scholarly articles on
African writing in English with particular
emphasis on research in new or under-researched
areas in African literature*

Submissions: invites contributions, including
unsolicited reviews, on all aspects of English
writing in Africa, as well as on the other
literatures of Africa, including oral traditions.

624   **Feminist Africa**
        African Gender Institute
        Strengthening Gender & Women's
        Studies for Africa's Transformation
        GWS Africa Project
        University of Cape Town
        All Africa House Middle Campus
        Private Bag
        Rondebosch 7701
Tel: +27-21-650 2970 Fax: +27-21-685 2142
Email: info@feministafrica.org or
agi@humanities.uct.ac.za
Web: http://www.feministafrica.org/
2003- Print (limited distribution) and online
ISSN 1726-460X 2Yr
Subs: print, apply to publisher
online: free
Eds: Amina Mama, Jane Bennett,
Elaine Salo, *et al*
*Provides a forum for progressive, cutting-edge
gender research and feminist dialogue focused on
the continent. By prioritising intellectual rigour,
the journal seeks to challenge the technocratic
fragmentation resulting from donor-driven and
narrowly developmentalist work on gender in
Africa. It also encourages innovation in terms of
style and subject matter as well as design and
layout. It promotes dialogue by stimulating
experimentation as well as new ways of engaging
with text for readers.*
Submissions: in accordance with themes
specified in the calls for contributions.
Feminist Africa has a submissions policy
determined by the continental focus and
capacity-building aims of the AGI's GWS
Project. All contributions must register the
centrality of gender analysis and politics to
past, present and ongoing processes of social,
political and cultural change in Africa.

625   **Green Dragon. Poetry and Prose**
        Dye Hard Press
        PO Box 783211
        Sandton 2146
Tel/Fax: n/a
Email: dyehardpress@iafrica.com
2003- Print [No ISSN] Ann
Subs: R24.00
Ed: Gary Cummiskey
A magazine of contemporary poetry and

prose.
Submissions: No more than 8 poems; if
prose is submitted, no more than 3pieces of a
maximum of 5,000 words.

626   **Historia. Journaal van die Historiese
        Genootskap van Suid-
        Afrika/Journal of the Historical
        Association of South Africa**
        Historical Association of South Africa
        Department of History and Cultural
        History
        University of Pretoria
        0002 Pretoria
Tel: +27-12-420 2323 Fax: +27-12-420 2656
Email: vniekerk@libarts.up.ac.za
Web: n/a
1956- Print (back issues on CD-ROM) ISSN
0018-229X 2Yr
Subs: print, in South Africa R80, elsewhere
R180
available via ➔ **SABINET Online (560)**
Ed: Johann Tempelhoff, School of Basic
Sciences, Potchefstroom University for
Christian Higher Education, Vaal Triangle
Campus, PO Box 1174, 1900 Vanderbijlpark,
Tel: +27-16-910 3502 Fax: +27-16-910 3503,
Email: gskjwnt@puknet.puk.ac.za
Book rev Book rev ed: Geoff Allen
*The official journal of the Historical Association of
South Africa, aimed at promoting current research
in South African and African history, historical
method, philosophy, theory and historiography.*
Submissions: on aspects of South African
history, methodology, historiography as well
as reviews and review articles in either
Afrikaans or English.
Note: issues covering the years 1956 to
November 2001 are now available on CD-
ROM, price R370 in South Africa, R470
elsewhere
H-Africa TOC

627   **Indilinga. African Journal of
        Indigenous Knowledge Systems**
        Private Bag X10
        Isipingo 4110
Tel: +27-31-907 7000 ext 2034
Fax +27-31-907 3011
Email: nmkabela@pan.uzulu.ac.za or
nmkabela@hotmail.com
Web: http://www.indilinga.org.za or
http://www.ajol.info/journals/indilin
ga or

http://www.journals.co.za/ej/ejour_finj.htm
l (SABINET Online)
2002- Print and online ISSN 1683-0296
2Yr
Subs: South Africa and elsewhere in Africa
R100 inst, elsewhere $50 inst
online version available via **SABINET
Online ➔ (560)**
Ed: Queeneth N. Mkabela
Book rev
*Indilinga stands for the "circular orientation" of
indigenous African communities exhibited in their
material culture and behaviour. The journal is
motivated by the need for a dependable expression
for critical and analytical writing on issues related
to production, dissemination and recognition of
Indigenous Knowledge Systems (IKS).*
Submissions: the journal represents a variety
of cross disciplinary interests in ethno-
methodology and in qualitative methods.
Debates and contributions on methodology,
epistemology, ethics, gender, education,
science and technology, arts, food systems
and social-cultural issues are invited.
AJOL

628   **Kleio. Journal of the Department of
        History, University of South Africa**
        Unisa Press
        University of South Africa
        PO Box 392
        Muckleneuk
        Pretoria 0003
Tel: +27-12-429 3081/429 2953
Fax:+27-12-426 4449
Email: unisa-press@unisa.ac.za or
delpoa@unisa.ac.za (Subscriptions)
Web:
http://www.unisa.ac.za/default.asp?Cmd=V
iewContent&ContentID=937
1969- Print and online (1998-)
ISSN 0023-2084 Ann
Subs: in South Africa R30, elsewhere $30
Ed: Johannes du Bruyn
Book rev Book rev ed: Julie Pridmore
*Articles in the journal are wide-ranging and
not confined to South African history. It also
serves as a forum for the publication of
articles by honours and MA students on a
wide range of subjects such as political,
environmental and gender issues.*
Submissions: as above

629   Journal for the Study of Religion
Department of Religious Studies
University of Cape Town
Private Bag
Rondebosch 7701
Tel/Fax: n/a
Email: tayob@humanities.uct.ac.za
Web: http://www.ajol.info/journals/jsr
(AJOL)
1988- Print ISSN 1011-7601 2Yr
Subscription to JSR only
Subs: in South Africa R125 inst R 100 indiv,
elsewhere in Africa R125 inst R75/$20 indiv,
outside Africa $50 inst $40 indiv
Eds: Abdulkader Tayob, Email
tayob@humanities.uct.ac.za, David Chidester
*Published by the Association for the Study of
Religion in Southern Africa, the journal provides
a forum for scholarly contributions on topics of
contemporary significance in the academic study
of religion.*
Submissions: as above
AJOL

630   Journal of African Elections
The Electoral Institute of Southern
Africa
PO Box 740
Auckland Park 2006
Tel: + 27-11-482 5495 Fax: +27-11-482 6163
Email: info@eisa.org.za
Web:
http://www.eisa.org.za/EISA/publications/
pubjournals.htm or
http://www.journals.co.za/ej/ejour_eisa_jae
.html (SABINET online)
2001- Print ISSN 1609-4700 2Yr
Subs: R80
online version available via **SABINET
Online ➜ (560)**
Ed: Jackie Kalley,
Email: jkalley@eisa.org.za
*An interdisciplinary biannual publication of
research and writing in the human sciences, which
seeks to promote scholarly understanding of
electoral developments and democratic change in
Africa. The aim of the journal is to supply a forum
for academic specialists and electoral professionals
to develop jointly insights into the practice,
conduct, administration and outcomes of elections
held throughout Africa.*
Submissions: as above; covers electoral issues
in all parts of Africa.

631   Journal of Psychology in Africa
NISC Pty Ltd
PO Box 377
Grahamstown 6140
Tel: +27-46-622 9698 Fax: +27-46-622 9550
Email: journals@nisc.co.za
Web:
http://www.nisc.co.za/JournalHome/jpa/h
ome.htm
1990- Print and online ISSN 1433-0237 2Yr
Subs: in South Africa R550 inst R225 indiv,
elsewhere in Africa R650 inst R254 indiv,
outside Africa $275 inst $116
Ed: Elias Mpofu, Department of Counsellor
Education, Counselling Psychology and
Rehabilitation Services, Pennsylvania State
University, 327 CEDAR Building, University
Park, PA 16802-3110, USA, Tel: +1-814-863
2411 Fax: +1-814-863 7750, Email:
exm31@psu.edu; Publication Managing ed:
Georgina Jones, (at NISC address above)
Email: editor@nisc.co.za
Book rev Book review ed: Tammy Shefer,
University of the Western Cape, South Africa
*A forum for dissemination and utilisation of
findings from psychological research in Africa and
related regions needs in the context of
development. Special emphasis is placed on the
consideration of African, African-American,
Asian, Caribbean, and Hispanic-Latino realities
and problems.*
Submissions: publishes original articles,
review articles, book reviews, commentaries,
special issues, case analyses, reports, special
announcements, etc. Contributions should
attempt a synthesis of emic and etic
methodologies and applications.
AJOL

**632   Language Matters: Studies in the
Languages of Southern Africa**
Department of Linguistics
University of South Africa
Theo van Wijk Building 9-76
Muckleneuk Hill
PO Box 392
Pretoria 0003
Tel: + 27-12-429 6687
Email: vzweeha@unisa.ac.za
Web:
http://www.journals.co.za/ej/ejour_langma
t.html
1969- Print and online ISSN 0256-5986 Ann
Subs: n/a

online version available via ➜ **SABINET Online (560)**
Ed: Lawrie Barnes, Email barnela@unisa.ac.za
Seeks to promote the dissemination of ideas, points of view, teaching strategies and research on different aspects of all the languages of southern Africa. The journal's primary focus is on issues related to multilingualism in the southern African context, and it aims to provide a forum for discussion on the whole spectrum of language usage and debate in southern Africa.
Submissions: as above

633   Lexikos
Buro van die WAT/Bureau of the WAT
PO Box 245
115 Banghoek Road
Stellenbosch 7599
Tel: +27-21-887 3113 Fax: +27-21-883 9492
Email: wat@sun.ac.za
Web:
http://www.up.ac.za/academic/libarts/afril ang/lexikos.htm
1991- Print ISSN 1684-4904
Ann
Subs: R360 inst, R190 indiv
Ed: W.F. Botha
A journal for lexicographic specialists, which also serves as the official mouthpiece of the African Association for Lexicography (AFRILEX)--an acronym for "lexicography in and for Africa". It is intended to stimulate lexicographical discourse in Africa and offers both research and contemplate articles, reports about new dictionary projects (including online dictionary projects), review articles, and book reviews.
Submissions: contributions are invited that deal with pure lexicography or with the intersection between lexicography on the one hand and related fields such as linguistics, general linguistics, computer science and management on the other hand
Note: an index of articles in all past issues is available at
http://www.sun.ac.za/wat/Engelse%20Web werf/Publications/Lexikos/lexindeks2.htm

634   Literator: Journal of Literary Criticism, Comparative Linguistics and Literary Studies/Tydskrif vir besondere en vergelykende taal- en literatuurstudie
Buro vir Wetenskaplike
Tydskrifte/Bureau for Scholarly

Journals
Private Bag X 6001
Potchefstroom 2520
Tel: +27-18-299 4082 Fax: +27-18-299 4084
Email: bwtes@puknet.puk.ac.za
Web: http://www.puk.ac.za/literator/
1980- Print and online ISSN 0258-2279 3Yr
Subs: print R190/$40
online version available via ➜ **SABINET Online (560)**
http://www.journals.co.za/ej/ejour_literat.h tml
Ed: H.M. Viljoen, Tel: +27-18-299 4081, Email: bwtscl@puknet.puk.ac.za
A journal of national and comparative linguistics and literature, publishing research articles on specific languages and specific literatures (like Afrikaans, English or Tswana), but also articles that compare different languages and literatures and other cultural phenomena across language and cultural boundaries.
Submissions: articles on special and comparative language and literary studies, both theoretical and applied.

635   New Coin Poetry
Institute for the Study of English in Africa
Rhodes University
PO Box 94
6140 Grahamstown
Tel: +27-46-622 6093 Fax: +27-46-603 8566
Email: J.King@ru.ac.za
Web:
http://www.ru.ac.za/institutes/isea/NewC oin/
1965- Print and online ISSN 0028-4459 2Yr
Subs: print: in South Africa R50, elsewhere in Africa R85, outside Africa $30/£17 (airmail)
online version available via ➜ **SABINET Online (560)**
http://www.journals.co.za/ej/ejour_iseacoin .html
Ed: Alan Finlay
Book rev
Publishes adventurous and outstanding poetry, and poetry-related reviews, commentary, and interviews. The journal places special emphasis on evolving forms and experimental use of the English language in poetry in the South African context. In this sense it has traced the most exciting trends and currents in contemporary poetry in South Africa for a decade or more.
Submissions: as above

636   New Contrast
PO Box 44844
Claremont 7735
Tel/Fax: n/a
Email: infofo@newcontrast.org (General
enquiries/Subscriptions)
submissions@newcontrast.org (Submissions)
Web: http://www.newcontrast.org/
1960- 1989 (as *Contrast*) 1990- (as *New
Contrast*, and merged with *Upstream*) Print
ISSN 0589-574X Qtly
Subs: in South Africa & SADEC countries
R150, in UK £35, North America and
elsewhere $65
Ed: Tom Eaton
Book rev
*A non-profit publication with a mandate to find
the best writing available in South Africa. The list
of contributors who have been published in*
Contrast *and* New Contrast *is a virtual who's
who of modern South African fiction and poetry,
all helping to set the standard for literary
excellence. Today the journal continues to unearth
new talent--writers who will develop into the stars
of the next generation.*
Submissions: unless a particular theme has
been advertised for a forthcoming issue, *New
Contrast* considers all genre and forms of
prose and poetry.

**637   Politeia. Journal for the Political
        Sciences**
Unisa Press
University of South Africa
PO Box 392
Muckleneuk
Pretoria 0003
Tel: +27-12-429 3081/429 2953
Fax: +27-12-426 4449
Email: unisa-press@unisa.ac.za or
delpoa@unisa.ac.za (Subscriptions)
Web:
http://www.unisa.ac.za/Default.asp?Cmd=
ViewContent&ContentID=941
or
http://www.unisa.ac.za/default.asp?Cmd=V
iewContent&ContentID=1625
1981- Print and online ISSN 0256-8845
3Yr
Subs: in South Africa R120 inst, R90 indiv,
elsewhere $100 inst $40 indiv
Ed: Clive Napier, Department of Political
Sciences, University of South Africa, PO Box
392, Unisa 0003, South Africa.
Tel: +27-12-429 6564

Email: napiecj@unisa.ac.za
Book rev Book review eds: Sarita Kant *et al*
*Promotes of the study of, and interest in, the
political sciences and the science of public
administration.*
Submissions: articles encompass a wide
spectrum of views and issues relating to
political science and public administration,
international politics, strategic studies, and
municipal government and administration.
H-Africa TOC

**638   Politikon. South African Journal of
        Political Studies**
Taylor & Francis Journals
4 Park Square
Milton Park
Abingdon OX14 4RN
UK
Tel: +44-(0)20-7017 6000
Fax: +44-(0)20-7017 6336
Email: tf.processing@tfinforma.com
Web:
http://www.tandf.co.uk/journals/carfax/02
589346.html
In the US:
Taylor & Francis Journals (US)
325 Chestnut Street Suite 800
Philadelphia PA 19106
Tel: +1-215-625 8900 Fax: +1-215-625 8914
1974- Print and online (2000-)
ISSN 0258-9346 2Yr
Subs: £151/$251 inst £36/$62 indiv
Ed: Stephen Louw, Department of Political
Studies, University of the Witwatersrand,
Private Bag 3, Wits 2050, South Africa
Book rev Book rev ed: Meenal Shrivastava,
Department of International Relations,
University of the Witwatersrand, PO Wits,
Private Bag 3, 2050, South Africa, Email:
shrivasta@social.wits.ac.za
Politikon, *the official journal of the South African
Association of Political Studies, focuses primarily
on South African politics, but not exclusively so.
In the last few years special issues have focused on
women and politics in South Africa, and the South
African election of 1999. Recent articles have
looked at the negotiated transition from apartheid
to democracy, aspects of identity politics in post-
apartheid South Africa, and issues of democratic
consolidation.*
Submissions: as above

639   Postamble
Centre for African Studies
University of Cape Town
Private Bag
Rondebosch, 7701
Cape Town
Tel: +27-21-650 2338 Fax: +27-21-689 7560
Email: amble@humanities.uct.ac.za
http://www.africanstudies.uct.ac.za/postam
ble/
2004- Online [No ISSN] 2Yr
Subs: free
Ed: Monique Whitaker
*A postgraduate journal of the Faculty of
Humanities located in the Centre for African
Studies, Postamble is committed to featuring
original post graduate student work of a high
academic standard which is of value to the
promotion of multi-disciplinary study of Africa
within the university environment.*
Submissions: submissions cover a wide range
of humanities, arts and social sciences topics
involving the study of public culture in
Africa. The journal encourages the
exploration of alternative forms of research
presentation that may include creative
writing, visual essays, the use of digital film
and sound, and digital photography
favouring works of an academic nature.

640   Social Dynamics
Centre for African Studies
Oppenheimer Building
University of Cape Town
Private Bag
Rondebosch 7701
Tel: +27-21-650 2308 Fax: +27-21-686 1505
Email africas@humanities.uct.ac.za
Web:
http://web.uct.ac.za/depts/cas/default.php
?pageName=social.php
1975- Print (recent issues partly online) ISSN
0253-3952 2Yr
Subs: in South Africa R180 inst R95 indiv,
elsewhere £100/$150 inst £25/$40 indiv
Ed: Jeremy Seekings, Email:
seekings@humanities.uct.ac.za; manuscripts
to Charmaine McBride, Social Dynamics,
Centre for African Studies, University of Cape
Town, Rondebosch 7701, Email:
cmcbride@humanities.uct.ac.za
Book rev
*An inter-disciplinary journal for African studies
that aims to problematize the ways in which
Africa has hitherto been studied through an inter-*
*disciplinary and comparative study of Africa. It
hopes to be a location for those who aim at
understanding the South African (or any other
regional) experience as part of the wider African
experience, without denying its specificity, but
also without the presumption of a South African
exceptionalism.*
Submissions: publishes rather more special
issues than general issues. Recent special
issues included 'AIDS and Society', 'Welfare
Reform' and an issue in commemoration of
the historian Leroy Vail.
H-Africa TOC
Note: for table of contents of all past issues *see*
http://web.uct.ac.za/depts/cas/pub2.html

641   South African Historical Journal
Unisa Press
PO Box 392
Muckleneuk
Pretoria 0003
Tel: +27-12-429 2953 Fax +27-12-429 3221
Email: delpoa@unisa.ac.za or
barnards@hum.uovs.ac.za
Web:
http://www.unisa.ac.za/default.asp?Cmd=V
iewContent&ContentID=930 or
http://web.uct.ac.za/depts/history/sahs/sa
hj.htm
1969- Print ISSN 0258-2473 2Yr
Subs: in South Africa R140 inst R120 indiv,
elsewhere $80 inst $60 indiv
available via ➔ **SABINET Online (560)**
Ed: John Lambert, Department of History, PO
Box 392, Unisa 0003,
Email: lambej@unisa.ac.za
*Published bi-annually by the South African
Historical Society, the journal is devoted to
articles on southern African history based on
original research, historiographical overviews,
critical reviews and review articles.*
Submissions: as above; the editorial team
also solicits articles for special features.
Recent issues have included features on
gender and history; the South African war;
the Internet; secrecy, lies and history; and
heritage in South Africa.
H-Africa TOC

**642   South African Journal of
        Agricultural Extension**
Dept LEVLO
University of Pretoria
Pretoria 0002
Tel: +27-12-420 3246 Fax +27-12-420 3247
Email: jcoertse@postino.up.ac.za

Web: http://www.ajol.info/journals/sajae
(AJOL)
1971- Print and online ISSN 0301-603X Ann
Subs: print: in southern Africa R100,
elsewhere $20;
online version available via → SABINET
Online (560)
http://www.journals.co.za/ej/ejour_agri.ht
ml
Ed: Fanie Terblanché
*Published by the South African Society for
Agricultural Extension, the journal aims to
advance and apply the science of extension and of
rural development as a discipline by stimulating
thought, study, research, discussion and the
publication and exchange of knowledge both
nationally and internationally.*
Submissions: original scientific contributions
relating to agricultural extension will be
considered for publication. Because of the
multi-disciplinary nature of agricultural
extension, contributions from other learned
disciplines can also be considered for
publication on condition that the articles
under consideration have sufficient bearing
on agricultural extension.
AJOL

643   **South African Journal of Cultural
        History/Suid-Afrikaanse Tydskrif
        vir Kultuurgeskiedenis**
        PO Box 11403
        0028 Hatfield
Tel: +27-12-346 0168 Fax: +27-12-346 8847
Email: Antonvv@tshwane.gov.za
1986- Print and online ISSN 1011-3053 2r
Subs: print: R60
online version available via → SABINET
Online (560)
http://www.journals.co.za/ej/ejour_culture.
html
Ed: Anton van Vollenhoven
Book rev
*Offers scientifically researched articles on of
Cultural historical significance.*
Submissions: publishes articles, review
articles and short communications in English
and Afrikaans; articles should contribute to
cultural history, including folk history.
H-Africa TOC

644   **South African Journal of Economic
        History**
        Economic History Society of Southern
        Africa
        Department of Economics

University of South Africa
PO Box 392
Unisa 0003
Fax: +27-12-429 3433
Email: inggsej@unisa.ac.za
http://home.intekom.com/joni/EHSOC.HT
M
1986- Print ISSN 1011-3436 2Yr
Subs: in South Africa R60, elsewhere R160
Eds: Stuart Jones and Jon Inggs
Book rev Book rev ed: Grietjie Verhoef
*The journal of the Economic History Society of
Southern Africa. Promotes the study of and
interest in economic and social history. Some
issues are devoted to specific topics.*
Submissions: on any economic or social
history topic, not restricted to southern Africa
only.
H-Africa TOC
Note: for table of contents of all issues
published to 1995 *see*
http://home.intekom.com/joni/VOL1-
19.HTM

645   **South African Journal of Higher
        Education**
        PO Box 392
        UNISA 0003
Tel: +27–12-429 4549 Fax: +27-12-429 4919
Email: higgsp@unisa.ac.za
Web: http://www.ajol.info/journals/sajhe
(AJOL)
1986- Print and online ISSN 1011-3487 3Yr
Subs: print: in southern Africa R150,
elsewhere $100
online version available via → SABINET
Online (560)
http://www.journals.co.za/ej/ejour_high.ht
ml
Ed: Philip Higgs, Email: higgsp@unisa.ac.za
*Published for the South African Association for
Research and Development in Higher Education,
the journal is a medium for articles of interest to
researchers and practitioners in higher education,
and provides a focal point for the publication of
educational research from throughout the world.
The journal is interdisciplinary in approach and
its purpose is to provide institutions of higher
education and professional readers with scholarly
information on major innovations in higher
education, research projects and trends.*
Submissions: articles in English or Afrikaans
are invited for consideration; the journal
publishes original contributions within any
field of higher education.
AJOL

646   South African Journal of International Affairs
Jan Smuts House East Campus
University of the Witwatersrand
PO Box 31596
Braamfontein 2017
Tel: +27-11-339 2021 Fax: +27-11-339 2154
Email: saiiagen@global.co.za
Web:
http://www.saiia.org.za/modules.php?op=
modload&name=News&file=article&sid=241
1993- Print ISSN 1022-0461 2Yr
Subs: in South Africa R250 inst 150 indiv, R75 stud, elsewhere $110 inst $69 indiv, $40 stud online available via ➔ **SABINET Online (560)**
Ed: Greg Mills
Book rev Book rev ed: Beverly Peters
The journal of the South African Institute of International Affairs, an independent NGO that aims to promote a wider and more informed understanding of international issues among South Africans, and which seeks to educate, inform and facilitate contact between people concerned with South Africa's place in the world. The journal covers international affairs, development, economics, and politics.
Submissions: while some contributions are specifically commissioned to fit the general themes of certain issues, the editors welcome unsolicited articles and briefings.
H-Africa TOC

647   Southern African Linguistics and Applied Languages Journal
NISC SA
22 Somerset Street
PO Box 377
Grahamstown 6140
Tel: +27-46-622 9698 Fax: +27-46-622 9550
Email: publishing@nisc.co.za
Web:
http://www.nisc.co.za/journals?id=9&PHPS
ESSID=13dcc61bd51424bfd18a803005d98d71
1983- Print ISSN 1607-3614 Qtly
Subs: in South Africa R399 inst R228 indiv, SADC countries (airmail) R399 inst R280 indiv, elsewhere (airmail) $220 inst $145 indiv
Ed: Marné Pienaar, Department of Linguistics and Literary Theory, University of Johannesburg, PO Box 524, Auckland Park 2006, Email: mpi@lw.rau.ac.za
Book Rev Book rev ed: Gerhard van Huyssteen, School of Languages, Potchefsroom University for CHE, Private

Bag X6000, Potchefstroom 2520, Email: afngbvh@puknet.puk.ac.za
The official combined journal of the Linguistics Society of Southern Africa and the Southern African Applied Linguistics Association. It publishes articles on a wide range of linguistic topics and acts as a forum for research into all the languages of southern Africa, including English and Afrikaans.
Submissions: contributions are welcomed on any of the core areas of linguistics, both theoretical (e.g. syntax, phonology, semantics) and applied (e.g. sociolinguistic topics, language teaching, and language policy). Contributions may be in any of the 11 official languages of South Africa.
AJOL

648   South African Theatre Journal
PO Box 6054
Uniedal 7612
Tel: +27-21-808 3216 Fax: +27-21-887 6566
Email: satj@sun.ac.za
Web:
http://academic.sun.ac.za/drama/English/
Centre/SATJ/satj.htm
2001- Print and online ISSN 1013-7548 Ann
Subs: print: in South Africa R60 inst R40 indiv, elsewhere $60 inst $40 indiv
online version available via ➔ **SABINET Online (560)**
http://www.journals.co.za/ej/ejour_theatre.html
Ed: Temple Haupfleisch
Book rev
Published by the Centre for Theatre and Performance Studies at the University of Stellenbosch, the journal provides a forum for the academic discussion of theatre and performance studies and the performing arts, especially as they manifest themselves in southern Africa. The publication features articles on the history, theory and practice of the performing arts, as well as the methodology of theatre research. It also contains theatre reports.
Submissions: the journal aims to foster multi- and inter-disciplinary study in the performing arts, and contributions are invited are invited from all writers interested in the subject, irrespective of their specific disciplines.
Note: an index to vol. 1 (1987) to vol. 15 (2001) can be freely accessed at http://academic.sun.ac.za/drama/English/
Centre/SATJ/index.htm

**649   Studies in Economics and
Econometrics**
Bureau for Economic Research
Private Bag 5050
Stellenbosch 7599
Tel: +27-21-887 2810 Fax: +27-21-883 9225
Email: hhman@ber.sun.ac.za
Web: http://www.ber.sun.ac.za/
1976- Print and online ISSN 0379–6205 3Yr
Subs: print: in South Africa R180, elsewhere
$40
online version available via ➔ **SABINET
Online (560)**
http://www.journals.co.za/ej/ejour_bersee.
html
Eds: Ben W. Smit, Email: bws@ber.sun.ac.za;
Murray Pellissier, Email: gmp@ber.sun.ac.za;
Correspondence and submissions to (Mrs) H.
Manefeldt, Email: hhman@ber.sun.ac.za
*A combined product of the Bureau of Economic
Research and the Graduate School of Business at
the University of Stellenbosch,* Studies in
Economics and Econometrics *is an
international journal publishing articles in the
field of study of economics, in the widest sense of
the word.*
Submissions: as above
AJOL

650   Tinabantu
Centre of Advanced Studies for
African Society (CASAS)
PO Box 352
Plumstead 7800
Fax +27-21-762 4452
Email: casas@casas.co.za
Web: http://www.casas.co.za/tinabantu.htm
2002- Print [No ISSN] 2Yr
Web:
Subs: in Africa, Asia, South America,
Caribbean R120/£12/$20, elsewhere £15/$25
Ed: Kwesi Kwaa Prah,
Email: kkprah@casas.co.za
Book rev
*Serves as a forum for the consideration of diverse
views, ideas and opinions reflecting differing
philosophical and political dispositions, but is
committed to the maintenance of high intellectual
standards and recognition of the historical and
cultural unity of Africa and its diaspora.*
Submissions: as above, papers in English,
French and in major African languages will
be considered for publication.

**651   Track Two. Constructive
Approaches to Community and
Political Conflict**
Centre for Conflict Resolution
UCT Hiddingh Campus
31-37 Orange Street
PO Box 1228
Cape Town 8000
Tel: +27-21-422 2512 Fax: +27-21-422 2622
Email: mailbox@ccr.uct.ac.za
Web:
http://ccrweb.ccr.uct.ac.za/index.php?id=9
or
http://www.journals.co.za/ej/ejour_track2.h
tml
1991- Print and (text only) online
ISSN 1019-7435 Qtly
Subs: print: in Africa R80 inst R60 stud,
elsewhere $50/£50 inst $35/£20 stud; online:
free (1996 onwards only)
available via ➔ **SABINET Online (560)**
Ed: Roshila Nair,
Email: rnair@ccr.uct.ac.za
*Quarterly publication of the Centre for Conflict
Resolution to promote innovative and constructive
approaches to community and political conflict as
an alternative to traditional adversarial tactics.
The term 'track two' refers to informal, unofficial
interaction outside the formal governmental power
structures, providing the means for historically
conflicting groups to improve communication and
gain a better understanding of each other's point
of view. Articles focus on conflicts and conflict
management in Africa.*
Submissions: articles fostering CCR's mission:
to contribute to a sustainable peace in South
Africa and other African countries by
promoting constructive, creative and cooperative approaches to the resolution of
conflict and the reduction of violence. Writers
from the African continent are prioritized.

652   Transformation
Programme of Economic History
University of Natal
Durban 4041
Tel: +27-31-260 1111 Fax: +27-31-260 2214
(University of Natal main tel/fax numbers)
Email: transform@nu.ac.za
Web:
http://www.transformation.und.ac.za/
available online, free of-charge, as part
of the ➔ **African e-Journals Project
(553)** or also at
http://muse.jhu.edu/journals/trn/
1987- Print and (partly) online

ISSN 0258-7696 (E-ISSN: 1726-1368) Qtly
Subs: print, in southern Africa R240 inst
R120 indiv, UK/Europe, £50 inst £40
indiv, North America $60 inst $75 indiv;
online, free
Eds: John Daniel *et al*, Programme of
Economic History, University of Natal,
Durban 4041, Email: transform@nu.ac.za
Serves as a forum for analysis and debate about
South African society in transition, as well as the
surrounding region, and the global context that
affects southern African developments. The
primary focus of the journal is on contemporary
society.
Submissions: papers that are academically
rigorous but that also clarify the implications
for social transformation of the issues
discussed.
Note: for an index to all articles published to
date *see*
http://www.transformation.und.ac.za/previ
ous_issues.htm#INDEX%20OF%20PAPERS%
20PUBLISHED%20IN%20TRANSFORMATI
ON
H-Africa TOC

Tanzania

653 Tanzania Zamani
Department of History
University of Dar es Salaam
PO ox 35050
Dar es Salaam
Tel: +255-22-241 0500/9
Fax: +255-22-241 0078/241 0514 (mark for
attn. Department of History)
Web: http://fass.udsm.ac.tz/TZZamani.htm
or
http://www.yale.edu/swahili/tsa/zamani.h
tml
in the US order from:
Gregory H. Maddox
Department of History, Geography &
Economics, Texas Southern University
3100 Cleburne, Houston TX 77004
1996- Print 0039-9507 2Yr
Subs: in Tanzania Tshs.4,000, elsewhere
$20/£12 inst $15/£8 indiv
Ed: Yusufu Q Lawi
The journal of the Historical Association of
Tanzania, covering the history and archaeology of
Tanzania, East Africa and Africa in general.
Submissions: as above, also welcomes
submissions of comparative and theoretical

articles on social science subjects taught in
Tanzanian schools and colleges. Emphasis
should be placed on historical knowledge
from research in the field, theoretical
discussions and clarifications.
Note: irregularly published, unable to verify
current availability.

Uganda

654 Eastern Africa Journal of Rural
Development
Department of Agricultural
Economics & Agribusiness
Makerere University
PO Box 7062
Kampala
Tel: + 256-41-531152 Fax +256-41-531641
Email: agecon@infocom.co.ug
Web: http://www.ajol.info/journals/eajrd
1985- Print ISSN 0377-7103 2Yr
Subs: in Africa $50 inst $30 indiv, elsewhere
$90 inst $75 indiv
Ed: Imelda Nalukenge, Email:
nalukenge@agric.mak.ac.ug
Book rev
Jointly published by the Ugandan Agricultural
Economics Association and the Department of
Agricultural Economics and Agribusiness at
Makerere University, the journal publishes
theoretical and empirical papers in the areas of
economics, agricultural economics, agribusiness,
agricultural extension education, rural sociology
and development, natural resources, and
environment studies.
Submissions: as above; while the primary
focus of the journal is eastern Africa, articles
originating from the rest of the world are
encouraged. Although the general orientation
of the journal is rural development,
interdisciplinary papers by researchers in
other closely related fields are welcomed.
AJOL

Zambia

→ **Quest. An African Journal of**
Philosophy/Revue Africaine de Philosophie
see under Netherlands, entry **719**

Zimbabwe

655   African Film & TV Magazine
Z Promotions Pvt Ltd
PO Box 6109
Harare
Tel: +263-4-726795 Fax: +263-4-726796
Email: info@africafilmtv.com
Web: http://www.africafilmtv.com
Published by:
Furco Ltd, 10 Jewry Street, Winchester,
SO23 8RZ, UK
Tel: +263-4-726795 Fax: +263-4-726796
Email: subs@africafilmtv.com
1994- Print [No ISSN] Qtly
Subs: various subscription packages are
offered, see Web site
Ed: Russell Honeyman, Email:
russellll@africafilmtv.com
An international journal of the moving image in
Africa: broadcasting, film and TV production,
distribution, media freedom & legislation,
investment; in Africa and globally.
Note: also publishes an annual *Africa*
Film & TV Yearbook/ Directory. Extracts
from the 2004 edition can be freely
accessed online at
http://www.africafilmtv.com/pages/archive
/yearbooks/af2004.pdf

656   Journal of Social Development in
Africa
PB 66022
Kopje
Harare
Tel: +263-4-751815 Fax: +263-4-751903
Email: zimreview@bigpond.com
Web: tables of contents and abstracts
are now available on Extenza
http://www.extenza-eps.com/WDG/loi/jall
1986- Print and online [from 2003] ISSN 1012-
1080 [E-ISSN 1726-3700] 2Yr
Subs: in Zimbabwe Z$300, developing world
$35, elsewhere $65 (airmail)
Ed: Edwin Kaseke
Email: sswprinc@samara.co.zw
Book rev
Critical analyses of social development issues as
they affect the poor and marginalized in African
societies. Seeks to enhance understanding of the
social development processes that contribute to the
planning and implementation of appropriate
intervention strategies at different levels.

Submissions: social development issues as
above, cross-disciplinarian.
AJOL

657   Moto Magazine
PO Box 890
Gweru
Tel: +263-54-28194 Fax: +263-54-21991
Web:
http://www.mambopress.co.zw/moto.php
Email: mambopress@telco.co.zw
1982- Print ISSN n/a Mon
Subs: see Web site (subs rates not
downloadable as at 07/11/05)
Ed: n/a
Long-established popular news magazine
that seeks to address economic, social,
political, cultural and religious issues. It
combines this with a consistent aspiration to
defend human rights and champion social justice.
Note: irregularly published, unable to verify
current availability.

658   Safere. Southern African Feminist
Review
SAPES Trust
2-6 Deary Avenue
Belgravia
PO Box MP 111
Mount Pleasant
Harare
Tel: +263-4-252962/3/5
Fax: 263-4-252964
Email: info@sapes.org.zw
Web: http://www.sapes.co.zw/index.htm
1995- Print ISSN 1024-9451 2Yr
Subs: in Zimbabwe Z$200, in Africa $45,
elsewhere $55
Ed: Gender Division, SAPES/SARIPS, 4
Deary Street, PO Box MP111, Mount Pleasant,
Harare,
Email: Administrator@sarips.co.zw
Book rev
Provides women with a writing platform that is
feminist in content and orientation, as well as
acting as a facilitator for African women to
express their ideas and interests through a
medium that is supportive and encouraging of
feminist opinions and positions.
Submissions: as above
AJOL
Note: irregularly published, unable to verify
current availability.

659 **Southern African Political and Economic Monthly**
SAPES Trust
2-6 Deary Avenue
Belgravia
PO Box MP 111
Mount Pleasant
Harare
Tel: +263-4-252962/3/5
Fax: 263-4-252964
Email: info@sapes.org.zw
Web: http://www.sapes.co.zw/index.htm
1987- Print ISSN n/a Mon
Subs: in Africa $120, elsewhere $160
Ed: Ibbo Mandaza (Ed.-in-chief), Email ibbo@sapes.org.zw ;
Allan Mushonga (Managing), Email: allan@sapes.org.zw
Book rev Book rev ed: Khabele Matlosa, Email: khabele@sapes.org.zw
Focuses on debate and analysis of political, economic and social developments, mainly in southern Africa. Contains comment, news briefs, feature articles, reviews, debates and viewpoints. Each issue has an overall cover story, and also includes an article on world issues.
Submissions: articles which fit the above guidelines and which focus on current political/economic issues in the southern African region.
Note: irregularly published, unable to verify current availability.

660 **Zambezia. The Journal of Humanities of the University of Zimbabwe**
University of Zimbabwe Publications
PO Box MP 203 Mount Pleasant
Harare
Tel: +263-4-303211, ext 1236/1662
Fax: +263-4-333407
Email: uzpub@admin.uz.ac.zw
1969- Print ISSN 0379-0622 2Yr
Subs: £20
Ed: Alois S. Mlambo
An interdisciplinary journal with a focus on the humanities in Zimbabwe and southern Africa.
Submissions: as above
AJOL
Note: irregularly published, last issue published vol. 30, no. 2, 2003.

ASIA

China

661 **West Asia and Africa**
PO Box 1120
Beijing 100007
Tel: +86-10-6403 9151/6403 9170
Fax: +86-10-6403 5718
Email: iwaas@public.fhnet.cn.net (General enquiries) or
panrx@isc.cass.net.cn (Administrator)
Web:
http://www.cass.cn/xiyafei/en/Publications/periodical.asp
1980- Print (English abstracts online) ISSN 1002-7122 6Yr
Subs: outside China ¥51/$6 (plus airmail postage)
Ed: Yang Guang,
Email: yangguang@cass.org.cn or waaa_2000@yahoo.com
Published bimonthly under the auspices of the → **Institute of West Asian and African Studies (1879)**, *Chinese Academy of Social Sciences, with articles primarily focusing on politics, economy and international relations concerning Africa and the Middle East. Since it started publication in 1980, the Journal has been the main forum for Chinese scholars engaged in study of Africa and the Middle East, and also provides a window for the Chinese government and Chinese enterprises to understand the issues in the two areas.*
Submissions: articles welcomed from all parts of the world. Articles should be in English, French or Arabic. The Journal is published in Chinese with English abstracts.

India

662 **Sephis**
c/o Samita Sen
Department of History
Calcutta University Alipore Campus
1 Reformatory Street
Kolkata 700 019 India
Email: sensamita@yahoo.co.uk
Web: http://www.sephis.org/htm/e-zine.htm
2004- Online [No E-ISSN] Qtly
Subs: free
Eds: Samita Sen (India), Email: sensamita@yahoo.co.uk

Shamil Jeppie (South Africa),
Email: sjeppie@humanities.uct.ac.za
Book rev
An interdisciplinary online magazine
dedicated to south-south exchange and to provide
a platform for scholars, researchers and students
based in countries of the south to engage in
conversations about their many visions of
development and history. The journal's focus is
both contemporary and historical events and
processes.
Submissions: articles on historical and
contemporary issues in "South" countries;
discussions of historical sources--written, oral
or visual. Contributors may focus on a single
source or a body of sources.

AUSTRALASIA & PACIFIC

Australia

663   The Australasian Review of
        African Studies
        c/o Tanya Lyons
        Globalisation Program
        Flinders University
        GPO Box 2100
        Adelaide SA 5001
Tel: +61-8-8201 3588
Email: tanya.lyons@flinders.edu.au
Email: hware@une.edu.au
Web:
http://www.ssn.flinders.edu.au/global/afsa
ap/publications/review.htm
1978- Print ISSN 1447-8420 2Yr
Subs: free to members of the African Studies
Association of Australasia & the Pacific;
others (same rates as membership fee) A$55
inst/indiv, A$15 stud
Ed: Helen Ware, School of Professional
Development and Leadership,
The University of New England, Armidale
NSW 2351, Australia
Tel: +61-2-6773 2442,
Email: hware@une.edu.au
Book rev Book rev ed: Jeremy Martens,
History Department, University of Western
Australia,
Email:
jmartens@arts.uwa.edu.au
The journal aims to contribute to a better
understanding of Africa in Australasia and the
western Pacific. It publishes both scholarly and

more generalist articles that provide authoritative,
informed, critical material that is both interesting
and readable on Africa and African affairs.
Submissions: the journal is inter-disciplinary
in scope and will consider articles across the
broad range of the humanities and social
sciences. Articles that explore the historical
context within which contemporary African
issues have to be situated are particularly
welcome. Short notes on contemporary
African affairs, research projects/reports,
professional involvement in Africa, etc. are
also welcome.
Affil: ➜ African Studies Association of
Australia and the Pacific (2754)

664   Mot Pluriels et Grands Themes de
        Notre Temps. Revue
        Electronique de Lettres à Caractère
        International
        c/o Jean-Marie Volet, Editor
        The University of Western Australia
        School of European Languages
        Department of French Studies
        Nedlands 6907
Tel/Fax: n/a
Email: jvolet@cyllene.uwa.edu.au
Web:
http://www.arts.uwa.edu.au/MotsPluriels/
MP.html
1996- Online ISSN 1327-6220 3Yr
Subs: free
Ed: Jean-Marie Volet
A refereed electronic and international journal
open to literary-minded scholars wishing to share
their points of view on important contemporary
world issues.
Submissions: each issue focuses on a special
theme.
Note: full-text archived issues published
between 1996 and 2003 still available at above
Web site, but no new issues have apparently
been published during 2004/2005.

Japan

665 **Afurika Kenkyu/Journal of African Studies**
c/o Shin'ichi Takeuchi,
Institute of Developing Economies
3-2-2 Wakaba
Mihama-ku, Chiba-City
261-8545 Chiba
Tel: +81-43-299 9620 Fax: +81-43-299 9731
Email: takeutis@ide.go.jp
Web: http://wwwsoc.nii.ac.jp/africa/index-e.html
1964- Print 2Yr ISSN 0065-4140
Subs: n/a
Ed: Shin'ichi Takeuchi
The journal of the Japan Association of African Studies, which aims to promote the study and research of society and culture, and the humanities of the continent of Africa, thus enhancing the interest in and the quality of African studies in Japan.
Affil: ➔ **Nihon Afurika Gakkai /Japan Association for African Studies (2778)**
Note: table of contents of back numbers with abstracts, are accessible on the Web site as from vol. 1, 1964 through vol. 65, 20054.

666 **Asian & African Area Studies**
Graduate School of Asian and African Area Studies
Kyoto University
Sakyo-ku
Kyoto 606-8501
Tel: +81-75-753 7161 Fax: +81-75-753 7161
Email: editor@asafas.kyoto-u.ac.jp
Web: http://www.asafas.kyoto-u.ac.jp/english/editoffice-e.html
2001- Print and (partly) online
ISSN n/a 2Yr
Subs: print: n/a online: free
Ed: Editorial Committee; all submissions to Editorial Committee at address above
Book rev
Publishes papers, research notes, and essays that aim to contribute to developing a new paradigm for the coexistence of the various regions in the world in the 21st century. Most issues focus on a special topic.
Submissions: welcomes submission of papers, research notes and book reviews that contribute to Asian and African area studies.

EUROPE

Belgium

667   **Afrika Focus**
Afrika Brug
Universiteitstraat 4
9000 Gent
Tel: +32-9-264 6911 Fax: +32-9-264 6985
Email: Bart.Crombez@rug.ac.be
Web:
http://cas1.elis.rug.ac.be/africa/menunederl
ands.htm
1985- Print ISSN 0772-084X 2Yr
Subs: BF2,000 inst BF750 indiv
Ed: Bart Crombez Book rev
*Provides a forum for the multidisciplinary study
of Africa. Text in Dutch, English, and French.*
Submissions: scholarly contributions dealing
with current trends and new developments in
this field. The articles should be based on
original research and should promote
interdisciplinary communication.

668   **ANB-BIA. African News
Bulletin/Bulletin d'Information
Africaine**
184 avenue Charles Woeste
1090 Brussels
Tel: +32-2-420 3436 Fax: +32-2-420 0549
Email: anb-bia@village.uunet.be
Web: http://www.peacelink.it/anb-bia.html
1982- Print [No ISSN] 2Mon; except in August
(22 issues pa)
Subs: in Africa €45/$50, elsewhere €55/$64
Ed: Paolo Costantini;
English desk: Richard Calcutt,
Rédaction Français: Frans Devillé
Book rev
*Information gathered from the press on the main
events in Africa during the previous two weeks.
Contains three sections: (1) press review,
providing a background to current events in
Africa, (2) short news items, (3) supplement of
articles written for ANB-BIA by African
journalists. Plus special issue annually devoted to
a particular theme.*
Submissions: analysis of current events,
background information and opinions.

669   **Forum**
c/o Mark van de Velde, Secretary
Belgische Vereniging van
Afrikanisten/Association belge des
Africanistes
Katholieke Universiteit Leven
Departement Linguistiek
Blijde-Inkomststraat 21
3000 Leuven
Tel: +32-16-324818
Email: bva@africana.be
Web:
http://home.scarlet.be/~hv980630/forum/fo
rum_nl.htm
1984- Online [No ISSN]
Subs: free
Ed: Geert Castryck et al, Nieuwste
Geschiedenis, Blandijnberg 2, 9000 Gent,
Tel: +32-9-264 4014;
Email: geert.castryck@UGent.be
Book rev
*Bulletin of the Belgische Vereniging van
Afrikanisten/Association belge des Africanistes,
containing news and short reports (in French and
English) about activities of the Association. Also
includes book reviews*
Affil: ➔ **Belgische Vereniging van
Afrikanisten/Association belge des
Africanistes (1783)**

Finland

➔ **Nordic Journal of African Studies** *see*
under Sweden, entry **732**

France

670   **Africa Energy Intelligence**
Indigo Publications
142 rue Montmartre
75002 Paris
Tel: + 33-1-44 88 26 10
Fax: + 33-1-44 88 26 15
Email: info@indigo-net.com
Web: http://www.africaintelligence.com/
2002- Print and online ISSN 1635-2742 Biwk
(23 issues annually)
Subs: print and online €790/$878
Ed: Phillipe Vasset, Email: desk@indigo-
net.com
*A leading publication on oil, gas and electricity in
Africa, that aims to cover energy news
"politically".*

**671 African Geopolitics/
Géopolitique Africaine**
ORIMA International
40 rue des Renaudes
75017 Paris
Tel: +33-1-42 67 12 13
Fax: +-33-1-48 88 05 00
Email: geoafric@wanadoo.fr
Web: http://www.african-geopolitics.org
In the US:
African Geopolitics/Géopolitique Africaine
236 East 5th Street
New York NY 10003
Tel: +1-212-477 6119 Fax: +1-212-674 9145
Email: admin@african-geopolitics.com
2001- Print ISSN 1632-3033 Qtly
Subs: €81/$77 inst, €70/$66 indiv, €58/$55 stud
Ed: Jean-Maurice Soussan, 2723 Denise Pelletier, Saint Laurent, Quebec, H4R 2T3, Canada, Tel: +1- 514 705 7090
Fax: + 1-514- 334 8713,
Email: geoafriccanada@aol.com
Book rev
An international, bi-lingual review on African affairs, containing articles, interviews, special reports and book reviews. Includes frequent contributions by African world leaders, expressing their views on current issues relating to African affairs.
Submissions: n/a

672 The Africa Report
Groupe Jeune Afrique
57 bis rue d'Auteuil
75016 Paris
Tel: +33-1-44 30 19 60
Fax: +33-1-45 20 09 67 (Sales/Subscriptions)
+33-1-44 30 19 30 (Editorial)
Email: sales@theafricareport.com (Sales/Subscriptions)
http://www.theafricareport.com/
2005- Print ISSN n/a Qtly
Subs: €7.50/$9.95 per issue (plus postage).
Eds: Patrick Smith, Richard Synge;
Managing ed: Nicholas Norbrook,
Email: editorial@theafricareport.com
A collaborative publication produced by anglophone and francophone journalists, offering incisive analysis of the continent's key issues in the area of politics, economics and culture.
Submissions: n/a
Note: the inaugural, 228-page issue of *The Africa Report* (published April 2005) is entitled "Africa Survey 2005", and is an in-depth

survey of all the 53 members states of the African Union.

673 Africultures. La revue des cultures africaines
L'Harmattan Edition Diffusion
5-7 rue de l'Ecole Polytechnique
75005 Paris
Tel: +33-1-40 46 79 11/40 46 79 20
Fax: +33-1 43 25 82 03
Email: karthala@wanadoo.fr
Web: http://www.editions-harmattan.fr/index.asp?navig=catalogue&obj=revue&no=1 (Subscription information)
http://www.africultures.com/index.asp (Main home page)
http://www.africultures.com/index.asp?menu=revue_sommaires&sous_menu=full_list (English version)
1998- Print and online ISSN 1276-2458 Qtly (print version)
Subs: print: in France €61, elsewhere €76 (€92 airmail)
online: €36 the first year, €15 in subsequent years years
(For non-subscribers access to "Dossiers" articles in the online version are subject to a fee; many articles are available in English or in English translation. Most articles cost €1.25)
Ed: Ayoko Mensah
Managing eds: Virginia Andriamirado & Olivier Barlet, Les Pilles, 26110 Nyons, France, Tel: +33-4-75 27 74 80,
Fax: +33-4-75 27 75 75,
Email: redaction@africultures.com
Monthly magazine (quarterly in print format) with each issue focusing on a particular aspect of the African arts and cultures, including literature, theatre, art, music, photography, cinema, etc. together with a calendar of African cultural events, reports about exhibitions, reviews, interviews, and more. At this time (August 2005) it offers access to over 3,500 articles, 64 "Dossiers", almost 3,000 reviews and notices of books, films, and CDs, Videos and DVDs.
Submissions: as above
Note: the Africultures Web site provides a forum of information and debate about African cultural expression, and a wide variety of information about the arts in Africa and elsewhere. A weekly newsletter, *La Lettre d'Information d'Africultures* (English version available as well), is available free on request, and includes a diary of forthcoming events

and the latest news provided by a network of 19 cultural associations throughout Africa.
See also ➜ **Afrilivres (392)**

674   Afrilex
Centre d'études et de recherches sur les droits africains et sur le développement institutionnel des pays en développement (CERDRADI)
Université Montesquieu Bordeaux IV
Avenue Léon Duguit
33608 Pessac
Tel: +33-5-56 84 85 14
Fax: +33-5-56 84 86 65
Email: cerdradi@u-bordeaux4.fr
Web: http://www.afrilex.u-bordeaux4.fr/
2002- Print and online ISSN 0998-6839 1-2Yr
Subs: online: free, print: price (per issue) on application
Ed: Alioune Badara Fall
Offers scholars specialising in African law a platform for debate and dissemination of research. Covers all aspects of African law, including administrative law and jurisprudence. Each number includes articles in two major sections: "Doctrines", for publication of research and analysis relating to points of law and legal problems in Africa, while the section "Jurisprudence" reports about significant decisions returned by the judicial authorities of African countries. Issues devoted to specific topics are also published, and some issues include annotated bibliographies.
Submissions: as above

675   Afrique Contemporaine
Agence Française de Développement
5 rue Roland-Barthes
75598 Paris Cedex 12
As from 2005 published by:
De Boeck Université
De Boeck Diffusion
rue de la Gare, 5-7
92130 Issy-les-Moulineaux
Tel: +33-1-41 90 94 94 Fax: +33-1-41 90 97 97
Email: commande@deboeckdiffusion.com
Web:
http://www.ladocumentationfrancaise.fr/catalogue/3303330100009/index.shtml or
http://universite.deboeck.com/livre/?GCOI=28011100243230&fa=sommaire
1962- Print ISSN: 0002-0478 Qtly
Subs: €72
Ed: François Gaulme,

Email: gaulmef@afd.fr
Book rev
Political, economic and social studies; extensive bibliographic section of new publications, including material in English.
Submissions: n/a

676   Afrique Education
3 rue Carvès
92120 Montrouge
Tel: +33-1-42 53 72 09 Fax: +33-1-46 56 88 08
Email: afriqueeducation@afriqueeducation.com
Web: http://www.afriqueeducation.com/
1993- Print and online ISSN 1247-5289 6Yr
Subs: see
http://www.afriqueeducation.com/abonnement/index.php
Ed: Paul Tedga
Book rev
News magazine covering African politics, economics, education, and culture.
Submissions: n/a

677   Afrique & Histoire. Revue internationale
Editions Verdier
234 rue du Faubourg-Saint-Antoine
75012 Paris
Tel: +33-1-43 79 20 45 Fax: +33-1-43 79 84 20
Email: contact@editions-verdier.fr
Web: http://www.editions-verdier.fr/v2/oeuvre-afriquehistoire.html
2003- Print [No ISSN, issues have individual ISBN's] Subs: issues individually priced, €25-€30 each
Eds: Bertrand Hirsch, Danielle de Lam, Ibrahima Thioub Managing ed: Jean-Pierre Chrétien, Centres de Recherches Africaines, Université Paris 1-Panthéon Sorbonne, 9 rue Malher, 75181 Paris Cedex 04,
Email: hafrique@univ-paris1.fr
A new journal devoted to Africa as well as to promote relations between Africa, Indian and Atlantic Oceans, and the Mediterranean Sea. It publishes essays dealing with North Africa and sub-Saharan Africa, and covering all historical eras, from antiquity to the present day.
Submissions: as above, in French or English

678   Afrique Express
SARL LB Presse
162 place du 19 Mars 1962
93100 Montreuil
Tel: +33-1-48 59 80 12 Fax: +33-1-48 59 80 12

Email: afrique.expr@magic.fr
Web:
http://www.afrique-express.com/
1993- Print and online ISSN n/a 24Yr
Subs: print €147/$153 (by email delivery/pdf €76/$79), online free
Ed: René Jacques Lique
Extensive coverage of African political,economic and industrial news by regions, with sections on health, human rights, religion, the environment, social life, and education.
Submissions: n/a

679   Afrique Magazine
Groupe Jeune Afrique
57 bis rue d'Auteuil
75016 Paris
Tel: +33-1-33 30 19 60 Fax: +33-1-44 30 18 87
1983- Print ISSN 0998-9307 8Yr (plus two double issues annually)
Email: afriquemagazine@cba.fr (General enquiries and subscriptions)
redaction@afriquemagazine.com (Editorial)
Web: http://www.afriquemagazine.com
Subs: in France €25, in Europe €35, in North America $50
Eds: Zyad Limam,
Email: zlimam@afriquemagazine.com
Emmanuelle Pontié
Email: epontie@afriquemagazine.com
Book rev
General interest and current affairs magazine for 'new generation' Africans. It aims to speak for all of Africa, including the Maghreb countries and the diasporas. Covers African societies, books, culture, music, fashion, health, travel, people and places, etc.
Submissions: n/a

680   Ankh. Revue d'Egyptologie et des Civilisations africaines
Association KHEPERA
BP 11
91192 Gif sur Yvette Cedex
Tel/Fax: n/a
Email: info-ankhonl@ankhonline.com
Web:
http://www.ankhonline.com/revue.htm
1992- Print ISSN 1164-6136 Ann
Subs: issues individually priced (available from ➔ **Librairie Présence Africaine (2316)** or from address above)
Eds: Theophilus Obenga et al

The journal takes its name from "Ankh", meaning "Life" in ancient Egyptian pharaonic. Is a journal of Egyptology and African civilizations, the human and exact sciences, classical African antiquities, and linguistics, particularly comparative historical linguistics. It also contains bibliographic and biographic contributions, especially of the work of the late Senegalese historian and scientist Cheikh Anta Diop.
Submissions: n/a

681   APAD Bulletin
Euro-African Association for the Anthropology of Social Change and Development/Association Euro-Africaine pour l'anthropologie du changement social et du développement (APAD)
c/o Giorgio Blundo
EHESS
Centre de la Vieille Charité
2 rue de la Charité
13002 Marseille
Tel: +33-91-140727/140754
Fax: +33-91-913401
Email: apad@ehess.cnrs-mrs.fr
Web: http://www.vcharite.univ-mrs.fr/shadyc/APAD/BULLETINSPARUS.html
1991- Print [No ISSN] 2Yr
Subs: €39 inst €19 ind €11 stud
Ed: Giorgio Blundo
Book rev
As the principal tool of APAD the Bulletin attempts to be as much a forum for intellectual debate as a vehicle for information. Contains reflections and debates on development anthropology, news of APAD activities, and reports on conferences, seminars, etc.
Submissions: as above
Affil: ➔ **Euro-African Association for the Anthropology of Social Change and Development/Association Euro Africaine pour l'anthropologie du changement social et du développement (2771)**

682   Autrepart. Revue de Sciences Sociales au Sud
Editions Armand Colin
11-15 rue Pierre Rigaud
94207 Ivry-sur-Seine cedex
Email: abonnement@editions-sedes.com
Web: http://www.bondy.ird.fr/autrepart/
1997- Print ISSN 1278-3986 Qtly
Subs: in France €66; elsewhere €79
Ed: Laurence Quinty, Institut de recherche pour le développement, 32 avenue Henri-Varagnat, 93143 Bondy Cedex,
Tel: +33-1-48 02 55 40,
Email: autrepart@bondy.ird.fr
Aims to promote discussions and debate on the complexity and the dynamic forces of the countries of the South and their economic, social, political, and ecological realities.
Submissions: as above, in the various disciplines of social sciences; contributions primarily in French, but with occasional papers in English. Many issues focus on a particular topic.

683   Cahiers d'Etudes Africaines
EHESS-Service Abonnement
5-7 rue Marcelin Berthelot
92762 Antony Cedex
Tel.: +33-1-55 59 52 53 Fax: +33-1-55 59 52 50
Email: abo.services@wanadoo.fr
Web: http://etudesafricaines.revues.org/
and
http://www.ehess.fr/html/html/378.html
1960- Print and online ISSN 0008-0055 Qtly
Subs: in Europe €72 inst/€46 indiv, elsewhere €83 inst €46 indiv
Ed: Jean-Loup Amselle, Ecoles hautes études sciences sociales, 54 boulevard Raspail, 75006 Paris, Tel: +33-1-49 54 24 69, Fax: +33-1-49 54 26 92,
Email: Cahiers-Afr@ehess.fr
Book rev
Multidisciplinary in scope, covering primarily anthropology, ethnology, history and sociology.
Submissions: as above, publishes papers in French and English
H-Africa TOC

684   Clio en Afrique: Bulletin d'Anthropologie et d'Histoire Africaines en langue française
Institut d'Etudes Africaines
Université de Provence
3 place Victor Hugo
1331 Marseille Cedex 03
Tel: +33-4-91 10 60 00
Email: wclio-af@newsup.univ-mrs.fr Web: http://www.up.univ-mrs.fr/~wclio-af/
2000- Online [No ISSN] Qtly
Subs: free
Ed: Editorial Committee, Jean-Louis Triaud *et al,*
Email: jlt@newsup.univ-mrs.fr;
A bulletin on research in the field of Africa anthropology, ethnology, and history. Aims to facilitate exchanges between historians in France and in francophone Africa.
Submissions: n/a
H-Africa TOC

685   Etudes Littéraires Africaines: Revue de l'Association pour l'Etude des Littératures Africaines
APELA
Université de Cergy-Pontoise
33 boulevard du Port
95001 Cergy-Pontoise Cedex
Tel: +33-1-34 25 64 22 Fax: +33-1-45 80 67 16
Email: delas@cergy.fr
Web: n/a (previous site at http://www.apela-asso.net has not been working for some time)
1996- Print ISSN 0769-4563 2Yr
Subs: €42 inst (reduced rates for APELA members)
Ed: Daniel Delas, Université de Cergy-Pontoise
Book rev Book rev ed: Pierre Halen, Email: phalen@zeus.lettres.univ-metz.fr
Book reviews, bibliographic section, association news, colloquium and conference dates; covers anglophone, francophone and lusophone Africa, and the West Indies.

686   Indian Ocean Newsletter
Indigo Publications
142 rue Montmartre
75002 Paris
Tel: + 33-1-44 88 26 10 Fax: + 33-1-44 88 26 15
Email: info@indigo-net.com
Web: http://www.africaintelligence.com/
1981- Print and online ISSN 0294-6475 Wk
Subs: print and online) €805/$894
Ed: Francis Soler,
Email: desk@indigo-net.com
Articles on politics, power-brokers, business networks, regional diplomacy and business intelligence in the Horn of Africa, East Africa, southern Africa and the islands of the Indian Ocean. Published in English and French editions.

687   **Jeune Afrique L'Intelligent**
(formerly Jeune Afrique)
Groupe Jeune Afrique
57 bis rue d'Auteuil
75016 Paris
Tel: +33-1-33 30 19 60 Fax: +33-1-44 30 19 30
Email: ventes@jeuneafrique.com
(Subscriptions)
Web: http://www.lintelligent.com/
1960- Print and online ISSN 0021-6089 Wk
(48Yr, plus two double issues)
Subs: in France €105, elsewhere in Europe
€135, North America $190,
CFA zone/Africa €150; online subs €9
monthly; for document delivery charges *see*
http://www.lintelligent.com/portefeuille/co
mpte.asp
Ed: Patrick Sandouly (Editor-in-chief)
Email: p.sandouly@jeuneafrique.com
Book rev
*Popular weekly news, current affairs, business
and cultural magazine.*
Submissions: n/a
Note: online archive provides access to over
60,000 articles.

688   **Journal des Africanistes**
Société des Africanistes Musée de
l'Homme
Palais de Chaillot
17 place du Trocadéro
75116 Paris
Tel: +33-01-47 27 72 55 Fax: +33-1-47 04 63 40
Email: africanistes@multimania.com
Web: http://www.mae.u-
paris10.fr/africanistes/journal.htm
http://www.mae.u-
paris10.fr/africanistes/journal_en.htm
(English text)
1930- Print ISSN 0399-0346 2Yr
Subs: €62
Ed: Paulette Roulon-Doko
Book rev
*Original articles on the human sciences in Africa:
ecology, geography, prehistory, history,
linguistics, physical, social and cultural
anthropology; sociological studies of relations
between Africa and the rest of the world.*
Submissions: as above
Affil: → **Société des Africanistes (2782)**

689   **Lusotopie. Enjeux contemporains
dans les espaces lusophones/
Desafios contemporâneos nos
espaços lusófonos/Contemporary
Challenges in Portuguese-Speaking
Worlds**
Editions Karthala
22-24 boulevard Arago
75013 Paris
Tel: +33-1-43 31 15 59 Fax: +33-1-45 35 27 05
Email: karthala@wanadoo.fr
Web:
http://www.lusotopie.sciencespobordeaux.fr
/ or http://www.karthala.com/
1994- Print and online No ISSN (Back issues
of annual volumes have individual ISBNs)
Ann to 2001 2Yr from 2002-
Subs: €78 (two issues)
Ed: Editorial Committee, Lusotopie
Centre d'étude d'Afrique noire, Maison des
Suds-CNRS, 12 Esplanade des Antilles,
33607 Pessac Cedex, France,
Tel: +33-5-56 84 42 82, Fax: +33-5-56 84 43 24
All submissions to Editorial Secretary,
Jaqueline Vivès,
Email: j.vives@sciencespobordeaux.fr
Book rev
*An international journal for political studies in
the social, human and environmental sciences, on
Portuguese and luso-creole historically linked and
official or national language places, countries and
communities.*
Submissions: in French, Portuguese, and
English.

690   **Maghreb Confidential**
Indigo Publications
142 rue Montmartre
75002 Paris
Tel: + 33-1-44 88 26 10 Fax: + 33-1-44 88 26 15
Email: info@indigo-net.com
Web: http://www.africaintelligence.com/
1990- Print and online ISSN 1210-4531 Wk (46
issues annually)
Subs: print and online €605/$672
Ed: Antoine Glaser,
Email: desk@indigo-net.com
*Tracks influential circles and corporate affairs in
which diplomacy, politics and business are inter-
connected in the countries of North Africa
Countries.*

691 Marchés Tropicaux et
Méditerranéens
Editions Moreux SA
11 rue du Faubourg Poissonieère
75009 Paris
Tel: +33-1-49 49 07 49 Fax: +33-1-49 49 07 45
Email: lelouvier@moreux.fr
Web: http://www.moreux.fr/
1945- Print and online ISSN 0025-2859 Wk
Subs: print only: in France and EU €550 ,
elsewhere €660; online only €550; print and
online €700
Ed: Bénédicte Chatel,
Email: b.chatel@moreux.fr
Fax: +33-1-49 49 07 50
Book rev
*Weekly magazine on the African economy,
industry, politics and development, and general
news, articles, and assessments on the economic
situation. Arranged by countries and by regions.*
Submissions: n/a

→ Notre Librairie: Revue des littératures du
Sud *see* 3 Current bibliographies, indexing
and abstracting services, and review media
entry **410**

692 Le Nouvel Afrique Asie
3 rue de Metz
75010 Paris
Tel: +33-1-40 22 06 72 Fax: +33-1-45 23 28 02
Email: africasi@wanadoo.fr
Web: http://www.afrique-asie.com/
1969- Print and online ISSN 1141-9946 Mon
Subs: print: in France €35, Europe €55, Africa
(airmail) €55, elsewhere (airmail) €70 (offers
some online articles for free)
Eds: Simon Malley and Barbara Malley, Ed-
in-chief–Africa: Francis Laloupo, Email:
francislaloupo@club-internet.fr
Book rev
*Monthly magazine of information, analysis, and
opinion on political, economic, social and cultural
events in Africa, the Arab world, Asia and Latin
America.*
Submissions: as above

693 Outre-mers: revue d'histoire
Société française d'histoire
d'outre-mer
15 rue Catulienne
93200 Saint-Denis
Tel: n/a
Fax: +33-145-826299
Email: shhom4@yahoo.fr

Web: http://sfhom.free.fr/Revue.php
2001- Print (continues *Revue française d'histoire
d'outre-mer*, 1959-2000) ISSN 1631-0438 2Yr
Subs: n/a
Eds: Bernard Droz, Lycée Louis-Le-Grand,
Paris; Jacques Frémaux, Université Paris IV-
Sorbonne
Book rev
*Publishes articles on the history of former French
colonies from the 18th century to the present,
together with book reviews, news, reports, and
conference announcements.*
Submissions: n/a
Affil: → **Société française d'histoire
d'outre-mer (2783)**

694 Politique Africaine
Editions Karthala
22-24 boulevard Arago
75013 Paris
Tel: +33-1-43 31 15 59 Fax: +33-1-45 35 27 05
Email: karthala@wanadoo.fr
Web:
http://www.politique-africaine.com/
or http://www.karthala.com/
1980- Print ISSN 0244-7837 Qtly Subs: in
France €60, elsewhere in Europe €70,
francophone Africa €70, elsewhere €85;
reduced rates for students
Issues also sold individually by Karthala with
individual ISBNs
Eds: Richard Banégas, Roland Marchal
(Managing editor), Centre d'études juridiques
et politiques du monde africain, 9, rue
Malher, 75181 Paris Cedex 04,
Tel: +33-1-44 78 33 23, Fax: +33-1-44 78 33 39
Email: politique.africaine@univ-paris1.fr
Book rev Book rev ed: Sandrine Perrot Centre
Mahler, 9 rue Malher, 75181 Paris Cedex 04
France
*A multidisciplinary journal of political analysis in
Africa, and French relations with Africa. Each
issue focuses on a special theme, country, social or
cultural topic.*
Submissions: as above, and on a given topic
H-Africa TOC

695 Présence Africaine. Revue Culturelle
du Monde Noire
25 bis rue des Ecoles
75005 Paris
Tel: +33-1-43 54 13 74 Fax: +33-1-43 54 96 67
Email: preaf@club-internet.fr
Web: n/a
1947- Print ISSN 0032-7638 2Yr

Subs: n/a
Ed: Yande Christiane Diop
Note: irregularly published, unable to verify
current availability status

**696   Revue Noire. Art Contemporain
          Africain/African Contemporary Art**
          8 rue Cels
          75014 Paris
Tel: +33-1-43 20 92 00 Fax: +33-1-43 22 92 60
Email: order@revuenoire.com
Web: http://www.revuenoire.com
1991- Print [No ISSN?] Qtly
Subs: issues individually priced, see Web site,
each no. €20-€30
Eds: Jean Loup Pivin, Simon Njami, Martin
Saint Leon; Email: redaction@revuenoire.com
*A review providing an alternative view of
contemporary Africa art and cultures. Published
in French and English, each issue is devoted to an
artistic theme, e.g. painting, sculpture,
architecture and design, photography, dance,
cinema, theatre, African artists, etc. or focussing
on an individual African country.*

**697   Takam Tikou. Le bulletin de la joie
          par les livres**
          Centre national du livre pour enfants
          25 boulevard de Strasbourg 75010
          Paris
Tel: +33-1-55 33 44 44 Fax: +33-1-55 33 44 55
Email: contact@lajoieparleslivres.com
Web: 1991- Print ISSN 1271-6103 1-2Yr
Subs: €20 per issue
Eds: Marie Laurentin, Email:
marie.laurentin@lajoieparleslivres.com
Viviana Quiñones, Email:
viviana.quinones@lajoieparleslivres.com
Hasmig Chahinian, Email:
hasmig.chahinian@lajoieparleslivres.com
*Focuses primarily on children's books from and
about Africa, but since issue no. 10 (February
2003) has expanded its scope to include articles
and special issues on African literature. Also
includes news and reports, interviews,
bibliographic listings, and extensive reviews of
new books.*

Germany

Note: for further, more general, non-academic
and cultural journals and magazines on
Africa published in Germany, Austria and
Switzerland *see* the ➔ **AfrikaHaus (2318)**
pages at
http://www.afrikahaus.de/page27.html

698   Afrikanistik Online
          Institut für Afrikanistik
          Universität zu Köln
          Meister-Ekkehart-Strasse
          750923 Cologne
Tel: +49-221-470 2708 Fax: +49-221-470 5158
Email: ama14@uni-koeln.de
http://www.dipp.nrw.de/afrika
2004- Online ISSN 1860-7462 Irregular (issues
not numbered; several articles and reports,
etc. annually)
Subs: free
Ed: Helma Pasch
Email: helma.pasch@koeln.de
Book rev
*A multilingual-journal that aims to represent
African studies in the spirit as propagated by
Diedrich Westerman: the people are always the
focus of research. The journal aims to enhance
international exchange and cooperation between
scholars of different Africa-related disciplines, e.g.
anthropology, theoretical and applied linguistics,
literature, communication studies.*
Submissions: as above; contributions with an
interdisciplinary perspective, or papers that
are the result of international online
cooperation, are particularly welcome.

699   Afrika Spectrum
          Institut für Afrika-Kunde
          Neuer Jungfernstieg 21
          20354 Hamburg
Tel: +49-40-42 825523 Fax: +49-40-42 825511
Email: iak@uni-hamburg.de
Web:
http://www.unihamburg.de/Wiss/FB/10/
AfrikaS/afrikauebersee.html or
http://www.duei.de/iak/shop/afrika_spect
rum.php?VID=Ev2pI0IDwwCtoDfc
1965- Print ISSN 0002-0397 3Yr
Subs: €55
Ed: Dirk Kohnert Book rev
*Interdisciplinary journal concentrating on
critical analyses of current issues in the
development of Africa. Articles in German,
English and French.*

Submissions: contributions from all social science disciplines, especially those of an empirical and problem-orientated nature.

700   Afrika und Übersee – Sprachen, Kulturen
Dietrich Reimer Verlag GmbH
Zimmerstrasse 26-27
10969 Berlin
Tel: +49-30-2591 73589
Fax: +49-30-2591 73537
Email: vertrieb-kunstverlage@reimer-verlag.de
Web: https://www.weltkunstverlag.de/
1910- Print ISSN 0002-0427 2Yr
Subs: €76
Eds: L. Gerhardt and T. Schumann, UHH - Asien-Afrika-Institut, Abteilung für Afrikanistik und Äthiopistik, Edmund-Siemers-Allee 1/ESA–OST 20146 Hamburg
Email: AfrikaundUebersee@uni-hamburg.de
Book rev Book rev ed: Hilke Meyer-Bahlburg
Articles mainly on African languages, on history in connection with languages, and on traditional literature in as it relates to languages.
Submissions: primarily those concerned with African languages and cultures, with an emphasis on the publication of original data on threatened languages, or on the cultural history of smaller ethnic groups.
H-Africa TOC

701   Frankfurter Afrikanistische Blätter
Rüdiger Köppe Verlag
Sprachen und Kulturen
Wendelinstrasse 73-75
Postfach 45 06 43
50881 Cologne
Tel: +49-221-491 1236/7
Fax: +49-221-499 4336
Email: info@koeppe.de
Web: http://www.koeppe.de/html/d_fab.htm
1988- Print [No ISSN, volumes have individual ISBNs) Ann
Subs: individually priced
Ed: Anne Storch, Institut für Afrikanische Sprachwissenschaften, Johann Wolfgang Goethe-Universität, Kettenhofweg 135, 60054 Frankfurt/Main,
Email: storch@em.uni-frankfurt.de
Book rev
The publication of the Institut Institut für Afrikanische Sprachwissenschaften, Johann

Wolfgang Goethe-Universität, Frankfurt. Papers on African language and linguistic studies.
Submissions: as above, contributions in German, English or French.

702   Lusorama. Zeitschrift für Lusitanistik/Revista de estudos sobre os Países de Língua Portuguesa
Axel Schönberger Verlag
Postfach 10 37 55
60107 Frankfurt am Main
Fax: +49- 69-5305 3846
Email: schoenberger@lusorama.de
Web: http://www.lusorama.de/
1985- Print ISSN 0931-9484 Qtly (2 issues as double numbers)
Subs: €45
Eds: Luciano Caetano da Rosa, Axel Schönberger, Michael Scotti-Rosin; contributions to: Axel Schönberger, Redaktion Lusorama, Postfach 10 37 55 60107 Frankfurt am Main,
Fax: +49-69 -5305 3846,
Email: schoenberger@uni-bremen.de
Book rev
Publishes a variety of contributions about Portugal, Brasil, and lusophone Africa covering literature, language, and cultural, political and social history.
Submissions: the emphasis is on Lusitanian studies and the areas of literary criticism and linguistics of Portuguese-speaking countries; contributions in German or Portuguese.
Note: index to volumes 1-30 available at http://www.lusorama.de/Inhalt/INDE1-50/inde1-50.htm

703   Matatu. Journal for African Culture and Society
Editions Rodopi B.V
Tijnmuiden 7
1046 AK Amsterdam
The Netherlands
Tel: +31-20-611 4821 Fax: +31-20-447 2979
Email: info@rodopi.nl
Web: http://www.rodopi.nl/senj.asp?SerieId =MATATU
In the US:
Editions Rodopi B.V.
906 Madison Avenue
Union, NJ 07083
Tel: +1-908-206 1166, Toll-free (US/Canada

only) 800-225 3998
Fax: +1-908-206 0820
1987- Print and online ISSN 0932-9714 1-2Yr
Subs: issues are individually priced (online
access bundled with print), and with
individual ISBNs, latest issue (vol. 29/30)
€55/$81
Founding ed: Holger G. Ehling
Eds: Gordon Collier, Geoffrey V. Davis, *et al.;*
contributions to Geoffrey V. Davis, Institut
für Anglistik, RWTH Aachen, Kármánstr. 17–
19, 52062 Aachen,
Email: davis@anglistik1.rwth-aachen.de
Book rev ed: Gordon Collier, Technical
Editor, Matatu, Department of English, Justus
Liebig Universität, Otto-Behaghel-Strasse 10,
35394 Giessen,
Email: Gordon.r.collier@anglistik.uni-
giessen.de
A journal on African literatures and societies
dedicated to interdisciplinary dialogue between
literary and cultural studies, historiography, the
social sciences and cultural anthropology. It
provides a forum for interchanges between African
and European critical debates, to overcoming
notions of absolute cultural, ethnic, or religious
alterity, and to promoting transnational
discussion on the future of African societies in a
wider world.
Submissions: although essays on all aspects of
African literature and culture are welcome –
as well as reports and interviews on topics of
pressing and current concern – individual
issues of the journal primarily focus on
specific themes. For a list of forthcoming
themes see Web site.

704   NTAMA. Journal of African Music
        and Popular Culture
        Institut für Ethnologie und Afrika-
        Studien
        Johannes Gutenberg-Universität
        Mainz
        55099 Mainz
Tel: +49-6131-392 2798
Fax: +49-6131-392 3730
Email: ntama@ntama.uni-mainz.de
Web: http://ntama.uni-mainz.de/
1998- Online [No ISSN] Ann
Subs: free
Book and music rev
Ed: Wolfgang Bender
A journal of African popular culture, African
music and musical life. Contains articles, portraits
of artists and musicians, discographies, news of
events, and reviews.

Submissions: on African popular culture and
African culture in general. The journal is
primarily addressed to a new generation of
academics publishing in the field of popular
culture and African music. It does not draw
strict lines, and contributions on so-called
"New African Art Music"are as welcome as
studies on African literature even if they are
not the focus of the journal.

705   Palabres. Revue d'Etudes
        Africaines
        Sélom Komlan Gbanou
        Lehrstuhl für romanische
        Literaturwissenschaft und
        Komparatistik, GSP Z. Nr. 435
        Universität Bayreuth
        D-95440 Bayreuth
Tel: +49-921-555170 Fax +49-921-553627
Email: selom.gbanou@uni-bayreuth.de
or selom@revuepalabres.com
Web: http://www.revuepalabres.com/
1996- Print ISSN 1767-8447 2Yr
Subs: €50/$50 inst, €40/€40 indiv
Ed: Sélom Komlan Gbanou
Devoted to the study of comparative literatures of
Africa and the Antilles, published in English and
French to provide a wider dialogue between
researchers from the two linguistic groups.
Submissions: as above

706   Recht in Africa/Law in Africa/Droit
        en Afrique
        Rüdiger Köppe Verlag
        Sprachen und Kulturen
        Wendelinstrasse 73-75
        Postfach 45 06 43
        50881 Cologne
Tel: +49-221-491 1236/7
Fax: +49-221-499 4336
Email: info@koeppe.de
Web:
http://www.koeppe.de/html/d_ria.htm
1998- Print ISSN 1435-0963 2Yr
Ed: Wilhelm J.G. Mölig, Institut für
Afrikanistik, Universität zu Köln,
50923 Cologne , Tel: +49-221-470 3884,
Fax: +49-221-470 5158,
Email: ama13@rrzk.Uni-Koeln.de
Book rev
The journal of the Gesellschaft für Afrikanisches
Recht, providing an information and discussion
forum for all areas relating to law on the African
continent.

Submissions: contributions in German, English or French.

707   SSUGIA. Sprache und Geschichte in Afrika
Rüdiger Köppe Verlag
Sprachen und Kulturen
Wendelinstrasse 73-75
Postfach 45 06 43
50881 Cologne
Tel: +49-221-491 1236/7
Fax: +49-221-499 4336
Email: info@koeppe.de
Web:
http://www.koeppe.de/html/d_sugia.htm
1985- Print ISSN 0170-5946 Ann (irregular)
Ed: Rainer Vossen *et al*, Institut für
Afrikanische Sprachwissenschaften, Johann
Wolfgang Goethe-Universität, Kettenhofweg
135, 60054 Frankfurt/Main,
Email: vossen@em.uni-frankfurt.de
Book rev
A joint publication of the Universities of Frankfurt and Cologne on language and history in Africa.
Submissions: contributions in German, English or French.

708   Swahili Forum
Institut für Ethnologie und
Afriakstudien
Forum Universitatis 6
55099 Mainz
Tel: +49-6131-392 2798
Fax: +49-6131-392 3730
Email: R.M.Beck@em.uni-frankfurt.de
Web: http://www.uni-mainz.de/~ifeas/SwaFo/
1994- Print and online (since June 2004) (Text on CD-ROM on request, for institutions in Africa) ISSN 1614-2373 Ann
Subs: print: n/a online: free
Eds: Rose Marie Beck, Lutz Diegner, Thomas Geider, Uta Reuster-Jahn
Email: thgeider@arcor.de or
R.M.Beck@em.uni-frankfurt.de
Book rev
Papers on all aspects of Swahili language, culture and society, as well as book reviews and bibliographic contributions pertaining to these topics.
Submissions: as above; publishes contributions in Swahili, English, French and German.

Note: vol. 10 (2003) contains *A Bibliography of Swahili Literature, Linguistics, Culture and History* compiled by Thomas Geider.

Italy

709   Africa e Mediterraneo
Via Gamberi 4
40037 Sasso Marconi
Bologna
Tel/Fax: +39-51-840166
Email: progetti@africaemediterraneo.it
Web: http://www.africaemediterraneo.it/
1992- Print ISSN 1121-8495 Qtly
Subs: €36 in Italy, €58 elsewhere
Ed: Sandra Federici Book rev
Aims to provide information about Africa, and to give a voice to African scholars and artists, and thus to promote and increase intercultural knowledge. Each number contains a monographic 'dossier' that focuses on a particular topic, together with information about events, articles on African literature, art, cinema, music, and sections devoted to intercultural projects, reviews of books, films, and exhibitions.
Submissions: welcomes contributions in English, Italian, French or Portuguese, provided they fit into one of the forthcoming 'dossiers' themes.
H-Africa TOC
Note: the complete list of themes of past individual 'dossiers' is available at
http://www.africaemediterraneo.it/ENG/magazine/dossiers.htm

**710   Africa. Missione e Cultura.
Rivista dei Missionari d'Africa**
Padri Bianchi
via Pordenone 1
20132 Milan
Tel: +39-2-215 1687
Email: (Economo provinciale):
frankpinna@libero.it (General enquiries at Milano office)
Email: Africa@padribianchi.it (Editorial and subscriptions)
Web:
http://www.missionaridafrica.org/pubblicazioni.htm
1922- Print and (partly) online ISSN n/a 6Yr
Subs: in Italy n/a, elsewhere CHFr 35
Ed: P. Vittorio Bonfanti (Editorial Director)
Eds: Antonio Scarin et al

Monthly journal of the Padri Bianchi (White Fathers), and the Ambrosian Center of Documentation for Religions. Covers current affairs, history, missionary work, religion, church history, Islam, and African social life and cultures. Submissions: n/a

711   Africa. Rivista Trimestriale di Studi e Documentazione
Istituto Italiano per l'Africa e l'Oriente
16 via Ulisse Aldrovandi
00197 Rome
Tel: +39-6-328 551 Fax: +39-6-322 5348
Email: info@isiao.it
Web: n/a
1946- Print and (partly) online
ISSN 0001-9747 Qtly
Subs: n/a
Ed: Gianluigi Rossi
Quarterly journal of studies and documentation of the Istituto Italiano per l'Africa e l'Oriente. Submissions: contributions in Italian and English.
Note: unable to verify current availability status, ceased?

712   African Societies/Societa Africane/Sociétés Africaines
Via Montezebio 32
00195 Rome
Tel: +39-6-323 25-5/3600 1480
Fax +39-6-322 1218
Email: info@africansocieties.org
Web: http://www.africansocieties.org/
2002- Online [No ISSN] Mon
Subs: free
Ed: Assouman Honoré Yao
Managing ed: Fabio Feudo
Promotes a modern vision of Africa referring to a plurality of societies that are little known. Deals with the theme of what may be called a dual reality of Africa. Africa is presented to the world in two guises: the first guise is of a virtual kind through the international media that offer a mainly negative picture of the continent. The second guise refers to a plurality of societies that are mostly little known, misunderstood and largely invisible. Submissions: published in English, Italian and French. Apart from the image of Africa in the international media, the main themes of the magazine are "social fates studies" in Africa, modernity, the legitimacy or risks of a unitary approach to Africa, the need to represent the social and cultural fabric of

African countries and the weight and historical role of the African diaspora.

713   Afriche e Orienti. Rivista di Studi ai Confini tra Africa Mediterraneo e Medio Oriente
Aiep Editore Snc
via Giacomini n. 86/A
47890 Repubblica di San Marino
Tel: +378-549-992389 Fax: +378-549-990398
Email: aiep@omniway.sm
Web:
http://www.comune.bologna.it/iperbol e/africheorienti/rivista.html
1999- Print [No ISSN] Qtly
Subs: in Europe and Africa €37, elsewhere €74
Eds: Maria Zamponi, Isabella Fabbri,
Via S. Mamolo 24, CP 41, 40100 Bologna Centro,
Tel/Fax: +39-51-333124
Email: africheorienti@hotmail.it
Presents analysis on the current situation in Africa, in the Mediterranean region and in the Middle East, especially on topics such as immigration, development, cooperation, multiculturalism and human rights. Submissions: as above

714   Nigrizia. Fatti e Problemi del Mondo Nero
Vicolo Pozzo 1
37129 Verona
Tel: +39-45-809 2390 Fax: +39-45-809 2391
Email: abbonamenti@nigrizia.it (Subscriptions)
Web: http://www.nigrizia.it/
1883- Print and online ISSN 0029-0173 11Yr
Subs: in Italy €23, Europe €40, Africa, North America and elsewhere €53
Ed: Carmine Curci, Email: redazione@nigrizia.it
Online ed: Michela Trevisan
Email: online@nigrizia.it
The long-established review of the Missionari Comboniani. Multidisciplinary, covering all aspects of African life, culture and religions etc., as well as social and economic development. Submissions: as above
H-Africa TOC

Netherlands

715 African and Asian Studies
Brill Academic Publishers
PO Box 9000
2300 PA Leiden
Tel: +31-71-53 53 500 Fax: +31-71-53 17 532
Email: cs@brill.nl
Web:
http://www.brill.nl/product.asp?ID=10254
2002- Print and online ISSN 1569-2094 Qtly
Subs: €192/$240 inst €89/$111 indiv
Ed: Tukumbi Lumumba-Kasongo, Chair,
Department of International Studies, Wells
College, Aurora, NY 13026;
Tel: +1-315-364 3220/607-255 6851
Fax: +1-315-3643257/607-255 6681
Email: tl-k@wells.edu
Presents a scholarly account of studies of
individuals and societies in Africa and Asia. The
journal focuses on problems and possibilities, past
and future. Where possible, comparisons are made
between countries and continents.
Submissions: publishes original research by
social scientists in the area of anthropology,
sociology, history, political science and
related social sciences about African and
Asian societies and cultures and their
relationships.

→ **African Studies Abstracts/African**
Studies Abstracts Online *see* 3
Current bibliographies, indexing and
abstracting services and review media
entry **396**

716 Itinerario. International Journal on
the History of European Expansion
and Global Interaction
History Department
Leiden University
PO Box 9515
2300 RA Leiden
Tel: +31-71-527 2767 Fax: +31-71-527 2615
Email: itinerario@let.leidenuniv.nl
Web: http://www.itinerario.nl/
1977- Print and online ISSB 0165-1153 3Yr
Subs: €58/$ 81 inst €44/$56indiv
Eds: Editorial collective, Hendrik E. Niemeijer
(Editor-in-chief)
Book rev Book rev ed: Markus Vink
Published by the Institute for the History of
European Expansion (IBEER of Leiden University
Itinerario *offers a publishing platform for*
research on the history of European expansion in
both its Western and non-Western contexts, and
its impact on World history in general.
Submissions: welcomes submissions dealing
with comparative dimensions of European
expansion and cultural interaction
worldwide. Articles from historians, ethno-
historians, literary critics, and
anthropologists, writing comparatively about
any dimension of either the establishment of,
or the responses to it, are welcome.

717 Journal of African Languages and
Linguistics
Walter de Gruyter GmbH & Co
Genthiner Strasse 13
10785 Berlin
Tel: +49-30-260 050 Fax: +49-30-260 05251
Email: wdg-info@deGruyter.de
Web:
http://www.degruyter.de/journals/jal
l/index.html
available via Extenza at
http://www.extenza-eps.com/WDG/loi/jall
In the US:
Walter de Gruyter Inc
500 Executive Boulevard
Ossining NY 10562
Tel: +1-914-762 5866 Fax: +1-914-762 0371
Email: info@degruyterny.com
1979- Print and online ISSN 0167-6164 (E-
ISSN 1613-3811) 2Yr
Subs: €98/$104 inst €25/$38 indiv
Ed: Felix K. Ameka and Maarten Mous,
Department of African Linguistics, Leiden
University, PO Box 9515, 2300 RA Leiden, Tel:
+31-71-527 2245,
Fax: +31-71-527 2615
Email: ameka@rullet.LeidenUniv.nl
or mous@rullet.LeidenUniv.nl
Book rev Book rev ed: James Essegbey
A forum for papers in African linguistics. Each
issue contains articles on different aspects of
African languages, an extensive book review
section, and list of recently published books on
African languages.
Submissions: original contributions on all
aspects of African language studies,
synchronic as well as diachronic, theoretical
as well as data-oriented.

718   **Journal of Language and Popular Culture in Africa**
Department of Sociology and Anthropology
University of Amsterdam
O.Z. Achterburgwal 185
1012 DK Amsterdam
Tel: +31-20-525 2615 Fax: +31-20-525 3010
Email: vderooij@pscw.uva.nl
Web:
http://www.pscw.uva.nl/lpca/jlpca/info.html
2001- Online ISSN 1570-016X Ann
Subs: free
Ed: Vincent A. de Rooij
Studies published in the journal describe and analyse materials from text collections available at this Web site or elsewhere.
Submissions: from a wide range of disciplines, including anthropology, sociology, African history, literary studies, philosophy, and socio-linguistics. Contributions to the journal will generally consist of densely annotated texts followed by a detailed analysis of the data presented (see Web site for further details), but other kinds of manuscripts will be published as well.

719   **Quest: An African Journal of Philosophy/Une Revue Africaine de Philosophie**
c/o Prof.dr Wim van Binsbergen
African Studies Centre
PO Box 9555
2300 RB Leiden
Tel: +31- 71-527 3677 Fax: +31-71-527 3344
Email: editor@quest-journal.net or quest_journal@yahoo.com
Web: http://quest-journal.net/
1987- Print and online [originally published in Zambia, re-launched March 2004] ISSN 1011-226X 2Yr
Subs: print, in Africa €20 inst €15 indiv, outside Africa €35 inst €25 indiv; online: free
Ed: Wim van Binsbergen
Aims to act as a channel of expression for thinkers in Africa and to stimulate philosophical discussion on problems that arise out of the radical transformations Africa and Africans are undergoing.
Submissions : in English or French ; the journal publishes materials on both current subjects related to Africa as well as subjects of general philosophical interest serving an international audience of professional philosophers and intellectuals in other disciplines with philosophical interest.
Note: originally published as *Quest. Philosophical Discussions* by the Department of Philosophy, University of Zambia, the journal has recently been resuscitated and is now published in the Netherlands; for free full text access to back volumes published, vol. 13, 1999-vol. 16, 2002 *see* http://www.quest-journal.net/access_to_volumes.htm

720   **Review of Contemporary African Art**
Tussen de Bogen 111
1013 JB Amsterdam
Tel: +31-20-531 8499
Fax: +31-20-531 8498
Email: review@vmcaa.nl
Web: http://www.vmcaa.nl/vm/index.html
2001- Online [No ISSN] Qtly [published irregularly]
Subs: free
Ed: Fons Geerlings *et al*
A quarterly review and virtual exhibition with discussions and commentary on contemporary African art, and also containing information about exhibitions and other African art events, both in the Netherlands and internationally. Additionally, there is an interactive bulletin board for announcements and postings, a who's who with links to African art resources and sites of African artists, and an exchange programme for African artists.
Submissions: as above

Norway

721   **Sudanic Africa. A Journal of Historical Sources**
Centre for Middle Eastern Studies
University of Bergen
Nygårdsgt. 5
5015 Bergen
Tel: +47-55-582711 Fax: +47-55-589891
Email: sylvia.liland@smi.uib.no
http://www.hf.uib.no/smi/sa/default.html
1990- Print and online ISSN 0803-0685
(E-ISSN 0806-7120)
Subs: £20/$30 inst £15/$20 indiv
Ed: Knut S. Vikør *et al,*
Email: knut.vikor@smi.uib.no

Devoted to the presentation and discussion of historical sources on the Sudanic belt, the area between the Sahara and the Bay of Niger, the Atlantic and the Indian Oceans. The journal typically presents such sources in the original language and in translation, with comments.
Submissions: as above
H-Africa TOC
Note: for a cumulative index of articles published in the journal (1990-) *see* http://www.hf.uib.no/smi/sa/default.html

Poland

722   Africana Bulletin
Institute of Developing Countries
Faculty of Geography and
Regional Studies
Warsaw University
Krakowskie Przedmiescie
3000-927 Warsaw
Tel: +48-22-552 0624 Fax: +48-22-552 1521
Email: africana@uw.edu.pl
http://www.orient.uw.edu.pl/~afrykanistyka/publications.html
1964- Print ISSN 0002-029X 2Yr
Subs: $30
Ed: Bogdan Stefanski
All subjects dealing with African affairs.
Submissions: as above, contributions in Polish, English or French.

Portugal

723   Africana Studia. Revista Internacional de Estudos Africanos
Centro de Estudos Africanos
Universidade do Porto
Via panorâmica s/n
4150-564 Porto
Tel: +351- 22-607 7141
Fax: +351-22-609 1610
Email: ceaup@letras.up.pt
Web: http://www.letras.up.pt/ceaup/
1999- Print ISSN 0874-2375 Ann
Subs: (issues individually priced, ca. €20 each)
Ed: António Custódio Gonçalves
Book rev
An international journal of African studies, with some focus on the history, cultures and literatures of the countries of lusophone Africa.
Submissions: articles in Portuguese, English and French.

724   Africa Debate
Associação Académica África Debate
Cacifo 19
ISCTE
Av das Forças Armadas
1649-026 Lisbon
Tel: +351-21-790 3000/+21-790-5000 (leave message for "Cacifo 19")
Email: africadebate@iscte.pt
Web: http://africadebate.iscte.pt
1999- Print and (partly) online [No ISSN] Ann
Subs: €5
Ed: Isabel Lopes Ferreira, Email: africadebate@yahoo.com
International, inter-universities African studies magazine; contains reports, articles, and dossiers, based mainly on masters or doctorate thesis.
Submissions: in Portuguese, English, French, and Spanish.
Affil: ➜ **Associação Académica África Debate (2762)**

725   Boletim Africanista
Estudos Sobre Africa
Centro Interdisciplinar de História,
Culturas e Sociedades (CIDEHUS)
Universidade de Évora
Palácio doVimioso Apartado 94
7001 Évora
Tel/Fax: n/a
Email: nesa@uevora.pt
Web:
http://www.cidehus.uevora.pt/nesa/bnesa/bsaout02.htm
1999- Online [no ISSN] Ann (irregular)
Subs: free
Eds: Núcleo de Estudos Sobre África do Centro Interdisciplinar de História, Culturas e Sociedades, Universidade de Évora
Africanist bulletin edited by the Group of Studies on Africa of the Interdisciplinary Centre of History, Cultures, and Societies of the University of Evora. The Bulletin contains African studies news and notices, news of events, meetings and conferences, book and journal reviews, etc.

Russia

726 **Vostok: Afro-aziatskie obshchestva:**
istoria i sovremennost'
(formerly Narodny Aziii Afriki)
MAIK Nauka-Interperiodica
Mezhdunarodnyi Otdel
10300 Moscow
Tel/Fax: n/a
Email: kvbun@maik.ru
Web: http://www.maik.rssi.ru/
1955- Print ISSN 0869-1908 2Yr
Subs: $180
Ed: L.B. Alaev, Institut vostokovedeniya
RAN, Spiridonovka, 30/1, Moscow
103001
History and political life of African and
Asian societies, political systems, economic
development and international relations.
Submissions: text in Russian, abstracts in
English.

Spain

727 **Mundo Negro**
Arturo Soria 101
28043 Madrid
Tel: +34-91-415 24 12 Fax: +34-91-519 25 50
Email: Mundonegro@combonianos.com
(Editorial and general enquiries)
edimune@combonianos.com (Subscriptions)
1960- Print Mon
Web: http://www.combonianos.com/mn/
Subs: in Spain €30 inst €24 indiv, elsewhere in
Europe €45, elsewhere €50
Eds: P. Francisco Carrera, Gerardo González
Calvo
Monthly magazine published by the Combonianos
Missionaries. Includes articles, news and reports
about Africa's social, political and religious life, as
well as contributions on African arts and cultures.

728 **Nova Africa**
Centro d'Estudis Africans (CEA)
Mare de Déu del Pilar 15 pral.
08003 Barcelona
Tel: +34-3-319 4008 Fax: +34-3-319 4008
Email: cea@pangea.org
Web:
http://www.estudisafricans.org/index2.htm
1995- Print ISSN 1136-0437 2Yr
Subs: €45, price includes subscription to
CEA's *Africa Actual* and ➜ **Studia Africana**
(729)
Ed: Antoni Castel,

Email: Antoni.Castel@uab.es
Book rev
A review of contemporary African affairs and
socio-political and economic analysis.
Submissions: in English (translated into
Spanish) and Spanish; contact Editor for more
details.

729 **Studia Africana**
Centro d'Estudis Africans (CEA)
Mare de Déu del Pilar 15 pral.
08003 Barcelona
Tel: +34-3-319 4008 Fax: -+34-3-319 4008
Email: cea@pangea.org
Web:
http://www.estudisafricans.org/index2.htm
1990- Print ISSN 1130-5703 Ann
Subs: €45, price includes subscription to
CEA's *Africa Actual* and ➜ **Nova Africa (728)**
Ed: Albert Roca, Email: roca@hahs.udl.es
Book rev
A bi-lingual journal devoted to African history,
anthropology, culture, religion, politics and the
economy.
Submissions: in English and Spanish; contact
Editor for more details.

Sweden

730 **Development Dialogue. A Journal**
of International Development
Cooperation
Dag Hammarskjöld Foundation
Övre Slottsgatan 2
753 10 Uppsala
Tel: +46-18-127272 Fax: +46-18-122072
Email: secretariat@dhf.uu.set
Web: http://www.dhf.uu.se
1972- Print and online ISSN 0345-2538 2Yr
Subs: free
Eds: Sven Hamrell, Niclas Hällström, Olle
Nordberg
Intended to provide a forum for critical discussion
of development priorities and problems facing the
21st century, international development
cooperation in general, and multilateralism in
particular.
Submissions: contains mainly material arising
from the seminars and workshops organized
by the ➜ **Dag Hammarskjöld Foundation**
(2687) However, the editors also, in certain
cases, commission articles. The issues often
feature a specific theme.

Note: full-text access (pdf) to all issues published from 1972-2002 available at the Web site.

731   News from the Nordic Africa Institute
Nordic Africa Institute
PO Box 1703
751 47 Uppsala
Tel +46-18-562200 Fax +46-18-562290
Email: nai@nai.uu.se
Web:
http://www.nai.uu.se/newsfromnai/newse
ng.html
1996- Print and online (online from no. 3, 2001) [No ISSN] 3Yr
Subs: free
Ed: Lennart Wohlgemuth
Contains news about the Institute and African studies related events and activities in the Nordic countries, short articles, (sometimes on special topics), commentary, interviews, conference reports, as well as listings and descriptions of recent NAI publications.
Note: issue no. 2, 2005, includes several articles on southern African archives and a number of digital projects.

732   Nordic Journal of African Studies
Abdulaziz Y. Lodhi, Publication Secretary
The Nordic Association of African Studies
Box 527
752 36 Uppsala
All correspondence to:
Professor Arvi Hurskainen
Institute for Asian and African Studies
Unioninkatu 38 B
Box 59
00014 University of Helsinki
Finland
Tel: +358-9-1912 2677 Fax: +358-9-1912 2094
Email: arvi.hurskainen@helsinki.fi
Web: http://www.njas.helsinki.fi/
1992- Print (to vol. 12, no. 2, 2003) Online only from vol. 13, no.1, 2004- ISSN 1235-4481 (E-ISSN 2004-, 1459-9465) 2Yr, Qtly for online version, 2004-
Subs: print edition/back issues (to vol. 12, 2003) €23 inst €18.50 indiv (free to members of the Nordic Association of African Studies); online (vol. 13, 2004-): free
Ed: Arvi Hurskainen, at address above,

Email: arvi.hurskainen@helsinki.fi
Book rev
An interdisciplinary journal published by the Nordic Association of African Studies with a focus on Africa, including the various fields of African language studies, literature, sociolinguistics, cultural and social anthropology, population, history, and art.
Submissions: the primary publication language is English, but articles written in French and Swahili will also be published.
Note: full-text access (pdf) to all issues published from vol. 1, no. 1, 1992 to current issue available at the Web site.

Switzerland

733   Le Fait Missionnaire. Pluridisciplinary Journal on the History and Heritage of Christian Missions
Observatoire des Religions en Suisse
Université de Lausanne
Bâtiment Provence
1015 Lausanne
Tel: +41-21-692 2700
Fax: +41-21-692 2705
Email: subscription@lefaitmissionnaire.com (Subscriptions) E-mail:
editors@lefaitmissionnaire.com (Editorial and submissions)
Web: http://www.lefaitmissionnaire.com
Eds: Eric Morier-Genoud and Didier Péclard
1995- Print and online ISSN 1420-2018 2Yr
Subs: print CHFr 40/$35
Aims to publish high quality academic work relating to the history and heritage of Christian missions, following a pluridisciplinary approach.
Submissions: as above, in English and French
H-Africa TOC
Note: full-text access (pdf) to all issues published from no. 1, 1995 to current issue available at
http://www2.unil.ch/lefaitmissionnaire/pag
es/issues.html

United Kingdom

734   Africa. The Journal of the
       International African Institute
       Edinburgh University Press
       22 George Square
       Edinburgh EH8 9LF
Tel: +44-(0)131-650 4218
Fax: +44-(0)131-662 0053
Email: journals@eup.ed.ac.uk
Web: http://www.eup.ed.ac.uk/ or
or: International African Institute SOAS,
Thornhaugh Street Russell Square,
London WC1H 0XG,
Tel: +44-(0)20-7898 4435
Web: http://www.iaionthe.net/africa.asp
Email: ed2@soas.ac.uk
1928- Print and online ISSN 0001-9720 Qtly
Subs: including annual → Africa
Bibliography (382): in UK and Europe £225
inst £90 indiv, North America $435 inst $118
indiv, elsewhere £242 inst £100 indiv
(includes online access); without annual
bibliography: £50/$95/£56 indiv only;
Ed: Richard Fardon, Department of
Anthropology and Sociology, School of
Oriental and African Studies, Thornhaugh
Street, Russell Square, London WC1H 0XG
Email: iai-africa@soas.ac.uk
Book rev Book rev ed: Paul Nugent, Centre
of African Studies, 21 George Square,
Edinburgh EH8 9LF
Email: paul.nugent@ed.ac.uk
*Devoted to the study of African societies and
cultures; encourages an interdisciplinary
approach, giving particular emphasis to historical
trends, issues of development, and links between
local and national levels of society.*
Submissions: social sciences, history,
environmental and life sciences, languages
and culture.
Affil: → International African Institute
(1622)
H-Africa TOC

735   Africa Analysis
       Africa Analysis Ltd.
       Diamond House Suite 2F
       36-38 Hatton Garden
       London EC1N 8EB
Tel: +44-(0)20-7404 4321
Fax: +44-(0)20-7404 4351
Email: aa@africaanalysis.com
Web: http://www.africaanalysis.com/
1986- Print and online ISSN 0950-902X 2Mon

Subs: print only £240/$466, pdf download
only £160/$315, print and Web access
£650/$1,240
Ed: Ahmed Rajab Book rev
*Fortnightly bulletin on African financial and
political trends; business, stock market and
corporate updates.*
Submissions: on African finance, economy,
and inside politics.

736   Africa Confidential
       Journal Customer Services
       Blackwell Publishing
       PO Box 1354
       9600 Garsington Road
       Oxford OX4 2XG
Tel: +44-(0)1865-778315
Fax: +44-(0)1865-471775
Email:
customerservices@oxon.blackwellpublishing.
com
Web:
http://www.blackwellpublishing.com/journ
al.asp?ref=0044-6483
or
http://www.africa-confidential.com
In the US:
Blackwell Publishing
350 Main Street
Malden MA 02148
Tel: +1-781-388 8200 Fax: +1-781-388 8210
1960- Print and online ISSN 0044-6483
25 times Yr
Subs: in EU £657.00, elsewhere outside Africa
$1,267, Africa £429 (Premium online service,
for other rates and options *see*
http://www.blackwellpublishing.com/subs.
asp?ref=0044-6483
Ed: Patrick Smith
Managing ed: Clare Tauben, Africa
Confidential, 73 Farringdon Road, London
ECIM 3JQ
Tel: +44-(0)20-7831 3511
Fax: +44-(0)20-7831 6778
Email: info@africa-confidential.com
Book rev
*Exclusive news, reports and sharp analysis on
African politics and economics, and relations
between Africa and the rest of the world, drawing
on an extensive network of independent
correspondents.*
Note: to browse articles by country or by
category *see*
http://www.africa-
confidential.com/index.aspx?pageid=10;

search results will display a short summary, and volume and issue date, but full-text access is subject to subscription and log-in; alternatively use the pay- per-view option.

737   Africa Investor Magazine
67-69 Whitfield Street
London W1T 4HF
Tel: +44-(0)20-7462 7550
Fax⁻ +44-(0)20-7462 7573
Email: subscriptions@africa-investor.com
editor@africa-investor.com (Editorial enquiries)
Web: http://www.africa-investor.com/index.html
2003- Print ISSN n/a Qtly
Subs: £32/$60
Eds: Katrina Manson,
Email: kmanson@africa-investor.com
Managing ed: Hubert Danso,
Email: hdanso@africa-investor.com
A joint initiative of the Commonwealth Business Council, the Friends of Africa Business Group, which mobilises international investment into Africa, and Africapractice, a public affairs agency dedicated to working with governments, international organizations and businesses to communicate their commitment to African development. The magazine aims to inform investors and policy makers involved in international investment business decisions, and to deepen understanding among international business and governments about Africa's investment opportunities, challenges and potential.

738   Africa Research Bulletin: Political, Social and Cultural Series/Africa Research Bulletin: Economic, Financial and Technical Series
Journal Customer Services
Blackwell Publishing
PO Box 1354
9600 Garsington Road
Oxford OX4 2XG
Tel: +44-(0)1865-778315
Fax: +44-(0)1865-471775
Email: customerservices@oxon.blackwellpublishing.com or info@africa-research-bulletin.com
Web: http://www.blackwellpublishing.com/journal.asp?ref=0044-6483 or http://www.africa-research-bulletin.com/
In the US:
Blackwell Publishing

350 Main Street
Malden MA 02148
Tel: +1-781-388 8200 Fax: +1-781-388 8210
Web (Political, social and cultural series): http://www.blackwellpublishing.com/journal.asp?ref=0001-9844&site=1
Web (Economic series): http://www.blackwellpublishing.com/journal.asp?ref=0001-9852&site=1
1964- Print and online ISSN A-political, social and cultural: 0001-9844 (E-ISSN 1467-825X) Mon (3 combined issues)
B-economic: 0001-9852 Mon (3 combined issues)
Subs: (premium online) in UK and Europe £696 inst £222 stud, Americas and the Caribbean $1,322 inst $288 stud, Africa: £452 inst £128 stud, elsewhere £787 inst £222 stud (reduced rate available if subscribing to both series, details from publisher); reduced rates also available for members of the ➔
African Studies Association of the UK (2757)
Ed: Pita Adams, Pines, Wykes Lane, Newton St Cyres, Devon EX5 5AX,
Tel: + 44-(0)-1392-851680,
Fax: + 44-(0)139-851680;
Email: P.B.Adams@exeter.ac.uk
Published in two separate parts. Provides impartial summaries of, and extensive reports on, political and economic developments throughout Africa, drawing on reports from local press, Web sites and radio, as well as international organizations and news agencies.
Submissions: does not accept non-commissioned material for publication.
H-Africa TOC

739   Africa Today
Afro Media (UK) Ltd
AMC House Suite 6
12 Cumberland Avenue
London NW10 7QL
Tel: +44-208-838 5900
Fax: +44-208-838 3700
Email: publisher@africatoday.com
Web: http://www.africatoday.com/cgi-bin/public.cgi
1995- Print and online ISSN 1357-311X Mon
Subs: print: in UK £40, Africa/Europe £60, USA/Canada/Caribbean $85
Online: free (requires registration)
Ed: Kayode Soyinka
A Pan-African news and current affairs magazine that provides information about Africa of assistance to the world of business, and to those

who have investments and commercial interests within the continent. The journal prides itself on its credibility as an independent journal of record for Africa and knowing Africa well.
Submissions: n/a

740 Africa Week
Transafrica Publishing Ltd
PO Box 50010
London SE6 2WJ
Tel: +44-(0)20-8285 1675
Fax: +44-(0)870 429 2026
Email: info@africaweekmagazine.com or admin@africaweekmagazine.com
Web:
http://www.africaweekmagazine.com/main.php
1917-2003 (as *West Africa*) 2004- (as *Africa Week*) Print and online [No ISSN] Wk (online, 50 issues), Mon (print, 12 issues)
Subs: online/print, 50 weekly issues online for one year plus 12 special monthly print editions £63/$100; print only £30/$65
Ed: Desmond Davies,
Email: ddavies@africaweekmagazine.com
Book rev
Supersedes [although is not connected with] the weekly West Africa *magazine published since 1917, providing commentary, analysis and news round ups, covering politics, business and finance, the environment, defence and security, health, human rights, industry, law and legislation, social affairs, as well as the arts, literature and culture. Also publishes special industrial and other reports on individual African countries, or on special topics.*
Submissions: n/a
For an insightful article, by one of *West Africa's* former Editors, Kay Whiteman, see "West Africa Magazine as an Historical Archive, 1917-1997", *African Research & Documentation,* no. 87 (2001): 19-28

741 African Affairs. Journal of the Royal African Society
Journals Subscription Department
Oxford University Press
Great Clarendon Street
Oxford OX2 6DP
Tel: +44-(0)1865-353907
Fax: +44-(0)1865-353485
Email: jnls.cust.serv@oupjournals.org
African.Affairs@ncl.ac.uk;
Web: http://afraf.oupjournals.org/
In the US:

Journals Customer Services
Oxford University Press
2001 Evans Road
Cary NC 27513
Tel: +1-919-677 0977, extn. 6686 Toll-free (USA/Canada only) 800-852 7323
USA/Canada) Fax: +1-919-677 1714
Email: jnlorders@oupjournals.org
1901- Print and online ISSN 0001-9909 (E-ISSN 1468-2621) Qtly
Subs: print and online £174/$296 inst, online only £157/$267 inst,
print only £165/$281 inst, £47/$80 indiv (special rates apply for African countries, print and online $20 indiv, and for members of the ➔ **African Studies Association of the UK (2757)**
Eds: Tim Kelsall, Department of Politics, University of Newcastle upon Tyne, 40-42 Great North Road, Newcastle upon Tyne NE 17RU, Tel: + 44-(0)191-222 8824,
Fax: +44-(0)191-222 5609;
Email: Tim.Kelsall@ncl.ac.uk;
Stephen Ellis, Afrika-Studiecentrum, PO Box 9555, 2300 RB Leiden; The Netherlands; Tel: +31-71 527 3362,
Fax: + 31-71-527 3344;
Email: ellis@fsw.leidenuniv.nl;
Submissions to Tim Kelsall
Book rev Book rev ed: JoAnn McGregor, Department of Geography, University of Reading, Whiteknights, PO Box 227, Reading RG6 6AB; Tel: +44-(0)118-931 8733; Fax: +44-(0)118-975 5865;
Email: J.Mcgregor@reading.ac.uk
Contains articles on recent political, social and economic developments in sub-Saharan African countries. Also included are historical, literary or scientific studies that illuminate current events in the continent.
Submissions: welcomes submissions from all over the world, in particular from Africa. It accepts articles not just from professional academics, but from authors in a variety of occupations.
Affil: ➔ **Royal African Society (2780)**
JSTOR Coverage: Vols. 43-98, 1944-1999
Journal URL:
http://www.jstor.org/journals/00019909.html
Vols. 1-43, 1901-1944
Journal URL:
http://www.jstor.org/journals/03684016.html

RSS RSS feed available, *see*
http://afraf.oxfordjournals.org/rss/

742   **African Archaeological Review**
Kluwer Academic Publishers
Van Godewijckstraat 30
PO Box 17
3300 AA Dordrecht
Netherlands
Tel.: +31-78-657 6000 Fax: +31-78-657 6254
Email: sales@wkap.nl
Web:
http://www.kluweronline.com/issn/02
63-0338
In the US:
Kluwer Academic Publishers
101 Philip Drive
Assinippi Park
Norwell MA 02061
Tel. +1-781-871 6600 Fax: +1-781 871 6528
Email: Teresa.Krauss@wkap.com
1983- Print and online ISSN 0263-0338
(E-ISSN 1572-9842) Qtly
Subs: see publisher Web site
Ed: Fekri H. Hassan, Department of
Egyptology, Institute of Archaeology,
University College, 31-34 Gordon Square,
London WC1H 0PY, Tel: +44-(0)20-7387-
7050 ext. 4429 Fax: + 44-(0)20-7383-2572
or +44-(0)20-7813-524;
Email: 1f.hassan@ucl.ac.uk
Book rev
Articles on African archaeology, highlighting the
outstanding contributions of this region's past as
they relate to key global issues. Important topics
include the emergence of modern humans, earliest
manifestations of human culture, and the origins
of African plant and animal domesticates.
Submissions: interregional studies, and new
field data, covering a wide research range,
including cultural continuities and
discontinuities, biocultural evolution; cultural
dynamics and ecology, the role of cultural
materials in politics and ideology; the
application of ethnohistorical, textual, and
ethnoarchaeological data in archaeological
interpretation; conservation, management of
cultural heritage, information technology,
and public archaeology.
Affil: ➔ **Society of Africanist Archaeologists**
(2785)

➔ **The African Book Publishing Record** *see* **3**
Current bibliographies, indexing and
abstracting services, and review media entry
384

743   **African Development Review**
Journal Customer Services
Blackwell Publishing
PO Box 1354
9600 Garsington Road
Oxford OX4 2XG
Tel: +44-(0)1865-778315
Fax: +44-(0)1865-471775
Email:
customerservices@oxon.blackwellpublishing.
com
Web:
http://www.blackwellpublishing.com/journ
al.asp?ref=1017-6772
In the US:
Blackwell Publishing
350 Main Street
Malden MA 02148
Tel: +1-781-388 8200 Fax: +1-781-388 8210
1988- Print and online ISSN 1017-6772
(E-ISSN 1467-8268) 3Yr
Subs: in Europe £120 inst £61 indiv, the
Americas $202 inst $69 indiv, elsewhere £120
inst £41 indiv (includes online access)
Ed: Mohammed Hussain, Temporary
Headquarters, African Development Bank
Group, Angle Des Trois Rues, BP 323, 1002
Tunis Belvedere,
Tunisia, Email: m.hussain@afdb.org
Managing ed: Barfour Osei,
Email: b.osei@afdb.org
Book rev Book rev ed: Obadiah Mailafia,
Email: O.Mailafia@afdb.org
Devoted to the study and analysis of development
policy in Africa. Emphasizes policy relevance of
research findings, rather than purely theoretical
and quantitative issues.
Submissions: papers, research notes, and
book reviews on development issues in
Africa. The journal focuses on quality policy-
oriented papers.
Affil: published on behalf of the ➔ **African**
Development Bank (2501)

744 **African Journal of International and Comparative Law** (New series)
Edinburgh University Press
22 George Square
Edinburgh EH8 9LF
Tel: +44-(0)131- 650 6207
Fax: +44-(0)131-662 0053
Email: journals@eup.ed.ac.uk
Web:
http://www.eup.ed.ac.uk/journals/content.aspx?pageId=1&journalId=12164
2005- (New series) Print ISSN 0954-8890 2Yr
Subs: in UK and Europe £90 inst, £40 indiv;
North America $160 inst, $70 indiv
Eds: Rachel Murray, School of Law,
University of Bristol, Wills Memorial
Building, Queens Road, Bristol BS6 5LD, Tel:
+44-(0)117-954 5374,
Fax: +44-(0)117-925 1870,
Email: Rachel.Murray@bristol.ac.uk;
Amazu Asouzu, School of Law, King's
College London, Strand, London WC2R 2LS,
Tel: +44-(0)20-7848 1159,
Fax: +44-(0)20-7848 2465,
Email amazu.asouzu@kcl.ac.uk
Provides refereed material in both international and comparative law on a pan-African basis.
Submissions: welcomes articles on public or private international law, either in English or French.

745 **African Literature Today**
James Currey Publishers
73 Botley Road
Oxford OX2 0BS
Tel: +44(0)1865-244111
Fax: +44(0)1865-246454
Email: sales@jamescurrey.co.uk
Web: http://www.jamescurrey.co.uk/
1968- Print ISSN 0852-5555 Ann (Irregular)
Subs: now sold individually, latest issue
no. 25, 2005, £14.95 (topic: New Directions in
African Literature)
Eds: Eldred Durosimi Jones & Marjorie Jones
(to no. 23, 2002); Ernest N. Emenyonu (no. 24,
2002-), Department of Africana Studies,
University of Michigan-Flint, 303 East
Kearsley Street, Flint MI 48502, USA; Fax: +1-
810-766 6719, Email: eernest@umich.edu
Book rev Book rev ed: James Gibbs,
8 Victoria Square, Bristol BS1 4ET, UK
Email: jamesgibbs@btinternet.com
Each volume focuses on a special aspect of African literature, such as Women's Writing, Poetry, Oral Literature, Drama, Prose, etc. which is announced in advance. Forthcoming titles, no. 26 War in African Literature, no. 27: New Novels in African Literature.
Submissions: welcomed, provided they fit into the announced topic.

746 **African News. Newsletter of the Centre of African Studies, University of London**
School of Oriental and African Studies
University of London
Thornhaugh Street
Russell Square
London WC1H 0XG
Tel: +44-(0)20-7898 4370
Fax: +44-(0)20-7898 4369
Email: cas@soas.ac.uk
Web:
http://www.soas.ac.uk/centres/centreinfo.cfm?navid=677 (issue 58)
1998- Online (html or pdf, or as an email
attachment) [No ISSN] 3Yr
Subs: free
Ed: Jackie Collis (Centre Organiser)
Contains a variety of news about events at the SOAS Centre of African Studies and Africa-related events, seminars, workshops, talks and lectures at other UK institutions, each item giving descriptive and contact information. Also includes news about graduate studentship and scholarship schemes.

747 **African Renaissance**
Adonis & Abbey Publishers Ltd
PO Box 43418
London SE14 4XZ
Tel: +44-(0)20-7793 8893/7463 2288
Email: sales@adonis-abbey.com
(Subscriptions) editor@adonis-abbey.com
(Editorial)
Web: http://www.adonis-abbey.com/journal_1.htm
2004- Print ISSN ISSN 1744-2532 6Yr [issues
also sold individually, with ISBNs]
Subs: UK and Europe £250 inst £120 indiv,
elsewhere £250 inst £150 indiv
Ed: Jideofor Adibe,
Email: editor@adonis-abbey.com
The magazine is a cross between an academic journal and a higher-end news features magazine, targeted principally at policy makers, policy moulders, professionals, intellectuals and 'stakeholders' in African affairs. The aim is to provide a platform "where Africanists can engage

in serious discussions without the sharp practises frequently associated with academic journals."
Submissions: articles can be on any topic of relevance to Africa, but written in ways to be of interest to policy makers. Lead articles may involve identifying major strands in a debate, and finding writers who represent each strand to write for us. These contributions are circulated to those invited to write on the topic for discussion.

748   African Research & Documentation
c/o Terry Barringer, Editor
70 Mortlock Avenue
Cambridge CB4 1TE
Tel: +44-(0)1223-424584
Email: tabarringe@aol.com
Web:
http://www.lse.ac.uk/library/scolma/ardm
ain.htm
1962- Print ISSN 0305-826X 3Yr
Subs: £24/$53 (surface mail) £30/$64 (airmail)
Subs orders to: Ian Cooke, Deputy Editor & Subscriptions Manager, ARD, Library, Institute of Commonwealth Studies, 28 Russell Square, London WC1B 5DS, Tel: +44-(0)20-7580 5876,
Email: Ian.Cooke@sas.ac.uk
Ed: Terry Barringer, at address above
Book rev Book rev ed: Terry Barringer (*see also* note below)
Articles and news items on all aspects of African studies, library and archive collections relating to Africa, and Africana bibliography.
Submissions: articles and information on all aspects of library, archive, and bibliographical matters relating to Africa and African studies.
Affil: ➜ **Standing Conference of Library Materials on Africa/SCOLMA (1892)**
H-Africa TOC
Note: references to a large number of reviews of African studies reference resources that have appeared in this journal are cited with book entries in section ➜ **2 The major general reference tools**

➜ **The African Review of Books** *see* **3 Current bibliographies, indexing and abstracting services, and review media** entry **407**

749   African Studies Association of the UK Newsletter
c/o Simon Heap, Editor
Plan International
Chobham House
Christchurch Way
Woking GU21 6JG
Fax: +44-(0)1483-756505
Web: http://www.asauk.net/news.html
1995- Print and online [No ISSN] Qtly Subs: free with membership of ASAUK and/or RAS, distributed with ➜ **African Affairs (741)**
Ed: Simon Heap, Email: simon.heap@plan-international.org
News and advance notices about Africanist activities throughout the UK.
Submissions: announcements of forthcoming meetings, workshops and conferences; brief reports of past conferences and events; announcements of appointments, links, exchanges, and new and forthcoming books by ASAUK/RAS members (but no book reviews); obituaries; prizes and awards; any news of general interest to Africanists.
Affil: ➜ **African Studies Association of the UK (2757)**

750   Bulletin of Francophone Africa
University of Westminster
Francophone ACP Research Group
School of Social Science, Humanities and Languages
309 Regent Street
London W1B 2UW
Tel: +44-(0)20-7911 5000 exts 2048, 2068,
Fax: +44-(0)20-7911 5001/5870
1992- Print ISSN 0966-1018 2Yr
Subs: n/a
Eds: Hélène Gill, Email: gillh@wmin.ac.uk; Ethel Tolansky
Book rev Book rev ed: Aline Cook, Email: cooka@wmin.ac.uk
Articles and reviews of books concerned with issues regarding the francophone Maghreb area of North Africa and francophone regions of sub-Saharan Africa, of a social, political, economic or literary nature.
Submissions: as above in English or French

751 Bulletin of the School of Oriental and African Studies
Cambridge University Press
The Edinburgh Building
Shaftesbury Road
Cambridge CB2 2RU
Tel: +44(0)1223-326070
Fax: +44(0)1223-325150
Email: journals@cambridge.org
In the US:
Cambridge University Press
100 Brook Hill Drive
West Nyack NY 10994-2133
Tel: +1-845-353 7500 (US/Canada only) 800-872-7423 Fax: +1-845-353-4141
Email: subscriptions_newyork@cambridge.org
Web:
http://titles.cambridge.org/journals/journal_catalogue.asp?mnemonic=bso
1917- Print and online ISSN 0041-977X (E-ISSN 1474-0699) 3Yr
Subs: print and online £119/$199 inst, print only, £115/$194 inst £45/$79 indiv
Ed: G. R. Hawting, School of Oriental and African Studies, History Department, University of London
Thornhaugh Street, Russell Square, London WC1H 0XG, Email: Bulletin@soas.ac.uk
Book rev
An interdisciplinary journal on the Near and Middle East, Asia and Africa. It carries articles and short notices on the languages, cultures and civilisations of these regions from ancient times to the present day, and also features an extensive book review section.
Submissions: articles and shorter communications, both scholarly and readable, on the history, religions and philosophies, literatures and languages, music, arts and archaeology, law, and anthropology.
H-Africa TOC
JSTOR Coverage: Vols. 10 - 62, 1940-1999
Journal URL:
http://www.jstor.org/journals/0041977X.html
Vols. 1-10, 1917-1940
Journal URL:
http://www.jstor.org/journals/13561898.html

752 Development and Change
Journal Customer Services
Blackwell Publishing
PO Box 1354
9600 Garsington Road
Oxford OX4 2XG
Tel: +44-(0)1865-778315
Fax: +44-(0)1865-471775
Email:
customerservices@oxon.blackwellpublishing.com
http://www.blackwellpublishing.com/journals/dech
1969- Print and online ISSN 0012-155X (E-ISSN: 1467-7660) 6Yr
Subs: Print and online £385/$647 inst €93/$104, online only £332/$558 inst; special rates apply for members of the Development Studies Association, for students, and for institutions and individuals in the developing world (see Web site for rates)
Eds: Ashwani Saith and Ben White, Institute of Social Studies, The Hague, The Netherlands;
Managing ed: Paula E. Bownas, Institute of Social Studies, PO Box 29776, 2502 LT The Hague, The Netherlands,
Tel: + 31-70-426 0491 Fax: + 31-70-426 0799, Email: bownas@iss.nl
Book rev Book review ed: Judith Treanor, Institute of Social Studies, PO Box 29776, 2502 LT The Hague, The Netherlands, Email: treanor@iss.nl
Covers a broad range of topics, publishing articles from all the social sciences and all intellectual persuasions concerned with development. With a mix of regular and special theme issues, Development and Change *is devoted to the critical analysis and discussion of the complete spectrum of development issues.*
Submissions: as above

753 Development Education Journal
Trentham Books Ltd
Westview House
734 London Road
Stoke on Trent ST4 5NP
Tel: +44-(0)1782-745567
Fax +44-(0)1782-745553
Email tb@trentham-books.co.uk
Web:
http://www.dea.org.uk/dea/pub_journal.html
1994- Print ISSN 1354-0742 3Yr

Subs: in UK £35 inst £30 indiv, elsewhere £41 inst £36 indiv
Ed: Gillian Symons, Development Education Association, 1st Floor, River House, 143-145 Farringdon Road, London EC1R 3AB, Tel: +44-(0)20-7812 1282, Fax: +44-(0)20-7812 1272 Email: dea@dea.org.uk; all submissions to Moira Jenkins, Journals Editorial Assistant, Email: moira.jenkins@dea.org.uk
Offers a forum for debate about development education theory and practice in the UK and overseas. Each issue or volume focuses on a key topic or debate in development education, inviting a leading figure in that field to introduce a series of in-depth articles.
Submissions: contributions are welcome from educators and others with an interest in development education, from agencies, DECs, academic institutions, schools, youth work, adult and community education, from Britain and overseas.

754   Development in Practice
Taylor & Francis Journals
4 Park Square
Milton Park
Abingdon OX14 4RN
Tel: +44-(0)20-7017 6000
Fax: +44-(0)20-7017 6336
Email: tf.processing@tfinforma.com
Web:
Web:
http://www.tandf.co.uk/journals/titles/096 14524.asp
In the US:
Taylor & Francis Journals (US)
325 Chestnut Street Suite 800
Philadelphia PA 19106
Tel: +1-215-625 8900 Fax: +1-215-625 8914
1991- Print and online ISSN 0961-4524 (E-ISSN 1364-9213) 6Yr
Ed: Deborah Eade, Oxfam GB, John Smith Drive, Oxford OX2 2JY,
Tel: +44(0)-1865 312149,
Fax: +44-(0)-1865 312600,
Email: editor@developmentinpractice.org
Book rev Book rev ed: Alina Rocha Menocal
Subs: £288/$475 inst £95/$158 indiv (includes online access for both inst and indiv); reduced rate $89 (available for subscribers in middle- and low-income countries as listed in the UNDP Human Development Report)
Offers practice-based analysis and research concerning the social dimensions of development

and humanitarianism, and provides a forum for debate and the exchange of ideas among practitioners, policy makers, and academics worldwide. The journal seeks to challenge current assumptions, stimulate new thinking, and seeks to shape future ways of working.
Submissions: contributions are welcome particularly from development practitioners and new writers. While the language of the journal is English, submissions for translation from French, Spanish or Portuguese are welcome.

755   Development Policy Review
Journal Customer Services
Blackwell Publishing
PO Box 1354
9600 Garsington Road
Oxford OX4 2XG
Tel: +44-(0)1865-778315
Fax: +44-(0)1865-471775
Email:
customerservices@oxon.blackwellpublishing.com
Web:
http://www.blackwellpublishers.co.uk/journal.asp?ref=0950-6764&site=1
In the US:
Blackwell Publishing
350 Main Street
Malden MA 02148
Tel: +1-781-388 8200 Fax: +1-781-388 8210
1982- Print and online ISSN 0950-6764 (E-ISSN 1467-7679) 6Yr
Subs: in Europe £268 inst £39 indiv, the Americas $450 inst $66 indiv, elsewhere £268 inst (special rates for IDS, SID and DSA members)
Ed: David Booth, Overseas Development Institute, 111 Westminster Bridge Road, London, SE1 7JD,
Tel: + 44-(0)20-7922 0300,
Fax: + 44-(0)20-7922 0399,
Email: dpr@odi.org.uk
Book rev
Edited by staff of the Overseas Development Institute, the London-based think-tank on international development and humanitarian issues. Coverage includes the latest thinking and research on poverty-reduction strategies, inequality and social exclusion, property rights and sustainable livelihoods, globalisation in trade and finance, and the reform of global governance.
Submissions: publishes single articles and theme issues on topics at the forefront of

current development policy debate. Invites contributions on all aspects of international development, from any discipline and all regions of the world, but the editors are looking particularly for research results and fresh ideas that extend or challenge the leading policy themes of the day.

756   Focus on Africa Magazine
Subscriptions Department
BBC Focus on Africa Magazine
PO Box 464
Berkhamsted HP4 2UR
Tel: +44-(0)1442-879097
Fax: +44-(0)1442-872279
Email: focus.magazine@webscribe.co.uk
Web:
http://www.bbc.co.uk/worldservice/africa/features/focus_magazine/index.shtml or
http://www.bbc.co.uk/worldservice/focusonafrica/
1990- Print and online ISSN 0959-957 Qtly
Subs: in UK £16, Europe €25, North America $32, Africa and elsewhere £18/$28 (some feature articles accessible for free at the online version)
Ed: Joseph Warungu, Focus On Africa BBC World Service, Bush House, Strand, London WC2B 4PH, Tel: +44-(0)20-7557 2400, Fax: +44-(0)20-7379 0519
Email: focus@bbc.co.uk
Published by the BBC World Service, each issue of Focus on Africa *covers the latest political, economical, social, cultural and sporting developments in Africa.*
Submissions: as above, welcomes contributions from readers across the continent.

757   Gender and Development
Taylor & Francis Journals
4 Park Square
Milton Park
Abingdon OX14 4RN
Tel: +44-(0)20-7017 6000
Fax: +44-(0)20-7017 6336
Email: tf.processing@tfinforma.com
Web:
http://www.tandf.co.uk/journals/carfax/13552074.html
In the US:
Taylor & Francis Journals (US)
325 Chestnut Street Suite 800
Philadelphia PA 19106
Tel: +1-215-625 8900 Fax: +1-215-625 8914

1993- Print and online ISSN 1355-2074 3Yr
Subs: £124/$207 inst £49/$82 indiv reduced rate $38 (available for subscribers in middle- and low-income countries as listed in the UNDP Human Development Report)
Ed: Caroline Sweetman, Oxfam GB, 274 Banbury Road, Oxford OX2 7DZ,
Tel: +44-(0)1865-312106,
Fax: +44(0)1865-312600,
Email: csweetman@oxfam.org.uk
Book rev
Published by ➜ **Oxfam GB (2719)**, Gender and Development *is the only journal to focus specifically on gender and development issues internationally, and to explore the connections between gender and development initiatives and feminist perspectives. It draws on Oxfam GB's strength as a leading NGO working to promote gender equality as an end in itself, and as an essential prerequisite for poverty eradication, peace and sustainable human development.*
Submissions: contributions are welcome from all involved in development initiatives: policy-makers and practitioners, researchers both inside and outside academia, and feminist activists. In recognition of common causes of poverty and marginalization across the world, writers focus on both southern and Northern contexts.

758   IDS Bulletin
Institute of Development Studies
University of Sussex
Brighton BN1 9RE
Tel: +44-(0)1273-606261
Fax: +44-(0)1273-621202/691647
Email: ids@ids.ac.uk
Web:
http://www.ids.ac.uk/ids/bookshop/bulletin/
1970- Print and online (online from 2002) 0265-5012 Qtly
Subs: £130 inst £85 indiv (includes Bulletin and Policy Briefing series)
Ed: each issue is edited by individual editors
Quarterly bulletin on development issues. Each number focuses on a particular topic. Recent topics, in 2004/2005, included: "Repositioning Feminisms in Development", "New Directions in African Agriculture", "Increased Aid: Minimising Problems, Maximising Gains", "Developing Rights".

759 Journal of African Cultural Studies
(formerly *African Languages and Cultures*)
Taylor & Francis Journals
4 Park Square
Milton Park
Abingdon OX14 4RN
Tel: +44-(0)20-7017 6000
Fax: +44-(0)20-7017 6336
Email: tf.processing@tfinforma.com
Web:
http://www.tandf.co.uk/journals/carfax/13
696815.html
In the US:
Taylor & Francis Journals (US)
325 Chestnut Street Suite 800
Philadelphia PA 19106
Tel: +1-215-625 8900 Fax: +1-215-625 8914
1988- Print and online ISSN 1369-6815
(E-ISSN: 1469-9346) 2Yr
Subs: £140/$234 inst £34/$61 indiv
Eds: Akin Oyètádé, Department of the
Languages and Cultures of Africa, School of
Oriental and African Studies, Thornhaugh
Street, Russell Square, London, WC1H OXG,
Tel: +44-(0)20-7898 4968, Fax: +44-(0)20-7898
4399, Email jacs@SOAS.ac.uk
*Focuses on dimensions of African culture
including literature (particularly African
language literatures), performance, art, music, the
role of the media, the relationship between culture
and power, as well as issues within fields such as
popular culture in Africa, sociolinguistic topics of
cultural interest, and culture and gender.*
Submissions: Africa-oriented papers in
descriptive linguistics, comparative
linguistics and classification; oral literature,
African writing in African and metropolitan
languages; African art and music.
H-Africa TOC
JTOR Coverage:
as *African Languages and Cultures* (ceased)
Vols. 1-10, 1988-1997
Journal URL:
http://www.jstor.org/journals/0954416X.ht
ml
as *African Languages and Cultures* Supplement
(ceased) Nos. 1-3, 1992-1996
Journal URL:
http://www.jstor.org/journals/14779366.ht
ml
as *Journal of African Cultural Studies*
Vols. 11-14, 1998-2001
http://www.jstor.org/journals/13696815.ht
ml

760 Journal of African Economies
Journals Subscription Department
Oxford University Press
Great Clarendon Street
Oxford OX2 6DP
Tel: +44-(0)1865-353907
Fax: +44-(0)1865-353485
Email: jnls.cust.serv@oupjournals.org
Web: http://jae.oxfordjournals.org/
In the US:
Journals Customer Services
Oxford University Press
2001 Evans Road
Cary NC 27513
Tel: +1-919-677 0977, extn. 6686 Toll-free
(USA/Canada only) 800-852 7323
USA/Canada) Fax: +1-919-677 1714
Email: jnlorders@oupjournals.org
1992- Print and online ISSN 0963-8024
(E-ISSN: 1464-3723) Qtly (with occasional
supplements)
Subs: print and online £228/$422 inst, online
only £205/$379 inst, print only £217/$401 inst
£49/$91 indiv (special rate for African
countries £30/$56 inst print only £49/$91
indiv, print and online)
Ed: Marcel Fafchamps, Centre for the Study
of African Economies, Department of
Economics, University of Oxford, Manor
Building, Manor Road, Oxford OX1 3UQ, Tel:
+44-(0)1865-271084, Fax: +44-(0)1865-281447,
Email: csaepub@economics.ox.ac.uk
Managing eds: Ernest Ayreety, University of
Ghana; Michael Bleaney, University of
Nottingham; Marcel Fafchamps, CSAE
Oxford; Augustin Fosu, AERC, Nairobi
Book rev
*A vehicle to carry rigorous economic
analysis, focused entirely on Africa, for
Africans and anyone interested in the continent –
be they consultants, policymakers, academics,
traders, financiers, development agents or aid
workers.*
Submissions: publishes theoretical,
methodological, and empirical contributions
to the understanding of African economies.
The emphasis is on original quantitative and
analytical research. Research papers on all
areas of economic analysis focused on Africa
are welcomed.

761 Journal of African History
Cambridge University Press
The Edinburgh Building
Shaftesbury Road
Cambridge CB2 2RU
Tel: +44(0)1223-326070
Fax: +44(0)1223-325150
Email: journals@cambridge.org
Web:
http://www.cambridge.org/uk/journals/journal_catalogue.asp?historylinks=ALPHA&mnemonic=AFH
In the US:
Cambridge University Press
100 Brook Hill Drive
West Nyack NY 10994-2133
Tel: +1-845-353 7500 (US/Canada only) 800-872-7423 Fax: +1-845-353-4141
Email:
subscriptions_newyork@cambridge.org
1960- Print and online ISSN 0021-8537 3Yr
(E-ISSN: 1469-5138) 3Yr
Subs: print and online £142/$224 inst, online only £120/$90 inst, print only £133/$210 inst; print and online £32/$48 indiv, print only £28/$42 indiv; special rates for members of the → **African Studies Association of the UK (2757)**
Eds: Gareth Austin *et al*, Department of Economic History, The London School of Economics and Political Science, Houghton Street, London WC2A 2AE, Email: g.m.austin@lse.ac.uk; for names of other editors and submissions information *see* http://assets.cambridge.org/AFH/AFH_ifc.pdf
Book rev
Publishes articles and book reviews ranging widely over the African past, from the late Stone Age to the 1970s. In recent years increasing prominence has been given to economic, cultural and social history and several articles have explored themes which are also of growing interest to historians of other regions such as: gender roles, demography, legal ideology, labour histories, environmental history, and photographs as historical sources.
Submissions: contributions dealing with pre-colonial historical relationships between Africa and the African diaspora are especially welcome. Articles on slavery, the slave trade and the interpretation of oral tradition are also included.
H-Africa TOC

JSTOR Coverage: Vols. 1-40, 1960-1999
Journal URL:
http://www.jstor.org/journals/00218537.html

762 Journal of African Law
Cambridge University Press
The Edinburgh Building
Shaftesbury Road
Cambridge CB2 2RU
Tel: +44(0)1223-326070
Fax: +44(0)1223-325150
Email: journals@cambridge.org
Web:
http://www.cambridge.org/uk/journals/journal_catalogue.asp?historylinks=ALPHA&mnemonic=JAL
In the US:
Cambridge University Press
100 Brook Hill Drive
West Nyack NY 10994-2133
Tel: +1-845-353 7500 (US/Canada only) 800-872-7423 Fax: +1-845-353-4141
Email:
subscriptions_newyork@cambridge.org
1956- Print and online ISSN 0021-8553
(E-ISSN: 1464-3731) 2Yr
Subs: print and online £88/$148 inst online only £76/$129 inst, print only £80/$135 inst, print only £30/$50 indiv
Eds: Fareda Banda *et al*, Department of Law, School of Oriental and African Studies, University of London, Thornhaugh Street, Russell Square, London WC1H 0XG, Email: fb9@soas.ac.uk; or John Hatchard at same address, Email: jh10@soas.ac.uk
The journal's wide coverage encompasses the laws of sub-Saharan African countries, and articles address contemporary legal issues and highlight issues of international and comparative significance. The journal contains a separate section on recent legislation, case-law, law reform proposals and recent international developments affecting Africa.
Submissions: as above
H-Africa TOC
JSTOR Coverage: Vols. 1 - 43, 1957 1999
Journal URL:
http://www.jstor.org/journals/00218553.html

763 Journal of Commonwealth Literature
Sage Publications
2455 Teller Road
Thousand Oaks CA 91320
USA
Tel: +1-805-499 9774 Fax: +1-805-499 0871
Email: use online form on Web site
Web: http://jcl.sagepub.com/
1965- Print and online ISSN 0021-9894 Qtly
Subs: print and online $451 inst, online only $428 inst, print only $433, print only $109 indiv
Eds: John Thieme, Ira Raja, Maria-Sabinu Alexandru
All correspondence and submissions to: John Thieme, English and American Studies, University of East Anglia, Norwich NR4 7TJ, Email: JohnThieme@aol.com
Book rev (annotated 'Books Received' section only in articles issues)
Critical studies and essays on literature written and published within the Commonwealth, post-colonial theory and related areas. Published in four issues, the first three contain critical studies and essays while the fourth is a bibliographic issue providing an annual bibliography of publications in several regions of the Commonwealth.
Submissions: as above; welcomes submissions (in English) on writing in languages other than English. The journal does not publish creative writing or book reviews, though the articles issues do include a Books Received section, which provide short notices of books sent to the Journal.

764 The Journal of Commonwealth and Comparative Politics
Taylor & Francis Journals
4 Park Square
Milton Park
Abingdon OX14 4RN
Tel: +44-(0)20-7017 6000
Fax: +44-(0)20-7017 6336
Email: tf.processing@tfinforma.com
Web: http://www.tandf.co.uk/journals/titles/146 62043.asp
In the US:
Taylor & Francis Journals (US)
325 Chestnut Street Suite 800
Philadelphia PA 19106
Tel: +1-215-625 8900 Fax: +1-215-625 8914
1962- Print and online ISSN 1466-2043 (E-ISSN 1743-9094) 3Yr

Subs: £213/$332 inst £52/$78 indiv
Eds: Vicky Randall, University of Essex, Roger Charlton, Caledonian University Glasgow, Email: vicky@essex.ac.uk
Book rev Book rev ed: Bruce Baker
Contains scholarly articles which both report original research on the politics of Commonwealth countries and relate their findings to issues of general significance for students of comparative politics. The journal also publishes work on the politics of other states where such work is of interest for comparative politics generally or where it enables comparisons to be made with Commonwealth countries.
Submissions: as above

765 Journal of Contemporary African Studies
Taylor & Francis Journals
4 Park Square
Milton Park
Abingdon OX14 4RN
Tel: +44-(0)20-7017 6000
Fax: +44-(0)20-7017 6336
Email: tf.processing@tfinforma.com
Web: http://www.tandf.co.uk/journals/titles/025 89001.asp
In the US:
Taylor & Francis Journals (US)
325 Chestnut Street Suite 800
Philadelphia PA 19106
Tel: +1-215-625 8900 Fax: +1-215-625 8914
1983- Print and online ISSN 0258-9001 (E-ISSN 1469-9397) 3Yr
Subs: £333/$549 inst £71/$115 indiv
Ed: Roger Southall, Human Sciences Research Council, South Africa; contributions to Journal of Contemporary African Studies, Institute of Social and Economic Research, Rhodes University, Grahamstown 6140, South Africa
Email: rsouthall@hsrc.ac.za
Book rev Book rev eds: Paul Maylam, Department of History, Rhodes University, South Africa; Rose Boswell, Department of Anthropology, Rhodes University, South Africa
An interdisciplinary journal of research and writing in the human sciences--economics, political science, international affairs, military strategy, modern history, law, sociology, education, industrial relations, urban studies, demography, social anthropology, literature, development studies and related fields. The journal seeks to promote a scholarly

understanding of developments and change in Africa.
Submissions: as above
H-Africa TOC

766   Journal of Modern African Studies
Cambridge University Press
The Edinburgh Building
Shaftesbury Road
Cambridge CB2 2RU
Tel: +44(0)1223-326070
Fax: +44(0)1223-325150
Email: journals@cambridge.org
Web:
http://www.cambridge.org/uk/journals/jo
urnal_catalogue.asp?historylinks=ALPHA&
mnemonic=MOA
In the US:
Cambridge University Press
100 Brook Hill Drive
West Nyack NY 10994-2133
Tel: +1-845-353 7500 (US/Canada only) 800-
872-7423 Fax: +1-845-353-4141
Email:
subscriptions_newyork@cambridge.org
1963- Print and online ISSN 0022-278X (E-
ISSN 1469-7777) Qtly
Subs: print and online £162/$262 inst, online
only £136/$220 inst, print only £148/$240 inst
£48/$76 indiv; special rates apply for
members of the ➔ **African Studies
Association of the UK (2757)**
Ed: Christopher Clapham, Centre of African
Studies, University of Cambridge, Free School
Lane, Cambridge. CB2 3RQ
Email: csc34@cam.ac.uk
Book rev Book rev ed: Rosaleen Duffy,
Department of Politics and International
Relations, Lancaster University, Lancaster
LA1 4YL,
Email: r.duffy@lancaster.ac.uk
*Offers a quarterly survey of developments in
modern African politics and society. Its main
emphasis is on current issues in African politics,
economies, societies and international relations. It
is intended not only for students and academic
specialists, but also for general readers and
practitioners with a concern for modern Africa,
living and working both inside and outside the
continent.*
Submissions: articles from specialists in
different academic disciplines whose
contributions can illuminate and cross-
fertilise one another. Editorial policy avoids
commitment to any political viewpoint or

ideology, but aims at a fair examination of
controversial issues in order to promote a
deeper understanding of what is happening
in Africa today.
H-Africa TOC
JSTOR Coverage: Vols. 1-37, 1963-1999
Journal URL:
http://www.jstor.org/journals/0022278X.ht
ml

**767   Journal of North African
         Studies**
Taylor & Francis Journals
4 Park Square
Milton Park
Abingdon OX14 4RN
Tel: +44-(0)20-7017 6000
Fax: +44-(0)20-7017 6336
Email: tf.processing@tfinforma.com
Web:
http://www.tandf.co.uk/journals/titles/136
29387.asp
Web: *In the US:*
Taylor & Francis Journals (US)
325 Chestnut Street Suite 800
Philadelphia PA 19106
Tel: +1-215-625 8900 Fax: +1-215-625 8914
1996- Print and online ISSN 1362- 9387 (E-
ISSN 1743-9345) Qtly
Subs: £219/$332 inst, £52/$78 indiv
Eds: John P. Entelis, Middle East Studies
Program-LL915A, Fordham University, 113
West 60th Street, New York, NY 10023, USA,
Email: entelis@fordham.edu;
George Joffé, Centre of North African Studies,
Centre for International Studies, 17 Mill Lane,
Cambridge CB2 1QZ,
Email: giris@msn.com
Book rev
*Published by the Centre of North African Studies
(CNAS), University of Cambridge and the
American Institute for Maghrib Studies, the
journal is a forum for scholars of and from the
region. Its contents cover both country-based and
regional themes, which range from historical
topics to sociological, anthropological, economic,
diplomatic and other issues.*
Submissions: as above

768   Journal of Religion in Africa
Brill Academic Publishers
PO Box 9000
Leiden
The Netherlands
Tel: +31-71-535 3566 Fax: +31-71-531 7532
Email: cs@brill.nl
Web:
http://www.brill.nl/product.asp?ID=73
22
or http://www.leeds.ac.uk/trs/jra/
In the US:
Brill Academic Publishers
112 Water Street Suite 601
Boston MA 02109
Tel: +1-617-263 2323 Fax: +1-617-263 2324
Email: cs@brillusa.com
1967- Print and online ISSN 0022-4200
Qtly
Subs: print and online €197/$247 inst
€100/$125 indiv, online only €177/$222 inst
€90/$113 indiv
Ed: David Maxwell, Email:
d.j.maxwell@keele.ac.uk
Brad Weiss; blweis@wm.edu all
contributions to Ingrid Lawrie, Journal of
Religion in Africa, The Mirfield Centre,
Stocksbank Road, Mirfield WF14 0BW, UK,
Email: jraedit@aol.com
Book rev Book rev ed: David Maxwell, Dept
of History, University of Keele, Keele, Staffs
ST5 5BG, UK
*Articles on all forms of religious tradition and
ritual practice in every part of Africa. Presents a
forum for the debate of theoretical issues in the
analysis of African religion past and present, the
journal also encourages the development of new
methodologies.*
Submissions: welcomes submission of
articles on all forms of religious tradition and
ritual practice in every part of Africa; from
scholars working in history, anthropology,
sociology, political science, missiology,
literature and related disciplines, and is open
to every methodology.
JSTOR Coverage: available shortly

769   Journal of Southern African Studies
Taylor & Francis Journals
4 Park Square
Milton Park
Abingdon OX14 4RN
Tel: +44-(0)20-7017 6000
Fax: +44-(0)20-7017 6336
Email: tf.processing@tfinforma.com

Web:
http://www.tandf.co.uk/journals/titles/030
57070.asp
In the US:
Taylor & Francis Journals (US)
325 Chestnut Street Suite 800
Philadelphia PA 19106
Tel: +1-215-625 8900 Fax: +1-215-625 8914
1974- Print and online ISSN 0305-7070 (E-
ISSN 1465-3893) Qtly
Subs: £262/$465 inst £71/$136
Eds: Deborah Gaitskell, Email:
rgaitskell@lineone.net, Lyn Schumaker,
Email: lynschumaker@yahoo.co.uk, David
Simon, Email: dsimon@rhul.ac.uk; all
contributions to Colin Stoneman, Editorial
Co-ordinator, Journal of Southern African
Studies, Old School, Swine, Hull, HU11 4JE,
Tel: +44-(0)1482-811227, Fax: +44-(0)1482-
815857, Email: jsas@stoneman.karoo.co.uk
Book rev Book rev ed: Paul la Hausse de
Lalouvière, Centre of African Studies,
University of Cambridge, Free School Lane,
Cambridge CB2 3RQ, Email:
p.delalouviere@dial.pipex.com
*Aims to generate fresh scholarly inquiry and
exposition in the fields of history, economics,
sociology, demography, social anthropology,
geography, administration, law, political science,
international relations, literature and the natural
sciences, in so far as they relate to the human
condition. It represents a deliberate effort to draw
together the various disciplines in social science
and its allied fields.*
Submissions: welcomes submissions that
reflects new theoretical approaches, and work
that discusses the methodological framework
in general use by students of the area. H-
Africa TOC JSTOR Coverage: Vols. 1-27,
1974-2001
Journal URL:
http://www.jstor.org/journals/03057070.ht
ml

770   New African
IC Publications
7 Coldbath Square
London EC1R 4LQ
Tel: +44-(0)20-7713 7711
Fax: +44-(0)20-7713 7898 (General)
Fax: +44-(0)20-7713 7970 (Editorial)
Email: icpubs@africasia.com (Generla)
subscriptions@africasia.com (Subscriptions)
Web:

http://www.africasia.com/newafrican/index.php
1966- ISSN 0142-9345 Mon
Subs: £40/€80/$90 inst/corp, £30/€60/$67 indiv
Ed: Baffour Ankomah Book rev
Offers a mix of political reporting, comment, economic and financial discussion, together with features on social affairs, the arts and culture. Also contains sections on the diaspora.
Submissions: commissioned work only

771   **New Internationalist**
Tower House
Lathkill Street
Market Harborough LE16 9EF
Tel: +44-(0)1858-438896
Fax: +44-(0)1858-461739
Email: newint@subscription.co.uk
Web: http://www.newint.org/
In the US:
PO Box 1143
Lewiston NY 14092
Tel: +1- 905-946 0407 Fax: +1-905-946-0410
Email: magazines@indas.on.ca
1972- Print ISSN 0305-9529 Mon
Subs: in the UK£33, Europe and North America £38
Eds: Katherine Ainger, Vanessa Baird, Dinyar Godreij, David Ransom
UK editorial office: 55 Rectory Road, Oxford OX4 1BW, Tel: +44-(0)1865-728181, Fax: +44-(0)1865-793152,
Email: ni@newint.org; for other editorial contacts worldwide see Web site
Book rev Book rev ed: Vanessa Baird,
Email: vanessab@newint.org
Exists to report on issues of world poverty and inequality; to focus attention on the unjust relationship between the powerful and the powerless in both rich and poor nations; to debate and campaign for the radical changes necessary if the basic material and spiritual needs of all are to be met.
Submissions: invites stories from an alternative viewpoint. The format of the *New Internationalist* always has the main body of the magazine dedicated to the theme of the month. This means that, in general, all pieces are commissioned for that particular theme. Contributors who would like to be considered for commissioning should write to the editorial team above.

772   **NewsAfrica**
321 City Road
London EC1V 1LJ
Tel: +44-(0)20-7713 8135
Fax: +44-(0)20-7713 8136
Email: subscriptions@newsafrica.net
Web: http://www.newsafrica.net/
2004-[?] Print ISSN n/a Biwk
Subs: n/a
Publ: Moffat Ekoriko,
Email: publisher@newsafrica.net
Ed: Mercy Ette, Email: editor@newsafrica.net
Aims to serve the news and information needs of Africa and Africans in the diaspora. It also provides news and intelligence on the continent to the international business community, and is a forum for objective reporting on a diverse and rapidly changing continent. It offers articles on politics, economics, commerce, social issues, tourism and culture
.Submissions: n/a

773   **Oxford Development Studies**
Taylor & Francis Journals
4 Park Square
Milton Park
Abingdon OX14 4RN
Tel: +44-(0)20-7017 6000
Fax: +44-(0)20-7017 6336
Email: tf.processing@tfinforma.com
Web:
http://www.tandf.co.uk/journals/titles/13600818.asp
In the US:
Taylor & Francis Journals (US)
325 Chestnut Street Suite 800
Philadelphia PA 19106
Tel: +1-215-625 8900 Fax: +1-215-625 8914
1996- Print and online ISSN 1360-0818 (E-ISSN 1469-9966) 3Yr
Subs: £474/$786 inst £57/$93 indiv
Eds: Sanjaya Lall, Nandini Gooptu and Raufu Mustapha, University of Oxford International Development Centre, Queen Elizabeth House, 21 St Giles, Oxford OX1 3LA, Tel: +44-(0)1865-273600, Fax: +44-(0)1865-273607,
Email: ocls@sable.ox.ac.uk
Multidisciplinary journal that provides a forum for rigorous and critical analysis of conventional theories and policy issues in all aspects of development, and that aims to contribute to new approaches. It covers a number of disciplines related to development, including economics, history, politics, anthropology and sociology.
Submissions: publishes relevant articles on worldwide development issues, quantitative

papers as well as surveys of literature, which are of interest to an international audience.

774   Review of African Political Economy
Taylor & Francis Journals
4 Park Square
Milton Park
Abingdon OX14 4RN
Tel: +44-(0)20-7017 6000
Fax: +44-(0)20-7017 6336
Email: tf.processing@tfinforma.com
Web:
http://www.tandf.co.uk/journals/titles
/03056244.asp or
http://www.roape.org/
In the US:
Taylor & Francis Journals (US)
325 Chestnut Street Suite 800
Philadelphia PA 19106
Tel: +1-215-625 8900 Fax: +1-215-625 8914
1974- Print and online ISSN 0305-6244
(E-ISSN 1740-1720) Qtly
Subs: £285/$496 inst £59/$101 indiv
Eds: Jan Burgess, Ray Bush; manuscript
submission to Ray Bush,
Email: rolov@freeuk.com, all other material to
Jan Burgess, ROAPE Publications, PO Box
678, Sheffield S1 1BF, Tel +44-(0)114-267-6880,
Fax +44-(0)-114 267 6881,
Email: editor@roape.org
Book rev Book and film rev eds: Carolyne
Dennis, Tunde Zack-Williams
*Has since 1974 provided radical analysis and
commentary on trends and issues in Africa. The
journal has paid particular attention to the
political economy of inequality, exploitation and
oppression, whether driven by global forces or
local ones (such as class, race, community and
gender) and to materialist interpretation of change
in Africa. It has sustained a critical analysis of the
nature of power and the state in Africa.*
Submissions: ROAPE is committed to
encouraging high quality research and
fostering intellectual excellence in the
understanding of African political economy.
In addition to articles, shorter, more news-
oriented or polemical pieces are equally
featured, as are contributions from grassroots
organizations, women's organizations, trade
unions and political groups.
Note: the searchable ROAPE database at
http://www.roape.org/ holds
all 1,597 abstracts from the Review and 1,443
other items of interest (as at August 2005).

**775   The Round Table. The
Commonwealth Journal
of International Affairs**
Taylor & Francis Journals
4 Park Square
Milton Park
Abingdon OX14 4RN
Tel: +44-(0)20-7017 6000
Fax: +44-(0)20-7017 6336
Email: tf.processing@tfinforma.com
Web:
http://www.tandf.co.uk/journals/titles/003
58533.asp
In the US:
Taylor & Francis Journals (US)
325 Chestnut Street Suite 800
Philadelphia PA 19106
Tel: +1-215-625 8900 Fax: +1-215-625 8914
1910- Print and online ISSN 0035-8533
(E-ISSN 1474-029X) 5Yr
Subs: £448/$833 inst £108/$190 indiv
Ed: Andrew Williams, Department of Politics
and International Relations University of
Kent, Kent, Email: A.J.Williams@kent.ac.uk;
all submissions to The Editor, The Round
Table, Institute of Commonwealth Studies,
University of London, 28 Russell Square,
London WC1B 5DS, UK.
Book rev Book rev ed: Terry Barringer
*Founded in 1910, The Round Table is Britain's
oldest international affairs journal, providing
analysis and commentary on all aspects of
international affairs. The journal is a major source
for coverage of the policy issues concerning the
contemporary Commonwealth and its role in
international affairs, with occasional articles on
themes of historical interest. The fifth issue of each
volume is a thematic special issue and covers
specific topics from a distinctive Commonwealth
perspective.*
Submissions: as above

776   Sable Litmag
S.A.K.S Media
PO Box 33504
London E9 7YE
Tel: n/a
Email: info@sablelitmag.org
(General enquiries/Subscriptions)
editorial@sablelitmag.org
(Editorial/Submissions)
Web: http://www.sablelitmag.org/
2001- Print and (partly) online ISSN n/a
Irregular to issue no. 3 Qtly (as from issue no.
4, Summer 2004-)

Subs: UK, Africa, Caribbean, Asia £35 inst £25 indiv, Europe £40 inst £35 indiv, elsewhere £45 inst 40 indiv
Ed: Kadija (George) Sesay; for full list of contacts for other editors (Poetry Editor, Fiction Editor, Non-Fiction Editor, etc.) *see* http://www.sablelitmag.org/biographies.html
Book rev
An international publication for writers of colour. Sable LitMag provides a space for new writers to showcase their work and to receive critical feedback in their chosen written language of expression.
Submissions: see Submitting to Sable http://www.sablelitmag.org/submissions.html
Note: this literary magazine has strong content on African writing (issue 3, for example, includes an interview with Niyi Osundare), and editorial advisors include Buchi Emecheta and Ngugi wa Thiongo.

777   SOAS Literary Review
AHRB Centre for Asian & African Literatures Room 399A
School of Oriental and African Studies
Thornhaugh Street
London WC1H 0XG
Tel: +44-(0)20-7898 4267
Fax: +44-(0)20-7898 4239
Email: soas.lit@soas.ac.uk
Web:
http://www.soas.ac.uk/soaslit/home.html
1999- Online [No ISSN] Ann
Subs: free
Eds: Duncan Adam, Irena Hayter, *et al*
Book rev
A journal of postgraduate research that seeks to provide an international forum for research students working on the literatures of Africa, Asia, and the Middle East.
Submissions: welcomes contributions on all aspects of postgraduate literary research, including articles, translations, fieldwork commentaries, and book and media reviews. Submissions are only accepted from current research students who have not yet received their doctoral award.

778   Social Identities. Journal for the Study of Race, Nation and Culture
Taylor & Francis Journals
4 Park Square
Milton Park
Abingdon OX14 4RN
Tel: +44-(0)20-7017 6000
Fax: +44-(0)20-7017 6336
Email: tf.processing@tfinforma.com
Web:
http://www.tandf.co.uk/journals/titles/13504630.asp
In the US:
Taylor & Francis Journals (US)
325 Chestnut Street Suite 800
Philadelphia PA 19106
Tel: +1-215-625 8900 Fax: +1-215-625 8914
1996- Print and online ISSN 1350-4630
Qtly
Subs: £453/$748 inst £133/$240 indiv
Eds: Pal Ahluwalia, Department of Politics, Goldsmiths College, University of London, UK, Email:
sss01pa@gold.ac.uk
University of California-Riverside, USA, Email: tobym@ucr.edu
Book rev Book Rev ed: Julia Maxted, Email: jemaxted@silwane.hsrc.ac.za
Aims to furnish an interdisciplinary and international focal point for theorizing issues at the interface of social identities. The journal is especially concerned to address these issues in the context of the transforming political economies and cultures of postmodern and postcolonial conditions. It is intended as a forum for contesting ideas and debates concerning the formations of, and transformations in, socially significant identities, their attendant forms of material exclusion and power, as well as the political and cultural possibilities opened up by these identifications.
Submissions: as above.

779   Third World Quarterly
Taylor & Francis Journals
4 Park Square
Milton Park
Abingdon OX14 4RN
Tel: +44-(0)20-7017 6000
Fax: +44-(0)20-7017 6336
Email: tf.processing@tfinforma.com
Web:
http://www.tandf.co.uk/journals/titles/01436597.asp
In the US:
Taylor & Francis Journals (US)

325 Chestnut Street Suite 800
Philadelphia PA 19106
Tel: +1-215-625 8900 Fax: +1-215-625 8914
1978- ISSN 0143-6597
(E-ISSN 1360-2241) 8Yr
Subs: Institutional: £632/$1,042 inst
£142/$235 indiv
Ed: Shahid Qadir, Department of Geography,
Royal Holloway College, Egham TW20 0EX,
Tel: +44-(0)1784-443579, Fax: +44-(0)1784-
472836,
Email: n/a
Book rev
A journal of scholarship and policy in the field of international studies providing detailed analysis of global affairs and a regular source of information on contemporary social, economic, and political issues. Coverage of the Asia/Pacific region, Latin America and the Caribbean, Africa and the Middle East
Submissions: analysis and commentary on contemporary issues and events of importance to the Third World.
H-Africa TOC

780   Timbuktu. The International Arts and Literary Journal Made in Wales
The Meeting Pool
13 Taliesin Street
Llandudno
Conwy LL30 2YE
Tel: n/a
Email: timbuktu_ed@tiscali.co.uk
Web:
http://myweb.tiscali.co.uk/meetingpool/
2004- Print, first issue only, thereafter online only [No ISSN] 2Yr
Subs: free
Eds: Bob Macintosh, Isabel Adonis
A literary and arts journal whose main concern is the exploration of culture and identity through literature and art. Contains articles, interviews, short stories, poetry, art, and photography.
Submissions: in general the editors are looking for pieces that speak *from* a culture rather than *for* one. Authorities, whether spiritual, academic, political or literary, are not acknowledged, so references are not required, though they may be included for interested readers.

781   Wasafiri
Department of English and
Drama
Queen Mary College
End Road
London E1 4NS
Tel/Fax: +44-(0)20-7882 3120
Email: wasafiri@qmul.ac.uk
Web: http://www.wasafiri.org
1984- Print ISSN 0269-0055 3Yr
Subs: in UK £50 inst £21 indiv, elsewhere £65
inst £27 indiv
Ed: Susheila Nasta,
Email: s.m.nasta@open.ac.uk
Managing ed: Richard Dyer, Email:
r.m.dyer@qmul.ac.uk
Book rev Book rev ed: Mark Stein, Email:
M.Stein@Wasafiri.Britishlibrary.net
New creative writing, critical coverage of new writing; a forum for current debate concerning the teaching of multicultural literature both at school and university level. Focus issues have been on the Caribbean, education and women, post-colonial writing, Africa, Asian diaspora, Black Britain.
Submissions: literature and education in Africa, the Caribbean, South-East Asia, Black British writing, interviews with writers, new creative writing

➔ **West Africa** *see* **Africa Week (740)**
Note: the long established *West Africa* magazine has ceased; the last issue published was issue no. 4384 July 13, 2003; it is superseded by *Africa Week* magazine, but which retains no connection with the owners of the previous *West Africa* magazine.

NORTH AMERICA

Canada

782 African Journal of Legal Studies
The Africa Law Institute
4523 Shoreline Drive
Ottawa ON K1V 1Y8
Tel: n/a
Email: ajls@africalawinstitute.org
Web:
http://www.africalawinstitute.org/ajls/
2004- Online ISSN 1708-7384 Qtly
Subs: free (requires registration)
Ed: Chernor Jalloh, Email:
ajlseditor@africalawinstitute.org
Book rev
Aims to provide an interdisciplinary forum for the thoughtful and scholarly engagement of a broad range of complex issues at the intersection of law, public policy and social change in Africa. The journal places emphasis on presenting a diversity of perspectives on fundamental, long-term, systemic problems of governance, as well as emerging issues, and possible solutions to them. Submissions: articles, notes and book reviews related to governance, democracy and the rule of law in Africa. The focus of the journal is on the interplay between law, public policy and social change in Africa.

783 Canadian Association of African Studies Newsletter
Canadian Association of African Studies/ Association Canadienne des Etudes Africaines CCASLS SB 115 c/o Concordia University 1455 de Maisonneuve O. Montréal Québec H3G 1M8
Tel: +1-514-848 2280 Fax: +1-514-848 4514
Email: caas@concordia.ca
Web:
http://caas.concordia.ca/htm/online.h tm
2000- 2Yr Online [No ISSN] 2Yr
Subs: free
Ed: Allison Goebel,
Email: goebela@post.queensu.ca
Contains news and announcements, advertised positions in African studies, campus news, details of new publications and new resources, new thesis in African studies, etc.
Affil: ➔ **Canadian Association of African Studies (2769)**

784 Canadian Journal of African Studies/Revue Canadienne des Etudes Africaines
Canadian Association of African Studies/ Association Canadienne des Etudes Africaines CCASLS SB 115 c /o Concordia University 1455 de Maisonneuve Ouest
Montréal Québec H3G 1M8
Tel: +1-514-848 2280 Fax: +1-514-848 4514
Email: caas@concordia.ca
Web:
http://caas.concordia.ca/CJAS/fr/homef.ht m (English version)
http://caas.concordia.ca/CJAS/fr/homef.ht m (French version)
1967- Print ISSN 0008-3968 3Yr
Subs: free to members of the Canadian Association of African Studies; others Can$100 inst Can$90 indiv
Ed: Roger Riendeau, Innis College, University of Toronto, 2 Sussex Avenue, Toronto, Ontario M5S 1J5, Tel: +1-416-978 7067, Email: roger.riendeau@utoronto.ca
Submissions in English to: J. Barry Riddell, Department of Geography, Mackintosh-Corry Hall, Queen's University, Kingston, Ontario, Canada K7L 3N6
Tel: +1-613-533 6037
Email: riddellb@post.queensu.ca or riddellb@kos.net
Submissions in French to: Marie-Nathalie LeBlanc, Département d'Anthopologie, et de Sociologie, Université Concordia 1455, de Maissoneuve Ouest Montréal, Québec, Canada H3G 1M8
Email: marienat@sympatico.ca
Book rev Book rev ed: Chris Youé, Head, Department of History, Memorial University, St. John's, Newfoundland, Canada A1C 5S7, Tel: +1-709-737 8420,
Email: cyoue@mun.ca
Publishes articles (in English and French) principally in the areas of anthropology, political economy, history, geography, and development of the continent. Many of the articles are interdisciplinary in approach, especially those which seek to assess the origins, nature, and success of development strategies. Special issues which bring together several research articles focused on a specific and pertinent theme.
Submissions: as above, in English and French
H-Africa TOC
JSTOR Coverage: Vols. 1-33, 1967-1999
Journal URL:

http://www.jstor.org/journals/000839
68.html
as *Bulletin of African Studies in Canada*
Vols. 1-3, 1963-1966
Journal URL:
http://www.jstor.org/journals/052513
70.html
Affil: → **Canadian Association of
African Studies (2769)**
H-Africa TOC
JSTOR Coverage: Vols. 1-30, 1967-1996
Journal URL:
http://www.jstor.org/journals/00083968.ht
ml
as *Bulletin of African Studies in Canada*
Vols. 1-3, 1963-1966
Journal URL:
http://www.jstor.org/journals/05251370.ht
ml

785   **Journal of Pan-African Wisdom**
Department of Political Science
Carleton University
1125 Colonel By Drive
Ottawa ON K1S 5B6
Tel: n/a
Email: dosabu@ccs.carleton.ca
Web:
http://www.carleton.ca/panafrica/journal/
home.htm
2001- [?] Online [No ISSN] Irregular
Subs: free
Ed: Daniel T. Osabu-Kle
*Dedicated to encouraging research and publication
by people of African descent everywhere, and in
any field of the social sciences.*
Submissions: n/a

786   **Journal of Asian and African Studies**
Sage Publications
2455 Teller Road
Thousand Oaks CA 91320
Tel: +1-805-499 9774 Fax: +1-805-499 0871
Email: journals@sagepub.com
Web: http://jas.sagepub.com/
1965- Print and online ISSN 0021-9096 (E-
ISSN 1745-2538) 6Yr
Subs: print and online $544 inst, online only
$516 inst, print only $522 inst/$77.00 indiv
Eds: Nigel C. Gibson, Institute of Liberal Arts,
Emerson College, 120 Boylston Street, Boston
MA 02116-4624, USA,
Email: Nigel_Gibson@emerson.edu
Book rev Book rev ed (Africa titles):

Richard Pithouse, Centre for Civil Society,
University of KwaZulu Natal, Durban, 4041,
South Africa, Email: Pithouser@ukzn.ac.za
Fax: +1-215-625 8914
*Aims to further research and study on Asia and
Africa. The journal unites contributions from all
the social sciences and covers a wide range of
cutting-edge events and topics.*
Submissions: from all the social sciences.

787   **Journal of Developing Societies**
Sage Publications
2455 Teller Road
Thousand Oaks CA 91320
Tel: +1-805-499 9774
Fax: +1-805-499 0871
Email: journals@sagepub.com
Web: http://jds.sagepub.com/
1984- Print and online ISSN 0169-796X
(E-ISSN1745-2546) Qtly
Subs: print and online $191 inst $ 109 indiv,
online only $55
Subs: print and online $357 inst, online only
$339 inst, print only $342 inst/$68 indiv
Ed: Richard L. Harris, California State
University Monterey Bay, Department of
Global Studies,
CSU Monterey Bay, 100 Campus Center,
Seaside, CA 93955-8001, USA
Tel: +1-831-582 4211,
Email: Richard_Harris@csumb.edu
Book rev
*Provides an interdisciplinary forum for the
publication of theoretical perspectives, research
findings, case studies, policy analyses and
normative critiques on the issues, problems and
policies associated with both mainstream and
alternative approaches to development.*
Submissions: contributions are welcome from
scholars and experts in any discipline or area,
provided the contributions fall within the
journal's broad focus.

United States

Note: several of the US-published journals listed here are available for electronic campus-wide access and combined print/electronic subscriptions via Project Muse, including access to archives, either as single title subscriptions or a basic subscription license package to all journal packages from participating publishers. For more details and current prices visit http://muse.jhu.edu/pricing.html.

788 **Abafazi: The Simmons College Journal of Women of African Descent**
Simmons College
Main College Building
Room C-319
300 The Fenway
Boston MA 02115
Tel: + 1-617-521 2256
Email: della.scott@simmons.edu
Web: http://www.simmons.edu/abafazi/
1991- Print ISSN 1078-1323 2Yr
Subs: $25 inst $15 indiv
Ed: Della Scott
The primary mission of Abafazi is to promote feminist scholarship in all fields of study in order to heighten readers' awareness of black women's intellectual traditions, "herstorieS", and socio-political, economic, and cultural issues throughout the African world; to discover emerging scholars, activists, writers, and artists; and to serve as an important resource to readers around the world.
Submissions: welcomes original manuscripts about women of African descent from scholars in all fields of study.

789 **ACAS Bulletin**
Association of Concerned Africa Scholars
c/o Daniel Volman
African Security Research Project
2627 Woodley Place, NW
Washington DC 20009
Tel/Fax: n/a
Email: dvolman@igc.org
Web: http://acas.prairienet.org/pubs.html
1987- Print and (partly) online
ISSN 1051-0842 Qtly
Subs: n/a
Eds: Daniel Volman, African Security Research Project , 2627 Woodley Place, NW,

Washington, DC 20009,
Email: dvolman@igc.org; Jesse Benjamin, Department of Human Relations and Multicultural Education
St. Cloud State University, 720 Fourth Avenue South, Saint Cloud, MN 56301, Email: benjamin@stcloudstate.edu
Strives to develop communications between peoples and scholars of Africa and the US; describes current, critical issues related to Africa.
Submissions: n/a
Affil: ➔ **Association of Concerned Africa Scholars (2767)**
H-Africa TOC

➔ **Africa Focus Bulletin. News-Analysis-Advocacy** *see* **1 General online resources on Africa and African studies: Academic and scholarly resources on African studies** entry **67**

790 **The Africa Journal**
Corporate Council on Africa
1100 17th Street NW Suite 1100
Washington DC 20036
Tel: +1-202-835 1115 Fax: +1-202-835 1117
Email: cca@africacncl.org
Web: http://www.africacncl.org/AfricaJournal/index.asp
2003-[?] Print and (partly) online [No ISSN] 6Yr
Subs: print $30
Ed: Luanne Grant
Provides information on current African issues related to African arts and culture, business, economy and policy, as well as editorials from members and others interested in African affairs.
Submissions: n/a

➔ **Africa News** (Durham, NC, 1973-1997), superseded by **AllAfrica.com** *see* **10 News sources for Africa** entry **851**

791 **The AFRican**
African Media Inc
146 West 29th Street no. 7E
New York NY 1000
Tel: +1-212-696 7407 Fax: +1-212-591 6064
Email: info@africanmag.com
Web: http://www.africanmag.com/
2001- Print and online [No ISSN] 6Yr

Subs: (for 2Yrs, 12 issues) print and online: in North America $19.99, elsewhere $39.99, $9.99 online only $9.99
Ed: Frankie Edozien
A bi-monthly publication primarily serving Africans from the diaspora. It strives to showcase the aspirations, successes and concerns of Africans living in the United States--whether it is recent continental/island immigrants adjusting to a new socio-political landscape, or those with longer historical ties.
Submissions: n/a

792   **Africa Renewal**
       (formerly Africa Recovery)
       Africa Section, DPI
       S-955
       United Nations
       New York NY 10017
Tel: +1-212-963 6857 Fax: 1-212-963 4556
Email: africarenewal@un.org
Web:
http://www.un.org/ecosocdev/geninfo/afr
ec/
1987- Print and online [No ISSN] Qtly
(Available in English or French; includes access to a series of 'Briefing Papers')
Subs: print $35 inst $20 indiv, online free
Ed: Julie I. Thompson (Editor-in-Chief),
Managing ed: Ernest Harsch,
Email: harsch@un.org
Seeks to provide timely and accurate news and analysis on the critical economic and development challenges facing the African continent, and examines the many issues that confront the people of Africa, its leaders and its international partners.

793   **Africa Today**
       Indiana University Press
       601 N Morton Street
       Bloomington IN 47404
Tel: +1-812-855 8817
Toll-free (US/Canada only) 800-842 6796
Email: journals@indiana.edu (General enquiries) iuporder@indiana.edu
(Subscription orders)
Web: http://iupjournals.org/africatoday/
1954- Print ISSN 0001-9887 Qtly
Subs: in US $110 inst $56 indiv, elsewhere (airmail) $140 inst $72 indiv
Eds: Gracia Clark, Maria Grosz-Ngate, John Hanson, Ruth Stone; Managing ed: Liz McMahon, Africa Today, 221 Woodburn Hall, Indiana University, Bloomington, IN 47405, Email: afrtoday@indiana.edu

Book rev Book rev ed: Marion Frank Wilson, Librarian for African Studies, Indiana University, Main Library E660, 1320 East 10th Street, Bloomington, IN 47405-3907,
Tel: +1-812-855-1481,
Email: mfrankwi@indiana.edu
Africa Today has been in the forefront in publishing Africanist reform minded research and provides access to the best scholarly work from around the world, on a full range of political, economic, and social issues. Multicultural in perspective, it provides an alternative forum for serious analysis and discussion, but offers positive solutions to the problems facing Africa today.
Submissions: all subject areas relating to contemporary Africa.
H-Africa TOC

794   **Africa Update**
       c/o Lisa-Marie Fellage
       International Affairs Center
       Central Connecticut State University
       PO Box 4010
       New Britain CT 06050-4010
Tel/Fax: n/a
Email: emeagwali@ccsu.edu
Web:
http://www.ccsu.edu/afstudy/archive.html
1993- Print and online [No ISSN] Qtly
Subs: print $25 inst $5 indiv, online free
Eds: Gloria T. Emeagwali *et al*, History Department, Central Connecticut State University, 1615 Stanley Street
New Britain, CT 06050
A quarterly newsletter of the African Studies Program at Central Connecticut State University. Aims promote an interdisciplinary approach to the study of Africa. Each issue focuses on a specific African country, region, topic, or current debate.
H-Africa TOC

795   **African Arts**
       MIT Press Journals Five
       Cambridge Center
       Cambridge MA 02142-1407
Tel: +1- 617-253 2889
Fax: +1-617-577 1545
Email: journals-orders@mit.edu
Web:
http://mitpress.mit.edu/catalog/item/defau
lt.asp?sid=40477E7C-F799-4EF2-83FF-
DB9B756B8830&ttype=4&tid=62
or
http://www.international.ucla.edu/africa/af
ricanarts/

1967- Print ISSN 0001-9933 Qtly Subs: (print only) In US $118 inst $72 indiv, elsewhere $135 inst, $102 indiv.
Eds: Marla C. Berns *et al*, The James S. Coleman African Studies Center, University of California-Los Angeles, PO Box 951310 Los Angeles, CA 90095-1310, Tel: +1-310-825 1218, Fax: +1-310-206 2250
Email: jscasc@international.ucla.edu (General) afriartsedit@international.ucla.edu (Editorial)
Executive ed: Leslie Ellen Jones, Email: lejones@ucla.edu
Book rev Book rev ed: Allen F. Roberts and Doran Ross Film and Video rev ed: Robert Cancel
Covers all the art forms of Africa, especially contemporary and traditional art, but not excluding dance, film, theatre and popular decorative forms. Publishes book and exhibition reviews relating to the above, and features on new museum acquisitions and current events. The African continent is the focus, occasionally pieces on the diaspora if there is a strong African connection.
Submissions: any areas, generally relating to specific field work or research; predominantly academics and specialist scholars
Notes: Archive/document delivery (at a charge) available through ProQuest;
RSS RSS feed available, *see* http://www.international.ucla.edu/africa/rss.asp

796 **African Economic History**
University of Wisconsin
African Studies Program - Publications
205 Ingraham Hall
1155 Observatory Drive
Madison WI 53706
Tel: +1-608-262 2493 Fax: +1-608-265 5851
Email: afpub@intl-institute.wisc.edu
Web: http://africa.wisc.edu/publications/aeh/
1972- Print ISSN 0145-2258 Ann
Subs: $38 inst $19.00 indiv
Eds: Toyin Falola *et al* Department of History, University of Texas, Austin, TX 78712
Fax +1-512-475 7222
toyin.falola@mail.utexas.edu,
Managing ed: David Henige,
Email: dhenige@library.wisc.edu

Book rev
Focuses on recent economic change in Africa as well as the colonial and precolonial economic history of the continent.
Submissions: in any areas of African economic history, in English and French.
H-Africa TOC
JSTOR Coverage: will become available shortly

→ **African Geopolitics/ Géopolitique Africaine** *see* under France, entry **671**

797 **African Issues**
African Studies Association
Rutgers University Douglass Campus
132 George Street
New Brunswick NJ 08901-1400
Tel: +1-732-932 8173 Fax: +1-732-932 3394
Email: callASA@rci.rutgers.edu
Web: http://www.africanstudies.org
1970- Print ISSN 0047-1607 2Yr
Subs: gratis to members of ASA
Eds: Cyril K. Daddieh, Political Science Department, Providence College, Providence, RI 02918 Email: daddieh@providence.edu; and Jo Ellen Fair, Journalism and Mass Communication, 5164 Vilas Hall, University of Wisconsin-Madison, Madison, WI 53706, Email: jefair@facstaff.wisc.edu
Multi-disciplinary journal that publishes short articles analysing and criticizing contemporary policies toward Africa, in Africa, and involving the Africanist community. Issues are generally organised thematically.
Submissions: political or policy-oriented questions relating to Africa or to African studies.
Affil: → **African Studies Association (2755)**
H-Africa-TOC
JSTOR Coverage: as *African Issues*
Vols. 28-29, 2000-2001
http://www.jstor.org/journals/15484505.html
as *Issue: a Journal of Opinion*
JSTOR Coverage: Vols. 1-27, 1971-1999
http://www.jstor.org/journals/00471607.html

African Literature Association Bulletin *see*
➔ ALA Bulletin (802)

798   African Rural and Urban Studies
Michigan State University Press
1405 South Harrison Road
Manly Miles Building Suite 25
East Lansing MI 48823-5202
Tel: +1-517-355 9543 Fax: +1-517-432 2611
Email: msupress@msu.edu
Web:
http://www.msu.edu/unit/msupress/journ
als/jour3.html
1978 [as African Rural and Urban Studies to
1983]- Print (online shortly) ISSN 1073-4600
3Yr
Subs: in USA $40 inst $30 indiv $20 stud,
elsewhere $60 inst $50 indiv
Ed: David Wiley, Director African Studies
Center, Michigan State University, 100
International Center, East Lansing, Michigan
48824-1035, Tel: +517- 353 1700 Fax: +1-517-
432 1209, Email: wiley@msu.edu
*A multidisciplinary journal published in
association with the African Studies Center at
Michigan State University. It focuses on
contemporary rural and urban Africa, including
urban society, urbanization, urban and regional
planning, and the urban institutions of the
world's most rapidly urbanizing continent; and
rural Africa, the rural society and economy,
agriculture, and the institutions of the world's
most rural continent.*
Submissions: n/a
H-Africa TOC

799   African Studies Quarterly. The
Online Journal of African Studies
PO Box 115560
427 Grinter Hall
PO Box 115560
Gainesville FL 32611
Tel: +1-352-392 9766/392 2187
Fax: +1-352-392 2435
Email: asq@africa.ufl.edu
Web:
http://web.africa.ufl.edu/asq/index.htm
1997- Online ISSN 1093-2658 Quarterly
Subs: free
Eds: Leonardo Villalón (Editor-in-chief),
Managing ed: Abubakar Alhassan, Center for
African Studies, 427 Grinter Hall, PO Box
115560, University of Florida, Gainesville FL
32611
Book rev

*An interdisciplinary, fully refereed, online journal
dedicated to publishing the finest scholarship
relating to the African continent.*
Submissions: invites submissions of
original manuscripts on a full range of
topics related to Africa in all disciplines.
As an electronic journal, it particularly
welcomes submissions that are of a
time-sensitive nature.

800   African Studies Review
African Studies Association
Rutgers University
Douglass Campus
132 George Street
New Brunswick NJ 08901-1400
Tel: +1-732-932 8173
Fax: +1-732-932 3394
Email: asapub@rci.rutgers.edu
(Renee Dutta, Publications and
Information Coordinator)
Web:
http://www.umass.edu/anthro/asr/
and
http://www.africanstudies.org/asa_publ
icationslist.htm
1957- Print ISSN 0002-0206 3Yr
Subs: gratis to ASA members only
Eds: Ralph Faulkingham Department of
Anthropology, University of Massachusetts,
Amherst, MA 01003-9278, Tel: +1-413-545
2065,
Fax: +1-413-545 9494
Email: faulkingham@anthro.umass.edu or
asr@anthro.umass.edu; Mitzi Goheen,
Amherst College,
Email: mrgoheen@amherst.edu,
Web: http://www.umass.edu/anthro/asr/
Book rev Book review ed: Eugenia Herbert,
African-American and African Studies
Program, Skinner Hall, Mount Holyoke
College, South Hadley, MA 01075-1450,
Tel: +1-413-538 2577,
Fax: +1-413-538 2513
Email: asrbook@mtholyoke.edu
Film rev ed: Samba Gadjigo, African-
American and African Studies Program,
Mount Holyoke College,
Email: asrfilm@mtholyoke.edu
*The principal academic and scholarly journal of
the African Studies Association, publishing
original research and analyses of Africa and book
reviews. Encourages scholarly debates across
disciplines.*

Submissions: welcomes high-quality articles and book reviews in all academic disciplines that are of interest to the interdisciplinary audience of ASA members. The editors welcome manuscript submissions from scholars everywhere, whether or not they are members of the ASA.

Affil: ➔ **African Studies Association (2755)**
See also ➔ **Index to the African Studies Review/Bulletin and the ASA Review of Books, 1958-1990 (413)**
JSTOR Coverage: Vols. 13-44, 1970-2001
Journal URL:
http://www.jstor.org/journals/00020206.html
as *ASA Review of Books* Vols. 1-6, 1975-1980
Journal URL:
http://www.jstor.org/journals/03641686.html as *African Studies Bulletin*
Vols. 1-12, 1958-1969
Journal URL:
http://www.jstor.org/journals/05681537.html

801   Africana Libraries Newsletter
Office of the Librarian for African Studies
Indiana University
Wells Library E-660
1320 East 10th Street
Bloomington IN 47405-3907
Tel: +1-812-855 1481 Fax: +1-812-855 8068
Email: mfrankwi@indiana.edu
Web:
http://www.indiana.edu/~libsalc/african/aln/alnindex.html
1975- Print and online ISSN 0148-7868
Qtly (3-4 times ann)
Subs: free
Eds: Marion-Frank Wilson, Bassey Irele
The newsletter of the (US) African Studies Association's Africana Librarians Council, with reports on meetings and other items of interest to Africana librarians and those concerned about information resources about or in Africa. Also publishes book reviews of new African studies reference resources, and notices about vendors, new serials, etc.
Book rev
Submissions: areas of interest to African studies librarians.
Affil: ➔ **Africana Librarians Council (1885)**
Note: print edition no longer available as from 2006, except for libraries in Africa, and subject to demand.

802   ALA Bulletin
Abioseh Michael Porter
Department of Humanities and Communications
Drexel University
Philadelphia PA 19104
Tel: +1-215-895 2448 Fax: +1-215-895 1071
Email: alabulletin@drexel.edu
Web: http://www.africanlit.org/ (access to Bulletin pages requires password)
1974- Print and online ISSN 0146-4965
Qtly
Subs: $50 (free to members of the African Literature Association); online version restricted to members of the ALA)
Ed: Abioseh Michael Porter
The publication of the African Literature Association, an independent professional society that exists primarily to facility the attempts of a world wide audience to appreciate the efforts of African writers and artists. The Bulletin contains news of ALA activities, articles, interviews, reports, and listings of new publications.
Submissions: conference reports, memorial tributes and historical occasions.
Affil: ➔ **African Literature Association (2753)**

803   ASA News
African Studies Association
Rutgers University Douglass Campus
132 George Street
New Brunswick NJ 08901-1400
Tel: +1-732-932 8173 Fax: +1-732-932 3394
Email: asapub@rci.rutgers.edu
Web: http://www.africanstudies.org
1967- Print ISSN 0278-2219 3Yr
Subs: gratis to ASA members
Ed: Carol L. Martin, Assoc ed: Renee Dutta, Email: clmasa@rci.rutgers.edu
Reports on current and future events of interest to members and Africanists, including notes and news, announcements, job vacancies, programme and panel information about the ASA annual meeting, election results, grants and fellowships, etc. Also includes a regular listing of recent doctoral dissertations in African studies.
Submissions: announcements, letters, notes on seminars and conferences.
Affil: ➔ **African Studies Association (2755)**

804 **Callalloo. A Journal of African Diaspora Arts and Letters**
The Johns Hopkins University Press
Journals Publishing Division
2715 North Charles Street
Baltimore MD 21218-4363
Tel: +1-410-516 6987 Toll-free
(US/Canada only) 800-548 1784
Fax: +1-410-516 6968
Web: https://www.press.jhu.edu/cgi-bin/order.cgi?oc_id=21 or
http://xroads.virginia.edu/~public/callaloo/home/callaloohome.htm
1976- Print and online ISSN 0161-2492 (E-ISSN: 1080-6512) Qtly
Subs: in US, print or online $120 inst $40 indiv, elsewhere $153 inst $66 indiv
Ed: Charles H. Rowell, Department of English, Texas A&M University, Blocker 249, TAMU 4227, College Station TX 77843, Tel: +1-979-458 3108, Fax: +1-979 458 3275, Email: callaloo@tamu.edu
Book rev
Offers a mixture of fiction, poetry, plays, critical essays, interviews, and visual art from the African diaspora. Frequent annotated bibliographies, special thematic issues drawing on people and places, and original art and photography, are some of the features of this international showcase of arts and letters.
Submissions: original submissions of essays, interviews, short fiction, poetry, drama, and visual art.
JSTOR Coverage: Nos. 1-41 (1976-1989), Vols. 13-17 (1990-1994), Links out to recent content: Vols. 18 - 27, 1995-2004
Journal URL:
http://www.jstor.org/journals/01612492.html

805 **Contours. A Journal of the African Diaspora**
University of Illinois Press
1325 South Oak Street
Champaign IL 61820
Tel: +1- 217-244 0626 Fax: +1-217-244 9910
Email: journals@uillinois.edu
Web:
http://www.press.uillinois.edu/journals/contours.html
2003- Print and online ISSN 1543-902X 2Yr
Subs: in US $45 inst $30 indiv, elsewhere $52 inst $37 indiv

Ed: D. Barry Gaspar, History Department, Duke University, 226 Carr Building, Durham NC 27708-0719, Tel: +1-919-684 2109, Fax: +1-919-681 7670
Email: dgaspar@duke.edu
Book rev Book rev ed: Sheila Smith McKoy, English Department, Vanderbilt University, Nashville TN 37235, Tel: +1-615-322 2541, Fax: +1-615-343 8028,
Email: SmithMcKoy@aol.com
A multidisciplinary and transnational journal that explores the ideas and experiences of people of African descent as they have globally dispersed. The journal publishes work primarily in the humanities and social sciences, much of it interdisciplinary. Also offers critical and informative commentary about society and culture in the African diaspora.
Submissions: as above; scholarly articles from a diverse range of disciplines, as well as fiction, poetry, and societal and cultural commentaries.
Note: free full-text access to the e-text version of volume 1, nos. 1-2, 2003 is available at the Web site.

→ **Eastern Africa Social Science Research Review** *see* under Ethiopia, entry **567**

806 **Electronic Journal of Africana Bibliography**
Scholarly Digital Resources Center
University of Iowa Libraries
Iowa City IA 52242-1420
Tel: +1-319-335 5299
Web:
http://sdrc.lib.uiowa.edu/ejab/index.html
1996- Online [No ISSN] Irregular
Eds: Afeworki Paulos, Email:
apaulos@umich.edu; Joseph S. Caruso, Email: caruso@columbia.edu; Edward Miner, Email: edward-miner@uiowa.edu; send submissions and proposals to Edward Miner, International Studies Bibliographer, University of Iowa Libraries, 100 Main Library, Iowa City, IA 52242-1420
A refereed online journal of bibliographies created by the late John Howell, University of Iowa Libraries. Coverage includes any aspect of Africa, its peoples, their homes, cities, towns, districts, states, countries, regions, including social, economic sustainable development, creative literature, the arts, and the diaspora.
Submissions: bibliographies must be at least 75 numbered entries, annotations preferred. Each bibliography must have an introduction

and/or preface. Essay bibliographies on specific topics are welcome.
Note: vols. 1-9 (1997-2004) published to date, all freely accessible at the Web site.

807   French Colonial History
Michigan State University Press
1405 South Harrison Road
Suite 25, Manly Miles Building
East Lansing MI 48823-5202
Tel: +1-517-355 9543 Fax: +1-517-432 2611
Email: msupress@msu.edu
Web:
http://msupress.msu.edu/bookTemplate.ph
p?bookID=694 or
http://www.frenchcolonial.org/
1995- Print ISSN 1539-3402 Ann
Subs: in US $35 inst $25 indiv, elsewhere $40
inst $35 indiv
Ed: Patricia Kay Galloway, Assistant
Professor, Archival Enterprise and Digital
Asset Management, School of Information,
University of Texas-Austin, 1 University
Station D7000, Austin, TX 78712-1276,
Tel: +1-512-232 9220, Fax: +1- 512-471 3971,
Email: galloway@ischool.utexas.edu
Sponsored by the French Colonial Historical
Society, French Colonial History is an annual
volume of refereed, scholarly articles selected from
the society's annual meetings. The journal covers
all aspects of French colonizing activity and the
history of all French colonies. Forthcoming articles
will reflect the temporal span, geographical
breadth, and diversity of subject matter that
characterize the scholarly interests of the society's
members.
Submissions: papers are selected from the
society's annual meetings.

808   GEFAME (incorporates *Passages: A*
Chronicle of the African Humanities)
Center for Afro-American and
African Studies
University of Michigan
505 S. State State
4700 Haven
Ann Arbor MI 48109-1045
[published in association with the
Scholarly Publishing Office,
University of Michgan]
Tel: +1-734-764 5513 Fax +1-734-763 0543
Email: gefame.editors@umich.edu or
passages.editors@umich.edu
Web: http://www.hti.umich.edu/g/gefame/
and

http://www.hti.umich.edu/p/passages/
2004- Online [print free on request to one
university in every African country with no
access to the Internet] ISSN 1053-1319 2Yr
Subs: free
Eds: Kofi Anyidoho, University of Ghana *et al*
Managing ed: Afeworki Paulos, University of
Michigan,
Email: passages.editors@umich.edu
Published jointly by the Scholarly Publishing
Office of the University of Michigan Library and
the Center for Afro-American and African Studies
at the University of Michigan, GEFAME
promotes scholarly communication in the field of
African studies. The journal aims to use the Web
to facilitate exchange of ideas between Africa-
based scholars and scholars outside the continent
of Africa. The Journal incorporates Passages: A
Chronicle of the African Humanities *originally*
published by the Program of African Studies at
Northwestern University. The Passages section
provides an online forum for commentary,
discussion, and the publication of writings that
are not necessarily peer-reviewed.
Submissions: *GEFAME*, as above; *Passages*:
welcomes readings, interpretations, reviews,
essays, debates, reports, news articles,
transcripts, as well as suggestions and
criticism.

809   History in Africa. A Journal of
        Method
Memorial Library
University of Wisconsin
728 State Street
Madison WI 53706
Tel: +1-608-262 6397 Fax: +1-608-265 2754
Email: dhenige@library.wisc.edu
Web:
http://www.africanstudies.org/asa_publicat
ionslist.htm
1974- Print ISSN 0361-5413 Ann
Subs: in US $50 inst $35 indiv, elsewhere $65
inst $50 indiv (reduced rates for members of
the ➔ **African Studies Association (2755)**
Ed: David Henige Book rev
Focuses on historiographical and methodological
concerns and publishes textual analysis and
criticism, historiographical essays, bibliographical
essays, archival reports, and articles on the role of
theory and non-historical data in historical
investigation.
Submissions: as above, and book review
essays.
H-Africa TOC

JSTOR Coverage: Vols. 1 - 28, 1974-2001
Journal URL:
http://www.jstor.org/journals/03615413.ht
ml

810   **Ijele: Art eJournal of the African**
       World
       Department of Africana Studies
       Binghamton University
       Vestal Parkway
       Binghamton NY 13902-6000
Tel/Fax: n/a
Email: nnzegwu@africaresource.com.
Web: http://www.ijele.com/
2000- Online ISSN 1525-447X 3Yr
Subs: free
Ed: Nkiru Nzegwu
Book rev Book rev ed: Julie L McGee
(Exhibition and Book Review Editor), Phyllis
J. Jackson (Film Review Editor)
*An online journal of contemporary art and
architecture, art history and criticism, focusing
exclusively on the visual creative expressions of
artists in Africa and other regions of the world.
The journal also highlights the work of non-
African/non-diaspora artists who use iconography
and symbolisms derived from any of the artistic
traditions of Africa.*
Submissions: original manuscripts, interviews
of artists, book and exhibition reviews, and
critical commentaries on any topical issue
related to the creative expressions of African
peoples, and the works of African artists and
artists of African descent in any region of the
world.
H-Africa TOC
Note: last issue published (as at September
2005) was issue 4, 2002.

811   **International Journal of African**
       Historical Studies
       African Studies Center
       Boston University
       270 Bay State Road
       Boston MA 02215
Tel: +1-617-353 7306 Fax: +1-617-353 4975
Email: ascpub@bu.edu
Web:
http://www.bu.edu/africa/publications/ija
hs/index.html
1968- Print ISSN 0361-7882 3Yr
Subs: in North America $120 inst $50 indiv,
elsewhere $130 inst $50 indiv
Ed: Jean Hay, Tel: +1-617-353 7306,
Email: jhay@bu.edu

Book rev
*Covers all aspects of the African past, including
interactions between Africa and the New World.*
Submissions: articles are accepted in English,
and the publication of original source
material is encouraged.
JSTOR Coverage: Vols. 5-35, 1972-2001
Journal URL:
http://www.jstor.org/journals/03617882.ht
ml
as *African Historical Studies*
Vols. 1-4, 1968-1971
Journal URL:
http://www.jstor.org/journals/00019992.ht
ml

812   **International Journal of African**
       Studies
       Global Publications
       Binghamton University, State
       University of New York
       Binghamton NY 13902-6000
Tel: +1-607-777 4495 Fax: +1-607-777 6132
Email: globlpub@binghamton.edu
Web:
http://www.centralstate.edu/africanstudies
/asj.html
1997- Print ISSN 1092-6399 2Yr (irregularly
published?)
Subs: $60 inst $30 indiv
Eds: Ebere Onwudiwe, Center for African
Studies, Central State University, Wilberforce,
OH 45384; Managing ed: Parvis Morewedge,
Office of the Schweitzer Chair, Institute of
Global Cultural Studies, Binghamton
University, PO Box 6000, Binghamton, NY
13902-6000,
Email: globlpub@binghamton.edu
Book rev Book rev ed: Minabere Ibelema,
Department of Journalism, University of
Alabama, Birmingham AL 35233
*Multidisciplinary journal published by the
National Resource Center for African Studies
Central State University, Wilberforce, Ohio,
containing articles of scholarship on socio-cultural
issues, history, and economic and political praxes
relating to Africa, and to African connections
through its diaspora.*
Submissions: as above

813   Ìrìnkèrindò: a Journal of African Migration
Mojúbàolú Olufúnké Okome
Brooklyn College CUNY
Department of Political Science
3413 James Hall
2900 Bedford Avenue
Brooklyn NY 11210-2889
Tel: +1-718-951 4318 Fax: +1-718-951 4833
Email: mokome@africamigration.com
Web: http://www.africamigration.com/
2002- Online ISSN 1540-7497 1-2Yr
Subs: free
Eds: Mojúbàolú Olufúnké Okome, Brooklyn College, CUNY, Department of Political Science, 3413 James Hall , 2900 Bedford Avenue Brooklyn NY 11210-2889, Email: mokome@africamigration.com; Bertrade Ngo-Ngijol Banoum, Lehman College, CUNY, Department of Black Studies, 285 Carman Hall, 250 Bedford Park Boulevard, Bronx, NY 10468-1589, Email: bertrade@lehman.cuny.edu
Ìrìnkèrindò is Yorùbá for 'incessant wanderings or travels', and the journal is devoted to the study of African migration and immigration to other parts of the world. It documents the relevance of African immigration to the world's social, political and economic systems as well as its historical effects on culture, and it will respond to the debates on immigration and problematize its assumed effects.
Submissions: contributions on contemporary issues and events of importance on African migration and immigration.

814   JCTAW. Journal of Culture and its Transmission in the African World
African World Studies Institute
Fort Valley State University
1005 University Drive
Fort Valley GA 31030
Tel: +1-478-825 6056
Fax: +1-478-825 6196
Email: dctaw@fvsu.edu
Web: http://www.dctaw.org/JCTAW.html
2002-[?] print ISSN 1542-7358 2Yr
Subs: in US $50 inst $25 indiv, elsewhere $66 inst $41 indiv
Ed: Sessi Aboh, Email: abohs@fvsu.edu
Seeks to promote the understanding of African cultural history as inclusive of the global experiences of Africans and their movements through time and space; encourage the exploration of the cultural continuities between Africa, the Americas and the Caribbean; and examine the factors that influence, encourage and/or disrupt
the transmission and retention of cultural knowledge and identity among African-descended people throughout the world.
Submissions: welcomes research papers, position papers, literature reviews, book reviews and essays related to the transmission and retention of African culture.

815   Jenda. A Journal of Culture and African Women Studies
Department of Africana Studies
Binghamton University
Vestal Parkway
Binghamton NY 13902-6000
Tel/Fax: n/a
Email: jen-editors@africaresource.com.
Web: http://www.jendajournal.com/
2000- Online ISSN 1530-5686 2Yr
Subs: free (requires registration)
Managing ed: Nkiru Nzegwu, Department of Africana Studies, Binghamton University, Email: panap@binghamton.edu
Co-eds: Mojubaolu Olufunke Okome, Brooklyn College, CUNY, Email: MOkome@brooklyn.cuny.edu, Oyeronke Oyewumi, SUNY-Stonybrook, New York, Email: ooyewumi@sunysb.edu
Book rev Book rev ed: Mary Dillard, Sarah Lawrence College, 1 Mead Way, Bronxville, NY 10708
Email: mdillard@mail.slc.edu
Devoted to the promotion of the research and scholarship of African women. JENdA documents and responds to debates on women's history and studies in African social, cultural, political, and economic systems. Provides a forum for African women scholars, analysts and activists.
Submissions: as above

816   The Journal of African Development
(formerly Journal of African Finance and Development)
c/o Leonard Wantchekon
African Studies Program
New York University
269 Mercer Street, Room 601E
New York NY 10003
Tel: +1-212-998 8533
Email: fas.jafed@nyu.edu
Web:
http://www.afea.org/jafed.html
1998- Print ISSN n/a 2Yr

Subs: in Europe/North America $100 inst $40 indiv, Africa/Latin America $50 inst $25 indiv
Ed: Leonard Wantchekon,
Email: leonard.wantchekon@nyu.edu
Book rev
Provides a forum for the exchange of ideas between academicians and practitioners and to disseminate the results of empirical and theoretical research, policy issues, and practical applications to as broad an audience as possible.
Submissions: although its principal contributors and audience consists largely of scholars, researchers, and other professionals interested in African finance and economic development, JAD strives to publish articles that are useful to officials in government and international organizations, as well as to business executives
Affil: ➔ **African Finance and Economics Association (2751)**

817   Journal of African Philosophy
Binghamton University
Vestal Parkway
Binghamton NY 13902-6000
Tel/Fax: n/a
Email: phil-editors@africaresource.com.
Web: http://www.africanphilosophy.com/
2000- Online ISSN 1533-1067 3Yr (irregularly published)
Subs: free (requires registration)
Eds: Olufemi Taiwo, Department of Philosophy, Seattle University, Seattle, WA; Ayotunde Bewaji, Department of Philosophy, University of the West Indies Jamaica; Pamela Abuya, Department of Philosophy, Moi University, Eldoret, Kenya
Managing ed: Nkiru Nzegwu, Email: panap@binghamton.edu;
Sponsored by the International Society for African Philosophy and Studies (ISAPS); promotes the study of African and African diaspora philosophy and studies worldwide from a broad, critical perspective.
Submissions: original manuscripts, book reviews, and critical commentaries on any topic on African philosophy, and substantive discussions of themes, orientations, traditions, schools, etc. on African philosophy, globally conceived.
Note: last issue published, as at September 2005, was issue 2, 2003.

818   Journal of African Policy Studies
Institute of African Affairs
PO Box X016
Middle Tennessee State University
Murfreesboro TN 37132
Tel: +1-615-898 5731 Fax: +1-615-898 5460
Email: mtesi@mtus.edu
Web: http://journalofafrica.tripod.com/
1995- Print ISSN 1958-5613 3Yr
Subs: in the US $78 inst $50 indiv, elsewhere $90 inst $62 indiv
Ed: Moses K. Tesi
An independent publication of The Institute of African Affairs concerned with global, regional, and domestic policy issues relating to Africa. Interdisciplinary in scope, the journal critically and analytically assesses a wide range of issues relating to African public policy.
Submissions: welcomes articles, review essays and research notes dealing with all levels of public policy as they relate to Africa, and which may be in the form of case studies, comparative analysis, or theory construction.

819   Journal of African Travel Writing
PO Box 346
Chapel Hill NC 27514
Tel/Fax: n/a
Email: ottotwo@email.unc.edu
Web: http://www.unc.edu/~ottotwo/
1996- Print and (partly) online
ISSN 1085-9527 2Yr
Ed: Amber Vogel
Book rev
Subs: in US $14 inst $10 indiv, elsewhere $18 inst $14 indiv
The journal presents and analyses accounts of past and contemporary African travel. Its specific aim is to explore Africa as a site of narrative. Contributors are writers, scholars, and travellers worldwide.
Submissions: scholarly articles related to African travel, including true narratives, primary materials, fiction, poetry, reviews, and related literary artefacts.
Note: the complete index to back issues is available on the Web site.

820   Journal of Colonialism and Colonial History
The Johns Hopkins University Press
2715 North Charles Street
Baltimore MD 21218-4363
Tel: +1-410-516 6987 Fax: +1-410-516 6968
Email: jlorder@jhupress.jhu.edu

Web:
http://www.press.jhu.edu/journals/journal
_of_colonialism_and_colonial_history/
2000- Online E-ISSN 1532-5768 3Yr
Subs: inst, apply to publisher (only available
as part of Project Muse), $25 indiv
Ed: Patricia W. Romero, Towson University,
Towson, MD 21252,
Email: promero@towson.edu,
Book rev Book rev ed: Antoinette Burton,
University of Illinois Urbana-Champaign
*Interdisciplinary in nature and global in scope the
journal publishes articles drawn from the tenth
century to modern times that deal with aspects of
colonialism and imperialism in the broadest sense
of these terms.*
Submissions: as above; the stance should be
narrative and empirical rather than
theoretical, although certain theoretical issues
such as post-colonialism are not excluded.

821   **Journal of Higher Education in
        Africa**
        The Johns Hopkins University Press
        2715 North Charles Street
        Baltimore MD 21218-4363
Tel: +1-410-516 6987
Fax: +1-410-516 6968
Email: jlorder@jhupress.jhu.edu
Web:
http://www.press.jhu.edu/journals/journal
_of_higher_education_in_africa/index.html
or
http://www.bc.edu/bc_org/avp/soe/cihe/
africaHEjournal/journal_home.htm
Joint publication with:
CODESRIA
Avenue Cheikh Anta Diop x Canal IV
BP 3304
Dakar
Tel: +221-825 98 22/23 Fax: +221-824 12 89
Email: codesria@codesria.sn
2003- Print ISSN 0851-7762 Qtly
Subs: free to African institutions
(orders/requests to CODESRIA address
below); outside Africa: $200 inst $60 indiv
Eds: Damtew Teferra, Center for International
Higher Education, Lynch School of
Education, Boston College, 140
Commonwealth Avenue, Campion Hall 240,
Chestnut Hill, MA 02467, USA
Tel: +1-617-552 4413 Fax: +1-617-552 8422,
Email: jhea@bc.edu;
Adebayo O. Olukoshi, CODESRIA,
PO Box 3304, Dakar, Senegal,

Tel: +221-825 98 22/23, Fax: +221-824 12 89,
Email: jhea@codesria.sn
Book rev
*Designed to serve as a multidisciplinary forum for
analysis and debate on the central issues in higher
education research, policy, and practice in Africa.
The JHEA strives to be a central element in the
"invisible college" of researchers, policymakers,
and others who have an interest in higher
education, and also help to stimulate additional
research on higher education in Africa.*
Submissions: the journal provides a
multidisciplinary forum for analysis and
debate on the central issues facing higher
education in Africa. Its concerns include not
only practical and applied topics, but also
broader issues such as globalization and the
role of higher education systems. The journal
welcomes contributions from different
theoretical, methodological, disciplinary, and
comparative perspectives. In addition to
researchers, contributions from policy
intellectuals are also encouraged.

822   **Journal of Sustainable Development
        in Africa**
        Valentine Udoh James
        College of Humanities and Social
        Sciences
        Fayetteville State University
        1200 Murchison Road
        Fayetteville NC 28301-4294
Tel: +1-910-672 1681 Fax: +1-910-672 1470
Email: valentineudohjames@yahoo.com
Web: http://www.jsd-africa.com/
1999- Online ISSN 1520-5509 2Yr
Subs: free
Ed: Valentine Udoh James
Book rev Book rev ed: Melanie Marshall
James
*The journal addresses the policy components of
Africa's development issues. It focuses on debates
of development; development paradigms; social,
cultural, economic, and ecological sustainability;
and the politics of sustainable development with
regard to governance.*
Submissions: welcomes and encourages
manuscripts that take holistic approaches in
tackling development issues from a scholarly
perspective.

**823   Journal of the African Language
Teachers Association**
Global Publications
Binghamton University State
University of New York
Binghamton NY 13902-6000
Tel: +1-607-777 4495 Fax: +1-607-777 6132
Email: globlpub@binghamton.edu
Web:
http://lang.nalrc.wisc.edu/alta/jalta.htm
1999- Print ISSN n/a Ann (irregularly
published)
Eds: Antonia Folarin Schleicher, Department
of African Languages & Literature, University
of Wisconsin-Madison, 1414 Van Hise, 1220
Linden Drive, Madison, WI 53706-1558,
Email: ayschlei@facstaff.wisc.edu; John
Hutchison, Boston University; Email:
hutch@bu.edu
Subs: $60 inst $30 indiv, $30 in Africa
*Dedicated to issues and concerns related to the
learning of African languages irrespective of the
educational level of the language with which
African language scholars are concerned. The
journal primarily seeks to address the interests of
African language teachers, administrators, and
researchers.*
Submissions: articles that describe innovative
and successful teaching methods, that are
relevant to the concerns and problems of the
profession, or that report about educational
research or experimentation in African
languages.
Affil: → **African Language Teachers
Association (2752)**
Note: last issue published (as at September
2005) vol. 1, 1999; vols. 2-4 reported to be
"in progress")

824   Journal of Third World Studies
Association of Third World
Studies Inc
PO Box 1232
Americus GA 31709
Tel: +1-229-931 2078
Email: hisaacs@canes.gsw.edu
Web:
http://itc.gsw.edu/atws/journal.htm
1984- ISSN 8755-3449 2Yr
Subs: $45
Ed: Harold Isaacs, Department of
History and Political Science, Georgia
Southwestern State University,

Americus GA 31709, Tel: +1-229-931 2078 Fax
+1-229-9312960, Email:
hisaacs@canes.gsw.edu
or hisaacs@americus.net
Book rev
*A scholarly and provocative periodical on
Third World problems and issues, published
by the Association of Third World Studies,
Inc. Includes frequent articles on African
politics and development and
socio-economic change.*
Submissions: as above

**825   Jouvert. A Journal of Postcolonial
Studies**
Department of English
Box 8105
North Carolina State University
Raleigh NC 27695-8105
Tel/Fax: n/a
Email: wyrick@social.chass.ncsu.edu
Web: http://social.chass.ncsu.edu/jouvert
1997- Online ISSN 1098-6944 3Yr
Subs: free
Eds: Deborah Wyrick,
Email: wyrick@social.chass.ncsu.edu;
Managing ed: Stephen Luyendyk,
Email: steve.luyendyk@interpath.net
Book rev Book rev ed: Andrea Mensch, Email
andreamo@unity.ncsu.edu
*A multi-disciplinary journal offering a widely
accessible forum for the interrogation of textual,
cultural and political postcolonialisms.*
Submissions: articles engaging in postcolonial
theory, literature, history, arts, and politics.
The journal is looking for work that opens
new perspectives on its subjects and poses
provocative questions about issues crucial to
postcolonial studies.
Note: latest online issue, as at September
2005, is vol. 7, issue 2 Winter/Spring 2003.

**826   Mande Studies. The Journal of the
Mande Studies Association**
African Studies Program
University of Wisconsin
205 Ingraham Hall
1155 Observatory Drive
Madison WI 53706
Tel: +1-608-262 2380 Fax: +1-608-265 5851
Email: africa@intl-institute.wisc.edu
Web:
http://uweb.txstate.edu/anthropology/man
sa/mande_studies.htm

http://www.swt.edu/anthropology/mansa/wisconu.html
1999- Print ISSN n/a Ann (irregularly published)
Subs: in US $30 inst $15 indiv, elsewhere $36 inst $18 indiv
Eds: Ariane Deluz, Laboratoire d'anthropologie sociale, College de France, 52 rue du Cardinal Lemoine, 75005 Paris, France, Email: Ariane.Deluz@ehess.fr;
Stephen Belcher, RD 1 Box 1000, Petersburg, PA 16669, Tel: +1-814-667 4490
Fax: +1-814-667 2493,
Email: spbelcher@mindspring.com
Articles on all aspects of the Mande world and the peoples and cultures who compose it. Most issues are devoted to a special topic of Mande studies.
Submissions: as above, in English or French.
Affil: ➔ **Mande Studies Association (2774)**
H-Africa TOC
Note: last volume published, as at September 2005, was vol. 4, 2002.

827   Meridians. Feminism, Race, Transnationalism
Indiana University Press
601 N Morton Street
Bloomington IN 47404
Tel: +1-812-855 8817
Toll-free (US/Canada only) 800-842 6796
Email: journals@indiana.edu (General enquiries) iuporder@indiana.edu (Subscription orders)
Web: http://iupjournals.org/meridians/ or http://www.smith.edu/meridians/
Ed: Paula Giddings, Editorial Office, Meridians, 146 Elm Street, Smith College, 98 Green Street Northampton, MA 01063, Tel: +1-413-585 3388, Fax: +1-413-585 3362, Email: meridians@smith.edu
2000- Print ISSN 1536-6936 2Yr
Subs: in US $85 inst $30 indiv $24 stud, elsewhere $101 inst $46 indiv
Provides a forum for scholarship and creative work by and about women of colour in US and international contexts. Recognizing that feminism, race, transnationalism, and women of colour are contested terms, the journal engages the complexity of these debates in a dialogue across ethnic and national boundaries, as well as across traditional disciplinary boundaries in the academy.
Submissions: invites submissions of essays, interviews, poetry, fiction, theatre, artwork, and photo-essays, as well as political manifestos, position papers, and archival documents of continuing interest.

828   Nka: Journal of Contemporary African Art
Suite 114
391 Pine Tree Road
Ithaca NY 14850-2820
Tel: +1- 607-255 0696 Fax: +1-607-254 4271
Email: nka_journal-mailbox@cornell.edu
Web: http://www.nkajournal.org/
1994- Print ISSN 1075-7163 2Yr
Subs: in US $43 inst $27 indiv, elsewhere $63 inst $47 indiv
Eds: Salah Hasan, Email: sh40@cornell.edu; Okwui Enwezor
Book rev
Places contemporary African art in a global perspective and brings significant aspects of contemporary African culture to the awareness of the world. Provides visibility and support for African artists, especially those living in the continent. Maintains contacts and connections with African-based artists and art critics, academics, museums and galleries. Also contains exhibition reviews.
Submissions: n/a

829   Northeast African Studies
Journals Division
Michigan State University Press
1405 South Harrison Rd., Suite 25
East Lansing MI 48823-5245
Tel: +1-517-355 9543 ext 130
Fax: +1-517-432 2611
Email: journals@msu.edu
Web: http://msupress.msu.edu/journals/neas/
1994- Print and online ISSN 0740-9133 (E-ISSN: 1535-6574) 3Yr
Subs: in US, print and online $77/$56 indiv, online only $55 inst $40 indiv, print only $55 inst $40 indiv
Eds: (transitional editorial team) Tim Carmichael, College of Charleston; Ezekiel Gebissa, Kettering University; Grover Hudson, Michigan State University; James McCann, Boston University; Jay Spaulding, Kean College
Book rev Book rev ed: Ezekiel Gebissa
Sponsored by Michigan State University African Studies Center's Northeast African Studies Committee, North East African Studies is the major North American academic journal concerning the Horn of Africa. It aims to publish widely across disciplines and thus to present a

panoramic and interrogative view of the political and cultural landscapes of the Horn of Africa. Submissions: not accepting new submissions at this time (September 2005). For questions regarding future submissions contact Grover Hudson hudson@msu.edu.

830   Philosophia Africana. Analysis of Philosophy and Issues in Africa and the Black Diaspora
Department of Philosophy
DePaul University
2352 North Clifton Avenue
Suite 150
Chicago IL 60614
Tel: +1-773-325 7265 Fax: +1-773-325 7268
Email: editors@philosophia-africana.org.
Web:
http://condor.depaul.edu/~africana/index.html
1998- Print ISSN 1369-6823 2Yr
Subs: $65
Ed: Emmanuel Chukwudi Eze
Book rev Book rev ed: Patrick Goodin, Department of Philosophy, College of Arts and Sciences, Howard University, 2441 6th Street, NW Washington, DC 20059;
Email: pgoodin@howard.edu.
Publishes philosophical or interdisciplinary works that explore the pluralistic experiences of Africa and the Black diaspora from both universal and comparative points of view. The journal also selectively publishes original or critical interpretations of creative and artistic works that reveal vibrant intellectual cultures of modern Africa, the Black diaspora traditions, and pluralistic, universally inclusive, systems of thought in the Americas, England, and Europe. Submissions: the journal is interested in advancing North-South international dialogues and welcomes contributions from anywhere on relevant philosophical issues; for example, philosophical issues in multiculturalism, philosophy of race and racism, postcolonial epistemologies, or philosophy and the new critical social and cultural theories.

831   Proudflesh. New Afrikan Journal of Culture, Politics and Consciousness
Department of Africana Studies
Binghampton University
Vestal Parkway
Binghamton NY 13902-6000
Tel: +1-607-777 4488 Fax: +1-607-777 6547
Email: pf-editors@africaresource.com.
Web: http://www.proudfleshjournal.com/
2002- Online ISSN 1543-0855 1-2Yr
Subs: free (requires registration)
Eds: Greg Thomas, English Department, 408 Hall of Languages, Syracuse University, Syracuse, NY 13244, Email: gthomas@syr.edu; Phyllis Lynne Burns, English Department, 201 Morrill Hall, Michigan State University, East Lansing, MI 48824, Email: burnsphy@pilot.msu.edu
Book rev Book review eds: Anthony Buisseret, Email: atbuisse@syr.edu; Aaron Kamugisha, Email: karakamu@yorku.ca
Peer-refereed academic journal of the Africa Resource Centre Inc. committed to disseminating to as wide an audience as possible, the research findings, analyses, and interpretations of scholars whose field is New Afrikan studies. Submissions: especially welcomes submissions that are critical and creative in its approach, "breaking as many intellectual barriers as possible". Material may consist of articles and essays, reviews of cutting-edge or historic books, music and film, as well as artistic texts, poetry, and fiction.

832   Research in African Literatures
Indiana University Press
601 N Morton Street
Bloomington IN 47404
Tel: +1-812-855 8817
Toll-free (US/Canada only) 800-842 6796
Email: journals@indiana.edu (General enquiries) iuporder@indiana.edu (Subscription orders)
Web: http://iupjournals.org/ral/
1970- ISSN 0034-5210 Qtly
Subs: in US $115 inst $55 indiv, elsewhere $145 inst $72 indiv (in Africa $62.50 inst)
Ed: John Conteh-Morgan, The Ohio State University, 361 Dulles Hall, 230 West 17th Avenue, Columbus, OH 43210-0789
Email: ral@osu.edu; Managing ed: Ruthmarie H. Mitsch, Email: ral@osu.edu
Book rev
Devoted to the publication of articles focusing on all aspects of the literatures of Africa, both oral

and written. The journal is open to a wide range of critical and theoretical approaches. Reviews of current scholarly books are included in every number, often presented as review essays, and a forum offers readers the opportunity to respond to issues raised in articles and book reviews. Special issues and clusters of articles reveal the broad interests of the readership.

Submissions: welcomes articles on topics including, but not limited to, African literatures and other forms of cultural expression, African literatures in an international context, and the relationship between African literatures and those of the metropole and of the recent and historical African diaspora.
H-Africa TOC

833   **Safundi. The Journal of South African and American Comparative Studies**
Andrew Offenburger
8650 East Via de La Escuela
Scottsdale AZ 85258
Tel: +1-480-239 9832
Email: offenburger@safundi.com
Web: http://www.safundi.com/
1999- Online ISSN 1543-1304 Qtly
Subs: $250 inst $49.95 indiv ("Safundi Scholar" rate, includes access to a comparative bibliographic database, an online member directory of over 2,000 scholars, and a course syllabi);
online access to individual issues (including back numbers): free
Found ed: Andrew Offenburger,
Eds: Rita Barnard, Christopher Saunders
Safundi is an online community of scholars, professionals, and others interested in comparing and contrasting the United States of America with the Republic of South Africa. The journal serves as the centrepiece of the online community, and in the belief that analysing the two countries in a comparative context enhances our perspective on each, individually.
Submissions: while new comparative research is the focus of the journal, it also publishes articles specifically addressing one country, provided the articles are of interest to the comparative scholar. Furthermore, the subject matter is as permeable as any country's border, and the journal will consider research addressing other colonial and postcolonial states in southern Africa and North America.
Note: Safundi also publishes a free monthly newsletter (pdf)

http://www.safundi.com/newsletter/ to facilitate comparative studies in South Africa and the United States.

834   **Saharan Studies Association Newsletter**
David Gutelius
Department of History
Stanford University
Stanford CA 94305-2152
Tel: +1-650-859 4861 Fax: +1-650-859 3668
Email: gutelius@stanford.edu
Web: http://www.ssa.sri.com/news/
1993- Online [No ISSN] 2Yr
Subs: free
Ed: David Gutelius
The Newsletter is the principal organ of the Saharan Studies Association, and is designed to be a forum for the exchange of news about publications, projects and scholarly debates.
Submissions: as above, in English and French.
Affil: → **Saharan Studies Association (2781)**
Note: all back issues of the Newsletter, are accessible free at the Association's Web site.

835   **SORAC Journal of African Studies**
French Department
Montclair State University
Upper Montclair NJ 07043
Tel: +1-973-655 5143 Fax: +1-973-655 7909
Email: mengarad@mail.montclair.edu
Web:
http://picard.montclair.edu/~sorac/publications/soracjas/
2000- Print ISSN 1542-1848 Ann (irregularly published)
Subs: $26
Ed: Daniel Mengara, SORAC, French Department, Montclair State University, Upper Montclair, NJ 07043
Published by SORAC (Society of Research on African Cultures) at Montclair State University as part of its contribution to a betterment of Africa's past, present and future through a clear understanding of where the continent is coming from, where it stands today, and where it should be going.
Submissions: the journal is intended as an opportunity for scholars to discuss subjects, theories and ideas pertaining to all areas of African studies, past, present and future, including all matters related to the African diaspora worldwide.
Note: last issue published, as at September 2005, vol. 2, November 2002.

836   Southern Africa Monthly Regional Bulletin – MRB
SouthScan Ltd
920 M Street SE
Washington DC 20003
Fax: +1-202-546 0676
Email: southscan@allafrica.com
Web: http://southscan.gn.apc.org/indexlinked/admin/mrbform.html
1992- Print and online ISSN 0966-8802 Mon
Subs: online only $425, print and online $525 (includes access to back issues, and e-mailed text files monthly, plus PDF file to print 16-page journal)
Ed: David Coetzee Book rev
Offers business and political intelligence on southern and central Africa. Analyses trends in regional integration, the impact of the new South Africa on other economies, relations between the EU, the US, the Far East and the region, foreign investment flows, internal and external trade, business opportunities, political shifts; backed with up-to-date statistical data and relevant charts and tables.
Submissions: conflict, policy issues, economy.

837   Southscan Bulletin
SouthScan Ltd
920 M Street SE
Washington DC 20003
Fax: +1-202-546 0676
Email: southscan@allafrica.com
Web: http://southscan.gn.apc.org/indexlinked/admin/scanform.html
1986- Online ISSN 0952-7542 2Wk
Subs: print and online $625 inst $300 indiv, online only $525 inst $200 indiv (includes access to back issues, and e-mailed text files monthly, plus PDF file to print 8-page journal)
Ed: David Coetzee Book rev
Bi-weekly political and economic analysis from South Africa and the southern and central African region.
Submissions: policy issues, politics, economics.

838   Studies in African Linguistics
Department of Linguistics
219 Oxley Hall
Ohio State University
Columbus OH 43210
Tel: +1-614-292 4052 (Subscriptions)
+1-614-292 2844 (Editorial)
Email: sal@ling.osu.edu
Web: http://www.ling.ohio-state.edu/sal/
1970- Print ISSN 0039-3533 2Yr
Subs: in the US $50 inst $25 indiv, elsewhere $60 inst $33 indiv
Ed: David Odden
Provides a public forum within the community of African language scholars for discourse and dialogue on issues of direct concern to the field of African linguistics. The journal seeks to publish African language data and analyses that might not find a place easily or suitably in more general journals.
Submissions: publishes articles focusing on issues of language structure in which the primary data come from African languages. Contributions are not expected to adhere to any particular theoretical framework or linguistic "school", but should be data-oriented and of potential theoretical interest. Contributions may also take the form of short, descriptive grammatical sketches of endangered African languages.
Note: an author, title, and language index to past volumes is available at http://www.ling.ohio-state.edu/sal/indices.htm

839   Transition. An International Review
Soft Skull Press
55 Washington Street
Suite 804
Brooklyn NY 11201
Email: transition@fas.harvard.edu (Editorial)
subscriptions@transitionmagazine.com (Subscriptions)
Tel: +1-718-643 1599 Fax: +1-866-881 4997
Web: http://www.softskull.com/ or http://www.TransitionMagazine.com
1961-1976, 1991- Print and (partly) online ISSN 0041-1191 Qtly
Subs: $90 inst $30 indiv (or $15 per issue)
Eds: Kwame Anthony Appiah, Henry Louis Gates, Jr.; Executive ed: Michael C. Vazquez
Managing ed: Nicole Lamy, Transition, 69 Dunster Street, Cambridge MA 02138, Tel: +1-617-496 2847, Fax: +1-617-496 2877,
Email: transition@fas.harvard.edu
Book rev
A quarterly, international review known for compelling and controversial writing on race, ethnicity, culture, and politics. Transition is a forum for black intellectuals, but is also for the general reader interested in current international

events and controversial perspectives on politics, art, literature, race, film, music, and religion. Submissions: the editors seek unconventional essays, memoirs, reviews, and short stories – especially by writers of colour. Submissions must be written in a lively, engaging, non-academic style free of jargon. The editors prefer work that is unpredictable and personal but nevertheless carefully crafted and stylistically tight.
JSTOR Coverage: No. 1 - No. 80, 1961-1999
Links out to recent content available for Vols. 9, [81/82] - 10, [88], 2000-2001
Journal URL:
http://www.jstor.org/journals/00411191.html

840   Ufahamu: A Journal of African Studies
The James S. Coleman African Studies Center
UCLA 10244 Bunche Hall
Box 951310
Los Angeles CA 90095-1310
Tel: +1-310-825 6059 Fax: +1-310-206 2250
Email: ufahamu@ucla.edu
Web:
http://www.international.ucla.edu/africa/ufahamu/
1970- Print ISSN 0041-5715 3Yr
Subs: in North America $23 indiv, $18 stud; Africa $18; elsewhere $36
Eds: Zachariah Mampilly, KimGeorge, Managing ed: Elizabeth Stein
Email: ufahamu@ucla.edu
Ufahamu is an interdisciplinary journal of African studies. Named after the Swahili word for comprehension, understanding or being, it is committed to views about social issues, addressing both the general reader and the scholar.
Submissions: publishes material supportive of the African revolution and socially significant works of African history, politics, economics, sociology, anthropology, law, planning and development, literature and other topics about the continent and the African diaspora. Contributions may include scholarly articles, commentaries, review articles, film and book reviews, poetry, prose fiction, and artwork.

841   USAID in Africa
Africa Bureau Information Center
10011 Pennsylvania Avenue NW
Suite 300 South
Washington DC 20004
Tel: +1-202-712 0500
Email: use contact form on Web site
Web: http://www.usaid.gov/locations/sub-saharan_africa/newsletters/docs/index/usaid_in_afr_sum05b.pdf
2002- Print and online [No ISSN] 3 Yr
Subs: free
Eds: Christine Chumbler and Patricia Manley
Provides news, updates, and resources from USAID's Bureau for Africa.
Submissions: articles must relate to USAID programs.

842   Voices. The Wisconsin Review of African Literatures
1414 Van Hise
1220 Liden Drive
University of Wisconsin
Madison WI 53706
Tel: +1-608-265 8746
Email: voices@studentorg.wisc.edu
Web: http://african.lss.wisc.edu/all/voices/
1999- Print ISSN n/a 2Yr (irregularly published)
Subs: $20 inst $15 indiv, in Africa $7.50 inst/indiv
Ed: Katrina Daly Thompson [?]
A forum for exploring issues of written and oral artistic production in Africa and the diaspora in relation to the continent.
Submissions: submissions that stretch and challenge such disciplinary boundaries are welcome, including articles, essays, book reviews of recently published works, translations and original creative writing. In addition to publishing work in English, French, Portuguese, and Spanish, *Voices* has a commitment to publishing work not only about but also in all languages of Africa.

843   West Africa Review
Department of Africana Studies
Binghamton University
Vestal Parkway
Binghamton NY 13902-6000
Tel/Fax: n/a
Email: editors@africaresource.com.
Web: http://www.westafricareview.com/
1999- Online ISSN 1525-4488 2Yr
Subs: free (requires registration)
Eds: Adeleke Adeeko; University of Colorado, Department of English, Campus Box 226, Boulder, CO 80309-0226, Email: adeleke@spot.colorado.edu;
Tejumola Olaniyan, University of Madison-

Wisconsin, Departments of English & African Languages and Literature, 1414 Van Hise Hall, 1220 Linden Drive, Madison, WI 53706, Email: tolaniyan@facstaff.wisc.edu; Olufemi Taiwo; Seattle University, Department of Philosophy, 900 Broadway, Seattle, WA 98122-4340 Email: taiwo@seattleu.edu. Managing ed: Nkiru Nzegwu, Binghamton University, Department of Africana Studies, Vestal Parkway, Binghamton, NY 13902-6000, Email: panap@binghamton.edu Book rev Book rev ed: Chiji Akoma; Department of English, St. Augustine Center, Villanova University, 800 Lancaster Avenue, Villanova, PA 19085, Email: chiji.akoma@villanova.edu *Devoted to the promotion of research and scholarship of importance to the global African community and friends of Africa.* Submissions: scholarly and scientific papers that further the understanding of the geography and life in the region.

844   West African Research Association Newsletter
African Studies Center
270 Bay State Road
Boston University
Boston MA 02215
Tel: +1-617-353 8902 Fax: +1-617-353 4915
Email: wara@bu.edu
Web:
http://www.africa.ufl.edu/WARA/news.htm
1995- Print and online [No ISSN] 2Yr
Subs: print, free with membership of WARA, online free
Ed: Adam D. Kiš, University of Florida, Email: adamkis@africa.ufl.edu
WARC promotes scholarly research on West Africa and the diaspora and works to foster cooperation between American and West African researchers, students and artists. Contains reports about WARC's activities, meetings, projects, announcements, opportunities, and partnerships.
Submissions: n/a
Affil: ➔ **West African Research Association (2787)**

845   World Development
Elsevier Journals
Customer Support Department
PO Box 211
1000 AE Amsterdam
The Netherlands
Tel: +31-20-485 3757 Fax: +31-20-485 3432
Email: nlinfo-f@elsevier.com
Web:
http://www.elsevier.com/wps/find/journaldescription.cws_home/386/description#description
In the US:
Elsevier Journals
6277 Sea Harbor Drive
Orlando FL 32887-4800
Tel: +1-407-345 4020 Toll-free
(USA/Canada only) +877-839 7126
Fax: +1 (407) 363-1354
Email: usjcs@elsevier.com
1973- Print ISSN 0305-750X Mon
Subs: €1,869/$2,090 inst, €277/$309 associate rate ("associated with institutions where a regular rate subscription is currently in place"), €81/$90 stud
Ed: Oliver Coomes, World Development, Department of Geography, McGill University, Room 705, Burnside Hall, 805 Sherbrooke Street West, Montréal, Quebec, H3A 2K6, Canada. Email: wd@mcgill.ca
A multi-disciplinary international journal devoted to the study and promotion of world development. It seeks to explore ways of improving standards of living, and the human condition generally, by examining potential solutions to problems such as poverty, unemployment, malnutrition, disease, lack of shelter, environmental degradation, inadequate scientific and technological resources, trade and payments imbalances, international debt, gender and ethnic discrimination, militarism and civil conflict, and lack of popular participation in economic and political life.
Submissions: any topic on international development, with a particular emphasis on comparative and policy-relevant papers.

SOUTH AMERICA/ CENTRAL AMERICA

Brazil

846 **Africa: Revista do Centro de Estudos Africanos**
CP 26097
05513-970 São Paulo
Tel/Fax: +55-11-3032 9416
Email: cea@usp.br
Web:
http://www.fflch.usp.br/cea/af_revista.html
1978- Print and online ISSN 0100-8153 Ann
Subs: outside Brazil available on exchange
only
Eds: Carlos Serrano, Kabengele Munanga,
Fernando A. Albuquerque Mourão
Book rev Book rev ed: Maria Odete Ferreira
*Presents results of research on Africa and Afro-Brazil conducted both in Brazil and elsewhere.
Covers history, sociology, law, literature,
philosophy, social anthropology and politics.*
Submissions: as above, articles are published
in Portuguese, French, English, Spanish and
Creole of Cabo Verde.

Cuba

847 **Revista de Africa y Medio Oriente**
Centro de Estudios sobre Africa y
Medio Oriente
Ave. 3ra, No. 1805, e/ 18 y 20
Miramar, Playa
La Habana
Tel: +53-7-221890 Fax: +53-3-57-221222
Email: ceamo@ceniai.inf.cu
Web: http://www.nodo50.org/ceamo/
1983- Print ISSN 0864-4403 2Yr
Subs: $40
Ed: David González López
*Mainly contains articles (in English and Spanish)
dealing with current events, along with papers
on historical and international topics and the
impact of African and Middle Eastern cultures in
the Americas.*
Submissions: basically embraces the work of
CEAMO´s researchers, collaborators and
other associates, but also invites contributions
from other specialists.

10
News sources for Africa

See also → **11 The African press**

This chapter provides details of the principal news sources for Africa, but it should be noted that Web sites that include African news sections as part of more general portals, mega sites, or directories are listed under → **1 General online resources on Africa and African studies, and the best of the Web.**

This fourth edition of the *African Studies Companion* includes links to RSS News feeds offered by news services and other information providers. A small orange RSS button is included with the entry to indicate availability of RSS feeds.

A note about RSS feeds

Many news services now offer delivery options by RSS feeds, and indicate this by displaying an RSS or XML pictogram on their Web pages. RSS (Really Simple Syndication) is a simple format for syndicating news headlines or other frequently updated content on the Web. (Another term used is RDF Site Summary "rich site summary".) Typically, a RSS message is short excerpt of text, for example the first sentence or line from a news bulletin, with a hyperlink to the original article, and which is then delivered directly to you. RSS feeds can be viewed for use on a Web site, as long as proper formatting is maintained and material is correctly credited.

In order to get started you first need to download an RSS reader. New versions are appearing all the time, some of which are accessed using browsers (including Firefox, Opera, and Safari, which have functionality to automatically pick up RSS feeds for you), while others are downloadable applications. Many RSS readers, some free, some available at a modest charge, are available to download (both for Windows or Mac OS X), for example:
RSS Reader http://www.rssreader.com/,
FeedReader http://www.feedreader.com,
Newz Crawler http://www.newzcrawler.com/,
or (for Mac OS X) NetNewsWire http://ranchero.com/netnewswire/.
Alternatively, check out the listing in the Open Directory, which can be found at
http://dmoz.org/Reference/Libraries/Library_and_Information_Science/T

echnical_Services/Cataloguing/Metadata/RDF/Applications/RSS/News_ Readers/.

Once the software is installed, you simply enter the addresses of RSS files that you are interested in and the programme will then regularly check each of them, alerting you to any new items it finds. The Reader will collect news in the background at user configurable intervals and warn with a little popup in the system tray that a news update has arrived. This makes it a convenient way of staying up-to-date with the content of your favourite Web sites (or Blog entries) without actually having to visit them.

For novices in RSS feeds there are many helpful resources available on the Web, among them the O'Reilly Network RSS DevCenter "Getting started" pages at http://www.oreillynet.com/topics/rss/getting_started, an annotated listing of links and resources on the topic. Good tutorials include Mark Nottingham's RSS Tutorial for Publishers and Web Masters, http://www.mnot.net/rss/tutorial/; Steve M. Cohen's RSS for Non-Techie Librarians http://www.llrx.com/features/rssforlibrarians.htm, or the Yahoo's Publisher's Guide to RSS http://publisher.yahoo.com/whatis.php. Yahoo http://news.yahoo.com/rssis has a special search engine that lets users search the content of RSS files (generating listings of the relevant Web pages), and is offering feeds in RSS formats for top news stories. You can now even create your own custom RSS feeds using Yahoo! News Search. The feeds are free of charge to use for individuals and non-profit organizations for non-commercial use. Attribution (included in each feed) is required.

A useful introduction to the topic, from the perspective of the Africanist librarian, "RSS–Newsfeeds and African Studies" by Lauris Olsen, appears in ➔ **Africana Libraries Newsletter (801)**, no. 117, July 2005 (pp. 5-7); available online at http://www.indiana.edu/~libsalc/african/aln/no117.pdf.

ⓘ **This symbol indicates "The editor's choice" of a particularly outstanding online information resource.**

---

848   Africa Daily
http://www.africadaily.com (Africa Daily)
http://www.wnafrica.com/ (WN Africa)
This is part of the impressive World News http://www.worldnews.com international news site. Supported by search facilities, it displays the latest headlines as they relate to the African continent, accompanied by pointers to related news items (politics, economy, human rights, media, business, etc.) and special reports,

plus a substantial number of links. Or, on the WN Africa pages, you can select an individual African country from the menu to receive the latest national news, together with links, for each country, to online newspapers, broadcasting media, and other news resources. A rich resource for African news. [03/09/05]

849   African News Dimension/AND Networkcom
http://www.andnetwork.com/app
RSS RSS feeds:
http://www.andnetwork.com/app;jsessionid=227D6B528582C1A2458F9DAAB8733 402?service=page/Feeds (available by top stories, recent stories, or by category feeds)
The AND network, with headquarters in Sandton, Johannesburg, was launched in September 2005 and promise to deliver, on a "second-by-second basis", African news services and financial information in the form of text, live video and audio. Top stories are on the front page. Access the latest news by region, or by ten broad categories: Business, Science and Technology, Natural Resources, Health, Politics, Education, Sport, Entertainment, Travel, and Crime & Justice. All content older than 24 hours is archived and is only available to view by premium subscribers at an annual subscription fee of $49. (Compare this with → **all.Africa.com (851)**, which allows free access to current news stories up to 30 days old before a subscription rate clicks in.) However, as at 18.00hrs GMT, 07 September 2005, top stories in, for example, the Education category, were all several days old, and therefore only accessible via subscription. The same was the case in the Travel section. Under the Politics category only two stories were less than 24hrs old; and in the regional West Africa section only one story was less than 24hrs old and thus freely accessible. In "Today's Top Stories" there were 4 current news stories, from Egypt, Ethiopia, Nigeria, and South Africa, that were less than 24hrs old, the remaining 11 featured on that page were 1-28 days old. A freely accessible video Africa Daily Brief Update, "your complete daily news update", all of 2 minutes long, is something less than impressive. Stories can be licensed for reproduction (prices are fairly high), and journalists from Africa are invited to join Andnetwork.com as contributors in all categories of news and current affairs, and will be paid a royalty of 15% each time their work is licensed for reproduction by an Andnetwork customer. Andnetwork.com aims to become the world's "preferred provider of fresh, ongoing and breaking African news content", but while this is an attractively presented portal and interactive Web site for African news, and the annual subscription rate is modest, it has a long way to go before it can seriously challenge other African news providers such as the → **BBC News - Africa /BBC World Service Network Africa (852, 853)** or → **allAfrica.com (851)**. [07/09/05]

850   Afrol.com/AfrolNews ⓘ
http://www.afrol.com/
Afrol News is an Oslo-based news agency established in 2000, working in partnership with a large number of independent news media in Africa, and in particular with MisaNet, a news exchange facilitated by the Windhoek-based → **Media Institute of Southern Africa (2612)**. A well-structured site, Afrol.com covers African news in English, Spanish and Portuguese, systematically analyzing the principal events on the continent and producing daily news articles. Access news

and news stories by country or by 15 broad topics. A searchable archives section, →Afrol documents - Centre for African Documentation (see separate entry 75), offers access to key historical documents, and updated reports and treaties of contemporary importance. The site also offers a large number of links and resources. [03/09/05]

851   allAfrica.com ⓘ
http://allafrica.com/ (English version)
http://fr.allafrica.com/ (French version)
RSS RSS news feeds available for current items.
http://allafrica.com/tools/headlines/rss.html (Current items in English and French are available across the 85 categories that are found on the allAfrica.com site.)
RDF/RSS Headline Modules http://allafrica.com/tools/headlines/rdf.html (allows Web sites to display up-to-the-minute, sorted, categorized news from the AllAfrica feeds.)
AllAfrica Global Media is a multi-media content service provider, systems technology developer and the largest electronic distributor of African news and information worldwide. Registered in Mauritius, with offices in Johannesburg, Dakar, Lagos and Washington, DC, it grew out of the former not-for-profit Africa News Online organization and was launched in 1993. Although now commercial – the basis of its business model includes several revenue streams including advertising, information sales and technology solutions – allAfrica.com has always been a company with a strong social vision. It aggregates and indexes content from over 125 African news organizations, plus more than 200 other sources, which include reports, speeches, press releases and announcements from governments, non-governmental organizations and other newsmakers, inside and outside of Africa. Winner of several awards, allAfrica.com is arguably the best pan-African news source currently available, posting over 1,000 stories daily in English and French and offering a diversity of multi-lingual streaming programming, as well as over 900,000 articles in its searchable archive. The home page provides access to the top news headlines of the day ranked for news value by the allAfrica editorial team, together with links to unranked stories posted as they become available. There are good and easy to use search facilities. News items can also be browsed by topics, covering economy, business and finance; the arts, culture and entertainment; education, environment, health, ICT and telecom, media, religion, science and biotech, travel, US Africa relations, Women, and more. The books pages at http://allafrica.com/books offer news stories and articles about a wide variety of book-related events in Africa (such as book launches, book development initiatives, book prizes, book fairs, news about literary and writers' events, etc.) as reported in African newspapers. There is also a separate section devoted to book reviews (published worldwide, *see also* entry → 408), and press releases relating to new book launches. The whole site is also available in a version français. allAfrica.com remains streets ahead of most of its competitors, and is highly recommended. [03/09/05]
Note: Current news stories on allAfrica.com (up to 30 days old) remain free and accessible without registration or subscription. Subscription to AllAfrica's Global Media's premium service is available for $95 annually. This offers unlimited access to AllAfrica's's archive of over 900,000 documents, a sophisticated search engine (to search by key word, publisher and/or category, by any range from one day to entire

archive, dating from 1996); and the option to choose from 15 categories of daily, customized email alerts of top news from allAfrica.com. For multi-user access and licenses, and pricing for library/institutional rates, apply to Publisher. The annual institutional rate is approximately $1,500.

852   BBC News – Africa (i)
http://news.bbc.co.uk/2/hi/africa/default.stm
853   BBC World Service Network Africa
http://www.bbc.co.uk/worldservice/networkafrica/
RSS RSS feeds:
http://newsrss.bbc.co.uk/rss/newsonline_world_edition/africa/rss.xml
RSS RSS feeds:
http://newsrss.bbc.co.uk/rss/newsonline_uk_edition/front_page/rss.xml
(UK edition)
http://newsrss.bbc.co.uk/rss/newsonline_world_edition/africa/rss.xml
(World edition)
An enormously rich resource, not only for the latest audio news bulletins on Africa (in English, French, Portuguese, Somali, Hausa, and Kiswahili), but also for audio files from the BBC's two major programmes on Africa, Network Africa (the morning programme) and Focus on Africa (the evening programme). The site also offers access to concise and up-to-date country profiles for each nation in Africa, with overviews and basic facts, current political leaders, and information about the media; and you can view a photo gallery of daily life in Africa. The Network Africa pages offer access to the more specialist BBC Africa programmes: Artbeat, Postmark Africa, African Perspective, Fast Track, Africa Live, This Week and Africa, and the → **Focus on Africa (756)** magazine. You can also find out what radio programmes are on the BBC African service, and how to tune into them. RSS feeds are available which allow you to stay up to date with the latest news and features you want from BBC News. [20/08/05]

854   Channel Africa
http://www.channelafrica.org/portal/site
Part of the South African Broadcasting Corporation, Channel Africa supplies daily news from Africa via short-wave radio, satellite and Internet radio. The shortwave broadcast covers southern, eastern, central and West Africa. The Satellite broadcast covers the sub-Saharan region although it can be picked up as far as London. The Internet broadcast covers the entire world. It provides a multi-lingual source of information about Africa – with news, music and sport, "free of subliminal agendas or foreign interpretations". Also offers videos on demand, live audio broadcasts, and access to a valuable audio archive. Channel Africa broadcasts in Chinyanja, English, French, Kiswahili, Portuguese, and Silozi. [03/09/05]

855   IPS Inter Press Service – Africa
http://www.ipsnews.net/africa.asp
RSS RSS feeds: http://www.ipsnews.net/rss/africa.xml
This is part of the → **IPS-Inter Press Service International Association, IPS-Africa (1094)**, a civil society news agency that aims to provide an independent voice from the South. From its headquarters in Johannesburg, IPS Africa coordinates a network

of correspondents and stringers in more than 30 African countries. This network of journalists provides news features and analyses on the events and processes affecting political, economic and social development of the people and nations in Africa—and "striving to go underneath to unearth that story about Africa that often remains untold." In addition to up-to-date news (in English, French and Kiswahili) and a "Rip & Read" Radio section, there are regional gateways offering news from East, West, southern and central Africa, supported by good search facilities. IPS Africa is also involved in a number of media and communication projects intended to broaden the scope of coverage and build the capacity of journalists throughout the continent. [29/06/05]

856   IRIN News.org ⓘ

http://www.irinnews.org/frontpage.asp

RSS RSS feeds: (daily updates) http://www.irinnews.org/Africa.xml

The Integrated Regional Information Networks (IRIN), are part of the ➔ **UN Office for the Coordination of Humanitarian Affairs/OCHA (2528)**. Its reporting focuses on "strengthening universal access to timely, strategic and non-partisan information so as to enhance the capacity of the humanitarian community to understand, respond to and avert emergencies." IRIN services are provided free-of-charge and are available in a range of forms, including analytical reports, fact sheets, interviews, daily country updates and weekly summaries in English, French and Kiswahili. IRIN does not seek to duplicate or redistribute the current news output of existing media organizations, but aims to enhance it with further analysis and details, and thus makes it of interest not only to humanitarian and disaster-relief organizations, but also to the African studies scholarly community. Select news by regions (East Africa, Great Lakes, Horn of Africa, southern Africa, West Africa), by themes such as Children, Democracy and Governance, Economy, Environment, Food Security, Gender Issues, Human Rights, etc. or by weekly round-ups. [10/04/05]

857   News from Africa (formerly Africa News)

http://www.newsfromafrica.org/

News from Africa publishes regular news, features, press reviews and editorials. It is the initiative of Koinonia Community, a not-for-profit development organization based in Nairobi, Kenya. It focuses primarily on culture, peace, justice, ecology, religion, gender issues, and sustainable development. All the articles published are written "from the perspective of the African grassroots people, and their struggle for freedom, dignity and justice." An archive of articles published from 2000 to 2004 is available at the Web site. [03/09/05]

➔ OneWorld – Africa *see* 1 General online resources on Africa and African studies, and the best starting points on the Web: Academic and scholarly resources on African studies entry 91

858   Pambazuka News

http://www.pambazuka.org/

RSS RSS feed: http://www.pambazuka.org/newsfeed.php

Pambazuka News ("Pambazuka" means arise or awaken in Kiswahili) is a tool for progressive social change in Africa. Produced by ➔ **Fahamu (2876)**, it is an informative forum and weekly news round-up on social justice in Africa, and is designed to serve as a tool for progressive social change. Each issue offers news, commentary, and analysis, with sections on conflict and emergencies, human rights, refugees and forced migration, women and gender, elections, health and HIV/Aids, media and freedom of expression, advocacy and campaigns, ICT, and more. There are also regular listings of e-newsletters and mailing lists, useful new online resources, courses, seminars, workshops, books and the arts. The bulk of the research and compilation for the weekly newsletter is done by Fahamu staff in South Africa with support from Fahamu's head office in Oxford, in the UK. Further input is made by editorial writers, content partners and volunteers from around the African continent [05/09/05]

859 Panapress.com
http://www.panapress.com (primarily subscription-based)
The African media pages of the Dakar-based → **Panafrican News Agency (1069)** (formerly Pan African News Agency/PANA) contain a rich selection of top African news stories, updated daily, and also browsable by 12 news topics. It is available in English, French, Portuguese and Arabic versions. The 24 hours news service is complemented by feature stories on important issues of the day and an extensive archive of African news stories from the Panapress wire service. Most access is subscription-based however; for more details of products and services contact Marketing@panapress.com. [05/09/05]

860 World News Connection
Springfield, VA: National Technical Information Service [Technology Administration, US Department of Commerce, Springfield, VA 22161], Online 1996- various subscriber options are offered; available through Dialog, http://www.dialog.com/ contact customer@dialog.com for subscription information, or see http://wnc.fedworld.gov/
World News Connection (WNC) is an online news service, accessible via the WWW, which offers a wide range of translated and English-language news and information, including material and current news from local media in sub-Saharan Africa. The material in WNC is provided to the National Technical Information Service (NTIS) by the Foreign Broadcast Information Service (FBIS), a US government agency. Coverage begins with 1996 (earlier FBIS material is available in microfiche, supported by an index on CD-ROM). The information is obtained from full text and summaries of newspaper articles, conference proceedings, television and radio broadcasts, periodicals, and non-classified technical reports. New information is entered into WNC database every business day, and usually becomes available within 24-72 hours from the time of original publication or broadcast. For a relatively modest monthly fee, WNC subscribers can conduct unlimited interactive searches and have the ability to set up automated searches known as "profiles". [04/09/05]

11
The African press

Introduction

An entirely new section in the 4th edition of *The African Studies Companion*, this is a directory of the African press. Arranged in country order, it provides essential information – including full contact details – about the continent's leading newspapers and news weeklies. Entries are restricted to newspapers published in English and French, and a small number in Portuguese, Afrikaans, and in Arabic (for which Arabic language browser software/Arabic text support will be required). When English or French versions (or condensed weekly versions) exist of newspapers in Arabic, we have listed the English or French versions only, but with links to the original Arabic version.

The majority of the papers listed are large circulation dailies and weeklies, but a number of small circulation independent media are included as well, especially for some of the smaller African countries. Most of the newspapers listed here now have online editions, although the Web sites of some of them can suffer from frequent down time (or have not been updated for a period of a year or more), either for technical reasons, or due to government harassment of sectors of the independent press—unfortunately an all too common occurrence in some parts of the continent. Sadly, it is still only a small proportion of the continent's press that can write and expose without fear of prosecution, imprisonment, or worse.

Exclusions

African-owned news weeklies, monthlies, etc. published outside Africa, or online newspapers hosted outside Africa – for example by Europe or US-based opposition parties, or news portals hosted by other exile groups – are *not* included here.

Newspapers entirely in African languages, e.g. a large number in Kiswahili published in the countries of East Africa, are not included. For listings of newspapers in African languages consult "Electronic Newspapers of Africa" http://www.columbia.edu/cu/lweb/indiv/africa/cuvl/newspapers which is part of → **Columbia University Libraries – African Studies Internet Resources (80)**; or the Stanford "African Newspapers on the Internet" at http://www-sul.stanford.edu/depts/ssrg/africa/current2.html, part of the Stanford → **Africa South of the Sahara – Selected Internet Resources (69)**, which is arranged by country.

Information provided

Each entry includes full address details, telephone/fax numbers, email addresses (general/subscription enquiries and editorial), Web site (where available); name of owner, chief executive and/or publisher (if information is available); name of editor-in-chief and/or other key editorial personnel; details of ownership and an indication of political orientation (i.e. independent or government owned/controlled); together with date founded/year first published, and frequency (daily, weekly, Sundays, or bi-weekly). Newspapers published less frequently than daily, weekly, or bi-weekly are not included.

In this section physical and postal addresses are given separately for most entries. However, written communications, letters to the editor of a newspaper, and press releases, should always be sent to the PO Box address.

Information about circulation figures, advertising rates, annual subscription rates, etc. can be found on the newspapers' Web sites, as can be details of additional editorial, advertising, or subscription sales contacts. It should be noted that while many of these online African newspapers provide free online access to full text, others allow free access to some sections, but require a subscription for access to the entire paper. Many of the newspapers and a number of the news weeklies listed here have informative arts/culture and book pages, and some publish regular book reviews.

All information provided is current (and all Web sites have been verified) as at July 2005. When it has not been possible to verify information, and/or where information is incomplete, this is indicated accordingly. To draw attention to any inaccuracies please email hanszell@hanszell.co.uk and we will correct or update the information in the online version.

Archives

Most of the newspapers offer access to an archive of (at least) recent issues. Each entry gives an indication if access to an archive is possible, with details of the commencement date of online archives. However, it should be noted that while some newspapers offer a fully searchable archive, others only offer access to (sometimes limited) back numbers without search facilities; or they may have a 'search site' facility, but no browsable archive at this time. In some cases access to searchable archives will require a subscription, and a number of the largest newspapers offer various subscription packages.

African news agencies
National press and news agencies for each country are listed as the first entry under each country heading. In some cases they are commercial agencies rather than government owned and controlled national press agencies.

Government-hosted general information services, portals, and directories are not included.

Other news sources for Africa
News sources for Africa, and listings of the major African news portals and Web sites, can be found in Section **10** ➔ **News sources for Africa**.

Other sources for African media
Listings of a number of other sources on African media and the press, and a new indexing project for Kenyan newspapers, can be found in Section **1** ➔ **General online resource on Africa and African studies: Guides to media and the press**.

Abbreviations and symbols used:

[?]	Indicates queried information that could not be verified
n/a	information not available/unable to ascertain
2001-	Year first published, e.g. since 2001 (Note: year first published is for *print* edition if print edition precedes the online version)
Archives	details of availability (if any) of online, searchable archives, and period available, e.g. 2003-, available from 2003 (to current)
Bi-wk	Bi-weekly (or 3Wk, three times weekly)
Chief exec	Chief Executive (or Director of Publication, Managing Director, or Executive Editor)
Dir	Director or Executive Director
Dir Gen	Director General
Dly	Daily (or 5 days weekly)
Ed	Editor or Editor-in-chief
Gov	Government owned/controlled, or pro-government
Ind	Independently owned, private, and/or opposition newspaper
Man ed	Managing Editor
News ed	News Editor
Publ	Name of publisher
Sun	Published on Sundays
Wk	Weekly (or Sundays)

Algeria

National press agency:

861 **Algérie Presse Service (APS)**
Avenue des frères Bouadou
Bir Mourad Rais
Algiers
Tel: +213-21-564444
Fax: +213-21-440312/541608
Email: aps@wissal.dz (General enquiries)
apsdi@aps.dz (News director) dcm@aps.dz
(Commercial section)
Web: http://www.aps.dz/fr/welcome.asp
(French version)
http://www.aps.dz/an/welcome.asp
(English version)
Dir Gen: Nacer Mehal

Newspapers:

862 **El-Khabar** (in Arabic)
Maison de la presse
1 rue Bachir Attar
Algiers 16016
Tel: +213-21-670705
Fax: +213-21- 670710
Email: admin@elkhabar.com
Web: http://www.elkhabar.com/ or
http://www.elkhabar.com/html/pageAngla
is.html   (English version, front page only;
also available in a French version)
1990- Dly Ind
Chief exec: Ali Djerri
Ed: n/a
Publ: El-Kahbar SPA

863 **El Moudjahid** (in French)
20 Rue de la Liberté
Alger
Tel: +213-21-737081 (General enquiries)
+213-21-737806 (Editorial)
Fax+213-21-738990/739043 (General
enquiries)
+213-21-739043 (Editorial)
Email: info@elmoudjahid.com (General
enquiries) or pub@elmoudjahid.com
(Sales/Subscriptions)
Web: http://www.elmoudjahid-dz.com/
1998- Dly Gov
Chief exec: Abdelmadjid Cherbal,
Email: elmoudja@elmoudjahid.com
Ed: Djamel Kaouane,
Email: kaouane@elmoudjahid.com

Man ed: Larbi Timizar,
Email: timizar@elmoudjahid.com
Publ: L'EPE-EURL el Moudjahid
Archives: fully searchable archive 2003[?]-

864 **El Watan** (in French)
Maison de la presse
1 rue Bachir Attar
Algiers 16016
Tel: +213-21-670705
Fax: +213-21- 670710
Email: admin@elwatan.com (General
enquiries)
redact@elwatan.com (Editorial)
Web: http://www.elwatan.com/
1990- Dly Ind
Chief exec/Publ: Omar Belouchet
Ed: Ali Bahmane, Email:
abahmane@elwatan.com
Publ: SPA El Watan
Archives: accessible three months in arrear

865 **Le Quotidien d'Oran**
1 rue Laid Ould Tayeb
63 avenue de l'ANP
Oran
Postal address:
BP 110
Oran
Tel : +213-41-326309/327278
Fax: +213-41-325136 (Editorial)
+213-41-326906 (Sales/Subscriptions)
Email : admin@quotidien-oran.com
Web: http://www.quotidien-
oran.com/html/home.html
2000- Dly Ind
Chief exec/Man ed: Mohamed Abdou
Benabbou
Publ: Oran-Presse SPA
Archives: accessible July 2002-

866 **Le Soir d'Algérie**
Maison de la presse
1 rue Bachir Attar
Algiers 1601
Tel.: +213-21670658/670651
Fax: +213-21-670656 (Administration/Sales)
+213-21-670679 (Editorial)
Email: info@lesoirdalgerie.com
(General/Editorial) pub@lesoirdalgerie.com
(Sales)
Web: http://www.lesoirdalgerie.com/
2000[?]- Dly Ind
Chief exec: Fouad Boughanem

Eds: Malika Boussouf (Editor-in-chief), Badr-Edine Manaa (Excecutive editor)
Publ: Le Soir d'Algérie.com
Archives: fully searchable archive March 2004-

867   Liberté
37 rue Larbi Ben M'hidi
Alger
Tel: +231-21-730489 (Sales)
+231-21-643555 (Editorial)
Fax: +231-21-730487
1992- Dly Ind
Chief exec: Ali Ouafek
Eds: Salim Tamani, Amar Ouali
Email: info@liberte-algerie.com
Web:
http://www.liberte-algerie.com/
Archives: fully searchable archive 2002-

868   La Tribune
Maison de la presse
1 rue Bachir Attar
Algiers 16016
Tel: +213-21-685421/+213-21-676331
Email: latribun@latribune-online.com
Web: http://www.latribune-online.com/
1991[?]- Dly Ind[?]
Chief exec: Hassen Bachir-Cherif
Ed: A. Ghezali
Publ: SARL Omnium maghrébin de presse
Archives: accessible October 2004-

Angola

National press agency:

869   Angola Press Agency/Agencia Angola Presse (ANGOP)
Rua Rei Katyavala 120/122
Luanda
Postal address:
PO Box 2181
Luanda
Tel: +244-2- 447343 Fax: +244-2- 447277
Email: for general enquiries complete online email form
Web: http://www.angolapress-angop.ao/ or http://www.angolapress-angop.ao/index-e.asp (English version)
Dir Gen: Manuel Miguel de Carvalho, Email: wadi@netangola.com
Newspapers:

870   Agora
rua Francisco A Pinto
6-8 Andar 21
Alvalade
Luanda
Tel: +244-2-323477 Fax: +244-2-323477
Email: n/a
1996- Wk Ind
Chief exec: Aguiar dos Santos
Ed: António José Freitas

871   Angolense
rua António Feliciano de Castilho 103
Luanda
Tel: +244-2-264915/263506
Email: info@semanarioangolense.net or
administrator@semanarioangolense.com
(General/Subscriptions)
editor@semanarioangolense.com (Editorial)
Web: http://www.semanarioangolense.net/
1997- Wk Ind
Email:
Chief exec/Man ed: Graça Campos, Email:
gracacampos@semanarioangolense.com
Archives: access subject to subscription

872   Jornal de Angola
Rua Rainha Ginga
CP 1312
Luanda
Tel: +244- 2-338947/335531
Fax: +244-2-333-342
2000- Dly Gov
Email: use email form on Web site
Web: http://www.jornaldeangola.com/
Chief exec: Dir Gen: Luís Fernando

Benin

National press agency:

873 Agence Bénin Presse (ABP)
01 BP 72
Cotonou
Tel: +229-312655 Fax: +229-311326
Email: abpben@bow.intnet.bj
Web:
http://www.gouv.bj/presse/abp/index.php
Dir Gen: Yaouvi Hounkponou
Ed: Joseph Vodounon

Newspapers:

874 L'Araignée
Face Cité Houéyiho
Point d'Accès à l'Information de
l'Ong Satin
Postal address:
01 BP 1357
Cotonou
Tel: +229-306412
Email: araignee@laraignee.org
Web: http://www.laraignee.org/
2000- Wk Ind
Chief exec: Félix Aniwanou Hounsa, Email:
direction@laraignee.org
Ed: Willéandre Houngbedji,
Email: willeandre@laraignee.org

875 Fraternité
Face station Menontin
Cotonou
Postal address:
05 BP 915
Cotonou
Tel: +229 38 47 70 Fax: +229-38 47 71
Email: fraternite@altern.org
Web:
http://www.webfirstplus.com/fraternite
(last issue posted 1025, 10 February 2004) or
http://www.fraternite.info/ (no info. as at
10/06/05)
2002[?]- Dly Ind
Chief exec: Malik Seibou Gomina
Ed: Brice U. Houssou
Archives: search site facility, but no
browsable archive at this time.

876 La Gazette du Golfe
03 BP 1624
Cotonou
Tel: +229-32408/09 Fax: +229-325226
Email: gazettedugolfe@serve.eit.bj
Web: http://www.eit.bj/gazettedugolfe.htm
1991- Wk Ind
Chief exec/Man ed: Modeste Gouthon
Publ: Groupe de presse la gazette du Golfe

877 Le Matinal
153-154 Atinkanmey
Cotonou
Postal address:
BP 1126
Cotonou
Tel: +229- 314920 Fax: +229-313428
Email: lematinal@h2com.com
Web: http://www.lematinalonline or
http://nt7.h2com.com/lmo_qui_lematinal.cf
m (site not updated after November 2004)
1997- Dly Ind[?]
Chief exec: Charles Toko
Ed: Napoléon Maforikan [?]
Archives: searchable for three months
retrospectively

878 La Nation
BP 1210
Cotonou
Tel: +229-300299 Fax: +229-303463
Email: onipben@intnet.bj
Web:
http://www.gouv.bj/presse/lanation/index.
php
1995[?]- Dly Gov
Chief exec: Akuété Assevi
Ed: Léon Brathier
Archives: searchable archive 2005-

Botswana

National press agency:

879 Botswana Press Agency (BOPA)
Private Bag 0060
Gaborone
Tel: +267-352541 Fax: +267-313601
Email: dailynews@gov.bw
Web: http://www.gov.bw/cgi-bin/news.cgi
Chief exec: Itumeleng Sabone
Ed: Epena Ngatangwe

Newspapers:

880   **Botswana Gazette**
125 Sedimosa House
Millennium Park
Kgale View
Gaborone
Postal address:
PO Box 1605
Gaborone
Tel: +267-3912833/3912774
Fax: +267-3972283
Email: editor@gazette.bw
Web: http://www.gazette.bw/
1985- Wk Ind
Chief exec/Man ed: Clara Olsen,
Email: colsen@gazette.bw
Ed: Batlhalefi Leagajang,
Email: bleagajang@gazette.bw

881   **Botswana Guardian**
Private Bag 00153
Gaborone
Tel: +267-352077
Fax: +267-355 2085
Email: guardsun@info.bw
1982- Wk Ind
Ed: Outsa Mokone,
Email outsa@guardiansun.oc.bw
Publ: Sun Publishing Ltd

882   **Daily News**
Department of Information and
Broadcasting
Private Bag 0060
Gaborone
Tel: +267-365 8000 (General enquiries)
+267-357792 (Editorial)
Fax: + 267-301675 (Editorial)
Email: dailynews@gov.bw
Web: http://www.gov.bw/cgi-bin/news.cgi
1975- Dly Gov
Ed: Lamong Leshaga,
Email: lleshaga@gov.bw
Archives: accessible for January 1999-

883   **Midweek Sun**
Private Bag 00153
Gaborone
Tel: +267-352077 Fax: +267-355 2085
Email: guardsun@info.bw
Web: http://www.midweeksun.co.bw/
1989- Wk Ind
Ed: Mike Mothibi
Email mike@guardiansun.oc.bw
Publ: Sun Publishing Ltd

Archives: under construction (not operational on 11/06/05)

884   **Mmegi/The Reporter**
Lot 8901
Segogwane Way
Gaborone
Postal address:
Private Bag BR 50
Gaborone
Tel: +267-397 4784 Fax: +267-390 5508
Email: dikgang@mmegi.bw (General
enquiries) editorial@mmegi.bw (Editor)
Web: http://www.mmegi.bw/
1984- Dly Ind
Ed: Mesh Moeti
Publ: Publishing Company (DPC)
Archives: access for 2002 only at this time.

Burkina Faso

National press agency:

885   **Agence d'Information du Burkina**
01 BP 2507
Ouagadougou
Tel: +226-324639/324640
Fax: +226-324640
Email: aib.redaction@mcc.gov.bf
Web: http://www.aib.bf/
Chief exec: (Mme) Mamina Sam

Newspapers:

886   **L'Hebdomadaire du Burkina**
01 BP 2075
Ouagadougou
Tel: +226-31 47 62
Email: hebdcom@fasonet.bf
Web: http://www.hebdo.bf/
1999- Wk Ind
Chief exec: Zephirin Kpoda
Ed: Djibril Touré
Archives: accessible February 2002-

887   **L'Indépendant**
01 BP 5663
Ouagadougou 01
Tel: +226-333775
Email: sebgo@fasonet.bf
Web:
http://www.independant.bf/semaine/frame
/f_sommaire.html
1993- Wk Ind

Chief exec: Liermé Dieudonné Somé
Ed: Talato Siid Saya
Archives: under construction

888   Journal du Jeudi
01 BP 3654
Ouagadougou 01
Tel: +226-50 31 41 08
Email: info@journaldujeudi.com
info@journaldujeudi.com
Web: http://www.journaldujeudi.com/
Publ & Ed: Boubakar Diallo
1991- Wk Ind
Archives: accessible for 1999-

889   L'Observateur Paalga
01 BP 584
Ouagadougou 01
Tel: +226-332705/305575 Fax: +226-314579
Email: lobservateur@zcp.bf
Web: http://www.lobservateur.bf/
1973- Dly (Sunday edition online) Ind
Chief exec/Ed: Edouard Ouédraogo
Archives: searchable archive January 2004-

890   L'Opinion
Ave. Dr. Kwamé Nkrumah
Ouagadougou
Tel: +226-308949
Email: zedcom@fasonet.bf
http://www.zedcom.bf/
2001- Wk Ind
Ed: Cheick Ahmed
Publ: Zénith Edition Communication
Archives: accessible October 2004-

891   Le Pays
Cité 1200 logements, face à CIJEF
Ouagadougou
Postal address:
01 BP 4577
Ouagadougou 01
Tel: +226-313546/361730 Fax: +226-360378
Email: ed.lepays@cenatrin.bf
Web: http://www.lepays.bf/
1991- Dly Ind
Chief exec: Boureima Jérémie Sigue
Ed: Mahorou Kanazoe
Publ: Groupe de Presse "Le Pays"
Archives: under construction

892   San Finna
01 BP 2061
Ouagadougou 01
Tel: +226-330909
Email: sanfinna@yahoo.fr (General enquiries)
maclau.y@fasonet.bf (Editorial)
Web: http://www.sanfinna.com/
2001- Wk Ind
Ed: Mathieu N'do (Editor imprisoned as at
May 2005)
Publ: Groupe San Finna Communication

893   Sidwaya
01 BP 507
Ouagadougou 01
Tel: +226-306306/07 Fax: +226-310362
Email: sidwaya84@yahoo.fr
Web: http://www.sidwaya.bf/
2000- Dly Gov
Ed: Bilele Benin
Publ: Les Editions Sidwaya
Archives: accessible for May 2004-

Burundi

National press agency:

894   Agence Burundaise de Presse (ABP)
Avenue Nicolas Mayugi
Bujumbura
Burundi
Postal address:
BP 2870
Bujumbura
Tel: +257-213083/213082
Fax +257-222282
Email: abp@cbinf.com
Web: http://www.abp.info.bi/
Chief execs: (Mme) Anne Rurerekana, Thadée
Barashikuza

Newspapers:

895   Le Renouveau
BP 2573
Bujumbura
Burundi
Tel: +257-225411/225487
Fax: +257-225894
Email: dgppb@cbinf.com
1978- Dly Gov
Chief exec: Siryuyumunsi Thaddée
Ed: Jean Nzeyimana
Publ: Publications de Presse Burundaise

Cameroon

National press agency:

896   Agence Camnews/ Cameroon News Agency (CAMNEWS)
Société de Presse et d'Editions du Cameroun
BP 1218
Yaoundé
Tel: +237-230 4012/230 4147
Fax: +237-230 4362
Email: cameroon-tribune@cameroon-tribune.cm
Web: http://www.cameroon-tribune.net/edition.php?lang=Fr&oled=j1506 2005#
Dir Gen: (Mme) Marie Claire Nnana

Newspapers:

897   Cameroon Tribune (in English and French)
Route de l'aéroport
Yaoundé
Postal address:
BP 1218
Yaoundé
Tel: +237-230 4147/230 3689
Fax: +237-230 4362
Email: cameroon-tribune@cameroon-tribune.cm
Web: http://www.cameroon-tribune.cm/
1974- Dly Gov
Chief exec: Marie Claire Nnana
Ed: Martin Badjang ba Nken
Publ: Société de Presse et d'Editions du Cameroun (SOPECAM)
Archives: accessible for 2004- (requires registration, but accessible free)

898   Dikalo (in French)
BP 4320
Yaoundé
Tel: +237-337 2122 Fax: +237-337 7552
Email: dikalo@fadilgroup.com
Web: http://www.iccnet.cm.dikalo/
(site down 25/11/05)
1991- Wk Ind
Ed: Célestin Biake Difana [?]
Publ: Groupe Saint-François

899   The Herald
BP 3659
Yaoundé
Tel: +237-231 8497 Fax: +237-231 8497
Email: contact@heraldnewspaper.org
Web: http://www.heraldnewspaper.org/
1992- 2Wk Ind
Chief exec/Man ed: Boniface Forbin
Ed: Asong Ndifor
Publ: Herald Newspaper Organisation
Archives: under construction

900   Le Messager
Rue des écoles
Douala
Postal address:
BP 5925
Douala
Tel: +237-342 0214 Fax: +237-342 0239
Email: messager@wagne.net
Web: http://www.lemessager.net/
1979- Bi-wk Ind
Chief exec: Pius N. Njawe
Ed: Jean Melvin Akam
Publ: Free Media Group
Archives: access subject to registration.

901   La Nouvelle Expression
BP 15333
Douala
Tel: +237-432227 Fax: +237-432669
Email: nouvelexpression@iccnet.cm
1991- 3Wk Ind
Chief exec: Séverin Tchounkeu
Ed: Edmond Kamguia
Publ: Groupe Saint-François

902   Ouest Echos
BP 767
Bafoussam
Tel: +237-344 1091 Fax: +237-344 6371
Email: ouechos@wagne.net
Web: http://www.wagne.net/ouestechos/
(site not updated 18 June 2002)
1994- BiWk Ind
Chief exec/Man ed: Michel Eclador Pekoua
Archives: accessible for December 1999-

903   The Post
GCE Board Entrance
Buea
Postal address:
PO Box 91
Buea
Tel: +237-332 3287

Email: thepostnp@yahoo.com or
wachefrancis@yahoo.co.uk
Web: http://www.postnewsline.com/
1997- Bi-wk Ind
Publ/Chief exec: Francis Wache
Ed: Charles Ndi Chia
Publ: The Post Newspaper Ltd

904   Le Quotidien Mutations
183 rue 1.055
Place Repiquet
Yaoundé
Postal address:
BP 12348
Yaoundé
Tel: +237-222 5104 Fax: +237-222 9635
Email: contact@quotidienmutations.net or
jmutations@yahoo.fr
Web: http://www.quotidienmutations.net/
1996- Dly Ind
Chief exec: Haman Mana
Ed: Alain B. Batongue
Publ: South Media Corporation
Archives: accessible three months in arrear

Central African Republic

Newspapers:

905   Centrafrique Presse
BP 1058
Bangui
Tel: +236-613957 Fax: +236-613957
Email: redaction@centrafrique-presse.com
Web: http://www.centrafrique-presse.com/
2000[?]- 2Wk Gov
Chief exec/Man ed: Prosper N'Douba

Chad

National press agency:

906   Agence Tchadienne de Presse (ATP)
BP 670
N'Djamena
Tel: +235-514253 [?]
Fax: + 235 516094
Email: n/a
Web: n/a
Dir Gen: Mahamat Hissène

Newspapers:

907   N'Djaména Hebdo
BP 4498
N'Djamena
Tel: +235-515314
Fax: +235-521498/521452
Email: ndjamenahebdo@intnet.td or
ndjb@intnet.td
Web:
http://www.chez.com/ndjamenahebdo/
(site not updated since October 2000, site
suspended?)
1989- 2Wk Ind
Chief exec: Yaldet Bégoto Oulatar
Ed: Dieudonné Djonabaye

908   L'Observateur
BP 2031
N'Djamena
Tel: +235-518005
Email: observer.presse@intnet.td
1997- Wk Ind
Chief exec. Sy Koumbo Singa Gali
Ed: Samory Ngaradoumbé

909   Le Progrès
BP 3055
N'Djamena
Tel: +235-515586/230094
Email: progres@intnet.td
2002[?]- Dly Ind
Chief exec: Abderamane Barka
Ed: Ramadan Sidjim

Comoros

Newspapers:

910   Al Watan
Dom 828
Des Comoros R.f.1
Grande Comore
Postal address:
BP 984
Moroni
Tel/Fax: n/a
Email: alwatwan@snpt.km
http://www.comores-online.com/al-
watwan/
1988- Wk Gov
Ed: n/a
Archives: under construction

911 **Le Matin des Comoros**
BP 1040
Moroni
Tel: +269-732955/732995
Email: lematin@snpt.km
2002[?]- Dly Ind
Publ & Ed: Aliloifa Mohamed Said

Congo (Brazzaville)

National press agency:

912 **Agence d'Information d'Afrique Centrale (ADIAC)**
Le Courrier d'Afrique Centrale
Hôtel Méridien
Brazzaville
Postal address:
BP 15457
Brazzaville
Tel/Fax: +242-764494
Email: direction@afrique-centrale.net
Web: http://www.afrique-centrale.net/
Chief exec: Jean-Paul Pigasse,
see also → **Le Courrier d'Afrique Centrale (913)**

Newspapers:

913 **Le Courrier d'Afrique Centrale**
Hôtel Méridien
Brazzaville
Postal address:
BP 15457
Brazzaville
Tel/Fax: +242-764494
Email: redaction@afrique-centrale.net or
belie@congonet.cg
Web: http://www.afrique-centrale.net/
1999- Wk[?] Gov
Chief exec: Jean-Paul Pigasse,
Email: direction@afrique-centrale.net
Ed: Belinda Ayessa
Email: belie@congonet.cg
Archives: search site facility, but no
searchable archives at this time.
Note: this publication also acts as a national
news agency, Agence d'Information
d'Afrique Centrale and publishes other
newspapers

914 **Les Dépêches de Brazaville**
Hôtel Méridien
Brazzaville
Postal address:
BP 15457
Brazzaville
Tel/Fax: +242-764494
Email: redaction@brazzaville-adiac.com
Web: http://www.brazzaville-adiac.com/
1994[?]- Wk Gov
Chief exec: Jean-Paul Pigasse
Ed: Belinda Ayessa, Email:
belie@congonet.cg
Archives: searchable archives 1998-

915 **La Semaine Africaine**
BP 2080
Brazzaville
Tel: +242-682283/812335 Fax: +242-828518
Email: lasemaineafricaine@yahoo.fr
Web: http://www.congo-site.info/index.php?action=rubrique&id_rubrique=5904
1952- Wk Ind
Ed: Joachim Mbanza
Publ: Episcopal Conference of the Congo

Congo Democratic Republic

National press agency:

916 **Agence Congolaise de Presse (ACP)**
44-48 Ave. Tombalbaye
Kinshasa 1
Congo Democratic Republic
Postal address:
BP 595
Kinshasa 1
Tel: +243-98 13 09 14/
+243-81-685 3105
Email: acprdcongo@yahoo.fr
Web: http://www.acpcongo.cd/
Chief exec: Laurent Masini Ntambu

Newspapers:

917 **L'Avenir**
873 Immeuble Ruzizi
Ave. Bas-Congo
Kinshasa-Gombe
Tel: +243-9818 3974/8168 84455
Email: presseecrite@groupelavenir.net
Web: http://www.groupelavenir.net/
1995[?]- Dly Gov

Chief exec: Pius Muabilu
Man ed: Joseph Mutambule
Publ: Groupe de Presse L'Avenir
Archives: limited archives for 2004 only

918   Journal Salongo Hebdo
10e rue
Kinshasa-Limete
Tel: +243-12-44038
Email: salongo@best.cd or
salongohebdo2003@yahoo.fr
Web: http://www.salongo.best.cd
1972- Dly Ind
Chief exec/Ed: Bondo Nsama
Archives: accessible for August 2004-

919   L'Observateur
Colonel Ebeya 4722A
Kinshasa-Gombe
Postal address:
BP 11505
Kinshasa 1
Tel: +243-81-502 5079/511 0278
Email: journalobservateur@hotmail.com
or observateur.mavo@laposte.net
Web: http://www.lobservateur.cd/
2002[?]- 2Wk Ind
Chief exec/Man ed: Mankenda Voka

920   Le Phare
Siege 2me niveau Building du 29 Juin
Ave. Colonel Lusaka Kinshasa 3392
Kinshasa-Gombe
Postal address:
BP 15662
Kinshasa 1
Tel: +243-884 5896/990 6352
Web: http://le-phare.com/
Email: info@le-phare.com
1983- Dly Ind
Chief exec: Polydor F. Muboyayi Mubanga
Ed: Kenge Mukengeshayi

921   Le Potentiel
873 Avenue du Bas-Congo
Kinshasa/Gombe
Postal address:
BP 11338
Kinshasa 1
Tel: +243-884 4456 Fax: +243-139 8472
Email: lepotentiel@yahoo.fr or
courrier@lepotentiel.com
Web: http://www.lepotentiel.com
1982- Dly Ind
Chief exec: F. Mulumba Kabuayi

Ed: Modeste Mutuishayi Mutinga
Publ: Les Editions Potentiel

922   La Tempete des Tropiques
90, Blvd du 30 Juin
Kinshasa Gombe
Postal address:
BP 10311
Kinshasa 1
Tel: +243-998 1017/992 0597
Fax: +243-884 3809
Email: contact@latempetedestropiques.tk
Web:
http://www.latempetedestropiques.tk/
2002- Dly Ind
Chief exec/Man ed: Alexis Mutanda
Archives: accessible six months in arrear

Côte d'Ivoire

National press agency:

923   Agence Ivoirienne de Presse (AIP)
Avenue Chardy
04 BP 312
Abidjan 04
Tel: +22520 22 64 13 (General enquiries)
+225-20 22 71 89 (Director General)
Fax : +25-20 21 57 12/20 21 35 99
Email: use online email form
Web: http://www.aip-ci.com/
Director Gen: Dalli Deby

Newspapers:

924   Fraternité Matin
Boulevard du Général de Gaulle
Abidjan – Adjamé
Postal address:
01 BP 1807
Abidjan 01
Tel: +225-20 37 06 66 Fax: +225-20 37 25 45
Email: use online email form on site
Web: http://www.fratmat.co.ci/ or
http://213.239.215.195/fratmat/content/ind
ex.php
1964- Dly Gov
Chief exec: Honorat de Yedagne
Ed: Jean-Baptiste Akroun
Man ed: Alred dan Moussa
Publ: Société Nouvelle de Presse et d'Edition
de Côte d'Ivoire (SNPECI)

Archives: fully searchable archive, free for articles published within the last six days (subscription-based for others)

925   Le Front
Havona Editions
Abidjan 220 Logts Immeuble Mistrale
Escalier D, 3ème étage
Abidjan
Postal address:
11 BP 2678
Abidjan 11
Tel: +225-20 38 13 24 Fax: +225-20 38 70 83
Email: quotidienlefront@yahoo.fr
Web: http://www.lefront.com/lf.asp
2003- Dly Ind
Chief exec/Man ed: (Mme) Fatoumata Coulibaly
Publ: Havona Editions
Archives: accessible for 2003-

926   L'Intelligent d'Abidjan
19 BP 1544
Abidjan 19
Tel: +225-22 42 71 61 (Editorial)
+ 225-07 99 42 43 (Sales/Subscriptions)
Email: intelliabidjan@whipmail.com or
Intelliabidjan@yahoo.fr
Web: http://www.lintelligentdabidjan.org/
2003- Dly Ind
Chief exec: W. Assé Alafé
Ed : Vicky Delore
Publ: Société de Communication, d'Edition, de Finances et des Nouvelles Technologies de l'Information et de la Communication (SOCEF-NTIC)
Archives: accessible 2003[?]-

927   L'Inter
Groupe de Presse Olympe
10 BP 2462
Abidjan
Tel: +225-253277 Fax: +225-358566
Email: inter@afnet.net
Web: http://www.presseci.com/linter/
1998- Dly Ind
Ed: Charles d'Almeida
Publ: Groupe de Presse Olympe
Archives: accessible (incomplete, some issues only) July 2004-

928   Le Jour
2 Plateaux
Abidjan
Postal address:
25 BP 1082
Abidjan 25
Web: http://www.lejourplus.com/
Tel: +225-219578/9
Email: lejour@africaonline.co.ci
1994- Wk Ind
Chief exec: Kouakou Kouame
Ed: Vicky Delore
Publ: Les Editions le Nere SARL

929   Notre Voie
Cocody les II-Plateaux 7è tranche
06 BP 2868
Abidjan 06
Tel: +225-22 42 63 27 Fax: 225-22 42 63 32
Email: gnh@africaonline.co.ci
Web: http://www.notrevoie.com/
1994- Wk Ind
Chief exec: Eugène Wanyou Allou
Ed: Diabaté A. Sidick
Archives: accessible for 2002-

930   Le Nouveau Réveil
Adjame-Sud Tours SICOGI, face Frat-Mat) Bat. A 2e étage P.6
Abidjan
Postal address:
04 BP 1947
Abidjan 04
Tel: +225 20 38 67 91 (General enquiries)
+225-07 84 64 32 (Editorial)
Fax: +225 20 38 67 91
Email: use email form on Web site
Web: http://www.lenouveaureveil.com/
2001- Dly Ind
Chief exec: Dénis Kah Zion
Ed: Gustave N'Guessan
Publ: Edition Le Sphinx
Archives: accessible 2004-

931   Le Patriote
23 rue Paul Langevin
Zone 4C
Abidjan
Postal address:
22 BP 509
Abidjan 22
Tel: +225-21 21 19 45/21 21 19 46
Fax: +225-21 35 11 83
Email: info@lepatriote.net
Web: http://lepatriote.net/

1999- Dly Ind
Chief exec: Sindou Meite
Ed: Moussa Toure
Publ: Mayama Editions et Productions
Archives: searchable archives 2003/2004-
(incomplete)

Djibouti

National press agency:

932   **Agence Djiboutienne d'Information**
1 Rue de Moscou
BP 32
Djibouti
Tel: +253-354013 Fax: +253-354037
Email: adi@intnet.dj
Web: http://www.adi.dj/
Dir Gen: n/a

Newspapers:

933   **La Nation**
BP 32
Djibouti
Tel: +253-358670
Email: lanation@intnet.dj
Web: http://www.lanation.dj/
2001- 3Wk Ind
Chief exec: AbdouRachid Idriss Nour, Email
rachididriss@yahoo.fr
Ed: Adil Ahmed Yousouf, Email:
adil_ahmedyoussouf@hotmail.com
Archives: accessible June 2001-

Egypt

National press agency:

934   **Middle East News Agency (MENA)**
17 Hoda Sharawi Street
Cairo
Egypt
Postal address:
PO Box 1165
Cairo
Tel: +20-2-393 3000 (General enquiries/Main
switchboard)
+20-2-394 1403 (Sales/Subscriptions)
+20-2-393 3559 (Central Editorial Desk)
Fax: +20-2-393 5055/393 7497
Email: webmaster@mena.org.eg
Web: http://www.mena.org.eg/

Chief exec: Mahfouz El-Ansari (Board
Chairman and Editor-in-chief)
See also → **Cairo Press Review (941)**

Newspapers:

Note: for more newspapers, weeklies, and
monthlies in Arabic *see* the Egyptian State
Information Service's "The Press in Egypt" at
http://www.sis.gov.eg/pressrev/html/presi
nfo.htm

935   **Al Ahaly**
Kareem Al-Dawla Street
Talaat Harb Square
Cairo
Tel: +20-2-778 6583 Fax: +20-2-390 0412
Email: n/a
Web: http://www.alahali.com/ (Site down
10/06/05)
1977- Dly Ind (National Progressive Party)
Ed: Abdel-Al Al-Baqouri
Publ: National Progressive Party

Al-Ahram (Daily) *see* → **Al-Ahram Weekly
(936)**

936   **Al-Ahram Weekly**
Al-Galaa Street
Cairo 11511
Tel: +20-2-5786100/5786200/5786300
Fax: +20-2-5782631/5786126/ 5786833
Email: weeklyweb@ahram.org.eg or
weeklyeditor@ahram.org.eg
Web: http://weekly.ahram.org.eg/ (English
version)
http://hebdo.ahram.org.eg/index.htm
(French version, *Al-Ahram Hebdo*)
1875- (Arabic daily version) 1991- (English
weekly version) Wk Ind
Chief exec: Ibrahim Nafie
Ed-in-chief: Hani Shukrallah, Email:
hshukrallah@ahram.org.eg
Man ed: Galal Nassar gnassar@ahram.org.eg
Ed: French version: Mohamed Salmawy
Publ: Al-Ahram Organisation
Archives: fully searchable archive 1998-
Note: this is weekly version of *Al-Ahram
Daily* http://www.ahram.org.eg/

937   **Al Ahraar**
58 Manshyet Al-Sadr
Kobry Al-Kobba
Cairo
Tel: +20-2- 482 3046/482 3072

Fax: +20-2-482 3027
Email: n/a
Web: n/a
1977- Dly Ind (Al Ahrar Party)
Chief exec: Mustapha Kamel Murad
Ed: Salah Qabadaya.
Publ: Publ: Al Ahrar Party

938   Al Akhbar
            Al Yom Foundation
            6 Al Sahafa Street
            Cairo
Tel: +20-2-578 2600/578 2500.
Fax: +20-2-578 2520/578 2510
Email: akhbarelyom@akhbarelyom.org
Web: http://www.elakhbar.org.eg/
1952- Dly Ind
Ed: Galal Dawidar.
Publ: Akhbar AlYom Foundation

939   Al Gomhoureya
            25 Zakaria Ahmed Street
            Cairo
Tel: +20-2-578 3333
Fax: +20-2578 1717
Email: eltahrir@eltahrir.net
Web:
http://www.algomhuria.net.eg/algomhuria
/today/fpage/
1953- Dly Ind
Chief exec/Man ed: Samir Ragab.
Publ: Al Tahrir Publishing and Printing
Group

940   Al Wafd
            1 Boulos Hanna Street
            Dokki
            Cairo
Tel: +20-2-348 2079/348 1863
Fax: +20-2-360 2007
Email: alwafd@alwafd.org
Web:
http://www.alwafd.org/front/index.php
1984- Dly Ind (AlWafd Party)
Chief exec: Nu'man Guma'a
Publ: Al Wafd Party

941   Cairo Press Review
            Middle East News Agency (MENA)
            17 Hoda Sharawi Street
            Cairo
            Postal address:
            PO Box 1165
            Cairo

Tel: +20-2-393 3000 (General enquiries/Main
switchboard)
+202-394 1403 (Sales/Subscriptions)
+20-2-393 3559 (Central Editorial Desk)
Fax: +20-2-393 5055/393 7497
Email: webmaster@mena.org.eg
Web: http://www.mena.org.eg/ or
http://www.sis.gov.eg/pressrev/html/fram
e.htm
1999- Dly (Daily summary of Egyptian press
translated into English) Gov (Egypt State
Information Service)
Chief exec: Mahfouz El-Ansari (Board
Chairman and Editor-in-chief)
Note: this service is subscription based.
Archives: accessible for 2004-

942   Cairo Times
            14 Al Saraya Al Kubra Street
            Suite 6
            Garden City
            Cairo
Tel/Fax: +20-2-794 3396
Email: caitimes@cairotimes.com
Web: http://www.cairotimes.com/
1997- Wk Ind
Chief exec/Publ: Hisham Kassem
Ed: Matthew Carrington
Man ed: Faye Wanchic
Archives: fully searchable archive, 2000-

943   Egyptian Gazette
            Dār al-Tahrīr lil-Tibā 'ah wa-al-Nashr
            Cairo
Tel: + 20-2-578 3333
Email: gazette@eltahrir.net
Web:
http://www.algomhuria.net.eg/gazette/1/
1880- Dly Ind
Chief exec: Samir Ragab
Ed: M. Ali Ibrahim
Note: part of the Algomhuria group, for main
site of daily paper in Arabic *see* ➜ **Al**
Gomhoureya (939).

944   Le Progrès Egyptien
            Dār al-Tahrīr lil-Tibā 'ah wa-al-Nashr
            Cairo
Tel: + 20-2-578-3333
Email: progress@eltahrir.net
Web:
http://www.algomhuria.net.eg/progres/1/
1893- Dly (also Sun as *Progrès Dimanche*) Ind
Chief exec: Samir Ragab
Ed: Ahmed El-Bardissi

Eritrea

National press agency:

945   Shabait.com
Ministry of Information of the State of
Eritrea
PO Box 872
Asmara
Tel: +291-1-120478/201820
Fax: +291-1-126747
Email: use email form on Web site
Web: http://shabait.com/articles-
new/publish/
Dir Gen: n/a

Newspapers:

946   Eritrea Profile Weekly/Shaebia
Ministry of Information of the State of
Eritrea
PO Box 872
Asmara
Tel: +291-1-120478/201820
Fax: +291-1-126747
Email: webmaster@shaebia.org
Web:
http://www.shaebia.org/artman/publish/in
dex.html
1995[?]- Wk Gov
Ed: n/a
Archives: limited number of 2002 issues
accessible

947   Hadas Eritrea (in English, Arabic and
Tigrinya)
Ministry of Information of the State of
Eritrea
PO Box 872
Asmara
Tel: +291-1-120478/201820
Fax: +291-1-126747
Email: use online form on Web site
Web:
http://www.shabait.com/articles/publish/c
at_index_12.html
1991[?]- 3Wk Gov
Ed: n/a

Ethiopia

National press agency:

948   Ethiopian News Agency (ENA)
Belay Zeleke Avenue
Addis Ababa
Postal address:
PO Box 530
Addis Ababa
Tel: +251-1-550011/565210
Fax: +251-1-551609/559931
Email: feedback@ena.gov.et or
ena@telecom.net.et
Web: http://www.ena.gov.et/
General Manager: Kefale Azeze

Newspapers:

949   Addis Fortune
PO Box 259 Code 1110
Addis Ababa
Tel: +251-1-627151 Fax: +251-1-627150
Contact: Tamrat G. Giorgis -
Publisher/ManEditor
Web: http://www.addisfortune.com/
2002[?]- Wk Ind
Ed: Tamrat Gebre Giorgis,
Email: tengirtt@hotmail.com
Archives: volume 4, issue 201 and 202 only.
Note: primarily business oriented

950   Addis Tribune
PO Box 2395
Addis Ababa
Ethiopia
Tel: +251-1-615228/29
Email: tambek@telecom.net.et
Web: http://www.addistribune.com/
1992- Wk Ind
Ed: Engidu Woldie
Publ: Tambek International
Archives: accessible 1996-

951   Ethiopian Herald
Ethiopian News Agency
PO Box 530
Addis Ababa
Tel: +251-1-550011/565210
Fax: +251-1-551609/559931
Email: ena@telecom.net.et or
enas@telecom.net.et
Web: http://www.ena.gov.et/
1943- Dly Gov
Ed: Tsegie Gebre-Amlak

952   The Monitor
Addis Ababa
PO Box 4502
Addis Ababa
Tel: +251-1-560518/560199
Fax: +251-1-552643
Email: themonitor@telecom.net.et
1993- Dly Ind
Chief exec: Lullit G. Michael
Ed: Namrud Berhane Tsahay

953   The Reporter
Media and Communications Centre
Woreda 19
Kebele 56 House No. 221
Addis Ababa
Postal address:
PO Box 7023
Addis Ababa
Tel: +2511-1-510665
Email: mcc@telecom.net.et
Web: http://www.ethiopianreporter.com/
1999- Wk Ind
Ed: Amare Aregawi
Publ: The Media and Communications Center
(MCC)
Archives: searchable archive January 2002-
Note: also published in Amharic

Gabon

National press agency:

954   Agence Gabonaise de Presse
BP 168
Libreville
Tel: +241-444782 Fax: +241-444781
Email: n/a
http://www.agpgabon.net/
Dir Gen: n/a

Newspapers:

955   L'Union
BP 826
Libreville
Tel: +241-729797 Fax: +241-764853
Email: n/a
Web:
http://www.internetgabon.com/gabon/actu
/actu.htm (Site down 10/06/05)
1974- Dly Gov
Ed: n/a
Publ: Sonapresse

The Gambia

National press agency:

956   Gambia News Agency (GAMNA)
Banjul
The Gambia
Tel: +220-226621
Email: gamna@gamtel.gm
Web: n/a
Chief exec: n/a

Newspapers:

957   The Daily Observer
Sait Matty Road
Banjul
Postal address:
PMB 131
Bakau
Banjul
Tel: +220-496608/496877
Fax: +220-496878
Email: info@observer.gm
Web: http://www.dailyobserver.gm/
1992- Dly Ind
Chief exec/Ed: Sheriff Bojang,
Email: md@observer.gm
Publ: The Observer Company (Gambia) Ltd

958   The Independent
PO Box 1106
Banjul
Tel: +220-374667/374665
Email: independent@qanet.gm
Web: http://www.qanet.gm/Independent/i
ndependent.html
1999- Bi-wk Ind
Ed: Abdoulie Sey

959   The Point
Garba Jahumpa Road
Bakau
Postal address:
PO Box 66
Banjul
Tel: +220-497441/497442
Web: http://www.qanet.gm/point/ or
http://www.qanet.gm/point/point.html
(both sites down as at 10/06/05)
Email: point@qanet.gm
1991- 3Wk Ind
Ed: n/a (previous Editor, Deyda Hydara,
murdered December 2004)

Ghana

National press agency:

960   Ghana News Agency (GNA)
PO Box 2118
Accra
Ghana
Tel: +233-21-662381/665135
Fax: +233-21-669841
Email: ghnews@ghana.com
Web: http://www.ghananewsagency.com
Chief exec: Rex Owusu-Ansah.
General Manager: Robert Kafui Johnson

Newspapers:

961   Accra Daily Mail
PO Box CT 4910
Cantonments
Accra
Tel: +233-21-771686
Email: accmail@africaonline.com.gh
Web: http://www.accra-mail.com/
1998- Dly Ind
Ed: Harruna Attah

962   Daily Graphic
Graphic Communications Group
Limited
PO Box 742
Accra
Tel: +233-21-228911/13 Fax: +233-21-234754
Email: info@graphicghana.com (General
enquiries)
online-editor@graphicghana.com (Online
editor)
Web: http://www.graphicghana.info/
1950- Dly Gov
Chief exec: Berfi Apenteng
Ed: Elvis D Aryeh
Publ: Graphic Communications Group Ltd
Archives: search site facility but no archives
at this time

963   The Dispatch
PO Box C1945
Cantonments
Accra
Tel: +233-21-763339
Fax: +233-21-761541
Email: news@daily-dispatch.com
Web: n/a
1999- Wk Ind
Chief exec/Man ed: Ben Ephson

964   Ghanaian Chronicle
Private Mail Bag
Accra – North
Tel: +233-21-232713/227789
Fax: +233-21-232 6208
Email: chronicl@africaonline.com.gh
Web: http://www.ghanaian-chronicle.com/
Supervising ed: Alex Lante-Lawson
Ed: Kojo Omaboe
1996- Dly Ind
Archives: accessible for 2002-

965   The Ghanaian Times
PO Box 2638
Accra
Tel: +233-21-223285 Fax: +233-21-229398
Email: newstimes@ghana.com
Web: http://www.ghanaweb.com/times/
1958- Dly Gov
Ed: Bob Bentil
Publ: New Times Corporation
Archives: access to limited number of back
issues for 2002 and 2005.

966   The Ghanaian Voice
PO Box 514
Mamprobi-Accra
Tel: +233-21-324644/314939
Fax: +233-21-314939
Email: GhanaianVoice@ghanaian-voice.com
(General enquiries)
ManagingEditor@ghanaianvoice.com
(Editorial)
Web:
http://www.ghanaianvoice.com/index.asp
1982- 3Wk Ind
Ed: Joris Jordan
Publ: Newstop Publications Ltd
Archives: search site facility, but no
browsable archives at this time.

967   The Independent
Clear Type Press Building Complex
off Graphic Road
Accra
Postal address:
PO Box 4031
Accra
Tel: +233-21-239338/850274
Fax: +233-21-66 10 91
Email: n/a
Web: http://www.independent-
gh.com/index.asp (last issue online, no. 050,
January 08, 2004)
1989- Wk Ind

Ed: Richmond Keelson
Publ: Trans Africa News

968 The Mirror
Graphic Communications Group Ltd
PO Box 742
Accra
Tel: +233-21-228911/13
Fax: +233-21-234754
Email: info@graphicghana.com (General enquiries)
online-editor@graphicghana.com (Online editor)
Web: http://www.graphic.com.gh/
1969- Wk Gov
Chief exec: Berfi Apenteng
Ed: E.N.O. Provencal
Publ: Graphic Communications Group Ltd
Archives: search site facility, but no searchable archive at this time.

969 The Statesman
PO Box 846
Accra
Tel: +233-21-553079/229875
1995[?]- Wk Ind
Email: n/a
Web: n/a
Chief exec: Nana Akufo Addo
Ed: Asare Otchere-Darko
Publ: Kinesic Communications

970 Weekly Insight
PO Box K272
Accra Newtown
Accra
Tel: +233-21-660148 Fax: +233-21-774338
Email: insight93@yahoo.com
2000- Wk Ind
Ed: Kwesi Pratt

Guinea

National press agency:

971 Agence Guinnée de Presse (AGP)
BP 1535
Conakry
Tel: +224-43059/454461
Fax: +224-454461
Email: agp@sotelgui.net.gn
Web: n/a
Man ed: Fode Kouyate
Newspapers:

972 Horoya
BP 191
Conakry
Tel: +224-413475 Fax: +224-414797
Email: n/a
1961- Dly Gov
Ed: n/a

973 Le Lynx
BP 1986
Conakry
Tel: +224-443214
Email: le-lynx@mirinet.net.gn
http://www.mirinet.net.gn/lynx/
1992- Wk Ind
Ed: Assan Abraham Keita [?]
Publ: Guicomed SARL
Archives: accessible for 1999 only

Guinea Bissau

National press agency:

974 Agência Bissau Media e Publicações
rua Eduardo Mondlane 52
CP 1069
Bissau
Tel: +245-206147
Email: agenciabissau@agenciabissau.com
Web: http://www.agenciabissau.com
Dir Gen: António Nhaga

Newspapers:

975 Correio de Bissau
rua Victorino Costa 8B
Bissau
Tel: +245-213264
1991- Dly Ind
Email: n/a
Web: n/a
Ed: Joao de Barros [?]
Note: may be currently dormant or prohibited; information not verifed

976 Nô Pintcha
Ministério da
Informação e Telecomunicações,
CP 200
Bissau
Tel: +245-212914 Fax: +245-211300
Email: n/a
Web: n/a
1975- Dly Gov

Dir Gen: Sotero Estanislau Andrade de Souza
Ed: Bibiano Baltazar

Kenya

National press agency:

977 **Kenya News Agency (KNA)**
Ministry of Information and
Communication
Directorate of Information
Utalii House off Uhuru Highway
Nairobi
Postal address:
PO Box 30025
Nairobi
Tel: +254-2-333555/313010
Fax: +254-2-318045
Email: kna1@insightkenya.com [?]
Web: n/a
Chief Information Officer: n/a

Press agencies:

978 **African Church Information Service**
PO Box 66878
Nairobi
Tel: +254-2-448541
Email: AfricaNN@inform-bbs.dk
Web: n/a
Ed: Noel Okoth
Note: this service if provided by the All
Africa Conference of Churches, Nairobi

Newspapers:

979 **Coastweek**
Coastweek Limited
Nkrumah Road / Mwenye Aboud
Road
Oriental Building 2nd Floor
Mombasa
Postal address:
PO Box 87270
Mombasa
Tel: +254-41-230125/230130
Fax: +254-41-225003
Email: coastwk@africaonline.co.ke
Web: http://www.coastweek.com/
1978- Wk Ind
Ed: Anjum Asodia
Publ: Coastweek Newspapers Ltd

Note: this paper is partly tourism and
business-related, and also includes articles in
German.

980 **Daily Nation**
Nation Media Group Ltd
Nation Centre
Kimathi Street
Nairobi
Postal address:
PO Box 49010 GPO
00100 Nairobi
Tel: +254-20-3208 8000 Fax: +254-20-214531
Email: syndicated@nation.co.ke
Web:
http://www.nationmedia.com/dailynation/
nmgindex.asp
1960- Dly (also Sun as *Sunday Nation*) Ind
Ed: Wangethi Mwangi
News ed: Mutegi Njau
Publ: Nation Media Group Ltd
Archives: fully searchable archive 1998-

981 **The East African**
Nation Centre
Kimathi Street
Nairobi
Postal address:
PO Box 49010
Nairobi
Tel: +254-2-221222/337710
Fax: +254-2-217112/214047
Email: eacomments@nation.co.ke
Web: http://www.nationmedia.com/eastafri
can/current/index.html
1993- Wk Ind
Ed: Wangethi Mwangi
Publ: Nation Media Group Ltd
Archives: fully searchable archive 1999-

982 **Kenya Times**
PO Box 30958
Nairobi
Tel: +254-2-652372 Fax: +254-2-218809
Email: kenyatimes@nbi.ispkenya.com
Web: http://www.kentimes.com/
Ed: Enock Wambua
2001- Dly (also Sun as *Sunday Times*) Gov
(Kenya African National Union party)
Publ: Kenya Times Media Trust
Archives: accessible for March 2003-

983 The People Daily
People Newspapers
PO Box 00100-10296
Nairobi
Tel: 253-2-431668 Fax: 254-2-223344
Email: editor@people.co.ke
Web: n/a
1993- Dly (also Wk as *People Weekly*) Ind
Chief exec/Man ed: Kenneth Matiba
Ed: n/a
News ed: Miwaga Oketch
Publ: Kalamka Ltd

984 The Standard (formerly *East African
Standard*)
I & M Building
Kenyatta Avenue
Nairobi
Postal address:
PO Box 30080
00100 GPO Nairobi
Tel: +254-20-322 2111
Fax: +254-20-214467 (General enquiries)
+254-20-322 2111 (Newsroom)
Email: online@eastandard.net (General
enquiries) editorial@eastandard.net
(Editorial)
Web: http://www.eastandard.net/
1902- Gov (also Sun as *Sunday Standard*) Ind
Ed: Wachira Waruru
Publ: The Standard Group
Archives: fully searchable archive 2002-

Lesotho

National press agency:

985 Lesotho News Agency (LENA)
Opposite Royal Palace
Lerotholi Road
Maseru
Postal address:
PO Box 36
Maseru 100
Tel: +266-2-232 5317 Fax: +266-2-232 6408
Email: use email form on Web site
Web: http://www.lena.gov.ls/
Chief exec: N. Thakali
Ed: (Ms) V. Maraisane

Newspapers:

986 Mopheme/The Survivor
PO Box 0772
Maseru West 105
Tel: + 266-311670
Email: mopheme@lesoff.co.za or
lawrence@mopheme.co.ls
Web: n/a
1993- Wk Ind
Ed: Lawrence Keketso

Liberia

National press agency:

987 Liberia News Agency (LINA)
Ministry of Information, Culture and
Tourism
1000 Monrovia 10
Tel: +231-226269 Fax: +231-226269
Email: lina@afrlink.com
Web: n/a
Chief exec: n/a

Newspapers:

988 The Analyst
Gibson Building
Carey Street
Opposite Central Bank of Liberia
Monrovia
Tel: +231-6-516334 (Publisher)
+231-6-512915 (Editor)
Email: info@analystliberia (General enquiries)
Web: http://www.analystliberia.com/
2000- Dly Ind
Chief exec: Stanley Seakor,
Email: publisher@analystliberia.com
Ed: Abdullai Dukuly, Email: news-
editor@analystliberia.com
News ed: Gibson Jerue
Publ: Liberia Analyst Corporation
Archives: search site facility, but no
searchable archive at this time.

989 The News
PO Box 3137
Monrovia
Tel: +231-227820
Email: lmms@afrlink.com
Web: http://www.liberia.net/news.htm
(site down 25/11/05)

1989- Wk Ind
Ed: Joseph G. Barkiah
Publ: Liberia Media & Marketing Services

Libya

National press agency:

990   **Al Jamahiriya News Agency (JANA)**
Al Fatah Road
Tripoli
Postal address:
PO Box 2303
Tripoli
Tel: +218-21-340 2606/340 2136
Fax: +218-21-340 2421
Email: mail@jamahiriyanews.com
Web:
http://www.jamahiriyanews.com/
Chief exec: n/a

Newspapers:

Note: the state owns and controls all media in
Libya, through the Al Jamahiriya News
Agency and the General Press Corporation;
more details at
http://www.libyanpress.com/
(this Web site requires Arabic browser
software)

991   **General Press Corporation**
Press Building
Al-Gomhoriya Street
Tripoli
Postal address:
PO Box 91291
Dat Al Eimad
Tel: + 218-21-3606393/94
Fax: +218-21 3605728
Email: n/a
Chief exec: n/a
Ed: n/a

Madagascar

National press agency:

992   **Agence de Presse MATERA. Agence
de Presse de l'Océan Indien**
c/o CITE Ambatonakanga
BP 74
Antananarivo
Tel: + 261-20-222 5386/226 0247
Fax: 261-20-223 3669
Email: matera@cite.mg
Web: http://www.ird.mg/matera/
(Site down as at 15/06/05)
Chief exec: n/a
Note: private press agency, electronic and
print services available by subscription only.

Newspapers:

993   **Dans les Media Demain/DMD**
58 rue Tsiombikibo
Ambatovinaky
Antananarivo 101
Postal address:
BP 1734
Antananarivo 101
Tel: +261-20-223 0754 Fax: +26120-223 0755
Email: dmd@wanadoo.mg
Web: http://www.dmd.mg/
1986- Wk Ind
Ed: Jean Eric Rakotoarisoa

994   **L'Express de Madagascar** (in French
and Malagasy)
BP 3893
Antananarivo 101
Tel: +261-20-222 1934 Fax: + 261-20-226 2894
Email: lexpress@malagasy.com
lexpress@malagasy.com
Web: http://www.lexpressmada.com/
1994- Dly Ind
Publ: Jean Jack Ramanabazafy
Ed: n/a
Archives: fully searchable archive 2003-

995   **La Gazette de la Grande Ile**
Lot IIW 23 L
Ankorahotra
Antananarivo
Postal address:
BP 8678
Antananarivo 101
Tel: +261-20-226 1377 Fax: +261-20-226 5188
Email: administration@lagazette-dgi.com

(General enquiries) redaction@lagazette-dgi.com (Editorial)
Web: http://www.lagazette-dgi.com/v2/index.php
1998- Dly Ind
Chief exec: Franck Raharison
Publ: Lola Rasoamaharo
Eds: Rolly Mercia, Christian Andrianarisoa
Man ed: James Ramarosaona
Publ: Groupe MPE
Archives: accessible 2004-

996   Madagascar Tribune
Immeuble SME
Rue Raroninahitriniarino
Ankoronahano
Antananarivo 101
Postal address:
BP 659
101 Antananarivo
Tel: +261-20-222 2635/223 2994
Fax: +261-20-222 2254
Email: tribune@bow.dts.mg
Web: http://www.madagascar-tribune.com/
1988- Dly Ind
Chief exec: Rahaga Ramaholimihaso
Ed: Frank Ramaroson [?]
Archives: searchable archives accessible three months in arrear.

997   Midi Madagasikara (in French and Malagasy)
BP 1414
Ankorondrano
Antananarivo
Tel: +261-20-226 9779
Fax: +261-20-222 7351
Email: infos@midi-madagasikara.mg (General enquiries) midi@midi-madagasikara.mg (Editorial)
Web: http://www.midi-madagasikara.mg/
1983- Dly Ind
Chief exec/Publ: Juliana Andriambelo Rakotoarivelo
Ed: Stéphane Jacob
Man ed: Zo Rakotoseheno
Archives: access for period 29 April to 22 August 2003 only

998   Les Nouvelles
8-10 rue Rainizanabololona
Antanimena
Antananarivo
Postal address:
BP 194
Antananarivo 191
Madagascar
Tel: +262-20-223 5433 (General/Subscriptions)
+262-20-223 2360 (Editorial)
Fax: +261-20-222 9993
Email: administration@les-nouvelles.com
Web: http://www.les-nouvelles.com/
2004- Dly Ind
Chief exec: Naina Andriantsitohaina
Publ: Bezo Andrianarivelo Razafy,
Email: dirpublication@les-nouvelles.com
Ed: Christian Chadefaux, Email: redacchef@les-nouvelles.com
Publ: Ultima Media
Archives: fully searchable archive 2004-

Malawi

National press agency:

999   Malawi News Agency (MANA)
Private Bag 28
Blantyre
Tel: +265-1-622122
Fax: +265-1-674138/621075
Email: manall@malawi.net
Web: http://www.information.gov.mw/maa.htm
Man ed: Anthony Chamveka

Newspapers:

1000   The Chronicle
111 Stansfield House
Kamuzu Proc. Road
Lilongwe
Postal address:
Private Bag 27
Lilongwe
Tel: + 265-1-756530/755715
Fax: +265-1-743086
Email: thechronicle@africa-online.net or chronicle@malawi.net
1994- (also Wk as *Weekly Chronicle*) Ind
Chief exec/Man ed: Rob Jamieson

1001 Daily Times
Scott Road
Blantyre
Postal address:
Blantyre Newspapers Ltd
Private Bag 39
Blantyre
Tel: +265-1-670115/671566
Fax: +265-1-671233
Email: use email form on Web site
Web: http://www.dailytimes.bppmw.com/
1895- Dly (also Wk as *Sunday Times*) Ind
(formerly Gov/Party)
Chief exec: Charles Simango
Ed: Vynn Phiri

1002 Malawi Standard (formerly The
Malawi Insider)
Trade Fair Grounds
Kamuzu Highway
Chichiri
Blantyre 3
Tel: +265-664770
Email: Malawi-Standard@africahome.net
Web: n/a
1999[?]- Dly Ind
Ed: Brian Ligomeka
Publ: Insider Publications

1003 The Nation (in English and
Chichewa)
PO Box Box 30408
Chichiri
Blantyre 3
Tel: +265-1-673703/673611
Fax: +265-1- 674343
Email: nation@nationmalawi.com
Web: http://www.nationmalawi.com/
Chief exec/Man ed: Alfred Mtonga
Ed: Mabvuto Banda
1993- Dly (also Wk as *Weekend Nation*) Ind
Publ: Nation Publications Ltd
Archives: search site facility, but no
browsable archives at this time

1004 The Star
PO Box 1240
Blantyre
Tel: +265-1-673470
Email: star@eo.wn.apc.org
2001[?]- Wk Ind
Ed: Lance Ngulube

Mali

National press agency:

**1005 Agence Malienne de Presse et de
Publicité (AMAP)**
Square Patrice Lumumba
BP 141
Bamako
Tel: +223-222 3683/222 57 67
Fax: +223-222 4774
Email: amap@afribone.net.ml
Dir: Souleymane Drabo
Newspapers:

1006 Les Echos
Hamdallaye Ave. Cheikh Zayed
Bamako
Postal address:
BP 2043
Bamako
Tel: +223-229 6289/229 4183
Fax: +223-229 7639
Email: jamana@malinet.ml
Web: http://www.les-echos.net/
1989- Wk Ind
Ed: Alexis Kalambry
Publ : Coopérative Jamana
Archives: searchable archive 2004-

1007 L'Essor
Square Patrice Lumumba
BP 141
Bamako
Tel: +223-222 3683/222 5767
Fax: +223-222 4774
Email: info@essor.gov.ml
Web: http://www.essor.gov.ml/
1961- Dly (also Wk) Gov
Ed: Souleymane Drabo [?]
Publ: Agence Malienne de Presse et de
Publicité
Archives: 'search site' facility but no
browsable archives at this time.

1008 L'Info Matin
350 Rue 56
Bamako-Coura
Postal address:
BP E 4020
Bamako
Tel: +223-222 8209 [?] Fax: + 223-222 8227 [?]
Email: info-matin@info-matin.com
Web: http://www.info-matin.com/
1997- Dly Ind[?]

Ed: Sambi Touré
Publ: Agence Mali Médias

1009   Le Reflet
Immeuble BEN
Boulkassoumbougou
Postal address:
BP E 1688
Bamako
Tel: +223 224 3953/54
Fax: +223-224 22308
Email: lereflet@afribone.net.ml
Web:
http://www.mediamali.org/reflet/index1.ht
m archives at
http://www.afribone.com/actualite/reflet/a
rchives.html
1997-   3Wk Ind
Ed: Abdoul Karim Dramé
Archives: accessible for 2003-

1010   Le Républicain
116 rue 400
Dravéla
Bolibana
Postal address:
BP 1484
Bamako
Tel +223-229 0900 Fax: +223 229 0933
Email: republicain@cefib.com
Web: http://www.lerepublicain.net.ml/
Archives at
http://www.afribone.com/actualite/republi
cain/archrep.html
1992- Wk Ind
Chief exec/Man ed: Salif Koné
Archives: accessible for 2003-

Mauritania

National press agency:

**1011   Agence Mauritanienne
d'Informations (AMI)**
1540 rue 22-006
Nouakchott
Postal address:
BP 467 - 371
Nouakchott
Tel: +222-253856/252916 Fax: +222-254587
Email: ami@mauritania.mr
Web: http://www.ami.mr/fr/defaultfr.htm
Chief exec: Mohamed Cheikh Ould Sidi
Mohamed

Newspapers:

Akhbar Nouakchott see ➜ **Nouakchott Info**
(1013)

1012   Horizons (in French)
BP 467 - 371
Nouakchott
Tel: +222-252940 Fax: +222-254587
Email: ami@mauritania.mr
1990- Dly Gov
Chief exec/Man ed: Mohamed Cheikh Ould
Sidi Mohamed
Publ: Agence Mauritanienne d'Information

1013   Nouakchott Info (in French)
Immeuble Abbas
Tevragh Zeina
Nouakchott
Postal address:
BP 1905
Nouakchott
Tel: +222-525 0271/524 2092
Fax: +222-525 5484/524 2093
Email: info@mapeci.com or
nouakchottinfo@yahoo.fr
http://www.nouakchottinfo.com/indexfr.ht
m or http://www.mapeci.com/
1999- Dly Ind
Chief exec/Publ: Cheikhna Ould Nenni
Ed: Isselmou O. Moustapha
Publ: La Mauritanienne de Presse d'Edition
de Communication et d'Impression
(MAPECI)
Archives: accessible July 2001-
Note: published as *Akhbar Nouakchott*
in Arabic.

Mauritius

National press agency:

1014   Government Information Service
New Government Centre
6th floor
Port Louis
Tel: +230-201 3558 Fax: +230-208-8243
Email: infserv@bow.intnet.mu
Web: http://www.gov.mu/portal/site/gio-
site
Director, Information Section:
C. P. Surajbali

Newspapers:

1015   5 Plus Dimanche
5 Plus Ltée
3 rue Brown Sequard
Port Louis
Tel: +230-213 5500 Fax: +230-213 5551
Email: comments@5plusLtdcom
Web:
http://www.5plusLtdcom/new/index.php
1990- Wk Ind
Chief exec: Darlhmah Naëck
Eds: Michaëlla Seblin, Jean-Claude Dedans
Publ: 5 Plus Ltée
Archives: accessible 2002-

1016   L'Express
Rue des Oursins
Baie-du-Tombeau
Port Louis
Postal address:
BP 247
Port Louis
Tel: + 230-206 8359
Fax: 230-247 1020/247 1010
Email: sentinelle@bow.intnet.mu
Web: http://www.lexpress.mu
1962- Dly Ind
Ed: Jean-Claude de l'Estrac
Publ: La Sentinelle Ltd
Archives: fully searchable archive 2003-

1017   Le Maurcien (in French and English)
8 rue St. Georges
Port Louis
Tel: +230-207 8200 Fax: +230-208 7059
Email: stefr@intnet.mu (General
enquiries/Subscriptions)
Web:
http://www.lemauricien.com/weekend/ind
ex.html
1907- Wk Ind
Chief exec: Jacques Rivet,
Email: jrivet@intnet.mu
Ed: Gilbert Ahnee, Email: marek@intnet.mu
Publ: Le Mauricien Ltd
Archives: accessible February 2005-

1018   Mauritius Times
23 Bourbon Street
Port Louis
Tel:: +230-212 1313 Fax: +230-212 1313
Email: mtimes@intnet.mu
Web: http://www.mauritiustimes.com/
1954- Wk Ind

Ed: Bickramsing Ramlallah
Publ: Mauritius Times Ltd
Archives: accessible October 2002-

1019   News on Sunday
St. James Court
rue Saint Denis
Port Louis
Tel: +230-211 5902 Fax: +230-211 7302
Email: newsonsunday@hotmail.com
1996- Wk (Sun) Ind
Ed: Mike Lynch
Publ: Caractère

1020   Star (in French)
38 rue Labourdonnais
Port Louis
Tel: +230-212 3086/212 6110
Fax: +230-211 7781
Email: starpress@intnet.mu
Web: http://www.mauriweb.com/star/
1973- Wk Ind
Chief exec/Man ed: Siddick Naudeer
Publ: Mauritius Star Press Co

Morocco

National press agency:

1021   Maghreb Arabe Presse (MAP)
122 Avenue Allal Ben Abdellah
Rabat
Postal address:
BP 1049
Rabat 10000
Tel: +212-37-764083/761673
Fax: +212-37-765005/702734
Email: webmap@map.co.ma
Web: http://www.map.co.ma/ or
http://www.map.ma/eng (English version;
French, Spanish and Arabic versions also
available)
Chief exec: Mohammed Khabbachi

Newspapers:

Note: a fuller listing of Moroccan newspapers
and magazines can be found at this
government Web site
http://www.mincom.gov.ma/french/adr_ut
il/adr_util.html

1022   **Al Anbaa** (in Arabic)
Ministère de la Communication
10 Rue Béni-Mellal
Rabat 10.000
Tel: +212-37-772412 Fax: +212-37-766908
Email: webmaster@mincom.gov.ma
Web:
http://www.mincom.gov.ma/alanbaa/
1992[?]- Dly Gov
Chief exec: M. Chakib Laroussi
(Director of Communication
and Press)
Ed: n/a
Archives: accessible 1997-2000

1023   **Assabah** (in Arabic)
201 Boulevard de Bordeaux
Casablanca
Tel: +212-22-271650
Fax: +212-22-297285/404016
Email: assabah@assabah.press.ma
Web: http://www.assabah.press.ma/
2001[?]- Dly Ind
Chief exec: Abdelmounaim Dilami
Ed: Talha Jibril
Publ: Le Groupe L'économiste
Archives: accessible 2002-

1024   **Aujourd'hui Le Maroc**
213 Rond-Point d'Europe
Casablanca
Tel: +212-22-262674
Fax: +212-22-262718 (Sales)
+212-22-262443 (Editorial)
Email: aaouachi@aujourdhui.ma
(Distribution)
kbendaoud@aujourdhui.ma (Editorial)
Web: http://www.aujourdhui.ma/
2001- Dly Ind
Chief exec:/Man ed: Khalil Hachimi Idrissi,
Email: kidrissi@aujourdhui.ma
Ed: Abdellah Chankou,
Email: achankou@aujourdhui.ma
Archives: fully searchable archives 2001-

1025   **L'Economiste**
201 Boulevard de Bordeaux
Casablanca
Tel: +212-22-271650
Fax : +212-22-2972 85/404016
Email : Info@leconomiste.com
Web: http://www.leconomiste.com/
1991[?]- Dly Ind
Chief exec: Abdelmounaim Dilami
Ed: Nadia Salah

Archives: accessible 1991-, requires
registration

1026   **Libération**
33 rue Amir Abdelkader
Casablanca
Postal address:
BP 2165
Casablanca
Tel: +212-22-619400 Fax: +212-22-620978
(Administration) +212-22-620972 (Editorial)
Email: infos@liberation.press.ma
Web: http://www.liberation.press.ma/
1995- Dly Ind
Chief exec/Publ: Mohamed El Yazghi
Ed: Mohamed El Gahs

1027   **Maroc Hebdo International**
4 rue des Flamants Rivièra
Casablanca
Tel: +212-22-238176
Fax: +212-22-981346
Email: mhi@maroc-hebdo.press.ma
Web: http://www.maroc-hebdo.press.ma/
1991- Wk Ind
Chief exec/Man ed: Mohamed Selhami,
Email: selhami@maroc-hebdo.press.ma
Archives: search site facility, but no
searchable archives at this time

1028   **Le Matin**
17 rue Othmane Ben Affane
Casablanca
Tel: +212-22-489100 Fax: +212-22-262969
Email: contact@lematin.press.ma
Web: http://www.lematin.ma/
1999[?]- Dly Ind
Chief exec: Hicham Senoussi,
Email: h.senoussi@lematin.ma
Ed: Said Abu-Sheleih (Directeur des systèmes
d'information),
Email: s.abusheleih@lematin.ma
Archives: search site facility but no searchable
archives at this time

1029   Nouvelle Tribune
320 bvd Zerktouni
angle rue Bouardel
Casablanca
Tel: +212-22-200030 Fax: +212-22-200031
Email: courrier@lanouvelletribune.com
Web: http://www.lanouvelletribune.com/
2000- Wk Ind
Chief exec/Man ed: Fahd Yata
Archives: accessible from no. 339, 2004-

1030   L'Opinion
Société Arrissala
Avenue Hassan II
Lotissement Vita
Rabat
Tel: +212-37-293002/3 Fax: +212-37-292639
Email: lopinion@lopinion.ma
Web: http://www.lopinion.ma/
2001- Wk Ind
Chief exec: Mohamed Idrissi Kaïtouni
Ed: Jamal Hajjam
Publ: Société Arrissala
Archives: search site facility but no searchable
archives at this time

Mozambique

National press agency:

**1031   Agência de Notícias. Agência de
Informação de Moçambique (AIM)**
CP 896
Maputo
Tel: +258-1-430795
Fax: +258-1-421906
Email: aimmoz@zebra.uem.mz
Web: http://www.sortmoz.com/aimnews/
Dir Gen: Gustavo Mavie

Newspapers:

1032   Diario de Moçambique
Esquina Rua Dom João Mascarenhas
e Major Cerpa Pinto
CP 81
Beira
or
Ave. 25 de Setembro 1509
2o. Andar Flat 12
Maputo
Tel: +258-3-326366/320765 (Beira)
+258-1-313629/313630 (Maputo)
Fax: +258-3-323405/329963 (Beira)

+258-1-427312 (Maputo)
Email: diario.moc@teledata.mz (Beira) or
diariomocmap@teledata.mz (Maputo)
Web: n/a
1981- Dly Gov
Ed: Artur Ricardo [?]

1033   Metical
Ave. Mártires da Machava 1002
Maputo
Postal address:
CP 4371
Maputo
Tel: +258-3-497385/497391
Fax: +253-1-497387
Email: metical@zebra.uem.mz
Web:
http://www.tropical.co.mz/%7Emetical/
(access requires subscription)
1997- Dly Ind
Chief exec/Man ed: n/a (Founder, Carlos
Cardoso, murdered in November 2000)
Note: this newspaper is currently dormant

1034   Jornal Notícias
Prédio Notícias
Rua Joaquim Lapa, 55
Maputo
Postal address:
CP 327
Maputo
Tel: +258-1-320119/320120
Fax: +258-1-320575
Email: domingo@teledata.mz [?]
Web: n/a
1956- Dly (also Sun as *Domingo*) Gov
Ed: Domingo Graça Machel

1035   Savana
Mediacoop
Ave. Amilcar Cabral, 1049
Maputo
Postal address:
CP 73
Maputo
Tel: +258-1-430106/301737
Fax: +258-1-302402
Email: savana@medcoop.uem.mz
Web: http://www.mediacoop.odline.com/
(site not updated since 14 November 2003,
currently dormant?)
1993- Wk Ind
Chief exec: Fernando Lima
Ed: Fernando Goncalves
Publ: Mediacoop

1036   **Zambeze**
Rua José Sidumo, 64
Maputo
Tel: +258-1-301717 Fax: +258-1-302019
Email: zambeze@tvcabo.co.mz
Web: n/a
2002- Wk Ind
Ed: Salomao Moiana

Namibia

National press agency:

1037   **Namibia Press Agency (NAMPA)**
Cnr Keller & Eugene Marais Street
Windhoek
Postal address:
PO Box 26185
Windhoek 9000
Tel: +264-61-374000
Fax: +264-1-221713/258262
Email: use email form on Web site
Web: http://www.nampa.org/
Chief exec: N. Hamunime

Newspapers:

1038   **Allgemeine Zeitung** (primarily in
German)
Omurambaweg 11
Windhoek
Postal address:
PO Box 86695
Windhoek
Tel: +264-61-225822 Fax: +264-61-220225
Email: azinfo@az.com.na
Web: http://www.az.com.na/
1916- Dly Ind
Chief exec/Man ed: Stefan Fischer,
Email: sfischer@az.com.na
Ed: Eberhard Hofmann,
Email: ehofmann@az.com.na
News ed: Marc Springer
Email: mspringer@az.com.na
Publ: Allgemeine Zeitung Verlag Pty
Ltd/Democratic Media Holdings (DMH)
Archives: searchable archive 2000-

1039   **The Namibian**
42 John Meinert Street
Windhoek
Postal address:
PO Box 20783
Windhoek
Tel: +264-61-279600 Fax: +264-61-279602
e-mail: info@namibian.com.na (General
enquiries) news@namibian.com.na
(Newsdesk)
Web: http://www.namibian.com.na/
1985- Dly Ind
Ed: Gwen Lister
Publ: Free Press of Namibia Ltd
Archives: fully searchable archive 1998-

1040   **The Namibia Economist**
Schuster Street
Windhoek
Postal address:
PO Box 49
Windhoek
Tel: + 264-61-221925 Fax: + 264-61-220615
Email: economist@economist.com.nam or
economist@nam.tia.net
Web: http://www.economist.com.na/
1998- Wk Ind
Ed: Daniel Steinmann,
Email: daniel@economist.com.na
News ed: Di-Anna Wahl,
Email: di-anna@economist.com.na
Archives: searchable archives January 2001-

1041   **New Era**
Daniel Tjongarero House
Dr. W .Kulz & Kerby Street
Near Game Shopping Centre
Windhoek
Tel: +264-61-273300 (General enquiries)
Fax: +264-61-220584
+264-61-273311 (Chief Executive)
+264-61-273310 (Editorial)
Email: info@newera.com.na
Web: http://www.newera.com.na/
1992- Dly Gov
Chief exec: Protasius Ndauendapo, Email:
md@newera.com.na
Ed: Rajah Munamava (Manager, Editorial
Services),
Email: editor@newera.com.na
Publ: New Era Publication Corporation
Archives: fully searchable archive May 2003-

1042   **Die Republikein** (primarily in
        Afrikaans)
        Omurambaweg 11
        Windhoek
        Postal address:
        PO Box 3436
        Windhoek
        Tel: +264-61-297 2000 Fax: +264-61-23721
        Email: republkn@republikein.com.na
        Web: http://www.republikein.com.na/ 1977-
        Dly Ind (DTA party)
        Chief exec/Man ed: Chris Jacobie,
        Email: chris@republikein.com.na
        Publ: Democratic Media Holdings (DMH)
        Archives: searchable archives 2000[?]-

Niger

National press agency:

1043   **Agence Nigerienne de Presse (ANP)**
        BP 11158
        Niamey
        Tel/Fax: +227-740809
        Email: n/a
        Web: n/a
        Chief exec: n/a

Newspapers:

1044   **Libération - Niger**
        Nouveau Marché
        rue NM-18
        Niamey
        Postal address:
        BP 10483
        Niamey
        Tel: +227-979622
        Email: liberation_niger@yahoo.fr
        Web:
        http://www.planeteafrique.com/liberation/
        or http://www.liberation-niger.uni.cc
        2004- Wk Ind
        Chief exec/Man ed: Boubacar A.H. Diallo,
        Email: boubacardiallo@caramail.com
        Archives: accessible October 2004-

1045   **Le Républicain**
        Nouvelle Imprimerie du Niger
        Place du Petit Marché
        Niamey
        Postal address:
        BP 12015
        Niamey

Tel: +227-734798 Fax: +227-734142
Email: webmasters@republicain-niger.com
(or use online email submission form)
Web: http://www.republicain-niger.com/
1991- Wk Ind
Chief exec/Man ed: Mman Abou
Publ: Nouvelle Imprimerie du Niger (NIN)
Archives: accessible January 2003-

Nigeria

National press agency:

1046   **News Agency of Nigeria
        (NAN)**
        Benue Crescent
        Area 1, Section 1
        Garki
        Abuja
        Tel: 234-9-234 1189/523 9054
        Fax: +234-9-234 3196
        Email: nan@gov.ng
        Web: n/a
        Chief exec: Akin Oshuntokun
        Ed: Malam Shehu Abui

Newspapers:

1047   **The Anchor**
        Anchor Newspapers
        100 Oregun Road
        Ikeja
        Lagos
        Tel: +234- 1-493 4169
        Email: n/a
        Web: http://www.anchoronline.com
        (Site not available as at 25/11/05)
        2003[?]- Dly Ind
        Chief exec: Niran Malaolu
        Publ: Anchor Newspapers

1048   **The Comet**
        The Comet Newspaper
        23-25 Ijora Causeway
        Ijora
        Lagos
        Postal address:
        PMB 12100
        Marina
        Lagos
        Tel: +234-1-545 5627
        Email: mail@cometnews.com.ng
        Web: http://www.cometnews.com.ng/
        (Site down as at 12/06/05)

1993[?]- Dly Ind
Chief exec: Lade Bonuola
Ed: Suleiman Husaini

1049 Daily Champion
Champion House
Isolo Industrial Estate
156/158 Oshodi/Apapa Expressway
Ilasamaja
Lagos
Postal address:
PO Box 2276
Oshodi
Lagos
Tel: +234-1-452 5807/452 5983
Fax: +234-1-452 4421/452 0424
Email: letters@champion-newspapers.com
Web: http://www.champion-newspapers.com/
1992- Dly (Sun as *Sunday Champion*) Ind
Ed: Emma Agu
Man ed: Augsten Adamu
Publ: Champion Newspapers Ltd
Archives: accessible for 2002-

1050 Daily Independent
Independent Newspapers Ltd
Block 5 Plot 7D
Wempco Road
Ogba
Ikeja
Lagos State
Postal address:
PMB 21777
Ikeja
Lagos State
Tel: +234-1-773 3489/496 2138 (General enquiries) +234-1-496 2136 (News room)
Fax: +234-1-496 2139
Email: info@dailyindependentng.com
Web: http://www.dailyindependentng.com/
2001- Dly (also Sun as *Sunday Independent*) Ind
Chief exec: Chief Abel K. Ubeku
Ed: Ted Iwere
Publ: Independent Newspapers Ltd

1051 Daily Times of Nigeria
3, 5 and 7 Kakawa Street
Lagos
Postal address:
PMB 21340
Ikeja
Lagos
Tel: +234-1-497 7280/3 Fax: +234-1-497 7284
Email: n/a
http://www.dailytimesofnigeria.com/ (Site not available 25/11/05)
1925- Dly Ind (formerly Gov)
Chief execs:
Fidelis Anosike (Chairman of the Board)
Chidi Amuta (Chair, Folio Communications)
Ed: Hakeem Bello
Publisher: Folio Communications
Note: under new ownership since February 2005, and to be jointly published in Nigeria and the US in the future, but no further information available at press time.

1052 Daily Triumph
Triumph Publishing Company Limited
Gidan Sa'adu Zungur
Kano
Postal address:
PMB 3155
Kano
Tel: +234-64-633875 Fax: +234-64-630273
Email: editor@triumphnewspapers.com
Web: http://www.triumphnewspapers.com/
Chief exec/Man ed: Mahmoud Adnan
Ed: Musa Ahmad Tijiani
1980- Dly (also Sun as *Weekend Triumph*) Gov
Archives: accessible July 2004-

1053 Daily Trust
14B Tunis Street
off Lusaka Street
Wuse Zone 6
Abuja
Tel: +234-9-523 8726 Fax: +234-9-523 8725
Email: mtrust1@skannet.com or dailytrust@yahoo.co.uk
Web:
http://www.gamji.com/daily_trust.htm or http://www.weeklytrust.com/
2002[?]- Dly (also Sun as *Weekly Trust*) Gov
Chief exec/Man ed: Kabiru A. Yusuf
Eds: Is'haq Modibbo Kawu (Daily Trust)
Garba Deen Muhammad (Weekly Trust)
Publ: Media Trust Ltd

Archives: accessible October 2002- at
http://www.gamji.com/

1054 Financial Standard
5 Iyalla Street
Alausa
Ikeja
Lagos
Postal address:
PO Box 11679
Ikeja
Lagos
Tel: +234-1-471 2337/470 0535
Fax: +234-1-493 4894
Email: info@financialstandardnews.com
Web:
http://www.financialstandardnews.com/
2001- Wk Ind
Chief exec: Ayo Arowolo (Chairman,
Editorial board)
Ed: Weneso Orogun

1055 The Guardian
Guardian Newspapers Ltd
Rutam House Isolo Expressway
Lagos
Postal address:
PMB 1217
Oshodi
Lagos
Tel: +234-1-452 4111/452 9183 (General
enquiries) +234-1-493 1793 (Editor)
Fax: +234-1-452 4080/493 1797
Email: letters@ngrguardiannews.com
(General enquiries)
editday@ngrguardiannews.com (Editorial,
comments/articles)
Web: http://www.ngrguardiannews.com/
1983- Dly (also Sun as *The Guardian on
Sunday*) Ind
Ed-in-chief: Emeka Izeze
Eds: Debo Adesina
Banji Adisa (Editor Saturday ed.)
Jahman Oladejo Anikulapo (Editor Sunday
ed.)
Publ: Guardian Newspapers Ltd
Archives: search site facility, but no
browsable archive at this time.

1056 New Age
Century Media Ltd
217/219 Moshood Abiola Way
Iganmu
Lagos
Tel: +234-1-791 1032/472 3021

Email: ebiz@newage-online.com
Web: http://www.newage-online.com/
2004[?]- Dly Ind
Chief exec/Man ed: Sully Abu
Ed: Steve Osuji
Publ: Century Media Limited
Archives: accessible 2004[?]-

1057 Newswatch
3 Billings Way
off Secretariat Road
Oregun Industrial Estate
Oregun
Lagos
Postal address:
PMB 21499
Ikeja
Lagos
Tel.: +234-1-493 5654 Fax: 234-1-496 0950
Email: newswatchngr@aol.com (General
enquiries)
Raydasoyak@aol.com (International
subscriptions)
Web: http://www.newswatchngr.com/
1985- Wk Ind
Chief exec: Ray Ekpu
Ed: Dan Agbese, Email:
editor@newswatchngr.com
Publ: Newswatch Communications Ltd
Archives: fully searchable archive 1998-
(requires subscription)
Note: access is subscription-based although
some articles are freely accessible.

1058 New Nigerian
New Nigerian Newspapers Ltd
Ahmadu Bello Way
Kaduna
Postal address:
PO Box 254
Kaduna
Tel: +234-62-244864 Fax: +234-62-214389
Email: n/a
http://www.newnigerian.com or
http://www.gamji.com/NNN.htm
(both sites down as at 12/08/05)
1966- Dly Gov
Ed: Mahmud Jega,
Email: mmjega@yahoo.com
Publ: New Nigerian Newspapers Ltd

1059   Nigerian Tribune
Tribune House
Imalefalafia Street
Oke-Ado
Ibadan
Postal address:
PO Box 78
Ibadan
Tel: +234-2-231 0000/231 1675
Fax: +234-2-231 7573/231 8709
Email: tribune_49@yahoo.com
Web: http://www.tribune.com.ng/
1949- Dly (also Wk as *Sunday Tribune*) Ind
Chief exec: Oluwole Awolowo (Publisher)
Ed: Akin Onipede
Publ: African Newspapers of Nigeria plc
Archives: accessible four months in arrear

1060   PM News
26 Ijaiye Road
Ogba Ikeja
Lagos
Postal address:
PMB 21531
Ikeja
Lagos
Tel: +234-1-492 4314/492 2499
Email: aonanuga@aol.com or
ijc@linkserve.com.ng
Web: n/a
1994- Dly Ind
Ed: Bayo Onanuga
Pub: Independent Communications Network

1061   The Punch
Punch (Nigeria) Ltd
1 Olu Aboderin Street
Onipetesi
Ikeja
Lagos
Tel: +234-1-492 0205 Fax: +234-1-497 2815
Email: enquiry@punchng.com
Web: http://www.punchng.com/
1973- Dly (also Sun as *Sunday Punch*)
Man ed: Gbemiga Ogunleye, Email:
dailyeditor@punchng.com
Publ: Punch Nigeria Ltd
Archives: search site facility, but no
browsable archives at this time

1062   The Sun
The Sun Publishing Limited
2 Coscharis Street
Kirikiri Industrial Layout
Apapa
Postal address:
PMB 21776
Ikeja
Lagos
Tel +234-1-587 5560/587 5561
or 234-1-7900632 (Hotline)
Fax: +234-1-587 5561
Email: editor@sunnewsonline.com or use
online email form
Web: http://www.sunnewsonline.com
2003- Dly (also Sun as *Sunday Sun*) Ind
Chief exec/Man ed: Mike Awoyinfa, Email:
mikeawoyinfa@sunnewsonline.com
Exec: Tony Onyima (Executive Director,
Operations), Email:
tony@sunnewsonline.com
Email:
Eds: Femi Adesina (Editor, daily edition),
Email: editor@sunnewsonline.com
Louis Odion (Editor, Sunday ed.)
Steve Nwosu (Editor, Saturday ed.)
Publ: Sun Publishing Ltd

1063   This Day
This Day Newspapers
35 Creek Road
Apapa
Lagos
Postal address:
PO Box 54749
Ikoyi
Lagos
Tel: +234-1-587 1432/587 2807
Fax: +234-1-587 1436
Email: thisday@nova.net.ng
Web: http://www.thisdayonline.com/
1995- Dly (also Sun as *This Day Sunday*) Ind
Chief exec: Nduka Obaigbena (Founding
Editor-in-Chief and Chairman)
Ed: Eniola Bello
Man ed: Kayode Komolafe
Publ: Leaders & Company Ltd
Archives: fully searchable archive 2001-
(requires subscription)

1064   Vanguard
Vanguard Media Ltd
Vanguard Avenue
Kirikiri Canal
Lagos
Postal address:
PMB 1007
Apapa
Tel: +234-1-587 2662/+234-1-264 5241
(General enquiries) +234-1-587 5847 (Sales)
+234-1-774 2861 (Editorial)
Email: vanguard@vanguardngr.com
Web: http://www.vanguardngr.com/
1984- Dly (also Sun) Ind
Ed: Gbenga Adefaye
Publ: Vanguard Media Ltd
Archives: 'search site' facility, but no
browsable archive at this time.

Rwanda

National press agency:

**1065   Office Rwandais d'Information
(ORINFOR)**
BP 83
Kigali
Tel: +250-575735/575218
Fax: +250-576539
Email: rna@rwanda1.com
Web: http://www.orinfor.gov.rw/index.htm
Chief exec: Jean Pierre Kagubare

Newspapers:

1066   New Times (in English)
PO Box 3215
Kigali
Tel: +250-584070 (General/Subscriptions)
+250-587533 (Editorial) Fax: +250-587534
Email: ivansaig@yahoo.com or
newtimes@rwanda1.com
Web: http://www.newtimes.co.rw/
2000[?]- 3Wk Gov (quasi-official)
Ed: Kennedy Ndahiro
Archives: available shortly

1067   La Nouvelle Releve (in French and
Kinywarwanda)
Office Rwandais d'Information
(ORINFOR)
BP 83
Kigali
Tel: +250-575735/575218 Fax: +250-576539

Email: n/a
http://www.orinfor.gov.rw/DOCS/lnr.htm
2003- Wk Gov
Chief exec: n/a
Publ: Office Rwandais d'Information
Archives: accessible 2004-

São Tomé e Príncipe

Newspapers:

1068   Diário Téla Nón
Largo Água
Grande Edifício Complexo Técnico da
C.S.T
Sao Tomé
Tel: +239-225099/100
Email: diario_digital@cstome.net
Web:
http://www.cstome.net/diario/index.htm
2002- Wk Ind
Ed: Abel Veiga
Publ: Sociedade Novas da Terra

Senegal

Pan-African press agency:

**1069   Panafrican News Agency/Panapress
(PANA)**
BP 4056
Dakar
Tel. +221-869 1234 Fax: +221-824 1390
Email: feedback@panapress.com (Newsroom)
marketing@panapress.com (Subscription
enquiries)
Web: http://www.panapress.com/ (English,
French, Portuguese, and Arabic versions)
Chief exec: Babacar Fall
Ed: Biava Seshie
Archives: fully searchable news archive
(requires subscription)
Note: most content, including access to full
text is fee-based, only available by
subscription. Summaries of news stories can
be accessed free.
See also → **News sources for Africa**, entry **859**

National news agency:

1070   Agence de Presse Sénégalaise (APS)
58 Blvd de la République
Dakar
Senegal
Postal address:
BP 117
Dakar
Tel: +221-821 1427/823 1667
Fax: +221-822 0767
Email: aps@aps.sn
Web: http://www.aps.sn/
Chief exec: Mamadou Koume

Newspapers:

1071   L'Observateur
Immeuble Elimane Ndour
Rue 15 X Corniche
Dakar
Tel: +221-849 1644/628 1414
Fax: +221-849 1645
Email: info@futursmedias.net
Web: http://www.lobservateur.sn/
2003- Dly Ind
Ed: n/a
Publ: Le Groupe FutursMédias
Archives: accessible for preceding seven days

1072   Le Quotidien
Sodida
Rue 14 prolongée
Dakar
Postal address:
BP 25221
Dakar Fann
Tel: +221-825 4920/22 Fax: +221-825 4930
Email: servicecom@lequotidien.sn
(Sales/Subscriptions)
lequotidien@lequotidien.sn (Editor)
Web: http://www.lequotidien.sn/
2003- Dly Ind
Chief exec: Madiambal Diagne
Ed: Mamadou Biaye (Editorial coordinator)
Publ: Groupe Avenir Communication

1073   Le Soleil
Route du Service géographique
Hann
Dakar
Postal address:
BP 92
Dakar
Tel: +221-859 5959 (General/Editorial)

+221- 859 5936 (Marketing/Sales)
Fax: +221-832 0886/859 6050
Email: lesoleil@lesoleil.sn
Web: http://www.lesoleil.sn/
1970- Dly Ind
Chief exec: El Hadji H. Kasse
Ed: Amadou Fall
Publ: Société Sénégalaise de Presse et de
Publications (SSPP),
Archives: fully searchable archive 1998 [?]-

1074   Sud Quotidien
Groupe Sud Communication
Immeuble Fahd Bd Djily Mbaye x rue
Macoudou Ndiaye
Dakar
Postal address:
BP 4130
Dakar
Tel: +221-822 5393/822-4205
Fax: +221-822 5260
Email: Sudquot@metissacana.sn
Web: http://www.sudonline.sn/
1993- Dly Ind
Chief exec: Abdoulaye Ndiaga Sylla [?]
Ed: Vieux Savane
Publ: Groupe Sud Communication
Archives: searchable archive (under
construction)

1075   Wal Fadjri/L'Aurore
Sicap Sacré Coeur # 8542
BP 576
Dakar
Tel: +221-824 2340/824 2343
Fax: +221-824 2346
Email: courrier@walf.sn
Web: http://www.walf.sn/
1993- Dly Ind
Ed: Ousseynou Gueye
Publ: Groupe Walf Fadjri
Archives: Searchable archive 2001-

Seychelles

National press agency:

1076   Seychelles Agence Press (SAP)
Information Division
Ministry of Communications
PO Box 800
Victoria
Tel: +248-225775 Fax: +248-321006

Email: seynat@seychelles.net
Web: http://www.nation.sc/
Chief exec: Denis Rose (Director of
Information)

Newspapers:

1077   The People (in English and Kreole)
PO Box 91 (or POB 1242)
Victoria Mahe
Tel: 248-324622/224455 Fax: +248-225070
Email admin@sppf.sc
http://www.thepeople.sc/index800.html
1976- Wk Gov (Seychelles People's
Progressive Front party)
Ed: Joel Albert

1078   Seychelles Nations (primarily in
English, with contributions in French
and Kreole)
Long Pier Road
Victoria Mahe
Postal address:
PO Box 800
Victoria Mahe
Tel: +248-225775/722680 Fax: +248-321006
Email: info@nationsonline.org
Web: http://www.nation.sc/
2001- Dly Gov
Ed: Denis Rose
Publ: Seychelles Nation
Archives: search site facility but no searchable
archive at this time.

Sierra Leone

National press agency:

1079   Sierra Leone News Agency (SLENA)
Office of the President
The Republic of Sierra Leone
State House
Freetown
Tel: +232-22-232101 Fax: +232-22-230565
Email: info@statehouse-sl.org
http://www.sierraleone.gov.sl/pages/slena
/slena1.htm
Director: Rod MacJohnson

Newspapers:

1080   Awoko
47 Percival Street
Freetown
Tel: +232-22-224927
Email: awoko71@hotmail.com
Web: http://www.awoko.com
1998- 2Wk Ind
Chief exec/Publ: Kelvin Lewis
Ed: Joseph Rahall

1081   Concord Times
9 Bathurst Street
Freetown
Tel: +232-22-229199
Email: concordtimes100@yahoo.com
Web: n/a
1992- Dly Ind
Chief exec: Kingsley Lington
Ed: Sulaiman Momodu
Publ: Concord Times Communications

1082   For di People
1 Short Street
Freetown
Tel: +232-22-228071
Email: fordipeople@hotmail.com
Web: n/a
1983- Dly Ind
Ed/Publ: Paul Kamara
Note: Editor currently (June 2005) imprisoned
and newspaper dormant

1083   The Pool Newspaper
1 Short Street 3rd floor
Freetown
Tel/Fax: +232-22-220102
Email: pool@justice.com
Web:
http://poolnewspaper.tripod.com/homepag
e.html (Web site not currently updated)
1992- 3Wk Ind
Ed: Osman F. Koroma
Man ed: Chernor Ojuku Sesay

1084   Punch
1 Short Street 5th floor
Freetown
Tel: +232-22-228803
Email: punchnewspaper@hotmail.com
Web: n/a
1999- 2Wk Ind
Chief exec/Man ed: David Tam Baryoh

1085   **Sierra News**
        15 Wallace Johnson Street
        Freetown
Tel: +232-22-224965/223127
Email: slena@sierratel.sl
2000- 3Wk Gov
Ed: Abdul Karim Jalloh
Publ: Government of Sierra Leone

1086   **Standard Times**
        2 Ascension Town
        Freetown
Tel: +232-22-229634/241273
Email: standardtimes@hotmail.com
Web: n/a
1995- 3Wk Ind
Chief exec: Philip Neville
Ed: Ibrahim Karim Sei
Publ: Standard Times Publications

1087   **New Vision**
        29 Rawdon Street
        Freetown
Tel: +232-22-229845
Email: visionnewspaper@hotmail.com
Web: n/a
1988- 3Wk Ind
Chief exec: Siaka Massaquoi
Ed: Sorie Fofanah
Publ: Vision Newspapers

Somalia/Somaliland

Newspapers:

1088   **Haatuf News** (primarily in Somali)
        Haatuf Media Network
        At Togdher Street
        Near Ged-deble Hotel
        Hargeisa
Tel: +252-2-253783/828 3783
2003- Dly Ind
Email: haatufnews@hotmail.com
Web: http://www.haatuf.net/
Ed: Yusuf Abdi Gabobe
Publ: Haatuf Media Network
Archives: accessible 2003-

1089   **The Somaliland Times** (in English)
        Haatuf Media Network
        At Togdher Street
        Near Ged-deble Hotel
        Hargeisa

Tel: +252-2-253783/828 3783
Email: feedback@somalilandtimes.net
Web: http://www.somalilandtimes.net/
2002- Wk Ind
Ed:
Publ: Haatuf Media Network
Archives: accessible 2002-July 2003

1090   **Wargeyska Dalka** (primarily in
        Somali, with weekly Arabic version)
        Dalka Newspaper
        SONNA
        Mogadishu
Tel: +252-1-500533/500532
Fax: 252-1-226874/932512
Email: dalka@somalinternet.com or
dalkaonline@hotmail.com,
Web: http://dalka-online.com/
2000[?]- Dly Gov
Ed: n/a

1091   **Wargeyska Jamhuuriya /
        The Republican** (in Somali, and in
        English as a weekly supplement)
        Maalinle ka soo baxa
        Hargeisa
Tel: + 252-2-223326 Fax: + 252-2-134501
Email: webmaster@jamhuuriya.info
Web: http://www.jamhuuriya.info/index.ph
p
1998- Dly Wk (English version) Ind
Ed: Hassan Heiss

South Africa

*Pan-African and South African news
agencies:*

1092   **African Eye News Service**
        PO Box 6896
        Nelspruit 1200
        Mpumalanga
Tel: +27-13-755 4117/8
Email: editor@africanpress.com
Web: n/a
Ed: Justin Arenstein
Note: mainly focuses mainly on
human rights issues in rural areas

1093 African News Dimension
183 Forest Drive Pine Slopes
Office Park Fourways Sandton
Johannesburg
2194 Gauteng
Postal address:
PO Box 782504
Sandton 2146
Email: breakingnews@andnetwork.com
(News/Editorial)
subscriptions@andnetwork.com
(Subscriptions)
Web: http://www.andnetwork.com/app
Tel: +27 11 467 5885
Fax: +27 11 705 1174
Chief exec: Ralston E. Smith

1094 IPS Inter Press Service - Africa
English network:
Media Mill
7 Quince Rd
Milpark 2092
Johannesburg
Postal address:
PO Box 1062
Auckland Park 2006
Tel: +27-11-727 7080
Fax: +27-11-727 7089
Email: (see individual contacts below)
Web:
http://www.ips.org/africa.shtml
Francophone service:
Immeubble Hounsou H. Pélagie Lot 213
Donaten
Cotonou
Benin
Postal address:
05 BP 1150
Cotonou
Benin
Tel/Fax: +229-330940
Regional Director, Africa: Farai Samhungu,
Email: farai@ips.org
Regional Editor (English network): Jacklynne
Hobbs, Email: jhobbs@ips.org
Regional Editor (Francophone service): Ali
Idrissou-Touré,
Email: ipscoo@intnet.bj
Note: part of IPS-Inter Press Service
International Association, with headquarters
in Rome, *see also* → **News sources for Africa**,
entry **855**)

1095 News24
Naspers Centre 14th floor
40 Heerengracht
Cape Town 8000
Postal address:
News24
PO Box 2271
Cape Town 8000
Tel: +27-21-406 2083 Fax: +27-21-406 3459
Email: use email form on Web site
Web: http://www.news24.com/
Publ: Elan Lohmann
Ed: Bryan Porter
Day ed: Jannie Momberg
Night ed: Elmarie Jack

1096 South African Press Association (SAPA)
Cotswold House
Greenacres Office Park
Cnr. Victory & Rustenburg Roads
Victoria Park
Johannesburg
Postal address:
PO Box 7766
Johannesburg 2000
Tel: +27-11-782 1600 Fax: +27+11-782 1587/8
Email: comms@sapa.org.za
Web: http://www.sapa.org.za/
Chief exec: Piet Greyling
Manager: William Davis
Ed: Mark van der Velden

Newspapers:

1097 Die Afrikaner (in Afrikaans)
PO Box/Posbus 1888
Pretoria 0001
Tel: +27-12-342 3410
Email: afrikaner@hnp.org.za
Web: http://www.hnp.org.za/afrikaner/
1976- Dly Ind (Herstige Nasionale Party)
Ed: J. L. Basson, Email:
jakkie@hnp.org.za
Publ: Herstige Nasionale Party

1098 Die Beeld (in Afrikaans)
MediaPark
Kingsway 69
Aucklandpark
Johannesburg 2000
Gauteng
Tel: +27-11-713 9000
Fax: +27-11-713 9961/9956
Email: briewe@beeld.com

Web:
http://www.news24.com/Beeld/Home/
1974- Dly Ind
Ed: Peet Kruger
Publ: Naspers Group
Archives: fully searchable archives 1997-

1099   Die Burger (in Afrikaans and English
versions)
Burger Western Cape:
40 Heerengracht
Cape Town 8001
Postal address:
PO Box 692
Cape Town 8000
Tel: +27-21-406 2121 (General enquiries)
Fax: +27 21-4062 911/3 (General enquiries)
Tel: +27-21-406 2222 (Editorial, Burger
Western Cape)
Email: webred@dieburger.co.za (Burger
Western Cape);
webred@burger.naspers.co.zam or
kontak@dieburger.com (General enquiries)
diens@dieburger.com (Subscriptions)
Burger Eastern Cape:
Ton Vosloo Media Centre
Ivor Benn Close
Port Elizabeth 6000
Postal address:
PO Box 525
Port Elizabeth 6000
Tel: +27-41-503 6111 (Editorial, Burger
Eastern Cape)
Email: oos@dieburger.com (Burger Eastern
Cape)
Web:
http://www.media24.co.za/index.html or
http://www.news24.com/Die_Burger/Hom
e/ (Afrikaans version)
http://www.media24.co.za/eng/newspaper
s/dieburger.html (English version)
1915- (as *Die Burger Eastern Cape* 1993-) Dly
Ind
Chief exec: Johann Botha (Publisher)
Ed: Arrie Rossouw (Burger Western Cape)
NewsEds:
Burger Western Cape:
Barnie Louw, Email: dbnred@dieburger.com
Burger Eastern Cape:
Nadia Sadovsky,
Email: nsadovsk@dieburger.com
Publ: Naspers Group
Archives: Archives: fully searchable archives
1997-

1100   Business Day
Johncom House
4 Biermann Avenue
Rosebank
2196 Johannesburg
Postal address:
PO Box 1745
Saxonworld 2132
Tel: +27-860-262626/860-522613
(Subscriptions)
Tel: +27-11-280 5503 Fax: +27-11-280 5505
(Editorial management)
Tel: +27-11-280 5601/5606/5609 Fax: +27-11-
280 5600 (Newsdesk)
Email: busday@bdfm.co.za
Web: http://www.bday.co.za/
1985- Dly Ind
Ed: Peter Bruce,
Email: brucep@bdfm.co.za
Man ed: Pearl Sebola,
Email: sebolaop@bdfm.co.za
Publ: Johnnic Communications
Archives: fully searchable archives 2002-

1101   Business Report
47 Sauer Street
Johannesburg
Postal address:
PO Box 1014
Johannesburg 2000
Tel: +27-11-633 2996 Fax: +27-11-838 2693
Email: niccc1@theinc.co.za
(Sales/Subscriptions)
editor@businessreport.co.za (Editorial)
http://www.businessreport.co.za/
1995- Wk Ind
Ed: Alide Dasnois, Email: adas@star.co.za
Man ed: Max Gebhardt,
Email: mge@star.co.za
Publ: Independent News and Media plc

1102   Cape Argus
PO Box 56
Cape Town 8000
Tel: +27-21-488 4911 (Main switchboard)
Tel: +27-21-488 4500 (Editor)
Fax: +27-21-488 4793 (Editor)
Tel: +27-21-488 4536/46 (News Editor) Fax:
+27-21-488 4156 (News Editor)
Email: feedback@iol.co.za
Web: http://www.capeargus.co.za
1857- Dly (also Sun as *Weekend Argus*) Ind
Ed: Ivan Fynn,

Email: lyntinaa@ctn.independent.co.za News
ed: Joseph Aranes, Email:
argusnews@ctn.independent.co.za
Publ: Independent News and Media plc
Archives: fully searchable archive 10
November, 2002-

1103   Cape Times
Newspaper House
St Georges Mall
Cape Town 8001
Tel: +27-21 488 4911
(General/Switchboard)
+27-21-488 4718 (Newsdesk)
Fax +27-21-488 793
Email: michaelv@ctn.independent.co.za
(Sales/Marketing)
Web: http://www.capetimes.co.za/
1876- Dly Ind
Ed: Chris Whitefield,
Email: chriswh@ctn.independent.co.za
Publ: Independent News and Media plc
Archives: fully searchable archive 2002-

1104   The Citizen
9 Wright Street Industria West
Johannesburg 2093
Postal address:
PO Box 43069
Industria
Johannesburg 2042
Tel: +27-11-248 6000 (General enquiries)
Tel: +27-11-248 6037 (News desk)
Fax: +27-11-248 6213
Email: citizen@citizen.co.za
Web: http://www.citizen.co.za/
1976- Dly Ind
Ed: (Acting) Martin Williams,
Email: letters@citizen.co.za
Publ: Caxton and CTP Printers and
Publishers
Archives: search site facility but no searchable
archives at this time.

1105   City Press
Media Park
69 Kingsway
Auckland Park 2006
Postal address:
PO Box 3413
Johannesburg 2000
Tel: +27+11-713 9001 (General enquiries)
+27-11-713 9592 (Editor)
+27-11-713 9591 (Editorial/News Editor)
Fax: +27-11-713 9985 (General enquiries)

Fax +27-11-713 9986 (Editor)
Email: news@citypress.co.za
Web:
http://www.news24.com/City_Press/Home
/ or
http://www.media24.co.za/eng/newspaper
s/citypress.html
1982- (as *Golden City Press*) Wk (Sun) Ind
Ed: Mathatha Tsedu,
Email: mtsedu@citypress.co.za
Man ed: Andre le Roux,
Email: aleroux@citypress.co.za
News ed: Chris Hlongwa,
Email: chlongwa@citypress.co.za
Publ: Naspers Group

1106   Daily Dispatch
35 Caxton Street
East London 5201
Postal address:
PO Box 131
East London 5200
Tel: +27-43-702 2000
Fax: +27 43 743 5155 (Editorial)
+27-43-743 5159 (Sales/Subscriptions)
Email: use online email forms
Web: http://www.dispatch.co.za/
1872- (as *East London Despatch)* Dly Ind
Chief exec: Thembela Sofisa (Publisher)
Ed: Phylicia Oppelt
Publ: Johnnic Communications
Archives: searchable archive 2001[?]-

1107   The Daily News
18 Osborne Street
Greyville
Durban 4001
Postal address:
PO Box 47549
Greyville 4023
Tel: +27-31-308 2911 (General enquiries)
+27-31-308 2107 (Editor)
Fax: +27-31-308 2111
Email: dnnews@nn.independent.co.za
Web: http://www.dailynews.co.za/
1878- (as *The Natal Mercantile Advertiser)* Dly
(also Sun as *Sunday Tribune)* Ind
Ed: Dennis Pather,
Email: pather@nn.independent.co.za
Man ed: Deon Delport,
Email: delport@nn.independent.co.za
Publ: Independent News and Media Ltd
Archives: fully searchable archives January
2002-

1108   Daily Sun
69 Kingsway
MediaPark
Auckland Park
Postal address:
PO Box 121
Auckland Park 2006
Tel +27-11-877 6000 (Main Switchboard)
Tel +27-11-877 6041 (News Editor)
Fax +27-11 877 6020 (New Editor)
Email: akoanaite@dailysun.co.za
(Sales/Distribution)
news@dailysun.co.za (News Editor)
Web: or
http://www.media24.co.za/eng/newspaper
s/dailysun.html
2002- (Sunday Sun 2001-) Dly (also Sun as
Sunday Sun, and in an Afrikaans version as
Son) Ind
News ed: Themba Khumalo,
Email: news@dailysun.co.za
Publ: Naspers Group

1109   Diamond Fields Advertiser
122 St Georges Mall
Newspaper House
Cape Town 8000
Postal address:
PO Box 4116
Cape Town 8001
Tel: +27-21-481 6200 (General enquiries)
Fax: +27-21-424 1088 (General enquiries)
+27-53-832 6261 (Editor)
Email: use online email form for general
enquiries
Web: http://www.iol.co.za/index
1878- Dly Ind
Chief exec: Howard Plaatjes (Managing
Director)
Ed: Johan du Plessis, Email: johanp@dfa.co.za
News ed: Patsy Beangstrom,
Email: pbe@dfa.co.za
Publ: Independent News & Media plc
Archives: search site facilitiy, but no
searchable archives at this time.

1110   East Cape News
East Cape News (Pty) Ltd,
Box 897
Grahamstown 6140
Tel: +27-46-636 1013
Email: editor@ecn.co.za
Web: http://www.ecn.co.za/
1997- Dly Ind
Ed: Mike Loewe

Publ: East Cape News (Pty) Ltd

1111   Financial Mail
Johnnic Publishing House
4th floor
Biermann Avenue
Rosebank
Postal address:
PO Box 1744
Saxonwold 2132
Johannesburg
Tel: +27-11-280-5808 Fax: +27-11-280-5800
Email: fmmail@fm.co.za
Web: http://free.financialmail.co.za/ (free
edition; full edition requires subscription)
1959- Wk Ind
Ed: Caroline Southey
Archives: fully searchable archives, subject to
subscription; free access to last four issues
Publ: BDFM Publishers (Pty) Ltd & Johnnic
Communications

1112   The Herald
Newspaper House
19 Baakens Street
Port Elizabeth
Postal address:
Private Bag X 6071
Port Elizabeth 6000
Tel: +27-41-504 7911 Fax: +27-41-585 4966
Email: theherald@johnnicec.co.za
Web: http://www.theherald.co.za/
1845- (and *Eastern Province Herald*) Dly Ind
Ed: Ric Wilson,
Email: rwilson@johnnicec.co.za
News ed: Pat Sydie,
Email: epherald@tmecl.co.za
Publ: Johnnic Communications

1113   The Independent
122 St Georges Mall
Newspaper House
Cape Town 8000
Postal address:
PO Box 4116
Cape Town 8001
Tel: +27-21-481 6200 Fax: +27-21-424 1088
Email: niccc1@theinc.co.za (Customer
services only; use email form on Web site for
communications to Editor or other personnel)
Web: http://www.iol.co.za/index.phpf
1996- Dly (also Sun as *Sunday Independent*)
Ind
Chief exec: Howard Plaatjes (Managing
Director)

Ed: Mahomed Saleh Abba Omar (Content
Manager)
Publ: Independent News and Media plc
Archives: search site facility, but no
browsable archives at this time.

1114   Mail & Guardian
Media Mill
7 Quince Road
Milpark
Johannesburg
Postal address:
PO Box 91667
Auckland Park
Johannesburg 2006
Tel: +27-11-727 7000 Fax: +27-11-727 7111
Email: letters@mg.co.za (General/Letters)
mgadvert@mg.co.za mgadvert@mg.co.za
(Advertising)
books@mg.co.za books@mg.co.za (Books
related)
amandac@mg.co.za (Subscriptions)
Web: http://www.mg.co.za/
1985- (originally published as *The Weekly
Mail*) Wk Ind
Eds: Ferial Haffajee,
Email: editor@mg.co.za
Matthew Buckland (Mail & Guardian Online
Editor),
Email: editoronline@mg.co.za
Publ: M&G Media (owned by Newtrust
Company Botswana Ltd), online ed: M&G
Media and M-Web
Archives: fully searchable archive 1994-

1115   The Mercury
Independent Newspapers Holdings
Ltd
18 Osborne Street
Greyville
Durban
Postal address:
PO Box 950
Durban 4000
Tel: +27-31-308 2500 (General enquiries)
+27-31-308 2306 (Editor)
Fax: +27-31-308 2355
Web: http://www.themercury.co.za/
1852- Dly Ind
Ed: David Canning,
Email: canning@nn.independent.co.za
Man ed: Thami Ngidi,
Email: thami@nn.independent.co.za
Publ: Independent News and Media plc

Archives: fully searchable archives January
2002-

1116   The Post
Independent Newspapers
19 Osborne Street
Greyville
Durban
Postal address:
PO Box 47549
Greyville 4023
Tel: +27-31-308 2424 (General enquiries)
+27-31-308 4000 (Editor)
+27-11-308 2411 (News Editor)
Fax: +27-31-308 2879
http://www.thepost.co.za/
1958- Wk (Wed) (also Wk as *Postweekend* on
Fridays) Ind
Ed: Brijlall Ramguthee,
Email: brijlall@nn.independent.co.za
News ed: Khalil Aniff,
Email: khalil@nn.independent.co.za
Publ: Independent News and Media plc

1117   The Pretoria News
216 Vermeulen Street
Pretoria
Postal address:
PO Box 439
Pretoria 0001
Tel: +27-12-300 2000 Fax: +27-12-328 7166
Email: ptanews@pretorianws.co.za
Web:
http://www.pretorianews.co.za/
Ed: Philani Mgwaba
1898- Dly (also Wk as *Pretoria News Weekend*)
Ind
Publ: The Pretoria News & Independent
News and Media Ltd
Archives: fully searchable archives June 2003-

1118   Rapport (in Afrikaans)
Media Park
69 Kingsway
Auckland Park
Postal address:
PO Box 8422
Johannesburg 2006
Tel: +27-11-713 9002 (General enquiries)
+27-11-713 9639 (Editorial/News Editor)
Fax: +27-11-713 9977
Email: rapport@rapport.co.za
Web:
http://www.news24.com/Rapport/Home/

http://www.media24.co.za/eng/newspaper
s/rapport.html
Ed: Tim du Plessis,
Email rapport@rapport.co.za
News ed: Lukas Meyer,
Email: lmeyer1@rapport.co.za
1970- Wk (Sun) Ind
Publ: Naspers Group
Archives: fully searchable archive 1997-

1119 The Sowetan
61 Commando Road
Industria West
Johannesburg
Postal address:
PO Box 6663
Johannesburg 2000
Tel: +27-11-471-4000 (Main switchboard)
+27-11-471 4035 (Editorial)
Fax: +27-11-474 2074
Email: taryn@sowetan.co.za
(Sales/Subscriptions)
editor@sowetan.co.za (Editorial)
Web: http://www.sowetan.co.za/
1981- Dly (also Wk as *Sunday World*) Ind
Chief exec: Andrew Gill
Ed: Thabo Leshilo,
Email: leshilot@sowetan.co.za
Man ed: Monk Nkomo,
Email: nkomom@sowetan.co.za
Publ: Johnnic Communications
Note: currently (August 2005) being
restructered by new owners Johnnic
Communications, *see*
http://www.johncom.co.za/

1120 The Star
48 Sauer Street
Johannesburg 2001
Postal address:
PO Box 1014
Johannesburg 2000
Tel: +27-11-633 2635
Fax: +27-11-838 3336 (Sales/Marketing)
Email: hca@star.co.za (Sales/Marketing)
Tel: +27-11-633-2139
Fax: +27 11 836-5593 (Editorial)
Web: http://www.thestar.co.za/
1887- Dly (Sat as *Saturday Star*) Ind
Chief exec: Peter Sullivan (Group Editor-in-Chief)
Ed: Moegsien Williams,
Email: editorpa@star.co.za
News ed: Mokone Moleti,
Email: starnews@star.co.za

Publ: The Star & Independent News and
Media Ltd
Archives: fully searchable archive January
2002-

1121 Sunday Times
Johnnic Publishing House
4 Biermann Avenue
Rosebank 2196
Tel: +27-11-280-3000 Fax: +27-11-280-5150/1
Email: suntimes@sundaytimes.co.za
(Editorial) leonm@johncom.co.za (Library
archive service)
Web: http://www.sundaytimes.co.za
1906- Wk (Sun) Ind
Chief exec: Connie Molusi
Ed: Mondli Makhanya
Publ: Johnnic Communications
Archives: fully searchable archive (requires
subscription)

1122 This Day (currently suspended, as at
October 2005)
3 Gwen Lane
Sandown
Sandton
Johannesburg 2196
Tel: +27-11-217 2000/2194
Fax: +27-11- 783 6737/ 8261
Email: thisday@thisdaysa.co.za
http://www.thisday.co.za (Web Site down as
at 03/10/05)
2003- (South African edition) Dly Ind
Chief exec: Nduka Obaigbena (Chairman)
Ed: Justice Malala
News ed: Vuyo Bavuma, Email
newsdesk@thisdaysa.co.za
Publ: Leaders & Company Ltd
Note: this is South African version of *This Day*
newspaper published in Nigeria, entry ➜
1063. Paper is currently (October 2005)
dormant; it suspended publication in October
2004, but plans relaunch sometime during the
course of 2006.

1123 Volksblad (in Afrikaans)
70 Nelson Mandela Drive
Bloemfontein 9300
Postal address:
PO Box 267
Bloemfontein 9300
Tel: +27-51-404 7600
(General/Sales)
+27 –51-404-7876 (Editor)

+27-51-404 7878 (News Editor)
Fax +27-51- 430 6949
Email: nuus@volksblad.com (General
enquiries) hvanniek@volksblad.com
(Subscriptions)
Web:
http://www.news24.com/Die_Volksblad/H
ome/ or
http://www.media24.co.za/eng/newspaper
s/volksblad.html
Ed: Jonathan Crowther,
Email: jcrowthe@volksblad.com
News ed: Mike van Rooyen, Email
mvanrooy@volksblad.com
Publ: Naspers Group
Archives: fully searchable archive January
1997-

1124 Die Wêreld (primarily in Afrikaans)
Posbus 76346
Lynnwoodrif 0040
Tel: +2-12-803 1539 Fax: +27-12-803 1538
Email: nuus@diewereld.co.za (News)
briewe@diewereld.co.za (Letters)
Web:
http://www.diewereld.co.za/
2005- Wk (Sun) Ind
Ed: Maryna Blomerus
Archives: searchable archives will become
available shortly

1125 The Witness
45 Willowton Road
Willowton
Pietermaritzburg 3201
Postal address:
PO Box 362
Pietermaritzburg 3200
Tel: +27-33-355 1111 (General enquiries)
Tel +27-33-355 1120 (Editor)
Tel +27-33-355 1127 (News Editor)
Fax: +27-33-551 1122
Email: newsed@witness.co.za (General
enquiries) echo@witness.co.za (Editorial,
communications to Editor)
Web: http://www.witness.co.za/identify.asp
(free access, but requires registration) or
http://www.media24.co.za/eng/newspaper
s/natalwitness.html
1846- (as *Natal Witness*) Dly Ind
Ed: John Conyngham,
Email: johnc@witness.co.za
News ed: Reggie Khumalo,
Email: newsed@witness.co.za

Publ: The Natal Witness (Pty) Ltd/ Naspers
Group
Archives: fully searchable archive January
1999-

Sudan

National press agency:

1126 Sudan News Agency (SUNA)
Foreign News Department
PO Box 1506
Khartoum
Tel: n/a
Fax: +24-11-780146
Email: n/a
http://www.sunanews.net/ (Arabic version)
http://www.suna-sd.net/Index_EN.htm
(English version, also available in a French
version)
Dir Gen: Aamar Ayoub Ahmad

Newspapers:

1127 Al Rayaam (in Arabic)
PO Box 363
Khartoum
Tel: +249-11-772176 Fax: +249-11-783279
Email: info@rayaam.net
Web: http://www.rayaam.net/
1945- Wk Ind
Chief exec/Man ed: Mahjoub Mohamed
Salah
Publ: AL Rayaam Newspapers

1128 Khartoum Monitor (currently
suspended, as at June 2005)
Street 61
New Extension
Khartoum
Tel: n/a
Email: n/a
Web:
http://www.khartoum-monitor.com/ (Web
site down 25/11/05)
2000- Dly Ind
Chief exec: Alfrid Tabban
Man ed: Nhial Bol
Ed: Albino Okely
Note: newspaper currently (June 2005)
suspended by the Sudanese government

1129   Sudan Vision
        PO Box 1506 [?]
        Khartoum
Tel: n/a
Email: info@sudanvisiondaily.com
Web: http://www.sudanvisiondaily.com/
2003- Dly (also Sun as *Sunday Vision)* Gov
Ed: n/a
Archives: fully searchable archives December
2003-
Note: a newspaper under this name was
originally launched by an independent
organization, the Sudan Development Trust,
but is now published in exile in Kenya, under
a new name, *Sudan Mirror*
http://www.sudanmirror.com/

Swaziland

National press agency:

1130   SmartNEWS
        Swaziland Broadcasting and
        Information Services
        Corner Gwamile & Msakato Street
        PO Box 338
        Mbabane H100
Tel: +268-404 2761/5
Fax: +268-404 2774
Email: n/a
Web:
http://www.gov.sz/home.asp?pid=3434
Director: Mandla Stan D. Motsa
News ed: Mr Welile Dlamini

Newspapers:

1131   Guardian of Swaziland
        PO Box 4747
        Mbabane
Tel: +268-404 8385
Email: info@theguardian.co.sz
Web: http://www.theguardian.co.sz/
(site down 25/11/05)
2001[?]- Wk Ind
Ed: n/a
Publ: The Guardian Media Group

1132   Swazi Observer
        Swazi Observer (Pty) Ltd
        3 West Street
        Mbabane
Tel: +268-404 9600 Fax: +268-404 5503
Email: info@observer.org.sz

Web: http://www.observer.org.sz/
1981- Dly (also Wk as *Weekend Observer*) Gov
Chief exec: (Mrs) S. M. Magagula
Eds: Wilton Mamba, Musa Ndlangamandla
Publ: Tibiyo Taka Ngwane/Swazi Observer
Newspaper Group

1133   The Times of Swaziland
        PO Box 628
        Mbabane
Tel: +268-404 1550
Email: info@times.co.sz
Web: http://www.times.co.sz/001.html
1897- Dly (also Wk/Sat as *Swazi News*, and
Sun as *Sunday Times*) Gov
Ed: Martin Dlamini, Email:
editor@times.co.sz
News ed: Nimrod Mabuza, Email:
news@times.co.sz
Publ: African Echo (Pty) Ltd

Tanzania

Press agencies:

1134   Press Services Tanzania Ltd (PST)
        PO Box 31042
        Dar es Salaam
        Tanzania
Tel: +255-22-211 9195/211 6077
Fax: +255-22-211 9195
Email: n/a
Web: n/a
Chief exec: n/a
Note: information not verified; this is a
privately-owned news agency service; the
former government agency, the Tanzania
News Agency (Shihata), was dissolved in
2002.

1135   TOMRIC News Agency
        PO Box 12994
        Dar es Salaam
Tel: +255-51-171008
Email: spaschal@linkmaster.com
Web: n/a
Ed: Sebastian Paschal
Note: unverified, currently dormant?

Newspapers:

1136   The African
PO Box 4793
Dar es Salaam
Tel: +255-22-391522 Fax: +255-22-246 1459
Email: mtanzania95@hotmail.com
Web:
http://www.tanserve.com/news/theafrican.
html (single page only)
1998- Dly Ind
Ed: n/a

1137   Arusha Times
AICC Building
Ngorongoro Block
First Floor Room 129
Arusha
Postal address:
PO Box 212
Arusha
Tel: +255-27-250 6438
Email: arushatimes@habari.co.tz
Web: http://www.arushatimes.co.tz/
1995- Wk Ind
Ed: William Lobolu,
Email: editor@arushatimes.co.tz
Publ: FM Arusha Ltd
Archives: fully searchable archive 2002-

1138   Business Times
Business Times Ltd
Adamjee Building
Bibi Titi Road
Dar es Salaam]
Postal address:
PO Box 71439
Dar es Salaam
Tel: +255-22-118379 Fax: +255-22-119430
Email: btimez@bcstimes.com
Web: http://www.bcstimes.com/btimes/ind
ex.shtml
2003- Wk Ind
Ed: Sammy Makilla
Publ: Business Times Ltd
Archives: search site facility, but no
browsable archive at this time.

1139   The Daily News
PO Box 9033
Dar es Salaam
Tel: +255-22-110595/116072
Fax: +255-22-112881
Web: http://www.dailynews.co.tz
(Site down as at 25/11/05)

Email: dailynews@raha.com
1930 - Dly (also Sun as *Sunday News*) Gov
Ed: n/a
News ed: Evarist Mwitumba

1140   Daily Times
Business Times Ltd
Adamjee Building
Bibi Titi Road
Dar es Salaam
Postal address:
PO Box 71439
Dar es Salaam
Tel: +255-22-213 0033 (General enquiries)
+255-748-732010 (Chief Editor)
+255-744-521458 (News Editor)
Email: webmaster@bcstimes.com
Web:
http://www.bcstimes.com/dailytimes/
Ed: Sammy Makilla
2003- Dly Ind
Ed: Bernard Mapalala
News ed: Egbert Mtui
Publ: Business Times Ltd
Archives: fully searchable archive 2001-

1141   The Express
Media Express Ltd
PO Box 20588
Dar es Salaam
Tel: +255-22-32451/33013 Fax: +255-22-46166
1997- Wk Ind
Email: editor@theexpress.com
Web: http://www.theexpress.com/
Man ed: Felix Kaiza [?]
Ed: John Ongeri
Publ: Media Holdings Ltd
Archives: accessible 2000[?]-

1142   Financial Times
The Guardian Ltd
PO Box 31042
Dar es Salaam
Tel: +255-22-270 0735/8
Fax: +255 22-277 3583/270 0146
Email: guardian@ipp.co.tz
Web:
http://www.ippmedia.com/ipp/newspaper
s/index.html
Ed: n/a
Publ: IPP Media Ltd

1143   The Guardian
The Guardian Ltd
PO Box 31042
Dar es Salaam
Tel: +255-22-270 0735/8
Fax: +255 22-277 3583/270 0146
Email: guardian@ipp.co.tz
Web:
http://www.ippmedia.com/ipp/newspaper
s/index.html
1993- Dly Ind
Chief exec: Vumi Urassa
Ed: n/a
News ed: Daodatus Mfugale
Publ: IPP Media Ltd

Togo

National press agency:

1144   Agence Togolaise de Presse (ATOP)
Ministère de la Communication et de
la Formation Civique
35 rue Des Medic
Lomé
Postal address:
BP 12941
Lomé
Tel: +228-221 2507 Fax: +228-221 4339
Email: n/a
Web: n/a
Chief exec: Sedeem M. Abassa

Newspapers:

1145   Le Combat du Peuple
BP 4682
Lomé
Tel: +228-904 5383/218845
Fax@ +228-222761
Email: combat@webmails.com
1994- Wk Ind
Chief exec/Publ: Lucien S. Messan
Ed: Denis Messan

1146   Crocodile
299 rue Kuévidjin no. 27 Bè
Lomé
Postal address:
BP 60087
Lomé
Tel: +228-221 3821 Fax: +228-222 2761
Email: crocodile.crocodile@caramail.com
Web: n/a

1993- 2Wk Ind
Chief exec/Man ed: Francis Pedro Amuzun
Ed: Franck Assah

1147   Sud Tribune
Face Stade de Kégué, non loin de la
boulangerie Boul'icon
Lomé
Tel: +228-261 1349/50
Email: info@sudtribune.info
Web: http://sudtribune.info/
2004- Wk Ind
Ed: n/a
Archives: searchable archives April-July 2004

1148   Le Temps
390 rue Assahoun
Tokoin Hôpital
Lomé
Postal address:
BP 81190
Lomé
Tel: +228-083690 Fax: +228-261370
Email: postmaster@letemps.net
Web: http://letemps.togo-ip.com/
(site down 25/11/05)
2004[?}- Dly Ind
Ed: n/a

1149   Togo-Presse
BP 891
Lomé
Tel: +228-216108 Fax: +228-223766
Email: n/a
1962- Dly Gov
Ed: n/a

Tunisia

National press agency:

1150   Tunis Afrique Presse (TAP)
7 Ave. Ben Sliman
2092 El Manar II
1002 Tunis
Tel: +216-71-889000 Fax: +216-71-76 61 50
Email: dg.tap@email.ati.tn
Web: n/a
Dir Gen: Mohamed Benazeddine

Newspapers:

Note: for additional Tunisian newspapers online *see* http://www.tunisie.com/nouvelles/

1151 Assabah (in Arabic)
Avenue 7 novembre 1987
1004 El Menzah
Postal address:
BP 441
1004 El Menzah
Tel: +216-71-717222 Fax: +216-71-723361
Email: info@assabah.com.tn
Web: http://www.tunisie.com/Assabah/
1997[?]- Dly (also Wk as *Assabah hébdo*) Ind
Ed: n/a
Publ: Dar Assabah-Société Tunisienne de
Presse, d'Impression, d'Edition, de Diffusion
et de Publicité

1152 La Presse
6 rue Ali Bach Hamba
1000 Tunis
Tel: +216-71-341066 Fax: +216-71-349720
Email: contact@lapresse.tn (General
enquiries) arfaoui.cherif@lapresse.tn
(Editorial)
Web: http://www.lapresse.tn
1936- Dly Ind
Chief exec: Zohra Ben Romdhane
Ed: Chérif Arfaqui (Editor of online edition)
Publ: Société Nouvelle d'Impression de
Presse et d'Edition
Archives: searchable archives January 2005-

1153 Le Quotidien
25 Ave. Jean Jaurès
Tunis 1000
Tel: +216-71-331000 Fax: +216-71-253024
Email: directiongenerale@lequotidien-tn.com
(General enquiries/Subscriptions)
redac-en-chef@lequotidien-tn.com (Editor)
Web: http://www.lequotidien-tn.com/
2002- Dly Ind
Ed: Dar Anwar
Publ: Dar Al Anwar
Archives: search site facility, but no
searchable archive at this time.

1154 Réalités
85 rue de Palestine
1002 Tunis Belvédère
Tel: +216-71-795140/788 313
Fax: +216-71-787160
Email : sof@realites.com.tn
Web:
http://www.realites.com.tn/index1.php
1998- Wk Ind
Chief exec/Man ed: Taïeb Zahar,
Email: Taïeb.Zahar@realites.com.tn
Ed: Zyed Krichen, Email:
redaction@realites.com.tn
Archives: fully searchable archive 2001-

1155 Le Renouveau
8 Rue de Rome
1000 Tunis
Tel: +216-1-352498/352168
Fax: +216-71-351927
Email: n/a
Web:
http://www.tunisieinfo.com/LeRenouveau/
(pdf)
1988- Dly Ind
Chief exec/Man ed: Nejib Ouerghi
Publ: Dar El Amal
Archives: one issue in arrear accessible in pdf
format

1156 Le Temps
Dar Assabah
Avenue 7 novembre 1987
1004 El Menzah
Postal address:
BP 441
1004 El Menzah
Tel: +216-71-717222 Fax: +216-71-723361
(General enquiries)
+216-71-719927 (Editorial)
Email: letemps@gnet.tn (General enquiries)
redaction@letemps.com.tn (Editorial)
Web: http://www.letemps.com.tn/
Chief exec/Man ed: Raouf Cheikhrouhou
Publ: Dar Assabah- Société Tunisienne de
Presse, d'Impression, d'Edition, de Diffusion
et de Publicité
Archives: under construction

1157 Tunis-Hebdo
1 Passage El Houdaibyah
1000 Tunis
Tel.: +216-71-344100
Fax: +216-71-355079

Email: tunishebdo@tunishebdo.com.tn
Web: http://www.tunishebdo.com.tn
Man ed: Mohamed Ben Youssef [?]
1988- Wk Ind
Archives: search site facility, but no
browsable archive at this time

Uganda

National press agency:

1158 **Uganda News Agency (UNA)**
Department of Information
Office of the President
PO Box 7041
Kampala
Tel: +256-41-254410
Fax: +256-41-256888/342259
Email: n/a
Web: n/a
Chief exec: J.P. Okullu-Mura (Director of
Information)

Newspapers:

1159 **The Monitor**
Monitor Publications Ltd
Plot 29-35, 8th Street
Industrial Area
Kampala
Postal address:
PO Box 12141
Kampala
Tel: +256-41-232367 Fax: +256-41-232369
Email: info@monitor.co.ug (General
enquiries) publications@monitor.co.ug
(Sales/Subscriptions)
editorial@monitor.co.ug (Editorial)
Web: http://www.monitor.co.ug/
1992- Dly Ind
Ed: Charles Onyango-Obbo
Publ: Monitor Publications/Nation Media
Group

1160 **New Vision**
Plot 14 Parliament Avenue
Jubilee Insurance Centre
1st Floor, Upper Podium
Kampala
Postal address:
PO Box 9815
Kampala
Tel: +256-41-344191/232058/232059/
Fax: +256-41-232050

Email: nvision@newvision.co.ug (General
enquiries) news@newvision.co.ug
(Editorial/News)
Web: http://www.newvision.co.ug/
1986- Dly (also Sun as *Sunday Vision*) Gov
Eds: William Pike (Managing Director &
Editor-in-chief),
Email: wpike@newvision.co.ug
News ed: John Kakande,
Email: jkakande@newvision.co.ug
Publ: New Vision Printing and Publishing
Corporation
Archives: fully searchable archive, access free,
but requires registration.

1161 **Weekly Observer**
The Observer Media Ltd
PO Box 1040
Kampala
Tel: +256-41-230433/230434
Fax: +256-41-230440
Email: editor@ugandaobserver.com
or letters@ugandaobserver.com
Web:
http://www.ugandaobserver.com/today/
2004- Wk Ind
Ed: James Tumusiime,
Email: jtumusiime@ugandaobserver.com
Publ: The Observer Media Ltd
Archives: select articles accessible 2004-

Western Sahara

National press agency: (located in Algeria)

1162 **Saharan Press Service/Agence de
Presse de la République Arabe
Sahraouie Démocratique (SPS)**
Chahid-el-Hafed
BP 12
DZ 37000 Tindouf
Algeria
Tel/Fax: +213-49 92 12 81
Email: sps@spsrasd.info
Web: http://www.spsrasd.info/index.html
Chief exec: n/a
Note: site of the Front Polisario; news in
English, French, Arabic and Spanish

Newspapers:

1163 Essahra El Hora/Sahrawi
(in Arabic)
Laayoune (El-Aaiun)
Tel: +213-49 92 23 96
Email: essahraelhora_tahrir@yahoo.fr
Web: http://www.essahraelhora.com/
1999-[?] Dly[?] Ind
Chief exec: n/a

Zambia

National press agency:

1164 Zambia News Agency (ZANA)
Mass Media Complex 2nd Floor
Alick Nkhata Road
Lusaka
Postal address:
PO Box 30007
Lusaka
Tel: +260-1-251240 (Newsroom)
+260-1-252338 (Ed-in-chief)
Fax: +260-1-251631
Email: zana@zamnet.zm
Web: http://www.zana.gov.zm/
Chief exec: Villie Lombanya (Editor-in chief)
Principal ed: Lewis Mwanangombe

Newspapers:

1165 The Post
36 Bwinjimfumu Road
Rhodes Park
Lusaka
Postal address:
Private Bag E352
Lusaka
Tel: +260-1-231092/224250 Fax: +260-1-229271
Email: post@zamnet.zm
Web: http://www.post.co.zm/
1991- Dly Ind
Ed: Fred M'membe
Publ: Post Newspaper Ltd

1166 The Mining Mirror
2567 Paragon Center President
Avenue
City Center
Kitwe
Copperbelt
Tel: +260-1-244164/224772

Fax: +260-1-1-222034
Email: miningm@zamnet.zm
Web: http://www.miningmirror.com
(site down 25/11/05)
1991[?]- Bi-Wk Ind
Ed: (Mrs) Pat Mwase [?]

1167 The Monitor
PO Box 31145
Lusaka
Tel: +260-1-236736 Fax: +260-1-231193
Email: monitor@zamnet.zm
Web: http://www.monitor.co.zm/
2000[?]- Wk Ind
Ed: Arthur Simuchoba [?]

1168 National Mirror
Bishops Road
Kabulonga
Lusaka
Postal address:
PO Box 320199
Lusaka
Tel: +260-1-263666/261193
Fax: +260-1-261193
Email: nmirror@zamnet.zm or
multimediazambia@zamnet.zm
Web: http://www.nationalmirror.com.zm/
or
http://www.nationalmirror.com.zm/nationa
l%20mirror.html
1973- Wk Ind
Chief exec: Jumbe Ngoma (Executive Director,
Multimedia Zambia Ltd)
Ed: Gideon Thole
Publ: Multimedia Zambia Ltd

1169 Synergy
Merlin Morpheus Creative Services
Ltd
Cnr Independence Avenue and
Dedan Kimathi Street
Tazara House 5th floor
Lusaka
Postal address:
PO Box 31738
Lusaka
Tel: +260-1-232738 Fax: +260-1-226657
Email: merlin@zamnet.zm
Web: http://www.synergy-africa.com/
(site not available 25/11/05)
2000- Wk Ind
Ed: Chilomo Mwondela [?]

Zimbabwe

National press agency:

1170   **New Ziana**
(formerly Zimbabwe Inter-Africa
News Agency/ZIANA)
Mass Media House
19 Selous Avenue
Harare
Postal address:
PO Box CY511
Causeway
Harare
Tel: +263-4-251750/4 Fax: +263-4-727146
Email: n/a
Web: n/a
Chief exec: Munacho Mutezo (Chairman of
the Board)
Man ed: Munyaradzi Matanyaire
Note: The New Ziana project was launched in
2001 to replace the disbanded Zimbabwe
Inter-Africa News Agency and to encompass
the Community Newspapers Group (CNG).
However we have been unable to verify
address and other information.

Newspapers:

1171   **The Chronicle**
Zimbabwe Newspapers Ltd
PO Box 585
Bulawayo
Tel: +263-9-650471 Fax: +263-9-75522
Email: webmaster@chronicle.co.zw
Web: http://www.zimbabwechronicle.com/
1894- Dly Gov
Ed: Stephen Ndlovu
Publ: Zimbabwe Newspapers (1980) Ltd

1172   **The Daily News** (currently banned)
Associated Newspapers of Zimbabwe
(Pvt) Ltd
18 Sam Nujoma Street corner Speke
Avenue
Harare
Tel: +263-4-753027 Fax: +263-4-753024
Email: editor@daily-news.co.za (Email
address in South Africa)
Web: http://www.daily-news.co.za/
(site hosted from South Africa)
2003- Dly (also Sun as *Sunday News*) Ind
Chief exec: S.S. Nkomo
Ed: Geoff Nyarota

Publ: Associated Newspapers of Zimbabwe
(Pvt) Ltd
Archives: fully searchable archive 2003-
Note: closed down by the Zimbabwean
government in September 2003, but may
recommence publication soon if its
application for a new license is granted.

1173   **The Financial Gazette**
Coal House
Cnr Nelson Mandela Ave/Leopold
Takawira Street
Harare
Tel: +263-478 1571-9
Email: newsdesk@fingaz.co.zw (Newsroom)
Web: http://www.fingaz.co.zw/
1969- Wk Ind
Chief exec: Jacob Chisese (General Manager),
Email: mgtserv@africaonline.co.zw
Ed: Sunsleey Chamunorwa, Email:
schamunorwa@fingaz.co.zw
News ed: Dumisani Ndlela, Email:
dndlela@fingaz.co.zw
Publ: Octadew (Pvt) Ltd
Archives: fully searchable archive 1999-

1174   **The Herald**
Herald House
George Silundika Ave/Second Street
PO Box 395
Harare
Tel: +263-4-795771 Fax: +263-4-791311
Email: n/a
Web: http://www.zimbabweherald.com/
1978- Dly (also Sun as *The Sunday Mail* and
Sunday News) Gov
Ed: Pikirayi Deketeke
Publ: Zimbabwe Newspapers (1999) Ltd

1175   **Sunday Mirror** (formerly *Zimbabwe
Mirror*)
Southern Africa Publishing House
109 Coventry Road
Workington
Harare
Postal address:
PO Box 1005
Mount Pleasant
Harare
Tel: +263-4-621681/621803 Fax: +263-4-666061
Email: sappho@zimmirror.co.zw
Web:
http://www.africaonline.co.zw/mirror/
1997- Wk (Sun) Ind

Chief exec: Ibbo Mandaza (Group Publisher
& Editor)
Ed: Innocent Chofamba Sithole
Publ: Southern African Printing & Publishing
House (SAPPHO)

1176   Zimbabwe Independent
Zimind Publishers (Private) Ltd
1st Block 3rd Floor
Ernst & Young Building
1 Kwame Nkrumah Avenue
Harare
Postal address:
PO Box BE 1165
Belvedere
Harare
Tel: +263-4-773934-8/755123/4
Fax: +263-4-773941
Email: newsdesk@zimind.mweb.co.zw
(Newsdesk) pubdis@mweb.co.zw
(Subscription enquiries)
Web: http://www.theindependent.co.zw/
1996- Wk (Fri) Ind
Chief exec: Trevor Ncube,
Email: tncube@zimind.mweb.co.zw
Ed: Iden Wetherell,
Email: idenw@zimind.mweb.co.zw
News ed: Vincent Kahiya,
Email: vincent@zimind.mweb.co.zw
Publ: Zimind Publishers (Private) Ltd
Archives: accessible for 2002-

1177   Zimbabwe Standard
Standard Press (Private) Ltd
Ernst & Young Building
1 Kwame Nkrumah Avenue
Harare
Postal address:
PO Box 661730
Kopje
Harare
Tel: +263-4- 750401/751351/755046
Fax: +263-4- 773854
Email: newsdesk@zimind.mweb.co.zw
(Newsdesk)
marketing@standard.mweb.co.zw
(Sales/Marketing) pubdis@mweb.co.zw
(Subscription enquiries)
Web: http://www.thestandard.co.zw/
1996[?]- Wk (Sun) Ind
Ed: Bornwell Chakaodza, Email:
chakaodzab@standard.mweb.co.zw
Man ed: Tendai Mutseyekwa,
Email: tendaim@standard.mweb.co.zw
Publ: Standard Press (Private) Ltd

12

Major African studies library collections in Europe, North America, and elsewhere outside Africa

This section identifies libraries worldwide (outside Africa) with substantial African studies collections, either maintained as separate Africa-related collections, or with significant holdings of Africana material, but not separately maintained. It includes entries for a small number of major archival collections, such as the National Archives in the UK, but more specialist archival collections are not included. In the USA, libraries with large African American/Black studies collections are only included if they also contain significant African studies holdings. Major academic and special libraries in Africa, and the national archives of each country, are listed in section ➜ **13 Major libraries and national archives in Africa**.

Each entry gives full name and address, telephone and fax numbers, email address, Web site, and details of the contact person in charge of the African studies collections (where appropriate). Please note that, where available, the Web page/URL specifically relating to the home page of the Africana collections is indicated, rather than the main university library. Unless otherwise indicated, email addresses given are those for the person in charge of the Africana collections, and/or the general email address for enquiries regarding the African studies collections. Other details, such as hours of opening, conditions of access, size of collection, loan and reference services, special collections, publications, resource materials, library staff, subject liaisons, etc. is accessible from each library's Web site. All libraries also offer access to their online catalogue from their Web site.

Libraries are listed alphabetically by countries. All information, including email addresses, Web sites, and contacts, has been completely updated and verified for this new edition and is current as at September 2005. A number of cross-references are included to guides to collections of some of these libraries, and/or major portals or other online resources hosted by a number of the libraries, and described in others sections of the *African Studies Companion*.

Listings included here are limited to academic, public and special libraries that hold sizeable collections of African studies material, generally a monograph collection of at least 20,000 volumes and/or significant holdings of other materials, although a few specialist libraries with smaller collections are also included. For other small, more specialist libraries with African studies collections, users should consult three other sources: for Europe, → **The SCOLMA Directory of Libraries and Special Collections on Africa in the United Kingdom and in Europe (317)** (a new 6th edition of which is currently in preparation); for the USA, the → **African Studies Information Resources Directory (297)**, which, although long out-of-print and now very dated, remains a valuable source, describing collections in libraries and in many other types of repositories in the United States. Additionally, and particularly useful for tracking down specialist archival and small special collections, there is an excellent online resource → **Africa Research Central. A Clearinghouse of African Primary Sources (1358)**, described elsewhere in this volume.

EUROPE

Austria

1178 **ÖFSE Bibliothek**
Österreichische Forschungsstiftung
für Entwicklungshilfe
Berggasse 7
1090 Vienna
Tel: +43-1-317 4010 Fax: +43-1-317 4015
Email: bibliothek@oefse.at (General enquiries)
g.bittner@oefse.at (Head of Library)
Web: http://www.oefse.at/bibliothek.htm
Contact: Gerhard Bittner, Head of Library

1179 **Universität Wien, Fachbibliothek
für Afrikanistik**
Universitätscampus Altes AKH Hof 5
Spitalgasse 2-4
1090 Vienna
Tel. +43-1-4277 16510 Fax: +43-1-4277 9431
Email: erich.sommerauer@univie.ac.at
Web: http://www.ub.univie.ac.at/fb-afrikanistik/
Contact: Erich René Sommerauer

Belgium

1180 **Aequatoria Archives**
Department of African Languages
and Cultures
Ghent University
Rozier 44
9000 Ghent
Tel.: +32-9-264 3808 Fax: +32-9-264 4180
Email: Michael.Meeuwis@rug.ac.be

Web:
http://www.aequatoria.be/archives_project
/index.html (English version)
http://www.aequatoria.be/archives_project
/French/FRindex.html (French version)
Contact: Michael Meeuwis
see also → **Centre Aequatoria, Congo
Democratic Republic (1378)**

1181 **Ghent University. De Bibliotheek
van de Vakgroep Afrikaanse Talen
en Culturen/Library of the
Department of African Languages
and Cultures**
Rozier 44
Ghent 9000
Tel: +32-9-264 3706 Fax: +32-9-264 4180
Email: afrikanistiek@ugent.be (General
enquiries) Greta.VanDaele@UGent.be (Head
of Library)
Web:
http://africana.rug.ac.be/texts/library/
(African Studies Library)
http://www.lib.ugent.be/ (Main Library)
Contact: Greta Van Daele, Head of Library

1182 **Ministry of Foreign Affairs,
Library/Archives**
Federal Public Service Foreign Affairs
Foreign Trade and Development
Cooperation
Service A62 – Library
Rue des Petits Carmes 15
1000 Brussels

Tel: +32-2-501 8098 (Africa desk) +32-2-501 3929 (International Cooperation Desk)
Fax: +32-2-501 3736
Email: biblio@diplobel.fed.be (General enquiries)
michel.erkens@diplobel.fed.be (Head of Library)
francoise.peemans@diplobel.fed.be (Head of Archives)
Web:
http://www.diplomatie.be/en/archives/arc hivesdetail.asp?TEXTID=2305 (Library)
Web:
http://www.diplomatie.be/en/archives/arc hivesdetail.asp?TEXTID=2295 (Archives)
Contacts: Michel Erkens, Library; Françoise Peemans, Archives
Note: this library's Africa Department collections incorporate the collections of the former Bibliothèque Africaine (formerly at 65 rue Belliard in Brussels).

1183   Koninklijk Museum voor Midden-Afrika/Musée Royal de l'Afrique Centrale
Leuvensesteenweg 13
3080 Tervuren
Tel: 32-2-769 56 00/+32-2-769 5603
Fax: +32-2-769 5642
Email: biblio@africamuseum.be (General enquiries) nathalie.de.vries@africamuseum.be (Head of Library Services)
Web:
http://www.africamuseum.be/visitor/librar ies
Contacts: Nathalie de Vries, Head of Library Services

Denmark

1184   Center for Afrikastudiers, Bibliotek
Københavns Universitet
Købmagergade 46 4 sal
1150 Copenhagen K
Tel: +45-3532 2587 Fax +45-3532 2590
Email: cas@teol.ku.dk (General enquiries)
css@teol.ku.dk (Librarian)
Web:
http://www.teol.ku.dk/cas/nyhomepage/H jemmeside_engelsk/index_engelsk.htm
Contact: Charlotte Støiberg Schmidt

→ **Centre for Development Research Library** *see* **Danish Centre for International Studies and Human Rights, DCISM Library** entry **1185**

1185   Danish Centre for International Studies and Human Rights DCISM Library
Strandgade 56
1401 Copenhagen K
Tel.: +45-3269 8676 (General enquiries)
+45 3269 8640 (Head of Library)
Fax: +45 32 69 86 00
bibliotek@dcism.dk (General enquiries)
sel@dcism.dk (Head of Library)
http://www.dcism.dk/library/Default.html
Contact: Svend Erik Lindberg-Hansen, Head of Library
Note: the library's street/visitor address is Wilders Plads 8K, Christianshavn, Copenhagen. The DCISM Library represents the merger of four previously independent libraries (including the Centre for Development Research Library), and Foreign Ministry libraries.

1186   Mellemfolkeligt Samvirke/ Danish Association for International Development, Library
Borgergade 10-14
1300 Copenhagen K
Tel: +45-7731 0000 Fax: +45-7731 0131
Email: library@ms.dk (General enquries)
Lethmoll@ms-dan.dk (Head of Library)
Web:
http://130.227.48.2/bibliotek/uk/default.ht m (English version)
Contact: Helle Leth-Møller, Head of Library

Finland

1187   Aasian ja Afrikan kielten ja kulttuurien laitos/Institute for Asian and African Studies, Library
Helsinki University
Unioninkatu 38 B
PO Box 59
00014 Helsinki
Tel: +358-9-1911 2244 Fax: +358-9-1912 2094
Email: Sylvia.Akar@Helsinki.Fi
Web: http://www.helsinki.fi/hum/aakkl/
Contact: Sylvia Akar, Institute Administrator; or Liisa Savolainen, Head User Services,

Helsinki University Library (no separate African studies collection maintained)

France

Note: for additional French libraries with African studies collections, including public libraries, *see* **Répertoire de bibliothèques à Paris et en régions dont les fonds présentent un intérêt pour la recherche sur l'Afrique (134)**

1188 **Académie des sciences d'outre-mer, Bibliothèque**
15 rue Lapérouse
75116 Paris
Tel: +33-1-47 20 87 93 Fax: +33-1-47 20 89 72
Email: bibliotheque@academiedoutremer.fr
Web: http://www.academiedoutremer.fr/biblioth
eque.php
Contact: Dominique Prince

1189 **Bibliothèque de documentation internationale contemporaine**
6 allée de l'Université
BP 106
92001 Nanterre Cedex
Tel: +33-1-40 97 79 00 (General enquiries) +33-1-40 97 79 01 (Bibliographic services and information) Fax: +33-1-40 97 79 40
Email: courrier@bdic.fr or bdic@u-paris10.fr
Web: http://www.bdic.fr/
Contact: Martine Lemaître-Demarquay

1190 **Bibliothèque de linguistique Africaine**
19 rue des Bernardins
75005 Paris
Tel: +33-1-44 32 05 87
Email: Prunelle.Charvet@univ-paris3.fr
Web: http://www.scd.univ-paris3.fr/La_acc.htm
Contacts: Raphaël Kaboré or Prunelle Charvet

1191 **Bibliothèque de recherches africaines**
Université Paris 1
Centre Malher
9 rue Malher
75181 Paris Cedex 04
Tel: +33-1-44 78 33 35
Email: daronian@univ-paris1.fr

Web: http://mald.univ-paris1.fr/bibliotheq/bib_actus.htm
Contact: Liliane Daronian, Librarian

1192 **Bibliothèque inter-universitaire des langues orientales**
4 rue de Lille
75007 Paris
Tel: +33-1-44 77 87 20 Fax: +33-1-44 77 87 30
Email: biulo@idf.ext.jussieu.fr
Web: http://www.univ-paris3.fr/bibliotheque/rattachees/langueorie
ntale/index.html
Contact: Nathalie Rodriguez

1193 **Bibliothèque Pierre Alexandre. Fonds de linguistique et d'ethnolinguistique africaines**
Université Lumière Lyon 2
5 Avenue Pierre Mendès France
69676 Bron Cedex
Tel: +33-4-78 77 43 82 Fax: +33-4-78 77 43 74
Email: nathalie.fargier@univ-lyon2.fr
Web: http://sophia.univ-lyon2.fr:8090/pierre.alexandre/index.php
Contact: Nathalie Fargier, Librarian

1194 **Bibliothèque nationale de France**
11 quai François Mauriac,
75706 Paris Cedex 13
and at:
58 rue de Richelieu
75002 Paris
Tel: +33-1-53 79 59 59 Fax: +33-1-53 79 41 80
Email: accueil@bnf.fr (General enquiries) orientation-lecteurs@bnf.fr (Enquiries regarding access to collections) coordination-bibliographique@bnf.fr (Bibliographic services); or use online enquiry form on Web site
Web: http://www.bnf.fr/ or http://www.bnf.fr/site_bnf_eng/index.html (English version)
Contacts: Valérie Tesnière, Head, Philosophy, History and Social Sciences Department; or Yann Fauchois, DCO/DI, same department
Note: to find collection holdings on African studies, African literatures and languages, etc. use search facility in online catalogue.

1195   Centre de recherche et d'etude sur
        les pays d'afrique orientale,
        Bibliothèque
        Université de Pau et des Pays de
        l'Adour
        Avenue du Doyen Poplawski
        Campus Universitaire
        BP 1633
        64016 Pau Cedex
Tel: +33-5-59 80 75 29
Fax: +33-5-59 80 75 07
Email: Francois.Constantin@univ-pau.fr or
claude.santini@univ-pau.fr
Web: http://www.univ-
pau.fr/RECHERCHE/CREPAO/lecrepao.ht
m
Contacts: Francois Constantin, Director; or
Claude Santini, Secretary

1196   Centre des archives d'outre-mer
        29 chemin du Moulin-Detesta
        13090 Aix-en-Provence
Tel: +33-4-42 93 38 50 Fax: +33-4-42 93 38 89
Email: caom.aix@culture.gouv.fr
Web:
http://www.archivesnationales.culture.gouv.
fr/caom/fr/
Contact: Marie T. Weiss-Litique

1197   Centre d'etude d'Afrique noire
        (CEAN), Bibliothèque/
        Documentation
        UMR 5115 CNRS
        Institut d'Etudes politiques
        11 Allée Ausone
        33607 Pessac Cedex
Tel. +33-5-56 84 42 86 Fax: +33-5-56 84 43 24
Email:
f.meynard@sciencespobordeaux.fr
Web:
http://www.cean.sciencespobordeaux.fr/
(Centre home page)
http://www.cean.sciencespobordeaux.fr/doc
umentation.htm (Library/Documentation)
Contact: Françoise Meynard,
Librarian/Documentalist

1198   Centre d'études africaines,
        Bibliothèque
        54 boulevard Raspail
        75006 Paris
Tel: +33-1- 49 54 25 62/2367
Fax: +33-1-49 54 26 92
Email: siroux@ehess.fr

Web:
http://www.ehess.fr/centres/ceaf/pages/bi
bliotheque.html
Contacts: Catherine Siroux, Head of Library;
Patricia Bleton

1199   Centre d'etudes africaines, arabes,
        asiatiques, Centre de
        Documentation (CEAAA)
        21 rue de la Fonderie
        31000 Toulouse
Tel: +33- 5-61 36 81 00 Fax: +33- 5-61 25 82 75
Email: documentation@ict-toulouse.asso.fr
Web: http://www.ict-
toulouse.asso.fr/istr/site/016.html or
http://www.ict-
toulouse.asso.fr/old/cea/s3p1.htm
Contact: Cathy Pretou

1200   Carrefour international francophone
        de documentation et d'information
        de l'agence intergouvernementale
        de la Francophonie, Centre de
        documentation et d'information
        (CIFDI)
        Agence intergouvernementale de la
        Francophonie
        Institut francophone des nouvelles
        technologies de l'information et de la
        formation (INTIF)
        15-16 Quai Louis XVIII
        33000 Bordeaux
Tel: +33-5-56 01 59 22 Fax: +33-5-56 51 78 51
Email: cifdi@francophonie.org (General
enquiries)
Danielle.Bouhajeb@francophonie.org
(Head of Documentation Centre)
Web: http://cifdi.francophonie.org
Contact: Danielle Bouhajeb, Head of
Documentation Centre

1201   La Documentation française, Centre
        de documentation internationale
        29 quai Voltaire
        75344 Paris Cedex 07
Tel: +33-1-40 15 72 18 Fax: +33-1-40 15 72 30
Email: cdi@ladocumentationfrancaise.fr or
bibliotheque@ladocumentationfrancaise.fr
Web:
http://www.ladocumentationfrancaise.fr/do
cumentation/documentation_internationale/
index.shtml
Contacts: see
http://www.ladocumentationfrancaise.fr/inf
ormations/nous-ecrire.shtml

Note: for a description of the collection, *see* "Le Fonds 'Afrique outré-mer de la bibliothèque de la Documentation française: etude des collections sur l'Afrique subsaharienne et perspectives de mise en valeur" by Céline Carrier. Paris: Bibliothèque de la Documentation française, 2002. 77 pp., also accessible online at http://www.enssib.fr/bibliotheque/docume nts/dcb/carrier.pdf

1202   **Fondation nationale des sciences politiques de Paris Bibliothèque/Services de documentation**
30 rue Saint-Guillaume
75007 Paris
Tel: +33-1-45 49 56 34/45 49 50 96
Fax: +33-1-42 22 99 80
Email: info@docum.sciences-po.fr
Web: http://www.sciences-po.fr/ (click on to Bibliothèque)
Contact: Joëlle Muller, Head, Documentation Services

1203   **Institut de recherche pour le développement (IRD), Secteur Documentation**
213 rue La Fayette
75480 Paris Cedex 10
Tel: +33-1-48 03 76 06 Fax: +33-1-48 03 08 29
Email: dominique.cavet@paris.ird.fr
Web: http://www.mpl.ird.fr/documentation
Contact: Dominique Cavet
For other documentation personnel *see* http://www.mpl.ird.fr/documentation/pers onnel_doc.php3
For full contact addresses at 9 documentation centres in Africa *see* http://www.mpl.ird.fr/documentation/cent re_doc.php3#Afrique)

1204   **Institut d'etudes portugaises, bresiliennes et d'afrique lusophone, Bibliothèque**
17 rue de la Sorbonne
Escalier C 2e étage
75005 Paris
Tel: +33-1- 40 46 29 19 Fax: +33-1-43 25 74 71
Email: Didier.Collet@univ-paris3.fr
Web: http://bucensier.univ-paris3.fr/Por_acc.htm
Contact: Didier Collet, Head of Library

1205   **L'Institut du Monde Arabe/Arab World Institute, Bibliothèque**
1 rue des Fossés-Saint-Bernard
Place Mohammed-V
75236 Paris Cedex 05
Tel: +33-1-40 51 38 38 Fax: +33-1-43 54 76 45Email: bib@imarabe.org
Web: http://www.imarabe.org/ang/perm/biblio_ id.html
Contact: The Librarian
See also ➔ **L'Institut du Monde Arabe/Arab World Institute** [Database] **(115)**

1206   **Laboratoire d'ethnologie et de sociologie comparative, Bibliothèque Éric de Dampierre**
Université Paris 10
Maison René Givouvès
21 allée de l'Université
92023 Nanterre Cedex
Tel: +33-1-46 69 24 00 Fax: +33-1-46 69 24 51
Email: baa@mae.u-paris10.fr
Web: http://web.mae.u-paris10.fr/recherche/beinforma.htm
Contact: Marie-Dominique Mouton

1207   **Maison provinciale des missionnaires d'Afrique, Pères Blancs, Bibliotheque**
5 rue Roger Verlomme
75003 Paris
Tel: +33-1-42 71 06 70 Fax: +33-1-48 04 39 67
Email: pierre.federle@wanadoo.fr
Web: http://peres-blancs.cef.fr/bibliothe.htm
Contact: Père Pierre Féderlé, Librarian

1208   **Musée de l'homme, Bibliothèque**
Palais de Chaillot 4e étage
Place du Trocadéro
75116 Paris
Tel: +33-1-44 05 72 03 Fax: +33-1-44 05 72 12
Email: bmhweb@mnhn.fr (General enquiries)
bidard@mnhn.fr (Librarian)
Web: http://www.mnhn.fr/mnhn/bmh/index.ht ml
Contact: Bidard Gaëlle, Librarian
See also ➔ **Musée du quai Branly, Médiathèque (1209)**

1209   Musée du quai Branly. Arts et
        civilisations d'Afrique, d'Asie,
        Océanie, et des Amériques,
        Médiathèque
        *Temporary address and tel/fax nos.
        only:*
        Hôtel industriel Le Berlier
        15 rue Jean-Baptiste Berlier
        75013 Paris
        Tel: +33-1-56 61 70 00 Fax: +33-1-56 61 70 01
        http://www.quaibranly.fr/index.php3 (Main
        site)
        http://www.quaibranly.fr/article.php3?id_a
        rticle=940 (Médiathèque advance
        information)
        Note: The Médiathèque in the new Musée du
        quai Branly, to be opened in quai Branly in
        Paris (7th arrondissement) in 2006, will bring
        together under one roof the collections
        (books, films, audio, photographs, maps, and
        archival material) of the → Musée de
        l'Homme (1208), and the Musée national des
        arts d'Afrique et d'Oceanie (entry 689 in the
        3rd edition).

1210   OECD Centre for Documentation &
        Information
        Organization for Economic
        Cooperation and Development
        2 rue André Pascal
        75775 Paris Cedex 16
        Tel: +33-1-45 24 82 00 (Main switchboard)
        Fax: +33-1-45 24 85 00
        Email: peter.raggett@oecd.org
        Web: http://puck.sourceoecd.org/
        Contact: Peter Raggett
        Note: this is not a physical library, but
        OECD's online library of statistical databases,
        books and periodicals, SourceOECD

1211   Réseau des centres de
        documentation pour le
        développement et la solidarité
        internationale/Network of
        Documentation Centers for
        Sustainable Development and
        International Solidarity
        21 ter rue Voltaire
        75011 Paris
        Tel: +33-1-44 64 74 14 Fax: +33-1-44 64 74 55
        Email: ritimo.voltaire@globenet.org
        Web: http://www.ritimo.org/anglais.html
        (English version)
        Note: *not* a physical library, but a network of
        documentation centres and shared databases.

1212   The UNESCO Library
        7 place de Fontenoy
        75352 Paris 07 SP
        Tel: +33-1-45 68 03 56
        Fax: +33-1-45 68 56 98 (Head, Reference
        Services)
        Email: library@unesco.org (General enquiries)
        p.van-den-born@unesco.org (Head,
        Reference Services)
        Web:
        http://www.unesco.org/general/eng/infose
        rv/doc/library.shtml
        Contact: Petra van den Born, Head, Reference
        Services

Germany

1213   Arnold-Bergsträsser Institut für
        Kulturwissenschaftliche Forschung,
        Bibliothek
        Windaustrasse 16
        79110 Freiburg
        Tel: +49-761-888 7821 Fax: +49-761-888 7878
        Email: bibliothek@abi.uni-freiburg.de
        Web: http://www.arnold-bergstraesser.de/
        (Click on to Library/
        Bibliothek)
        Contacts: Ilse Buschman, Stefanie Gerum

1214   Asien-Afrika-Institut, Abteilung für
        Afrikanistik und Äthiopistik,
        Bibliothek
        (Universität Hamburg)
        Edmund-Siemers-Allee
        1 Flügel Ost
        20146 Hamburg
        Tel: +49-40-42838 4874
        Fax: +49-40-42838 5675
        Email: afrikanistik@uni-hamburg.de
        Web: http://www.uni-
        hamburg.de/Wiss/FB/10/AfrikaS/biblio.ht
        ml
        Contact: Prof. Dr. Gerhardt

1215   Bayerische Staatsbibliothek
        Ludwigstrasse 16
        80539 Munich
        Tel: +49-89-28638 0 (General enquiries)
        +49-89-28638 2784 (User services)
        +49-89-28638-2773 (Information Services)
        Fax: +49-89-28638 2200
        Email: benutzungsdienste@bsb-
        muenchen.de (General enquiries, User

Services) maneval@bsb-muenchen.de
Information services)
Web: http://www.bsb-muenchen.de/
Contact: Renate Maneval, Head of
Information Services

**1216 Bibliothek der Institute am
Englischen Garden**
(Universität München)
Oettingenstrasse 67
80538 Munich
Tel. +49-89-2180 9753 (General enquiries) +49-89-2180 9756 (Librarian)
Fax +49-89-2180 9759
Email: beg@lrz.uni-muenchen.de (General
enquiries) (Head of Library)
j.mackenzie@lrz.uni-muenchen.de
Web: http://beg.ub.uni-muenchen.de/#
Contact: Janet MacKenzie, Head of Library
Note: this library forms part of the University
Library of Ludwig-Maximilians-Universität
in Munich, and brings together the former
separate collections of eight Institute libraries,
including that of the Institut für Völkerkunde
und Afrikanistik.

**1217 Deutsche Zentralbibliothek für
Wirtschaftswissenschaften,
Bibliothek des Instituts für
Weltwirtschaft**
Düsternbrooker Weg 120
24105 Kiel
Tel: +49-431-8814 383/555
Fax: +49-431-8814 520
Email: info@zbw.ifw-kiel.de (General
enquiries) h.thomsen@zbw.ifw-kiel.de
(Head of Library)
Web: http://www.uni-kiel.de/ifw/zbw/econis.htm
Contact: Horst Thomsen, Head of Library

**1218 Deutsches Institut für
Entwicklungspolitik/German
Development Institute, Bibliothek**
Tulpenfeld 4
53113 Bonn
Tel.: +49-228-94927 140/141
Fax: +49-228-94927 130
Email: DIE@die-gdi.de (General enquiries)
Renate.Scholten@die-gdi.de
(Head of Library)
Web: http://www.die-gdi.de/die_homepage.nsf/FSdbib?OpenFrameset
Contact: Renate Scholten, Head of Library

**1219 Deutsches Institut für Tropische
und Subtropische
Landwirtschaft/German Institute
for Tropical and Subtropical
Agriculture, Bibliothek**
Steinstrasse 19
Postfach 1652
37213 Witzenhausen
Tel: +49-5542-60713 Fax: +49-5542-60739
Email: bibliothek@ditsl.de
http://www.wiz.uni-kassel.de/ditsl/de/biblio.html
Contact: Claudia Blau, Librarian

Deutsches Uebersee Institut *see* → **Institut
für Afrika-Kunde (1224)**

**1220 Frobenius-Institut an der Johann
Wolfgang Goethe-Universität,
Bibliothek**
Grüneburgplatz 1
60323 Frankfurt am Main
Tel: +49-69-798 33050/51 (General enquiries)
+49-69-798-33240 (Librarian)
Fax: +49-69-798 33101
Email: frobenius@em.uni-frankfurt.de
(General) Platte@em.uni-frankfurt.de
(Librarian)
Web: http://www.frobenius-institut.de/
Contact: Editha Platte, Librarian

**1221 Humboldt-Universität zu Berlin,
Universitätsbibliothek.
Zweigbibliothek Asien- und
Afrikawissenschaften**
Invalidenstrasse 118
Eingang über Schlegelstr. 26
10115 Berlin
Tel: +49-30-2093 6693 (General enquiries) +49-30-2093-6691 (Head of Library)
Fax: +49-30-2093-6666
Email: asa@ub.hu-berlin.de (General
enquiries) (Head of Branch Library)
uta.freiburger@ub.hu-berlin.de
Web: http://www.ub.hu-berlin.de/
(Main university library home page)
http://www.ub.hu-berlin.de/bibliothek/zweigbibliotheken/asienaf/asienaf.html (Zweigbibliothek Asien-
und Afrikawissenschaften)
Contact: Uta Freiburger, Head of Branch
Library

1222   Ifo-Institut für
        Wirtschaftsforschung,
        Ifo-Bibliothek/
        Informationszentrum
        Poschingerstrasse 5
        81679 Munich
        Tel: +49-89-9224 1350 Fax: +49-89-985369
        Email: ifo@ifo.de (General enquiries)
        braitacher@ifo.de (Head, Library Services)
        Web: http://www.ifo.de/
        Contact: Petra Braitacher, Head, Library
        Services

1223   Informationsstelle Südliches Afrika
        e.V., Archiv/Bibliothek
        Königswinterer Strasse 116
        53227 Bonn
        Tel: +49-228-464 369 Fax: +49-228-468 177
        Email: issa@comlink.org
        Web: http://www.issa-bonn.org/
        Contact: Hein Möllers

1224   Institut für Afrika-Kunde,
        Bibliothek
        (Deutsches Übersee-Institut/DÜI)
        Neuer Jungfernstieg 21
        20354 Hamburg
        Tel: +49-40-42 825 523 (General enquiries)
        Tel. +49-40- 42-825 569 (Library)
        Fax: +49-40-42 825 511
        Email: bibliothek@iak.duei.de
        Web:
        http://www.duei.de/iak/show.php/de/con
        tent/bibliothek/bibliothek.html (German
        version)
        http://www.duei.de/iak/show.php/en/con
        tent/library/library.html
        (English version)
        Contact: Christine Hoffendahl, Head of
        Library

1225   Institut für Afrikanistik, Bibliothek
        (Universität zu Köln)
        Meister-Ekkehart-Strasse 7
        50923 Cologne
        Tel: +49-221-470 2708 (General enquiries) +49-
        221-470 3885 (Library)
        Fax: +49-221-470 5158
        Email: helga.krueger@uni-koeln.de
        Web: http://www.uni-koeln.de/phil-
        fak/afrikanistik/
        Contact: Helga Krüger, Librarian

1226   Institut für Auslandsbeziehungen,
        Bibliothek/Dokumentation
        Charlottenplatz 17
        70173 Stuttgart
        Tel: +49-711-222 5147 (General enquiries) +49-
        711-222 5148 (Librarian)
        Fax: +49-711-222 5131
        Email: bibliothek@ifa.de (General enquiries)
        czekalla@ifa.de (Librarian)
        Web: http://www.ifa.de/b/index.htm
        Contact: Gudrun Czekalla

1227   Institut für Ethnologie, Bibliothek
        (Freie Universität Berlin)
        Drosselweg 1-3
        14195 Berlin
        Tel: +49-30-838 52693/54152
        Fax: +49-30-838 52382
        Email: use online email form on Web site
        Web: http://userpage.fu-
        berlin.de/~ethnolog/
        Contacts: Sibylle Alsayad, Michael Brauer

1228   Institute für Ethnologie und
        Afrikastudien, Institutsbibliothek
        (Johannes Gutenberg-Universität)
        Forum 6
        55099 Mainz
        Tel: +49-6131-392 0119 (Institute Library)
        Fax: +49-6131-392 3730 (Institute Library)
        Tel.: +49-6131-392 5933 (Jahn-Bibliothek)
        Fax: +49-6131-392 3730 (Jahn-Bibliothek)
        Email: brandste@mail.uni-mainz.de (Institute
        Library) aoed@uni-mainz.de (Janheinz Jahn
        Library)
        Web: http://www.ifeas.uni-
        mainz.de/info/bib_sam.html (Institute
        Library) or
        http://www.jahn-bibliothek.ifeas.uni-
        mainz.de/ (Janheinz Jahn-Bibliothek für
        Afrikanische Literatur)
        Contacts: Anna-Maria Brandstetter Institute
        Librarian; Anja Oed, Librarian, Janheinz Jahn-
        Bibliothek für Afrikanische Literatur

1229   Institut für Völkerkunde,
        Fachbereichsbibliothek Geographie
        und Völkerkunde
        (Albert-Ludwigs Universität
        Freiburg)
        Werderring 10
        79085 Freiburg
        Tel.: +49-761-203 3593 (General enquiries)
        +49-761-203 3561 (Library)

Fax: +49-761-203 3581
Email: sekretariat@ethno.uni-freiburg.de
(General enquiries) molz@ub.uni-freiburg.de
(Head of Library)
Web: http://www.ethno.uni-
freiburg.de/anfang.html (click on to
Bibliothek)
Contacts: Winfried Molz, Head of Library

→ Institut für Völkerkunde und
Afrikanistik, Universität München see
Bibliothek der Institute am Englischen
Garden (1216)

→ Ludwig-Maximilians-Universität
Bibliothek, Munich see
Bibliothek der Institute am Englischen
Garden (1216)

1230   Max Planck Institute for Social
        Anthropology, Library
        Advokatenweg 36
        PO Box 110351
        06017 Halle/S.
Tel: +49-345-2927 503 Fax: +49-345-2927 502
Email: neumann@eth.mpg.de
Web: http://www.eth.mpg.de/ (click on to
Library)
Contact: Anja Neumann, Head Librarian

1231   Staatsbibliothek zu Berlin
        Preussischer Kulturbesitz
        Orientabteilung
        Potsdamer Strasse 33
        Haus 2
        10785 Berlin
Tel: +49-30-266 2489 (General enquiries) +49-
30-266 2415 (Head of Orientabteilung)
Fax: +49-30-264 5955
Email: orientabt@sbb.spk-berlin.de (General
enquiries) meline.pehlivanian@sbb.spk-
berlin.de (African studies specialist)
Web: http://www.sbb.spk-
berlin.de/deutsch/sondersammelgebiete/ori
entalistik/
Contacts: Harmut-Ortwin Feistel,
Head, Sondersammelgebiet Orientalistik;
Meliné Pehlivanian, African studies specialist

1232   Stadt-und-Universitätsbibliothek
        Frankfurt am Main
        Sondersammelgebiet
        Afrika südlich der Sahara
        Bockenheimer Landstrasse 134- 138
        60325 Frankfurt am Main
Tel: +49-69-798-39247
Email: a.kasper@ub.uni-frankfurt.de
Web: http://www.ub.uni-
frankfurt.de/ssg/afrika.html
Contacts: Anne-Marie Kasper, Lesesaal Afrika
See also entries → 128, 131

1233   Übersee-Museum, Bibliothek
        Bahnhofsplatz 13
        28195 Bremen
Tel: +49-421-1603 8180 Fax: +49-421-160 3899
Email: office@uebersee-museum.de (General
enquiries) w.steenken-eisert@uebersee-
museum.de   (Head of Library)
Web: http://www.uebersee-
museum.de/bib_bibliothek.htm
Wilfried Steenken-Eisert, Head of Library

1234   Universitätsbibliothek Bayreuth
        Universität Bayreuth
        95440 Bayreuth
Tel: +49-921-553420 (General enquiries) +49-
921-553436 (Reader Services)
Fax: +49-921-553442 Email:
Wolfgang.Bilgeri@ub.uni-bayreuth.de
(Reader Services)
 rainer-maria.kiel@ub.uni-bayreuth.de (Public
Relations)
Web: http://www.ub.uni-bayreuth.de/
Contacts: Wolfgang Bilgeri, Head, Reader
Services; Rainer-Maria Kiel, Public Relations

1235   Universitätsbibliothek Bielefeld
        Universitätsstrasse 25
        Postfach 100291
        33502 Bielefeld
Tel: +49-521-106 4114/4051
Fax: +49-521-106 4052
Email: info@ub.uni-bielefeld.de (General
enquiries) ute.wiessner@uni-bielefeld.de
(Head, Central User Services)
Web: http://www.ub.uni-bielefeld.de
Contact: Ute Wiessner
Head, Central User Services

1236   Universitätsbibliothek Tübingen
Orientalistik
Wilhelmstrasse 32
Postfach 2620
72016 Tübingen
Tel: +49-7071-2972 846 (General enquiries)
+49-7071-297 3430 (Head, Orientabteilung)
Fax: +49-7071-293123
Email: info-zentrum@ub.uni-tuebingen.de
(General enquiries)
walter.werkmeister@ub.uni-tuebingen.de
(Head, Orientalistik
Web: http://www.uni-tuebingen.de/ub/
Contact: Walter Werkmeister, Head
Orientalistik

Italy

**1237   Biblioteca del Dipartimento
Politica, istitizioni, storia,
Università Bologna**
Palazzo Hercolani
Strada Maggiore 45
40125 Bologna
Tel: +39-51-209 2532 Fax: +39-51-209 2536
Email: mafessanti@spbo.unibo.it
Web:
http://www2.spbo.unibo.it/bologna/diparti
m/dist/biblioteca/index.html
Contact: Mariangela Mafessanti, Head of
Library

**1238   Biblioteca Nazionale Centrale di
Firenze**
Piazza Cavalleggeri 1
50122 Florence
Tel: +39-55-249191 Fax: +39-55-234 2482
Email: info@bncf.firenze.sbn.it
Web: http://www.bncf.firenze.sbn.it/
Contact: Antonia Ida Fontana, Director

**1239   Food and Agriculture Organization
of the United Nations (FAO), David
Lubin Memorial Library**
Library and Documentation Systems
Division
Via delle Terme di Caracalle
00100 Rome
Tel: +39-6-5705 3703 Fax: +39-6-5225 2002
Email: FAO-Library-Reference@fao.org
(General enquiries) Jane.Wu@FAO.org
(Chief Librarian)
Web:

http://www.fao.org/library/_info_services/
Index.asp
Contact: Jane Wu, Chief Librarian

**1240   Istituto Italiano per l'Africa e
l'Oriente, Biblioteca**
Via Ulisse Alovandi 16
00197 Rome
Tel: +39-6-328 551/322 1258
Fax: +39-6-322 5348
Email: info@isiao.it
Web: http://www.isiao.it/ (click on to
Biblioteca)
Contact: The Librarian

**1241   Istituto per le Relazioni tra l'Italia e
i Paesi dell'Africa, America Latina e
Medio Oriente, Biblioteca**
Via Degli Scipioni 147
00192 Rome
Tel: +39-6-3269 9738 Fax: +39-6-3269 9750
Email: ipalmo@ipalmo.com
Web:
http://www.ipalmo.com/biblio_sede.html
Contact: Cristina Luciani, Librarian and Head
of Documentation Centre

**1242   Istituto Universitario Orientale di
Napoli, Biblioteca del Dipartimento
di Studi e Ricerche su Africa e Paesi
Arabi**
Palazzo Corigliano
Piazza San Domingo Maggiore 12
80134 Naples
Tel: +39-81-909714 Fax: +39-81-551 7901
Email: dibrapa@iuo.it
Web:
http://www.iuo.it/diprapa/DSRAPA/dsrap
a_default.htm
Contacts: Enrico Catemario, Director of the
Library

→ **Padri Bianchi** see **Societa' dei Missionari
d'Africa (1244)**

**1243   Pontificia Universitas Urbaniana,
Biblioteca**
Via Urbano VIII 16
00120 Città del Vaticano
Tel: +39-6-6988 9676 Fax: +39-6-6989 663
Email: puu@puu.urbe.it (General
enquiries) marek@puu.urbe.it (Director
of Library Services)
Web:
http://www.urbaniana.edu/biblio/it/

index.htm
Contact: Fr. Marek Rostkowski, Director
of Library Services

**1244   Societa' dei Missionari d'Africa
(Padri Bianchi)**
Service Bibliothèque--Archives
Via Aurelia 269
CP 9078
00100 Roma
Tel: +39-6-39 36 34 1 (General enquiries) +39-6-39 36 34 99 (Director of Library Services)
Fax: +39-6-39 36 34 79
Email: archivio@mafroma.org or
biblioteca@mafroma.org (Library A-Books)
biblioteca.b@mafroma.org (Library B-Periodicals) archivio.annexe@mafroma.org
(Archives)
Web: http://www.africamission-mafr.org/archivesdocgb.htm (English version)
Contacts: Father Ivan Page, Director of
Library Services; Father Johannes Tappeser,
Archivist; Father Jean-Marie Gabioud,
Librarian (Books)

Netherlands

1245   Afrika Centrum Library
Rijksweg 15
6267 AC Cadier en Keer
Tel: +31-43-407 7383 Fax: +31-43-407 7374
Email: bibliotheek@afrikacentrum.nl
Web:
http://www.afrikacentrum.nl/bibliotheek_en.htm (English version)
Contact: B. Oek, Librarian

**1246   Afrika-Studiecentrum, African
Studies Centre Library**
Wassenaarseweg 52
PO Box 9555
2300 RB Leiden
Tel: +31-71-527 3354 (General enquiries)
+31-71-527 3352 (Head of Library)
Fax: +31-71-527 3350
Email: vanderwerf@fsw.LeidenUniv.nl
Web: http://www.ascleiden.nl/Library/
Contact: Titia van der Werf-Davelaar, Head,
Library, Documentation and Information
Department
See also entries ➜ 72, 87, 109, 535, 1894-1896

**1247   Institute of Social Studies,
ISS Library Services**
Kortenaerkade 12
2518 AX The Hague
Tel: +31-70-426 0460 (General enquiries)
+ 31-70-426 0447 (Head of Library)
Fax: +31-70-426 0799
Email: wesseling@iss.nl
Web: http://www.iss.nl
Contact: Michel Wesseling, Head, Office of
Library and Information Technology Services

**1248   Netherlands Institute for Southern
Africa, Library, Information and
Documentation Centre**
Prins Hendrikkade 33
PO Box 10707
1001 ES Amsterdam
Tel: +31-20-520 6210 Fax: +31-20-520 6249
Email: bidoc@niza.nl
Web: http://www.niza.nl/ (click on to
Documentatie)
Contacts: Kier Schuringa or Anton Dekker,
Documentalists

**1249   Royal Tropical Institute, KIT
Library**
Mauritskade 63
PO Box 95001
1090 HA Amsterdam
Tel: +31-20-568 8462 Fax: +31-20-665 4423
Email: library@kit.nl
Web:
http://www.kit.nl/frameset.asp?TargetURL
=/information_services/default.asp
Contact: Hans van Hartevelt, Head, KIT
Library & Information Services

➜ **South Africa House** see **Zuid Afrikahus**
(1251)

**1250   Universiteit Utrecht, Bibliotheek
Centrum Uithof**
Heidelberglaan 2
PB 80124
3508 TC Utrecht
Tel: +31-30-253 2197/5595
Fax: +31-30-253 1357
Email: info.bcu@library.uu.nl (General
enquiries) or w.karreman@ubu.ruu.nl
Web:
http://www.library.uu.nl/182main.html
Contact: W. M. Karreman, Librarian

1251 Zuid Afrikahus/South Africa House, Bibliotheek
Keizersgracht 141
1015 CK Amsterdam
Tel: +31-20-624 9318 Fax: +31-20-638 2596
Email: bibliotheek@zuidafrikahuis.nl
Web:
http://www.zuidafrikahuis.nl/main.php?ite
m=library&nexpand=3
Contact: Corine de Maijer

Norway

1252 Bergen University Library
Social Science Library
Herman Foss Gate 6
5007 Bergen
Tel: +47-55-583261 Fax: +47-55-588380
Email: ubbsv@ub.uib.no (General enquiries)
tom.johnsen@ub.uib.no (Faculty Librarian)
Web: http://www.ub.uib.no/eng-index.htm
(English version)
Contact: Tom Johnsen, Faculty Librarian

1253 Chr. Michelsen Institute Library
Fantoftvegen 38
PO Box 6033 Postterminalen
5892 Bergen
Tel: +47-55-574191 (General enquiries) +47-55-574187 (Head of Library)
Fax: +47-55-574166
Email: biblio@cmi.no (General enquiries)
kirsti.andersen@cmi.no (Head of Library and Documentation)
Web: http://www.cmi.no/library/index.cfm
(English version)
Contact: Kirsti Hagen Andersen, Head of Library and Documentation

Portugal

1254 Arquivo Historico Ultramarino
Instituto de Investigação
Científica Tropical
Rua da Junqueira, n°. 86 - 1°
1300-344 Lisbon
Tel: +351-21-361 6340 Fax: +351-21-363 1460
Email: iict@iict.pt
Web:
http://www.iict.pt/estrutura/vest02.asp?div
isao=255 or
http://lanic.utexas.edu/project/tavera/port
ugal/ultramarino.html

Contact: Ana Canas, Head

1255 Biblioteca Nacional do Portugal
Campo Grande 83
1749-081 Lisbon
Tel: +351-21-798 200 (General enquiries) +351-21-798 2470 (Bibliographic Information) +351-21-798 2182 (Head, Direcção de Serviços de Colecções e Acesso)
Fax: +351-21-798 2138
Email: bn@bn.pt (General enquiries)
bnref@bn.pt (Reference Department)
rgalvao@bn.pt (Head, Direcção de Serviços de Colecções e Acesso)
Web: http://www.bn.pt
Contact: Rosa Maria Marcelino Galvão, Head, Direcção de Serviços de Colecções e Acesso

1256 Instituto de Investigação Científica Tropical, Centro de Documentação e Informação
Rua da Junqueira n° 86 - 1°
1300-344 Lisbon
Tel: +351-21-361 9730 Fax: +351-21-363 8218
Email: cdi@iict.pt
Web:
http://www.iict.pt/pgn/pagpgn/vcgr01xx.a
sp?cod=5
Contact: Maria Virgínia Aires Magriço, Head of Documentation and Information Centre

Russia

1257 Institute of African Studies Library Russian Academy of Sciences
Spiridonovka 30/1
103001 Moscow
Tel: +7-95-290 6385 Fax: +7-95-202 0786
Email: info@inafr.ru
Web: http://eng.inafr.ru/ (English version)
Contact: Natalia B. Kaptereva, Chief Librarian

Spain

1258   Biblioteca Nacional
        Sección de Africa y Mundo Arabe
        Paseo de Recoletos 20
        28071 Madrid
        Tel: +34-91-580 7800 (Main switchboard)
        Email: info@bne.es or
        (General enquiries) acceso@bne.es (Access
        services) bib@bne.es (Bibliographic
        Information Services) director.tecnico@bne.es
        (Head, Technical Services)
        Web: http://www.bne.es/ (Spanish version)
        http://www.bne.es/ingles/indice-fra.htm
        (English version)
        Contact: Head of Access Services

1259   Centro de Información y
        Documentación Africanas,
        Biblioteca
        C/. Gaztambide 31
        28015 Madrid
        Tel.: +34-91-544 1818
        Email: cidaf@planalfa.es
        Web:
        http://www3.planalfa.es/cidaf/bibliote1.ht
        m (English version)
        Contact: The Librarian

Sweden

1260   Nordiska Afrikainstitutet/The
        Nordic Africa Institute Library
        Kungsgatan 38
        PO Box 1703
        75147 Uppsala
        Tel: +46-18-562270 (General enquiries)
        +46-18-562272 (Chief Librarian)
        Fax: +46-18-562291
        Email: library@nai.uu.se (General enquiries)
        asa.lund-moberg@nai.uu.se (Chief Librarian)
        Web:
        http://www.nai.uu.se/bibl/bibleng.html
        (English version)
        Contact: Åsa Lund Moberg, Chief Librarian
        See also entries ➔ 76, 83

1261   Utrikespolitiska Institutet/The
        Swedish Institute of International
        Affairs, Anna Lindh Library
        Drottning Kristinas väg 37
        PO Box 27805
        11593 Stockholm
        Tel: +46-8-553 42560 Fax: +46-8-553 42568

Email: info@annalindhbiblioteket.se (General
enquiries)
ann-kristin.forsberg@fhs.se (Chief Librarian)
Web:
http://www.annalindhbiblioteket.se/english
/index.asp
Contact: Ann-Kristin Forsberg, Chief
Librarian

Switzerland

1262   Basler Afrika Bibliographien.
        Namibia Resource Centre-Southern
        Africa Library
        Klosterberg 21
        PO Box 2037
        4051 Basle
        Tel: +41-61-228 93 33 Fax: +41-61-228 93 30
        Email: library.bab@bluewin.ch
        Web:
        http://www.baslerafrika.ch/Bab_libr.html
        Contact: Dag Henrichsen
        See also entry ➔ 312

1263   Institut universitaire d'études du
        développement, Bibliothèque
        Roy Adrian Preiswerk
        20 rue Rothschild
        CP 136
        1211 Geneva 21
        Tel: +41-22-906 5940 (General enquiries)
        +41-22- 906 5920 (Head of Library)
        Fax: +41-22-906 5969/5947
        Email: biblio@iued.unige.ch (General
        enquiries) christine.wehrli@iued.unige.ch
        (Head of Library)
        Web:
        http://www.unige.ch/iued/new/informatio
        n/bibliotheque/
        Contact: Christine Wehrli, Head of Library

1264   International Labour Office, Central
        Library
        4 route des Morillons
        1211 Geneva 22
        Tel: +41-22-799 8682 (Information desk)
        +41-22-799 8625 (Director of the Library)
        Fax: +41-22-799 6516
        Email: inform@ilo.org
        Web:
        http://www.ilo.org/public/english/support
        /lib/index.htm (English version)

Contact: (Ms.) L. Dryden, Acting Chief of Library Services

1265   Mission 21, Bibliothek
Evangelisches Missionswerk Basel
Missionsstrasse 21
4003 Basle
Tel: +41-61-260 2121 (General enquiries)
+41-61-260 2241 (Library)
Fax: +41-61 260 21 22
Email: info@mission-21.org (General enquiries) marcus.buess@mission-21.org (Librarian) guy.thomas@mission-21.org (Head of Archives)
Web: http://www.mission-21.org/deutsch/50_bildung/40_archiv.php
Contacts: Marcus C. Buess, Librarian; Guy Thomas, Head of Archives

1266   Stadtbibliothek Winterthur Studienbibliothek
Museumstrasse 52
Postfach 132
8401 Winterthur
Tel: +41-52-267 5149/+41-52-267 5145
Fax: +41-52-267 5140
Email: stadtbibliothek@win.ch (General enquiries) harry.joelson@win.ch (Head of Studienbibliothek)
Web: http://www.winbib.ch/
Contacts: Harry Joelson-Strohbach, André Gasser

1267   United Nations Library at Geneva (UNOG Library)
Palais des Nations
1211 Geneva 10
Tel: +41-22-917 4181 (General enquiries)
+41-22-917 3615 (Chief, User Services and Documentation)
+41-22-917 2634 (UNOG Archives)
Fax: +41-22-917 0418 (UNOG Library)
+41-22-917 0664 (UNOG Archives)
Email: library@unog.ch (UNOG Library)
libraryarchives@unog.ch (UNOG Archives)
Web: http://www.unog.ch/library/start.htm
Contact: Chief, User Services and Documentation

1268   Zentralbibliothek Zürich
Zähringerplatz 6
80001 Zurich
Tel: +41-44-268 3100 Fax: +41-44-268 3290
Email: zb@zb.unizh.ch (General enquiries)
ludwig.kohler@zb.unizh.ch (Head, User Services)
Web: http://www-zb.unizh.ch/
Contact: Ludwig Kohler, Head, User Services

United Kingdom

1269   Bodleian Library of Commonwealth and African Studies at Rhodes House
South Parks Road
Oxford OX1 3RG
Tel: +44-(0)1865-270908 (General enquiries)
+44-(0)1865-282701 (Librarian)
Fax: +44-(0)1865-270912
Email: rhodes.house.library@bodley.ox.ac.uk (General enquiries)
john.pinfold@bodley.ox.ac.uk (Librarian)
Web: http://www.bodley.ox.ac.uk/dept/rhl/
Contact: John Pinfold, Librarian
See also entry ➔ **315**

1270   British Empire and Commonwealth Museum and Archives
British Empire & Commonwealth Museum
Clock Tower Yard
Temple Meads
Bristol BS1 6QH
Tel: +44-(0)117-925 4983
Fax: +44-(0)117-925 4980
Email: admin@empiremuseum.co.uk (General enquiries) archives@empiremuseum.co.uk (Paper and Oral History Archives) (resources@empiremuseum.co.uk Resource Centre
photo@empiremuseum.co.uk (Photographic Archive)
film@empiremuseum.co.uk (Film Archive)
Web: http://www.empiremuseum.co.uk/
Contacts: Mary Ingoldby, Oral history archive; Pippa Griffith, Artefacts & documents collections; Joanna Hopkins, Photographic archive; Jan Vaughan, Film archive

1271 British Library, Asia, Pacific & Africa Collections
(formerly Oriental & India Office Collections)
St. Pancras
96 Euston Road
London NW1 2DB
Tel: +44-(0)20-7412 7873 (General enquiries)
Fax: +44-(0)20-7412 7563
Tel: +44-(0)20-7412 7829 (Curator of African Collections)
Email: oioc-enquiries@bl.uk (Asia, Pacific & Africa Collections (General enquiries)
Marion.Wallace@bl.uk (Curator of African Collections)
Web:
http://www.bl.uk/collections/african.html
Contact: Marion Wallace, Curator of African Collections
Note: this Web site relates specifically to Africana collections, including printed books and newspapers, audio, maps, pictures, photographs, stamps, bibliography, manuscripts and archives.

1272 British Library for Development Studies
Institute for Development Studies
University of Sussex
Brighton BN1 9RE
Tel: +44-(0)1273-678263
Fax: +44-(0)1273-621202/691647
Email: blds@ids.ac.uk (General enquiries)
m.g.bloom@ids.ac.uk (Head of Library)
Web: http://www.ids.ac.uk/blds/index.html
Contact: Michael Bloom, Head of Library

1273 British Museum Anthropology Library (formerly British Museum Ethnography Library)
Department of Africa, Oceania and the Americas
The British Museum
Great Russell Street
London WC1B 3DG
Tel: +44-(0)20-7323 8041/44 (General enquiries) +44-(0)20-7323 8069 (Senior Librarian) Fax: +44(0)20-7323 8013
Email: ethnography@thebritishmuseum.ac.uk (General enquiries)
smackie@thebritishmuseum.ac.uk (Senior Librarian)
Web:
http://www.thebritishmuseum.ac.uk/ethno/ethservlib.html
Contact: Sheila Mackie, Senior Librarian

1274 Commonwealth Secretariat Library
Marlborough House
Pall Mall
London SW1Y 5HX
Tel: +44-(0)20-7747 6253 (Librarian)
+44-(0)20-7747 6167 (Archivist)
Fax: +44-(0)20-7747 6168
Email: library@commonwealth.int (General enquiries) d.blake@commonwealth.int (Librarian)
Web:
http://www.thecommonwealth.org/Templates/Internal.asp?NodeID=36252 (Library and Archives pages)
Contacts: David Blake, Librarian; Matti Watton, Archivist

1275 Department of International Development, DFID Library
Room AH 219
Abercrombie House
Eaglesham Road
East Kilbride
Glasgow G75 8EA
Tel: +44-(0)1355-843880/843272
Fax: +44-(0)1355-843632
Email: library@dfid.gov.uk (main DFID home page)
Web: http://www.dfid.gov.uk
Contact: R. Martin, Librarian

1276 Durham University Library
Stockton Road
Durham DH1 3LY
Tel: +44-(0)191-334 2968
Fax: +44-(0)191-334 2971
Email: main.library@durham.ac.uk (General enquiries) m.a.sunuodula@durham.ac.uk (Area Studies Librarian)
Web: http://www.dur.ac.uk/library/
Contact: Mamtimyn Sunuodula, Area Studies Librarian

1277 Edinburgh University Library
George Square
Edinburgh EH8 9LJ
Tel: +44-(0)131-650 3409/3384
Fax: +44-(0)131-667 9780
Email: Library@ed.ac.uk (General enquiries) or f.abercromby@ed.ac.uk (Librarian, College of Humanities and Social Sciences)
Denny.Colledge@ed.ac.uk (African Studies Liaison Librarian)

Web: http://www.lib.ed.ac.uk
Contacts: Frances Abercromby, Librarian,
College of Humanities and Social Sciences;
Denny Colledge, African Studies Liaison
Librarian

**1278 Foreign and Commonwealth Office
Library**
Room E213
King Charles Street
London SW1A 2AH
Tel: +44-(0)20-7008 3925
Fax: +44-(0)20-7008 3270
Email: library.enquiries@fco.gov.uk
Web:
http://www.fco.gov.uk/servlet/Front?page
name=OpenMarket/Xcelerate/ShowPage&c
=Page&cid=1056724715645
Contact: Stephen Latham, Chief Librarian

**1279 Institute of Commonwealth Studies
Library**
University of London School of
Advanced Studies
28 Russell Square
London WC1B 5DS
Tel: +44-(0)20-7862 8842 (Library reading
room desk)
Fax: +44-(0)20-7862 8820
Email: icommlib@sas.ac.uk
Web:
http://www.sas.ac.uk/commonwealthstudie
s/library.htm
Contacts: David Parker, Collections Librarian;
Julie McCaffery Resources Development
Librarian

**1280 Institute of Education, Library &
Information Services**
University of London
20 Bedford Way
London WC1H 0AL
Tel: +44-(0)20-7612 6080/6087
Fax: +44-(0)20-7612 6093
Email: lib.enquiries@ioe.ac.uk (General
enquiries) stan.smith@ioe.ac.uk (Head of
Information Services) d.guthrie@ioe.ac.uk
(Comparative Education Librarian)
Web:
http://ioewebserver.ioe.ac.uk/ioe/cms/get.a
sp?cid=10713
Contacts: Stan Smith, Head of Information
Services
Diana Guthrie, Comparative Education
Librarian

→ **International Development Centre
Library, Queen Elizabeth House,
Oxford** see **Oxford University. Social
Science Library (1284)**

**1281 London School of Economics &
Political Science. British Library of
Political and Economic Science**
10 Portugal Street
London WC2A 2HD
Tel.: +44-(0)20-7955 7229
Fax: +44-(0)20-7955 7454
Email: library@lse.ac.uk
Web: http://www.lse.ac.uk/library/
Contacts: Jean Sykes, Librarian and Director
of Information Services; or Clive Wilson,
Librarian

1282 The National Archives
(formerly Public Record Office)
Kew
Richmond TW9 4DU
Tel: +44-(0)20-8876 3444
Fax: +44-(0)-20-8392 5286
Email: use contact form on Web site
Web: http://www.nationalarchives.gov.uk/
(Main home page)
http://www.nationalarchives.gov.uk/partne
rprojects/casbah/default.htm (Caribbean
Studies and Black and Asian
History/CASBAH pages, see also
http://www.nationalarchives.gov.uk/pathw
ays/blackhistory/about.htm (Black Presence
pages)
Contact: Natalie Ceeney, Chief Executive;
Mandy Banton, Research, Knowledge and
Academic Services Department; or see
departmental information at
http://www.nationalarchives.gov.uk/contac
t/departments.htm
Note: The National Archives of England,
Wales and the United Kingdom was formed
in April 2003 by bringing together the Public
Record Office and the Historical Manuscripts
Commission. It has one of the largest archival
collections in the world, spanning 1,000 years
of British history, from the Domesday Book of
1086 to government papers recently released
to the public. Under the Freedom of
Information Act, anyone in the world can
request information held at The National
Archives. There is also a separate Web site of
the National Archives of Scotland at
http://www.nas.gov.uk/.

1283   National Maritime Museum,
        Caird Library
        Park Row
        Greenwich
        London SE10 9NF
Tel: +44-(0)20-8312 6528 (General library
enquiries)
Tel: +44-(0)20-8312 6516 (E-Library)
Email:library@nmm.ac.uk (Library items)
manuscripts@nmm.ac.uk (Manuscript items)
bdthyn@nmm.ac.uk (Charts and maps)
Web:
http://www.nmm.ac.uk/server/show/con
WebDoc.11602
Contact: Margarette Lincoln, Director of
Research for Collections and Curatorial
Development

1284   Oxford University. Social
        Science Library
        Centre for Advanced Studies in the
        Social Sciences
        Manor Road Building
        Manor Road
        Oxford OX1 3UQ
Tel: +44-(0)1865-271093
Fax: +44-(0)1865-271072
Email: library@ssl.ox.ac.uk (General
enquiries) margaret.robb@ssl.ox.ac.uk
(Social Sciences Librarian)
susan.pemberton@ssl.ox.ac.uk International
Development Subject Consultant
Web: http://www.ssl.ox.ac.uk/default.htm
Contacts: Margaret Robb, Social Sciences
Librarian; Susan Pemberton, International
Development Subject Consultant
Note: the Social Science Library now
incorporates the collections of the former
International Development Centre Library at
Queen Elizabeth House, Oxford.

1285   Overseas Development Institute
        Library
        111 Westminster Bridge Road
        London SE1 7JD
Tel: +44-(0)20-7922 0300
Fax: +44-(0)20-7922 0399
Email: library@odi.org.uk
Web: http://www.odi.org.uk/library.html
Contact: Kate Kwafo-Akoto, Librarian

1286   Oxfam Library
        Oxfam House
        John Smith Drive
        Cowley
        Oxford OX4 2JY
Tel: +44-(0)-1865 473757
Email: rbuck@oxfam.org.uk
http://www.oxfam.org.uk/about_us/library
.htm
Contact: Ros Buck, Librarian

→ Public Record Office *see* The National
Archives (1282)

→ Rhodes House Library *see* Bodleian
Library of Commonwealth and African
Studies at Rhodes House (1269)

1287   Royal Commonwealth Society
        Collections
        Cambridge University Library
        West Road
        Cambridge CB3 9
Tel: +44-(0)1223-333000/333198
Fax: +44(0)1223-333160
Email: library@lib.cam.ac.uk
Web:
http://www.lib.cam.ac.uk/Handbook/D2.ht
ml
Contact: The Librarian
see also → University of Cambridge. African
Studies Centre Library (1291)

1288   Royal Institute of International
        Affairs, Library
        Chatham House
        10 St James Square
        London SW1Y 4LE
Tel: +44-(0)20-7957 5723 (General enquiries)
+44-(0)20-7957 5720 (Librarian)
Fax: +44-(0)20-7957 5710
Email: libenquire@chathamhouse.org.uk
Web: http://www.riia.org/index.php?id=8
Contacts: Catherine Hume, Sue Franks

1289   School of Oriental and African
        Studies, Library
        University of London
        Thornhaugh Street
        Russell Square
        London WC1H 0XG
Tel: +44-(0)20-7898 4163 (General enquiries)
Tel: +44-(0)20-7898 4157 (African Studies
Librarian) Fax: +44-(0)20-7898 4159
Email: libenquiry@soas.ac.uk (General

enquiries) bs24@soas.ac.uk (African Studies Librarian)
Web: http://lib.soas.ac.uk/
Contact: Barbara Spina, African Studies Librarian (and Faculty Librarian: Law & Social Sciences)
See also entries ➔ 444, 460

1290   University of Birmingham,
Main Library
Information Services
Edgbaston
Birmingham B15 2TT
Tel: +44(0)121-414 5828
Fax: +44(0)121-471 4691
Email: library@bham.ac.uk (General enquiries) k.j.jackson@bham.ac.uk (Arts Liaison Librarian)
Web: http://www.is.bham.ac.uk/mainlib/ (Main library home page)
http://www.bham.ac.uk/WestAfricanStudies/cwaslib.htm   (Centre of West African Studies)
Contact: Karen Jackson, Arts Liaison Librarian

1291   University of Cambridge,
Centre of African Studies Library
Free School Lane
Cambridge CB2 3RQ
Tel: +44-(0)1223-334398
Fax: +44-(0)1223-334396
Email: afrlib@hermes.cam.ac.uk (General enquiries) meg23@cam.ac.uk (Librarian)
Web:
http://www.african.cam.ac.uk/library/
Contact: Marilyn Glanfield, Librarian
See also ➔ **Royal Commonwealth Society Collections (1287)**

1292   University of Leeds,
The Brotherton Library
Leeds LS2 9JT
Tel: +44-(0)1133-343 5663 (General enquiries)
Fax: +44(0)1133-343 5561
Email: libraryenquiries@leeds.ac.uk (General enquiries) j.wilkinson@leeds.ac.uk (University Librarian)
Web:
http://www.leeds.ac.uk/library/news/newsite.htm
Contact: Janet Morton, Social Sciences Faculty Team Librarian

1293   University of Manchester,
John Rylands Library
Oxford Road
Manchester M13 9PP
Tel: +44-(0)161-275 3751 (General enquiries)
+44-(0)161-275 3737 (Deputy Librarian and Head, Information Resources and Services)
+44-(0)161-275 3769 (Academic Liaison Librarian for Government, International Politics and Philosophy)
Fax: +44-(0)161-273 7488
Email: libtalk@man.ac.uk (General enquiries) diana.leitch@man.ac.uk (Deputy Librarian and Head, Information Resources and Services) hector.blackhurst@man.ac.uk (Academic Liaison Librarian for Government, International Politics and Philosophy)
Web: http://www.library.manchester.ac.uk/
Contacts: Diana Leitch, Deputy Librarian and Head, Information Resources and Services; Hector Blackhurst, Academic Liaison Librarian for Government, International Politics and Philosophy

1294   University of Portsmouth,
Frewen Library
Cambridge Road
Portsmouth PO1 2ST
Tel: +44-(0)23-9284 3222
Fax: +44--(0)23-9284 3233
Email: library@port.ac.uk (General enquiries) anne.worden@port.ac.uk (Subject Librarian)
Web: http://www.libr.port.ac.uk/
Contact: Anne Worden, Subject Librarian, Languages and Area Studies, Social and Political Studies, Geography

NORTH AMERICA

Canada

1295   Carleton University,
Maxwell MacOdrum Library
1125 Colonel By Drive
Ottawa ON K1S 5B6
Tel: +1-613-520 2735 (Information desk)
+1-613-520 8148 (Reference Services
Department) Fax: +1-613-520 2750
Email: joanne_cameron@carleton.ca
Web: http://www.library.carleton.ca
Contact: Joanne Cameron, Reference Services
Department

1296   International Development
Research Center Library
250 Albert Street 9th floor
PO Box 8500
Ottawa ON K1G 3H9
Tel: +1-613-236 6163 ext 2578
Fax: +1-613-563 3858
Email: reference@idrc.ca
Web: http://www.idrc.ca/en/ev-8564-201-1-
DO_TOPIC.html (English version)
Contact: Hélène De Celles, Research Librarian

1297   McGill University Libraries,
Humanities and Social Sciences
Library
3459 McTavish Street
Montréal QC H3A 1Y1
Tel: +1-514-398 4734 Fax: +1-514-398 7184
Email: mclennan.library@mcgill.ca (General
enquiries) anastassia.khouri@mcgill.ca
(Access Services Librarian)
Web:
http://www.library.mcgill.ca/human/hssl.h
tm
Contact: Anastassia Khouri, Access Services
Librarian

1298   York University Libraries
4700 Keele Street
Toronto ON M3J 1P3
Tel: +1-416-736 5150
Email: library@yorku.ca
Web:
http://www.library.yorku.ca/Home/About
/index.htm
Contact: Lisa Sloniowski, Reference Librarian
See also entry ➔ **43**

United States

1299   Atlanta University Centre,
Robert W. Woodruff Library
111 James P. Brawley Drive S
Atlanta GA 30314
Tel: +1-404-522 8980 ext 1171
Fax: +1-404-577 5158
Email: akilah@auctr.edu
Web: http://www.auctr.edu/
Contact: Akilah S. Nosakhere, Special
Collections Librarian

1300   Boston University,
African Studies Library
Mugar Memorial Library 6th floor
771 Commonwealth Avenue
Boston MA 02215
Tel: +1-617-353 3726 Fax: +1-617-353 2084
Email: gwalsh@bu.edu
Web:
http://www.bu.edu/library/asl/index.html
Contact: Gretchen Walsh, Head, African
Studies Library
See also entries ➔ **65, 126, 501**

1301   Brown University,
John D. Rockefeller Library
10 Prospect Street
Box A
Providence RI 02912-9109
Tel: +401-863 2165 (General enquiries)
+1-401-863-2976/863 2515 (Reference
Librarian/Africana Studies Specialist)
Fax: +1-401-863 1272
Email: Steven_L_Thompson@brown.edu
(Reference Librarian/Africana Studies
Specialist)
Web:
http://www.brown.edu/Facilities/Universit
y_Library/
Contact: Steven L. Thompson, Reference
Librarian/Africana Studies Specialist

1302   Center for Research Libraries
6050 South Kenwood Avenue
Chicago IL 60637-2804
Tel: +1-773-955 4545 ext 324
Fax: +1-773-955 4339
Email: simon@crl.edu
Web: http://www.crl.edu/
Contact: James T. Simon, Director of
International Studies (and Collaborative
Collection Development Programs)

Note: CRL is a consortium of North American universities, colleges, and independent research libraries. The consortium acquires and preserves traditional and digital resources for research and teaching and makes them available to member institutions through interlibrary loan and electronic delivery.
See also entries ➜ **92, 139, 1899**

1303   Columbia University,
           Lehman Library
           308 Lehman Library
           International Affairs Building
           Mail Code 3301
           420 West 118th Street
           New York NY 10027
Tel: +1-212-854 8045 Fax: +1-212-854 3834
Email: africa@libraries.cul.columbia.edu
(General enquiries) caruso@columbia.edu
(African Studies Librarian)
Web:
http://www.columbia.edu/cu/lweb/indiv/africa/
Contact: Joseph Caruso, African Studies Librarian
See also entries ➜ **80, 140, 181**

1304   Cornell University, Africana Studies
           and Research Center, J.H. Clarke
           Africana Library
           University Library
           310 Triphammer Road
           Ithaca NY 14850-2599
Tel: +1-607-255 3822 (General enquiries)
+1-607-255 5229 (Librarian)
Fax: +1-607-255 0784
Email: afrlib@cornell.edu (J.H. Clarke Africana Library)
Web:
http://www.library.cornell.edu/africana
Contact: Eric Kofi Acree, Librarian, J.H. Clarke Africana Library
See also entry➜ **531**

1305   Dartmouth College,
           Baker/Berry Library
           Hinman Box 6025
           Hanover NH 03755-3525
Tel: +1-603-646 2560 (General enquiries)
+1-603-646 2560 (Head of Access Services)
Fax: +1-603-646 3702
Email: jennifer.taxman@dartmouth.edu
(Head of Access Services) or use online email enquiry form

Web: http://diglib.dartmouth.edu/
Contacts: Jennifer Taxman, Head of Access Services; Amy Witzel, African/African American Studies Subject Specialist

1306   Duke University, Perkins Library
           International and Area Studies
           Perkins Library
           Box 90195
           Durham NC 27708
Tel: +1-919-660 5922 Fax: +1-919-684 2855
Email: k.j.hunt@duke.edu
Web: http://www.lib.duke.edu/ias/africa/
Contact: Karen Jean Hunt, Subject Librarian for African and African American Studies
(and Director, John Hope Franklin Collection)

1307   Emory University,
           Robert W. Woodruff Library
           540 Asbury Circle
           Atlanta GA 30322
Tel: +1-404-727 6875 (General enquiries)
+1-404-727 6953 (Librarian for African Studies and Sociology)
Fax: +1-404-727 0408
Email: libemb@emory.edu
Web: http://web.library.emory.edu/
Contact: Elizabeth A. McBride, Librarian for African Studies and Sociology
See also entry➜ **529**

1308   Georgia State University,
           William Russell Pullen Library
           100 Decatur Street SE
           Atlanta GA 30303-3202
Tel: +1-404-651 2422 (General enquiries) Tel:
+1-404-463 9940 (African American Studies Liaison Librarian)
Fax: +1-404-651 2508
Email: libmeh@gsu.edu (African American Studies Liaison Librarian)
Web: http://wwwlib.gsu.edu/
Contact: Elaine Hughes, African American Studies Liaison Librarian

1309   Harvard College Library,
           Widener Library
           Sub-Saharan Africa Collection
           Development Department
           Widener Library Room 197
           Cambridge MA 02138
Tel: +1-617-495 3559 Fax: +1-617-495 0403
Email: jcoelho@fas.harvard.edu
Web:

http://hcl.harvard.edu/libraries/widener/c
ollections/subsaharan.html
Contact: Jill Young Coelho, Librarian for Sub-
Saharan Africa

**1310   Harvard University,
          Tozzer Library**
          21 Divinity Avenue
          Cambridge MA 02138-2089
Tel: +1-617-495 2253
Fax: +1-617-496 2741
Email: tozref@fas.harvard.edu (General
enquiries)
gregory_finnegan@harvard.edu
(Associate Librarian for Public Services and
Head of Reference)
Web: http://hcl.harvard.edu/tozzer
Contact: Gregory A. Finnegan, Associate
Librarian for Public Services and Head of
Reference

→ Hoover Institution Library and Archives
see **Stanford University Libraries (1327)**

**1311   Howard University,
          Founders Library**
          500 Howard Place NW
          Washington DC 20059
Tel: +1-202-806 7234 (Main Library)
+1-202-806 7252 (Reference Desk)
Fax: +1-202-806 6405
Email: cguyton@howard.edu (Manager,
Access Services) sfauntroy@howard.edu
(African Studies subject specialist)
Web: http://www.howard.edu/library/
Contacts: Clara L. Guyton, Manager, Access
Services; Sarah Fauntroy, African Studies
subject specialist

**1312   Howard University, Moorland
          Springarn Research Center**
          500 Howard Place NW
          Washington DC 20059
Tel: +1-202-806 7240 Fax: +1-202-806 6405
Email: jchurch@howard.edu
Web:
http://www.founders.howard.edu/moorlan
d-spingarn/
Contact: Jean Currie Church, Chief Librarian

**1313   Indiana University Libraries,
          Wells Library**
          Wells Library E 660
          1320 East 10th Street
          Bloomington IN 47405-3907

Tel: +1-812-855 1481 Fax: +1-812-855 8068
Email: mfrankwi@indiana.edu
Web:
http://www.libraries.iub.edu/index.php?pa
geId=322
Contact: Marion Frank-Wilson, Librarian for
African Studies
See also entries **→ 354, 439, 450, 506, 1917**

**1314   Johns Hopkins University
          Paul H. Nitze School of Advanced
          International Studies
          Sydney R. and Elsa W. Mason
          Library**
          1740 Massachusetts Ave. NW
          Washington DC 20036
Tel: +1-202-663 5900 (General enquiries)
+1-202-663-5905 (Director of the Library)
Email: saislibrary@jhu.edu (General
enquiries)
sthalhimer@jhu.edu (Director of the Library)
Web: http://www.sais-
jhu.edu/library/index.html
Contact: Sheila Thalhimer, Director of the
Library

1315   Joint Bank Fund Library
          International Monetary Fund and
          World Bank Group Libraries
          700 19th Street NW
          Room IMF C-700
          Washington DC 20431
Tel: +1-202-623 7054 (Information desk)
Fax: +1-202-623 6417
Email: libsyssupport@imf.org (General
enquiries) ianderson@imf.org (Librarian)
Web:
http://jolis.worldbankimflib.org/external.ht
m (Main home page)
http://jolis.worldbankimflib.org/e-
nldirect.htm (Links to the 11 libraries
that belong to the Library Network at the
World Bank Group and IMF Headquarters
Contact: Iris W. Anderson, Document
Delivery Team Leader and Librarian, Joint
World Bank-International Monetary Fund

**1316   Library of Congress, African and
          Middle Eastern Division**
          Room LJ 220
          Thomas Jefferson Building
          101 Independence Avenue SE
          Washington DC 20540-4820
Tel: +1-202-707 7937 (Administrative offices),
+1-202-707 4188 (Reading room),

+1-202-707 5528 (African section)
Fax: +1-202-252 3180/1724
Email: amed@loc.gov
Web: http://lcweb.loc.gov/rr/amed/
(African & Middle Eastern Division home
page)
http://www.loc.gov/rr/amed/afs/afshome.
html (African section)
Contacts: Mary-Jane Deeb, Chief; Area
Specialists, African section: Angel Batiste,
Marieta L. Harper, Mattye Laverne Page,
Joanne Zellers
Note: for email addresses/telephone contacts
and staff assignments for African countries *see*
http://www.loc.gov/rr/amed/afs/afsrefac.
html
See also entries ➔ **88, 89, 94, 133, 309, 389**
➔ **Library of Congress Office, Nairobi** (and
Cairo) *see* **1890**

**1317   Michigan State University Libraries,
Africana Library**
East Lansing MI 48824-1048
Tel: +1-517-432 6123 exts 237/239
Fax: +1-517-432 3532
Email: lauer@msu.edu (Africana Librarian)
limb@msu.edu (Bibliographer)
Web:
http://www.lib.msu.edu/coll/main/african
a
Contacts: Joe Lauer, Africana Librarian; Peter
Limb, Bibliographer
See also entries ➔ **77, 112, 125, 161, 528**

**1318   National Museum of African Art,
Warren M. Robbins Library**
Smithsonian Institution
Room   2138
950 Independence Avenue SW
Washington DC 20560
Tel: +1-202-633 4680 (General enquiries,
appointments) Tel: +1-202-633 4681 (Head of
Library) Fax: +1-202-357 4879
Email: libmail@si.edu (General enquiries)
jstanley@nmafa.si.edu (Head of Library)
Web:
http://www.sil.si.edu/libraries/nmafa/
Contact: Janet L. Stanley, Head of Library
See also entry ➔ **53**

**1319   New York Public Library,
Schomburg Center for Research in
Black Culture**
515 Malcolm X Blvd
New York NY 10037-1801
Tel: +1-212-491 2200 (General enquiries)
+1-212-491 2218 Associate Chief Librarian,
General Research and Reference Division
Fax: +1-212-491 6760
Email: scgenref@nypl.org (General enquiries)
gmclaurin@nypl.org (Associate Chief
Librarian, General Research and Reference
Division)
Web:
http://www.nypl.org/research/sc/sc.html
Contact: G. McLaurin, Associate Chief
Librarian, General Research and Reference
Division
See also entries ➔ **220, 313**

**1320   New York University,
Elmer Holmes Bobst Library**
70 Washington Square South
New York NY 10012
Tel: +1-212-998 2505 (General enquiries)
 +1-212-998 2436 (Librarian for Africana
Studies) Fax: +1-212-995 4366
Email: timothy.johnson@nyu.edu
Web:
http://www.nyu.edu/library/bobst/researc
h/soc/africa/
Contact: Timothy Johnson, Librarian for
Africana Studies, Anthropology and Food
Studies

**1321   Northern Illinois University,
Founders Memorial Library**
DeKalb IL 60115-2868
Tel: +1-815-753 1995 (Main switchboard)
+1-815-753-1689 (Social Sciences and
Humanities)
Fax: +1-815-753 9845
Email: lib-admin@niu.edu
Web: http://www.niulib.niu.edu/
Contacts: Charles Larry, Department Head,
Social Sciences and Humanities;
Robert Ridinger, Electronic Info Resources
Management

1322   Northwestern University Library,
        Melville J. Herskovits Library of
        African Studies
        1970 Campus Drive Evanston
        IL 60208-2300
Tel: +1-847-467 3084 (Reference desk) +1-847-
491 7684 (Office) +1-847-491 4549 (Curator)
+1-847-491 2936 (Librarian of Africana)
+1-847-491 3941 (Africana Bibliographer) Fax:
+1-847-467 1233
Email: africana@northwestern.edu (General
enquiries) dleaster@northwestern.edu
(George and Mary LeCron Foster Curator)
p-ogedengbe@northwestern.edu (Librarian of
Africana) ekale@northwestern.edu (Africana
Bibliographer)
Web:
http://www.library.northwestern.edu/africa
na/
Contacts: David L. Easterbrook, George and
Mary LeCron Foster Curator; Patricia
Ogedengbe, Librarian of Africana; Esmeralda
M. Kale, Africana Bibliographer
See also entries ➜ 42, 155, 159, 230, 394, 395,
440, 534

1323   Ohio State University Libraries,
        Black Studies Library
        William Oxley Thompson
        Library Room 240
        1858 Neil Avenue Mall
        Columbus OH 43210-1286
Tel: +1-614-688 8676
Fax: +1-614-292 7859
Email: conteh-morgan.2@osu.edu (African
Studies Collection Manager)
krikos.1@osu.edu (African American Studies
Collection Manager)
Web:
http://library.osu.edu/sites/blackstudies/In
dex.html
Contacts: Miriam Conteh-Morgan, African
Studies Collection Manager; Linda Krikos,
African American Studies Collection Manager
Note: the future of the Black Studies Library,
as an independent unit of OSU libraries, is
apparently under threat see
http://library.osu.edu/sites/blackstudies/B
SLDisolution.html

1324   Ohio University Libraries,
        Alden Library
        Center for International Collections
        Athens OH 45701-2978
Tel: +1-740-593 2699 (General enquiries)
+1-740-597 1317 (Africana Bibliographer) Fax:
+1-740-593 2708
Email: mbabu@ohiou.edu
Web:
http://www.library.ohiou.edu/subjects/afri
ca/asubmain.htm
Contact: Loyd Mbabu, Africana Bibliographer
See also entry ➜ 63

1325   Princeton University Library,
        Firestone Library
        Princeton NJ 08544-2098
Tel: +1-609- 609 258 1470 (General enquiries)
+1-609-258 5962 (African Studies Selector)
Fax: +1-609-258 0441/4105
Email: pressman@princeton.edu
Web:
http://libweb.princeton.edu/libraries/firesto
ne.php and
http://www.princeton.edu/~pressman/afric
a.html
Contact: Nancy Pressman Levy, Librarian,
General and Humanities Reference, and
African Studies Selector

1326   Rutgers University,
        Archibald S. Alexander Library
        169 College Avenue
        New Brunswick NJ 08901-1163
Tel: +1-732-932 7851 (General enquiries)
+1-732-932 7129 (Latin America, Spanish &
Portuguese, and Africa Librarian)
Fax: +1-732- 932 1101
Email: lvazquez@rci.rutgers.edu
Web:
http://www.libraries.rutgers.edu/rul/libs/a
lex_lib/alex_lib.shtml
and
http://www.libraries.rutgers.edu/rul/rr_gat
eway/research_guides/africana/africana.sht
ml
Contact: Lourdes Vazquez, Latin America,
Spanish & Portuguese, and Africa Librarian

1327   Stanford University Libraries/
        Hoover Institution Library and
        Archives
        African Collection
        Green Library SSRC 121
        Stanford CA 94305-6004
Tel: +1-650-725 3505
Fax: +1-650-723 9348
Email: kfung@stanford.edu
Web: http://www-
sul.stanford.edu/depts/ssrg/africa/africa.ht
ml
and http://www.hoover.org/hila/africa.htm
Contact: Karen Fung, Curator, African
Collection
See also entries → **69, 493**

→ **State University of New York at Albany
Libraries** *see* **University at Albany Libraries,
The State University of New York (1331)**

→ **State University of New York at Buffalo
Libraries** *see* **University at Buffalo Libraries,
The State University of New York (1332)**

1328   State University of New York at
        New Paltz, Sojourner Truth Library
        75 South Manheim Boulevard
        New Paltz NY 12561-2493
Tel: +1-845-257 3700 (General enquiries)
+1-845-257 3681 (Interlibrary Loan Librarian)
Fax: +1-845-257 3712
Email: nyquistc@newpaltz.edu
Web: http://lib.newpaltz.edu/
Contact: Corinne Nyquist, Interlibrary Loan
Librarian

1329   Syracuse University,
        Ernest Stevenson Bird Library
        222 Waverly Avenue
        Syracuse NY 13244-2010
        and
        Martin Luther King, jr. Memorial
        Library
        Department of African American
        Studies
        200 Sims Hall V
        Syracuse NY 13244-1230
Tel: +1-315-443 2093 (Bird Library)
+1-315-443 9349 (Martin Luther King jr.
Memorial Library) +1-315-443 9349 (Africa
and African-American Bibliographer) Fax: +1-
315-443 9510 (Bird Library) +1- 315-443 1725
(Martin Luther King jr. Memorial Library)

Email: bcryan@library.syr.edu (Associate
Librarian, African/African-American Studies)
MLK@cas.syr.edu (Martin Luther King jr.
Memorial Library, General enquiries)
aawillia@mailbox.syr.edu (Librarian,)
Web: http://libwww.syr.edu/ (Bird Library)
http://aas.syr.edu/mlk/index.html (Martin
Luther King jr. Memorial Library)
Contacts: Bonnie Ryan, Associate Librarian,
African/African-American Studies, E.S. Bird
Library; Angela Williams, Librarian, Martin
Luther King jr. Memorial Library

1330   United Nations,
        Dag Hammarskjöld Library
        Consortium & Collections Unit,
        Room L-360
        405 East 42nd Street
        New York NY 10017
Tel: +1-212-963 1457 (Help line for
non-United Nations users) +1-212 963
5321 (UN related queries only)
Fax: +1-212-963 8861 (Chief Users Services
Section) +1- 212-963 7394 (Reference desk,
authorized users only)
Email: for general enquiries use email form
on Web site; Dickstein@un.org (Head
Librarian) dhluss@un.org (Chief, Users
Services Section)
Web: http://www.un.org/Depts/dhl/
Contact: as above; or Phyllis Dickstein, Head
Librarian

1331   University at Albany Libraries
        State University of New York
        1400 Washington Avenue
        Albany NY 12222-0001
Tel: +1-518-442 3599
Fax: +1-518-442 3567
Email: dlafond@uamail.albany.edu
Web:
http://library.albany.edu/subject/africana_
main.html
Contact: Deborah M. LaFond, Social Sciences
Bibliographer
See also entry → **62**

1332   University at Buffalo Libraries
        The State University of New York
        321 Lockwood Library North
        Campus
        Buffalo NY 14260
Tel: +1-716-645 645 2814 ext 424
Fax: +1-716-645 3859
Email: lclcharl@buffalo.edu

Web:
http://ublib.buffalo.edu/libraries/
Contact: Charles D'Aniello, Associate
Librarian, Arts and Science Libraries

1333 **University of California-Berkeley,**
Doe Library
224 Doe Library
Berkeley CA 94720
Tel: +1-510-643 0398 Fax: +1-510-643 6650
Email: akautzma@library.berkeley.edu
Web:
http://www.lib.berkeley.edu/doemoff/afric
ana/
Contact: Amy Kautzman, Library Liaison,
African Studies, & Head, Reference, Research
and Collections
See also entries ➜ **64, 124, 503, 532, 533**

1334 **University of California-Irvine,**
Main Library
Main Library – Zot 8100
PO Box 19557
Irvine CA 92623-9557
Tel: +1-949-824 6836 (General enquiries)
+1-949-824 4969 (Social Sciences Librarian)
Email: pdmanaka@uci.edu
Web: http://www.lib.uci.edu/
Contact: Pauline Manaka, Social Sciences
Librarian, Langson Library, Reference

1335 **University of California-Los**
Angeles, Charles E. Young Research
Library
PO Box 951575
Los Angeles CA 90095-1575
Tel: +1-310-825 1201 (General enquiries)
+1-310-825 1518 (African Studies &
Development Studies Bibliographer)
+1-310-825-5096 (Librarian for African
American Studies)
Fax: +1-310-206 4974
Email: rbellgam@library.ucla.edu or
miki@library.ucla.edu
Web:
http://www.library.ucla.edu/libraries/yrl/
Contacts: Ruby Bell-Gam, African Studies &
Development Studies Bibliographer; Miki
Goral, Librarian for African American
Studies, World Arts & Cultures & Public
Services Coordinator, Reference Department

1336 **University of California-Santa**
Barbara, Information Services/
Library
Santa Barbara CA 93106-9010
Tel: +1-805- 893 2478 (General enquiries)
+1-805-893 8022 (Collection Manager for
Black Studies)
Fax: +1-805-893 4676
Email: ask@library.ucsb.edu (General
enquiries) curtis@library.ucsb.edu (Black
Studies Librarian)
Web: http://www.library.ucsb.edu/
Contact: Sylvia Y. Curtis, Collection Manager
for Black Studies and Dance

1337 **University of Florida, George A.**
Smathers Libraries
Library East, 2nd floor
University of Florida
PO Box 117001
Gainesville FL 32611-7001
Tel: +1-352-392 9075 exts 109 & 110
Fax: +1-352-846 2746/2762
Email: petmala@uflib.ufl.edu or
danrebo@uflib.ufl.edu
Web:
http://www.uflib.ufl.edu/cm/africana/
Contacts: Peter Malanchuk, Africana and
Political Science Bibliographer; Daniel A.
Reboussin, Assistant in African Area Studies
Note: Library West closed in December 2003
for two years.
See also entry ➜ **435**

1338 **University of Illinois Urbana-**
Champaign Library
Africana Room 328 Library
1408 West Gregory Drive
Urbana IL 61801
Tel: +1-217-333 6519 Fax: +1-217-333 2214
Email: akagan@uiuc.edu
Web: http://www.afrst.uiuc.edu/lib.html
Contact: Alfred Kagan, Africana
Bibliographer
See also entries ➜ **78, 136, 492**

1339 **University of Iowa Libraries**
100 Main Library
Iowa City IA 52242-1420
Tel: +1-319-335 5299 (Information Desk)
+1-319- 335 5867 (Administrative offices)
+1-319-335 5883 (International Studies
Librarian)
Fax: +1-319-335 5900

Email: edward-miner@uiowa.edu
Web: http://www.lib.uiowa.edu
Contact: Edward A. Miner, International
Studies Librarian
See also entries ➔ 29, 79

1340   University of Kansas,
        Anschutz Library
        1425 Jayhawk Boulevard
        Lawrence KS 66045-7544
Tel: +1-785-864 3506 (General enquiries)
+1-785-864 4593 (Africana Bibliographer) Fax:
+1-785-864-5311
Email: libweb@ku.edu (General enquiries)
klohrentz@ukansas.edu (African/African
American Studies Librarian)
Web: http://www.lib.ku.edu/
Contact: Kenneth P. Lohrentz,
African/African American Studies Librarian
See also entry➔ 68

1341   University of Michigan,
        Harlan Hatcher Graduate Library
        214-C Graduate Library
        920 North University
        Ann Arbor MI 48109-1205
Tel: +1-734-764 0400 (General enquiries)
+1-734-764 7289 (African Studies Librarian)
Fax: +1-734-764 0259
Email: apaulos@umich.edu
Web: http://www.lib.umich.edu/grad/
Contact: Afeworki Paulos, African Studies
Librarian

1342   University of Pennsylvania,
        Van Pelt Library
        3420 Walnut Street
        Philadelphia PA 19104-6206
Tel: +1-215-898 0119 Fax: +1-215-898 0559
Email: olson@pobox.upenn.edu
Web:
http://www.library.upenn.edu/home.html
(Main library home page)
http://www.library.upenn.edu/sitedocs/pro
totypes/africa.html (African Collection)
Contact: Lauris Olson, African Studies
Bibliographer

1343   The University of Texas
        Libraries, Perry-Castañeda
        Library
        Austin TX 78713-8916
Tel: +1-512-495 4330 (Main Switchboard)
+1-512-495 4250 (Reference & Information

Services) +1-512-495 4270 (African American
Studies Librarian)
Fax: +1-512-495 4397
Email: tongate@mail.utexas.edu (Head,
Reference & Information Services)
draaijer@mail.utexas.edu (African American
Studies Librarian)
Web: http://www.lib.utexas.edu/
Contacts: John Tongate, Head Librarian,
Reference & Information Services; Gera
Draaijer, African American Studies Librarian
See also entry ➔ 510

1344   University of Virginia,
        Alderman Library
        PO Box 400114
        Charlottesville VA 22904-4114
Tel: +1-434-924 3021 (Reference and
Information Services) +1-434-924 4984
(Subject Librarian/Africana Bibliographer)
Fax: +1-434-924 1431
Email: gtc@virginia.edu
Web:
http://www.lib.virginia.edu/alderman/
Contact: George T. Crafts, Subject
Librarian/Africana Bibliographer

1345   University of Wisconsin,
        Memorial Library
        728 State Street
        Madison WI 53706-1494
Tel: +1-608-262 2357/3193 (General enquiries)
+1-608-262 6397 (Subject Librarian,
Africa/Middle East & Anthropology)
Fax: +1-608-265 2754
Email: dhenige@library.wisc.edu
Web: http://www.library.wisc.edu
Contact: David Henige, Subject Librarian,
Africa/Middle East & Anthropology
See also entries ➔ 10, 169

1346   Yale University, Sterling Memorial
        Library, African Collection
        Room 317
        PO Box 208240-130
        130 Wall Street
        New Haven CT 06520-8240
Tel: +1-203-432 1883 Fax: +1-203-432 7231
Email: dorothy.woodson@yale.edu
Web: http://www.library.yale.edu/african/
Contact: Dorothy C. Woodson, Curator,
African Collection

ASIA & MIDDLE EAST

China

1347   **Institute of West Asian and African Studies Library**
3 Zhang Zhizhong Lu
Dongcheng District
Beijing 100007
Tel: +86-10-6403 9168/6403 9171
Fax: +86-10-6403 5718
Email: iwaas@public.fhnet.cn.net (General enquiries)
chengh@isc.cass.net.cn (Senior Librarian)
Web: http://www.cass.cn/xiyafei/en/others/library.asp
Contact: (Ms) Cheng Hong, Senior Librarian

India

1348   **Centre of African Studies Library, University of Mumbai**
Ranade Bhavan
Vidyanagari Campus
Mumbai 400 098
Tel: +91-22-652 6091 ext 329/+91-22-652 6388 ext 330, 427
Fax: +91-22-652 6893
Email: director@cas.mu.ac.in
Web: http://www.mu.ac.in/libsub.html
Contact: S. R. Ganpule, University Librarian

Israel

1349   **Moshe Dayan Center for Middle Eastern and African Studies Library**
Room 419 Gilman Building
Tel Aviv University
Tel Aviv 69978
Tel: +972-3-640 9646/640 9100
Fax: +972-3-641 5802
Email: dayanlib@post.tau.ac.il, (General enquiries)
marion@ccsg.tau.ac.il (Librarian)
Web: http://www.dayan.org/framelib.htm
Contact: Marion Gliksberg, Librarian

AUSTRALASIA/PACIFIC

Australia

1350   **La Trobe University, Borchardt Library**
Plenty Road
Bundoora
Victoria 3086
Tel: +61-3-9479 2922 (Information Desk)
Fax: +61-3-9479 3018
Email: l.burke@latrobe.edu.au (Reference and Information Services Librarian)
Web: http://www.lib.latrobe.edu.au/home/
Contact: Liz Burke, Reference and Information Services Librarian

1351   **University of Western Australia, Reid Library**
Humanities and Social Sciences Library M209
35 Stirling Highway
Crawley WA 6009
Tel: +61-8-9380 2342 Fax: +61-8-9380 1012
Email: HSS-ref@library.uwa.edu (General enquiries) efraser@library.uwa.edu.au (HSS Librarian)
Web: http://www.library.uwa.edu.au/services/libraries/hss.html
Contact: (Ms) Erin Fraser, HSS Librarian

Japan

1352   **Kyoto Daigaku Afurika Chiiki Kenkyu Senta/Center for African Area Studies, Library**
Graduate School of Asian and African Area Studies
Kyoto University
46 Yoshida Shimoadachi-cho
Sakyo-ku
Kyoto 606-8501
Tel: +81-75-753 7800 Fax: +81-75-753 7810
Email: info@jambo.africa.kyoto-u.ac.jp or comm@asafas.kyoto-u.ac.jp
Web: http://jambo.africa.kyoto-u.ac.jp/display_e.htm (Main home page)
http://www.asafas.kyoto-u.ac.jp/econtent.html (English version)
Contacts: The Librarian; or Tsuyoshi Kato, Dean, Graduate School of Asian and African Area Studies

1353   Research Institute for the Study of
        Languages and Cultures of Asia and
        Africa, Information Resources
        Centre
        Fuchu-shi Asahi-cho 3-11-1
        Tokyo 183-8534
Tel: +81-42-330 5600 Fax +81-42-330 5610
Email: ilcadj1@aa.tufs.ac.jp (General
enquiries) mmine@aa.tufs.ac.jp (Director,
Information Resources Centre)
Web: http://irc.aa.tufs.ac.jp/index_e.html
Contact: Makoto Minegishi, Director,
Information Resources Centre

1354   Institute of Developing Economies,
        JETRO-IDE Library
        3-2-2 Wakaba Mihama-ku
        Chiba-shi
        Chiba 261-8545
Tel: +81-43-299 9716 (Reference)
+81-43-299 9706 (General enquiries about the
library) Fax: +81-43-299 9734
Email: sonobe@ide.go.jp
Web:
http://www.ide.go.jp/English/Library/inde
x.html
Contact: (Ms) Masuko Sonobe, Information
Services Office, The Library

New Zealand

1355   National Library of New Zealand/
        Te Puna Mātauranga o Aotearoa,
        Alexander Turnbull Library
        Cnr Molesworth and Aitken Streets
        PO Box 1467
        Wellington
Tel: +64-4-474 3000/3006 Fax: +64-4-474 3035
Email: information@natlib.govt.nz (General
enquiries) atl@natlib.govt.nz (Alexander
Turnbull Library) reference@natlib.govt.nz
(Reference Services)
Web: http://www.natlib.govt.nz/
Contact: Reference Services; or Murray
Stevens, Director, People, Culture and
Resources

SOUTH AMERICA

Brazil

1356   Centro de Estudos Afro-
        Orientais (CEAO), Biblioteca
        Praça 15 de novembro, 17
        Terreiro de Jesus - CEP 40 025
        0010 Salvador-Bahia
Tel: +55-71-322-6742 Fax: +55-71-322-8070
Email: ceao@ufba.br
Web: http://www.ceao.ufba.br/biblioteca-
ing.htm
Contact: Maria José S.Costa Sodré,
Administrative Secretary

Mexico

1357   Centro de Estudios de Asia y
        Africa El Colegio de México,
        Biblioteca
        Camino al Ajusco 20
        Col. Pedregal de Sta. Teresa
        10740 México DF
Tel. + 52-5449 2934 Fax: +52-5645 4584
Email: jramirez@colmex.mx or
biblio@colmex.mx
Web: http://www.colmex.mx/centros/ceaa/
(Centre Web site) http://biblio.colmex.mx/
(Main Library)
Contact: Jannette Ramírez Arámburo,
Librarian

13

Major academic libraries and national archives in Africa

Online guides and directories of African libraries and archives

> ⓘ This symbol indicates "The editor's choice" of a particularly outstanding online information resource.

1358   Africa Research Central. A Clearinghouse of African Primary Sources ⓘ
http://www.africa-research.org/mainframe.html (English version)
http://www.africa-research.org/mainframeFR.html (French version)
Created in 1998 and maintained by Susan Tschabrun and Kathryn Green at California State University-Fullerton, this is a very ambitious undertaking. Africa Research Central "has as its goal to centralize and constantly update information about institutions with African primary source collections so as to facilitate international research in African studies." The core of the site is a *Repositories* section with a searchable database of African archives, libraries, and museums with primary source collections. Additionally, Africa Research Central also hosts a *Repository Wish List*, which allows institutions in Africa to publicize their preservation needs, and which also features a gateway to potential sources of international funding, where African institutions may search an International Funding Agencies database to locate possible international funders.

The *Repositories* database currently has close to 500 entries covering the whole of Africa, and there are also links to repositories in Europe and in North America (albeit with quite a large number of dead links). It can be searched by type of repository, country, repository name, type of primary sources, or holdings. It can also be browsed in alphabetical order by country. For some repositories the information is still a bit patchy at this time (and may consist of only a name and address, contact/name of director, telephone/fax numbers, and email addresses and Web sites for a number of them), but for many others information can be very full. This can include access information, details about available finding tools, nature of collections (holdings, types of material, languages, size of collections), as well as publications issued, or references to published articles about the collections. Some even have pictures of the archives. During the 2003-04 periods, the database was refreshed based on new data gathered as part of a major new survey of repositories. In addition to updating and expanding the contact, access and collections information in the *Repositories* section, thousands of pages of finding aids, guides, brochures, and other materials received in the course of 2003-04 have been linked to the relevant repository records. All those included in the database, but which lack fuller information at this time, are encouraged to contact Africa Research Central to ensure a full entry. This is an excellent resource. [21/09/05]

1359 Africa South of the Sahara-Topics: Libraries and Archives
http://www-sul.stanford.edu/depts/ssrg/africa/libaf.html
This is part of the Stanford ➔ **Africa South of the Sahara (69)** site, an 18-page annotated listing of African academic and special libraries, national libraries, national archives, and African library associations who have Web sites at this time, together with some links to other African libraries-related sources. A separate 9-page section on South African libraries and archives can be found at http://www-sul.stanford.edu/depts/ssrg/africa/rsalibs.html. [21/09/05]

The Book Chain in Anglophone Africa. A Survey and Directory (print and online) *see* ➔ **2 The major general reference tools: Directories of libraries, publishers, and museums** entry **260**

1360 A Directory of Archival Repositories 1999 [South Africa]
http://www.national.archives.gov.za/dir_repository1999.htm
Seeks to provide essential information to users of archives and other repositories in South Africa. Lists repositories in alphabetical order, providing details of access, acquisitions policies, areas of specialisation, core holdings, finding aids, publications, and indicates whether participating in the National Archives' *National Register,* which covers manuscripts, photographs, audio-visual materials and oral sources that are accessible for online searching at a number of participating institutions. [21/09/05]

1361 Directory of University Libraries in Africa
http://www.ru.ac.za/library/otherlibraries/africa/
Compiled by library staff at ➔ **Rhodes University Library (1460)** in Grahamstown, this directory is arranged by country, and covers the whole of Africa, including francophone and North Africa. For each library listed it provides full address details, telephone and fax numbers, and email addresses and Web sites for a small number. Also included for most entries are names of the university librarian at each institution. Originally based on a survey undertaken in 1998, the compilers caution that some information may now be dated, although several country pages have been updated and/or modified as at June 2003. [21/09/05]

Major academic and special libraries in Africa with African studies collections

This listing is confined to the major, for the most part long-established university and special libraries in Africa that hold collections of at least 50,000 volumes, including sizeable Africana collections. For listings of other African academic and tertiary-level special libraries, national and public libraries, consult the directory sections of ➔ **The Book Chain in Anglophone Africa. A Survey and Directory (260)**. For listings of more specialist collections and repositories, small collections in archives or museums, as well as national and public libraries, consult ➔**Africa Research Central (1358)**.

All Web sites, where they exist, have been verified and are current as at September 2005. It should be noted, however, that the Web pages of several African university libraries are still under various stages of construction; and, secondly, that some of them suffer from frequent, and sometimes prolonged down times. Thus a "Not found" error message does *not* necessarily mean that the site doesn't exist any longer, or has migrated elsewhere. If the site has moved, e.g. from an externally hosted site to its own domain, it is usually easy enough to track it down via Google.

Where available, we have indicated the telephone/fax numbers of the library for each institution listed, together with library email address(es) and Web sites. However, it should be noted that, particularly in some francophone African countries, and those in North Africa, the telephone numbers, email addresses, and Web site URLs are those of the university institution (i.e. its main home page), rather than the university library. While most university institutions now have their own Web site, with links to departments, faculty, centres and institutes, etc., many are – somewhat surprisingly – still without pages offering information about their libraries.

Names of principal librarians, or other contacts, are indicated where we have been successful in tracking down this information, either pulled from Web sites or from other current sources.

A question mark [?] indicates queried/unverified information.

Algeria

1362   Bibliothèque universitaire d'Alger
2 rue Didouche Mourad
BP 488
Algiers 16000
Tel: +213-21-637101 Fax: +213-21- 637629
Email: bu@univ-alger.dz
Web: http://bu.univ-alger.dz/
Contact: Abdellah Abdi, Conservateur en Chef

1363   Université 'Badji Mohhtar'-Annaba, Bibliothèque
BP 12
23200 Sidi-Ammar
Tel: + 213-38-872678 (Main switchboard)
+213-38-878907 (Library)
Fax: +213-38-872436
Email: rectorat@univ-annaba.net
Web: http://www.univ-annaba.org/
Contact: M. le Bibliothécaire-en-chef

1364   Université d'Oran es-Senia, Bibliothèque
BP 1524
Oran El-M'Naouer 31000
Tel: : +213-41-416939/416644
Fax: +213-41-416021
Email: IGMO@UNIV-ORAN.DZ
Web: http://www.univ-oran.dz/
Contact: Kechar Bouabdellah, Chef de Centre des Ressources Informatiques

1365   Université Mentouri Constantine, Bibliothèque
Rue Äin-El-Bey
BP 325
Constantine 25000
Tel: +213-31-614348 Fax: +213-31-614349
Email: univ-constantine@fr.fm
Web: http://www.univ-constantine.dz
Contact: M. le Bibliothécaire-en-chef

Angola

1366   Universidade Agostinho Neto, Biblioteca
Endereço Av. 4 de Fevereiro 7 - 2
CP 815
Luanda
Tel: +244-2-311 125/310 341

Fax +244-2-310 283/330 520
Email: info@uan.ao
Web: http://www.uan.ao
Contact: n/a

1367   Universidade Católica de Angola, Biblioteca
Endereço R. Nossa Senhora da Muxima
CP 2064
Luanda
Tel: +244-2-233 1973
Fax: +244-2-239 8759
Email: info@ucan.edu
Web:
http://www.ucan.edu/biblioteca/index.php
Contact: José A. Cachadinha, Director of the Library

Benin

1368   Université d'Abomey-Calavi, Bibliothèque universitaire
01 BP 526
Cotonou
Tel: +229-360074/360126
Fax: +229-360028/301638
Email: pgandaho@syfed.bj.refer.org
(University Librarian)
Web: http://www.uac.bj.refer.org/
(University home page) http://uac-bu.bj.refer.org/ (University Library) or
http://www.bj.refer.org/benin_ct/edu/univ
-be/bu/bu.htm (University Library)
Contact: Pascal Gandaho, University Librarian

Botswana

1369   University of Botswana Library Services
Private Bag 00390
Gaborone
Tel: +267-355 5229/355 2304 (General Enquiries) +267-355 2620 (Director of Library Services)
Fax: +267-395 7291/395 6591
Email: directorlibrary@mopipi.ub.bw
(General enquiries) raseroka@mopipi.ub.bw
(Director of Library Services)
Web: http://www.ub.bw/library/
Contact: (Mrs) Kay Raseroka, Director of Library Services

1370   SADC Secretariat Library
        Southern African Development
        Community
        Private Bag 0095
        Gaborone
        Tel.: +267-351863 Fax: +267-372848
        Email: registry@sadc.int (General enquiries)
        mtali@sadc.int (Librarian)
        Web:
        http://www.sadc.int/index.php?action=a100
        1&page_id=library_about
        Contact: Maria Tali, Librarian

Burkina Faso

1371   Université de Ouagadougou,
        Bibliothèque
        03 7021 Ouagadougou 03
        Tel: +226-307064/65 Fax: +226-307242
        Email: info@univ-ouaga.bf
        Web: http://www.univ-
        ouaga.bf/html/bibliotheque/frbibliotheque.
        html (site under construction)
        Contact: (Mme) Maïmouna Sanok, University
        Librarian

Burundi

1372   Université du Burundi,
        Bibliothèque
        BP 1550
        Bujumbura
        Tel: +257-22-2059 Fax: +257-22-3288
        Email: rectorat@biblio.ub.edu.bi
        Web: http://www.ub.edu.bi/ or
        http://www.univ-tlse2.fr/gril/Buja.html
        (hosted by University of Trieste)
        Contact: M. le Bibliothécaire-en-chef

Cameroon

1373   Université de Yaoundé,
        Bibliothèque
        BP 1312
        Yaoundé
        Tel: +237-222 0744 Fax: +237-223 5388
        Email: mouen@yahoo.com
        Web: http://www.uninet.cm/biblio.html
        Contact: Peter Chateh, University Librarian

1374   University of Buea Library
        PO Box 63
        Buea
        Tel: +237-332 2134 ext 203
        Fax: +237-332 2272
        Email: unibu@iccnet2000.com or
        ubue@uycduuninet.cm
        Web: http://www.ub.com (not operational as
        at September 21005)
        Contact: Rosemary M. Shafack, Head
        Librarian

Central African Republic

1375   Université de Bangui, Bibliothèque
        universitaire
        Avenue des Martyrs
        BP 1450
        Bangui
        Tel: +236-612005/611767 Fax: +236-617890
        Email: univ-bangui@yahoo.fr
        Web: http://www.univ-bangui.cf/
        Contact: Joseph Goma-Bouanga, Director of
        the Library

Chad

1376   Université de N'Djamena,
        Bibliothèque centrale
        BP 1117
        N'Djamena
        Tel: +235-514444/515946 Fax: +235-514581
        Email: rectorat@intnet.td
        Web: n/a
        Contact: Doumtangar Koulassim, Head of
        Library

Congo (Brazzaville)

1377   Université Marien Ngouabi,
        Bibliothèque
        BP 69
        Brazzaville
        Tel: 242-814207/812436 Fax: 242-814207
        Email: n/a
        Web: n/a
        Contact: Innocent Mabiala, University
        Librarian

Congo Democratic Republic

1378 Centre Aequatoria
Centre Æquatoria
BP 276
Mbandaka
Email: vinck.aequatoria@belgacom.net
Web:
http://www.aequatoria.be/HomeEnglishFra
meSet.html
Contacts: Honoré Vinck, Director; G.I. Essalo,
Librarian and Archivist
(*Note:* contact in Belgium: Centre Aequatoria,
Stationsstraat 48, 3360 Lovenjoel, Belgium.
Tel./Fax: +32-16-464484. Email as above)
See also →**Aequatoria Archives, Ghent
University (1180)**

**1379 Université de Kinshasa,
Bibliothèque**
BP 127
Kinshasa 11
Tel: +243-12-27793 Fax: +243-12-21360
Email:
unikin@kinpost.ccmail.compuserve.com
Web n/a
Contact: Paul Tete Wersey
Bibliothécaire en chef adjoint

**1380 Université de Lubumbashi,
Bibliothèque centrale**
BP 1825
Lubumbashi
Tel: +243-22-5285/5403
Fax: +243-22-8099
Email: unilu@unilu.net
Web: http://www.unilu.net/
Contact: Bilonda Lwanba, University
Librarian

Côte d'Ivoire

**1381 Institut africain pour le
développement économique et
social (INADES), Centre de
documentation**
15 rue Jean Mermoz
08 BP 2088
Cocody
Abidjan 08
Tel: +225-22 40 02 16 Fax: +225-22 40 02 30
Email: ifsiege@inadesfo.ci
Web: http://www.inadesfo.org/
Contact: Nicole Vial, Head of Documentation
Centre

**1382 Université d'Abidjan-Cocody,
Bibliothèque**
BP V34
Abidjan 01
Tel: +225—22-440895/443900
Fax: +225-22-448751/443531
Email: accueil@ucocody.ci
Web: http://www.ucocody.ci/index.php
Contact: Françoise N'Goran, University
Librarian

**1383 Université d'Abobo-Adjamé,
Bibliothèque**
02 BP 801
Abidjan 02
Tel: +225-20-304211 Fax: +225-20-378118
Email: info@uabobo.ci
Web:
http://www.uabobo.ci/pages/bibliotheque.
htm
Contact: n/a

1384 Université de Bouaké, Bibliothèque
01 BP V18
Bouaké 01
Tel: +225-31-633242/634857
Fax: +225-31-632513/635984
Email: p-infor@africaonline.co.ci
Web:
http://roland.adjovi.free.fr/bouake.htm
(single page only)
Contact: Mian Kouakou Agniman

Egypt

**1385 Ain Shams University, Central
Library**
PO Box 11566
Abassia
11566 Cairo
Tel: +20-2-482 0230/683 1231
Fax: +20-2-2847824
Email: info@asunet.shams.edu.eg
Web: http://net.shams.edu.eg/
Contact: Nasr El-Din Abdel Rahman,
University Librarian

1386   Alexandria University, Central
        Library
        163 El-Horia Ave
        Elshatby
        Alexandria
        Postal address:
        233 El-Ebrahemia
        Alexandria
        Tel: +20-3-428 2928
        Fax: +20-3-428 2927
        Email: auclib@auclib.edu.eg
        Web: http://www.auclib.edu.eg/
        Contact: (Mrs) Soheir Gamal, General
        Manager of Library Affairs

1387   The American University in Cairo
        Libraries
        11 Youcef El Guindi Street
        Bab el Louk
        Cairo
        Postal address:
        PO Box 2511
        11511 Cairo
        Tel: +20-2-797 6904 (General
        enquiries/Reference desk)
        Fax: +20-2-792 3824
        Email: library@aucegypt.edu (General
        enquiries/Reference questions)
        mKenerson@aucegypt.edu (Head of
        Reference and Information Literacy)
        selsawy@aucegypt.edu (Dean of Libraries
        and Learning Technologies)
        Web: http://lib.aucegypt.edu/
        Contacts: Shahira El Sawy Dean of Libraries
        and Learning Technologies;
        Murle Kenerson, Head of Reference and
        Information Literacy

1388   Assiut University, Documentation
        and Libraries Department
        Assiut 71515
        Tel: +20-88-234 3704/2343 705
        Fax: +20-88-234 3703
        Email: sup@aun.eun.eg
        Web:
        http://www.aun.edu.eg/iiddsc/n1.htm
        Contact: n/a

1389   Bibliotheca Alexandrina –
        The Library of Alexandria
        El Shatby
        Alexandria 21526
        Postal address:
        PO Box 138
        Chatby

        Alexandria
        Tel: +20-3-4839999/4830334
        Fax: +20-3-4830327 (Library Services
        Department) +20-3-4830339 (Director
        Bibliotheca Alexandrina)
        Email: secretariat@bibalex.org (General
        enquiries) InfoDesks@bibalex.org (Library
        Information Services)
        youssef.ziedan@bibalex.org
        (Manuscripts, Rare Books and Microfilm
        Collections)
        youssef.ziedan@bibalex.org
        Web:
        http://www.bibalex.org/English/index.aspx
        Contact: Ismail Serageldin, Librarian of
        Alexandria; Youseff Ziedan Manuscripts,
        Rare Books and Microfilm Collections
        Note: Library collections consist of the Arts &
        Multimedia Library and the Taha Hussein
        Library (a library for the blind and visually
        impaired). However, Bibliotheca
        Alexandrina is not only a library; it is an
        integrated cultural complex, with libraries,
        museums, exhibition areas, educational
        centres, and an international conference
        centre.

1390   Cairo University,
        Central Library
        Nahdet Misr Street Orman
        PO Box 12613
        Cairo
        Tel: +20-2-572 9584 Fax: +20-2-568 8884
        Email: mailmaster@main-scc.cairo.eun.eg or
        postmaster@cairo.eun.eg
        Web:
        http://www.cu.edu.eg/General%20Info/Ma
        p%20and%20Campus/Central_Library.asp
        Contact: Fatima Ibrahim Mahmoud,
        University Librarian [?]

1391   Helwan University, Central Library
        Ein Helwan
        Cairo
        Tel: +20-2-344 6441 Fax: +20-2-345 5461
        Email: info@helwan.edu
        Web: http://www.helwan.edu.eg/
        Contact: Kharya El-Rafey, University
        Librarian

1392   Mansoura University Library
        60 El Gomhoria Street
        Mansoura 35516
        Tel: +20-50-247054/347054

Fax: +20-50-347900/353584
Email: mua@mans.edu.eg
Web: http://www.mans.edu.eg/
Contact: Madiha Mahmoud Elemam, Chief
Librarian

1393   Menoufia University Library
Gamal Abdel Nasser Street
Shebin el-Kom
Tel: +20-48-222 4216/222 4155
Fax: +20-48-222 6454
Email: menofia@mailer.menofia.edu.eg
Web: http://www.menofia.edu.eg/
Contact: Hamid Arafa [?]

1394   Tanta University Library
El-Geish Street
PO Box 31512
Tanta
Al-Gharbia
Tel: +20-40-317929 Fax: +20-40-331800
Email: tanta@frcu.eun.eg
Web: http://www.tanta.edu.eg/index.asp
(Main home page, English version)
http://www.tanta.edu.eg/liberary/Index1.ht
m (Library, in Arabic only)
Contact: Mohamed El Seteha, University
Librarian

Eritrea

1395   University of Asmara Library
PO Box 1220
Asmara
Tel: +291-1-162553/161926 ext 245
Fax: +291-1-162236
Email: assefawa@asmara.uoa.edu.er
Web: http://www.uoa.edu.er/
Contact: Atto Assefaw Abraha, Director,
Library and Information Service

Ethiopia

**1396   Addis Ababa University
Kennedy Library**
PO Box 1176
Addis Ababa
Tel: +251-1-115220 Fax: +251-1-560442
Email: infolib@lib.aau.edu.et or
kennedy.aau@telecom.net.et (General
enquiries) girmaj@lib.aau.edu.et (University
Librarian)

Web:
http://www.aau.edu.et/libraries/index.html
Contacts: Ato Girma Makonnen, University
Librarian; Ato Getahun Semeon, Assistant
University Librarian

**1397   African Union Library and
Archives**
(formerly OAU Library)
PO Box 3234
Addis Ababa
Tel: +251-1-517700 exts 332/211
Fax: +251-1-517844
Email: tpst@africa-union.org
Web: http://www.africa-union.org
Contact: The Chief Librarian (vacant)

1398   ECA Library
United Nations Economic
Commission for Africa
PO Box 3001
Addis Ababa
Tel: +251-1-51 72 00 ext 35510
+251-1-510280 (Chief Librarian)
Fax: +251-1-51 22 33
+251-1-51 03 65 (Chief Librarian
Email: ecalibadmin@uneca.org or
ecainfo@uneca.org
pamonoo@uneca.org (Chief Librarian)
http://www.uneca.org/eca_resources/librar
y/ or
http://www.uneca.org/disd/library/index.
html/
Contact: Petrina Amonoo, Chief Librarian

**1399   International Livestock Research
Institute, ILRI InfoCentre**
PO Box 5689
Addis Ababa
Tel: +251-1-463215 Fax: +251-1-461252
Email: Ilri-information@cgiar.org
Web:
http://www.ilri.cgiar.org/pageselflink.asp?p
ageid=315&menuid=38
Contact: Azeb Abraham, Head of InfoCentre
Note: The ILRI Library in Kenya specializes
in biological sciences, and is at Old Naivasha
Road, PO Box 30709, Nairobi 00100
Tel: +254-20-22 3000 Fax: +254-20-223001,
Email: Library@cgiar.org

Gabon

1400   Université Omar Bongo,
        Bibliothèque Centrale
        Boulevard Léon M'Ba
        BP 13131
        Libreville
Tel: +241-726910/732045
Fax: +241-730417/734530
Email: uob@internetgabon.com
Web: http://www.uob.ga/
Contact: M. Aboghe-Obiang [?]

The Gambia

1401   University of the Gambia Library
        Administration Building
        Kanifing
        PO Box 3530
        Serrekunda
Tel: +220-372213/395062/5
Fax: +220-395064
Email: unigambia@qanet.gm
Web: http://www.unigambia.gm/
(site down 25/11/05)
Contact: n/a

Ghana

1402   Kwame Nkrumah University of
        Science and Technology, KNUST
        Library
        University Post Office
        Kumasi
Tel: +233-51-60199 (General enquiries)
+233-51-60133 (University Librarian)
Fax: +233-51-60358
Email: lib@knust.edu.gh (General enquiries)
ul@knust.edu.gh (University Librarian)
Web:
http://www.knust.edu.gh/academics/librar
y.htm
Contact: Helena R. Asamoah-Hassan,
University Librarian

1403   University of Cape Coast Library
        University Post Office
        Cape Coast
Tel: +233-42-32481/30952
Fax: +233-42-32485
Email: ucclib@libr.ug.edu.gh

Web: http://www.uccghana.net/default.asp
(Home page, new university Web site, no
library pages as yet)
http://nanayaa.8m.com/libr.html (Old
library Web site)
Contact: Richard Arkaifie, University
Librarian

1404   University of Ghana,
        Balme Library
        PO Box LG 24
        Legon
        Accra
Tel: +233-21-500309 Fax: +233-21-502701
Email: pad@ug.edu.gh or balme@ug.edu.gh
(General enquiries)
aalemna@ug.edu.gh (University Librarian)
Web: http://www.ug.edu.gh/library.php
Contact: Anaba A. Alemna, University
Librarian

Guinea

1405   Université Gamal Abdel Nasser de
        Conakry, Bibliothèque
        Universitaire
        BP 1147
        Conakry
Tel: +224-460181/464689
Fax: +224-460101/464808
Email: uganc@mirinet.net.gn
Web:
http://www.un.org/french/Depts/dpi/Abi
djan99/edu_guinee/
Contact: Mansa Kanté, Librarian

Kenya

1406   Catholic University of Eastern
        Africa, CUEA Library
        Lang'ata Road
        PO Box 62157
        City Square
        Nairobi 00200
Tel: +254-20-891601/6 (General enquiries)
+254-20-891601-6 ext 2319 (Head Librarian)
Fax: +254-20-891261/891084
Email: library@cuea.edu
Web:
http://www.cuea.edu/facilities/lib.htm
Contact: Rev. Fr. M Kisenyi, Head Librarian

1407   Egerton University Library
        PO Box 536
        Njoro 20107
Tel: +254-37-62265/62277 Fax: +254-37-61389
Email: eujdrlib@africaonline.co.ke
Email:
Web:
http://www.egerton.ac.ke/academics/librar
y/library.php
Contact: S.C. Otenya, Librarian

1408   International Centre for Insect
        Physiology and Ecology-
        (ICIPE), Library/Information
        Resources Centre
        PO Box 30772
        Nairobi
Tel: +254-20-863 2000
Fax: +254-2-863 2001/8632002
Email: dg@icipe.org (General enquiries)
amengech@icipe.org (Head, Information
Services Unit)
Web:
http://www.icipe.org/research_support_uni
ts/information_and_publications_unit/index
.html
Contact: Annalee Ng'eny-Mengech
Head, Information Services Unit

International Livestock Research Institute
(ILRI), Kenya see → International Livestock
Research Institute (ILRI), Ethiopia (1399)

1409   Kenyatta University Library
        Thika Road
        PO Box 43844
        Nairobi
Tel: +254-2-810187
Fax: +254-2-811455/810759
Email: dvcadm@ku.ac.ke (General enquiries)
rgitachu@avu.org (Social Sciences Librarian)
Web: http://www.ku.ac.ke/
Contacts: James Nganga, Librarian; Rosemary
W. Gitachu, Social Sciences Librarian

1410   Moi University,
        Margaret Thatcher Library
        PO Box 3900
        Eldoret
        Tel: +254-321-43001/43309
        Fax: +254-321-43047/43275
Email: libusers@moiuniversity.ac.ke (General
enquiries) tanui@moiuniversity.ac.ke
(University Librarian)
Web: http://www.mu.ac.ke/library/mtl.htm

Contact: Tirong arap Tanui, University
Librarian

1411   University of Nairobi Library
        PO Box 30197
        00100 Nairobi
Tel: +254-2-334244/63 (General enquiries)
+254-2-210642 (University Librarian)
Fax: +254-2-336885
Email: salma@uonbi.ac.ke (University
Librarian) kingorigm@yahoo.com (Librarian,
Institute of African Studies)
Web: http://library.uonbi.ac.ke/ (site down
15/10/05)
http://www.uonbi.ac.ke/ (Main university
home page)
Contacts: Salome W. Mathangani, University
Librarian; Jacinta Were, Senior Librarian
G.M. King'ori, Librarian, Institute of African
Studies

Lesotho

1412   National University of Lesotho,
        Thomas Mofolo Library
        PO Roma
        Roma 180
Tel: +266-340601/213426 Fax: +266-340000
Email: m.moshoeshoe-chadzingwa@nul.ls
Web: http://www.nul.ls/library
Contact: (Mrs) Matselio Mamahlape
Moshoeshoe-Chadzingwa, Head,
Documentation Centre, Institute of Southern
African Studies, University of Lesotho, and
Ag. University Librarian

Liberia

1413   University of Liberia Libraries
        Capitol Hill
        PO Box 9020
        Monrovia
Tel: +231-6-224670 (General enquiries)
+231-6-422304 (Office of the President)
Fax: +231-6-226418
Email: n/a
Web:
http://members.aol.com/_ht_a/drconteh/m
yhomepage/
Note: this Web site provides information
about the current status and rehabilitation of
the University of Liberia, hosted by Al-
Hassan Conteh.

Libya

1414 African Centre for Applied
Research and Training in Social
Development (ACARTSOD),
Library
Africa Centre Wahda Quarter
Zawia Road
PO Box 80606
Tripoli
Tel: +218-21-833640/833228
Fax: +218-22-832367
Email: fituri_acartsod@hotmail.com
Web: n/a
Contact: (Mrs) Lamis Gabsi, Head,
Information Services

1415 Al-Fateh University, Central Library
PO Box 13482
Tripoli Sedi El-Masri
Tel: +218-22-605441 Fax: +218-22-605460
Email: n/a
Web: http://www.alfateh-univ-engg.org/
Contact: Mohamed Abdul Jaleel [?]

1416 Garyounis University, Central
Library
PO Box 1308
Benghazi
Tel: +218-61-25007/20148
Fax: +218-61-20051
Email: garyounisuniv@ittnet.net
Web:
http://www.garyounis.edu/English/index.h
tm (University home page, English version)
http://www.garyounis.edu/e/central_librar
y/index.html (Central Library, these pages
not accessible 22/11/05)
Contact: Ahmed M. Gallal

Madagascar

1417 Bibliothèque universitaire
d'Antananarivo
Division Madagascar et Océan Indien
Campus Universitaire
d'Ambohitsaina
BP 908
Antananarivo 101
Tel: +261-20-64654/61228
Fax: +261-20-21103
Email: bu-tana@syfed.refer.mg (General
enquiries) adrianiaina@minitel.refer.org.
(Head of Library)
Web: http://www.univ-antananarivo.mg/
(Main university home page)
www.refer.mg/madag_ct/edu/tana/bu/bua
c.htm (Library pages on old Web site)
Contact: Jean-Marie R. Andrianiaina, Head of
Library

Malawi

1418 University of Malawi Library
PO Box 280
Zomba
Tel: +265-525935/524222
Fax: +265-525225/524046
Email: rmasanjika@medcol.mw or
rmasanjika@yahoo.com
Web: http://www.unima.mw/
Contact: Contact: Ralph Masanjika, Librarian,
College of Medicine, and Acting University
Librarian

Mali

1419 Université du Mali, Bibliothèque
Rue Baba Diarra Porte 113
BP 2528
Bamako
Tel: +223-221933/229302
Fax: +223-221932
Email: universiteaml@refer.org
Web:
http://www.ml.refer.org/mali_ct/edu/univ
mali.htm
Contact: n/a

Mauritania

1420   Université de Nouakchott,
        Bibliothèque
        BP 633
        Nouakchott
Tel: +222-255381 ext 221
Fax: +222-251945
Email: BU@univ-nkc.mr
Web: http://www.univ-nkc.mr/BU/
Contact: Issa Ould Mohamed Ahmed

Mauritius

1421   University of Mauritius Library
        Reduit
Tel: +230-454 1041 ext 1229
Fax: +230-454 0905
Email: l.dassyne@uom.ac.mu
Web:
http://www.uom.ac.mu/Library/libhomepa
ge.htm
Contact: I. Dassyne, Chief Librarian

Morocco

1422   Centre Africain de formation et de
        recherche administratives pour le
        développement/The African
        Training and Research Centre in
        Administration for Development,
        CAFRAD Library
        PO Box 310
        Tangier 90001
Tel : +212-61 30 72 69 Fax: +212-39 32 57 85
Email : cafrad@cafrad.org
Web: http://www.cafrad.org/
Contact: n/a

1423   Fondation du Roi Abdul Aziz Saoud
        pour les etudes islamiques et les
        sciences humaines,
        Bibliothèque/Centre de
        Documentation
        Blvd de la Corniche
        Ain Diab - Anfa
        BP 12585
        Casablanca 20052
Tel: +212-22 39 10 27/30
Fax: +212-22 39 10 31
Email: secretariat@fondation.org.ma

Web:
http://www.fondation.org.ma/fondlatin/bi
blioth.htm
Contact: n/a

1424   Université Hassan II, Faculté des
        Lettres et de Sciences Humaines de
        Mohammedia, Service de la
        Bibliothèque et de la
        Documentation
        Avenue Hassan II
        BP 546
        Mohammedia
Tel: +212-23-324873/74 Fax: +212-23-325377
Email: flsh-uh2m@fusion.net.ma
http://www.univh2m.ac.ma/fac02_presentat
ion.htm (Main faculty site) http://www.fsjes-
uh2c.ac.ma/biblio.html (Main library home
page)
Contact: Amina Ait Hmad, Head of Library
and Documentation Services

1425   Université Mohamed 1er/Jami'at
        Muhammad al_Awwal,
        Bibliothèque
        Complexe Universitaire
        Hay El Qods
        BP 724
        Oujda 60000
Tel: +212-56 50 06 12/14
Fax: +212-56 50 06 09
Email: rectorat@univ-oujda.ac.ma (Main
university email address) fm@univ-
oujda.ac.ma (University Librarian)
Web: http://www.univ-oujda.ac.ma/
(Main University home page)
http://wwwdroit.univ-oujda.ac.ma/ (Faculté
des sciences juridiques, économiques, et
socials)
Contact: Fouad Mehdaoui, University
Librarian

1426   Université Mohammed V-Rabat-
        Chellah, Bibliothèque
        3 rue Michlifen Agdal
        BP 554
        Rabat-Chellah
Tel: +212-37-671318/671324
Fax: +212-37-671401/673318
Email: belkeziz@onpt.net.ma
Web: http://www.emi.ac.ma or
http://www.emi.ac.ma/univ-MdV/
Contact: Hassan Quazzani [?], Librarian

1427   Université Mohamed V-Souissi
        Rabat, Bibliothèque
        Angle avenue Allal El Fassi et Mfadel
        Cherkaoui
        8007 N.U. Rabat
        Tel: +212-37 77 43 87/37 77 43 96
        Fax: +212-37 68 11 63
        Email: presidence@um5s.ac.ma (Main
        university email address)
        Web: http://www.um5s.ac.ma/fr/index.php
        or
        http://www.emi.ac.ma/univ-
        MdV/rectorat.html
        Contact: Mme Nadia Belhaj, University
        Librarian

Mozambique

1428   Universidade Eduardo Mondlane
        Direcção dos Serviços de
        Documentação
        Campus Universitario Principal
        Edificio 6
        CP 1169
        Maputo
        Tel: +258-1-492875 Fax: +258-1-493174
        Email: bibweb@nambu.uem.mz (General
        enquiries) aissa@dsdoc.uem.mz (Head,
        Departamento de Formação e Informação)
        Web: http://www.uem.mz/dsd/index.htm
        Contacts: Policarpo Camilo Matiquite,
        Director, Direcção dos Serviços de
        Documentação; (Ms) Aissa Isaak, Head,
        Departamento de Formação e Informação

Namibia

1429   University of Namibia
        Library/Information and Learning
        Resource Centre
        340 Mandume Ndemufayo Avenue
        Pioneers Park
        Private Bag 13301
        Windhoek
        Tel: +264-61-206 3874 (General enquiries)
        +264-61-2063873 (University Librarian) Fax:
        +264-61-206 3876
        Email: library@unam.na (General enquiries)
        rviljoen@unam.na (University Librarian)
        Web:
        http://www.unam.na/ilrc/library/index.ht
        ml (New page) or
        http://library.unam.na/ (Old page)

Contact: (Ms) Ria Viljoen, University
Librarian

Niger

1430   Université Abdou Moumouni,
        Bibliothèque centrale
        BP 237
        Niamey 10896
        Tel: +227-732713/732714
        Fax: +227-733862
        Email: resadep@ilimi.uam.ne
        Web:
        http://www.ird.ne/partenariat/resadep/
        (Pages for Réseau Sahélien de Recherche et de
        Publication)
        http://www.georgetown.edu/programs/oip
        /os/sites/africa/niamey.htm (Pages hosted
        by Georgetown University)
        Contact: M. Seydou Harouna, Curator

Nigeria

1431   Abubakar Tafawa Balewa
        University Library
        PMB 0248
        Bauchi
        Bauchi State
        Tel: +234-77-543500/592964
        Fax: +234-77-542065
        Email: info@atbunet.org (General enquiries)
        zubairum2001@yahoo.com (University
        Librarian)
        ekojai@yahoo.com (Principal Librarian)
        Web:
        http://www.atbunet.org/pages/University
        %20Library_01.htm
        Contacts: Mohammed Zubairu, University
        Librarian; Innocent Ekoja, Principal Librarian

1432   Ahmadu Bello University, Kashim
        Ibrahim Library
        Zaria
        Kano State
        Tel: +234-69-550553/601280
        Fax: +234-69-550022
        Email: KIL@abu.edu.ng (General enquiries)
        dobozimo@infoweb.abs.net (University
        Librarian)
        Web:
        http://www.widernet.org/nigeriaconsult/ab
        u.htm (Note: this is not an official Web site,
        but more in the nature of an article)

Contact: Doris O. Bozimo, Professor of Library Science and University Librarian

1433   Bayero University Library
PMB 3011
Kano
Kano State
Tel: +234-64-317560/+234-64-661026
Fax: +234-64-666021/+234-64-665904
Email: buklibrarian@yahoo.com or librarian@buk.edu.ng
Web:
http://www.kanoonline.com/buk/library/index.htm
Contact: Mallam Misbahu Na'iya, University Librarian

1434   International Institute of Tropical Agriculture (IITA), Library & Documentation Centre
Oyo Road
PMB 5320
Ibadan
Oyo State
Tel: +234-2-241 2626 Fax: +234-2-241 2221
Email: IITA@cgiar.org (General enquiries)
E.Ezomo@cgiar.org (Principal Librarian)
Web: http://www.iita.org/info/libsrv.htm
Contact: E.O. Ezomo, Principal Librarian

1435   Nigerian Institute of International Affairs.
NIIA Library
13/15 Kofo Abayomi Road
Victoria Island
GPO Box 1727
Lagos
Lagos State
Tel: +234-1-261 5606/5607 exts 112 or 129
Fax: +234-1-261 1360
Email: library@niianigeria.org
qcoker@niianet.org (Head, Library and Documentation Services)
Web: http://www.niianet.org/library.htm
Contact: (Mrs) Q. F. Coker, Head, Library and Documentation Services

1436   Obafemi Awolowo University, Hezekiah Oluwasanmi Library
Ile-Ife
Osun State
Tel: +234-36-230290/231822
Fax: +234-36-233974/233128
Email: oauife@oauife.edu.ng (General

enquiries) omole@oauife.edu.ng (University Librarian)
kjagboro@library.oauife.edu.ng (Library staff)
Web: http://www.oauife.edu.ng/index.php (Main university home page)
http://elibrary.oauife.edu.ng/ (University Library) (these pages not accessible 25/11/05)
Contacts: M.O. Ofolabi, University Librarian; B.O. Omotayo, Senior Librarian

1437   University of Benin, John Harris Library
Ugbowo-Lagos Road Ugbowo
PMB 1154
Benin City
Edo State
Telephone: +234-52-600443
Fax: +234-52-602370
Email: info&pr@uniben.edu
Web:
http://www.uniben.edu/library/index.htm
Contact: S.A. Ogunrombi, University Librarian

1438   University of Calabar Library
PMB 1115
Calabar
Cross River State
Tel: +234-87- 221697/234748
Fax: +234-87-221766
Email: olulaw@unical.anpa.net.ng
Web: n/a
Contact: Olufunmilayo Olatunde Lawal, University Librarian

1439   University of Ibadan, Kenneth Dike Library
Ibadan
Oyo State
Tel: +234-22-810 1100-4/412668
Fax: +234-22-810 3034
Email: librarian@mail.ui.edu.ng
Web:
http://www.ui.edu.ng/unitslibrary.htm
Contact: Georgina D. Ekpenyong, Acting University Librarian

1440   University of Ilorin Library
PMB 1515
Ilorin
Kwara State
Tel: +234-31-221552/22991
Fax: +234-31-22561/221593
Email: fhsilorin@anpa.net.ng
Web: n/a
Contacts: Matthew Ajibero
University Librarian; Joseph O. Aina, Deputy
University Librarian

1441   University of Jos Library
PMB 2084
Jos
Plateau State
Tel: +234-73-53724/44952
Fax: +234-73-610514
Email: mailbox@unijos.edu.ng (General
enquiries) ochai@unijos.edu.ng (University
Librarian) akins@unijos.edu.ng (Deputy
University Librarian-Systems)
Web:
http://128.255.135.155/libraries/index.htm
(Library home page)
http://www.uiowa.edu/intlinet/unijos/dep
artments/libraries/index.htm (Mirror site
hosted by University of Iowa)
Contacts: A.Ochai, Ag. University Librarian;
Stephen A. Akintunde, Deputy University
Librarian-Systems

1442   University of Lagos Library
Akoka
Yaba
Lagos
Lagos State
Tel: +234-1-8921273/492652
Fax: +234-1-822644
Email: library@unilag.edu
Web site: http://www.unilag.edu Contacts:
K. Adeniji, University Librarian; S. Olajire
Olanlokun - University of Lagos, Librarian

**1443   University of Maiduguri,
          Ramat Library**
Barma Road
PMB 1069
Maiduguri
Borno State
Tel: +234-76-231725 Fax: +234-76-822644
Email: n/a
Web: http://www.unimaid.org/
Contact: Margaret Hamza, Librarian

**1444   University of Nigeria,
          Nnamdi Azikiwe Library**
Nsukka
Enugu State
Tel: +234-42-770709/771911
Fax: +234-42-770644
Email: misunn@aol.com
Web: http://www.unizikonline.net (site
down 25/11/05)
Contact: Celestine C. Uwaechie [?]
Note: The domain "University of Nigeria" at
http://www.universityofnigeria.com/ is a
actually a spoof site created to parody the
Nigerian 4-1-9 (Advance fee) frauds and other
scams.

1445   University of Port Harcourt Library
PMB 5323
Port Harcourt 50004
Rivers State
Tel: +234-84-230 8909 ext 2564
Email: uniport@phca.linkserve.com or
uniportlibrary@yahoo.com
Web: http://www.uniport.edu.ng/gi/tl.htm
Contact: Nathaniel Patrick Obokoh,
University Librarian

Réunion

**1446   Université de la Réunion,
          Service Commun de la
          Documentation**
BP 7152
Saint-Denis Cedex 97715
Tel : +262-938383 (General enquiries)
+262-938361 (Librarian)
Fax : +262-938364
Email : anne-christine.girard@univ-reunion.fr
(General enquiries)
Email: Anne-Marie.Blanc@univ-reunion.fr
(Director, Service Commun de la
Documentation)
Web: http://bu.univ-reunion.fr/index.html
Contact: Anne-Marie Blanc, Director, Service
Commun de la Documentation

Rwanda

**1447   Université nationale du Rwanda,
          Bibliothèque centrale**
BP 117
Butare
Tel: +250-530330 ext 1050
Fax: +250-530210

Email: biblio@nur.ac.rw
Web: http://www.lib.nur.ac.rw/ (site down 25/11/05)
Contact: Emmanuel Serugendo, Director of Library Services

Senegal

1448   **African Institute for Economic Development and Planning (IDEP)/Institut Africain de Développement Economique et de Planification, Bibliothèque**
BP 3186
Dakar
Tel.: +221-823 1020 Fax: +221-822 2964
Email: idep@unidep.org or unidep@unidep.org (General enquiries)
micnageri@unidep.org (Head of Library Services)
Web:
http://www.unidep.org/francais/indexfranc ais.html (French version)
http://www.unidep.org/homepage.htm (English version)
Contact: Michael Nageri, Head of Library Services

1449   **Bureau Régional de l'UNESCO pour l'éducation en Afrique (BREDA), Centre de Documentation**
12 avenue L.S. Senghor
Dakar
Tel.: +221-849 2342 Fax: +221-823 8393
Email: m.zormelo@unesco.org
Web:
http://www.dakar.unesco.org/centre_doc_fr /doc.shtml
Contact: (Mme) Magna Zormelo, Documentalist

1450   **Council for the Development of Social Science Research in Africa/Conseil pour le développement de la recherche en sciences sociales en Afrique, CODESRIA Documentation and Information Centre (CODICE)**
Ave. Cheikh Anta Diop x Canal IV
BP 3304
Dakar
Tel: +221-825 9822/23 Fax: +221-824 1289

Email: codesria@codesria.sn (General enquiries) abou.ndongo@codesria.sn (Chief Librarian)
Web:
http://www.codesria.org/Documentation.ht m
Contact: Abou Moussa Ndongo, Chief Librarian

1451   **Institut Fondamental d'Afrique Noire Cheikh Anta Diop, Bibliothèque/Documentation**
Université Cheikh Anta Diop de Dakar
BP 2006
Dakar
Tel: +221-250090/259890 Fax: +221-244918
Email: bifan@telecomplus.ns
http://www.ucad.sn/
Web:
http://www.ucad.sn/article.php3?id_article =386
Contact: Gora Dia, Head of Library and Documentation

1452   **Université Cheikh Anta Diop, Bibliothèque universitaire**
BP 2006
Dakar
Tel: 221-824 6981 Fax: +221-824 2379
Email: biblicat@ucad.sn (General enquiries)
hsene@ucad.sn (University Librarian)
Web: http://www.bu.ucad.sn/ (site down 22/11/05) or
http://www.ucad.sn/article.php3?id_article =17
Contact: Henri Sene, University Librarian

Sierra Leone

1453   **Fourah Bay College Library**
University of Sierra Leone
Mount Aureol
Private Mail Bag
Freetown
Tel: +232-22-227924/229471
Fax: +232-22-224260
Email: fbcadmin@sierratel.sl
Web: http://fbcusl.8k.com/
Contact: Oliver Harding, Librarian

South Africa

1454   Africa Institute of South Africa Library
Nipilar House, Corner of Hamilton and Vermeulen Streets
Arcadia
PO Box 630
Pretoria 0001
Tel: +27-12-328 6970 Fax: +27-12-323 8153
Email: ai@ai.org.za (General enquiries)
amanda@ai.org.za (Library)
Web: http://www.ai.org.za/library.asp
Contacts: Amanda Wortman, Librarian

1455   The Brenthurst Library
PO Box 87184
Houghton 2041
Tel: +27-11-646 6024 Fax: +27-11-486 1651
Email: marcelle.graham@brenthurst.co.za
Web:
http://www.brenthurst.org.za/library.htm
Contact: Marcelle Graham, Librarian and Director of the Brenthurst Press

1456   Don Africana Library
Libert Towers 10th floor
West Street
PO Box 917
Durban 4000
Tel: 27-31-332 0586/3374700
Fax: 27-31-337 4700
Email: phyllisc@crsu.durban.gov.za
Web:
http://www.durban.gov.za/eThekwini/Services/libraries/services/dona
Contact: Phyllis Connerty, Head of Library

1457   National English Literary Museum, Research Department/Information Services
87 Beaufort Street
Private Bag 1019
Grahamstown 6140
Tel: +27-46-622 7042 Fax: +27-46-622 2582
Email: nefp@kudu.ru.ac.za (General enquiries) C.Warren@ru.ac.za (Research queries)
Web:
http://www.ru.ac.za/affiliates/nelm/nelmhome.html
Contacts: Anne Warring, Crystal Warren

1458   Potchefstroom University for Christian Higher Education, Ferdinand Postma Library
Private Bag X05
Noordbrug 2520
Tel: +27-18-299 2000 Fax: +27-48-299 2999
Email: fpbalg@puk.ac.za
Web:
http://www.puk.ac.za/biblioteek/index_e.html
Contact: Tom Larney Director

1459   Rand Afrikaans University Library
PO Box 524
Auckland Park
Johannesburg 2006
Tel: +27-11-489 2171 (General enquiries)
+27-11-489 2170 (Director of the Library)
Fax: +27-11-489 2164
Email: info@bib.rau.ac.za
Web:
http://general.rau.ac.za/library/bibweb/HTML/
Contact: (Ms) J. Sander, Chief Director

1460   Rhodes University Library
PO Box 184
Grahamstown 6140
Tel: +27-46-603 8436 Fax: +27-46-622 3487
Email: library@ru.ac.za (General enquiries)
V.Botha@ru.ac.za (Head, Public Services)
Web: http://www.ru.ac.za/library
Contact: Vivien Botha, Head, Public Services

1461   The South African Library
Queen Victoria Street
PO Box 496
8000 Cape Town
Tel: +27-21-424 6320 Fax: +27-21-423 3359
Head Office address:
National Library of South Africa
Private Bag X990
Tel: +27-12-401 9782 Fax: 27-12-321 1128
Email: Infodesk@nlsa.ac.za (General enquiries) john.tsebe@nlsa.ac.za (National Librarian of South Africa and CEO)
joan.debeer@nlsa.ac.za (Deputy National Librarian)
Web: http://www.nlsa.ac.za/
Contact: John Kgwale Tsebe, National Librarian of South Africa and CEO;
Joan Frances de Beer, Deputy National Librarian
Note: The South African Library is now part of the National Library of South Africa

1462   University of Cape Town Libraries,
        African Studies Library
        Private Bag
        Rondebosch 7701
Tel: +27-21-650-3107/6 Fax: +27-21-689-7568
Email: asl@uctlib.uct.ac.za (General enquiries)
bev@uctlib.uct.ac.za (Head, African Studies
Library)
Web: http://www.lib.uct.ac.za/asl/
Contact: Bev Angus, Head, African Studies
Library

1463   University of Fort Hare,
        Howard Pim Library
        Private Bag X1322
        Alice 5700
Tel: +27-40-602 2612 (General enquiries)
+27-40-602-2515 (Librarian, Howard Pim
Library) Fax: +27-40-653-1423
Email: ysoul@ufh.ac.za (University Librarian)
msnyders@ufh.ac.za (Librarian, Howard Pim
Library)
Web:
http://www.ufh.ac.za/library/index.html
Contacts: Yolisa Soul, University Librarian;
Mark P. Snyders, Librarian, Howard Pim
Library/Africana Librarian

1464   University of Kwazulu-Natal,
        Howard College Libraries
        220 Marriott Road
        Private Bag X10
        Dalbridge
        Durban 4041
Tel: +27-31-260 2317 Fax: +27-31-260 2051
Email: webster@lib.und.ac.za (General
enquiries) buchanan@nu.ac.za (Campus
Librarian) dubbeld@nu.ac.za (Head,
Information Services)
Web: http://www.library.und.ac.za/
Contacts: Nora Buchanan, Campus Librarian;
Catherine Dubbeld, Head, Information
Services

1465   University of Kwazulu-Natal,
        Killie Campbell Africana Library
        220 Marriott Road
        Durban 4001
Tel: +27-31-260 1720 Fax: +27-31-209 1622
Email: somers@ukzn.ac.za (General
enquiries/Reading room)
seleti@kcc.und.ac.za (Director)
Web: http://khozi2.nu.ac.za/kcafricana.htm
Contacts: Yonah N. Seleti, Director;
Anne Somers, Library Information Officer

1466   University of Kwazulu-Natal,
        Pietermaritzburg Library/
        Alan Paton Centre and Struggle
        Archive
        Private Bag X014
        Scottsville 3209
Tel: +27-33-260 5896 (General enquiries)
+27-33-260 5054 (Acting University Librarian)
+27-33-260 5926 (Alan Paton Centre and
Struggle Archive)
Fax: +27-33-260 5260
Email: brammage@nu.ac.za (Acting
University Librarian) koopmanj@nu.ac.za
(Alan Paton Centre and Struggle Archive))
Web: http://www.library.unp.ac.za (Main
library home page)
http://www.library.unp.ac.za/paton/ (The
Alan Paton Centre and Struggle Archive)
Contacts: Carol Brammage, Acting Librarian
and Deputy Librarian; Jewel Koopman, Alan
Paton Centre and Struggle Archive

1467   University of Limpopo,
        Africana Library
        (formerly University of the North)
        Private Bag X1112
        Sovenga 0727
Tel: +27-15-268 2463 (General enquiries)
+27-15-268 2968 (Africana Library)
+27-15-268 4656 (University
Librarian) Fax: +27-15-268 2198
Email: matshayap@ul.ac.za (University
Librarian) modibad@unin.unorth.ac.za
(Africana Librarian)
Web:
http://www.unorth.ac.za/Library/index.ht
ml (Main home page)
http://www.unorth.ac.za/Library/lib-
specialcol.htm (Africana Library)
Contacts: (Ms) Pateka Matshaya,
University Librarian; M.D. Ledwaba,
Africana Librarian

1468   University of Port Elizabeth,
        Albertus Delport Library
        Private Bag X6058
        Port Elizabeth 6000
Tel: +27-41-504 2281 Fax: +27-41-504 2280
Email: library@upe.ac.za (General enquiries)
marjorie.eales@nmmu.ac.za (Interim Director)
Web: http://www.upe.ac.za/library/
Contact: Marjorie Eales, Interim Director

1469   University of Pretoria Academic
        Information Service (University
        Library)
        Pretoria 0002
Tel: +27-12-420 2235/2236 (General
enquiries/Help desk) +27-12 4203 631
(Service Unit Coordinator, General Services)
Fax: +27-12-362 5100
Email: helpdesksk@ais.up.ac.za (Help desk)
delports@ais.up.ac.za (Service Unit
Coordinator, General Services)
Hennie.muller@up.ac.za (Main Counter,
Academic Information Service)
Web: http://www.ais.up.ac.za
Contacts:
Sonja Delport, Service Unit Coordinator,
General Services; Hennie Muller, Main
Counter, Academic Information Service

1470   University of South Africa,
        UNISA Library
        PO Box 392
        Unisa 0003
Tel: +27-12-429 3206 Fax: +27-12-429 2925
Email: bib-circ@unisa.ac.za (General
enquiries) hennijc@unisa.ac.za (Head of
Technical Services and Acting Executive
Director) pearcrj@unisa.ac.za (Head, Client
Services)
Web:
http://www.unisa.ac.za/library/index.html
Contacts: Judy Henning, Head of Technical
Services and Acting Executive Director;
Robert Pearce, Head, Client Services

1471   University of Stellenbosch,
        JS Gericke Library
        Private Bag X5036
        Stellenbosch 7599
Tel: +27-21-808 4385 (General enquiries)
+27-21-808 2346 (Head, Client Services)
Fax: +27-21-808 4336
Email: asn@sun.ac.za (General
enquiries/Secretary) jhvi@sun.ac.za (Senior
Director) ean@sun.ac.za (Head, Client
Services)
Web:
http://www.sun.ac.za/library/index.htm
(English version)
Contacts: Hennie Viljoen, Senior Director;
Elda Nolte, Head, Client Services

1472   University of the Free State, Library
        and Information Services
        PO Box 339
        Bloemfontein 9300
Tel: +27-51-401 9393/488
Fax: +27-51-430 6976
Email: maretha@hbib.uovs.ac.za (Senior
Librarian, Librarian and Information
Services) crn@hbib.uovs.ac.za (Director of the
Library)
Web:
http://www.uovs.ac.za/support/library/E_l
ibrary.php
Contacts: Clemence Namponya, Director of
the Library, Maretha Stapelberg, Senior
Librarian, Library and Information Services

1473   University of the Western Cape
        Libraries
        Modderdam Road
        Private Bag X17
        Bellville 7535
Tel: +27-21- 959-2911 (General enquiries) +27-
21-959 2947 (University Librarian) +27-21-959
2916 (Faculty/Africana Librarian)
Email: Etise@uwc.ac.z (University Librarian)
Jfortuin@uwc.ac.za (Africana Librarian)
Web: http://www.uwc.ac.za/library/
Contacts: (Ms) E.R. Tise, University Librarian;
Joan Fortuin, Faculty/Africana Librarian
See also → UWC-Robben Island Mayibuye
Archives (1474)

1474   UWC-Robben Island Mayibuye
        Archives
        Modderdam Road
        Private Bag X17
        Bellville 7535
Tel: +27-21-959 2939/2954
Fax: +27-21-959 3411
Email: mayib@uwc.ac.za
Web: http://www.mayibuye.org/
Contact: André Odendaal

1475   University of the Witwatersrand
        Libraries
        Wartenweiler Library
        Private Bag X1
        Wits 2050
Tel: +27-11-717 1944/1917 (General enquiries)
+27-11-717 1901/3 (University Librarian)
+27-11-717 1955 (Africana Librarian)
Fax: +27-11-339 7559
Email: mandlan@library.wits.ac.za (General
enquiries)

406 MAJOR ACADEMIC LIBRARIES & NATIONAL ARCHIVES IN AFRICA

felixu@library.wits.ac.za University
Librarian)
margaren@library.wits.ac.za (Africana
Librarian) http://www.wits.ac.za/library/
Contacts: Felix Ubogu, University Librarian;
Margaret Northey, Africana Librarian
Note: Africana is now housed in the William
Cullen Library; Reference is in Wartenweiler

1476   University of Zululand Library
Private Bag X1001
KwaDlangezwa 3886
Tel: +27-35-9026462/3 (General
enquiries) +27-35-902 6462 (University
Librarian) Fax: +27-35-902 6451
Email: use email online form on Web site
Web: http://www.uzulu.ac.za/lib355.aspx
Contact: (Ms) L. Vahed, University Librarian;
(Ms) B.H. Khumalo, Subject Librarian, Social
Sciences

Sudan

1477   El Neelain University Library
PO Box 12702
Khartoum
Tel: +249-11-776433 Fax: +249-11-776338
Email: Alageed_Seedahmed@hotmail.com
Web: n/a
Contact: S.E. Alageed, Dean of Libraries

1478   University of Gezira Library
PO Box 20
Wad Medani 2667
Tel: +249-511-40023/41355
Fax: +249-511-46237/40466
Email: abuobeida-h@yahoo-com
Web: http://www.gezirauniversity.net/
Contact: A.M. Hamouda

1479   University of Juba Library
PO Box 321/1
Khartoum Centre 80295
(or PO Box 82, Juba)
Tel: +249-11-451352 Fax: +249-11-451351
Email: jucs@sudanet.net
Web: http://www.mei.com.jo/juba.htm
(hosted by Majdalawi Educational Institute,
Jordan)
Contact: Alfred D. Lado [?], University
Librarian

1480   University of Khartoum Library
PO Box 321
Khartoum 1115
Tel: +249-11-770022/447448
Fax: +249-11-780295
Email: library@uofk.edu
Web:
http://www.uofk.edu/library/index.htm
Contact: (Prof.) Muna Mahgoub Mohamed
Ahmed, University Librarian

Swaziland

1481   University of Swaziland Library
Private Bag 4
Kwaluseni M201
Tel: +268-518 5886 Fax: +268-518 5276
Email: mmavuso@uniswacc.uniswa.sz
(University Librarian)
zngcobo@uniswacc.uniswa.sz   (General
enquiries/Head, Reader services)
Web: http://library.uniswa.sz
Contacts: M. Mavuso, University Librarian; Z.
G. Ngcobo, Head, Reader Services;

Tanzania

**1482   Sokoine National Agricultural
Library**
Chuo Kikuu
PO Box 3022
Morogoro 23
Tel: +255-33-260 3511/241 0500
Fax: +255-23-260 4639/604651
Email: library@suanet.ac.tz or snal@sua.ac.tz
Web: http://www.suanet.ac.tz/library.htm
Contact: F. Dulle, Ag. Director of Library

1483   University of Dar es Salaam Library
PO Box 35092
Dar es Salaam
Tel: +255-22-241 0241/43241
Fax: +255-22-241 0241/43241
Email: libdirec@udsm.ac.tz (General
enquiries) director@libis.udsm.ac.tz (Director
of Library Services)
mukangara@libis.udsm.ac.tz (Head, East
Africana Collection)
Web: http://www.udsm.ac.tz/library/ (site
down)
Contacts: (Ms) Julita Nawe, Director of
Library Services; F.E.Mukangara, Head, East
Africana Collection

Togo

1484 **Université de Lomé, Bibliothèque**
BP 1515
Lomé
Tel: +228-254843/213027 Fax: +228-218595
Email: cafmicro@ub.tg (General enquiries)
biblio-ub@syfed.tg.refer.org (University
Library)
Web: http://www.ub.tg
Contact: Atsufui Brigitte Fiatuwo Gbiki-
Benissan

Tunisia

1485 **Institut de Recherche sur le**
Maghreb Contemporain (IRM),
Bibliothèque
20 rue Mohamed Ali Tahar
Mutuelleville
1002 Tunis
Tel: +216-71-796722 Fax: +216-71-797376
Email: bib@irmcmaghreb.org Web:
http://www.irmcmaghreb.org/biblio/
Contact: Patrick Pollet, Head of Library

1486 **Université de La Manouba,**
Bibliothèque
Campus Universitaire
2010 La Manouba 2
Tel: +216-71-601499/602996
Fax: +216-71-602 211/601499
Email: mail@uma.rnu.tn
Web: http://www.uma.rnu.tn/index.htm
(site hosted by the Ministry of Education)
Contact: n/a

1487 **Université de Tunis I,**
Bibliothèque de la faculté des
sciences humaines et sociales
92 avenue du 9 avril 1938
1007 Tunis
Tel: +216-71-567322/261272
Fax: +216-71-560633
Email : universite.tunis@utunis.rnu.tn
Web: http://www.utunis.rnu.tn/
Contact: n/a

1488 **Université de Sousse, Bibliothèque**
43 bis avenue Mohamed El
Karoui
4002 Sousse
Tel: +216-73-368129/368130
Fax: +216-73-368126/368128

Email: universite.centre@uc.rnu.tn
(University email address)
flsh.sousse@fls.rnu.tn (Faculté de letters et
des sciences humaines)
Web: http://www.uc.rnu.tn/ (Main
university home page)
http://www.mes.tn/flshs/welcome.htm
(Faculté de letters et des sciences humaines)
Contact: n/a

1489 **Université de Sfax pour le Sud,**
Bibliothèque
Rue de l'A'erodrome Km 0.5
3029 Sfax
Tel: +216-74-244423/240678
Fax: +216-74-240913/240986
Email: uss@uss.rnu.tn
Web: http://www.mes.tn/uss/index.htm
Contact: n/a

1490 **Université de Tunis el Manar,**
Bibliothèque
Campus Universitaire
BP 94
2092 Tunis
Tel: +216-71-873366/873228
Fax: +216-71-872055
Email: unitumanar@tun2.mu.tn (Main
university email address)
Web: http://www.utm.rnu.tn/ (Main
university home page)
Contact: n/a

1491 **Université du 7 novembre à**
Carthage, Bibliothèque
29 rue Asdrubal
1002 Tunis
Tel: +216-1-787502/1841353
Fax: +216-1-788768
Email: Adel.Gammoudi@univ7nc.rnu.tn
Web:
http://www.universites.tn/univ_7_nov/
Contact: Adel Gammoudi, Head, Information
Services

1492 **Université libre de Tunis,**
Bibliothèque
30 avenue Khéreddine Pacha
1002 Tunis
Tel: +216-71-841411/890393
Fax: +216-71-782260
Email: intac.ult@planet.tn
Web: http://www.ult.ens.tn/htm/index.asp
Contact: n/a

Uganda

1493   Makerere University Library
PO Box 7062
Kampala
Tel: +256-41-531041/2 (General enquiries)
+256-41-533735 (University Librarian)
Fax: +256-41-540374
Email: info@mulib.mak.ac.ug (General
enquiries) mmusoke@med.mak.ac.ug
(University Librarian)
kigozid@mulib.mak.ac.ug (Senior Librarian &
Head, Africana/Special Collections Section)
Web: http://www.makerere.ac.ug/mulib/
Contacts: Maria G. N. Musoke University
Librarian; (Mrs) Dorcas Kigozi, Senior
Librarian & Head, Africana/Special
Collections Section

**1494   Uganda Martyrs University,
African Research &
Documentation Centre**
PO Box 5498
Kampala
Tel: +256-78-410611 or +256-481-21894/5
Fax: +256- 78-410 100
Email: ardc@umu.ac.ug
Web:
http://www.fiuc.org/umu/faculty/ardc/in
dex.html
Contact: Peter Kanyandago, Director

Zambia

1495   Copperbelt University Library
PO Box 21692
Kitwe
Tel: +260-2-223972 Fax: +260-223972
Email: library@cbu.ac.zm (General enquiries)
cbmlungu@cbu.ac.zm (University Librarian)
Web:
http://www.cbu.edu.zm/units/library/libra
ry.htm
Contact: Charles B.M. Lungu, University
Librarian

1496   University of Zambia Library
Great East Road Campus
PO Box 32379
Lusaka 10101
Tel: +260-1-250845 Fax: +260-1-253952
Email: librarian@library.unza.zm (General
enquiries)

mwacalimba@library.unza.zm (University
Librarian) msimui@library.unza.zm (Deputy
Librarian)
Web:
http://www.unza.zm.library/Library.html
(site down 22/11/05)
Contacts: Hudwell Mwacalimba, University
Librarian; (Mrs) Muyoyeta Simiu, Deputy
Librarian

Zimbabwe

**1497   Southern African Research and
Documentation Centre (SARDC)**
15 Downie Avenue Belgravia
PO Box 5690
Harare
Tel: +263-4-791141/791143Fax: +263-4-791271
Email: sardc@sardc.net (General enquiries)
pjohnson@sardc.net (Director)
cmuvezwa@sardc.net (Chief Documentalist)
Web: http://www.sardc.net (Main home
page)
http://databases.sardc.net/ (Virtual Library)
Contacts: Phyllis Johnson, Executive Director;
(Ms) Chipo Muvezwa, Chief Documentalist

**1498   University of Zimbabwe
Libraries**
PO Box MP 167
Mount Pleasant
Harare
Tel: +263-4-303211 (General enquiries)
+263-4-303211 ext 1164 (University
Librarian)
Fax: +263-4-335383
Email: infocentre@uzlib.uz.ac.zw or
library@uzlib.uz.ac.zw (General enquiries)
bmbambo@uzlib.uz.ac.zw (University
Librarian)
Web: http://www.uz.ac.zw/library/
Contact: Buhle Mbambo, University
Librarian

National archives

Algeria

1499 **Archives nationales d'Algerie**
BP 61
Alger Gare
Tel: +213-2-542160/61 Fax: +213-2-541616
Email: dgan@ist.cerist.dz
Web: http://www.archives-dgan.gov.dz/
Contact: Abdelmadjid Chikhi, Director
General

Angola

1500 **Arquivo Histórico Nacional, Centro
National de Documentação e
Investigação**
Rua Pedro Félix Machado 49
CP 2468
Luanda
Tel: +244-2-334416/333512
Fax: +244-2-334410
Email: n/a
Contact: Rosa Cruz e Silva, Head

Benin

1501 **Archives nationales du Bénin**
rue de Ouando
Face à l'Ecole Régionale de la
Magistrature
BP 629
Porto-Novo
Tel: +229-213079/226609 Fax: +229-213079
Email: anbenin@intnet.bj
Web: http://www.anbenin.bj/ or
http://www.unesco.org/webworld/archives
/benin/anb.htm (site hosted by UNESCO,
not updated since 1997)
Contact: Elise Paraiso, Director

Botswana

1502 **Botswana National Archives and
Records Service**
Khama Crescent Government
Enclave
PO Box 239
Gaborone
Tel: 267-391 1820 Fax: +267-390 8545

Email: archives@gov.bw (General enquiries)
kkgabi@gov.bw (Director)
Web:
http://www.gov.bw/government/ministry_
of_labour_and_home_affairs.html (part of
Ministry of Labour and home affairs pages)
Contact: (Ms) Kelebogile Kgabi, Director

Burkina Faso

1503 **Centre national des archives**
Présidence de Faso
BP 7030
Ouagadougou
Tel: +226-336196/32472 Fax: +226-314926
Email: assaned49@yahoo.fr
Contact: (Lt Colonel) Assane Sawadogo,
Director General

Burundi

1504 **Archives nationales**
Ministère de la Jeunesse, de la
Culture et des Sports
BP 1095
Bujumbura
Tel: + 257-225051/51257
Fax: +257-226231/219295
Email: niconyandwi@yahoo.fr
Contact: Nicodème Nyandwi, Director

Cameroon

1505 **Archives nationales du
Cameroun/National Archives of
Cameroon**
Ministère de la Culture
Direction du Patrimoine culturel
BP Box 1053
Yaoundé
Tel: +237-223 2010/223 0078
Fax: +237-222 8078
Email: pokekoa@yahoo.fr
Contact: Amadou Pokeko, Head of Archives

Cape Verde

1506 **Arquivo Histórico Nacional**
CP 321
Praia
Tel: +238-612125/613962

Fax: +238-613964
Email: ahn.praia@mail.cvtelecom.cv
Web: http://www.ahn.cv/ (site under
construction)
Contact: Claudia Correia, Director

Central African Republic

1507   Archives nationales de la
        République centrafricaine
        BP 881
        Bangui
Tel: +236-613871 Fax: +236-615787
Email: dan@intnet.cf
Contact: Célestin Dimanche, Director

Chad

1508   Direction des archives nationales
        BP 638
        N'djamena
Tel: +235-523375/282056 Fax: +235-525536
Email: n/a
Contact: Narayam Ndissedibaye,
Director

Comoros

1509   Archives nationales. Centre national
        de documentation et de recherche
        scientifique
        Musée national des Comores
        BP 169
        Moroni
        Grande Comore
Tel: +269-732615/74487 Fax: +269-731550
Email: cndrs@snpt.km
Contact: Ainouddine Sidi, Director General

Congo (Brazzaville)

1510   Centre national des archives et de
        la documentation
        BP 1489
        Brazzaville
Tel: +242-663 1259 Fax: +242-815009
Email: fetrasseic_congo@yahoo.fr
Contact: Edouard Nzino, Director

Congo Democratic Republic

1511   Archives nationales du Congo
        42A avenue de la Justice
        BP 11122
        Kinshasa 1
Tel: +243-12-33433/31083
Email: prof_lumenganeso@yahoo.fr
Contact: Antoine Kobe Lumenga-Neso,
Director General

Côte d'Ivoire

1512   Archives nationales de Côte d'Ivoire
        BP V-126
        Abidjan
Tel: +225-217578 Fax: +225-215013
Email: n/a
Contact: Missa Kouassi, Director

Djibouti

1513   Institut supérieur d'études et de
        recherches scientifiques et
        techniques
        BP 486
        Djibouti
Tel: +253-352795 Fax: +253-354812
Email: n/a
Contact: Mohamed Anis Abdallah, Director

Egypt

1514   National Library and Archives of
        Egypt
        Corniche El-Nil, Ramlet Boulac
        PO Box 8 - Sabttiya
        Cairo 11638
Tel: +202-575 0886/575 1078
Fax: +202-576 5634
Email: info@darelkotob.org (Public services)
libmang@darelkotob.org (Head of National
Library) archmang@darelkotob.org (Head of
National Archives)
Web: http://www.darelkotob.org/ (Main
home page)
http://www.darelkotob.org/ENGLISH/HT
ML/NATIONAL%20_ARCHIVE.HTM
(National Archives Sector, English)

Contacts: Galal Ghandour, Head of the
National Library; Mohamed Saber Arab,
Head of the National Archives

Equatorial Guinea

1515   Consejo de Investigaciones
        Cientificas y Tecnologicas
        (incorporates the National Archives)
        Malabo Bioko Norte
Tel: +240-93313, 94535
Fax: +240-93313
Email: n/a
Contacts: Garcia Bolekia, Director; Saturnino
Obama Nsí, National Archives

Eritrea

1516   Research and Documentation
        Centre
        PO Box 897
        Asmara
Tel: +291-1-122808 Fax: +291-1-122902
Email: rdc@eol.com.er
Web:
http://denden.com/EritreanArchives/main.
html
Contact: Azieb Tewolde, Director
Note: the above likely to be designated as the
National Archives shortly.

Ethiopia

1517   National Archives & Library of
        Ethiopia
        PO Box 717
        Addis Ababa
Tel: +251-1-516532
Fax: +251-1-526411
Email: nale@telecom.net.et or
nale@ethionet.et (General enquiries)
atkilt2001@yahoo.com (Director General)
Web: http://www.nale.gov.et/
Contact: Atkilt Assefa, Director General

Gabon

1518   Archives nationales du Gabon
        BP 1188
        Libreville
Tel: +241-730239 Fax: +241-732871
Email: jangoune_nzoghe@yahoo.fr
Contact: Jérôme Angoune-Nzoghe, Director

The Gambia

1519   National Records Service/
        Gambia National Archives
        Departmental Mail Bag
        The Quadrangle
        Banjul
Tel: +220-226700/22351 Fax: +220-202086
Email: nrs@gamtel.gm
http://www.nrs.gm/
Contacts: (Ms) Penda E. Bah, Acting Director,
National Records Service;
Andrew O. Evborokhai, Gambia Naitonal
Archives
Note: the above Web site includes the
National Records Service Slave Trade Archive
pages.

Ghana

1520   Public Records and Archives
        Administration Department
        (formerly Ghana National Archives)
        PO Box 3056
        Accra
Tel: +233-21-221234 Fax: 233-21-220014
Email: praad@internetghana.com
Web: http://www.praadgh-gov.org or
www.internetghana.com/praad/index.htm
(both sites down 25/11/05)
Contact: Cletus Azangweo, Director

Guinea

1521   Archives nationales de Guinée
        Avenue du Port
        Almamya
        BP 1005
        Conakry
Tel: +224-444297/414297 Fax: +224-411119
Email: n/a

Contact: Almamy Stell Conté, Director
General

Guinea Bissau

1522 Instituto Nacional de Estudos e Pesquisa, Arquivo Histórico
Complexo Escolar 14 de Novembro
BP 112
Bairro Cobornel
Bissau
Tel: +245-251867/223032 Fax: +245-251125
Email: inep@sol.gtelecom.gw or
mama_jao@hotmail.com
Contact: Mamadu Jao, Director

Kenya

1523 Kenya National Archives and Documentation Service
Moi Avenue
PO Box 49210
00100 Nairobi
Tel: +254-2-228959/223977
Fax: +254-2-742424
Email: knarchives@kenyaweb.com
Web: http://www.kenyarchives.go.ke/
Contact: Musila Musembi, Director & Chief Archivist

Lesotho

1524 National Archives of Lesotho
Minstry of Tourism, Environment
and Culture
PO Box 52
Maseru 100
Tel: +266-313034 ext 45 Fax: +266-310194
Email: n/a
Contact: Ntina Quobosheane, Head

Liberia

1525 Center for National Documents and Records/Liberian National Archives
PO Box 9046
Monrovia
Tel: +231-221296
Email: n/a
Contact: G. Narrison Toulee, Director General

Libya

1526 National Archives
Castello
Tripoli
Tel: +218-61-40166
Email: n/a
Contact: n/a

Madagascar

1527 Archives nationales de Madagascar
23 Karije Street
PO Box 3384
Anatananarivo
Tel: +261-20-223534 Fax: +261-20-223534
Email: rijandriamihamina@malagasy.com
Contact: (Mme) Sahondra Andriamihamina Ravoniharoson, Director

Malawi

1528 National Archives of Malawi
Mkulichi Road
PO Box 62
Zomba
Tel: +265-1-525240
Fax: +265-1-525240/524089
Email: archives@sdnp.org.mw
Web: http://chambo.sdnp.org.mw/ruleoflaw/archives/
Contact: Paul Lihoma, Director

Mali

1529 Archives nationales du Mali
BP 159
Koulouba
Bamako
Tel: +223-229420/225644 Fax: +223-227050
Email: dnambko@afribone.net.ml (General enquiries) alyongoiba@yahoo.fr (Director)
Contact: Aly Ongoï Ba, Director

Mauritania

1530   Archives nationales
BP 77
Nouakchott
Tel: +222-2-52317/53753
Fax: +222-2-52636/51945
Email: n/a
Contact: Nagi Ould Mohamed Mahmoud

Mauritius

1531   Mauritius Archives
Development Bank of Mauritius
Complex
Coromandel
Petite Rivière
Tel: +230-233 4469/233 7341
Fax: + 230-233 4299
Email: arcmail.gov.mu
Web:
http://www.gov.mu/portal/site/mac/men
uitem.adf2c4b1e2d8d5aea6597adaa0208a0c/
Contact: Gheeandut Suneechur, Acting
Director

Morocco

**1532   Bibliothèque générale et archives
du Maroc**
5 avenue Ibn Batouta
BP 1003
Rabat
Tel: +212-7-771890/772152
Fax: +212-7-776062
Email: n/a
Web: http://www.bga.org.ma/ (site down
22/11/05) or
http://www.minculture.gov.ma/fr/Biblioth
%E8que%20G%E9n%E9rale%20et%20Archive
s%20de%20Rabat.htm (Ministry of Culture
pages)
Contact: Ahmed Toufik, Director

Mozambique

1533   Arquivo Histórico de Moçambique
Avenida Filipe Magaia 715
CP 2033
Maputo
Tel: +258-1-421177 Fax: +258-1-423428

Email: ahm@ahm.mz or
JNeves@zebra.uem.mz or
joeltembe@hotmail.com
Contact: Joel das Neves Tembe, Director

Namibia

1534   National Archives of Namibia
4 Lüderitz Street
Private Bag 13250
Windhoek
Tel: +264-61-293 4308/5300+264-61-
293042/5308
Email: natarch@natarch.mec.gov.na   (General
enquires)
kutzner@mec.gov.na or
jochen@natarch.mec.gov.na (Chief Archivist)
Web: http://www.natarch.mec.gov.na or
http://witbooi.natarch.mec.gov.na/
(both sites down 25/11/05)
Contact: Jochen Kutzner, Chief Archivist

Niger

1535   Archives nationales du Niger
BP 550
Niamey
Tel: +227-722682
Fax: +227-723654
Email: n/a
Conact: Idrissa Yansambou, Director

Nigeria

1536   National Archives Department
Federal Ministry of Information and
Culture
Ikoyi Road
PMB 12897
Lagos
Tel: +234-1-686469 Fax: +234-1-269 4642
Email: n/a
Web:
http://www.nigeria.gov.ng/nationalarchives
.aspx
Contact: Comfort Aina Ukwu

1537   National Archives of Nigeria, Enugu
        Branch
        3 Colliery Avenue
        PMB 01050
        Enugu
        Enugu State
        Tel: +234-42-259700
        Email: uesse@enugu.nipost.com.ng
        Web: http://www2.rz.hu-
        berlin.de/inside/orient/nae
        (Web site hosted by the Center for Modern
        Oriental Studies, Berlin)
        Contact: U.O.A. Esse, Assistant Director

1538   National Archives of Nigeria,
        Zonal Office Ibadan
        PMB 4
        University Post Office
        University of Ibadan
        Ibadan
        Oyo State
        Tel/Fax: n/a
        Email: n/a
        Contact: Comfort Aina Ukwu

Rwanda

1539   Archives nationales
        Ministère de l'enseignement
        supérieur, de la recherche
        scientifique et de la culture
        BP 1044
        Kigali
        Tel: +250-83525/73086 Fax: +250-83518
        Email: kizarie@yahoo.fr
        Contact: Elias Kizari, Director

São Tomé e Príncipe

1540   Arquivo Histórico de São Tomé e
        Príncipe
        CP 87
        1012 São Tomé
        Tel: +239-21630
        Email: n/a
        Contact: Maria Nazaré de Ceita

Senegal

1541   Archives Nationales du Sénégal
        Immeuble Administratif
        Avenue L.S. Senghor Dakar
        Tel: +221-821 7021/849 7483
        Fax: +221-821 7021
        Email: Bdas@telecomplus.sn (General
        enquiries) pmarchi@primature.sn (Director)
        ssissoko@hotmail.com (Conservator of
        Archives)
        Web:
        http://www.archivesdusenegal.gouv.sn/
        Contact: Papa Momar Diop, Director;
        Saliou Amadi Sissoko, Conservator of
        Archives

Seychelles

1542   National Archives of Seychelles
        BP 720
        La Bastille
        Mahé
        Tel: +248-224777 Fax: +248-322113
        Email: seymus@seychelles.net
        Contact: Alain Lucas, Joint Director

Sierra Leone

1543   National Archives of Sierra Leone
        Fourah Bay College
        Mount Aureol
        Freetown
        Tel: +232-22-227509
        Email: bert_moore90@hotmail.com or moore-
        albert20@hotmail.com
        Contact: Bert Moore, National Government
        Archivist

South Africa

1544   National Archives and Records
        Service of South Africa
        24 Hamilton Street Arcadia
        Private Bag X236
        Pretoria 0001
        Tel: +27-12- 323 5300 Fax: +27-12-323 5287
        Email: enquiries@dac.gov.za (General
        enquiries)
        archives@dac.gov.za (Chief
        Director/National Archivist)

Mandy.Gilder@dac.gov.za
enquiries2@dac.gov.za Genealogical and
family history enquiries)
Web: http://www.national.archives.gov.za/
Contacts: Graham Dominy, Chief Director;
(Ms) Boatametse Mandy Gilder, Director,
National Archives and Records Service
Note: for contact details of other offices that
form part of the National Archives and
Records Service of South Africa see Web site.

Sudan

1545   National Record Office
PO Box 1914
Khartoum
Tel: +249-81995/80567
Email: n/a
Contact: The Director (vacant)

Swaziland

1546   Swaziland National Archives
Parliament Road
Lobamba
PO Box 946
Mbabane H100
Tel: +268-416 1278/1276
Fax: +268-416 1241
Email: sdnationalarchive@realnet.co.sz
Web:
http://www.gov.sz/home.asp?pid=2002
Contact: (Mrs) D.F.K.Mthethwa, Acting
Director

Tanzania

**1547   Records and Archives Management
Division**
(formerly National Archives of
Tanzania)
Vijibweni Street
PO Box 2006
Dar es Salaam
Tel: +255-22-215 0634
Email: records@intafrica.com
Contact: Peter J. Mlyansi, Director

1548   Zanzibar National Archives
Department of Antiquities, Archives
and Museums
PO Box 116
Zanzibar
Tel: +255-230342 Fax: +255-235241/233722
Email: dama@zitec.org
Web: http://www.zanzibar-
archive.org/content.htm
Contact: Hamad H. Omar, Director, National
Archives and Museums

Togo

1549   Archives nationales du Togo
41 avenue Sarakauva
BP 1002
Lomé
Tel: +228-221 6367/221 0410
Fax: +228-222 0783
Email: dban@tg.refer.org or mabcoul@voila.fr
Contact: Wénmi-Agore M. Coulibaly,
Director

Tunisia

1550   Archives nationales de Tunisie
122 Boulevard 9 avril 1938
1030 Tunis
Tel: +216-71-576800/576500
Fax: +216-1-569175
Email: archives.nationales@email.ati.tn
Web: http://www.archives.nat.tn/
Contact: Moncef Fakhfakh, Director General

Uganda

1551   Uganda National Archives
Ministry of Public Service
Department for Records and
Information Technology
PO Box 7003
76 Buganda Road
Kampala
Tel: +256-41-251003/255651
Fax: +256-41-255463/4
Email: info@publicservice.go.ug
Web:
http://www.publicservice.go.ug/record-
mgt.html

Contact: Jacques Charles Etomet, Principal
Archivist

Zambia

1552   National Archives of Zambia
Government Road Ridgeway
PO Box 50010
Lusaka
Tel: +260-1-254080/250446
Fax: +260-1-254081
Email: naz@zamnet.zm
Contact: Chrispin Hamooya, Director

Zimbabwe

1553   National Archives of Zimbabwe
Head Office
Borrowdale Road Gunhill
PO Box 7729
Causeway
Harare
Tel: +263-4-792741/795696
Fax: +263-4-792398
Email: archives@gta.gov.zw
Contact: Ivan Munhamu Murambiwa,
Director

14
Centres of African studies & African studies programmes and courses worldwide
(including African American & Black studies programmes)

This directory – a new feature in this 4th edition of the *African Studies Companion* – provides short profiles and essential address and contact details of 330 centres of African studies, and university institutions offering African studies programmes and courses, in all parts of the world. In the US it also includes the leading Africana and African American/Black studies programmes – major and minor – all of which include African studies and/or African arts, literatures and cultures as a component of their Master's, Bachelor's, or certificate degree programmes. Ethnic studies programmes are included if African or African American studies forms a significant component of the programme. A small number of the major institutes of development studies, with strong African teaching and research interests, are included as well.

Organizations and institutions that promote African arts and cultures through special events, public lectures, exhibitions, etc., such as for example → **The Africa Centre (2551)** in London, are not included here.

Each entry includes the full postal address, telephone/fax numbers with international dialling codes, Web site, and email address(es). Unless otherwise indicated, this is either the main email contact address, the email of the administrative coordinator or departmental secretary, or the email of the Director of the programme if no other email contact is available. Each entry also includes the name of the current Director (or Head, Chair, or Coordinator) of the centre or programme, with email address if available. The links to Web sites lead to full information about faculty and staff, degree programmes and courses offered, admission requirements, scholarships and fellowships, events calendars, and publications if available. Some of the Web sites also offer information about exchange and study abroad programmes, and affiliations with university institutions in Africa.

All information has been verified and is current as at July 2005. However, it should be noted that department chairs, or coordinators, can change from year to year. If there are any inaccuracies in our listings we shall be grateful if these could be brought to our attention. Please email us at hanszell@hanszell.co.uk and we will put this right in one of our regular online updates.

Cross-references to libraries at some of these institutions – i.e. those with substantial African studies collections – are indicated by a ➔ symbol followed by the entry number. However, please note that cross-references to library resources relate to *African studies material only*, not those in e.g. the field of African American or diaspora studies.

EUROPE

Austria

1554 **Institute für Afrikanistik**
Universität Wien
Universitätscampus Altes AKH
Spitalgasse 2-4 Hof 5
A-1090 Wien
Tel.: +43-1-4277/432-01 Fax: +43-1-4277/9432
Email: Afrikanistik@univie.ac.at
Web:
http://www.univie.ac.at/afrikanistik/home
pageneu/index.htm
Director: Prof. Dr. Norbert Cyffer
Library resources: see → **1179**

Belgium

1555 **Brussels Centre for African Studies**
c/o Centre d'Anthropologie
Culturelle
Institut de Sociologie
44 avenue Jeanne
1050 Elsene
Tel: +32-2-650 3425 Fax: +32-2-650 4337
Email: bcas@ulb.ac.be or
svhoyweg@vub.ac.be
Web: http://www.vub.ac.be/BCAS/
Board: Dr Jan Gorus *et al*
See
http://www.vub.ac.be/BCAS/about.html
for complete list of board members.

1556 **Centre Æquatoria. Centre de**
Recherches Culturelles
Africanistes
Stationsstraat 48
3360 Lovenjoel
Tel/Fax: +32-16-464484
Email: vinck.aequatoria@skynet.be
Web:
http://www.aequatoria.be/French/HomeFr
enchFrameSet.html (French version)
http://www.aequatoria.be/English/HomeE
nglishFrameSet.html (English version)
Director: Honoré Vinck,
Library resources: see → **1180**
Note: also at Centre Æquatoria, BP 276,
Mbandaka, Democratic Republic of the
Congo

1557 **Centre for Liberation Theologies**
Katholieke Universiteit Leuven
Faculty of Theology
Sint-Michielsstraat 6
3000 Leuven
Tel: +32-16-32 38 03 Fax: +32-16-32 38 58
Email:
liberation.theology@theo.kuleuven.ac.be
(General enquiries)
Jacques.Haers@theo.kuleuven.be (Chair)
Web:
http://www.theo.kuleuven.ac.be/clt/net_afr
icaine.htm
Chair: Prof. Dr. Jacques Haers, sj

1558 **Centrum voor de Studie van**
het Gebied van de Grote Meren
in Afrika/Centre d'étude de
la region des grands lacs
d'afrique
Université d'Anvers
Venusstraat 35 / 207
2000 Antwerp
Tel: +32-3-220 4842 Fax: +32-3-220 4787
Email: gralac@ua.ac.be (General enquiries)
stefaan.marysse@ufsia.ac.be (Chair)
Web: http://www.gralac.org/home_f.htm
(French version)
http://www.gralac.org/home_e.htm
(English version)
Chair: Stefaan Marysse, chairman

1559 **Department of African Languages**
and Cultures
Ghent University
Rozier 44
9000 Ghent
Tel: +32-9-264 3706 Fax: +32-9-264 4180
Email: Freddy.Mortier@UGent.be
Web: http://africana.UGent,be
Head: Dr. Freddy Mortier
Library resources: see → **1181**

1560 **Koninklijk Museum voor Midden –**
Afrika/Royal Museum for Central
Africa (KMMA/RMCA)
Research Department
Leuvensesteenweg 13
3080 Tervuren
Tel: +32-2-769 52 84 (Reception,
Research Department)
Email: paula.lamal@africamuseum.be
(Reception, General enquiries)
guido.gryseels@africamuseum.be
(Director)

Web:
http://www.africamuseum.be/muse
m (Dutch version)
http://www.africamuseum.be/research
(English version)
Fax: +32 2 767 02 42
Director: Dr. Guido Gryseels
Library resources: *see* ➔ **1183**

Denmark

1561   Center for Afrikastudiers
Københavns Universitet
Købmagergade 46 4 sal
1150 Copenhagen K
Tel: +45-3532 2585 Fax +45-3532 2590
Email: cas@teol.ku.dk (General enquiries)
hbh@teol.ku.dk (Director)
Web:
http://www.teol.ku.dk/cas/nyhomepage/H
jemmeside_engelsk/index_engelsk.htm
(English version)
Director: Prof. Holger Bernt Hansen
Library resources: *see* ➔ **1184**

Finland

1562   Aasian ja Afrikan kielten
jakulttuurien laitos/Institute for
Asian and African Studies
Helsinki University
Department of African Studies
Room B222
Unioninkatu 38 B
PO Box 59
00014 Helsinki
Tel: +358-9-191 22224 Fax: +358-9-191 22224
Email: Harry.Halen@Helsinki.Fi (Institute)
Arvi.Hurskainen@Helsinki.Fi
(Chair, Dept. of African Studies)
Web: http://www.helsinki.fi/hum/aakkl/
and
http://www.helsinki.fi/hum/aakkl/d_africa
.html
Chair: Prof. Arvi Hurskainen
Library resources: *see* ➔ **1187**

France

1563   Centre de recherches africaines
(CRA)
Université Paris 1
Centre Malher 2e étage
Bureau 201
9 rue Malher
75181 Paris Cedex 04
Tel: +33-1-44 78 33 32 Fax: +33-1-44 78 33 39
Email: cra@univ-paris1.fr
Web: http://mald.univ-
paris1.fr/centres/cra.htm
Director: Prof. Bertrand Hirsch
Library resources: *see* ➔ **1191**

1564   Centre d'études africaines arabes et
asiatiques (CEA)
31 rue de la Fonderie
BP 7012
31068 Toulouse Cedex
Tel: +33-5-61 36 81 25
Email: documentation@ict-toulouse.asso.fr
Web: http://www.ict-toulouse.asso.fr/cea/
Director: Dr. Robert Chuquet

1565   Centre d'étude d'afrique noire/
CEAN – IEP de Bordeaux
11 allée Ausone
Domaine Universitaire
33607 Pessac Cedex
Tel: +33-5-56 84 42 82 Fax: +33-56 84 43 24
Email: info@cean.u-bordeaux.fr (General
enquiries) d.darbon@sciencespobordeaux.fr
(Director)
 Web: http://www.cean.u-bordeaux.fr/
(French version) http://www.cean.u-
bordeaux.fr/anglais/index.html (English
version)
Director: Dr. Dominique Darbon
Library resources: *see* ➔ **1197**

1566   Centre d'études africaines
de l'Ecole des hautes etudes en
sciences socials (EHESS)
54 boulevard Raspail
75006 Paris
Tel: +33-1-49 54 23 93 Fax: +33-1-49 54 26 92
Email: stceaf@ehess.fr (General enquiries)
agier@ehess.fr (Director)
Web:
http://www.ehess.fr/centres/ceaf/index.ht
ml
Director: Dr. Michel Agier
Library resources: *see* ➔ **1198**

1567 Centre d'études et de recherches sur les pays du Commonwealth (CERPAC)
Département d'Etudes Anglophones
Université Paul Valéry Montpellier III
3 route de Mende
34199 Montpellier Cedex 5
Tel: +33-4-67 14 20 00 (Main university switchboard)
Email: judith.misrahi-barak@univ-montp3.fr
Web: http://alor.univ-montp3.fr/cerpac/
Contact: Judith Misrahi-Barak
Note: formerly Centre d'Études et de Recherches sur les Pays d'Afrique Noire Anglophone

1568 Centre d'étude juridiques et politiques du monde africain (CEJPMA)
Université Paris 1
Centre Malher 2e étage
Bureau 202A
9 rue Malher
75181 Paris Cedex 04
Tel: +33-1-44 78 33 23 Fax: +33-1-44 78 33 39
Email: banegas@aol.com
Web: http://mald.univ-paris1.fr/centres/cejpma.htm
Director: Dr. Richard Banégas
Library resources: *see* ➔ **1191**

1569 Centre de recherche et d'étude sur les pays d'afrique orientale Université de Pau et des Pays de l'Adour (CREPAO)
Avenue du Doyen Poplawski
Campus Universitaire
BP 1633
64016 Pau Cedex
Tel: +33-5- 59 40 80 49 Fax: +33-5-59 40 80 50
Email: claude.santini@univ-pau.fr (General enquiries)
Francois.Constantin@univ-pau.fr (Director)
Web: http://www.univ-pau.fr/RECHERCHE/CREPAO/lecrepao.htm
Director: Prof. François Constantin

1570 Groupe de recherche afrique noire et océan indien (SEDET)
Université Paris 7 Denis-Diderot
2 place Jussieu
75251 Paris Cedex 05
Tel: +33-1-44 27 47 01/44 27 46 21
Fax: +33-1-44 27 79 87

Email: sedet@ccr.jussieu.fr
Web:
http://www.sedet.cicrp.jussieu.fr/sedet/Afrilab/Afrhome.htm
Coordinator: Mme Far Rajaonah

1571 Institut d'etudes africaines d'Aix-en-Provence (IEA)
Université de Provence
Maison Méditerranéenne des Sciences de l'Homme (MMSH)
5 rue du Château de l'Horloge
BP 647
13094 Aix-en-Provence Cedex 02
Tel: +33-4-42 52 40 61
Fax: +33-4-42 52 43 61
Email: testaniere@mmsh.univ-aix.fr (General enquiries)
Jean-Louis.Triaud@mmsh.univ-aix.fr (Director)
Web: http://www.mmsh.univ-aix.fr/iea/index.html
Director: Prof. Jean-Louis Triaud

1572 L'institut de recherche pour le développement (IRD)
213 rue La Fayette
75480 Paris Cedex 10
Tel: +33 -1-48 03 77 77
Fax: +33-1-48 03 08 29
Email: corlay@paris.ird.fr (Research enquiries)
Web: http://www.ird.fr/ (French version)
http://www.ird.fr/us/ (English version)
Director General: Serge Calabre
Secretary General: Christine d'Argouges
Contact: (Bureau des concours/Research)
Hélène Corlay *Note:* For IRD offices in Africa see
http://www.ird.fr/fr/monde/afrique.htm

1573 Laboratoire d'anthropologie juridique de Paris (LAJP)
Université Paris 1
Centre Malher, 5e étage,
Bureau 508
9 rue Malher
75181 Paris Cedex 04
Tel: +33-1-44 78 33 80 Fax: +33-1-44 78 33 33
Email: lajp@univ-paris1.fr
Web: http://mald.univ-paris1.fr/centres/lajp.htm
Director: Prof. Etienne Le Roy
Library resources: *see* ➔ **1191**

1574 Laboratoire sociologie, histoire, anthropologie des dynamiques culturelles (SHADYC)
Centre de la Vieille-Charité
2 rue de la Charité
13002 Marseille
Tel: +33-4-91 14 07 20/91 14 07 58
Fax: +33-4-91 91 34 01
Email: wmshadyc@ehess.cnrs-mrs.fr (Administration/Deputy Director)
boutier@ehess.univ-mrs.fr (Director)
Web: http://www.vcharite.univ-mrs.fr/shadyc/
Prof. Jean Boutier, Director

1575 La Maison René Ginouvès d'Archéologie et d'Ethnologie
21 allée de l'Université
92023 Nanterre Cedex
Tel: +33-1-46 69 24 00 Fax: +33-1-46 69 24 51
Email: vidal@mae.u-paris10.fr
Web: http://www.mae.u-paris10.fr/accueil/index.htm (French version) http://web.mae.u-paris10.fr/traduction/gbindex.html (English version)
Director: Pierre Rouillard
Library resources: *see* ➜ 1206

1576 Mutations africaines dans la longue durée (MALD)
Université Paris 1
1 Centre Malher 2e étage
Bureau 210
9 rue Malher
75181 Paris Cedex 04
Tel: +33-1-44 78 33 41 Fax: +33-1-44 78 33 39
Email : mald@univ-paris1.fr
Web: http://mald.univ-paris1.fr/index.htm
Director of the Unit: Pierre Boilley
Joint Director: Dominique Beaulaton
Note: this is the umbrella body of **CEJPMA (1568)**, **CRA (1563)**, and **LAJP (1573)** listed above.

Germany

1577 Arnold-Bergsträsser-Institut für kulturwissenschaftliche Forschung
Windausstr. 16
79110 Freiburg im Breisgau
Tel: +49-761-888780

Fax: +49-761-888 7878
Email: abifr@abi.uni-freiburg.de (General enquiries)
heribert.weiland@abi.uni-freiburg.de (Executive Director)
Web: http://www.arnold-bergstraesser.de/
Executive Director: Prof. Dr. Heribert Weiland
Library resources: *see* ➜ 1213

1578 Asien-Afrika-Institut, Abteilung für Afrikanistik und Äthiopistik,
(Universität Hamburg)
Edmund-Siemers-Allee 1
1 Flügel Ost
20146 Hamburg
Tel: +49-40-42838 4873/74
Fax: +49-40-42838 5675
Email: afrikanistik@uni-hamburg.de or mreh@uni-hamburg.de
Web: http://www.uni-hamburg.de/Wiss/FB/10/AfrikaS/index.html
Contacts: Prof. Dr. Mechthild Reh; Dr. Verena Böll
Library resources: *see* ➜ 1214

1579 Deutsches Institut für Entwicklungspolitik (DIE)/ German Development Institute
Tulpenfeld 4
53113 Bonn
Tel.: +49-228-949 270 Fax: +49-228-949 27130
Email: DIE@die-gdi.de (General enquiries)
dirk.messner@die-gdi.de (Director)
Gabriele.Kahnert@die-gdi.de (Head of Administration)
Web: http://www.die-gdi.de/die_homepage.nsf/Pstartd?OpenPage (German version) http://www.die-gdi.de/die_homepage.nsf/FSStartE?OpenFrameset (English version)
Director: Dr. Dirk Messner
Contact, Head of Administration: Gabriele Kahnert
Library resources: *see* ➜ 1218

1580 Institut für Afrika-Kunde (IAK)
Neuer Jungfernstieg 21
20354 Hamburg
Tel: +49-40-4282 5523 Fax: +49-40-4282 5511
Email: iak@iak.duei.de (General)
mehler@iak.duei.de (Director)
Web: http://www.duei.de/iak/show.php (German version)

http://www.duei.de/iak/show.php/en/con
tent/welcome/welcome.html (English
version)
Director: Dr. Andreas Mehler, Director
Library resources: see → 1224

**1581 Institut für Afrika-Studien
Universität Bayreuth**
Iwalewa-Haus
Münzgasse 9
95444 Bayreuth
Tel: +49-921-552088 Fax: +49-921-552085
Email: IAS@uni-bayreuth.de (General
enquiries) herbert.popp@uni-bayreuth.de
(Director)
Web: http://www.uni-
bayreuth.de/Afrikanologie/IAS/ (German
version) http://www.uni-
bayreuth.de/Afrikanologie/IAS/e-
index.html (English version)
Director: Dr. Herbert Popp
Library resources: see → 1234

**1582 Institut für Afrikanische
Sprachwissenschaften (IfAS)
Goethe-Universität Frankfurt am
Main**
Kettenhofweg 135
60054 Frankfurt am Main
Tel: +49-69-798 28261
Fax: +49-69-747046
Email: ifas@uni-frankfurt.de
Web: http://web.uni-frankfurt.de/fb09/afr/
Chair: Prof. Dr. Rainer Vossen

**1583 Institut für Afrikanistik
Universität zu Köln**
Philosophische Fakultät
Meister-Ekkehart-Str. 7
50923 Cologne
Tel: +49-221-470 2708 Fax: +49-221-470 5158
Email: d.jansen@uni-koeln.de
Web: http://www.uni-koeln.de/phil-
fak/afrikanistik/ (German version)
http://www.uni-koeln.de/phil-
fak/afrikanistik/index_e.shtml (English
version)
Managing Committee: Prof. Dr. Heike
Behrend *et al* see
http://www.uni-koeln.de/phil-
fak/afrikanistik/mitarbeit/
Library resources: see → 1225

**1584 Institut für Afrikanistik
Universität Leipzig**
Geisteswissenschaftlichen Zentrum
Beethovenstr. 15
04107 Leipzig
Tel: +49-341-973 7030
Fax: +49-341-973 7048
Email: mgrosze@uni-leipzig.de
Web: http://www.uni-leipzig.de/~afrika/
Head of Secretariat: Monika Grosse (for list of
teaching staff see Web site)

**1585 Institut für Asien- &
Afrikawissenschaften
Humboldt-Universität zu Berlin**
Unter den Linden 6
10099 Berlin
Tel: +49-30- 2093 6601 Fax: +49-30-2093 6649
Email: iaawsekretariat@staff.hu-berlin.de
(General enquiries)
iaawdir1@cms.hu-berlin.de (Director)
flora.veit-wild@rz.hu-berlin.de (Executive
Director)
Web: http://www2.hu-berlin.de/asaf/iaaw/
(Main Institute home page)
http://www2.hu-
berlin.de/asaf/Afrika/index.html (Seminar
für Afrikawissenschaften)
Director: Dr. Vincent J.H. Houben
Deputy Director & Executive Director: Prof.
Dr. Flora Veit-Wild
Library resources: see → 1221

**1586 Institut für Ethnologie
der Freien Universität Berlin
Regionalbereich Afrika**
Drosselweg 1-3 Raum 123
14195 Berlin
Tel +49-30-838 56505/838 56727
Fax: +49-30-838 52382
Email: luig@zedat.fu-berlin.de
Web: http://www.fu-berlin.de/ethnologie/
Director: Prof. Dr. Ute Luig
Library resources: see → 1227

**1587 Institut für Ethnologie und
Afrikastudien
Johannes Gutenberg Universität**
Forum Universitatis 6
55099 Mainz
Tel: +49-6131-392 2798 Fax: +49-6131-392 3730
Email: ifeas@mail.uni-mainz.de (General
enquiries) biersche@mail.uni-mainz.de
(Chair)

Web: http://www.ifeas.uni-mainz.de/
(German version) http://www.ifeas.uni-
mainz.de/english/Department.html
(English version)
Chair: Prof. Dr. Thomas Bierschenk *et al*
Library resources: *see* ➔ **1228**

**1588   Institut für Ethnologie
            Westfälische Wilhelms-
            Universität Münster**
            Studtstrasse 21
            48149 Münster
Te.: +49-251-924 010 Fax: +49-251-9240113
Email: ifethno@uni-muenster.de
Web: http://www.uni-
muenster.de/Ethnologie/
Head, and Chair of Social Anthropology:
Prof. Dr. Josephus Platenkamp

**1589   Institut für Völkerkunde und
            Afrikanistik**
            Flügel B Raum B 0.12
            Oettingenstr. 67
            80538 Munich
Tel: +49-89-2180 9601 Fax: +49-89-2180 9602
Email: ethnologie@vka.fak12.uni-
muenchen.de (General enquiries)
Matthias.Laubscher@vka.fak12.uni-
muenchen.de (Chair)
Web: http://www.fak12.uni-
muenchen.de/vka/
Director: Prof. Dr. Matthias S. Laubscher
Library resources: *see* ➔ **1216**

**1590   Zentrum für interdisziplinäre
            Afrikaforschung (ZIAF)
            Johann Wolfgang Goethe-
            Universität**
            Campus Westend Raum 6.418
            Grüneburgplatz 1
            60323 Frankfurt am Main
Tel: +49-69-7983 2097
Fax: +49-69-7983 3098
Email: info@ziaf.de
Web: http://www.ziaf.de/
Coordinator: Dr. Stefan Schmid

Italy

**1591   Istituto Italiano per l'Africa e
            l'Oriente**
            Via Ulisse Alovandi 16
            00197 Rome
Tel: +39-6-3285 5216 Fax: +39-6-322 5348

Email: info@isiao.it or uff.stampa@isiao.it
Web: http://www.isiao.it/
Director General: Prof. Giancarlo Gargaruti
Executive Director: Giorgio Torchia
Library resources: *see* ➔ **1240**

**1592   Istituto per le Relazioni tra l'Italia e i
            Paesi dell'Africa, America Latina e
            Medio Oriente**
            Via degli Scipioni 147
            00192 Rome
Tel: +39-6-679 2321/2311 Fax: +39-6-679 7849
Email: ipalmo@ipalmo.com (General
enquiries) triulzizi@ipalmo.com (Executive
Director)
Web: http://www.ipalmo.com (Italian
version)
http://www.ipalmo.com/eng/default.htm
(English version)
Executive Director: Dr. Umberto Triulizi
Library resources: *see* ➔ **1241**

**1593   Istituto Universitario Orientale di
            Napoli. Dipartimento di Studi e
            Ricerche su Africa e Paesi Arabi**
            Piazza San Domenico Maggiore 12
            Palazzo Corigliano
            80134 Naples
Tel: +39-81-690 9622 Fax: +39-81-551 5386
Email: diprapa@iuo.it (General enquiries)
a.triulzi@agora.stm.it (Coordinator, African
studies)
Web:
http://www.iuo.it/diprapa/DSRAPA/dsrap
a_default.htm
Director: Prof. Giorgio Banti
Coordinator, African studies: Prof.
Alessandro Triulzi
Library resources: *see* ➔ **1242**

Netherlands

1594   African Studies Centre (ASC)
            Pieter de la Courtgebouw/
            Faculty of Social Sciences
            Wassenaarseweg 52
            2333 AK Leiden
            Postal address:
            PO Box 9555
            2300 RB Leiden
Tel: +31-71-527 3372 Fax +31-71-527 3344
Email: asc@ascleiden.nl (Secretariat/General
enquiries) lhaan@ascleiden.nl (Director)

Web: http://www.ascleiden.nl/
Director: Prof. Dr L.J. de Haan
Note: **RSS** RSS feed (all seminar, calendar, and topical items) at http://www.ascleiden.nl/RssFeeds/Channel Version1.xml
Library resources: *see* ➔ **1246**

Norway

1595   **Chr. Michelsen Institute**
Fantoftvegen 38
Fantoft
Postal address:
PO Box 6033 Postterminalen
5892 Bergen
Tel: +47-55-574000 Fax: +47-55-574166
E-mail: cmi@cmi.no (General enquiries)
gunnar.sorbo@cmi.no (Director)
Web: http://www.cmi.no/
Director: Dr. Gunnar M. Sørbø
Library resources: *see* ➔ **1253**

1596   **Programme of African Studies Norwegian University of Science and Technology**
SVT-Fakultetet
Bygg 1 Nivå 4
NTNU Dragvoll
7491 Trondheim
Tel: +47-73-59 19 00 Fax: +47-73 59 19 01
Email: gunn.hilde.garte@svt.ntnu.no
Web:
http://www.svt.ntnu.no/afrika/default_eng .htm (English version) or
http://www.svt.ntnu.no/adm/eng/stud/fa gbeskrivelser/afrikastudier/bachelor.htm
Programme Coordinator: Gunn Hilde Garte

Poland

1597   **Department of African Languages and Cultures. Institute of Oriental Studies, Warsaw University**
Faculty of Modern Languages and Oriental Studies
ul. Krakowskie Przedmieście 26/28
00927 Warsaw
Tel: + 48-22-552 0517 Fax: + 48-22-826 3683
Email:
afrykanistyka.orient@uw.edu.pl (General enquiries)

j.mantel-niecko@uw.edu.pl (Chair)
Web:
http://www.orient.uw.edu.pl/~afrykanistyk a/
Chair: Prof. Joanna Mantel-Niećko

Portugal

1598   **Centro de Estudos Africanos (ISCTE)**
Avenida das Forças Armadas
Sala 2N17
1600 Lisbon
Tel: +351-21-790 30 67 Fax: +351-21-795 53 61
Email: cea@iscte.pt
http://www.cea.iscte.pt/
President: José Fialho Feliciano
Executive Director: Prof. Franz Heimer

1599   **Centro de Estudos Africanos Universidade do Porto**
Via panorâmica s/n
4150-564 Porto
Tel: +351- 22-607 7141 Fax: +351-22-609 1610
Email: ceaup@letras.up.pt
Web: http://www.letras.up.pt/ceaup/
Director: Prof. António Custódio Gonçalves

1600   **Centro de Estudos Africanos e Asiáticos Instituto de Investigação Científica Tropical (IICT)**
R. da Junqueira 30 - 1°
1349-007 Lisbon
Tel: +351-21-360 05 81/361 63 40
Fax: 21 363 14 60 (Main ICCT fax)
Email: iict@iict.pt (IICT General enquiries)
jbmacedo@fe.unl.pt (President. IICT)
cestaa@iict.pt (Centre of African and Asian Studies)
Web: http://www.iict.pt/ (Main IICT page)
http://www.iict.pt/actividades/254/viict254 .asp (Centre of African and Asian Studies pages)
President, IICT: Prof. Jorge Braga de Macedo
Centre contact: Dr. Jill Dias
Library resources: *see* ➔ **1256**

1601   **Centro de Estudos sobre Africa e do Desenvolvimento. Instituto Superior de Economia e Gestão Universidade Técnia de Lisboa**
R. Miguel Lupi 20
1249-078 Lisbon

Tel: + 351-21-392 5983
Fax: + 351-21-397 6271
Email: cesa@iseg.utl.pt (General enquiries)
jochen@iseg.utl.pt (Director)
Web: http://pascal.iseg.utl.pt/~cesa/ (in
Portuguese and English versions at same
URL)
Director: Prof. Jochen Oppenheimer

1602   Centro Interdisciplinar de
        História, Culturas e Sociedades da
        Universidade de Évora
        Núcleo de Estudos Sobre África
        (CIDEHUS/NESA)
        Palácio do Vimioso Apartado 94
        7002-554 Évora
Tel: +351-266-706581 Fax: +351-26-744677
Email: cidehus@uevora.pt
Web:
http://www.cidehus.uevora.pt/indexn.htm
Director, CIDEHUS: Prof. Mafalda Soares da
Cunha
Director, NESA: Prof. Eduardo da Conceição
Medeiros

Russia

1603   Institute of Asian and African
        Studies
        Lomonsov Moscow State University
        Vorobjevy Gory
        Moscow 119992
Tel: +7-95-203 2741 Fax: +7-95-203 3647
Email: office@polit.isaa.msu.su
Web:
http://www.ied.msu.ru/faculties/isaa.html
Dean: Prof. Mickail S. Meyer

1604   Institute for African Studies
        Russian Academy of Sciences
        Spiridonovka 30/1
        Moscow 103001
Tel: +7-95-290 6385 Fax: +7-95-202 0786
Email: info@inafr.ru
Web: http://www.inafr.ru/ (Russian
version) http://eng.inafr.ru/
(English version)
Director: Prof. Alexei Vassiliev
Library resources: *see* ➔ **1257**

1605   Department of African Studies
        Saint Petersburg State University
        Faculty of Oriental and African
        Studies
        Universitetskaja emb. 7/9
        199034 Street Petersburg
Tel: +7-812-328 2982
Email: orient@vk4589.spb.edu
Web: http://www.orient.pu.ru/eorient.htm
Head: Prof. Andrey Alekseevich Zhukov

Spain

1606   Catedra UNESCO de Estudios
        Afroiberoamericanos
        Universidad de Alcalá
        Dpto. de Fundamentos de
        Economía e Hª Económica
        Plaza de Dan Diego
        28801 Alcalá de Henares
Tel: +34-91-885 4085 Fax: +34-91-885 4130
Email: luis.beltran@uah.es
Web:
http://www.um.es/gtiweb/unitwin/cuahea
.htm#contacto
Director: Prof. Luis Beltrán

1607   Centro de Información y
        Documentación Africanas (CIDAF)
        C/. Gaztambide 31
        28015 Madrid
Tel: +34-91-1544 1818
Email: cidaf@planalfa.es
Web: http://www3.planalfa.es/cidaf/
(Spanish version)
http://www3.planalfa.es/cidaf/eng.htm
(English version)
Director: Dr. Bartolomé Burgos
Library resources: *see* ➔ **1259**

1608   Centro d'Estudis Africans (CEA)
        Mare de Déu del Pilar 15 pral.
        08003 Barcelona
Tel: +34-3-319 4008 Fax: +34-3-319 4008
Email: cea@pangea.org
Web:
http://www.estudisafricans.org/index2.htm
Projects Director: Eduard Gargallo

1609   Colegio Mayor Universitario
        "Nuestra Señora de Africa"
        Ramiro de Maeztu 8
        Ciudad Universitaria
        28040 Madrid

Tel: +34-91-554 0104
Fax: +34-91-554 0401
Email: africa@guadanet.org
Web: http://www.aeci.es/fcm/africa/
Director: Dr. Basilio Rodríguez Cañada

Sweden

1610   Centre for Africa Studies
Seminariegatan 1
PO Box 700
SE 405 30 Gothenburg
Tel: +46 31-773 1309 Fax: +46-31-773 49 33
Email: info@ovs.gu.se (General enquiries)
j.ewald@padrigu.gu.se (Director)
Web:
http://www.africastudies.gu.se/english/def
ault.html (English version)
Director: Jonas Ewald

1611   Nordiska Afrikainstitutet/
Nordic Africa Institute (NAI)
Kungsgatan 38
75321 Uppsala
Postal address:
PO Box 1703
75147 Uppsala
Tel +46-18-562200 Fax: +46-18-562290
Email: nai@nai.uu.se (General enquiries)
carin.norberg@nai.uu.se (Director)
Web: http://www.nai.uu.se/index.html
(Swedish version)
http://www.nai.uu.se/indexeng.html
(English version)
Director: Dr. Carin Norberg
Library resources: *see* ➜ **1260**

Switzerland

1612   Fach Afrikanistik
Universität Zürich
Allgemeine Sprachwissenschaft
Plattenstrasse 54
8032 Zurich
Tel: +41-1-634 2185 Fax +41-1-634 4357
Email: babel@spw.unizh.ch (General
enquiries) ebert@spw.unizh.ch (Head)
Web: http://www.unizh.ch/spw/afrling/
Head: Prof. Dr. Karen Ebert

1613   Institut Universitaire d'études du
développement (IUED)
20 rue Rothschild
CP 136
1211 Geneva 21
Tel: +41-22-906 5940 Fax: +41-22-906 5947
Email: iued@unige.ch (General
enquiries) Michel.Carton@iued.unige.ch
(Director)
http://www.unige.ch/iued/new/ (French
version)
http://www.unige.ch/iued/en/institut/ind
ex.html (English version)
Director: Prof. Michel Carton
Library resources: *see* ➜ **1263**

1614   Zentrum für Afrikastudien
(ZASB)/Centre for African Studies
Universität Basel
Rheinsprung 9
4051 Basle
Tel. +41-61-267 2742 Fax +41-61-267 4469
Email: zasb@unibas.ch (General enquiries)
veit.arlt@unibas.ch (Coordinator)
Web: http://www.unibas-
zasb.ch/deutsch/index.php (German
version) http://www.unibas-
zasb.ch/english/index.php (English version)
Coordinator: Dr. Veit Arlt

United Kingdom

1615   African Studies Centre
Coventry Business School
Coventry University
Priory Street
Coventry CV1 5FB
Tel: +44-(0)24-7688 8213
Email: lsx061@coventry.ac.uk (General
enquiries) R.May@coventry.ac.uk (Director)
Web:
http://www.stile.cov.ac.uk/public/rcon/cas
/ and
http://corporate.coventry.ac.uk/cms/jsp/po
lopoly.jsp?d=1001&a=872
Director: Prof. Roy May

1616   Centre for the Study of African
Economies
University of Oxford
Department of Economics
Manor Road
Oxford OX1 3UQ
Tel: +44-(0)1865-271084

Fax: +44-(0)1865-281447
Email: csae.enquiries@economics.ox.ac.uk
(General enquiries)
paul.collier@economics.ox.ac.uk (Director)
Web: http://www.csae.ox.ac.uk/
Director Prof. Paul Collier, Director
Library resources: *see* ➔ **1284**

1617   Centre of African Studies
Edinburgh University
21 George Square
Edinburgh EH8 9LD
Tel: +44-(0)131-650 3878
Fax: +44-(0)131-650 6535
Email: African.Studies@ed.ac.uk (General
enquiries)
Kenneth.King@ed.ac.uk (Director)
Web: http://www.ed.ac.uk/centas/
Director: Prof. Kenneth King
Library resources: *see* ➔ **1277**

1618   Centre of African Studies
University of Cambridge
Free School Lane
Cambridge CB2 3RQ
Tel/Fax: +44-(0)1223-334396
Email: african-studies@lists.cam.ac.uk
(General enquiries) laq10@cam.ac.uk
(Director)
Web: http://www.african.cam.ac.uk/
Director: Dr Ato Quayson
Library resources: *see* ➔ **1291**

1619   Centre of West African Studies
The University of Birmingham
(CWAS)
Edgbaston
School of Historical Studies
Edgbaston
Birmingham B15 2TT
Fax +44-(0)121-414 3228
Tel: +44-(0)121-414 5128
Email: CWAS@bham.ac.uk (General
enquiries) S.Brown@bham.ac.uk (Director)
Web: http://www.cwas.bham.ac.uk/
Director: Dr. Stewart Brown
Library resources: *see* ➔ **1290**

1620   The Ferguson Centre for African
and Asian Studies
The Open University
Faculty of Arts
Walton Hall
Milton Keynes MK7 6AA

Tel: +44-(0)1908-655244
Fax: +44-(0)1908-653973
Email: arts-ferguson-centre-
enquiries@open.ac.uk (General enquiries)
david.richards@open.ac.uk (Director)
Web:
http://www.open.ac.uk/Arts/ferguson-
centre/index.html
Director: Dr. David Richards

1621   Institute of Development Studies
University of Sussex (IDS)
Falmer
Brighton BN1 9RE
Tel: +44-(0)1273-606261
Fax: +44-(0)1273-621202/691647
E-mail: ids@ids.ac.uk (General enquiries)
bookshop@ids.ac.uk (Publications)
L.Haddad@ids.ac.uk (Director)
Web: http://www.ids.ac.uk/ids/
Director: Dr. Lawrence Haddad
Library resources: *see* ➔ **1272**

1622   International African Institute/
Institut Africain International
School of Oriental and African
Studies
Thornhaugh Street
Russell Square
London WC1H 0XG
Tel: +44-(0)20-7898 4420
Fax: +44-(0)20-7898 4419
Email: iai@soas.ac.uk (General enquiries)
ed2@soas.ac.uk (Publications)
Web: http://www.iaionthe.net/
Chair: Prof .Y. Mudimbe
Hon. Director: Prof. Philip Burnham

1623   The Leeds University Centre for
African Studies (LUCAS)
University of Leeds
Leeds LS2 9JT
Tel: +44-(0)113-233 5069
Fax: +44-(0)113-233 4400
Email: ipiafric@leeds.ac.uk (General
enquiries) lrcliffe@leeds.ac.uk (Director)
Web: http://www.leeds.ac.uk/lucas/
Director: Emeritus Prof. Lionel Cliffe
Library resources: *see* ➔ **1292**
See also Information for Students from Africa
http://www.leeds.ac.uk/international/eafric
a.htm

1624 National Institute of African Studies
112 Burnham Lane
Slough SL1 6LZ
Tel: +44-(0)1628-666476
Fax: +44 (0)1753-551956
Email: admin@africanstudies.co.uk
Web:
http://home.btconnect.com/NATIONAL-INSTITU/nias.html
Director: Dr. Dele Williams
Note: also at 3rd Floor, 22-24 Cross Street, Reading, RG1 1SN

1625 School of Oriental & African Studies
University of London (SOAS)
Thornhaugh Street
Russell Square
London WC1H 0XG
Tel: +44-(0)20-7637 2388
Fax: +44-(0)20-7436 3844
Email: study@soas.ac.uk (General enquiries) cb3@soas.ac.uk (Director & Principal) *see*
http://www.soas.ac.uk/contact/index.cfm?navid=1133 for other email contacts
Web: http://www.soas.ac.uk/
Director & Principal: Prof. Colin Bundy
Library resources: *see* ➔ **1289**

1626 University Centre for African Studies (University of Oxford)
St Antony's College
62 Woodstock Road
Oxford OX2 6JF
Tel: +44-(0)1865-284996/274554
Fax: +44-(0)1865)-274478
Email: african.studies@sant.ox.ac.uk
Web:
http://www.sant.ox.ac.uk/areastudies/african.shtml#contact and
http://www.africanstudies.ox.ac.uk/
Chair, African Studies Committee:
Prof. William Beinart
Contact: Secretary of African Studies
Library resources: *see* ➔ **1284**

1627 University of Oxford Centre for Development Studies/Queen Elizabeth House
Mansfield Road
Oxford OX1 3TB
Tel: +44-1865-281800 Fax +44-1865-281801
Email: *see* Staff list at
http://www.qeh.ox.ac.uk/people/staffliStreethtml?type=1
Web: http://www.qeh.ox.ac.uk/
Director: Frances Stewart
Library resources: *see* ➔ **1284**

NORTH AMERICA

Canada

Note: Canadian African studies programmes and institutes, etc. are listed in alphabetical order *by name of main institution.*

1628 Middle Eastern and African Studies Programme University of Alberta
Office of Interdisciplinary Studies
6-30 Humanities Centre
Edmonton AB T6G 2E5
Tel: +1-780-4924802/492 6606
Email: ann.mcdougall@ualberta.ca
Web: http://www.arts.ualberta.ca/~cmeas/index.htm
Director: Dr. E. Ann McDougall

1629 African Studies Research Group University of Calgary
Department of Anthropology
Social Sciences Room 854
2500 University Drive NW
Calgary AB T2N 1N4
Tel: +1-403-220 6516 Fax: +1-403-284 5467
Email: tcheuyap@ucalgary.ca
Web: http://www.anth.ucalgary.ca/afstgp/Default.htm
Coordinator: Dr. Alexie Tcheuyap

1630 African Studies Committee Carleton University
Department of Political Science
D685 Loeb Building
Carleton University
1125 Colonel By Drive
Ottawa ON K1S 5B6
Tel: +1- 613-520 2764 Fax: +1- 613-520 4064
Email: Edward_OseiKwadwoPrempeh@carleton.ca
Web: http://www.carleton.ca/iis/african_studies.html
Coordinator: Edward Osei Kwadwo Prempeh
Library resources: *see* ➜ **1295**

1631 Centre for African Studies Dalhousie University
Multidisciplinary Studies Centre
Henry Hicks Building Room 339
Dalhousie University
6299 South Street
Halifax NS B3H 4H6
Tel: + 1-902-494 3814 Fax: +1-902-494 2105
Email: parpart@is.dal.ca
Web: http://artsandsocialsciences.dal.ca/Research%20Services/Centre_for_African_S.html
Director: Dr. Jane Parpart

1632 African Studies Program McGill University
Peterson Hall Room 318
3460 McTavish Street
Montréal QC H3A 1X9
Tel: +1-514-398 4301
Email: faye.scrim@mcgill.ca
Web: http://www.mcgill.ca/africanstudies/
Chair: Prof. Myron Echenberg
Library resources: *see* ➜ **1297**

1633 Groupe d'étude et de recherche sur les sociétés africaines (GERSA) Université Laval
École de psychologie Pavillon Félix-Antoine-Savard
Faculté des sciences sociales
Université Laval QC G1K 7P4
Tel: +1- 418-656 5383 (Faculty Secretary)
Fax: +1-418-656 3646
Email: psy@psy.ulaval.ca (Faculty Secretary)
Web: http://www.fss.ulaval.ca/gersa/
Faculty Coordinator and Vice-Dean of Research: Dr. Michel Loranger

1634 African Studies Program York University
Division of Social Science
Faculty of Arts
322 Founders College
4700 Keele Street
Toronto ON M3J 1P3
Tel: +1-416-7362100 ext 20260/66939
Email: parris@yorku.ca (General enquiries)
pidahosa@yorku.ca (Coordinator)
Web: http://www.arts.yorku.ca/sosc/african/index.html
Coordinator: Prof. Pablo Idahosa
Library resources: *see* ➜ **1298**

United States

Note: US African and African American/Black studies programmes and institutes, etc. are listed in alphabetical order *by name of main institution.*

1635   **Department of Black Studies**
Amherst College
108 Cooper House
PO Box 5000
Amherst MA 01002-5000
Tel: +1-413-542 5800 Fax: +1-413-542-2133
Email: blackstudies@amherStreetedu
Web:
http://www.amherStreetedu/~blackstudies
/
Chair: Prof. Rowland O. Abiodun

Amherst College *see also* → **Five Colleges**
African Studies Certificate Program (1681)

1636   **African and African American**
Studies Program
Arizona State University
PO Box 873802
Cowden Family Resources Building
224
Tempe AZ 85287-3802
Tel: +1-480-965 4399 Fax: +1-480-965 7229
Email: aframstu@asu.edu (General enquiries)
okey.iheduru@asu.edu (Director)
Web: http://www.asu.edu/clas/aframstu/
Director: Prof. Okey Chris Iheduru

1637   **Africana Studies**
Bard College
PO Box 5000
Annandale-on-Hudson
NY 12504-5000
Tel: +1-845-758 7201
Email: shipley@bard.edu
Web:
http://inside.bard.edu/academic/programs
/aads/index.html
Director: Dr. Jesse Weaver Shipley

1638   **African American Studies**
Bates College
2 Andrews Road
73/75 Campus Avenue Room 5
Lewiston ME 04240-6028
Tel: +1-207-786 6407

Email: mbruce@bates.edu
Web: http://www.bates.edu/AAS.xml
Chair: Prof. Marcus C. Bruce

1639   **The Institute of Global Cultural**
Studies (IGCS)
Binghamton University
State University of New York
PO Box 6000 LNG-100
Binghamton NY 13902
Tel: +1-607-777 4494
Email: igcs@binghamton.edu (General
enquiries) amazrui@binghamton.edu
(Director)
Web:
http://www.binghamton.edu/igcs/index.ht
m
Director: Prof. Ali A. Mazrui

1640   **African American Studies**
Boston University
138 Mountfort Street
Brookline MA 02446 446
Tel: +1-617-353 2795 Fax: +1- 617-353-0455
afam@bu.edu (General enquiries)
HDarodius@aol.com (Director)
Web: http://www.bu.edu/afam/
Director: Donald K. Richardson

1641   **African Studies Center**
Boston University
College of Arts and Sciences
270 Bay State Road
Boston MA 02215
Tel: +1-617-353 7311/617-353 7308
Email: johart@bu.edu (Program
administrator/General enquiries)
mccann@bu.edu (Director)
Web: http://www.bu.edu/africa/
Director: Dr. James C. McCann
Library resources: *see* → **1300**

1642   **Africana Studies Program**
Bowdoin College
Russwurm House
6-8 College Street
7200 College Station
Brunswick ME 04011-8472
Tel: +1-207-725 3272 Fax: +1-207-725 3766
Email: richards@henry.bowdoin.edu
Web:
http://academic.bowdoin.edu/africana_stud
ies/
Coordinator: Dr. Harriet Richards

1643 Africana Studies
Bowling Green State University
132 Shatzel Hall
Bowling Green OH 43403
Tel: +1-419-372 7914/371 2269
Email: lashcra@bgnet.bgsu.edu
Web:
http://www.bgsu.edu/departments/african
a/index.html
Director: Dr. Lillian Ashcraft-Eason

1644 Department of African and Afro-
American Studies
Brandeis University
116 Rabb MS 004
PO Box 549110
Waltham MA 02454-9110
Tel: +1-781-736 2090 Fax: +1-781-736 2095
Email: krakauer@brandeis.edu (General
enquiries) fsmith@brandeis.edu (Chair)
Web:
http://www.brandeis.edu/departments/afr
o_amer_studies/
Director: Prof. Faith L. Smith

1645 Africana Studies Department
Brown University
Box 1904 Churchill House
155 Angell Street 2nd Floor
Providence RI 02912
Tel: +1-401-863 3137
Email: sheila_grant@brown.edu (General
enquiries) barrymore_bogues@brown.edu
(Chair)
Web:
http://www.brown.edu/Departments/Afric
an_American_Studies/
Chair: Prof. Anthony Bogues
Library resources: *see* ➔ **1301**

1646 Africana Studies
Bryn Mawr College
101 North Merion Avenue
Bryn Mawr PA 19010-2899
Tel: +1-610-526 5000 ext 5318
Email: lbeard@brynmawr.edu
Web: http://www.brynmawr.edu/africana/
Coordinator: Dr. Linda-Susan Beard

1647 Department of Africana Studies
California State University-
Dominguez Hills
1000 E. Victoria Street
Carson CA 90747
Tel: +1-310-243 3420

Email: WLittle@csudh.edu
Web:
http://www.csudh.edu/Africana/
Chair: Prof. William Alexander Little

1648 Afro-Ethnic Studies
California State University-
Fullerton
PO Box 6868
Fullerton CA 92834-6868
Tel: +1-714-278 3848 Fax +1-714-278 3306
Email: bgreen@fullerton.edu (General
enquiries)
wgethaiga@fullerton.edu (Chair)
Web: http://hss.fullerton.edu/afro/
Chair: Dr. Wacira Gethaiga

1649 Department of Black Studies
California State University-Long
Beach
College of Liberal Arts
1250 Bellflower Boulevard
Long Beach CA 90840-0905
Tel: +1-562-985 4624
Fax: +1-562-985 5599
Email: mkarenga@csulb.edu
Web: http://www.csulb.edu/~africana/
Chair: Dr. Maulana Karenga

1650 Department of Pan-African Studies
California State University-Los
Angeles
King Hall C3095
5151 State University Drive
Los Angeles CA 90032
Tel: +1-323-343 2290 Fax: +1-323-343 5485
Email: pas@calstatela.edu
Web:
http://www.calstatela.edu/academic/
pas/
Chair: Dr. C.R.D. Halisi

1651 Pan-African Studies Department
California State University-
Northridge
18111 Nordhoff Street
Northridge CA 91330-8315
Tel: +1-818-677 3311 Fax: +1-818-677 3619
Email: tom.spencer.walters@csun.edu
Web: http://www.csun.edu/~pasafdep/
Chair: Prof. Tom Spencer-Walters

1652   African/African American Studies
        Program
        Carleton College
        One North College Street
        Northfield MN 55057
Tel: +1-507-646 4000
Email: kowusu@carleton.edu
Web:
http://www.carleton.edu/curricular/AFAM
/index.html
Director: Dr. Kofi Owusu

1653   African Studies Program
        Central Connecticut State University
        Psychology Department
        1615 Stanley Street
        New Britain CT 06050
Tel: +1-860-832 3105
Email: matekolec@ccsu.edu
Web: http://www.ccsu.edu/Afstudy/
Coordinator: Prof. Charles Mate-Kole

1654   Center for African Studies
        Central State University
        PO Box 1004
        Wilberforce OH 45384
Tel: +1-937-376-6011
Email: info@csu.ces.educ (General enquiries)
eonwudiwe@cesvxa.ces.edu (Director)
http://www.centralstate.edu/africanstudies
/
Director: Prof. Ebere Onwudiwe

1655   Department of African American
        Studies
        Chicago State University
        9501 South King Drive
        Chicago IL 60628-1598
Tel:+1-773 995–2192
Email: ebradbur@csu.edu
Web:
http://www.csu.edu/AfricanAmericanStudi
es/facultyA.htm
Chair (Acting): Dr. Emmett L. Bradbury

1656   Intercollegiate Department of Black
        Studies (IDBS), The Claremont
        Colleges
        102 Fletcher Hall
        Pitzer College
        1050 N Mills Avenue
        Claremont CA 91711
Tel: +1-909-607 3070
Email: sonya_young@pitzer.edu

Web:
http://www.pitzer.edu/academics/idbs/
Chair: Dr. Rita Roberts (Scripps)

→ Claremont McKenna College see
Intercollegiate Department of Black
Studies, The Claremont Colleges (1656)

1657   Department of African and African
        American Studies &
        Africana Women's Studies
        Clark Atlanta University
        McPheeters-Dennis Hall
        Rooms 11 and 14
        223 James P. Brawley Drive SW
        Atlanta GA 30314
Tel: +1-404-880 8533/880-6810
Fax: +1-404-880 8534
Email: jbradley@cau.edu
Web:
http://www.cau.edu/acad_prog/afr_am_stu
d/afram_right.html
Head: Dr. Josephine B. Bradley

1658   African American Studies
        Coe College
        Hickok Hall 304C
        1220 First Avenue NE
        Cedar Rapids IA 52402
Tel: +1-319-399-8500 ext 8593
Email: jrandall@coe.edu
Web:
http://www.coe.edu/catalog/africanameric
anstudies.htm
Coordinator: Prof. James Randall

1659   African American Studies
        Colby College
        4705 Mayflower Hill Drive
        Waterville ME 04901
Tel: +1-207-872 3133 Fax: +1-207-872 3752
Email: ctgilkes@colby.edu
Web:
http://www.colby.edu/afr.amer/
Chair: Dr. Cheryl Townsend Gilkes

1660   Department of Africana & Latin
        American Studies
        Colgate University
        Alumni Hall
        13 Oak Drive
        Hamilton NT 13346
Tel: +1- 315-228 7546 Fax: + 315-228 7098
Email: cjmartin@mail.colgate.edu

Web:
http://cwis.colgate.edu/faculty/default.asp?
department=african
Head: Prof. Clarice Martin

1661 African American Studies Program
College of Charleston
66 George Street
Charleston SC 29424
Tel: +1-843-953 5929
Email: dulaneyw@cofc.edu
Web: http://www.cofc.edu/~aast/
Coordinator: Dr. W. Marvin Dulaney

1662 African American Studies
College of Staten Island
The City University of New York
History/Political Science, Economics,
and Philosophy Building Room 210
2800 Victory Boulevard
Staten Island NY10314
Tel: +1-718-982 2880
Email: holder@mail.csi.cuny.edu
Web:
http://www.csi.cuny.edu/catalog/undergra
duate/programs/africanamerican.php3
Coordinator: Prof. Calvin Holder

1663 Department of Africana Studies
The College of Wooster
Wooster OH 44691
Tel: +1-330-263-2465
Email: mbanks@wooster.edu
Web:
http://academics.wooster.edu/progra
ms/africana_studies/
Head: Prof. Martha E. Banks

1664 Black Studies Program
College of William and Mary
112 Tucker Hall
PO Box 8795
Williamsburg VA 23187-8795
Tel: +1-757-221 1634
Email: jymcle@wm.edu
Web: http://www.wm.edu/blackstudies/
Director: Prof. Jacqueline McLendon

1665 Institute for Research in African-
American Studies
Columbia University
1200 Amsterdam Avenue
758 Schermerhorn Extension
Mail Code 5512
New York NY 10027

Tel: +1-212-854 7080 Fax: +1-212-854 7060
Email: iraas@columbia.edu (General
enquiries) fjg8@columbia.edu (Director)
Web:
http://www.columbia.edu/cu/iraas/
Director: Prof. Farah Griffin

1666 Institute of African Studies
Columbia University
School of International and Public
Affairs
1103 International Affairs Building
420 West 118th Street
Mail Code 3331
New York NY 10027
Tel: +1-212-854 4633 Fax: +1-212-854 4639
Email: africa-institute@columbia.edu
Web:
http://www.columbia.edu/cu/sipa/REGIO
NAL/IAS/
Director (Acting): Dr. Gail Gerhart
Library resources: *see* ➔ **1303**

1667 Africana Studies and Research
Center
Cornell University
310 Triphammer Road
Ithaca NY 14853-2599
Tel: +1-607 255-4625 Fax: +1-607-255 0784
Email: spt1@cornell.edu (General enquiries)
sh40@cornell.edu (Director)
Web: http://www.asrc.cornell.edu/
Director: Prof. Salah Hassan
Library resources: *see* ➔ **1304**

1668 Institute for African Development
Cornell University
170 Uris Hall
Tower Road
Ithaca NY 14853-7601
Tel: +1-607-255 5499
Fax: +1-607-254 5000
Email: ciad@cornell.edu (General enquiries)
mbn5@cornell.edu (Director)
Web:
http://www.einaudi.cornell.edu/Africa/
Director: Prof. Muna Ndulo
Library resources: *see* ➔ **1304**

1669 **African and African American**
Studies
Dartmouth College
121 Silsby Hall   HB 6134
Hanover NH 03755
Tel: +1-603-646 3397 Fax: +1-603-646 1680
Email: Rita.G.Hall@Dartmouth.edu (Program
Administrator/General enquiries)
J.Martin.Favor@Dartmouth.edu (Chair)
Web: http://www.dartmouth.edu/~african/
Chair: Prof. J. Martin Favor
Library resources: *see* ➔ **1305**

1670 **Center for Black Studies**
Denison University
Knapp Hall
Granville OH 43023
Tel: +1-740-587 6594 Fax: +1-740-587 5759
Email: jackson@denison.edu
Web:
http://www.denison.edu/departments/blst
/
Director: Prof. John L. Jackson

1671 **African & Black Diaspora Studies**
Program
DePaul University
College of Liberal Arts and Sciences
SAC 551 / 554
1 E. Jackson Boulevard
Chicago IL 60604
Tel: +1-773-325 7176
Email: dmoore1@depaul.edu
Web: http://condor.depaul.edu/~abds/
Director: Dr. Darrell Moore, Director

1672 **Black Studies Department**
DePauw University
PO Box 37
313 S. Locust Street
Greencastle IN 46135-0037
Tel: +1-765-658 4680
Email: sbates@depauw.edu (General
enquiries) vdickerson@depauw.edu
(Director)
Web:
http://www.depauw.edu/acad/black/
Director: Prof. Vanessa Dickerson

1673 **African & African American Studies**
Duke University
John Hope Franklin Center
Box 90252
2204 Erwin Road
Durham NC 27708

Tel: +1-919-684 2830 Fax: +1- 919-684 2832
Email: blackmor@duke.edu (General
enquiries) cmpayne@duke.edu (Director)
Web:
http://www.duke.edu/web/africanameric/
Director: Dr. Charles M. Payne
Library resources: *see* ➔ **1306**

1674 **African and African American**
Studies
Earlham College
801 National Road West
Richmond IN 47374-4095
Tel: +1- 765-983 1661
Email: washibo@earlham.edu
Web: http://www.earlham.edu/~aaas/
Associate Dean: Dr. Bonia Washington-Lacey

1675 **African Studies Committee**
East Carolina University
Greenville NC 27858
Tel: +1-252-328 6131 (Main university
switchboard)
Email: eribof@mail.ecu.edu
Web:
http://www.ecu.edu/african/homepage.ht
m
Coordinator: Dr. Festus Eribo

1676 **African American Studies**
Eastern Illinois University
College of Arts and Humanities
2140 Blair Hall
Charleston IL 61920
Tel: +1-217-581 5719 Fax: +1-217-581 6598
Email: cssgb@eiu.edu (General enquiries)
cfowo@eiu.edu (Chair)
Web: http://www.eiu.edu/~afriamer/
Director: Dr. Onaiwu W. Ogbomo

1677 **Department of African American**
Studies
Eastern Michigan University
620 Pray-Harrold
Ypsilanti MI 48197
Tel: +1-734-487-3460 Fax: +1-734-487-6891
Email: ronald.woods@emich.edu
Web:
http://www.emich.edu/public/daas/
Head (Interim): Prof. Ronald C. Woods

1678   African and African American
        Studies
        Elon University
        College of Arts and Sciences
        2700 Campus Box
        Elon NC 27244-2010
Tel: +1-800-334 8448
Email: n/a
Web:
http://www.elon.edu/catalog/courses/aaa/
Coordinator: n/a (vacant)

1679   Institute of African Studies
        Emory University
        1385 Oxford Road
        Atlanta GA 30322
Tel: +1- 404-727 6402 Fax: +1-404-727 6724
Email: ybamps@emory.edu (General
enquiries) ebay@learnlink.emory.edu
(Director)
Web:
http://www.emory.edu/COLLEGE/IAS/
Director: Prof. Edna Bay
Library resources: see ➔ 1307

1680   Program of African American
        Studies
        Emory University
        Atlanta GA 30322
Tel: +1-404-727 6847 Fax: +1-404-727 6848
Email: aas@emory.edu (General enquiries)
msander@emory.edu (Director)
Web:
http://www.aas.emory.edu/aasindex.html
Director: Prof. Mark Sanders
Library resources: see ➔ 1307

1681   Five Colleges African Studies
        Certificate Program
        Five Colleges, Inc
        97 Spring Street
        Amherst MA 01002
Tel: +1-413-256 8316
Email: ntherien@fivecolleges.edu (Director
for Academic Programs)
Web:
http://www.fivecolleges.edu/sites/african/i
ndex.php
African Studies Council Chair: Joye Bowman
Director for Academic Programs, Five
Colleges, Inc.: Nathan A. Therien

1682   Five Colleges African Scholars
        Program
        706 Herter Hall
        University of Massachusetts
        Amherst MA 01003
Tel: +1-413-577 3778 Fax: +1-413-577 3781
Email: asp@fivecolleges.edu
Web:
http://www.fivecolleges.edu/sites/asp/
Director: John Lemly
Program Coordinator: Tina Barsby

1683   African New World Studies
        Florida International University
        Biscayne Bay
        3000 NE 151st Street
        North Miami FL 33181
Tel: +1-305-919 5521 Fax +1-305-919 5267
Email: africana@fiu.edu (General enquiries)
cboyced@fiu.edu (Director)
Web: http://www.fiu.edu/~africana/
Director: Dr. Carole Boyce Davies

1684   African American Studies Program
        Florida State University
        211 Bellamy Bldg.
        Florida State University
        Tallahassee FL 32306-2151
Tel: +1-850-644 4418
blkstudy@mailer.fsu.edu (General enquiries)
pmason@garnet.fsu.edu
Web: http://www.fsu.edu/~aas/index.htm
Director: Patrick L. Mason

1685   Department of African American
        Studies
        Fordham University
        113 W. 60th Street Room 414
        New York NY 10023
Tel: +1-212-636 6363
Email: chapman@fordham.edu
Web:
http://www.fordham.edu/Academics/Prog
rams_at_Fordham_/African_and_African_/
Chair: Prof. Mark L. Chapman, Chair

1686   African World Studies Institute
        Fort Valley State University
        1005 University Drive
        Fort Valley GA 31030
Tel: +1-478-825 6056 Fax: +1-478-825 6196
Email: dctaw@fvsu.edu

Web:
http://www.fvsu.edu/aws/african_studies.a
sp
Director: Dr. Mwalimu J. Shujaa

1687   Africana Studies Department
Franklin & Marshall College
PO Box 3003
Lancaster PA 17604-3003
Tel: +1-717-291 3911 (Main university
switchboard)
Email: Misty.Bastian@fandm.edu
Web:
http://www.fandm.edu/Departments/Afric
anaStudies/
Chair: Prof. Misty Bastian

1688   Centre for Africana Studies
Georgia Southern University
College of Liberal Arts and Social
Sciences
Forest Drive Suite 1116
PO Box 8049
Statesboro GA 30460-8049
Tel: +1-912-681 5387 Fax: +1-912-871 1596
Email: africana@gsaix2.cc.GaSoU.edu
(General enquiries)
sjallow@georgiasouthern.edu (Chair)
Web:
http://academics.georgiasouthern.edu/afric
ana/
Chair: Dr. Saba Jallow

1689   Department of African American
Studies
Georgia State University
One Park Place Suite 962
Atlanta GA 30303-3083
Tel: +1-404-651 2157 Fax: +1-404-651 4883
Email: cjones@gsu.edu
Web:
http://www.gsu.edu/~aadbsf/index.htm#
Menu
Chair: Dr. Charles E. Jones
Library resources: *see* ➜ **1308**

1690   African American Studies
Guilford College
229 King Hall
5800 West Friendly Avenue
Greensboro NC 27410
Tel: +1-336-316-2318
Email: ktinsley@guilford.edu

Web:
http://www.guilford.edu/academics/index.
cfm?ID=100002770
Coordinator: Dr. Karen Tinsley

1691   Africana Studies
Hamilton College
198 College Hill Road
Clinton NY 13323
Tel: +1-315-859 4210
Email: vodamtte@hamilton.edu
Web:
http://www.hamilton.edu/academics/africa
n/default.html
Chair: Dr. Vincent Odamtten

Hampshire College *see* ➜ **Five Colleges**
African Studies Certificate Program (1681)

1692   Committee on African Studies
Harvard University
1033 Massachusetts Avenue
Room 216A
Cambridge MA 02138
Tel: +1-617-495 5265 Fax: +1-617-496 5183
Email: cafrica@fas.harvard.edu (General
enquiries) rbreen@fas.harvard.edu (Executive
Officer and Executive Director)
akyeamp@fas.harvard.edu (Chair)
Web: http://www.fas.harvard.edu/~cafrica/
Chair: Prof. Emmanuel K. Akyeampong
Executive Officer and Executive Director: Rita
M. Breen
Library resources: *see* ➜ **1309, 1310**

1693   Department of African and African
American Studies
Harvard University
12 Quincy Street
Barker Center 2nd Floor
Cambridge MA 02138
Tel: +1- 617-495 4113 Fax: +1-617-496 2871
Email: jackson6@fas.harvard.edu
(Department Administrator /General
enquiries)
kcdalton@fas.harvard.edu (Assistant
Director)
Web:
http://www.fas.harvard.edu/~afroam/
Chair: Henry Louis Gates, Jr.
Assistant Director: Karen C. C. Dalton
Library resources: *see* ➜ **1309, 1310**

1694 Africana and African Studies
Haverford College
Department of Religion
370 Lancaster Avenue
Haverford PA 19041-1392
Tel: +1-610-896 1486
Email: thucks@haverford.edu
Web:
http://www.haverford.edu/catalog/africana
_african_studies.htm
Joint Coordinators: Prof. Tracey E. Hucks
(Haverford College)
Prof. Robert Washington (Bryn Mawr)
Note: bi-college programme with
Bryn Mawr College.

1695 Africana Studies Program
Hofstra University
104 Hofstra University
Hempstead NY 11549-1040
Tel: +1-516-463 5588
Email:
africanastudies@hofstra.edu
(General enquiries) soccbm@hofstra.edu
(Chair)
Web:
http://www.hofstra.edu/Academics/HCLA
S/Africana/index_Africana.cfm
Chair: Dr. Cheryl Mwaria

1696 Department of African Studies
Howard University
Washington DC 20059
Tel: +1-202-806 7115
Email: rcummings@howard.edu
Web:
http://www.founders.howard.edu/african/
Chair: Prof. Robert J. Cummings
Library resources: *see* ➜ 1311

1697 Department of Africana and Puerto-
Rican-Latino Studies
Hunter College
City University of New York
1711 HW
695 Park Avenue
New York NY 10021
Tel: +1-212-772 5035 Fax: +212-650 3596
Email: eiwerieb@hunter.cuny.edu
Chair: Dr. Ehiedu Iweriebor
Web:
http://www.hunter.cuny.edu/blpr/index.ht
ml

1698 African American Studies Program
Indiana University-Purdue
University-Indianapolis
425 University Boulevard
Cavanaugh Hall 540
Indianapolis IN 46202
Tel: +1-317-274 8662/274 7611
Fax: +1-317-278 2347
Email: dabjenki@iupui.edu (General
enquiries) mlittle@iupui.edu (Director)
Web: http://www.iupui.edu/~afam/
Director: Prof. Monroe H. Little, Jr.

1699 African Studies Program
Indiana University
Woodburn Hall 221
Bloomington IN 47405
Tel: +1-812-855 6825 Fax: +1-812-855 6734
Email: afrist@indiana.edu (General enquiries)
jhhanson@indiana.edu (Director)
Web: http://www.indiana.edu/~afrist/
Director: Prof. John Hanson
Library resources: *see* ➜ 1313

1700 Department of African and African
American Studies
Indiana State University
A236 Root Hall
Indiana State University
Terre Haute IN 47809
Tel: +1-812-237 2550 Fax: +1-812-237 2549
Email: abellen@isugw.indstate.edu (General
enquiries) ascsaue@isugw.indstate.edu
(Chair)
Web: http://www.indstate.edu/afri/
Chair (Interim): Dr. Tom Sauer

1701 African Studies Program
School of Advanced International
Studies (SAIS)
Johns Hopkins University
Rome Building
1619 Massachusetts Avenue NW
Washington DC 20036
Tel: +1-202-663 5676 Fax: +1-202-663-5676
Email: tsimmons@jhu.edu.
Web:
http://www.sais-
jhu.edu/programs/africa/index.html
Director (Acting): Dr. Gilbert M. Khadiagala
Library resources: *see* ➜ 1314

**1702 Department of African American
Studies
John Jay College of Criminal Justice**
City University of New York
Room 3226 North Hall
City University of New York
899 Tenth Avenue
New York NY 10019
Tel: +1-212-237 8757 Fax: +1-212-237 8099
Email: diaspora@jjay.cuny.edu
Web: http://web.jjay.cuny.edu/~aas/
Chair: Dr. Jannette Domingo

**1703 Department of Pan-African Studies
Kent State University**
Ritchie Hall
PO Box 5190
Kent OH 44242-0001
Tel: +1-330-672 2300 Fax: +1-330-672 4837
Email: dbadejo@kent.edu (Chair)
Web: http://dept.kent.edu/pas/
Chair: Prof. Diedre L. Badejo

**1704 African Studies Department
Kalamazoo College**
Dewing Hall 303F
1200 Academy Street
Kalamazoo MI 49006
Tel: +1-269-337 5789 Fax: +1-269-337 7251
Email: wickstro@kzoo.edu
Web: http://www.kzoo.edu/africa/
Chair: Prof. John B. Wickstrom

**1705 African American Studies
Kenyon College**
Department of English
Gambier OH 43022-9623
Tel: +1-740-427 5000/5204
Fax: +1-740-427 5214
Email: masonte@kenyon.edu
Web:
http://www.kenyon.edu/academics/cos/20
01-02/courses/afamer.phtml
Director: Prof. Theodore O. Mason Jr.

**1706 Black Studies Program
Knox College**
2 East South Street
Galesburg IL 61401-4999
Tel: +1-309-341 7224
Email: fhord@knox.edu
Web:
http://www.knox.edu/blackstudies.xml
Chair: Prof. Fred L. Hord

**1707 Department of Black Studies
Lehman College**
City University of New York
CA-285
250 Bedford Park Boulevard W
Bronx NY 10468
Tel: +1-718-960 8283
Email: jervis@lehman.cuny.edu
Web:
http://humanities.lehman.cuny.edu/blackst
udies/
Chair: Dr. James Jervis

**1708 African American Studies
Department
Loyola Marymount University**
University Hall 4319
7900 Loyola Boulevard
Los Angeles CA 90045
Tel: +1-310-338 2810
Email: tlewis@lmu.edu (General enquiries)
JDavis@lmu.edu (Chair)
Web: http://bellarmine.lmu.edu/AFAM/
Chair: Prof. John A. Davis

**1709 African American Studies
Mercer University**
Department of English
1400 Coleman Avenue
Macon GA 31207
Tel: +1-912-752 2562 Fax: +1-912-752 2457
Email: fontenot_cj@mercer.edu
Web:
http://www2.mercer.edu/Admissions/Acad
emicPrograms/AfricanAmerican.htm
Chair: Chester J. Fontenot, Jr.

**1710 African Studies Center
Michigan State University**
100 Center for International Programs
East Lansing MI 48824-1035
Tel: +1-517-353 1700 Fax: +1-517-432 1209
Email: Africa@msu.edu (General enquiries)
wiley@msu.edu (Director)
Web:
http://www.isp.msu.edu/AfricanStudies/
Director: Prof. David Wiley
Library resources: see → 1317

**1711 African American Studies Program
Middle Tennessee State University**
Peck Hall 223
1301 East Main Street
Murfreesboro TN 37132-0001
Tel: +1-615-898 2536

Email: abakari@mtsu.edu
Web:
http://www.mtsu.edu/ucat/academics/aas.
html
Director: Prof. Adonijah L. Bakari

1712 Society of Research on African Culture
Montclair State University
French Department
1 Normal Avenue
Upper Montclair NJ 07043
Tel: +1-973-655 5143 Fax: +973-655 7909
Email: mengarad@mail.montclair.edu
Web:
http://picard.montclair.edu/%7Esorac/
Director: Dr. Daniel Mengara

1713 African American Studies Program
Morehouse College
Brawley Hall 212
830 Westview Drive SW
Atlanta GA 30314
Tel: +1-404-681 2800, ext 2528
Fax: +1-404-215 3480
Email: mbarksda@morehouse.edu
Web:
http://www.morehouse.edu/academics/hu
msocsci/africanamericanstudies/
Chair: Dr. Marcellus C. Barksdale

1714 Master of Arts-African American Studies with a Concentration in African Diaspora History
Morgan State University
School of Graduate Studies
Holmes Hall Room 326-I
1700 E. Cold Spring Lane
Baltimore MD 21251
Tel: +1-443-885-3185/885 3190
Fax: +1-443-885 8226/885 8227
Email: terborgpenn@moac.morgan.edu
(General enquiries)
apalmer@moac.morgan.edu (Chair)
Web:
http://www.morgan.edu/academics/Grad-
Studies/programs/aframer.asp
Chair: Dr. Annette Palmer

Mount Holyoke *see* ➔ **Five Colleges African Studies Certificate Program (1681)**

1715 National Consortium for Study in Africa (NCSA)
c/o African Studies Center
Michigan State University
100 Center for International Programs
East Lansing MI 48824-1035
Tel: +1-517-353 1700 Fax: +1-517-432 1209
Email: NCSA@msu.edu
Web: http://www.isp.msu.edu/ncsa/
Director: Dr. David Wiley (Director, African
Studies Center, MSU)

1716 Africana Studies Program
New York University
269 Mercer Street, Suite 601
New York NY 10003-6687
Tel: +1-212-998 2130 Fax: +1-212-995 4109
Email:
Web: rbk1@nyu.edu (General enquiries)
robert.hinton@nyu.edu (Director)
http://www.nyu.edu/gsas/dept/africana/
Director: Prof. Robert Hinton
Library resources: *see* ➔ **1320**

1717 Department of African American Studies
Northeastern University
132 Nightingale Hall
Boston MA 02115
Tel: +1-617-373 3148 Fax: +1-617-373 2625
Email: aas@neu.edu (General enquiries)
k.panford@neu.edu (Chair)
Web: http://www.afrostudies.neu.edu/
Chair: Prof. Kwamina Panford

1718 Department of African American Studies
Northwestern University
Weinberg College of Arts and
Sciences
2-320 Kresge Hall
Evanston IL 60208-2209
Tel: +1- 847-491 5122/491 5123
Fax: +1- 847-491 4803
Email: af-amstudies@northwestern.edu
Web: http://www.afam.northwestern.edu/
Chair (Interim): Dr. Darlene Clark Hine

1719 Program of African Studies
Northwestern University
620 Library Place
Evanston IL 60208-4110
Tel: +1-847-491 7323 Fax: +1-847-491 3739
Email:

african-studies@northwestern.edu (General enquiries) v-delancey@northwestern.edu (Academic Coordinator)
r-joseph@northwestern.edu (Director)
Web:
http://www.northwestern.edu/african-studies/
Director: Dr. Richard A. Joseph
Academic Coordinator: Virginia DeLancey
Library resources: *see* → **1322**

1720   Department of African American Studies
Oberlin College
Rice Hall Room 214
Oberlin OH 44074
Tel: +1-440-775 8923 Fax: +1-440-775 6485
Email: rejoice.acolatse@oberlin.edu
Web:
http://www.oberlin.edu/afamstud/courses/Dep_Info_Maj_Req.html#Menu
Chair: Prof. James Millette

1721   Center for African Studies
Department of African American and African Studies
Ohio State University
486 University Hall
230 North Oval Mall
Columbus OH 43210
Tel: +1-614-292 3700 Fax: +1-614-292 2293
Email: wilks.1@osu.edu (General enquiries)
goings.14@osu.edu
(Chair)
Web: http://aaas.ohio-state.edu/
Director: Prof. Kenneth W. Goings
Library resources: *see* → **1323**

1722   African Studies Program
Ohio University
Center for International Studies
Yamada International House
Athens OH 45701
Tel: +1-740-597 1511 Fax: +1-740-593 1837
Email: african.studies@ohio.edu (General enquiries)
howard@ohio.edu (Director)
Web:
http://www.cats.ohiou.edu/~african/main.htm
Director: Dr. W. Stephen Howard
Library resources: *see* → **1324**

1723   Department of African American Studies
Ohio University
Lindley Hall Room 300
Athens OH 45701
Tel: +1-740-593 4546 Fax: +1-740-5930671
Email: african.american.studies@ohio.edu (General enquiries)
cambridg@ohio.edu (Chair)
Web: http://www.ohio.edu/aas/
Chair: Dr. Vibert C. Cambridge
Library resources: *see* → **1324**

1724   Department of African and African American Studies
The Pennsylvania State University
214 Willard Building
University Park PA 16802
Tel: +1-814-863 4243 Fax: +1-814-863 3578
Email: mas73@psu.edu (General enquiries)
kim3@psu.edu (Head)
Web: http://aaas.la.psu.edu/
Head: Prof. Kidane Mengisteab

1725   Multicultural Studies Department
Palomar College
1140 West Mission Road
San Marcos CA 92069-1487
Tel: +1-760-744-1150, ext. 2206
Fax: +1-760-744 2932
Email: ssivert@palomar.edu
Web:
http://www.palomar.edu/multicultural/
Advisor: Prof. Wilma Docket-McLeod, Africana Studies

Pfitzer College *see* → **Intercollegiate Department of Black Studies, The Claremont Colleges (1656)**

Pomona College *see* → **Intercollegiate Department of Black Studies, The Claremont Colleges (1656)**

1726   Department of Black Studies
Portland State University
308 Neuberger Hall
PO Box 751
Portland OR 97207
Tel: +1-503-725 3472
Email: millerjonesd@pdx.edu,
Web: http://www.blackstudies.pdx.edu/
Chair: Prof. Dalton Miller-Jones

1727   **Princeton in Africa**
        Princeton University
        83 Prospect Avenue
        Room 202
        Princeton NJ 08544
        Tel: +1-609-258 7215
        Email: PiAf@princeton.edu
        Web: http://www.princeton.edu/~piaf/
        Executive Director: Dr. Holly Sanderson
        Schade
        Library resources: *see* ➜ **1325**

1728   **Program in African American**
        Studies
        Princeton University
        112 Dickinson Hall
        Princeton NJ 08544
        Tel: +1-609-258 4270 Fax: +1-609-258 5095
        Email: jeanw@princeton.edu
        Web:
        http://www.princeton.edu/~aasprog/home
        page.html
        Director: Prof. Valerie Smith
        Library resources: *see* ➜ **1325**

1729   **Program in African Studies**
        Princeton University
        Princeton Institute for International
        and Regional Studies
        Bendheim Hall
        Princeton NJ 08544-1022
        Tel: +1-609-258 4851 Fax: +1-609-258 3988
        Email: jslack@princeton.edu (Programs
        Manager, PIIRS) dir@Princeton.EDU
        (Director)
        Web:
        http://www.princeton.edu/%7Epiirs/progr
        ams/african_studies.html
        Director: Daniel I. Rubenstein
        Library resources: *see* ➜ **1325**

1730   **Program in Black Studies**
        Providence College
        Howley Hall 301
        Providence RI 02918
        Tel: +1-401-865 1229
        Email: daddieh@providence.edu
        Web:
        http://www.providence.edu/afro/index.ht
        ml
        Director: Prof. Cyril K. Daddieh

1731   **African American Studies &**
        Research Center
        Purdue University
        Beering Hall of Liberal Arts and
        Education (BRNG) Room 6182
        100 North University Street
        West Lafayette IN 47907-2067
        Tel: +1-765-494 5680 Fax: +1-765-496 1581
        Email: aasrc@sla.purdue.edu (General
        enquiries) vpatton@purdue.edu (Director)
        Web:
        http://www.sla.purdue.edu/academic/idis/
        African American/
        Director: Dr. Venetria K Patton

1732   **The St Clair Drake Center for**
        African and African-American
        Studies
        Roosevelt University
        School of Liberal Studies
        College of Arts and Sciences
        430 S. Michigan Avenue
        Chicago IL 60605
        Tel: +1-312-341 3500/341 3864
        Email: use online form at
        http://www.roosevelt.edu/drake/contact.ht
        m (General enquiries)
        abennett@roosevelt.edu (Director)
        Web:
        http://www.roosevelt.edu/drake/default.ht
        m
        Director: Albert L. Bennett

1733   **African American Studies Program**
        Rutgers University-Camden
        355 Armitage Hall
        311 North 5th Street
        Camden NJ 08102
        Tel: +1- 856-225 6220
        Email: glasker@crab.rutgers.edu
        Web:
        http://www.camden.rutgers.edu/dept-
        pages/afro_american/AfroAmericanStreetht
        ml
        Chair: Dr. Wayne Glasker

1734   **Department of African-American**
        and African Studies
        Rutgers University-Newark
        323 Conklin Hall
        175 University Avenue
        Newark NJ 07102
        Tel: +1- 973-353 5528 Fax: +1-973-353 1193
        Email: cstras@andromeda.rutgers.edu
        (General enquiries)

wholbrok@andromeda.rutgers.edu (Chair)
Web: http://www.afam.rutgers.edu/
Chair: Prof. Wendell Holbrook
Library resources: *see* ➔ **1326**

1735   Center for African Studies
Rutgers University-
Piscataway/New Brunswick
99 Avenue E Livingston College
Beck Hall Room 206
Piscataway NJ 08854-8045
Tel: +1-732-445 1192 Fax: +1-732-445 6637
Email: bacooper@rci.rutgers.edu
Web: http://ruafrica.rutgers.edu
Director: Prof. Barbara Cooper
Library resources: *see* ➔ **1326**

1736   Department of Africana Studies
Rutgers University-Piscataway/New
Brunswick
Beck Hall Room 112
Piscataway NJ 08854-8045
Tel: +1-732-445 3334 Fax: +1-732-445 0076
Email: kbutler@rci.rutgers.edu
http://africanastudies.rutgers.edu/
Chair: Dr. Kim D. Butler
Library resources: *see* ➔ **1326**

1737   Department of Africana Studies
San Diego State University
AH-3131
5500 Campanile Drive
San Diego CA 92182
Tel: +1-619-594 6531
Email: africana@mail.sdsu.edu (General
enquiries)
weber2@mail.sdsu.edu (Chair)
Web: http://www-
rohan.sdsu.edu/dept/afras/
Chair: Dr. Shirley N. Weber

1738   African American Studies
Department
San José State University
College of Social Work
1 Washington Square WSQ 216
San Jose CA 95192-0108
Tel: +1-408-924 5871 Fax: +1-408-924 5872
Email: afamstud@email.sjsu.edu (General
enquiries)
smillner@sjsu.edu (Chair)
Web:
http://www.sjsu.edu/depts/afamstudy/
Chair: Dr. Steven M. Millner

1739   Department of Black Studies
San Francisco State University
College of Ethnic Studies
1600 Holloway Avenue
San Francisco CA 94132
Tel: +1-415-338 2352
Email: bls@sfsu.edu
Web:
http://www.sfsu.edu/~ethnicst/BLS.html
Chair: Dr. Dorthy Tsuruta

1740   Africana Studies
Savannah State University
International Education Center
King-Frazier Student Center
Room 246
PO Box 20187
3219 College Street
Savannah GA 31404
Tel: +1-912-353 4942 Fax: +1-912-353 4946
Email: stmarkc@savstate.edu
http://www.savstate.edu/iec/Africa/astudy
.htm
Director: Dr. Cornelius Street Mark

Scripps College see ➔ **Intercollegiate**
Department of Black Studies (IDBS),
The Claremont Colleges (1656)

1741   Department of African American
Studies
Seton Hall University
Arts and Sciences Hall
400 South Orange Avenue
South Orange NJ 07079
Tel: +1-973-761 9411/9415
Email: n/a
Web: http://artsci.shu.edu/afam/
Chair: Dr. William W. Sales

1742   Africana Studies
Simmons College
Room E-319
300 The Fenway
Boston MA 02115-5898
Tel: +1-617-521 2183 Fax: +1-617-521 3199
Email: kristin.carroll@simmons.edu (General
enquiries) janie.ward@simmons.edu
(Chair)
Web:
http://www.simmons.edu/academics/unde
rgraduate/africana_studies/programs/social
_justice.shtml
Chair: Prof. Janie Ward

→ School of International Training- SIT
Study Abroad: African Studies *see* 202

1743 Afro-American Studies
Smith College
130 Wright Hall
Northampton MA 01063
Tel: +1-413-585-3572
Email: pgiddings@smith.edu
Web:
http://www.smith.edu/aas/index.html
Chair: Prof. Paula Giddings
see also → **Five Colleges African Studies**
Certificate Program (1681)

1744 Ethnic Studies Program
Southern Methodist University
Dedman College
6425 Boaz Lane
Dallas TX 75205
Tel: +1-216-768 2000 (Main university
switchboard)
Email: kmarvin@smu.edu
Web:
http://www.smu.edu/dedman/majors/ethn
icstudies/default.asp
Director: Prof. Kenneth Hamilton

1745 African American Studies
Southwestern College
School of Social Sciences and
International Studies
Building 470 Room 0750D
900 Otay Lakes Road
Chula Vista CA 91910
Tel: +1-619-421 6700 ext 5637
Email: sjames@swc.cc.ca.us
Web:
http://www.swc.cc.ca.us/~ssis/Disciplines/
index.asp?D30
Chair: Prof. Stanley James

1746 African Studies Undergraduate
Programs
St Cloud State University
273 Stewart Hall
720 Fourth Avenue South
St Cloud MN 56301-4498
Tel: +1-320-308-2003/308-3165
Email: pfnayenga@stcloudstate.edu
Web:
http://bulletin.stcloudstate.edu/ugb/progra
ms/afStreetasp
Director: Dr. Peter F. Nayenga

1747 African Studies Progam
Street Lawrence University
23 Romoda Drive
Canton NY 13617
Tel: +1-315-229 5011 (Main university
switchboard)
Email: blewett@stlawu.edu
Web:
http://web.stlawu.edu/programs/african_st
udies.html
Chair: Prof. Robert Allen Blewett

1748 Center for African Studies
Stanford University
Building 240 Room 104
Stanford CA 94305-2152
Tel: +1-650-723 0295 Fax: +1-650-723 8528
Email: ccapper@leland.stanford.edu (General
enquiries) rroberts@stanford.edu (Director)
http://www.stanford.edu/dept/AFR/
Director: Prof. Richard Roberts
Library resources: *see* → **1327**

1749 African & African American Studies
Stanford University
450 Serra Mall Bldg. 240
Stanford CA 94305-2084
Tel: +1-650-723 3782 /2088
Fax: +1- 650-723 8528
Email: rickford@csli.stanford.edu
Web:
http://www.stanford.edu/dept/AAAS/
Director: Prof. John R. Rickford
Library resources: *see* → **1327**

1750 Department of African and
Afro-American Studies
State University of New York-
Brockport
112 Faculty Office Building
350 New Campus Drive
Brockport NY 14420
Tel: +1-585-395 2470
Email: jmarah@brockport.edu
Web:
http://www.brockport.edu/catalogs/
undergraduate/chapter7/aas.html
Chair: Prof. John K. Marah

1751 Africana Studies Department
Stony Brook University
State University of New York
SBS Bldg. Room S-249
Stony Brook NY 11794
Tel: +1-631-632 7470 Fax: +1-631-632 5703

Email: Lorraine.Geiger@stonybrook.edu
Web:
http://naples.cc.sunysb.edu/CAS/afric
ana.nsf
Chair: Prof. Floris Barnett Cash

1752   Black Studies Program
          Swathmore College
          Department of English Literature
          500 College Avenue
          Swathmore PA 19081-1397
Tel: +1- 610-328-8000 (Main University
switchboard)
Email: ggiffor1@swarthmore.edu (General
enquiries)
cjames1@swarthmore.edu (Coordinator)
Web:
http://www.swarthmore.edu/Humanit
ies/blackstudies/
Coordinator: Dr. Charles James

1753   Department of African American
          Studies
          Syracuse University
          College of Arts and Science
          200 Simms Hall
          Syracuse NY 13244-4100
Tel: +1-315-443 4302 Fax: +1-315-443 1725
Email: aas@syr.edu (General enquiries)
lcarty@syr.edu (Chair)
Web: http://aas.syr.edu/
Chair: Dr. Linda Carty
Library resources: see ➔ 1329

1754   Department of African American
          Studies
          Temple University
          828 Gladfelter Hall
          1115 W. Berks Street
          Philadelphia PA 19122
Tel: +1-215-204 8491 Fax: +1-215-204 5953
Email: afro-am@temple.edu (General
enquiries) nathaniel.norment@temple.edu
(Chair)
Web:
http://www.temple.edu/AAS/index.htm
Chair: Prof. Nathaniel Norment, Jr.

1755   Africana Studies Department
          Tennessee State University
          College of Arts and Sciences
          3500 John A. Merritt Blvd
          Nashville TN 37209-1561
Tel: +1-615-963 5561 Fax: +1-615-963 7472
Email: al-hadid@harpo.tnstate.edu

Web:
http://www.tnstate.edu/arts_science/africa
na.html
Head: Dr. Amiri Y. Al-Hadid

1756   African & Diaspora Studies
          Tulane University
          119 Mayer Hall
          New Orleans LA 70118
Tel: +1-504-862 3550 Fax: +1-504-862 8677
Email: adst@tulane.edu (General enquiries)
felipes@tulane.edu (Chair)
Web: http://www.tulane.edu/~adst/
Chair: Prof. Felipe Smith

1757   African American Studies Program
          University of Alabama-Birmingham
          15th Street Office Bldg. Suite 151
          Birmingham AL 35294-2060
Tel: +1-205-975-9652 Fax: +1-205-975 9649
Email: niyi@uab.edu
Web:
http://www.uab.edu/african/
Director: Dr. Niyi Coker

1758   African American Studies Program
          University of Alabama-Tuscaloosa
          Box 870214
          Tuscaloosa AL 35487-0214
Tel: +1-205-348 2532 Fax: +1-205-348 9766
Email: amilcar@bama.ua.edu
Web:
http://www.as.ua.edu/amstud/aasthome.ht
m
Chair: Prof. Amilcar Shabazz

1759   Department of Africana Studies
          University at Albany
          State University of New York
          1400 Washington Avenue
          Business Admin. Bldg.   115
          Albany NY 12222
Tel: +1-518-442 4730 Fax: +1-518-442 2569
Email: africana@albany.edu (General
enquiries) lslade@albany.edu (Chair)
Email: rms99@cnsunix.albany.edu
Web:
http://www.albany.edu/africana/index.htm
l
Chair: Dr. Leonard Slade, jr.
Library resources: see ➔ 1331

1760   Department of African American
        Studies
        University at Buffalo
        State University of New York
        732 Clemens Hall
        Box 604680
        Buffalo NY 14260-4680
Tel: +1- 716-645 2082 ext 1126
Fax: +1-716-645 5976
Email: dpierce@buffalo.edu (Departmental
Secretary/General enquiries)
lsw4@buffalo.edu (Chair)
Web:
http://wings.buffalo.edu/academic/depart
ment/AandL/aas/
Chair: Prof. Lillian S. Williams
Library resources: *see* ➔ 1332

1761   Center for African Studies
        University of California-Berkeley
        Stephens Hall Room 342
        Berkeley CA 94720-2314
Tel: +1-510-642 8338 Fax: +1-510-642 0721
Email: ascsc@uclink.berkeley.edu (General
enquiries) mcf@berkeley.edu (Director)
Web: http://www.ias.berkeley.edu/africa/
Director: Prof. Mariane Ferme
Library resources: *see* ➔ 1333

1762   Department of African American
        Studies
        University of California-Berkeley
        660 Barrows Hall Room 2572
        Berkeley CA 94720
Tel: +1- 510-642 7084 Fax: +1-510-642 0318
Email: africam@berkeley.edu (General
enquiries) small@socrates.berkeley.edu
(Chair)
Web:
http://violet.berkeley.edu/~africam/
Chair: Prof. Stephen A. Small
Library resources: *see* ➔ 1333

1763   Program in African American and
        African Studies
        University of California-Davis
        2205 Hart Hall
        One Shields Avenue
        Davis CA 95616
Tel: +1-530-752 1548
Email: aas@ucdavis.edu (General enquiries)
jkolupona@ucdavis.edu (Chair)
Web: http://aas.ucdavis.edu/
Chair: Dr. Jacob K. Olupona

1764   Program in African American
        Studies
        University of California-Irvine
        300A Murray Krieger Hall
        Irvine CA 92697-6850
Tel: +1-949-824 2376 Fax: +1-949-824 7006
Email: djbaham@uci.edu
Web:
http://www.humanities.uci.edu//afam/
Program Manager: Dr. Donna Iliescu
Library resources: *see* ➔ 1334

1765   The James S. Coleman African
        Studies Center
        University of California-
        Los Angeles
        10244 Bunche Hall
        PO Box 951310
        Los Angeles CA 90095-1310
Tel: +1-310-825 3686 Fax: +1-310-206 2250
Email: jscasc@isop.ucla.edu (General
enquiries) aroberts@arts.ucla.edu (Chair)
Web: http://www.isop.ucla.edu/africa/
Director: Prof. Allen S. Roberts
UCLA African Studies Center
RSS RSS feed
http://www.international.ucla.edu/africa/rs
s.asp
Library resources: *see* ➔ 1335

1766   Ralph J. Bunche Center for African
        American Studies at UCLA
        Interdepartmental Program in Afro-
        American Studies
        160 Haines Hall
        Box 951545
        Los Angeles CA 90095-1545
Tel: +1-310-8257403 Fax: +1-310-825 3776
Email: lbritton@bunche.ucla.edu
Web:
http://www.bunchecenter.ucla.edu/
Center Director: Prof. Darnell M. Hunt
IDP Chair: Prof. Brenda Stevenson
Library resources: *see* ➔ 1335

1767   African American Studies
        University of California- Riverside
        Department of Ethnic Studies
        3606 HMNSS
        Riverside CA 92521
Tel: +1- 951-827 4577 ext 11823
Fax: +1-951-827 4344
Email: karen.tolbert@ucr.edu (General
enquiries) alfredo.mirande@ucr.edu (Chair)

Web:
http://www.ethnicstudies.ucr.edu/program
s/afas.html
Chair: Prof. Alfredo M. Mirandé

1768   Department of Black Studies
        University of California-Santa
        Barbara
        3631 South Hall
        Santa Barbara CA 93106-3150
Tel: +1-805-893 3800 Fax: +1-805-893 3597
Email: stowe@blackstudies.ucsb.edu
(General) lomeli@blackstudies.ucsb.edu
(Chair)
Web: http://www.blackstudies.ucsb.edu/
Chair: Prof. Francisco A. Lomelí
Library resources: see ➜ 1336

1769   African & African American Studies
        Research Project
        University of California-San Diego
        Arts & Humanities
        9500 Gilman Drive
        La Jolla CA 92093-0406
Tel: +1-858-822 0265
Email: bjulesrosette@ucsd.edu
Web: n/a
Chair: Prof. Bennetta Jules-Rosette

1770   African and African-American
        Studies
        University of Chicago
        Graham School of General Studies
        1427 E. 60th Street
        Chicago IL 60637
Tel: +1-773-702 8821 Fax: 1-773-702 3562
Email: rschultz@uchicago.edu
Web:
http://grahamschool.uchicago.edu/has/sub
program.cfm?subprogramid=341&forcredit=
2
Coordinator: Dr. Bart Schultz

1771   Department of African American
        Studies
        University of Cincinnati
        609 Old Chemistry Building
        PO Box 210370
        Cincinnati OH 45221-0370
Tel: +1-513-556 0350
Fax: +1-513-556 4595
Email: afam.studies@uc.edu (General)
john.brackett@uc.edu (Head)
Web:
http://asweb.artsci.uc.edu/afamstudies

Head: Professor John K. Brackett

1772   Center for Contemporary African
        Studies
        University of Connecticut
        843 Bolton Road Unit 1182
        Storrs CT 06269-1182
Tel: +1-860-486 2908 Fax: +1-860-486 2963
Email: Elizabeth.Mahan@uconn.edu
Web: http://www.ia.uconn.edu/CCAS/
Associate Executive Director, Office of
International Affairs & Program Advisor for
African Studies: Prof. Elizabeth Mahan

1773   Afro-American Studies
        The Department of Ethnic Studies
        University of Colorado
        Ketchum 30
        Campus Box 339
        Boulder CO 80309
Tel: +1-303-492 8852 Fax: +1-303-492 7799
Email: Ethnic.Studies@Colorado.EDU
(General departmental enquiries)
kingwm@spot.Colorado.EDU (Head, Afro-
American Studies)
Web:
http://www.colorado.edu/EthnicStudies/af
ro_american/index.html
Head (Afro-American Studies):
Dr. William M. King

1774   Center for African Studies
        University of Florida
        427 Grinter Hall
        PO Box 115560
        Gainesville FL 32611
Tel: +1-352-392 2183 Fax: +1-352-392 2435
Email: cgreene@africa.ufl.edu (Office
Manager/General enquiries)
villalon@africa.ufl.edu (Director)
Web: http://www.africa.ufl.edu/index.html
Director: Dr. Leonardo Villalón
Library resources: see ➜ 1337

1775   African Studies Institute
        University of Georgia
        321 Holmes/Hunter Academic
        Building
        Athens GA 30602
Tel: +1-706-542 5314 Fax: +1-706-583 0482
Email: africa@uga.edu (General enquiries)
moshi@uga.edu (Director)
Web:
http://www.uga.edu/~afrstu/index.htm
Director: Prof. Lioba Moshi

1776   Department of African American
        Studies
        University of Illinois at Chicago
        1223 University Hall (M/C 069)
        601 South Morgan Street
        Chicago IL 60607-7112
Tel: +1-312-996 2950 Fax: +1-312-996 5799
Email: carlap@uic.edu (General enquiries)
brichie@uic.edu (Head)
Web:
http://www.uic.edu/las/afam/aasthome.ht
ml
Head: Prof. Beth. E. Richie

1777   Centre for African Studies
        University of Illinois at Urbana-
        Champaign
        210 International Studies Building
        (MC-485)
        910 South Fifth Street
        Champaign IL 61820
Tel: +1-217-333 6335 Fax: +1-217-244 2429
Email: african@uiuc.edu
Web:
http://www.afrStreetuiuc.edu/center.html
Director: Prof. Jean Allman
Library resources: see ➜ 1338

1778   African Studies Program
        The University of Iowa
        120 International Center
        Iowa City IA 52242
Tel: +1-319-353 5700
Email: walter-jahava@uiowa.edu (General
enquiries)
rex-honey@uiowa.edu (Chair)
Web: http://intl-
programs.uiowa.edu/academic/asp/index.h
tm
Director: Prof. Rex Honey
Library resources: see ➜ 1339

1779   Department of African and African
        American Studies
        University of Kansas
        1440 Jayhawk Boulevard
        9 Bailey Hall Room 9
        Lawrence KS 66045-7574
Tel: +1-785-864 3054 Fax: +1-785-864 5330
Email: afs@ku.edu
Web: http://www.ku.edu/~afs/
Chair: Prof. Peter Ukpokodu
Library resources: see ➜ 1340

1780   Department of Pan-African Studies
        University of Louisville
        Strickler Hall Room 445
        Louisville KY 40292
Tel: +1-502-852 5985 Fax: +1-502-852 5954
Email: rljone01@gwise.louisville.edu
Web: http://www.louisville.edu/a-s/pas
Chair: Dr. Ricky Jones

1781   Africana Studies Department
        University of Maryland-Baltimore
        County
        1000 Hilltop Circle
        Baltimore MD 21250
Tel: +1- 410-455-1000 (Main university
switchboard)
Email: lamouses@umbc.edu
Web:
http://www.research.umbc.edu/africana/
Chair: Prof. Willie B. Lamouse-Smith

1782   David C. Driskell Center for the
        Study of the African Diaspora
        University of Maryland-
        College Park
        2114 Tawes Fine Arts Building
        College Park MD 20742-1211
Tel: +1-301-314 2615 Fax: +1-301-314 0679
Email: driskellcenter@umail.umd.edu
Web: http://www.driskellcenter.umd.edu/
Executive Director: Dr. Robert E. Steele

➜ **University of Massachusetts-Amherst** see
Five Colleges African Studies Certificate
Program (1681)

1783   The William Monroe Trotter
        Institute for the Study of Black
        Culture
        University of Massachusetts-Boston
        100 Morrissey Boulevard
        Boston MA 02125-3393
Tel: +1-617-287 5880 Fax: +1-617-2875865
Email: trotterinstitute@umb.edu (General
enquiries)
barbara.lewis@umb.edu (Chair)
Web: http://www.trotter.umb.edu/
Director: Dr. Barbara Lewis

1784   African and African American
        Studies
        University of Memphis
        Scates Hall 107
        Memphis TN 38152-3520
Tel: +1-901-678 3550

Email: bgbond@memphis.edu
Web: http://cas.memphis.edu/isc/aaas/index.html
Director: Dr. Beverly Bond

**1785   Africana Studies
University of Miami-Coral Cables**
College of Arts and Sciences
Building 21-V
5600 Merrick Drive
Coral Gables FL 33124
Tel: +1-305-284 6340 Fax: +1-305-2846127
Email: lbarza@miami.edu
(General enquiries)
eabaka@mail.as.miami.edu (Director)
Web:
http://www.as.miami.edu/africanastudies/
Director: Dr. Edmund Abaka

**1786   Center for Afroamerican and
African Studies
University of Michigan-Ann Arbor**
505 South State Street
4700 Haven
Ann Arbor MI 48109-1092
Tel: +1-734-764 5513 Fax: +1-734-763 0543
Email: caas-info@umich.edu (General
enquiries) gaineskk@umich.edu (Director)
Web:
http://www.umich.edu/~iinet/caas/
Director: Prof. Kevin Gaines
Library resources: *see* ➔ **1341**

**1787   Center for Middle Eastern and
North African Studies (CMENAS)
University of Michigan-Ann Arbor**
1080 South University Avenue Suite
4640
Ann Arbor MI 48109-1106
Tel: +1-734-764 0350 Fax: +1-734-764 8523
Email cmenas@umich.edu (General
enquiries) minhorn@umich.edu (Director)
http://www.umich.edu/~iinet/cmenas/
Director: Prof. Marcia C. Inhorn
Library resources: *see* ➔ **1341**

**1788   Department of Africana Studies
University of Michigan-Flint**
346 David M. French Hall
303 East Kearsley Street
Flint MI 48502-1950
Tel: +1-810-762 3353 Fax: +1-810-766 6719
Email: judyj@umflint.edu (General enquiries)
eernest@umflint.edu (Chair)

Web:
http://www.umflint.edu/departments/africana/
Chair: Prof. Ernest N. Emenyonu

**1789   Department of African American &
African Studies
University of Minnesota-Twin
Cities**
College of Liberal Arts
808 Social Science Building (West
Bank)
267 19th Avenue South
Minneapolis MN 55455
Tel: +1-612-624 9847 Fax: +1-612-624 9383
Email: afroam@umn.edu (General enquiries)
atkin013@umn.edu (Chair)
Web: http://www.afroam.umn.edu/
Chair: Prof. Keletso Atkins
http://www.afroam.umn.edu/

**1790   Department of Black Studies
University of Nebraska at Omaha**
6001 Dodge Street
184 Arts and Sciences Hall
Omaha NE 68182
Tel: +1- 402-554 2412 Fax: +1-402-554 3883
Email: n/a
Web:
http://www.unomaha.edu/wwwblst/index.htm
Chair: Prof. Robert Chrisman

**1791   Afro-American Studies
Program
University of Nevada**
Anthropology Department
Mail stop 5003
4505 Maryland Parkway
Las Vegas NV 89154
Tel: +1-702-8950943
Email: rspencer@ccmail.nevada.edu
Web:
http://www.unlv.edu/programs/afram/
Director: Dr. Rainier Spencer

**1792   Division of African American
Studies
University of New Mexico**
Mesa Vista Hall Room 4023
Albuquerque NM 87131-1581
Tel: +1-505-277 5644
Email: afamsts@unm.edu (General enquiries)
shiame@unm.edu (Director)

Web: http://www.unm.edu/~afamstds/
Director: Dr. Shiame Okonor

**1793   Department of African and
American Studies
University of North Carolina at
Chapel Hill**
109 Battle Hall CB# 3395
Chapel Hill NC 27599-3395
Tel: +1-919-966 5496 Fax: +1-919-962 2694
Email: dacrowde@email.unc.edu (General
enquiries) jen321@email.unc.edu (Chair)
Web:
http://www.unc.edu/depts/afriafam/afriaf
am.html
Chair: Dr. Julius E. Nyang'oro

**1794   Department of African American
and African Studies
University of North Carolina at
Charlotte**
9201 University City Boulevard
Macy 204B
Charlotte NC 28223-0001
Tel: +1- 704-687 2371 Fax: +1-704-687 3888
Email: ejbyrd@email.uncc.edu
(General enquiries)
mjazeved@email.uncc.edu (Chair)
Web: http://www.aaas.uncc.edu/index.html
Chair: Prof. Mario Azevedo

**1795   African American Studies Program
University of North Carolina-
Greensboro**
200 Foust Building
PO Box 26170
Greensboro NC 27402-6170
Tel: +1-336-334 5507/334 889
Email: nfwoods@uncg.edu
Web: http://www.uncg.edu/afs/
Director: Dr. Frank Woods

**1796   Department of Africana Studies
University of Northern Colorado**
Campus Box 159
Greeley CO 80639
Tel: +1-970-351 2685 Fax: +1-970-351 2898
Email: jhjunne@aol.com
Web: http://www.unco.edu/afs/index.htm
Chair: Prof. George Junne

**1797   African & African-American Studies
Program
University of Oklahoma**
Ellison Hall
633 Elm Avenue Room 233
Norman OK 73019-3120
Tel: +1-405-325 2327 Fax: +1-405-325 0842
Email: jrdavidson@ou.edu
Web: http://www.ou.edu/cas/afam/
Director: Dr. Jeanette Davidson

**1798   African Studies Committee
University of Oregon**
International Studies Program
175 Prince Lucien Campbell Hall
University of Oregon
Eugene OR 97403-5206
Tel: +1-541- 346-5051/346 5052
Fax: +1-541- 346 5041
Email: isp@uoregon.edu (General enquiries)
dgalvan@uoregon.edu (Chair)
Web:
http://darkwing.uoregon.edu/~dgalvan/asc
/asc.html
Chair: Prof. Dennis Galvan

**1799   African Studies Center
University of Pennsylvania**
School of Arts & Sciences
255 South 36th Street
647 Williams Hall
Philadelphia PA 19104-6305
Tel: +1-215-898 6971 Fax +1-215- 573-7379
Email: africa@sas.upenn.edu (General
enquiries) moudilen@sas.upenn.edu
(Director)
Web:
http://www.sas.upenn.edu/African_Studies
/AS.html
Director: Dr. Lydie Esther Moudileno
Library resources: *see* ➔ **1342**

**1800   African Studies Program
University of Pittsburgh**
University Center for International
Studies
3T Posvar Hall
Pittsburgh PA 15260
Tel: +1-412-648 2058 Fax: +1-412-648 7214
Email: africast@ucis.pitt.edu
(General enquiries) jadjaye@pitt.edu (Chair)
Web:
http://www.ucis.pitt.edu/africa/index.html
Chair: Prof. Joseph K. Adjaye

1801 **African and African American**
Studies
University of Rhode Island
90 Lower College Road
Roosevelt Hall
Kingston RI 02881
Tel: +1-401-874 2536 Fax: +1-401-874 4527
Email: cmh@uriacc.uri.edu
Web:
http://www.uri.edu/artsci/afr/index.html
Chair: Dr. Cynthia Hamilton

1802 **Frederick Douglass Institute for**
African and African American
Studies
University of Rochester
Morey 302
Rochester NY 14627
Tel: +1-585-275 7235 Fax: +1-585-256 2594
Email: fdi@troi.cc.rochester.edu (General
enquiries)
fredrick.harris@rochester.edu (Director)
Web:
http://www.rochester.edu/College/AAS/
Director: Prof. Fredrick C. Harris

1803 **African American Studies Program**
University of South Carolina
202 Flinn Hall
Columbia SC 29208
Tel: +1-803-777 7248 Fax: +1-803-777 1785
Email: csutton@gwm.sc.edu (General
enquiries)
cleve@gwm.sc.edu
Web: http://www.cla.sc.edu/AFRA/
Chair: Dr. Cleveland Sellers

1804 **Department of Africana Studies**
University of South Florida
4202 East Fowler Avenue
FAO 175
Tampa FL 33620
Tel: +1-813-974 2427 Fax: +1-813-974 4434
Email: yeisenha@cas.usf.edu (General
enquiries) purcell@cas.usf.edu (Chair)
Web:
http://www.cas.usf.edu/african_studies/
Chair: Prof. Trevor W. Purcell

1805 **The Africa Program**
University of Texas at Arlington
301 S. Center Suite 420
PO Box 19991
Arlington TX 76019-0991
Tel: +1-817-272 5302 Fax: +1-817-272 5210

Email: africaprogram@uta.edu (General
enquiries) Jalloh@uta.edu (Chair)
http://www.uta.edu/africaprogram/
Dr. Alusine Jalloh, Director

1806 **Center for African & African**
American Studies
University of Texas
Jester Center A232A
Campus Code D7200
Austin TX 78705
Tel: +1-512-471 1784 Fax: +1-512-471 1798
Email: caaas@uts.cc.utexas.edu (General
enquiries) etgordon@mail.utexas.edu (Chair)
Web:
http://www.utexas.edu/cola/depts/caaas/
Director: Dr. Edmund T. Gordon
Library resources: *see* ➔ **1343**

1807 **Africana Studies Program**
University of Tuledo
University Hall 2370
2801 West Bancroft Street
Toledo OH 43606
Tel: +1-419-530 7252 Fax +1-419-530 4739
Email: kathy.arquette@utoledo.edu (General
enquiries)
abdul.alkalimat@utoledo.edu (Director)
Web:
http://www.africa.utoledo.edu/#faculty
Director: Prof. Abdul Alkalimat

1808 **The Carter G. Woodson Institute for**
African American and African
Studies
University of Virginia
108 Minor Hall
PO Box 400162
Charlottesville VA 22904-4162
Tel: +1-434-924 3109 Fax: +1-434-924 8820
Email: woodson@gwis.virginia.edu (General
enquiries) rdb6d@virginia.edu (Chair)
Web: http://www.virginia.edu/woodson/
Director: Dr. Regional D. Butler
Library resources: *see* ➔ **1344**

1809 **Program of African Studies**
University of Washington
Thomson Hall 308
Box 353650
Seattle WA 98195
Tel: +1-206-616 0998 Fax: +1-206-616 2465
Email: africa1@u.washington.edu (General
enquiries) lynnmt@u.washington.edu (Chair)
Web:

http://depts.washington.edu/africa1/
Chair: Dr. Lynn M. Thomas

1810   African Studies Program
University of Wisconsin-Madison
205A Ingraham Hall
1155 Observatory Drive
Madison WI 53706
Tel: +1-608-262 2380 Fax: +1-608-265 5851
Email: asp@africa.wisc.edu (General
enquiries) schatzberg@polisci.wisc.edu
(Director)
Web: http://africa.wisc.edu/
Director: Dr. Michael G. Schatzberg
Library resources: *see* ➜ **1345**

1811   Department of Afro-American
Studies
University of Wisconsin-Madison
4145 HC White
600 N. Park
Madison WI 53706
Tel: +1-608-263 2332 Fax: +1-608-263 7198
Email: rjdaniel@facstaff.wisc.edu (General
enquiries) smjames@wisc.edu (Chair)
Web:
http://polyglot.lss.wisc.edu/aas/
Chair: Prof. Stanlie M. James
Library resources: *see* ➜ **1345**

1812   Department of Africology
University of Wisconsin-Milwaukee
PO Box 413
Milwaukee WI 53201
Tel: +1-414-229 4155 Fax: +1-414-229 4607
Email: dmbalia@uwm.edu (General
enquiries) lemelle@uwm.edu (Chair)
Web:
http://www.uwm.edu/Dept/Africology/in
dex.html
Chair: Prof. Anthony J. Lemelle

1813   Program in African American and
Diaspora Studies
Vanderbilt University
018-C Furman Hall
VU Station B Box 351516
2301 Vanderbilt Place
Nashville TN 37235-1516
Tel: +1-615-343 6390 Fax: +1-615-343 1444
Email:
africanamericanstudies@vanderbilt.edu
(General enquiries)
t.sharpley-whiting@vanderbilt.edu (Director)

Web:
http://sitemason.vanderbilt.edu/aframst/ho
me
Director: Dr. T. Denean Sharpley-Whiting

1814   Africana Studies Program
Vassar College
Box 739
124 Raymond Avenue
Poughkeepsie NY 12604
Tel: +1-845-437 7490 Fax: +1-845-437 5925
Email: africastudies@vassar.edu
Web: http://africanastudies.vassar.edu/
Director (Acting): Judith Weisenfeld

1815   African American Studies Program
Virginia Commonwealth University
Scherer Hall Room 105
915 W. Franklin Street
Richmond VA 23284-2509
Tel: +1-804-828 1384 Fax: +1-804-828 4983
Email: drthomas@vcu.edu (General
enquiries) mjackson@vcu.edu (Director)
Web: http://www.has.vcu.edu/aas/
Director: Dr. M. Njeri Jackson

1816   African and African American
Studies Program
Washington University in Saint
Louis
One Brookings Drive Box 1109
226 McMillan Hall
Saint Louis MO 63130
Tel: +1-314-935 5690 Fax: +1-314-935 5631
Email: afas@artsci.wustl.edu
Web: http://www.artsci.wustl.edu/~afas/
Director: Prof. John Baugh

1817   Africana Studies Department
Wayne State University
5057 Woodward
Detroit MI 48220
Tel: +1-313-577 2321 Fax: +1-313-577 3407
Email: ae5016@wayne.edu (General
enquiries)
EboeHutchf@aol.com (Head)
Web:
http://www.cla.wayne.edu/africanastudies/
Head: Prof. Eboe Hutchful

1818   Africana Studies Department
Wellesley College
106 Central Street
Wellesley MA 02481
Tel: +1-781-283 2563

Email: fsteady@wellesley.edu
Web:
http://www.wellesley.edu/Africana/african
a.html
Chair: Prof. Filomina Steady

1819   Center for African American Studies
African American Studies Program
Wesleyan University
343 High Street
Middletown CT 06459
Tel: +1-860-685 2190 Fax: +1-860-685 2041
Email: arushdy@wesleyan.edu
Web: http://www.wesleyan.edu/afam/
Chair: Prof. Ashraf Rushdy

1820   The Center for Black Culture and
Research
West Virginia University
590 Spruce Street
PO Box 6417
Morgantown WV 26506-6417
Tel: +1-304-293 7029 Fax: +1-304-293 2967
Email: lynnmarie.kuntz@mail.wvu.edu
(General enquiries)
katherine.bankole@mail.wvu.edu (Director)
Web: http://www.wvu.edu/~cbcr/
Director: Dr. Katherine Olukemi Bankole

1821   Department of African American
Studies
Western Illinois University
College of Arts & Sciences
1 University Circle
Morgan Hall 232
Macomb IL 61455
Tel: +1-309-2981181 Fax: +1-309-298 2181
Email: aas@wiu.edu (General enquiries)
A-Naallah@wiu.edu (Chair)
Web: http://www.wiu.edu/AAS/
Chair: Prof. Abdul-Rasheed Na'Allah

1822   Africana Studies Program
Western Michigan University
1903 West Michigan Avenue
Kalamazoo MI 49008
Tel: +1-269-3872665
Email: patty.deloach@wmich.edu (General
enquiries)
lpotter@wmich.edu (Chair)
Web:
http://www.wmich.edu/blackamericanastu
dies/
Director: Dr. Lawrence T. Potter

1823   African, African American &
Caribbean Studies Program
William Paterson University
Atrium 227
300 Pompton Road
Wayne NJ 07470
Tel: +1-973-720 3927/3027
Email: falonef@wpunj.edu (General
enquiries) mbogonil@wpunj.edu (Director)
Web: http://www.wpunj.edu/cohss/aacs/
Chair: Dr. Lawrence Mbogoni

1824   Africa Program
Woodrow Wilson Center
One Woodrow Wilson Plaza
1300 Pennsylvania Avenue, NW
Washington DC 20004-3027
Tel: +1-202-691 4097
Email: africa@wwic.si.edu (General enquiries)
wolpehe@wwic.si.edu (Director)
http://www.wilsoncenter.org/index.cfm?fus
eaction=topics.home&topic_id=1417
Director: Dr. Howard Wolpe

1825   African and African American
Studies
Wright State University
144 Millett Hall
Wright State University
Dayton OH 45435-0001
Tel: +1-937-775 5532
Email: African_AfricanAmerican@wright.edu
(General enquiries)
paul.griffin@wright.edu (Director
Web:
http://www.cola.wright.edu/Prog/AFS/
Director: Dr. Paul Griffin

1826   African American Studies Program
Yale University
493 College Street
Yale Station
PO Box 203388
New Haven CT 06520-3388
Tel: +1-203-432 1170 Fax: +1-203-432 2102
Email: geneva.melvin@yale.edu (General
enquiries) paul.gilroy@yale.edu
paul.gilroy@yale.edu (Chair)
Web: http://www.yale.edu/afamstudies/
Chair: Prof. Paul Gilroy
Library resources: see ➔ **1346**

1827   Council on African Studies
Yale University
Yale Center for International and
Area Studies
34 Hillhouse Avenue
PO Box 208206
New Haven CT 06520-8206
Tel: +1-203-432 3436 Fax: +1-203-432 5963
Email: african.studies@yale.edu (General
enquiries) robert.harms@yale.edu (Chair)
http://www.cis.yale.edu/ycias/african/
Chair: Prof. Robert Harms
Library resources: *see* ➔ **1346**

1828   Africana Studies Program
Youngstown State University
DeBartolo Building Room 422
One University Plaza
Youngstown OH 44555
Tel: +1-330-941 3097
Email: afrst@cc.ysu.edu
Web: http://www.as.ysu.edu/~afrst/
Director: Prof. Victor Wan-Tatah

AFRICA

Note: courses on Africa studies topics
are offered at most university
institutions in Africa. However, the
listing below is restricted to African
studies institutes, and university
institutions with departments of African
Studies as individual units.

Egypt

1829   Office of African Studies
The American University in Cairo
PO Box 2511
113 Sharia Kasr El Aini
Cairo
Tel: +20-2-797 6922/23 Fax: +20-2-797 6628
http://www.aucegypt.edu/academic/oas/
Email: oas@aucegypt.edu (General enquiries)
myambo@aucegypt.edu   (Director)
Web:
http://www.aucegypt.edu/academic/oas/
Director (Acting): Dr. Kathleen Myambo
Library resources: *see* ➔ **1387**

1830   Institute of African Research and
Studies (IARS)
Cairo University
12613 Giza
Cairo
Tel: +20-2-567 5549/392 4804
Fax: +20-2-578 0979
Email: n/a
Web:
http://www.cu.edu.eg/Faculties/a&sr.asp
Director: Dr Sayyid Ali Feleyfel
Library resources: *see* ➔ **1390**

Cameroon

1831   Pan-African Institute for
Development (PAID)
PO Box 133
Buea
Tel: +237-32806/421061 Fax: +237-424335
Email: info@paid-wa.org
Web: n/a (http://www.pai-wa.org
not accessible as at September 2005)
Mrs Rosetta B Thompson, Director

Côte d'Ivoire

➔ Institut africain pour le développement économique et social/African Institute for Economic and Social Development (INADES) *see* 18 Major African and international organizations entry 2598

Eritrea

1832   Institute of African Studies
       Asmara University
       PO Box 1220
       Asmara
Tel: +291-1-161926 Fax: +291-1-162236
Email: n/a
Web: http://www.uoa.edu.er/ (Main
university Web site)
Director: n/a
Library resources: *see* ➔ 1395

Ethiopia

1833   Organization for Social Science
       Research in Eastern and Southern
       Africa (OSSREA)
       PO Box 31971
       Addis Ababa
Tel: +251-1-239484 Fax: +251-1-223921
Email: ossrea@telecom.net.et (General
enquiries) executive.secretary@ossrea.net
(Executive Secretary)
Web: http://www.ossrea.net/
Executive Secretary: Dr. Alfred G. Nhema
Note: see also ➔ 275

Ghana

1834   Department of African and General
       Studies
       University of Cape Coast
       University Post Office
       Cape Coast
Tel: +233-42-32480/83
Email: n/a
Web:
http://www.uccghana.net/Departments/De
partment_Of_African_And_Gen_Studies.Ht
m
Head: Dr. J.H. Addai-Sundiata
Library resources: *see* ➔ 1403

1835   Department of African Studies
       University for Development Studies
       Tamale
Tel/Fax: +233-71-22080
Email: uds@ug.gn.apc.org
Web:
http://www.ghanauniversities.com/universi
ty_for_development_stud.htm
Director: n/a

1836   Institute of African Studies
       University of Ghana
       PO Box 73
       Legon
       Accra
Tel: +233-21-513390 Fax: +233-21-500512
Email: iasgen@ug.edu.gh (General enquiries)
dir-ias@ug.edu.gh (Director)
Web: http://www.ug.edu.gh/ (Main
university home page)
http://www.ug.edu.gh/ias/Index.htm
(Institute pages not accessible as at September
2005)
Director: Prof. Takyiwaa Manuh
Library resources: *see* ➔ 1404

Kenya

1837   French Institute for Research in
       Africa/Institute Français de
       recherche en Afrique (IFRA)
       Maendeleo House 4th floor
       Monrovia Street
       Nairobi
       Postal address:
       PO Box 58480
       00200 City Square
       Nairobi
Tel: +254-20-221922 Fax: +254-20-336253
Email: ifra3@iconnect.co.ke (General
enquiries)
ifra1@iconnect.co.ke (Director)
Web: http://www.ifra-nairobi.net/ (English
version) http://www.ifra-
nairobi.net/defaultfr.htm (French version)
Director: Charlery de la Masselière
Note: see also ➔ **IFRA, Ibadan, Nigeria (1844)**

1838   Institute of African Studies
       University of Nairobi
       PO Box 30197
       Nairobi
       Kenya
Tel: +254-20-742080 Fax: +254-2-744123

Email: directorias@insightkenya.com
(General enquiries) nama@insightkenya.com
(Director)
Web:
http://www.uonbi.ac.ke/faculties/ias/index
.htm?letter=I
Director: Dr. Isaac K. Nyamongo
Library resources: see ➔ 1411

1839   Institute for Development Studies
        University of Nairobi (IDS)
        Gandhi Wing 5th floor
        Main Campus University Way
        PO Box 30197
        Nairobi 00100 GPO
Tel: +254-20-338741/337436
Fax: +254-20-222036
Email: idsdirector@swiftkenya.com or
ids@nbnet.co.ke or uonids@nbnet.co.ke
Web:
http://www.uonbi.ac.ke/faculties/ids/?lette
r=I
or http://www.ids-nairobi.ac.ke/ (this site
not accessible as at September 2005)
Director: Prof. Dorothy McCormick

1840   Maryknoll Institute of African
        Studies
        PO Box 15199
        Lang'ata 00509
Tel: +254-20-890765 Fax: +254-20-91145
Email: miasmu@tangaza.org or
MIAS@maf.or.ke
Web: http://www.mias.edu
Director: Fr. Michael Kirwen

Lesotho

1841   Institute of Southern African Studies
        The National University of Lesotho
        PO Roma 180
        Lesotho
Tel: +266-22-340247 Fax: +266-223 40000
Email: m.mochebelele@nul.ls
Web:
http://www.nul.ls/institutes/isas.htm
Director: Dr. M. Mochebelele
Library resources: see ➔ 1412

Morocco

1842   L'Institut des Etudes Africaines/
        Institute of African Studies
        Université Mohamed V-Agdal
        3 bis rue Innaouen
        BP 8968
        Agdal-Rabat
Tel: +212-37-776579 /776576
Fax: +212-37-778425
Email: iea@enssup.gov.ma
Web: http://www.emi.ac.ma/univ-
MdV/IEA.html
Director: Prof. Fatima Harrak
Library resources: see ➔ 1426

Mozambique

1843   Centro de Estudos Africanos
        Universidade Eduardo Mondlane
        (CEA)
        Campus Universitário principal
        Caixa Postal 1993
        Maputo
Tel: +258-1-490828/491896 Fax: +258-1-491896
Email: ceadir@zebra.uem.mz
Web: http://www.cea.uem.mz/ (not
accessible as at September 2005)
http://www.uem.mz/ (Main university Web
site)
Director: Prof. Teresa Cruz e Silva
Library resources: see ➔ 1428

Nigeria

1844   French Institute for Research in
        Africa/Institute Français de
        recherche en Afrique (IFRA)
        Institute of African Studies
        University of Ibadan
        UI PO Box 21540
        Ibadan Oyo State
Tel/Fax: +234-2-810 4077
Email: ifra@skannet.com
Web: http://ifra-ng.org
Director: Gérard Pescheux
Note: see also ➔ IFRA, Nairobi, Kenya (1838)

1845   Institute of Cultural Studies
        Obafemi Awolowo University
        Ile-Ife Osun State
Tel: +234-36-230290

Fax: +234-36-233971
Email:
Web: http://www.oauife.edu.ng/ (Main
university Web site)
Director: Dr. A. Ogunba
Library resources: *see* → **1436**

1846   Institute of African Studies
University of Ibadan
U I PO Box 21540
Ibadan Oyo State
Tel/Fax: +234-2-810 4077
Email: n/a
Web: http://www.ui.edu.ng (Main
university Web site)
Director: Dr. S. A. Ademuyiwa
Library resources: *see* → **1439**

1847   Institute of African Studies
University of Nigeria
Nsukka
Enugu State
Tel: +234-42-771911 (Main university
switchboard) Fax: +234-42-770644
Email: n/a
Web: http://www.unnportal.com/
http://www.uem.mz/ (Main university Web
site)
Head: Osmond Enekwe
Library resources: *see* → **1444**

1848   Nigerian Institute of International
Affairs (NIIA)
13-15 Kofo Abayomi Road
Victoria Island
Lagos
Postal address:
GPO Box 1727 Marina
Lagos
Tel: +234-1-261 5606/7 Fax: +234-1-261 1360
Email: dgeneral@niianet.org (General
enquiries)
jogwu@niianet.org (Director General)
Web: http://www.niianet.org/
Director-General: Prof. U. Joy Ogwu
Library resources: *see* → **1435**

Senegal

1849   Centre de Recherche Ouest Africain/
West African Research Center
Avenue E x Leon G. Damas
Fann Residence

BP 5456
Dakar-Fann
Tel: +221-865 2277/+221-824 2062
Fax: +221-824 2058
Email: warc_croa@yahoo.fr
Web: http://www.warc-croa.org/
President, AROA, Senegal:
Dr. Ibrahima Thioub
Director: Prof. Ousmane Sène
Director of Administration &
Telecommunication: Abdoulaye Niang

1850   Council for the Development of
Social Science Research in
Africa/Conseil pour le
développement de la recherche en
sciences sociales en Afrique
(CODESRIA)
Avenue Cheikh Anta Diop x Canal IV
BP 3304
Dakar 18524
Tel: +221-825 9822/23 Fax: +221- 824 1289
Email: codesria@codesria.sn (General
enquiries)
executive.secretary@codesria.sn
(Executive Secretary's Office)
Web: http://www.codesria.org/
Executive Secretary: Dr. Adebayo Olukoshi
Library resources: *see* → **1450**

1851   Institut Fondamental d'Afrique
Noire Cheikh Anta Diop (IFAN)
Université Cheikh Anta Diop de
Dakar
BP 2006
Dakar
Tel: +221-250090/259890 Fax: +221-244918
Email: bifan@telecomplus.ns
Web:
http://www.ucad.sn/rubrique.php3?id_rubr
ique=169
Director: Prof. Djibril Samb
Library resources: *see* → **1451**

Sierra Leone

1852   Institute of African and Cultural
Studies
Fourah Bay College
University of Sierra Leone
Mount Aureol
Freetown
Tel: +232-22-227924/224260
Fax: +232-22-224260

Email: fbcadmin@sierratel.sl (General university email)
Web: http://fbcusl.8k.com/index.html (Main university Web site)
Director: Dr. G. Anthony
Library resources: *see* ➔ **1453**

South Africa

1853 Africa Institute of South Africa
1 Embassy House
Cnr Edmond and Bailey Streets
Arcadia
Pretoria
Postal address:
PO Box 630
Pretoria 0001
Tel: +27-12-328 6970 Fax: +27-12-323 8153
Email: ai@ai.org.za
Web: http://www.ai.org.za/
Executive Director: Dr. Eddy Maloka
Library resources: *see* ➔ **1454**

1854 Centre of Advanced Studies for African Society (CASAS)
7 Nursery Road
PO Box 359
Rondebosch 7701
Fax +27-21-685 0332 Tel: +27-21-689 9217
Email:
casas@casas.co.za (General enquiries)
kkprah@casas.co.za (Director)
Web: http://www.casas.co.za/index.htm
Director Prof. Kwesi Kwaa Prah

1855 Centre for Southern African Studies University of the Western Cape
School of Government
Private Bag X17
Bellville 7535
Tel: +27-21-959 2911 (Main university switchboard)
Email: lthompso@uwc.ac.za
Web:
http://www.uwc.ac.za/ems/sog/CSAS/
Director: Prof. Christo de Koning
Library resources: *see* ➔ **1473**

1856 Centre of African Studies University of Cape Town
Harry Oppenheimer Institute
Building Level 3
Private Bag
Rondebosch 7701

Tel: +27-21-650 2338 Fax: +27-21-689 7560
Email: cmcbride@humanities.uct.ac.za
cmcbride@humanities.uct.ac.za
Email: brenda@humanities.uct.ac.za
(Director)
Web: http://www.africanstudies.uct.ac.za/
Director: Prof. Brenda Cooper
Library resources: *see* ➔ **1462**

1857 Human Sciences Research Council of South Africa (HSRC)
134 Pretorius Street
Pretoria
Postal address:
Private Bag X41
Pretoria 001
Tel: +27-12-302 2000 Fax: +27-12-302 2001
Email: JEBotha@hsrc.ac.za (General enquiries/Council Secretariat)
rmaharaj@hsrc.ac.za (Chief Executive Officer)
http://www.hsrc.ac.za/
Chief Executive Officer: Dr. Romilla Maharaj

1858 The Institute for the Study of Mankind in Africa (ISMA) University of the Witwatersrand Medical School
School of Anatomical Sciences
7 York Road
2193 Parktown
Tel: +27-11-647 2203 Fax: +27-11-643 4318
Email: kuykendallkl@anatomy.wits.ac.za
Web: http://www.wits.ac.za/isma/
President: Dr Kevin Kuykendall

1859 Institute of Social and Economic Research Rhodes University
PO Box 94
Grahamstown 6140
Tel: +27-46-603 8550 Fax: +2746-622 3948
Email: iser-sec@ru.ac.za
Web: http://www.ru.ac.za/institutes/iser/
Director: Dr. Valerie Møller
Library resources: *see* ➔ **1460**

1860 School of Development Studies University of KwaZulu-Natal
Durban 4041
Tel: +27-31-260 2363
Fax: +27-31-260 2359
Email: csds@ukzn.ac.za (General enquiries)
mayj@ukzn.ac.za (Head)
Web: http://www.nu.ac.za/cs ds/Index.htm

Head: Prof. Julian May
Library resources: *see* ➔ **1465**

**1861   South African Institute of
        International Affairs (SAIIA)**
        Jan Smuts House East Campus
        University of the Witwatersrand
        Postal address:
        PO Box 31596
        Braamfontein 2017
Tel: +27-11-339 2021
Fax: +27-11-339 2154
Email: saiiagen@global.co.za (General
enquiries)
sidiropoulose@saiia.wits.ac.za (National
Director)
Web: http://www.wits.ac.za/saiia/
National Director: Elizabeth Sidiropoulos

**1862   Wits Institute for Social & Economic
        Research (WISER)**
        6th Floor Richard Ward Building
        East Campus
        University of the Witwatersrand
        Postal address:
        University of the Witwatersrand
        Private Bag 3
        PO Box Wits 2050
Tel: +27-11-717 4220 Fax: + 27-11-717 4235
Email: admin2@wiser.wits.ac.za (General
enquiries) poseld@wiser.wits.ac.za (Director)
Web: http://wiserweb.wits.ac.za/
Director: Prof. Deborah Posel
Library resources: *see* ➔ **1475**

Sudan

**1863   Institute of African and Asian
        Studies
        University of Khartoum**
        PO Box 321
        Khartoum
Tel: +249-11-775820 Fax: +249-11-777 0444
Email: Abumanga2000@yahoo.com
Web:
http://www.uofk.edu/institutes/african/ab
ouIAAS.html
Director: Dr. Al-Amin Abu-Manga
Mohamed
Library resources: *see* ➔ **1480**

Tunisia

**1864   Institut de Recherche sur le
        Maghreb Contemporain (IRM)**
        20 rue Mohamed Ali Tahar
        Mutuelleville
        1002 Tunis
Tel: +216-71-796722 Fax: +216-71-797376
Email: direction@irmcmaghreb.org
Web:
http://www.irmcmaghreb.org/index.htm
Director: Pierre Robert Baduel, Director
Library resources: *see* ➔ **1485**

Uganda

**1865   Makerere Institute of Social
        Research (MISR)**
        Makerere University
        PO Box 16022
        Kampala
Tel: 256+41-532830/554582
Fax: +256-41-532821
Email: misrlib@imul.com
Web: http://www.uganda.co.ug/misr/
Director: Dr. Nakanyike B. Musisi
Library resources: *see* ➔ **1493**

CENTRAL & SOUTH AMERICA

Argentina

1866   Facultad de Filosofía y Letras,
        Sección Interdisciplinaria de
        Estudios de Asia y Africa
        Universidad de Buenos Aires
        Moreno 350
        1002 Buenos Aires
        Tel: +54-11-4345 8196
        Email: africayasia@yahoo.com.ar
        Web: http://www.filo.uba.ar/ (Faculty
        pages)
        Director: Prof. Marisa Pinneau

Brazil

1867   Centro de Estudos Africanos
        Universidade de São Paulo
        Av. Prof. Luciano Gualberto 315
        Sala 1087
        São Paulo
        Postal address:
        CP 26097 - C. Universitaria
        São Paulo 05513-970
        Tel: +55-11-3091 3744 Fax: +55-11-3032 9416
        Email: cea@edu.usp.br
        Web: http://www.fflch.usp.br/cea/
        Director: Prof. Fernando A.A. Mourão

1868   Centro de Estudos Afro-Asiáticos
        Instituto de Humanidades
        Praça Pio X 7 – 9º Andar
        CEP 20040-020 – Centro
        Rio de Janeiro – RJ
        Tel: +55-21-2233 9039 Fax: +55-21-2518 2798
        Email: f.antonio@candidomendes.edu.br
        Web: http://www.candidomendes.br/ceaa/
        Director: Dr. Amauri Mendes Pereira

1869   Centro de Estudos Afro-Orientais
        (CEAO)
        Praça 15 de novembro 17
        CEP 40 025 010 - Terreiro de Jesus
        Salvador-Bahia
        Tel: +55-71-322-6742 Fax: +55-71-322-8070
        Email: ceao@ufba.br (General enquiries)
        jocelio@ufba.br (Director)
        Web: http://www.ceao.ufba.br/
        Director: Jocélio Teles dos Santos, Director
        Library resources: *see* → 1356

See also: Programa Multidisciplinar de Pós-Graduação em Estudos Étnicos e Africanos
http://www.posafro.ufba.br/

Columbia

1870   African Studies Group
        University Externado de Colombia
        Centre for Research and Special
        Projects - CIPE
        Faculty of Finance, Government and
        International Relations
        Calle 12 # 0-85 Este
        Bogotá DC
        Tel: +57-1-342 0288 ext. 2009
        Fax: +57-1-341 8715
        Email: africa@uexternado.edu.co
        Web:
        http://cursos.uexternado.edu.co/africa/ingles.htm
        Coordinator: Prof. Madeleine Labeu
        Andebeng Alingué

Cuba

1871   Centro de Estudios sobre Africa y
        Medio Oriente (CEAMO)
        Avenue 3ra, Nº 1805, e/ 18 y 20
        Miramar Playa
        Havanna
        Tel: +53-221222/221890 Fax: +53-357-221222
        Email: ceamo@ceniai.inf.cu
        Web: http://www.nodo50.org/ceamo/
        Director: Prof. David González López

Mexico

1872   Centro de Estudios de Asia y Africa
        El Colegio de México
        Camino al Ajusco 20
        Col. Pedregal de Sta. Teresa
        10740 México DF
        Tel. + 52-5449 3000 ext 4101
        Fax: +52-5645 0464
        Email: coord.acad.ceaa@colmex.mx (General
        enquiries) jramirez@colmex.mx (Director)
        Web: http://www.colmex.mx/centros/ceaa/
        Director: Dr. Juan José Ramírez Bonilla
        Library resources: *see* → 1357

AUSTRALASIA & PACIFIC

Australia

1873 **African Research Institute**
La Trobe University
History Program
Bundoora Campus
VIC 3086 Victoria
Tel: +61-3-9479 2430 Fax: +61-3-9479 1942
Email: history@latrobe.edu.au (General enquiries) d.dorward@latrobe.edu.au (Director)
Web: http://www.latrobe.edu.au/african/
Director: Prof. David Dorward
Library resources: *see* ➜ **1350**

Japan

1874 **Center for African Area Studies/**
Graduate School of Asian and
African Area Studies (ASFAS)
Kyoto University
46 Shimoadachi-cho
Yoshida Sakyo-ku
Kyoto 606-8501
Tel: +81-75-753 7374/7375
Fax: +81-75-753 7350
Email: info@asafas.kyoto-u.ac.jp
Web: http://www.asafas.kyoto-u.ac.jp/
http://www.asafas.kyoto-u.ac.jp/econtent.html (English pages)
Director: Dr. Jiro Tanaka
Library resources: *see* ➜ **1352**

1875 **The Institute of Developing**
Economies (JETRO)
3-2-2 Wakaba Mihama-ku
Chiba-shi
Chiba 261-8545
Tel: +81-43-299 9500 (General information)
+81-43-299 9536 (Information division)
Fax: +81-43-299 9726
Email: info@ide.go.jp
Web: http://www.ide.go.jp/English/index4.html
President: Dr. Masahisa Fujita
Library resources: *see* ➜ **1354**

1876 **Research Institute for the Languages**
and Cultures of Asia and Africa
Tokyo University of Foreign Studies
Fuchu-shi Asahi-cho 3-11-1
Tokyo 183-8534
Tel: +81-42-330 5600 Fax +81-42-330 5610
Email: director@aa.tufs.ac.jp
Web: http://www.aa.tufs.ac.jp/index_e.html
Director: Prof. Koji Miyazaki
Library resources: *see* ➜ **1353**

ASIA & MIDDLE EAST

China

1877 **Center for African Studies**
Peking University
Beijing 100871
Tel: +86-10-6275 1246/6275 1242 (Office of International Relations)
Fax: +86-10-6275 1240 (Office of International Relations)
Email: oir@pku.edu.cn (Office of International Relations)
Web: http://www.pku.edu.cn/ (Main university home page)
http://en.pku.edu.cn/ (Main university home page, English version)
Dean: Prof. Lu Ting'en

1878 **Institute of African Studies**
Xiangtan University
Xiangtan
Hunan Province 411105
Email: iec@xtu.edu.cn (International exchange centre)
Tel: +86-732-829 2130/829 3966 (International exchange centre)
Fax: +86-732-829 2282
Web: http://www.xtu.edu.cn (Main university home page)
http://www.xtu.edu.cn/xtu_en/ (Main university home page, English version)
Director: n/a

1879 **Institute of West Asian and**
African Studies (IWAAS)
Chinese Academy of Social Sciences
3 Zhang Zhizhong Lu
Dongcheng District
Peking 100007

Tel: +86-10-6403 9168/6403 9171
Fax: +86-10-6403 5718
Email: iwaas@public.fhnet.cn.net (General enquiries) or panrx@isc.cass.net.cn (Administrator)
yangguang@cass.org.cn (Director)
Web:
http://www.cass.cn/xiyafei/en/others/about.asp
Director: Prof. Yang Guang
Library resources: *see* ➔ **1347**

India

1880 **Centre of African Studies**
University of Mumbai
Ranade Bhavan
Vidyanagari Campus
Mumbai 400 098
Tel: +91-22-652 6091 ext 329/91-22-652 6388 ext 330 Fax: +91-22-652 6893
Email: director@cas.mu.ac.in (General enquiries) svanaraj@cas.mu.ac.in or sheth47@yahoo.com (Director)
Web:
http://www.mu.ac.in/african/profile.html
Director: Dr. (Mrs) Aparajita Biswas
Library resources: *see* ➔ **1348**

1881 **Centre for West Asian and**
African Studies (CWAAS)
School of International Studies
Jawaharlal Nehru University
New Mehrauli Road
New Delhi 110 067
Tel: +91-11-610 7676 ext. 2607
Fax: +91-11-618 5886/619 8234
Email: akdubey@mail.jnu.ac.in
Web:
http://www.jnu.ac.in/Academics/Schools/SchoolOfInternationalStudies/AfricanCenter.htm
Chair: Dr. Ajay K. Dubey

1882 **Department of African Studies**
University of Delhi
Delhi 110007
Tel: +91-11-2766 6673
Fax: +91-11-2766 7126 (Main university fax number)
Email: n/a (use email form on Web site)
Web:
http://www.du.ac.in/show_department.html?department_id=African+Studies Head:
Head: Prof. Sneh Lata Tandon

Israel

1883 **The Institute of Asian and African**
Studies
Department of African Studies
The Hebrew University of Jerusalem
Mt. Scopus
Jerusalem 91905
Tel: +972-2-588 3516/588 3659
Fax: +972-2-588 3658
Email: AsiaAfrica@h2.hum.huji.ac.il (General enquiries)
barasher@h2.hum.huji.ac.il (Director)
Web:
http://asiafrica.huji.ac.il/eng/index.html

1884 **The Moshe Dayan Center**
for Middle Eastern and African
Studies
Tel Aviv University
Ramat Aviv
Tel Aviv 69978
Tel: +972-3-640 9646/640 9100
Fax: +972-3-641 5802
Email: dayancen@ccsg.tau.ac.il (General enquiries) susser@poStreettau.ac.il (Director)
Web: http://www.dayan.org/
Director: Prof. Asher Susser
Library resources: *see* ➔ **1349**
Director: Prof. Meir M. Bar-Asher

15
Africanist documentation
and African studies bibliography

This section provides details of organizations and associations involved in Africanist documentation and also lists a select number of books and articles on African studies bibliography, Africana librarianship, and on the acquisition of African-published material. However, it does not contain listings of books and articles on the topic of libraries and librarianship in Africa, for which there are other several other sources, for example the second edition of Alfred Kagan's ➔ **Reference Guide to Africa (225)**, chapter 16 "Libraries and Librarianship". Particularly valuable are the various books and documents on African academic and public libraries published by the ➔ **International Network for the Availability of Scientific Publications/INASP (2218, 2608)**, including research reports, info-briefs, training manuals, directories, and bibliographic resources. Many of them are available as freely accessible full-text documents and e-books, for the complete list *see* http://www.inasp.info/pubs/index.shtml.

Organizations

1885　**Africana Librarians Council (ALC)**
　　　Chair: (2005-2006)
　　　Lauris Olson
　　　Social Sciences Bibliographer
　　　University of Pennsylvania Library
　　　3420 Walnut Street
　　　Philadelphia PA 19104-6206
　　　USA
Tel: +1-215-898 0119 Fax: +1-215-898 0559 Email: olson@pobox.upenn.edu
Secretary:
Esmeralda M. Kale
Africana Bibliographer
Northwestern University Library
Melville J. Herskovits Library of African Studies
1970 Campus Drive
Evanston IL 60208-2300
USA
Tel: +1-847-491 3941 Fax: 847-467 1233 Email: ekale@northwestern.edu
Web: http://www.loc.gov/rr/amed/afs/alc/

A constituent organization of the [US] →African Studies Association (2755), devoted to Africana libraries and African studies collection development, and providing a forum for African and Africanist librarians. It is open to librarians and scholars worldwide who are interested in Africana librarianship, and the ALC makes a particular effort to reach out to colleagues in Africa.
Prizes and awards: → Conover-Porter Award (2828)
Mailing list: → ALCASA List (2806) a (restricted) discussion list to facilitate the work of the Africana Librarians Council. To subscribe: send email to majordomo@lists.stanford.edu with the following command: subscribe alcasalist
Publications: → Africana Libraries Newsletter (801), → Africana Librarians Council Directory (255), → Directory of Book Donation Programs (163)
Note: an essay by Gregory Finnegan, "The Africana Librarians Council and the Cooperative Africana Microform Project Since 1989" appears in →**Africanist Librarianship in an Era of Change (1904)**, pp. 29-47.

1886   Arbeitskreis der deutschen Afrika-Forschungs-und Dokumentationstellen (ADAF)
(Working Group of German African Research and Documentation Centres)
c/o Institut für Afrika-Kunde
Neuer Jungfernstieg 21
20354 Hamburg
Germany
Tel: +49-40-4282 5523 Fax: +49-40-4282 5511 Email: iak@iak.duei.de
Web: http://www.duei.de/iak/show.php/de/content/forschung/adaf.html
Founded: 1967
ADAF is a loose network of institutions in Germany with Africa-related research and/or documentation activities and interests. Its main objective is to facilitate the exchange of information about on-going activities in the field of African studies and Africanist documentation.
Membership dues: none
Publications: *ADAF-Rundbrief* (Newsletter)
Note: a complete list of the members of the Working Group, with their full addresses, including email addresses for most, can be found at the above Web site.

1887   Asian, African, and Middle Eastern Section ACRL (AAMES)
Chair (2005-2006)
Cynthia Tysick
Senior Assistant Librarian
State University of New York
221 D Lockwood Library North Campus
Amherst NY 14260-2200
USA
Tel: +1-716-645-2814 ext 458 Fax: +1-716-645 3859 Email: cat2@buffalo.edu
Web:
http://www.ala.org/ala/acrl/aboutacrl/acrlsections/aames/aameshomepage.htm
Secretary: (2005–2007)
Chengzhi Wang
Librarian, Columbia University East Asian Library

Kent Hall
1140 Amsterdam Avenue
New York NY 10027
USA
Tel: +1-212-854 3721 Fax: +1-212-6626286 Email: cw2165@columbia.edu
Founded: 1969
Created in 1969, AAMES represents librarians and specialists in the fields of Asian,
African, and Middle Eastern studies and acts for the Association of College and
Research Libraries in those areas of library service that require knowledge of Asian,
African and Middle Eastern languages and cultures.
Mailing list: AAMES-L, to facilitate and encourage discussion of important issues
amongst Section members and non-members across the spectrum of the area studies
librarian's groups represented. To subscribe: send email to listproc@ala1.ala.org with
the following command: subscribe AAMESL
Publications: *AAMES Newsletter* (twice yearly)
http://www.ala.org/ala/acrl/aboutacrl/acrlsections/aames/Document.pdf
Editor: Muhammad al-Faruque, Asian Library, University of Illinois at Urbana-
Champaign, 1408 West Gregory Drive, Urbana IL 61801, USA,
Email: Faruque@uiuc.edu

1888   Black Caucus of the American Library Association (BCALA)
President: (to 2006)
Andrew P. Jackson (Sekou Molefi Baako)
Executive Director
Langston Hughes Community Library Cultural Center
Queens Borough Public Library
100-01 Northern Boulevard
Corona NY 11368
USA
Tel: +1-718 651 1100 ext 210 Fax: +1-718-651 6258
Email: andrew.p.jackson@queenslibrary.org
Web: http://www.bcala.org/
Secretary:
Ira Revels
Instruction Librarian
309 Uris Library
Cornell University
Ithaca NY 14850
USA
Tel: +1-607-255 1569 Fax: +1-607-255 7922 Email: ir33@cornell.edu
Serves as an advocate for the development, promotion, and improvement of library
services and resources to the nation's African American community, and provides
leadership for the recruitment and professional development of African American
librarians.
Prizes, awards, and scholarships: BCALA Literary Awards, The BCALA E.J. Josey
Scholarship Award, DEMCO/ALA Black Caucus Award for Excellence in
Librarianship, BCALA Trailblazer's Award

Publications: *BCLA Newsletter* (six times yearly) Editor: Roland Barksdale-Hall, 939 Baldwin Avenue, Suite 1, Sharon, PA 16146, USA, Tel: +1-724-346 0459, Fax: +1-724-342-1808, Email: newsletter@bcala.org Web: http://www.bcala.org/newsletter.htm

1889 Cooperative Africana Microform Project (CAMP)
Chair: (2004-2006)
Peter Malanchuk
Africana and Political Science Bibliographer
University of Florida
George A. Smathers Libraries
PO Box 117001
Gainesville FL 32611
USA
Tel: +1-352-392 4919 Fax: +1-352-392-8118 Email: permala@mail.uflib.ufl.edu
Web: http://www.crl.edu/areastudies/CAMP/index.htm
Secretary: (2003-2005)
Edward Miner
International Studies Librarian
100 Main Library University of Iowa Libraries
Iowa City IA 52242-1420
USA
Tel: +1-319-335 5883 Fax: +1-319-335 5900 Email: edward-miner@uiowa.edu
Founded in 1963, CAMP is a joint effort by research libraries throughout the world and the ➔ **Center for Research Libraries/CRL (1302)** to promote the preservation of publications and archives concerning the nearly fifty nations of sub-Saharan Africa, and to make these materials available to researchers in microform. CAMP acquires expensive microform sets and authorises original filming of unique research materials in North America, Africa, and Europe. CAMP collects microform copies of such material as selected newspapers, journals, government publications, personal and corporate archives, and personal papers.
Note: for additional information see also an article by Gregory Finnegan, "The Africana Librarians Council and the Cooperative Africana Microform Project Since 1989" in ➔**Africanist Librarianship in an Era of Change (1904)**, pp. 29-47; and "Cooperative Africana Microform Project (CAMP): Forty Years of Collaboration and Scholarship", The Center for Research Libraries, *Focus* 23, no. 4 (Summer 2004): 3-4. http://www.crl.edu/FocusArticles/CAMP_Forty_Years.htm. The full issue can be accessed at http://www.crl.edu/PDF/pdfFocus/Summer-04.pdf (pdf). This informative issue also contains other articles and reports about other archival and e-resources projects in the African studies field.

1890 Library of Congress Office Nairobi
Director for East and Central Africa:
Pamela Howard-Reguindin
US Embassy Building Room 003
PO Box 30598
00100 Nairobi GPO
Kenya
Tel: +254-2-363 6300/6153 Fax: +254-2-363 6321

Email: nairobi@libcon-kenya.org (General enquiries) PamelaHR@loc.gov(Director)
Web: http://www.loc.gov/acq/ovop/nairobi/
The → **Library of Congress (1316)** Office in Nairobi, Kenya, is one of six overseas offices administered by the African/Asian Acquisitions and Overseas Operations Division of the Library. Established in 1966, the Library of Congress Office acquires and catalogues publications in all subjects (except clinical medicine and technical agriculture) from commercial, government, and non-trade sources from 29 African countries. Publications are acquired not only for the Library of Congress, but also for more than 35 institutions that participate in the Cooperative Acquisitions Program. Participants are primarily US university libraries. Another aspect of the Nairobi office program is the preservation of African newspapers. The approximately 300 newspaper titles being received are being preserved on microfilm.
Publications: → **Quarterly Index to African Periodical Literature (404)**;
→ **Accessions List of the Library of Congress Office, Nairobi, Kenya (381**)
(formerly *Accessions List, Eastern and Southern Africa)*, with the biennial *Serial Supplement* (available on CD-ROM), and the *Annual Publishers Directory.*
Note: the other LC overseas office in Africa is located in Cairo, Egypt. Contact details are as follows:
James Gentner, Acting Field Director
Library of Congress
US Embassy
8 Kamal El-Din Salah Street
Garden City
Cairo
Egypt
Tel: +20-2-797 2206 Fax: +20-2-796 0233
Email: cairo@loc.gov (General enquiries) jgen@loc.gov (Director)
Web: http://www.loc.gov/acq/ovop/cairo/

1891 Mountain-Plains Africana Libraries Association (MPALA)
Convener:
Kenneth P. Lohrentz
University of Kansas Libraries
Lawrence KS 66045-7537
USA
Tel: +1-785-864 4593 Fax: +1-785-864 5705 Email: klohrentz@ukans.edu
Secretary:
Gloria Creed-Dikeogu
Topeka and Shawnee County Public Library
1515 SW 10th Avenue
Topeka KS 66604-1374
USA
Tel: +1-785-580 4677 Email: gcdikeog@tscpl.lib.ks.us
Founded in April 2002, MPALA has the following objectives: (1) sharing information about Africana resources, Web sites, databases, and other information resources; (2) undertaking projects of mutual interest and benefit for staff development such as mentoring and increased awareness of Africana collections; (3) working as an interest group to improve the infrastructure for shared access to library materials throughout the region.

1892   **Standing Conference on Library Materials on Africa (SCOLMA)**
Chair: (2005-2006)
David Blake
Librarian
Commonwealth Secretariat
Marlborough House
Pall Mall
London SW1Y 5HX
UK
Tel: +44-(0)20-7747 6164 Fax: +44-(0)20-7747 6168 Email: scolma@hotmail.com
Web: http://www.lse.ac.uk/library/scolma/
Secretary:
Ian Cooke
The Library
Institute of Commonwealth Studies
28 Russell Square
London WC1B 5DS
UK
Tel: +44-(0)20-7580 5876 Email: Ian.Cooke@sas.ac.uk
Provides a forum for librarians and others concerned with the provision of materials for African studies in libraries in the United Kingdom. Monitors, co-ordinates and improves the acquisition of library materials on and from Africa, especially through its Co-operative Area Specialisation Scheme. Sponsors bibliographical projects, publishes bibliographical works and a journal, and organizes conferences and seminars on African bibliographical topics.
Publications: ➜ **African Research & Documentation (748)**, ➜ **SCOLMA Directory of Libraries and Special Collections on Africa in the United Kingdom and Europe (317)**, ➜ Theses on Africa (376, 377), ➜ **Writings on African Archives (310),** as well as other reference works and conference proceedings.
Note: for a recent account and chronology of SCOLMA's history see "SCOLMA: A Chronology of Forty Years, 1962 to 2002" by John McIlwaine, *African Research & Documentation*, no. 88 (2002): 3-17.

Resources and publications (print and online)

See also ➜ **2 The major general reference tools. Guides to library collections and archival sources**

➜Africana Libraries Newsletter *see* **9 Journals and magazines** entry **801**

➜ African Research & Documentation *see* **9 Journals and magazines** entry **748**

1893   **African Research and Documentation in the New Millenium. Papers Presented at the SCOLMA 40th Anniversary Conference, Oxford, June 2002.**
African Research & Documentation [Special issue], no. 90 (2002): 1-107.
Contains the text of eight of the papers that were delivered at 40th anniversary conference of the ➜ **Standing Conference on Library Materials on Africa (1892)**,

held in Oxford in June 2002. Papers include overviews of the growth and current state African scholarship and African studies by Colin Bundy (Director, School of Oriental and African Studies, University of London) and Anthony Kirk-Greene (St. Antony's College, Oxford) respectively, while Alvaro Correia de Nobrega contributes a paper on African studies in Portugal and the lusophone world. Papers by Africana librarians include "Accessing African Archives, Libraries and Journals: Partnerships, Ethics and Equity in the 21st Century" by Peter Limb; "New Directions in Reference and Collections Management in Africana Collections in the US" by Laverne Page; "Africana Collections in South Africa" by Lesley Hart; and "On Documenting Africa in the Netherlands" by Marlene van Doorn (also available online, *see* ➜ separate entry **1918** in this section).

1894   ASC Thesaurus for African Studies: Thesaurus of African Languages ⓘ
http://www.ascleiden.nl/Library/Thesauri/Languages/
1895   ASC Thesaurus for African Studies: Thesaurus of African Peoples ⓘ
http://www.ascleiden.nl/Library/Thesauri/Peoples/
1896   ASC Thesaurus for African Studies: Thesaurus of African Polities ⓘ
http://www.ascleiden.nl/Library/Thesauri/Polities/
This valuable resource from the Library of the ➜ **African Studies Centre (1246)** in Leiden is designed to assist improved access to national and international information resources in the field of African studies, for use by all those seeking information on Africa. To facilitate topical access, the UDC-based classification currently used for subject indexing has been converted into a more user-friendly word-based indexing system, and the aim is to construct a thesaurus for African studies using the library's UDC codes as a starting point. To date the UDC codes for African languages, African peoples, and African polities have been translated, and three provisional thesauri are accessible for experimental use: the ASC Thesaurus of African Languages (350 preferred terms), the ASC Thesaurus of African Peoples (1,200 preferred terms), and the ASC Thesaurus of African Polities (300 preferred terms). In the course of the project the ASC Library plans to put more subject thesauri on to the Web as more UDC codes are converted into thesaurus equivalents. Each thesaurus can be searched, or browsed alphabetically. [25/09/05]

1897   Bertelsen, Cynthia "Issues in Cataloging Non-Western Materials: Special Problems with African Language Materials."
http://filebox.vt.edu/users/bertel/africana.html 15 pp. 10 March 1996
An examination of the issues and problems of cataloguing African language materials, providing a literature review and a discussion of the issues, with examples of access point selection, and links to other resources on cataloguing of African language materials, names of African ethnic groups, and African geographic names. [25/09/05]

1898   Bibliophilia Africana 8 Conference Proceedings. From Papyrus to Print-out: The Book in Africa Yesterday, Today and Tomorrow. Centre of the Book Cape Town, 11-14 May 2005. Pretoria and Cape Town: National Library of South Africa/Centre of the Book [PO Box 496, 8000 Cape Town, orders to Publications Department, Email: Mandla.Hermanus@nlsa.ac.za], 2005. R200.00
Some papers online at http://www.nlsa.ac.za/b8_late_papers.html#l

[not examined/not available for examination at press time]

1899   The Center for Research Libraries, *Focus* **23, no. 4 (Summer 2004): 1-16.**
http://www.crl.edu/PDF/pdfFocus/Summer-04.pdf (pdf)
This informative issue of the ➔ **Center for Research Libraries (1302)** *Focus*
newsletter concentrates on Africa collections, cooperative collection programs and
initiatives, and e-resources in the field. It includes reports on the ➔ **Cooperative**
Africana Microform Project (1889), a microfilming project at the ➔**Archives**
Nationales du Sénégal (1541), two archival microfilm projects of southern African
materials, together with an article by James Simon about the Political
Communications Web Archiving project, which examined the Web sites by Nigerian
political parties and candidates for presidential and gubernatorial elections in
December 1993. There is also a survey by Peter Limb of recent developments in
African scholarly e-resources. [06/09/05]

1900   Coelho, Jill Young "Once, Present (and Always?) Africana Acquisitions
Policies." In *Africanist Librarianship in an Era of Change,* edited by Victoria K. Evalds
and David Henige. Lanham, MD: Scarecrow Press, 2005, 13-30.
Reviews the methods and strategies by which Africana librarians have acquired
materials during the last decades of the 20th century, and the manifold problems,
obstacles, and pitfalls that are associated with the acquisition of sub-Saharan African
imprints. The author – who is Librarian for sub-Saharan Africa at Harvard's ➔
Widener Library (1309) – notes that purchasing African-published material
continues to be a major topic of meetings and conversations among Africana
librarians; that there are no easy solutions, but by "learning about and using the
available tools makes it possible to create a good basic collection; persistence, luck
and curiosity will do the rest."

1901   Dilevko, Juris, and Lisa Gottlieb "Book Titles Published in Africa Held by
North American University Research Libraries and Review Sources for African-
published Books." *Library & Information Science Research* 25 (2003): 177-206.
A well-documented article that offers some interesting analysis about the presence of
African books on the shelves of major North America research libraries (especially
institutions participating in the Association of Research Libraries/ARL), as well as
gauging the percentage of African-published non-fiction titles that are reviewed by
scholarly journals and major library reviewing tools such as *Choice,* to ascertain
whether the presence of such reviews is related to the number of African-published
non-fiction titles owned by North American libraries. It finds that although ARL
university libraries at institutions with well-established African studies programmes
in stand-alone academic units typically have strong collections of sub-Saharan
African-published titles, ARL university libraries at institutions not meeting such
criteria have relatively weak collections of such material. The authors also urge
Choice to revisit some of their current practices and policies that unintentionally
exclude African-published titles from their review pages, thus assuring wider
visibility of African publishing output.

1902   Easterbrook, David L. **"African Theses and Dissertations in Academic Libraries in the United States: Background and Current Practices."**
http://www.aau.org/datad/reports/2004workshop/easterbrook.pdf 12 pp. 2004 also at http://www.crl.edu/PDF/datadeasterbrook.pdf
A paper presented at the Association of African Universities ➔ **DATAD (203)** workshop on Intellectual Property, Governance, Dissemination and Funding Strategies, Accra, Ghana, February 19-20, 2004. After setting out some background information, the paper describes the US interest in publications, theses and dissertations from African universities and the manner in which the emerging vendor scene did or did not offer these materials (ethical and otherwise); strategies in North American institutions to acquire university publications, theses and dissertations (especially that of ➔ **Northwestern University Library (1322)**; developing/changing inter-institutional cooperation with African universities; the role of Africanist professional organizations; the importance of access to research coming from African universities and programmes to share American research, especially theses. Finally, the paper shows how during the present time North American institutions acquire African theses and dissertations, how they are used in Africanist scholarship today, and how their availability influences Africanist scholarship and graduate studies. [22/08/05]
Note: also of interest, and presented to the same workshop, is "Historical Practice in Managing Theses and Dissertations at African Universities and University Libraries", by Elizabeth Kondo, Director, University of Dar es Salaam University Library Services http://www.aau.org/datad/reports/2004workshop/kiondo.pdf [22/08/05] also at http://www.crl.edu/PDF/datadkiondo.pdf [22/08/05]

1903   Easterbrook, David L. **"American Libraries, American Markets, African Books."** In *Indaba 2000. Millennium Marketplace,* edited by the Zimbabwe International Book Fair Trust. Harare: Zimbabwe International Book Fair Trust, 2001, 164-169.
The curator of the ➔ **Melville J. Herskovits Library of African Studies (1322)** at Northwestern University looks at the acquisition methods for African books by American libraries, discusses some of the selection tools and resources they use, and offers some suggestions of what African publishers might do to make their books more easily available in North America, in particular in use of the Internet and postings to online mailing lists and discussion groups.

➔ **Electronic Journal of Africana Bibliography** *see* **9 Journals and magazines** entry **806**

1904   Evalds, Victoria K., and David Henige, eds. **Africanist Librarianship in an Era of Change.** Lanham, MD, and Oxford: Scarecrow Press, 2005, 248 pp. $35.00/£22.99/€39.44 pap.
Published in memory of the late Dan Britz, former Africana Bibliographer at ➔ **Northwestern University Libraries (1322)**, this collection of essays discuss current issues, problems, and challenges facing area studies librarians, with the aim of placing Africanist librarianship "in the bewildering context of our times." Themes include information and reference services in African studies, bibliographic instruction and provision of resources, cataloguing, Africana serials, electronic

publishing and African studies, outreach activities, establishing partnerships with African institutions, and the acquisition of African-published material. Following an introductory essay by David Henige, and a professional chronology and appreciation of Dan Britz by David Easterbrook, the collection includes the following papers (some of which are also listed as separate entries, as indicated):

Jill Young Coelho, "Once, Present (and Always?) Africana Acquisitions Policies." (*see also* separate entry ➜ **1900**)

Gregory Finnegan, "The ➜**Africana Librarians Council (1885)** and the ➜ **Cooperative Africana Microform Project (1889)** Since 1989."

Marion Frank-Wilson, "Electronic Publishing and African Studies: A Way to Bridge the Information Gap?"

Miki Goral, "Africana Reference for the Generalist."

Alfred Kagan, "Teaching African Studies Bibliography."

Patricia S. Kuntz, "US-African University Library Partnerships."

Joseph J. Lauer, "Trends in North American Theses Production."

Robert W. Lesh, "Continuing Developments in Africana Cataloging in the United States, 1989-2002."

Peter Limb, "Africana Periodicals: Problems and Progress of Collection and Publication." (*see also* separate entry ➜ **1907**)

Patricia Ukoli Ogedengbe, "Africa Matters: Outreach Programs and Bringing Africa to the American Academy and Public."

Gretchen Walsh, "Library Instruction and Reference for Undergraduates: Opening a Faculty-Library Partnership."

David Westley, "WorldCat and African Lexicography Since 1980." (*see also* separate entry ➜ **448**)

Hans Zell, "The Perilous Business of Reference Publishing in African Studies."

Nancy Lawler and Ivor Wilks, "Remembering Dan."

➜ Kagan, Alfred **"Sources for African Language Materials from the Countries of Anglophone Africa."** *see* **5 Guides to African language resources** entry **443**

1905 LaFond, Deborah M., and Gretchen Walsh, eds. **Research, Reference Service, and Resources for the Study of Africa.** Special issue of *The Reference Librarian*, edited by Bill Katz, volume 42, issue 87/88. Binghamton, NY: The Haworth Press, 2004. Print and online. (accessible online if part of subscription to *The Reference Librarian*) 314 pp. $39.95 cased $29.95 pap. (as individual issue)

A wide ranging collection of essays that examine reference service in terms of research on Africa on the one hand, and libraries in Africa on the other. In addition to the print edition, the introduction and individual articles contained in this special issue of *Reference Librarian* can be accessed online as follows (abstracts are freely accessible):

Gretchen Walsh, Deborah M. LaFond, Introduction
http://www.haworthpress.com/store/ArticleAbstract.asp?ID=39244

Gretchen Walsh, ""Can We Get There from Here?": Negotiating the Washouts, Cave-ins, Dead Ends, and Other Hazards on the Road to Research on Africa."
http://www.haworthpress.com/store/ArticleAbstract.asp?ID=39245

Marion Frank-Wilson, "Teaching African Studies Bibliography-Information Literacy for 21st Century Scholars."

http://www.haworthpress.com/store/ArticleAbstract.asp?ID=39246
Angel D. Batiste, "African Business and Economic Resource Index: Selected Internet Resources." (*see also* separate entry ➔ **465**)
http://www.haworthpress.com/store/ArticleAbstract.asp?ID=39247
Peter Limb, "Partnership as a New Paradigm for Reference Librarians in African Studies" http://www.haworthpress.com/store/ArticleAbstract.asp?ID=39248
Miriam Conteh-Morgan, "Reading African Women's Writing: The Role of Librarians in Expanding the Canon."
http://www.haworthpress.com/store/ArticleAbstract.asp?ID=39249
Akilah Shukura Nosakhere, "Designing an Anglophone University Undergraduate Library Collection for a Francophone West African Environment."
http://www.haworthpress.com/store/ArticleAbstract.asp?ID=39250
Colin Darch, "Frog Voices, Whispers, and Silences: Problems and Issues in Collecting for an African Studies Library in Africa."
http://www.haworthpress.com/store/ArticleAbstract.asp?ID=39252
Deborah M. LaFond, "Library Capacity Building in Africa or the Exportation of Technolust? Discerning Partnership Models and Revitalization Efforts in the Age of Globalization."
http://www.haworthpress.com/store/ArticleAbstract.asp?ID=39253
Mark Stover, "The Reference Librarian as Non-Expert: A Postmodern Approach to Expertise." http://www.haworthpress.com/store/ArticleAbstract.asp?ID=39254
Brice Austin, "Should There be "Privilege" in the Relationship Between Reference Librarian and Patron?"
http://www.haworthpress.com/store/ArticleAbstract.asp?ID=39255

1906 Kistler, John M. **"Special Acquisitions: Collecting African Materials."** *The Acquisitions Librarian* 15, no. 29 (2003): 31-50.
A new project to begin a depository of Benin resources at West Virginia State College (as part of a partnership with the ➔ **National University of Benin (1368)** may offer ideas for other libraries wishing to do special acquisitions in Africana materials. This article addresses language and cultural barriers, the need for early planning, methods of acquisition, and collection maintenance concerns. The author, Acquisitions Librarian at Utah State University, has worked in acquisitions for special, public, and academic libraries, but has only recently begun to learn the complex issues in Africana acquisitions. [Not examined]

1907 Limb, Peter **"Africana Periodicals: Problems and Progress of Collection and Publication."** In *Africanist Librarianship in an Era of Change,* edited by Victoria K. Evalds and David Henige. Lanham, MD: Scarecrow Press, 2005, 125-140.
Examines the problems associated with Africana journals and their collection, giving particular attention to journals published in Africa. Starts off with a review of current trends in periodical publishing and usage, the profound changes created by the impact of digital technology and the new scholarly communications environment, the proliferation of e-journals, and escalating journal prices. Thereafter the author turns his attention to the problems of identifying and acquiring African-published serials – most still only published in print format at this time – and the perennial problems usually associated with the process, including regularity (or the lack of it) and viability of Africa-based journals, inadequate marketing and distribution,

sometimes poor production quality, breakdowns in communications, and other logistical problems. He also describes some recent digital initiatives designed to improve the visibility and accessibility of African journals, but which, while useful and beneficial in the short run, "have not greatly succeeded in helping African journals achieve greater viability." The author states that "improving the acquisition of African serials relates closely to their own fate, which in turn rests on the wider African political economy." He calls for more international collaboration, and solid, mutually beneficial partnerships bringing together all stake holders in the journal chain; and argues that Western libraries could do more to serve their primary users and help African journals survive "by organizing and coordinating their acquisition of African journals better, and by doing this in closer conjunction with publishers; but this must be a two-way process."

1908   Matovelo, Doris S., and Inese A. Smith **"A Study on Africana Collections in UK Libraries: present state and future scenarios."** *Library Collections, Acquisitions & Technical Services* 25 (2001): 21-36.
Based on a questionnaire survey and interviews with librarians and suppliers of Africana materials in the UK, the authors attempt to shed some light on the current situation relating to the demand, acquisitions policies, extent and adequacy of Africana acquisitions, and the tools and sources used by libraries in the selection process. The study found that 41% of academic libraries surveyed acquired African-published material, but many were affected by budgetary constraints. It also found that, surprisingly, well-established bibliographic services covering African book publishing output, such as the quarterly ➔ **African Book Publishing Record (384)**, were only used as a buying and acquisitions tool by 21% of the libraries surveyed.

1909   McIlwaine, John **"Current State of Publishing and Bibliography of African Materials."** In *The Love of Books. Proceedings of the Seventh South African Conference of Bibliophiles held at The South African Library, Cape Town, 8-10 May 1996*, edited by Pieter E. Westra and Leonie Twentyman Jones. Cape Town: South African Library (Bibliophilia Africana VII, South African Library General Series, 26), 1997, 3-14.
An overview of the issues relating to publishing and bibliographic control of and in Africa, considering both materials published in Africa itself, and also the wider field of Africa-related materials published outside Africa. Reviews the major current bibliographies and continuing sources, national bibliographies, books-in-print, indexes and abstracting services, and some other materials. Also looks at the need and prospects of bibliographic tools in electronic formats.

1910   McIlwaine, John **"*Plus ça change:* Four Decades of African Studies Bibliography."** In *Africa Bibliography. Works on Africa published during 1999*, edited by T.A. Barringer. Edinburgh: Edinburgh University Press; London: International African Institute, 2001, vii-xix.
An informative article in which the author reviews progress in Africana bibliography, and the various attempts that have been made to improve bibliographic control of sources emanating from and relating to Africa, over a period of some forty years. Taking the International Conference on African Bibliography held at University College, Nairobi, in December 1967 as a starting point, he examines projects, bibliographies and bibliographic services, other reference tools

and publication of archival resources, publishers and publishing activities in the field of African studies bibliography, the development of databases, Pan-African documentation activities, current awareness services and bibliographic serial publications, and electronic sources. He also provides information about the activities of organizations and groups of librarians devoted to Africana libraries and African studies collection development. The author describes the article as "a largely personal tour of aspects of African bibliography that have particularly struck or influenced me over the years." He concludes that "much valuable work has been done, but failures have been at least as numerous as successes", citing lack of resources, both human and financial, as one of the main reasons for failed initiatives.

1911   Otchere, Freda **African Studies Thesaurus. Subject Headings for Library Users.** Westport, CO: Greenwood Press, (Bibliographies and Indexes in Afro-American and African Studies, 29) 1992. 480 pp. $120.95/£69.50
A thesaurus of some 4,000 subject headings used by the Library of Congress for sub-Saharan Africa, including classification numbers for most headings and cross-references. It includes the names of over 600 African ethnic groups and nearly 600 African language headings, together with geographical, historical and other terms, and instructions about use of the LCSH. Useful for subject searches in library catalogues that use the LC subject headings.
Choice review:
Choice February 1993 (reviewed by Gretchen Walsh)

1912   Pinfold, John **"Acquiring Books from Southern Africa: A Librarian's View."** *Focus on International & Comparative Librarianship* 27, no. 2 (10 September 1996): 100-106. [Also in *African Research & Documentation*, no. 72 (1996): 54-59]
The Head of the ➜ **Rhodes House Library (1269)** in Oxford provides a librarian's perspective how librarians find out what has been published in southern Africa, how they go about acquiring such material, the kind of budgetary constraints they are working under, and how they are coping with it. Reviews the various selection tools available and describes policies governing the acquisitions process.

1913   Pinfold, J., Barringer, T., and C. Holden, eds. **Images of Africa: The Pictorial Record. Papers presented at the SCOLMA Conference, London, 9-10 June 1994.** 114 pp. £7.50 (reduced price)
Brings together the papers presented at a ➜ **SCOLMA (1892)** conference held in 1994. Twelve contributors consider a wide variety of visual images of Africa, including paintings, drawings, etchings and engravings, still photographs, films and television, and discuss issues ranging from the role of images – and the motives of those creating them – to the practical problems involved in storing, conserving and cataloguing such materials. Half the papers are devoted to describing the collections of visual images of Africa in major library and archival collections in Britain, such as the Royal Geographical Society, the National Army Museum, Kew Gardens, and the Royal Commonwealth Society.

1914   Raseroka, H.K. **"Acquisition of African-published Materials by Libraries in Botswana - and Elsewhere in Africa."** *Focus on International & Comparative*

Librarianship 27, no. 2 (10 September) 1996: 86-95. [Also in *African Research & Documentation*, no. 72 (1996): 45-53]
The Librarian at the ➜ **University of Botswana (1502)** examines the problems facing acquisitions librarians in Africa in obtaining regular information of new African-published books, and the purchase of this material. Reviews collection development policies at the University of Botswana and then provides a detailed analysis of sources for selection for African-published material. The author is critical of African publishers' marketing strategies and the failure by some publishers to provide regular advance information and other promotional material, which are essential selection tools for librarians. The absence of effective distribution outlets, and bookselling methods which are not responsive to public needs, further aggravates the problem.

1915 Schmidt, Nancy J., ed. **Africana Librarianship in the 21st Century: Treasuring the Past and Building the Future. Proceedings of the 40th Anniversary Conference of the Africana Librarians Council, November 13, 1997**. Bloomington, In: African Studies Program, Indiana University (Monographs on Africana Librarianship, 6), 1998. 96 pp. $8.00 pap. ($10.00 overseas, incl. postage) [Order from: Publications, African Studies Program, 221 Woodburn Hall, Indiana University, Bloomington, IN 47405, USA, email: jecole@indiana.edu]
A publication to mark the 40th anniversary of the ➜ **Africana Librarians Council (1885)**, containing the papers presented at an ALC conference in 1997, and which attracted a mix of speakers from Africa, North America and Europe. A keynote address by Kay Raseroka, Librarian at the ➜ **University of Botswana (1502)**, sets the tone and in which she discusses Vision 2010, the initiative launched in 1996 by the ➜ **UN Economic Commission for Africa (2523)** to achieve a sustainable information society in Africa by the year 2010, the implications, and challenges, for sub-Saharan African library and information services, and the possibilities for partnerships with libraries in the developed world. Following the keynote address, thirteen papers were presented in three panels, covering collection development, cooperation, and reference and bibliographic instruction. Contributors include many prominent Africana librarians from the US and in Europe, who discuss a wide range of issues confronting Africana librarianship from an international perspective.

1916 Sternberg, Ilse, and Patricia M. Larby, eds. **African Studies. Papers Presented at a Colloquium at the British Library, 7-9 January 1985.** London: The British Library in association with SCOLMA, 1986. 351 pp. £14.95 (British Library Occasional papers, 6)
An overview of the state of African studies and Africana library services in the UK and (to some extent) in Africa in the mid 1980s. The papers describe the resources available to researchers, the currency of guides and indexes to those resources, publishing and distribution problems for African studies in the UK, and international library and archival collaboration in the African studies field.

1917 **Title VI Africana Librarians Web site**
http://www.indiana.edu/~libsalc/african/TitleVI.html
Maintained at ➜ **Indiana University's (1313)** African Studies Collection Web pages, this site provides details of the activities of Title VI librarians among the ➜ **Africana**

Librarians Council (1885), and includes minutes of past meetings going back to 2001. There are also progress reports about a number of cooperative projects, including the ➔ **Senegal National Archives (1541)** Project (a joint CAMP/Title VI project *see* http://www.crl.edu/areastudies/CAMP/relatedprojects/t6archives.htm); the ➔ **Cooperative African Newspapers Project (139)**; the International Union List of Africana Microfilm Collections; and two potential new projects, the Liberian Presidential Archives and the ➔ **Arquivo Historico de Mocambique (1533)** historical archives. [06/09/05]

1918 van Doorn, Marlene **"On Documenting Africa in the Netherlands."** *African Research & Documentation*, no. 90 (2002): 43-52.
online http://www.ascleiden.nl/pdf/scolma.pdf June 2002 10 pp.
A paper presented at the 40th annual conference of the ➔ **Standing Conference on Library Materials on Africa (1892)**, Oxford, 25-26 June 2002. It provides an overview of the state of Africanist documentation in the Netherlands and, more specifically, outlines the work of the African Studies Centre (ASC) in Leiden, its origins and objects, its research programme, the work of the ➔ **African Studies Centre Library's Documentation and Information Department (1246)**, and access to African studies resources through the ASC's OPAC (➔ *see* **72**). The paper also describes the ASC's abstracting journal ➔ **African Studies Abstracts (396)** and the Centre's partnerships with commercial publishers. [25/09/05]

1919 Walsh, Gretchen **"Opportunities and Challenges in Africana Library Service."** http://people.bu.edu/gwalsh/alc-coop.html 08 November 2001 8 pp.
A working document (in draft from) prepared for the ➔ **Africana Librarians Council (1885)**, which describes the work of the ALC and the ➔ **Cooperative Africana Microform Project (1889)** in five areas of concern for the Africana library community. A brief list of the challenges and concerns for each area is followed by a description of current, past and planned projects, covering collection development, access (including cataloguing, bibliography and indexes, and document delivery), reference and bibliographic instruction, preservation, and advocacy and capacity building in Africa. [25/09/05]

1920 Wilson, Paul **"Out-of-Print and Secondhand: A View of the Antiquarian Book Trade."** In *Africa Bibliography. Works on Africa published during* 2001 edited by T.A. Barringer. Edinburgh: Edinburgh University Press; London: International African Institute, 2002, vii-xiii.
The proprietor of ➔ **Oriental and African Books (2346)** in Shrewsbury describes some of the workings of the secondhand and antiquarian book trade relating to Africa and the development of his firm, which specializes in putting together collections on a particular area or theme.

1921 Witherell, Julian, ed. **Africana Resources and Collections. Three Decades of Development and Achievement. A Festschrift in Honor of Hans Panofsky.**
Metuchen, NJ: Scarecrow Press, 1989. 265 pp. $35.00/£32.50/€55.75
Published to honour Hans Panofsky (former Curator of Africana at Northwestern University), this is a collection of essays on various aspects of Africana librarianship, past, present, and future. It also contains biographic portrait of Panofsky and a bibliography of his work.

1922   Zaccaria, Massimo **Photography and African Studies. A Bibliography.** Pavia: Department of Political and Social Studies in the University of Pavia, 2001. 175 pp. [Available on an exchange basis only, contact the author, Massimo Zaccaria , Email: zaccaria@unipv.it]

Building on the work by Judith Kisor, John McIlwaine and Andrew Roberts – who published a preliminary bibliography on "Photographs of Africa" in *African Research & Documentation* in 1996 (no. 72, pp. 16-39) – this valuable annotated bibliography contains 1,503 references, divided into two parts: the first part lists articles relating to specific African countries covering bibliographies, anthropology and photography, colonial photography (in France, Germany, Great Britain and Italy), missionary photography, photojournalism, and postcards. Part two lists specific collections of African photographs in libraries and archives, arranged by continent and thereafter by countries, and includes 199 entries. A subject and author index facilitate access to the entries.

ARD review:
African Research & Documentation no. 88 (2002): 87-89 (reviewed by Terry Barringer)
Online review:
Sudanic Africa 12 (2001): 179-181.
http://www.hf.uib.no/smi/sa/12/12Zaccaria.pdf (reviewed by Heather J. Sharkey)

1923   Zell, Hans M. **"The Rise and Rise of Journal Subscription Prices in African Studies."** *Africana Libraries Newsletter*, no. 111 (June/September 2003): 7-9
online at http://www.indiana.edu/~libsalc/african/aln/no112.pdf [25/09/05]

An analysis comparing subscription prices for African studies journals and how they have increased between 1989 to 2003. The analysis is based on 13 leading, multidisciplinary African studies journals published in English, plus two journals that are primarily bibliographic in nature. It showed that subscription rates for a total of six journals increased at a relatively modest pace, by up to 50%, or an average of about 10% annually; another three increased rates by between 64-87% in the five year period 1998 to-2003, or by about 13-17% annually. The rest were all above 100%, two by more than 120%, two by over 200%, and one by an astonishing 410%.

1924   Zurbrugg, Tony **"A Perspective on the Trade in Books from and about Africa in Anglophone Europe."** In *Africa Bibliography. Works on Africa published during 2002*, edited by T.A. Barringer. Edinburgh: Edinburgh University Press; London International African Institute, 2003. vii-xvii.

A useful survey of bookshops in "Anglophone Europe" (a term the author identifies as "broadly non-Latin western Europe"), who hold some kind of stocks of books on Africa, principally in the UK but also covering the Netherlands, Belgium, and Denmark. There is especially good coverage of bookshops in London, which includes full addresses, telephone numbers, and a short description of stocks held and/or areas of specialization. Also covers some "off the High Street" distributors, library suppliers and online booksellers, although it is puzzling that there is no mention at all of the Oxford-based ➔ **African Books Collective (2332).** The author is Managing Director of the ➔ **Africa Book Centre (2331)** in London.

16

Publishers with African studies lists in Africa, Europe and North America

This section offers a comprehensive directory of almost 400 publishers worldwide with active African studies lists. It covers publishers who produce scholarly and academic works on Africa (both monographs and reference works), and textbooks at tertiary level. Also included are those publishing creative writing by African authors or critical studies on African literature. However, a number of prominent European publishers, for example those in France, who publish occasional works of fiction by African writers, or publish African fiction in translation, are *not* included here, unless they are also active in non-fiction publishing in the African studies field.

Publishers of general and trade titles on Africa, such as coffee-table type of books, or travel and guidebooks, are not included.

It should also be noted that some institutional publishers, especially those in Africa, publish only work originating from their own institutions, and/or research undertaken by their own staff. Research institutions whose publishing activities are restricted to publishing occasional papers, short research reports, or policy briefing papers, etc. are not included, nor are research institutions in Africa publishing *national* research studies only.

Arrangement and information provided
Publishers are grouped by continent: Africa, Europe, and North America, and within each region arrangement is alphabetical by country. The new edition includes a much more substantial number of publishers in Africa, primarily those publishing in English, but also including a large number of imprints in francophone Africa producing scholarly books, or creative writing by African authors.

Information for each entry includes full name and postal address, telephone and fax number, email address, Web site (where available), name of chief executive and/or name of commissioning editor or other contact person responsible for the publisher's African studies list, and areas of publishing. It should be noted that some African publishers' Web sites, where available, can suffer from frequent down time.

Where available both physical and postal addresses are indicated, but communications to publishers, or orders, etc. should always be sent to the postal (PO Box) address in preference.

Areas of publishing (see also below) are only indicative as it relates to publishing activities *within the field of African studies*, and most academic and scholarly publishers do of course have active lists in many other disciplines.

All information has been verified and updated as far as has been possible, and is current as at October 2005.

Manuscript submissions

Many publishers' Web sites provide helpful and detailed guidelines for submitting proposals, the manuscript review process, and points to note in the preparation of manuscripts. Some of them also provide online proposal forms. For a number of publishers we have included details of submission restrictions as it relates to preliminary enquiries; for example, some publishers will not accept manuscript proposals, or sample chapters, submitted by email.

Although multiple contacts are indicated for many entries (including the names of chief executives, or the directors of university presses), book proposals should normally be addressed to the acquisitions or commissioning editors indicated.

Initial submissions should always be letter of enquiry and/or proposal with an outline and table of contents, and accompanied by a CV or other brief biographical information. Do *not* submit unsolicited manuscripts. Before submitting a proposal become familiar with the publisher's imprint and their list, to ensure that your work would be compatible with their programme (and see Publishing areas below).

Publishing areas/Indexes to fields of activity

Using a numerical coding system, each entry is classified to indicate fields of activity and area(s) of publishing within the African studies field (and a number in the field of agriculture, environmental studies, health studies and health care, natural history, and the sciences), covering a total of 45 disciplines. Publishers' areas of activities have been primarily identified through examination of their print and/or online catalogues, information about the scope of the publishing list and manuscript submissions policies provided on Web sites, and, for African publishers, on the basis of listings in the quarterly ➔ **African Book Publishing Record (384)**, the subject index of the cumulative ➔**African Books in Print (385)**, as well as print/online catalogues and new title information from distributors such as ➔ **African**

Books Collective (2332), the ➔Africa Book Centre (2331), ➔ Global Book Marketing (2338), the ➔ Afrilivres (392) online catalogue database, as well as some other sources.

If a press has a special interest in a particular topic or area of study not covered by the broader subject categories, this area of specialization is indicated separately, as part of the entry.

A key to subject codes appears at the beginning of each regional section, together with indexes to fields of activity by publishers in Africa, Europe, and in North America. It should be noted, however, that some publishers may well be willing to consider manuscripts of outstanding quality in areas other than those listed.

At the end of each regional index there is a separate index of publishers of electronic and online products, ebooks, CD-ROM, and microfiche/microfilm.

Using the online version database search to find publishers
Authors looking for publishers in their fields of interest will find that the online version of the *African Studies Companion* can track down relevant publishers very quickly: (1) In any of the three regional sections, click on to the link "Index and key to publisher subject areas". (2) This will then display a menu of all 45 subject codes grouped by AFRICA, EUROPE, and NORTH AMERICA, with hyperlinks to the relevant entry numbers for the subject category chosen. (3) Clicking on to any of them will display the full entry of the publishers. For example, in category *1 African art and art history* - NORTH AMERICA, the entries of all publishers active in this area will be shown as a result of the database search, in this example 12 North American publishers, while Europe will display 7 matches, and Africa 29.

Distributors/Online catalogues
Where available, North American distributors of European publishers and, vice-versa, European/UK distributors of North American publishers, are indicated as part of the entry.

European/US distributors of African publishers are also indicated, i.e. those distributed by ➔African Books Collective Ltd/ABC (2332) – now distributed in the US by ➔ Michigan State University Press (2271) – ➔ Africa Book Centre/Global Book Marketing/ (2331, 2338), ➔ L'Harmattan (2314) or ➔ Khartala (2171) in Paris, and some other agents.

AFRICA

Please note that fields of activity indicated under 'Publishing areas' refer to publishing activities either in the field of African studies, or African literature. However, many of the African publishers listed here are also involved in publishing activities *other than* academic and scholarly books, for example publishing educational and schoolbooks, and books for children. Many publishers in Africa are also active in publishing creative writing in African languages.

While the *African Studies Companion* includes imprints with scholarly publishing output in francophone Africa (or publishing African literature in French), coverage of publishers in North Africa is limited to a small number of academic publishers producing African studies titles in French. For a more comprehensive listing of publishers in the countries of the Maghreb consult "Edition et éditeurs au Maghreb", compiled by the → **Fondation du Roi Abdul Aziz Saoud pour les Etudes Islamiques et les Sciences Humaines (1423)** http://www.fondation.org.ma/Maghareb/editeurs.htm.

A rapidly increasing number of African publishers now have their own Web sites and URLs are indicated where available, although some sites tend to suffer from frequent and sometimes prolonged down time.

The output of a sizeable number of publishers in francophone Africa can now also be accessed at two collective Web sites: → **Afrilivres (392)** and **L'Alliance des éditeurs indépendents pour une autre mondalisation (393)**. Where applicable, this is indicated as part of the entry. However, it should be noted that titles listed online on these sites may only represent *extracts* from the publisher's list.

AFRICA

Africa: Index and key to publisher subject areas

1   African art and art history
1925, 1953, 1957, 1960, 1962, 1992, 2011, 2014, 2022, 2053, 2054, 2061, 2070, 2072, 2080, 2081, 2098, 2099, 2104, 2111, 2113, 2114, 2118, 2119, 2121, 2129, 2135, 2138, 2144

**2   African cultural studies
(in general)**
1926, 1927, 1930, 1940, 1941, 1942, 1943, 1946, 1949, 1951, 1952, 1953, 1954, 1957, 1962, 1967, 1978, 1979, 1992, 2006, 2007, 2007, 2011, 2012, 2016, 2020, 2022, 2029, 2030, 2035, 2036, 2040, 2044, 2047, 2050, 2059, 2061, 2064, 2065, 2070, 2081, 2092, 2098, 2099, 2104, 2117, 2119, 2121, 2123, 2124, 2128, 2129, 2132, 2143, 2152, 2154, 2156, 2157, 2159

3   African film and cinema
2078, 2112

4   African languages and linguistics
1932, 1934, 1944, 1949, 1952, 1953, 1962, 1963, 1974, 1979, 1989, 1991, 1992, 1993, 1997, 2033, 2035, 2036, 2040, 2045, 2052, 2055, 2056, 2057, 2061, 2090, 2092, 2098, 2102, 2103, 2107, 2117, 2119, 2120, 2127, 2128, 2129, 2133, 2140, 2144 2158, 2161

**5   African literature:
Critical studies and collections**
1925, 1926, 1927, 1930, 1941, 1943, 1946, 1948, 1953, 1956, 1957, 1960, 1961, 1962, 1963, 1967, 1974, 1979, 1987, 1988, 1989, 1991, 1992, 1996, 2004, 2007, 2010, 2011, 2013, 2013, 2014, 2015, 2016, 2020, 2022, 2024, 2029, 2030, 2031, 2034, 2035, 2036, 2038, 2039, 2042, 2044, 2046, 2049, 2051, 2052, 2053, 2056, 2061, 2064, 2068, 2070, 2074, 2080, 2082, 2083, 2085, 2089, 2096, 2098, 2099, 2104, 2111, 2112, 2117, 2118, 2119, 2121, 2123, 2124, 2128, 2129, 2132, 2133, 2134, 2138, 2139, 2144, 2148, 2150, 2151, 2154, 2158, 2159, 2161, 2162

6   African literature: Fiction
1926, 1928, 1929, 1930, 1937, 1938, 1939, 1941, 1943, 1946, 1947, 1948, 1950, 1952, 1953, 1954, 1955, 1957, 1960, 1969, 1970, 1974, 1976, 1977, 1978, 1979, 1980, 1987, 1988, 1991, 1992, 1993, 1995, 1996, 2004, 2006, 2007, 2012, 2014, 2017,

2022, 2029, 2030, 2034, 2035, 2036, 2038, 2042, 2043, 2044, 2046, 2051, 2053, 2056, 2061, 2064, 2065, 2068, 2080, 2082, 2083, 2085, 2089, 2092, 2095, 2098, 2101, 2104, 2107, 2111, 2112, 2113, 2116, 2128, 2129, 2130, 2132, 2133, 2134, 2135, 2136, 2139, 2140, 2142, 2148, 2150, 2151, 2152, 2153, 2154, 2159, 2161, 2161

7   African literature: Drama
1929, 1941, 1943, 1952, 1953, 1957, 1974, 1976, 1987, 2007, 2034, 2035, 2036, 2038, 2039, 2043, 2044, 2046, 2050, 2051, 2053, 2056, 2064, 2979 2098, 2104, 2119, 2132, 2135, 2142, 2151, 2152

8   African literature: Poetry
1926, 1930, 1938, 1939, 1941, 1946, 1952, 1953, 1957, 1962, 1970, 1974, 1976, 1977, 1978, 1979, 1987, 2004, 2011, 2029, 2030, 2034, 2035, 2036, 2039, 2043, 2044, 2046, 2051, 2053, 2055, 2061, 2064, 2071, 2077, 2079, 2083, 2085, 2089, 2092, 2098, 2104, 2107, 2111, 2112, 2113, 2116, 2118, 2119, 2132, 2134, 2135, 2139, 2148, 2151, 2152, 2152, 2161

9   African music
1925, 1927, 1967, 1970, 1974, 2049, 2053, 2054, 2077, 2098, 2140

**10   Agricultural sciences and
agricultural development**
1956, 1965, 1966, 1968, 1974, 1981, 1982, 1984, 1990, 1995, 2003, 2012, 2013, 2028, 2031, 2041, 2062, 2074, 2097, 2107, 2127, 2140, 2154, 2158,

11   Anthropology and ethnology
1927, 1932, 1936, 1942, 1949, 1951, 1952, 1957, 1966, 1969, 1974, 1979, 1987, 2007, 2010, 2011, 2012, 2017, 2021, 2022, 2026, 2027, 2028, 2035, 2050, 2057, 2058, 2064, 2074, 2075, 2088, 2098, 2099, 2117, 2119, 2121, 2129, 2132, 2135, 2137, 2147, 2154

12   Archaeology and pre-history
1925, 1927, 1960, 2028, 2050, 2074, 2104, 2117, 2127

13   Architecture
1960, 2098, 2117, 2119

14   Biography and autobiography
1926, 1934, 1967, 1970, 1977, 1989, 2000, 2001, 2007, 2010, 2032, 2035, 2037, 2043, 2053, 2068, 2077, 2092, 2098, 2099, 2101, 2105, 2106, 2111, 2112, 2113, 2116, 2118, 2121, 2124, 2129, 2132, 2140, 2151

15   Constitutional and land law
2060, 2091, 2093

16   Diaspora studies
----

17   Economics and development studies
1929, 1932, 1940, 1941, 1944, 1945, 1947, 1951,
1953, 1956, 1957, 1958, 1962, 1964, 1966, 1969,
1971, 1974, 1978, 1978, 1984, 1987, 1991, 1995,
1997, 1998, 1999, 2010, 2012, 2018, 2019, 2020,
2021, 2022, 2024, 2028, 2031, 2035, 2036, 2044,
2048, 2049, 2050, 2053, 2055, 2056, 2059, 2064,
2066, 2069, 2074, 2083, 2084, 2086, 2088, 2090,
2094, 2098, 2100, 2102, 2107, 2108, 2112, 2113,
2117, 2119, 2120, 2121, 2124, 2127, 2129, 2130,
2131, 2138, 2140, 2141, 2143, 2147, 2155, 2156,
2157, 2158, 2159, 2161

18   Education
1926, 1931, 1932, 1933, 1935, 1945, 1947, 1951,
1953, 1956, 1957, 1958, 1966, 1970, 1972, 1974,
1975, 1978, 1979, 1981, 1982, 1987, 1991, 1997,
1998, 2011, 2017, 2020, 2021, 2024, 2027, 2035,
2036, 2040, 2053, 2054, 2055, 2056, 2057, 2059,
2064, 2069, 2083, 2084, 2086, 2090, 2094, 2095,
2098, 2102, 2104, 2107, 2112, 2117, 2127, 2128,
2129, 2130, 2131, 2132, 2133, 2137, 2140, 2142,
2145, 2149, 2151, 2152, 2156

19   Entomology
1927, 1929, 1965, 1990, 2012, 2013, 2115

20   Environmental studies
1932, 1954, 1965, 1966, 1967, 1968, 1978, 1981,
1982, 1985, 1990, 2014, 2031, 2062, 2073, 2090,
2098, 2104, 2106, 2108, 2115, 2117, 2118, 2126,
2129, 2143, 2156, 2157, 2159

21   Flora and fauna of Africa
1956, 1958, 1959, 1963, 1965, 1968, 1982, 2024,
2061, 2073, 2099, 2110, 2118, 2121, 2129

22   Folklore and oral cultures
1939, 1946, 1948, 1949, 1955, 1957, 1967, 1969,
1970, 1979, 1987, 1993, 1997, 2007, 2010, 2011,
2012, 2016, 2029, 2034, 2047, 2052, 2053, 2064,
2065, 2089, 2104, 2113, 2119, 2121, 2123, 2129,
2132, 2133, 2142, 2149, 2154

23   Food studies and food security
2020, 2024, 2041, 2062, 2099, 2119

24   Geography
1963, 1996, 2019, 2022, 2024, 2035, 2036, 2053,
2069, 2074, 2084, 2095, 2098, 2099, 2135, 2137,
2147

25   Geology and earth sciences
1956, 2035, 2049

**26   Government and public
administration**
1933, 1944, 1987, 2012, 2013, 2036, 2048, 2053,
2056, 2057, 2059, 2069, 2086, 2090, 2102, 2108,
2119, 2120, 2140, 2156, 2157

27   History
1925, 1927, 1929, 1932, 1936, 1940, 1943, 1944,
1945, 1948, 1951, 1953, 1955, 1956, 1957, 1958,
1960, 1961, 1962, 1963, 1964, 1967, 1974, 1975,
1976, 1977, 1978, 1979, 1980, 1987, 1991, 1992,
1996, 1997, 1998, 1999, 2003, 2005, 2006, 2007,
2010, 2011, 2015, 2016, 2017, 2018, 2019, 2020,
2021, 2022, 2024, 2024, 2027, 2031, 2032, 2035,
2037, 2040, 2044, 2049, 2050, 2052, 2058, 2059,
2064, 2065, 2066, 2070, 2074, 2076, 2077, 2080,
2081, 2084, 2094, 2096, 2098, 2099, 2102, 2104,
2105, 2111, 2113, 2117, 2118, 2124, 2131, 2132,
2133, 2134, 2135, 2136, 2137, 2138, 2140, 2144,
2147, 2150, 2152, 2152, 2154, 2156, 2161

28   Human rights
1932, 1933, 1964, 2000, 2003, 2024, 2035, 2048,
2049, 2059, 2060, 2074, 2086, 2090, 2129, 2140,
2147, 2156

29   Labour studies
1984, 2016, 2060, 2088, 2118, 2120, 2122, 2156,
2158, 2159

30   Law
1932, 1934, 1939, 1944, 1951, 1953, 1955, 1956,
1957, 1973, 1976, 1986, 1987, 1994, 2035, 2036,
2040, 2044, 2049, 2053, 2060, 2063, 2066, 2091,
2093, 2102, 2119, 2120, 2121, 2127, 2129, 2137,
2138, 2140, 2158, 2160

**31   Library and information
sciences/Information technology**
1974, 1982, 2031, 2054, 2055, 2061, 2156

32   Media and communication
1933, 1934, 1956, 1983, 2000, 2025, 2068, 2078,
2080, 2086, 2090, 2112, 2146, 2159

33 Medical and health studies/ Health care (including HIV/AIDS)
1941, 1956, 1965, 1967, 1974, 1985, 1987, 1995, 1998, 2016, 2027, 2053, 2062, 2075, 2083, 2084, 2086, 2088, 2090, 2097, 2098, 2102, 2107, 2111, 2112, 2117, 2118, 2120, 2121, 2158

34 Natural history
2006, 2024, 2061, 2073, 2074, 2081, 2105, 2113, 2115, 2125, 2129

35 Philosophy
1929, 1941, 1944, 1951, 1987, 2030, 2040, 2049, 2054, 2055, 2057, 2059, 2065, 2083, 2117, 2119, 2132, 2138, 2152, 2155

36 Politics, political economy, and international relations
1926, 1927, 1929, 1932, 1933, 1939, 1940, 1941, 1942, 1944, 1945, 1947, 1951, 1953, 1955, 1957, 1958, 1960, 1962, 1969, 1970, 1974, 1976, 1981, 1987, 1991, 1998, 1999, 2003, 2005, 2007, 2007, 2010, 2011, 2012, 2012, 2013, 2014, 2015, 2016, 2017, 2018, 2019, 2022, 2027, 2028, 2029, 2031, 2032, 2035, 2036, 2040, 2044, 2048, 2049, 2050, 2053, 2055, 2057, 2058, 2059, 2061, 2064, 2066, 2069, 2070, 2074, 2077, 2080, 2084, 2086, 2087, 2088, 2090, 2094, 2096, 2098, 2099, 2102, 2104, 2105, 2106, 2108, 2109, 2111, 2112, 2113, 2117, 2118, 2119, 2120, 2121, 2122, 2124, 2127, 2129, 2130, 2131, 2134, 2135, 2137, 2138, 2140, 2140, 2142, 2143, 2146, 2147, 2151, 2154, 2156, 2157, 2158, 2159, 2161

37 Psychology
1956, 1979, 1987, 2017, 2027, 2074, 2084, 2090, 2098, 2102, 2104, 2106, 2119, 2120, 2127, 2147

38 Reference
1932, 1933, 1949, 1960, 1961, 1967, 1972, 1979, 1980, 1981, 1989, 1995, 2002, 2004, 2006, 2010, 2013, 2018, 2021, 2022, 2024, 2025, 2027, 2033, 2035, 2037, 2040, 2045, 2048, 2053, 2054, 2056, 2069, 2070, 2074, 2075, 2082, 2084, 2094, 2095, 2097, 2098, 2099, 2102, 2103, 2106, 2107, 2112, 2113, 2120, 2121, 2133, 2140, 2151, 2152, 2154

39 Refugee and migration studies
2074

40 Religion and theology
1934, 1941, 1949, 1950, 1952, 1957, 1960, 1962, 1969, 1974, 1977, 1987, 2000, 2002, 2004, 2008, 2007, 2017, 2021, 2030, 2031, 2047, 2052, 2053, 2061, 2066, 2070, 2074, 2075, 2098, 2099, 2104, 2107, 2113, 2117, 2119, 2120, 2132, 2133, 2144, 2154, 2158

41 Rural development
1974, 1984, 1997, 2003, 2028, 2036, 2040, 2049, 2069, 2127, 2149, 2159

42 Science and technology
1956, 1959, 1981, 1982, 1990, 2013, 2035, 2061, 2066, 2083, 2090, 2098, 2106, 2107, 2112, 2117, 2126, 2158

43 Sociology
1925, 1926, 1927, 1931, 1939, 1942, 1943, 1944, 1945, 1951, 1957, 1960, 1966, 1974, 1977, 1981, 1987, 1999, 2002, 2003, 2005, 2007, 2014, 2016, 2017, 2018, 2019, 2021, 2024, 2027, 2028, 2035, 2040, 2049, 2053, 2054, 2055, 2056, 2057, 2059, 2061, 2062, 2064, 2067, 2083, 2084, 2086, 2088, 2090, 2092, 2094, 2096, 2102, 2104, 2108, 2109, 2112, 2118, 2119, 2121, 2127, 2128, 2133, 2135, 2137, 2138, 2146, 2147, 2149, 2152, 2155, 2156, 2158, 2159

44 Urban studies
1956, 1978, 2003, 2005, 2021, 2074, 2084, 2098, 2102, 2127

45 Women's and gender studies
1926, 1932, 1939, 1950, 1952, 1955, 1957, 1960, 1962, 1966, 1974, 1977, 1978, 1979, 1981, 1986, 1988, 1989, 1993, 2000, 2003, 2007, 2010, 2011, 2012, 2012, 2016, 2017, 2018, 2021, 2024, 2035, 2042, 2053, 2054, 2055, 2057, 2059, 2061, 2062, 2065, 2069, 2075, 2084, 2086, 2090, 2094, 2098, 2099, 2100, 2101, 2102, 2104, 2109, 2117, 2118, 2119, 2121, 2122, 2127, 2128, 2133, 2138, 2139, 2140, 2147, 2156, 2157, 2158, 2159, 2160, 2161

Publishers of electronic & online products, ebooks, CD-ROM, and microfiche/ microfilm
1972, 1992, 1994, 2063, 2069, 2084, 2091, 2093, 2097, 2103, 2108,

Algeria

1925   Editions du Tell
3 Rue des Frères Yacoub Torki
09000 Blida
Tel: +213-25-311035 Fax: +213-25-311036
Email: contact@editions-du-tell.com
Web: http://www.editions-du-tell.com/
Contact: Djamel Souidi
Publishing areas: 1, 5, 9, 12, 27, 43 (primarily
on Algeria and the Maghreb countries)

Angola

1926   Editorial Nzila
Avenida Commander Eurico
nº45-2°/B
CP 3462
Luanda
Tel: +244-2-331362 Fax: +244-2-441613
Email: nzila@ebonet.net
Web: n/a
Contact: Isabel Arlindo
Publishing areas: 2, 5, 6, 8, 14, 17, 18, 36, 43, 45

Benin

1927   AFRIDIC
01 BP 269
01 Porto-Novo
Tel: +229-223 228
Email: afridic@caramail.com
Web: n/a
Contact: Jean-Baptiste Adjibi
Publishing areas: 8, 11, 12, 27, 36, 43
Online catalogue: Afrilivres

1928   Editions Ruisseaux d'Afrique
C/2186 Kindonou
04 BP 1154
04 Cotonou
Tel/Fax: +229-383186/947925
Email: ruisseau@mail.leland.bj
Web: n/a
Contact: Béatrice Lalinon Gbado
Publishing areas: 6 (publishes
primarily children's books)
Online catalogue: Afrilivres, Alliance

1929   Editions du Flamboyant
BP 08-271
Cotonou
Tel: +229-310220/350472 Fax: +229-946628
Email: zoundin@yahoo.fr or
joachimomega@yahoo.fr
Web: n/a
Contacts: Oscar de Suza, Joachim
Adjovi
Publishing areas: 2, 5, 6, 7, 17, 19, 27, 35, 36
Online catalogue: Afrilivres, Alliance

1930   Editions Souvenir
Carrefour du Bd Cachi von 1 Ghe
01 BP 2589
Porto-Novo
Tel: +229-884904/888013
Email: editsouvenir@voila.fr
Web: n/a
Contact: Jean-Baptiste Kunda Li
Fumu'Nsamu
Publishing areas: 2, 5, 6, 8
Online catalogue: Afrilivres

Botswana

**1931   Foundation for Education with
Production**
PO Box 20906
001 Gaborone
Also at:
PO Box 53565
Troyville
2139 Johannesburg
South Africa
Tel: +267-391 4311 Fax: +267-318 4296
(Botswana) Tel: +27-11-618 2132
Fax: + 27-11-618 1297
Email: n/a
Web: n/a
Contact: Patrick van Rensburg
Overseas distr: ABC
Publishing areas: 18, 43

**1932   Lentswe La Lesedi (Pty)
Ltd/Lightbooks Publishers**
Digitec House
685 Botswana Road
The Mall
PO Box 2365
Gaborone
Tel: +267-390 3994 Fax: + 267- 391 4017
Email: lightbooks@it.bw or
bewlay@lightbooks.net

Web: http://www.lightbooks.net
Contact: Charles Bewlay, Publisher
Publishing areas: 4, 11, 17, 18, 20, 27, 28, 30, 36, 38, 45
Overseas distr: ABC

1933 Morula Publishers
PO Box 70404
Gaborone
Tel: +267-352199 Fax: +267-351299
Email: seb2roxide@yahoo.com
Web: n/a
Contact: Barolong Seboni
Publishing areas: 18, 26, 28, 32, 36, 38

1934 Pula Press
c/o Botswana Book Centre
PO Box 91
Gaborone
Tel: +267-352931 Fax: +267- 374315
Email: bbcbot@global.bw
Web: n/a
Contact: M.S. Johnson
Publishing areas: 4, 14, 30, 32, 40
Overseas distr: Africa Book Centre

1935 Pyramid Publishing (Pty) Ltd
Unit 12 Plot 20743 Block 3
PO Box 403092
Gaborone
Tel/Fax: +267-3902244 /+267-565194
Email: pyramid@botsnet.bw (General enquiries) lucyclarke@botsnet.bw or 4lucylu@gmail.com (Publisher)
Web: http://www.pyramidpublishing.net/ (site under construction)
Contact: Lucy Dixon-Clarke, Publisher
Publishing areas: 18
Overseas distr: ABC

Burkina Faso

1936 Editions Découvertes du Burkina Faso
06 BP 9237
Ouagadougou 06
Tel: +226-362238/254269
Email: jacques@liptinfor.bf
Web: n/a
Contact: Jacques Guégané, Director
Publishing areas: 11, 27
Online catalogue: Afrilivres

1937 Editions G.T.I (Graphic Technic International)
01 BP 3230
Ouagadougou 01
Tel: +226-316769 Fax: +226-316769
Email: tass@fasonet.bf or hien.ignace@fasonet.bf
Web: n/a
Contacts: Tasséré N. Sawadogo, Ansomwin Ignace Hien
Publishing areas: 6
Online catalogue: Afrilivres

1938 Editions La Muse
01 BP 3531
Ouagadougou 01
Tel: +226-430417/317907
Fax: +226-316769
Email: hien.ignace@fasonet.bf
Web: n/a
Contact: Ansomwin Ignace Hien, Managing Director
Publishing areas: 6, 8
Online catalogue: Afrilivres

1939 Editions Sankofa & Gurli
01 BP 3811
Ouagadougou 01
Tel: +226-50 36 43 44
Email: sankogur@yahoo.fr or samourai@yahoo.fr
Web: n/a
Contact: Jean Claude Naba
Publishing areas: 6, 8, 22, 30, 36, 43, 45
Online catalogue: Afrilivres, Alliance

Cameroon

1940 Buma Kor Publishers Ltd
BP 727
Yaoundé
Tel: +237-756 3268
Email: bkor2000@yahoo.com or b.kor@iccnet.cm
Web: http://www.bumakorbook.com (site not accessible October 21005)
Contact: Buma Kor, Managing Director
Publishing areas: 2, 17, 27, 36
Note: publishes under the imprint DeScholar Press.

1941   Editions CLE
BP 1501
Yaoundé
Tel: +237-222 3554
Fax: +237-223 2709
Email: cle@camnet.cm or Gatwatw@yahoo.fr
Web: http://www.wagne.net/cle/
Contact: Tharcisse Gatwa, Director
Publishing areas: 2, 5, 6, 7, 8, 17, 33, 35, 36, 40
Online catalogue: Afrilivres

1942   Editions Demos
BP 12257
Yaoundé
Tel: +237-222 1209
Email: jm_tchegho@yahoo.fr
Web:
http://www.megasoftcm.com/~racine/
Contact: Jean Marie Tchegho
Publishing areas: 2, 11, 36, 43

1943   Editions Ndzé
BP 647
Bertua
Cameroon
also at:
BP 188
Libreville
Tel: +237-950 9295 Fax: +237-224 2585
Email: editions@ndze.com (General enquiries)
cadence@ndze.com (Director)
Web: http://www.ndze.com/
Contact: Michel Cadence, Director
Publishing areas: 2, 5, 6, 7, 27, 43
Overseas distr: Association Littéraire
Francophone d'Afrique, 55 blvd Soult, 75012
Paris, France

1944   Presses Universitaires d'Afrique
22 place Elig Essono
BP 8106
Yaoundé
Tel: +237-220030 Fax: +237-222325
Email: aes@iccnet.cm
Web: n/a
Contact: Serge Dontchueng Kouam
Publishing areas: 4, 17, 26, 27, 30, 35, 36, 43
Online catalogue: Alliance

1945   Presses Universitaires de Yaoundé
22 Place Elig-Essono
BP 8106
Yaoundé
Tel: +237-222 1320/222 2325
Email: uy1@uycdc.uninet.cm

Web: n/a
Publishing areas: 17, 18, 27, 36, 43

Congo (Brazzaville)

1946   Editions Lemba
BP 2351
Brazzaville
Tel: +242-676558 Fax: +242-810017
Email: editions_lemba@yahoo.fr
Contact: Apollinaire Singou-Basseha
Publishing areas: 2, 5, 6, 8, 22
Online catalogue: Afrilivres

**1947   Les Presses Universitaires de
          Brazzaville**
BP 2150
Brazzaville
Tel:/Fax: +242-81170
Email: n/a
Web: n/a
Contact: Jean Mouaya
Publishing areas: 6, 17, 18, 36

Congo Democratic Republic

1948   Afrique Editions
51 avenue Mfumu Lutuno
Kinshasa-Gombé
Tel: +243-884 3202 Fax: +243-880 3812
Email: afde@raga.net
Web: n/a
Publishing areas: 5, 6, 22, 27
Overseas distr: Éditions Hurtubise HMH
1815, avenue De Lorimier, Montréal, Québec,
H2K 3W6, Canada Email:
hurtubisehmh@hurtubisehmh.com

**1949   Centre d'etudes ethnologiques/
          Institut de culture africaine de
          Bandundu**
BP 8631
Kinshasa 1
Tel/Fax: n/a
Email: bfansaka@yahoo.it or ceeba@steyler.at
Web: http://www.ceeba.at/
Contacts: (Prof.) Bernard Fansaka,
(Prof.) Herman Hochegger
Publishing areas: 2, 4, 11, 22, 38, 40
Overseas distr/enquiries: (Prof.) Hermann
Hochegger, Antenne d'Autriche, St. Gabriel,
A-2340 Mödling, Austria,
Email: Hochegger@steyler.at

1950   Editions La Perle
8 Parc de Virunga
BP 752
Kinshasa XI
Tel: + 243-88-48493/45529
Email: odiomarg@yahoo.fr
Web: n/a
Contact: M. Odio
Publishing areas: 6, 40, 45

1951   Les Presses Universitaires du DRC
BP 1632
Kinshasa 1
Tel: +243-12-30562
Email: n/a
Web: n/a
Contact: Ependa Nkumu
Publishing areas: 2, 11, 17, 18, 27, 30, 35, 36, 43

Côte d'Ivoire

1952   EDILIS, Les Editions Livres du Sud
Biétry, rue du Canal 10 lot 137
BP 477 Abidjan 10
Tel: +225-21 24 46 50 Fax: +225-21 24 46 51
Email: edilis@africaonline.co.ci
Web: http://www.edilis-ci.com/ (site down
15/10/05)
Contact: (Mme) Mical Dréhi Lorougnon
Publishing areas: 2, 4, 6, 7, 8, 11, 40, 45
Other: publications in African languages
Online catalogue: Afrilivres, Alliance

1953   Editions CEDA
Centre d'édition et de diffusion
africaines
Immeuble Jeceda
Abidjan Plateau
04 BP 541
Abidjan 04
Tel: +225-21 24 65 10/21 24 65 11
Fax: +225-21 25 05 67 (General enquiries)
+225-20 31 60 30/44 (Editorial)
Email: infos@ceda-ci.com (General enquiries)
direction@ceda-ci.com (Managing Director)
editions@ceda-ci.com (Editorial Director)
Web: http://www.ceda-ci.com
Contacts: Venance Kacou, Managing Director;
Omar Sylla, Editorial Director
Publishing areas: 1, 2, 4, 5, 6, 7, 8, 17,
18, 27, 30, 36
Online catalogue: Afrilivres
Overseas distr: Éditions Hurtubise HMH
1815, avenue De Lorimier, Montréal, Québec,

H2K 3W6, Canada Email:
hurtubisehmh@hurtubisehmh.com

1954   Editions Eburnie
01 BP 1984
Abidjan 01
Tel: +225-20 21 64 65/+225-20-215758
Fax: +225-20-21 45 46
Email: eburnie@aviso.ci or
amoikon.ma@aviso.ci
Web:
Contact: Marie Agathe Amoikon
Fauquembergue
Publishing areas: 2, 6, 20

1955   Editions Neter
01 BP 7370
Abidjan 01
Tel: +225-525268/216490
Email: n/a
Web: n/a
Contacts: Richard Ta Bi Senin,
Susanne Loucou
Publishing areas: 6, 22, 27, 30, 36, 45
Online catalogue: Afrilivres

**1956   Editions Universitaires de Côte
d'Ivoire**
Locaux UFR Sciences
Pharmaceutiques de l'Université
de Cocody
BP V 34
Abidjan
Tel/Fax: +225-22 44 48 35
Email: educiabj@yahoo.fr
Web:
http://www.ucocody.ci/educi/index.php
Contact: Pr. Kattie A. Louka, Director
Publishing areas: 5, 10, 17, 18, 21, 25, 27, 30,
32, 33, 37, 42, 44

1957   Les Nouvelles Editions Ivoiriennes
1 boulevard de Marseille
01 BP 1818
Abidjan 01
Tel: +225-21 24 07 66/21 24 08 25
Fax: +225-21 24 24 56
Email: edition@nei-ci.com
Web: http://www.nei-ci.com
Contacts: Guy Lambin, Managing Director;
Roger G. Oze, Commercial Director; Isaïe
Biton Koulibali, Editorial Director
Publishing areas: 1, 2, 5, 6, 7, 8, 11, 17, 18, 22,
27, 30, 36, 40, 43, 45
Online catalogue: Afrilivres

1958   Presses Universitaires et Scolaires
        d'Afrique
        08 BP 177
        Abidjan Plateau 08
Tel: +225-22 41 12 71 Fax: +225-449858
Email: aes@iccnet.cm
Web: n/a
Contact: Cissé Daniel Amara
Publishing areas: 17, 18, 21, 27, 36
Online catalogue: Afrilivres, Alliance

Djibouti

1959   Couleur Locale SARL
        BP 3500
        Djibouti
Tel: +253-352121 Fax: +253-353996
Email: couleurloc@intnet.dj
Contact: Véronique Carton, Director
Publishing areas: 21, 42
Other photographic works; travel guides
Online catalogue: Afrilivres
Overseas distr: l'Harmattan

Egypt (of scholarly titles in English only)

1960   American University in Cairo Press
        113 Sharia Kasr El Aini Street
        PO Box 2511
        Cairo 11511
Tel: +20-2-797 6926 (General) +20-2-797 6888
(Director) Fax: +20-2-794-1440
Email: aucpress@aucegypt.edu (General)
linz@aucegypt.edu
(Director) rnh@aucegypt.edu (Associate
Director for Editorial Programs)
Web: http://aucpress.com
US office:
420 Fifth Avenue
New York 10018-2729
Tel: +1-212-730 8800 Fax: +1-212-730 1600
Email: cterry@aucegypt.edu
Contacts (Cairo): Mark Linz, Director; Neil
Hewison, Associate Director for Editorial
Programs;
Publishing areas: 1, 5, 6, 12, 13, 27, 36, 38, 40,
43, 45
Other: Modern Arabic writing, ancient Egypt
Overseas distr:
US: The American University in Cairo Press,
c/o Books International (BI), PO Box 605,
Hendon, VA 20172, Email orders:
bimail@presswarehouse.com

Europe: The American University in Cairo
Press, c/o Eurospan (EDS), 3 Henrietta Street,
London WC2E 8LU, Email orders:
orders@edspubs.co.uk
Web: http://www.eurospan.co.uk

1961   Boustany's Publishing House
        4 Aly Tawfik Shousha Str.
        11371 Nasr City
        Cairo
Tel: +20-2-262 3085/590 8025
Fax: +202-262 3085
Email: boustany@link.net
Web: http://www.boustanys.com/
Publishing areas: 5, 27, 38 (publishes books
both in English and in Arabic)
Other: Arabic studies and Arabic literature;
company is also a retailer and library supplier
(see ➔ 2395)

Eritrea

1962   Africa World Press/The Red Sea
        Press Inc
        Via Teferi Yazew 19-21
        PO Box 48
        Asmara
Tel: +291-1-120707 Fax: +291-1-123369
Email: awpsrp@eol.com.er or
awprsp@africanworld.com
Web site: http://www.africanworld.com/
(site down 28/10/05)
Contact: Mulubirhan Kidan Kassahun
Publishing areas: 1, 2, 4, 5, 8, 17, 27, 36, 40, 45
Overseas distr and US office: ➔ Africa World
Press Inc/The Red Sea Press Inc (2246)

Ethiopia

1963   Addis Ababa University Press
        POB 1176
        Addis Ababa
Tel: +251-1-119148/+251- 1-111044
Fax: +251-1-550655
Web: http://www.aau.edu.et/index.php
(Main university home page, no details as yet
of University Press)
Contacts: Darge Wole, Director;
(Ms) Messelech Habte, Editor
Publishing areas: 4, 5, 21, 24, 27

1964   **The Ethiopian Institute of**
        International Peace & Development
        PO Box 115
        Area Code 1110/18528
        Addis Ababa
Tel: +251-1-531955 Fax: +251-1-533398
Email: sophia@telecom.net.et or
eiipd@telecom.net.et
Web: http://www.eiipd.org
Contact: Kinfe Abraham
Publishing areas: 17, 27, 28
Other: peace and conflict studies (especially
Ethiopia and Horn of Africa)
Overseas distr: ABC

1965   **International Livestock Research**
        Institute
        (formerly International Livestock
        Centre for Africa)
        PO Box 5689
        Addis Ababa
Tel: +251-1-338290 Fax: +251-1-338755
Email: ILRI-debre-zeit@cgiar.org or
ilri-information@cgiar.org (General enquiries)
b.scott@cgiar.org (Director of Partnerships
and Communication)
h.ibrahim@cgiar.org (Head of Publications)
Web: http://www.ilri.cgiar.org/default.asp
(Main home page)
http://www.ilri.cgiar.org/pageselflink.asp?p
ageid=319&menuid=38 (Publications)
Contacts: R. Bruce Scott, Director of
Partnerships and Communication;
H. Ibrahim [?], Head of Publications; Areas of
publishing: 10, 19, 21, 20, 33
Other: dairy production, genetics, livestock
research, veterinary sciences

1966   **Organisation for Social Science**
        Research in Eastern and
        Southern Africa (OSSREA)
        PO Box 31971
        Addis Ababa
Tel: 251-11-123 9484/123 9717
Fax: 251-11-122 3921
Email: pubunit@ossrea.net (General enquiries)
sami@ossrea.net (Head, Publishing Unit)
Web:
http://www.ossrea.org/publications/public
ation.htm
Contacts: (Dr.) Alfred Nhema, Executive
Secretary; Etalem Engeda, Head Publishing
Unit
Publishing areas: 10, 11, 17, 18, 20, 43, 45
Overseas distr: ABC

1967   **Shama Books**
        PO Box 8153
        Addis Ababa
Tel: + 251-1-553959 Fax: +251-1-551010
Email: Shamabooks@telecom.net.et
Web: http://www.shamabooks.com (site not
accessible October 2005)
Contact: Jonathan W. Niehaus, Publishing
Director
Publishing areas: 2, 5, 9, 14, 20, 22, 27, 33, 38
Overseas distr: Transaction Publishers
Distributors, 390 Campus Drive, Somerset, NJ
08893, USA, Email:
orders@transactionpub.com

Gabon

1968   **Editions ECOFAC**
        Conservation et utilisation
        rationnelle des Ecosystèmes   Forestiers
        d'Afrique Centrale
        Batterie 4 - Face groupe scolaire Gros
        Bouquet 2
        BP 15115
        Libreville
Tel: +241-732343/732344
Fax: +241-732345
Email: coordination@ecofac.org
Web: http://www.ecofac.org (General)
http://www.ecofac.org/Biblio/GabonBiblio.htm
(Online catalogue)
Contact: J. Roggeri (Europaid Cooperation Office,
EU, Brussels),
Email: paolo.roggeri@cec.eu.int
Publishing areas: 10, 20, 21
Other: forest conservation

1969   **Editions du Silence**
        292 avenue du Colonel Parent
        BP 13822
        Libreville
Tel: +241-239797 Fax: +241-729548
Email:
moussiroumouyama@yahoo.fr
Web: n/a
Contact: Auguste Moussirou
Mouyama
Publishing areas: 6, 11, 17, 22, 36, 40
Online catalogue: Afrilivres, Alliance

Ghana

1970   AFRAM Publications (Ghana) Ltd
C 184/22 Midway Lane
Abofu-Achimota
PO Box M18
Accra
Tel: 233-21-412561 Fax: 233-24-278844/55
Email: aframpub@punchgh.com (General
enquiries) or ericofei@yahoo.co.uk (Publisher)
Web:
http://www.aframpublications.com.gh/
(site not accessible October 2005)
Contact: Eric Ofei, Publisher
Publishing areas: 6, 8, 9, 14, 18, 22, 36
Overseas distr: ABC

1971   African Capital Markets Forum
Trust Towers 4th floor
PO Box CT 5789
Accra
Tel: +233-21-701 0249/235421
Fax: +233-21-701 0248
Email: acmf@african-cap.org (General)
namu@african-cap.org (Programme Officer)
Web: http://www.african-
cap.org/publications.htm (Publications pages)
Contact: Nora Amu, Programme Officer
Publishing areas: 17
Other: finance, investment
Overseas distr: ABC

**1972   Association of African Universities
Press**
African Universities House
11 Aviation Road Extension
Airport Residential Area
PO Box AN 5744
Accra
Tel: +233-21-774495 Fax: +233-21-774821
Email: taye@aau.org
Web:
http://www.aau.org/english/publications.htm
(English version)
Contacts: Pashal Hoba, Head, Communications
and Services Department; Victoria Duah,
Operations Assistant, Publications
Publishing areas: 18, 38
Other: databases *see* ➔ **DATAD**, entry **203**
Overseas distr: ABC

1973   Blackmask Ltd.
17 Watson Avenue
Daybreak Behind Holy Spirit
Cathedral.
PO Box CT 770
Accra
Tel: +233 -21-34577
Email: blackmask@internetghana.com
Web: n/a
Contact: Yaw Owusu Asante, Managing
Director
Publishing areas: 30
Overseas distr: ABC

1974   Ghana Universities Press
PO Box GP 4219
Accra
Tel/Fax: +233-21-513401 (General enquiries)
+233-21-513383 (Director)
Email: drkwakuganu@yahoo.com
Web: n/a
Contact: Kwaku Mensah Ganu, Director
Publishing areas: 4, 5, 6, 9, 10, 11, 17, 18, 27,
31, 33, 36, 40, 41, 43, 45
Overseas distr: ABC

1975   Sankofa Educational Publishers
PO Box C 1234
Cantonments
Accra
Tel: +233-21-777866 Fax: 233-21-778839
Email: n/a
Web: n/a
Contact: (Prof.) Adu Boahen, Director
Publishing areas: 18, 27
Overseas distr: ABC

1976   Sedco Publishing Ltd
Sedco House
5 Tabon Street Off Ring Road Central
North Ridge
POB 2051
Accra
Tel: +233-21-221332 Fax: +233-21-220107
Email: sedco@africaonline.com.gh
Web: n/a
Contact: Courage Kwami Segbawu,
Chairman/Publisher
Publishing areas: 6, 7, 8, 27, 30, 36
Overseas distr: ABC

1977   Sub-Saharan Publishers
Korama Ice Cream Building
9 Goodwill Building
PO Box 358
Legon
Accra
Tel/Fax: +233-21-234251
Email: saharanp@africaonline.com.gh
Contact: Akoss Ofori-Mensah, Managing Director
Publishing areas: 6, 8, 14, 27, 40, 43, 45
Overseas distr: ABC

1978   Woeli Publishing Services
PO Box NT 601
Accra New Town
Tel: +233-21-229294/227182
Fax: +233-21-229294
Email: woeli@libr.ug.edu.gh
Web: n/a
Contact: Woeli Dekutsey, Managing Director
Publishing areas: 2, 6, 8, 17, 18, 20, 27, 44, 45
Other: travel guides
Overseas distr: ABC

Guinea

1979   Editions Ganndal
BP 542
Conakry
Tel: +224-463507 Fax: +224-463507
Email: ganndal@mirinet.net.gn
Web: http://www.editionsganndal.com/
Contacst: Mamadou Aliou Sow, Director General; Yaya Satina Diallo, Editor
Publishing areas: 2, 4, 5, 6, 8, 11, 18, 22, 27, 36, 38, 45
Online catalogue: Afrilivres, Alliance

1980   Société Africaine d'Edition et de Communication
BP 6826
Belle-vue
Commune de Dixinn
Conakry
Tel: 224-297141/423444
Email: dtniane@biasy.com or ntniane@eti.bull.net
Web: n/a
Contact: Oumar Tall
Publishing areas: 6, 27, 38
Online catalogue: Afrilivres

Kenya

1981   Academy Science Publishers/African Academy of Sciences
Miotoni Lane off Miotoni Road
PO Box 14798
Nairobi
Tel: +254-20-884401/2/3/4/5
Fax: +254-20-884406
Email: asp@africaonline.co.ke
Web: http://www.aasciences.org/publications.htm
Contact: (Prof.) Samuel O. Akatch, Publishing Manager
Publishing areas: 10, 18, 20, 36, 38, 42, 43, 45
Overseas distr: ABC

1982   African Centre for Technology Studies (ACTS)
ICRAF Campus
United Nations Avenue, Gigiri
PO Box 45917
Nairobi
Tel: +254-20-722 4700/722 4000
Fax: +254-20-722 4701/722 4001
Email: acts@cgiar.org (General enquiries)
j.wakhungu@cgiar.org (Executive Director)
Web: http://www.acts.or.ke/publications/publications.html
Contacts: Judi Wakhungu, Executive Director; Patricia Kameri-Mbote, Director of Research and Policy Outreach; Harrison Maganga, Communications & Publications Officer
Publishing areas: 10, 18, 20, 21, 31, 42
Other: biotechnology, biodiversity, drylands development, indigenous knowledge, environmental law, natural and energy resources management

1983   African Council for Communication Education (ACCE)
University of Nairobi
Education Building 3rd Floor
PO Box 47495
Nairobi
Tel: +254-20-215270/227043
Fax: +254-20-216135
Email: acceb@arcc.or.ke
Web: http://www.africancouncilcomed.org/publications.html
Contact: Carol Kagunda, Documentalist
Publishing areas: 32
Overseas distr: ABC

1984 African Economic Research Consortium (AERC)
3rd Floor-Middle East BankTowers Building
Milimani Road
PO Box 62882
Nairobi 00200 City Square
Tel: +254-20-2734150
Fax: +254-20-2734170
Email: admin@aercafrica.org (General enquiries) exec.dir@aercafrica.org (Executive Director) publications@aercafrica.org (Publications Administrator)
Web: http://www.aercafrica.org/publications/index.asp
Contacts: (Prof.) William Lyakurwa, Executive Director; (Prof.) Olusanya Ajakaiye, Director of Research; Charles Owino, Publications Administrator
Publishing areas: 10, 17, 29, 41
Other: finance, macroeconomic policies, regional integration and sectoral policies, stabilization and growth, resource mobilization and investment, trade

1985 African Medical & Research Foundation
Book Distribution Unit
PO Box 27691
Wilson Airport
Nairobi 00506
Tel: +254-20-699 3000
Fax: +254-20-609518
Email: janei@amrefhq.org (Book Distribution Unit)
Web: http://www.amref.org/index.asp?PageID=28 (Bookshop/Publications pages)
Contacts: Michael Smalley, Director General and Director of Programmes; Head, Book Distribution Unit
Publishing areas: 20, 33
Other: health-related behaviour, health information systems, health learning manuals, hydatid disease, sexual and reproductive health, malaria

1986 Center for Law and Research International (CLARION)
PO Box 46991
Nairobi 00100 GPO
Tel: +254-20-571614/570740
Fax: +254-20-571857
Email: info@clarionkenya.org
Web: http://www.clarionkenya.org/ :
Contact: Lawrence Mute, Director
Publishing areas: 30, 45

1987 East African Educational Publishers Ltd
Mpaka Road/Woodvale Grove
PO Box 45314
Nairobi 00100 GPO
Tel: +254-20-444700/445260
Fax: +254-20-448753/532095
Email: eaep@africaonline.co.ke or eaep@nbnet.co.ke
Web: http://www.eastafricanpublishers.com
Contacts: Henry Chakava, Chairman; Muriuki Njero, Managing Director; Anne Mithamo, Publishing Manager
Publishing areas: 5, 6, 7, 8, 11, 17, 18, 22, 26, 27, 30, 33, 35, 36, 37, 40, 43
Overseas distr: ABC

1988 Femart/Gadece
Impala Walk
Aga Khan Road
PO Box 1588
Kisumu
Tel: +254-35-22791 Fax: +254-35-22791
Email: gadod@arcc.or.ke
Web: n/a
Contact: Lilian Odero
Publishing areas: 5, 6, 45

1989 Focus Publications Ltd
Howse & McGeorge
Factory Street off Bunyala Road
Industrial Area
PO Box 28176
Nairobi 00200
Tel: +254-20-559296/559515
Fax: +254-20-559123
Email: focus@africaonline.co.ke
Contact: Sarah Mwangi, Managing Director
Publishing areas: 4, 6 (primarily by women writers) 14, 38, 45

1990 ICIPE Science Press
The International Centre of Insect Physiology and Ecology
PO Box 30772-00100
Nyayo Stadium
Nairobi
Tel: +254-20-8632000
Fax: +254-20-8632001/8632002
Email: dg@icipe.org (General)

douya@icipe.org (Science Editor,
Information Services Unit)
Web:
http://www.icipe.org/research_support_uni
ts/information_and_publications_unit/index
.html (Information and Publications Unit) or
http://www.icipe.org/publications/index.ht
ml
Contact: Daisy Wairimu Ouya, Science Editor,
Information and Publications Unit
Publishing areas: 10, 19, 20, 42
Other: agricultural biodiversity, animal and
plant pests and diseases, population ecology,
socioeconomic aspects of arthropod-related
development issues

1991   Jomo Kenyatta Foundation
Enterprise Road Industrial Area
PO Box 30533
Nairobi 00100 GPO
Tel: +254-2-557222/531965
Fax: +254-2-531966
Email: sales@jomokenyattaf.com or
publish@jomokenyattaf.com
Contacts: Idris M. Farah, Chief Executive;
Nancy W. Karimi
Publishing areas: 4, 5, 6, 17, 18, 27, 36
Overseas distr: ABC

1992   Kwani Trust
Madonna House Suite 1S
Westlands Road
Westlands
PO Box 2895
Nairobi 00100
Tel: +254-20-445 1383
Email: info@kwani.org (General enquiries)
submissions@kwani.org (Submissions)
Web: http://www.kwani.org/index.htm
Contacts: Binyavanga Wainaina, Founder and
Editor; Kairo Kiarie, General Manager
Publishing areas: 1, 2, 4, 5, 6, 27
Note: publishes both in print and online
formats, and on cassette
see also ➔ **Kwani? (577)**

1993   Lake Publishers and Enterprises
Jomo Kenyatta Highway
PO Box 1743
Kisumu
Tel: +254-35-22291
Fax: +254-35-22291/22707
Email: gadod@swiftkisumu.com or
info@lakepublishers.com

Web site: http://www.lakepublishers.com
(site down 25/10/05)
Contact: Asenath Bole Odaga
Publishing areas: 4, 6, 22, 45
Overseas distr: ABC

1994   Law Africa Publishing Ltd
Co-op Trust Plaza 1st Floor
Lower Hill Road
PO Box 4260
Nairobi 00100 GPO
Tel: +254-20-272257/80 Fax: +254-20-2722592
Email: info@lawafrica.com
ormillie.ollows@lawafrica.com
(General enquiries)
katarina.juma@lawafrica.com (Director)
Web: http://www.lawafrica.com/
Contact: Katarina Juma , Director, or Millicent
Ollows
Publishing areas: 30 (in print format and on CD-
ROM)
Other: law reports for East Africa
Overseas distr: ABC

1995   Longhorn Publishers
Kenya Commercial Bank Building
Funzi Road
PO Box 18033
Nairobi 00100 GPO
Tel: +254-2-532579/80/81
Fax: +254-2-540037
Email: longhorn@iconnect.co.ke (General)
jnjoroge@longhornbooks.co.ke (Managing
Director)
Web: n/a
Contact: Janet Njoroge, Managing
Director
Publishing areas: 6, 10, 17, 33, 38

1996   Macmillan Kenya (Publishers) Ltd
Kijabe Street
PO Box 30797
Nairobi 00100 GPO
Tel: +245-20-220012/ 224485
Fax: +254-20-212179
Email: dmuita@macken.co.ke
Web: http://www.macmillan-
africa.com/Contacts/Kenya.htm
Contact: David Muita, Managing Director
Publishing areas: 5, 6 24, 27

1997   Nairobi University Press
University of Nairobi
Jomo Kenyatta Memorial Library
PO Box 30197
Nairobi
Tel: +254-20-334244 ext 28581
Fax: +254-20-336885
Email: nup@uonbi.ac.ke or
mbugua@uonbi.ac.ke
Web: www.uonbi.ac.ke/comps_projects/press
Contacts: J. Kimaita Kirimania, Ag. Secretary;
Pauline W. Mahugu, Senior Editor
Publishing areas: 4, 17, 18, 22, 27, 41
Overseas distr: ABC

1998   Moi University Press
Moi University
PO Box 3900
Eldoret
Tel: +254-321-43720/43620
Fax: +254-321-43047
Email:
fismembers@rinaf.mufis.mooiuniversity.ac.ke
Web:
http://www.mu.ac.ke/finform/finform.htm
(Single page only, Faculty of Information
Science)
Contacts: Felix Muriithi, Ag. Head,
Department of Publishing and
Booktrade; Tom O.Ouko, Senior Editor
Publishing areas: 17, 18, 27, 33, 36

**1999   Oxford University Press–Eastern
Africa**
Waiyaki Way
ABC Place 2nd floor
PO Box 72532
Nairobi 00100 GPO
Tel: +254-20-440555/446376
Fax: +254-20-443972/444938
Web: n/a
Email: amwangi@oxford.co.ke
Contact: Abdulla Ismaily, Regional Director,
Eastern Africa
Publishing areas: 17, 27, 36, 43

2000   Paulines Publications - Africa
Daughters of St Paul
PO Box 49026
Nairobi 00100 GPO
Tel: +254-20-442202/3 Fax: +254-20-442097
Email: publications@paulinesafrica.org or
distribution@paulinesafrica.org
Web: http://www.paulinesafrica.org/
Contact: Sister Carmel

Areas of publishing: 14, 28, 32, 40, 45

2001   Sasa Sema Publications Ltd
PO Box 13956
Nairobi
Tel: +254-20-550400/399 or 254-20-72-522310
(Mobile)
Email: sasasema@wananchi.com or
info@sasasema.com
Web: http://www.sasasema.com/
Contact: Lila Luce, Managing Director
Publishing areas: 14 (at junior level)
Other: political cartoons and comic strips
(including titles in Kiswahili)
Overseas distr: Peppercorn Books & Press, PO
Box 693, Snow Camp, NC 27349, USA
Email: post@peppercornbooks.com

**2002   Zapf Chancery Research
Consultants and Publishers**
PO Box 4988
Eldoret
Tel: +254-321-31413 Fax: +254-321-63043
Email: zapfchancerykenya@yahoo.co.uk
Web: n/a
Contact: C.B. Peter
Areas of publishing: 38, 40, 43

Lesotho

2003   Institute of Southern African Studies
The National University of Lesotho
PO Roma 180
Tel: +266-340601/340247 Fax: 266-340004
Email: isas@nul.ls (General enquiries)
t.khalanyane@nul.ls (Publications Officer)
Web: http://www.nul.ls/institutes/isas.htm
Contact: Tankie Khalanyane, Publications
Officer
Publishing areas: 10, 27, 28, 36, 41, 43, 44, 45
Overseas distr: ABC

Madagascar

**2004   Trano Printy Fiangonana Loterana
Malagasy (TPFLM)**
9 rue Général Ramanantsoa
BP 538
Antananarivo
Tel: +261-2-222 3340 /222 4569
Fax: +261-2-226 2643
Email: impluth@dts.mg or
impluth@hotmail.com

Web: n/a
Contact: Raymond Randrianatoandro,
Director General
Publishing areas: 5, 6, 8, 38, 40
Online catalogue: Afrilivres

2005   Tsipika SARL
5 rue Laroche Amparibe
101 Antananarivo
Tel: +261-20-226 2315
Fax: +261-20-222 4595
Email: tsipika@malagasy.com
Web: n/a
Contact: Claude Rabenord
Publishing areas: 27, 36, 43, 44
Online catalogue: Alliance

Malawi

2006   Central Africana Ltd
PO Box 631
Victoria Avenue
Blantyre
Tel: +265-1-676110 Fax: +265-1-676102
Email: africana@iafrica.com or
centralafricana@africa-online.net
Web: http://www.centralafricana.com/
Contact: Frank Johnston, Publisher
Publishing areas: 2, 6, 27, 34, 38
Other: travel and guide books
Overseas distr: ABC
Note: also has bookshop operation, *see* entry
➔ **2425**

2007   Chancellor College Publications
PO Box 280
Zomba
Tel/Fax: n/a
Email: publications@chanco.unima.mw
Contact: Kingsley Jika, Book Editor
Publishing areas: 2, 5, 6, 7, 36, 43
Overseas distr: ABC

2008   E & V Publications
PO Box 131
Ngumbe 27 Zaleva Road (M1)
Opp. GDC Chileka
Blantyre
Tel: +265-991 9665 Fax: +265-164 0569
Email: egmpanga@yahoo.com
Contact: Egidio Mpanga, Publishing Director
Publishing areas: 40
Overseas distr: ABC

2009   Kachere Series
PO Box 1037
Zomba
Tel/Fax: +265-524705
Email: fiedler@africa-online.net or
kachere@globemw.net
Web:
http://www.sdnp.org.mw/kachereseries/
Contact: Klaus Fiedler, Publisher
Publishing areas: 2, 11, 14, 22, 27, 36, 40, 45
Overseas distr: ABC

Mali

2010   Editions Donniya
Cité du Niger
BP 1273
Bamako
Tel: +223-2-214646/214599
Fax: +223-2-219031
Email: donniya@malinet.ml or
donniya@msgto.com
Web:
http://www.cefib.com/impcolor/donniya.ht
m
Contact: Abdoulaye Sylla
Publishing areas: 5, 11, 14, 17, 22, 27, 36, 38, 45
Online catalogue: Afrilivres
Overseas distr: Editions Menaibuc-Dila,
3 rue de Palestine, 75019 Paris, France

2011   Editions Jamana
Coopérative Culturelle Multimédia
Avenue Cheick Zayed
Porte 2694 Hamdallaye
BP 2043
Bamako
Tel: +223-229 6289 Fax: +223-229 7639
Email: jamcom@jamana.org
Web: http://www.jamana.org/edition.html
Contact: Hamidou Konate, Director General;
Ba Maïra Sow, Editorial Director
Publishing areas: 1, 2, 5, 8, 11, 18, 22, 27, 36,,
45
Online catalogue: Afrilivres, Alliance

2012   Le Figuier
151 rue 56
Sema 1
Tel: +223-223 32 11
Fax: +223-223 32 11
Email: lefiguier@afribone.net.ml or
konatem@wanadoo.fr
Contact: Moussa Konate

Publishing areas: 2, 6, 11, 17, 22, 36, 45
Other: photographic collections, children's
and youth literature
Online catalogue: Alliance

Mauritius

2013   Editions de l'Océan Indien
Stanley
Rose Hill
Tel: +230-464 6761/464 3959
Fax: +230-464 3445
Email: eoibooks@intnet.mu
Web: n/a
Contacts: Sadhna Ramlallah, Nazal Rosunally
Publishing areas: 5, 10, 19, 26, 36, 38, 43

2014   Editions Le Printemps
4 Club Road
Vacoas
Tel: +230-686 2647/696 2505
Email: elp@bow.intnet.mu
Web: n/a
Contact: Ahomud Islam Sulliman, Director
Publishing areas: 1, 5, 6, 20, 36, 43

2015   Editions Vizavi
9 rue St Georges
Port Louis
Tel: +230-208 0983/211 2435
Fax: +230 211 3047
Email: vizavi@intnet.mu
Web: n/a
Contact: Pascale Siew, Director
Publishing areas: 6, 27, 36
Online catalogue: Afrilivres

2016   Mahatma Gandhi Institute
Site Office
Moka
Mauritius
Tel: +230-403 2000 Fax: +230-433 2235
Email: asibmgi@intnet.mu
Web:
http://mgi.intnet.mu/research/index.html
(Research and Publications pages)
Contact: (Mrs) S. D. Chengalrayen-Frederic,
Head, Department of Publishing and Printing
Areas of publishing: 2, 5, 22, 27, 29, 33, 36, 43,
45

Morocco

2017   Editions le Fennec
89 bis Boulevard d'Anfa 14ᵉ étage
Appartement 30
20000 Casablanca
Tel: +212-22-209314/209268
Fax: +212-22-277702
Email: info@lefennec.com (General enquiries)
laylachaouni@lefennec.com (Director)
Web: http://www.lefennec.com/
Contact: Layla B. Chaouni, Director
Publishing areas: 6, 11, 18, 27, 36, 37, 40, 43, 45

2018   Les Editions Maghrébines
EDIMA Quartier Industrial
Rue E, No.15
Aïn Sebaâ
Casablanca
Tel: +212-22-351707/353230
Fax: +212-22-357892
Email: n/a
Web: n/a
Contact: S. Abdelmoumni, Managing Director
Publishing areas: 17, 27, 36, 38, 43, 45

2019   Editions Tarik
321 route d'El Jadida
Casablanca
Tel: +212-22-259007 Fax: +212-22-232550
Email: tarik.edition@wanadoo.net.ma
Contact: Bichr Bennani
Publishing areas: 17, 24, 27, 36, 43
Online catalogue: Alliance

**2020   Faculté des Lettres et de Sciences
Humaines de Mohammedia
Université Hassan II**
Avenue Hassan II
BP 546
Mohammedia
Tel: +212-324873/74 Fax: +212-325377
Email: flsh-uh2m@fusion.net.ma
Web:
http://www.univh2m.ac.ma/fac02_presentat
ion.htm
Contact: Souad Charradi, Service des
Publications, de Diffusion et des Relations
Extérieures
Publishing areas: 2, 5, 17, 18, 23, 27
Other: Arabic literature studies

2021   **Fondation du Roi Abdul Aziz Saoud**
        pour les etudes islamiques et les
        sciences humaines
        Blvd de la Corniche
        Ain Diab - Anfa
        BP 12585
        Casablanca 20052
Tel: +212-22-391027/30
Fax: +212-22-391031
Email: secretariat@fondation.org.ma
Web: http://www.fondation.org.ma/
Publishing areas: 11, 17, 27, 28, 38, 40, 43, 44,
45
Other: Arab and Islamic studies

2022   **L'Institut des Etudes Africaines/**
        Institute of African Studies
        Université Mohamed V-Agdal
        3 bis rue Innaouen
        BP 8968
        Agdal-Rabat
Tel: +212-37-776579 /776576
Fax: +212-37-778425
Email: iea@enssup.gov.ma
Web: http://www.emi.ac.ma/univ-
MdV/IEA.html
Publishing areas: 1, 2, 5, 6, 11, 17, 24,
27, 36, 38
Other: Arab studies

Mozambique

2023   **Moçambique Editora**
        Rua Armando Tivane
        1430 Bairro da Polana
        Maputo
Tel: +258-1-499071/483422/495017
Fax: +258-1-498648
Email: info@ME.co.mz (General enquiries)
comercial@ME.co.mz (Sales)
professor@ME.co.mz (Editorial, scholarly
titles)
Web: http://www.me.co.mz
Contact: Editorial Director
Publishing areas: 2, 4, 18, 22, 27, 38
Note: Main area of publishing is educational
and school books.

Namibia

2024   **Gamsberg Macmillan Publishers**
        (Pty) Ltd
        19 Faraday Street
        PO Box 22830
        Windhoek
Tel: +264-61-232165 Fax: +264-61-233538
Email: gmp@iafrica.com.na (General
enquiries) gmpubl@iafrica.com.na (Head of
Publishing)
Web: http://www.macmillan-
africa.com/contacts/namibia.htm ·
Contacts: Herman van Wyk, Chief Executive;
Peter Reiner, Head of Publishing
Publishing areas: 5, 17, 18, 21, 23, 24, 27, 28,
34, 38, 43, 45
Note: now incorporates New Namibia Books.

2025   **Media Institute of Southern Africa**
        21 Johann Albrecht Street
        Private Bag 13386
        Windhoek
Tel: +264-61-232975 Fax: +264-61-248016
Email: webmaster@misa.org.na (General
enquiries) director@misa.org (Regional
Director) resource@misa.org (Programme
Officer, Publications)
Web: http://www.misa.org/
Contacts: Luckson Chipare, Regional
Director; Eric Libongani, Programme Officer,
Publications
Publishing areas: 32, 38

→ **New Namibia Books** *see* **Gamsberg**
Macmillan Publishers (Pty) Ltd (2024)

2026   **Out of Africa (Pty) Ltd**
        POB 21841
        Windhoek
Tel: +264-61-221494 Fax: +264-61-221270
Email: n/a
Web: n/a
Chief executive: Wide Lochner, Managing
Director
Publishing areas: 11, 27

2027   **University of Namibia Press**
        University of Namibia
        Private Bag 13301
        Windhoek
Tel: +264-206 3312/3313
Fax: +264-61-206 3320
Email botaala@unam.na

Web: http://www.unam.na/ (University
home page)
Contact: (Prof.) Barnabus Otaala
Publishing areas: 11, 18, 27, 33, 36, 37, 38, 43
Overseas distr: ABC

Nigeria

→ **African Heritage Press** *see* under United
States, entry **2245**

2028   African BookBuilders Ltd
2 Awosika Avenue
UI POB 20222
University of Ibadan
Ibadan
Oyo State
Tel: +234-2-810 1113
Email: n/a
Web: n/a
Contact: Chris W. Bankole
Publishing areas: 10, 11, 12, 17, 36, 41, 43
Note: publishes on behalf of the → **Institut
français de recherche en Afrique/IFRA
(1845)**

2029   Bookcraft Ltd
29 Moremi Road
New Bodija
PO Box 16270
Ibadan
Oyo State
Tel: +234-2-810 3238
Email: oziengbe@skannet.com or
info@bookcraft.com
Web: http://www.bookcraftafrica.com/
Contact: (Mrs) J O Maduka, Chief Executive;
Bankole Olayebi, Publishing Director
Publishing areas: 2, 5, 6, 8, 22, 36
Overseas distr: ABC

2030   Cogito Publishers
PO Box 4203
Enugu
Tel/Fax: +234-42-250522/+234-805-234 7667
Email: info@cogitopublishers.com or
chielozona@hotmail.com
pawlikm@cogitobooks.com
Web: http://www.cogitopublishers.com/
Contact: Chielozona Eze, Publisher
Publishing areas: 2, 5, 6, 8, 35, 40
Overseas distr: ABC

2031   College Press Publishers
ESC Campus
5A Baale Akintayo Road
Jericho GRA
Secretariat PO Box 30678
Ibadan
Oyo State
Tel: +234-2-810 4165/810 5630
Fax: +234-2-810 4165/241 1339
Email: lizzyadeopa@yahoo.co.uk or
Collegepresspublishers@yahoo.com
Web: n/a
Contact: (Mrs) Taiwo T. Owoeye
Publishing areas: 5, 10, 17, 20, 27, 31, 36, 40
Overseas distr: ABC

2032   CSS Limited
Bookshop House
4th Floor
50/52 Broad Street
PO Box 174
Lagos
Tel: +234-1-2633081/2637009
Fax: +234-1-2637089
Email: cssbookshops@skannet.com.ng
Web: n/a
Contacts: Chief Fola B. Osibo, Managing
Director; Dotun Adegboyega, General Manager
Publishing areas: 14, 27, 36
Overseas distr: ABC

2033   Enicrownfit Publishers
23 Ireakari Street
Mokola Roundabout
PO Box 14580 UI Post Office
Ibadan
Oyo State
Tel: +234-2-713312 Fax: + 234-2-8103043
Email: ecfp2002@yahoo.com
Web: n/a
Contact: Olusegun Babajide, Director of
Publications
Publishing areas: 4, 38
Overseas distr: ABC

2034   Farafina
25 Military Street Onikan
Lagos
PO Box 73940
Victoria Island
Lagos
Tel+ 234-1-263 7895/264 7527
Email: info@farafina-online.com (General
enquiries) subscriptions@farafina-online.com
(Subscriptions)

Web: http://www.farafina-online.com/
Contact: Muhtar Bakare, Managing Director
Publishing areas: 5, 6, 7, 8, 22
Note: a new company, part of Kachifo
Limited, launched in 2005, who
also publish reissues, under license, of
African literary works published outside
Nigeria.

2035   Fourth Dimension Publishing Co Ltd
16 Fifth Avenue   City Layout
PMB 01164
Enugu
Enugu State
Tel: + 234-42-459969/453739
Fax: +234-42-456904/453298
Email: fdpbooks@aol.com or
info@fdpbooks.com (General enquiries)
nwankwov@infoweb.abs.net or
aanwankwo@yahoo.co.uk
(Chairman), evaigwilo@yahoo.com (Managing
Editor)
Web site: http://www.fdpbooks.com (site not
accessible October 2005)
Contacts: Chief Arthur Nwankwo, Chairman;
Evaristus Igwilo, Managing Editor
Publishing areas: 2, 4, 5, 6, 7, 8, 11, 14, 17, 18,
24, 25, 27, 28, 30, 36, 38, 42, 43, 45
Overseas distr: ABC

**2036   Heinemann Educational Books
(Nigeria) Plc**
1 Ighodaro Road Jericho Layout
PMB 5205
Ibadan
Oyo State
Tel: 234-2-241 2268/241 3237
Fax: 234-2-241 3237/241 1089
Email: info@heinemannbooks.com or
heinemannbooks@yahoo.com (General)
ayojen@skannet.com (Managing Director)
afueriolawepo@yahoo.com (Assistant General
Manager, Editorial; for manuscript
submissions)
Web: http://www.heinemannbooks.com/
Contacts: Ayo Ojeniyi, Managing
Director/Chief Executive; Chief Aigboje Higo,
Chairman; (Mrs) Olawepo Afueri Sogo,
Assistant General Manager, Editorial
Publishing areas: 2, 4, 5, 6, 7, 8, 17, 18, 24, 26,
30, 36, 41
Overseas distr: ABC

2037   Hugo Books Ltd
Plot 1 Alhaji Basheer Shittu Avenue
Magodo Phase 1
PO Box 51743
Falomo
Lagos
Tel: +234-1-473 0599
Fax: +234-802-304 7317
Email: hugopublications@yahoo.com
Web: n/a
Contact: Osahon Ugowe
Publishing areas: 14, 27, 38

2038   Humanities Publishers
University of Ibadan
PO Box 14177
Ibadan
Tel/Fax: n/a
Email: infohumpub@yahoo.co.uk or
Infohumanities@yahoo.com
Web: n/a
Contact: Segun Ogunleye, Director
Publishing areas: 5, 6, 7
Overseas distr: ABC

2039   Hybun Books
ANA House
26 Olodipo Labinjo Crescent
off Akinsemoyin Street
Surulere
Lagos
Tel/Fax: n/a
Email: hgnl2000@yahoo.com
Web: n/a
Contact: Hyacinth Obunseh
Publishing areas: 5, 7, 8

2040   Ibadan University Press
University of Ibadan
PMB 16 UI Post Office
Ibadan
Oyo State
Tel: +234 02-810 1100-4 exts 2161/1244/1042
Fax: +234-02-810 3043/810 3118
Email: iup_unibadan@yahoo.com
Web: http://www.ui.edu.ng/unitspress.htm
(single Web page only)
Contacts: (Prof.) S.O. Asein, Chairman; (Mrs)
Chinwe A. Adigwe, Ag. Deputy Director of
Publishing
Publishing areas: 2, 4, 18, 27, 30, 35, 36, 38, 41,
43

2041 International Institute of Tropical Agriculture
Oyo Road
PMB 5320
Ibadan
Oyo State
Tel: +234-2-241 2626 Fax: +234-2-241 2221
Email: W4G@cgiar.org (General enquiries)
EKoper@cgiar.org (Head, Communciation and Information Services)
Web: http://www.iita.org/info/info.htm (Publications pages)
Contacts: E. Koper, Head, Communication and Information Services; A. Oyetunde, Coordinating Editor
Publishing areas: 10, 23
Other: biotechnology, biological control, crops and crops management, farming systems, soil science

2042 Mary Kolawole Publications
Department of English
Obafemi Awolowo University
Ile-Ife
Oyo State
Tel: +234-36-232365
Email: mkolawo@oauife.edu.ng
Web: n/a
Contact: Mary Kolawole, Publisher
Publishing areas: 5, 6, 45
Overseas distr: ABC

2043 Kraft Books
6A Polytechnic Road Sango
PO Box 22084
UI Post Office
Ibadan
Oyo State
Tel: +234-90-8042 108 712 (mobile)
+1-617-598 1048 ext 2228 (US number)
Email: krabooks@onebox.com or kraftobooks@yahoo.com
Web: n/a
Contact: Steva Shaba
Publishing areas: 6, 7, 8, 14
Overseas distr: ABC

2044 Malthouse Press Ltd
11B Goriola Street
off Adeola Odeku Street
Victoria Island
PO Box 500
Ikeja
Lagos
Lagos State
Tel: +234-1-820358 Fax: +234-1-2690985
Email: malthouse_lagos@yahoo.co.uk
Web: n/a
Contact: (Prof.) Dafe Otobo
Publishing areas: 2, 5, 6, 7, 8, 17, 27, 30, 36,
Overseas distr: ABC

2045 New Generation Books
Shop 51 Nnamdi Azikiwe Stadium Shopping Mall
Ogui Road
PO Box 3472
Enugu
Anambra State
Tel: +234-803 473 7947 (Mobile)
Email: newgenbooks@yahoo.com or latzchukwukelu@yahoo.com
Web: n/a
Contact: Chukwukelu Lazarus, President
Publishing areas: 4, 38
Overseas distr: ABC

2046 New Gong Publishers
11 Abiona Close
Off Falolu Road
Surulere
Lagos
Tel/Fax: +234-1-894 8824
Email: newgong@newgong.com
Web:
http://www.thenewgong.com/index.html
Contact: Bashir Olanrewaju, Publications Manager
Publishing areas: 5, 6, 7, 8
US distr: Adibooks.com, 181 Industrial Avenue, Lowell, MA 01852-5147 Email: Sales@adibooks.com Web:
http://www.adibooks.com/
Note: this is a new imprint set up in 2005, which functions as a cooperative of writers leveraging on their own editorial, managerial and technical skills to run a publishing house.

2047 NIDD Publishing and Printing Ltd
PO Box 26
Oyo
Oyo State
Tel: +234-38-241091
Email: nidd_nidds@hotmail.com;
ogunmat@yahoo.com
Web: n/a
Contact: Dewumi Adediran, Publisher
Publishing areas: 2, 22, 40
Overseas distr: ABC

2048   Nigerian Institute of International Affairs
13/15 Kofo Abayomi Road
Victoria Island
PMB 12750
Lagos
Lagos State
Tel: +234-1-261 5606/7 Fax: +234-1-261 1360
Email: info@niianet.org (General enquiries)
dgeneral@niianet.org (Director General)
Web:
http://www.niianet.org/publications1.htm
(Publications pages)
Contacts: (Prof.) U. Joy Ogwu, Director
General (Ms) E.A Ude, Publications section
Publishing areas: 17, 26, 28, 36, 38

2049   Obafemi Awolowo University Press Ltd
PMB 004 OAU Post Office
Obafemi Awolowo University
Ile-Ife
Osun State
Tel: +234-36-230284 Fax: +234-36-233442
Email: oaupress@oauife.edu.ng
Web: http://www.oauife.edu.ng/index.php
(Main univeresity home page, no pages as yet
for press)
Contact: Akin Fatokun, General Manager
Publishing areas: 5, 9, 17, 25, 27, 28, 30, 35, 36, 41, 43
Overseas distr: ABC

2050   Onyoma Research Publications
11 Orogbum Crescent
G.R.A. Phase II
Port Harcourt
Rivers State
Tel: +234-803-308 3385
Email: kala_joe@yahoo.com
or alagoa@ph.rcl.nig.com
Web: http://www.onyoma.org (site not
accessible October 2005)
Contact: (Prof.) E.J. Alagoa, Publisher
Publishing areas: 2, 7, 11, 12, 17, 27, 36
Overseas distr: ABC

2051   Opon Ifa Readers
49 Bourdillon Road
Ikoyi
Lagos
Tel/Fax: n/a
Email: okinbalaunko@yahoo.com
Web: n/a
Contact: (Prof.) Femi Osofisan
Publishing areas: 5, 6, 7, 8

2052   Sefer Books Ltd
2 Alayande Street
Bodija Estate
Ibadan
Tel/Fax: n/a
Email: sefer@skannet.com
Web: http://www.sefer-nigeria.com
Contact: Modupe Oduyoye
Publishing areas: 4, 5, 22, 27, 40
Other: Islam; relationships between the Indo-
European and Afro-Asiatic family of
languages
Distr: Able Press, 94B Aladelola St, Ikosi
Ketu, Lagos, Tel: +234-1-288 0395/+234-802-
322 7748

2053   Spectrum Books Ltd
Spectrum House
Ring Road
PMB 5612
Ibadan
Oyo State
Tel: +234-2-2310145/2311215/2310058
Fax: +234-2-2312705/2318502
Email: admin1@spectrumbooksonline.com
(General enquiries)
joopberkhout@spectrum.co.ng or
Chiefberkhout@aol.com (Chairman/Managing
Director)
Web:
http://www.spectrumbooksonline.com/cgi-
bin/cart.plx
Contact: Chief Joop Berkhout,
Chairman/Managing Director
Publishing areas: 1, 5, 6, 7, 8, 9, 14, 17, 18, 22, 24, 26, 30, 33, 36, 38, 40, 43, 45
Overseas distr: ABC

2054   Stirling-Holden Publishers Ltd
110-113 GAAF Building
UI-Oyo Road Orogun
PO Box 20984
Ibadan
Email: horden@skannet.com
Web: n/a

Tel: +234-802-351 9154/+234-803-390 3034
Contact: Oshoitse A. Okwilagwe
Publishing areas: 1, 9, 18, 31, 35, 38, 43, 45
Other: publishing and book industries

2055   University of Lagos Press
University of Lagos
Commercial Road
PO Box 132
Unilag Post Office
Akoka Yaba
Lagos State
Tel/Fax: +234-1-825048
Email: library@unilag.edu or
books@infoweb.abs.net
Web: http://www.unilag.edu (Main university
home page, no pages as yet for press)
Contact: (Ms) O.A. Oshin
Publishing areas: 4, 8, 17, 18, 31, 33, 36, 42, 43
Overseas distr: ABC

2056   University Press Plc
Three Crowns Building Jericho
PMB 5095
Ibadan
Oyo State
Tel: +234-22-241 2056/241 0105
Fax: +234-22-41-2056
Email: unipress@skannet.com.ng (General
enquiries) Aso@skannet.com (Executive
Director)
Web: n/a
Contacts: Samuel Kolawole, Managing
Director; Sunday O. Adebogun, Executive
Director
Publishing areas: 4, 5, 6, 7, 17, 18, 26, 38, 43
Overseas distr: ABC

2057   Vantage Publishers (Int) Ltd
POB 7669 Secretariat
Ibadan
Oyo State
Tel: +234-2-810 0341
Email: vantagepublishers@skannet.com.ng
Web: n/a
Contact: 'Poju Amori, Chairman
Publishing areas: 4, 11, 18, 26, 35, 36, 43, 45

2058   West African Book Publishers
Plot D Block 1 Industrial Estate
PO Box 3445
Ilupeju
Lagos State
Tel: +234-1-497 0196/900 7604
Fax: +234-1-616702/824-858

Email: wabp@academypressplc.com
Web: n/a
Contact: (Mrs) Shade Omo-Eboh
Publishing areas: 11, 27, 36
Note: company is part of Academy
Press.

Senegal

**2059   Council for the Development of Social
Science Research in Africa/Conseil
pour le développement de la
recherche en sciences sociales en
Afrique (CODESRIA)**
Department of Publications and
Communication
Ave Cheikh Anta Diop x Canal IV
BP 3304
Dakar
Tel: +221-825 9822/23
Fax: +221-824 1289 (General enquiries)
Tel.: +221-825 721
Fax: +221-864 0143/82412 89 (Head,
Department of Publications & Communication)
Email: codesria@codesria.sn (General
enquiries) francis.nyamnjoh@codesria.sn
(Head, Department of Publications &
Communication)
Web:
http://www.codesria.org/Publications.htm
(Department of Publications & Communication)
Contact: Francis Nyamnjoh, Head,
Department of Publications &
Communication
Publishing areas: 2, 17, 18, 26, 27, 28, 35, 36,
43, 45
Overseas distr:
Titles in English: ABC
Titles in French: Editions Karthala, 22-24
Boulevard Arago, 75013 Paris, France

2060   Les Editions Juridiques Africaines
8 rue Raffenel
P 22420
Dakar - Ponty
Tel: + 221-821 6689/823 0071
Fax: +221-823 2753
Email: edja.ed@sentoo.sn
Web: n/a
Contact: Salimata Ngom Diop
Publishing areas: 15, 28, 29, 30
Online catalogue: Afrilivres

2061   Editions Xamal
P 380
Saint-Louis
Tel:/Fax: +221-961 722 Fax: +221-961519
Email: xamal@sentoo.sn
Web:
http://www.arts.uwa.edu.au/AFLIT/Editio
nsXamal.html (site hosted by the University
of Western Australia)
Contact: Aboubakar Diop, Managing Director
Publishing areas: 1, 2, 4, 5, 6, 8, 21, 31, 34, 36,
40, 42, 43, 45
Online catalogue: Afrilivres

2062   Enda Editions
Environmental Development Action
in the Third World
Département Diffusion
54 rue Carnot
BP 3370
Dakar
Tel: +221-822 9890/823 6491
Fax: +221-822 2695/823 5772
Email: editions@enda.sn
Web:
http://www.enda.sn/editions/accueil.htm
Contact: Jacques Bugnicourt, Director of
Publications; Gideon Prinsler Omolu,
Publisher
Publishing areas: 10, 20, 23, 33, 43, 45

**2063   Informatique Documentaire Edition
Electronique (IDEE)**
32 rue Lulu Sicap Fann Hock
BP 22823
Dakar-Ponty
Tel: +221-823 5380
Email: idee@sentoo.sn
Web: http://www.idee.sn/
(site not accessible October 2005)
Publishing areas: 30
Contact: Marc-André Ledoux
Other: CD-ROM and print titles on laws
and jurisprudence in Senegal and
Cameroon, as well as regional laws from
other French speaking African countries.

**2064   Les Nouvelles Editions Africaines
du Sénégal**
10 rue Amadou Assane Ndoye
BP 260
Dakar
Tel: +221-821 1381/822 1580
Fax: +221-822 3604
Email: neas@sentoo.sn

Web:
http://www.soumbala.com/site/pageneas1.
htm (pages hosted by Soumbala.com)
Contacts: François Boirot, Madieyna Ndiaje,
Aminata Sy
Publishing areas: 2, 5, 6, 7, 8, 11, 17, 18, 22, 27,
36, 43
Online catalogue: Afrilivres

**2065   Per Ankh SARL/
Per Ankh Publishers**
PER ANKH Building
Popenguine Village
BP 2
Popenguine
Dakar
Tel: +221-957 7113 Fax: +221-957 7114
Email: perankheditions@arc.sn
Web: http://www.perankh.info/
Contacts: Ama Gueye, Ayi Kwei Armah
Publishing areas: 2, 6, 22, 27, 35
Note: Per Ankh is an African publishing co-
operative. In addition to book publishing
activities it also runs writers' workshops and
hands-on seminars on the use of current
technology for literary productivity.

2066   Presses Universitaires de Dakar
Camp Jérémy
Avenue Cheikh Anta Diop
BP 5713
Dakar-Fann
Tel: +221- 824 2448
Email: djiibagne@refer.sn
Web: http://membres.lycos.fr/pud/
(several pages not accessible October 2005)
Contact: Djibril Agne
Publishing areas: 17, 27, 30, 36, 40, 42

**2067   Union pour l'Etude de la
Population Africaine/
Union for African Population
Studies (UPS)**
Stele Memoz – Km7.5
Avenue Cheikh Anta Diop
BP 21 007
Dakar-Ponty
Tel: +221-824 3528/825 5951
Fax: +221-8255955
Email: aziz@uaps.org or uaps@sentoo.sn
Web: http://www.uaps.org
Contact: Abdoul Aziz Ly, Head of
Publications
Publishing areas: 43, 45

Other: demography and population studies; also publishes a reports series in English and French
Other: Demography/Population studies

Sierra Leone

2068   PenPoint Publishers
International Pen Sierra Leone
14A Wallace Johnson Street
Freetown
Tel: +232-22-7666 5556/7662 8345
Email: sierraleonepen@yahoo.co.uk
Contact: Michael Butscher, Executive Secretary
Publishing areas: 5, 6, 14, 32
Overseas distr: ABC

South Africa

2069   Africa Institute of South Africa
Nipilar House crn Hamilton and Vermeulen Streets
Arcadia
PO Box 630
Pretoria 0001
Tel: +27-12-328 6970 Fax: +27-12-323 8153
Email: ai@ai.org.za
Web: http://www.ai.org.za/
Contacts: Eddy Maloka, Executive Director; or Head of Publications
Publishing areas 17, 18, 24, 26, 36, 38, 41, 45
Other: maps; online publications and electronic monographs
Overseas distr: ABC

2070   Jonathan Ball Publishers
POB 33977
Jeppestown 2043
Tel: +27-11-622 2900
Fax: +27-11-622 3553/622 7610
Email orders@jonathanball.co.za (Orders)
fblum@jonathanball.co.za (Editorial)
Web: http://www.jonathanball.co.za/ or http://www.viaafrika.com/eng_new/jonathan.asp (English version)
Contacts: Jonathan Ball, Managing Director; Barry Streek, Editor-in-chief; Francine Blum, Editor
Publishing areas: 1, 2, 5, 27, 36, 38, 40
Note: part of the Naspers group, incorporates Ad Donker Publisher.

2071   Barefoot Press
PO Box 532
Aukland Park 2006
Tel: +27-82-659 3165
Email: roy@royblumenthal.com
Web: http://www.pix.za/barefoot.press/
Contact: Roy Blumenthal, Managing Editor
Publishing areas: 8
Note: distributes free poetry pamphlets featuring South African poets, also making their work available online

2072   Bell-Roberts Publishing
Bell-Roberts Contemporary Art Gallery
199 Loop Street
Cape Town 8001
Tel: +27-21-422 1100 Fax: +27-21-423 3135
Email: brendon@bell-roberts.com
Web: http://www.bell-roberts.com/frameset_publishing.htm
Contact: Brendon Bell-Roberts
Publishing areas: 1
Other: contemporary South African art

2073   Briza Publications
PO Box 56569
Arcadia 0007
Tel: +27-12-329 3896 Fax: +27-12-329 4525
Email: books@briza.co.za
Web: http://www.briza.co.za/
Contact: Christo Reitz
Publishing areas: 20, 21, 34
Other: specialises in botanical books, and guides to mammals and reptiles of southern Africa
Overseas distr: Global Book Marketing

2074   Cambridge University Press
Nautica Building The Water Club
Beach Road Granger Bay
PO Box 50017 V & A Waterfront
Cape Town 8002
Tel: +27-21-412 7800 Fax: +27 21-419 0594
Email: capetown@cambridge.org or directcustserve@cambridge.org (Orders)
http://www.cambridge.org/africa/south_africa/
Contact: Colleen McCallum, Excecutive Director; Hennette Calitz, Publishing Manager
Publishing areas: 5, 10, 11, 12, 17, 24, 27, 28, 34, 36, 37, 38, 39, 40, 44

Note: the South African branch of Cambridge University Press publishes primarily educational and text books.

2075   Cluster Publications
PO Box 2400
Pietermaritzburg 3200
Tel/Fax: +27-33-345 9897
Email: cluster@futurenet.co.za
Web:
http://www.hs.unp.ac.za/theology/cluspub.
htm
Contact: Editorial Director
Publishing areas: 11, 33, 38, 40, 45

2076   Corporal Publications
PO Box 8945
Centurion 0046
Tel: +27-12-664 6340 Fax: +27-12-664 2241
Email: corporalafrica@mweb.co.za
Web:
http://www.mazoe.com/aboutcorporal.html
Contact: n/a
Publishing areas: 27
Other: specialises in books on Southern African history and military history

2077   Covos Day Books
PO Box 6996
Weltevredenpark 1715
Tel: +27-11-888 1407 Fax: +27-11-475 8974
Email: covos@global.co.za (General enquiries) orders@ibs.co.za (Orders)
Web: http://www.covosdaybooks.co.za/
Contacts: Chris Cocks, Martyn Day
Publishing areas: 8, 9, 14, 27, 36
UK/European distr:
Verulam Publishing, 152a Park Street Lane, Park Street, St Albans, AL2 2AU, UK, Email: verulam.pub@ntlworld.com
US distr: BHB International, Inc., 108 East North 1st Street, Suite G, Seneca, SC 29678, Email: bhbbooks@aol.com

2078   Culture, Communication and Media Studies (CCMS)
(formerly Centre for Cultural and Media Studies)
University of Kwa-Zulu Natal
King George V Avenue
Durban 4001
Tel: +27-31-260 2505 Fax: +27-31 260 1519
Email: ccms@mtb.und.ac.za or govends@ukzn.ac.za

Web:
http://www.nu.ac.za/ccms/publications/pu
blications_default.asp (Publications pages)
Contacts: Keyan Tomaselli, Director; Susan Govender
Publishing areas: 3, 32

2079   Deep South Publishing
PO Box 6082
Grahamstown 6140
Tel: n/a
Email: contact@deepsouth.co.za
Web: http://www.deepsouth.co.za
Contacts: Robert Berold, Paul Wessels
Publishing areas: 7, 8
Submission restrictions: does not accept unsolicited manuscripts/submissions
Distr: → **University of Kwazulu-Natal Press (2118)**

2080   Double Storey Books
Mercury Crescent
Wetton
PO Box 24309
Lansdowne 7779
Tel: +27-21-763 3500 Fax: +27-21-762 4523
Email: doublestorey@juta.co.za (General enquiries) bimpey@juta.co.za (Managing Director)
Web:
http://www.juta.co.za/doublestoreybooks/
default.asp
Contact: Bridget Impey, Managing Director
Publishing areas: 1, 5, 6, 27, 32, 36
Overseas distr: Global Book Marketing
Note: an imprint of Juta; primarily publishes general books, humour, political cartoons, and travel titles.

2081   Fernwood Press
PO Box 15344
Vlaeberg 8018
Tel: +27-21-786 2460 Fax: +27-21-786 2478
Email: ferpress@iafrica.com
Web: http://www.fernwoodpress.co.za
Contacts: Pieter Struik, Pam Struik, Directors
Publishing areas: 1, 2, 27, 34
Other: limited editions of fine art books; photography; pictorial works
Overseas distr: Global Book Marketing

2082   Francolin Publishers (Pty) Ltd
PO Box 18726
Wynberg
Cape Town 7824
Tel: +27-21-712 0373 Fax: +27-21-755001
Email: francolin@iafrica.com
Web: n/a
Publishing areas: 5, 6, 38

**2083   Heinemann Higher and Further
Education (Pty) Ltd**
POB 781940
Sandton 2146
Tel: +27-11-322 8600 Fax: +27-11-322 8715/16
Email: customerliaison@heinemann.co.za or
heininfo@heinemann.co.za
debrap@heinemann.co.za (Publisher, Social
Sciences)
Web: http://www.heinemann.co.za
Contact: Tanya Reinders, Managing Editor;
Debra Primo, Publisher, Social Sciences
Publishing areas: 5, 6, 8, 17, 18, 33, 35, 42, 43

2084   HSRC Publishers
Human Sciences Research Council
Pleinpark Building 16th floor
69-83 Plein Street
Private Bag X9182
Cape Town 8000
Tel: +27-21-466 8000 Fax: +27-21-461 0836
Email: publishing@hsrc.ac.za (General
enquiries) grosenberg@hsrc.ac.za (Publishing
Director)
Web: http://www.hsrcpublishers.co.za/
Contact: Garry Rosenberg, Publishing
Director
Publishing areas: 17, 18, 24, 27, 33, 36, 37, 38,
43, 44, 45
Distr in UK & Europe: Eurospan, 3 Henrietta
Street, Covent Garden, London WC2E 8LU,
Email: info@eurospan.co.uk
Web: http://www.eurospanonline.com
Note: the Press has a dual publishing
philosophy; academic research material is
offered both in print and online formats.
Printed copies of HSRC publications are
available for purchase, while online versions
can be downloaded at no cost (either as
specific chapters or as entire publications) via
the HSRC Press Web site.

2085   Human & Rousseau
PO Box 5050
Cape Town 8000
Tel: +27-21-406 3033 Fax: +27-21-406 3812

Email: humanhk@humanrousseau.com
Web: http://www.humanrousseau.com
Contacts: (Mrs) A. Potgieter, E. Bloemhof
(Literature)
Publishing areas: 5, 6, 8
Note: part of NB Publishers group; primarily
a general and children's book publisher, but
with an extensive literary list; publishes in
English and in Afrikaans.
Overseas distr: Global Book Marketing

2086   IDASA Publishing
The Institute for Democracy in South
Africa (IDASA)
Cape Town Democracy Centre
6 Spin Street
Cape Town 8001
Tel/Fax: +27-21-467 5600/461 5615
Email: shahieda@idasact.org.za
(Sales/Bookstore) moira@idasact.org.za
(Publishing Manager)
Web: http://www.idasa.org.za
Contact: Moira Levy, Publishing Manager;
Bronwen Muller, Editor
Publishing areas: 17, 18, 26, 28, 32, 33,
36, 43, 45
Other: budget briefs, conference reports, media
briefings, fact sheets, expenditure monitoring
reports, Afrobarometer working papers
Overseas distr: ABC

2087   Institute for Security Studies
Veale Street
Block C, Brooklyn Court
New Muckleneuk
PO Box 1787 Brooklyn Square
Pretoria 0075
Tel: +27-12-346 9500 Fax: +27-12-460 0998
Email: iss@iss.co.za (General enquiries)
JKC@iss.co.za (Executive Director)
Andre@iss.co.za (Publications
Coordinator)
Web: http://www.iss.co.za
Contacts: Jakkie Cilliers, Executive Director;
Andre Snyders, Publications Coordinator
Publishing areas: 36
Other: crime prevention, peacekeeping,
security studies

**2088   Institute for Social and Economic
Research**
Rhodes University
PO Box 94
Grahamstown 6140
Tel: +27-46-603 8550 Fax: +27-46-622 3948

Email: iser-sec@ru.ac.za
Web:
http://www.ru.ac.za/community/ISER/ or
http://www.ru.ac.za/institutes/iser/index.h
tml
Contacts: Valerie Møller, Director; Nova de
Villiers, Publications Officer
Publishing areas: 11, 17, 29, 33, 36, 43

**2089   Institute for the Study of English in
           Africa**
           Rhodes University
           PO Box 94
           Grahamstown 6140
Tel: +27-46-603 8565/622 6093
Fax: +27-46-603 8566
Email: J.King@ru.ac.za (General enquiries)
L.Wright@ru.ac.za (Director)
B.Cummings@ru.ac.za (Publications Officer)
Web:
http://www.ru.ac.za/institutes/isea/
Contact: (Prof.) Lawrence Wright, Director;
Bev Cummings, Publications Officer
Publishing areas: 5, 6, 8, 22

2090   Juta Academic
           PO Box 24309
           Lansdowne 7779
Tel: +27-21-763 3500/797 5101
Fax: +27-21-761 5861/762 4523
Email: ejserv@juta.co.za (Orders/Customer
services)
gyounge@juta.co.za (Publishing Director,
Academic)
Web: http://www.juta.co.za
Contacts: Glenda Younge, Publishing
Director, Academic
Areas of publishing: 4, 17, 18, 20, 26, 28, 32,
33, 36, 37, 42, 43, 45
Other: adult education, banking, computing
Overseas distr: Global Book Marketing
Note: includes the ➜ **UCT Press (2117)**
imprint; also maintains retail outlets.

2091   Juta Law
           PO Box 24299
           Lansdowne 7780
Tel: +27-21-797 5101 Fax: +27-21-797 0121
Email: http://www.jutalaw.co.za/ (General)
(Publishing Director Law/International
Projects Director) rdekock@juta.co.za (Print
Publishing Director),
Web:
http://www.juta.co.za/academic/default.as
p

Contacts: Ciaran MacGlinchey, Publishing
Director Law and International Projects
Director; Ria de Kock, Print Publishing
Director; Chipo Chipidza, Publisher,
Corporate and Business titles; Ute Kuhlman,
Publisher, Practitioner titles
Publishing areas: 15, 30
Note: publishes in all areas of law and
taxation, including law reports, loose-leaf
publications, books, journals and CD-ROM
and Internet publications; also maintains
retail outlets.

➜ **David Krut Publishing** *see* **Taxi Art Books
(2114)**

2092   Kwela Books
           Naspers 12th floor
           40 Heerengracht
           PO Box 6525
           Roggebaai 8012
Tel: +27-21-406 3605 Fax: +27-21-406 3712
Web:
http://www.nb.co.za/Kwela/kSplash.asp
Email: kwela@kwela.com
Contact: Nelleke de Jager
Areas of publishing: 2, 4, 6, 8*, 14, 43
(*poetry is published in association with
Snailpress)
Note: part of NB Publishers group.
Overseas distr: Global Book Marketing

2093   LexisNexis Butterworth Publishers
           215 North Ridge Road
           Morningside 4001
           PO Box 792
           Durban 4000
Tel: +27-31-268 3111 Fax: +27-31-268 3110
Email: customercare@lexisnexis.co.za
(Customer Services Centre)
lucy.gosai@lexisnexis.co.za (Professional
Legal Publishing Manager)
ingrid.fernihough@lexisnexis.co.za
(Africa Publishing Manager)
Web:
http://www.butterworths.co.za/index.php
Contacts: Lucy Gosai, Professional Legal
Publishing Manager; Ingrid Fernihough,
Africa Publishing Manager
Publishing areas: 15, 30
Other: accounting, business, taxation; online
legal products and services

2094   Macmillan Academic Southern Africa/Pan MacMillan SA (Pty) Ltd
PO Box 31487
Braamfontein 2017
Tel: +27-11-731 3440/325 5220
Fax: +27-11-731 3540/325 5225
Email: roshni@panmacmillan.co.za or academic@panmacmillan.co.za
Web: http://www.panmacmillan.co.za or http://www.macmillan.co.za/ or
Contact: Dusanka Stojakovic, Managing Director
Publishing areas: 17, 18, 27, 36, 38, 43, 45

2095   Maskew Miller Longman (Pty) Ltd
Corner Logan Way and Forest Drive
Pinelands
PO Box 396
Cape Town 8000
Tel: + 27-21-532 6000/531 7750
Fax: + 27-21-531 4049 (Orders)
+ 27-21-531 7236 (Editorial)
Email: webmaster@mml.co.za
Web: http://www.mml.co.za/ (site not accessible October 2005; being upgraded)
Contacts: Fathima Dada, Chief Executive; Nikki Clarke, Higher Education, Adult and Trade Director
Publishing areas: 6, 18, 24, 38
Other: adult education, atlases and maps; primarily an educational publisher
Overseas distr: Global Book Marketing

2096   Mayibuye Publications
University of the Western Cape
Private Bag X17
Bellville 7535
Tel: +27-21-959 2935/54 Fax: +27-21-959 3411
Email: mayib@uwc.ac.za
Web: http://www.mayibuye.org/
Contact: Barry Feinberg, Head of Publications Division
Publishing areas: 5, 27, 36, 43
Overseas distr: Global Book Marketing

2097   NISC (Pty) Ltd
19 Worcester Street
PO Box 377
Grahamstown 6140
Tel: +27-46-622 9698 Fax: +27-46-622 9550
Email: sales@nisc.co.za (Orders)
info@nisc.co.za (Managing Director)
Web: http://www.nisc.co.za
Contact: Margaret Crampton, Managing Director

Publishing areas: 10, 33, 38
Other: fish and fisheries, water resources; database publishing in African studies on CD-ROM and the Internet.
Note: part of NISC International, Inc.

2098   New Africa Books (Pty) Ltd/ New Africa Education
99 Garfield Road
Claremont
PO Box 46962
Glosderry 7702
Tel: +27-21- 674 4136 Fax: +27-21-674 3358
Email: info@newafricabooks.co.za (General)
bwafa@mweb.co.za (Managing Director)
carolyn@newafricabooks.co.za (Manuscript submissions)
Web: http://www.newafricabooks.co.za
Contacts: Brian Wafawarowa, Managing Director; Arabella Koopman, Publishing Director; Nkululeko Ndiki, Publishing Manager, African Languages
Areas of publishing: 1, 2, 4, 5, 6, 7, 8, 9, 11, 13, 14, 17, 18, 20, 24, 27, 33, 36, 37, 38, 40, 42, 44, 45
Other: atlases and maps
Overseas distr: Global Book Marketing
See also ➔ David Philip (2104), ➔ Spearhead (2111)

2099   New Holland Publishing (South Africa) (Pty) Ltd/Struik Books for Africa
80 McKenzie Street Gardens
PO Box 1144
Cape Town 8000
Tel: +27-21-462 4360 Fax: +27-21-461 9378
Email: books@struik.co.za (General enquiries)
stevec@struik.co.za (Managing Director)
georginah@struik.co.za (General Manager, Publishing) pippap@struik.co.za (Publisher, Natural History) helendv@struik.co.za (Managing Editor)
marlenef@zebrapress.co.za (Zebra Press imprint)
Web: http://www.struik.co.za
Contacts: Steve Connolly, Managing Director; Georgina Hatch, General Manager, Publishing; Helen de Villiers, Managing Editor; Pippa Parker, Publisher, Natural History; Marlene Fryer, Publisher Zebra Press imprint (see below)
Areas of publishing: 1, 2, 11, 14, 21, 23, 24, 27, 34, 36, 40

Other: atlases and maps, cultural diversity, photography, wildlife and conservation
Zebra Press imprint: 5, 14, 27, 36, 38
See also ➔ **Map Studio (516)**
Note: part of Johnnic Publishing

2100   Olive (O D & T)
Olive-Organisation, Development and Training
21 Sycamore Road
Glenwood
Durban 4001
Tel: +27-31-206 1534 Fax: +27-31-205 2114
Email: olive@oliveodt.co.za (General enquiries) evangeline@oliveodt.co.za (Publishing and Distribution Administrator)
Web:
http://www.oliveodt.co.za/pubs/ideas.html (Publications pages)
Contact: Evangeline Govender, Publishing and Distribution Administrator
Publishing areas: 17, 45
Other: change management, leadership, organisation and people development

2101   Oshun Books
80 McKenzie Street
Gardens
PO Box 1144
Cape Town 8000
Tel: +27-21-462 4360 Fax: +27-21-462 4379
Web:
http://www.struiknews.co.za/oshunbooks/
Email: bevc@struik.co.za (Export sales)
michellem@oshunbooks.co.za (Publishing Manager)
ceridwenm@struik.co.za (Editor)
Contacts: Michelle Matthews, Publishing Manager; Ceridwen Morris, Editor
Publishing areas: 6 (by South African women writers), 14 (of women), 45
Other: gift and resource books aimed specifically at women and written in English.
Note: a division of ➔ **Struik Books/New Holland Publishing (2099)**

2102   Oxford University Press Southern Africa
Vasco Boulevard
N1 City Goodwood
PO Box 12119
N1 City
Cape Town 7463
Tel: +27-21-596 2300 Fax: +27-21-596 1234

Email: oxford.za@oup.com (General enquiries) orders.za@oup.com (Orders)
Web: http://www.oup.com/za/
Contacts: Lieze Kotze, Managing Director; Judy Spoor, Publishing Director; address manuscript submissions to The Commissioning Editor, Academic Division
Publishing areas: 4, 17, 18, 26, 27, 30, 32, 33, 36, 37, 38, 43, 44, 45
Other: research methodology

2103   Pharos Dictionaries/Pharos Woordeboeke
PO Box 879
Cape Town 8000
Tel +27-21-406 3033 Fax +27-21-406 3812
Email: pharos@pharos.co.za
Web:
http://www.nb.co.za/Pharos/phSplash.asp
Contact: H.D. Büttner, Manager
Publishing areas: 4, 38
Overseas distr: Global Book Marketing
Note: part of the NB Publishers group; also publishes out-of-print hard-copy dictionaries electronically and on demand.

2104   David Philip
An imprint of New Africa Books
PO Box 46962
Glosderry 7702
Tel: +27-21-674 4136 Fax: +27-21-674 3358
Email: info@newafricabooks.co.za (General enquiries)
carolyn@newafricabooks.co.za (Manuscript submissions)
Web: http://www.newafricabooks.co.za
Contacts: Brian Wafawarowa, Managing Director; Arabella Koopman, Publishing Director, Commissioning Editor: Jeanne Hromnik, Commissioning Editor
Publishing areas: 1, 2, 5, 6, 7, 8, 12, 18, 20, 22, 27, 36, 37, 40, 43, 45
Note: formerly David Phillip Publishers; now owned by ➔ **New Africa Books (Pty) Ltd/New Africa Education (2098)**.
Overseas distr: Global Book Marketing

2105   Stephan Phillips (Pty) Ltd
Unit 014 Old Castle Brewery Building
6 Beach Road Woodstock
PO Box 12246
Mill Street

Cape Town 8010
Tel: +27-21-448 9839 Fax: +27-21-447 9879
Email: info@stephanphillips.com
Web: http://www.stephanphillips.com
Contact: Harry Stephan
Publishing areas: 14, 27, 34, 36
Other: photography, popular art, wildlife and
conservation
Note: books on the list are primarily sourced
from publishers in the USA, UK, Europe, and
from some countries in Africa, but the
company also publishes its own books from
time to time.

2106   Random House South Africa Pty Ltd
Endulini East Wing
5A Jubilee Road
Parktown
Sandton 2193
Tel: +27-11-484 3538 Fax: +27-11-484 6180
Email: mail@randomhouse.co.za (General
enquiries) fmchardy@randomhouse.co.za
(Managing Director)
Web: n/a
Contact: Françoise McHardy, Managing
Director
Publishing areas: 14, 20, 36, 37, 38, 42
Overseas distr: Global Book Marketing

**2107   Shuter & Shooter Publishers (Pty)
Ltd**
21C Cascades Crescent
Cascades Pietermaritzburg
PO Box 13016
Cascades
Pietermaritzburg 3202
Tel: +27-33-347 6100 Fax: +27-33-347 6120
Email: dryder@shuters.com (Managing
Director) thenjie@shuters.com (Regional
Manager)
Web: http://www.shuter.co.za
Contact: David Ryder, Managing Director;
 (Mrs) L.Williamson, Publishing Manager; R
Wela, African languages publishing
Publishing areas: 4, 6, 8 (in South African
languages), 10, 17, 18, 28, 33, 38, 40, 42
Other: Afrikaans language and literature;
primarily an educational publisher

**2108   South African Institute of
International Affairs**
Jan Smuts House East Campus
University of the Witwatersrand
POB 31596
Braamfontein 2017

Tel: +27-11-339 2021 Fax: +27-11-339 2154
Email: saiiagen@global.co.za
Web: http://www.saiia.org.za/ (click on to
Publications)
Conact: Elizabeth Sidiropoulos, National
Director; or Head of Publications
Publishing areas: 17, 20, 26, 36, 38, 43
Other: digital publishing; all recent
publications are available for purchase in
digital format from I-Net Bridge
http://www.inet.co.za

**2109   South African Institute of Race
Relations**
PO Box 31044
Braamfontein 2017
Tel: +27-11-403 3600
Fax: +27-11-403 3671/339-2061
Email: sairrinfo@pcb.co.za
Web: http://www.sairr.org.za/publications/
(Publication pages)
Contact: Joe Mpye, Marketing Manager
Publishing areas: 36, 43, 45

**2110   South African National Biodiversity
Institute (SANBI)**
(formerly National Botanical
Institute)
Private Bag X101
Pretoria 0001
Tel: +27-12-843 5000 Fax: +27-12-78043211
Email: info@sanbi.org (General enquiries)
bookshop@sanbi.org
(Bookshop/Publications)
Web:
http://www.nbi.ac.za/frames/productsfram
.htm (Publications)
Contacts: (Prof.) Brian J. Huntley, Acting
Chief Executive Offier; (Prof.) Gideon Smith,
Director, Research and Scientific Services
Publishing areas: 21

2111   Spearhead
An imprint of New Africa Books
PO Box 46962
Glosderry 7702
Tel: +27-21- 674 4136 Fax: +27-21-674 3358
Email: info@newafricabooks.co.za
(General enquiries)
carolyn@newafricabooks.co.za (Manuscript
submissions)
Web: http://www.newafricabooks.co.za
Contacts: Brian Wafawarowa, Managing
Director; Arabella Koopman, Publishing
Director; Margaret Matthews, Publisher

Publishing areas: 1, 5, 6, 8, 14, 20, 27, 33, 36
Overseas distr: Global Book Marketing

2112   STE Publishers
Sunnyside Ridge 4th floor
Sunnyside Park
32 Prince of Wales Terrace
Park Town
PO Box 3371
Houghton 2041
Tel: +27 11 484-7824 Fax: +27 11 484-4296
Email: angela@ste.co.za (Sales)
reedi@ste.co.za (Director)
Web: http://www.ste.co.za/
Contacts: Reedwaan Vally, Director
Publishing areas: 3, 5, 6, 8, 14, 17, 18,
32, 33, 36, 38, 42, 43

➔ **Struk Books for Africa** *see* **New Holland Publishing (2099)**

**2113   Tafelberg-Uitgewer Bpk/
Tafelberg Publishers Ltd**
Naspers 12th Floor
40 Heerengracht
Roggebaai
PO Box 879
Cape Town 8000
Tel: +27-21- 406 3033 Fax: +27-21-406 3812
Email: tafelbrg@tafelberg.com
Web:
http://www.nb.co.za/Tafelberg/tbSplash.as
p
Contact: Louise Steyn, Editor/Publisher
Publishing areas: 1, 6 (in Afrikaans), 8 (in
Afrikaans) 14, 17, 22, 27, 34, 36, 38, 40
Note: part of NB Publishers group; primarily
a publisher of general and trade books, and
children's books.

**2114   Taxi Art Books/David Krut
Publishing**
140 Jan Smuts Avenue
Parkwood
PO Box 892
Houghton 2041
Johannesburg
Tel: +27-11-880 4242 Fax: +27-11-880 6368
Email: dkrut@icon.co.za
Web: http://www.taxiartbooks.com/
Contact: David Krut, Publisher; Brenda
Atkinson, Editor
Publishing areas: 1 (contemporary South
African art and photography); also CDs
and videos

2115   Umdaus Press (Pvt) Ltd
PO Box 11059
Hatfield 0028
Tel: +27-11-880 0273 Fax: +27-11-788 1498
Email: umdaus@succulents.net or
gariep@succulents.net
Web:
http://www.succulents.net/umdaus/index.
html
Contact: n/a
Publishing areas: 19, 20, 34
Other: Botany; specialises in the publication
of fine books on natural history of Southern
Africa and environs with emphasis on
succulent plants.

2116   Umuzi Press
Safmarine House 3rd floor
22 Riebeck Street
Cape Town
PO Box 6810
Roggebai 8012
Tel: +27-21-410 8785 Fax: +27-21-410 8711
Email:
umuzi@randomhouse.co.za (General
enquiries) annari.umuzi@randomhouse.co.za
(Publishing Director)
Contact: Annari van der Merwe, Publishing
Director
Web: http://www.umuzi-
randomhouse.co.za/
Publishing areas: 6, 8, 14
Other: crime fiction, photographic works,
travel writing
Note: this is a new imprint recently launched
by ➔ **Random House South Africa Pty Ltd
(2106)**

**2117   University of Cape Town Press
(UCT Press)**
PO Box 24309
Lansdowne 7779
Tel: +27-21-797 5101 Fax: +27-21-762 7854
Email: GYounge@juta.co.za (Publisher)
Web:
http://www.juta.co.za/academic/UCTPress.
htm or
http://www.juta.co.za/academic/default.as
p
Contact: Glenda Younge, Publisher
Publishing areas: 2, 4, 5, 11, 12, 13, 17, 18, 20,
27, 33, 35, 36, 40, 42, 45
Other: natural sciences
Note: part-owned by ➔ **Juta Academic (2090)**
Overseas distr: Global Book Marketing

2118   University of KwaZulu Natal Press
(formerly University of Natal Press)
Private Bag X01
Scotsville 3209
Tel: +27-33-260 5226 Fax: +27-33-260 5801
Email: books@ukzn.ac.za (General)
cowleyg@nu.ac.za (Publisher)
Web: http://www.unpress.co.za/
Contacts: Glenn Cowley, Publisher
Publishing areas: 1, 5, 8, 14, 20, 21, 27, 29, 33, 36, 43, 45
Other: atlases and maps, natural sciences, ornithology, Zulu people
Overseas distr:
UK & Europe: Eurospan, 3 Henrietta Street, Covent Garden, London WC2E 8LU, Email: info@eurospan.co.uk
Web: http://www.eurospanonline.com
USA: ISBS, 5804 NE Hassalo Street, Portland OR 97213-3644, USA

2119   UNISA Press
University of South Africa
PO Box 392
UNISA Muckleneuk Campus
Pretoria 0003
Tel: +27-12-429 308 (General enquiries)
Tel: +27-12-429 3316 (Manuscript proposals)
Fax: +27-12-429 3221
Email: unisa-press@unisa.ac.za (General enquiries)
zegeya@unisa.ac.za (Director)
boshosm@unisa.ac.za (Manuscript proposals)
Web:
http://www.unisa.ac.za/dept/press/index.html or
http://www.unisa.ac.za/default.asp?Cmd=ViewContent&ContentID=247
Contacts: (Prof.) Abebe Zegeye, Director; manuscript proposals to Sharon Boshoff
Publishing areas: 1, 2, 4, 5, 7, 8, 11, 13, 17, 22, 23, 26, 30, 35, 36, 37, 40, 43, 45
Other: research methodology
Overseas distr: ABC (select titles only)

2120   Van Schaik Publishers/
Van Schaik Uitgewers
1064 Arcadia Street
PO Box 12681
Hatfield 0028
Tel: +27-12-342 2765 Fax: +27-12-430 3563
Email: vanschaik@vanschaiknet.com (General enquiries)
lmartini@vanschaiknet.com (Publishing Manager) jread@vanschaiknet.com

(Publisher, Education, Social and Human sciences) lreid@vanschaiknet.com (Publisher, (Development & public administration, communication, media, fine arts & languages, law & IT)
Web: http://www.vanschaiknet.com
Contacts: Leanne Martini, Publishing Manager; Julia Read, Publisher (Education, Social and Human sciences); Lydia Reid, Publisher (Development & public administration, communication, media, fine arts & languages, law & IT)
Publishing areas: 4, 17, 26, 29, 30, 33, 36, 37, 38, 40
Other: natural sciences
Note: also maintains retail outlets.
Overseas distr: Global Book Marketing

2121   Witwatersrand University Press
23 Junction Avenue
Parktown
PO Wits
Johannesburg 2050
Tel: +27-11-484 5907/8/9/10
Fax: +27-11-484 5971
Email: klippv@wup.wits.ac.za (Publisher)
mostertm@wup.wits.ac.za (Commissioning Editor)
Web: http://witspress.wits.ac.za/default.asp
Contacts: Veronica Klipp, Publisher; Marguerethe Mostert, Commissioning Editor
Publishing areas: 1, 2, 5, 11, 12, 14, 17, 21, 22, 27, 30, 33, 36, 38, 43, 45
Other: natural sciences
Overseas distr:
UK & Europe: Eurospan, 3 Henrietta Street, Covent Garden, London WC2E 8LU, Email: info@eurospan.co.uk
Web: http://www.eurospanonline.com
USA: Transaction Publishers Distribution, 390 Campus Drive, Somerset, NJ 08873, USA, Email: orders@transactionpub.com

2122   Zabalaza Books
Postnet Suite 116
Private Bag X42
Braamfontein 2017
Tel: +27-881-220416 (leave message)
Email: zabalaza@zabalaza.net
Web: http://www.zabalaza.net/zababooks/
Contact: n/a
Publishing areas: 29, 36, 45
Other: anarchism/African anarchism, women's liberation

Swaziland

2123   Academic Publishers (Swaziland)
8 Manzini
Box 2223
Matsapha M202
Tel/Fax: n/a
Email: academic.pubsz@executivemail.co.za
Web:
Contact: c/o Foluke Ogunleye,
(Email: segfoleye@yahoo.com)
Publishing areas: 2, 5, 22

2124   JANyeko Publishing Centre Ltd
PO Box 6699
Manzini
also at:
Opidi Cottage
Kisasi Road Ntinda
PO Box 25613
Kampala
Uganda
Tel: +268-518 4617/+268-604 7192 (Mobile)
Email: janetnyeko@yahoo.com
Web: http://www.geocities.com/janpcentre/
Contact: Janet Nyeko, Managing Director
Publishing areas: 2, 5, 14, 17, 27, 36
Overseas distr: ABC

Tanzania

2125   Blue Mango Ltd
PO Box 70045
Dar es Salaam
Tel: +255-22-266 6383
Email: pjh@bluemango.co.tz
Web: n/a
Contact: Paul Joynson-Hicks
Publishing areas: 34
Other: wildlife, photographic works
Overseas distr: Global Book Marketing

**2126   Centre for Energy, Environment,
Science & Technology (CEEST)**
B3-16 TIRDO Estates
Morogoro Stores
Oysterbay
PO Box 5511
Dar es Salaam
Tel: +255-51-667569 Fax: +255-51-666079
Email: ceest@ceest.com
Web: http://www.ceest.com/ (Home page)
http://www.ceest.com/publications.html
(Publications)

Contacts: (Prof.) M.J. Mwandosya, (Prof.)
M.L. Luhanga, Directors
Publishing areas: 20, 42
Other: biological diversity, climate change,
conservation, energy
Overseas distr: ABC

2127   Dar es Salaam University Press
University of Dar es Salaam
Uvumbuzi Road
PO Box 35182
Dar es Salaam
Tel: +255-22-241 0093/300
Fax: +255-22-241 0137
Email: dup@udsm.ac.tz (General enquiries)
bernhard-sanyagi@yahoo.co.uk (Publications
Manager)
Web: http://www.dup.co.tz/
Publishing areas: 4, 10, 12, 17, 18, 27, 30, 36,
37, 41, 43, 44, 45
Contacts: Lipangala Minzi, Director; Bernard
Sanyagi, Publications Manager
Overseas distr: ABC

2128   E & D Ltd
PO Box 4460
Dar es Salaam
Tel: +255-22-277 5361
Email: ed@ud.co.tz
Web: n/a
Contact: Elieshi Lema, Publisher
Publishing areas: 2, 4, 5, 6, 18, 43, 45
Overseas distr: ABC

2129   Mkuki na Nyota Publishers
6 Muhonda Street
Mission Quarter
Opp. Kanisa Katoliki Kariakoo
Ilala
PO Box 4246
Dar es Salaam
Tel: +255-22-218 0479 (General and Sales
Department) +255-22-276 0408/276 0409
(Editorial Department)
Fax: +255-22-212 1416
Email: sales.mauzo@mkukinanyota.com
(Sales)
editorial.uhariri@mkukinanyota.com
(Editorial submissions)
walter@mkukinanyota.com (Managing
Director)
Web:
http://www.mkukinanyota.com/home.html
Contact: Walter Bgoya, Managing Director

Publishing areas: 1, 2, 4, 5, 6, 11, 14, 17, 18, 20, 21, 22, 28, 30, 34, 36
Note: physical address of editorial department is at Plot # 50/29, Apartment #311, Mwinjuma Road, Mwananyamala, Kinondoni, Dar es Salaam
Overseas distr: ABC

2130   Tanzania Publishing House
47 Samora Machel Avenue
PO Box 2138
Dar es Salaam
Tel: +255-22-213 7402/3
Email: tphouse@yahoo.com
Web: n/a
Contact: Primus Isidor Karugendo, General Manager
Publishing areas: 6, 17, 18, 36
Overseas distr: ABC

2131   Tema Publishing
2nd Floor Diamond Jubilee Building
Jamhuri Street/ Upanga Road
PO Box 63115
Dar es Salaam
Tel: +255-22-2110472
Email: temapubs@hotmail.com
Web: n/a
Contact: Todo Maliyamkono, Managing Director
Publishing areas: 17, 18, 27, 36
Overseas distr: ABC

Togo

2132   Editions Akpagnon
BP 3531
Lomé
Tel: +228-220244 Fax: +228-220244
Email: yedobge@hotmail.com
Web: n/a
Contact: Yves-Emmanuel Dogbé, Managing Director
Publishing areas: 2, 5, 6, 7, 8, 11, 14, 18, 22, 27, 36, 40
Online catalogue: Afrilivres

2133   Editions HaHo
Centre d'Editions Evangéliques
1 rue du Commerce
BP 378
Lomé
Tel: +228-221 4582 Fax: +228-211 2967
Email: ctce@café.tg

Web: n/a
Contact: Kodjo Mawuli Etsé
Publishing areas: 4, 5, 6, 18, 22, 27, 38, 40, 43, 44, 45
Online catalogue: Afrilivres

2134   Les Editions de la Rose Bleue
5 ter Rue du Maréchal Bugeaud
BP 12452
Lomé
Tel: +228-222 9339 Fax: +228-222 9669
Email: edit@larosebleue.net (General enquiries) dorkenoo_ephrem@yahoo.fr (Director)
Web: http://www.larosebleue.net/
Contact: Ephrem Seth Dorkenoo, Director
Publishing areas: 5, 6, 8, 27, 36

2135   Nouvelles Editions Africaines du Togo
239 Boulevard du 13 Janvier
BP 4862
Lomé
Tel: +228-216761/216527 Fax: +228-221003
Email: ctekue@yahoo.fr
Web: n/a
Contact: Christine T. Ekue, Managing Director
Publishing areas: 1, 6, 7, 8, 11, 24, 27, 36, 43

Tunisia

2136   Alyssa Editions
7 rue H. Thameur
Sidi Bou Saïd 2026
Tel/Fax: n/a
Email: alys@planet.tn
Web: n/a
Contact: Nicole ben Youssef, Editorial Director
Publishing areas: 6, 27

2137   Centre d'etudes de recherches et du publications
Campus Universitaire
BP 255
1002 Tunis Cedex
Tel: +216-71-510307/874426
Fax: +216-71-511677/871677
Email: n/a
Web: n/a
Contact: Khadija Djellouli Zahouano
Publishing areas: 11, 18, 24, 27, 30, 36, 43

2138   Cérès Editions
6 rue Alain Savary
BP 56 Belvédère
Tunis 1002
Tel: +216-71-280505 Fax: +216-71 287216
Email: info@ceres-editions.com
Email: nbk.ceres@planet.tn
Web: http://www.ceres-editions.com
Contact: Karim Ben Smail
Publishing areas: 1, 5, 17, 27, 30, 35, 36, 43, 45
Other: Arabic language and literature;
reference and photographic works on
Carthage's mosaics and Tunisian painters

Uganda

2139   Femrite Publications Ltd
Plot 147 Kira Road
PO Box 705
Kampala
Tel: +256-41-543943
Email: femrite@infocom.co.ug
Web:
http://www.wworld.org/about/affiliates/fe
mrite.htm (hosted by Women's World)
Contact: Goretti Kyomuhendo, Director
Publishing areas: 5, 6 (by women writers), 8,
45
Overseas distr: ABC

2140   Fountain Publishers
Fountain House
Plot 55 Nkrumah Road
PO Box 488
Kampala
Tel: +256-41-259163/251112
Fax: +256-41-251160/534973
Email: fountain@starcom.co.ug or
fountain@africaonline.co.ug Web:
http://www.fountainpublishers.co.ug/
Contact: James Tumusiime, Managing
Director
Publishing areas: 4, 6, 9, 10, 14, 17, 18, 26, 27,
28, 30, 36, 38, 45
Other: travel and guide books
Overseas distr: ABC

➜ **JANyeko Publishing Centre Ltd** see under
Swaziland, entry **2124**

2141   Makerere University Press
PO Box 7062
Kampala
Tel: +256-41-531530/532631 ext 290/ +256-41-
545160 Fax: +256-41-541068
Email: easl@mukla.gn.apc.org
Web: http://www.makerere.ac.ug/
(University home page, no pages as yet for
the Press)
Contact: n/a
Publishing areas: 17, 36

2142   MK Publishers (U) Ltd
Kibuye Kampala – Entebbe Road
PO Box 12385
Kampala
Tel: +256-41-271615/262584
Fax: +256-41-271615
Email: mkpub@mkpublishers.com or
mkpub@utlonline.com
Web: http://www.mkpublishers.com/
Contacts: Samuel Majwega Musoke,
Chairman/Chief Executive Director;
Samuel Serwange, Editorial Manager
(Scholarly publications)
Publishing areas: 6, 7, 18, 22, 36

**2143   Uganda Martyrs University-African
            Research and Documentation
            Centre (ARDC)**
PO Box 5498
Kampala
Tel: +256-78-410 611/+256-481-21894/5
Fax: +256-78-410100
Email: umu@umu.ac.ug
Web: http://www.fiuc.org/iaup/ssi/PDF-
doc/UMU-doc/mtafiti/bottom.html
Publishing areas: 2, 17, 20, 36

Zambia

2144   Bookworld Publishers
PO Box 32581
Lusaka
Tel: +260-1-222688/225282
Fax: +260-1-225195
Email: Gadsden@zamnet.zn
Web: n/a
Contact: Fay Gadsden, Publisher
Publishing areas: 1, 4, 5, 27, 40

2145   Image Publishers Ltd
PO Box 35033
Lusaka
Tel: 260-1-295049/260-1-97-779672 (Mobile)
Email: chrischirwa@yahoo.co.uk or
chrischirwa@zamtel.zm
Web: n/a
Contact: Chris Chirwa, Publisher
Publishing areas: 18
Overseas distr.: ABC

2146   Multimedia Zambia
Bishops Road Kabulonga
PO Box 320199
Woodlands
Lusaka
Tel/Fax: +260-1-261193
Email: rbczam@zamnet.zm
Web: http://www.nationalmirror.com.zm/
Contacts: Jumbe Ngoma, Executive Director;
E.M. Mbozi, Book Publishing Manager
Publishing areas: 32, 36, 43
Overseas distr: ABC

2147   University of Zambia Press
University of Zambia
POB 32379
Lusaka
Tel: +260-1-291777 Fax: +260-1-253952
Email: press@admin.unza.zm
Web: http://www.unza.zm (University home
page, no pages as yet for the Press)
Contact: (Ms) Monde Sifuniso, Director
Publishing areas: 11, 17, 24, 27, 28, 36, 37, 43,
45

**2148   Zambia Women Writers
Association (ZAWWA)**
PO Box 38388
Lusaka
Zambia
Tel: +26-97-848 134
Email: hhmusunsa81@hotmail.com
Web: n/a
Contact: Hilda H. Musunsa, President
Publishing areas: 5, 6 (by women writers), 7, 8
Overseas distr: ABC

Zimbabwe

**2149   Africa Community Publishing &
Development Trust**
59 Glenara Avenue North Highlands
PO Box 7250
Harare
Tel: +263-4-743739/743740
Fax: +263-4-743741
Email: bookteam@icon.co.zw or
bookteam@mweb.co.zw
Web: http://www.icon.co.zw/acpdt
Contact: Maxwell Muchemwa, Publisher
Publishing areas: 18, 22, 41, 43
Other: community publishing (books based
on and developed through participatory
methods); local governance and participation
Overseas distr: ABC

2150   Baobab Books
An imprint of Academic Books (Pvt)
Ltd
2 Pat Dunn Close
PO Box 567
New Ardbennie
Harare
Tel: +263-4-665187/661642
Fax: +263-4-665155
Email: academic@mweb.co.zw
Web: n/a
Contact: Nigel Hattle, Manager
Publishing areas: 5, 6, 27
Note: Baobab Books, formerly a leading
scholarly and literary publisher in Zimbabwe,
is now primarily active in educational
publishing.

2151   College Press Publishers (Pvt) Ltd
15 Douglas Road Workington
POB 3041
Harare
Tel: +263-4-754145/754255
Fax: +263-4-754256
Email: nellym@collegepress.co.zw
Web: http://www.macmillan-africa.com/
(Macmillan Africa site)
Contact: Ben Mugabe, Managing Director
Publishing areas: 5, 6, 7, 8, 14, 18, 36, 38

2152   Kimaathi Publishing House
53 Harare Drive
Greendale
Harare
Tel: + 263-4-244022

Email: info@kimaathipublishing.com
(General) w_ngugi@yahoo.com (Publisher)
Web: http://www.kimaathipublishing.com/
Contact: Wanjiku Ngugi, Publisher
Publishing areas: 2, 6, 8, 18, 27, 35, 36, 38, 43
Other: photographic works
Overseas distr: ABC

**2153   Longman Zimbabwe Publishers
(Pvt) Ltd**
POB ST125
Southerton
Harare
Tel: +263-4-621611-617
Fax: +263-4-621670
Email: cs@longman.co.zw (General enquiries)
ob@longman.co.zw (Editorial)
Web: n/a
Contacts: Nda Dlodlo, Managing Director;
Obey Bvute (Editorial)
Publishing areas: 6, 7, 8, 27

2154   Mambo Press
PO Box 779
Senga Road
Gweru 054
Tel: +263-54-224016/7 Fax: +263-54-221991
Emal: mambopress@telco.co.zw
Web: http://www.mambopress.co.zw
Contacts: Constantino Mashonganyika,
Managing Director; Emmanuel Makadho,
Managing Editor
Publishing areas: 2, 5, 6, 10, 11, 22, 27, 36, 38,
40
Overseas distr: ABC

2155   Nehanda Publishers (Pvt) Ltd
11 Buckingham Road Eastlea
PO Box UA 517
Union Avenue
Harare
Tel: +263-4-776964 Fax: +263-4-795393
Email: bethule@africaonline.com
Web: n/a
Contact: Bethule Nyamambi
Publishing areas: 17, 35, 43

**2156   Southern Africa Printing and
Publishing House/SAPES Trust**
109 Coventry Road
Workington
PO Box MP 1005
Harare
Tel: +263-4-621681-6/621803-7
Fax: +263-4-666061/621687

Email: sappho@samara.co.zw (General
enquiries) ibbo@sapes.org.zw (Chairperson,
SAPES Trust) mafa@sapes.org.zw (Executive
Director)
Web:
http://www.sapes.co.zw/webfiles/sapes_bo
oks.htm (SAPES Books)
Contacts: (Prof.) Ibbo Mandaza, Chairperson,
SAPES Trust; Mafa Sejanamane, Executive
Director; Trevor Harris, Editorial & Production
Manager
Publishing areas: 2, 17, 18, 20, 26, 27, 28, 29,
31, 36, 43, 45
Overseas distr: ABC

**2157   Southern African Research and
Documentation Centre (SARDC)**
15 Downie Avenue Belgravia
PO Box MP 5690
Harare
Tel: +263-4-791141/3 Fax: 263-4-791271
Email: sardc@sardc.net or smapasure@sardc.net
pjohnson@sardc.net (Director)
Web: http://www.sardc.net
Contacts: Phyllis Johnson, Director; Sabelo
Mapasure, Head of Programme (Information
and Knowledge Programme)
Publishing areas: 2, 17, 20, 26, 36, 45
Other: governance, water management and
resources
Overseas distr: ABC

2158   University of Zimbabwe Publications
PO Box MP 203
Harare
Tel: +263-4-303211 ext 1236
Fax: +263-4-333407/335249
Email: uzpub@admin.uz.ac.zw (General)
mtetwam@admin.uz.ac.zw (Director)
Web:
http://uzweb.uz.ac.zw/publications/books/
Publishing areas: 4, 5, 10, 17, 24, 27, 29, 30, 33, 36,
40, 42, 43, 45
Other: natural sciences
Contact: Munani S. Mtetwa, Director
Overseas distr: ABC

2159   Weaver Press Ltd
PO Box A1922
Avondale
Harare
Tel: +263-4-308330 Fax: +263-4-339645
Email: weaver@pci.co.zw or
weaver@mango.zw
Web: http://www.weaverpresszimbabwe.com

Contacts: Murray McCartney, Director; Irene Staunton, Director
Publishing: 2, 5, 6, 17, 20, 29, 32, 36, 41, 43, 44, 45
Other: child studies and child welfare, conservation
Overseas distr: ABC

2160   Women and Law in Southern Africa Research Trust
16 Lawson Avenue Milton Park
PO Box UA 171
Union Avenue
Harare
Tel: +263-4-253001/79340
Fax: +263-4-252884
Email: wlsa@samara.co.zw or
Wlsasly@africanonline.co.zw
Web: http://www.wlsa.co.zw/about.htm
Contacts: Sylvia Chirawu, National Co-ordinator; Sara Mvududu, Regional Coordinator
Publishing areas: 30, 45
Overseas distr: ABC

2161   Zimbabwe Women Writers
2 Harvey Brown Road
Milton Park
Private Bag A256
Harare
Tel: +263-4-796374 Fax: 263-4-751202
Email: zww@telco.co.zw
Web:
http://www.ecoweb.co.zw/entertainment/zim
_womenwriters.asp (site note accessible October 2005)
Contacts: Chiedza Musengezi, Director; Virginia Phiri, National Co-ordinator
Publishing areas: 4, 5, 6 (by women writers), 8, 45
Overseas distr: ABC

2162   ZPH Publishers (Pvt) Ltd
(formerly Zimbabwe Publishing House)
188 Arcturus Road
Kamfinsa
PO Box GD 510
Greendale
Harare
Tel: +263-497555-8/497548
Fax: +263-4-497554
Email: ndai@zph.co.zw

http://www.grace-notes.com/apg/default.html (African Publishing Group pages only)
Contacts: (Mrs) Ndai Nyamakura, Managing Director
Publishing areas: 5, 6, 8, 17, 27, 36
Other: a series of African travel guides under the company's African Publishing Group imprint.
Overseas distr: ABC
African Publishing Group: Global Book Marketing

EUROPE

Europe: Index and key to publisher subject areas

1   African art and art history
2173, 2174, 2179, 2181, 2185, 2187, 2228

2   African cultural studies (in general)
2165, 2169, 2173, 2174, 2177, 2179, 2181, 2184, 2187, 2193, 2194, 2196, 2197, 2198, 2199, 2201, 2203, 2208, 2210, 2219, 2227, 2228, 2231, 2238

3   African film and cinema
2174, 2194, 2196, 2210, 2238

4   African languages and linguistics
2171, 2174, 2181, 2184, 2185, 2186, 2194, 2204, 2212, 2219, 2222, 2228, 2233

5   African literature: Critical studies and collections
2164, 2165, 2165, 2169, 2171, 2173, 2174, 2175, 2177, 2179, 2180, 2181, 2184, 2185, 2193, 2194, 2198, 2199, 2206, 2208, 2210, 2212, 2214, 2219, 2222, 2227, 2228, 2230, 2233

6   African literature: Fiction
2165, 2166, 2169, 2171, 2172, 2173, 2174, 2177, 2178, 2180, 2199, 2200, 2208, 2214, 2223, 2237

7   African literature: Drama
2169, 2177

8   African literature: Poetry
2169, 2174, 2177, 2208

9   African music
2164, 2174, 2181, 2182, 2185, 2194, 2197, 2199, 2228

10   Agricultural sciences and agricultural development
2171, 2175, 2176, 2179, 2183, 2191, 2192, 2196, 2197, 2203, 2205, 2206, 2207, 2209, 2210, 2211, 2212, 2216, 2218, 2219, 2222, 2223, 2227, 2230, 2233, 2236, 2238

11   Anthropology and ethnology
2164, 2168, 2170, 2173, 2174, 2184, 2185, 2187, 2189, 2192, 2196, 2198, 2203, 2205, 2206, 2209, 2210, 2212, 2215, 2219, 2228, 2231, 2233, 2238

12   Archaeology and pre-history
2166, 2173, 2185, 2193, 2206, 2210, 2234

13   Architecture
2173, 2187, 2228, 2234

14   Biography and autobiography
2173, 2174, 2178, 2199, 2215, 2229, 2234

15   Constitutional and land law
2184, 2192, 2203, 2219

16   Diaspora studies
2171, 2174, 2178, 2185, 2209

17   Economics and development studies
2172, 2174, 2176, 2177, 2179, 2183, 2185, 2190, 2191, 2192, 2193, 2196, 2197, 2200, 2203, 2205, 2206, 2207, 2209, 2210, 2211, 2215, 2216, 2218, 2219, 2222, 2226, 2227, 2228, 2230, 2233, 2234, 2236, 2238

18   Education
2171, 2174, 2176, 2179, 2181, 2183, 2197, 2203, 2210, 2216, 2219, 2223, 2230, 2233, 2236, 2238

19   Entomology
–

20   Environmental studies
2171, 2176, 2191, 2192, 2197, 2199, 2203, 2210, 2211, 2218, 2222, 2227, 2231, 2233, 2238

21   Flora and fauna of Africa
2192, 2227

22   Folklore and oral cultures
2166, 2169, 2172, 2173, 2174, 2175, 2177, 2184, 2194, 2197, 2200, 2201, 2219, 2227

23   Food studies and food security
2191, 2192, 2197, 2207, 2219

24   Geography
2174, 2179, 2198, 2203, 2206, 2211, 2223, 2227, 2230, 2233, 2234

25   Geology and earth sciences
2179, 2198

26   Government and public administration
2222, 2223, 2230

27 History
2166, 2168, 2170, 2171, 2173, 2174, 2175, 2177, 2179, 2184, 2185, 2186, 2192, 2193, 2198, 2199, 2201, 2205, 2206, 2210, 2212, 2215, 2219, 2220, 2222, 2227, 2228, 2229, 2230, 2231, 2234, 2235, 2238

28 Human rights
2163, 2197, 2206, 2207, 2221, 2227, 2238

29 Labour studies
2176, 2192, 2197, 2203, 2210, 2219, 2222

30 Law
2163, 2184, 2185, 2192, 2219, 2228

31 Library and information sciences/Information technology
2179, 2188, 2198, 2217, 2236

32 Media and communication
2171, 2179, 2183, 2184, 2185, 2194, 2209, 2227, 2231, 2239

33 Medical and health studies/ Health care (including HIV/AIDS)
2171, 2176, 2179, 2181, 2184, 2185, 2192, 2196, 2197, 2207, 2211, 2216, 2222, 2223, 2226, 2227, 2233, 2236, 2238

34 Natural history
2206

35 Philosophy
2174, 2177, 2179, 2185, 2200, 2212, 2219, 2231

36 Politics, political economy, and international relations
2163, 2164, 2169, 2171, 2172, 2173, 2174, 2175, 2176, 2177, 2178, 2183, 2190, 2192, 2193, 2196, 2197, 2199, 2200, 2203, 2203, 2205, 2206, 2207, 2209, 2210, 2215, 2219, 2221, 2222, 2227, 2228, 2229, 2230, 2233, 2234, 2238

37 Psychology
2170, 2185, 2196, 2206

38 Reference
2171, 2173, 2174, 2176, 2179, 2183, 2184, 2187, 2188, 2192, 2193, 2198, 2205, 2206, 2210, 2211, 2212, 2213, 2216, 2217, 2219, 2222, 2227, 2232, 2233, 2234, 2235, 2239

39 Refugee and migration studies
2168, 2174, 2189, 2192, 2196, 2197, 2203, 2203 2206, 2209, 2210

40 Religion and theology
2170, 2171, 2174, 2177, 2181, 2185, 2192, 2193, 2197, 2198, 2200, 2206, 2207, 2209, 2212, 2215, 2219, 2222, 2227, 2228, 2234

41 Rural development
2174, 2176, 2191, 2192, 2196, 2197, 2203, 2216, 2222, 2226, 2236, 2238

42 Science and technology
2176

43 Sociology
2163, 2164, 2168, 2171, 2173, 2174, 2175, 2176, 2177, 2179, 2181, 2183, 2184, 2185, 2192, 2196, 2197, 2198, 2199, 2200, 2203, 2205, 2207, 2209, 2210, 2211, 2212, 2215, 2216, 2218, 2219, 2221, 2226, 2228, 2231, 2233, 2234, 2238

44 Urban studies
2168, 2171, 2174, 2176, 2183, 2192, 2196, 2197, 2203, 2206, 2210, 2211, 2219, 2233

45 Women's and gender studies
2168, 2171, 2173, 2174, 2177, 2179, 2181, 2185, 2189, 2192, 2196, 2197, 2199, 2203, 2205, 2207, 2209, 2210, 2212, 2216, 2218, 2219, 2226, 2231, 2233, 2238

Publishers of electronic & online products, ebooks, CD-ROM, and microfiche/ microfilm
2176, 2179, 2184, 2188, 2192, 2193, 2195, 2206, 2217, 2224, 2225, 2227, 2232, 2239

Belgium

2163 Académia Bruylant SA
Grand Place 29
1348 Louvain-la-Neuve
Tel +32-10-452395 Fax: +32-10-454480
Email: academia.bruylant@skynet.be
Web: http://www.academia-bruylant.be
Contact: Yves Wellemans, Managing
Director
Publishing areas: 28, 30, 36, 43
Other: Islamic studies

France

Note: major French publishers such as
Gallimard, Juillard, Albin Michel,
Seuil, etc. who publish occasional works
of African fiction, but who do not
publish non-fiction titles in African
studies, are not included here.

2164 Actes Sud
Le Méjan
BP 90038
13633 Arles Cedex
Tel: +33-4-90 49 86 91 Fax: +34-4-90 96 95 25
Email: contact@actes-sud.fr
Web: http://www.actes-sud.fr
Contact: Bertrand Py, Editorial director
Publishing areas: 5, 9, 11, 36, 43
Other: Islamic studies, photography

2165 Ana Éditions
BP 36
33019 Bordeaux - Cedex
Tel: +33-6-21 05 86 47
Email: ana.editions@free.fr
Web: http://ana.editions.free.fr/
Contact: n/a
Publishing areas: 2, 5, 6

2166 Les Classiques Africains
Saint-Paul France SA
3 rue Porte de Buc
BP 652
78006 Versailles Cedex
Tel: +33-1-39 67 16 00 Fax: +33-1-39 20 02 13
Email: n/a
Web: http://www.stpaulfrance.fr/ (site
under construction)
Contact: Daniel Beaudat, Director
Publishing areas: 6, 11, 12, 22, 27

2167 EDICEF
58 rue Jean-Bleuzen
92178 Vanves
75008 Paris
Tel: +33-1-46 62 10 01/55 00 11 89
Fax: +33-1-40 95 10 74
Email: smigne@hachette-livre.fr
Contact: Laurent Loric, Director
Publishing areas: 2, 5, 17, 18, 27, 36
Note: primarily an educational publisher,
part of the Hachette group.

2168 Editions Bouchène
113/115 rue Danielle Casanova
93200 Saint Denis
Tel: +33-1-48 20 93 75 Fax: +33-1-48 20 20 78
Email: edbouchene@wanadoo.fr
Web: http://www.bouchene.com
Contact: Abderrahmane Bouchène
Publishing areas: 6 (North African literature),
11, 27, 38, 43, 44, 45
Other: specialists on books on the countries
(and by authors) from the Maghreb.

2169 Editions Klanba
3 avenue Villemain
Paris 75014
Tel/Fax: +33-1-45 40 47 36
Email: klanba.editions@laposte.net
Web:
http://derives.free.fr/editions.htm
Contact: n/a
Publishing areas: 2, 5, 6, 7, 8, 22, 36

2170 Editions EHESS
(Éditions de l'École des Hautes
Études en Sciences Sociales)
131 boulevard Saint-Michel
75005 Paris
Tel: +33-1-53 10 53 55 Fax: +33-1-44 07 08 89
Email: edition@ehess.fr
Contacts: Pierre-Antoine Fabre, Jean-Yves
Grenier, Alice Ingold, Editorial department
Web:
http://www.ehess.fr/html/html/155.html
Publishing areas: 11, 27, 37, 40

2171 Editions Karthala
22-24 boulevard Arago
75013 Paris
Tel: +33-1-43 31 15 59 Fax: +33-1-45 35 27 05
Email:karthala@wanadoo.fr (General
enquiries) jeanf.leguilbayart@ceri.sciences-
pro.fr (Editor, African studies and
international relations)

georges.courade@bondy.ird.fr (Editor, Economics and development studies)
tourneux@vjf.cnrs.fr (Editor, Literature/Languages, Caribbean studies)
Web: http://www.karthala.com/
Contacts: Robert Agenau, Managing Director; Jean-Francois Bayart, Editor (African studies and international relations); Georges Courade, Editor (Economics and development studies); Henry Tourneux, Editor (Literature/Languages, Caribbean studies); for other contacts/subject areas *see* http://www.karthala.com/rubrique/contact.php
Publishing areas: 4, 5, 6, 10, 16, 18, 20, 27, 32, 33, 36, 38, 40, 43, 44, 45

2172 Editions Moreux
11 rue du Faubourgh Poissonière
75009 Paris
Tel: +33-1-49 49 07 49 Fax: +33-1-49 49 07 45
Email: webmaster-mtm@moreux.fr
Web: http://www.moreux.fr/
Contact: n/a
Publishing areas: 6, 17, 22, 36
Note: publishes primarily serial publications.

2173 Editions SEPIA
6 ave du Gouverneur Général Binger
94100 Saint-Maur-des-Fossés
Tel: +33-1-43 97 22 14 Fax: +33-1-43 97 32 62
Email: sepia@editions-sepia.com
Web: http://www.editions-sepia.com/
Contact: Patrick Mérand, Publisher and Chief Executive
Publishing areas: 1, 2, 5, 6, 11, 12, 13, 14, 22, 27, 36, 38, 43, 45
Other: African arts and crafts, travel and guide books, photographic works, children's books

2174 L'Harmattan, Edition-Diffusion
7 rue de l'Ecole Polytechnique
75005 Paris
Tel: +33-1-40 46 11 20(Orders/General)
Fax: +33-1-43 25 82 03 (Orders/General)
Tel: +33-1-40 46 79 14 (Editorial)
Fax: +33-1-43 29 86 20 (Editorial)
Email: harmattan1@wanadoo.fr (General/Editorial enquiries)
diffusion@harmattan@wanadoo.fr (Orders)
Web:
http://www.editions-harmattan.fr/
Contact: Denis Pryen, Managing Director; and editors of individual series (and see

online proposal form on Web site; publishes some 1,500 new titles annually)
Publishing areas: 1, 2, 3, 4, 5, 6, 8, 9, 11, 14, 16, 17, 18, 22, 24, 27, 35, 36, 38, 39, 40, 41, 43, 44, 45
Note: also a bookseller and distributor, *see* ➜ **2314**

2175 Maisoneuve et Larose
15 rue Victor-Cousin
75005 Paris
Tel: +33-1-1-44 41 49 37
Fax: +33-1-1-43 25 77 41
Email: servedit@wanadoo.fr
Web: http://perso.wanadoo.fr/marque-pages11/MaisonneuveLarose1.htm (site under construction) or
http://www.bibliomonde.net/pages/fiche-editeurs.php3?id_editeur=89
Publishing areas: 5, 10, 22, 27, 36, 43
Other: Arab, Islamic, and Oriental studies

2176 OEDC Publishing
Organisation for Economic Co-operation and Development
PAC Editorial and Rights
2 rue André Pascal
75775 Paris Cedex 16
Tel: +33-1-45 24 82 00
Fax: +33-1-45 24 13 91 (Rights enquiries)
Email: rights@oecd.org (Right enquiries)
Web:
http://www.oecd.org/EN/home/0,,EN-home-592-17-no-no-no-592,00.html (Editorial and Rights) publisher@oecd.orgm (Senior Editor)
Web: http://www.oecd.org/publications
OECD Paris Bookshop:
19, rue de Franqueville
75775 Paris Cedex 16
Tel: + 33-1-45 24 81 67 Fax: +33-1-45 24 19 50
Email: bookshop@oecd.org or sales@oecd.org. (Order enquiries, Online bookshop)
Web:
http://www.oecdbookshop.org/oecd/index.asp?lang=EN
Contact: Patrice Maubourguet, Publisher; Catherine Candea, Catherine Candea, Head of Editorial and Rights
Publishing areas: 10, 17, 18, 20, 29, 33, 36, 38, 41, 42, 43, 44
Other: electronic publications; statistical annuals, yearbooks and databases
UK distr: OECD, c/o Turpin Distribution Services Ltd, PO Box 22, Blackhorse Road,

Letchworth SG6 1YT, UK, Email:
books@turpinltd.com
North American distr: OECD Turpin North
America, PO Box 194, Downingtown, PA
19335-0194, USA. Email:
Bookscustomer@turpinna.com

2177 Présence Africaine
25 bis rue des Ecoles
75005 Paris
Tel: +33-1-43 54 13 74 Fax: +33-1-43 25 96 67
Contact: (Mme) Yandé Christiane Diop, Chief
executive
Email: presaf@club-internet.fr
Web: n/a
Publishing areas: 2, 5, 6, 7, 8, 17, 22, 27, 35, 36,
40, 43, 45
Note: also maintains a bookshop at the same
address, *see* **2316**

2178 Le Serpent à Plumes
20 rue des Petits Champs
75002 Paris
Tel: +33-1-55 35 95 85 Fax: +33-1-42 61 17 46
Email: contact@serpentaplumes.com (General
enquiries) p.astier@serpentaplumes.com
(Editorial Director)
Web: http://www.serpentaplumes.com/
(site not accessible October 2005)
Contact: Pierre Astier, Editorial Director
Publishing areas: 6, 14, 36

2179 UNESCO Publishing
7 place de Fontenoy
75352 Paris 07 SP
Tel: +33-1-45-68 43 37 (General enquiries)
Tel: +33-1-45 68 49 92 (Rights department)
Fax: +33-1-33-1-4568 55 89/45 68 57 41
Email: publishing.promotion@unesco.org
(General/Sales enquiries)
m.tanaka@unesco.org (Head
Publishing Section-BPI/PUB)
m.couratier@unesco.org (Chief, Publications,
Information and Documentation Section)
p.almeida@unesco.org (Rights and
permissions)
Web: http://upo.unesco.org/
Contacts: (Ms) Michiko Tanaka, Head
Publishing Section (BPI/PUB); Monique
Couratier, Chief, Publications, Information
and Documentation Section; Georgina
Almeida, Rights and Permissions
Publishing areas: 1, 2, 5, 10, 17, 18, 24, 25, 27,
31, 32, 33, 35, 38, 43, 45

Other: atlases and maps; online publications
and e-books
Note: although most books from UNESCO
Publishing are collective works written by
experts in different countries, a few titles are
also commissioned to specific leading
specialists on a given subject related to one of
UNESCO's fields of competence.
Distr: for distributors of UNESCO
publications worldwide *see*
http://publishing.unesco.org/distributors.as
px

2180 Vents d'ailleurs
11 route de Sainte-Anne
13640 La Roque d'Anthéron
Tel: +33-4-42 50 59 92 Fax: +33-4-42 50 58 03
Email: info@ventsdailleurs.com (General
enquiries) jhepke@ventsdailleurs.com
(Editor)
Web: http://www.ventsdailleurs.com/
Contacts: Jutta Hepke, Gilles Colleu
Publishing areas: 5, 6
Other: studies on Haiti and French Guyana;
photographic collections; children's books

Germany

Note: publishers in Germany producing
German translations of African works of
literature are not included here unless
they also publish non-fiction African
studies titles. For a listing of links to
German publishers offering African
writing in German translation visit the
links collection of the ➔ **Gesellschaft
zur Förderung der Literatur aus Afrika,
Asien, und Latinamerika e.V./Society
for the Promotion of African, Asian
and Latin American Literature (2596)**,
which can be found at
http://www.litprom.de/sites/dialog_e
nfrm.htm, click on to "Verlage mit
interessanten Übersetzungen".

2181   Bayreuth African Studies
Universität Bayreuth
95440 Bayreuth
Fax: +49-921-553627
Email: eckhard.breitinger@uni-bayreuth.de
Web: http://www.uni-bayreuth.de/Afrikanologie/publikationen/
Contact: (Prof.) Eckhard Breitinger
Publishing areas: 1, 2, 4, 5, 9, 18, 33, 40, 43, 45
UK distr: ➔ **Global Book Marketing (2338)**

2182   CWJEF Music Publications
Lerchenstrasse 85
70176 Stuttgart
Tel: +49-711-3582634
Fax: +49-711-3582632
Email: info@cwjefmusic.com
Web: http://www.cwjefmusic.com
Publishing areas: 9
Other: scores, sheet music, contemporary and traditional, by African composers and musicians
Note: formerly based in Vancouver, Canada

2183   Institut für Afrika-Kunde
Neuer Jungfernstieg 21
20354 Hamburg
Tel: +49-40-42 825 523
Fax: +49-40-42 825 511
Email: iak@iak.duei.de (General enquiries)
mehler@iak.duei.de (Director)
baumann@iak.duei.de (Publications)
Web:
http://www.duei.de/iak/show.php/de/content/publikationen/publikationen.html
(Publication pages, German)
http://www.duei.de/iak/show.php/en/content/publications/publications.html
(Publications pages, English) or
http://www.duei.de/iak/shop/en/
(Bookshop)
Contacts: (Dr.) Andreas Mehler, Director;
Ellen Baumann, Head of Publications
Publishing areas: 10, 17, 18, 32, 36, 38, 43, 44
Other: electronic publications

2184   Rüdiger Köppe Verlag
Sprachen und Kulturen
Wendelinstrasse 73-75
Postfach 45 06 43
50881 Cologne
Tel: +49-22-4911236/4911237
Fax: +49-221-4 99 4336
Email: info@koeppe.de

Web: http://www.koeppe.de/ (German version) http://www.koeppe.de/indexe.htm (English version)
Contact: Rüdiger Köppe, Managing Director
Publishing areas: 2, 4, 5, 11, 15, 22, 27, 30, 32, 33, 38, 43
Other: electronic publications; CD-ROMs; Berber Studies, Khoisan Studies; *Archiv afrikanistischer Manuskripte* (devoted to hitherto unpublished manuscripts and documents on the languages and literatures of Africa deposited in private and institutional libraries, which are now being rescued from obscurity and made available to the public through this series).
Note: publishes both in German and in English, and works in association with numerous research institutions in Germany active in the field of African studies, linguistics, and ethnology.

2185   LIT Verlag
Lektorat Afrika
Grevener Strasse 179
48159 Münster
Tel: +49-251-235091 Fax: +49-251-231972
Email: lit@lit-verlag.de (General enquiries)
vertrieb@lit-verlag.de (Orders) berlin@lit-verlag.de (Berlin office, for editorial proposals/submissions)
Web: http://www.lit-verlag.de/ also
http://www.lit-verlag.de/berlin/
Berlin Office (for editorial submissions):
Calvinstrasse 19
10557 Berlin
Tel: +49-30-610 7434 Fax: +49-30-610 74341
Contact: Veit-Dietrich Hopf, Director, Lektorat Afrika (Berlin Office)
Publishing areas: 1, 4, 5, 9, 11, 12, 16, 17, 27, 30, 32, 33, 35, 37 40, 43, 45
Note: publishes both in English and in German; editorial proposals and submissions to Berlin office.
US distr: Transaction Publishers Distributors, 390 Campus Drive, Somerset, NJ 08893 Email: orders@transactionpub.com

2186   Mouton de Gruyter
Genthiner Strasse 13
10785 Berlin
Tel: +49-30-260 050 Fax: +49-30-260 05251
Email: wdg-info@deGruyter.de (General enquiries) Anke.Beck@deGruyter.com
(Publishing Director, Linguistics /Communications, Literary Studies)

Web:
http://www.degruyter.de/index.html
(English version)
In the US:
Walter de Gruyter Inc
500 Executive Boulevard
Ossining NY 10562
Tel: +1-914-762 5866 Fax: +1-914-762 0371
Email: info@degruyterny.com (General
enquiries)
degruytermail@presswarehouse.com (Orders)
Contact: Anke Beck, Publishing Director,
Linguistics/Communications, Literary
Studies (and see online proposal form on Web
site)
Publishing areas:
4, 27
Other: Egyptology

2187   **Prestel Verlag/Prestel Publishing**
        Königinstrasse 9
        80539 Munich
Tel: +49-89-3817090 (General/Orders)
Tel: +49-89-381709 56 (Editorial)
Fax: +49-89-335175
Email: sales@prestel.de
(General/Orders) bauer@prestel.de
(Editorial)
Web: http://www.prestel.com/
In the UK: (Sales and editorial)
Prestel Publishing Ltd.
4 Bloomsbury Place
London WC1A 2QA
Tel: +44-(0)20-7323 5004
Fax: + 44-(0)20-7636-8004
Email: sales@prestel-uk.co.uk
In the US: (Sales and editorial)
Prestel Publishing
900 Broadway Suite 603
New York NY 10003
Phone: +1-212-995 27 20
Fax: +1-212-995 27 33
Email: sales@prestel-usa.com
Contact: Claudia Bauer (at Munich
headquarters)
Publishing areas: 1, 2, 11, 13, 38
Other: exhibition catalogues, museum guides,
photography, pictorial works
UK distr: Marston Book Services Ltd, PO Box
269, 160 Milton Park Estate, Abingdon OX14
4YN, Email: direct.orders@marston.co.uk

2188   **K.G. Saur Verlag GmbH**
        A Gale/Thomson Learning
        Company
        Ortlerstrasse 8
        Postfach 70 16 20
        81316 Munich
Tel. +49-89-769 020 Fax +49-89-769 02150
Email: saur.info@thomson.com (General
enquiries)
Clara.Waldrich@thomson.com (Publishing
Director)
Web: http://www.saur.de/
Contacts: Clara Waldrich, Publishing
Director; Barbara Fischer, Editor/Lektorat
Publishing areas: 31, 38
Other: → **African Biographical Archive (415)**
on microfiche; publisher of →**The African
Book Publishing Record (384)**,
→ **International African Bibliography (387)**
and → **African Books in Print (385)**
Distr: for details *see*
http://www.saur.de/index.cfm?content=ser
vice/01_howtoorder/frameset02.htm&menu
=service1

2189   **Transcript. Verlag für
        Kommunikation, Kultur und
        Soziale Praxis**
        Mühlenstrasse 47
        33607 Bielefeld
Tel: +49-5-216 3454 Fax +49-5-216 1040
Email: live@transcript-verlag.de
Web: http://www.transcript-verlag.de/
Contacts: Roswitha Gost, Editor-in-chief
Publishing areas: 11, 39, 45
Other: Islamic studies

2190   **Weltforum Verlag**
        Am Kreuter 8
        53177 Bonn
Tel: + 49-228-368 2430 Fax: +49-228-368 2439
Email: n/a
Web:
http://www.internationalesafrikaforum.de/
WfV/weltforum.html
Contact: Rena Sutor
Publishing areas: 17, 36
Notes: publishes on behalf of the Ifo-Institut
für Wirtschaftsforschung, Munich; →
**Bundesministerium für wirtschaftliche
Zusammenarbeit und Entwicklung (2657)**,
Berlin; and the Deutsches Institut für
Entwicklungspolitik.

The journal *Internationales Afrikaforum*, published by this company since 1964, ceased in 2004.

Italy

2191   Food and Agriculture Organization of the United Nations (FAO)
Sales and Marketing Group
Information Division
Viale delle Terme di Caracalla
00100 Rome
Tel: +39-6-5705 3215 Fax: +39-6-5705 3360
Email: publications-sales@fao.org (Orders)
Alain.Savary@fao.org (Head, Publishing section)
Web: http://www.fao.org/icatalog/inter-e.htm (Publications, English version)
Contact: Alain Savary (no submissions, FAO-commissioned material only)
Publishing areas: 10, 17, 20, 23, 41
Other: fisheries, food standard and commodities trade, forestry, genetics, land and water development, nutrition, legislation and investment, plant and animal protection; online publications, statistical data
US distr: Bernan Associates, 4611/F Assembly Drive, Lanham MD 20706-4391, Email: query@bernan.com Web: http://www.bernan.com; and The United Nations Bookshop, General Assembly Building Room 32 New York, NY 10017 Email: bookshop@un.org ; for sales agents elsewhere see Web site

Netherlands

2192   African Studies Centre
Pieter de la Courtgebouw Building
Faculty of Social Sciences
Wassenaarseweg 52
Postal address:
PO Box 9555
2300 RB Leiden
Tel: +31-71-527 3372/76 Fax +31-71-527 3344
Email: asc@ascleiden.nl (General enquiries)
lhaan@ascleiden.nl (Director)
reeves@ascleiden.nl (Publications Editor/Administrator)
Web:
http://www.ascleiden.nl/Publications/ (Publications)

Contacts: (Prof.) L.J. de Haan, Director;
Ann Reeves, Publications Editor/Administrator
Publishing areas: 10, 11, 15, 17, 20, 21, 23, 27, 29, 30, 33, 36, 38, 39, 40, 41, 43, 44, 45
Note: publisher of ➔ **African Studies Abstracts/African Studies Abstracts Online (396)**

2193   Brill Academic Publishers
Plantijnstraat 2
PO Box 9000
2300 PA Leiden
Tel: +31-71-535 3500 Fax: +31-71-531 7532
Email: cs@brill.nl (General enquiries)
wissink@brill.nl (Publishing Director, Social Sciences & Religion) bruinsma@brill.nl (History Publishing Unit Manager)
In the US:
Brill Academic Publishers Inc.
112 Water Street Suite 601
Boston MA 02109
Tel: +1-617-263 2323 Fax: +1-617-263 2324
Email: cs@brillusa.com (General enquiries)
Web: http://www.brill.nl/
Contacts: Jan-Peter Wissink, Publishing Director, Social Sciences and Religion; Sam Bruinsma, History Publishing Unit Manager, for other contacts *see*
http://www.brill.nl/m_brill.asp?sub=6
Publishing areas: 2, 5, 12, 17, 27, 36, 38, 40
Other: Arabic literature of Africa, Islamic studies, Oriental studies; electronic products

2194   Editions Rodopi BV
Tijnmuiden 7
1046 AK Amsterdam
Tel: +31-20-611 4821 Fax: +31-20-447 2979
In the US:
906 Madison Avenue
Union NJ 07083
Tel: +1- 908- 206 1166 Toll-free (US/Canada only) 800-225-3998
Fax: +1-908-206 0820
Email: info@rodopi.nl (General enquiries)
E.van.Broekhuizen@rodopi.nl (Publisher)
Web: http://www.rodopi.nl/
Contact: Eric van Broekhuizen, Publisher
Publishing areas: 2, 3, 4, 5, 9, 22, 32
Note: the main language of publication is English, but the list includes titles in German, French, and Spanish.

2195   IDC Publishers
Hogewoerd 151
POB 11205
2301 EE Leiden
Tel: +31-71-514 2700 Fax: +31-71-513 1721
Email: info@idc.nl
In the US:
IDC Publishers Inc.
350 Fifth Avenue Suite 1801
Empire State Building
New York NY 10118
Tel: +1-212-271 5945 Toll-free (USA/Canada only) 800-757-7441
Email: info@idcpublishers.com
Web: http://www.idc.nl/
Contacts: Victor van Beijnum, Managing Director, IDC Publishers, Netherlands; Todd Bludeau; Managing Director, IDC Publishers Inc, North America
Frans Havekes, Director, Publishing (Bibliographic Department)
Publishing areas: primary sources and rare archival materials on microform and in electronic formats.

2196   KIT Publishers
Mauritskade 63
PO Box 95001
1090 HA Amsterdam
Tel: +31-20-568 8272 Fax: +31-20-568 8286
Email: publishers@kit.nl (General enquiries)
r.smit@kit.nl (Head of Publishing)
l.schouten@kit.nl (Chief Editor)
Web: http://www.kit.nl/
Contacts: Ron Smith, Head of Publishing; Liesbeth Schouten, Chief Editor
Publishing areas: 2, 3, 10, 11, 17, 33, 36, 37, 39, 41, 43, 44, 45
Other: community management, intercultural communication, natural resources management, small-scale enterprises
UK distr: Marston Book Services, PO Box 269, Abingdon, OX14 4SD,
Email: orders@marston.co.uk
US distr: Stylus Publishing, PO Box 605, Herndon, VA 20172-0605 Email: stylusmail@presswarehouse.com
Web: http://www.styluspub.com

Sweden

2197   Nordiska Afrikainstitutet/ Nordic Africa Institute
Kungsgatan 38
POB 1703
751 47 Uppsala
Tel: +46-18-562200 Fax: +46-18-18-562290
Email: nai@nai.uu.se (General enquiries)
orders@nai.uu.se (Orders)
Lennart.Wohlgemuth@nai.uu.se (Director)
sonja.johansson@nai.uu.se (Editorial Manager)
Web: http://www.nai.uu.se/publ/publeng.html (English version)
Contact: Sonja Johansson, Editorial Manager
Publishing areas: 2, 9, 10, 17, 18, 20, 22, 23, 28, 29, 33, 36, 39, 40, 41, 43, 44, 45
Other: electronic publications (freely downloadable)
Note: publishes books in English, French and Swedish.
UK distr: ➜ **Global Book Marketing (2338)**
US distr: Stylus Publishing LLC
PO Box 605, Herndon VA 20172-0605
Email: stylusmail@presswarehouse.com
Web: http://www.styluspub.com

Switzerland

2198   Basler Afrika Bibliographien
Klosterberg 21-23
PO Box 2037
4001 Basel
Tel: +41-61-228 9333 Fax: +41-61-228 9330
Email: bab@bluewin.ch
Web: http://www.baslerafrika.ch/
Contacts: Dag Henrichsen, Pierrette Schlettwein
Publishing areas: 2, 5, 11, 24, 25, 27, 32, 38, 40, 43
Other: specializes in Namibian studies
Notes: also publishes under the imprint P. Schlettwein Publishing; maintains a library/resource centre (*see* ➜ **1262**) and an antiquarian bookshop (*see* ➜ **2329**).

2199   Éditions d'en bas
12 rue du Tunnel
Case Postale 304
1000 Lausanne 17
Tel: +41-21-323 3918 Fax: +41-21-312 3240
Email: enbas@bluewin.ch

Web: http://www.enbas.ch
Contact: Jean Richard
Publishing areas: 2, 5, 6, 9, 14, 20, 27, 36, 43, 45
Other: children's books by African authors

→ **Peter Lang European Academic Publishers** *see* under United States, entry **2266**

United Kingdom

2200   **Adonis & Abbey Publishers Ltd**
PO Box 43418
London SE11 4XZ
Tel: +44-(0)20-7793 8893/7463 2288
Email: editor@adonis-abbey.com
Web: http://www.adonis-abbey.com
Contact: Jideofor Adibe
Publishing areas: 6, 17, 22. 35, 36, 40 43

2201   **Akada Press**
Unit 24
Millmead Business Centre
Millmead Road
London N17 9QU
Tel: +44-(0)20-8801 2211
Fax: +44-(0)20-8801 2211
Email: info@akadapress.com
http://www.akadapress.com/home.htm
Publishing areas: 2, 22, 27
Other: Caribbean studies
Contact: David Benson

2202   **Ashgate Publishing Ltd**
Gower House
Croft Road
Aldershot GU11 3HR
Tel: +44-(0)1252-331551
Fax: +44-(0)1252-344405
Email: info@ashgatepub.co.uk (General enquiries)
In the US:
Ashgate Publishing Company
101 Cherry Street Suite 420
Burlington VT 05401-4405
Tel: +1-802-865 7641 Fax: +1-802-865 7847
Email: info@ashgate.com
khowgate@ashgatepub.co.uk (Senior Editor, International Relations and Politics);
bgeorge@ashgatepub.co.uk (Senior Editor, Academic Business, Economics)
cwintersgill@ashgatepub.co.uk (Editor, Sociology, Ethnic and Gender Studies, Social Policy and Social Work)

Web: http://www.ashgate.com/
Contacts: Kirstin Howgate, Senior Editor, International Relations and Politics; Brendan George, Senior Editor, Academic Business, Economics; Caroline Wintersgill, Editor, Sociology, Ethnic and Gender Studies, Social Policy and Social Work; for the complete list of editorial contacts *see*
http://www.ashgate.com/contact.htm
Publishing areas: 2, 10, 15, 17, 18, 20, 24, 29, 36, 39, 41, 43, 44, 45
US distr: Ashgate Publishing Company, PO Box 2225, Williston, VT 05495-2225
Email: orders@ashgate.com

2203   **Berghahn Books**
3 Newtec Place
Magdalen Road
Oxford OX4 1RE
Tel: +44(0)1865-250011
Fax: +44(0)1865-250056
In the US:
Berghahn Books Inc
150 Broadway Suite 812
New York NY 10038
Tel: +1-212-222 6502 Fax: +1-212-222 5209
Email: publicityUK@berghahnbooks.
(General/Sales, UK)
productionUK@berghahnbooks.com
(Editorial, UK)
publisher@berghahnbooks.com (Publisher, UK) productionUS@berghahnbooks.com
(Editorial, US)
Web: http://www.berghahnbooks.com/
Contact: Marion Berghahn, Publisher
Publishing areas: 11, 36, 39

2204   **Joseph Biddulph Publisher**
32 Stryd Ebeneser
Pontypridd CF37 5PB
Cymru/Wales
Tel: +44-1443-662559
Email: n/a
Web:
http://www.cs.vu.nl/~dick/biddulph/
(hosted in the Netherlands)
Contact: Joseph Biddulph
Publishing areas: 4 (published in simple formats)

2205 Blackwell Publishing Ltd
9600 Garsington Road
Oxford OX4 2DQ
Tel: +44-(0)1865-776868
Fax: +(0)44-1865- 714591
customerservices@blackwellpublishing.com
or direct.orders@marston.co.uk
(General/Orders)
philip.carpenter@oxon.blackwellpublishing.com
(Academic & Science Books Director)
nigel.balmforth@oxon.blackwellpublishing.com (Publisher, Aquaculture and Fisheries, Nutrition, Food Science, Agriculture)
tessa.harvey@oxon.blackwellpublishing.com (Associate Editorial Director, History)
justin.vaughan@oxon.blackwellpublishing.com (Publisher, Human Geography, Sociology and Politics}; for other editorial contacts *see* http://www.blackwellpublishing.com/contacts/employee.asp?site=1#ukbooked (in UK)
http://www.blackwellpublishing.com/contacts/employee.asp?site=1#usbooked (in US)
In the US:
Blackwell Publishing
350 Main Street
Malden MA 02148
Tel: +1-781-388 8200 Fax: +1-781-388 8210
mlloyd@bos.blackwellpublishing.com
Web: http://www.blackwellpublishing.com/
Contacts: Philip Carpenter, Academic & Science Books Director; Nigel Balmforth Publisher, Aquaculture and Fisheries, Nutrition, Food Science, Agriculture; Tessa Harvey, Associate Editorial Director, History; Justin Vaughan, Publisher Human Geography, Sociology and Politics
Publishing areas: 10, 11, 17, 27, 36, 38, 43, 45

2206 Cambridge University Press
The Edinburgh Building
Cambridge CB2 2RU
Tel: +44-(0)1223-312393
Fax: +44-(0)1223-315052
Email information@cambridge.org (General enquiries) ukcustserve@cambridge.org (Orders, UK) intcustserve@cambridge.org (Orders, International)
editorial@cambridge.org (Editorial, UK)
Web: http://www.cambridge.org/
In the US:
Cambridge University Press
40 West 20th Street
New York NY 10011-4221
Tel: +1-212-924 3900 Fax: +1-212-691 3239

Email: information@cup.org (General enquiries) orders@cup.org (Orders) macland@cambridge.org (Editorial, History and Area Studies) jhaslam@cambridge.org (Editorial, Politics and International Relations and Sociology)
Web: http://www.cambridge.org/us/
Contacts, in the UK: Marigold Acland, History and Area Studies; John Haslam, Politics and International Relations and Sociology; for contacts in other subject areas *see* https://authornet.cambridge.org/information/proposaluk/hss/#editorial
Contacts, in the US: Alia Winters, African Studies, Criminology, Sociology, Email: awinters@cup.org
for contacts in other subject areas *see* http://us.cambridge.org/information/authors.htm
Publishing areas: 5, 10, 11, 12, 17, 24, 27, 28, 34, 36, 37, 38, 39, 40, 44
Other: electronic products

➔ **Frank Cass & Co Ltd** *see* **Routledge (2233)**

2207 Catholic Institute for International Relations (CIIR)
Unit 3 Canonbury Yard
190a New North Road
London N1 7BJ
Tel: +44-(0)20-7354 0883
Fax: +44-(0)20-7359 0017
Email: ciir@ciir.org (General enquiries) sales@ciir.org (Orders) christine@ciir.org (Executive Director) judith@ciir.org (Regional Manager, Africa/Middle East)
Web: http://www.ciir.org/Templates/system/basket.asp?nodeid=89630 (Publications pages)
Contacts: Christine Allen, Executive Director; Judith Gardner, Regional Manager, Africa/Middle East
Publishing areas: 10, 17, 23, 28, 33, 36, 40, 43, 45
Submission restrictions: commissioned work only.

2208 Ayebia Clarke Literary Agency & Publishing Ltd
7 Syringa Walk
Banbury OX16 1FR
Tel: +44-(0)1295-709228 (Editorial/Submissions) Tel: +44-(0)208-829 3008 (Customer Services/Orders)

Fax: +44 (0)1295-267681 (Editorial/
Submissions)
Fax: +44-(0)208-881 50887
(Customer Services/Orders)
Email: info@ayebia.co.uk
(Editorial/Submissions)
orders@turnaround-uk.com
(Customer Services/Orders)
Web: http://www.ayebia.co.uk/
Contacts: Becky Ayebia, David Clarke
Publishing areas: 2, 5, 6, 8
Other: Caribbean writing

2209   The Continuum International
Publishing Group
The Tower Building
11 York Road
London SE1 7NX
Tel: +44-(0)207-922 0880
Fax: +44-(0)207-922 0881
Email: info@continuum-books.com (General)
ahaynes@continuumbooks.com (Publishing
Director, Academic lists)
awebster@continuumbooks.com (Senior
Commissioning Editor, Education & Social
Sciences) asandeman@continuumbooks.com
(Senior Commissioning Editor Humanities)
In the US:
The Continuum International Publishing
Group
Madison Square Park
15 East 26th Street, Suite 1703
New York NY 10010
 info@continuum-books.com
Tel: +1-212-953 5858 Fax: +1-212-953 5944
Email: info@continuum-books.com (General)
Web:
http://www.continuumbooks.com/(ptq24i45
15htro45id3y25rx)/Location.aspx
Contacts, in the UK: Anthony Haynes,
Publishing Director, Academic lists;
Alexandra Webster, Senior Commissioning
Editor Education & Social Sciences; Anna
Sandeman, Senior Commissioning Editor
Humanities
Contacts, in the US: Frank Oveis, VP and
Senior Editor Catholic Studies, Spirituality,
Judaica, and Current Affairs, Email:
 frank@continuum-books.com
Evander Lomke, VP and Senior Editor
Literary Criticism, Performing Arts, Social
Thought, and Women's Studies, Email:
evander@continuum-books.com
Publishing areas: 10, 11, 16, 17, 32, 36, 39, 40,
43, 45

Note: Continuum London continues the
academic publishing lists of Cassell/Cassell
Academic, including the Pinter, Mansell, and
Leicester University Press imprints, as well as
➔ **Thoemmes Press (2235).** Continuum also
publish a small number of titles from
the ➔ **Institute of Commonwealth Studies**
(1279)
Distr: for distributors worldwide (and
additional editorial contacts) *see*
http://www.continuumbooks.com/(ptq24i45
15htro45id3y25rx)/Contact.aspx#UKedit

2210   James Currey Publishers Ltd
73 Botley Road
Oxford OX2 0BS
Tel: +44-(0)1865-244111
Fax: +44-(0)1865-246454
Email: mary.tinker@jamescurrey.co.uk
(General enquiries/Office Administrator)
Email: editorial@jamescurrey.co.uk (Editorial,
general enquiries)
douglas.johnson@jamescurrey.co.uk
(Editorial Director)
lynn.taylor@jamescurrey.co.uk (Editorial
Manager)
sales@jamescurrey.co.uk (Orders) or
info@globalbookmarketing.co.uk
Web: http://www.jamescurrey.co.uk/
Contacts: James Currey, Chairman; Douglas
H. Johnson, Managing Director and Editorial
Director (manuscript submissions for
anthropology, archaeology, economics,
development, history, politics); Lynn Taylor,
Editorial Manager (manuscript submissions
for literary criticism, theatre and film,
Caribbean studies)
Publishing areas: 2, 3, 5, 10, 11, 12, 17, 18, 20,
27, 29, 36, 38, 39, 43, 44, 45
Other: Caribbean studies
Submission restrictions: initial enquiries may
be sent by post or email. Email attachments
not accepted unless requested by the
publisher; entire manuscripts or sample
chapters by email not accepted.
Note: ➔ **The Africa Book Centre (2331)**
holds stocks of a full range of James Currey
titles.
Distr (trade orders): Marston Book Services
Ltd, PO Box 269, Abingdon, Oxon, OX14
4YN, Email: trade.orders@marston.co.uk

2211   Earthscan/James & James
8-12 Camden High Street
London NW1 0JH
Tel: +44-(0)20-7387 8558
Fax: +44-(0)20-7387 8998
Email: orders@earthscan.co.uk (General and
orders) publisher@earthscan.co.uk
(Editorial/Book proposals)
Web: http://www.earthscan.co.uk
Contact: Jonathan Sinclair Wilson, Director;
Frances MacDermott, Publishing Manager
Publishing areas: 10, 17, 20, 24, 33,
38, 43, 44, 45

2212   Edinburgh University Press
22 George Square
Edinburgh EH8 9LF
Tel: +44-(0)131-650 4218
Fax: +44-(0)131-662 0053
Email: marketing@eup.ed.ac.uk
(Sales/Marketing) editorial@eup.ed.ac.uk
(Editorial) Jackie.Jones@eup.ed.ac.uk
(Editorial Director)
Web: http://www.eup.ed.ac.uk/
Contacts: Jackie Jones, Editorial Director;
submit proposals to Alison Bowden
Publishing areas: 4, 5, 10, 11, 27, 35, 38, 40, 43,
44, 45
Submission note: publishes on behalf of the
➔ **International African Institute (1622,
2217)**; all ms. proposals for IAI must be
submitted through International African
Institute, School of Oriental and African
Studies, Thornhaugh Street, Russell Square,
London, WC1A 0XG.
UK distr: Marston Book Services Ltd, PO Box
269, Abingdon, Oxon, OX14 4YN,
Email: trade.sales@marston.co.uk
US distr: Columbia University Press, 136
South Broadway, Irvington NY 10533
Email: cup_book@columbia.edu

2213   Europa Publications
Taylor & Francis Group Ltd
11 New Fetter Lane
London EC4P 4EE
Tel: +44-(0)20-7842 2133
Fax: +44-(0)20-7842 2249
Email: info.europa@tandf.co.uk (General
enquiries) sales.europa@tandf.co.uk
(Sales/Orders) edit.europa@tandf.co.uk
(Editorial)
Web:
http://www.europapublications.co.uk/

Contact: Paul Kelly, Editorial Director; send
manuscript proposals to The Development
Projects Editors
Publishing areas: 38
Other: electronic products
Note: part of Routledge Reference, in the
Taylor & Francis Group.

2214   Heinemann International
Halley Court
Jordan Hill
Oxford OX2 8EJ
Tel: +44-(0)1865-888084
Fax: +44-(0)1865-314169
Email: orders@heinemann.co.uk
or international@harcourteducation.co.uk
In the US: (see also ➔ *entry* **2261**)
Heinemann Publishers
361 Hanover Street
Portsmouth NH 03801-3912
Tel: +1-603-431 7894 Fax: +1-603-431-7840
Email: custserv@heinemann.com (Customer
Services/Orders)
Web:
http://www.heinemann.co.uk or
http://www.harcourteducation.co.uk/
http://www.africanwriters.com (African
Writers Series)
Contacts: Nigel Kelly, Publishing Director,
International Division; any queries regarding
submissions to "African Writers Series" to
Robert Sulley or Charlotte Rosen-Svenson,
but see note below.
Publishing areas: 5, 6*
Note: in November 2002 Heinemann's
decided not to pursue new titles for the
"African Writers Series" at the present time,
although the backlist will continue to be
maintained and actively promoted. The series
is now also available in full-text digital format
(as an add-on to *Literature Online*) from ➔
ProQuest/Chadwyck Healey (2232), *see*
http://www.proquest.com/products/pd-
product-aws

2215   C. Hurst & Co (Publishers)
38 King Street
Covent Garden
London WC2E 8JT
Tel: +44-(0)20-7240 2666
Fax: +44-(0)20-7240 2667
Email: hurst@atlas.co.uk
Web: http://www.hurstpub.co.uk/
(site not accessible 20/10/05, being
reconstructed)

Contacts: Christopher Hurst, Managing Director; Michael J. Dwyer, Director
Publishing areas: 11, 14, 17, 27, 36, 40, 43
Other: Islamic and Middle Eastern studies

2216   Institute of Development Studies
University of Sussex
Publications Office
Brighton BN1 9RE
Tel: +44-(0)1273-678269/606261
Fax: +44(0)1273-621202/691647
Email: publications@ids.ac.uk or
G.Edwards@ids.ac.uk
Web: http://www.ids.ac.uk/ids/ (Home page)
http://www.ids.ac.uk/ids/bookshop/index.html (Bookshop/Publications)
Contacts: Gary Edwards, Publications Office
Publishing areas: 10, 17, 18, 33, 38, 41, 43, 45
Other: working/discussion papers, research reports, policy briefings
Submission restrictions: commissioned ms submissions from IDS Fellowship only.

**2217   International African Institute/
           Institut africain international**
SOAS
Thornhaugh Street
Russell Square,
London WC1H OXG
Tel: +44-(0)20-7898 4420 (General)
Tel: +44-(0)20-7898 4435 (Publications)
Fax: +44-(0)20-7898 4419
Email: iai@soas.ac.uk (General enquiries)
ed2@soas.ac.uk (Editorial)
Web: http://www.iaionthe.net
Contact: Robert Molteno, Chairman, Publications Committee
Publishing areas: 2, 4, 5, 10, 11, 15, 17, 18, 22, 23, 27, 29, 30, 35, 36, 38, 40, 43, 44, 45
Other: business/enterprise
Note: publishes in association with ➔
Edinburgh University Press (2212), ➔ James
Currey Publishers (2210), and ➔ **LIT Verlag
(2185)**.

**2218   International Network for the
           Availability of Scientific
           Publications (INASP)**
58 St. Aldates
PO Box 516
Oxford OX1 1WG
Tel: +44-(0)1865-249909
Fax: +44-(0)1865-251060

Email: psmart@inasp.info
Web:
http://www.inasp.info/pubs/index.html
Contact: Pippa Smart, Senior Programme Manager (Publishing)
Publishing areas: 31, 38
Other: African publishing and booktrade; electronic book and journal publishing; IT training materials and resources

2219   ITDG Publishing
Bourton Hall
Bourton-on-Dunsmore
Rugby CV23 9QZ
Tel +44-(0)1926-634501
Fax +44-(0)1926-634502
Email: proposals@itpubs.org.uk
Web: http://www.itdgpublishing.org.uk/ (Publishing)
http://www.developmentbookshop.com/ (Bookshop) toby.milner@itdg.org.uk (Managing Director)
Contact: Toby Milner, Managing Director
Publishing areas: 10, 17, 20, 43, 45
Other: alternative finance, appropriate technology, building, business, child issues, fisheries, food processing, energy, transport, water

2220   Ituri Publications
4 Chestnut Close
Woodford Halse NN11 3NB
Tel/Fax: 44-(0)1327-264725
Email: rick@pulfordmedia.co.uk
Web:
http://www.pulfordmedia.co.uk/ituri/ituriframe.htm
Contact: Cedric Pulford
Publishing areas: 27

2221   Justice Africa
1C Leroy House
436 Essex Road
London N1 3QP
Tel: +44-(0)207-354 8400
Fax: +44-(0)207-354 8736
Email: enquiries@justiceafrica.org or
Tajudeen28@yahoo.com
Web:
http://www.justiceafrica.org/books.html
Contact: Tajudeen Abdul Raheem
Publishing areas: 28, 36, 43
Other: HIV/AIDS; specializes in publications and occasional papers on the Sudan, the Horn of Africa, and the Great Lakes region

2222   Kegan Paul International Ltd
POB 256
London WC1B 3SW
Tel: +44(0)20-7580 5511
Fax: +44(0)20-7436 0899
Email: books@keganpaul.com
Web: http://www.keganpaul.com/
Contacts: Peter Hopkins, Chairman and
Managing Director; Kaori O'Connor, Editorial
Director
Publishing areas: 4, 5, 10, 17, 20, 26, 27, 29, 33,
36, 38, 40, 41

→ **Longman** see **Pearson Education (2230)**

2223   Macmillan Africa
Macmillan (Oxford)
Between Towns Road
Oxford OX4 3PP
Tel: +44-(0)1865-405700
Fax: +44-(0)1865-405701
Email: MacmillanAfrica@macmillan.co.uk
(General enquiries) alison.hubert@mhelt.com
(Manuscript proposals)
Web: http://www.macmillan-africa.com/
Contact: Alison Hubert
Publishing areas: 6, 10, 18, 24, 26, 33,
Other: fiction for teenagers and young adults;
maps, wall charts
Note: primarily a publisher of educational
textbooks and supplementary reading
materials; for academic titles see → **Palgrave
Macmillan (2228).**

→ **Macmillan Education** see **Palgrave
Macmillan (2228)**

2224   Adam Matthew Publications Ltd
Pelham House
London Road
Marlborough SN8 2AA
Tel: +44-(0)1672-511921
Fax: +44-(0)1672-511663
Email: info@ampltd.co.uk (General enquiries)
orders@ampltd.co.uk (Orders)
Web: http://www.adam-matthew-
publications.co.uk/index.htm
Contacts: William Pidduck, Director/
Publisher; David Tyler, Director/Publisher
Publishing areas: original manuscript
collections, rare printed books and other
primary source material on microform and in
electronic format, including African colonial
journals, abolition and anti-slavery papers,
Church Missionary Society archives, and

original manuscripts from the Royal
Commonwealth Society

**2225   Microform Imaging Ltd/
Microform Academic Publishers**
Main Street
East Ardsley
Wakefield WF3 2AT
Tel: +44-(0)1924-825700
Fax: +44-(0)1924-871005
Email: MAP@microform.co.uk (General
enquiries/Orders) pknights@microform.co.uk
(Editor)
Web: http://www.microform.co.uk/
(General)
http://www.microform.co.uk/academic/ind
ex.php
Contacts: Michelle Mortimer, Publishing
Manager; Paul Knights, Editor
Publishing areas: titles on microfilm,
microfiche and on CD-ROM, covering
African/African studies journals and
magazines, archival papers and collections,
catalogues, reports, accounts, government
publications, and parliamentary papers

2226   Oxfam Publishing
Oxfam House
John Smith Drive
Cowley
Oxford OX4 2JY
Tel: +44-(0)1865-472255
Fax: +44-(0)1865-472393
Email: publish@oxfam.org.uk
Web:
http://publications.oxfam.org.uk/oxfam/def
ault.asp?TAG=&CID=
Contact: Robert Cornford, Sales and
Marketing Manager and Deputy Team
Leader
Publishing areas: 17, 33, 41, 43, 45
Other: development management,
emergency work and humanitarian
issues, NGO policy and practice
Distr: for a list of Oxfam Publishing's agents
and distributors worldwide see
http://publications.oxfam.org.uk/oxfam/dis
tributors.asp#1
Note: most of Oxfam's published material is
written and developed by Oxfam staff and
partners.

2227 Oxford University Press
Great Clarendon Street
Oxford OX2 6DP
Tel: +44-(0)1865-556767
Fax: +44-(0)1865-267741
Email: bookorders.uk@oup.com
(Customer Services/orders)
highereducation.europe@oup.com (Higher
education textbook proposals); for other
email contacts *see*
http://www.oup.co.uk/contactus/ukcontact
s/
Web: http://www.oup.co.uk/
In the US:
Oxford University Press Inc USA
198 Madison Avenue
New York NY10016
Tel: +1-212-726 6000
Fax: +1-212-726 6440
Email custserv@oup-usa.org (Customer
service)
Web: http://www.oup.com/us/?view=usa
Contacts, in the UK: Sarah Caro, Publisher,
Economics; Christopher Wheeler, Publisher,
History; Andrew McNeillie, Senior
Commissioning Editor, Literature; Dominic
Byatt, Chief Editor, Politics, International
Relations, and Sociology
for contacts of commissioning editors in other
areas, and for email addresses for some of the
above, *see*
http://www.oup.co.uk/contactus/ukcontact
s/
Contacts, in the US: *see*
http://www.us.oup.com/us/information/ed
itors/higher.education/?view=usa (Higher
education textbooks) or
http://www.us.oup.com/us/corporate/cont
acteditor/scholarlypopular/?view=usa
(Scholarly and popular titles)
Submission restrictions: does not accept
unsolicited academic submissions by email
Publishing areas: 2, 5, 10, 17, 20, 21, 22, 24, 27,
28, 32, 33, 36, 38, 40
Other: electronic products

2228 Palgrave Macmillan
Houndmills
Basingstoke RG21 6XS
Tel: +44-(0)1256-329242 (General)
Fax: +44-(0)1256-479476
Email: bookenquiries@palgrave.com (General
enquiries) orders@palgrave.com (Orders)
s.burridge@palgrave.com (Scholarly &
Reference Director)

f.arnold@palgrave.com (Publishing Director,
College Division)
Web: http://www.palgrave.com/
In the US:
Palgrave Macmillan/St. Martin's Press
175 Fifth Avenue
New York NY 10010
Tel: +212-982 3900 Toll-free (USA/Canada
only) 800-221-7945
Fax: +212-777 6359
Web: http://www.palgrave-usa.com/
Contacts, in the UK: Samantha Burridge,
Scholarly & Reference Director; France
Arnold, Publishing Director, College
Division; for Publishers and Commissioning
Editors by subject area see
http://www.palgrave.com/contactus/contac
ts/editorial.htm#Academic
Contacts, in the US:
Ella Pearce, Commissioning Editor, African
Studies & Latino & Latin American Studies
for other contacts *see* http://www.palgrave-
usa.com/Info/Submissions.aspx
Publishing areas: 1, 2, 4, 5, 9, 11, 13, 17, 27, 30,
36, 40, 43
Submission restrictions: does accept
unsolicited submissions by email or
telephone.
Note: Palgrave combines the publishing lists
of the former Macmillan Press, UK, and St.
Martin's Press in the United States.

2229 Panaf Books
75 Weston Street
London SE1 3RS
Orders to:
19 Muirfield
Great Denham
Bedford MK40 4FB
Tel: +44-(0)870-333 1192
Fax: +44-(0)870-333 1196
Email: zakakembo@yahoo.co.uk
Web: http://www.panafbooks.com/
Contact: June Milne Director, and
Literary Executrix of Kwame Nkrumah
Publishing areas: 14, 27, 36
Other: specialists in books on Pan
Africanism and the writings of Kwame
Nkrumah

→ **Pathfinder Press** *see* under United States,
entry **2280**

2230   Pearson Education
Edinburgh Gate
Harlow CM20 2JE
Tel: +44(0)1279-623928
Fax: +44(0)1279-414130
Email: HEEnquiriesUK@pearsoned-ema.com
(General enquiries)
christina.wipf-perry@pearson.com
(Commissioning Editor, History)
philip.langeskov@pearson.com
(Commissioning Editor, Literature and
Linguistics) morten.fuglevand@pearson.com
(Commissioning Editor, Psychology and
Politics)
Web: http://www.pearsoned.co.uk/ or
http://vig.pearsoned.co.uk/
In the US:
Pearson Education
One Lake Street
Upper Saddle River NJ 07458
Tel: 1-201-236 7000
Email: Communications@pearsoned.com
Web: http://www.pearsoned.com/
Contacts: Christina Wipf-Perry,
Commissioning Editor, History;
Philip Langeskov, Commissioning Editor,
Literature and Linguistics; Morten
Fuglevand, Commissioning Editor,
Psychology and Politics; for additional
professional and higher education editorial
contacts see
http://vig.pearsoned.co.uk/getContent/0,29
48,aHR0cDovL3d3dy5wZWФyc29uZWQuY28
udWsvQWNhZGVtaWMvQXV0aG9ycy9Db2
50YWN0cy8=,00.html
Publishing areas: 5, 10, 17, 18, 24, 26, 27, 36
Other: electronic products
Note: Pearson Education was created in
November 1998 through the merger of
Addison Wesley Longman, Prentice Hall
Europe and Financial Times Management;
now primarily an educational publisher
(further and higher education).

2231   Pluto Press
Pluto Publishing Ltd
345 Archway Road
London N6 5AA
Tel: +44-(0)20-8348 2724
Fax: +44-(0)20-8348 9133
Email: pluto@plutobooks.com (General
enquiries/Orders) rogervz@plutobooks.com
(Chairman) robert.webb@plutobooks.com
(Managing Editor)
Web: http://www.plutobooks.com/

Contacts: Roger van Zwanenberg, Chairman;
Robert Webb, Managing Editor
Publishing areas: 2, 11, 20, 27, 32, 36, 43, 45
US distributor: University of Michigan Press,
c/o Chicago Distribution Center, 11030 South
Langley Avenue, Chicago IL 60628, Email:
custserv@press.uchicago.edu

2232   ProQuest Information and Learning
(incorporating Chadwyck-Healey)
The Quorum
Barnwell Road
Cambridge CB5 8SW
Tel: +44(0)-1223-215 512
Fax:+44 (0)-1223-215 514
Email: marketing@proquest.co.uk
(Sales/Orders) julie.carroll-
davis@proquest.co.uk (Vice-President of
Publishing) dan.burnstone@proquest.co.uk
(Senior Publisher, Academic)
tom.jackson@proquest.co.uk (Senior
Publisher, Reference & Schools)
Web: http://www.proquest.co.uk/pr
ducts/index.asp
In the US:
ProQuest Information and Learning
300 North Zeeb Road
PO Box 1346
Ann Arbor MI 48106–1346
Tel: +1-734-761 4700 Toll-free (US/Canada
only) 800-521 0600 Fax: +1-734-975 6430
Email: info@il.proquest.com or
pqsales@il.proquest.com
http://www.il.proquest.com
Contacts, in UK: Julie Carroll David, Vice
President of Publishing; Dan Burnstone,
Senior Publisher, Academic; Tom Jackson,
Senior Publisher, Reference & Schools
Publishing areas: 38 (including
national library catalogues, catalogues of
archival collections, periodical indexes,
statistical serials, etc. on CD ROM,
microfiche, microfilm, and print)
Other: Web-based online information
systems
Notes: includes Chadwyck-Healey, UMI,
XanEdu, and ➔ **Norman Ross Publishing
(2284);**
 ProQuest/Chadwyck-Healey is now also
offering full-text access to 66 titles in the
➔ **Heinemann (2214)** *African Writers
Series* (1962 to present), integrated as
an add-on to its *Literature Online* product,
enabling users cross-searching with 350,000

other literary works, and critical and reference material support; *see also* http://www.proquest.com/products/pd-product-aws

→ **Radcliffe Press** *see* **I.B. Tauris (2234)**

2233 Routledge
Routledge Books
2 Park Square
Milton Park
Abingdon OX14 4RN
Tel: +44-(0)20-7017 6000
Fax: +44 (0)20-7017 6699
Email: info@routledge.co.uk
Web: http://www.routledge.com/
In the US: (Editorial & Marketing Offices)
Routledge
270 Madison Avenue
New York NY 10016-0602
Tel: +1-212-216 7800
Fax: +1-212-564 7854
Email: info@taylorandfrancis.com
 (General enquiries) cserve@routledge-ny.com (Customer Services)
specialsales@taylorandfrancis.com (Trade and library orders)
Web: http://www.routledge-ny.com
Contacts: Routledge UK: n/a (address proposals to relevant Commissioning Editor, e.g. Editor: Politics, International Relations)
Contacts, in US: *see* http://www.routledge-ny.com/util/resources.asp?filename=publish_with_us.htm
Publishing areas: 4, 5, 10, 11, 17, 18, 20, 24, 33, 36, 38, 43, 44, 45
Submission restrictions: does not accept proposals by email
Note: a member of the Taylor & Francis Group, includes Garland Publishing and → **Fitzroy Dearborn Publishers (2258)**; and from 2005 also includes new titles published under the former Frank Cass imprint.

2234 I.B. Tauris & Co Ltd
6 Salem Road
London W2 4BU
Tel: +44-(0)20-7243 1225
Fax: +44-(0)20-7243 1226
In the US:
I.B.Tauris & Co Ltd
St Martin's Press
175 Fifth Avenue

New York NY 10010
Tel: +1-212-982 3900 Fax: +1-212-777 6359
Email: mail@ibtauris.com (General enquiries)
sales@ibtauris.com (Orders)
lestercrook@hotmail.com (Commissioning Editor, History and Regional Studies)
100674.3022@compuserve.com (Commissioning Editor, Geography and Reference) brewster@dircon.co.uk (Commissioning Editor, Film and Cultural Studies) isteer@ibtauris.com (US Publishing Manager)
Web: http://www.ibtauris.com
Contacts, in the UK: Lester Crook, Commissioning Editor, History and Regional Studies; Stonestreet, Commissioing Editor, Geography and Reference; Philippa Brester, Commissioning Editor, Film and Cultural Studies;
Contact, in the US: Isabella Steer, US Publishing Manager
For Commissioning Editors in other subject areas *see* http://213.253.134.2/ibtauris/whos_who.asp?TAG=&CID=
Publishing areas: 12, 13, 14 (Radcliffe Press imprint) 17, 24, 27, 36, 38, 40, 43
Other: Islam

2235 Thoemmes Press
11 Great George Street
Bristol BS1 5RR
Tel: +44-(0)117-929 1377
Fax: +44-(0)117-922 1918
Email info@Thoemmes.com (Customer services/Orders)
ahaynes@continuumbooks.com (Publishing Director) rudi@thoemmes.com (Editorial Director)
Web: http://www.thoemmes.com/
Contacts: Anthony Haynes, Publishing Director; Rudi Thoemmes, Editorial Director
Publishing areas: 27, 38
Other: History of African Thought series, collections of writings by early African nationalist leaders
Note: part of the Continuum International Publishing GrouP

2236 VSO Books
Voluntary Service Overseas
317 Putney Bridge Road
London SW15 2PN
Tel: +44(0)20-8780 7200/8780 7314
Email: response@vso.org.uk

Web:
http://www.vso.org.uk/resources/books/
Contact: VSO Books Editor
Publishing areas: 10, 17, 18, 31, 33, 41,
Other: adult literacy
Submission restrictions: book proposals
should draw upon or be able to include
practical examples and information based on
VSO volunteers' and their overseas
colleagues' professional experience.

2237   The Women's Press
27 Goodge Street
London W1T 2LD
Tel: +44-(0)20-7636 3992
Fax: +44-(0)20-7637 1866
Email: sales@the-womens-press.com
Web: http://www.the-womens-press.com/
Contact: Submission Department
Publishing areas: 6 (by women writers)
Other: feminist fiction and non-fiction by
outstanding women writers from all around
the world.
Submission restrictions: does not accept
editorial submissions via the Internet.
US distr: Trafalgar Square Books, Howe Hill
Road, North Pomfret VT 05053
Web:
http://www.trafalgarsquarebooks.com/

→ **Yale University Press** *see* under United
States, entry **2306**

2238   Zed Books
7 Cynthia Street
London N1 9JF
Tel: +44-(0)20-837 4014
Fax: +44-(0)20-833 3960
Email: n/a; use online email form on Web site
Web: http://zedbooks.co.uk/
Contact: Robert Molteno, Publisher and
Managing Director; or mail proposals to
Editorial Department
Publishing areas: 2, 3, 10, 11, 17, 18, 20, 27, 28,
33, 36, 41, 43, 45
Other: energy policy/renewable energy,
transport
US distr (trade): Palgrave, 175 Fifth Avenue,
New York, NY 10010

2239   Hans Zell Publishing
Glais Bheinn
Lochcarron IV54 8YB
Ross-shire
Scotland
Tel: +44-(0)1520-722951
Fax: +44-(0)1520-722953
Email: hanszell@hanszell.co.uk or
hzell@btopenworld.com
Web: http://www.hanszell.co.uk
also at
http://www.africanstudiescompanion.com/
Contact: Hans M. Zell, Publisher
Publishing areas: 32, 38
Other: information resources (print and
electronic) on African studies, and African
publishing and book development
Note: continues the publishing programme of
the former Hans Zell Publishers imprint
under Bowker-Saur/Reed Reference
Publishing.

NORTH AMERICA

North America: Index and key to publisher subject areas

1 African art and art history
2240, 2246, 2247, 2252, 2262, 2264, 2275, 2287, 2290, 2291, 2296, 2306

2 African cultural studies (in general)
2246, 2249, 2261, 2264, 2274, 2275, 2277, 2285, 2287, 2288, 2295, 2299

3 African film and cinema
2264, 2290

4 African languages and linguistics
2246, 2250, 2255, 2266, 2270, 2271, 2273, 2298

5 African literature: Critical studies and collections
2242, 2245, 2246, 2250, 2252, 2253, 2254, 2257, 2259, 2260, 2261, 2263, 2264, 2266, 2267, 2270, 2277, 2283, 2290, 2291, 2292, 2298, 2299, 2300, 2302

6 African literature: Fiction
2245, 2248, 2257, 2261, 2274, 2295, 2300

7 African literature: Drama
2245, 2246, 2300

8 African literature: Poetry
2242, 2245, 2246, 2250, 2300

9 African music
2240, 2246, 2247, 2264, 2291, 2303

10 Agricultural sciences and agricultural development
2241, 2261, 2266, 2270, 2272, 2275, 2276, 2277, 2283, 2288, 2298, 2301, 2305

11 Anthropology and ethnology
2243, 2246, 2248, 2253, 2254, 2260, 2261, 2262, 2264, 2266, 2270, 2271, 2277, 2283, 2287, 2288, 2290, 2291, 2292, 2293, 2296, 2297, 2299, 2302, 2306

12 Archaeology and pre-history
2243, 2248, 2264, 2271, 2287, 2290, 2295, 2299, 2304

13 Architecture
2291

14 Biography and autobiography
2247, 2263, 2264

15 Constitutional and land law
--

16 Diaspora studies
2246, 2250, 2263, 2264, 2266, 2270, 2271, 2274, 2294, 2296

17 Economics and development studies
2241, 2246, 2251, 2254, 2260, 2261, 2263, 2265, 2266, 2267, 2270, 2272, 2276, 2279, 2283, 2288, 2289, 2298, 2301, 2302, 2305

18 Education
2250, 2251, 2252, 2260, 2261, 2264, 2266, 2270, 2276, 2288, 2289, 2298, 2301, 2305

19 Entomology
--

20 Environmental studies
2241, 2254, 2265, 2267, 2269, 2270, 2271, 2272, 2277, 2289, 2290, 2293, 2296, 2299, 2301, 2302, 2305, 2306

21 Flora and fauna of Africa
2290, 2306

22 Folklore and oral cultures
2246, 2252, 2257, 2260, 2261, 2263, 2264, 2270, 2271, 2277, 2290, 2292, 2297

23 Food studies and food security
2241, 2246, 2265, 2289, 2305

24 Geography
2270, 2299, 2305

25 Geology and earth sciences
--

26 Government and public administration
2243, 2251, 2301, 2302

27 History
2243, 2246, 2247, 2248, 2252, 2253, 2254, 2260, 2261, 2262, 2263, 2264, 2270, 2274, 2276, 2277, 2279, 2282, 2283, 2288, 2290, 2291, 2292, 2293, 2294, 2295, 2297, 2298, 2299, 2302, 2304, 2306

28   Human rights
2289, 2298

29   Labour studies
2246, 2253, 2260, 2261, 2272, 2277, 2280, 2289, 2290, 2302, 2305

30   Law
2289

31   Library and information sciences/Information technology
2241, 2269, 2270, 2286

32   Media and communication
2241, 2250, 2260, 2266, 2267, 2270, 2276, 2277, 2288, 2293, 2298

33   Medical and health studies/ Health care (including HIV/AIDS)
2241, 2246, 2247, 2252, 2260, 2261, 2265, 2270, 2289, 2290, 2298, 2301, 2305

34   Natural history
2290

35   Philosophy
2248, 2264, 2272, 2277, 2298

36   Politics, political economy, and international relations
2241, 2243, 2246, 2250, 2251, 2252, 2253, 2254, 2260, 2261, 2263, 2264, 2265, 2266, 2267, 2270, 2272, 2274, 2275, 2276, 2277, 2279, 2280, 2282, 2283, 2285, 2289, 2290, 2293, 2298, 2299, 2301, 2302, 2304, 2306

37   Psychology
2252, 2276

38   Reference
2244, 2247, 2249, 2255, 2256, 2258, 2259, 2260, 2262, 2266, 2268, 2269, 2286, 2288, 2302, 2305, 2306

39   Refugee and migration studies
2289, 2302

40   Religion and theology
2246, 2260, 2261, 2264, 2266, 2270, 2276, 2277, 2278, 2283, 2288, 2298, 2299, 2302, 2304, 2306

41   Rural development
2241, 2261, 2265, 2298, 2302, 2305

42   Science and technology
2241 2289,

43   Sociology
2246, 2252, 2253, 2260, 2261, 2264, 2270, 2271, 2276, 2283, 2289, 2290, 2293, 2298, 2306

44   Urban studies
2241, 2246, 2252, 2261, 2266, 2289, 2290, 2293, 2298, 2302, 2305

45   Women's and gender studies
2241, 2246, 2252, 2253, 2257, 2260, 2261, 2263, 2264, 2265, 2266, 2270, 2271, 2272, 2275, 2277, 2280, 2283, 2285, 2289, 2290, 2291, 2301, 2302, 2304, 2305, 2306

Publishers of electronic & online products, ebooks, CD-ROM, and microfiche/ microfilm
2241, 2243, 2244, 2256, 2259, 2260, 2268, 2284, 2289, 2290, 2291, 2295, 2301, 2303, 2305

Canada

2240 Galerie Amrad African Arts Publications
2104 Chartier Avenue
Dorval OC H9P 1H2
Tel: +1-514- 631-4496
Email: gmanager@simplcom.ca
Web: http://www.simplcom.ca/gaaap/
Contact: Esther A. Dagan, Publisher
Publishing areas: 1, 9
Other: specializes in publishing highly
illustrated books on African art

2241 International Development Research Centre-IDRC Books
24 Albert Street
PO Box 8500
Ottawa ON K1G 3H9
Tel: +1-613-236 6163
Fax: +1-613-238 7230
Email: pub@idrc.ca
Web: http://www.idrc.ca/books/ or
http://www.idrc.ca/books/ev-8574-201-1-
DO_TOPIC.html
Contacts: Bill Carman, Senior
Communications Advisor, Publishing
Publishing areas: 10, 17, 20, 23, 31, 32, 33, 36,
41, 42, 44, 45 (in English and French)
Other: biodiversity, natural resources
Submission restrictions: will consider only
manuscripts that are the direct result of
IDRC-funded research; or that report, wholly
or partially, on an IDRC-funded project. Will
consider for publication any manuscript that
is the result of an activity administered by
IDRC or produced by IDRC staff.

2242 Tsar Publications
PO Box 6996 Station A
Toronto ON M5W 1X7
Tel: +1-416-483 7191
Fax: +1-416-486 0706
Email: inquiries@tsarbooks.com (General
enquiries) naziz@tsarbooks.com (Publisher)
Web: http://www.tsarbooks.com/
Contact: Nurjehan Aziz, Publisher
Publishing areas: 5, 6, 8
Other: Caribbean and Asian writing
Distr: LitDistCo100, Armstrong Avenue
Georgetown, Ontario L7G 5S4
Email: orders@lpg.ca
US distr: Small Press Distribution Inc.
1341 Seventh Street, Berkeley CA 94710
2243 University of Calgary Press

2500 University Drive NW
Calgary AL T2N 1N4
Tel: +1-403-220 7578 (General)
Fax: +1-403-282 0085
Email: ucpmail@ucalgary.ca (General
enquiries) orders@gtwcanada.com (Orders)
whildebr@ucalgary.ca (Director)
jking@ucalgary.ca (Senior Editor
Web: http://www.uofcpress.com/
Contact: Walter Hildebrandt, Director; John
King, Senior Editor
Publishing areas: 11, 12, 26, 27, 36
Other: Diaspora studies; electronic
publications
US distr: →**Michigan State University Press
(2271)**
UK and European distr: Gazelle Book
Services, White Cross Mills, High Town.
Lancaster LA1 4XS,
Email: sales@gazellebooks.co.uk

United States

2244 ABC-CLIO
130 Cremona Drive
Santa Barbara CA 93117
Tel: +1-805-968 1911 Toll-free (US/Canada
only) 800-368 6868
Fax: +1-805-685 9685
Email: sales@abc-clio.com
Web: http://www.abc-clio.com/
In the UK:
ABC-CLIO
7200 Quorum
Oxford Business Park North
PO Box 651
Oxford OX1 9BP
Tel: +44-(0)1865-481403
Fax +44-(0)1865-481482
Email: DHarman@abc-clio.com
UK & European distr: EDS, 3 Henrietta
Street, Covent Garden, London
WC2E 8LU, Email: orders@edspubs.co.uk
Web: http://www.europspan.co.uk
Contacts: Ron Boehm, President & CEO
Heather Cameron, Editor
Publishing areas: 38
Other: focus is in the area of history reference;
electronic products/e-books; ABC-Clio also
have significant publication lists in the
subjects of politics, law, government,
geography, popular and traditional culture,
religion, and current issues.

2245   African Heritage Press
(formerly Africana Legacy Press)
PO Box 1433
New Rochelle NY 10802
Tel: +1-718-862-3262 Fax: +1-718-862-1440
Email: afroheritage9760@aol.com (General
enquiries) onwuemto@uwec.edu (President)
Web:
http://www.africanheritagepress.com/ahp/
base.asp
Contact: Tess Osonye Onwueme, President
Publishing areas: 2, 5, 6, 7, 8
Note: Nigerian headquarters at 23 Unity
Road, Ikeja, Lagos, Tel: +234-1-497 2044

**2246   Africa World Press Inc/
The Red Sea Press Inc**
541 West Ingham Avenue Suite B
Trenton NJ 08638
Tel: +1-609-695 3200 Fax: +1-609-695 6466
Email: awprsp@verizon.net
Web: http://www.africanworld.com/ (site
down 25/11/05 and earlier; new site to be
launched shortly, details not available at
press time)
http://store.yahoo.com/africanworld/redsea
press.html (Red Sea Press online store, site
also down 25/11/05)
Contacts: Kassahun Checole, President;
Nanjiku Ngugi, Editor
Publishing areas: 1, 2, 4, 5, 6, 8, 9, 11, 14, 16,
17, 22, 23, 27, 29, 33, 36, 40, 43, 44, 45
Other: Caribbean studies and Caribbean
literature, Eritrean studies
See also ➔ **Africa World Press, Eritrea (1962)**

2247   African Studies Association
Rutgers, The State University of New
Jersey
Douglass Campus
132 George Street
New Brunswick NJ 08901-1400
Tel: +1-732-932 8173 Fax: +1-732-932 3394
Email: asapub@rci.rutgers.edu (Publications
and Information Coordinator
asaed@rci.rutgers.edu (Executive Director)
Web:
http://www.africanstudies.org/asa_publicat
ionslist.htm
Contacts: Carol L. Martin, Executive Director;
Renee Dutta, Publications and Information
Coordinator
Publishing areas: 1, 9, 14, 27, 33, 38
Note: the ➔ African Studies Association's

(2755) book publishing programme is
currently dormant and no new titles have
been published since 1999.

2248   Altamira Press
A Division of Rowman & Littlefield
Publishers, Inc.
4501 Forbes Boulevard, Suite 200
Lanham MD 20706
Tel: +1-301-459 3366 Fax: +1-301-429-5748
Email: explore@altamirapress.com (General
enquiries rrobertson@altamirapress.com
(Senior Editor, Anthropology, Ethnic Studies,
Criminology)
Web: http://www.altamirapress.com/
Also at: (Editorial)
AltaMira Press
A Division of Rowman & Littlefield
Publishers
1563 Solano Avenue #364
Berkeley CA 94707
Tel: +1-510-526 5315 Fax: +1-510-526 5340
Contacts: Rosalie M. Robertson, Senior Editor,
Anthropology, Ethnic Studies, Criminology
Publishing areas: 6, 11, 12, 27, 35
Other: Ethnic studies, African American
studies
Note: a division of the Rowman and
Littlefield publishing group.

2249   Basic Civitas Books
387 Park Avenue South
12th Floor
New York NY 10016-8810
Tel: +1-212-340 8100
Email: perseus.orders@perseusbooks.com
(Perseus Group, Orders/Customer Service)
Web: http://www.basiccivitasbooks.com/
In the UK: Perseus Running Press
69-70 Temple Chambers
3-7 Temple Avenue
London, EC4Y 0HP
Tel: +44-(0)207-353 7771
Fax: +44-(0)207-353 7786
Email: victoria.gilder@perseusbooks.co.uk
John Donatich, Publishing Director; Elizabeth
Maguire; Vice-President, Associate Publisher
and Editorial Director
Publishing areas: 2, 38
Other: African American studies
Note: part of the Perseus Group.
UK/European distributors: Marston Book
Services, 160 Milton Park, PO Box 269,
Abingdon, OX14 4YN,
Email: direct.order@marston.co.uk

→ **Berghan Books** *see* under United Kingdom, entry **2203**

2250 Black Academy Press
229 East North Avenue
Baltimore MD 21202
Tel: 1-443-857 1953 Fax: +1-410-602 3939
Email: bapress@aol.com
Web: http://www.blackacademypress.com/
Contacts: S. Okechukwu Mezu, Publisher;
Rose Ure Mezu
Publishing areas: 4, 5, 8, 16, 18, 32, 36
Other: African American studies, Diaspora
studies

2251 The Brookings Institution Press
1775 Massachusetts Avenue NW
Washington DC 20036-2188
Tel: +1-202-797 6252 Fax: +1-202-797 6195
Email: BIBooks@brookings.edu
(General/Orders)
ckelaher@brookings.edu (Acquisitions Editor)
Web: http://brookings.nap.edu/
Contacts: Robert L. Faherty, Vice President
and Director; Christopher Kelaher,
Acquisitions Editor
Publishing areas: 17, 18, 26, 36
Other: public policy issues in business
Note: the Press publishes both books that
result from the Institution's own research and
books of a similar nature written by outside
authors.

→ **Boydell & Brewer Inc** *see*
University of Rochester Press (2294)

→ **Cambridge University Press** *see*
under United Kingdom, entry **2206**

2252 Carolina Academic Press
700 Kent Street
Durham NC 27701
Tel: +1-919-489 7486 Fax: +1-919-493 5668
Email: cap@cap-press.com (General
enquiries) orders@cap-press.com (Orders)
ksipe@cap-press.com (Publisher) linda@cap-
press.com (Senior Editor)
Web: http://www.cap-press.com/
Contacts: Keith Sipe, Publisher; Linda Lacy,
Senior Editor
Publishing areas: 1, 5, 18, 22, 27, 33, 36, 37, 43,
44, 45

→ **Continuum International Publishing Group** *see* under United Kingdom, entry **2209**

2253 Cornell University Press
Box 6525
750 Cascadilla Street
Ithaca NY 14851-6525
Tel: +1-607-277 2211 Fax: +1-607-277 6292
cupressinfo@cornell.edu (General enquiries)
jga4@cornell.edu (Director)
fgb2@cornell.edu (Editorial Director)
Web:
http://www.cornellpress.cornell.edu/
Also at: (Editorial/Manuscript Proposals)
Sage House
512 East State Street
Ithaca NY 14850
Tel: +1-607-277 2338 Fax: +1-607-277 2374
Contacts: John G. Ackerman, Director;
Frances Benson, Editorial Director; for a
complete list of Acquisitions Editors and their
areas of expertise *see*
http://www.cornellpress.cornell.edu/cup_co
ntact.html
Publishing areas: 11, 27, 29, 36, 43, 45
Other: minority studies, Oriental studies

2254 Duke University Press
905 West Main Street
POB 90660
Durham NC 27708-0660
Tel: +1-919-687 3600 Fax: +1-919-688 4574
Email: orders@dukeupress.edu (Customer
Services/Orders) kwissoker@dukeupress.edu
(Editor-in-Chief) rsmith@dukeupress.edu
(Executive Editor)
Web: http://www.dukeupress.edu/
Contacts: Ken Wissoker, Editor-in-Chief; J.
Reynolds Smith, Executive Editor
Publishing areas: 5, 11, 17, 20, 27, 36
Other: African American studies, Caribbean
studies
Submission restrictions: do not submit full
proposal electronically, unless asked to do so.

2255 Dunwoody Press
A division of McNeil Technologies
McNeil Multilingual, Inc.
6564 Loisdale Court Suite 800
Springfield VA 22150
Tel: +1-703-797 7400/703-921 1600
Fax: +1-703-921 1610
Email: dpadmin@mcneiltech.com
Web: http://www.dunwoodypress.com/

Contact: all editorial proposals to University of Maryland Eastern Shore, African Language Research Project, Department of English and Modern Languages, Princess Anne, MD 21853
Tel: +1-410-651 6909
Web: http://www.umes.edu/english/newalp/index.html
Publishing areas: 4, 38
Other: specializes in publishing language instruction materials for less commonly taught languages, including African languages; also publishes bilingual dictionaries, grammars, textbooks, readers, and handbooks of common expressions.

2256   Facts On File Inc
132 West 31st Street 17th Floor
New York NY 10001
Tel: +1-212-967 8800
Toll-free (US/Canada only) 800-322 8755
Fax: Toll-free (US/Canada only) 800–678 3633
Email: CustServ@factsonfile.com (Customer Services/Orders) editorial@factsonfile.com (Editorial Director)
llikoff@factsonfile.com (Manuscript Guidelines/Submissions)
Web: http://www.factsonfile.com/
Contact: Laurie Likoff, Manuscript Guidelines/Submissions
Publishing areas: 38 (print and electronic)
Orders from Non-US customers: contact bjacobs@factsonfile.com to place an order.

2257   The Feminist Press at the City University of New York
The Graduate Center
365 Fifth Avenue Suite 5406
New York NY 10016
Tel: +1-212-817 7925 Fax: +1-212-817 1593
Email: jishmon@gc.cuny.edu (General enquiries) fhowe@gc.cuny.edu (Director)
Web: http://www.feministpress.org/
Contact: Florence Howe, Executive and Editorial Director
Publishing areas: 5, 6 (by African women writers), 22, 45
Other: dedicated to publishing work by and about women.
Note: For more details about the Feminist Press "Women Writing Africa" project *see* http://www.feministpress.org/about/index.cfm?fa=special#womenwritingafrica

2258   Fitzroy Dearborn Publishers
Routledge
Taylor & Francis Group
29 West 35th Street 10th Floor
New York NY10001
Tel: +1- 212-216 7800 Fax: +1-212-564 7854
Email: reference@routledge-ny.com
Web: http://www.routledge-ny.com/default.asp or
http://www.fitzroydearborn.com/index.html (title list)
Contact: Sylvia K. Miller, Publishing Director, Routledge Reference
Publishing areas: 38
Note: Fitzroy Dearborn is now an imprint of Routledge, a division of Taylor and Francis. Its London office closed in August 2002 and new projects are now being developed in the Routledge New York office.
Distr: c/o Taylor & Francis, 325 Chestnut Street, Suite 800, Philadelphia, PA 19106

2259   Gale Group/The Thomson Corporation
27500 Drake Road
Farmington Hills MI 48331
Tel: +1-248-699 4253
Toll-free (US/Canada only) 800-877 GALE
Fax: +1-248-699 8035
Email: galeord@gale.com (General enquiries) international@gale.com (Outside US and Canada)
Web: http://www.galegroup.com/
In the UK:
Thomson Learning Library Reference EMEA
High Holborn House
50/51 Bedford Row
London WC1R 4LR
Tel: +44(0)20-7067 2500
Fax: +44-(0)20-7067 2600
Email: enquiries@thomson.com or tlemea.customerservices@thomson.com
http://www.galegroup.com/world/index.htm (World site)
For other contacts and addresses outside the UK *see*
http://lr.thomsonlearning.co.uk/contactus/index.html
Contact: Allen W. Paschal, Chief Executive Officer; proposals to Editorial Department; and/or see Contacts information on the Web sites of individual imprints below
Publishing areas: 5 (Twayne imprint only), 38 (print and electronic)
Note: imprints include

Macmillan Reference USA
http://www.gale.com/macmillan/
Charles Scribners's Sons
http://www.gale.com/scribners/
K.G. Saur
http://www.gale.com/psm/ (*see also* **2259**)
Twayne Publishers
http://www.gale.com/twayne/
UXL http://www.gale.com/uxl/
Distr outside the US: (UK, Europe and
elsewhere) see
http://www.galegroup.com/world/distribu
tors/index.htm

➜ **Garland Publishing** *see* **Routledge (2233)**

2260   Greenwood Publishing Group Inc
88 Post Road West
POB 5007
Westport CT 06881-5007
Tel: +1-203-226 3571
Toll-free (US/Canada only) 800-225 5800
Fax: +1-203-750 9790
Email: customer-service@greenwood.com
(Customer Services)
editorial@greenwood.com (Editorial, General
enquiries)
wschnauf@greenwood.com (Area Studies,
Cultural Studies, Ethnic Studies)
mhermann@greenwood.com (Current Events,
History, International Affairs, Politics)
Web: http://www.greenwood.com/
Contacts: Wendi Schnaufer, Area Studies,
Cultural Studies, Ethnic Studies;
Michael Hermann, Current Events, History,
International Affairs, Politics; for other
contacts, Reference and Non-Reference
(Praeger imprint) *see*
http://www.greenwood.com/author/prosp
ect/editorial_contacts_by_subject.asp
Note: includes ➜ **Heinemann US (2261)**,
Praeger Publishers, and Oryx.
Publishing areas: 5, 11, 17, 18, 22, 27, 29, 32,
33, 36, 38, 40, 43, 45
UK & European distr: Greenwood Publishing
Group, Customer Service, Linacre House,
Oxford, OX2 8DP, Email:
Greenwood.enquiries@harcourteducation.co.
uk

2261   Heinemann
361 Hanover Street
PO Box 6926
Portsmouth NH 03802-6926
Tel: +1-603-431 7894 Toll-free (US/Canada
only) 800-225 5800
Fax: +1-603-431 7840
Email: custserv@heinemann.com (Customer
Services/Orders) info@heinemann.com
(General enquiries)
proposals@heinemann.com (Manuscript
proposals) leigh.peake@heinemann.com
(Editorial Director)
lisa.fowler@heinemann.com (Managing
Editor)
Web: http://www.heinemann.com/
Contacts: Leigh Peake, Editorial Director; Lisa
Fowler, Managing Editor
Publishing areas: 2, 5, 6*, 10, 11, 17, 18, 22, 27,
29, 33, 36, 40, 41, 43, 44, 45
*Note: in November 2002 ➜ **Heinemann** UK
(2214) decided not to pursue new titles for the
African Writers Series at the present time,
although the backlist will continue to be
maintained and actively promoted.
UK/European distr: Greenwood
International, Linacre House, Oxford OX2
8DP, Email:
greenwood.enquiries@harcourteducation.co.u
k
See also ➜ **Heinemann International (2214)**

2262   Holmes & Meier Publishers
PO Box 943
Teaneck NJ 07666
Tel: +1-201-833 2270 Fax: +1-201-833 2272
Email: info@holmesandmeier.com
Web: http://www.holmesandmeier.com/
Publishing areas: 1, 11, 27, 38
Contact: Miriam Holmes, President
UK distr: Dan Levey, BR&D, 244a London
Road, Hadleigh SS7 2DE,
Email: info@bookreps.com
Note: includes the former Africana Publishing
Company imprint.

2263   Howard University Press
2225 Georgia Avenue NW
Suite 718
Washington DC 20059
Tel: +1-202-238 2570 Fax: +1-202-588-9849
Email: howardupress@howard.edu (General
enquiries) danderson@howard.edu (Director)
Web: http://www.hupress.howard.edu/

Contact: D. Kamili Anderson, Director;
address all proposals to Editorial Department
Publishing areas: 5, 14, 16, 17, 22, 27, 36, 45
Other: African American studies

2264   Indiana University Press
601 North Morton Street
Bloomington IN 47404-3797
Tel: +1-812-855 8817 (General enquiries) Toll-
free (US/Canada only) 800-842 6796
Fax: +1-812-855 8507
Email: iupress@indiana.edu (Customer
Services/Orders) jrabinow@indiana.edu
(Director) rjsloan@indiana.edu (Editorial
Director)
mortense@indiana.edu (Sponsoring Editor,
African studies, Middle East studies, and
Philosophy)
Web: http://www.indiana.edu/~iupress
Contacts: Janet Rabinowitch, Director; Robert
Sloan, Editorial Director; Dee Mortensen,
Sponsoring Editor, African studies,.
Publishing areas: 1, 2, 3, 5, 9, 11, 12, 14, 16, 18,
22, 27, 35, 36, 40, 43, 45
Other: African American studies, Caribbean
studies; electronic products

2265   Kumarian Press Inc
1294 Blue Hills Avenue
Bloomfield CT 06002
Tel: +1- 860-243 2098 Toll-free (US/Canada
only) 800-289 2664 Fax: +1-860-243 2867
Email: kpbooks@kpbooks.com (General
enquiries) jlance@kpbooks.com (Editor and
Associate Publisher
Web: http://www.kpbooks.com/
Contacts: Krishna K. Sondhi, President and
Publisher; submissions to Jim Lance
Editor and Associate Publisher
Publishing areas: 17, 20, 23, 33, 36, 41, 45

2266   Peter Lang Publishing Inc
275 Seventh Avenue 28th floor
New York NY 10001-6708
Tel.: +1-212-647 7700 Toll-free (US/Canada
only) 800-770 5264 Fax: +1-212-647 7707
Tel: +1-410- 879 6300 (Maryland office)
Fax: +1-410-836 9550 (Maryland office)
Email: customerservice@plang.com
(Customer Services/Orders)
Hburnsplp@aol.com (Senior Editor)
PhyllisK@plang.com (Senior Editor)
Web: http://www.peterlangusa.com/
In Switzerland:
Peter Lang AG

Hochfeldstrasse 32
Postfach 746
3000 Berne 9
Tel.: +41-31-306 1717 Fax: +41-31-306 1727
Email: info@peterlang.com
Web: http://www.peterlang.net
In the UK:
Peter Lang AG
International Academic Publishers
Evenlode Court
Main Road
Long Hanborough
Witney OX29 8SZ
Tel: +44-(0)1993-880088
Fax: +44 (0)1993-882040
Email: oxford@peterlang.com
Web:
http://www.peterlang.net/Index.cfm?vUR=
8&vLang=E
Contacts, in US: Heidi Burns, Senior
Editor (at Maryland office: Peter Lang
Publishing, PO Box 1246, Bel Air, MD
21014-1246); Phyllis Korper, Senior Editor
Contacts, in UK: Graham Speake, Publisher;
Alexis Kirschbaum, Commissioning Editor
Publishing areas: 4, 5, 10, 11, 16, 17, 18, 32, 36,
38, 40, 44, 45
Other: African American studies
Note: publishes in English, German, and
French, and also has offices in Berlin,
Brussels, Frankfurt, and Vienna, for contact
details at these offices *see*
http://www.peterlang.net/Index.cfm?vHR=
4&vLang=E

2267   Lexington Books
4501 Forbes Blvd Suite 200
Lanham MD 20706
Tel: +1-301-459 3366
Toll-free (US/Canada only) 800-462
6420
Email: custserv@rowman.com (Customer
Services/Orders)
jsisk@rowmanlittlefield.com (Publisher)
skrombach@rowman.com (Editorial
Acquisitions Editor and Director)
Web: http://www.lexingtonbooks.com/
Contacts: John Sisk, Publisher; submissions to
Serena Leigh Krombach, Editorial
Acquisitions Editor and Director
Publishing areas: 5, 17, 20, 32, 36
Note: a division of the Rowman and
Littlefield publishing group.

2268 **LexisNexis Academic & Library Solutions**
7500 Old Georgetown Road
Suite 1300
Bethesda MD 20814-6126
Tel: +1-301-654 1550 Toll-free (US/Canada only) 800-638 8380 Fax +1-301-657 3203
Email: academicinfo@lexisnexis.com or academicinternational@lexisnexis.com (International sales information)
Web: http://www.lexisnexis.com/academic/
Publishing areas: 38 (reference, research, and archival collections in electronic and traditional media, and Web services)
Other: African American studies (see http://www.lexisnexis.com/academic/2upa/Aaas/default.asp)
Note: includes the University Publications of America list

2269 **McFarland & Company, Publishers**
Box 611
Jefferson NC 28640
Tel: +1-336-246 4460 Fax: +1-336-246 5018
Email: info@mcfarlandpub.com (General enquiries) editorial@mcfarlandpub.com (Editorial/Submissions) swilson@mcfarlandpub.com (Executive Editor) vtobiassen@mcfarlandpub.com (Editorial Development Chief)
Web: www.mcfarlandpub.com/
Contact: Steve Wilson, Executive Editor; Virginia Tobiassen, Editorial Development Chief
Publishing areas: 20, 31, 38
Other: African American studies

➔ **Macmillan Reference US** see **Gale Group/The Thomson Corporation (2259)**

2270 **Edwin Mellen Press**
415 Ridge Street
PO Box 450
Lewiston NY 14902-0450
Tel: +1-716-754 2266 Fax: +1-716-754 4056
Email: cservice@mellenpress.com (Orders) jrupnow@mellenpress.com (Acquisitions Director)
Web: http://www.mellenpress.com/
In the UK:
Mellen House
Unit 17 Llambed Business Park
Ceredigion SA48 8LT
Tel: +44-(0)1570-423356

Fax: +44-(0)1570-423775
Email: iwilliams@mellenpress.com
Publishing areas: 4, 5, 10, 11, 16, 17, 18, 20, 22, 24, 27, 31, 32, 33, 36, 40, 43, 45
Contact, in the US: John Rupnow, Acquisitions Director
Contact, in the UK: Iona Williams

2271 **Michigan State University Press**
1405 South Harrison Road
Manly Miles Building Suite 25
East Lansing MI 48823-5245
Tel: +1-517-335 9543 (Toll free, US/Canada only) 800-678 2120 Fax: +1-517-432 2611
Email: msupress@msu.edu (General enquiries) bohm@msu.edu (Director) batesmar@msu.edu (Acquisitions Editor)
Web: http://www.msupress.msu.edu
Contacts: Fredric C. Bohm, Director; Martha Bates, Acquisitions Editor
Publishing areas: 4, 11, 12, 16, 20, 22, 43, 45
Other: electronic products, books on CD-ROM
Note: MSU Press is the distributor in North America of ➔ **African Books Collective (2332)** see
http://www.msupress.msu.edu/series.php?seriesID=22
Distr in UK & Europe: Eurospan, 3 Henrietta Street, Covent Garden, London WC2E 8LU, Email: info@eurospan.co.uk
Web: http://www.eurospanonline.com

2272 **Monthly Review Press**
122 West 27th Street
New York NY 10001
Tel: +1-212-791 2555 Toll-free (US/Canada only) 800-670 9499
Fax: +1 212-727 3676
Email: promo@monthlyreview.org (General enquiries) bookorder@monthlyreview.org (Orders) anash@monthlyreview.org (Submissions)
Web: http://www.monthlyreview.org/mrpress.htm
Contact: Andrew Nash
Publishing areas: 10, 17, 20, 29, 35, 36, 45
Other: race, culture and class struggle, socialist theory

2273 **Mother Tongue Editions**
511 Main Street
West Newbury MA 01985
Tel: +1-617-353 7305 (at Boston University)

Email: hutchisonjohn@hotmail.com or
hutch@bu.edu
Web: http://www.mothertongue.us/
Contacts: John Hutchison, Kassim Kone
Publishing areas: 4
Note: this is a non-profit publishing
organization whose purpose is to facilitate
and encourage African language literacy both
in Africa and abroad. The services of Mother
Tongue Editions are available to authors who
would like to prepare a book or manual for
publication in an African language.

→ **National Information Services
Corporation (NISC)** *see* under South Africa,
entry **2097**

2274   The New World African Press
        1958 Matador Way #35
        Northridge CA 91330
Tel: +1-818-642 8061
Fax: +1-818-363 1734
Email: info@newworldafricanpress.com
(General enquiries)
orders@newworldafricanpress.com (Orders)
Web:
http://www.newworldafricanpress.com/ind
ex.htm
Contact: Joseph E. Holloway, Editor-in-chief
Publishing areas: 2, 6, 16, 27, 36
Other: African American studies

2275   W.W. Norton & Company Inc
        500 Fifth Avenue
        New York NY 10110
Tel: +1- 212-354 5500 Toll-free (US/Canada
only) 800-233 4830 Fax: +1-212-869 0856
Email: n/a (Orders)
manuscripts@wwnorton.com (proposals,
outline only)
Web: http://www.wwnorton.com/
Contact: W. Drake McFeely, President;
proposals to Editorial Department,
College Division
Publishing areas: 1, 2, 10, 36, 45
Other: African American studies
Submission restrictions: "due to
concerns about unsolicited mail,
manuscripts/proposals sent by mail will
not be opened"; no telephone calls; no
attachments in email proposals

2276   Nova Publishers
        400 Oser Avenue Suite 1600
        Hauppauge NY 11788-3619
Tel: +1-631-231 7269
Fax: +1-631-231 8175
Email: Novascience@earthlink.net or
nova@novapublisher.com (General)
novaeditorial@earthlink.net (Editorial)
or editorial@novapublisher.com
Web: http://novapublishers.com/catalog/
Contact: n/a; send submissions to Editor-in-
Chief
Publishing areas: 10, 17, 18, 27, 32, 36, 37, 40,
43

2277   Ohio University Press
        19 Circle Drive
        The Ridges
        Athens OH 45701-2979
Tel: +1-740-593 1158 Fax: +1-740-593 4536
Email: wilsonj@ohio.edu (General/Orders)
sandersd@ohio.edu (Director)
berchowi@ohio.edu (Senior Editor)
Web: http://www.ohiou.edu/oupress/
Contacts: David Sanders, Director; all
submissions to Gillian Berchowitz, Senior
Editor
Publishing areas: 2, 5, 11, 20, 22, 27, 29, 32, 35,
36, 40, 45
UK/European distr: Eurospan Group, 3
Henrietta Street, Covent Garden, London
WC2E 8LU, Email: orders@edspubs.co.uk
Web: http://www.eurospan.co.uk

2278   Orbis Books
        POB 308
        Maryknoll NY 10545-0308
Tel: +1-914-941 7636 (General enquiries)
Toll-free (US/Canada only) 800-258 5838
Tel: +1-914-941 7636 ext 2487 (Editorial
Department) Fax: +1-914-945 0670
Email: orbisbooks@maryknoll.org
Web:
http://www.maryknoll.org/MALL/ORBIS/i
ndex.htm
Contact: Karin Volpe
Publishing areas: 40

→ **Oxford University Press Inc, USA** *see*
under United Kingdom, entry **2227**

→ **Palgrave Macmillan/St. Martin's Press** *see*
under United Kingdom, entry **2228**

2279 Pan-African Books
National Academic Press
341 Eastern Avenue NE
First Floor
Grand Rapids MI 49503
Tel: n/a
Email:
panafricanbooks@panafricanbooks.com
or napress@altelco.net
Web: http://napress1.tripod.com/
Contact: Godfrey Mwakikagile
Publishing areas: 17, 27, 36

2280 Pathfinder Press
PO Box 162767
Atlanta GA 30321-2767
Tel: +1-404-669 0600
Fax: +1-707-667 1141
Email: pathfinder@pathfinderpress.com
Web: http://www.pathfinderpress.com/
In the UK:
Pathfinder Press
120 Bethnal Green Road Lane
London E2 6DG.
Tel: +44(0)20-7613 3855
Fax: +44(0)20-7613 3855
Email: pathfinderlondon@compuserve.com
Contact: n/a, submissions to Editorial
Director
Publishing areas: 29, 36, 45
Other: Black history, Cuban revolution,
Marxism

2281 Perseus Publishing/Perseus Group
Headquarters and editorial:
387 Park Avenue South 12th Floor
New York NY 10016
Customer Services:
1094 Flex Drive
Jackson TN 38301
Tel: +1-212-340 8100 (Headquarters)
Tel: Toll-free (US/Canada only) 800-371-1669
(Customer services)
Fax: Toll-free (US/Canada only) 800-453-2884
(Customer services)
Email: perseus.orders@perseusbooks.com
Email: info@perseuspublishing.com (General
enquiries) wvproposal@perseusbooks.com
(Editorial proposals)
Web:
http://www.perseusbooksgroup.com/perse
us/home.jsp
Contacts and publishing areas: see entries for
➜ **Basic Civitas Books (2249), Public Affairs
Books (2282),** and ➜ **Westview Press (2302)**

Note: imprints include ➜ **Basic Civitas
Books (2249),** Da Capo Press, **Public Affairs
Books (2282),** and ➜ **Westview Press (2302).**
UK & European distr: Marston Book Services,
160 Milton Park, PO Box 269, Abingdon,
OX14 4YN, Email:
direct.order@marston.co.uk

➜ **Praeger Publishers** *see* **Greenwood
Publishing Group Inc (2260)**

➜ **Prestel Publishing** *see* under **Germany,**
entry **(2187)**

➜ **ProQuest Information and Learning** *see*
under United Kingdom, entry **(2232)**

2282 Public Affairs Books
250 West 57th Street Suite 1321
New York NY 10107
Tel: +1-212-397 6666 Fax: +1-212-397 4277
Email: PublicAffairs@perseusbooks.com
http://www.publicaffairsbooks.com/
Contacts: Susan Weinberg, Publisher
Clive Priddle, Executive Editor
Publishing areas: 27, 36
Note: part of the Perseus Group.

2283 Lynne Rienner Publishers Inc
1800 30th Street Suite 314
Boulder CO 80301
Tel: +1-303-444 6684 Fax: +1-303-444 0824
Email: questions@rienner.com (General and
editorial enquiries) cservice@rienner.com
(Orders)
Web: http://www.rienner.com/
In the UK:
Lynne Rienner Publishers
3 Henrietta Street
Covent Garden
London WC2E 8LU
Tel: +44-(0)20-7240 0856
Fax: +44 -(0)20-7379 0609
Email: orders@edspubs.co.uk
Web: http://www.eurospanonline.com
Contact, in the US: Lynne Rienner, President;
Contact, in the UK: Elisabetta Linton, 30 Lake
Road, Wimbledon, London SW19 7EX;
Tel/Fax: +44-(0)20-8286 0803
Publishing areas: 5, 10, 11, 17, 27, 36, 40, 43, 45
Submission restrictions: proposals by email
not accepted.

2284   Norman Ross Publishing Inc
330 West 58th Street Suite 306
New York NY 10019-5878
Tel: +1-212-765 8200 Fax: +1-212-765 8296
Email: info@rosspub.com
Web: http://www.rosspub.com/ or
http://www.nross.com
Contact: Norman Ross, Executive Director,
UMI Division, ProQuest Information and
Learning
Publishing areas: Microfiche/microfilm
products, including products on African art,
African studies, collections of newspapers,
etc.
Note: now part of ➜ **Pro-Quest Information
and Learning (2232)**

➜ **Routledge** *see* under United Kingdom,
entry **2233**

➜ **Rowman & Littlefield Publishing Group**
see **Altamira Press (2248) Lexington Books
(2267), Scarecrow Press (2286), University
Press of America (2298)**

2285   Rutgers University Press
100 Joyce Kilmer Avenue
Piscataway NJ 08854-8099
Tel: +1-732-445-7762 Toll-free
(US/Canada only) 800-446
9323 ext 630 Fax: +1-732-445-7039
Email: bksales@rci.rutgers.edu
(Customer Services/Orders)
marlie@rutgers.edu (Director)
lmitch@rutgers.edu (Editor-in-Chief and
Associate Director)
anadkarn@rutgers.edu (Proposals,
Humanities) bkres@rci.rutgers.edu
(Proposals, Social sciences)
Web: http://rutgerspress.rutgers.edu/
Contacts: Marlie Wasserman, Director;
Leslie Mitchner, Editor-in-Chief and
Associate Director; send manuscript
submissions to: Alicia Nadkarni, Editorial
Assistant (Proposals, Humanities); Beth
Kressel, Editorial Assistant (Proposals, Social
sciences)
Publishing areas: 2, 36, 45
Other: African American studies

St. Martin's Press Inc *see* ➜ **Palgrave/
Macmillan**, under United Kingdom, entry
2228

K.G. Saur *see* ➜ **Gale Group/The Thomson
Corporation (2259)** and ➜ **K.G. Saur Verlag
(2188)**

2286   Scarecrow Press Inc
4501 Forbes Blvd. Suite 200
Lanham MD 20706
Tel: +1-301-459-3366 Toll-free (US/Canada
only) 800-462 6420 Fax: +1-301-429 5748
Email: custserv@rowman.com (Customer
Services/Orders)
ekurdyla@scarecrowpress.com (Publisher and
Editorial Director)
mdillon@scarecrowpress.com (Acquisitions
Editor, Academic Reference, Library &
Information Science)
Contacts: Edward Kurdyla, Publisher and
Editorial Director; Martin Dillon, Acquisitions
Editor, Academic Reference, Library &
Information Science
mdillon@scarecrowpress.com
Web: http://www.scarecrowpress.com/
Publishing areas: 31, 38
UK & European distr: NBN International
Estover Road, Plymouth PL6 7PY
Email: orders@nbninternational.com
Note: a division of the Rowman and
Littlefield publishing group.

Charles Scribner's Sons *see* ➜ **Gale
Group/The Thomson Corporation (2259)**

**2287   Smithsonian Institution Scholarly
            Press**
PO Box 37012
SI Building Room 153
MRC 010
Washington DC 20013-7012
Tel: +1-202-633 3017 (Press) +1-212-207 7950
(Smithsonian Books)
Toll-free (US/Canada only) 800-242 7737
(Orders) Fax: +1-202-275-2274
Email: schol.press@si.edu (General enquiries)
dfehr@sipress.si.edu (Director)
Web: http://www.si.edu/publications/
Contacts: Don Fehr, Director, Smithsonian
Books; proposals to Scott Mahler,
Anthropology Editor
Publishing areas: 1, 2, 11, 12
Other: biocultural diversity, material culture

2288 Transaction Publishers
Rutgers – The State University of
New Jersey
35 Berrue Circle
Piscataway NJ 08854-8042
Tel: +1-732-445 2280 Toll-free (US/Canada
only) 888-999 6778 Fax: +1-732-445 3138
(*Orders to:* Transaction Publishers, 390
Campus Drive, Somerset, NJ 07830)
Email: trans@transactionpub.com (General
enquiries) orders@transactionpub.com
(Orders)
ihorowitz@transactionpub.com (Chairman &
Editorial Director)
lmintz@transactionpub.com
(Editorial/Submissions)
Web: http://www.transactionpub.com/cgi-
bin/transactionpublishers.storefront
Contacts: Irving Louis Horowitz , Chairman;
Mary E. Curtis, President; L. Mintz, Editorial
Department Books):
Publishing areas: 2, 10, 11, 17, 18, 27, 32, 36, 40
Other: African American studies

→ **Twayne Publishers** *see* **Gale Group/The
Thomson Corporation (2259)**

2289 United Nations Publications
Room DC2-853
2 UN Plaza
New York NY 10017
Tel: +1- 212-963 8302 Toll-free (US/Canada
only) 1-800-253 9646 Fax: +1-212-963 3489
Email: publications@un.org
Web:
https://unp.un.org/ (Main home page) or
https://unp.un.org/bookshop/ (United
Nations Bookshop)
In Switzerland:
United Nations Publications
Sales and Marketing Section
Bureau E-4
1211 Geneva 10
Tel: +41-22-917-2614/2600 (General enquiries)
+41-22-917 2615 (Orders)
Fax: +41-22-917 0027
Email: unpubli@unog.ch
Contact: no submissions, UN
commissioned work only;
Contact for rights & permissions enquiries:
Renata Morteo, UN Publications, 2 UN Plaza,
Room DC2-856, New York, NY 10017, Tel: +1-
212-963 5455 Fax: +1-212-963 3489,
Email: unprights@un.org (and *see also*

https://unp.un.org/programmes_permission
s.aspx)
Publishing areas: 17, 18, 20, 23, 28, 29,
30, 33, 36, 38, 39, 42, 43, 44, 45
Other: business and trade; electronic
and microfiche products
Distr: for worldwide list of distributors of UN
Publications *see*
https://unp.un.org/howto_distributors.aspx

→ **University Microfilms/UMI** *see* **ProQuest
Information and Learning (2232)**

2290 University of California Press
2120 Berkeley Way
Berkeley CA 94720
Tel: +1-510- 642 4247 Fax: +1-510-643 7127
Email: askucp@ucpress.edu (General
enquiries) orders@cpfs.pupress.princeton.edu
(Customer Services/Orders)
sheila.levine@ucpress.edu (Submissions for
regional studies)
Web: http://www.ucpress.edu/
Contacts: Lynne Withey, Director; Naomi
Schneider, Executive Editor; submissions to
Sheila Levine, Associate Director and
Publisher (Areas of acquisition: Food Studies,
Regional Studies) Randy Heyman: Regional
Studies
for contacts for other areas *see*
http://www.ucpress.edu/press/MsSubmissi
on.html
Publishing areas: 1, 3, 5, 11, 12, 20, 21, 22, 27,
29, 33, 34, 36, 43, 44, 45
Other: African American studies, biodiversity
Submission restrictions: proposals via email
or by telephone not accepted.
UK & European distr: University Presses of
California, Columbia, & Princeton Ltd, 1
Oldlands Way, Bognor Regis, PO22 9SA, UK,
Email: lois@upccp.demon.co.uk
Note: for the University of California
International and Area Studies (UCIAS)
Digital Collection, a peer-reviewed electronic
publications programme, *see*
http://repositories.cdlib.org/uciaspubs/
Contact: Laura Cerruti, Acquisitions Editor
and Editorial Director for Digital Publishing,
Books Division, Email:
laura.cerruti@ucpress.edu

2291   University of Chicago Press
1427 East 60th Street
Chicago IL 60637
Tel: +1-773-702 7700 Toll-free (US/Canada only) 800-621 2736 Fax: +1-773-702 9756
Email: custserv@press.uchicago.edu (Customer Services/Orders)
Web: http://www.press.uchicago.edu
Contact: Paula Barker Duffy, Director; submissions to John Tryneski, Editorial Director, Social Sciences and Paperback Publishing (Areas of acquisition: Political science, law and society); T. David Brent, Executive Editor (Areas of acquisition: Anthropology, Music, Paleoanthropology, Philosophy, Psychology); for other contacts *see*
http://www.press.uchicago.edu/Misc/Chicago/infopage.html
Publishing areas: 1, 5, 9, 11, 13, 27, 45
Other: electronic products
Submission restrictions: proposals by email or by fax not accepted.
UK & European distr: The University of Chicago Press, c/o John Wiley & Sons Ltd Distribution Centre, 1 Oldlands Way, Bognor Regis, PO22 9SA, UK,
Email: cs-books@wiley.co.uk

2292   University of Massachusetts Press
671 North Pleasant Street
PO Box 429
Amherst MA 01004
Tel: +1-413-545 2219 (General/Orders)
+1-413-545 2217 (Editorial offices)
Fax: +1-413-545 1226
Email: info@umpress.umass.edu (General enquiries) wilcox@umpress.umass.edu (Director) cdougan@umpress.umass.edu (Senior Editor)
Web: http://www.umass.edu/umpress/
Contacts: Bruce Wilcox, Director; proposals to Clark Dougan, Senior Editor
Publishing areas: 5, 11, 22, 27
Other: African American studies
Submission restrictions: email attachments not accepted in proposals by email
UK & European distr: Eurospan, 3 Henrietta Street, Covent Garden, London WC2E 8LU, Email: orders@edspubs.co.uk
Web: http://www.eurospan.co.uk

2293   University of Minnesota Press
Suite 290
111 Third Avenue South
Minneapolis MN 55401
Tel: +1-612-627 1970 (General)
+1-612-627-1973/74 (Editorial)
Fax: +1-612-627 1980
Email: ump@umn.edu (General enquiries) morri094@umn.edu (Senior Editor for Humanities and Social Sciences) t-orja@umn.edu (Senior Editor for Regional Studies and Contemporary Affairs)
Web: http://www.upress.umn.edu/
Contacts: Richard Morrison, Senior Editor for Humanities and Social Sciences; Todd Orjala, Senior Editor for Regional Studies and Contemporary Affairs
Publishing areas: 11, 20, 27, 32, 36, 43, 44
Other: African American studies, Caribbean studies

2294   University of Rochester Press /Boydell & Brewer Inc
668 Mount Hope Avenue
Rochester NY 14620-2731
Tel: +1-585-275 0419Fax: +1-585-271 8778
Email: urpress@mail.rochester.edu or boydell@boydellusa.net (General enquiries) Klemens@boydellusa.net (US Director) guiod@uofrochesterpress.net (Editorial Director)
Web: http://www.urpress.com/ or http://www.boydellandbrewer.com/
In the UK:
Boydell & Brewer Ltd
PO Box 9
Woodbridge IP12 3DF
Tel: +44-(0)1394-610600
Fax: +44-(0)1394 -610316
Email: boydell@boydell.co.uk
Contacts: Mark Klemens, US Director; Suzanne Guiod, Editorial Director
Publishing areas: 16, 27

2295   University of Virginia Press
PO Box 400318
Charlottesville VA 22904-4318
Tel: +1-434-924 3361 Toll-free (US/Canada only) 800-831 3406
Email: upressva@virginia.edu (General enquiries) pkaiserlian@virginia.edu (Director) cib8b@virginia.edu (Humanities Editor) rkh2a@virginia.edu (History and Social Sciences Editor)
Web: http://www.upress.virginia.edu/

Contacts: Penelope J. Kaiserlian, Director; Cathie Brettschneider, Humanities Editor; Richard K. Holway; History and Social Sciences Editor
Publishing areas: 5, 6 (African literature translated from the French), 10, 12, 27
Other: African American studies, Caribbean studies; electronic publications
U & European distr: Eurospan, 3 Henrietta Street, Covent Garden, London WC2E 8LU, UK, Email: orders@edspubs.co.uk Web: http://www.eurospan.co.uk

2296   University of Washington Press
1326 Fifth Avenue Suite 555
PO Box 50096
Seattle WA 98145-5096
Tel: +1-206-543 4050 Toll-free (US/Canada only) 800-441 4115 Fax: +1-206-543-3932
Email: uwpord@u.washington.edu (General enquiries) patsoden@u.washington.edu (Director) michaeld@u.washington.edu (Executive Editor)
Web: http://www.washington.edu/uwpress/
Contacts: Pat Soden, Director; Michael Duckworth, Executive Editor
Publishing areas: 1, 11, 16, 20
UK & European distr: Combined Academic Publishers Ltd/Marston Book Services Ltd, PO Box 269, 160 Milton Park Estate, Abingdon OX14 4YN, Email: direct.orders@marston.co.uk

2297   University of Wisconsin Press
1930 Monroe Street
Madison WI 53711-2059
Tel: +1-608-263 1110 Fax: +1-608-263 1120
Email: uwiscpress@uwpress.wisc.edu (General enquiries) smleary@wisc.edu (Interim Director) subreckenrid@wisc.edu (Managing Director)
kadushin@wisc.edu (Acquisitions Editor)
Web: http://www.wisc.edu/wisconsinpress/
Contacts: Sheila Leary, Interim, Director; Sue Breckenridge, Managing Editor; submissions to Raphael Kadushin, Acquisitions Editor
Publishing areas: 11, 22, 27
U & European distr: Eurospan, 3 Henrietta Street, Covent Garden, London WC2E 8LU, UK, Email: orders@edspubs.co.uk
Web: http://www.eurospan.co.uk

2298   University Press of America Inc
4501 Forbes Boulevard Suite 200
Lanham MD 20706
Tel: +1- 301-459 3366 Toll-free (US/Canada only) 800-462 6420 Fax: +1-301-429 5748
Email: custserv@rowman.com (Customer Services/Orders) submitupa@univpress.com (Submissions, general)
mmarino@univpress.com (Manager, Editorial Administration) dchao@univpress.com (Acquisitions Editor)
Web: http://www.univpress.com/
Contacts: Michael Marino, Manager, Editorial Administration; David Chao, Acquisitions
Publishing areas: 4, 5, 10, 17, 18, 27, 28, 32, 33, 35, 36, 38, 40, 41, 43, 45
Other: African American studies, Caribbean studies
UK & European distr: NBN International, Estover Road, Plymouth, PL6 7PY, UK, Email: orders@nbninternational.com
Note: a division of the Rowman and Littlefield publishing group.

2299   University Press of Florida
15 NW 15th Street
Gainesville FL 32611-2079
Tle: +1-352-392 1351 Toll-free (US/Canada only) 800-226 3822 Fax: +1-352-392 7302
Email: info@upf.com (General enquiries) mb@upf.com (Director))
Web: http://www.upf.com/
Contacts: Meredith Morris-Babb, Director; submissions to John Byram, Associate Director & Editor-in-Chief
Publishing areas: 2, 5, 11, 12, 20, 24, 27, 36, 40
UK/European distr: Eurospan, 3 Henrietta Street, Covent Garden, London WC2E 8LU, UK, Email: orders@edspubs.co.uk
Web: http://www.eurospan.co.uk

2300   US-Africa Writers Foundation
c/o Chimdi Maduagwu
Executive Director
1681 San Gabriel Ave
Decatur, GA 30032
Tel/Fax: +1-216-274 9003
Email: AfricanWriters@bowwave.org (General enquiries) Usalf@bowwave.com (Submissions)
Web: http://www.bowwave.org/AfricanWriters
Contact in Africa:
Dr. Bode Osanyin, Chairman

Department of Creative Arts
University of Lagos
Akoka Yaba
Lagos
Nigeria
Tel: +234-1-545 4891/2 ext 1363
+234-802-306-5924 (Mobile), Email:
bodeosanyin@yahoo.com
Contact: Chimdi Maduagwu, Executive
Director
Publishing areas: 5, 6, 7, 8
Note: seeks to work in association with
AuthorHouse.com
http://www.authorhouse.com, the US-based
print-on-demand publisher, and aims to serve
authors throughout Africa.

2301   US Agency for International
Development. Africa Bureau
Information Center
1331 Pennsylvania Avenue NW
Suite 1425
Washington DC 20004-1703
Tel: +1-202-661 5827
Fax: +1-202-661 5890
Email: abic@dis.cdie.org (General enquiries)
lpierson@usaid.gov (Assistant Administrator,
Africa Bureau)
Web: http://www.usaid.gov/locations/sub-
saharan_africa/publications/ (Publication
resources)
Order documents from: (and see also Note below)
USAID Development Experience
Clearinghouse
Document Distribution Unit
8403 Colesville Road Suite 210
Silver Spring MD 20910
Tel: +1-301-562 0641
Fax: +1-301-588 7787
Email: docorder@dec.cdie.org
Contact: Lloyd O. Pierson, Assistant
Administrator, Africa Bureau
(no submissions; USAID commissioned work
only)
Publishing areas: 10, 17, 18, 20, 26, 33, 36, 45
Other: Humanitarian response
Note: USAID documents, reports and
publications can also be viewed and ordered
by using the agency's Development
Experiment Clearing House (DEC/DEXS), an
online database of over 124,000 USAID
technical and program documents, with over
19,000 available for electronic download. It
can be found at http://www.dec.org/.

2302   Westview Press
5500 Central Avenue
Boulder CO 80301-2877
Tel: +1-303-444 3541 Toll-free
(US/Canada only) 800-386 5656
Fax: +1-303-449 3356
(Orders to: Perseus Books, Order Department,
1094 Flex Drive, Jackson,
TN 38301)
Email: westview.orders@perseusbooks.com
(Customer Services/Orders)
holly.hodder@perseusbooks.com (Publisher)
karl.yambert@perseusbooks.com (Senior
Editor, African studies)
Web:
http://www.perseusbooksgroup.com/westv
iew/home.jsp
In the UK: (General information, publicity
and promotion)
OPP
PO Box 317
Oxford OX2 9RU
Tel: +44-(0)-1865 860960
Fax: +44-(0)-1865 862763
Email: sue.miller@perseusbooks.com
Contacts: Cathleen Tetro
Associate Publisher; Steve Catalano,
Senior Editor; send submissions to
The Acquisitions Editor
Publishing areas: 5, 11, 17, 20, 26, 27, 29, 36,
38, 39, 40, 41, 44, 45
Other: Islamic studies
Submission restrictions: no submissions by
email accepted.
Note: part of the Perseus Group.

2303   White Cliffs Media
PO Box 6083
Incline Village NV 89450
Tel: +1-775-831 4899 Toll-free (US/Canada
only) 800-345-6665 (Orders)
Fax: +1-760-8756062
Email: wcm@wcmedia.com (General
enquiries) pbs@pathwaybook.com (Orders)
Web:
http://www.wcmedia.com/wcm/wcm.htm
Contact: Lawrence Aynesmith, Founder and
Publisher
Publishing areas: 9
Other: specialist publisher of books and CDs
about African, world, folk and popular music.
Distr: White Cliffs Media, Inc, c/o Pathway
Book Service, 4 White Brook Road, Gilsum,
NH 03448

2304 Markus Wiener Publishing Inc
231 Nassau Street
Princeton NJ 08542
Tel: +1-609-921 1141 Fax: +1-609-921 1140
Email: info@markuswiener.com
Web: http://www.markuswiener.com
Contact: Markus Wiener, President
Publishing areas: 12, 27, 36, 40, 45
Other: African American studies, Caribbean
studies, Islamic studies

2305 The World Bank-Publications
The World Bank
PO Box 960
Herndon VA 20172-0960
Tel: +1-703-661 1580 Toll-free (US/Canada
only) 800-645 7247 Fax: +1-703-661 1501
Office of the Publisher:
1818 H Street NW
Washington DC 20433
Tel+1-202-473 1153 Fax: +1-202-522 2631
Email: books@worldbank.org (Orders)
infoshop@worldbank.org (Development
Gateway Bookstore)
pubdistributors@worldbank.org (Marketing
and Sales department)
pubrights@worldbank.org (Rights
department)
Web:
http://publications.worldbank.org/ecommer
ce/ or
http://www.worldbankinfoshop.org/ecomm
erce/ (Development Gateway Bookstore)
Contact: Dirk Koehler, Office of the Publisher
(no submissions, World Bank-commissioned
material only)
Publishing areas: 10, 17, 18, 20, 23, 24, 29, 33,
38, 41, 44, 45
Other: biodiversity, energy, water resources;
electronic products
Notes:
(i) search and download more than 14,000
World Bank publications at
http://www-wds.worldbank.org/.
(ii) For details about the World Bank
e-Library, an online, fully indexed and cross-
searchable portal of over 3,000 World Bank
documents, *see*
http://elibrary.worldbank.org
This subscription-based research and
reference tool (hosted by Ingenta) consists of
over 1,400 World Bank publications and over
2,000 Policy Research Working Papers.

2306 Yale University Press
302 Temple Street
PO Box 209040
New Haven CT 06520-9040
Tel: +1-203-432 0960 Toll-free
(US/Canada only) 800-405 1619
Fax: +1-203-432 0948
Email: customer.care@triliteral.org
(Customer Services/Orders)
jonathan.brent@yale.edu (Editorial
Director)
Web: http://www.yale.edu/yup/
In the UK:
47 Bedford Square
London WC1B 3DP
Tel: +44-(0)20-7079 4900
Fax: +44-(0)20-7079 4901
Email: sales@yaleup.co.uk (Orders)
robert.baldock@yaleup.co.uk (Editorial
Director, Humanities, UK)
Web:
http://www.yalebooks.co.uk/yale/default.a
sp
Contacts, in the US: Jonathan Brent, Editorial
Director; John Kulka, Senior Editor
(Literature, Literary studies, Philosophy,
Political science); Christopher Rogers,
Executive Editor (History, Current Events)
For other contacts *see*
http://yalepress.yale.edu/yupbooks/submis
sions.asp
Contacts, in the UK: Robert Baldock,
Managing Director & Editorial Director
(Humanities); Gillian Malpass, Editorial
Director, (Art and Architecture); Heather
McCallum, Publisher (History, Politics,
International Affairs, Biography)
Publishing areas: 1, 11, 20, 21, 27, 36,
38, 40, 43, 45
Other: photography
Submissions restrictions: no submissions by
email accepted.

17

Dealers and distributors of African studies materials

This is a selective listing of the principal dealers, booksellers and distributors of books and other materials on African studies in Europe, North America, Africa, and a small number elsewhere. It includes vendors dealing exclusively with rare and antiquarian Africana, although it is by no means a complete listing of antiquarian booksellers.

While there are entries for some suppliers of multicultural materials, more general retailers, such as Foyle's in London, or bookshops elsewhere in the UK or in the USA that stock a small range of African or African American studies materials, are not included. Also not included are major library suppliers such as Blackwell's, Book House Inc, Coutts Information Services, Dawson's, the Eastern Book Company, or YBP Book Services/Lindsay & Croft, although these vendors will supply books from most publishers, large and small, and include African studies material as part of their approval plans. One or two of the top library suppliers, for example YBP, now include African imprints in their approval plan programmes, although the number of titles is still very small.

Most of the dealers listed here primarily stock books, but some also carry stocks of videos and maps. However for a listing of specialist vendors in African maps see the separate section ➔ 7 Cartographic and geographic information sources/Maps sales and map vendors. For distributors of African films and videos see ➔ 8 Guides to film and video/DVD resources: Vendors and distributors.

Many booksellers in Africa concentrate primarily in the supply of school textbooks and educational materials, although there are a number of university bookshops and library suppliers that aim to serve the tertiary and library markets, and will also supply to customers outside Africa. Listings of booksellers in Africa are therefore confined to a relatively small number of firms that will handle orders from overseas (and can be reached by email), although we have not been able to verify in every case that they are in fact willing to do so, nor of course can we guarantee reliability of services offered. We have, however, tried to list at least one source in most countries of the continent. A more comprehensive listing of over 200 African booksellers and library/educational suppliers is available in ➔ The African Publishing Companion: A Resource Guide (259). More bookshops in francophone Africa can also be found on the ➜ **Afrilivres (392)** site under the "Fiche d'éditeur" profiles, which lists "Diffuseurs/distributeurs" for each publisher, including links to address information for local bookshops.

For helpful guidance and tips on how to acquire material in African languages – including blanket and approval plan dealers, bookshops and publishers – consult Alfred Kagan's paper presented to the 61st IFLA General Conference in 1995, ➜ **"Sources for African Language Materials from the Countries of Anglophone Africa" (443)**.

Another helpful source, for those interested in African art books, is *Book Dealers Specializing in African Art*, a directory compiled by the staff of the Smithsonian Institution ➜ **National Museum of African Art Library (1318)**, Washington, DC. First published in 1997, it was last updated in June 2003; it is at http://www.sil.si.edu/SILPublications/dealers.htm.

Disclaimer:
Listings of dealers and distributors in the *African Studies Companion* does not amount to an endorsement of the quality, or reliability, of their services and products.

EUROPE

Belgium

2307   Black Label
Maréestraat 33
2140 Borgerhout (Antwerp)
Tel/Fax: +32-3-236 0212
Email: blacklabel@wol.be
Web: http://www.blacklabel.be
Mail order supplier of books on African literature and the arts in Dutch, English and French; also children's, cookery, dictionaries, etc. Offers online and print catalogues.

2308   De Groene Waterman
Woolstraat 7
Antwerp 2000
Tel: +32-3-232 9394
Email: use email form on Web site
Web: http://www.groenewaterman.be/
Carries the most extensive stocks of books on Africa in Belgium.

Denmark

2309   ALOA. Centre for Literature from Africa, Asia, Latin America and Oceania
Bakkegårdsalle 9 kld
1804 Frederiksberg C
Tel: +45-31-310900 Fax: +45-31-310900
Email: aloa@get2net.dk
Web: http://www.aloa.nu/
Mainly stocks literary titles. Catalogues issued (in Swedish and Norwegian). Also a publisher.

France

➜ **Afrilivres** *see* 3 **Current bibliographies, indexing and abstracting services, and review media** entry 392

2310   Aux Amateurs du Livre
62 avenue de Suffren
75015 Paris
Tel: +33-1-45 67 18 38 Fax: +33-1-45 66 50 70
Email: aal@auxam.fr

Web: http://www.auxam.fr
In the US:
Aux Amateurs du Livres North American
Representative
1855 Wildhaven Crest
Bellingham WA 98226
Tel: +1-360-714 0622 Fax: +1-360-714 0715
Email: jmaddox@auxam.fr
Well-established French library supplier and
wholesaler, who can obtain some
francophone African-published material, and
also offers standing order services.

2311   Les Classiques Africains
3 rue Porte-de-Buc
BP 652
70006 Versailles Cedex
Tel: +33-1-39 67 16 00 Fax: +33-1-3920 02 13
Email: St.PaulFr@aol.com
Distributes and stocks a range of titles from
publishers in Cameroon, Côte d'Ivoire,
Senegal, and Togo.

2312   Librairie Michéle Dhennequin
76 rue du Cherche-Midi
75006 Paris
Tel: +33-1-42 22 18 53 Fax: +33-1-45 44 08 79
Email: slam@franceantiq.fr
Antiquarian bookseller specializing in books
relating to the former French overseas
territories and French-speaking countries,
including Madagascar, as well as ethnology
and ethnography, and colonial literature.

2313   Librairie Kongo
Chantal Delhougne-Miller
BP 65
08600 Givet
Tel: +33-3-24 42 05 92 Fax: +33-3-24 42 01 97
Email: librairie-kongo@wanadoo.fr
Web: http://www.librairie-kongo-
africa.com/
Specialist dealer in rare and antiquarian
African books in French, especially
exploration, ethnography, history, linguistics,
flora and fauna. Catalogues available on
request.

2314   L'Harmattan Edition-Diffusion
Librairie-Centre:
16 rue des Ecoles
75005 Paris
Tel: +33-1-40 46 79 11
also at:
Librairie Sciences Humaines:

21 bis rue des Ecoles
75005 Paris
Tel: +33-1-46 34 13 71
Fax: +33-1-43 29 86 20/43 25 82 03
Email: harmattan1@wanadoo.fr
Web:
http://www.librairieharmattan.com/V1/ind
exM.php3?MAG_ID=2194&oid=1 or
http://www.editions-
harmattan.fr/index.asp?navig=harmattan&sr
=1
A leading Africanist bookshop in France with
the most extensive stocks of African studies
materials, both in French and in English.
Maintains three bookshops, or which two are
in the university area of central Paris. Regular
catalogues issued. Offers an online ordering
facility at its Web site. L'Harmattan is also a
major publisher, *see* ➜ **2174**.

2315   Librairie Picard
82 rue Bonaparte
75006 Paris
Tel: +33-1-43 26 96 73 Fax: +33-1-43 26 42 64
Email: livres@librairie-picard.com
Web:
http://www.abebooks.com/home/libpicard
or http://www.galaxidion.com/picard/
Stocks both new and out-of-print books,
specializing in the field of archaeology, art
and art history, history, philosophy, religion
and fine arts. Searchable online catalogue
available.

2316   Librairie Présence Africaine
25 bis rue des Ecoles
75005 Paris
Tel: +33-1-43 54 15 88/43 54 13 74
Fax: +33-1-43 25 96 67/43 54 96 67
Email: presaf@club-internet.fr
Long established specialist bookshop in the
heart of the Quartier Latin district in Paris,
with an extensive stock of titles on African
studies, and African arts, culture and
literatures, including African-published
material. Présence Africaine is also a
publisher *see* ➜ **2177**.

**2317   Soumbala.com. Librairie
africaniste/Africana bookseller**
ZAE
Les Baronnes
34730 Prades Le Lez
Tel: +33-4-67 59 85 90 Fax: +33-4-67 59 85 91
Email: contact@soumbala.com

Web: http://www.soumbala.com
French online bookseller for African books.
Has an excellent Web site in French, English,
and German. New titles as well as ancient,
rare, or second-hand books on sub-Saharan
Africa, and African journals back issues.
Offers a range of online catalogues, with
secure online ordering facilities, and an email
new title notification service. Browse by new
titles, publishers, journals, authors, broad
subject groups, or African ethnic groups.

Germany

2318   **Afrikahaus - Bücher**
        Remsfelder Strasse 4
        Postfach 1214
        34568 Homburg
Tel: +49-5681-930999 Fax: +49-5681-930977
Email: buecher@afrikahaus.de or
Info@afrikahaus.de
Web: http://www.afrikahaus.de/
This multicultural organization combines a
Web site – providing a variety of information
about African culture and cultural events in
Germany, Austria and Switzerland – with a
book supply service for a large number of
titles listed on the site (primarily in German),
available by mail order. The site also offers
book and film reviews and a number of
useful resources.

2319   **Buchhandlung Fremde Welten**
        Konstantin von Harder
        Lena-Christ-Strasse 50
        82152 Martinsried
Tel: +49-89-85661626 Fax: +49-89-8566 1636
Email: info@fremdewelten.de
Web: http://www.fremdewelten.de
Non-profit organization near Munich; offers
total stocks of over 750,000 titles, including
materials from the countries of the South, also
stocks videos, CDs, maps, children's books,
and more.

2320   **Missing Link**
        Versandbuchhandlung
        Westerstrasse 114-116
        28199 Bremen
Tel: +49-421-504348 Fax: +49-421-504316
Email: info@missing-link.de
Web: http://www.missing-link.de

Major mail order supplier and book importer
for English-language publications, including
publications from Africa.

2321   **Timbuktu African Art & Culture**
        Ladenburgerstrasse 50
        69120 Heidelberg Neuenheim
Tel: +49-6221-411861 Fax: +49-6221-473946
Email: jbeduaddo@aol.com
Web: http://www.heidelberg-
guide.de/afrika-timbuktu/index_e.shtml
In addition to African writing, guidebooks
and volumes of art and poetry, stocks
academic titles on many countries and topics
from the African world. Also carries CDs and
cassettes of African music, African arts and
crafts, musical instruments, and gift items.
Also has a small publishing programme of its
own.

2322   **Tropical Scientific Books (TRIOPS)**
        S. Toeche-Mittler
        Verlagsbuchhandlung GmbH
        Hindenburgstrasse 33
        64295 Darmstadt
Tel: +49-6151-33665 Fax: +49-6151-314048
Email: info@net-library.de or orders@net-
library.de
Web:
http://www.triops.de/index_triops.htm
A leading supplier of specialist literature in
the field of natural sciences for tropical and
subtropical scientific books, and literature
regarding development studies. Search an
online catalogue of more than 5,000 titles.

Ireland

2323   **Kennys Bookshop and Art Galleries**
        High Street
        Galway City
        Galway
Tel: +353-91-709350 Fax: +353-91-709351
Email: queries@kennys.ie
Web: http://www.kennys.ie/
Specializes in building and supplying subject
collections of rare and out-of-print books,
including African anthropology, history,
travel, culture, colonialism/imperialism,
literature, etc. Has substantial stocks of
antiquarian books on Africa. Advanced
search facilities available on the Web site.
Note: also operates as Kennys Book
Collections and Library Services.

Netherlands

2324 Boekhandel De Verre Volken
Steenstraat 1a
2312 BS Leiden
Tel: +31-71-516 8706 Fax: +31-71 5289128
Email: info@ethnographicartbooks.com
Web:
http://www.ethnographicartbooks.com/
Part of the Rijksmuseum voor
Volkenkunde/National Museum of
Ethnology at Leiden. Specializes in books on
the material culture of non-Western
civilizations, including African art and
anthropology.

2325 Matthys de Jongh
Groenmarkt 11
7201 HW Zutphen
Tel +31-575-543 136 Fax +31-575-543 182
Email: matthys@mdejongh.com
Web: http://www.mdejongh.com/
Old, rare and scholarly books, including
offerings of books on sub-Saharan Africa, and
North Africa/Middle East, in various
languages. Specializes in books on economics
and social history.

2326 Gerits & Sons
Prinsengracht 445
1016 HN Amsterdam
Tel. +31-20-627 2285 Fax +31-20-625 8970
Email: a.gerits@inter.nl.net
Web: http://www.nvva.nl/gerits/
Antiquarian bookseller specializing in
economics, law, philosophy, political and
social history, travel and voyages. Offers
catalogues on Africa, Asia and Australia,
among other subject selections.

Portugal

2327 Livraria Académica
rua Martires da Liberdade 10
4050-358 Porto
Tel: +351-22-200 5988 Fax: +351-22-208 9239
Email: academica@mail.telepac.pt
Web: http://www.livraria-academica.com/
The leading Africana dealer in Portugal;
mostly antiquarian. Catalogues issued
regularly.

2328 Livraria Sousa & Almeida
Rua da Fábrica 42
4050-245 Porto
Tel/Fax: +351-222-050073
Email: geral@sousaealmeida.com (New
books)
sousaealmeida@net.sapo.pt (Antiquarian)
Web: http://www.sousaealmeida.com/
Regular catalogues issued (and also available
online) covering both new and antiquarian
books, including a substantial number of
titles on lusophone/former Portuguese
Africa.

Switzerland

2329 Basler Afrika Bibliographien
Klosterberg 21-23
PO Box 2037
4001 Basel
Tel: +41-61-228 9333 Fax: +41-61-228 9330
Email: bab@bluewin.ch
Web: http://www.baslerafrika.ch/antiq.html
New and secondhand books from/on all
parts of Africa; specialist in books on
Namibia and southern Africa. Online
catalogues offered. Also publishers *see*
→ **2198.**

United Kingdom

2330 Afribilia Limited
16 Bury Place
London WC1A 2JL
Tel: +44-(0)20-7404 7137
Fax: +44-(0)20-7404 7138
Email: info@afribilia.com
Web: http://www.afribilia.com
African art, both contemporary and tribal;
Historical memorabilia and printed
ephemera; militaria; also bank notes, coins,
stamps, and mineral specimens.

2331 The Africa Book Centre Ltd
Preston Park Business Centre
36 Robertson Road
Brighton BN1 5NL
Tel: +44-(0)1273 560 474
Fax: +44-(0)1273 500 650
Email: info@africabookcentre.com or
orders@africabookcentre.com.
Web: http://www.africabookcentre.com

Specialist dealer and library supplier of books on Africa. Maintains a database of about 35,000 titles and stocks of some 5,000 books are carried, including an extensive range of African-published material. The company provides a series of bibliographic and information services, including the ➔ **Africa Book Centre Book Review (405)**, and a weekly email notification service for new titles. Usefully, the company also offers a classified online catalogue to material in a large number of African languages (including dictionaries, grammars, self-teaching, phrasebooks, and creative writing in African languages), which can be found at http://www.africabookcentre.com/acatalog /index.html. Also runs a Reading Group, a space for the discussion and appreciation of African fiction and non-fiction. To join, send email to africareadinggroup@hotmail.co.uk. *Note:* formerly located in the building of ➔ **The Africa Centre (2551)** in Covent Garden in central London, which is currently being redeveloped. It hopes to recreate a bookshop there in late 2007. Africa Book Centre Ltd is affiliated with ➔**Global Book Marketing Ltd (2338)**
See also entry ➔ **390**

2332   African Books Collective Ltd (ABC)
Unit 13 Kings Meadow
Ferry Hinksey Road
Oxford OX2 0DP
Tel: +44-(0)1865-726686
Fax: +44-(0)1865-793298
Email: abc@africanbookscollective.com
Web: http://www.africanbookscollective.com
Founded in 1989, African Books Collective (ABC) is a major self-help initiative by a group of African publishers to promote their books in Europe, North America, and in Commonwealth countries outside Africa. ABC is collectively owned by its founding member publishers. It is donor supported and non-profit making on its own behalf. From an initial 17 founder member publishers in 1989, membership has grown rapidly and ABC now provides a single source of supply for the books from 109 African publishers, in 18 African countries, with a stock inventory of some 1,600 titles. A wide range of catalogues are issued, and the complete stock list can be accessed at the ABC

Web site, which provides a secure ordering environment. ABC also offers standing order plans for libraries, and an email notification service for new titles. The complete list of publishers currently distributed by ABC is provided below. Since January 2003 ABC books are exclusively marketed and distributed in North America by ➔ **Michigan State University Press (2271)**, 1405 South Harrison Road, 25 Manly Miles Building, East Lansing, MI 48823-5202, USA. Tel: +1-517-335 9543 (Toll free, North America only) 800-678 2120, Fax: +1-517-432 2611. Email: msupress@msu.edu, Web: http://www.msupress.msu.edu or http://msupress.msu.edu/series.php?seriesI D=22
ABC is now also producing many titles on a print-on-demand basis (POD) on behalf of its publishers, with over 220 titles produced by this method and for sale in northern markets. *See also* entry ➔ **391**

African publishers distributed by African Books Collective Ltd:

Botswana
Foundation for Education with Production, Gaborone
Lightbooks Publishers, Gaborone
Pyramid Publishing, Gaborone

Ethiopia
Development Policy Management Forum, Addis Ababa
Organisation for Social Science Research in Eastern and Southern Africa (OSSREA), Addis Ababa

Ghana
Afram Publications (Ghana) Ltd, Accra
African Capital Markets Forum, Accra
Africa Christian Press, Accra
Association of African Universities Press, Accra
Blackmask Ltd, Accra
Freedom Publications, Accra
Ghana Universities Press, Accra
Sankofa Educational Publishers, Accra
Sedco Publishing, Accra
SEM Financial Training Centre Ltd, Accra
Sub-Saharan Publishers, Accra
Woeli Publishing Services, Accra

Kenya
Academy Science Publishers, Nairobi
Chrisley Ltd, Nairobi
East African Educational Publishers, Nairobi
Focus Publications, Nairobi
Kwani Trust, Nairobi
Law Africa Publishing Ltd, Nairobi
Nairobi University Press, Nairobi
Noni's Publicity, Nairobi
P-J Kenya, Nairobi

Lesotho
Institute of Southern African Studies,
    National University of Lesotho, Roma
Law Society of Lesotho, Maseru

Malawi
Central Africana, Blantyre
Chancellor College Publications, Zomba
E & V Publications, Blantyre
Kachere Series, Zomba
Writers Advisory Services International
    (WASI), Zomba

Nambia
Department of Sociology, University of
    Namibia, Windhoek
University of Namibia Press, Windhoek

Nigeria
African Heritage Press, Lagos
Apex Books, Lagos
The Book Company Ltd, Lagos
Bookcraft Ltd, Ibadan
Bolabay Publishers, Lagos
Cogito Publishers, Enugu
College Press Publishers, Ibadan
CSS Bookshops, Lagos
Dokun Publishing House, Ibadan
Enicrownfit Publishers, Lagos
Epik Books, Lagos
Fourth Dimension Publishing Co Ltd, Enugu
Heinemann Educational Books (Nigeria) plc,
    Ibadan
Humanities Publishers, Ibadan
Ibadan University Press, Ibadan
Kraft Books, Lagos
Maiyati Chambers, Lagos
Malthouse Press Ltd, Lagos
Mary Kolawole Publications, Lagos
New Horn Press, Ibadan
Nidd Publishing and Printing, Oyo
Obafemi Awolowo University Press, Ile-Ife
Onyoma Research Publications, Port

Harcourt
Opon Ifa Readers, Lagos
Saros International Publishers, Port Harcourt
Spectrum Books Ltd, Ibadan
University of Lagos Press, Lagos
University Press Ltd, Ibadan
Urhobo Historical Society, Lagos
Women's Health and Action Research, Benin

Senegal
African Renaissance, Dakar
Council for the Development of Social
    Science Research in Africa (CODESRIA),
    Dakar
Union for African Population Studies, Dakar

Sierra Leone
Penpoint Publishers, Freetown

South Africa
Africa Institute of South Africa, Pretoria
Frank Horley Books, Johannesburg
IDASA Publishing, Cape Town
Mail and Guardian Books, Johannesburg
University of South Africa Press (UNISA
    Press), Pretoria

Swaziland
Academic Publishers, Manzini
JAN Publishing Centre, Mbabane
TTI Publishers, Manzini

Tanzania
Centre for Energy, Environment, Science &
    Technology (CEEST), Dar es Salaam
Dar es Salaam University Press, Dar es
    Salaam
E & D Ltd, Dar es Salaam
Mkuki na Nyota Publishers, Dar es Salaam
Tanzania Publishing House, Dar es Salaam
Tema Publishing, Dar es Salaam

Uganda
Fountain Publishers Ltd, Kampala
FEMRITE (Uganda Women Writers'
    Association), Kampala

Zambia
Bookworld Publishers, Lusaka
Image Publishers Ltd, Lusaka
Multimedia Zambia, Lusaka
University of Zambia Press
Zambia Women Writers Association

Zimbabwe

Africa Community Publishing &
  Development Trust, Harare
Baobab Books, Harare
Kimathi Publishing House
Mambo Press, Gweru
Southern Africa Printing and Publishing
  House/SAPES Trust, Harare
Southern African Research and
  Documentation Centre (SARDC), Harare
Southern and Eastern African Trade,
  Information and Negotiation Institute
  (SEATINI), Harare
University of Zimbabwe Publications, Harare
Weaver Press Ltd, Harare
Women and Law in Southern Africa
  Research Trust, Harare
Zimbabwe International Book Fair Trust,
  Harare
Zimbabwe Publishing House, Harare
Zimbabwe Women Writers, Harare

**2333   African Shop for African Books/
         African Online Shop**
         2 Surrenden Road
         Brighton
         BN1 6PP
Tel: +44-(0)1273-236746
Fax: 44-(0)1273-236748
Email: sales@over2u.com
Web: http://www.over2u.com/
UK dealer in African books and magazines
(mostly Nigerian), music, video, films, fabrics
and textiles, drama, and gospel music.
Note: US address is at PO Box 922335,
Norcross GA 30010, Tel: +1-530-684 7455

2334   Allsworth Rare Books
         235 Earls Court Road
         PO Box 134
         London SW5 9FE
Tel/Fax: +44-(0)20-7377 0552
jenny@allsworthbooks.com (General
enquiries) or travel@allsworthbooks.com
(Travel titles)
Web: http://www.allsworthbooks.com/
Specializes in fine travel books and
nineteenth century photographs, with a
particular emphasis on Africa and the Far
East.

2335   Peter J. Ayre
         Greenham Hall nr. Wellington
         TA21 0JJ
Tel: +44-(0)1823-672603

Fax: +44-(0)1823-672307
Email: PeterJAyre@aol.com
http://www.abebooks.com/home/TREMLE
TT/
New and secondhand books on Kenya/East
Africa, and big game hunting.

2336   Cyclamen Books
         PO Box 69
         Leicester LE1 9EW
Fax: +44-(0)116-270 4623
Email: rara@cyclamenbooks.com
Web: n/a
Offers antiquarian books (and an email
notification service) on Islamic studies,
including books on North Africa and the
Sudan.

**2337   The Development Bookshop/
         Development Bookshop Online**
         ITDG Publishing
         Bourton Hall
         Bourton-on-Dunsmore
         Rugby CV23 9QZ
Tel: +44-(0)1926-634501
Fax: +44 (0)1926-634502
Email: admin@developmentbookshop.com or
marketing@itpubs.org.uk
Web:
http://www.developmentbookshop.com
Operated by ➔ ITDG Publishing (2219),
Development Bookshop.com offers a wide
range of key titles on international
development from around the world.
Operates a worldwide mail-order service and
provides mail-order catalogues. Browse by
categories on the Web site, or search for
books by author, title, etc. Specializes in
books with practical information for a range
of professionals, including community
development workers, agricultural extension
specialists, engineers and technicians,
enterprise development specialists, and
humanitarian workers.

2338   Global Book Marketing Ltd (GBM)
         99B Wallis Road
         London E9 5LN
Tel +44-(0)20-8533 5800
or (UK only) 0845-458 1580
Email: tz@globalbookmarketing.co.uk
Web:
http://www.centralbooks.co.uk/acatalog/se
arch.html (online catalogue search)
Distribution and order fulfilment:

Central Books Ltd
99 Wallis Road
London E9 5LN
Tel: +44-(0)20-8986 4854
Fax: +44-(0)20-533 5821
Email: orders@centralbooks.com
Partnering with the ➔ **Africa Book Centre
(2231)**, GBM promotes, markets, and manages
distribution in Europe for some thirty
publishers. It is an African studies specialist,
and its services include provision of book
information by subject and by region,
printing book bar codes, supplying select
mailing lists, and exhibiting at African studies
events. GBM sells the lists of ➔ **Bayreuth
African Studies (2181)**, the ➔ **Nordic Africa
Institute (2197)**, and ➔ **James Currey
Publishers (2210)**, together with the African-
based publishers listed below. To find out if a
book is in stock, visit the online catalogue.

*African publishers distributed by Global Book
Marketing Ltd:*

Kenya
Camerapix Publishers, Nairobi

South Africa
Blue Weaver, Cape Town (and its agencies)
Briza Publishers, Pretoria
Double Storey, Cape Town
Fernwood Press, Vlaeberg
Human and Rousseau, Cape Town
Jacana, Johannesburg
Juta, Cape Town
Kwela Books, Cape Town
New Africa Books, Claremont (and affiliated
   imprints)
New Africa Education Publishing, Claremont
NB Group, Cape Town (and affiliated
   imprints)
Pan-Macmillan South Africa, Craighall
Pharos, Cape Town
David Philip Publishers, Cape Town
STE Publishers, Johannesburg
Stromberg Publishers, Cape Town
University of Cape Town Press, Cape Town

Tanzania
Blue Mango, Dar es Salaam
Gallery and HSP Publications, Zanzibar

Zimbabwe
African Publishing Group, Harare

2339   Michael Graves-Johnston
54 Stockwell Park Road
London SW9 ODR
Tel: +44-(0)20-7274 2069
Fax: +44-(0)20-7738 3747
Email: Info@Graves-Johnston.com
Web: http://www.graves-johnston.com/
Specializing in ancient tribal cultures and also
carries extensive stocks of works on travel,
anthropology, ethnology, art, archaeology
and colonial literature. Catalogues issued
frequently; recent catalogues accessible
online.

**2340   Hogarth Representation/
            Meabooks Inc**
Unit 54 Millmead Business Centre
Millmead Road
Tottenham Hale
London N17 9QU
Tel: +44-(0)20-8365 1515
Fax: +44-(0)20-8808 7090
Email: hogarth@hogarthrep.fsnet.co.uk
Web:
http://www.meabooks.com/default.htm
In Canada:
Meabooks Inc
34 Chemin du Boise
Lac-Beaufort OC G0A 2C0
Email: info@meabooks.com
Tel: 1-418-841 3237 Fax: 1-418-841 1644
Largely a library supplier, and one of the
leading blanket order/approval plan dealers
for African imprints, including government
and official publications, serial publications,
and grey literature. Also offers a search
service. Extensive range of lists and
catalogues issued. The Web site provides
access to a searchable and browsable Africana
online catalogue. Now works primarily in
association with the Canada-based ➔
Meabooks Inc (2353) and ➔ **Options Book
Centre (2456)** in Nigeria.

**2341   Kenya Books. Books on Kenya and
            Africa**
31 Southdown Avenue
Brighton BN1 6EH
Tel:/Fax: +44-(0)1273-556029
Email: info@kenyabooks.com
Web:
http://www.abebooks.com/home/kenyaboo
ks
Holds an inventory of approximately 6,000
out-of-print books on Africa, principally on

Kenya and East Africa, and secondly central and southern Africa, but also many titles on African languages, linguistics, and ethnography. Inventory can be searched online.

2342 Maggs Rare Books
Maggs Bros Ltd
50 Berkeley Square
London W1J 5BA
Tel: +44-(0)20-7493 7160
Fax: +44-(0)20-7499 2007
Email: enquiries@maggs.com or (for travel books department) travel@maggs.com
Web: http://www.maggs.com/
RSS RSS feed
http://www.maggs.com/rss/au.asp
Founded in 1853, Maggs Bros is one of the world's largest antiquarian booksellers and dealer in rare books, manuscripts, and first editions. Areas of specialization include travel and exploration in Africa, the Boer War, and natural history.

2343 Multicultural Books Ltd
PO Box 107
Greenford UB6 9XY
Tel/Fax: +44-(0)20-8813 1978
Email: multicultural@btconnect.com or blossom.jackson@btconnect.com
Web: http://www.multiculturalbooks.co.uk
Supplies and promotes multicultural books from around the world, primarily by mail order. The Web site offers access to an annotated catalogue.

2344 New Beacon Books
76 Stroud Green Road
Finsbury Park
London N4 3EN
Tel: +44-(0)20-7272 4889
Fax: +44-(0)20-7281 4662
Email: newbeaconbooks@lineone.net
Web: http://www.newbeaconbooks.co.uk/
Well-known bookshop (and publisher) in North London, founded by John la Rose in 1966. Extensive stocks of over 20,000 titles covering fiction and non-fiction from/about Africa, the Caribbean, Afro-America and Black Britain. Also stocks multi-ethnic children's books.

2345 One World Book Co
8 Rickett Street
West Brompton
London SW6 1RU
Tel: +44-(0)20-7381 4994
Fax: +44-(0)20-7385 0534
Email: br@one-world-books.demon.co.uk
Web: http://www.one-world-books.demon.co.uk
Suppliers of books on the Black perspective and multicultural materials to libraries and educational institutions. Showrooms located in West London.

2346 Oriental and African Books
33 Whitehall Street
Shrewsbury SY2 5AD
Tel: +44-(0)1743-752575
Fax: +44-(0)1743-363432
Email: paul@africana.co.uk
Web: http://www.africana.co.uk/
Specializes in rare, antiquarian and out-of-print books on Africa and the Middle East, with smaller holdings relating to Asia. The company has also developed a particular interest in putting together collections on specific areas or subjects relating to Africa and the Middle East. These are primarily intended for library or institutional use.
See also → Wilson, Paul **"Out-of-Print and Secondhand: A View of the Antiquarian Book Trade."** in section **15 Africanist documentation and African studies bibliography**, entry **1920**.

2347 Passionet.net
537 Norwood Rd
Entrance 1 Chestnut Road
West Norwood
London SE27 9DL
Tel: +44-(0)845-330 9498
Fax: +44-(0)208-761 1469
Email: info@passionet.net
Web: http://www.passionet.net/default.asp
This online bookseller stocks a large range of black and urban books for all levels of reading, including educational and children's books. The emphasis is on African American and Black British writers.

2348 Arthur Probsthain Oriental Bookseller
41 Great Russell Street
London WC1B 3PE
Tel: +44(0)20-7636 1096
Fax: +44(0)20-7636 1096
Email: ap@oriental-african-books.com (Main shop)
ms61@soas.ac.uk (SOAS Bookshop)
Web: http://www.oriental-african-books.com/
Long established firm, and one of the oldest bookshops in central London, located opposite the British Museum, and specialising in Asian, African and Middle Eastern studies. Catalogues issued in print formats and online. Also has a branch at the
→ **School of Oriental and African Studies (1289)**, which is located in the Brunei Gallery.

2349 Risborough Books
E.T. Funnell
81 Manor Park Avenue
Princes Risborough HP27 9AR
Tel: +44(0)-1844-343165
Web: n/a
Specializes in books on East and Central Africa. Regular lists issued.

2350 Shapero Gallery
32 Saint George Street
London W1S 2EA
Tel: +44-(0)20-7493 0876
Fax: +44-(0)20-7229 7860
Email: rarebooks@shapero.com
Web: http://www.shapero.com/php/
Among other subjects, specializes in travel books, natural history, colour plate books, maps, and decorative books. A catalogue of books relating to Africa and travel in Africa was issued in 2003 and is still available for download. Also has a large collection of old photographs from North and sub-Saharan Africa.

NORTH AMERICA

Canada

2351 CMG Books & Art
2455 Cawthra Road Unit 31
Mississauga ON L5A 3P1
Tel: +1-905-275 2665 Fax: +1-905-275 1366
Email: info@CMGBooksandArt.com
Web: http://www.cmgbooksandart.com/
Specialist dealer in books on the arts of Africa, Oceania, Native American, Latin America, and Islamic. Also offers a large selection of books on textiles, folk and decorative art. Browse Web site by category or use the online search service.

2352 A Different Booklist
746 Bathurst Street
Toronto ON M5S 2RG
Tel: +1-416-538 0889 Fax: +1-416-538 3224
Email: info@adifferentbooklist.com
Web: http://www.adifferentbooklist.com/
Progressive Toronto bookstore offering culturally diverse general, academic, and children's titles.

2353 Meabooks Inc
34 Chemin du Boise
Lac-Beauport QC G0A 2C0
Tel: +1-418-841 3237 Fax: +1-418-841 1644
Email: info@meabooks.com
Web:
http://www.meabooks.com/default.htm
Offers stocks, and an online database, of over 3,000 recent titles from Africa, all obtained through personal visits to Africa. Works in association with the UK dealer → **Hogarth Representation (2340)**. Sells books, periodicals, and audiovisual materials from Africa, Central Asia, Russia and parts of the Middle East. Browse or search the Africana online catalogue.

United States

2354 African Imprint Library Services (AILS)
8122 Reynard Road
Chapel Hill NC 27516
Tel: +1-919-968 9417 Fax: +1-919-932 5341
Email: ailscils@msn.com
Web: http://www.africanbooks.com

Primarily a library supplier and blanket order dealer for virtually all printed materials published anywhere in Africa, including government and official publications and more elusive material. Numerous lists issued, and posted on AILS's Web site. Searchable online catalogue. Also supplies publications from the Caribbean.

2355 Axis Gallery
453 West 17th Street 4th Floor
New York NY 10011
Tel: +1-212-741-2582 Fax: +1-212-924-2522
Email: axisgallery@aol.com
Web: http://www.axisgallery.com/store/
Specializes in books (in print and out-of-print) films, CDs, and CDROMS on contemporary South African art.

2356 Bennett-Penvenne Livros
162 Oak Street
Duxbury MA 02332
Tel: +1-781-934 0961
Email: normanbennett@earthlink.net
Web: n/a
Books and pamphlets on lusophone Africa, and the Portuguese and Spanish worlds. Catalogues issued.

2357 Dandemutande Gifts
1122 East Pike Street #1163
Seattle WA 98122-3934
Tel:/Fax: n/a
Email: email@dandemutande.com
Web: http://www.dandemutande.com
Seattle-based specialist supplier of Zimbabwean music, books and other materials.

2358 Ethnographic Arts Publications/ Tribal Arts Books.com
1040 Erica Road
Mill Valley CA 94941
Tel: +1-415-383 2998 Fax: +1-415-388 8708
Email: orders@tribalartbooks.com
Web: http://www.tribalartbooks.com
Specializes in books on African art, artefacts, ethnography and material culture. Holds an inventory of more than 12,000 rare and out of print books, catalogues, and journals.

2359 Great Epic Books
15918 20th Place West
Lynnwood WA 98037
Tel: +1-425-745 3113 Fax +1-425-745 9520

Email: africabooks@worldnet.att.net
Web: http://www.greatepicbooks.com/
Rare and scarce antiquarian books about the continent of Africa. Has an inventory of more than 40,000 African books, maps, documents, manuscripts and other collectibles.

2360 Indian Ocean Books, Maps, and Prints (Larry W. Bowman)
PO Box 232
Storrs CT 06268-0232
Tel: +1-860-429 4289 Fax: +1-860-486 3347
Email: indianoceanbooks@earthlink.net
Web: http://www.indianoceanbooks.com
Specialist dealer in (primarily) rare and antiquarian books, maps, and prints from the entire Indian Ocean region.

2361 Luso-Brazilian Books
560 West 180th Street Suite 304
New York, NY 10033
Tel: +1- 212-568-0151 Fax: +1-212-568 0147
Email: info@lusobraz.com
Web: http://www.lusobraz.com/index.php3
An American source for books in Portuguese, both from Brazil and Portugal. Stocks include some African literature titles, scholarly titles on lusophone Africa, and children's books.

2362 McBlain Books
PO Box 185062
2348 Whitney Avenue
Hamden CT 06518
Tel: +1-203-281 0400 Fax: +1-203-230 1629
Email: books@mcblainbooks.com
Web: http://www.mcblainbooks.com
Primarily antiquarian dealer specializing in African Americana; sub-Saharan Africa; North Africa and the Middle East; and also some other areas. Regular catalogues issued, in print and electronic formats.

2363 Multilingual Books
1309 NE Ravenna Boulevard
Seattle WA 98105
Tel: +1-206-328 7922 Toll-free (US/Canada only) 800-218-2737 Fax: +1-206-328 7445
Email: info@multlingualbooks.com
Web: http://www.multilingualbooks.com/index.html
Offers courses, tapes, videos, and software in over 100 languages including African language material. Also has a very useful links collection to African Internet Radio and

Online News Radio at
http://www.multilingualbooks.com/online-radio-african.html.

**2364 National Museum of African
Art Museum Shop**
Smithsonian Institution
950 Independence Avenue SW
Washington DC 20560-0708
Tel: +1-202-786 2147
Web:
http://www.nmafa.si.edu/geninfo/genshop.htm
The Museum Shop has a large selection of
books for adults and children on African art,
culture, and history. The shop also carries
African crafts, posters, note cards, records,
and tapes. *See also* entry ➜ **53**.

2365 Océanie-Afrique-Noire
15 West 39th Street 2nd floor
New York NY 10018-3806
Tel: +1-212-840 8844 Fax: +1-212-840 3304
Email: oan@computer.net
Web: http://www.oanbooks.com or
http://www.ambook.org/bookstore/oanartbooks/ (neither site accessible as at November
2005)
Specializes in art, ethnology and related
publications of Africa, Oceania, the Americas
and Southeast Asia, both foreign and US
published, and covering in-print and out-of-print titles, periodicals, exhibition and
auction catalogues. Catalogues issued.

2366 Peaceworks Educational Inc
3812 N First Street
Fresno CA 93726
Tel: +1-559-435 8092 Fax: +1-559-439 9009
Email: peacwrk@aol.com
Web: n/a
Stocks and distributes books in indigenous
African languages, including (at this time),
Bambara, Kiswahili, Twi, and Tagawa.

2367 Peppercorn Books & Press Inc
PO Box 693
Snow Camp NC 27349
Tel: +1-336-574 1634 Toll-free (US/Canada
only) 877 574 1634
Fax: +1-336-376 9099
Email: post@peppercornbooks.com
Web: http://www.peppercornbooks.com/
Distributes the titles of a small number of
South African publishers.

2368 Revolution Books
9 West 19th Street
New York NY 10011
Tel: +1-212-691 3345
Email: n/a
Web: n/a
Long-established leftist bookshop just off 5th
Avenue in central Manhattan. Carries small
stocks of African and African American
studies material.

2369 Terra Media Books
12 Leighton Road
Wellesley MA 02482
Tel: +1-781-237 6485 Fax: +1-781-416 2083
Email: terram@attbi.com
Web:
http://www.abebooks.com/home/ESAADBKS/
Specializes in Africa and African exploration,
Arabia, the Middle East, and Islam. Has
stocks of about 15,000 titles.

2370 TomFolio.com
PO Box 392
Readville MA 02137
Email: n/a (use online email form on Web
site)
Web: http://www.tomfolio.com/default.asp
A Web site for buying and selling used, rare
and collectible books, ephemera, and
periodicals, operated by A Book CoOp as a
cooperative venture, jointly owned by
independent member booksellers. There are
good search facilities, and more than 1,000
titles on Africa and African studies are on
offer from various booksellers.

2371 Women Ink
777 UN Plaza 3rd floor
New York NY 10017
Tel: +1-212-687 8633 ext 204
Fax: +1-212-661 2704
Email: wink@womenink.org or
alicequinn@womenink.org
Web: http://www.womenink.org/
Distributes resources on women and
development from over 60 publishers
worldwide, including books on African
gender studies, African women's writing, and
African-published material. Offers an email
notification service for new titles.

AFRICA

Listed below are a select number of what, arguably, are some of the leading booksellers, library and educational suppliers, and book distributors in Africa, who may be willing to handle mail orders from overseas for locally published material. A small number of them can provide new locally-published titles on a standing order basis.

Where available, and verifiable, we have added a short description indicating the range of stocks carried, and/or areas of specialization. Only a small number of bookshops currently have Web sites, but most have an email address.

For a more comprehensive listing of African booksellers consult ➔ **The African Publishing Companion (259)**

Disclaimer:
Listings of dealers and distributors in the *African Studies Companion* does not amount to an endorsement of the quality, or reliability, of their services and products.

Algeria

2372 Maison des Livres
12 rue Maître Ali Boumendjel
Alger 16000
Tel: +213-21-736523 Fax: +213-21-921610
Email: maison-livres@hotmail.com

2373 Algiers International Study Centre-EURL AISC Librairie/Booksellers
Cité 134 logts. Bat 5A
BP 050 Bouchaoui
16803 Cheraga
Algiers
Email: n/a
Tel: +213-21 39 55 02 Fax: +213-21 94 43 72/73
Suppliers of academic books in French and English.

Benin

2374 Librairie Notre Dame
Avenue Clozel
BP 307
Cotonou
Tel: +229-313015/314094 Fax: +229-310719
Email: libdame@intnet.bj or lnd@bj.refer.org
Web: n/a

2375 Librairie SONAEC
01 BP 2042
Cotonou
Tel: +229-312242 Fax: +229-312058
Email: libfadoul@firstnet.bj or pointlpp@intnet.bj

Botswana

2376 Bobi Books
Plot 514 Southring Road
Private Bag X010
Village Post Office
Gaborone
Tel: +267-375860 Fax: +267-375803

Email: bobi@info.bw
General, educational, children's and tertiary-level books; also music and CDs.

2377   Botswana Book Centre
The Main Mall
PO Box 91
Gaborone
Tel: +267-352931 Fax: +267-374315
Email: bookcentre@botsnet.bw
Web: http://www.bbc.co.bw/
Well-stocked general bookshop in Gaborone's central shopping precinct. Suppliers of a wide range of books of an educational and general nature. Stock guides and catalogues issued. Has branches throughout the country.

2378   Ngwato Stationers and Bookshop
Main Mall
PO Box 923
Serowe
Central District
Tel: +267-431178 Fax: +267-430480
Email: n/a
Educational and library suppliers.

2379   University of Botswana Bookstore
Private Bag 0022
Gaborone
Tel: +267-355 2272 Fax: +267-355 2272
Email: modukan@ub.bw

Burkina Faso

2380   Librairie Jeunesse d'Afrique
01 BP 1471
Ouagadougou 01
Tel: +226-333625 Fax: +226-307275/307251
Email: lja@liptinfor.bf
Primarily educational, religious, and children's books.

2381   Librairie Universitaire
01 BP 7021
Ouagadougou 03
Tel: +226-308820 Fax: +226-307242
Email: lu@univ-ouaga.bf

Cameroon

2382   Librairie des Editions CLE
BP 1501
Yaoundé
Tel: +237-222 3554 Fax: +237-223 2709
Email: cle@wagne.net or cle@camnet.cm
Web: http://www.wagne.net/cle/
Retail outlet of one of Cameroon's leading publishers, stocking ➔ **Editions CLE (1941)** as well as other publications, primarily general and educational books, African fiction and drama, and children's books.

2383   Librairie Euréka
Carrefour CES
Ngola Ekele
BP 8275
Yaoundé
Tel: +237-223 1895 Fax: +237-223 1873
Email: eureka@camnet.cm
Web: n/a

2384   Librairie Saint-Paul
BP 763
Yaoundé
Tel: +237-222 3404 Fax: +237-231 8896
Email: lib.sp@refinedet.net
Primarily educational and religious books, but also stocks and distributes Cameroonian imprints.

2385   Librairie Universitaire Sapiencia
PO Box 7835
Douala
Tel/Fax: +237-340 4417
Email: sapiencia@francemail.com
Stocks university-level textbooks and other titles for tertiary education.

Congo Democratic Republic

2386   Librairie Paulines
BP 335
Kinshasa-Limete
Tel/Fax: +243-88-41670
Email: fspkin@maf.org
Stocks primarily religious and educational titles.

2387   Livres de l'Afrique Centrale
BP 3366
Kinshasa-Gombe
Tel/Fax: n/a
Email: ntiakulu_isaac@yahoo.fr
Well-established library supplier of
publications from the Congo (Democratic
Republic) and Congo-Brazzaville. Catalogues
issued.

Côte d'Ivoire

2388   Arte Lettres Librairie-Papeterie
Rivièra face Leader Price
BP 1970
Abidjan 25
Tel: +225-22 43 20 36 /90 44 28
Fax: + 225-22 43 21 46
Email: arte@aviso.ci
A well-stocked general bookshop in Abidjan.

**2389   Centre d'Edition et de Diffusion
Africaines (CEDA)**
04 BP 541
Abidjan 04
Tel: +225-21-246510Fax: +225- 21-250567
Email: info@ceda-ci.com
Web: http://www.ceda-ci.com
Primarily a publisher (*see* ➔ 1953) at this
time, but also plans to become a distributor.

**2390   Edicom SA/Librairie Forum des
Livres**
16 BP 466
Abidjan 16
Tel: +225-21-227856 Fax: +225-21-417711
Email: n/a
Retailer and distributor of francophone
African-published materials to libraries and
other book buyers in the countries in the
North, especially for books published in the
Côte d'Ivoire.

2391   Ex Libris Abidjan
Boulevard La Trille
Abidjan 06
Tel: + 225-21-2242 8796
Fax: + 225-21-2242 8797
Email: Libris@Africa-online

2392   Librairie de France Group
Avenue Chardy
Immeuble Alpha 2000
01 BP 587
Abidjan 01
Tel: +225-20 30 63 63 Fax: +225-20 30 63 64
Email: ldf@africaonline.co.ci or
barnoin@ci.refer.org
Web:
http://www.ci.refer.org/ivoir_ct/eco/ent/b
ar/horaire.htm (site down as at 01/11/05)
Leading Ivoirien bookseller with several
branches throughout the country. However, it
reportedly suffered serious fire damage in
November 2004, during civil disturbances,
and its current status has not been verified.

Djibouti

2393   Librairie Couleur Locales
BP 3500
Djibouti
Tel: +253-352121 Fax: +253-353996
Email: couleurloc@intnet.dj
Both bookseller and publisher, *see* ➔ 1959

Egypt

**2394   Alex Centre for Multimedia &
Libraries**
181-183 Ahmed Shawky St.
Roushdy
Alexandria
Postal address:
PO Box 115
Al-Saray
21411 Alexandria
Tel: +203-541 1741/541 1109
Fax: +203-541 1742
Email: periodicals@acml-egypt.com (Serials)
books@acml-egypt.com (Books)
lib-supplies@acml-egypt.com (Library
supplies in general)
Web: http://www.acml-egypt.com/
A leading library supplier and subscription
agent in the Arab world. Also supplies
articles and dissertations.

2395   Boustany's
4 Aly Tawfik Shousha Street
11371 Nasr City
Cairo
Tel: +202-2-262 3085/590 8025
Fax: +20-2-262 3085
Email: boustany@link.net or
boustany@boustanys.com
Web: http://www.boustanys.com
Both a publishing house (*see* ➔ **1961**) and a
bookseller, established in 1900. Supplies
current publications, as well as rare and out-
of-print books. Offers catalogues and a
worldwide delivery service for any
monographs, newspapers and/or periodicals
that are published in Egypt and the Middle
East.

2396   Leila Books
39 Kasr El-Nil Street
Floor 2 Office 12
Cairo
Postal address:
Leila Books
PO Box 31
Daher 11271
Bookshop at:
Leila Bookshop
17 Gawad Hosny Street
Cairo
Tel: +20-2-393 4402/395 9747
Fax: +20-2-392 4475
Email: info@leilabooks.com (General
enquiries) sales@leilabooks.com
(Sales/Orders)
Web: http://www.leilabooks.com/index.php
Established in 1961 Leila Books is one of the
leading vendors for monographs and
periodicals from Egypt and the Middle East.
Offers standing-order plans and provides
catalogue and bibliographic services.

2397   Madbouly Bookshop
6 Talaat Harb Square
Cairo
Tel: +20-2-575 6421 Fax: +20-2-575 2854
Email: madbouly@madbouly.com
Web: http://www.madbouly.com/ (site
down as at 01/11/05)
Operated by the Madbouly family for over 50
years, this one of Egypt's most prominent
publishing enterprises and bookshop.

2398   Les Livres de France
Kasr el Nil Street
Immeuble Immobilia
Cairo
Tel: +20-2-393 5512 Fax: +20-2-393 0804
Email: farazli@link.com.eg
A small well-stocked bookshop in downtown
Cairo. As well as French books, stocks
include titles in English, particularly on
Egyptology.

Eritrea

2399   Awget Bookshop
PO Box 1299
Zoba Maekel
Asmara
Tel: +291-1-122359 Fax: +291-1-114918
Email: awget@eol.com.er
The bookshop outlet of the Popular Front for
Democracy and Justice. Stocks and distributes
local, government, and international
publications.

2400   Mediatech Bookshop
PO Box 4412
Asmara
Tel: +291-1-184632 Fax: +291-1-184631
Email: mediatech@eol.com.er
Wholesaler and retailer of educational and
general books. Also offers subscription
services.

Ethiopia

2401   Ethiopia Book Centre
King George Street
PO Box 1024
Addis Ababa
Tel: +251-1-123336
Email: n/a
Well-established retail bookshop in the centre
of Addis Ababa.

2402   Image International
PO Box 80766
Addis Ababa
Tel: +251-1-665269 Fax: +251-1-665272
Email: image@telecom.net.et
Wholesale and retail bookseller with
branches throughout the country.

2403 **Mega Distribution Enterprise**
PO Box 914
Addis Ababa
Tel: +1- 251-1-550688 Fax: +1-251-1-550868
Email: mde@telecom.net.et
A leading private bookseller and distributor, primarily stocking general and educational titles.

Gabon

2404 **Librairie Comete**
BP 6794
Libreville
Tel: +241-724401 Fax: + 241-724401
Email: comete.informatique@inet.ga

The Gambia

2405 **M & B Bookshop**
4 Rene Blain Street
Banjul
Tel: +220-223755 Fax: +220-228004
Email: m&bbookshop@yahoo.com
Small bookshop in central Banjul selling general and educational books and African fiction.

2406 **Timbooktoo Bookshop**
120 Kairaba Avenue
Kakau Newtown Junction
PO Box 273
Banjul
Tel: +220-494345/6 Fax: +220-494242
Email: timbooktoo@gamtel.gm
Recently established modern bookshop offering a wide range of stocks, including both fiction and non-fiction, African-interest titles, and academic books.

Ghana

2407 **EPP Book Services (Ghana) Ltd**
44 A/7 La Education,
PO Box TF 490
Trade Fair
Accra
Tel: +233-21-784849/778853
Fax: +233-21-779099
Email: epp@eppbookservices.com
Web: http://www.eppbookservices.com/

Major retailer and library supplier with headquarters near the Ghana Trade Fair Centre, and branches in Accra (adjacent to the Ghana Law School near Makola), Achimota, Kumasi, Tema, and Takoradi. Specializes in books for tertiary education, but also carries a wide range of general stocks.

2408 **Omari Bookshop**
85 Ring Road East Extension
Labone
PO Box 0468
Osu-Accra
Tel: +223-21-776212 Fax: +233-21-778798
Email: omari@ighmail.com
Carries a good range of stocks of Ghanaian-published materials, and other titles on African studies.

2409 **University Bookshop**
University of Ghana
University Square
PO Box 1
Legon
Tel: +223-21-500398 Fax: +223-21-500774
Email: bookshop@ug.edu.gh
Web: http://www.ug.edu.gh/index.php
(University home page)
The premier university bookshop in the country. Extensive stocks of books on or published in Ghana, including titles from many Ghanaian publishers. Lists and catalogues issued.

Guinea

2410 **Librairie Ganndal (Librairie de Guinée)**
BP 542
Conakry
Tel: +224-463507/447624 Fax: +224-412012
Email: ganndal@mirinet.net.gn
Web: http://www.editionsganndal.com/
The bookshop of Guinea's leading publisher, → **Editions Ganndal (1979)**. Wide range of stocks carried.

2411 **Sogudip**
545 rue KA 020
Boulbinet
BP 4517
Conakry
Tel: +224 -413119 Fax: +224-414740
Email: cheick.soguidip@mirinet.net.gn

Kenya

2412   Books First Ltd
Ukay Centre
Ring Road Parklands
PO Box 2384
Nairobi
Tel: +254-20-742735/742253/742526
Email: booksfirst@nbi.ispkenya.com
General bookshop, part of a chain bookstore.

2413   Inter-Africa Book Distributors Ltd
Kencom House
Moi Avenue
PO Box 73586
Nairobi
Tel: +254-20-330232/211183
Fax: +254-20-214618/213025
Email: n/a
Stockists and distributors of educational,
tertiary, business and law books.

2414   Keswick Books and Gifts Ltd
PO Box 10242
Nairobi
Tel: +254-20-226047 Fax: +254-20-728557
Email: Keswick@swiftkenya.com
Well-established general, educational, and
religious booksellers.

2415   Legacy Books and Distributors
Yaya Centre 2nd floor
PO Box 68077
Nairobi
Tel: +254-2-387 3991 Fax: +254-20-387 3993
Email: info@legacybookshop.com
Web: http://www.legacybookshop.com/
A 'Development Bookshop' distributing
books, self-help manuals, videos and tapes;
specialists in development and professional
books. The Web site offers access to a large
number of titles on African studies
(particularly on East Africa), as well as titles
in African languages and children's books.
Online ordering facilities and email
notification service for new titles. Also
maintains a bookshop in The Mall,
Westlands.

2416   Moi University Bookshop
Main Campus off Kesses Road
PO Box 3900
Eldoret
Tel: +254-53-43259/43122

Fax: +254-53-43259/43047
Email: bookshop@moi_university.ac.ke or
lnyariki@yahoo.com
The campus bookshop at Moi University,
with a good range of stocks of Kenyan and
other African-published titles.

**2417   Suba Books and Periodicals
Distributors Ltd**
PO Box 51336
Nairobi
Kenya
Tel: +254-22-449231 Fax: +254-22-444110
Email: subabooks@iconnect.co.ke
Web: http://www.subabooks.com/(Web site
down 03/11/05)
Describes itself as a "stockist, distributor and
agent of Africana books and journals
worldwide."

2418   Text Book Centre Ltd
Kijabe Street
PO Box 47540
Nairobi
Tel: +254-22-330340/45 Fax: +254-22-225779
Email: admin@tbc.co.ke
Web:
http://www.textbookcentre.com/index.htm
Kenya's largest bookshop and the leading
educational and library supplier, with
extensive stocks. Headquartered in Kijabe
Street, it also maintains a modern general
bookshop in the Sarit Centre in Nairobi, as
well as an academic bookshop on the same
premises.

**2419   Zapf Chancery African
Dissertation Service**
PO Box 4988
Eldoret
Tel: n/a
Fax: +254-321-63043
Email: rotij@net2000ke.com or
zapfchancerykenya@yahoo.co.uk
Does not supply books, but provides an on-
demand dissertation publishing service that
aims to supply libraries overseas with
original and previously unpublished masters'
theses and dissertations by African scholars.
A complete list of titles that can currently be
supplied is available on request.

Lesotho

2420   NUL Bookshop
National University of Lesotho
PO Box 180
Roma
Tel: +266-340601 Fax: +266-340000
Email: mnmohapi@nul.ls
University-level and educational books.

Madagascar

2421   Espace Loisirs
11 rue Ratsimilaho
Antaninarenina
BP 4028
Antananarivo
Tel: +261-20-222 1475 Fax: +261-20-226 1899
Email: espace.loisirs@simicro.mg
General, educational, and academic
bookshop; also children's books.

2422   Librairie de Madagascar
38 avenue de l'Indépendance
Antananarivo
Tel: +261-20-222 2454
Fax: +261-20-226 4395/222 5117
Email: n/a
Long-established bookshop with a broad
selection of titles about the island.

2423   Librairie Mixte
37 bis, av 26 Jona Analakely
Antananarivo 101
Tel: +261-20-22 251 30 Fax: +261-20-223 7616
Email: librairiemixte@dts.mg
Academic bookseller.

2424   Librairie Tsipika
5 rue Ratsimilaho
Antaninarenina
Antananarivo 101
Tel: +261-20-226 2315 Fax: +261-20-222 4595
Email: tsipika@malagasy.com
General and academic bookshop, specializing
in books about Madagascar. Also carries
stocks of children's books.

Malawi

2425   Central Africana Ltd/
Victoria Avenue
PO Box 631
Blantyre
Tel: +265-1-623227 Fax: +265-1-620533
Email: centralafricana@africa-online.net
Web: http://www.centralafricana.com/
Operates bookshops and art galleries in
Blantyre and Lilongwe, with a
comprehensive selection of both new and
antiquarian books on the history and the
cultures, exploration, and development of
Africa, Central Africa, and Nyasaland/
Malawi, as well as guidebooks, maps and
Malawi fiction. Also a publisher, *see* ➔ **2006**.

**2426   Dzuka Publishing Company
Bookshops**
Salmin Amour Road
Private Bag 39
Blantyre
Tel: +265-584694
Email: dzuka@malawi.net
Concentrates on sales of its own publications,
but also stocks other educational
publications, and material in Chichewa.

2427   Times Bookshop
Victoria Avenue
BP 39
Blantyre
Tel: +265-670000 Fax: +265-670318
Email: timesbookshop@sdnp.org.mw
The oldest bookshop chain in Malawi,
stocking a wide range of general/trade,
educational, and children's books. Branches
in Lilongwe and elsewhere in the country.

Mali

2428   Librairie Jamana
Avenue Cheick Zayed Porte 2694
Hamdalaye
BP 2043
Bamako
Tel: +223-226289/77156 Fax: +223-227639
Email: jamana@jamana.org
Web: http://www.jamana.org/edition.html
The retail outlet of Mali's leading publisher
(and publishing cooperative) ➔ **Editions
Jamana (2011)**

2429 Publimage
BP 3249
Bamako
Tel/Fax: +223-225366 Fax: +223-225366
Email: Pimage@malinet.ml

Mauritius

2430 Bookcourt
Caudan Waterfront
Port Louis
Tel: +230-211 9262 Fax: +230-211 9263
Email: andre@intnet.mu

2431 Librairie Allot
Sir W.Newton Street
Port Louis
Tel: +230-212 7132 Fax: +230-212 7539
Email: liballot@intnet.mu
Major bookseller, with a branch in Curepipe.

2432 Librairie Trèfle
BP 183
Port Louis
Tel: +230-212 1106 Fax: +230-670 2441
Email: n/a
Long-established bookstore with good selection of locally published material.

2433 Noble Books Ltd
Atrium Building
Vandermeersch Street
Rose Hill
Tel: +230-454 5293 Fax: +230-464 0293
Email: twaher@intnet.mu

Morocco

2434 Carrefour des Livres
Angle des rues des Landes et
Vignemale
Maârif
Casablanca 20000
Tel: +212-2-258781 Fax: +212-2-234665
Web: http://carrefour.casanet.net.ma/ (site down 04/11/05)
One of Morocco's leading booksellers. General, educational, and academic books, and children's literature.

2435 Hassoune-Librairie Papeterie
4 merstane, 4 americh
Marrakech 40002
Tel: +212-4-313648 Fax: +212-4-313647
Email: jhassoune@caramail.com

2436 Kalila wa Dimma
344 boulevard Mohamed V
Rabat
Tel: + 212-37-723106 Fax: + 212-37-722478
Email: sobado@mtds.com

2437 Librairie des Colonnes
54 rue Pasteur
Tangier
Tel: +212-39-936955 Fax: +212-39-936955
Email: n/a
The famous and much celebrated bookshop in the heart of Tangier.

2438 Livre Service
11 rue Poincaré
Casablanca
Tel: +212-2-262072
Email: livser@iam.net.ma

2439 Marylene Benvel
26 bis, Rue Med Taha, Oasis
Casablanca 20100
Tel: +212-2-257420 Fax: +212-2-257420
Email: marylene@q-texte.net.ma

Mozambique

2440 Eduardo Mondlane Bookshop
Universidade Eduardo Mondlane
Campus Universidade
Edf-3 Av Julius Nyerere
CP 1840
Maputo
Tel: +258-1-493426 Fax: +258-1-492869
Email: luem@zebra.uem.mz
Web: http://www.uem.mz/ (University home page)
The campus bookstore at the Universidade Eduardo Mondlane, carrying primarily academic and tertiary-level titles, but also some general books and locally-published material.

Namibia

2441   The Book Cellar
Carl List Building
Peter Müller Street
PO Box 1074
Windhoek
Tel: +264-61-231615 Fax: 264-61-236164
Email: bookcellar@nam.lia.net
Well-stocked general bookshop in central
Windhoek.

2442   The Book Den
PO Box 3469
Windhoek
Tel: +264-61-239976 Fax: +264-61-234248
Email: wbd@olfitra.com.na
General retailer.

2443   Gamsberg Macmillan Bookshop
19 Faraday Street
PO Box 22830
Windhoek
Tel: +264-61-232165 Fax: +264-61-233538
Email: gmp@iafrica.com.na
Major retailer and library supplier, associated
with ➜ **Gamsberg Macmillan Publishers
(2024)**

2444   Onganda y'Omambo Bookshop
Shop 28
Post Street Mall
Windhoek
Tel: +264-61-235796
Fax: +264-61-235796/221114
Email: omambo@iafrica.com.na
This bookshop in central Windhoek offers
extensive stocks of books published in
Namibia, and well as a wide range of other
publications on Africa and by African writers.
Also acts as distributor for some African
publishers.

Nigeria

2445   Abiola Bookshops Ltd
362 Herbert Macaulay Street
Yaba
Lagos
Tel: +234-1-800450 Fax: +234-1-520360
Email: n/a
Specializes in the supply of scholarly and
professional books.

2446   The Book Company Ltd
1 Alabi Okumagbe Street
Off Lagos Road Ikorodu
PO Box 1608
Shomolu
Lagos
Tel: + 234-1-778340 Fax: +234-1-7780340
Email: thebookcom@skannet.com
Web: http://www.thebookcom.com/
New company recently set up by the former
Managing Director of CSS Bookshops in
Lagos; supplier of imported and local books,
including all those from major Nigerian
publishers.

2447   Books and Prints Ltd
PO Box 4060
49 Lawani Street
Onitiri
Yaba
Lagos
Tel: +234-1-822297 Fax: +234-1-825789
Email: books@infoweb.abs.net or
booksandp@yahoo.com
New bookshop set up by the former Manager
of the University of Lagos Bookshop, Ronke
Orimalade, stocking a wide range of
professional and tertiary-level books, as well
as general and trade books, and children's
books. The firm describes itself as a
"development bookshop", and also acts as a
library supplier, offering Nigerian-published
material to overseas libraries.

2448   Chelis Bookazine Ltd
3 Remilekun Street
off Ogunlana Drive
Surulere
Lagos
Tel: +234-1-583 7212/774 2241
Fax: +234-1-585 0732/583 2374
Email: info@chelisbookazine.com (General
enquiries) sales@chelisbookazine.com
(Sales/Orders)
Web: http://www.chelisbookazine.com
Supplier of educational, professional and
library books; primarily school book supplies.

2449   CSS Bookshops Ltd
Bookshop House
50/52 Broad Street
PO Box 174
Lagos
Tel: +234-1-263 3081 Fax: +234-1-267089
Email: cssbookshop@skannet.com.ng or

Nigeria's oldest (established in 1869) and largest bookshop group, with branches throughout the country. Stocks a very wide range of titles, including books in Nigerian languages.

2450   Elite and Professional Books
Cornershop
Plot 4
Sudary Lusaka Street
Abuja
Tel: +234-9-523 7098 Fax: 234-9-523 6099
Email: maduabum@m.Istn.com
Retail bookseller and library supplier.

2451   Glendora International (Nigeria) Ltd
Shop C4
Falomo Shopping Centre
PO Box 50914
168 Awolowo Road
Ikoji
Lagos
Tel: +234-1-269 2762
Fax: +234-1-261 8083
Email: 105271.11@compuserve.com
Web: http://www.glendora-eCulture.com
(site down as at 04/11/05)
One of Nigeria's leading bookshops, carrying a large selection of books and magazines. Specializes in books on African art, African literature, philosophy, history, tradition and culture.

2452   Igwegbe International Bookshops Ltd
71 Zik Avenue
PO Box 626 Uwani
Enugu
Tel: +234-42-257924/256112
Fax: +234-42-254385
Email: igwegbebooks@yahoo.com
Stockist of tertiary level books and reference materials in all disciplines. International library agent.

2453   Mosuro: The Booksellers
52 Magazine Road
Jericho
PO Box 30201
Ibadan
Tel: +234-2-241 3375 Fax: +234-2-241 3374
Email: mosuro@skannet.com or
kmosuro@linkserve.com.ng
Web: http://www.mosuro.com/prof.htm
(site down 04/11/05)

Widely considered to be one of the best bookshops in Nigeria, with extensive stocks, in large premises.

2454   Odusote Bookstores Ltd
68 Obafemi Awolowo Way
Oke-Ado
PO Box 244
Ibadan
Tel: +234-2-231 6451 Fax: +234-2-23 18781
Email: odubooks@infoweb.abs.net
Long-established family firm with large stocks of general, educational, tertiary-level, and children's books. Retail outlets in Ibadan and in Lagos.

2455   Oma International Booksellers
15 Adewunmi Layout Agbowo
PO Box 22073
UI Post Office
Ibadan
Tel: +234-0803-123896 (Mobile)
Email: oma@booksellers.com or
omabooksellers@yahoo.com
Web: http://www.omabooksellers.com (site down/suspended 04/11/05)
Exporter and library supplier of Nigerian scholarly and academic books and journals. Standing Order and search services offered. Good Web site, browsable by subject areas.

2456   Options Book Centre
B1 GAAF Building
110/112 Oyo Road Orogun
PO Box 21259
UI Post Office
Ibadan
Tel/Fax: n/a
Email: optionsbook@justice.com
Recently established new bookshop in Ibadan, dealing in educational, tertiary level, professional, and general books. Offers blanket order plans for new Nigerian-published materials, and collaborates with ➔ **Hogarth Representation (2340)** in the UK and ➔ **Meabooks (2353)** in Canada.

2457   University Bookshop (Nigeria) Ltd
PMB 2
University of Ibadan Post Office
Ibadan
Tel: +234-2-810 1100 exts 1208, 1047
Fax: n/a
Email: n/a

Web:
http://www.ui.edu.ng/unitsbookshop.htm
In addition to undergraduate texts, carries
fairly substantial stocks of Africana and
Nigeriana materials. However, what used to
be one of the finest university bookshops in
Africa is currently a far cry from its former
glory days.

2458   **University of Abuja Bookshop**
        University of Abuja
        PMB 117
        Abuja
Tel: +234-9-882 0385 ext. 255
Fax: +234-9-882 1605
Email: n/a

2459   **University of Lagos Bookshop**
        PMB 1013
        University of Lagos Post Office
        Akoka
        Yaba
        Lagos State
Tel: +234-1-820279 Fax: +234-1-822644
Email: n/a
Web: http://www.unilag.edu/ (University
home page)
Nowadays probably the best university
bookshop in Nigeria.

Rwanda

2460   **Librairie Ikirezi**
        Avenue de la Paix
        BP 443
        Kigali
Tel: +250-70298/71314 Fax: +250-71314
Email: ikirezi@rwandatel1.rwanda1.com

Senegal

2461   **Librairie Clairafrique**
        2 rue El Hadj Mbaye Gueye
        Place de l'Indépendance
        BP 2005
        Dakar
Tel: +221-822 2169 Fax: +221-821 8408/9
Email: clafrique@le-senegal.com or
clairaf@telecomplus.sn
Web: http://www.le-
senegal.com/clairafrique/ (site down
04/11/05)

Long-established bookshop in the centre of
Dakar with a wide selection of titles in most
areas, including locally-published material.
Also stocks videos, and African arts and
crafts.

2662   **Librairie Aux Quatre Vents**
        55 rue Felix Faure
        BP 1820
        Dakar
Tel: +221-822 1346/821 8083
Fax: +221-822 9536
Email: quatrevents@arc.sn
Carries a good range of titles about Senegal
and West Africa.

South Africa

2463   **Adams Campus Bookshop**
        Adams Campus Bookshop
        University of Natal
        King George V Avenue
        PO Box 17221
        Congella 4013
Tel: +27-31-261 2320 Fax: +27-31-261 6053
Email: undcampus@adamsbooks.co.za
Web: http://www.adamsbooks.co.za
This campus bookshop at the University of
Natal, Durban, offers comprehensive South
African stocks. Publishes a newsletter
notifying customers of new titles. There is
also an Adams general bookshop at 341 West
Street in Durban.

2464   **African Book Centre**
        139 Smit Street
        Fairland
        Johannesburg 2195
Tel/Fax: +27-11-476 5431
Email: rosner@afrobook.co.za
Recently-established company distributing
new and out-of-print books and serials
published in Africa, and African titles
published elsewhere.

2465   **Christison Books**
        PO Box 100245
        Scotsville 3209
Tel: +27-33-386 4911 Fax: +27-33-386 4911
Email: antiquarian@antiquarian.co.za
Web: http://www.antiquarian.co.za
Specialist dealer in Africa-interest books,
primarily out-of-print and antiquarian.
Online catalogues.

2466   Clarke's Bookshop
211 Long Street
Cape Town 8001
Tel: +27-21-423 5739 Fax: +27-21-423 6441
Email: books@clarkesbooks.co.za
Web: http://www.clarkesbooks.co.za
Established in 1956, Clarke's Bookshop is a
leading dealer of new and secondhand books
on southern Africa. It maintains a fine
bookshop in central Cape Town, which offers
a very large selection of new and antiquarian
books. Catalogues are issued twice yearly and
since 1998 are also available online. Offers
standing order plans, and a search service for
out-of-print titles.

2467   Constantine's Africana Bookstore
PO Box 2321
Clareinch 7740
Tel: +27-21-671 3980
Email: capeinst@new.co.za
Web:
http://www.geocities.com/Eureka/7064/cat
index.htm
Antiquarian titles on South Africa (especially
on the Boer War) and southern Africa.

2468   Exclusive Books (Pty) Ltd
Mutual Place 1st floor
Mutual Road
Rivonia
Postal address:
PO Box 605
Rivonia 2128
Tel: +27-11-797 3888 Fax: +27-11-807 1063
Email: info@exclusivebooks.com or
orders@exclusivebooks.com
Web: http://www.exclusivebooks.com
Chain bookstore and South African Internet
bookseller, with over 30 stores throughout
South Africa. Its flagship store is at Hyde
Park, Johannesburg, reputedly the biggest
general bookshop in Africa. The Web site
features book-related news items, details of
award winners, author interviews,
competitions and auctions, together with
search facilities.

2469   Fables Bookshop
119 High Street
Grahamstown 6139
Tel/Fax: +27-46-636 1525/622 2474
Email: aesop@fables.co.za
Web: http://www.fables.co.za/

A general out of print bookshop with
academic and specialist stock. Specializes in
Africana, books and ephemera mainly related
to Southern Africa.

**2470   Hargraves Library Services (Pty)
Ltd**
5 & 7 Speke Street
Observatory
Cape Town 7924
Tel: +27-21-423 7015 Fax: +27-21-447 5792
Email: Richard@hargraves.co.za
http://www.hargraves.co.za/ (site under
construction)
One of the leading South African library
suppliers.

2471   Maroelaboeke
Maroelastraat 3
Tygerbergheuwels
Bellville 7530
Tel: +27-21-913 1713
Email: pclou@netactive.co.za
Web: http://maroelaboeke.co.za/ (site is
entirely in Afrikaans)
Antiquarian books on South Africa (and
Namibia and Zimbabwe to a lesser extent),
covering architecture, genealogy, flora and
fauna, history, travel, and literature.
Catalogues issued, and offers a search service.

**2472   Oneworldbooks/Blue Weaver
Marketing and Distribution**
4 Lily Rd 1st Floor
Retreat
Cape Town
Postal address:
PO Box 30370
Tokai
Cape Town 7966
Tel: +27-21-701 4477/701 7302
Fax: +27-21-701 7302
Email: blueweav@mweb.co.za (Blue Weaver
Marketing and Distribution)
info@oneworldbooks.com (Oneworldbooks,
general enquiries)
orders@oneworldbooks.com
(Oneworldbooks, orders)
Web: http://www.oneworldbooks.com
Cape Town-based online bookshop for
publications from African and international
publishers and research organizations
(primarily South African NGOs), offering a
searchable catalogue, secure purchasing, an

email notification service about new titles, and delivery worldwide.

Distributes titles from the following South African publishers and NGOs:
Africa Institute of South Africa
African Minds
Centre for the Study of Higher Education
Council for Higher Education Transformation
Environmental Education Association of
  Southern Africa
Human Sciences Research Council
Institute for Democracy in Africa
Institute for Global Dialogue
Institute for Justice and Reconciliation
Programme for Land and Agrarian Studies
Public Service Accountability Monitor
SiberInk
South African Institute of International
  Affairs
University of Cape Town, South African
  College of Music
University of the Western Cape, Faculty of
  Education
Volunteer and Service Enquiry Southern
  Africa

**2473   Thorold's Africana & Legal
         Booksellers**
         Meischke's Building
         42 Harrison Street 3rd Floor
         PO Box 241
         Johannesburg 2000
Tel: +27-11-838-5903/838-6031
Fax: +27-11-838-4715
Email: thorolds@icon.co.za
Major library supplier for southern African-published materials; antiquarian and current imprints.

2474   Van Schaik Bookstore/Boekhandel
         Head Office:
         On-the-Dot Building
         Sacks Circle
         Bellville South
         PO Box 2355
         Bellville 7535
Tel: +27-21-918 8500 Fax: +27-21-951 1470
Hilton@vanschaik.com or
vst@vanschaik.com
Email: vsonline@vanschaik.com
Web:
http://www.vanschaik.com/books/index.asp?lang=eng (English version)

http://www.kalahari.net/vs/front.asp?toolbar=mweb (Online bookstore)
Major South African retail outlet and online bookseller, specializing in academic and medical books. The company has 35 branches countrywide.

Swaziland

2475   Websters Bookshop
         PO Box 292
         Mbabane
Tel: +268-42560/42242
Fax: +268-4044897/374315
Email: webstersbooks@africaonline.co.sz
The leading bookshop in the country, with several branches. Stocks cover educational and school books, academic books, as well as general titles.

Tanzania

2476   General Booksellers
         PO Box 20468
         Dar es Salaam
Tel: +255-22-213 5582 Fax: +255-22-212 1455
Email: gbs@cats-net.com
Educational and general/trade books.

2477   Mathews Bookstore & Stationers
         PO Box 7252
         Dar es Salaam
         Tanzania
Tel: +255-22-286 1281 Fax: +255-22-276 1562
Email: ipyanam@yahoo.com
Stocks primarily educational and textbooks.

2478   A Novel Idea
         PO Box 76513
         Dar es Salaam
Tel: +255-22-2601088/2134353
Email: books@anovelidea-africa.com or
novel@twiga.com
Web: http://www.anovelidea-africa.com/
Describes itself as "possibly the best bookshop in East Africa." Located at The Slipway, Msasani Peninsula, and at Steers Complex. The Web site offers general interest as well as scholarly titles, fiction, and children's books. Also acts as educational and library supplier.

**2479   Shirika la Kikristo la
         Maandiko/SKM
         (Dar es Salaam Bookshop)**
PO Box 11041
Dar es Salaam
Tel: +255-22-212 3813/+ 255-744 283544 (Cell)
Email: act@anglican.or.tz (General Secretary)
Web: http://www.anglican.or.tz/skm.htm
This is the bookshop of the Anglican Church
of Tanzania, also known as the Dar es Salaam
Bookshop. While primarily a religious
bookseller, it also stocks general titles.

2480   TEPUSA Bookshop
The Network of Technical
Publications in Africa
PO Box 22638
Dar es Salaam
Tel: +255-51-114 876 Fax: +255-51-112 434
Email: tepusa@intafrica.com
The bookshop maintained by the Network of
Technical Publications in Africa (TEPUSA),
stocking educational, general, scholarly, and
scientific and technical titles.

**2481   University of Dar es Salaam
         Bookshop**
PO Box 35090
Dar es Salaam
Tel: +255-51-49192/48300 ext 2388/2389
Email: n/a
Web: http://www.udsm.ac.tz/ (University
home page)
Tertiary-level and scholarly books.

Togo

2482   Librairie Bon Pasteur
Rue de l'église-rue Aniko Palako
BP 1164
Lomé
Tel/Fax: +228-213628 Fax: +228-213279
Email: bonpasteur@netcom.tg
General, educational and children's books.

2483   Librairie Maldis
13 rue Bonaparte
Lomé
Tel: +228 –217776 Fax: +228-218056/221824
Email: malidis@email.com
Web: http://www.malidis.com/ (site down
07/11/05)

Tunisia

2484   La Grande Librairie Spécialisée/GLS
Rue Mohsen Kallel
Immeuble Abdelkafi
Sfax 3000
Tel: +216-74-296 855 Fax: + 216-74-298 270
Email: contact@grande-librairie.com
Web: http://www.grande-librairie.com/
Major academic and education bookseller and
library supplier. Also journal subscription
agent.

2485   Librairie Clairfontaine
5 bis rue Pierre Mendès-France
Mutuelleville
1082 Tunis 1082
Tel: 216-71-254471 Fax: 216-71-894502
Email: clairefontaine@planet.tn

2486   L'Univers du Livre
39 rue Naplouse
Tunis 1002
Tel: +216-71-830561 Fax: +216-71-835001
Email: houssem.ammar@planet.tn
http://www.univers-livre.com/indexfr.asp
Leading general, educational, professional
and academic bookseller. Offers over 8,000
titles online.

Uganda

2487   Alphamat Bookworld
UCIL House UMA Showground
Lugogo
PO Box 25492
Kampala
Tel: +256-41-222982 Fax: +256-77-428812
Email: alphamat@infopoint.co.ug or
alphamat@africaonline.co.ug
Carries primarily stocks of general/trade and
educational books.

2488   Artistoc Booklex Ltd
OAR-001 Diamond Trust Building
PO Box 5180
Kampala
Tel: +256-41-244381/349052
Fax: +256-41-254867/254968
Email: abluga@swiftug.com
Textbooks and other titles on most subjects
and levels.

2489   **University Bookshop Makerere**
PO Box 7062
Kampala
Tel: +256-41-531288 Fax: +256-41-534973
Email: ubm@mak.ac.ug or
ubm@africaonline.com.ug
Web:
http://www.makerere.ac.ug/index.php?p=h
ome (University home page)
The campus bookstore at Makerere
University, stocking general and academic
titles.

Zambia

2490   **Bookworld**
Cairo Road North-End
PO Box 31383
Lusaka
Tel: +260-1-225282/228209
Fax: +260-1-225195
Email: bookwld@zamtel.zm
Web:
http://www.zamtel.zm/bookworld/index.h
tm
A leading general bookshop, with four retail
outlets, whose stocks includes locally-
published material.

2491   **Gadsden Books**
Plot 3798 Kwacha Road
Olympia Parks
PO Box 32581
Lusaka
Tel: +260-1-222486/290331
Fax: +260-1-221549
Email: Gadsden@zamnet.zm
Recently established general bookshop in
central Lusaka.

2492   **University of Zambia Bookshop**
Great East Road Campus
University of Zambia
PO Box 32379
Lusaka
Tel/Fax: +260-1-294690/290319
Fax: +260-1-290319/253952
Email: bookshop@admin.unza.zm or
hudsonunene@yahoo.com
Web: http://www.unza.zm/ (University
home page)
Stocks educational, professional, academic, as
well as general interest titles. Has a branch in
downtown Lusaka and in Livingstone.

Zimbabwe

2493   **The Book Café**
Five Avenue Shopping Centre
Fife Ave/6th St
PO Box A 267
Harare
Tel: +263-4-792551/728191
Fax: +263-4-793182
Email: bricks@mweb.co.zw or
pamberit@mweb.co.zw or
artslive@mweb.co.zw
The Book Café, now under the umbrella of
the welfare arts organization Pamberi Trust,
consists of restaurant and bar, performance
space, venue for meetings and public debates,
and a small development oriented bookshop
specialising in African fiction, history, and
social life. The Book Café is one of the liveliest
multicultural meeting places in Harare, and
has also provided an important platform for
local musicians, writers, and performers.

2494   **LICS Bookshop Pvt Ltd**
Kopje Plaza Shop no. 10
1 Jason Moyo Avenue
PO Box 7230
Harare
Tel: +263-4-775524 Fax: +263-4-790730
Email: lics@samara.co.zw

2495   **Mambo Press Bookshop**
Senga Road
PO Box 779
Gweru
Tel: +263-54-24016/7 Fax: +263-54-21991
Email: mambopress@telco.co.zw
Web: http://www.mambopress.co.zw/ or
http://www.geocities.com/wchitirobho/mai
n.html
Retail outlet of one of the country's leading
publishers, stocking ➔ **Mambo Press (2154)**
titles as well as books from other publishers.

2496   **Model Educational Suppliers**
Corner Speke Avenue/Mbuya
Nehanda Street
PO Box 568
Harare
Tel: +263-4-750768 Fax: +263-4-773641
Email: modeledu@pci.co.za
Primarily supplier of school and tertiary-level
textbooks, scientific equipment, and
educational materials.

2497   **Townsend Booksellers**
Suite 2
Blandford Court
47 Fife Avenue/Corner Leopold
Takawira Street
PO Box 3281
Harare
Tel/Fax: +263-4-727732
Email: booktown@harare.iafrica.com
Academic and professional booksellers, and
library suppliers.

ELSEWHERE

India

2498   **Books and Periodicals Agency**
B-1 Inder Puri
New Delhi 110012
Tel: +91-11-575 5096/578 6046
Fax: +91-11-579 5554
US agent Fax: 1+-603-947 7786
Email: bpage@del2.vsnl.net.in
Web: http://www.bpagency.com/
International bookseller who offers lists of
scholarly titles – including books on Africa
and African studies – published in India and
in the southern Asia region. Online catalogue
and email notification service for new titles.

Japan

2499   **Biblio Limited**
2-12 Misakicho 2-chome
Chiyoda-ku
Tokyo 101-0061
Tel: +81-3-3263 7189 Fax: +81-3-3263 7180
Email: bibliobk@eagle.ocn.ne.jp
Web: http://www7.ocn.ne.jp/~biblio/
Specialist Japanese dealer in Africa and Asia-
related materials.

2500   **Hotaka Book Co Ltd**
1-15 Kanda Jinbo-cho
Chiyoda-ku
Tokyo 101-0051
Tel: +81-3-3233 0331 Fax: +81-3-3233 0332
Email: info@hotakabooks.com
Web: http://www.hotakabooks.com/
Retail bookseller and library supplier.

18

Major African and international organizations

See also ➜ **19 Major foundations, donors, government and aid agencies**

African and international organizations listed here are grouped under four
sections:
(1)   the major African-based organizations;
(2)   United Nations agencies and related organizations;
(3)   the World Bank Group and similar agencies; and
(4)   other international organizations, development agencies, associations,
        policy institutes, NGOs, networks, and advocacy bodies, who are
        either active in Africa, and/or support research and activities in the
        arts, humanities and social sciences, agriculture, science and
        technology, human rights and civil society, or in other areas.

Information provided includes full postal address details, telephone/fax
numbers, email address, and Web sites, together with the names of principal
contacts, i.e. names of executive personnel, presidents or chairpersons of the
organizations listed, Director General or Secretary General, or other chief
executive. All contact details have been verified and are current as at late
2005.

Agencies relating to the Commonwealth of Nations, the European Union,
and the Francophone Community can be found under section ➜ **19 Major
foundations, donors, government and aid agencies**.

Fuller information about most of these organizations' activities, their
history, structure, objectives, officers, finance, membership, and
publications, can be found on their Web sites, as well as in several print
resources, notably the annual ➜ **Africa South of the Sahara (211)**, or the ➜
**Historical Dictionary of International Organizations in Sub-Saharan
Africa (262)**. For more details about organizations that support publishing
and book development in Africa consult the ➜ **African Publishing
Companion (259)**.

Major Africa-based organizations

2501 African Development Bank Group/Banque Africaine de développement (ADB)
BP 1387
Abidjan 01
Côte d'Ivoire
Tel: +225-20-204444 Fax: +225-20-204959
Email: afdb@afdb.org
Web: http://www.afdb.org
President: Donald Kaberuka
Secretary General: Cheikh Ibrahima Fall
Note: the above are the Bank's statutory headquarters. Its temporary relocation address is as follows:
ADB Temporary Relocation Agency (Tunis)
African Development Bank Angle des trois rues: Avenue du Ghana, Rue Pierre de Coubertin, Rue Hedi Nouira
BP 323 1002
Tunis Belvedère
Tunisia
Tel: +216-71-333511/71-103450
Fax: +216-71-351933
Email: afdb@afdb.org

2502 African Export-Import Bank (AFREXIMBANK)
World Trade Cente
1191 Corniche El-Nil
PO Box 404 Gezira
Cairo 11568
Tel: +20-2-578 0281 Fax: +20-2-578 0276
Email: mail@afreximbank.co or info@afreximbank.com
Web: http://www.afreximbank.com/
President and Chairman to the Board: Jean-Louis Ekra
Board Secretariat: Getachew Telahun

2503 African Leadership Forum (ALF)
ALF Plaza 1 Bells Drive Km 9
Idiroko Road
PO Box 2286
Ota Ogun State
Nigeria
Tel: +234-39-722730/722731
Fax: +234-39-722521
Email: info@africaleadership.org,
Web: http://www.africaleadership.org/
Chair: Francis Deng
Executive Director: Ayodele Aderinwale

2504 African Union/Union Africaine (AU)
(formerly Organization of African Unity)
POB 3243
Addis Ababa
Ethiopia
Tel: +251-1-517700 Fax: +251-1-517844
Email tpst@africa-union.org
Web: http://www.africa-union.org/
Chair (changes annually)
2005: HE Mr. Alpha Oumar Konare
Director, Bureau of the Chairperson:
Margaret Vogt, Email: VogtM@africa-union.org
Directorate of Administration:
(Ms) Ennet N. Nkambule,
Email: dadmin@africa-union.org
Press Attaché: Adam Thiam,
Email: ThiamA@africa-union.org

2505 Arab Bank for Economic Development in Africa/Banque arabe pour le développement économique en Afrique (BADEA)
Sayed Abdel Rahmann El-Mahdi Street
POB 2640 Khartoum
Sudan
Tel: +249-11-73646/773709
Fax: +249-11-70600/770498
Email: badea@badea.org
Web: http://www.badea.org
Chairman: HE Mr. Ahmed Abdallah El-Akeil
Director General: HE Medhat Sami Lofty

2506 Arab Maghreb Union/L'Union du Maghreb Arabe (UMO)
14 rue Zalagh
Rabat-Agadal
Morocco
Tel: +212-37-671274/278 Fax: +212-37-671253
Email: sg.uma@maghrebarabe.org
Web: http://www.maghrebarabe.org
Secretary General: Habib Boulares

2507 Common Market for Eastern and Southern Africa (COMESA)/Marche Commun de l'Afrique de l'Est et de l'Afrique Australe/Mercado Comum Para Africa Oriental e Austral
COMESA Centre
Ben Bella Road
PO Box 30051
10101 Lusaka
Zambia

Tel: +260-1-229725 Fax: +260-1-225107
Email: comesa@comesa.int (General
enquiries) jmwencha@comesa.int (Secretary
General)
Web: http://www.comesa.int
Chairperson: HE Mr. Yoweri K. Museveni,
President of the Republic of Uganda
Chairperson, Council of Ministers:
Hon. Edward Rugumayo
Secretary General:
Erastus J.O. Mwencha

2508 Council for the Development of
Social Science Research in
Africa/Conseil pour le
développement de la recherche en
sciences sociales en Afrique
(CODESRIA)
Avenue Cheikh Anta Diop x Canal IV
BP 3304
Dakar
Senegal
Tel: +221-825 9822/23 Fax: +22- 824 1289
(General enquiries)
Tel.: +221-824 0374 Fax: +221-824 5795
(Executive Secretary's Office)
Email: codesria@sentoo.sn (General
enquiries) adebayo.olukoshi@codesria.sn
(Executive Secretary's Office)
Web: http://www.codesria.org/
President: Zenebeworke Tadesse
Vice-President: Paulin Hountondji
Executive Secretary: Adebayo Olukoshi
See also → CODESRIA (Publications) (2059);
and entry 1851

2509 East African Community
(EAC)/Jumuiya Ya Afrika Mashariki
Arusha International Conference
Centre AICC Building
Kilimanjaro Wing 5th Floor
PO Box 1096
Arusha
Tanzania
Tel: +255-27-250 4253 Fax +255-27-250 4255
Email: eac@eachq.org (General enquiries)
mushega@eachq.org (Secretary General)
Web: http://www.eachq.org
Secretary General:
Hon. Nuwe Amanya-Mushega

2510 East African Development Bank
4 Nile Avenue
PO Box 7128
Kampala
Uganda
Tel: 256-41-230021 Fax: +256-41-259763
Email: admin@eadb.com (General enquiries)
dg@eadb.org
Web: http://www.eadb.org/
Chairman of the Board: Hon. Chris Kassami
Director General: Godfrey Tumusiime

2511 Economic and Monetary Community
of Central Africa
(EMCCA/Communauté économique
et monétaire d'Afrique centrale
(CEMAC)
BP 969
Bangui
Central African Republic
Tel: +236-611885/612179 Fax: +236-612135
Email: sgudeac@intnet.cf
Web:
http://www.izf.net/izf/FicheIdentite/CEM
AC.htm
Executive Secretary: Jean Nkuete

2512 Economic Community of West
African States (ECOWAS)/
Communauté Economique des Etats
de l'Afrique de l'Ouest (CEDEAO)
Executive Secretariat
6 King George V Road
Lagos
Nigeria
Tel: +234-1-636841 Fax: +234-1-636822
Email: info@ecowas.info
Web: http://www.ecowas.info/
Executive Secretary: Lansana Kouyate

2513 Economic, Social and Cultural
Council of the African Union
(ECOSOCC)
African Union
PO Box 3243
Addis Ababa
Ethiopia
Tel: +251-1-517700 Fax: +251-1-517844
Email: n/a
Web: http://www.africa-
union.org/organs/ecosocc/home.htm
President: Wangari Maathi
Vice President, Interim Standing Committee:
Ayodele Aderinwale

2514   Indian Ocean Commission (IOC)/Commission de l'océan Indien
Q4 Avenue Sir Guy Forget
Quatre Bornes
Mauritius
Tel: +230-425 1652/425 9564
Fax: +230-425 2709
Email: coi7@intnet.mu (General enquiries)
M.Andreas@coi.intnet.mu (Secretary General)
Web: http://www.coi-info.org
Secretary General:
Monique Andreas Esoavelomandroso

2515   Intergovernmental Authority on Development (IGAD)
PO Box 2653
Djibouti
Republic of Djibouti
Tel: +253-354050 Fax: +253-356994
Email: igad@intnet.dj (General enquiries)
attalla.bashir@igad.org (Executive Secretary)
afeworki.abraham@igad.org (Director,
Economic Cooperation & Social Development
Division)
Web: http://www.igad.org/
Executive Secretary: Attalla H. Bashir
Director, Economic Cooperation & Social
Development Division: Afeworki Abraham
Programme Manager, Documentation and
Information: Juliet Kamara

2516   New Partnership for African Development (NEPAD)
NEPAD Secretariat
PO Box 1234
Halfway House
Midrand 1685
South Africa
Tel: +27-11-313 3716/3776
Fax: +27-11-313 3684/3778
Email: thaningas@nepad.org
Web: http://www.nepad.org/
Executive Head: Wiseman Nkuhlu
General Manager, Communications &
Marketing: (Ms) Thaninga Shope-Linney

➔ **Organization of African Unity** see **African Union/Union Africaine (2504)**

2517   Pan-African Parliament
PO Box 31293
Dar es Salaam
Tanzania
Tel /Fax: +255-22-2451 308
Email: awa@ud.co.tz (General enquiries
MongellaG@africa-union.org (President)
Web: http://www.africa-union.org/home/Welcome.htm (click on to Organs)
President: Hon. Gertrude Mongella
Note: the Pan-African Parliament is an organ of the ➔ **African Union/Union Africaine (2504)**

2518   Southern African Development Community (SADC)
SADC House Government Enclave
Private Bag 0095
Gaborone
Botswana
Tel: +267-351863 Fax: +267-397 2848
Email: registry@sadc.int
Web: http://www.sadc.int
Chair: The Hon. Paul Raymond Berenger, Prime Minister of Mauritius
Executive Secretary: Prega Ramsamy

2519   Unesco Nairobi Office
UN Complex Gigiri Block C
United Nations Avenue
PO Box 30592
00100 GPO Nairobi
Kenya
Tel: +254-20-621234 Fax: +254-20-622750
Email: nairobi@unesco.org
Web: http://www.unesco-nairobi.org/
Director: Joseph M.G. Massaquoi

2520   Unesco Regional Office for Education in Africa/ Bureau régional de l'Unesco pour l'éducation en Afrique (BREDA)
12 avenue L.S. Senghor
BP 3318
Dakar
Senegal
Tel: +221-849 2323 Fax: +221-823 8393
Email: dakar@unesco.org (General enquiries)
la.ben-barka@unesco.org (Director)
Web:
http://www.dakar.unesco.org/bureau_reg_en/breda.shtml
Director: (Mrs) Lalla Aïcha Ben Barka

→ **Unesco Regional Office for Science and Technology in Africa (ROSTA)**
see **Unesco Nairobi Office (2519)**

2521   Union économique et monétaire ouest-africaine/West African Economic and Monetary Union (UEMOA)
380 rue Agostino Neto
01 BP 543
Ouagadougou 01
Burkina Faso
Tel: +226-318873 Fax: +226-318872
Email: commission@uemoa.int
Web: http://www.uemoa.int/Index.htm
President: Soumaïla Cisse

2522   United Nations African Institute for Economic Development and Planning/Nations Unies, Institut Africain de développement économique et de planification (IDEP)
Rue du 18 juin
BP 3186 CP 18524
Dakar
Senegal
Tel: +221-823 1020 Fax: +221-822 2964
Email: unidep@unidep.org or idep@unidep.org (General enquiries)
dseck@unidep.org(Director)
Web: http://www.unidep.org/
Director: Diéry Seck

2523   United Nations Economic Commission for Africa (UNECA)/Nations Unies commission économique pour l'Afrique (CEA)
Menelik II Ave
PO Box 3001
Addis Ababa
Ethiopia
Tel: +251-1-517200 (General enquiries) +251-1-511167 (Officer in charge, Development Information Services Division) Fax: +251-1-514416 (General enquiries) Fax: 251-1-443562 (Officer in charge, Development Information Services Division)
Email: ecainfo@uneca.org (General enquiries)
aopoku-mensah@uneca.org (Officer in charge, Development Information Services Division)
Web: http://www.uneca.org
Executive Secretary: K.Y. Amoako

Officer in charge, Development Information Services Division: (Ms) Aida Opoku-Mensah
Note: for other contacts, and for contact details for ECA regional offices in Africa, see http://www.uneca.org/era2004/

2524   United Nations Human Settlements Programme/UN Habitat. Regional Office for Africa and Arab States (ROASS)
PO Box 30030
Nairobi
Kenya
Tel: +254-20-623221 Fax: +254-20-623904
Email: roaas@unhabitat.org (General enquiries) Alioune.Badiane@unhabitat.org (Director, ROASS)
Web:
http://www.unhabitat.org/roaas/ (English version)
http://www.unhabitat.org/offices/roaas/index.htm (French version)
Executive Director: Anna Kajumulo Tibaijuka
Director, ROAAS: Alioune Badiane

2525   West African Development Bank (WADB)/Banque Ouest Africaine de développement (BOAD)
68 Avenue de la Libération
BP 1172
Lomé
Togo
Tel: +228-221 5906/4244
Fax: +228-221 5267/7269
Email: boadsiege@boad.org
Web: http://www.boad.org/
President: Boni Yayi
Administrative Director: Issoufou Kanda

United Nations agencies and related organizations

Note: this is *not* a complete listing of all UN agencies and specialized bodies.

➔ **African Ministerial Conference on the Environment (AMCEN)** *see* **2534**

2526   Food and Agriculture Organization of the United Nations (FAO)/Organisation des Nations Unies pour l'alimentation et l'agriculture/ Organización de las Naciones Unidas para la Agricultura y la Alimentación
Viale delle Terme di Caracalla
00100 Rome
Italy
Tel: +39-6-57051 Fax: +39-6-5705 3152
Email: telex-room@fao.org
Web: http://www.fao.org
Director General: Jacques Diouf
Note: for regional and sub-regional offices *see* http://www.fao.org/english/departments/index.html

2527   International Labour Organization (ILO)/ Organisation internationale du travail (OIT)
4 route des Morillons
1211 Geneva 22
Switzerland
Tel: +41-22-799 6111 Fax: +41-22-798 8685
Email: ilo@ilo.org. (General enquiries)
ducci@ilo.org (Executive Director, Office of the Director General) abidjan@ilo.org (Regional Director, Field Programmes in Africa)
Web: http://www.ilo.org/
Director General: Juan Somavia
Executive Director: Kari Tapiola
Executive Director, Office of the Director General: María Angélica Ducci
Regional Director, Field Programmes in Africa (Abidjan): Regina Amadi-Njoku
Note: for regional offices in Africa *see* http://www.ilo.org/public/english/depts/dir_afri.htm

2528   Office for the Coordination of Humanitarian Affairs (OCHA)
New York office:
United Nations
S-3600
New York NY 10017
USA
Tel: +1-212-963 1234 (General enquiries)
Tel: +1 212-963 3759/963 4832 (Press contact/Advocay and External Relations)
Fax:+1-212-963 1312/963 9489
Email: ochany@un.org
(General enquiries) tsui@un.org (Director, New York Office)
Web: http://ochaonline.un.org/index.asp
Under-Secretary-General for Humanitarian Affairs and Emergency Relief Coordinator: Jan Egeland
Director, New York office: Ed Tsui
Director of African Humanities Action: Dawitt Zawide
Press contact: Advocacy and External Relations Section
Geneva office:
Office for the Coordination of Humanitarian Affairs
United Nations
Palais des Nations
8-14 ave de la Paix
1211 Geneva 10
Switzerland
Tel: +41-22-917 1234 (General enquiries)
+41-22-917 3518 (Press contact)
Fax:+41-22-917 0023
Email: ochagva@un.org
Director, Geneva office: Yvette Stevens
Press contact: Sergio Piazzi

2529   The United Nations
UN Headquarters:
First Avenue at 46th Street
New York NY 10017
Department of Public Information:
Room S-1070 L
New York NY 10017
USA
Tel: +1-212-963 4475 (Department of Public Information)
+1-212-963 7162 (Office of the Spokesman for the Secretary General)
Fax: +1-212-963 6914 (General)
+1-212-963 7055 (Press/media enquiries)
Email: inquiries@un.org (General enquiries)
dpingo@un.org (Department of Public Information)

stevens@un.org (Director, Office of the Special Advisor on Africa)
Web: http://www.un.org/english/
Secretary General: Kofi A. Annan
Spokesman for the Secretary General: Stephane Dujarric
Director, Office of the Special Advisor on Africa (OSSA): Yvette Stevens
See also
➜ **United Nations, Dag Hammarskjöld Library (1330)**
➜ **United Nations Publications (2289)**
Note: for index to departments and offices *see* http://www.un.org/Depts/index.html

➜ **United Nations African Institute for Economic Development and Planning/ Nations Unies, Institut Africain de développement économique et de planification (IDEP)** *see* **2522**

2530   United Nations Children's Fund (UNICEF)
3 UN Plaza
New York NY 10017
USA
Tel: +1-212-326 7000 Fax: 1-212-303-7992
Email: information@unicefusa.org (General enquiries) media@unicef.org (Press Centre)
aironside@unicef.org   (Media Chief)
Web: http://www.unicef.org/
Executive Director: Ann N. Veneman
Media Chief: Alfred Ironside
Note: for Africa regional offices *see* http://www.unicef.org/infobycountry/index.html

2531   United Nations Conference on Trade and Development (UNCTAD)/Conférence des Nations Unies sur le commerce et le développement (CNUCED)
Palais des Nations
1211 Geneva 10
Switzerland
Tel: +41-22-917 5809 Fax: +41-22-917 0051
Email: info@unctad.org (General enquiries)
sgo@unctad.org (Secretary General)
Web: http://www.unctad.org/
Secretary General (Acting): Edna dos Santos
See also ➜ **International Trade Centre UNCTAD/WTO (2545)**

2532   United Nations Development Programme (UNDP)/Programme des Nations Unies pour le développement (PNUD)/ Programa de las Naciones Unidas para el Desarrollo (PNUD)
One United Nations Plaza
New York NY 10017
USA
Tel: +1-212-906 5295/+1-212-906 5558 (General enquiries) +1-212-906 5576 (Executive Board Secretariat)
Fax: +1-212-906 5634
Email: aboutundp@undp.org (General enquiries)
Web: http://www.undp.org
Chair, Executive Board/President: Ambassador Extraordinary and Plenipotentiary Permanent Representative HE Ms. Carmen María Gallardo-Hernández
Director, Executive Board Secretariat and Secretary, UNDP/UNFPA Executive Board: Rekha Thapa
UNDP Administrator: Mark Malloch Brown
Note: for UNDP offices and Resident Coordinators in Africa *see* http://www.undp.org/regions/africa/

➜ **United Nations Economic Commission for Africa (UNECA)/ Nations Unies commission économique pour l'Afrique (CEA)** *see* **2523**

2533   United Nations Educational, Scientific and Cultural Organization (UNESCO)/ Organisation des Nations Unies pour l'education, la science et la culture (UNESCO)
7 Place de Fontenoy
75352 Paris 07 SP
France
and at:
1 rue Miollis
75732 Paris Cedex 15
Tel: +33-1-45 68 10 00 Fax: +33-1-45 67 16 90
Email: bpiweb@unesco.org or use email form on Web site
Web: http://www.unesco.org (Main home page) http://portal.unesco.org/en/ev.php-URL_ID=19521&URL_DO=DO_TOPIC&URL_SECTION=201.html (Africa Department home page)
Director General: Koïchiro Matsuura
Head, Office of the Director General: Françoise Rivière

Director, Bureau of Public Information: Saturnino Muñoz Gomez
Head, Africa Department: Noureni Tidjani-Serpos
Note: for other Service and Sector contacts *see* the Organigramme at http://oberon.unesco.org/orgchart/en/ORG_vis_files/ORG_vis_frames.htm
For contact details of UNESCO National Commissions in Africa, and Permanent Delegations to UNESCO for African countries *see*
http://portal.unesco.org/en/ev.php-URL_ID=11151&URL_DO=DO_TOPIC&URL_SECTION=201.html and then select Africa from the Regions/Country menu
See also → UNESCO Publishing 2179

2534   United Nations Environment Programme. Regional Office for Africa (UNEP-ROA)
PO Box 30552
Nairobi
Kenya
Tel: +254-20-624292 Fax: +254-20-623928
Email: roainfo@unep.org (General enquiries)
Sekou.Toure@unep.org (Director)
Peter.Acguah@unep.org (Senior Programme Officer) Angele.Luh@unep.org (Regional Information Officer)
Web: http://www.unep.org/roa/index.asp
Director: Sekou Toure
Senior Programme Officer and Secretary to AMCEN: Peter Acquah
Regional Information Officer: Angele Luh Sy
Note: the Web pages of the African Ministerial Conference on the Environment (AMCEN) are at http://www.unep.org/roa/amcen/about.asp

→ Unesco Nairobi Office *see* 2519

→ Unesco Regional Office for Education in Africa/ Bureau regional de l'Unesco pour l'éducation en Afrique (BREDA) *see* 2520

→ Unesco Regional Office for Science and Technology in Africa/ Bureau régional de l'Unesco pour la science et la technologie en Afrique (ROSTA) *see* Unesco Nairobi Office (2519)

2535   United Nations High Commissioner for Refugees (UNHCR)
CP 2500
1211 Geneva 2 Dépôt
Switzerland
Tel: +41-22-739 8111
Email: usawa@unhcr.ch
Web: http://www.unhcr.ch
Chair: HE Ambassador Juan Martabit (Chile)
High Commissioner: António Guterres

→ United Nations Human Settlements Programme/UN Habitat *see* United Nations Human Settlements Programme/UN Habitat, Regional Office for Africa and Arab States (ROASS) (2524)

2536   United Nations Office of the High Representative for the Least Developed Countries, Landlocked Developing Countries and Small Island Developing States (UN-OHRLLS)
United Nations
Room UH-900
New York NY 10017
USA
Tel: +1-212-963 7778/963 5051
Fax: +1-917-367 3415
Email: OHRLLS-UNHQ@un.org
Web: http://www.un.org/special-rep/ohrlls/ohrlls/default.htm
United Nations Under-Secretary General and High Representative UN-OHRLLS: Ambassador Anwarul K. Chowdhury

2537   United Nations Population Fund (UNFPA)
220 East 42nd Street
New York NY 10017
USA
Tel: +212-297 5000 Fax: +212-730 0201
Web: http://www.unfpa.org (Main home page)
http://www.unfpa.org/africa/index.htm (Sub-Saharan Africa pages)
Chair, Executive Board/President: Ambassador Extraordinary and Plenipotentiary Permanent Representative HE Ms. Carmen María Gallardo-Hernández
Executive Director and UN Under Secretary General: (Ms) Thoraya Obaid
Director, Executive Board Secretariat and Secretary, UNDP/UNFPA
Executive Board: Rekha Thapa

2538 United Nations Programme on HIV/AIDS (UNAIDS)
20 avenue Appia
1211 Geneva 27
Switzerland
Tel: +41-22-791 3666 Fax: +41-22-791 4187
Email: unaids@unaids.org
Web: http://www.unaids.org/(Main home page)
http://www.unaids.org/en/geographical+area/by+region/sub-saharan+africa.asp (Sub-Saharan Africa pages)
Executive Director and Under Secretary General of the United Nations:
Peter Piot
Director, Social Mobilization and Information (SMI): Marika Fahlen
Director, Country and Regional Support Department (CRE): Michel Sidibe
Associate Director, Division for Africa (AFR): Meskerem Grunitzky-Bekele

2539 World Health Organization (WHO)/Organisation mondiale de la santé (OMS)
Avenue Appia 20
1211 Geneva 27
Switzerland
Tel: +41-22-791 2111 Fax: + 41-22-791 3111
Email: info@who.int (General information about WHO, events, etc.)
library@who.int (for WHO health information and documentation)
mediainquiries@who.int (Media enquiries)
Web: http://www.who.int (Main home page) http://www.afro.who.int/
(Regional office in Africa)
Director General: Lee Jong-Wook
Chef de Cabinet, Office of the Director General: Denis Aitken
Regional Director, Africa: Luís Gomes Sambo

2540 World Food Programme (WFP)
Via Cesare Giulio Viola 68/70
Parco dei Medici
00148 Rome
Italy
Tel: +39-6-65131/6531 2602
Fax: +39-6-6513 2840
Email: wfpinfo@wfp.org (General enquiries)
brenda.barton@wfp.org (Deputy Director, Communications)
Web: http://www.wfp.org/
Executive Director: James T. Morris
Deputy Executive Director (Administration): Susana Malcorra
Deputy Director, Communications: Brenda Barton

The World Bank group of organizations, and similar agencies

2541   Consultative Group on International Agricultural Research (CGIAR)
CGIAR Secretariat
The World Bank
MSN G6-601
1818 H Street NW
Washington, DC 20433 USA
Tel: +1-202-473 8951 Fax: +1-202-473 8110
Email: cgiar@cgiar.org (General enquiries)
f.douglas@cgiar.org (Media enquiries)
Web: http://www.cgiar.org
Chair: Ian Johnson
Director: Francisco Reifschneider

→ **International Bank for Reconstruction and Development (IBRD)** *see* **The World Bank Group (2548)**

→ **International Development Association (IDA)** *see* **The World Bank Group (2548)**

2542   International Finance Corporation (IFC)
2121 Pennsylvania Avenue NW
Washington DC 20433
USA
Tel: +1-202-473 1000 (General enquiries)
Tel: +1-202-473 0319 Fax: +1-202-974 4332 (Sub-Saharan Africa Department)
Tel: +1-202-473 6864
Fax: +1-202-974 4396 (Middle East & North Africa Department)
Email: webmaster@ifc.org
Web: http://www.ifc.org
http://www.ifc.org/africa (IFC in Sub-Saharan Africa page)
http://www.ifc.org/mena
(IFC in Middle East & North Africa pages)
President: Paul Wolfowitz
Vice President, Operations: Assaad J. Jabre
Director, Sub-Saharan Africa Field Office: Richard Ranken (Johannesburg)
Director, Middle East & North Africa Field Office: Sami Haddad (Cairo)

2543   International Fund for Agricultural Development (IFAD)
107 via del Serafico
00142 Rome
Italy
Tel: +39-6-54591 Fax: +39-6-504 3463
Email: ifad@ifad.org (General enquiries)
pamailbox@ifad.org (Western and Central Africa Division)
pfmailbox@ifad.org (Eastern and Southern Africa Division)
Web: http://www.ifad.org/
President: Lennart Båge
Director, Western and Central Africa Division: Mohamed Beavogui
Director, Eastern and Southern Africa Division: Gary Howe

2544   International Monetary Fund (IMF)
700 19th Street NW
Washington DC 20431
USA
Tel: +1-202-623-7000/7300 (General enquiries)
+1-202623 6660 (Scholarship & external training program inquiries)
Fax: +1-202-623-4661/6278
Email: publicaffairs@imf.org (General enquiries) insinfo@imf.org (Scholarship & external training program inquiries)
Web: http://www.imf.org/
Managing Director:
Rodrigo de Rato y Figaredo
Director, Africa Department:
Abdoulaye Bio-Tchané

2545   International Trade Centre (UNCTAD/WTO)
54-56 rue de Montbrillant
Palais des Nations
1211 Geneva 10
Switzerland
Tel: +41-22-730 0111 Fax: +41-22-733 4439
Email: itcreg@intracen.org
Web: http://www.intracen.org/
Executive Director: J. Denis Bélisle
Director, Department of Operations and Deputy Executive Director: J. Smadja
Chief, Division of Trade Support Services: R. Badrinath
Chief, Division of Technical Cooperation Coordination: S. Sok
Head, Trade Information Section: vacant
Head, Office for Africa: M. Farahat
See also → **The World Trade Organization/WTO (2549)**

2546   Multilateral Investment Guarantee Agency (MIDA)
1800 G Street NW Suite 1200
Washington DC 20433
USA
Tel: +1-202-473-1000 (General enquiries)
Fax: +1-202-522 2650 (Africa operations)
Email: migaguarantees@worldbank.org
(Guarantee applications)
migainquiry@worldbank.org (Marketing inquiries)
dbridgman@worldbank.org (Africa Operations)
Web: http://www.miga.org/
Executive Vice President:
(Ms) Yukiko Omura
Contact, Sub-Saharan Africa Operations:
David Bridgman

2547   The OPEC Fund for International Development
Parkring 8
1010 Vienna
Austria
Tel: +43-1-515640 Fax: +43-1-513 9238
Email: Info@opec.org
Web: http://www.opecfund.org/
Director General: Suleiman J. Al-Herbish

2548   The World Bank Group
1818 H Street NW
Washington DC 20433
USA
Tel: +1-202-473 1000 (General enquiries)
1-202-473 4467 (Africa region)
Fax: +1-202-477 6391
Email: use feedback email form on Web site for general enquiries
Email for Africa region:
africainfo@worldbank.org
Web: http://www.worldbank.org/ (Main home page) http://www.worldbank.org/afr (Sub-Saharan Africa pages)
http://www.worldbank.org/mena (Middle East and North Africa pages)
President of the World Bank Group:
Paul Wolfowitz
Managing Director: Shengman Zhang
Chief Economist and Senior Vice President, Development Economics:
Francois Bourguignon
Vice President and Corporate Secretary for the World Bank Group:
W. Paatii Ofosu-Amaah
Vice President, Africa region:

Gobind Nankani
Vice President, Middle East and North Africa region: Christiaan J. Poortman
Note: for country office information and Country Directors in Africa *see*
http://web.worldbank.org/WBSITE/EXTERNAL/COUNTRIES/AFRICAEXT/0,,contentMDK:20234094~menuPK:485641~pagePK:146736~piPK:226340~theSitePK:258644,00.html
For organizational chart for country departments in Africa, sector units, and regional contacts *see*
http://web.worldbank.org/WBSITE/EXTERNAL/COUNTRIES/AFRICAEXT/0,,contentMDK:20234083~menuPK:485643~pagePK:146736~piPK:226340~theSitePK:258644,00.html
See also ➔ **The World Bank-Publications (2305)**, and entry ➔ **81**

2549   The World Trade Organization (WTO)
Centre William Rappard
Rue de Lausanne 154
1211 Geneva 21
Switzerland
Tel: +41-22-739 5111 Fax: +41-22-731 4206
Email: enquiries@wto.org
Web: http://www.wto.org
Chair, WTO General Council:
HE Ms Amina Chawahir Mohamed
Director General: Pascal Lamy

Some other international organizations, associations, institutes, NGOs, and networks (in Africa and elsewhere)

See also → **19 Major foundations, donors, government and aid agencies**

The directory below lists regional or international organizations, major research and policy institutes, NGOs, associations, networks, advocacy bodies or campaigning organizations, who are either active in Africa, and/or support research and activities in the arts, humanities and social sciences, agriculture, science and technology, human rights and civil society, media and communication, or in other areas.

2550   Africa Action
1634 Eye Street NW #810 Washington
DC 20006
USA
Tel: +1-202-546 7961 Fax: +202-546 1545
Email: africaaction@igc.org (General
enquiries) sbooker@africaaction.org
(Executive Director)
Web:
http://www.africaaction.org/index.php
President, Board of Directors:
James Early
Executive Director: Salih Booker
Note: incorporates the former American
Committee on Africa (ACOA), The Africa
Fund, and the Africa Policy Information
Center (APIC).

2551   The Africa Centre
38 King Street
London WC2E 8JT
UK
Tel: +44-(0)20-7836 1973
Fax: +44-(0)20-7836 1975
Email: info@africacentre.org.uk (General
enquiries) admin@africacentre.org.uk
(Administrator)
director@africacentre.org.uk (Director)
resources@africacentre.org.uk (General
Manager)

Web: http://www.africacentre.org.uk/
Director: Adotey Bing
General Manager: Mo Jonah
Administrator: Susan Odamtten
See also → **Contemporary Africa Database
(437)**

Africa-America Institute *see* → **19 Major
foundations, donors, government and aid
agencies** entry **2727**

Africa Educational Trust *see* → **19 Major
foundations, donors, government and aid
agencies** entry **2699**

2552   Africa Faith and Justice Network
3035 Fourth Street NE
Washington DC 20017
USA
Tel: +1-202-832 3412 Fax: +1-202-832 9051
Email: afjn@afjn.org
Web: http://afjn.cua.edu/
Chair: Robert A. Dowd
Executive Director: Fr. William Dyer

**2553   Africa Free Media Foundation
(AFMF)**
(formerly The Network for the
Defence of Independent Media in
Africa)
PO Box 70147 – 00400
Nairobi
Kenya
Tel: 254-66-51118 Fax: +254-66-50836
Email: afmf@freemediafoundation.org
(General enquiries)
sambure@africaonline.co.ke (Director)
emily@ndima.org (Programme Coordinator)
Web: http://www.freemediafoundation.org/
Director: Sam Mbure
Programme Coordinator and
Administrator: Emily Nyanjugu

Africa Fund → *see* **Africa Action (2550)**

**2554   Africa Grantmakers' Affinity
Group (AGAG)**
437 Madison Avenue 37th floor
New York NY 10022-7001
USA
Tel: +1-212-812 4212 Fax: +1-212-812 4299
Email: agag@africagrantmakers.org
Web: http://www.africagrantmakers.org
Director: Niamani Mutima

Note: AGAG does *not* give grants nor is AGAG staff able to provide fundraising assistance.
See also entry ➔ **191**

➔ **Africa Policy Information Center** *see* **Africa Action (2550)**

2555   African Academy of Sciences (AAS)
Miotoni Lane
Karen
PO Box 14798
Nairobi
Kenya
Tel: +254-20-884401/884620
Fax: 254-20-884406
Email: aas@africaonline.co.ke
Web: http://www.aasciences.org/
President: Mohamed H. A. Hassan
Secretary General and Ag. Executive Director: G.B.A. Okelo
See also ➔ **Academy Science Publishers (1981)**

➔ **African Association for Political Science/Association africaine de science politique** *see* ➔ **20 African studies associations and societies**, entry **2750**

2556   African Association for Public Administration and Management (AAPAM)
British American Centre
Ragati & Mara Roads
PO Box 48677
Nairobi 00100 GPO
Kenya
Tel: +254-20-273 0505
Tel/Fax: +254 20-273 0555
Email: aapam@africaonline.co.ke
or info@aapam.org
Web: http://www.aapam.org/
President: John Mitala (Uganda)
Secretary General: Yolamu R. Barongo

2557   African Capacity Building Foundation (ACBF)
Intermarket Life Towers Cnr.
Jason Moyo/Sam Nujoma Street
PO Box 1562
Harare
Zimbabwe
Tel: +263-4-790398/700208
Fax: +263-4-702915/738520
Email: root@acbf-pact.org

Web: http://www.acbf-pact.org
Chair: Emmanuel Tumusiime-Mutebile (Uganda)
Executive Secretary: Soumana Sako

2558   African Centre for Applied Research and Training in Development (ACARTSOD)
Wahda Quarter
Zawia Road
POB 80606
Tripoli
Libya
Tel: +218-21-833640/833228
Fax: 218-21-832357
Email: fituri_acartsod@hotmail.com
Executive Director: Ahmed Said Fituri

2559   African Centre for Gender and Development (ACGD)
African Centre for Women
Economic Commission for Africa
PO Box 3001
Addis Ababa
Ethiopia
Tel: +251-1-517200 exts 33300/33301
Fax: 251-1-512785/514416
Email: ouedraogoj@un.org
Web: http://www.uneca.org/fr/acgd/en/1024x768/acgd.htm
Director: Josephine Ouédraogo

2560   African Council for Communication Education (ACCE)
University of Nairobi
Education Building 3rd Floor
PO Box 47495
Nairobi
Kenya
Tel: +254-20-215270/227043
Fax: +254-20-216135
Email: acceb@arcc.or.ke
Web: http://www.africancouncilcomed.org/
President: Ikechukwu Nwosu
Executive Secretary: Wilson Ugangu

2561   The African Development Institute Inc
PO Box 1644
New York NY 10185
USA
Tel: +1-201-838 7900 (Toll free, US & Canada only) 888-619 7535 Fax: +1-201-944 7773
Email: ca498@bfn.org

Web:
http://www.africainstitute.com/index.html
Board of Directors: Enock Mensah, Kwame
Akonor, *et al*

→ **African Economic Research Consortium
(AERC)** *see* **19 Major foundations, donors,
government and aid agencies** entry **2672**

**2562   African Energy Policy
Research Network (AFREPREN)**
Elgeyo Marakwet Close
Kilimani
PO Box 30979
Nairobi 00100 GPO
Kenya
Tel: +254-20-5660032/571467
Fax: +254-20-561465/566231
Email: afrepren@africaonline.co.ke or
StephenK@africaonline.co.ke or
skarekezi@form-net.com
Web: http://www.afrepren.org
Director: Stephen Karekezi

**2563   African Forum and Network on
Debt and Development
(AFRODAD)**
31 Atkinson Drive Hillside
PO Box CY1517
Causeway
Harare
Zimbabwe
Tel: +263-4-778531/778536
Fax: 263-4-747878
Email: afrodad@afrodad.co.zw
(General enquiries) charles@afrodad.co.zw
(Ag. Executive Director)
Web: http://www.afrodad.org/
Chairman of the Board: Opa Kapijimpanga
Executive Director (Acting): Charles Mutasa

**2564   African Medical and Research
Foundation (AMREF)**
AMREF Headquarters
Langata Road
PO Box 27691 – 00506
Nairobi
Kenya
Tel: +254-20-605220 Fax + 254-20-609518
Email: info@amrefke.org
Web: http://www.amref.org/
Director General: Michael Smalley
Country Director, Kenya: (Ms) Mette Kjaer;
for Country Directors elsewhere in Africa *see*

http://www.amref.org/index.asp?PageID=1
02
AMREF UK:
Kensington Charity Centre
4th Floor Charles House
375 Kensington High Street
London W14 8QH
Tel: +44-(0)20-7471 6755
Fax: +44-(0)20-7471 6756
Director: Alexander Heroys
AMREF USA:
19 West 44th Street
Room 710
New York
NY 10036
Tel: +1-212-768 2440 Fax: +1-212-768 4230
Email: amrefusa@amrefusa.org
Executive Director: Lisa K.Meadowcroft
Note: for country offices elsewhere *see*
http://www.amref.org/index.asp?PageID=1
04
See also → **African Medical & Research
Foundation** (Publishing unit) **1985**

**2565   African Network of Scientific and
Technological Institutions
(ANSTI)/Reseau africaine
d'institutions scientifiques et
technologiques**
UNESCO Nairobi Office
POB 30592
Nairobi
Kenya
Tel: +254-20-622619 Fax: +254-20-622750
Email: info@ansti.org (General enquiries)
Joseph.Massaquoi@unesco.unon.org (ANSTI
Coordinator)
Web: http://www.ansti.org/
Cooordinator: Joseph Massaquoi

**2566   African Publishers' Network
(APNET)**
Temporary address:
c/o Ghana Book Publishers
Association (GBPA)
Accra Workers College 3rd floor
Adabraka
PO Box 1176 Cantonments
Accra
Ghana
Tel: +233-21 229178
Fax: +233-21 220107/234251
Email: *(temporary)* apnettraining@yahoo.fr
(Executive Secretary) apnettrade@yahoo.com
(Trade promotion)

Email: *(permanent)* secretariat@apnet.org
(General enquiries) es@apnet.org (Executive
Secretary) tpo@apnet.org (Trade Promotion)
Web:
http://www.apnet.org/home.html
(available in English, French and Portuguese
versions)
Chair: vacant (Chair interim APNET task
team: Brian Wafawarowa)
Executive Secretary: Alice M. Nga Minkala
Note: at press time (November 2005) APNET
was in the course of relocating from their
Abidjan offices to new headquarters in Accra.

2567   **African Regional Centre for
        Technology (ARCT)**
        FAHD Building 17th Floor
        Boulevard Djily Mbaye
        BP 2435
        Dakar
        Senegal
Tel: +221-823 7712 Fax: +221-823 7713
Email: arct@sonatel.senet.net
Executive Director: Ousmane Kane

2568   **African Wildlife Foundation (AWS)**
        1400 16th Street NW Suite 120
        Washington DC 20036
        USA
Tel: +1- 202-939 3333 Fax: +1-202-939 3332
Email: africanwildlife@awf.org
Web: http://www.awf.org/
Chair, Board of Trustees: Leila S. Green
President and CEO: Patrick J. Bergin
Note: for AWS regional centres in Africa, and
for African senior staff, *see*
http://www.awf.org/about/contactus.php,
and
http://www.awf.org/about/seniorstaff.php

2569   **African Women's Development and
        Communication Network/ Résau de
        développement et de
        communication des femmes
        africaines (FEMNET)**
        Off Westlands Road
        PO Box 54562
        00200 Nairobi
        Kenya
Tel: +254-20-374 1301/20
Fax: +254-20-3742927
Email: admin@femnet.or.ke
Web: http://www.femnet.or.ke/
Chair, Board of Trustees: (Ms) Kibre Dawit
Executive Director: Lynne Muthoni Wanyeki

Note: for a complete list of FEMNET regional
and country contacts *see*
http://www.femnet.or.ke/about.asp

2570   **The Africa Society of the National
        Summit on Africa**
        Carnegie Endowment for
        International Peace
        1779 Massachusetts Avenue NW
        Suite 510-A
        Washington DC 20036
        USA
Tel: +1-202-232 3862 Fax: +1-202-232 3870
Email: Fdoumbia@africasummit.org (General
enquiries)
pbaine@africasummit.org (Program
Administrator)
leonardrobinson@africasummit.org
(President and Chief Executive Officer)
Web:
http://www.africasummit.org/index.html
President and Chief Executive Officer:
Leonard H. Robinson, Jr
Program Administrator: Patrica Baine

2571   **AfriMAP. Africa Governance
        Monitoring and Advocacy Project**
        6-8 Amwell St
        London EC1R 1UQ
Tel: +44-(0)20-7837 5006
Fax: +44-(0)20-7278 7660
Email: info@afrimap.org
http://www.afrimap.org/
Director: Bronwen Manby (London)
Deputy Director: Ozias Tungwarara
(Johannesburg)
Advocacy Director: Pascal Kambale
(Washington DC)
Note: AfriMAP is part of the ➜ **Open Society
Institute (2742)** network, and has staff based
in London, Johannesburg, and Washington,
DC.

2572   **Afro-Asian Peoples Solidarity
        Organization/Organisation de la
        solidarité des peuples afro-
        asiatiques (AAPSO)**
        89 Abdel Aziz Al Saoud Street Manial
        el Roda
        PO Box 61
        Cairo 11451-61
        Egypt
Tel: +20-2-362 2946/363 6081
Fax: +20-2-363 7361
Email: aapso@idsc.net.eg

Secretary General: Nouri Abdul Razzak

→ **American Committee on Africa** *see* **Africa Action (2550)**

2573 All Africa Conference of Churches/ Conférence des églises de toute l'Afrique (AACC)
Melaku Kifle Waiyaki Way
POB 14205 Westlands
Nairobi
Kenya
Tel: +254-20-444 1338/9
Fax: +254-20-444 3241
Email: secretariat@aacc-ceta.org (General enquiries)
mvume@aacc-ceta.org (General Secretary)
Web: http://www.aacc-ceta.org/
General Secretary: Rev. Muvume Dandala

2574 Alliance française
101 boulevard Raspail
75270 Paris Cedex
France
Tel: +33-1-42 84 90 00
Fax: +33-1-42 84 91 00 (General enquiries) +33-1-42 84 91 02
(Service pédagogique)
Email: info@alliancefr.org
Web:
http://www.alliancefr.org/sommaire.php3?l
ang=fr (French version)
Web: http://www.alliancefr.org
(English version)
Secretary General: Jean-Claude Jacq
Note: for Alliance française offices and contact details in Africa *see*
http://www.alliancefr.org/rubrique.php3?id
_rubrique=231

2575 American Association for the Advancement of Science, Sub-Saharan Africa Program (AAAS)
AAAS International Office
1200 New York Avenue NW
Washington DC 20005
USA
Tel: +1-202-326 6650 Fax: +1-202-289 4958
Email: sabbott@aaas.org
Web:
http://www.aaas.org/international/africa/s
td.shtml
Chief International Officer: Shere Abbott

2576 Amnesty International
International Secretariat
1 Easton Street
London WC1X 0DW
UK
Tel: +44-(0)20-7413 5500
Fax: +44-(0)20-7956 1157
Email: info@amnesty.org.uk (General enquiries) press@amnesty.org.uk (Press Officer, UK)
Web: http://www.amnesty.org/
http://news.amnesty.org/regions/AFR
(Africa regional pages)
In the US:
Amnesty International USA
5 Penn Plaza 14th floor
New York NY 10001
Tel: +1-212-807 8400
Fax: +1-212- 627 1451
Email: admin-us@aiusa.org
Web: http://www.amnestyusa.org/
Secretary General, Amnesty International: Irene Khan
Chair, Amnesty International UK: Linda Wilkinson
Chair, Amnesty International UK Business Group: Chris Marsden
Executive Director, Amnesty International USA: William F. Schulz
Press Officer (UK) Africa and Asia: Sarah Green
Media Director (USA): (Ms) Wende Gozan

2577 Article 19
6-8 Amwell Street
London EC1R 1UQ
UK
Tel: +44-(0)20-7278 9292
Fax: +44-(0)20 7278 7660
Email: info@article19.org
Web: http://www.article19.org/index.html
Executive Director: Agnès Callamard
Africa Programme Officer: Fatou Jagne-Senghore

2578 Association for the Development of African Education/ L'association pour le développement de l'éducation en Afrique (ADEA)
7-9 rue Eugène-Delacroix
75116 Paris
France
Tel: +33-1-45 03 77 57 Fax: +33-1-45 03 39 65
Email: adea@iiep.unesco.org
Web: http://www.ADEAnet.org

Chair, Steering Committee:
Ahlin Byll-Cataria
Executive Secretary: Mamadou Ndoye
Note: for contacts of various Working
Groups *see*
http://www.adeanet.org/workgroups
/en_workgroups.html

**2579   Association for Progressive
         Communications (APC)**
         APC Secretariat
         Presidio Building 1012
         Torney Avenue
         PO Box 29904
         San Francisco CA 94129
         USA
Tel: +1-416-516 8138 Fax: +1-416-516 0131
(*Note*: these are Toronto, Canada numbers)
Executive Director's Office:
PO Box 29755
Melville 2109
South Africa
Tel: +27-11-726 1692
Fax: +27-11-726 1692
Email: webeditor@apc.org (General
enquiries) apc-africa@apc.org (APC
Africa apcwomen@apc.org (Women's
Networking Support Program)
africa.rights@sn.apc.org (Africa Internet
Rights Team) apc-policy@apc.org
(Communications Policy Awareness and
Internet Rights)
Web: http://www.apc.org (Main home
page)
http://www.apc.org/english/rights/a
frica/ (Africa pages)
Chair, Executive Board:
Julián Casasbuenas (Colombia)
Executive Director: Anriette Esterhuysen
(South Africa)
Project Manager, Africa Internet Rights
Team: Emmanuel Njenga

**2580   Association of African Universities/
         Association des universités
         africaines (AAU)**
         PO Box 5744
         Accra North
         Ghana
Tel: +233-21-774495/761588
Fax: +233-21-774821
Email: info@aau.org (General enquiries,
administration and services)

secgen@aau.org (Secretary General)
research@aau.org (Research
Department/Director of Research)
Web: http://www.aau.org/
Secretary General: Akilagpa Sawyerr
Director of Research and Programmes:
Paschal Mihyo
Head, Communication and Services:
Pashal Hoba
Note: for contacts of project coordinators *see*
http://www.aau.org/english/secretariat.ht
m

**2581   Association of African Women for
         Research and Development
         (AAWORD)/Association des
         femmes africaines pour la recherche
         et le développement (AFARD)**
         Sicap Sacré-Coeur I no. 8798
         BP 15367
         Dakar-Fann
         Senegal
Tel: +221- 824 2053/825 2349
Fax: +221-824 2056
Email: aaword@sentoo.sn
Web: http://www.afard.org/
President: Malika Benradi (Morocco)
Vice-President: Stella Y. Erinosho
(Nigeria)
Executive Secretary: Aicha Tamboura
Note: for contact addresses of AFARD groups
throughout Africa *see* Web site (click on to
Members et organisations partenaires)

**2582   Association pour la diffusion de la
         pensée française (ADPF)**
         Ministère des Affaires Etrangères
         6 rue Ferrus
         75683 Paris Cedex 14
         France
Tel: +33-1-43 13 11 00 Fax: +33-1-43 13 11 25
Email: ecrire@adpf.asso.fr (General enquiries)
francois.neuville@adpf.asso.fr (Director)
Web: http://www.adpf.asso.fr/
President: Jacques Blot
Director: François Neuville
Secretary General: Nicole Lamarque

**2583   Bellagio Publishing Network
         Secretariat**
         PO Box 1369
         Oxford OX4 4ZR
         UK
Tel/Fax: +44-(0)1865-250024

Email: info@bellagiopublishingnetwork.org
(General enquiries)
ks@bellagiopublishingnetwork.org
(Coordinator)
Web:
http://www.bellagiopublishingnetwork.org
Coordinator: Katherine Salahi

2584   Bellanet International Secretariat
c/o IDRC
PO Box 8500
Ottawa
Ontario K1G 3H9
Canada
Tel: +1-613-236 6163 ext 2398
Fax: +1-613-238 7230
Email: info@bellanet.org
Web: http://www.bellanet.org/
Senior Program Officer and Interim
Executive Director: Michael Roberts
Secretariat Coordinator: Aida Sullivan

2585   Book Aid International (BAI)
39-41 Coldharbour Lane
Camberwell
London SE5 9NR
UK
Tel: +44-(0)20-7733 3577
Fax: +44-(0)20-7978 8006
Email: info@bookaid.org
Web: http://www.bookaid.org
Chair: Tim Rix
Director: Sara Harrity

→ The British Council see Major
foundations, donors, government and aid
agencies, entry 2702

**2586   British Overseas NGOs for
Development**
Regent's Wharf
8 All Saint's Street
London N1 9RL
UK
Tel: +44-(0)20-7837 8344
Fax: +44-(0)20-7837 4220
Email: bond@bond.org.uk
Web: http://www.bond.org.uk/
General Secretary: Richard Bennett

**2587   Centre africain de formation et de
recherches administratives pour le
développement/African Training
and Research Centre in Training for
Development (CAFRAD)**
Avenue Mohamed V
BP 310
Tangier 90001
Morocco
Tel: +212-61-32 27 07/30 72 69
Fax: + 212-39-32 57 85
Email: cafrad@cafrad.org
Web: http://www.cafrad.org
Director General:
Simon Lelo Mamosi

**2588   Centre for Black and African Arts
and Civilisation**
National Theatre
PMB 12794
Lagos
Nigeria
Tel: 234-1-470 5667/585 2173
Email: jbaac@cbaac.org
Web: http://www.cbaac.com/
Director General: Duro Oni

**2589   Centre international des civilisations
Bantu (CICIBA)**
BP 770
Libreville
Gabon
Tel: +241-739650 Fax: +241-775090
Email: ciciba@caramail.com
Web: n/a
Secretary General: Marie Helene Mathey-Boo

2590   Commission for Africa Secretariat
Public Enquiry Point
Department for International
Development
Abercrombie House
Eaglesham Road
East Kilbride
Glasgow G75 8EA
UK
Tel: 0845-300 4100 (local call rate from within
the UK)
Tel: +44-1355-843132 (from outside the UK)
Fax: +44-(0)-1355-843632
Email: enquiry@dfid.gov.uk
http://www.commissionforafrica.org/
(English version; archive only)

Chair of Commissioners: The Rt. Hon. Tony Blair, MP, Prime Minister of the United Kingdom
Director of Policy and Research: Sir Nicholas Stern
Head of Secretariat: Myles Wickstead
Note: the Secretariat to the Commission for Africa closed on 31 July 2005 having finished its work. The above Web site is a permanent archive of the Commission's work. Any further general requests for information about the Commission should be directed to the DFID address above.
See also entries ➜ **33, 34**

2591   The Corporate Council on Africa (CCA)
1100 17th Street NW Suite 1100
Washington DC 20036
USA
Tel: +1-202-835 1115 Fax: +1-202-835 1117
Email: cca@africacncl.org (General enquiries)
shayes@africacncl.org (President)
Web: http://www.africacncl.org/
Chairman of the Board: W. Frank Fountain
President: Stephen Hayes
Vice President for Programs: Robert C. Perry

2592   Council on Foreign Relations (CFR)
The Harold Pratt House
58 East 68th Street
New York NY 10021
USA
Tel: +1-212-434 9400 Fax: +1-212-434 9800
Email: communications@cfr.org (General enquiries) lshields@cfr.org (Director of Communications) asiebenaler@cfr.org (Assistant Director of Studies)
plyman@cfr.org (Director, Africa Studies Program)
Web: http://www.cfr.org/ (Main home page)
http://www.cfr.org/reg_index.php?id=1 | | | 1 (Africa pages)
http://www.cfr.org/program.php?id=31 (Studies Program Africa)
President: Richard N. Haass
Vice President and Director of Membership and Fellowship Affairs:
Elise Carlson Lewis
Vice President, Office of Communications:
Lisa Shields
Assistant Director of Studies:
Alicia Siebenaler
Director, Africa Studies Program and Ralph

Bunche Senior Fellow in Africa Policy Studies: Princeton N. Lyman

2593   European Association of Development Research and Training Institutes/Association Européenne des Instituts de Recherche et de Formation en Matière de Développement (EADI)
Kaiser-Friedrich-Strasse 11
53115 Bonn
Germany
Tel: +49-228-261 8101 Fax: +49-228-261 8103
Email: postmaster@eadi.org (General enquiries) lawo@eadi.org (Executive Secretary)
Web: http://www.eadi.org/
President: Louk de la Rive Box
Executive Secretary: Thomas Lawo

2594   Forum for African Women Educationalists (FAWE)
FAWE House on Chania Avenue off Wood Avenue
PO Box 21394
Ngong Road
Nairobi 00505
Kenya
Telephone: +254-2-573131/573351
Fax: +254-2-574150
Email: fawe@fawe.org
Web: http://www.fawe.org/
Executive Director: Penina Mlama

2595   The Free Africa Foundation
910 17th Street NW Suite 419
Washington DC 20006
USA
Tel: +1-202-296 7081 Fax: +1-202-2965909
Email: info@freeafrica.org or africa@erols.com
Web: http://www.freeafrica.org/
President: George B.N. Ayittey
Secretary: Kate Anderson

2596   Gesellschaft zur Förderung der Literatur aus Afrika, Asien, und Latinamerika e.V./Society for the Promotion of African, Asian and Latin American Literatures
Reineckstrasse 3
PO Box 10 01 16
60001 Frankfurt am Main
Germany
Tel: +49-69-210 2247/210 2250

Fax: +49-69-210 2227/210 2277
Email: litprom@book-fair.com or
mayenburg@book-fair.com
Web: http://www.litprom.de/(German
version)
http://www.litprom.de/sites/dialog_enfrm.
htm (English version; also in French and
Spanish)
Chairman of the Governing Board:
Peter Weidhaas
Contacts: Peter Ripken, Director; or Corry
von Mayenburg

→ Goethe Institut *see* 18 Major African and
international organizations entry 2663

**2597   Innovations et réseaux pour le
         développement/Development
         Innovations and Network (IRED)**
         Case 116
         3 rue de Varembé
         1211 Geneva 20
         Switzerland
Tel: +41-22-734 1716 Fax: +41-22-740 0011
Email: ired@ired.org
Web: http://www.ired.org/
Secretary General: Fernand Vincent

**2598   Institut africain pour le
         développement économique et
         social/African Institute for Economic
         and Social Development (INADES)**
         15 rue Jean Mermoz
         08 BP 2088
         Abidjan 08
         Côte d'Ivoire
Tel: +225-22 40 02 16 Fax: +225-22 40 02 30
Email: ifsiege@inadesfo.ci (General enquiries)
ibrahim.ouedraogo@inadesfo.org (Secretary
General)
Web: http://www.inadesfo.org/
Secretary General: Ibrahim Ouédraogo
Note: for INADES African regional offices *see*
http://www.inadesfo.org/presentation/bn/i
ndex.htm

→ Institut fondamental d'Afrique
Noire Cheikh Anta Diop (IFAN) *see* 14
Centres of African studies & African
studies programmes worldwide, entry
1852

→ Institut de recherche pour le
développement (IRD) *see* 14 Centres
of African studies & African studies
programmes worldwide, entry 1572

**2599   Institute for African Alternatives
         (IFAA)**
         Lyndhurst Hall
         London NW5 4RE
Tel: +44-(0)20-7482 4660
Fax: +44-(0)20-7482 4662
Email: ifaanet@gn.apc.org
Web: http://www.ifaanet.org/index.htm
Chair: Mohammed Suliman

2600   Institute for the African Child
         Ohio University
         Center for International Studies
         RTEC Building 3rd Floor
         Athens OH 45701
         USA
Tel: +1-740-597 1368 Fax: +1-740-593 1837
Email: afrchild@www.ohio.edu (General
enquiries)
howard@ohio.edu (Director)
owusu-kw@ohio.edu (Coordinator)
http://www.ohiou.edu/afrchild/Index.htm
Director: Stephen Howard
Assistant Director and Coordinator:
Nana Kwaku Owusu-Kwarteng

**2601   Institut Panos Afrique de l'Ouest /
         The Panos Institute West Africa
         (IPAO)**
         6 rue Calmette
         BP 21132 Dakar Ponty
         Dakar
         Senegal
Tel : +221-849 1666 Fax : +221-822 1761
Email : panos_(auo)_panos-ao.org
Web : http://www.panos-ao.org
President : Gaston Zongo (Burkina Faso)
Director General: Diana Senghor
see also → The Panos Institute (2720)

→ International African Institute/
Institut Africain International *see*
14 Centres of African studies & African
studies programmes worldwide, entry
1622

2602   International Centre of Insect Physiology and Ecology (ICIPE)
PO Box 30772
Nairobi 00100 GPO
Kenya
Tel: +254-20-863 2000
Fax: +254-20-863 2001/8632002
Email: dg@icipe.org
Web: http://www.icipe.org/
Chair, Governing Council: Peter Esbjerg
Director General & Chief Executive Officer:
Christian Borgemeister
Director of Research and Partnerships:
Onesmo Ole-MoiYoi

2603   International Centre for Research in Agroforestry (ICRAF)
World Agroforestry Centre
United Nations Avenue Gigiri
PO Box 30677
Nairobi 00100 GPO
Kenya
Tel: +254-20-722 4000
or via USA +1-650-833 6645
Fax: +254-20-722 4001
or via USA +1-650-833 6646
Email: ICRAF@cgiar.org (General enquiries)
d.garrity@cgiar.org
(Director General) j.laarman@cgiar.org
(Deputy Director General-Programmes)
Web:
http://www.worldagroforestrycentre.org
Chair, Board of Trustees: Eugene Terry
Director General: Dennis Garrity
Deputy Director General-Programmes:
Jan Laarman

2604   International Council of African Museums/Conseil International des Musées Africains (AFRICOM)
PO Box 38706 Ngara
Nairobi 00600
Kenya
Tel: +254-20-374 8668 Fax: +254-20-374 8928
Email: africom@africom.museum (General
enquiries) l.abungu@africom.museum
(Executive Director)
a.namodi@africom.museum (Program
Manager)
Web: http://www.africom.museum/
(English version)
Executive Director: Lorna L. Abungu
Program Manager: Alphas Namodi
See also entry ➔ **147**

2605   International Institute for Environment and Development (IIED)
3 Endsleigh Street,
London WC1H 0DD
UK
Telephone: +44-(0)20-7388 2117
Fax: +44-(0)20-7388 2826
Email: info@iied.org (General enquiries)
camilla.toulmin@iied.org (Director)
Web: http://www.iied.org/index.html
Chair: Mary Robinson
Director: Camilla Toulmin

2606   International Institute of Tropical Agriculture (IITA)
Oyo Road
PMB 5320
Ibadan
Oyo State
Tel: +234-2-241 2626 Fax: +234-2-241 2221
International mailing address:
IITA
c/o Lambourn (UK) Limited
Carolyn House
26 Dingwall Road
Croydon CR9 3EE
UK
Email: iita@cgiar.org (General enquiries)
p.hartmann@cgiar.org (Director General)
J.Cramer@cgiar.org (Executive Assistant to
the Director General)
Web: http://www.iita.org/
Director General: P. Hartmann
Executive Assistant to the Director
General/Governing Board Secretary:
J. Cramer
See also ➔ **International Institute of Tropical Agriculture** (Publishing unit) **(2041)**

International Laboratory for Research on Animal Diseases (ILRAD) now part of ➔ **International Livestock Research Institute (2607)**

➔ **International Livestock Centre for Africa (ILCA)** now part of **International Livestock Research Institute (2607)**

2607 **International Livestock Research Institute (ILRI)**
ILRI-Kenya:
Old Naivasha Road
PO Box 30709
Nairobi 00100
Kenya
Tel: +254-20-422 3000 or
1-650 833 6660 (USA direct)
Fax: +254-20-422 3001 or
+1-650 833 6661 (USA direct)
Email: ILRI-Kenya@cgiar.org
ILRI-Ethiopia: (Debre Zeit Research Station)
PO Box 5689
Addis Ababa
Ethiopia
Tel: +251-1-338 290 Fax: +251-1-338 755
Email: ilri@cgnet.com (General enquiries)
c.sere@cgiar.org (Director General)
b.scott@cgiar.org (Director, Corporate Services)
ILRI-debre-zeit@cgiar.org (Debre Zeit Research Station)
Web: http://www.cgiar.org/ilri/
Board Chair: John Vercoe
Director General: Carlos Seré
Director, Corporate Services: Bruce Scott
See also ➔ **International Livestock Research Institute** (Publishing unit) **(1965)**

2608 **International Network for the Availability of Scientific Publications (INASP)**
58 St Aldates
Oxford OX1 1ST
UK
Tel: +44-(0)1865-249909
Fax: +44-(0)1865-251060
Email: inasp@inasp.info
Web: http://www.inasp.info
Chair, Board of Trustees: Robert Campbell
Director: Carol Priestley
Office Manager: Anne Powell
Note: for complete staff list, including Senior Programme Managers, *see*
http://www.inasp.info/info/people.shtml
See also entry **264**, and ➔ **International Network for the Availability of Scientific Publications** (Publishing unit) **(2218)**

2609 **International Reading Association (IRA)**
800 Barksdale Road
PO Box 8139
Newark DE 19714-8139
USA
Tel: +1- 302-731 1600 Fax: +1-302-731 1057
Email: pubinfo@reading.org (General enquiries) afarstrup@reading.org (Executive Director)
Web: http://www.reading.org
President: Timothy Shanahan
Executive Director: Alan E. Farstrup

2610 **Justice Africa**
1C Leroy House
436 Essex Road
London N1 3QP
UK
Tel: +44-(0)207-354 8400
Fax: +44-(0)207-354 8736
Email: enquiries@justiceafrica.org
Web: http://www.justiceafrica.org/
Directors: Alex de Waal, Tajudeen Abdul Raheem, Yoanes Ajawin, Abdul Mohamed
Office contacts: (Ms) Kiiza Ngonzi, Hafiz Moham
See also ➔ **Justice Africa** (Publications) **(2221)**

2611 **Ithaka**
New York office:
120 Fifth Avenue 5th Floor
New York NY 10011
USA
Tel: +1-212-229 1211 Fax: +1-212-229 6841
Email: info@ithaka.org
Web: http://www.ithaka.org/index.htm
Princeton office:
228 Alexander Street
Princeton NJ 08540
Tel: +1-609- 258 9700 Fax: +1-609-258 5778
Chair, Board of Trustees: William G. Bowen
President: Kevin M. Guthrie
See also entry ➔ **2907**

2612 Media Institute of Southern Africa
21 Johann Albrecht Street
Private Bag 13386
Windhoek
Namibia
Tel: + 264-61-232975 Fax: +264-61-248016
Email: infor@misa.org (General enquiries)
director@misa.org (Director)
Web: http://www.misa.org/index.html
Director: Luckson Chipare
See also entry ➜ **143**

➜ **Nigerian Institute of International Affairs (NIIA) see 14 Centres of African studies & African studies programmes worldwide**, entry **1849**

2613 Observatory of Cultural Policies in Africa (OCPA)
11 rua Comandante Augusto Cardoso
Maputo
CP 1207
Maputo
Mozambique
Tel: +258-1-301015 Fax +258+1-312272
Email: secretariat@ocpanet.org or
ocpa@tvcabo.co.mz (Secretariat)
director@ocpanet.org (Executive Director)
Web: http://www.ocpanet.org/
Chair: Pierre Dandjinou (Benin)
Executive Director: Lupwishi Mbuyamba
See also entry ➜ **70**

2614 OneWorld International
River House 2nd floor
143-145 Farringdon Road
London EC1R 3AB
UK
Tel: +44-(0)-20-7239 1400
Fax: +44-(0)-20-7833 3347
Email: justice@oneworld.net (General enquiries) partnership@oneworld.net (Partnership enquiries)
media@oneworld.net (Press and media; but *not* a newsdesk address)
Chair of Trustees: Larry Kirkman
Director, OneWorld International Foundation, and Project Manager, OneWorld UK: Anuradha Vittachi
General Manager, OneWorld International Foundation: Miles Litvinoff
Director, OneWorld International Ltd: Peter Armstrong
Network & Communications Director: Pete Cranston

Web: http://www.oneworld.net/ (Main home page)
http://africa.oneworld.net/article/frontpage/151/509 (OneWorld Africa)
OneWorld Africa:
OneWorld Africa
Plot Number 6499 Suite 4
Kasangula Road Roma
PO Box 37011
Lusaka
Zambia
Tel: + 260-1-292740 Fax: +260-1-294188
Email: africa@oneworld.net
Centre Director: Priscilla Jere
Email: priscilla.jere@oneworld.net
OneWorld US:
OneWorld United States
3201 New Mexico Avenue NW
Suite 395
Washington DC 20016
USA
Tel: +1-202-885 2679 Fax: +1-202-885 1309
Email: us@oneworld.net
Web: http://us.oneworld.net
Centre Director: Michael Litz
Email: michael.litz@oneworld.net
Note: the OneWorld Global Database, covering more than 1,500 organizations from across the globe, can be found at
http://www.oneworld.net/section/partners/
See also entry ➜ **91**

2615 Operation Crossroads Africa
PO Box 5570
New York NY 10027
USA
Tel: +1-212-289 1949 Fax: +1-212-289 2526
Email: oca@igc.apc.org
Web: http://operationcrossroadsafrica.org/
Director: LaVerne Brown

2616 Pan African Association for Literacy and Adult Education (PAALAE)
Rue 10 Immeuble 306
BP 10358
Dakar
Senegal
Fax: +221-824 4413
Email: anafa@sentoo.sn (General enquiries) kane_lamine@hotmail.com (Steering Committee Coordinator)
Web: n/a
Steering Committee Coordinator: Lamine Kane

→ **Pan-African Institute for Development/Institut panafricain pour le développement (PAID)** see **14 Centres of African studies & African studies programmes worldwide,** entry **1831**

→ **Panafrican News Agency/Panapress** see **11 The African press** entry **1069**

2617 Pan-African Writers Association (PAWA)
PAWA House Roman Bridge
POB C456 Cantonments
Accra
Ghana
Tel: +233-21-773062 Fax: +233-21-773042
Email: pawa@ghana.com
Web: n/a
Secretary General: Atukwei Okai

2618 Peace Corps
The Paul D. Coverdell Peace Corps Headquarters
1111 20th Street NW
Washington DC 20526
USA
Tel: Toll-free (US/Canada only) 800-424 8580; for other see regional contact information at http://www.peacecorps.gov/index.cfm?shell =contact.regcon
Email: see URL above
Web: http://www.peacecorps.gov/ (Main home page)
http://www.peacecorps.gov/index.cfm?shell =learn.wherepc.africa Sub-Saharan Africa pages)

http://www.peacecorps.gov/index.cfm?shell =learn.wherepc.northafr (Middle East and North Africa pages)
Director: Gaddi Vasquez

**2619 SIT Study Abroad
The School for International Training**
Kipling Road
PO Box 676
Brattleboro VT 05302-0676
USA
Tel: +1-802-257 7751 toll free (US only) 800-257-7751 Fax: +1-802-258 3248
Email: studyabroad@sit.edu
Web: http://www.sit.edu/index.html (Main home page)
http://sit.edu/studyabroad/themes/Africa.html (Africa pages)
Senior Vice President, World Learning for International Development: Pamela Baldwin
Director International Student and Scholar Services: Janet Hulnick
Senior Administrative Director: Zelma Harrison
Note: for Faculty *see* http://www.sit.edu/graduate/faculty/index .html;
for Study Abroad coordinators: *see* http://216.204.215.30/directory/sit/FMPro
See also entry → **202**

2620 Southern African Book Development Education Trust
c/o Margaret Ling
25 Endymion Road
London N4 1EE
UK
Tel +44-(0)20-8348 8463
Fax: +44-(0)20-8348 4403
Email: margaret.ling@geo2.poptel.org.uk
Web: http://www.sabdet.com/index.htm
Chair: Kelvin Smith
Hon. Secretary: Margaret Ling

2621   Support Africa International Inc
Association for the Support of Higher
Schools for Applied Sciences,
Colleges and Universities Inc
Alte Strasse 19
56357 Berg/Taunus
Germany
Tel: +49-6772-1480 Fax +49-6772-8680
Email: supportafrica@t-online.de
Web: http://www.support-
africa.de/English/english.html
President: B. Ed. Pfeiffer
General Secretary: Joachim Hoelzl
Head of Administration:
Monika Weiler-Helbach

2622   TransAfrica Forum
1426 21st Street NW 2nd floor
Washington DC 20036
USA
Tel: +1-202-223 1960 Fax: +1-202-223 1966
Email: info@transafricaforum.org (General
enquiries) bfletcher@transafricaforum.org
(President) sms@transafricaforum.org
(Executive Vice President)
mmunthali@transafricaforum.org (Director of
Information)
Web: http://www.transafricaforum.org/
Chairman, Board of Directors: Danny Glover
President: Bill Fletcher
Executive Vice President:
Selena Mendy Singleton
Director of Information: Mwiza Munthali

**2623   United States Agency for International
Development (USAID). Bureau for
Africa**
Ronald Reagan Building
Washington DC 20523-1000
USA
Tel: +1-202-712 4810 (General enquiries; for
individual telephone numbers *see* under
USAID Africa Bureau contacts below)
Fax: +1-202-216 3524
Email: *see* under contacts below
Web: http://www.usaid.gov/ (Main home
page)
http://www.usaid.gov/locations/sub-
saharan_africa/ (Sub-Saharan Africa pages)
http://www.afr-sd.org/ (Office of
Sustainable Development)
USAID Administrator:
Andrew S. Natsios
Assistant Administrator-Bureau for Africa:
Lloyd O. Pierson

Tel: +1-202-712-0500
Email: lpierson@usaid.gov
Director, Office of Sustainable Development:
Harry M. Lightfoot, Sr.
Tel: +1-202-712 5534
Email: hlightfoot@usaid.gov
Director, Office of Development Planning:
Wade Warren
Tel: +1-202-712 1660
Email: wwarren@usaid.gov
Director, Office of West African Affairs:
Carol Grigsby
Tel: +1-202-712 0220
Email: cgrigsby@usaid.gov
Director, Office of Eastern Africa Affairs:
Jeff Borns
Tel: +1-202-712 4195
Email: jborns@usaid.gov
Director, Office of Southern Africa Affairs:
Patrick Fleuret
Tel: +1-202-712 1803
Email: pfleuret@usaid.gov
Director, Office of Sudan Programs:
Curt Reintsma
Tel: +1-202-712 4018
Email: creintsma@usaid.gov
Note: for Country Desk Officers contacts *see*
http://www.usaid.gov/locations/sub-
saharan_africa/utility/directory.html

2624   Voluntary Service Overseas (VSO)
317 Putney Bridge Road
London SW15 2PN
UK
Tel: +44-(0)20-8780 7200
Fax: +44-(0)20-8780 7300
Email: enquiry@vso.org.uk (General
enquiries) neera.dhingra@vso.org.uk (Media)
Web: http://www.vso.org.uk (VSO UK)
http://www.vsocan.org/ (VSO Canada)
Chair, Board of Trustees, VSO UK:
Keith Bezanson
Chief Executive: Mark Goldring
Director, VSO Canada: Shelag Savage
Note: for UK regional contacts *see*
http://www.vso.org.uk/about/contact/local
.asp

2625   Washington Office on Africa (WOA)
212 East Capitol Street
Washington DC 20003
USA
Tel: +1-202-547 7503 Fax: +1-202-547 7505
Email: woa@igc.org
Web: http://www.woaafrica.org/

President: Jon Chapman
Interim Executive Director:
Jennifer Davis

2626   West African Museums Programme
11 Route du Front de Terre
BP 357 - CP18524
Dakar
Senegal
Tel: +221-827 3389 Fax: +221- 827 3369
Email: wamp@wamponline.org or
wamp@sentoo.sn (General enquiries)
bdiamitani-wamp@sentoo.sn (Director)
Web: http://www.wamponline.org/
(English and French versions)
Chair: Anthonia K. Fatunsin
Director: Boureïma Tiékoroni Diamitani
See also entry ➔ **257**

2627   World Council of Churches (WCC)
150 route de Ferney
PO Box 2100
1211 Geneva 2
Switzerland
Tel: +41-22-791 6111 Fax: +41-22-791 0361
Email: infowcc@wcc-coe.org
Web: http://www.wcc-coe.org/
In the US:
475 Riverside Drive Room 915
New York NY 10115
USA
Tel: +1-212-870 3260 Fax: +1-212-870 2528
Web:
http://www.ecumenismnow.org/
General Secretary: Rev. Samuel Kobia
Director of Programmes:
Geneviève Jacques
Executive Secretary: Rev. Sabine Udodesku
Programme Executive, US office:
Rev. Deborah de Winter

**2628   World Intellectual Property
Organization (WIPO)**
34 chemin des Colombettes
PO Box 181211
Geneva 20
Switzerland
Tel: +41-22-338 9111 Fax: +41-22-733 5428
Email: wipo.mail@wipo.int (General
enquiries) publicinf@wipo.int (Media
Relations & Public Affairs Section)
information.center@wipo.int (WIPO
Information Centre)
Web:
http://www.wipo.int/portal/index.html.en
Director General: Kamil Idris
Executive Director, Office of Strategic
Planning and Policy Development, and the
WIPO Worldwide Academy (WWA):
Yoshiyuki Takagi
Administrative Support Services and General
Assembly Affairs: (Ms) Wang Binying
Director, Economic Development Bureau for
Africa: Geoffrey Onyeama

2629   World Resources Institute
10 G Street NE Suite 800
Washington DC 20002
USA
Tel: +1-202-729-7600 Fax: +1-202-729 7610
Email: lauralee@wri.org
Web: http://www.wri.org/
Chairman of the Board: James A. Harmon
President: Jonathan Lash
Executive Vice President and Managing
Director: Paul Faeth

19

Major foundations, donors, government and aid agencies

See also ➔ 1 General online resources on Africa and African studies and the best starting points on the Web: Guides to funding sources

➔ 18 Major African and international organizations

This section identifies the major foundations, donors, development assistance, and government agencies working on Africa, supporting research in Africa, or otherwise active in Africa. This includes donors and foundations supporting economic or social development programmes, arts and cultural activities, libraries, scholarly communication initiatives, museums and art conservation, IT and Internet development; or those providing support for specific activities and projects, for example in education and culture, or in the field of agriculture, governance, health, human rights, rural development, science and technology, social justice, or women's empowerment. Also included are some of the leading relief support and multilateral aid agencies, and a number of institutions or organizations supporting bilateral research cooperation, and/or providing support for training, workshops and conferences, publications, scholarship programmes, fellowships, and exchange and visitor programmes.

The listing includes agencies relating to the Commonwealth of Nations, the European Union, and the Francophone Community, but UN agencies, and organizations within the World Bank Group are listed under section ➔ 18 **Major African and international organizations**.

Book donation organizations, and those involved in book or journal assistance programmes in Africa, are *not* included. Full information about such organizations can be found in the ➔**INASP Directory (264)**, and the ➔ **Africana Librarians Council (1885)** Book Donation Committee's ➔ **Directory of Book Donation Programs (163)**.

Entries are listed by country, providing full contact addresses, telephone/fax numbers, email addresses (except see note below), and Web sites. Names of key personnel (Chair of the Board of Trustees, President, Executive Director or Chief Executive, Director General, Secretary General, etc.) and/or other senior staff contact information is also included, and is current as at November 2005. Please note that titles such as Prof. or Dr. are not included.

For more detailed information about each organization's principal objectives and activities, their organizational structure, the nature of their support, range of programmes, and countries in which it operates, click on to the Web site addresses indicated. Most Web sites also include names of programme officers, policies and procedures relating to applications or submission of proposals (where appropriate), and details of grants or awards made (if applicable).

Important note:
Many of the agencies and organizations listed here are *not* grant-making bodies, or only support projects through NGOs, or through bilateral programmes with individual African countries. Moreover, many donors or foundations listed here do *not* provide grants, fellowships, or other support to individuals, and unsolicited proposals are rarely funded. While some will accept general enquiries by email, others do not, and will only consider proposals made in writing. Some of them do not wish to publicize an email address for general enquiries – and email addresses are therefore not indicated for a number of entries – but may have an 'Ask a question' email response form as part of their Web pages.

Australia

2631 **Australian Council for International Development (ACFID)**
(formerly the Australian Council for Overseas Aid/AFOA)
Private Bag 3
Deakin ACT 2600
Tel: +61 2-6285 1816 Fax: +61-2-6285 1720
Email: cdignan@acfid.asn.au (Secretariat contact for Africa-related support)
krichards@acfid.asn.au (Africa related policies)
Web: http://www.acfid.asn.au/index.html (Main home page)
http://www.acfid.asn.au/campaigns/africa.htm (Africa pages)
President: Margaret Reid
Executive Director: Paul O'Callaghan
Executive Coordinator: Vanessa Weiss
Policy Coordinator, Human Rights and Governance (including Africa):
Kathy Richards
Deputy Director, Development Policy and Practice Team (including Africa-related

support): Cecile Dignan
Note: ACFID is an independent national association of NGOs working in the field of international aid and development.
For a listing of Australian NGOs supporting projects and operations in Africa *see* http://members.acfid.asn.au/projectDetails.php?c=Africa&PHPSESSID=25476b03c26bda7c1f8ca985e6954e64

Austria

2632 **Österreichische Entwicklungszusammenarbeit / Austrian Development Agency (ADA)**
Informationsbüro
Zelinkagasse 2
1010 Vienna
Tel: +43-1-903 990/903 99411
Fax: +43-1-5011 59277
Email: office@ada.gv.at (General enquiries)
oeza.info@ada.gv.at (Information Bureau)

Web:
http://www.ada.gv.at/view.php3?r_id=3042
&LNG=en&version (English version)
Head: Ambassador Michael Linhart
Director, Programmes and Projects: Robert
Zeiner
Director, Administration: Rudolf Holzer

**2633   Österreichische Forschungsstiftung
        für Entwicklungshilfe**
        Berggasse 7
        1090 Vienna
Tel: +43-1-317 4010 Fax: +43-1-317 4015
Email: office@oefse.at
Web: http://www.oefse.at/
Chair: Klaus Zapotoczky
Chief Executive: Gerhard Bittner

**2634   Wiener Institut für
        Entwicklungsfragen und
        Zusammenarbeit/Vienna Institute
        for Development and Cooperation
        (VIDC)**
        Möllwaldplatz 5/3
        1040 Vienna
Tel: +43-1-713 3594 Fax: +43-1-713 3594/73
Email: office@vidc.org (General enquiries)
andrlik@vidc.org (Executive Director)
Web: http://www.vidc.org/
President: Franz Vranitzky
Executive Director: Erich Andrlik

Belgium

**2535   Coopération par l'education et la
        culture (CEC)**
        18 rue Joseph II
        1000 Brussels
Tel: +32-2-217 9071 Fax: +32-2-217 8402
Email: info@cec-ong.org or cec-
ong@yucom.be
Web: http://www.cec-ong.org/
President: Joseph Boly
Administratrice Déléguée/Chief Executive:
Ann Gerrard

2636   The European Commission
        Rue de la Loi/Wetstraat 200
        1049 Brussels
Tel: +32-2-299 1111 (General switchboard)
Email/Contacts: use mailbox form on Web
site at http://europedirect-
cc.cec.eu.int/websubmit/?lang=en

or see
http://europa.eu.int/comm/contact/index_e
n.htm or (General conact information);
http://europa.eu.int/comm/commission_ba
rroso/president/team/index_en.htm
(President's Team);
http://europa.eu.int/comm/commission_ba
rroso/index_en.htm (Commissioners);
http://europa.eu.int/comm/contact/dg_en.
htm (Contact guide by Commission activity)
Web:
http://europa.eu.int/comm/index_en.htm
ACP-EU trade sites:
http://www.acp-eu-trade.org/ and
http://www.ecdpm.org/Web_ECDPM/Web
/Content/Navigation.nsf/index2?ReadForm
President: José Manuel Barroso
Head of Cabinet: João Vale de Almeida
See also ➔ **Secrétariat général du groupe des
Etats d'Afrique, des Caraibes et du
Pacifique/General Secretariat of the African,
Caribbean and Pacific Group of States** entry
2637

**2637   Secrétariat général du groupe
        des Etats d'Afrique, des
        Caraibes et du Pacifique/
        General Secretariat of the African,
        Caribbean and Pacific Group of
        States (ACP)**
        Avenue Georges Henri 451
        1200 Brussels
Tel.: +32-2-743 0600 (General enquiries)
+32-2-743 0601 (Secretary General)
Fax: +32-2-735 5573
Email: info@acp.int
Web: http://www.acpsec.org/index.htm
Secretary General: HE Sir John Kaputin
Chief of Cabinet: Henry Okole
Executive Secretary to the Secretary General:
Bernadette Eveedang-Mbozoo

Canada

**2638   Agence universitaire de la
        Francophonie, Rectorat**
        BP 400
        Succursale Côte-des-Neiges
        Montréal QC H3S 2S7
Tel. +1-514-343 6630
Fax: +1-514-343 2107/5783
Email: rectorat@auf.org or
info@auf.org
Web: http://www.auf.org/

http://www.afrique-ouest.auf.org/
Executive Director:
Michèle Gendreau-Massaloux
Director of Programmes (Paris):
Georges Malamoud
Director of Information Resources:
Christophe Villemer
Note: for contact details of AUF regional and
national offices in Africa see
http://www.auf.org/contacts/liste.html?typ
e=cai

**2639   Canadian International
         Development Agency (CIDA)**
200 Promenade du Portage
Hull QC K1A 0G4
Tel: +1-819-997 5006 Toll free (US and Canada
only) 800-230 6349
Fax: +1-819-953 6088
Email: info@acdi-cida.gc.ca
Web: http://www.acdi-cida.gc.ca/home
(Main home page) http://www.acdi-
cida.gc.ca/cidaweb/webcountry.nsf/africa_e
.html (Africa and Middle East branch)
Vice President, Africa Branch: Paul Hunt
Director General, Policy, Strategic Planning
and Technical Services: Nadia Kostiuk
Director General, Sahel and Senegal, Central
Africa, Great Lakes, Gulf of Guinea: Barbara
Brown
Director General, Eastern Africa, Horn of
Africa, Southern Africa: Michael Lemelin
Director, Canada Fund for Africa Secretariat:
Brian Pagan
Director, Pan African Program:
Louise Clément

**2640   Centre canadien d'étude et de
         coopération internationale/
         Canadian Centre for International
         Studies and Cooperation (CECI)**
3000, rue Omer-Lavallée
Montréal QC H1Y 3R8
Tel: +1-514-875 9911 Fax: +1-514-875 6469
Email: info@ceci.ca
Web: http://www.ceci.ca/index.asp or
http://www.ceci.ca/eng/accueileng.html
(English version)
Executive Director: Michel Chaurette
Regional Director, Africa: Phillipe Jean
Africa Coordinator: Susanne Dumouchel

**2641   Code Canada (Canadian
         Organization for Development
         through Education)**
321 Chapel Street
Ottawa ON K1N 7Z2
Tel: +1-613-232 3569 Toll free (USA and
Canada only) 800-661 2633
Fax: +1-613-232 7435
Email: codehq@codecan.org
Web site: http://www.codecan.org/
Chair, Board of Directors: Christopher Bredt
Executive Director: Yvonne Appiah

**2442   International Development Research
         Center (IDRC)**
250 Albert Street
PO Box 8500
Ottawa ON K1G 3H9
Tel: +1-613-236 6163 Fax: +1-613-238 7230
Email: info@idrc.ca
Web: http://www.idrc.ca/
Chair, IDRC: Gordon Smith
President: Maureen O'Neill
Director, Regional Office for Eastern and
Southern Africa (Nairobi):
Constance Freeman
Director, Regional Office for the Middle East
and North Africa (Cairo): Eglal Rached
Director, Regional Office for West and
Central Africa (Dakar): Gilles Forget
Note: for contact details for regional offices in
Africa *see*
http://www.idrc.ca/en/ev-26269-201-1-
DO_TOPIC.html

2643   World University Service of Canada
1404 Scott Street
Ottawa
ON K1Y 4M8
Tel: +1-613-798 7477 Fax: +1-613-798 0990
Email: wusc@wusc.ca (General enquiries)
paul@wusc.ca (Executive Director)
Web: http://www.wusc.ca/
http://www.wusc.ca/expertise/worldwide/
africa/ (Africa pages)
Chair, Executive Committee, Board of
Directors: Dr Judith Woodsworth
Executive Director: Paul Davidson

Denmark

2644 Center for Kultursamarbejde med
Udviklingslandene/
Danish Centre for Culture and
Development (DCCD)
Nytorv 17
1450 Copenhagen K
Tel: +45-33-179700 Fax: +45-33-179701
Email: info@dcc.dk (General enquiries)
ogh@dccd.dk (Director) jh@dccd.dk (Director
of Projects) mgp@dccd.dk (Head of Culture
and Development Projects)
Web: http://www.dccd.dk
Director: Olaf Gerlach Hansen
Director of Projects: Jutta Helles
Head of Culture and Development Projects:
Morten Gøbel Poulsen

2645 Danish International Development
Assistance/DANIDA
Ministry of Foreign Affairs
Asiatisk Plads 2
1448 Copenhagen K
Tel: +45-33-920000 Fax: +45-33-540533
Email: um@um.dk
Web:
http://www.um.dk/da/menu/Udviklingsp
olitik/ (Main home page)
http://www.um.dk/en (English version) and
http://www.um.dk/en/menu/Development
Policy/DanishDevelopmentPolicy/DanishDe
velopmentPolicy (Danish Development
Policy)
Minister for Foreign Affairs: Per Stig Møller
Minister for Development Cooperation:
Ulla Tørnaes
State Secretary, Head of the South Group:
Carsten Staur
Head of Communications & Information:
Eva Egesborg Hansen

2646 Mellemfolkeligt Samvirke (MS)
Borgergade 10-14
1300 Copenhagen K
Tel: +45-7731 0000 Fax: +45-7731 0101
Email: ms@ms.dk (General enquiries)
udsholt@ms.dk (Secretary General)
Web: http://www.ms.dk/sw13950.asp
Chair: Søren Hougaard
Secretary General: Lars Udsholt
Note: for MS offices in Africa see
http://www.ms.dk/sw3833.asp

Finland

2647 Ministry for Foreign Affairs,
Department for International
Development Cooperation
Information Unit
Division for Africa and the Middle
East
Kanavakatu 4 a
PO Box 176
00160 Helsinki
Tel. +358-9 -1605 6370/1605 6349
Fax +358-9-1605 6375
Email: kyoinfo@formin.fi (General enquiries)
globaltoimitus@formin.fi (Editor-in-chief,
Development Policy Information Unit)
Web:
http://global.finland.fi/index.php?kieli=3
(English version)
Director General, Department for Africa and
the Middle East: Aapo Pölhö
Head, Unit for East and West Africa:
Heli Sirve
Head, Unit for Southern Africa: Riikka Laatu
Head, Unit for the Middle East and North
Africa: Eija Rotinen
Editor-in-chief, Development Policy
Information Unit: Christian Sundgren

France

2648 Agence française de développement
(AFD)
5 rue Roland Barthes
75598 Paris Cedex 12
Tel: +33-1-53 44 31 31 Fax: + 33-1-44 87 99 39
Email: com@afd.fr
Web: http://www.afd.fr/
President: Jean-Didier Roisin
Director General: Jean-Michel Severino
Head of Communications: Henry de Cazotte

2649 Agence intergouvernementale de la
Francophonie (AIF)
13, quai André Citroën
75015 Paris
Tel: +33-1-44 37 33 00 Fax: +33-1-45 79 14 98
Email: agence@francophonie.org
(General enquiries)
Roger.DEHAYBE@francophonie.org
(Administrator General)
Nafissa.seck@francophonie.org (Personal
Assistant to the Administrator General)
Web: http://agence.francophonie.org/ or

http://www.francophonie.org/acteurs/aif/
Secretary General, Organisation
Internationale de la Francophonie:
Abdou Diouf
Administrator General, AIF: Roger Dehaybe
Personal Assistant to the Administrator
Genral: Nafissa Seck
Web: http://www.francophonie.org/oif.cfm
Note: AIF is part of the Organisation
internationale de la Francophonie.
For regional Bureaux in Africa *see*
http://agence.francophonie.org/agence/adr
esses.cfm;
for national correspondents in Africa *see*
http://agence.francophonie.org/agence/coo
rdonnees/correspondants.cfm

➔ **Agence universitaire de la francophonie**
see under Canada, entry **2638**

2650   Fondation Charles Léopold Mayer
Executive Office:
38 rue Saint Sabin
75011 Paris
Tel: +33-1-43 14 75 75 Fax: +33-1-43 14 75 99
Email: paris@fph.fr (General enquiries)
pic@fph.fr Director General) morgane@fph.fr
(Territoires, économie et société Afrique)
Headquarters and Swiss office:
Chemin de Longeraie 9
1006 Lausanne
Tel: +33-21-342 5010 Fax: +33-21-342 5011
Email : lausanne@fph.ch
Web: http://www.fph.ch/
President of the Council: Françoise Astier
Vice-President of the Council: Paulette
Calame (Responsable de la gestion mobilière
et immobilière de la foundation)
Director General: Pierre Calame
Contact for Africa-related activities:
Morgane Iserte (Territoires, économie et
société Afrique)

2651   Ministère des affaires étrangères.
Direction générale de la
internationale et du développement
244 boulevard Saint-Germain
75303 Paris 07SP
Tel: +33-1-43 17 90 00
Email: cooperation.dgcid@diplomatie.gouv.fr
Web: http://www.diplomatie.gouv.fr/fr/ or
http://www.diplomatie.gouv.fr/fr/minister
e_817/missions-organisations_823/structure-
administration-centrale_808/direction-
generale-cooperation-internationale-du-

developpement_3146/dgcid-au-coeur-du-
dispositif-francais-cooperation_7424.html
Minister of Foreign Affairs:
Philippe Douste-Blazy
Director General: Bruno Delaye
Director, Direction de la coopération
culturelle et du français: Xavier North

2652   International Institute for
Educational Planning (IIEP)
7-9 rue Eugène-Delacroix
75116 Paris
Tel: +33-1-45 03 77 00 Fax: +33-1-40 72 83 66
Email: info@iiep.unesco.org (General
enquiries) g.hernes@iiep.unesco.org
(Director)
k.mahshi@iiep.unesco.org (Information on
operational activities)
Web: http://www.unesco.org/iiep/
Chair: Dato'Asiah bt.Abu Samah
Director: Gudmund Hernes
Chief, Communication and publications: Ian
Denison
Note: for training and research staff *see*
http://www.unesco.org/iiep/eng/about/sta
ff/restr.htm

2653   Organisation for Economic Co-
operation and Development (OECD)
2 rue André Pascal
75775 Paris Cedex 16
Tel: +33-1-45 24 82 00 Fax: +33-1-45 24 85 00
Email: webmaster@oecd.org (General
information) news.contact@oecd.org (Media
enquiries) cendev.contact@oecd.org (OECD
Development Centre)
Web: http://www.oecd.org/ (Headquarters
home page)
http://www.oecd.org/department/0,2688,en
_2649_33721_1_1_1_1_1,00.html
(Development Co-operation Directorate)
http://www.oecd.org/department/0,2688,en
_2649_33711_1_1_1_1_1,00.html (Sahel &
West Africa Club)
OECD Washington Center:
2001 L Street NW Suite 650
Washington DC 20036-4922
Tel: +1-202-785 6323 Fax: +1-202-785 0350
Email: washington.contact@oecd.org
Web:
http://www.oecdwash.org/DATA/online.ht
m
Secretary General: Donald J. Johnston
Note: for OECD Departments, Directorates,
Centres, and Agencies *see*

http://www.oecd.org/maindepartment/0,26
19,en_2649_201185_1_1_1_1_1,00.html

→ **Organisation internationale de la**
Francophonie *see* **Agence**
intergouvernementale de la Francophonie
(2649)

→ **United Nations Educational, Scientific,**
and Cultural Organization (UNESCO) *see* **17**
Major African and international
organizations entry **2533**

Germany

2654   Konrad Adenauer Stiftung
Rathausallee 12
53757 Sankt Augustin
Tel: +49-22-412460 Fax: +49-22-4124 6591
Email: zentrale@kas.de (General enquiries)
wilhelm.staudacher@kas.de (Secretary
General) gerhard.wahlers@kas.de
(Head, Section Internationale
Zusammenarbeit)
Web: http://www.kas.de/
Secretary General: Wilhelm Staudacher
Head, Section Internationale
Zusammenarbeit: Gerhard Wahlers
Note: for contact addresses and activities in
Africa see
http://www.kas.de/international/laender/a
frika/124_webseite.html

2655   Heinrich Böll Stiftung
Hackesche Höfe
Rosenthaler Strasse 40/41
10178 Berlin
Tel: +49-30-285340 Fax: +49-30-2853 4109
Email: info@boell.de
Web site: http://www.boell.de (General
enquiries) nord@boell.de (Head, Regional
Referat Afrika)
Executive Director: Birgit Laubach
Head, Regional Referat Internationale Politik:
Ingrid Spiller
Head, Regional Referat Afrika: Antonie Nord

2656   Brot für die Welt
Stafflenbergstrasse76
70184 Stuttgart
Tel: +49-711-2590 Fax: +49-711-215 9110
Email: bfdwpresse@brot-fuer-die-welt.org
(General) bfdwprojektinfo@brot-fuer-die-
welt.org (Project information)

Web: http://www.brot-fuer-die-welt.de/
Chairman of the Board:
Parson Jürgen Gohde
Head, Projects and Programmes:
Joachim Lindau

2657   Bundesministerium für
wirtschaftliche Zusammenarbeit
und Entwicklung/German Federal
Ministry for Economic Cooperation
and Development (BMZ)
Friedrich-Ebert-Allee 40
53113 Bonn
Tel: +49-1888-535 0/535 2456
Fax: +49-1888-535 3500/535 2535
Email: info@bmz.bund.de (General enquiries)
presse-kontakt@bmz.bund.de (Press
enquiries)
Web: http://www.bmz.de/
Chair: Federal Minister Heidemarie
Wieczorek-Zeul (Bundesministerin für
wirtschaftliche Zusammenarbeit und
Entwicklung)
G8 Afrika-Beauftragte of the Federal
Chancellor, and Secretary of State: Uschi Eid
Chair of Governing Council, and Secretary of
State for Economic Cooperation and
Development: Erich Stather
Contact for general enquiries:
Elisabeth Kirfel-Rühle

2658   Deutsche Gesellschaft für
Technische Zusammenarbeit (GTZ)
Dag-Hammarskjöld-Weg 1-5
65760 Eschborn
Tel: +49-6196-79 0 Fax: +49-6196-791115
Email: info@gtz.de
Web: http://www.gtz.de/de/index.htm
Executive Directors: Bernd Eisenblätter,
Wolfgang Schmitt
Head, Africa region: Peter Conze
Note: for contacts for individual African
regions *see*
http://www.gtz.de/de/dokumente/orga-
e.pdf

→ **Deutsche Stiftung für Internationale**
Entwicklung/ German Foundation for
International Development *see* **InWEnt –**
Internationale Weiterbildung und
Entwicklung gGmbH (2664)

2659   Deutsche Stiftung Weltbevölkerung
        Göttinger Chaussee 115
        30459 Hannover
        Tel: +49-511-943730 Fax: +49-511-2345051
        Email: info@dsw-hannover.de (General
        enquiries) joerg.maas@dsw-hannover.de
        (Chief Executive)
        Web: http://www.dsw-online.de
        Chairman of the Board of Trustees:
        Erhard Schreiber
        Chief Executive: Jörg F. Maas

2660   Deutsches Zentralinstitut für soziale
        Fragen (DZI)
        Bernadottestrasse 94
        14195 Berlin
        Tel: +49-30-839 0010 Fax: +49-30-831 4750
        Email: sozialinfo@dzi.de
        Web: http://www.dzi.de
        Chief Executive: Burkhard Wilke

2661   Friedrich Ebert Stiftung/Friedrich
        Ebert Foundation
        Godesberger Allee 149
        53175 Bonn
        Tel. +49-228-883-0 Fax: +49-228-883396
        Email: presse@fes.de (General enquiries)
        MATAMBALYAS@fes.de (Referat Afrika)
        Web: http://www.fes.de (Main home page)
        http://www.fes.de/international/afrika/ind
        ex.html (Africa home page)
        Chairperson: Anke Fuchs
        Chief Executive: Roland Schmidt
        Head of Secretariat: Ingrid Humber
        Head, Referat Afrika: Werner Puschra
        Note: for other contacts relating to projects in
        Africa see the organizational chart on the
        Referat Afrika Web pages.

2662   Evangelischer Entwicklungsdienst
        e.V./Church Development Services
        (EED)
        Ulrich-von Hassell-Strasse 76
        53123 Bonn
        Tel: +49-228-81010 Fax: +49-228-810 1160
        Email: eed@eed.de (General enquiries)
        sigrid.liebeck@eed.de (Head of Secretariat)
        Web: http://www.eed.de
        Head, Board of Trustees:
        Bishop Christian Krause
        Chairman of the Board: Konrad von Bonin
        Contact/Head of Secretariat: Sigrid Liebeck

German Foundation for International
Development *see* → InWEnt –
Internationale Weiterbildung und
Entwicklung gGmbH (2664)

2663   Goethe Institut
        Dachauer Strasse 122
        Postfach 19 04 19
        80604 Munich
        Tel: +49-89-159210 Fax: +49-89-1592 1450
        Email: info@goethe.de (General enquiries)
        generalsekretaer@goethe.de (General
        Secretary)
        Web: http://www.goethe.de
        President: Jutta Limbach
        Secretary General: Hans-Georg Knopp
        Head of Public Relations Office:
        Ulrich Sacker
        Notes: includes the former Inter Nationes,
        which merged with the Goethe Institute in
        2001.
        For departmental and sectional contacts *see*
        http://www.goethe.de/uun/adr/zen/prt/d
        eindex.htm;
        for Goethe Institutes worldwide, including
        those in Africa, with full contact information,
        see
        http://www.goethe.de/ins/wwt/sta/deinde
        x.htm.
        A complete address register can also be
        downloaded at
        http://www.goethe.de/mmo/priv/155454-
        STANDARD.pdf

→ Inter Nationes *see* Goethe Institut (2663)

2664   InWEnt – Internationale
        Weiterbildung und Entwicklung
        gGmbH. Capacity Building
        International
        (formerly Deutsche Stiftung für
        Internationale Entwicklung/
        German Foundation for International
        Development)
        Tulpenfeld 5
        53113 Bonn
        Tel: +49-228-24345/228-243 4771
        Fax: +49-228-243 4855
        Email: info@inwent.org (General enquiries)
        presse@inwent.org (Press enquiries)
        Web: http://www.inwent.org/
        Chairman, Board of Directors/Advisory
        Board: Erich Strather
        Chief Executive Director: Ulrich Popp
        Contact, general enquiries: Andreas Baaden

2665   **Friedrich-Naumann-Stiftung/Friedrich Naumann Foundation**
Karl-Marx-Strasse 2
14482 Potsdam
Tel: +49-331-70190 Fax: +49-331-701 9188
Email: fnst@fnst.org (General enquiries)
fnst.vorstand@fnst.org (Chief Executive)
africa@africa.fnst.org (Head, Regional Bureau for Africa, Johannesburg)
Web: http://www.fnst.de/ (Main home page)
http://www.fnst.org/webcom/show_article.php/_c-1011/_lkm-1426/i.html (Friedrich Naumann Foundation Africa)
Chairman, Board of Trustees: Otto Graf Lambsdorff
Chief Executive: Rolf Berndt
Head, Regional Bureau for Africa (Johannesburg): Eva-Maria Köhler-Renfordt
Note: for offices in Africa *see* http://www.fnst.org/webcom/show_page.php/_c-1015/_nr-1/_lkm-1430/i.html

2666   **Alexander von Humboldt Stiftung/Alexander von Humboldt Foundation**
Jean-Paul-Strasse 12
53173 Bonn
Tel.: +49-228-8330 Fax: +49-228-833199
Email: info@avh.de or post@avh.de
Web: http://www.avh.de/en/index.htm
President: Wolfgang Frühwald
Secretary General: Georg Schütte

Hungary

→ **The Open Society Institute/The Soros Foundation** *see* under United States, entry 2742

Ireland

2667   **Concern Worldwide**
52-55 Lower Camden Street
Dublin 2
Tel: -353-1-417 7700 Fax: +353-1-475 7362
Email: use email form on Web site
Web: http://www.concern.net/indexD.php
Chief Executive: Tom Arnold

Italy

2668   **Caritas Internationalis**
Palazzo San Calisto
00120 Vatican City
Tel: +39-6-698 79799 Fax: +39-6-698 87237
Email: caritas.internationalis@caritas.va
Web: http://www.caritas.org/
President: Denis Viénot
Secretary General: Duncan MacLaren
Regional Desk Officer, Africa:
Father Pierre Cibambo Ntakobaflra

2669   **Centro Interfacoltà per la Cooperazione con i Paesi in Via di Sviluppo/Centre for Cooperation with the Developing Countries**
Università degli Studi di Pavia
Ufficio Affari Internazionali
Corso Strada Nuova 65
27100 Pavia
Tel. +39-382-504694 Fax: +39-382-504695
Email: catfox@unipv.it
Web: http://www.unipv.it/cicops/index.html
Chair: Gianni Vaggi
Secretary General: Marco Mozzati
Administrative Director: Piero Zanello

Japan

2670   **Japan International Cooperation Agency/Institute for International Cooperation (JICA)**
6-13F Shinjuku Maynds Tower
1-1 Yoyogi 2-chome
Shibuya-ku
Tokyo 151-8558
Tel: +81-3-5352 5311/5312/5313/5314
Institute for International Cooperation:
10-5 Ichigaya Honmura-cho
Shinjuku-ku
Tokyo 162-0845
Tel: +81-3-3269 2911
Email: Email: jicagap-opinion@jica.go.jp
Web: http://www.jica.go.jp/ (Main home page)
http://www.jica.go.jp/english/contact/ific/index.html (English version, Institute for International Cooperation)
http://www.jica.go.jp/english/about/policy/south/projects/africa.html (South-South Coperation, Africa pages)

http://www.jica.go.jp/english/countries/af/index.html (Africa pages)
President: Sadako Ogata
Note: for JICA offices in Africa *see*
http://www.jica.go.jp/english/contact/afric a.html

2671   The Toyota Foundation
Shinjuku Mitsui Building 37F
2-1-1 Nishi-Shinjuku
Shinjuku-ku
Tokyo 163-0437
Tel: +81-3-3344 1701 Fax: +81-3-3342 6911
Email: admin@toyotafound.or.jp
Web:
http://www.toyotafound.or.jp/etop.htm
Chair, Board of Directors: Tatsuro Toyoda
President: Shosaburo Kimura
Managing Director: Norio Kanie
Secretary General: Keisuke Sasaki
Chief Program Officer: Yumiko Himemoto

Kenya

**2672   African Economic Research
Consortium (AERC)**
3rd Floor-Middle East Bank Towers
Building 3rd floor Milimani Road
PO Box 62882
00200 Nairobi
Kenya
Tel: +254-20-273 4150 Fax: +254-20-273 4170
Email: admin@aercafrica.org (General
enquiries) exec.dir@aercafrica.org (Executive
Director) research@aercafrica.org (Enquiries
about research) training@aercafrica.org
(Enquiries about training)
Web: http://www.aercafrica.org
Chair, AERC Board: Caroline Pestiau
Executive Director: William Lyakurwa
Director of Research: Olusanya Ajakaiye
Director of Training: Njuguna S. Ndung'u

➔ **Agency for Cooperation and Research in
Development (ACORD)** *see* under United
Kingdom, entry **2700**

Netherlands

➔ **Centre Technique de Coopération
Agricole et Rurale ACP-UE (CTA)**
see **Technical Centre for Agricultural and
Rural Cooperation ACP-EU (2680)**

**2673   Humanistisch Instituut voor
Ontwikkelingssamenwerking
(HIVOS)**
Raamweg 16
PO Box 85565
2508 CG The Hague
Tel: +31-70-376 5500 Fax: +31-70-362 4600
Email: info@hivos.nl (General enquiries)
dirse@hivos.nl (Director for Programmes and
Projects, or Executive Director)
Web:
http://www.hivos.nl/english/index.html
(English version) http://www.hivos.org/
(Hivos Virtual Office)
Executive Director: (Ms) Manuela Monteiro
Director for Programmes and Projects:
A.P. van den Ham
Director, External relations: J.J. Dijkstra
Head, Africa Desk: Karel Chambille
Note: for regional offices in Africa and
elsewhere *see*
http://www.hivos.nl/english/english/about
_hivos/addresses

**2674   The International Institute for
Communication and Development
(IICD)**
Raamweg 5
PO Box 11586
2502 AN The Hague
Tel: +31-70-311 7311 Fax: +31-70-311 7322
Email: information@iicd.org (General
enquiries) skrogt@iicd.org (Team Leader,
Country Programmes)
Web: http://www.iicd.org/ (Main home
page) http://www.iicd.org/countries/
(Country programmes in Africa, and
elsewhere)
Chairman, Board of Trustees:
(Ms) Hella Voûte-Droste
Managing Director: Jac Stienen
Team Leader, Country Programmes:
Stijn van der Krogt

2675 Netherlands Institute of
International Relations
'Clingendael'
Clingendael 7
PO Box 93080
2509 AB The Hague
Tel +31-70-324 5384 Fax: 31-70-328 2002
Email: info@clingendael.nl (General
enquiries) jzwaan@clingendael.nl (Director)
Web: http://www.clingendael.nl/
President, Board of Governors:
Hans van den Broek
Director: Jaap de Zwaan

2676 Netherlands Ministry of Foreign
Affairs. Directorate-General for
International Cooperation (DGIS)
Bezuidenhoutseweg 67
PO Box 20061
2500 EB The Hague
Tel: +31-70-348 6486 Fax: +31-70-348 4848
Email: daf@minbuza.nl (Sub-Saharan Africa
Department)
Web: http://www.bz.minbuza.nl (Main
home page)
http://www.minbuza.nl/default.asp?CMS_I
TEM=7C8EB095BEFE42C0A0ED2385B434B42
4X1X56192X15 (Directorate-General for
International Cooperation-DGIS)
http://www.minbuza.nl/default.asp?CMS_I
TEM=MBZ419296 (Africa pages)
http://www.minbuza.nl/default.asp?CMS_I
TEM=177A80CF1BE2440DA84FAF7E23E6651
9X3X44485X04 (Focus on Africa pages)
Minister of Foreign Affairs: Bernard R. Bot
Minister for Development Cooperation:
Agnes van Ardenne
Contact: use email form on Web site, or
telephone Information Desk +31-70-348 6789

2677 Netherlands Organization for
International Cooperation in
Higher Education (NUFFIC)
Kortenaerkade 11
PO Box 29777
2502 LT The Hague
Tel: +31-70-4260 260 Fax: +31-70-4260 399
Email: nuffic@nuffic.nl (General enquiries)
jvvliet@nuffic.nl (Director, International
Marketing and Communication)
aboeren@nuffic.nl (Acting Head, Cooperation
Programmes Section)
Web: http://www.nuffic.nl
Chair, Board of Trustees:
Trude Maas-de Brouwer

President: Sander van Eijnden
Acting Head, Cooperation Programmes
Section: Ad Boeren
Director, International Marketing and
Communication: Jacques van Fliet
Note: for a complete NUFFIC staff list and
Who's Who *see*
http://www.nuffic.net/TGU_nuffic/ListVie
w.asp?Id=1&lang=1

2678 Prince Claus Fund
Hoge Nieuwstraat 30
2514 EL The Hague
Tel: +31-70-427 4303 Fax: +31-70-427 4277
Email: info@princeclausfund.nl
Web site:
http://www.princeclausfund.org/en/index.
html
Hon. Chairs: His Royal Highness Prince
Johan Friso, His Royal Highness Prince
Constantijn
Chair: Lilian Gonçalves-Ho Kang You
Director: Els van der Plas

2679 The South-South Exchange
Programme for Research on the
History of Development
Cruquiusweg 31
1019 AT Amsterdam
Tel: +31-20-463 6395 Fax: +31-20-463 6385
Email: sephis@iisg.nl
Web: http://www.iisg.nl/~sephis/index.htm
Director: n/a (governed by an International
Steering Committee)
Note: Sephis is an independent research and
exchange programme under the aegis of an
international Steering Committee.

2680 Technical Centre for Agricultural
and Rural Cooperation ACP-EU
(CTA)/Centre technique de
coopération agricole et rurale ACP-
UE
Agro Business Park 2
Postbus 380
6700 AJ Wageningen
Tel: +31-317-467100 Fax: +31-317-460067
Email: cta@cta.nl
Web: http://www.cta.nl/
Director: Carl B. Greenidge

2681   Bernard van Leer Foundation
Eisenhowerlaan 156
PO Box 82334
2508 EH The Hague
Tel: 31-70-331 2200 Fax: +31-70350 2373
Email: registry@bvleerf.nl (General enquiries)
proposal.administration@bvleerf.nl
(Proposals/Grant seeking)
Web: http://www.bernardvanleer.org
Executive Director: Rien van Gendt

Norway

**2682   Fellesrådet for Afrika/
The Norwegian Council for Africa**
Osterhausgt. 27
0183 Oslo
Tel: +47-22-989311 Fax: +47-22-989301
Email: afrika@afrika.no (General enquiries)
Camilla@afrika.no (Executive Director)
Web: http://www.afrika.no/
Executive Director: Camilla Houeland

**2683   Norwegian Agency for
Development Co-operation
(NORAD)**
Ruseløkkveien 26
Postboks 8034 Dep
0030 Oslo
Tel+ 47-22-242030 Fax: +47-22-242031
Email: postmottak@norad.no
Web:
http://www.norad.no/default.asp?V_ITEM_
ID=1139&V_LANG_ID=0 (English version)
Minister of Foreign Affairs: Jonas Gahr Støre
Minister of International Development:
Erik Solheim
Director General: Ingunn Klepsvik
Head of Information Department: Jon Bech
Project Leader, Information Department:
Thore G. Hem

**2684   Stiftelsen Imtec/International
Movement Towards Educational
Change/IMTEC Foundation**
Sognsveien 4
0451 Oslo
Tel: +47-22-2320 3900 Fax: +47-22-2320 3901
Email: imtec@imtec.org (General enquiries)
kstranden@imtec.org (Director)
Web: http://www.imtec.org
Director: Knut Stranden
Project Secretary: Anne Mortensen

Portugal

**2685   Fundação Calouste
Gulbenkian/Calouste Gulbenkian
Foundation**
Av de Berna 45A
1067-001 Lisbon
Tel: +351- 21782 3000 Fax: +351-21-782 3021
Email: info@gulbenkian.pt
Web: http://www.gulbenkian.pt/
Chair, Board of Trustees: Emílio Rui Vilar
Directors Diogo de Lucena, Isabel Mota,
Eduardo Marçal Grilo *et al*

Senegal

➔ **Council for the Development of
Social Science Research in Africa/
Conseil pour le développement de la
recherche en sciences socials en Afrique
(CODESRIA)** *see* **18 Major African and
international organizations: Major Africa-
based organizations** entry **2508**

South Africa

➔ **ActionAid International** *see* under United
Kingdom, entry **2698**

2686   Nelson Mandela Foundation
Nelson Mandela House
107 Central Avenue
Private Bag X 70 000
Houghton 2041
Tel: +27-11-728 1000
Email: nmf@nelsonmandela.org
Web: http://www.nelsonmandela.org/
Chief Executive: John Samuel
Administrative Manager: Heather Henriques
Programme Managers, Education:
Kenny Boshego, Merlyn van Voore
Senior Project Officer, Centre of Memory and
Commemoration: Anthea Josias

Sweden

2687   Dag Hammarskjöld Foundation
Övre Slottsgatan 2
75310 Uppsala
Tel: +46-18-102772 Fax: +46-18-122072

Email: secretariat@dhf.uu.se (General
enquiries) olle.nordberg@dhf.uu.se
(Executive Director)
Web: http://www.dhf.uu.se
Chair, Board of Trustees: Göran Hydén
Executive Director: Olle Nordberg
Associate Director: Niclas Hällström

**2688   International Foundation for Science
(IFS)**
Karlavägen 108 5th floor
11526 Stockholm
Tel: +46-8-5458 1800 Fax: +46-8-5458 1801
Email: info@ifs.se
Web: http://www.ifs.se/
Chairman, Board of Trustees: Pierre Roger
Director: Michael Ståhl
Deputy Director and Scientific Programme
Coordinator: Richard Hall
Programme Administrator, Social Sciences:
Maria Dutarte

➜ **Sida** *see* **Swedish International
Development Co-Operation Agency/Sida
(2689)**

**2689   Swedish International Development
Co-Operation Agency/Sida**
Sveavägen 20
10525 Stockholm
Tel: +46-8-698 5000 Fax: +46-8-208864
Email: info@sida.se
Web: http://www.sida.se (Swedish version)
http://www.sida.se/Sida/jsp/Crosslink.jsp?
d=107 (Main site, English version)
http://www.sida.se/Sida/jsp/polopoly.jsp?
d=2278&a=19661&pfLang=en (Department
for Africa pages)
Chairperson and Director General of Sida:
Maria Norrfalk
Head, Department for Africa (AFRA):
Lotta Sylwander
Head, Department for Democracy and Social
Development (DESO): Maria Stridsman
Head, Department for Infrastructure and
Economic Cooperation (INEC): Rolf Carlman
Head, Department for Research Cooperation
(SAREC): Berit Olsson
Head, Co-operation with NGOs,
Humanitarian Assistance and Conflict
Management: Eva Asplund
Note: for other departmental heads *see*
http://www.sida.se/Sida/jsp/polopoly.jsp?
d=160&a=19910#organigram13

Switzerland

2690   The Aga Khan Foundation
The Aga Khan Development
Network
Avenue de la Paix 1-3
PO Box 2049
1211 Geneva
Tel: +41-22-909 7200 Fax: +41-22-909 7292
Email: information@aiglemont.org
Web:
http://www.akdn.org/agency/akf.html
Founder and Chairman: His Highness Prince
Karim Aga Khan

➜ **CARE International** *see* under United
Kingdom, entry **2704**

**2691   Direktion für Entwicklung und
Zusammenarbeit/Direction du
développement et la
coopération/Swiss Agency for
Development and Cooperation
(DEZA/SDC)**
DEZA Hauptsitz
Freiburgstrasse 130
3003 Berne
Tel: +41-31-322 3475 Fax: +41-31-324 13 48
Email: info@deza.admin.ch
Web: http://www.deza.ch/
(German version)
http://www.deza.ch/index.php?userhash?35
318401&navID=1&l=e (English version)
Director General: Walter Fust
Deputy Director: Remo Gautschi
Head, Middle East and North Africa Division:
Annick Tonti
Head, West Africa Division: Sabine Schenk
Head, Eastern and Southern Africa Division:
Paul Peter

**2692   Federation terre des hommes/
Terre des hommes Foundation**
International Secretariat:
31 chemin Frank-Thomas
1208 Geneva
Tel: +41-22-736 3372 Fax: +41-22-736 1510
Email: info@terredeshommes.org
Web: http://www.terredeshommes.org/
Terre des hommes Foundation:
Stiftung Terre des hommes
Head Office
En Budron C8
1052 Le Mont-sur-Lausanne
Tel: +41-21-654 6666 Fax: +41-21-654 6677

Email: info@tdh.ch (General enquiries)
pbr@tdh.ch (Secretary General)
President, Terre des Hommes Foundation:
Heinrich von Grünigen
President, Executive Committee:
Raffaele Salinari
Secretary General of the Terre des Hommes
Foundation, Lausanne, and Vice-President of
the International Federation Terre des
Hommes: Peter Brey
Programme Director I: Phillippe Buchs

➔ **Fondation Charles Léopold Mayer** *see*
under France, entry **2650**

**2693   Helvetas. Schweizer Gesellschaft für
internationale Zusammenarbeit/
Swiss Association for International
Cooperation/ Association Suisse
pour la coopération internationale**
St Moritzstrasse 15
8042 Zurich
Tel: +41-1-368 6500 Fax: +41-1-368 6580
Email: info@helvetas.ch (General enquiries)
melchior.lengsfeld@helvetas.ch (Secretary
General)
Web: http://www.helvetas.ch/
President: Peter Arbenz
Secretary General: Melchior Lengsfeld
Head, International Programmes: Remo Gesù
Note: for other contacts for International
Programmes *see*
http://www.helvetas.ch/wEnglish/about_us
/people/International_Programmes.asp

**2694   International Committee of the
Red Cross/Comité internationale
de la Croix-Rouge**
19 avenue de la Paix
1202 Geneva
Tel: +41-22-734 6001
Fax: + 41-22-733 2057 (General)
+41-22-730 2768 (Production, Marketing,
Distribution Division)
Email: webmaster.gva@icrc.org (General
information) press.gva@icrc.org (For press or
operational information)
Web: http://www.icrc.org/
President, ICRC Assembly:
Jakob Kellenberger
Director General: Angelo Gnaedinger
Director of Operations: Pierre Kraehenbuehl
Director for International Law and
Cooperation within the Movement:
François Bugnion

Director of Communication: Yves Daccord
Note: for contact information for heads of
ICRC delegations in Africa *see*
http://www.icrc.org/Web/eng/siteeng0.nsf
/iwpList85/7FDCE918A3A833D1C1256B660
059218B

**2695   Médecins Sans Frontières
Doctors without Borders,
MSF International Office**
Rue de Lausanne 78
CP 116 - 1211
1211 Geneva 21
Tel: +41-22-849 8484 Fax: +41-22-849 8488
Email: office-gva@geneva.msf.org
Web: http://www.msf.org/
Secretary General MSF International:
Jean-Marie Kindermans
Note: for MSF offices and contacts in
individual countries *see*
http://www.doctorswithoutborders.org/msf
offices.cfm

**2696   Swiss Academy for
Development/Swiss Institute for
Development (SID)**
Lindenhof
Bözingenstrasse 71
2502 Biel
Tel: +41-32-344 3050 Fax: +41-32-341 0 810
Email: info@sad.ch (General enquiries)
schwery@sad.ch (Director)
Web: http://www.sad.ch
President of the Board: Roland Gröbli
Chief Executive: Rolf Schwery

**2697   Swisscontact. Schweizerische
Stiftung für technische
Entwicklungszusammenarbeit/
Swiss Foundation for Technical
Cooperation**
Döltschiweg 39
Postfach
8055 Zurich
Tel: +41-1-454 1717 Fax: +41-1-454 1797
Email: sc@swisscontact.ch
Web: http://www.swisscontact.org/
Chair: Peter Grüschow
Executive Director: Urs Egger
Project Management: Markus Kupper

United Kingdom

2698   ActionAid
Hamlyn House
Macdonald Road
Archway
London N19 5PG
Tel: +44-(0)20-7561 7561
Fax: +44-(0)20-7272 0899
Email: mail@action.aid.org.uk
Web: http://www.actionaid.org/index.asp
International Head Office:
ActionAid International
Postnet Suite 248
Private Bag X31
Saxonwold 2132
Johannesburg
South Africa
Tel: +27-11-880 0008 Fax: +27-11-8808082
Email: mail.jhb@actionaid.org
Web: http://www.actionaid.org/index.asp
Chair, Board of Trustees, UK: Karen Brown
Chair, Board of Trustees ActionAid
International: Noerine Kaleeba
UK Director: Richard Miller
Chief Executive: Salil Shetty
Regional Director, Africa:
Alegresia Akwi Ogojo

2699   Africa Educational Trust
38 King Street
London WC2E 8JS
Tel: +44-(0)20-7836 5075/7940
Fax: +44-(0)20-7379 0090
Email: info@africaeducationaltrust.org
Web:
http://www.africaeducationaltrust.org/hom
e.html
Chair: Sally Tomlinson
Director: Michael Brophy

**2700   Agency for Cooperation and
         Research in Development (ACORD)**
Development House
56-64 Leonard Street
London EC2A 4JX
Tel: +44-(0)20-7065 0850
Fax: +44-(0)20-7065 0851
Email: info@acord.org.uk (General enquiries)
kenb@acord.org.uk (Northern Director)
In Nairobi:
ACK Garden House
1st Ngong Avenue 1st Floor Wing C
PO Box 61216
Nairobi 00200

Tel: + 254-20-272 1172 /1185
Fax: + 254-20-272 1166
Email: info@acordnairobi.org
ongum@acordnairobi.org (Executive Director,
Nairobi)
Web: http://www.acord.org.uk
Executive Director (Nairobi):
Ousainou Ngum
Northern Director (London): Ken Bluestone
Programming Director (Nairobi):
Bonaventure Wakana
Note: for contacts at programme offices in
Africa *see*
http://www.acord.org.uk/b-contactus.htm

2701   The Arts Council of England
London Office:
2 Pear Tree Court
London EC1R 0DS
Tel: +44-(0)845-300 6200
Fax: +44-(0)20-7608 4100
Email: use email form on Web site for general
enquiries; david.mcneill@artscouncil.org.uk
(Director of Press & Public Affairs)
Web: http://www.artscouncil.org.uk
Chief Executive: Peter Hewitt
Director of Press & Public Affairs:
David McNeill
Director, Development: Moira Sinclair
Head of Literature: Nick McDowell
Diversity Department (including Africa-
related events and activities):
Gus Casely Hayford
Note: for complete list of London staff,
departments, and job titles, *see*
http://www.artscouncil.org.uk/documents/
regions/StaffLondon_phpkXZPuQ.doc;
for UK regional Executive Directors *see*
http://www.artscouncil.org.uk/aboutus/exe
cutive.php

2702   The British Council
Headquarters:
10 Spring Gardens
London SW1A 2BN
Tel: +44-(0)20-7930 8466
Fax +44-(0)20-7839 6347
British Council Information Centre:
Tel: +44-(0)161-957 7755
Fax: +44 (0)161-957 7762
Development Services Headquarters:
The British Council
Bridgewater House
58 Whitworth Street
Manchester M1 6BB

Tel: +44-(0)161-957 7894
Fax: +44-(0)161-957 7616
Email: general.enquiries@britishcouncil.org
(General enquiries)
developmentservices@britishcouncil.org
(Development Services)
Web: http://www.britishcouncil.org (Main
home page)
http://www.britishcouncil.org/development
.htm (Development Services pages)
http://www.britishcouncil.org/ism.htm
(Knowledge and Information Services pages)
http://www.britishcouncil.org/ukrn-
scholars-bc-scholars.htm (British Council
Scholars pages)
Chair, Board of Trustees: The Rt. Hon. Lord
(Neil) Kinnock of Bedwellty
Director General: Sir David Green
Director, Film, Literature and New Media:
Susanna Nicklin
Director of Performing Arts/Head of Music:
John Kieffer
Director, Africa and Asia: Cathy Stephens
Director, Grant-Funded Services:
Paul De Quincey
Director Development Services: Mike Hardy
Regional Information Co-ordinator, Sub-
Saharan Africa (Manchester-based):
Chaudhry Javed Iqbal
Note: for British Council offices in Africa and
worldwide, including full contact
information, *see*
http://www.britishcouncil.org/home-
contact-worldwide.htm; the complete list of
British Council offices in the UK is at
http://www.britishcouncil.org/home-
contact-uk.htm

2703   CAB International
Nosworthy Way
Wallingford
Oxon OX10 8DE
Tel: +44-(0)1491-832111
Fax: +44-(0)1491-833508
Email: corporate@cabi.org
Africa Regional Centre:
CABI Africa Regional Centre
ICRA Complex
PO Box 633 Village Market
Tel: +254-20-722 4450 Fax: +254-20-712 2150
Email: cabi-arc@cabi.org
Web: http://www.cabi.org
Chair, Governing Board: John Regazzi
Chief Executive Officer: Trevor Nicholls

2704   CARE International UK
10-13 Rushworth Street
London SE 1 0RB
Tel: +44-(0)20-7934 9334
Fax: +44-(0)20-7934 9335
Email: info@uk.care.org
Web:
http://www.careinternational.org.uk
CARE International USA:
151 Ellis Street NE
Atlanta GA 30303-2440
Tel: +1-404-681-2552 (Toll-free,
US/Canada only) 1-800-521 2273
Fax: +1-404-589 2651
Email: info@care.org
Web: http://www.careusa.org/
International Secretariat:
CARE International Secretariat
Chemin de Balexert 7-9
1219 Chatelaine Geneva
Switzerland
Tel: +41-22-795 1020 Fax: +41-22-795 1029
http://www.care-international.org/
Chair, UK Board of Trustees:
Richard Greenhalgh
Chief Executive: Geoffrey Dennis
Programme Director, CARE International UK:
Raja Jarrah
Chair, US Board of Trustees: Lincoln C. Chen
President and Chief Executive Officer, CARE
USA: Peter D. Bell
Note: for contact information about Care
International Offices worldwide *see*
http://www.care-
international.org/contactinfo.html

**2705   Catholic Agency for Overseas
          Development (CAFOD)**
Romero Close
Stockwell Road
London SW9 9TY
Tel: +44-(0)20-7733 7900
Fax: +44-(0)20-7274 9630
Email: cafod@cafod.org.uk
Web: http://www.cafod.org.uk/
Director: Chris Bain

2706 **Catholic Institute for International**
Relations (CIIR)
Unit 3
Canonbury Yard
190a New North Road
London N1 7BJ
Tel: +44-(0)20-7354 0883
Fax: +44-(0)20-7359 0017
Email: ciir@ciir.org (General enquiries)
davidb@ciir.org (Acting Executive Director)
rod@ciir.org (International Programmes
Director) cathy@ciir.org (Regional manager,
Africa/Middle East)
Web: http://www.ciir.org/
Acting Executive Director: David Bedford
International Programmes Director:
Rod MacLeod
Regional Manager, Africa/Middle East:
Catherine Scott

2707 **Christian Aid**
35 Lower Marsh
Waterloo
London SE1 7RL
Tel: +44-(0)20-7620 4444
Fax: +44(0)20-7620 0719
Email: info@christian-aid.org
Web: http://www.christianaid.org.uk/
Chair: The Rt. Rev. John Gladwin, Bishop of
Chelmsford
Director: Daleep Mukarji

2708 **Department for International**
Development (DIFD)
1 Palace Street
London SW1E 5HE
Tel: +44-(0)20-7023 0000 (General numbers)
Fax: +44 (0)20-7023 0019
Tel: +44-(0)-1355-843132 (Public enquiry
points from outside the UK)
Fax: +44-(0)-1355-843632
Email: enquiry@dfid.gov.uk
Web: http://www.dfid.gov.uk Secretary of
State, Department for International
Development: Hilary Benn MP
Director General for Regional Programmes:
(Ms) Nemat Shafik
Director General for Policy and International
Development: Masood Ahmed
Director, Africa Division: Dave Fish
Note: for Country Profiles-Africa, and full
contact information for DFID offices in Africa,
see
http://www.dfid.gov.uk/countries/africa/

2709 **CDC Capital Partners**
6 Duke Street
St James's
London SW1Y 6BN
Tel: +44-(0)20-7484 7700
Fax: +44-(0)-20-7484 7750
Email: enquiries@cdcgroup.com
Web: http://www.cdcgroup.com/
Chair: Malcolm Williamson
Chief executive: Richard Laing
Corporate Communications Director:
Miriam de Lacy

2710 **Comic Relief UK**
89 Albert Embankment 5th floor
London SE1 7TP
Tel: +44-(0)20-7820 5555
Fax: +44-(0)20-7820 5500
Email: red@comicrelief.org.uk (General
enquiries) k.conway@comicrelief.org.uk
(Media enquiries)
Web: http://www.comicrelief.com/ (Main
home page) http://www.rednoseday.com/
(Red Nose Day, annual event)
Chair, Board of Trustees: Peter Bennett-Jones
Chief Executive: Kevin Cahill
Director of International Grants:
Richard Graham
Contact for media enquiries: Kate Conway

2711 **The Commonwealth Foundation**
Marlborough House
Pall Mall
London SW1Y 5HY
Tel: +44-(0)20-7930 3783
Fax: +44-(0)20-7839 8157
Email: geninfo@commonwealth.int
Web:
http://www.commonwealthfoundation.com
/
Chairperson: Guido de Marco
Director: Mark Collins
Director of Programmes: Leo Bashyam
Programme Manager, Governance and
Democracy: Seth Lartey
Programme Manager, Culture and Diversity:
Andrew Firmin
Civil Society Liaison Officer:
Sharon Robinson

2712   The Commonwealth Institute
New Zealand House
80 Haymarket
London SW1Y 4TQ
Tel: +44-(0)-207-024 9822
Fax: +44 (0)-207-024 9833
Email: information@commonwealth-institute.org
Web: http://www.commonwealth.org.uk/
Chair, Board of Trustees: Judith Hanratty
Note: the status of the original Commonwealth Institute building in Kensington High Street is currently (November 2005) uncertain. It was closed in 2004 as it had fallen into disrepair; *see* statement by the Trustees
http://www.commonwealth.org.uk/theCI/2 6%20July%2005%20media%20statement.doc

2713   The Commonwealth Secretariat
Marlborough House
Pall Mall
London SW1Y 5HX
Tel: +44-(0)20-7747 6500
Fax: +44-(0)20-7930 0827
Email: info@commonwealth.int
Web: http://www.thecommonwealth.org/
Commonwealth Secretary General:
Rt. Hon. Donald C McKinnon
Deputy Secretary General: Winston A Cox
Deputy Secretary General:
Florence Mugasha
Director of Communications and Public Affairs: Joel Kibazo

2714   The Doyle Foundation
41 St Germains
Bearsden
Glasgow G61 2RS
Email: info@doylefoundation.org (General enquiries) g.persley@doylefoundation.org (Chair)
Web: http://www.doylefoundation.org/
Director and Chair: Gabrielle J Persley
Director and Treasurer: Simon Best

2715   European Bank for Reconstruction and Development (EBRD)
1 Exchange Square
London EC2A 2JN
Tel: +44-(0)20-7338 6000
Fax: +44-(0)20-7338 6100
Email: generalenquiries@ebrd.com (General enquiries) newbusiness@ebrd.com (Project proposals)

Web: http://www.ebrd.com/
President: Jean Lemierre
Secretary General: Horst Reichenbach
Acting Chief Economist: Steven Fries
General Counsel: Emmanuel Maurice
Head of Unit, Project proposals:
Bruno Balvanera
Note: for other contacts *see*
http://www.ebrd.com/about/structure/index.htm

2716   The Hunter Foundation
Marathon House
Olympic Business Park
Drybridge Road
Dundonald
Ayrshire KA2 9AE
Tel: +44-(0)7803-904769
Email: info@thehunterfoundation.co.uk
Web:
http://www.thehunterfoundation.co.uk/
Chair: Sir Tom Hunter
Chief Executive: Ewan Hunter

2717   The Leverhulme Trust
1 Pemberton Row
London EC4A 3BG
Tel: +44-(0)20-7822 5220
Fax: +44-(0)20-7822 5084
Email: enquiries@leverhulme.org.uk (General enquiries) gdupin@leverhulme.ac.uk (Enquiries for the Director, and programme grants) bkerr@leverhulme.ac.uk (Research Fellowships)
Web: http://www.leverhulme.org.uk/
Director: Sir Richard Brook
Contact for general enquiries and programme grants: Gillian Dupin
Contact for research fellowships:
Bridget Kerr
Note: for other contacts *see*
http://www.leverhulme.org.uk/about/contact/

2718   Overseas Development Institute (ODI)
Public Affairs
111 Westminster Bridge Road
London SE1 7JD
Tel: +44-(0)20-7922 0300
Fax: +44-(0)20-7922 0399
Email: media@odi.org.uk (General enquiries) s.maxwell@odi.org.uk (Director)
Web: http://www.odi.org.uk/
Chair of Council: Baroness Jay

Director: Simon Maxwell
Research Officer & Head of Fellowship
Scheme: Adrian Hewitt
Programme Officer, Fellowship Scheme:
Susan Barron
Note: for complete staff list *see*
http://www.odi.org.uk/staff/alphabetical.ht
ml

2719   Oxfam
        Oxfam UK:
        Oxfam House
        John Smith Drive
        Cowley
        Oxford OX4 2JY
Tel: +44-(0)1865-473727
Fax: +44-(0)1865-472600
Contact: use email form on Web site
Web: http://www.oxfam.org.uk/
International Secretariat:
Oxfam International Secretariat
274 Banbury Road Suite 20
Oxford OX2 7DL
Tel: +44-(0)1865-339100
Fax: +44-(0)1865-339101
Email: information@oxfaminternational.org
Web: http://www.oxfam.org/eng/
Oxfam America:
26 West Street
Boston MA 02111-1206
Tel: +1-617-482 1211 Fax: +1-617-728 2594
Email: info@oxfamamerica.org
Web: http://www.oxfamamerica.org/
Chair, Oxfam International: David Bryer
Executive Director, Oxfam International:
Jeremy Hobbs
Chair, Oxfam UK: Rosemary Thorp
Director, Oxfam UK: Barbara Stocking
Chair, Oxfam America: Barbara Fiorito
Director, Oxfam America:
Raymond Offenheiser
Note: for offices and contacts elsewhere *see*
http://www.oxfam.org/eng/contacts.htm

2720   The Panos Institute
        9 White Lion Street
        London N1 9PD
Tel: +44-(0)20-7278 1111
Fax: +44-(0)20-7278 0345
Email info@panos.org.uk
Web: http://www.panos.org.uk/
Executive Director: Mark Wilson
Director of Programmes: Teresa Hanley
Communications Director: Mark Covey

Note: for heads of programmes and
programme officers in different areas *see*
http://www.panos.org.uk/about/contact.as
p;
for Panos offices in Africa, and elsewhere
worldwide, *see*
http://www.panos.org.uk/about/worldwid
e.asp
See also ➔ **Institut Panos Afrique de l'Ouest /
The Panos Institute West Africa (2601)**

2721   PLAN International
        Chobham House
        Christchurch Way
        Woking GU21 6JG
Tel: +44-(0)1483-755155
Fax: +44-(0)1483-756505
Email: info@plan-international.org
Web:
http://www.plan-international.org(Main
home page)
http://www.plan-
international.org/wherewework/westafrica/
(West Africa pages)
Chair, International Board of Directors:
Steinar Sivertsen
International Executive Director:
John Greensmith
Note: for PLAN offices in Africa, and
elsewhere worldwide, *see*
http://www.plan-
international.org/about/planoffices/

2722   The Plunkett Foundation
        The Quadrangle
        Woodstock OX20 1LH
Tel: +44-(0)1993-810730
Fax: +44-(0)1993-810849
E-mail: info@plunkett.co.uk
Web: http://www.plunkett.co.uk/
Chair: David Button
Chief Executive: Richard Moreton

**2723   The Joseph Rowntree Charitable
        Trust**
        The Garden House Water End
        York YO30 6WQ
Tel: +44-(0)1904 627810
Fax: +44-(0)1904 651990
Email: info@jrct.org.uk (General enquiries)
stephen.pittam@jrct.org.uk (Trust Secretary)
Web: http://www.jrct.org.uk/
Chair, Board of Trustees: Andrew Gunn
Trust Secretary: Stephen Pittam
Project Manager, Visionaries: Di Stubbs

2724   War on Want
Fenner Brockway House
37-39 Great Guildford Street
London SE1 OES
Tel: +44-(0)0845-193 1952
Fax: +44-(0)20-7261 9291
Email: mailroom@waronwant.org (General
enquiries) lrichards@waronwant.org
(Chief Executive) jhilary@wsaronwant.org
(Campaigns & Policy Director)
grogel@waronwant.org (Director of
International Programmes)
Web: http://www.waronwant.org
Chief Executive: Louise Richards
Campaigns & Policy Director: John Hilary
Director of International Programmes:
Guillermo Rogel

**2725   World Association for Christian
Communication (WACC)**
357 Kennington Lane
London SE11 5QY
(see *Note* about relocation to Canada)
Tel: +44-(0) 20-7582 9139
Fax: +44-(0) 20-7735 0340
Email: wacc@wacc.org.uk (General enquiries)
rn@wacc.org.uk (General Secretary)
lm@wacc.org.uk (Director, Regional
Development) jm@wacc.org.uk (Regional
Coordinator: Africa and Middle East)
Web: http://www.wacc.org.uk/ (Main home
page)
http://www.wacc.org.uk/wacc/network/af
rica (Africa pages)
President: Musimbi Kanyoro
General Secretary: Randy Naylor
(As from 2006: Amany Latif)
Director, Regional Development:
Lavinia Mohr
Interim Director, Global Studies Programme
and Regional Coordinator Europe:
Philip Lee
Regional Coordinator, Africa and Middle
East: Julienne Munyaneza
Note: during the course of 2006 the WACC
will relocate to new headquarters in Toronto,
Canada.

United States

2726   Acumen Fund Inc
74 Trinity Place 9th Floor
New York NY 10006
Tel: +1- 212-566 8821 Fax: +1-212-566 8817
Email: use email enquiry form on Web site
Web: http://www.acumenfund.org/
Chair, Board of Directors: Margo Alexander
Chief Executive Officer:
Jacqueline Novogratz
Chief Investment Officer / Chief Operating
Officer: David Kyle
Health Portfolio Manager: Denise Ciesielka
Housing Portfolio Manager: Helen Ng
Water Portfolio Manager: Yasmina Zaidman

2727   Africa-America Institute
Graybar Building
420 Lexington Avenue Suite 1706
New York NY 10170-0002
Tel: +1-212-949 5666 Fax: +1-212-682 6174
Email: aainy@aaionline.org
Washington office:
The Africa-America Institute
1625 Massachusetts Avenue NW Suite 400
Washington DC 20036
Tel: +1-202-667 5636 Fax: +1-202-265 6332
Web: http://www.aaionline.org
President and Chief Executive Officer:
Mora McLean
Chief Operations Officer: Kofi A. Boateng
Note: for contact details of offices in Africa *see*
http://www.aaionline.org/about_aai/whoC
ontact.asp

2728   Africare
Africare House
440 R Street NW
Washington DC 20001
Tel: + 1-202-462 3614 Fax: +1-202-387 1034
Email: africare@africare.org
Web: http://www.africare.org
Honorary Chairman: Nelson Mandela
Chair: George A. Dalley
President: Julius E. Cole
Secretary: Joseph C. Kennedy
Regional Director, Anglophone East and West
Africa: Alan C. Alemian
Regional Director, Francophone West and
Central Africa: Myron Golden
Regional Director, Southern Africa:
Kevin G. Lowther
Note: for contact details of offices in Africa *see*

http://www.africare.org/about/where-we-work/where-we-work.html

2729 Benton Foundation
1625 K Street NW 11th Floor
Washington DC 20006
Tel: +1-202-638 5770 Fax: +1-202-638 5771
Email: benton@benton.org (General enquiries) karenm@benton.org (Executive Vice President)
Web: http://www.benton.org/
Chair, Board of Directors and Trustee: Charles Benton
Executive Vice President: Karen Menichelli
Director of Policy Research: Kevin Taglang

➔ **CARE International USA** *see* under United Kingdom, entry **2704**

2730 Carnegie Corporation of New York
437 Madison Avenue
New York NY 10022
Tel: +1-212-371 3200 Fax: +1-212-754 4073
Email: www@carnegie.org. (General enquiries only, no proposals are accepted via email)
Web: http://www.carnegie.org (Main home page)
http://www.carnegie.org/sub/program/intl_development.html (International Development Program)
Chair, Board of Trustees: Helene L. Kaplan
President: Vartan Gregorian
Program Chair, Education: Daniel Fallon
Program Chair, International Development: Narciso Matos
Chair, Carnegie Scholars Program, Special Advisor to the Vice President and Director for Strategic Planning and Program Coordination: Patricia L. Rosenfield
Director of Public Affairs and Publications: Eleanor Lerman

2731 The Christensen Fund
394 University Avenue
Palo Alto CA 94301
USA
Tel: 650-462-8600
Email: info@christensenfund.org (General Information) ken@christensenfund.org (Executive Director)
wolde@christensenfund.org (Program Officer, The African Rift Valley)

Web:
http://www.christensenfund.org/index.html
President and Chair: C. Diane Christensen
Executive Director: Kenneth Wilson
Program Officer, The African Rift Valley (Ethiopia): Wolde Gossa Tadesse

2732 Council for International Exchange of Scholars. Fulbright Scholar Program
3007 Tilden Street NW Suite 5L
Washington DC 20008-3009
Tel: +1-202-686 4000 (General enquiries)
Fax: +1-202-362 3442
General program enquiries, awards, application materials: Tel: +1-202-686 7877
Email: scholars@cies.iie.org
Web: http://www.cies.org/ (Main home page)
http://www.cies.org/award_book/award2006/country/AfrAfr10.htm (Africa. Sub-Saharan African Region Research Program)
Fulbright Student Programs (Pre-Doctoral):
Program Manager: Walter Jackson (for general enquiries)
Email: wjackson@iie.org Tel: +1-212-984-5327
Africa & the Near East Program Manager: Jermaine Jones Email: jjones@iie.org
Tel: +1-212-984-5341
US Program Staff Africa/Western Hemisphere:
Assistant Director: Debra Egan
Email: degan@cies.iie.org
Tel: +1-202-686 6230
Senior Program Coordinator: Jenai Green
Email: jgreen2@cies.iie.org
Tel: +1-202-686 6239
Visiting (Non-US) Program Staff Unit:
Assistant Director: Debra Egan Email: degan@cies.iie.org Tel: +1-202-686 6230
Senior Program Coordinator: Michelle Grant
Email: mgrant@cies.iie.org Tel: +1-202-686 4029
Note: for complete list of contacts for US program staff for Africa/Western Hemisphere *see*
http://www.cies.org/amstaff.htm
see also ➔ **Institute of International Education (2736)**

2733   The Ford Foundation
320 East 43rd Street
New York NY 10017
Tel: +1-212-573 5000 Fax: +1-212-351 3677
Email:
office-communications@fordfound.org
(General information)
office-secretary@fordfound.org (Grant
enquiries)
Web: http://www.fordfound.org (Main
home page)
http://www.fordfound.org/program/asset_
main.cfm (Asset Building and Community
Development program; includes Economic
Development)
http://www.fordfound.org/program/peace
_main.cfm (Peace and Social Justice Program)
http://www.fordfound.org/program/edu_
main.cfm (Knowledge, Creativity and
Freedom program; includes Media, Arts and
Culture)
http://www.fordifp.net/ (International
Fellowship Programs/IFP)
http://leadershipforchange.org/
(Leadership for a Changing World Program)
Chair, Board of Trustees: Kathryn S. Fuller
President: Susan V. Berresford
Executive Vice President, Secretary, and
General Counsel: Barron M. Tenny
Vice President for Communications:
Marta L. Tellado
Director, Economic Development unit:
Frank DeGiovanni
Director, Community and Resource
Development unit: Suzanne Siskel
Director, Human Rights unit: Sara Rios
Director, Governance and Civil Society unit:
Michael A. Edwards
Director, Education, Sexuality, Religion unit:
Janice Petrovich
Director, Media, Arts and Culture unit:
Margaret B. Wilkerson
Executive Director, International Fellowship
Programs: Dr Joan Dassin
Director for Africa, International Fellowship
Programs: Joyce Malombe
Note: for addresses of regional offices in
Africa, and elsewhere, *see*
http://www.fordfound.org/about/address.c
fm;
for the International Fellowship Program *see*
also ➔ **Institute of International Education
(2736)**
See also ➔ **The Ford Foundation –
Guidelines for Grant Seekers** entry 198

➔ **Fulbright Scholar Programme** *see* **Council
for International Exchange of Scholars
(2732)**

2734   Bill & Melinda Gates Foundation
PO Box 23350
Seattle WA 98102
Tel: +1-206-709 3100 (General enquiries)
Tel: +1-206-709 3140 (Grant enquiries)
Fax: +1-206-709 3280
Email: info@gatesfoundation.org (General or
grant enquiries) edinfo@gatesfoundation.org
(Education Programs)
libraryinfo@gatesfoundation.org (Library
Programs) media@gatesfoundation.org
(Media enquiries)
Web: http://www.gatesfoundation.org/
Co-founders: William (Bill) H. Gates, III;
Melinda French Gates
Co-chair: William H. Gates Sr
Co-chair & President: Patty Stonesifer
Chief Operating Officer and Executive
Director, Libraries, Pacific Northwest and
Special Projects: Sylvia M. Mathews
Executive Director, Education Program:
Tom Vander Ark
Executive Director, Global Health Program:
Richard D. Klausner
Director, Global Libraries Program:
Martha Choe

**2735   Google.org/Google Foundation
Google Inc**
1600 Amphitheatre Parkway
Mountain View CA 94043
USA
Tel: +1-650-253 0000 Fax: +1-650-618 1499
Email: info@google.org
Web: http://www.google.org/ (Google.org)
http://www.google.com/grants/ (Google
Grants)
Note: Google.org is *not* accepting funding
requests and unsolicited proposals at this
time (November 2005). Google.org. is a new
umbrella body that includes the work of the
Google Foundation, as well as partnerships
and contributions to for-profit and non-profit
entities. Its future work will focus on several
areas, including global poverty alleviation,
energy, and the environment. Google is
currently partnering with ➔ **Acumen Fund
Inc (2726)** and working with ➔**TechnoServe
(2745)**, on a project in Ghana. It also plans to
support research in western Kenya to identify

ways to prevent child deaths caused by poor water quality.

2736   Institute of International Education
Headquarters:
809 UN Plaza
New York NY 10017-3580
Tel: +1-212-883 8200 Fax: +1-212-984 5452
Web: http://www.iie.org (Main Home page)
http://www.iie.org/Content/ContentGroup
s/Exchange1/IVLP/IVLP.htm (International
Visitor Leadership Program)
Europe Office:
Institute of International Education – Europe
Vigyazo Ferenc utca 4 II/1
1051 Budapest
Hungary
Tel: +36-1-472 2250 Fax: 36-1-472 2255
Email: iie@iie.hu
http://www.iie.org//Content/NavigationM
enu/Locations/Europe/Europe_Hungary.ht
m
Chair, Board of Trustees: Thomas S. Johnson
President and Chief Executive Officer:
Allan E. Goodman
Executive Vice President, COO and Vice
President of Educational Services:
Peggy Blumenthal
Chair, Executive Committee:
Thomas A. Russo
Director Institute of International Education-
Europe: Christopher Medalis
Note: the IIE cannot respond to general
requests for information on IIE programs at
the above addresses. Please use IIE's Program
Search to find contact information on
individual programs, at
http://www.iie.org/Template.cfm?Section=
About_IIE&template=/Activity/SearchActivi
ty.cfm.
For IEE offices worldwide *see*
http://www.iie.org/Template.cfm?section=L
ocations
See also → **Council for International
Exchange of Scholars (2732)**

2737   W.K. Kellogg Foundation
1 Michigan Avenue East
Battle Creek MI 49017-4012
Tel: +1-269-968 1611 Fax: +1-269-968 0413
Web: http://www.wkkf.org/
President and Chief Executive Officer:
William C. Richardson
Chair of the Board: Wenda Weekes Moore

Program Director and Senior Advisor to
President: Dan Moore
Senior Vice President for Programs (Interim):
Jim McHale
Director of Communication: Karen Lake
Regional Director, Africa Programs:
Malusi Mpumlwana
Proposals to Deborah A. Rey, Project
Manager and Liaison
Note: for complete staff list *see*
http://www.wkkf.org/WhoWeAre/Staff.asp
x

**2738   The John D. and Catherine T.
MacArthur Foundation**
Office of Grants Management
140 South Dearborn Street
Suite 1100
Chicago IL 60603-5285
Tel: +1-312-726 8000 Fax: +1-312-920 6258
Email: 4answers@macfound.org
Web: http://www.macfound.org/
Chair of the Board:
Sara Lawrence-Lightfoot
President: Jonathan F. Fanton
Chief of Staff: Elizabeth T. Kane
Program Officer and Co-Director, Africa Task
Group: Raoul J. Davion
Director, Africa Office (Nigeria):
Kole A. Shettima
Note: for the complete list of Foundation staff,
and Directors of different programs, *see*
http://www.macfound.org/about_us/staff.h
tm

2739   The Andrew W. Mellon Foundation
140 East 62nd Street
New York NY 10021
Tel: +1-212-838 8400 Fax: +1-212-223 2778
Email: wr@mellon.org
Web: http://www.mellon.org/
Chair of Trustees: Anne M. Tatlock,
President: Don Michael Randel
General Counsel and Secretary:
Michele S. Warman
Senior Administrator, Office of the President:
Patricia T. Woodford
Programme Officer and Director Mellon
Mays Undergraduate Fellowship Program:
Lydia L. English
Program Officer, Scholarly Communications:
Donald J. Waters
Program Officer, Higher Education:
Joseph S. Meisel

Program Officer, Museums and Art Conservations: Angelica Zander Rudenstine

2740   National Endowment for the Humanities (NEH)
1100 Pennsylvania Avenue NW
Washington, DC 20506
Tel: +1-202-606-8400 (General enquiries) Toll free (US/Canada only) 800-NEH 1121
Email: info@neh.gov
Web: http://www.neh.fed.us (Main home page)
http://www.neh.fed.us/manage/index.html (Information for NEH Award Recipients
http://www.neh.fed.us/grants/grantsbydivision.html (Activity areas)
Chair of the Board: Bruce Cole
Acting Deputy Chair: Thomas Mallon
Note: for contacts at different NEH Divisions, Offices, and Programs *see*
http://www.neh.fed.us/whoweare/officedirectory.html, and the Staff Directory at
http://www.neh.fed.us/whoweare/staffdirectory.html

2741   Robert S. McNamara Scholarship and Fellowship Program
Resources and Operations Unit
World Bank Institute
1818 H Street NW
Washington DC 20433
Tel: +1-202-458-2498
Email: wbi_infoline@worldbank.org
Web: http://www.worldbank.org/wbi/scholarships/
Note: the Program has been restructured into a Master's degree in Public Policy at the Woodrow Wilson School of Public and International Affairs; all enquiries to:
The Woodrow Wilson School of Public and International Affairs
Master's Degree in Public Policy
Robertson Hall
Princeton University
Princeton NJ 08544-1013
Tel: +1-609-258 4836 (Graduate Admissions)
For additional telephone contacts and other information *see*
http://www.wws.princeton.edu/contact.html
Email: wwswww@princeton.edu or mpp@wws.princeton.edu

Web: http://www.wws.princeton.edu/acad-adm/programs/mpp.html
Faculty Chair of the M.P.P. Program; Professor of Politics and Public Affairs: Charles M. Cameron

2742   The Open Society Institute/ The Soros Foundation
400 West 59th Street
New York NY 10019
Tel: +1-212-548-0600 Fax: +1-212-548-4600
Washington Office:
OSI-Washington DC
1120 19th Street NW 8th Floor
Washington DC 20036
Tel: 1-202-721 5600 Fax: 1-202-530 0128
Email: use email form on Web site
Web: http://www.soros.org/ (Open Society Institute)
http://www.soros.org/about/foundations (Soros Foundations)
http://www.soros.org/initiatives/regions/africa (Africa region pages)
http://www.osiwa.org/en/node (Open Society Initiative for West Africa/OWISA)
Founder and Chair: George Soros
Executive Vice President: Stewart J. Paperin
President of the Open Society Institute and Soros Foundations Network: Aryeh Neier
Vice President and Director of US Programs for the Open Society Institute:
Gara LaMarche
Director of International Operations: Robert Kushen
Regional Director, Office of Africa: Julie Hayes (New York-based)
Chair, OSIWA Board of Directors: Abdul Tejan-Cole (Freetown-based)
Senior Policy Analyst for Africa: Akwe Amosu (Washington-based)
Notes: for contacts of individual networks, support and scholarship programmes, *see* the Foundation's Web site and staff directory at http://www.soros.org/about/staff.
OSI also maintains offices elsewhere in Europe and North America, for details *see* http://www.soros.org/about/offices.
OSI-New York and OSI-Budapest are separate organizations that operate independently yet cooperate informally with each other.

2743   The Rockefeller Foundation
420 Fifth Avenue
New York NY 10018
Tel: +1-212-869 8500 (General enquiries)
Toll free (US/Canada only) (800) 645-1133
Fax: (212) 764-3468
Email: media@rockfound.org (Media
enquiries only)
Regional Office in Africa:
The Rockefeller Foundation
Eastern & Southern Africa Program
PO Box 47543
GPO
Nairobi 00100
Kenya
Tel: +254-20-326 2000/228061
Fax: +254-20-326 2269/218840
Email: info@rockfound.or.ke
Web:
http://www.rockfound.org/iandr/EasternA
ndSouthernAfrica
Web: http://www.rockfound.org (Main
home page)
http://www.rockfound.org/Grantmaking/A
griculture (Agriculture/Food Security)
http://www.rockfound.org/Grantmaking/A
rtsAndCulture (Arts and Culture)
http://www.rockfound.org/Grantmaking/G
lobalization (Globalization/Global Inclusion)
http://www.rockfound.org/Grantmaking/H
ealth (Health Equity)
Chair of the Board: James F. Orr III
President: Judith Rodin
Associate Vice President, Human and
Institutional Capacity Building:
Joyce Moock
Director, Communications: André Oliver
Director, Health Equity: George Brown
Director, Food Security: Gary Toenniessen
Director, Creativity & Culture: Morris Vogel
Director, Working Communities:
Darren Walker
Director, Africa Regional Program (Nairobi):
Peter Matlon
Note: for contacting the above *see*
http://www.rockfound.org/Grantmaking/F
undingPrograms, and
http://www.rockfound.org/Grantmaking/I
nquiry

**2744   Social Science Research Council
(SSRC)**
810 Seventh Avenue
New York NY 10019
Tel: +1-212-377 2700 Fax: +1-212-377 2727
Email: info@ssrc.org (General enquiries)
exec@ssrc.org (Executive Director); and *see
also* email addresses of individual Program
Directors below
Web: http://www.ssrc.org
Chair of the Board: Lisa Anderson
President: Craig Calhoun
Executive Director/SSRC Program Director:
Mary Byrne McDonnell
Program Director, Africa; Emergencies and
Humanitarian Action, International
Dissertation Field Research Fellowships,
Youth Activism and Citizenship: Ronald
Kassimir Email: kassimir@ssrc.org
Program Director, Children and Armed
Conflict; Africa: Alcinda Honwana
Email: honwana@ssrc.org
Program Director: Eurasia, Middle East and
North Africa, International Collaboration:
Seteney Shami Email: shami@ssrc.org
Programme Director, HIV/AIDS and Social
Transformation, Emergencies and
Humanitarian Action: Alex deWaal
Email: dewaal@ssrc.org
Program Director, Culture, Creativity and
Information Technology, Arts;
Communication as a Right and a Public
Good, Media and Democracy: Joe Karaganis
Email: karaganis@ssrc.org
Note: for other Program Directors and
Officers *see*
http://www.ssrc.org/staff/viewstaffgroup.p
erl?group=pgm_directors_officers

→ **Soros Foundation** *see* **The Open Society
Institute/The Soros Foundation (2742)**

2745   TechnoServe
49 Day Street
Norwalk CT 06854
Tel: +1-203-852 0377 Fax: +1-203-838 6717
Email: TechnoServe@tns.org (General
enquiries) lvangelova@tns.org
(Media enquiries)
Web:
http://www.technoserve.org/home.html
(Main Home Page)
http://www.technoserve.org/africa/africa-
1.html (Africa pages)

President and Chief Executive Officer: Bruce McNamer
General Counsel and Director, Human Resources and Administration:
Stacey Daves-Ohlin
Vice President and Regional Director, Africa: Simon Winter
Director of Marketing and Communications: Luba Vangelova
Note: for offices and contacts in Africa, and elsewhere worldwide, *see* http://www.technoserve.org/about-staff.html#addresses

→ **United States Agency for International Development (USAID)** *see* **2623**

2746   Wenner-Gren Foundation for Anthropological Research, Inc
470 Park Avenue South 8th Floor
New York NY 10016-6819
Tel: +1-212-683 5000 Fax: +-212-683 9151
Email: inquiries@wennergren.org
Web: http://www.wennergren.org/
Chair, Board of Trustees:
Richard C. Hackney, Jr
President: Leslie Aiello
International Programs Administrator:
Pamela Smith
Grants Curator: Mary Beth Moss

2747   World Education
World Education Headquarters
44 Farnsworth Street
Boston MA 02210-1211
Tel: +1-617-482 9485 Fax: +1-617-482 0617
Email: wei@worlded.org
Web: http://www.worlded.org (Main home pages)
http://www.worlded.org/weiinternet/Projects/ListProjects.cfm?Select=Region&ID=2
(Africa region pages)
Chair, Board: Charles H. Trout
President: Joel H. Lamstein
Note: for field offices in Africa *see* http://www.worlded.org/weiinternet/contact/index.cfm; and for Program Officers for individual countries/projects *see* http://www.worlded.org/weiinternet/Projects/ListProjects.cfm?Select=Region&ID=2

2748   World Neighbors
World Neighbors International Headquarters
4127 NW 122 Street
Oklahoma City OK 73120
Tel: +1-405-752 9700 Fax: +1-405-752 9393
Email: info@wn.org (General enquiries)
mmacdonald@wn.org (President and Chief Executive Officer) pgubbels@wn.org (Vice President, International Programs)
wnghana@africaonline.com.gh (Regional Office, Accra)
Web: http://www.wn.org
Chair, Board of Trustees: Anthea George
President and Chief Executive Officer:
Melanie Macdonald
Vice President, International Programs:
Peter Gubbels
Regional Director, West Africa:
Donald Amuah

20

African studies associations, societies and networks

This chapter offers profiles of active African studies associations and societies worldwide, and also includes a number of networking organizations. Associations devoted to the study of a single African country, for example the Liberian Studies Association, the Tanzania Studies Association, or the Uganda Society, etc., are not included.

Research institutes, such as for example the International African Institute in London, are not listed here, and full address and contact information may be found in section ➔ **14 Centres of African studies and African studies programmes worldwide**.

Details provided (officers, membership dues, etc.) are current as at November 2005.

2749   **Africa-Europe Group for Interdisciplinary Studies in Social Sciences and Humanities (AEGIS)**
AEGIS Secretariat
Centre of African Studies
School of Oriental and African Studies
Thornhaugh Street
Russell Square
London WC1H 0XG
UK
Tel: +44-(0)20 7898 4370 Fax: +44-(0)20 7898 4369 Email: cas@soas.ac.uk
Web: http://www.aegis-eu.org/
Founded: 1991
Mission:/Objectives: a research network of European studies centres that aims to create synergies between experts and institutions. With primary emphasis on the social sciences and the humanities, AEGIS' main goal is to improve understanding about contemporary African societies. The AEGIS Web site offers access to information about each institution's research programmes, library online catalogues and other resources, and also provides links to events, activities, research vacancies, and newsletters at these institutions.
President/Chair: Patrick Chabal, King's College, Email: patrick.chabal@kcl.ac.uk
Administrator: Jackie Collins Email: cas@soas.ac.uk
Meetings: 1st European Conference on African Studies was held from June 29 - July 3, 2005 at the School of Oriental and African Studies and the Institute of Commonwealth Studies, London (*see* http://www.nomadit.co.uk/~aegis/ for

updates and downloads). Next AEGIS thematic conference to be held in Edinburgh, UK, June 15-16, 2006.
Publications: discussion list ➜ AEGIS-L (2795)

2750   **African Association of Political Science/Association africaine de science politique (AAPS)**
195 Beckett Street
Arcadia
Pretoria 0083
Postal address:
PO Box 13995
The Tramshed 0126
Pretoria
South Africa
Tel: +27-12-343 0409 Fax: +27-12-344 3622 Email: program@aaps.org.za
Web: http://www.aaps.org.za/
Founded: 1973
Mission/Objectives: a pan-African organization of scholars whose mandate is to promote the study and application of political science in and about Africa, the AAPS is open to individual scholars of African descent specialising in political science, public policy, and related disciplines. It has a student membership, and admits scholars of non-African descent and institutions as associate and corporate members, respectively.
President: Luc Sindjoun (Cameroon), Email: cpsr@hotmail.com
Executive Secretary: Adekunle Amuwo, Email: amuwo@aaps.org.za
Programme Officer: Vivian Nain Kuma, Email: kuma@aaps.org.za
Membership dues: in Africa $40 individuals, $120 institutional/corporate $30 students, elsewhere $60 individual $150 institutional/corporate
Meetings: biennial congress held; workshops.
Publications: ➜ **African Journal of Political Science (611)**, *AAPS Newsletter,* monographs and occasional papers

2751   **African Finance and Economic Association (AFEA)**
c/o Albert A. Okunade
Professor of Economics
The University of Memphis
Memphis TN 38152
USA
Tel: +1- 901-678 2672 Fax: +1-901-678 2685 Email: aokunade@memphis.edu
Web: http://www.afea.org/
Founded: 1998
Mission/Objectives: a professional association for academicians and practitioners of finance and economics with scholarly or professional interests in the development of Africa.
President/Chair: Sylvain Boko, Department of Economics, Wake Forest University, Box 7505 Reynolda Station, Winston-Salem, NC 27109, USA
Tel: +1-336-758 4461/336-758 5334 Fax: +1-336-7586028 bokosh@wfu.edu
Secretary: Albert A. Okunade (address as above)

Membership dues: $25 (if affiliated with an African-based institution), others $50, students $25
Meetings: AFEA annual meeting held.
2007: January 5-7, Chicago, IL
2008: January 4-6, New Orleans, LA
Publications: → **Journal of African Development (816)**, discussion list, JAD Online Forum, to subscribe send email to fas.jafed@nyu.edu

2752 African Language Teachers Association (ALTA)
c/o Dr. Alwiya Omar
ALTA Membership Chair
Department of Linguistics
Indiana University
Memorial Hall 326
Bloomington IN 47405
USA
Tel: +1-812-855 3323 Fax: +1-812-855 5363 Email: aomar@indiana.edu
Web: http://lang.nalrc.wisc.edu/alta/mission.htm or
http://www.councilnet.org/pages/FrameALTAtext.html
Founded: 1997
Mission/Objectives: dedicated to the teaching and learning of African languages. ALTA's membership is open to individuals and organizations that share this interest. The Association aims to develop a field of African language teachers where members can share common interests and concerns having to do with the study of African languages; to identify for each African language (with priority given to those most commonly studied) sets of learning materials for beginning, intermediate and advanced study; and to establish needs and priorities for new learning materials and resources, both generic and for specific languages.
President/Chair: Alwiya S. Omar, Indiana University, Email: aomar@indiana.edu
Secretary: Audrey Mbeje, University of Pennsylvania, Email: mbeje@sas.upenn.edu
Membership dues: $50 institutional, $35 individual, $20 student
Meetings: annual meeting/conference held.
Publications: → **Journal of the African Language Teachers Association (823)**; discussion list http://www.ohiou.edu/alta/altalistserv.htm

2753 African Literature Association (ALA)
c/o Jo Anne Cornwell
ALA Headquarters Director
French and Africana Studies
San Diego State University
San Diego CA 92182-8132
USA
Tel: +1-619-594 4131 Email: cornwel@mail.sdsu.edu
Web: http://www.africanlit.org/
Founded: 1974
Mission/Objectives: an independent non-profit professional society open to scholars, teachers and writers from every country. It exists primarily to facilitate the attempts of a worldwide audience to appreciate the efforts of African writers and artists. The organization welcomes the participation of all who produce the object of its study

and hopes for a constructive interaction between scholars and artists. The ALA as an organization affirms the primacy of the African peoples in shaping the future of African literature and actively supports the African peoples in their struggle for liberation.

President/Chair: (2005-2006) Debra Boyd-Buggs, PO Box 16405, Winston-Salem, NC 27115-6405, USA, Tel: +1-336-765 7651, Email: seletta1@yahoo.com

Secretary: Amy Elder, Dept. of English & Comparartive Literature, University of Cincinnati, Cincinnati OH 45219, USA; Tel: +1-513-556 3517, Email: elder2@fuse.net

Membership dues: $15-$80 depending on annual income, $50 institutional, $100 sponsor, $1,000 lifetime member, $5African students in Africa

Meetings: annual meeting held; one meeting in Africa every five years; 2006: May 17-21, Accra, Ghana, University of Ghana.

Publications: ➔ ALA Bulletin (802); membership directory is printed in the summer issue of the ALA Bulletin; conference papers (published with various publishers)

2754   African Studies Association of Australasia and the Pacific (AFSAAP)
c/o Dr. Tanya Lyons
Globalisation Program
Flinders University
Beford Park
GPO Box 2100
Adelaide SA 5001
Australia

Tel: +61-8-8201 3588 Email: tanya.lyons@flinders.edu.au

Web: http://www.ssn.flinders.edu.au/global/afsaap/

Founded: 1978

Mission/Objectives: promotes research and teaching of African studies in Australia and the Pacific and facilitates contact among scholars and students in the field of African studies through conferences, regional meetings, and publications. Membership is not conceived as narrowly academic and from its inception membership has included members of aid and NGO organizations, government departments, local African communities, and others.

President/Chair: Deryck Schreuder, Vice-Chancellor, University of Western Australia, Email: vc@acs.uwa.edu.au

Vice President: Geoffrey Hawker, Senior Lecturer, Department of Politics, Division of Humanities, Macquarie University, NSW 2109, Australia, Email: geoffrey.hawker@mq.edu.au

Secretary: Graeme Counsel, University of Melbourne, Email: g.counsel@umpa.unimelb.edu.au

Membership dues: A$65 institutional A$40 individual A$20 student (these rates outside Australasia, reduced rates for Australia/Pacific region),

Meetings: organizes annual conference; also holds small groups meetings, informally, in a number of universities.

Publications: ➔**The Australasian Review of African Studies (663)**, ➔ **Directory of Africanists in Australasia and the Pacific (269)**; conference papers (print and microfiche), and occasional publications

2755 African Studies Association (ASA)
Rutgers, The State University of New Jersey
Douglass College
132 George Street
New Brunswick NJ 08901-1400
USA
Tel: +1-732-932 8173 Fax: +1-732-932 3394 Email: callASA@rci.rutgers.edu
Web: http://www.africanstudies.org/
Founded: 1957
Mission/Objectives: founded in 1957 as a non-profit membership corporation, the ASA is open to all individuals and institutions interested in African affairs. Its mission is to bring together people with a scholarly and professional interest in Africa. The ASA also provides a range of useful services to the Africanist community, and publishes and distributes scholarly Africanist materials.
President/Chair: (to 2006) Bruce Berman, Department of Political Science, Queen's University, Kingston, ON K7L 3N6, Canada, Email: bermanb@qsilver.queensu.ca
Vice President-elect: Pearl T. Robinson, Department of Political Science, Tufts University, Medford, MA 02155, USA, Email: pearl.robinson@tufts.edu
Executive Director: Carol L. Martin, Email: asaed@rci.rutgers.edu
Executive Administrator: Margaret McLaughlin, Email: members@rci.rutgers.edu
Annual Meeting Coordinator/*ASA News,* Associate Editor: Kimme Carlos
Email: asaamc@rci.rutgers.edu
Membership Coordinator: Leigh-Anne M. Cobb, Email: lcobb@rci.rutgers.edu
Membership dues: $75-$135 individuals depending on income;
$120 institutional in US and overseas; $55 African institutions and individuals
Meetings: meeting held annually in the autumn, in different regions of the US each year, and providing an occasion for panels, plenary sessions and discussion groups, exhibits and films (see forthcoming meeting dates and venues below).
Awards: Book Donation Award, Children's Africana Award, ➜ **Claude Ake Award (2826)** ➜ **Conover Porter Award (2828)**, ➜ **Distinguished Africanist Award (2829)**, ➜ **Graduate Student Paper Prize (2830)**, ➜ **Melville J. Herskovits Award (2832)**, International Visitors Award
Publications: ➜ **African Issues (797)**, ➜ **African Studies Review (800)**, ➜ **ASA News (803)**, ➜ **History in Africa (809)**; also occasional publications, monographs, reference works, etc. published under the ASA Press imprint. (*Note:* this imprint is currently dormant and no new monographic titles have been published in recent years. However, several backlist titles are still in print and available from the ASA)
ASA meeting dates and venues to 2011:
2006: November 16-19, San Francisco, Westin St. Francis Hotel
2007: October 18-21, New York, Sheraton New York Hotel & Towers
2008: November 13-16, Chicago, Sheraton Chicago Hotel & Towers
2009: November 19-22, New Orleans, New Orleans Marriott
2010: November 18-21, San Francisco, Westin St. Francis Hotel
2011: November 17-20, Washington DC, Marriot Wardman Park Hotel

2756 African Studies Association of Ireland (ASAI)
c/o Íde Corley, Hon Secretary
1/5 Beaumont House
60 Terenure Road East
Dublin 6
Ireland
Tel/Fax: n/a Email: ide.corley@eircom.net
Web: http://quis.qub.ac.uk/asai/
President/Chair: Vincent Durac, Trinity College, Dublin Email: vincent.durac@ucd.ie
Honorary Secretary: (Ms) Íde Corley, Trinity College, Dublin, Email:
ide.corley@eircom.net
Founded: 2000
Mission/Objectives: the objective of the Association is to advance African studies in
Ireland, particularly in higher education.
Meetings: annual meeting held
Publications: *A.S.A.I Newsletter*
http://quis.qub.ac.uk/asai/ASAI%20Newsletter%205.pdf; research database
(forthcoming, on Web site)
Membership dues: €12.50/£8 full members, €6/£4 students

2757 African Studies Association of the UK (ASAUK)
School of Oriental and African Studies
Thornhaugh Street
Russell Square
London WC1H 0XG
Tel: +44-(0)20-7898 4390 Fax: +44-(0)20-7898 4389 Email: info@asauk.net
Web: http://www.asauk.net/
Founded: 1963
Mission/Objectives: to promote lively debate in the academic study of Africa. The
Association is open to anyone with an interest in African studies. It seeks to foster the
dissemination of knowledge and public awareness of African issues, and to build
and strengthen links with African universities and related institutions.
President/Chair: Graham Furniss, SOAS, London
Honorary Secretary: Insa Nolte, Centre of West African Studies, University of
Birmingham, Email: M.I.Nolte@bham.ac.uk
Secretary: Lindsay Allen
Membership dues: joint ASAUK/Royal African Society £37, Student joint
ASAUK/Royal African Society £15, Corporate £75, Associate (no Journal) £6
Meetings: annual general meeting; biennial conference, and regular conferences and
symposia which explore the frontiers of teaching and research in Africa
Next biennial conference:
2006: September, School of Oriental and African Studies, University of London, more
details to become available at http://www.asauk.net/conf.htm
Awards: ➔ **Audrey Richards Prize (2836)**, Distinguished Africanist Award
Publications: ➔**ASAUK Newsletter (749)**.

Africana Librarians Council/ALC *see* ➔ **14 Africanist documentation and African
studies bibliography** entry **1885**

2758 Afriche e Orienti
Via S. Mamolo 24
CP 41
40100 Bologna Centro
Italy
Tel/Fax: n/a Email: africheorienti@hotmail.it
Web:
http://www.comune.bologna.it/iperbole/africheorienti/english/associazione.html
Founded: 1999
Mission/Objectives: a cultural non-profit association working to inform and raise awareness about development, international solidarity and multiculturalism. It focuses on Africa, the Mediterranean region and the Near and Middle East. Undertakes research and organizes workshops, conferences and courses, and promotes cultural initiatives including exhibitions.
President/Chair: n/a (governed by an advisory committee)
Membership dues: n/a
Publications: ➜ **Afriche e Orienti. Rivista di studi ai confini tra Africa mediterraneo e medio oriente (713);** monograph series

Arbeitskreis der deutschen Afrika-Forschungs-und Dokumentationstellen/ADAF
see ➜ **14 Africanist documentation and African studies bibliography** entry 1886

2759 Arts Council of the African Studies Association (ACASA)
c/o Tavy D. Aherne, ACASA Secretary/Treasurer
2261 Bent Tree Drive
Bloomington IN 47401
USA
Tel: +1-812-323 9173 Email: taherne@indiana.edu or tavy@mymy.com.
Web: http://www.h-net.org/~artsweb/welcome/acasa.html
Founded: 1982
Mission/Objectives: an independent non-profit professional association affiliated with the ➜**African Studies Association (2755)** in the United States. The organization exists to facilitate communication among scholars, teachers, artists, museum specialists and all others interested in the arts of Africa and the African Diaspora. Its goals are to promote greater understanding of African material and expressive culture in all its many forms, and to encourage contact and collaboration with African and diaspora, artists and scholars.
President/Chair: Robin Poynor, Email: RPoynor@arts.ufl.edu
Secretary/Treasurer: Tavy D. Aherne, Email: taherne@indiana.edu or tavy@mymy.com.
Meetings: as an ASA-sponsored association, ACASA recommends panels for inclusion in the ASA annual meeting program on a wide range of topics. ACASA is also an affiliated society of the College Art Association, and meets on an ad hoc basis at its annual conference. ACASA sponsors a Triennial Symposium on African Art hosted each time by a different institution.
Next symposium:
2007: 14th Symposium on African Art, University of Florida, 2007, more details available shortly at http://www.h-net.org/~artsweb/conferences/index.html

Awards: recognizes significant contributions to the field through the presentation of two major awards. The Leadership Award is conferred upon individuals whose accomplishments best exemplify intellectual excellence and leadership in the study of African and African diaspora art. Two Arnold Rubin Outstanding Publication Awards are given in recognition of books of original scholarship and excellence in visual presentation, which enhance our understanding of the arts and material culture of Africa and the diaspora.

Other: through a Book Distribution Program, complimentary subscriptions to the journal ➜ African Arts (795), select exhibition catalogues, and books are sent to 125 museums, libraries and research institutions in Africa and the Caribbean.
Membership dues: $75 institutions, $50 regular/individuals, $20 students
Publications: ACASA Newsletter, three times yearly; Ed: Rebecca Nagy, Email: rnagy@uf.edu.

2760   Asociacion Española de Africanistas (AEA)
c/o Ramiro de Maezetu,
s/n Colegio Mayor "Na. Sa. de Africa"
Ciudad Universitaria
28040 Madrid
Spain
Tel: +34-91-554 0104 Fax: +34-91-554 0401 Email: n/a
Web: n/a
Founded: 1984
Mission/Objectives: to encourage the study of every aspect of the African continent; to promote interest in African subjects; to collaborate with African institute overseas; to improve focus in Spain on the Sub-Saharan region as well as the Maghreb; to stimulate the level of consciousness of the African contribution to Hispanic culture.
President/Chair: Basilio Rodríguez Cañada
Secretary: Belén Pozuelo Mascaraque [?]
Membership dues: n/a
Meetings: annual courses on African history
Publications: Estudios Africanos, Boletin de la AEA, cuadernas monograficos
Note: unable to verify above information

2761   Asociación Latinoamericana de Estudios de Asia y Africa (ALADAA)
Centro de Estudios de Asia y África
El Colegio de México
Camino al Ajusco No. 20
CP 10740
México DF
Mexico
Tel. +52-55-54 49 30 00 ext 4056 Fax: +52-55-56 45 04 64 Email: aladaa@colmex.mx
Web: http://www.colmex.mx/centros/ceaa/aladaa/
Found: 1976
Mission/Objectives: The Latin American Association for Asian and African Studies unites scholars involved in the study of these regions, encourages and promotes research, aims to increase awareness about the peoples and countries of Asia and Africa, and facilitates international collaboration. The Association maintains regional affiliates at university institutions throughout Latin America.

Secretary General: Walburga Wiesheu Forster
Membership dues: n/a
Meetings: Annual congress held.
Publications: conference proceedings; *Boletín, Correo de ALADAA* Newsletter, Ed:
Paulina Ponce Vargas

2762   Associação Académica África Debate
        Cacifo 19
        ISCTE
        Av. das Forças Armadas
        1649-026 Lisbon
        Portugal
Tel: +351-21-790 3000 Email: africadebate@yahoo.com
Web: http://africadebate.iscte.pt
Founded: 1999
Mission/Objectives: an independent academic association on African studies at the
Interdisciplinary Centre of History, Cultures and Societies (ISCTE), Lisbon.
President/Chair: Isabel Lopes Ferreira
Secretary/Treasurer: Ana Célia Calapez Gomes
Membership dues: none
Meetings: organizes conferences, colloquiums, and debates
Publications: → **Africa Debate (724)**, → **Boletim Africanista (725)**, *África Lusófona*
(popular magazine)

→ **Association Belge des Africanistes** *see* **Belgische Vereniging van Afrikanisten
(2768)**

→ **Association Canadienne des etudes africaines** *see* **Canadian Association of
African Studies (2769)**

→ **Association de Recherche Ouest Africaine** *see* **West African Research
Association (2787)**

2763   Association for the Publication of African Historical Sources (APAHS)
        c/o John H. Hanson, Director
        African Studies Program
        Indiana University
        Woodburn 221
        Bloomington IN 47405
        USA
Tel: +1- 812-855 8284 Fax: +1-812-855 6734 Email: jhhanson@indiana.edu
Web: n/a
Found: 1982
Mission/Objectives: to identify important unpublished source materials, to assign
them to appropriate translators and annotators, to publish finished works, and to act
as the US affiliate of the *Fontes Historiae Africanae* of the International Academic
Union.

Co-coordinators: John H. Hanson, Associate Professor, History Department &
Director, African Studies Program, Indiana University, Woodburn 221, Bloomington,
IN 47405, USA, Email: jhhanson@indiana.edu;
Dimitri van den Bersselaar, Department of Politics, University of Liverpool,
Liverpool L69 3BX, UK, Email: dvdb@liv.ac.uk
Membership dues: $5
Meetings: annual meeting held concurrently with that of the ➔ **African Studies
Association (2755)**; organizes panels at the annual ASA meetings
Awards: ➔ **Paul Hair Text Prize (2834)**
Publications: *Newsletter*

2764   Association for the Study of the Worldwide African Diaspora (ASWAD)
Department of History
New York University
53 Washington Square South 7th Floor
New York NY 10012-1098
Tel/Fax: n/a Email: admin@aswadiaspora.org
Web: http://www.aswadiaspora.org/
Founded: 2000
Mission/Objectives: an organization of international scholars seeking to further our
understanding of the African diaspora. Through the examination of history, dance,
anthropology, literature, women's studies, education, geology, political science,
sociology, language, art, music, film, theater, biology, photography, etc., ASWAD
seeks to share the most recent research both within and across disciplinary and other
conventional boundaries.
Chair/President: Michael A. Gomez, Professor of History and Middle Eastern
Studies, New York University
Secretary: n/a
Treasurer: Barbara Krauthamer, Department of History, New York University
Membership dues: (optional) $25 full academic, $15 general/student
Meetings: conferences and symposia held periodically.
Publications: discussion list, ASWAD Forum, (available shortly), ASWAD
announcements mailing list announcements@aswadiaspora.org.

2765   Association for Africanist Anthropology (AFAA)
c/o Michael Lambert
Department of African and Afro-American Studies
University of North Carolina
102 Battle Hall CB# 3395
Chapel Hill NC 27599
USA
Tel/Fax: n/a Email: mlambert@unc.edu
Web: http://www.ibiblio.org/afaa/
President/Chair: Gracia Clark, Indiana Unversity Email: gclark@indiana.edu
Secretary: Elisha Renne, University of Michigan, Email: erenne@umich.edu
Objectives/Description: the Association for Africanist Anthropology aims to
stimulate, strengthen, and advance anthropology by promoting the study of Africa,

as well as Africanist scholarship and the professional interests of Africanist anthropologists in the US, both in and outside of the African continent.
Membership dues: n/a
Awards: Distinguished Lecturers Award, African Scholars Travel Grant (not awarded since 1999); occasional grant-in-aid awards to help enable a scholar of African nationality to present a paper on the anthropology of Africa at the annual meeting of the American Anthropological Association.

2766 Association of African Women Scholars (AAWS)
　　　　c/o Obioma Nnaemeka
　　　　French & Women's Studies
　　　　Cavanaugh Hall 001C
　　　　Indiana University
　　　　425 University Boulevard
　　　　Indianapolis IN 46202
　　　　USA
Tel: +1-317-278 2038 or +1-317-274-0062 (messages) Fax: +1-317-274 2347
Email: aaws@iupui.edu
Web: http://www.iupui.edu/~aaws/ (site last updated April 2001)
Founded: 1995
Mission/Objectives: the AAWS is a worldwide organization dedicated to promoting and encouraging scholarship on African women in African studies, forging intellectual links and networks with scholars, activists, students, and policy makers inside and outside Africa, and participating actively in continental and global debates on issues specifically relevant or related to African women.
President/Chair: Obioma Nnaemeka
Secretary: Pamela Smith, Associate Professor of English and Humanities, The Goodrich Scholarship Program, Annex 24, University of Nebraska at Omaha, Omaha, NE 68182 , USA, Tel: +1-402-554 3463 Fax: +1-402-554 3776,
Email: Pam_Smith@unomaha.edu
Membership dues: $40-$80 depending on annual income; $10 institutional, $10 students in Africa
Meetings: conferences and symposia held periodically.
Publications: *AAWS Newletter*, discussion list, AFWOSCHO, to subscribe listserv@listserv.iupui.edu, or send request to nnaemeka@iupui.edu.

2767 Association of Concerned Africa Scholars (ACAS)
　　　　c/o Meredeth Turshen (co-chair)
　　　　School of Planning and Public Policy
　　　　Rutgers University
　　　　New Brunswick NJ 08903
　　　　USA
Tel: +1-732-932-4101 ext 681 Email: turshen@rci.rutgers.edu
Web: http://www.prairienet.org/acas/
Founded: 1977
Mission/Objectives: dedicated to formulating alternative analyses of Africa and US government policy, developing communication and action networks between the peoples and scholars of Africa and those in the USA, and mobilizing support in the United States on critical, current issues related to Africa.

Chair/President (co-chairs): Meredeth Turshen, School of Planning and Public Policy, Rutgers University, New Brunswick, NJ 08903, USA, Email: turshen@rci.rutgers.edu; Michael O. West, Department of Sociology, Binghamton University, Binghamton, NY 13902-6000, USA, Email: mwest@mail.binghamton.edu
Treasurer and Membership Secretary: Kristin Peterson, Center for Afroamerican and African Studies, University of Michigan
505 South State Street, 4700 Haven Hall, #4663
Ann Arbor, MI 48109-1045, USA, Email krisp@umich.edu
Membership dues: $10-$45 depending on income; $60 institutional, $15 African scholars or libraries
Publications: ➜ **ACAS Bulletin (789)**; also commentaries, action alerts, pamphlets, briefing papers, and a series of brochures on the National Security Education Program (NSEP), highlighting the dangers of military and intelligence agencies' control over African studies.

2768   **Belgische Vereniging van Afrikanisten (BVA)/Association Belge des Africanistes (ABA)**
        c/o Mark van de Velde, Secretary
        Katholieke Universiteit Leuven
        Department Linguïstiek
        Blijde-Inkomstraat 21
        3000 Leuven
        Belgium
Tel: +32-16-324818 Email: mark.vandevelde@arts.kuleuven.ac.be (Secretary)
aba@africana.be (Membership applications)
Web: http://www.africana.be/
Founded: 1984
Mission/Objectives: the BVA/ABA unites Africanist researchers of different disciplines across the linguistic borders in Belgium. The Association regularly organizes meetings and an international colloquium in alternate years.
President/Chair: Boris Wastiau, MRAC, Section d'ethnographie, Leuvensesteenweg 13, 3080 Tervuren, Belgium, Tel: +32-2-769 5680 Email: wastiau@africamuseum.be
Secretary: Mark van de Velde, at address above
Membership dues: €12 regular, €25 supporting members, €7 students
Meetings: international conferences and colloquia
Publications: ➜ **Forum (669)** ➜ **Afrika-studies in België, Sociale en Humane Wetenschappen/ Etudes africaines en Belgique, Sciences Sociales et Humaines (177)**

2769   **Canadian Association of African Studies/**
        Association Canadienne des Etudes Africaines
        CCASLS SB 115
        c/o Concordia University
        1455 de Maisonneuve Ouest
        Montréal Québec H3G 1M8
        Canada
Tel: +1-514-848 2280 Fax: +1-514-848 4514 Email: caas@concordia.ca
Web: http://caas.concordia.ca/htm/indexe.htm (English version)

http://caas.concordia.ca/htm/indexf.htm (French version)
Founded: 1970
Mission/Objectives: the objectives of the Canadian Association of African Studies
are: (1) to promote the study of Africa in Canada; (2) to improve Canadian
knowledge and awareness of Africa, including the problems and aspirations of its
peoples; (3) to facilitate scholarly and scientific exchange as well as to strengthen
linkages between the Canadian and African scholarly and scientific communities,
particularly by the publication of the *Canadian Journal of African Studies*.
Chair/President: Phil Zachernuk, Department of History, Dalhousie University,
Halifax, Nova Scotia, Canada B3H 4P9
Tel: +1-902-494 2011 Fax: +1-902-494 3349 Email: philip.zachernuk@dal.ca
Executive Director: Annamaria Piccioni, Email: ampiccio@alcor.concordia.ca
Membership dues: $90 regular, $55 retired, $45 students
Meetings: conferences, seminars; annual meeting held at a different Canadian
university each year, usually held in May/June.
Publications: → **Canadian Association of African Studies Newsletter (783)**
→ **Canadian Journal of African Studies (784); → Canadian Association of African
Studies — List of members (178)**

2770 **Deutsch-Afrikanische Gesellschaft e.V. (DAFRIG)**
(German Africa Society)
DAFRIG-Berlin:
c/o Jugendhaus Marzahn Ost
12679 Berlin
Germany
Tel: +49-30-543 4533 Email: quart.elis@web.de
Web: http://www.vineta.com/dafrig/index.shtml
DAFRIG-Leipzig:
Sternwartenstrasse 4
04103 Leipzig
Germany
Tel/Fax: +49-341-257 7237 Email: dafrigleipzig@t-online.de
Founded: 1990
Mission/Objectives: based in Berlin and Leipzig, the German Africa Society is an
independent NGO that seeks to promote and strengthen relations between Germany
and Africa, through projects, advocacy, information dissemination, and publications.
President/Chair: Joachim Oelssner (Berlin)
Deputy Chair: Jürgen Kunze (Leipzig)
Membership dues: no dues
Meetings: organizes meetings, talks, lectures and symposia.
Publications: online news reports accessible on the Association's Web site: *Beiträge
zur Politik, Beiträge zu Bildung und Erziehung, Beiträge zur Wirtschaft, Beiträge zur
Wirtschaft.*

2771 Euro-African Association for the Anthropology of Social Change and Development/Association Euro-Africaine pour l'anthropologie du changement social et du développement (APAD)
Shadyc – Centre de la Vieille Charité
2 rue de la Charité
13002 Marseille
France
Tel: +33-4-91 14 07 77 Fax: +33-4-91 91 34 01 Email: apad@ehess.cnrs-mrs
Web: http://www.vcharite.univ-mrs.fr/shadyc/APAD/APAD1.html
http://www.vcharite.univ-mrs.fr/shadyc/APAD/APADAng.html (English version)
Founded: 1991
Mission/Objectives: to stimulate Euro-African partnerships in order to exchange ideas and experiences within the national scholarly communities, on a development approach-based, broad understanding of social change. Encourages debate on methods and know-how within anthropology and the social sciences, as well as within other disciplines.
President/Chair: Giorgio Blundo, EHESS, Centre de la Vieille Charité, 13002 Marseille, France, Email: blundo@ehess.cnrs-mrs.fr
Secretary General: J. Bouju, Université Aix-Marseille II, Centre de la Vieille Charité, 13002 Marseille, France, Email: bouju@ehess.cnrs-mrs.fr
Meetings: organizes biennial symposium, thematic meetings, and workshops.
Publications: ➔ **APAD Bulletin (681)**, *APAD Newsletter;* and two monograph series published by ➔ **Editions Khartala (2171)** and ➔ **Lit Verlag (2185)**

2772 Indian Society for Afro-Asian Studies (ISAAS)
297 Saraswati Kunj
Indraprastha Extension Mother Dairy Road
New Delhi 110092
India
Tel: +91-11-224 8246/22722801 Fax: +91-11-242 5698/ 332 9273 Email: isaas@vsnl.com or dp@isaas.delnet.ren.nic.in
Founded: 1980
Mission/Objectives: engaged in studies, seminars, surveys, publications, to increase awareness about the peoples and countries of Africa and Asia, and Afro-Asian perspectives and viewpoints.
President/Chair: Shri Lalit Bhasin
Secretary: Dharam Pal
Membership dues: Rs1,000 SAARC region; $100 overseas
Meetings: international conference on cooperation held every two years on issues concerning this region; also seminars, training courses, conferences-conventions.
Publications: *Newsletter*, IRAA; proceedings of seminars/conferences, various monographs

Japan Association for African Studies *see* ➔ **Nihon Afurika Gakkai (2778)**

2773 Lusophone African Studies Organization (LASO)
c/o Kathleen Sheldon
925 14th Street # 24
Santa Monica CA 90403
USA
Tel/Fax: n/a Email: ksheldon@ucla.edu
Founded: 2000
Mission/Objectives: open to all scholars with an interest in the Portuguese-speaking countries of Africa. Affiliated with the → **African Studies Association (1773)**, the organization promotes scholarly research about lusophone Africa, encourages cooperation among persons engaged in research on lusophone Africa, and organizes panels and conference on lusophone Africa.
President/Chair: Kathleen Sheldon
Membership dues: $10-$20 depending on income, $5 students
Publications: discussion list, H-Luso-Africa, http://www.h-net.org/~lusoafri/

2774 Mande Studies Association (MANSA)
c/o Dr. Catherine Bogosian
Department of History
Wayne State University
3094 Faculty/Administration Building
Detroit MI 48202
USA
Tel: +1-313-577 6148 Email: ao0184@wayne.edu
Web: http://uweb.txstate.edu/anthropology/mansa/
Founded: 1986
Mission/Objectives: an independent society with membership open to all individuals with an academic or professional interest in the Mande region of West Africa. The organization is international and multidisciplinary, with members across the globe and across the academic-intellectual spectrum. A primary goal of MANSA has been to promote the participation of our West African colleagues, and an important part of MANSA membership is a commitment by our American and European participants to return the results of their research to Africa.
President/Chair: David C. Conrad, State University of New York at Oswego, History Department, SUNY-Oswego, Oswego, NY 13126, USA, Tel: +1-315-341 3443 Fax: +1-315-312 5444, Email: basitigi@earthlink.net
Secretary/Treasurer: Catherine Bogosian, Department of History, Wayne State University, 3094 Faculty/Administration Building, Detroit, MI 48202, USA Email: AO0184@wayne.edu
Membership dues: $25 institutional/individual, $20 students
Meetings: conferences held periodically (six held to date)
Publications: → **Mande Studies (826)**, *MANSA Newsletter*

2775 The Mid-America Alliance for African Studies (MAAAS)
c/o Margaret Buckner - MAAAS 05
Sociology and Anthropology SMSU
901 South National Avenue
Springfield MO 65804
USA

Tel: +1-417-836 6165 Email: mlb211f@smsu.edu
Web: http://www.ku.edu/~asrc/programs/conferences/maaas/about/ and
http://www.missouristate.edu/anthropology/MAAAS05.html (annual conference
Web site, 2005 conference)
Founded: 1995
Mission/Objectives: an organization for the promotion of African studies in mid-
America, including in particular the region between the Mississippi River and the
frontal range of the Rocky Mountains. MAAAS seeks to encourage scholarship and
teaching in African studies regionally and sub-regionally through conferences,
seminars, workshops, consortia, faculty and student exchanges, cooperative relations
between libraries, and promotion of African language teaching, among other
endeavours.
Secretary: Margaret Buckner
Membership dues: $30 institutional, $20 individual, $10 students
Meetings: annual conference held

**2776 Netherlands African Studies Association/
Nederlandse Vereniging voor Afrika Studies (NVAS)**
PO Box 9555
2300 RB Leiden
The Netherlands
Tel: +31-71-527 3358 Fax: +31-71-527 3344 Email: winden@ascleiden.nl
Web: http://www.afrikastudies.nl/ (English version)
Founded: 1997
Mission/Objectives: provides a forum for Africanists working in the Netherlands.
The NVAS aims to promote and coordinate the study of the social sciences on Africa
by maintaining close links with universities and research institutes. It is
multidisciplinary in composition, with the following disciplines currently being
represented: cultural anthropology, non-western sociology, archaeology, pre- and
proto-history, social geography, economics, linguistics, literature, political science,
social administration, law, environmental studies, comparative religious studies and
women's studies. The NVAS cooperates closely with the ➜ **African Studies Centre
(1594)** in Leiden.
President/Chair: G.J. Abbink, Email: abbink@fsw.leidenuniv.nl
Secretary: L. Pelckmans
Membership administration: Marieke van Winden
Membership dues: €11.50, €4.50 students
Meetings: every two years the NVAS organizes a conference about Africa-related
research in the Netherlands from different disciplines. It also organizes an annual
study day about a typical, original or controversial theme in contemporary African
research.
Publications/Databases: **Digital Africana Repositories Community/Connecting
Africa (109)** (in association with the ➜ **African Studies Centre (1594)** in Leiden)
NVAS Nieuwsbrief/Newsletter (in Dutch, 3Yr), Ed: Fiona Klein Klouwenberg, Email:
fionakk@zonnet.nl, online (latest issue as at November 2005)
http://www.afrikastudies.nl/downloads-newsletters/nvasnieuwsbriefmei2005.pdf

2777   New York Association for African Studies
c/o Seth N. Asumah
SUNY Cortland
Old Main 208-B
Cortland NY 13045
USA
Tel: +1-607-753 2064 Email: info@nyasa.org (General enquiries)
membership@nyasa.org (Membership information)
Web: http://www.nyasa.org/
Founded: 1967
President/Chair: John Marah, Department of African and Afro-American Studies,
SUNY Brockport, 350 New Campus Drive, Brockport, NY 14420-2964,
Tel: +1-716-395-5571, Fax: +1-716 395-5085, Email: marah@nyasa.org
Executive Secretary: Ibipo Johnston-Anumonwo, SUNY Cortland,
Email: johnston@nyasa.org
Mission/Objectives: a non-profit membership association dedicated to advancing the discipline of Africana Studies. NYASA encompasses Africanists who are faculty members at colleges and universities, researchers, professionals, and students. As a regional organization, the Association promotes the visibility and advancement of the discipline in New York State and surrounding areas, and offers opportunities for the scholarly and professional development of educators, and enhanced education for community members, leaders and activists.
Membership dues: $25 Elder $15 Student $10
Awards: Distinguished Africanist Award, awarded to an academic by the NYASA Executive Board for outstanding contributions to the field of Africana Studies; also Distinguished Teacher Award, and NYASA Service Award.
Meetings: annual conference held
Publications: *The NYASA Newsletter*, Co-eds: Roger Gocking, Mercy College; Thomas Nyquist, SUNY New Paltz (irregularly published)

2778   Nihon Afurika Gakkai
(Japan Association for African Studies)
Dogura & Co.
1-8 Nishihanaikecho
Koyama Kita-ku
Kyoto 603
Japan
Tel: +81-75-451 4844 Fax: +81-75-451 0436 Email: AEI04761@nifty.com
Web: http://wwwsoc.nii.ac.jp/africa/index-e.html (English version)
Founded: 1964
Mission/Objectives: to promote and conduct studies and field research on nature, society, and the humanities of the continent of Africa and its nearby islands. The Association aims to enhance the standards and teaching of African studies in Japan, promotes academic exchanges with other related associations inside and outside the country, and conducts study seminars in the African studies field.
President/Chair: Katsuhiko Kitagawa
Director in Charge of General Affairs: Motoji Matsuda
Membership dues: Yen 6,000

Meetings: annual conference held on the last Saturday and Sunday of May every year. Several seminars are held by four branches of the Association (Kanto area, Kansai area, Chubu area, and Tohoku area) each year.
Publications: ➜ **Afurika Kenkyu/Journal of African Studies (665)**, *Nihon Africa Gakkai Kaiho* (Newsletter of the Japan Association for African Studies)

2779 Oxford University Africa Society
 c/o Michael Lokale, General Secretary
 Hertford College
 Catte Street
 Oxford OX1 3BW
 UK
Tel: n/a Email: afrisoc@herald.ox.ac.uk
Web: http://users.ox.ac.uk/~Afrisoc/index.html
Founded: 2004
President/Chair: Julie Sisenda, Email: jsisenda@yahoo.com
General Secretary: Michael Lokale, Email: michael.lokale@physiol.ox.ac.uk
Mission/Objectives: dedicated to promoting and encouraging dialogue and the appreciation of the economic, social and cultural depth and potential of Africa and her diaspora. The Society has served to inform, entertain and unite Africans and friends of Africa in Oxford through various activities such as debates, discussions, film screenings, speaker events, and cultural festivals.
Membership dues: £7, all members of the university community are eligible for an Afrisoc membership, and the society can extend membership to a limited number of individuals who are not members of the University.

2780 The Royal African Society
 School of African and Oriental Studies
 University of London
 Thornhaugh Street
 Russell Square
 London WC1H 0XG
 UK
Tel: +44-(0)20-7898 4390 Fax: +44-(0)20-7898 4389 Email: ras@soas.ac.uk
Web: http://www.royalafricansociety.org/
Founded: 1901
Mission/Objectives:
Now more than 100 years old, the Royal African Society today is Britain's primary Africa organization, promoting Africa's cause. Through its journal, *African Affairs*, and by organizing meetings, discussions and other activities, the Society strengthens links between Africa and Britain and encourages understanding of Africa and its relations with the rest of the world. The Society has about 1,000 members at present with branches in Bristol and Scotland. To help keep Africa high on the agenda in Government and at Parliament, the Society supports the The Africa All-Party Parliamentary Group, providing it with research and administrative assistance (*see* http://www.royalafricansociety.org/what_we_do/africa_appg).
Chair: Chief Emeka Anyaoku, Secretary-General of the Commonwealth
President: Rt. Hon. the Lord Holme of Cheltenham

Director: Richard Dowden
Secretary: Lindsay Allan
Membership dues: £32 ordinary, £37/€58/80 (includes joint membership of the ➔
African Studies Association of the UK (2757); £15/€27/$32 student
(jointmembership with ASAUK), £300/€430/$600 corporate
Meetings: discussion meetings and conferences with distinguished politicians,
diplomats, aid officials, academics and journalists; normally about 25 meetings are
held each year.
Publications: ➔ **African Affairs (741)**, ➔ **A Directory of Africanists in Britain (270)**,
"African Arguments" monograph series published in association with ➔**Zed Books
(2238)**, the ➔ **International African Institute (2217)**, and ➔ **Justice Africa (2221)**;
also reports and other publications.
See also ➔ **Voices from Africa: A Letter to World Leaders (58)**

2781   Saharan Studies Association (SSA)
c/o John Hunwick
Department of History
Northwestern University
Evanston IL 60208
USA
Tel: +1-847-491 7323 Fax: +1- 847-467 1393 Email: j-hunwick@nwu.edu
Web: http://www.ssa.sri.com/
Founded: 1992
Mission/Objectives: supports the study of the people, cultures and environment of
the Sahara Desert. The aim of the Association is to foster collaboration and exchange
of information between interested scholars in a variety of disciplines ranging through
the arts, the humanities, the social sciences and the natural sciences, as they
encounter new research materials, engage with local fieldwork problems and seek
avenues for bringing the results of their research to a wider circle of colleagues.
President/Chair: (co-Chairs) John Hunwick, Department of History, Northwestern
University, Evanston IL 60208, Fax: +1- 847-467 1393, Email: j-hunwick@nwu.edu;
David Gutelius, Department of History, Stanford University, Stanford, CA 94305-
2152, USA, Tel: +1- 650-859 4861, Fax: +1-650-859 3668
Email: gutelius@stanford.edu
Membership dues: no dues (free)
Publications: ➔ **Saharan Studies Association Newsletter (834)**

2782   Société des Africanistes (SDA)
Musée de l'Homme
17 Place du Trocadéro et 11 novembre
75116 Paris
France
Tel: +33-1-47 27 72 55 Fax: +33-1-47 04 63 40 Email: africanistes@multimania.com
Web: http://www.mae.u-paris10.fr/africanistes/ (French version)
http://www.mae.u-paris10.fr/africanistes/index_en.htm (English version)
Founded: 1930
Mission/Objectives: a French African studies society devoted to the
multidisciplinary, scholarly study of, and dissemination of knowledge about, the

African continent and its inhabitants from prehistoric times to the present day.
President/Chair: Jean-Louis Boppe
Secretary: Catherine Baroin
Membership dues: €45 regular, €20 students, and in Africa
Meetings: monthly lecture series/conferences from October to June.
Publications: ➔ **Journal des Africanistes (688)**, Mémoires de la Société des Africanistes
Note: the complete list of SDA members can be found at http://www.mae.u-paris10.fr/africanistes/membres.htm#haut, with a subject index to research interests of individual members at http://africanistes.free.fr/activite/listhematique.htm

2783   Société française d'histoire d'outre-mer (SFHOM)
15 rue Catulienne
93200 Saint-Denis
France
Tel: n/a Fax: +33-145-826299 Email: shhom4@yahoo.fr
Web: http://sfhom.free.fr/Presentation.php
Founded: 1912
Mission/Objectives: An association which brings together academics, scholars and professionals with an interest in the history and development in the countries that formed the former French overseas territories.
Secretary-General: Josette Rivallain, 169 avenue de Choisy, 75013 Paris, France
Hon. President: Charles-Robert Ageron
President/Chair: Hélène d'Almieda-Topor
Membership dues: n/a
Meetings: annual conference held.
Publications: ➔ **Outre-mers: revue d'histoire (693)**, Les Tables de la SFHOM

2784   Société Suisse d'études africaines/Schweizerische Afrika-Gesellschaft/ Swiss Society of African Studies (SAG/SSEA/SSAS)
Postfach 8212
3001 Berne
Switzerland
(or use contacts below)
Tel/Email: see under Co-Presidents and Coordinators below
Web: http://www.sagw.ch/dt/Mitglieder/outer.asp?id=49
Founded: 1974
Mission/Objectives: promotes research on Africa in the context of specific disciplines and encourages pluri-disciplinary exchanges. The Society advocates an area studies centered approach. It collaborates with other academic institutions in Switzerland and abroad, and with public and private donor agencies, and provides documentation and information about Africa.
Co-Presidents and Coordinators: Lilo Roost Vischer, Zentrum für Afrikastudien, Universität Basel, Rheinsprung 9, 4051 Basle, Switzerland, Tel: +41-61-267 2742, Email: lilo.roost-vischer@unibas.ch;
Yvan Droz, Institut Universitaire d'études du développement, Université de Genève, 24 rue Rothschild, 1211 Geneva 21, Switzerland, Tel: +41-22-906 5966, Email: yvan.droz@iued.unige.ch
Membership dues: CHF75 ordinary, CHF150 corporate, CHF35 students

Meetings: annual general meeting held; also hosts forums, colloquia, and symposia. Publications: *Schweizerische Afrika-Bibliographie/Bibliographie africaine suisse* (annual), *Bibliography of Swiss Doctoral Dissertations on sub-Saharan Africa, 1897-1996;* monographs and occasional publications, monograph series and collections published with ➔**Lit Verlag (2185),** *Newsletter SGAS-SSEA* (downloadable on Web site), Ed: Didier Péclard: Avenue d. Echallens 8, 1004 Lausanne, Switzerland.

2785 Society of Africanist Archaeologists (SAFA)
c/o Jeffrey Fleisher (Treasurer-SAFA)
Department of Sociology and Anthropology
Lehigh University
681 Taylor St.
Bethlehem PA 18015
USA
Tel/Fax: n/a Email: safa@rice.edu (General enquiries)
fleisher@lehigh.edu (Membership enquiries/Treasurer)
Web: http://safa.rice.edu/
Founded: 1972
Mission/Objectives: an organization of archaeologists, researchers from associated disciplines, and others who share an interest in African archaeology and African societies. Membership is international, with participation from Africa, the Americas, Europe and Asia, and the Society is actively involved in research in many African countries.
President/Chair: Peter Mitchell, St. Hugh's College, Oxford, UK
peter.mitchell@st-hughs.oxford.ac.uk
Organizing Secretary: Diane Lyons, University of Calgary, Canada
Email: dlyons@ucalgary.ca
Membership dues: various options are offered, including print/online subscriptions to the Society's journals, with special rates for members in Africa, *see* http://cohesion.rice.edu/CentersAndInst/SAFA/emplibrary/2006_Membership_Fo rm.pdf
Meetings: biennial meeting held.
Awards: book prize in African archaeology, *see* http://cohesion.rice.edu/CentersAndInst/SAFA/emplibrary/SAfA%20Book%20Pri ze.pdf
Publications: ➔ **African Archaeological Review (742),** *Nyame Akuma. Bulletin of the Society of Africanist Archaeologists,* Ed: Pam Willoughby
Email: pam.willoughby@ualberta.ca online at http://safa.rice.edu/bulletin.cfm; discussion list http://safa.rice.edu/forums/index.cfm

Standing Conference on Library Materials on Africa/SCOLMA *see* ➔ **14 Africanist documentation and African studies bibliography** entry **1892**

Swiss Society of African Studies *see* ➔ **Société Suisse d'études africaines/ Schweizerische Afrika-Gesellschaft/Swiss Society of African Studies (2784)**

2786   **Vereinigung von Afrikanisten in Deutschland**
(Association of Africanists in Germany)
VAD Geschäftsstelle
Institut für Afrika-Kunde
Neuer Jungfernstieg 21
20354 Hamburg
Germany
Tel: +49-40-42 825 523 Fax: +49-40-42 825 511 Email: info@vad-ev.de
Web: http://www.vad-ev.de/
Founded: 1968
Mission/Objectives: an academic grouping of Africanists dedicated to analysis of current problems of development in Africa as well as the continent's historical roots. It aims to promote interdisciplinary research and international cooperation between scholars concerned with African development, on an equitable basis.
Chair of the Board: Rainer Vossen, Institut für Afrikanische Sprachwissenschaften, Dantestrasse 4-6, 60054 Frankfurt am Main, Germany,
Email: vossen@em.uni-frankfurt.de
Deputy Chair and Treasurer: Andreas Mehler, Institut für Afrika-Kunde, Neuer Jungfernstieg 21, 20354 Hamburg, Germany, Email: andreas.mehler@vad-ev.de
Membership dues: €35
Meetings: a multi-disciplinary conference on Africa is held every two years.
Next biennial meeting:
2006: July 24-27, Frankfurt am Main
Publications: Schriften der VAD (monograph series), published with ➔ **Lit Verlag (2185)**

2787   **West African Research Association (WARA)/**
Association de Recherche Ouest Africaine (AROA)
Programs, grants, or administrative matters:
WARA
Boston University
African Studies Center
270 Bay State Road
Boston MA 02215
USA
Tel: +1-617-353 8902 Fax: +1- 617-353 4915 Email: wara@bu.edu
Newsletter and membership enquiries:
WARA
University of Florida
Center for African Studies
427 Grinter Hall
PO Box 115560
Gainesville FL 32611-5560
USA
Tel: +1-352-392 2183 Fax: +1-352-392 2435 Email: wara@africa.ufl.edu
West African Research Centre/CROA:

WARC/AROA
BP 5456 Fann-Residence
Dakar
Senegal
Tel: +221-824 2062 Fax: +221-824 2058 Email: warc_croa@yahoo.fr
Web: http://www.africa.ufl.edu/WARA/index.htm
Founded: 1989
Mission/Objectives: the mission of the West African Research Association is to enhance US and West African scholarship and increase interest in international affairs among Americans through a reciprocal program of research exchange between American and West African scholars and institutions. The association's overseas research centre, the → **Centre de Recherche Ouest Africaine/West African Research Center (1849)** in Dakar, provides an institutional presence and lends continuity and stability to programmes sponsored by postsecondary US institutions.
President/Chair: Catherine Boone Associate Professor of Government, University of Texas, Austin, USA
Director (US): Jennifer Yanco, African Studies Center, Boston University, USA
Director (West Africa, Dakar) Ousmane Sène, Associate Professor of Literature, Department of English, Université Cheikh Anta Diop, Dakar, Senegal
Secretary: Wendy Wilson Fall, Associate Professor in Pan African Studies, Kent State University
Membership dues: $250 institutions, $30 individuals, $15 students
Meetings: sponsors panels at the annual meetings of the → **African Studies Association (2755)**
Publications: → **West African Research Association Newsletter (844)**

21
Online forums and mailing lists

Mailing lists continue to be one of the primary forms of interaction on the Internet, and there are now a very substantial number of online forums that discuss issues relating to Africa and African studies, not to mention thousands of newsgroups. However, several discussion lists started over the last few years have now fizzled out to a trickle in terms of postings, and some list archives show that there have been no further postings over the past two or more years, while others served a temporary purpose – e.g. as a follow-up to conferences and meetings – but are now dormant. Accordingly, some forums listed in the previous edition have been dropped.

The listing below provides a small selection of what, arguably, are some of the most popular and most widely subscribed lists of interest to Africanists and Africana librarians. Newsgroups or newsletters are *not* included. For additional guides to online discussion groups, and newsgroups, consult some of the directories and guides listed below.

For discussions groups and newsletters devoted to Internet access and ICT in Africa *see* ➔ **22 Information and communication development in Africa: a guide to Web sites and resources: E-journals, newsletters, and discussion forums**.

Directories and guides to discussion groups

2788   Africa South of the Sahara. Topic Discussion Lists
http://www-sul.stanford.edu/depts/ssrg/africa/email.html
Part of the ➔ **Africa South of the Sahara – Selected Internet Resources (69),** listing a number of online forums – and some newsletters – whose coverage is continent-wide, and which are listed by keyword. (For lists that only concern one country, see the site's Countries section). The site also provides some helpful guidance how to subscribe or unsubscribe to a list. [21/11/05]

2789   Bellanet Forums
http://www.bellanet.org/lyris/helper/index.cfm?fuseaction=Home
Lists a large number of email forums hosted by ➔ Bellanet (2584), focussing primarily on development issues and ICT. Archives of open/moderated public lists are available here. There are also details of closed lists. [21/11/05]

2790   CatList Reference Site
http://www.lsoft.com/lists/listref.html
This is the catalogue of Listserv lists, from where you can browse over 61,500 public Listsserv lists on the Internet and get additional information on the host sites. (It is restricted to those that use the Listserv software programme and excludes, e.g those running on Majordomo). You can search for a particular mailing list of interest, view lists by host country, by those with 10,000 subscribers or more, or those with 1,000 or more subscribers. You can also views sites by country. Search results display the host name, number of subscribers, features (e.g. spam filters), and you can view the list's configuration or contact the list owner. You can also directly subscribe by sending an email message to the host and with a command (the CatList reference number) pasted into the message, for example a number of discussion groups hosted by the School of Oriental and African Studies at the University of London. It has to be added, however, that a good number of Africa/African studies related lists include some with very few subscribers—and a few show no current subscribers at all! [21/11/05]

➜ **Google Groups** http://groups.google.com/*see* the section on Google Groups – and sub-section Google Groups vs. Yahoo! Groups – in chapter **25 Using Google for African studies research: a guide to effective Web searching. Google's other search services: Google Groups**

2791   H-Net Discussion Networks
http://www.h-net.org/lists/
These pages provide access to all of the H-Net Humanities & Social Sciences Online discussion networks (including discussion logs), of which a substantial number are on African studies topics, *see* ➜ **H-Africa (85, 2810)** and entries **2811-2821**. Search discussion logs from here, or subscribe to any of the lists. [21/11/05]

2792   Listservs & Discussion Groups
http://www.sas.upenn.edu/African_Studies/Listserv/menu_Listserv.html
This is part of the University of Pennsylvania ➜ **African Studies WWW (73)**, which provides details of a large number of discussion groups. However, there is no indication when these pages were last updated and several groups listed here may be currently dormant or no longer active. [21/11/05]

2793   Topica
http://lists.topica.com/
Quite a sizeable number of Africa-related groups can be found here, although it is irritating that any searching using "Africa" or "African" as part of keywords always seem to be classified under "Regional and Travel", e.g. "Regional and travel-Regions-Africa-Arts". [21/11/05]]

➜ **Yahoo! Groups** http://groups.yahoo.com/ *see* the section on Google Groups – and sub-section Google Groups vs. Yahoo! Groups – in chapter **25 Using Google for African studies research: a guide to effective Web searching. Google's other search services: Google Groups-Google Groups vs. Yahoo! Groups**

Select discussion groups and mailing lists

Most of the groups that are listed here have their own home page on the Web, or have a sign-in home page as part of, for example Yahoo! Groups. To subscribe click on to 'Subscribe' on the home page menu, and which in most cases will lead to a form that is to be completed. For others send a message to the listserv address indicated. Groups devoted to discussions about individual African countries are not included here.

2794 ADF - African Development Forum III: Defining Priorities for Regional Integration
http://www.uneca.org/adfiii/discuss.htm
The African Development Forum is an initiative led by the ➔ **United Nations Economic Commission for Africa (2523)** to position an African-driven development agenda that reflects a consensus among major partners, and that leads to specific programmes for country implementation. [21/11/05]

2795 AEGIS-L
https://listserv.surfnet.nl/archives/aegis-l.html
The discussion list of the ➔**Africa-Europe Group for Interdisciplinary Studies (2749)**.

2796 Af-Aids/Safco
http://www.hivnet.ch/fdp/forums.html
Hosted by the Geneva-based Fondation du Présent, which brings together a multisectoral community of over 10,000 members (more than half of them in developing countries) to raise and jointly address health-related issues, particularly HIV/AIDS. The forums are organized into four major categories: Global, Regional, National and Topic specific; for Africa there are two regional lists AF-AIDS sub-Saharan Africa (in English), and SAFCO, sub-Saharan (West and Central) Africa (in French). [21/11/05]

2797 Aflib-L – African Libraries List Serv
http://mailman.nlsa.ac.za/mailman/listinfo/aflib-l
A forum for the exchange of ideas for African librarians, and their colleagues elsewhere, who seek to overcome the professional isolation among professionals on the continent. Its aim is to encourage contact between and communication among professionals on the continent. This is a closed list, to subscribe contact the administrator of the list, Hester van der Walt, Hester.vanderWalt@nlsa.ac.za at the National Library of South Africa. [21/11/05]

2798 Africa Distance Education
http://www.physics.ncat.edu/~michael/adla/ or
http://groups.yahoo.com/group/africa_distance_education/
Co-ordinates existing educational technologies and the skill of African expatriates to assist African scientific and social institutions via traditional collaborations, volunteer teaching, information, and student exchange. [21/11/05]

2799   Africadiv – Africa Diversity Mailing List
http://www.nuffic.nl/ik-pages/lists.html#africadiv
Devoted to the sustainable use and conservation of biological diversity and indigenous knowledge in Africa. [21/11/05]

2800   Africa Network Mail List
http://www.open.ac.uk/Arts/ferguson-centre/text-africa-network/maillist.htm
Sponsored by ➔ **The Ferguson Centre for African and Asian Studies at the Open University (1620)**, this is a discussion forum for a range of topics in African studies, focusing in the first instance on 'The Idea of Africa'. [08/09/05]

2801   African Librarians' Advocacy Group
http://www.dgroups.org/groups/avlin-l/index.cfm
Provides an advocacy forum for African library and information science professionals. To subscribe contact the administrator of the list at avlin-l-owner@dgroups.org. [21/11/05]

2802   Africa-Talk
http://www.africa-talk.com/
Hosted by West Africans living in the US, this list aims to provide a platform for discussions "on everything relating to Africa", including music, politics, and business. [21/11/05]

2803   AfricaWorld
http://groups.yahoo.com/group/africaworld/
An African diaspora network and mailing list with news about jobs, events, conferences, travel, study, internships, volunteer work, research, exchange programmes, festivals, news, and more. [21/11/05]

2804   Afri-Phil
http://pegasus.cc.ucf.edu/~janzb/afphil/afri-phil.htm
Devoted to the philosophy of African society, its current issues and future directions. Offers a forum for the exchange of views, experiences, techniques, and professional information pertaining to the teaching and study of the philosophical thought of African and African diaspora cultures. [21/11/05]

2805   Ahenet – African Higher Education Network
http://www.aufoundation.org/listserv_files/ahenet.html
Designed to promote the exchange of ideas, experiences, visions, comments, and other information relating to African higher education. To subscribe ahenet@aufoundation.org. [21/11/05]

2806   ALCASA List – Africana Librarians Council
alcasalist@lists.stanford.edu
A discussion list to facilitate the work of the ➔ **Africana Librarians Council (1885)**. To subscribe send email to Majordomo@lists.Stanford.edu. The administrator of the list is Karen Fung at Stanford University Libraries, kfung@stanford.edu. [21/11/05]

2807   Afro-Nets
http://www.afronets.org/
The electronic conference for the African Networks for Health Research & Development (AFRO-NETS), established to facilitate exchange of information among different networks active in health research for development in anglophone Africa, and to facilitate collaboration in the fields of capacity building, planning, and research. To subscribe afro-nets-join@healthnet.org. [21/11/05]

2808   ASAWomen
The discussion list for members of the ➔ **African Studies Association's (2755)** Women's Caucus. The list is maintained by Kathleen Sheldon at the University of California-Los Angeles Center for the Study of Women. To subscribe, send a message to LISTSERV@listserv.ucla.edu (indicating subscribe ASAWOMEN). [21/11/05]

2809   Bellpubnet – Bellagio Publishing Network
http://www.bellagiopublishingnetwork.org/forum.htm
http://www.topica.com/lists/BellagioPublishingNetwork/ (Archives)
Provides a forum for engaging questions around publishing in the South, especially in Africa. Encourages contributions from every perspective and persuasion, from all the book professions and the international book community, including librarians, publishers, booksellers, writers and scholars, and readers. However, the list seems to be currently dormant. [21/11/05]

2810   H-Africa – Africa's History, Culture and African Studies
http://www.h-net.org/~africa/
RSS RSS feed: http://h-net.msu.edu/rss/H-Africa.rss
An international scholarly online discussion list on African culture and the African past. H-Africa encourages discussions of research interests, teaching methods, and historiography. H-Africa is especially interested in the teaching of history to graduate and undergraduate students in diverse settings. In addition, H-Africa publishes course materials, announcements of conferences and fellowships, book reviews, and the H-Net job guide. From this page you can also search all the logs of the H-Africa lists below. [21/11/05] *See also* further H-Africa lists in entries below.

2811   H-AfrArts – Expressive Cultures of Africa
http://www.h-net.org/~artsweb/
H-AfrArts is composed of two parts, a discussion list and a Web site, co-sponsored by Humanities and Social Sciences OnLine (H-Net) and the Arts Council of the ➔ Arts Council of the African Studies Association (2759). Its content focuses on the expressive cultures of Africa and the African diaspora. [21/11/05]

2812   H-AfrLitCine – African Literature and Cinema
http://www.h-net.org/~aflitweb/
A H-Net Network discussing African literature and cinema. [22/11/05]

2813   H-AfrPol – Educated Discussions on African Politics
http://www.h-net.org/~afrpol/
H-AfrPol is sponsored by H-Net Humanities and Social Sciences Online, Michigan State University, the American Political Science Association, and the ➔ **African**

Association of Political Science (2750). It encourages scholarly discussion of African political history. [22/11/05]

2814 H-AfResearch – Research in African Primary Resources
http://www.h-net.org/~afrsrch/
RSS RSS feed: http://h-net.msu.edu/rss/H-AfResearch.rss
Dedicated to enhancing scholarly communication about the use of primary sources in African humanities and social sciences research. [22/11/05]

2815 H-AfrTeach – Teaching about Africa
http://www.h-net.org/~afrteach/
A discussion list whose mission is to provide a stimulating forum for considering the possibilities and problems involved in teaching about Africa. It is intended for a wide audience, encompassing educators, students and others with an interest in teaching about Africa at all educational levels. [22/11/05]

2816 H-French-Colonial
http://www.h-net.org/~frenchco/
An international online discussion list on French colonial history and cultural studies, as well as examining links between metropolitan France and its colonies, past and present. It encourages discussions of research interests, teaching methods, and historiography. [22/11/05]

2817 H-Hausa
http://www.h-net.org/~hausa/
A platform for the discussion of issues related to Hausa language, literature and culture. [22/11/05]

2818 H-Luso-Africa
http://www.h-net.org/~lusoafri/
The official discussion list initiated by the ➔ **Lusophone African Studies Organization (2773)**, an independent professional society established in the United States that is open to all scholars with an interest in lusophone Africa. [22/11/05]

2819 H-SAfrica
http://www.h-net.org/~safrica/
An international electronic discussion group dedicated to the promotion of all aspects of South and southern Africa history and culture, and southern African studies in general. [22/11/05]

2820 H-Swahili – Network on Swahili Language and Culture
http://www.h-net.org/~swahili/
RSS RSS feed: http://h-net.msu.edu/rss/H-Swahili.rss
Conducts its business in Swahili and in English as the primary languages on topical issues related to the use, teaching, promotion and general advancement of the Swahili language and culture. [21/11/05]

2821   H-West-Africa
http://www.h-net.org/~wafrica/
RSS RSS feed: http://h-net.msu.edu/rss/H-West-Africa.rss
Dedicated to enhancing research and teaching on the West African region, its history, culture, science and development. [22/11/05]

→ **Pambazuka News** *see* **10 News sources for Africa** entry **858**

2822   Panafricanist Forum
http://groups.yahoo.com/group/panafricanistforum/
A forum "for discussion of African subjects spanning the entire range of the ideological spectrum." The focus is on African politics, economics and history, from a Pan-Africanist perspective. [22/11/05]

2823   Unicode-Afrique
http://fr.groups.yahoo.com/group/Unicode-Afrique/
A discussion forum (in French) on Unicode – a standard that provides a unique number for every character, no matter what the platform, the program, or the language – designed to publicize African projects using Unicode and to share experiences. [22/11/05]

22

Awards and prizes in African studies

This chapter provides details of annual or biennial international awards offered in the African studies field. 'Closed' prizes, awarded to nationals of a particular country, are not included, nor are prizes linked to a particular university or other institutions and that are only open to students or faculty of these institutions. Literary prizes are also not included; details of African book and literary awards can be found in ➔ **The African Publishing Companion: A Resource Guide (259)**, and in an online resource freely available ➔**Awards for Books about Africa** (*see* entry **2824** below), which also includes details of children's and young writers awards.

For organizations that fund fellowship schemes or provide endowment assistance *see* ➔ **19 Major foundations, donors, government and aid agencies**.

Information given includes full name and contact address, year founded or first awarded, amount of prize or award money, the sponsors of the award, a description of the aims and objectives of each award, details of the selection process and/or conditions of entry and criteria, the closing date for submitting entries or nominations, and details of past (or recent) winners of these awards.

Other sources

2824   Awards for Books about Africa
http://www.indiana.edu/%7Elibsalc/african/awards/
Compiled by library staff at ➔ **Indiana University Libraries (1313)** this is a directory of awards for books about Africa and published in Africa, both for adult books and children/young adult books. For each competition the principal conditions of entry are indicated, together with contact details of the award's administrators, sponsors, and prize money. Additionally it provides a complete chronological listing of past winners, and details about current and past jury members. Although the site has not been updated since April 2000, it is still useful as an archival source. [22/11/05]

Awards and prizes

Note: details of 2005 winners were not available at press time for a number of awards and prizes, but information on the most recent winners will updated in the online version of the *African Studies Companion* when they become available.

2825   **The Aidoo-Snyder Prize for Scholarly and Creative Work**
c/o Prof. Gwendolyn Mikell
Department of Sociology and Anthropology
ICC 305
Georgetown University
Washington DC 20057-1036
USA
Tel: +1-202-687 4306 Fax: +1-202-687 7326 Email: mikellg@georgetown.edu
Contact: for social science works: Gwendolyn Mikell, Email:
mikellg@georgetown.edu; for creative works: Omofolabo Ajayi, Email:
omofola@ku.edu
Administered by the Women's Caucus of the ➔**African Studies Association (2755)**
Year founded: 2005 Award: $500
Objectives/Description: given in alternate years to (1) an outstanding work in social science – in English or in English translation – that prioritizes the experiences of African women; (2) a creative/literary work by an African woman, which may include novels, poetry, exhibition catalogues, books of drawings, photographs, or other expressions of art.

Conditions of entry: the first prize was awarded in 2005 in the social science category; the second prize, in the literary/creative works category, will be given in 2006, and books published from 2002-2005 will be eligible for entry. In 2007, in the social science category, books published in 2005 or 2006 will be eligible for entry. Three non-returnable copies of each title nominated must be submitted. Submissions for the prize may be made by publishers, authors, or other interested individuals.

Closing date: May 1 each year.

Recent past winners: information not available at press time

2826   **The Claude Ake Memorial Awards Program**
The Africa-America Institute
Graybar Building
420 Lexington Avenue Suite 1706
New York NY 10170
USA
Tel: +1-212-739-7870 Email: rachelminka@aaionline.org
Web: http://www.aaionline.org/whatwedo/whatClaudeAke.asp
Administered by: ➔ **The Africa America Institute (2727)**, in conjunction with the
➔**African Studies Association (2755)**

Contact: Vivian Awumey, Director, Professional Training and Advanced Degree
Programs
Year founded: 2001 Award: $6,000 per stipend
Sponsors: funded by the → **Ford Foundation (2733)**
Objectives/Description: funded by the Ford Foundation, the Claude Ake Memorial
Awards Program seeks to encourage young and mid-career African scholars and
activists to develop research-based project ideas directed at addressing some of
Africa's most pressing challenges. The award is intended for Africans, working either
on the continent or in the US, who are engaged in knowledge-based and reality-
informed problem solving, in the tradition of Claude Ake, an activist for democracy,
a visionary and a scholar of global standing. The fellows – three women, and three
men – will each receive a one-year $6,000 stipend to further their innovative and
practical research into resolving Africa's developmental problems. Fellows travel to
the United States to participate in study tours tailored to their specific research
interests, then present their findings at the annual meeting of the African Studies
Association. The Africa-America Institute will compile a resource book with
syntheses of the Ake Scholars' research and distribute it widely to academic and
other audiences.

Conditions of entry: the program is intended primarily for African scholar/activists
residing on the continent of Africa. Awards may also be made to select African
applicants residing outside of Africa. Preference is given to individuals who have not
recently visited North America. Proficiency in written and spoken English is
required. Applications will be reviewed by an award committee comprised of noted
Africanists from the ASA and senior AAI and ASA staff members, who select the
fellows each year. Applications (see application form downloadable at the Web site)
must be received in hard copy at the Africa America Institute no later than by mid-
January each year. Fax and email applications will not be accepted. Notification of
the awards usually takes place at the end of March each year.

Closing date: mid-January each year

2001 Claude Ake scholars:
Wale Adebanwi (Nigeria)
Research topic: Impact of Technology on Socio-Political Structures
Mumed Abdurahman Ame (Ethiopia)
Research topic: Afar Pastoralism and Land Management Policies in Ethiopia
Adeniyi Sulaiman Gbadegesin (Nigeria)
Research topic: Resource Management in the Nigerian Delta
Josephine Hombarume (Zimbabwe)
Research topic: Needs of Unaccompanied Refugee Children
Ifeoma Stella Madueme (Nigeria)
Research topic: Conflict Resolution in Traditional Igbo Society
Rebecca Njoki Wanjiku (Kenya)
Research topic: Coping Strategies of Women Refugees and Disrupted Communities

2002 Claude Ake scholars:
John Sorana Akama (Kenya)

Research topic: The Efficacy of Tourism as a Tool for Socio-Economic Development in Kenya: A Cultural Perspective
Caroline Wanjiku Kihato (Kenya)
Research topic: Moving Beyond the Rhetoric? South Africa's Experience in Strengthening Civil Society
Tendayi Mutimukuru (Zimbabwe)
Research topic: Managing Conflicts for Sustainable Forest Management. Lessons from Mafungautsi Forest, in Gokwe Communal Area, Zimbabwe
Ubong Samuel Nda (Nigeria)
Research topic: Theatre for Environmental Sensitization
Charles Uzodimma Ogbulogo (Nigeria)
Research topic: Igbo-English Medical Dictionary
Owen Ziwoya (Malawi)
Research topic: Radio as a Rendezvous for Socio-Economic Development in Malawi

2003 Claude Ake scholars:
Ebrahim Harvey (South Africa)
Research topic: Perceptions, Views, and Concerns about the Planned Installation of Pre-Paid Water Meters in Soweto, Johannesbug, (South Africa)
Annet Koote (Uganda)
Research topic: A Situational Analysis of Child headed Families in Luwero District (Uganda)
Gidion Kaino Mandesi (Tanzania)
Research topic: An Investigation into the Plight of Disabled People in Politics and Elections in Tanzania
Adebobola Nathaniel-Imeh (Nigeria)
Integration of Indigenous Knowledge of Rural Women in Sustainable Ecology, Agricultural Productivity and Environmental Conservation: a Nigerian Case Study
Richard Nyirenda (Zimbabwe)
Research topic: Committee or User Based Forestry Management? Alternative Approaches to Community Involvement in Community Based Forest Management: Case Studies from Mafungautsi Forest, Zimbabwe
Abdoulaye Tall (Senegal)
Research topic: Begging Children, their Hope, their Future. Do Children's Rights Mean Anything to Them?

2004 Claude Ake scholars:
Leah Kimathi (Kenya)
Research topic: Traditional Non-State Political Organization as a Basis of State Reconstruction: The Case of Southern Sudan
Monga Alphonse Maindo (Democratic Republic of the Congo)
Research topic: Militia Recruitment in the Democratic Republic of Congo: the Restructuring of the Local Political Ground by Way of Violence
Ogochukwu Nzewi (Nigeria)
Research topic: Sounds and Voices: Very Open Inspiring Communication: Expending the Scourge
Francis Orech (Kenya)
Research topic: The Domestication and Promotion of Nutritious and Safe Traditional

Leafy Vegetables in the Farming Systems of Nyang'oma Division, Bondo District, Western Kenya
Kudzai Shava (Zimbabwe)
Research topic: The Use of Peer Education and its Impact on HIV/AIDS Awareness Among Visually Impaired Adolescents at Copota School for the Blind in Masvingo, Zimbabwe
Paul Tarus (Kenya)
Research topic: Search for Bioactive Phytochemicals with Antimalarial Activity from Selected Kenyan Indigenous Medicinal Plants from the *Euphorbiaceae* Family

2005 Claude Ake scholars:
no competition held

2827   CODESRIA Prize for Doctoral Theses
Council for the Development of Social Science Research in Africa
BP 3304
Dakar
Senegal
Tel: +221-825 9822/23 Fax: +221-824 1289 Email: virginie.niang@codesria.sn
Web:
http://www.codesria.org/Links/Training_and_Grants/prize%20for%20doctoral%20theses.htm
Administered by: ➜ **CODESRIA (2508)**
Year founded: 2002 Award: $1,000 each, and the publication of a suitably revised version of the selected thesis in the CODESRIA Book Series
Objectives/Description: a new CODESRIA initiative designed to encourage excellence in post-graduate research in Africa by offering three prizes annually for the best doctoral theses produced within Africa. In determining the best theses produced, emphasis is placed on originality, rigour, innovation and relevance. Beneficiaries of the CODESRIA Small Grants Programme (for more details *see* http://www.codesria.org/Links/Training_and_Grants/Small%20Grants.htm)   are encouraged to participate in the competition for the award of the prizes, but the initiative is not limited to them as all postgraduate students involved in social research are encouraged to enter the competition. Any African student registered in a doctoral programme in an African university who has produced a thesis in the social sciences that has been accepted after due examination is eligible to enter. To be considered, the thesis should have been submitted and successfully defended in the period between 01 June of any one year and 31 May of the subsequent year.

The award process is managed by an independent jury of eminent scholars

Conditions of entry/Closing dates: the submission date is 31 July of each year, for other details and application procedures *see*
http://www.codesria.org/Links/News/announcements_2004/prize_doctoral_thesis04.pdf (Call for Applications 2004) Call for Applications 2005 or 2006 not available at press time.

2828   Conover-Porter Award
c/o Peter Limb, Africana Bibliographer
Michigan State University
100 Library
East Lansing MI 48824-1048
USA
Tel: +1517-432-6123 ext 239 Fax: +1-517-432 3532 Email: limb@msu.edu
Web: http://www.loc.gov/rr/amed/afs/alc/conport2.html
Administered by: ➔ **Africana Librarians Council (1885)** of the ➔ **African Studies Association (2755)**
Year founded: 1980 Award: $300
Sponsors: Africana Librarians Council of the African Studies Association
Contact: Peter Limb, Conover Award Committee Chair (2005/06), at above address
Objectives/Description: established in 1980 to honour outstanding publications in Africana bibliography and reference works, the award is named after two pioneers in African studies librarianship, Helen F. Conover and Dorothy B. Porter. Award winners are selected every two years by the Africana Librarians Council of the African Studies Association. Awarded biennially (in even-numbered years) at the African Studies Association's annual meeting.

Conditions of entry: any Africa-related reference work, bibliography or bibliographic essay published separately or as part of a larger work, published during the previous two years, may be submitted for the competition. Books may be nominated by individuals or by publishers. Nominations must be accompanied by a brief justification and at least one review.

Members of the Conover Award Committee select the biennial winner of the Award. In addition to the main prize winner, further titles are cited for 'Honourable mention'.

Closing date for nominations: 1 January in alternate years. Application form (2006 Award) at http://www.loc.gov/rr/amed/afs/alc/c-pform.html

Complete list of past winners:
1980: Julian Witherell *The United States and Africa: Guide to US Official Documents and Government-Sponsored Publications on Africa, 1785-1975* (Library of Congress)
1982: Roger Hilbert and Christian Oehlmann *Foreign Direct Investments and Multinational Corporations in Sub-Saharan Africa: A Bibliography* (Campus Verlag)
1984: Hans M. Zell, Caroline Bundy, and Virginia Coulon *A New Reader's Guide to African Literature* (Heinemann/Africana Publishing Corporation)
1986: Tore Linne Eriksen *The Political Economy of Namibia: An Annotated Critical Bibliography* (Scandinavian Institute of African Studies)
1988: (joint winners) Jean E. Meeh Gosebrink *African Studies Information Resources Directory* (Hans Zell Publishers); and Daniel P. Biebuyck *The Arts of Central Africa: An Annotated Bibliography* (G.K. Hall)
1990: Yvette Scheven *Bibliographies for African Studies, 1970-1986* (Hans Zell Publishers)

1992: Carol Sicherman *Ngugi wa Thiong'o: The Making of a Rebel: A Source Book in Kenyan Literature and Resistance*; and Carol Sicherman *Ngugi wa Thiong'o: A Bibliography of Primary and Secondary Sources, 1957-1987* (both Hans Zell Publishers)
1994: (joint winners) Thomas George Barton *Sexuality and Health in Sub-Saharan Africa: An Annotated Bibliography* (AMREF); and Hans M. Zell, editor *African Books in Print*, 4th ed. (Hans Zell Publishers)
1996: (joint winners) Bernth Lindfors *Black African Literature in English, 1987-1991* (Hans Zell Publishers); and Nancy J. Schmidt *Sub-Saharan African Films and Filmmakers, 1987-1992: An Annotated bibliography* (Hans Zell Publishers)
1998: (joint winners) Amélia Neves de Souto *Guia bibliográfico para o estudante de história de Moçambique* (Centro de Estudos Africanos, Universidade Eduardo Mondlane); and John McIlwaine *Writings on African Archives* (Hans Zell Publishers, on behalf of the Standing Conference on Library Materials on Africa)
2000: John Middleton, editor-in-chief *Encyclopedia of Africa South of the Sahara* (Charles Scribner's Sons, New York)
2002: (joint winners) Thomas J. Bassett and Yvette Scheven *Maps of Africa to 1900: A Checklist of Maps in Atlases and Geographical Journals in the Collections of the University of Illinois, Urbana-Champaign* (The Graduate School of Library and Information Science, University of Illinois at Urbana-Champaign); and David W. Bade, compiler *Books in African Languages in the Melville J. Herskovits Library of African Studies, Northwestern University: A Catalog* (Program of African Studies, Northwestern University)
2004: A.J. Christopher *The Atlas of Changing South Africa* (Routledge)

2829 Distinguished Africanist Award
African Studies Association
Rutgers, The State University of New Jersey
Douglass Campus
132 George Street
New Brunswick NJ 08901-1400
USA
Tel: +1-732-932 8173 ext 10 Fax: +1-732-932 3394 Email: members@rci.rutgers.edu
Web: http://www.africanstudies.org/asa_awardsdistinguished.html
Contact: Margaret McLaughlin, Executive Administrator
Administered by: ➔ **African Studies Association (2755)**
Year founded 1988   Award: not a cash award; award consists of a plaque and a Certificate of Lifetime Membership of the African Studies Association
Sponsors: African Studies Association
Objectives/Description: the ASA Distinguished Africanist Award was established to recognize and honour scholars who have contributed a lifetime record of outstanding scholarship in their respective field of African studies and service to the Africanist community. Criteria for the Award are the distinction of contribution to Africanist scholarship, as measured by a lifetime of accomplishment and service in the field of African studies. Contributions to scholarship within and without the academic community are considered. The Award is presented at the annual meeting awards ceremony, and consists of a plaque and a lifetime membership of the African Studies Association.

Conditions of entry: any member of the Association is eligible to propose a candidate. The nomination must include CV of the nominee, a detailed letter of nomination justifying the candidature in terms of the criteria for the Award, and three similar letters from ASA members seconding the nomination. At least two of the latter must be affiliated with institutions other than that of the nominee.

The Distinguished Africanist Award Committee for the Award is composed of the Past President, the President, the Vice President, and two ASA members designated by the Executive Committee of the ASA Board of Directors. The non-Board members of the committee serve three-year terms. The recommendation of the Committee is presented to the Board of Directors at its Spring Meeting, and the final choice is made by the Board.

Closing date: the complete dossier of the candidate must be submitted to the ASA Executive Office by February 15 each year.

Complete list of past winners:
1984: Gwendolyn M. Carter
1985: Elliot Skinner
1986: Jan Vansina
1987: Joseph Greenberg
1988: Elizabeth Colson
1989: Roland Oliver
1990: M. Crawford Young
1992: Philip D. Curtin
1993: J. Ade Ajayi
1995: Ali A. Mazrui
1996: not awarded
1997: Akin Mabogunji
1998: Ivor G. Wilks
1999: Catherine Coquery-Vidrovitch
2000: Bernth Lindfors
        J.H. Kwabena Nketia
        Roy Sieber
2001: Martin Klein
        Bethwell Ogot
2002: Peter Geschiere
2003: Joseph E. Harris
2004: Francis M. Deng
2005: John Hunwick

2830 Graduate Student Paper Prize
        African Studies Association
        Rutgers, The State University of New Jersey
        Douglass Campus
        132 George Street
        New Brunswick NJ 08901-1400
        USA
Tel: +1-732-932 8173 ext 10 Fax: +1-732-932 3394 Email: members@rci.rutgers.edu
Web: http://www.africanstudies.org/asa_awardsdistinguished.html

Contact: Margaret McLaughlin, Executive Administrator
Administered by: ➜ **African Studies Association (2755)**
Year founded: 2001 Award: competition, not a monetary award
Objectives/Description: a new annual prize for the best graduate student paper presented at the previous year's annual meeting of the African Studies Association. All papers presented by graduate students at each year's annual meeting are eligible for the prize, which is awarded at the Association's annual meeting. The winning paper is published in the Association's ➜ **African Studies Review (800)**.

Closing date: graduate students may submit their papers with a letter of recommendation from their advisor by January 15 each year. Submissions to the ASA Executive Office.

Recent winners:
2004: Kristen E. Cheney, University of California, Santa Cruz, for *Village Life is Better than Town Life: Identity, Migration, and Development in the Lives of Ugandan Child Citizens*
2005: details not available at press time

2831 Joel Gregory Prize
Canadian Association of African Studies/
Association Canadienne des Etudes Africaines
c/o Cétase
Université de Montréal
CP 6128 Succ A
Montréal Quebec H3C 3J7
Canada
Tel: +1-513-343 65 69 Fax: +1-514-343 7716 Email: caas@cetase.umontreal.ca
Web: http://caas.concordia.ca/htm/joelgregprize.htm
Administered by: ➜ **Canadian Association of African Studies (2769)**
Year founded: 1989
Contact: Annamaria Piccioni, Executive Director or Chris Youe, Head, Department of History, Memorial University, St. John's, Newfoundland A1C 5S7,
Email: cyoue@mun.ca
Objectives/Description: The Joel Gregory was established in 1989 in memory of one of the Association's outstanding members, Joel Gregory, who, in addition to being an internationally acclaimed demographer, served as co-editor of the *Canadian Journal of African Studies* and, at various times, member of the CAAS Executive, and as President. The prize is awarded biennially for the best book on Africa in the area of the social sciences and humanities published by a Canadian author, a landed immigrant, or an African who has studied in Canada.

Conditions of entry: Books in English and in French are considered. In edited collections, all the contributors must fulfil the criteria above. The book must be published in the preceding three calendar years prior to each biennial prize.

Closing date: 31 December in alternate years; for next (2006 prize) books must be published between 1 July 2002 and 31 December 2005.

Complete list of past winners:

1990: Jonathan Crush *The Struggle for Swazi Labor 1890-1920* (McGill and Queen's University Press)

1992: Bruce Berman *Control and Conflict in Colonial Kenya* (Ohio University Press)

1996: Dan O'Meara *Forty Lost Years: The Apartheid State and the Politics of the National Party, 1948-1994* (Ohio University Press)

1998: Fiona Mackenzie *Land, Ecology and Resistance in Kenya, 1880-1952* (Edinburgh University Press/International African Institute, and Heinemann US)

2000: Lisa Mcnee *Selfish Gifts: Senegalese Women's Autobiographical Discourses* (State University of New York Press)

2002 to 2005: details not available at press time; for details of nominees for the 2006 Joel Gregory Prize see http://caas.concordia.ca/htm/joelgregprize.htm#news

2832   Melville J. Herskovits Award
African Studies Association
Rutgers, The State University of New Jersey
Douglass Campus
132 George Street
New Brunswick NJ 08901-1400
USA
Tel: +1-732-932 8173 ext 10 Fax: +1-732-932 3394 Email: members@rci.rutgers.edu
Web: http://www.africanstudies.org/asa_herskovits.html
Contact: Margaret McLaughlin, Executive Administrator
Administered by: → **African Studies Association (2755)**
Year founded: 1965   Award: $500
Sponsors: African Studies Association
Objectives/Description: the Award is named in honour of Melville J. Herskovits, one of the original founders of the ASA. It is presented annually for the best scholarly work on Africa published in English in the previous year and distributed in the US. The Award consists of a plaque and $500 and is presented at the awards ceremony at the ASA's annual meeting. The selection committee for the Herskovits Award consists of five senior scholars chosen to represent as broad a spectrum as possible of the disciplines associated with the study of Africa. Committee terms are staggered so that new members join the committee each year. The ASA Board recommends a prioritized list of several individuals to serve on the Committee, one of whom will be named to membership of the Committee for a term to begin in the following calendar year. The ASA Executive Director invites individuals to serve in the order of priority determined by the Board.

Conditions of entry: nominations for the Herskovits Award are made directly by publishers who may nominate as many separate titles in a given year as they desire. All nominations must meet the following criteria: they must be original non-fiction scholarly works published in English in the year prior to the competition and distributed in the United States. The subject matter must deal with Africa and/or related areas (Cape Verde, Madagascar, or Indian Ocean Islands off the East African coast). Collections and compilations, proceedings of symposia, new editions of previously published books, bibliographies, and dictionaries are not eligible for the competition. A copy of the book(s) nominated must be sent to each member of the

Herskovits Committee appointed by the African Studies Association (*see* Web site for details). A form or letter indicating the publisher, address, email address, telephone, fax, and titles nominated must be sent to the Executive Director of the Association.

Closing date: May 1 each year.

Complete list of past winners:

1965: Ruth Schachter Morgenthau *Political Parties in French-speaking West Africa* (Oxford University Press)
1966: Leo Kuper *An African Bourgeoisie* (Yale University Press)
1967: Jan Vansina *Kingdoms of the Savanna* (University of Wisconsin Press)
1968: Herbert Weiss *Political Protest in the Congo* (Princeton University Press)
1969: Paul and Laura Bohannan *Tiv Economy* (Northwestern University Press)
1970: Stanlake Samkange *Origins of Rhodesia* (Praeger Publishers)
1971: René Lemarchand *Rwanda and Burundi* (Praeger Publishers)
1972: Francis Deng *Tradition and Modernization* (Yale University Press)
1973: Allen F. Isaacman *Mozambique - the Africanization of a European Institution: the Zambezi Prazos, 1750-1902* (University of Wisconsin Press)
1974: John N. Paden *Religion and Political Culture in Kano* (University of California Press)
1975: Lansine Kaba Wahhabiyya: *Islamic Reform and Politics in French West Africa* (Northwestern University Press)
1976: Ivor Wilks *Asante in the Nineteenth Century* (Cambridge University Press)
1977: M. Crawford Young *The Politics of Cultural Pluralism* (University of Wisconsin Press)
1978: William Y. Adams *Nubia: Corridor to Africa* (Princeton University Press)
1979: Hoyt Alverson *Mind in the Heart of Darkness: Value and Self-Identity Among the Tswana of Southern Africa* (Yale University Press)
1980: Richard B. Lee *The !Kung San* (Cambridge University Press)
1981: Gavin Kitching *Class and Economic Change in Kenya: The Making of an African Petite Bourgeoisie, 1905-1970* (Yale University Press)
1982: (joint winners) Frederick Cooper *From Slaves to Squatters: Plantation Labor and Agriculture in Zanzibar and Coastal Kenya, 1890-1925* (Yale University Press); and Sylvia Scribner and Michael Cole *The Psychology of Literacy* (Harvard University Press)
1983: James W. Fernandez *Bwitti: An Ethnography of the Religious Imagination in Africa* (Princeton University Press)
1984: (joint winners) Paulin Hontoundji *African Philosophy* (Hutchinson/Indiana University Press); and J.D.Y. Peel *Ijeshas and Nigerians: the Incorporation of a Yoruba Kingdom* (Cambridge University Press)
1985: Claire Robertson *Sharing the Same Bowl* (Indiana University Press)
1986: Sara Berry *Fathers Work for their Sons: Accumulation, Mobility, and Class Formation in an Extended Yoruba Community* (University of California Press)
1987: (joint winners) Paul M. Lubeck *Islam and Urban Labour in Northern Nigeria: The Making of a Muslim Working Class* (Cambridge University Press); and T.O. Beidelman *Moral Imagination in Kaguru Modes of Thought* (Indiana University Press)
1988: John Iliffe *The African Poor: A History* (Cambridge University Press)

1989: (joint winners) Joseph C. Miller *Way of Death: Merchant Capitalism and the Angolan Slave Trade, 1730-1830* (University of Wisconsin Press); and V.S. Mudimbe *The Invention of Africa: Gnosis, Philosophy and the Order of Knowledge* (Indiana University Press)

1990: Edwin Wilmsen *Land Filled with Flies: A Political Economy of the Kalahari* (University of Chicago Press)

1991: (joint winners) Johannes Fabian *Power and Performance: Ethnographic Exploration through Proverbial Wisdom and Theater in Sahba, Zaire* (University of Wisconsin Press); and Luise White *The Comforts of Home: Prostitution in Colonial Nairobi* (University of Chicago Press)

1992: Myron Echenberg *Colonial Conscripts: The Tirailleurs Sénégalais in French West Africa* (Heinemann)

1993: Kwame Anthony Appiah *In My Father's House: Africa in the Philosophy of Culture* (Oxford University Press)

1994: Keleso Atkins *The Moon is Dead! Give Us Our Money! The Cultural Origins of an African Work Ethic, Natal, South Africa, 1843-1900* (Heinemann)

1995: Henrietta L. Moore and Megan Vaughn *Cutting Down Trees: Gender, Nutrition, and Agricultural Change in the Northern Province of Zambia, 1890-1990* (Heinemann/James Currey/University of Zambia Press)

1996: Jonathon Glassman *Feasts and Riot: Revelry, Rebellions and Popular Consciousness on the Swahili Coast, 1856-1888* (Heinemann/James Currey)

1997: Mahmood Mamdani *Citizen and Subject: Contemporary Africa and the Legacy of Late Colonialism* (Princeton University Press)

1998: Susan Mullin Vogel *Baule: African Art Western Eyes* (Yale University Press).

1999: Peter Uvin *Aiding Violence: The Development Enterprise in Rwanda* (Kumarian Press)

2000: Nancy Rose Hunt *A Colonial Lexicon: Of Birth Ritual, Medicalization, and Mobility in the Congo* (Duke University Press).

2001: (joint winners) Karin Barber *Generation of Plays* (Indiana University Press); and J.D.Y. Peel *Religious Encounter and the Making of the Yoruba* (Indiana University Press)

2002: (joint winners) Judith Carney *Black Rice* (Harvard University Press); and Diana Wylie *Starving on a Full Stomach: Hunger and the Triumph of Cultural Racism in Modern South Africa* (University of Virginia Press)

2003: Joseph Inikori *Africans in the Industrial Revolution in England: A Study in International Trade and Economic Development* (Cambridge University Press)

2004: Allen F. Roberts and Mary Nooter Roberts *A Saint in the City: Sufi Art in Urban Senegal* (University of California-Los Angeles, Fowler Museum of Cultural History)

2005: (joint winners) Adam Ashforth *Witchcraft, Violence and Democracy in South Africa* (University of Chicago Press); and Jan Vansina *How Societies Are Born: Governance in West Central Africa Before 1600* (University of Virginia Press)

2833   The Noma Award for Publishing in Africa
PO Box 128
Witney OX8 5XU
UK
Tel: +44-(0)1993-775235 Fax: +44-(0)1993-709265
Email: maryljay@aol.com
Web: http://www.nomaward.org (Main home page)
http://www.nomaaward.org/noma.pdf (Brochure 1980-2002)
Contact: Mary Jay, Secretary to the Noma Award Managing Committee
Administered by: Secretariat, Noma Award Managing Committee
Year founded: 1979 Award: US$10,000
Sponsor: Shoichi Noma (deceased)/Kodansha Publishers, Tokyo
Objectives/Description: established in 1979, the Noma Award is open to African writers and scholars whose work is published in Africa. The $10,000 prize is given annually for an outstanding new book in any of these three categories: (i) scholarly or academic, (ii) books for children, and (iii) literature and creative writing. Books are admissible in any of the languages of Africa, both local and European.

The Noma Award is administered by a Secretariat in Oxford, UK. An impartial committee, or jury, currently (2005) chaired by the Tanzanian publisher Walter Bgoya, comprising African scholars and book experts, and representatives of the international book community, is entrusted with the selection of the annual prize. The jury is assisted by independent opinion and assessments from a large and distinguished pool of subject specialists from throughout the world, including many scholars in Africa. An original work first published in Africa is selected each year as the winner. Occasionally, there have been joint winners. In order to recognise the merits of other deserving titles, the jury also singles out books for 'Special commendation' and/or 'Honourable mention'. The Noma Award is presented at a special ceremony each year, usually held in Africa, and traditionally linked with a book promotion event such as a book fair.

Conditions of entry: the Noma Award is given for an outstanding new book in any of the three categories eligible for the competition. Publishers – who must be fully autonomous African publishers within the spirit of the Award – may submit a maximum number of three titles. Books entered for the prize must be first published in Africa, and the African publisher submitting the entry must hold the original rights if also published, or co-published, elsewhere and/or outside Africa. Entries must be works published during the twelve months calendar period prior to each year's annual award. Six non-returnable copies of a published work must be submitted and should be accompanied by an entry form, providing a short résumé of the work and an outline justifying its submission.

For the full conditions of entry *see* http://www.nomaaward.org/entry.shtml

Closing date: 31 March each year.

Complete list of past winners:
1980: Mariama Bâ *Une si longue lettre* (Nouvelles Editions Africaines)

1981: Felix C. Adi *Health Education for the Community* (Nwamife Publishers)
1982: Meshack Asare *The Brassman's Secret* (Educational Press & Manufacturers)
1983: A.N.E. Amissah *Criminal Procedure in Ghana* (Sedco Publishing)
1984: (joint winners) Gakaara wa Wanjau *Mwandiki wa Mau Mau ithaamirio-ini* (Heinemann Educational Books East Africa); and Njabulo Simakhale Ndebele *Fools and Other Stories* (Ravan Press)
1985: Bernard Nanga *La Trahison de Marianne* (Nouvelles Editions Africaines)
1986: Antònio Jacinto *Sobreviver em Tarrafal de Santiago* (Instituto Nacional do Livro e do Disco)
1987: Pierre Kipré *Villes de Côte d'Ivoire, 1893-1940* (Nouvelles Editions Africaines)
1988: Luli Callinicos *Working Life. Factories, Townships, and Popular Culture on the Rand, 1886-1940* (Ravan Press)
1989: Chenjerai Hove *Bones. A Novel* (Baobab Books)
1990: Francis Wilson and Mamphela Ramphele *Uprooting Poverty: The South African Challenge* (David Philip)
1991: Niyi Osundare *Waiting Laughters. A Long Song in Many Voices* (Malthouse Press)
1992: (joint winners) Souad Khodja *A comme Algériennes* (Entreprise Nationale du Livre); and Charles Mungoshi *One Day, Long Ago. More Stories from a Shona Childhood* (Baobab Books)
1993: Mongane Wally Serote *Third World Express* (David Philip)
1994: Paul Tiyambe Zeleza *A Modern Economic History of Africa. Volume 1: The Nineteenth Century* (CODESRIA)
1995: Marlene van Niekerk *Triomf* (Queillerie Publishers)
1996: Kitia Touré *Destins parallèles* (Nouvelles Editions Ivoiriennes)
1997: A. Adu Boahen *Mfantsipim and the Making of Ghana: A Centenary History, 1876-1976* (Sankofa Educational Publishers)
1998: Peter Adwok Nyaba *The Politics of Liberation in South Sudan. An Insider's View* (Fountain Publishers)
1999: Djibril Samb *L'interprétation des rêves dans la région Sénégambienne. Suivi de la clef des songes de la Sénégambie, de l'Egypte pharaonique et de la tradition islamique* (Les Nouvelles Editions Africaines du Sénégal)
2000: Kimani Njogu and Rocha Chimerah *Ufundishaji wa Fasihi. Nadharia na Mbinu* [The Teaching of Literature: Theory and Methods] (The Jomo Kenyatta Foundation)
2001: Abosede Emanuel *Odun Ifa/Ifa Festival* (West African Book Publishers)
2002: Hamdi Sakkut *The Arabic Novel: Bibliography and Critical Introduction, 1865-1995*, 6 vols. (American University in Cairo Press)
2003: Elinor Sisulu *Walter and Albertina Sisulu. In our Lifetime* (David Philip Publishers, an imprint of New Africa Books Pty Ltd, Cape Town)
2004: no award made
2005: Werewere-Liking *La mémoire amputee. Chant-Roman* (Nouvelles Editions Ivoiriennes)

2834 **The Paul Hair Prize** (formerly The Text Prize)
The Paul Hair Prize Committee
c/o Dmitri van den Bersselaar
School of History
University of Liverpool
9 Abercromby Square
Liverpool L69 7WZ
UK
Tel. +44-(0)151-794 2420 Fax. +44(0)151-794 2366 Email: dvdb@liv.ac.uk
Web: n/a
Contact: Dmitri van den Bersselaar
Administered by: → **Association for the Publication of African Historical Sources/APAHS (2763)**
Year founded: 2005 Award: $300
Objectives/Description: presented in odd-numbered years the Paul Hair Prize is offered in recognition of the best critical edition or translation into English of primary source materials on Africa published during the preceding two years. The name of the winner is announced at the → **African Studies Association (2755)** annual meeting.

Conditions of entry: eligible for consideration are texts dealing with the history, literature, and other aspects of the cultures of Africa, whether in African or European languages, from oral or written traditions, or whether the text is published for the first time or in a new edition. Evaluation for the prize is based on the importance of the text, its presentation, its critical apparatus, and the utility of the work as a whole for scholars and teachers of Africa. Works edited by a single individual or jointly edited by more than one author are eligible for consideration. Anthologies with separate contributions by different authors, children's books, and straightforward texts are not eligible. Works submitted must be of minimum length of 10,000 words, excluding the documentary apparatus. The Paul Hair Prize Committee consists of three scholars identified by the Board of APAHS.

Closing date: texts published in 2005 or 2006 will be eligible for the 2007 award, for which nominations must be received by May 1, 2007. To nominate a text, three copies of the publication must be sent to the administrators of the prize.

2835 **Trevor Reese Memorial Prize**
Institute of Commonwealth Studies
University of London
28 Russell Square
London WC1B 5DS
UK
Tel: +44-(0)20-7862 8844 Fax: +44-(0)20-7862 8820 Email: ics@sas.ac.uk
Web: http://www2.sas.ac.uk/commonwealthstudies/reese.htm
Contact: Mary Sanver, Events & Publicity Officer
Administered by: Institute of Commonwealth Studies
Year founded: 1979 Award: £1,000

Objectives/Description: the Trevor Reese Memorial prize was established by the Institute of Commonwealth Studies of the University of London in 1979. Dr Trevor Reese, a distinguished scholar of imperial history, was Reader in Imperial Studies at the Institute up to his death in 1976. He was founder and first editor of the *Journal of Imperial and Commonwealth History*. The Prize was established with the proceeds of contributions to a memorial fund from scholars in Britain and a large number of overseas countries. The £1,000 prize is awarded every two years, and honours an outstanding work of scholarship in the field of Imperial and Commonwealth history published in the preceding two years.

Conditions of entry: the adjudicators are interested in wide-ranging publications, but the terms of the Prize specifically apply to scholarly works, usually by a single author, in the field of Imperial and Commonwealth history. The next award will be in 2007, for books published during the course of 2005 and 2006. Publishers or authors willing to submit titles for consideration should send one copy to the Events and Publicity Officer, Institute of Commonwealth Studies, at the address above, any time up to the end of May 2006. No other form of entry is required.

Closing date: (for 2007 Award) 31 May, 2006.
Recent past winners:
1994: Bruce Berman and John Lonsdale *Unhappy Valley: Conflict in Kenya and Africa*, Book One: *State and Class*, Book Two: *Violence and Ethnicity* (James Currey/Ohio University Press/Heinemann Kenya)
1996: D.K. Fieldhouse *Merchant Capital and Economic Decolonization: The United States Africa Company, 1929-1987* (Clarendon Press)
1998: Rod Emond *Representing the South Pacific. Colonial Discourse from Cook to Gauguin* (Cambridge University Press)
2000: (joint winners) Terence Ranger *Voices from the Rocks* (James Currey/Indiana University Press); and Samita Sen *Women and Labour in Late Colonial India* (Cambridge University Press)
2003: Catherine Hall *Civilising Subjects: Metropole and Colony in the English Imagination, 1830-1867* (Polity Press in association with Blackwell Publishers)
2005: details not available at press time

2836   Audrey Richards Prize
African Studies Association of the UK (ASAUK)
c/o School of Oriental and African Studies
Thornhaugh Street
Russell Square
London WC1H 0XG
UK
Tel: +44-(0)20-7898 4390 Fax: +44-(0)20-7898 4389 Email: info@asauk.net or asa@soas.ac.uk
Web: http://www.asauk.net/awards.htm
Contact: Lindsay Allen, Hon. Secretary
Administered by: ➔ **African Studies Association of the UK (2757)**
Year founded: 2001 Award: consists of books, and an invitation to participate free of charge at the ASAUK's next biennial conference

Objectives/Description: awarded biennially to the best doctoral thesis on an African or Africa-related topic accepted by a UK university that has been successfully examined in a UK institution of higher education in the two calendar years preceding each ASAUK conference.

Conditions of entry: nominations should be made by the supervisor, with the permission of the candidate (normally not more than one nomination from each person). The letter of nomination must be accompanied by a copy of the thesis, together with a cover letter from the supervisor. The recommendation of the Award will be made by a Prize Committee of up to three persons appointed by the Council of the ASAUK.

Closing date: (for next award, the best thesis on Africa 2004 and 2005) 14 June, 2006.

Most recent winners:
2002: Helen Tilley
2004: Joost Fontein

2837   The Amaury Talbot Prize for African Anthropology
Royal Anthropological Institute
50 Fitzroy Street
London W1T 5BT
UK
Tel: +44-(0)20-7387 0455 Fax +44-(0)20-7383 4235 Email: admin@therai.org.uk
Web: http://www.therai.org.uk/prizes/prizes.html#amaurytalbot
Contact: Therese Kearns, Office Manager
Administered by: the Royal Anthropological Institute on behalf of the trustees,
Barclays Bank Trust Company Ltd.
Year founded: 1960 Award: £500
Objectives/Description: annual prize awarded to the author or authors of the most valuable of the work of anthropological research that is submitted in the competition.

Conditions of entry: only works published in the calendar year prior to the submission date are eligible for the award. Preference will be given to works relating in the first place to Nigeria and in the second place to any other part of West Africa in general. Works relating to other regions of Africa are, however, also eligible for submission. All applications, together with three non-returnable copies of the book, article or work in question, must be received by 31st March of the year following publication of the book and must be sent to the Amaury Talbot Prize Co-ordinator, Royal Anthropological Institute.

Closing date: 31 March each year.

Recent past winners:
1991: (joint winners) Karin Barber *I Could Speak Until Tomorrow: Oriki Women and the Past in Yoruba Towns* (Edinburgh University Press); and Richard Werbner *Tears of the Dead: the Social Biography of an African Family* (Edinburgh University Press/International African Institute, and Smithsonian Institution Press)

1992: Robert Launay *Beyond the Stream* (University of California Press)

1993: Christopher B Stiner *African Art in Transit* (Cambridge University Press)

1994: (joint winners) Geoffrey A Fadiman *When We Began they Were Witchmen: An Oral History from Mount Kenya* (University of California Press); and Douglas H. Johnson *Nuer Prophets* (Clarendon Press)

1995: Liisa Malkki *Purity and Exile: Violence, Memory and National Cosmology among the Hutu Refugees in Tanzania* (Clarendon Press)

1996: (joint winners) James Fairhead and Melissa Leach *Misreading the African Landscape: Society and Ecology in a Forest-Savannah Mosaic* (Cambridge University Press); and Sharon Hutchinson *Nuer Dilemmas: Coping with Money, War and the State* (University of California Press)

1997: Susan R. Whyte *The Pragmatics of Uncertainty in Eastern Uganda* (Cambridge University Press)

1998: Silla, Eric *People Are Not the Same: Leprosy and Identity in Twentieth-Century Mali* (Heinemann)

1999: (joint winners) Donald Donham *Marxist Modern: An Ethnographic History of the Ethiopian Revolution* (University of California Press/James Currey); and Charles Piot *Remotely Global: Village Modernity in West Africa* (University of Chicago Press)

2000: Mahir Saul and Patrick Royer *West African Challenge to Empire Culture and History in the Volta-Bani Anticolonial War* (Ohio University Press/James Currey)

2001: J.D.Y. Peel *Religious Encounter and the Making of the Yoruba* (Indiana University Press)

2002: Caroline H. Bledsoe *Contingent Lives: Fertility, Time and Ageing in West Africa* (University of Chicago Press)

2003: (joint winners) Peter D. Little *Somalia: Economy without State* (James Currey); and Daniel P. Reed *Dan Ge Performance: Masks and Music in Contemporary Cote d'Ivoire* (Indiana University Press)

2004: (joint winners) Frank Willett *The Art of Ife* (submitted as CD-ROM); and Alma Gottlieb *The Afterlife Is Where We Come From: The Culture of Infancy in West Africa* (University of Chicago Press)

2005: details not available at press time

23

Information and communication development in Africa: a guide to Web sites and resources

The development of ICT infrastructure in Africa continues to be crucially important for the dissemination of African research and scholarship, and access to electronic information resources by scholars in the countries of Africa has far-reaching consequences for the equity of so-called 'globalization'.

In this section we offer a selection of a number of Web sites and resources devoted to information and communication development in Africa, including newsletters and discussion groups, sources for analysis of Internet connectivity and ICT infrastructure in Africa, and Web sites of major communication initiatives and networking communities. Also included is a small selection of recent articles and reports that will be of particular interest to the Africanist community and Africana librarians. However, several articles and reports that were included in the previous edition of the *African Studies Companion*, published before 2002, are now inevitably rather dated, and have been deleted for the most part. Instead we have added details of a number of important more recent studies, reports, and articles, and there is also a new sub-section on digital libraries. All information is current as at October 2005, and the date last accessed is indicated for each Web resource.

Africa on the Internet: General sources and learning materials

See also ➔ **Communication initiatives and networking communities**

2838   Africa Digital Net
http://www.afridigital.net/
This new site merges the ➔ **Balancing Act (2840)** site with Mike Jensen's ➔ **African Internet Status Report/African Internet Connectivity (2864)** in order to offer readers the opportunity to obtain ICT information and profiles on a country-by-country basis. All merged information resources are being been turned into a searchable database. The new site offers free downloads of articles and reports, providing an overview of the state of the Internet in each African country, including the state of the telecommunications industry, communication costs, national and organizational ICT activities, and more. The individual country profiles are very useful, although one curious omission is the fact that no dates when the information was current are indicated for any of them. Most seem to date back to the 1999/2000 period. For those

seeking more detailed and more current information on the Internet in each country of Africa, Balancing Act also offers a series of subscription-based ➔ **African Internet Country Market Profiles (2839),** published in four parts and supplemented with a quarterly updating service. [09/09/05]

2839 African Internet Country Market Profiles (subscription based)
http://www.balancingact-africa.com/publications.html
Edited by Paul Hamilton, Mike Jensen, and Russell Southwood
Part 1: West Africa, Part 2: East Africa, Part 3: Southern and Central Africa, Part 4: North Africa; plus quarterly updating service.
Complete set of four parts: £180/$330 in Africa, £500/$900 elsewhere (commercial purchasers); reduced price for universities and NGOs £90/$170 (can also be purchased as individual parts, see Web site for price information, or contact Balancing Act, 71 Crescent Lane, London, SW4 9PT, UK, Tel: +44-(0)20-7720 5993 Email: editorial@balancingact-africa.com)
From the publishers of the ➔ **Balancing Act (2840),** this is a comprehensive series of Internet country profiles that summarize the current state of the Internet in each country of Africa, identifying growth opportunities and relevant industry issues. The reports contain the following information for each country: (1) Key Statistics: summary data on the status of ITC and the telecommunications industry; (2) Key Issues: a summary of the main issues affecting each country; (3) Country Background Data: a brief description of main features of the country, including geography and highlights of the economy; (4) Number of ISPs: providing details of the numbers of ISPs and identifies the main players with their market share. (5) Dial-up Subs: provides estimates of individual dial-up subscribers and (where available) the same for users; (6) Cost of Access; (7) Geographic Coverage; (8) Cyber-cafes, (9) Local Web content: information on the Web content and design sector as well services provided locally on the Web. (10) Current Status of Regulation: a summary of the regulatory position in relation to key Internet/IT issues; (11) Digital Divide Initiatives: a summary of some of the more significant digital divide initiatives in countries where these projects exist.; (13) Other Forms of Connectivity: describing different types of connectivity that are available. [Not examined]

2840 Balancing Act
http://www.balancingact-africa.com/
Working in association with a number of African partner organizations, Balancing Act aims to facilitate the development of content for the Internet and other new media technologies in Africa, in the three fields of economic, social and cultural development. The site provides access to a series of 'News update' with reports about the growth of the Internet in Africa, and the development of content "that will support things that people will want to use." This is a valuable information source on IT and Internet developments in Africa. The news updates are also provided as an Email service ➔ **Balancing Act News Update (2858).** [11/10/05]
See also ➔ **2838, 2839**

2841   Licensing Digital Information: Developing Nations Initiatives
http://www.library.yale.edu/~llicense/develop.shtml
In the year 2001, a number of organizations began to develop or publicize programs to bring high quality, peer-reviewed science journals for free (or very cheaply) to developing nations. This site from Yale University Library identifies the programs that have been set up to date, and provides links to the Web sites where readers can learn more about these initiatives. [12/10/05]

2842   NCIC in Africa
http://www.uneca.org/aisi/nici/
These are the ➔ UN Economic Commission on Africa's (2523) Web pages on developing national information and communications infrastructure (NCIC) in Africa. Provides details of plans, policies, and strategies, together with reports and analysis of the status of NCIC in Africa, together with NICI country profiles, NCIC Web resources, and some basic statistical data. [12/10/05]

2843   LearnLink
http://learnlink.aed.org/
Funded by ➔ USAID (2623), LearnLink uses information, communication and educational technologies to strengthen learning systems essential for sustainable development. The site offers a helpful range of online resources that pertain to the use of modern communication technology and multimedia, including computer assisted instruction, distance education, community communication centres, and e-commerce online. There are also free downloads for publications, e.g. *Digital Opportunities for Development: A Sourcebook for Access and Applications* http://learnlink.aed.org/Publications/Sourcebook/home.htm, which features six "models-of-use" that describe technology applications, and provide practical guidelines and strategies for assessing, implementing, monitoring, evaluating, and institutionalizing ICT-based activities, supported by illustrative examples within each model. [15/10/05]

2844   Network Startup Resource Centre (NSRC)
http://www.nsrc.org/AFRICA/africa.html
The NSRC provides technical and engineering assistance to international networking initiatives in developing countries; the Africa pages provide reports and papers about networking in Africa, connectivity and topology maps, and relevant links. Information can also be accessed through an alphabetical index by country. However, most of the resources offered here are now rather dated. [12/10/05]

2845   SchoolNet Africa/African Education Knowledge Warehouse (AEKW)
http://www.schoolnetafrica.net/1500.0.html
The African Education Knowledge Warehouse is a pan-African education portal which services African SchoolNet practitioners, policymakers and school-based communities on ICTs in education across Africa. It is one of Africa's first African-led, African-based non-government organizations that operates across the continent, in its endeavour to improve education access, quality and efficiency through the use of information and communication technologies in African schools. One of its publications is the *African Schoolnet Toolkit*, a practical resource designed to help education planners and practitioners integrate information and communication

technologies into education systems. Published in two parts, it can be freely downloaded (pdf) at
African_SchoolNet_Toolkit_-_I_01.pdf
and at African_SchoolNet_Toolkit_-_II_01.pdf. [03/08/05]
See also ➔ **SchoolNet Namibia (2880)**

2846   Time to Get Online. Simple Steps to Success on the Internet
http://www.ttgo.kabissa.org/
Developed by ➔ **Kabissa (2878)**, *Time to Get Online* is an Internet capacity-building project for West African civil society organizations, designed to assist civil society activists and organizers to get online and to integrate the Internet into their organizations. The project has two main components: (1) a set of self-learning materials that can be used as both a self-taught curriculum and as a reference guide for users with varying levels of Internet experience and expertise. (2) Local workshops serve as a supplement to the learning materials and give organizations the opportunity for hands-on learning. The 150-page *Time to Get Online* can be downloaded for free (in pdf), and is also available in a print version. The materials centre around the five essential "steps to success on the Internet". The first half of the materials is geared towards creating Internet-savvy activists. The second half aims to help them to become effective Internet champions, capable of leading their organizations through the challenging process of integrating the Internet into everything they do. The appendices and accompanying CD-ROM (with print version only) contain a wealth of additional resources for continued learning, freely distributable computer software, and more. This is an excellent resource. [09/09/05]

2847   UNESCO-Webworld — Communication and Information Sector
http://www.unesco.org/webworld/ (Main home page)
http://portal.unesco.org/ci/en/ev.php-
URL_ID=1300&URL_DO=DO_TOPIC&URL_SECTION=201.html (UNESCO's activities in communication and information in Africa)
➔ **UNESCO's (2533)** Communication and Information Sector aims to promote the free flow of ideas and universal access to information, promoting the expression of pluralism and cultural diversity in the media and world information networks, and to promote access for all to ICTs. These pages provide information about regional and country programmes, activities by theme, news about conferences, meetings, workshops, and training courses, as well as providing a Web portal for African libraries and archives. [12/10/05]

2848   World66-Net Café Guide [Africa]
http://www.world66.com/ (click on to Africa)
Originally hosted by a Norwegian organization, the former *Internet Café Guide* has recently been acquired by World66, an open content travel guide (still in a Beta version) where every part of the travel guide can be edited directly by those who use it, or anyone can add details of their favourite watering holes, etc. Search or browse by country or city, and information provided includes full address, Web site (where available), email, telephone and fax numbers, prices charged, opening hours, together with other information such as the type of Internet connection used, bandwidth, and number of work stations, etc. and most entries have a short description about services offered. It lists Internet cafés in virtually every African

country, although listings for some countries and cities, for example Tanzania and Zimbabwe, seem to have dropped significantly from the original version, and for some "Destination" cities there are none. [11/10/05]

E-journals, newsletters, and discussion groups

2849   ADF4 ICT Focus Group Discussion List
http://www.dgroups.org/groups/adf4ictfg/index.cfm?op=info
The discussion list aims to provide members of the ADF4 ICT Focus Group with a platform to discuss issues related to the theme of the 4th African Development Forum (ADF4): "Governance for Progressing Africa", and the roles that ICTs play in achieving good governance in Africa. ADF4 took place from 11 to 15 October 2004 in Addis Ababa, Ethiopia.

2850   Africana-L
http://www.sdgateway.net/mailinglists/list16.htm
Discusses problems and issues related to information technology planning, distribution, access and policies that promote and/or retard use on the African continent. [12/10/05]

2851   Africa Web Content Owner
http://groups.yahoo.com/group/africa_web_content_owner/
An online discussion forum designed to encourage the quality and quantity of Web content in Africa, to promote localisation of Web content development and hosting, the production of Web-based subject gateways to information primarily developed in Africa, and the democratisation of access to Internet technologies in Africa. No activity since October 2003. [12/10/05]

2852   Afrik-IT
https://listserv.heanet.ie/archives/afrik-it.html
An African network of IT experts and professionals devoted to the use of information technology in Africa. To subscribe send email to listserv, afrik-it@listserv.heanet.ie. [12/10/05]

2853   AICP African Internet Connectivity Project
http://www.lsoft.com/scripts/wl.exe?SL1=AICP&H=H-NET.MSU.EDU
H-Net discussion group for the African Internet Connectivity Project. To subscribe send email to listserv, AICP@H-Net.msu.edu. [12/10/05]

2854   AISI-academia-l. Online Discussion on the African Academia and the Information Society
http://www.uneca.org/aisi/discuss.htm
The general aim of this discussion forum is to determine how universities and other higher education institutions see their involvement in the development of information societies, and in which particular areas. To subscribe contact: aopoku-mensah@uneca.org. [12/10/05]

2855 AISI-L African Information Society Initiative/Harnessing Information
Technology for Development
http://www.uneca.org/aisi/discuss.htm and
http://www.bellanet.org/lyris/helper/index.cfm?fuseaction=Visit&listname=aisi-l
A discussion list for general information exchange among the principal organizations
and individuals involved in the implementation of the AISI programmes (*see also* ➔
2869). To subscribe contact aopoku-mensah@uneca.org. [12/10/05]

2856 AISI-Media-l. Online Discussion on the African Media and the Information
Society
http://www.dgroups.org/groups/aisi-media-l/
This online discussion list provides a platform and space for African media
practitioners to reflect on the many issues for enhancing the role of the media
(journalists and institutions) in the information society. It also serves as a forum for
exchange of knowledge, information, lessons, and resources on information society
issues in Africa. [12/10/05]

2857 AVLIN-L. Online Discussion on the African Virtual Library and
Information Network
http://www.dgroups.org/groups/avlin-l/
A forum providing a platform to share experience and discuss strategies for
advocating for the role of libraries in development in Africa, and the development of
the ➔ **African Virtual University Library (2906).** [12/10/05]

2858 Balancing Act's News Update
http://www.balancingact-africa.com/contact.html
Newsletter from ➔ **Balancing Act (2840),** covering Internet connectivity and
developments in Africa. Each issue includes African Web, telecoms and Internet
news, reports and analysis about new initiatives, profiles of IT entrepreneurs, and
there are frequent special issues focussing on particular African countries, or
particular topics. An archive of almost 300 issues can be consulted and searched at
the site. One of the best newsletters about IT developments in Africa. [13/10/05]

2859 The Drum Beat. Communication and Change News and Issues
http://www.comminit.com/drum_beat.html
Part of ➔ **The Communication Initiative (2872)** each issue of Drum Beat offers
descriptive links in support of communication for change programming. Over 300
issues have been published to date (October 2005) and the entire archive can be
searched by keyword. A rich resource. [13/10/05]

2860 Electronic Journal on Information Systems in Developing Countries
http://www.ejisdc.org/
Edited by Robert Davison at the University of Hong Kong, this is a forum for
practitioners, teachers, researchers and policy makers to share their knowledge and
experience in the design, development, implementation, management and evaluation
of information systems and technologies in developing countries. 22 issues have been
published to date (October 2005) with frequent contributions on ICT in Africa.
Articles are freely accessible as full-text documents, as is the complete archive.
[13/10/05]

2861   iConnect Africa
http://www.uneca.org/aisi/IConnectAfrica/index.htm
Published by the → **UN Economic Commission for Africa (2523)**, and the **International Institute for Communication and Development/IICD (2877)**, this is a quarterly email service that aims to raise awareness in the wider African development community regarding the possibilities offered by ICTs in development. Published since 2002, early issues primarily reported on activities forming part of the → **African Information Society Initiative (2869** and its Building Digital Opportunities Programme, but the site was revamped in 2005 based on a new strategy. In collaboration with IICD, it now offers a series of locally written, qualitative articles on the impact and use of ICTs for development. The articles have a strong focus on facts on the ground, with a developing world's perspective, and content written by local people. [13/10/05]

2862   Kabissa Mailing Lists
http://lists.kabissa.org/mailman/listinfo
From the → **Kabissa (2878)** organization, this page provides a listing of all the public mailing lists on lists.kabissa.org, including working groups, networks, newsletters and conferences, and from this page you can also set up a new list. [13/10/05]

2863   Soul Beat Africa – e-newsletter
http://www.comminit.com/africa/soul-beat.html
A project of Soul City at the Institute for Health and Development Communication, South Africa and → **Soul Beat Africa Communication for Change (2882)**, this lively electronic newsletter (often theme-based) focuses on development communication issues, and access of libraries to information communication technologies in Africa. [09/09/05]

Internet access and ICT infrastructure in Africa

2864   African Internet Status Reports/African Internet Connectivity
Mike Jensen's ongoing monitoring and reports on the state of Internet access and connectivity in Africa have been among the most authoritative sources about Internet use in Africa. Although no longer updated since 2002, we retain the links here as they still provide valuable background information. The status reports have now been superseded by → **Africa Digital Net (2838)**, and a series of (subscription-based) → **African Internet Country Market Profiles (2839)**. [13/10/05]

The original reports consist of six different components, all still accessible as follows:

The African Internet - A Status Report (Updated July 2002)
http://demiurge.wn.apc.org/africa/afstat.htm
A detailed and informative 16-page document reporting about the growth of hosts, number of Internet users, ISPs, access costs, international bandwidth, and use of ICT hardware and software, as well as including information on the status of the broadcasting and telecommunications infrastructure in Africa.
Continent-wide Connectivity Indicators (July 2002)
http://demiurge.wn.apc.org/africa/afstat.htm
An inventory and analysis of continental Internet connectivity for all the countries of Africa.

African Internet Connectivity. Information & Communication Technologies (ICTs), Telecommunications, Internet and Computer Infrastructure inAfrica
http://www3.sn.apc.org/africa/index.html
An annual status report and overview together with links to further resources for articles and data on connectivity and access to the Internet, summaries of current Internet projects in Africa, and a calendar of events and meetings.
African Internet Connectivity. Maps and Tables
http://www3.sn.apc.org/africa/afrmain.htm
A range of tables, clickable maps, bar graphs, and pie charts, showing international bandwidth, national access, access costs, and country status summaries.
List of African Internet Service Providers (July 2002)
http://www3.sn.apc.org/africa/af-isps.htm
An annual list by country showing local ISPs with links to their Web sites.
African Internet Connectivity – Resources
http://www3.sn.apc.org/africa/resources.html
A collection of links to resources and articles on ICT in Africa.

2865   African Tertiary Institutions Connectivity Survey (ATICS)
http://www.atics.info/
An ➔ **African Virtual University (2906)** initiative that aims to enhance Internet connectivity in Africa's tertiary sector. As part of its activities it conducted a survey of Internet connectivity needs in tertiary institutions across Africa, which was completed late in 2004 and for which 80 responses were received. Initial studies undertaken by various agencies had indicated that if a large group of African universities and other higher education and research institutions can club together to buy satellite bandwidth in bulk, very considerable cost savings could be made, and it was one of the objectives of the survey to discover African tertiary institution's needs, and their willingness to participate in a "bandwidth purchasing club". The full report (pdf, 11 pages) can be downloaded from this site, or you can view completed survey forms submitted by individual African tertiary institutions. Some other documents relating to ICT issues, Internet connectivity, and bandwidth optimization in Africa, can also be downloaded from this site. [09/09/05]

2866   ITU Digital Access Index
http://www.itu.int/newsroom/press_releases/2003/30.html
Part of the International Telecommunication Union's *World Telecommunications Development Report 2003*, this is a global ICT ranking report on the ability of 178 countries to exploit the digital revolution. The Digital Access Index (DAI) measures the overall ability of individuals in a country to access and use information and communication technology. It consists of eight variables organized into five categories. Each variable is converted to an indicator with a value between zero and one by dividing it by the maximum value or "goalpost". Each indicator is then weighted within its category and the resulting category index values are averaged to obtain the overall DAI value. Countries are classified into one of four digital access categories: high, upper, medium, and low. The Scandinavian countries (the highest is Sweden with a DAI rating of 0.85), together with Korea, the Netherlands, and Hong Kong dominate the top of the chart. Taiwan, Canada, the USA, the UK, and Switzerland also score highly. Most African countries dominate the bottom section of the table, although the Seychelles (0.54), Mauritius (0.50), South Africa (0.45), Botswana (0.43) do relatively well, as do Libya (0.42), Tunisia (0.41), Egypt (0.40)

Namibia (0.39), Cape Verde (0.39), and Algeria (0.37). Zimbabwe scores 0.29, but most other African countries are below the 0.20 level, e.g. Zambia 0.17, Ghana 0.16, Nigeria 0.15, or Senegal 0.14, while Mali (0.09), Burkina Faso (0.08), and Niger (0.04) make up the bottom three of the global table. [08/08/05]

Note: ITU Digital Access Index for later periods not available at press time.

2867   Nua.com Internet Surveys. How Many Online? Africa

http://www.nua.ie/surveys/how_many_online/africa.html

Nua.com is one of the world's leading analysts of Internet trends and statistics worldwide. Find out here how many people in Africa are online The site provides analysis by country showing the estimates on top (the most recent is December 2001), comparative figures for 2000, 1999, and 1998, the total number that are online, percentage of population, and the source for the analysis. Unfortunately there would not appear to have been any updates of these estimates, although more up-to-date (but less detailed) stats on Global Online Populations can be found at http://clickz.com/stats/web_worldwide/ including projections for 2006 and 2007. [13/10/05]

Communication initiatives and networking communities

2868   The Acacia Initiative

http://www.idrc.ca/acacia/

A project of the ➔ **International Development Research Centre (2442),** the Acacia Initiative is an international effort to empower sub-Saharan African communities with the ability to apply information and communication technologies to their own social and economic development. It is designed as an integrated program of research and development, and includes demonstration projects to address issues of applications, technology, infrastructure, policy and governance. The site includes a useful resources section of articles (freely accessible in their full-text versions) on ICT in Africa, although most articles relate to the 1999-2002 period, with the most recent published in May 2002. [14/10/05]

2869   African Information Society Initiative (AISI)

http://www.uneca.org/aisi/

Hosted by the ➔ **UN Economic Commission for Africa (2523),** AISI is an action framework to build Africa's information and communication network that aims to provide an enabling environment to facilitate the development of Africa's information society. The site provides details about AISI's activities, partners, programmes, and briefing papers. It also offers access to a number of discussion lists, including ➔ **Iconnect Africa (2861).** [14/10/05]

2870   African Network Information Centre (AfriNIC)

http://www.afrinic.net

AfriNIC is a non-government, not-for-profit, membership based organization based in Mauritius to serve the African Internet community. It is composed of network operators and Internet professionals from the whole African continent and is guided by self-governing principle. In April 2005 it became the 5th regional Internet

Registry, with the responsibility for assignment of Internet addresses within the continent. The Web site and the AfriNIC database provides access to a number of policy documents and resources. [09/09/05]

→ **African Virtual University (AVU)** *see* **2906**

2871   Bellanet
http://home.bellanet.org/index.php
RSS RSS feed http://blogs.bellanet.org/index.php?/feeds/index.rss (for Bellanet Blogs)
→ **Bellanet (2584)** works to assist development partners in the South and in the North improve their use of ICTs and knowledge to achieve their goals, and to connect with the global development community, thus leading to better policies, a more coordinated approach to development, and ultimately measurably greater impact. The Web site provides details about Bellanet's projects and activities, and at Bellanet Blogs the Bellanet Document Corner offers a collection of documents that relate to Bellanet's research activities. [14/10/05]

→ **Bioline International** *see* **9 Journals and magazines. Table of contents alterting services and other journal resources** entry **555**

2872   The Communication Initiative
http://www.comminit.com/
Advocates the importance of communication for sustainable development, and encourages dialogue and debate of key communication issues and programmes. It is an email and Web network of selected programmes, data, materials, people, and media sources from communication, development and change organizations. Also offers an informative newsletter, → **Soul Beat Africa (2882),** which seeks to cover the full range of communication for development activities. [14/10/05]

2873   Digital Dividend Clearinghouse
http://wriws1.digitaldividend.org/wri/app/index.jsp
Created by the → **World Resources Institute (2629)** in Washington DC, this Web resource is dedicated to exploring innovative business approaches, public-private partnerships, and other sustainable ways to bridge the global digital divide. The Clearinghouse serves as a repository for information and shared experience on digital and digitally enabled projects providing services to underserved populations in developing countries. A 'Project Finder' lets you follow your interests and navigate through the project database over 1,000 digital or digitally enabled projects, seeking a specific type of project to partner with or assist, or tracking activity in a particular sector or country. [14/10/05]

2874   Electronic Information for Libraries
http://www.eifl.net/index.html
Electronic Information for Libraries (eIFL) is an initiative of → **The Open Society Institute (2742),** a private grant-making and operating foundation that is part of the Soros Foundation network. It endeavours to lead, negotiate, support and advocate for the wide availability of electronic resources by library users in transition and developing countries, including those in Africa. Its main focus is on negotiating

affordable subscriptions on a multi-country consortia basis, while supporting the enhancement of emerging national library consortia in member countries. The core service of eIFL.net is the provision of access to commercially produced electronic journals and databases. The Web site also offers a useful "Consortium Basics Resource List", and access to current and past issues of an informative monthly newsletter. There is also a link to a *Directory of Open Access Journals* at http://www.doaj.org/, hosted and developed by the University of Lund Libraries in Sweden, currently (September 2005) including 1,748 journals, of which 421 are searchable at article level, and now consisting of a database of almost 77,000 articles. [09/09/05]

2875   ESAP Project: Electronic Supply of Academic Publications to and from Universities in Developing Regions
http://www.fiuc.org/esap/index2.php?page=esaphome
A project of the International Association of University Presidents in cooperation with the International Federation of Catholic Universities, ESAP aims to set up a sustainable electronic document delivery systems for scholarly publications between universities in the North and the South as well as on a South-South basis, and thus assist in the supply of academic publications to as well as from the developing world. In Africa the project has 10 participating universities. One of the aims of ESAP is to provide the participating African universities with a possibility to electronically publish their articles and reports on the Internet and thus to make their academic work known and available to the world. [15/10/05]

2876   Fahamu
http://www.fahamu.org.uk/
Fahamu (the Kiswahili word for 'understanding') seeks to exploit the developments in ICT to support the work of not-for-profit and other NGOs, and is committed to supporting progressive social change in the South through using information and communication technologies. The site features a rich links and resources section, and Fahamu also publishes a series of training manuals and courses, available online or on CD-ROM, including an excellent *Writing for Change,* designed for those in the not-for-profit sector to improve their writing and communication skills, and writing for advocacy, and thus more likely to stand a chance to influence others. [15/10/05]
See also ➔ **Pambazuka News,** section **10 News sources for Africa,** entry **858**

➔ **The Freedom Toaster** *see* **The Shuttleworth Foundation (2881)**

2877   International Institute for Communication and Development (IICD)
http://www.iicd.org/
Established in 1997 and financially supported by Dutch, British and Swiss donors, the International Institute for Communication and Development assists developing countries to realise locally owned sustainable development by harnessing the potential of information and communication technologies. IICD works with its partner organisations in selected countries, helping local stakeholders to assess the potential uses of ICTs in development. Its focus is on traditional development sectors, such as education, governance, health, livelihood opportunities (especially agriculture) and the environment. [15/10/05]

2878   Kabissa—Space for Change in Africa
http://www.kabissa.org/
Kabissa (meaning 'complete' in Kiswahili) uses technology to strengthen African non-profit organizations working to improve the lives of people in Africa. It provides Internet services for the African non-profit sector and NGOs, including free space, domain hosting, linking networks, organizing workshops, and by promoting capacity-building initiatives. The site is also a good source for news and information about ICT in Africa, and offers access to a bulletin board, learning resources, links to a very large number of member profiles (which can be browsed by sector, region, or country, or searched by keywords), as well as several publicly accessible mailing lists and e-newsletters. [15/10/05] *See also* ➔**Kabissa Mailing Lists (2862)**.

2879   SANGOnet
http://www.sangonet.org.za/
SANGONeT is a facilitator in the effective and empowering use of information and communication technology tools by development and social justice actors in Africa. It aims to share information, build capacity and link people and organizations through the use of ICTs. It publishes the excellent ➔ **PRODDER Directory (167).** [17/10/05]

2880   SchoolNet Namibia
http://www.schoolnet.na/
SchoolNet Namibia is an innovative initiative that provides Internet services, computers, and training for schools in Namibia, and which has had enjoyed considerable success in supplying and training people in open-source software. Since February 2000, close to 450 schools have received free hardware, free training on the OpenLab operating system and subsidized telephone service, to help get the nation's young people online and to empower youth through Internet access. [17/10/05]
See also ➔ **SchoolNet Africa/African Education Knowledge Warehouse (2845)**

2881   The Shuttleworth Foundation
http://www.tsf.org.za/
The Freedom Toaster
http://www.freedomtoaster.co.za/
Established by South African entrepreneur Mark Shuttleworh, the Foundation invests in projects which offer unique and innovative, albeit high-risk, solutions to educational challenges in an African society, focussing in the areas of science, technology, entrepreneurship and Maths (STEM) in education, and open source software. One of its projects is the Freedom Toaster, a vending-machine shaped, conveniently located, self-contained "Bring 'n Burn" facility, where users bring their own blank discs and make copies of any open source software they require. It takes its name from the open-source community's word for creating or burning a CD, known as "toasting". Through a simple touch screen interface, it offers access to open-source software with free licences for those who might have a computer but have no Internet access. It encapsulates the spirit of open source software: that everybody should have the freedom to choose which software they use, and the freedom to share it with anyone else, for free. There are currently Freedom Toasters in 14 South African cities, as well as one in Namibia. [08/10/05]

2882   Soul Beat Africa – Communication for Change
http://www.comminit.com/africa/
Soul Beat Africa, part of ➔ **The Communication Initiative (2872)** is an information-sharing Web site that aims to provide a forum for communicators across Africa to share experiences, materials, strategic thinking and events, and to engage in discussion and debate. The site is meant for all those interested in communication for change in Africa, and provides an opportunity for the experiences and issues of the continent to be shared and debated, while helping to strengthen communication for development. Content includes project and NGO presentations, materials and resources, events and training opportunities, awards and funding, as well as summaries of research documents, findings, reports and articles that facilitate strategic planning for development communication work. An Africa-specific e-newsletter (*see* ➔ entry **2863**), based on the information summarised on Soul Beat Africa, is offered free-of-charge. [20/07/05]

2883   UAICT- Africa Gateway
http://celi.lub.lu.se/cgi-bin/search.pl?form=simple
The Use and Application of ICT in Education and Information Provision in Africa (UAICT-Africa) project is a joint venture by 10 university libraries in southern Africa and the R&D department of Lund University Libraries in Sweden, and is financially supported by ➔ **Sida (2689)**. Using content contributed by the various university libraries, it aims to provide a comprehensive information resource and database on ICT use and application in education and information provision in sub-Saharan Africa. Thus far about 200 resources are accessible, with summaries and full-text, and browsable under two broad headings, Education (i.e. ICTs in Education, etc.) and Information and Libraries (including areas such as ICT projects, information literacy, information policy, information services, library technology, etc.) It was last updated in December 2003. [02/08/05]

2884   The WiderNet Project
http://www.widernet.org/
WiderNet.Org – a partnership between the University of Iowa and the University of Jos and University of Ibadan in Nigeria – aims to improve digital communication for people in developing countries and, in particular, help to build digital technical capacity at Nigerian universities through technical, financial and organizational coaching, and by providing faculty and students with access to computers, email facilities, and the Internet. The site provides details about the organization and its current projects. [17/10/05]

2885   The World Summit on the Information Society:
            Geneva, 10-12 December 2003/Tunis, 13-15 November Tunis 2005
http://www.itu.int/wsis/index.html (Main home page)
http://www.itu.int/wsis/documents/doc_multi.asp?lang=en&id=1161 | 1160
(Declaration of Principles and a Plan for Action)
The World Summit on the Information Society (WSIS) was organized under the auspices of the ➔ **United Nations (2529)**, in cooperation with other interested UN agencies, and with the International Telecommunication Union (ITU) taking a leading role. WSIS was held in two phases, the first phase of the summit took place in Geneva, hosted by the government of Switzerland, from December 10-12, 2003. It

addressed a broad range of themes and participants from 175 countries adopted a "Declaration of Principles and a Plan of Action"—a set of principles and rules of conduct aimed at establishing a more inclusive and equitable information society, supported with a plan of action that formulates operations proposals and concrete measures to be taken, so that people all over the world will benefit more equitably from the opportunities presented by the information society. The second phase of the World Summit took place in Tunis, hosted by the government of Tunisia, in November 2005. The Web site provides access to the report about the Tunis phase, preparatory documents submitted, statements and speeches during the summit, the complete list of speakers, and other documents. Among documents submitted for the Phase 2 summit, there is a report about the outcome of a WSIS Regional Conference, held in February 2005 in Accra in preparation for the Tunis meeting, which is at http://www.itu.int/wsis/docs2/regional/outcome-accra.html. [17/10/05; updated 28/12/05]

Some recent studies, reports and articles

Note: this listing is restricted to online articles and reports that are freely accessible. Articles in subscription-based scholarly journals are not included.

2886   Access to ICT in Sub-Saharan Africa, Civil Society and Governance
by Lishan Adam [November 2003]
http://www.ssrc.org/programs/itic/publications/knowledge_report/memos/ada
mmemo.pdf
Seeks to elaborate on a report submitted to the Social Science Research Council (SSRC) **Global Governance of Information and Communication Technologies: Implications for Transnational Civil Society Networking** by Seán Ó. Siochrú. (*see* ➔ **2894** below). Examines various perspectives of access to IT in Africa, the issue of the digital divide and access, regional cooperation and national ICT policies, and the civil society response to the challenges of access. The author argues that the role of trans-national civil society organizations and governance "should be seen within the context of national policies, the contribution of international cooperation to ICT development in Africa and the digital opportunities movement." [09/09/05]
Note: More response papers to the SSRC report can be found at
http://www.ssrc.org/programs/itic/governance_report/memos_gov.page.

2887   "African Journals Online: Improving Awareness and Access"
by Diana Rosenberg, *Learned Publishing*, vol. 15, January 2002: 51-57 freely available online at
http://taddeo.ingentaselect.com/vl=981465/cl=132/nw=1/rpsv/cgi-
bin/linker?ini=alpsp&reqidx=/cw/alpsp/09531513/v15n1/s7/p51
Describes the scope and development of INASP's ➔**African Journals Online (554)** project, a free service that provides online access to the tables of contents and abstracts of scholarly journals published in Africa, backed by a document delivery service. Greatly expanded in recent years to become a major showcase for African journal publishing, the article reviews the objectives of the expanded programme, its coverage and components, management, current usage, and the benefits to

participating journal publishers. It also examines aspects of the scheme's long-term sustainability, and draws attention to areas of African journal publishing that require improvement, notably journal management, marketing, and improvements in quality of content. The author concludes that it is equally important that "the profile of the journals and their value to scholarship in their own country must be raised and acknowledged" as a first step towards getting them better used and read. [17/10/05]

2888   Agence de la francophonie et la Communauté française de Belgique.
Cahiers du Rifal, **"Le traitement informatique des langues africaines".**
(Special issue, no. 23, November 2003)
http://www.rifal.org/cahiers_rifal/rifal23.pdf 109 pp. pdf
This informative special thematic issue of the *Cahiers du Rifal* (Résau international francophone d'aménagement linguistique) is devoted to data processing aspects of African languages. It contains eight papers, both of a more general or technical nature, as well as contributions on matters of orthography and other aspects of individual African languages, including Hausa, Kiwswahili, isiXhosa, Lingala, Malagasy, and Somali. [09/09/05]

2889   CODESRIA Conference on Electronic Publishing and Dissemination,
1st -2nd September 2004, Dakar, Senegal
http://www.codesria.org/Links/conferences/el_publ/elpubl_papers.htm
The papers from this CODESRIA conference offer a rich source of information about current thinking and analysis of the state of electronic publishing in Africa, the dissemination of African scholarship through digital media, the growth of open access journals, and the development of digital libraries. Papers (in English and French, all freely available in pdf or PowerPoint formats) are grouped under six major themes: Employing ICTs for the Advancement of Research; Access and Visibility of African Scholarship in the Digital Age; Electronic Theses and Dissertations: The Experiences and Opportunities; Digital Libraries: Rising to the Challenge, and Digitising for Academic Outreach, Quality Control and Social Policy. Among papers in English are:
Maria A. Beebe, "Impact of the ICT Revolution on the African Academic Landscape"; Andrew Offenburger and Christopher J. Lee, "The Challenges and Possibilities of New Media in African Scholarship: The Case of *Safundi* and US-South African Comparative Studies" (*see also* ➜ **833**); Margaret Crampton, "Online Access to the Research Output from and about Africa through Database Aggregation and Full Text Linking" (*see also* ➜ **217**); Segun Ogunleye, "Free Access and Reasonable Remuneration: Electronic Publishing and the Copyright Question"; Eve Gray, "Digital Publishing and Open Access for Social Science Research Dissemination: a Case Study"; Pippa Smart, "Access to African Journals: The African Journals Online (AJOL) Initiative"(*see also* ➜ **554**); Allison Möller, "The Rise of Open Access Journals: Their Viability and their Prospects for the African Scholarly Community"; Mary Materu-Behitsa, "The Database of African Theses and Dissertations (DATAD)" (*see also* ➜ **203**); Alexander Schunka, "Digitising Historical Information from Hand-Written Sources in Databases: Possible Solutions for Small-size Research Projects"; Marie-Louise Fendin, "Digital Libraries in the Nordic countries"; Titia van der Werf-Davelaar, "Connecting Africa: Under Construction"; Williams E. Nwagwu, "Options for Peer-Reviewing the Electronic Journal, Opportunities for the Participation of

Developing Countries' Scientists in Main Stream Science", and Manji Firoze, "Using ICTs for Social Justice in Africa". [09/09/05]

2890   Confronting the Digital Divide: An Interrogation of the African Initiatives at Bridging the Gap
by Y.Z. Ya'u [2002]
http://www.codesria.org/Links/conferences/Nepad/yau.pdf
Provides a critical examination of the initiatives by various organizations such as the
➔ **United Nations Economic Commission on Africa (2523)** to improve ICT development in Africa and help to bridge the digital divide. It assesses the level of implementation of these initiatives and projects, their impact and progress made to date, and what needs to be learned from these efforts to speedily bridge the digital gap. The author recognizes that ICTs have the potential to improve social and economic equality in Africa, but argues that it has not done so. "Instead, ICTs development is following the historical patterns of uneven development with the developing world being ICT poor." He states that a new kind of imperialism has emerged "based on the monopolization of knowledge through an unequal access to ICTs and the use of WTO instruments such as those relating to the protection of intellectual property rights", and that in this process new media multinational corporations control the news industry globally, and have acquired a knowledge and information monopoly. He concludes that "for the potentials of the ICTs to be translated into reality, the current paradigm must change. The current asymmetry has to be eliminated. But this can only be done if human beings rather than the market at the focus of development." [09/09/05]

2891   Digital Media and African Publishing
by Hans M. Zell *The Book & the Computer*, November 12, 2003
http://www.honco.net/os/index_0310.html
The digital age and innovations in printing and publishing technologies offer many opportunities and challenges for the African book professions. This article examines the problems faced in different aspects of African book culture and how technology might address them. It reports about a number of new ICT initiatives and partnerships, looks at the current (October 2003) use of the Web by the African book sector, the prospects of online publishing in Africa, the promise of print-on-demand and e-books, and the challenges that lie ahead. [09/09/05]

2892   E-journals: Developing Country Access Survey
by Pippa Smart, *INASP Newsletter*, no. 22, February 2003: 13
online http://www.inasp.info/newslet/feb03.html#14
Reports about a survey conducted in 2002 by the ➔**International Network for the Availability of Scientific Publications (2608)** to identify the interest in initiatives to promote and deliver information into the developing world. It highlighted a number of small publisher-specific programmes already in place, mostly associated with learned societies and society membership. It also drew attention to the complexities of the publishing environment, where involvement in any initiatives to promote readership are frequently dependent on other partnerships. The survey confirmed that there is a desire by publishers (both commercial and non-commercial) to make their content more visible and more available in the developing world. However, it also showed that there were some concerns about the costs to societies and

publishers. Collaborative, continent-wide initiatives were perceived as an opportunity to improve the reach into less developed countries, whilst reducing the burden on publishers. The complete INASP report can be found at http://www.inasp.info/pubs/survey.html. [17/10/05]

2893   Global Diffusion of the Internet IV: The Internet in Ghana
by William Foster, Seymour Goodman, Eric Osiakwan, and Adam Bernstein
Communications of AIS, vol. 13, article 38, June 2004
http://www.afridigital.net/downloads/GhanaGDI.pdf
An interesting article and case study published by the Association of Information Systems. It looks at the growth and development of the Internet in Ghana – one of the first countries in Sub-Saharan Africa to gain Internet access, although development has been slow recently after relative boom years from 1980-2000 – and how policy-makers are currently struggling with the question of how to fund telecommunications deployment in rural Ghana. It examines Internet diffusion in the country along six dimensions: pervasiveness, geographical dispersion, sectoral absorption, connectivity infrastructure, organizational infrastructure, and sophistication of use. The study concludes by suggesting ways the Ghanaian government can influence, and reinvigorate, the evolution of the Internet in Ghana. [09/09/05]

2894   Global Governance of Information and Communication Technologies: Implications for Transnational Civil Society Networking
by Seán Ó. Siochrú, November 2003
http://www.ssrc.org/programs/itic/governance_report/index.page
Sets out to examine whether governance processes and institutions hinder or constrain transnational civil society organizations in their use of ICT for networking purposes. The report focuses on the impact of governance on ICT access and use in so far as these are used by civil society organizations in their networking activities. It explores the constraints and the underlying trends, examines their impact on networking, and considers what might be done about it. [09/09/05]

2895   Information and Communication Technologies for Development in Africa
Volume 1: **Opportunities and Challenges for Community Development**
Edited by Ramata Molo Thioune
http://web.idrc.ca/en/ev-33000-201-1-DO_TOPIC.html (description)
http://web.idrc.ca/openebooks/001-2/ (free download as e-book)
(Print: CODESRIA/IDRC 2003 220 pp. $30.00)
Volume 2: **The Experience with Community Telecentres**
Edited by Florence Etta and Shiela Parvyn-Wamahiu
http://web.idrc.ca/en/ev-33004-201-1-DO_TOPIC.html (description)
http://web.idrc.ca/openebooks/006-3/ (free download as e-book)
(Print: CODESRIA/IDRC 2003 230 pp. $30.00)
Volume 3: **Networking Institutions of Learning -- SchoolNet**
Edited by Tina James
http://web.idrc.ca/en/ev-33006-201-1-DO_TOPIC.html (description)
http://web.idrc.ca/openebooks/008-x/ (free download as e-book)
(Print: CODESRIA/IDRC 2004, 294 pp. $30.00)

These are three important studies on the current status of ICTs in a development context in Africa. Jointly published by the ➜ International Development Research Centre /IDRC (2442) and the ➜ Council for the Development of Social Science Research in Africa/CODESRIA (2059) can be freely downloaded as e-books in their entirety. The executive summaries, individual chapters, conclusions, appendices, etc. can also be downloaded individually, and all three volumes are also available in French versions. Volume 1 looks at the introduction, adoption, and utilization of ICTs at the community level. In various contexts – geographical, technological, socioeconomic, cultural, and institutional – the book explores the questions of community participation. It looks at how communities in sub-Saharan Africa have reacted to the changes brought about by the introduction of these new ICTs and reviews both the opportunities and the challenges that ICTs present for community development. Volume 2 examines the setting, operations, and effects of community telecentres. It describes the telecentre experiences of a variety of local and often rural communities, exploring the management structures and mechanisms that have been established to support these telecentres. The book provides profiles of telecentre usage and discusses the potential and challenges of setting up and maintaining community telecentres in the context of poor information infrastructure and limited human capacity. Volume 3 documents the processes used, and institutions created, to bring computers and connectivity into schools, as a means of enhancing the use and integration of ICTs in teaching and learning. A range of project, administrative, and cultural settings are explored, as are a wide variety of technical solutions. [09/09/05]

2896   New Scenarios on Africa, African Studies and the Internet
by Peter Limb, *Mots Pluriel*, no. 18, August 2001
http://www.arts.uwa.edu.au/MotsPluriels/MP1801pl.html
Taking into account recent trends in publishing, new technologies, and developments in scholarly communication, the author reviews the many and diverse problems facing African scholars seeking to publish or communicate. It looks at the current (as at 2001) state of Internet connectivity in Africa, and examines how people are seeking to harness new technologies in the face of severe material limitations and other constraints. The author concludes that, with the spread of the Internet, economic and cultural domination of Africa by the West and transnational corporations is likely to remain a problem, and will even intensify. [17/10/05].

2897   Old Wine in New Wine Bottle: The Internet and the Techolonization of
Africa
by Bosah Ebo, *Mots Pluriel*, no. 20, February 2002
http://www.arts.uwa.edu.au/MotsPluriels/MP2002be.html
An interesting article (albeit now a bit dated), presenting a somewhat pessimistic view of the prospects of the Internet in Africa. The author concedes that digital communication technology has enormous potential to create sustainable national development for the countries in the South, but while the potential of the Internet shows exciting promise "the characteristics and tendencies of the technology as they have manifested tell a different story"; and that the Internet relies on technology that is much less accessible and much more expensive in Africa and other parts of the developing world than in the industrialized countries. The author is wary of some of the hype surrounding the Internet and its rapid growth, warns about the danger of "cyberimperialism", and questions whether Western corporations are digitizing

Africa to bring the continent into the new global economy or to create more markets for Western products and services. [17/10/05]

2898   Online Journals Feasibility Study
[No date indicated]
http://www.aaas.org/international/africa/oljreport/
The → **American Association for the Advancement of Science (2575)** Africa Project has had a long-standing interest in projects to improve information access for scientists in Africa. This feasibility study (no date is indicated when the study was conducted) addresses the technical issues of online access to journals, as the foundation for a future project to address the larger question of how African universities can formulate sustainable and effective information strategies. It involved a two-person team travelling to four African universities in order to test the downloading of articles from online journals, and to evaluate a range of technical and other factors that affect the overall feasibility of online journals accessibility. These pages provide a summary of the report, a closer look at the current status at each university, and the recommendations and conclusions. [17/10/05]

2899   Open Access Scholarly Communication in South Africa: A Role for National Information Policy in the National System of Innovation
by Jennifer A. De Beer, February 2005
http://eprints.rclis.org/archive/00003110/ (Abstract)
http://www.jenniferdebeer.net/research/DeBeerJenniferThesisMPhil2004.pdf (full text)
This thesis is structured around two core sections: a theoretical framework based in the literature, and an empirical study. Its aims are two-fold: to assess levels of awareness of and investment in open access modes of scholarly communication within defined scholarly communities; and to create a benchmark document of South Africa's involvement to date in various open access initiatives. While the author favours open access, she argues that the disparate and uncoordinated nature of open access in South Africa needs a policy intervention. The author recommends the amendment of the current statutory reporting mechanism – used by scholars to report and obtain publication rate subsidies – which would require that scholars make their research available via an open access mode of scholarly communication, and would also require scholars to report that they have done so. [10/08/05]

2900   Rowing Upstream. Snapshots of Pioneers in the Information Age in Africa
edited by Lisbeth A. Levey and Stacey Young, May 2002
http://www.piac.org/rowing_upstream/
Print version: Johannesburg: Sharp Sharp Media [48 Rothesay Avenue, Craighall Park 2196], 2002. 126 pp. with CD-ROM in pocket gratis on request
This site provides access to the full text of the book with the above name, that grew out of the work of the Project for Information Access and Connectivity (PIAC), established in 1997 in Nairobi with the support of the → **Ford Foundation (2733)** and the → **Rockefeller Foundation (2743)**. PIAC assisted grantees of the two foundations to enhance their ability to use email effectively, access and evaluate information on the Internet, disseminate African programmatic content, and strengthened African institutions with ICT capacity. The book is an attempt to celebrate the achievments of these institutions, and to "document some of the most salient lessons learned form

the experience of more than five years work undertaken." The book contains six chapers, together with a number of appendixes. Particularly useful, in the online version, is Appendix Two, which is an index, and provides links to, selected Web sites listed in the chapters. This an interesting account of the early development of email and the Internet in Africa. [17/10/05].

2901   Spam Issues in Developing Countries
by Suresh Ramasubramanian, 26 May 2005
Organisation for Economic Co-operation and Development/Organisation de Coopération et de Développement Economiques. Committee for Information, Computer and Communications Policy. Task Force on Spam
Document DSTI/CP/ICCP/SPAM(2005)6/FINAL
http://www.oecd.org/dataoecd/5/47/34935342.pdf
Spam and net abuse are bleeding the Internet economy in developing countries of scarce and costly bandwidth, and many countries are ill equipped to deal with these issues, both in terms of technical know-how, and money and equipment for ISPs to deal with it. This paper discusses the challenges faced by developing economies in fighting spam, with an emphasis on the issues facing Internet Service Providers. Beginning with a review of the economic and technical issues of spam, it goes on to suggest several technical and legislative solutions, backed by the education and empowerment of users, giving them access to secure computing resources, and making them more sensitized to net abuse issues. The paper thereafter goes on to examine what developing economies can do to combat spam on their own. [03/08/05]

2902   Telecentres in Libraries. Email Discussion 2004
http://www.bookaid.org/resources/downloads/Issue5_Transcript.PDF
An lively discussion among African librarians, ➔ **Book Aid International (2585)** staff, and others, which followed an article in BAI's *BookLinks* issue no. 5, 2004, http://www.bookaid.org/resources/downloads/BookLinks_5.pdf, "Tele-centres in Libraries: Increasing Access to Information for All" by Paul Zulu, Chief Librarian of the Zambia National Library Service. The subsequent discussion conducted by email looks at the challenges, constraints, costs, and problems associated with setting up telecentres in libraries across Africa – especially as an appropriate method of introducing ICTs in the rural community – and asks "how can libraries join the telecentre revolution." [09/09/05]

2903   Towards the Digital Library: Findings of an Investigation to Establish the Current Status of University Libraries in Africa
by Diana Rosenberg, July 2005
http://www.inasp.info/pubs/INASPdigitallib.pdf
(also available in print format, Oxford, INASP, 2005, 36 pp.)
Over the past fifteen years libraries worldwide have very substantially increased their holdings of electronic information and automated their operations, but within Africa digital development has been uneven. In 2004 ➔ the **International Network for the Availability of Scientific Publications (2608)** commissioned a survey of the current status of digital libraries in sub-Saharan anglophone Africa. The investigation aimed to provide an overview of the progress made in establishing digital libraries, explore the current priorities and plans of African university libraries, ascertain

which support interventions have worked best, and identify where and what support is required. [09/09/05]

2904   Workshop on International ICT Policies, 20-21 September 2004, Mbodiene (Senegal)
http://www.cipaco.org/article.php3?id_article=8&lang=en
A report (and some documents) about a workshop on international ICT policies for central and West Africa convened by the Centre for International ITC Policies Central and West Africa (CIPACO), designed to develop a strategy to increase African capacities for a better participation in international ICT decision-making. Some fifty ICT experts and institutions working in that field in West and central Africa participated in the workshop, from all sectors: private, public, civil society, and development partners. The workshop helped identify priority issues on which CIPACO will focus its future activities. [09/09/05]

Digital libraries

➔ *See also* **1 General online resources on Africa and African studies and the best starting points on the Web: Sources for e-books**

➔ **African Digital Library** *see* **1 General online resources on Africa and African studies and the best starting points on the Web** entry 18

2905   African Online Digital Library (AODL)
http://www.africandl.org/index.php
Developed by MATRIX, Michigan State University's humanities and technology research centre, in cooperation with the MSU ➔**African Studies Center (1710)** and in partnership research institutions in Africa, the goal of this online repository is to adopt the emerging best practices of the American digital library community and apply them in an African context. AODL aims to serve scholars and students conducting research and teaching about West and South Africa, while at the same time providing a model for creating and distributing a diverse array of materials in a region with very limited electronic connectivity. At this time (September 2005) material in seven thematic "galleries" can be browsed or searched: (1) a sampling of images held at the ➔ **Institute Fondamental d'Afrique Noire (1852)** in Dakar, the largest repository of francophone West African culture and civilization in Africa; (2) Phil Curtin collection, a gallery of images from years of fieldwork from Phillip Curtin's personal collection; (3) Collection Boubacar Barry, Professor of History at the University of Dakar, the leading figure in collecting and publishing historical materials on Futa Jalon; (4) selections from the extensive work in AIDS research and the history of medicine by the French scholar Charles Becker; (5) Fifty Photographs from "Passport to Paradise": Sufi Arts of Senegal and Beyond, based on an exhibition created by the Fowler Museum of Cultural History at the University of California, Los Angeles; (6) Mosques of Bondoukou, a series of sample photographs of some of the mosques of Bondoukou and its environs, capital of the pre-colonial state of Akan and part of the Asante empire, taken by art historian Ray Silverman in 1987; and (7) The History and Culture of Futa Toro, Senegal and Mauritania, a range of interviews

undertaken in the middle valley of the Senegal River by historian David Robinson during 1968 and 1969, which describe the emergence of the Islamic state Futa Toro in the 18th and 19th centuries, its varied fortunes, and eventual conquest by the French, and the Muslim culture for which it became known. [10/09/05]

2906   African Virtual University (AVU)
http://www.avu.org/
The objective of the AVU is to build capacity and support economic development by leveraging the power of modern telecommunications technology to provide high quality education and training programmes to students and professionals in Africa. Initially supported by (and run as a project of) the → **World Bank (2548),** it is now an independent inter-governmental organization based in Nairobi, with over 34 learning centres in 19 African countries. It works in collaboration with African universities to identify the most essential training programmes needed for Africa's development, and now offers undergraduate and postgraduate courses based on what are considered to be the priority needs of students and educational institutions at tertiary level. Certificate and diploma programmes are offered in specialist areas. [05/08/05]

2907   Aluka
http://www.ithaka.org/aluka/
Aluka is a project of → **Ithaka (2611),** a not-for-profit organization with a mission to accelerate the productive uses of information technologies for the benefit of higher education around the world. The word Aluka is based on the Zulu "to weave", reflecting Aluka's mission of digitally aggregating scholarly content from around the world, and to build and support a sustainable online database of scholarly resources from the developing world, beginning in Africa. One initial project will be an African Cultural Heritage Sites collection, designed to create a permanent record of African heritage sites and their cultural landscapes in digital form, which will consist of high-level computer visualization models, GIS mappings, and site-related materials for 10-20 sites. Among materials offered will be scholarly and scientific papers, excavation reports, research papers, cultural objects, nineteenth century ethnologies, etc. Content selection and digitization for the first three content areas in Africa is currently (September 2005) underway. By early 2006, it is expected that testing will begin on a beta version of the Web application with initial content from all three African collections. [04/09/05]

2908   eGranary Digital Library
http://www.widernet.org/digitalLibrary/
The eGranary Digital Library provides Internet resources off-line to institutions in Africa (and in other parts of the developing world) who either have no Internet connection, or, if they do, have such limited bandwidth that they cannot offer free Web browsing to the majority of their staff and students. Through a process of garnering permissions, copying Web sites and delivering them to Intranet Web servers inside eGranary's partner institutions, the project is able to deliver millions of documents that can be instantly accessed over local area networks. The project is supported by volunteer librarians and includes the collective contributions of hundreds of authors and publishers. [09/09/05]

24

Abbreviations and acronyms in African studies

The abbreviations and acronyms listed below include all the organizations, institutions, networks, associations, projects, press agencies, etc. listed in the *African Studies Companion*, plus those of some other bodies. Also included are a number of other acronyms commonly used in African and development studies. Acronyms for online databases and electronic information services are excluded, as are acronyms for names of journals.

The ➜ **Review of African Political Economy (774)** has a useful *ROAPE African Acronym Demystifier* at http://www.roape.org/acronym1.html, which identifies some lesser well known acronyms, and giving sources where referred to.

AAAS	American Association for the Advancement of Science
AACC	All Africa Conference of Churches
AALAE	African Association for Literacy and Adult Education
AAPAM	African Association for Public Administration and Management
AAPS	African Association of Political Science
AAPSO	Afro-Asian Peoples Solidarity Organization
AAS	African Academy of Sciences
AAU	Association of African Universities
AAWORD	Association of African Women for Research and Development
AAWS	Association of African Women Scholars
ABA	Association Belge des Africanistes
ABC	African Books Collective Ltd
ABIP	*African Books in Print*
ABN	Autorité du Bassin du Niger
ABP	Agence Bénin Presse
ABPR	*The African Book Publishing Record*
ACARTSOD	African Centre for Applied Research and Training in Development
ACAS	Association of Concerned Africa Scholars
ACASA	Arts Council of the African Studies Association
ACBF	African Capacity Building Foundation
ACCE	African Council for Communication Education
ACCT	Agence de coopération culturelle et technique
ACEA	Association Canadienne des études africaines
ACFID	Australian Council for International Development
ACGD	African Centre for Gender and Development
ACORD	Agency for Cooperation and Research in Development
ACP (1)	African, Caribbean and Pacific Countries Group of States (European Union – The Lomé Convention)
ACP (2)	Agence Congolaise de Presse

ADAF	Arbeitskreis der deutschen Afrika-Forschungs- und Dokumentationsstellen
ADB	African Development Bank
ADC	Austrian Development Corporation
ADEA	Association for the Development of African Education
ADF	African Development Fund
ADIAC	Agence d'Information d'Afrique Centrale
ADPF	Association pour la diffusion de la penseé française
AEA	Asociacion Española de Africanistas
AEC	African Economic Community
AEGIS	Africa-Europe Group for Interdisciplinary Studies in Social Sciences and Humanities
AEIDP	African Institute for Economic Development and Planning
AEJ	African Economics Journalists Forum
AEKW	African Education Knowledge Warehouse
AERC	African Economic Research Consortium
AFAA	Association of Africanist Anthropologists
AFD	Agence française de développement
AFEA	African Finance and Economic Association
AFESD	Arab Fund for Economic and Social Development
AFMF	Africa Free Media Foundation
AFREPREN	African Energy Policy Research Network
AFREXIMBANK	Africa Export-Import Bank
AFRICOM	Conseil Internationaldes Musées Africains/International Council of African Museums
AFRINIC	African Network Information Centre
AFRINUL	African Newspapers Union List
AFRISTATE	L'Observatoire Economique et Statistique d'Afrique Subsaharienne
AFRODAD	African Forum and Network on Debt and Development
AFSAAP	African Studies Association of Australasia and the Pacific
AGAG	Africa Grantmakers' Affinity Group
AGP	Agence Guinnée de Presse
AIC	Africa Information Centre (UK)
AID	Agency for International Development
AIEDP	African Institute for Economic Development and Planning
AIP	Agence Ivoirienne de Presse
AIM	Agência de Notícias. Agência de Informação de Moçambique
ALA	African Literature Association
ALADAA	Asociación Latinoamericana de Estudios de Asia y Africa
ALC	Africana Librarians Council
ALF	African Leadership Forum
ALTA	African Language Teachers Association
AMAP	Agence Malienne de Presse et de Publicité
AMI	Agence Mauritanienne d'Informations
AMREF	African Medical and Research Foundation
AMU	Arab Maghreb Union
ANC	African National Congress
ANGOP	Angola Press Agency/Agencia Angola Presse
ANP	Agence Nigerienne de Presse
ANSTI	African Network of Scientific and Technological Institutions
APAD	Association Euro-Africaine pour l'anthropologie du changement social et du développement

APAHS	Association for the Publication of African Historical Sources
APARC	African Presidential Archives and Research Center
APNET	African Publishers' Network
ABPRM	African Peer Review Mechanism
APS (1)	Algérie Presse Service
APS (2)	Agence de Presse Sénégalaise
ARB	*The Africa Review of Books* (Dakar)
ARCT	African Regional Centre for Technology
ARD	*African Research and Documentation*
AROB	*The African Review of Books* (Laverstock, UK)
ASA	African Studies Association (US)
ASAI	African Studies Association of Ireland
ASAUK	African Studies Association of the United Kingdom
ASC	African Studies Centre (Leiden)
ASFAS	Center for African Area Studies/Graduate School of Asian and African Area Studies (Kyoto)
ASICL	African Society of International and Comparative Law
ASWAD	Association for the Study of the Worldwide African Diaspora
ATICS	African Tertiary Institutions Connectivity Survey
ATOP	Agence Togolaise de Presse
ATP	Agence Tchadienne de Presse
ATRCW	African Training and Research Centre for Women
AU	African Union (formerly OAU)
AUF	Agence universitaire de la francophonie
AUPELF	Association des universités partiellement ou entièrement de langue française
AVU	African Virtual University
AWF	African Wildlife Foundation
BADEA	Banque Arabe pour le développement économique en Afrique
BAI	Book Aid International
BCEAO	Banque centrale des états de l'Afrique de l'Ouest
BLDS	British Library for Development Studies
BMZ	Bundesministerium für wirtschaftliche Zusammenarbeit und Entwicklung (Germany)
BOPA	Botswana Press Agency
BREDA	Bureau régional de l'UNESCO pour l'éducation en Afrique
CASAS	Centre of Advanced Studies for African Society (Rondebosch)
CAB	Commonwealth Agricultural Bureaux
CACEU	Central African Customs and Economic Union
CAFRAD	Centre africain de formation et de recherches administratives pour le développement
CAMNEWS	Cameroon News Agency/Agence Camnews
CAMP	Cooperative Africana Microform Project
CAS	Canadian Association of African Studies
CASAS	Centre of Advanced Studies for African Society (Rondebosch)
CBLT	Commission du Bassin du Lac Tchad
CCA	Corporate Council on Africa
CEA (1)	Centro d'Estudis Africans (Barcelona)
CEA (2)	Centro de Estudos Africanos (Lisbon)
CEA (3)	Centro de Estudos Africanos Universidade Eduardo Mondlane
CEA (4)	Centre d'études africaines arabes et asiatiques (Toulouse)
CEAMO	Centro de Estudios sobre Africa y Medio Oriente (Havanna)

CEAN	Centre d'étude d'afrique noire (Bordeaux)
CEAO	Centro de Estudos Afro-Orientais (Salvador-Bahia)
CEC	Coopération par l'education et la culture
CECI	Centre canadien d'étude et de coopération internationale/ Canadian Centre for International Studies and Cooperation
CEEA	Conseil européen des études africaines
CEIJPMA	Centre d'étude juridiques et politiques du monde africain (Université Paris 1)
CERPAC	Centre d'études et de recherches sur les pays du Commonwealth
CFA	Communauté financière africaine
CFR	Council on Foreign Relations
CGIAR	Consultative Group on International Agricultural Research
CICIBA	Centre international des civilisations Bantu
CIDA	Canadian International Development Agency
CIDAF	Centro de Información y Documentación Africanas (Madrid)
CIDEHUS/NESA	Centro Interdisciplinar de História, Culturas e Sociedades da Universidade de Évora Núcleo de Estudos Sobre África
CIIR	Catholic Institute for International Relations
CMEA	Council for Mutual Economic Assistance
CMENAS	Center for Middle Eastern and North African Studies (University of Michigan-Ann Arbor)
CODE	Canadian Organization for Development through Education
CODESRIA	Conseil pour le développement de la recherche en sciences sociales en Afrique/Council for the Development of Social Science Research in Africa
COMESA	Common Market for Eastern and Southern Africa
CPLP	Comunidade dos Paises de Lingua Portuguesa
CRA	Centre de recherches africaines (Université Paris 1)
CRDI	Centre de recherches pour le développement international
CREPAO	Centre de recherche et d'étude sur les pays d'afrique orientale (Pau)
CSI	civil society initative
CSO	civil society organization
CTA	Centre technique de coopération agricole et rurale/Technical Centre for Agricultural and Rural Cooperation ACP-EU
CWAAS	Centre for West Asian and African Studies (Jawaharlal Nehru University, Bombai)
CWAS	Centre of West African Studies (Birmingham)
DAC	Development Assistance Committee
DAFRIG	Deutsche-Afrikanische Gesellschaft
DANIDA	Danish International Development Assistance
DARC	Digital Africana Repositories Community
DEZA	Direktion für Entwicklung und Zusammenarbeit (Switzerland)
DIE	Deutsches Institut für Entwicklungspolitik
DIFD	Department for International Development (UK)
DSE	Deutsche Stiftung für Internationale Entwicklung
DÜI	Deutsches Übersee-Institut
DZI	Deutsches Zentralinstitut für soziale Fragen
EAC	East African Community
EBRD	European Bank for Reconstruction and Development
EC	European Community
ECA	Economic Commission for Africa

ECAS	European Council on African Studies (currently dormant)
ECOSOCC	Economic, Social and Cultural Council of the African Union
ECOWAS	Economic Community of West African States
EDF	European Development Fund
EED	Evangelischer Entwicklungsdienst
EFA	education for all
EHESS	Centre d'études africaines de l'Ecole des hautes etudes en sciences socials (Paris)
EIB	European Investment Bank
EIU	Economist Intelligence Unit
EMCCA	Economic and Monetary Community of Central Africa
ENA	Ethiopian News Agency
EPA	economic partnership agreement
ESAF	Enhanced Structural Adjustment Facility (IMF)
EU	European Union
FAO	Food and Agriculture Organization of the United Nations
FAWE	Forum for African Women Educationalists
FDI	foreign direct investment
FRELIMO	Mozambique Liberation Front
FTA	free trade area
GAMNA	Gambia News Agency
GATT	General Agreement on Tariffs and Trade
GBM	Global Book Marketing Ltd
GDP	gross domestic product
GNA	Ghana News Agency
GNP	Gross National Product
GTZ	Deutsche Gesellschaft für Technische Zusammenarbeit
HABITAT	United Nations Centre for Human Settlements
HELVETAS	Swiss Association for International Cooperation
HDI	human development index
HFA	health for all
HIPC	highly indebted poor countries
HIVOS	Humanist Institute for Cooperation with Developing Countries
HSRC	Human Sciences Research Council of South Africa
IAB	*International African Bibliography*
IAI	International African Institute
IAK	Institut für Afrika-Kunde (Hamburg)
IARS	Institute of African Research and Studies (Cairo)
IBRD	International Bank for Reconstruction and Development (World Bank)
ICAS	International Congress of African Studies
ICIPE	International Centre for Insect Physiology and Ecology
ICRAF	International Council for Research in Agroforestry
ICS	Institute of Commonwealth Studies (University of London)
ICT	information and communication technologies
IDA	International Development Association (World Bank)
IDBS	Intercollegiate Department of Black Studies, The Claremont Colleges
IDC	International Development Centre (University of Oxford)
IDEP	Institut africain pour le développement économique et de planification

IDP	internally displaced person
IDRC	International Development Research Centre
IDS (1)	Institute for Development Studies (University of Sussex)
IDS (2)	Institute for Development Studies (University of Nairobi)
IEA (1)	Institute of Economic Affairs (Accra)
IEA (2)	Institut d'etudes africaines d'Aix-en-Provence
IFAA	Institute for African Alternatives
IFAD	International Fund for Agricultural Development
IFAN	Institut fondamental de l'Afrique noire
IFAS	Institut für Afrikanische Sprachwissenschaften (Goethe-Universität Frankfurt am Main)
IFC	International Finance Corporation
IFRA	Institute Français de recherche en Afrique / French Institute for Research in Africa
IFS	International Foundation for Science
IGAD	Intergovernmental Authority on Development
IGCS	Institute of Global Cultural Studies (Binghamton University)
IIAR	International Institute for African Research
IICD	International Institute for Communication and Development
IIE	Institute of International Education
IICT	Instituto de Investigação Científica Tropical (IICT) (Lisbon)
IIED	International Institute for Environment and Development
IIEP	International Institute for Educational Planning
IITA	International Institute for Tropical Agriculture
IJNet	International Journalists' Network
ILCA	International Livestock Centre for Africa (now ILRI)
ILO	International Labour Office
ILRAD	International Laboratory for Research on Animal Diseases
ILRI	International Livestock Research Institute
IMF	International Monetary Fund
IMTEC	International Movements Towards Educational Change
INADES	Institut africain pour le développement économique et social (Abidjan)
INASP	International Network for the Availability of Scientific Publications
INHEA	International Network for Higher Education in Africa
IOC	Indian Ocean Commission
IPAO	Institut Panos Afrique de l'Ouest/The Panos Institute West Africa
IPS	Inter Press Service
IRA	International Reading Association
IRD	Institut de recherche pour le développement (formerly ORSTOM)
IRED	Innovations et réseaux pour le développement
IRM	Institut de Recherche sur le Maghreb Contemporain
ISAAS	Indian Society for Afro-Asian Studies
ISIC	International Standard Industrial Classification
ISMA	Institute for the Study of Mankind in Africa
IOUED	Institut Universitaire d'études du développement (Geneva)
IWAAS	Institute of West Asian and African Studies (Peking)
JANA	Al Jamahiriya News Agency
JASPA	Jobs and Skills Programme for Africa (ILO)
JETRO	Institute of Developing Economies (Chiba, Japan)
JICA	Japan International Cooperation Agency

KIT	Koninklijk Instituut voor de Tropen
KMMA	Koninklijk Museum voor Midden–Afrika/Royal Museum for Central Africa
KNA	Kenya News Agency
LAJP	Laboratoire d'anthropologie juridique de Paris (Université Paris 1)
LASO	Lusophone African Studies Organization
LC	Library of Congress
LDC	least developed countries
LENA	Lesotho News Agency
LINA	Liberia News Agency
LUCAS	Leeds University Centre for African Studies
MAAAS	Mid-America Alliance for African Studies
MALD	Mutations africaines dans la ongue durée (Université Paris 1)
MANA	Malawi News Agency
MANSA	Mande Studies Association
MAP	Maghreb Arabe Presse
MENA	Middle East News Agency
MIDA	Multilateral Investment Guarantee Agency
MISR	Makerere Institute of Social Research
MDG	millennium development goals
MS	Mellemfolkeligt Samvirke
NAI	Nordiska Afrikainstitutet/Nordic Africa Institute
NAMPA	Namibia Press Agency
NAN	News Agency of Nigeria
NCSA	National Consortium for Study in Africa
NEH	National Endowment for the Humanities
NEPAD	New Partnership for African Development
NGO	non-governmental organization
NIEO	new international economic order
NIIA	Nigerian Institute of International Affairs
NORAD	Norwegian Agency for Development Cooperation
NOVIP	Netherlands Organization for International Development Cooperation
NUFFIC	Netherlands Organization for International Cooperation in Higher Education
NVAS	Nederlandse Vereniging voor Afrika Studies/ Netherlands African Studies Association
OAU	Organization of African Unity (now African Union)
OCAM	Organisation commune africaine et mauricienne
OCHA	Office for the Coordination of Humanitarian Affairs
OCPA	Observatory of African Cultural Policies
ODA	Overseas Development Administration
ODI	Overseas Development Institute
ODS	United Nations Official Document System
OECD	Organization for Economic Cooperation and Development
OIC	Organization of the Islamic Conference
OPEC	Organisation of Petroleum Exporting Countries
ORINFOR	Office Rwandais d'Information
OSSREA	Organization for Social Science Research in Eastern and Southern Africa

OXFAM	Oxford Committee for Famine Relief
PAALAE	Pan African Association for Literacy and Adult Education
PACA	Pan-African Circle of Artists
PADIS	Pan African Documentation and Information System
PAID	Pan African Institute for Development
PANA	Pan African News Agency (now Panapress)
PAUST	Pan-African Union of Science and Technology
PAWA	Pan African Writers Association
PRO	Public Record Office (UK, now The National Archives)
PRS	poverty reduction strategy paper
PST	Press Services Tanzania Ltd
PTA	Preferential Trade Area for East and Southern Africa
REC	regional economic commission
RENAMO	Mozambique National Resistance
RSM	Robert S. McNamara Fellowship Program
ROSTA	Bureau régional de l'UNESCO pour la science et la technologie en Afrique
SACU	Southern African Customs Union
SADC	Southern African Development Community
SADCC	Southern African Development Coordination Conference
SAF	structural adjustment facility (IMF)
SAFA	Society of Africanist Archaeologists
SAG/SSEA	Schweizerische Afrika-Gesellschaft/ Société Suisse d'études africaines
SAIIA	South African Institute of International Affairs
SAIS	School of Advanced International Studies (Johns Hopkins University)
SAP (1)	structural adjustment programme
SAP (2)	Seychelles Agence Press
SAPA	South African Press Association
SARAP	South African Research and Archival Project
SAREC	Swedish Agency for Research Cooperation with Developing Countries (now part of SIDA)
SCOLMA	Standing Conference on Library Materials on Africa
SDA	Société des africanistes
SDR	special drawing rights (IMF)
SEDET	Groupe de recherche afrique noire et océan indien (Université Paris 7)
SHADYC	Laboratoire sociologie, histoire, anthropologie des dynamiques culturelles (Marseille)
SIDA	Swedish International Development Cooperation Agency
SLENA	Sierra Leone News Agency
SOAS	School of Oriental and African Studies (University of London)
SPLA	Sudan People's Liberation Army
SPLM	Sudan People's Liberation Movement
SSLM	Southern Sudan Liberation Movement
SPS	Saharan Press Service/Agence de Presse de la République Arabe Sahraouie Démocratique
SSA	Saharan Studies Association
SSRC	Social Science Research Council
STIC	Standard International Trade Classification
SUNA	Sudan News Agency

SWAPO	Southwest African People's Organization
TAP	Tunis Afrique Presse
TPLF	Tigrayan People's Liberation Front
UAICT	Use and Application of ICT in Education and Information Provision in Africa Project
UDEAC	Union douanière et économique de l'Afrique Centrale
UEMOA	Union économique et monétaire ouest-africaine
UMA	Union du Maghreb Arabe
UMAC	Central African Monetary Union
UN	United Nations
UNA	Uganda News Agency
UNCTAD	United Nations Conference on Trade and Development
UNDP	United Nations Development Programme
UNEP	United Nations Environment Programme
UNEP-ROA	United Nations Environment Programme, Regional Office for Africa
UNESCO	United Nations Educational, Scientific and Cultural Organization
UNFPA	United Nations Population Fund
UNHCR	United Nations High Commissioner for Refugees
UNICEF	United Nations Children's Fund
UNIDO	United Nations Industrial Development Organization
UNNDAF	New Agenda for the Development of Africa in the 1990s (UN)
UN-OHRLLS	United Nations Office of the High Representative for the Least Developed Countries, Landlocked Developing Countries, and Small Island Developing States
UNSO	United Nations Sudano-Sahelian Office
USAID	United States Agency for International Development
VAD	Vereinigung von Afrikanisten in Deutschland
VIDC	Vienna Institute of Development
VSO	Voluntary Services Overseas
WABD	West African Development Bank
WACC	World Association for Christian Communication
WAMP	West African Museums Programme
WAO	Washington Office on Africa
WARA	West African Research Association
WB	The World Bank
WCC	World Council of Churches
WFP	World Food Programme
WHO	World Health Organization
WIPO	World Intellectual Property Organization
WISER	Wits Institute for Social and Economic Research
WRI	World Resources Institute
WTO	World Trade Organization
ZANA	Zambia News Agency
ZIAF	Zentrum für interdisziplinäre Afrikaforschung (Johann Wolfgang Goethe-Universität Frankfurt am Main)
ZIANA	Zimbabwe Inter-Africa New Agency (now new ZIANA)

25

Using Google for African studies research: a guide to effective Web searching

Contents

Do you have any comments or suggestions?
Critical comments or suggestions about this guide are most welcome, especially from African studies scholars and Africana librarians. Please email these to Hans Zell at hanszell@hanszell.co.uk.

Introduction to the condensed and updated version

This a fully updated but much condensed version of a guide previously published as a pilot edition at http://www.hanszell.co.uk/google/. The pilot edition was published in September 2004, just after Google had become a public corporation and its shares began trading on the Nasdaq Stock Market on 19 August 2004.

The much longer pilot edition included a broad overview of Google and an examination of its extraordinary growth and popularity, its page ranking and indexing system (*see* http://www.google.com/technology/index.html), concerns about privacy issues, the matter of cookies, and the Google privacy policy (*see* http://www.google.com/privacy.html), while a chapter entitled "Google doesn't know it all" looked at Google as an 'answer machine' vs. library reference services. Additionally, the pilot edition contained a detailed analysis of Google Answers (*see* http://answers.google.com/answers/), and how it performed on African studies topics. The fairly extensive chapter on search strategies, and evaluating search results, is also not included here, but it can still be viewed at http://www.hanszell.co.uk/google/chapter5.shtml.

The pilot edition will remain freely accessible, but will not be updated any longer. A number of cross-references to information contained in the pilot edition are included in this condensed version.

The guide is designed to help the user get the most out of Google's Web searching techniques and at the same time provides a critical evaluation of Google's many Web search features, services and tools. The updated version now also devotes some space to a number of new Google services launched since publication of the pilot edition, → **Google Book Search/Google Books Library Project,** → **Google Earth,** and → **Google Scholar**.

However, it is difficult to keep up-to-date with Google, and in addition to the above Google has launched almost 20 new search offerings, tools, and free software since the pilot edition of this guide was published. They include, but are *not* examined here:

Google Base (Beta) – "put stuff on Google", a competitor to eBay? http://base.google.com/

Google Blog Search – search for blog posts, blog names, authors or a specific date range http://blogsearch.google.com/

Google Desktop/Google Desktop Search – an application that gives you easy access to information on your computer http://desktop.google.com/

Google Local – enter a particular location or post/ZIP code, and then conduct a search in whatever interests you http://local.google.com/, and also **Google Local UK** (Beta) http://local.google.co.uk/

Google Maps – part of Google Local above http://maps.google.com/, and also **Google UK Maps** http://maps.google.co.uk/

Google Mini – delivers results, in both Intranet and public site deployments
http://www.google.com/enterprise/mini/

Google News Feeds – part of ➜ **Google News**
http://news.google.com/intl/en_us/news_feed_terms.html

Google Pack – free collection of software http://pack.google.com

Google Personalized Search (Beta) – originally launched as Google–My Search History; enables users to add and customize their favourite content to their main Google.com page
http://www.google.com/psearch

Google Personalized for Mobile – to go with Google Personalized above
http://mobile.google.com/personalized/

Google Personalized Search: Trends – offers graphics and lists detailing your own search activities; to use Trends you need to have Personalized Search (see above) turned on and be signed in to your Google account http://www.google.com/psearch/trends

Google Reader – a Web-based feed reader, as a companion to go with Google News Feeds
http://www.reader.google.com

Google Suggest (Beta) – as you type into the search box Google Suggest guesses what you're typing and offers suggestions in real time
http://www.google.com/webhp?complete=1&hl=en;

Google Talk – Internet telephone programme and instant messaging system; requires Gmail username and password http://www.google.com/talk/;

Google Video/Google Video Search (Beta) – http://video.google.com/

Google Web Accelerator (Beta) – an application that uses the power of Google's global computer network to make Web pages load faster http://webaccelerator.google.com/

Picasa – freely downloadable software that helps you to find, organize, edit and share digital pictures on your PC http://picasa.google.com/index.html

Nowadays Google is in the news or makes headlines almost every day. The story that broke in late January 2006, that Google's new Chinese Internet server at http://www.google.cn/ would be subject to Chinese government censorship and block Web access to politically sensitive content – e.g. searches containing the words "Tibet", or "human rights", and even for words such as "democracy" – caused dismay not only among free speech advocates, human rights organizations, and Internet activists, but even among the most ardent Google enthusiasts.

As you do a search in the new, censored version of Google in China, you will find a message at the foot of the results page that translates something like this: "In accordance with local law, regulations, and government policies, a portion of search results are not shown." This censorship is hard to reconcile with Google's always high moral ground, its stated mission to provide all information to everyone, and make the world a better place. Some observers feel that, sadly, the Google of today is not the same company as it was only a very short while ago—the underdog and humble pre-flotation version of Google.

The company's motto is "Don't be evil", but censorship is apparently OK. Or, as John Lanchester has rather caustically put it in a recent article in *The Guardian* http://technology.guardian.co.uk/online/story/0,,1695167,00.html, perhaps its real motto is "Don't be evil except when there's serious money in it".

About this guide
While the guide is primarily intended for students, we hope post-graduate Africanist scholars, and Africana librarians, will also find it helpful. The guide is not meant to serve as a tutorial, and assumes that users have some basic experience in using search tools on the Web, nor does it cover the full range of Google's constantly expanding search services. It covers only those aspects that are relevant for academic research and, more specifically, for research on Africa and African studies, primarily in the humanities and the social sciences.

The guide is interspersed with examples of searches relating to Africa or African studies topics. Most searches for the examples shown were originally conducted during the period March to July 2004, but have now been updated for this condensed version, and the results re-evaluated (as at January/February 2006). However in terms of the number of links found, the search results at time of the publication of the 4th edition of the *African Studies Companion* are likely to be at least marginally different. Examples of search terms appear in *italic* typeface.

All cross-references to the various Google search services are hyperlinked in the online edition to facilitate quick navigation.

Google's limitations
Web search engines, and especially Google, can sometimes generate excellent results for the African studies researcher, and are now well recognized as significant research tools across all disciplines. Google can do simple or more advanced searches quickly, and can come up with remarkably good results. One downside of this is that some students, impressed by Google's capabilities and sophisticated search offerings, tend to think that the extent of their research need not go beyond clicking on to Google.

Nowadays most researchers will include the Web as part of a research strategy, but much will depend on the nature of the research. There are occasions when Google can do the job best, but while Google's search results can be a very helpful gateway and starting point for tracking down information, one must always be aware of its limitations. Google doesn't know it all, and any researcher must always apply careful critical judgment in the choice and evaluation of links to information and Internet resources which Google, or other Web search engines, are able to provide.

The first thing to remember is that, at this time at least, Google searches are limited to publicly available network resources on the Web and the "open Web", also called the "visible Web", and those it is allowed to search and index by arrangement with publishers (*see also* ➔ **Google Book Search** and ➔ **Google Scholar**). While Google lets you search freely accessible pages on the Web, including Word documents, the text (or at least part of the text) of most freely accessible PDF files, and files in other formats such as PowerPoint or Excel, the Google robots cannot reach, or are prevented from reaching – and are therefore unable to index – password-protected online resources and databases that are available only by subscription or under licence, and/or require registration before access is granted. Additionally, there are Web pages and databases, often containing high-quality and authoritative information, which search engines will not index for technical reasons or limitations of their Web crawlers, or will not add to their indices as a matter of deliberate policy. (For more information on this topic *see also* ➔ **Pilot edition, Google's page ranking and indexing system** http://www.hanszell.co.uk/google/chapter1.shtml#3.)

There are a vast number of valuable online information sources that are part of the "invisible Web" or also called the "deep Web". The BrightPlanet™ Corporation has published a listing of the 60 known, largest "deep Web" sites http://www.brightplanet.com/infocenter/largest_deepweb_sites.asp that contain data of about 750 terabytes, which amounts to roughly 40 times the size of the known surface of the Web. These sites appear in a broad array of domains, from science to law to images and commerce. BrightPlanet™ estimates the total number of records or documents within this group to be about 85 billion, and it is constantly growing.

This invisible Web includes not only a huge number of proprietary (fee-based) databases and online information services, but also numerous openly accessible government and public records in digital formats, statistical and image databases, archives of newspapers and magazines, digital library projects, as well as, for the most part freely accessible, content-rich databases from libraries and educational institutions around the globe. Although it is not specifically devoted to African studies resources, a useful launch pad for invisible Web research, and to discover the Web's hidden information sources that are not picked up by general-purpose search engines, is The Invisible Web at http://invisible-web.net.

For example, in the African studies field, Google does not index searchable databases such as David Bullwinkle's massive *Bibliography of Africana Periodical Literature Database*, which is part of his ➔ **Africabib (102)** Web resource, nor it does not cover indexing services such as the ➔ **Africana Conference Paper Index (394).** Moreover, as indicated above, any Web site or resource that requires a user name and/or password is out of bounds to search engine robots, and that includes a very large number of scholarly journals. Thus Google's ability to index articles in African studies periodicals is limited, although in the new ➔ **Google Book Search** and ➔ **Google Scholar** you will now be allowed to view *extracts* and *sample pages* from books and periodical articles, but not full-text, unless it is freely accessible as open source, or covers books in the public domain.

As another example: Google will have indexed the pages of the *African Studies Companion* that can be accessed for free, namely the preface, table of contents, and the Introduction, but not the listings and resources contained in the database itself, which require subscription access.

The second important point to remember is that although Google is clever, as are some other sophisticated search engines, none of them will interpret your question. Google says it believes in instant gratification: "You want answers and you want them right now" it says in its *Google Ten Things* credo http://www.google.com/corporate/tenthings.html. However, interpreting Google search results as "answers" could be fallacious and merely amount to a quick-fix solution. The fact is that Google will simply find the words or terms you are looking for on Web pages. The links it finds and the search results it generates are not the same as answers, much less authoritative and reliable answers, although it might eventually lead to answers or authoritative sources. But Google does not, and cannot be expected to, either interpret search or enhance the information it tracks down.

For some basic questions – for example, brief factual information and statistical data, current population figures, GDP, literacy rates, life expectancy, etc. – consulting an authoritative and current print or online resource may well be quicker than conducting a search in Google. It is therefore important to have at least broad knowledge of the major reference tools and information sources that are available in your university or college library, in both print and electronic formats. This includes the major current bibliographies and continuing sources, and the guides to sources (e.g. bibliographies of bibliographies, directories, encyclopaedias, handbooks, etc.), thus enabling you to quickly identify the most appropriate research tools for finding answers to your questions. There are annotated listings of some of these sources in Section ➜ **2 The major general reference tools** of the *African Studies Companion*, although they are restricted to general and multidisciplinary sources for the most part.

This could also apply, for example, when searching for basic information about African governments and government agencies – including current heads of state, ministers for the different government ministries, specialized agencies, etc – which can be quickly tracked down by using some of the online resources listed in Section ➜ **1 General online resources on Africa and African studies, and the best starting points on the Web**. Moreover, for more general lines of enquiry relating to African studies – for example, the major publishers, vendors, journals, libraries, associations, organizations, online forums, degree programmes, etc. – it will probably be quicker to consult the appropriate sections in either the print or online version of the *African Studies Companion*, or find information quickly on some of the best African studies gateways such as the Stanford ➜ **Africa South of the Sahara – Selected Internet Resources (69)** or the ➜ **Columbia University Libraries – African Studies Internet Resources (80)**.

Always remember there is life beyond Google: for any more complex research questions consult your reference or specialist subject librarians, who have the knowledge and skills to put you in the right direction, and they can facilitate access to authoritative and trusted sources both in print and digital formats.

And finally, while this guide focuses on Google, we must make it clear that we are not of course suggesting that African studies students and scholars should exclusively rely on Google for their Web search. Try to use other search engines on a regular basis; some of them are suggested in the section ➔ **Other search engines worth a try**. Test them with search queries, and compare their results with Google. If you want to run a comparison between what Google finds and what other search engines find, you can also use comparison tools, which include, for example, Grab All http://www.graball.com/, or the interesting Double Trust http://sushil01.securesites.net/~ashish/doubletrust/. Alternatively, run a search on a multi-search engine such as eZ2Find http://ez2find.com or Turbo Scout http://www.turboscout.com/, which will give you comparative search results from several leading search engines.

A word of caution: the nuisance of Web spam

Search engine optimization (SEO) is a perfectly legitimate practice used by Webmasters to improve a Web site's visibility, making it search engine-friendly, and thus boosting its position in search engine results. However, the rather less ethical SEO practice, that of search engine Web *spamming*, is unfortunately on the increase. Web spammers constantly find new tricks and techniques to influence page ranking, and to circumvent search engines' ranking algorithms and their efforts to protect the quality and integrity of their search services.

Web spamming – not to be confused with email spamming – is defined as the practice of manipulating Web pages for commercial ends, and introducing artificial text and links into Web pages in order to rank some Web pages higher than they would without manipulation. The activities of these unscrupulous spin doctors are not only a serious problem for Google and other search engines, but also a problem for users because they may not be alert to this. Google is well aware of the various deceptive tactics to try to trick its indexing and ranking system and is taking an aggressive attitude toward spam and the various dubious practices that are associated with it (*see also* http://www.google.com/webmasters/seo.html).

Web spamming inevitably raises questions of information reliability, and the trustworthiness, or otherwise, of search results. While spammers probably have little motivation to influence Web search results as it applies to African studies research, it can nevertheless be a serious nuisance. Most of all perhaps, it can be enormously time-wasting, in as far as Web spam may lead you up the garden path by making you click on to links that sound very promising and relevant but which turn out to be a complete waste of time. When you enter a query into the Google search box, some of the "results" you see may in fact turn out to be the result of putting the search terms into the search fields of databases (e.g. directories) on Web pages, because Google finds pages of relevant searchable databases, into which the search terms go. That's about as much as Google does, and can do, and it is only when you follow the link that you then see the result of the search in that database – which may or may not find anything relevant, or contain anything relevant. Therefore most of these search results are of no use whatsoever because Google is not finding the result of the search on the database it retrieves, it is simply finding a database that says it contains data related to the search terms entered.

Google's Web Search

Many of those seeking information through Google don't use it to maximum effect and make no attempt to improve their search techniques, or to gain a good grasp of Google's many features, how its search engine works, and how to use the different search operators to fine tune search queries. Many users of Google could significantly improve their search efforts and track down the information they seek by learning a bit more about the many simple and advanced strategies that Google offers to narrow or broaden searching and to refine search terms.

The tips and examples below, together with the checklists of the important points to bear in mind as you commence a search, will enable more effective Google Web searching, and help you find information more rapidly.

How to search with Google & the Google Toolbar

You can search with Google

(i)   from the Google home page at http://www.google.com.
(ii)   By making the Google search page your browser's home default page.
(iii) If you use Windows, via the Google Toolbar in Microsoft Internet Explorer (System requirements: Windows 98/ME/2000/XP; Internet Explorer 5.5 or later versions);
(iv)   If you use Macintosh OS X, via the Google Toolbar now compatible with Firefox 1.5, the free cross-platform Web browser developed by the Mozilla Foundation, (System requirements: Windows XP/2000 SP3+, Mac OS X 10.2+, or Red Hat Linux 8.0+; Firefox 1.0+, 1.5); or
(v)   via the integrated Google search box in Apple's Safari browser (*see also* the Macintosh Search Google service at http://gu.st/proj/SearchGoogle.service/).

You can download the Google Toolbar for Microsoft Internet Explorer for Windows at http://www.toolbar.google.com (the latest version, December 2005, is 3.0.128.1) and install it with or without its advanced features. A Firefox extension (the latest version, December 2005, is 1.0.20051104) can be downloaded at http://www.toolbar.google.com/firefox/. The Google Toolbar updates itself automatically, and so you never need to install a newer version as long as you use the Toolbar.

If you don't want to install the Google Toolbar, or if you don't use Internet Explorer or Safari and prefer other browsers (e.g. Mozilla, or Netscape 7.0 and higher), there are a number of alternative options. For example, the Mozilla browser has a built-in Googlebar at http://googlebar.mozdev.org. Mozilla's current release (version 0.9) emulates all of the basic search functionality of the Google Toolbar, allowing users to access easily almost all of Google's specialty searches from one toolbar.

The Google Toolbar is available in a number of languages (including Arabic, in a Beta version), *see* http://toolbar.google.com/. For more information generally, visit the Google Toolbar Help pages at http://www.google.com/support/toolbar?hl=en.

The Toolbar's advanced features give you access (i.e. extra search buttons) to other Google search services such as the → **Google Directory,** → **Google Groups,** → **Google Image Search,** → **Google News**, and the → **I'm feeling lucky** button; and you can use its highlighting and word-finding features to quickly locate terms within the pages of the search results. A useful feature is a Search History, which lets you repeat previous recent searches without having to type the words in again. (Please note that this will include search queries made on all Google search forms). Additionally, you can use the toolbar to block pop-up windows (including those irritating pop-up ads), but you can still view any pop-ups you want to see by holding down the Control (CTRL) key, and you can tell the Google blocker to allow pop-ups from particular sites. (Safari has its own pop-up blocker, independent from the Google Toolbar.) More recently Google has added WordTranslator and SpellCheck as extra features for the Google Toolbar.

The advanced functionality in the toolbar is optional, and by going to the Google Toolbar menu, selecting "Help", and then selecting "Privacy Information" you can disable it by deactivating the "Page Rank Display" features. With the advanced features disabled no information about the page you are viewing will be sent to Google unless you explicitly request more information about that page (such as with the "Cached Snapshot", "Backward Links" or "Similar Pages" features).

The Toolbar also displays the Google page ranking and page information features such as a "Translate Page into English". How many of the advanced features you want to include in the Toolbar is entirely up to you, and you can set your preferences in the Toolbar Options menu.

Setting your preferences

- On the Google Preferences page http://www.google.com/preferences you can customize your searching preferences, which can be adjusted at any time later on. All it takes is a click of the "Save Preferences" button each time you make changes – but you will need to remember that these are global preferences, applying across most of Google's services such as → **Google Groups,** → **Google News**, etc. (*Note*: setting or re-setting preferences will work only if cookies are enabled in the preferences in your browser.)

- *Interface language:* this relates to the language in which Google displays its search page, display tips, and buttons. The default is English, but you can select your preferred language for the Google interface. Google currently (January 2006) offers over 100 interface languages – including, tongue-in-cheek, "languages" such Bork Bork Bork! (ze language of ze Sweedish chef who puts ze cheeken in de oven in de Muppet show); Elmer Fudd (the cartoon character in Looney Tunes, who tells you to be vewy vewy quiet because he is hunting a wabbit); Klingon (the language of the aliens in Star

Trek), or Pig Latin (the language for adults who want to be daft, or the language choice of children who don't want their parents to know what they're talking about.)

- *African interface languages:* African interface languages for the Google home page (including buttons, display messages, and the Advanced Search page) currently offered (January 2006) are Afrikaans, Amharic, Lingala, Sesotho, Shona, Somali, Swahili, Tigrinya, Twi, Xhosa, Yoruba, and Zulu.

- *Search language:* not to be confused with ➜ *Interface language* above, restricts the languages that should be considered for searches (the default is "any language"). *See* ➜ **Language tools and local Google sites in African countries** below. Google currently (January 2006) supports 35 languages, including Arabic.

- *SafeSearch filtering:* blocks pages with explicit sexual content. The default is "Use moderate filtering" which blocks explicit images but not explicit language. Other choices are strict filtering or no filtering.

- *Number of results:* Google displays 10 results per page in default mode, and for more results you click on the results page 1, 2, 3, etc., at the foot of the page. However, if you expect a fairly large number of results this can be a bit tedious, and to increase the number of results for rapid scrolling click on Advanced Search, where you can increase them up to 100. While Google's default of 10 results per page provides the fastest results, if you prefer a larger number as default – and it won't take much longer to load, even if you are using a relatively slow dial-up connection – you can set this in the Google Preferences; or you can do so temporarily for a series of searches for which you want to see a larger number of results per page, and then later revert to the default setting.

  A setting of at least 50 results is recommended, as important and relevant results may well be found beyond the first 10 results. An additional problem with just viewing 10 results could be that search engine spammers, and others pursuing shady practices, may have muscled their way into the top 10 results due to aggressive search engine optimization, or manipulation rather, often relegating important and relevant results to lower positions (*see also* ➜ **A word of caution: the nuisance of Web spam**, and ➜ **Pilot edition, Google's page ranking and indexing system** http://www.hanszell.co.uk/google/chapter1.shtml#3).

- *Results window:* enabling this feature in Google Preferences will open the search results in a new window when clicked on. This can be useful, especially when conducting prolonged research, as it prevents you from losing your place, and it will always leave the Google window open to return to the search results.

Language tools and local Google sites in African countries
You can translate foreign-language pages into English using Google's "Translate this page" tool next to the search results. On Google's Language Tools page at http://www.google.com/language_tools?hl=en you can also translate entire pages, or parts of text, written in French, German, Italian, Portuguese and Spanish into English, or vice versa. Beta versions of machine translation programmes for (Simplified) Chinese, Japanese, and Korean are now also available.

Bear in mind, though, that this is translation by machine and you can't rely on it for accuracy. At best, it may be a passable translation; at worst, it may be only vaguely comprehensible, but will give you just about the gist of what appears on a foreign-language Web page. Relatively short phrases or sentences translate better on the whole, single word translations work very well for the most part, but translations of entire Web sites can be more comical than accurate.

From Google's Language Tools pages you can also visit Google local domains for individual countries: for Africa, in English or French, currently (January 2006) those in Burundi, Côte d'Ivoire, Democratic Republic of the Congo, Congo (Brazzaville), Djibouti, Egypt (this seems to be temporarily unavailable as at January 2006), The Gambia, Kenya (also offered in Kiswahili), Lesotho (also offered in IsiZulu), Malawi, Mauritius, Namibia (also offered in Afrikaans), Rwanda, Saint Helena, Seychelles, South Africa (also offered in Afrikaans, Sesotho, IsiZulu, and IsiXhosa), and Uganda. Keep in mind that if you use one of these local domains for searching, any preferences you will have set for the main Google.com domain will not be operative, as each local domain is configured separately.

Google and foreign language characters
Assuming you are using an English keyboard, and using Windows, searches in Google for terms containing special language characters such as German umlauts or French accents (diacritics) can be a bit cumbersome. Unlike in some other search engines, in Google, and until recently at least, a term with an accent does not necessarily match a term without one, or vice versa.

So, if you are a Windows user – Macintosh users are rather better served here, as accents are typed easily from the keyboard – you will need to copy and paste characters with accents into the search form (or enter them via the ALT key) etc., to find all relevant results. However, for the most comprehensive search, it is best to search with and without the diacritics if you want more than an exact match, or add the OR search operator (*see* ➜ **Using the OR operator** below).

Alternatively, if you are conducting a search consisting primarily of terms in, say, French and/or published in French-speaking countries, it may well be the best strategy, initially at least, to restrict your search to pages in French in Google Preferences (*see* ➜ **Setting your preferences**). At the completion of this search exercise you will need to remember to set them back to "any language" and press "Save Preferences".

However, the picture seems to be changing. While Google, in their general FAQ at http://www.google.com/help/faq.html#foreign_char, still states that its technology is sensitive to the precise spelling of foreign words, and that spelling the word correctly with the appropriate foreign characters will significantly improve the quality of search results as well as the number of hits, tests conducted in December 2005 would seem to contradict this. Several test searches with identical search terms, but searched with or without accents, generated search results that were not significantly different.

Similarly, for searches for European organizations or institutions, with or without foreign language characters, it doesn't seem to make much difference.

Some general points to bear in mind

- With its superior page ranking methods and criteria, and with its consistent cycle of Web crawling, a Google search will not only lead to sources of interest, but can also bring up links to unpublished material cited on Web pages, for example unpublished papers cited in academics' CVs.

- Google does not only search content, it can also become a launching pad to online Usenet newsgroups covered by ➔ **Google Groups**, where specialist questions might possibly be answered by someone with detailed knowledge of the field, albeit always with the proviso that the answers may not necessarily be reliable.

- Google presents your search results in order of relevance based on its Web crawling, indexing, and sophisticated page ranking techniques (*see also* ➔ **Pilot edition, Google's page ranking and indexing system** http://www.hanszell.co.uk/google/chapter1.shtml#3), which computes a score for each page, and which in turn is based on numerous factors and what Google calls metrics, i.e. a piece of information about a page. This includes, for example, where and how the search terms appear on a page and its prominence, the frequency with which your search terms appears on a page and factors such as word proximity, as well as more arcane metrics as they relate to information retrieval and analysis. To compute a score for a page Google says that it combines more than a hundred metrics in order to determine page rank.

- What Google considers to be the most relevant result will be shown as search result no. 1, and at the top of the page it shows how many results it has found. In default mode it gives you ten results per page. You can browse through the search results ten results at a time and then hit the > next at the foot of the page, but it may be quicker to click on the Advanced Search menu and change the number of search results to a larger number which can then be scrolled more rapidly. (Or you can adjust it in the Preferences, *see* ➔ **Setting your preferences:** *Number of results*).

- Number of results you can view: although Google can report tens of thousands or millions of hits for many search queries, the number of results it displays, and which you can actually view for any query, is usually a maximum of 800-900 as, in practice, few people will scroll through more than the first few pages of results. However, if you click on to "Search within results" at the foot of the results page, it will open a new search form which allows you to search *within* the total number of results reported.

It should also be noted in this connection that the number of results for identical queries are very rarely exactly the same each time they are keyed into the Google search box, even on the same day. Sometimes there will be relatively insignificant temporary variations in the search results (as well as page rankings), but occasionally there can be startlingly different number of results over a matter of just a few days. This is due to Google's use of different data centres that it searches. Google has over 100,000 computers in data centres throughout the world. Normally the search request is processed by a server geographically closest to the origin of the request, but if a server is down, or overloaded, Google will redirect your query to another data centre. Thus, when a search query switches between data centres you will be seeing a different cache of the Web, and the results may vary considerably, although it is nothing to be unduly concerned about.

▪ File size: on the search results Google shows the file size of the text portion of the Web pages it has found for the search, which sometimes can be a useful indicator of content. It is important to note, however, that Google only indexes the first 101kb of text on a Web page (and the first 120kb of pdf files).

▪ Cache: each Google search results page offers links to the latest cached version as part of the search, and, additionally, it gives you an option to view the cached page showing only text, without images. The cached version is an exact replica of the page when it was last indexed by Google. For some African-based Web sites suffering from poor server performance, clicking on to the cached link instead of the title link can sometimes be a quicker way to access such sites.

Important points to remember – and the dos and the don'ts

▪ Much will depend on how you choose your search terms, which will determine which pages will appear in the result, and the order in which they appear. Imagine what result you want, and search for words that are likely to appear on the pages you want, not for a description of the page, or the Web site, unless you want to track down names of Web sites that contain precisely the same words as your search terms (*see* ➔ **intitle:** search).

▪ Try to pick words that are unique to the topic you are investigating, and construct your query as precisely as possible. Try to visualize how answers to your search query might be expressed on Web pages.

- For example, a good approach is to try to think of search terms that are specific or unique enough to avoid your being inundated with too many irrelevant results, but at the same time that are broad enough not to miss anything that might be useful and relevant to the enquiry.

- While using search terms that are unique, i.e. that relate only to the specific topic of the search, may not be practical in many cases, narrowing the search to an exact phrase (or part of a phrase) that might appear in the pages or documents you're searching for could lead to more satisfactory results (*see* ➔ **Using quotation marks below**).

- Experiment by using search terms with or without quotation marks, and refine your searches by using alternative search terms that are either more or less specific.

- Always bear in mind that Google may not be able to differentiate between words that have multiple meanings.

- Don't use questions as search queries, as you might do for some other search engines, such as Ask Jeeves.

- For the most part, it is prudent to avoid search terms describing the form in which you want information, e.g. "papers on", "articles about", "discussion of", etc.

- Google lets you search for up to a maximum of 32 words; until recently it was only 10 words, but the 32 words limit now also includes the advanced search commands in any query (*see* ➔ **Advanced Search & Google search operators** below). However for better results confine your search to a few precise terms.

- Bear in mind that Google's Boolean default is AND. This means that if you enter multiple search words without modifiers such as OR – what Google calls search operators (*see* ➔ **Advanced Search & Google search operators** below) – it will search and display results for pages matching *all* the search terms appearing somewhere on a page.

- Google ignores certain common words that appear in virtually every Web page, such as "a", "about", "an", "are", "at" "by", "from", "I", "in", "of", "that", "the", "this", "to", "what", "when", "where", "who" or "will", etc., which it calls stop words. If you are looking for something specific that contains a stop word put the search terms in quotation marks (*see* ➔ **Using quotation marks** below), which tells Google to treat them as one unit.

- Google is not case sensitive, i.e. it does not distinguish between CAPITAL and lower-case letters in search terms (except for the OR operator, *see* ➔ **Using the OR operator** below): it assumes that all your search terms are lower case. However, if by force of habit you key in certain words in both upper and lower case (e.g. "African Studies" vs. "african studies") it won't affect the search results.

- Google ignores most punctuation in a search query except for apostrophes, and the double quotation marks used as Google search operators. Hyphenation is not important and it will find the words with or without hyphens.

- It will search for some characters, e.g. the ampersand &, and has recently started searching for the Dollar $ sign when it precedes a number. It can also search for a range of numbers (with or without commas), and number searches can be combined with other search terms.

- Singular vs. plural form: Google will search for either the singular or plural form of search terms you enter. However, it is not always entirely consistent, and may in fact search for singular/plural variants without telling you. This is probably the result of its stemming (word variations) technology, which means it will search not only for your search terms but also for words that are similar to some or all of them. Overall, it is probably better to use the singular form, but if in doubt use both, or conduct separate searches for each form.

Other factors to consider

- *Search term order and proximity:* the search term order for multi-term queries can affect results. Google tends to retrieve the results of the search by listing pages containing the search terms in the same order as they appear in your search query. It also considers the proximity of search terms within a page, and will favour results that have your search terms near to each other on the Web pages it finds.

- *Multiple results:* when you look at your search results you will notice that some results are indented. Google does this because many sites would produce thousands of occurrences of a search term, and so, instead of attempting to display them all, Google shows only the first two from each site. It adds a link that offers "More results from ..." that site; click this to see all the results from that particular site.

- *First 50 results:* be mindful that if the first three or four pages of 10 results, or the first page of 50 results, don't show very satisfactory results, the chances of turning up anything relevant and worthwhile on subsequent pages are probably not very good, and it is better that you refine your query using some of the special Google search operators (*see* ➔ **Advanced Search & Google search operators**) discussed below.

- *Millions of results*: if Google reports millions of results – which it does very frequently – and if you can't find relevant information on the first 50-100 search results, refine your search with more focused search terms.

- *Wildcards:* Google supports a wildcard word – using an asterisk [*] sign – inserted into a phrase, or what they call "stemming" (to mean anything) in other computer programmes. The wildcard will act as substitutes for any whole word you don't know – for example, in a book title, quotations or poetry – but not as a stand-in for part of a word. You can also use two or more asterisks [**] to signify two or more missing words, but you must be careful to include enough words in the phrase or quotation to find unique results, e.g. *"why the chicken ***"*.

- *Accuracy of spelling:* there may be occasions when you are not sure of the correct spelling (especially of proper names), or when you make a mistake typing in the words. If Google can't find a precise match for the spelling you provided and thinks you have misspelled it, it may offer a suggestion for an alternative spelling, "Did you mean …", which will appear at the top of the search results page. Bear in mind, though, that if the names are actually spelt incorrectly on Web pages, Google will of course show those results. Google can also get it wrong if enough people misspell the word on the Web!

I'm feeling lucky search

If you click this search method or button (which you will need to activate under Options if you are using the Google Toolbar) it will lead you to the page of the first search result, i.e. the page that Google considers most relevant. It won't actually show a search result, but it will take you straight to the relevant home page, if a home page exists.

"I'm feeling lucky" is quite useful if you know the precise name of an organization, institution, library, company or association, etc.

Examples:
The search terms
african studies association
will lead you direct to the [US] African Studies Association's home page at http://www.africanstudies.org/, although it finds it just as easily in ordinary search mode where it comes up as the first result of over 29 million hits, picking up other occurrences of "African", "studies" and "association".

Exactly the same happens, for example, for
african literature association
african studies companion
or *africa confidential.*

It is slightly different, for example for
journal of modern african studies
for which the first search result shows the ➔ **JSTOR (558)** page for the archived issues of the journal, and the second result the Cambridge University Press's pages devoted to this journal. Similarly, "I'm feeling lucky" also leads to the JSTOR pages because it is the top result in regular Web search mode.

Two further examples:
university of florida libraries
"I'm feeling lucky" sends you straight to the home page at
http://web.uflib.ufl.edu/, while ordinary Google Web Search also shows it as result no. 1.

scarecrow press
will lead you direct to the home page of this North American publisher at http://www.scarecrowpress.com/, and which, again, is also the first result in regular search mode.

If you are fairly certain that a Web site does exist for an organization or institution, and that the name is spelt correctly in your search, "I'm feeling lucky" is pretty dependable on the whole.

university of ibadan
or
university ibadan
comes up as the first result in the search results, or takes you directly to the University of Ibadan Web site if you hit "I'm feeling lucky".

Another example:
Want to go straight to the top? Entering the words
president sierra leone
will take you to the Sierra Leone State House site and the Office of the President of Sierra Leone Ahmad Tejan Kabbah http://www.statehouse-sl.org/; while
president kenya
will lead you to the Web site of the Office of the President of Kenya, Mwai Kibaki, at http://www.officeofthepresident.go.ke/, although I haven't tested to see whether this works equally well for the presidents of all African countries!

Advanced Search & Google search operators

Below I set out some of the many Google search operators and how they work. However, it is not really essential to learn them by heart. All you need to do is to click on to Google's Advanced Search page. This brings up a form with drop-down menu choices for most types of advanced searches. Thus even the novice Web searcher can perform quite complex searches without the need to acquire Boolean search skills. From the Advanced Search page you can also restrict results to specific languages, domains, file formats, and more (*see* ➔ **Additional commands and special syntaxes** below). Moreover, you can mix advanced search operators and word filters for a single query, e.g. you can type in search terms in four advanced search fields, (i) with "all the words", (ii) with the "exact phrase", (iii) with "at least one of the words", or (iv) "without" the words.

First, a word about search term order and word proximity:

As indicated earlier under ➔ **Other factors to consider** above, Google says that word order can affect multi-term queries, and that the order in which the terms are typed will affect the search results. Unfortunately, it doesn't tell you how to formulate a search query to take advantage of this fact. However, for searches containing both geographic terms (e.g. the name of an African country) and subject/topic terms, it doesn't seem to make a significant difference, certainly not for the first 50 results.

Example:
sierra leone women rights legal status
finds 454,000 results (using the apostrophe, i.e. *sierra leone women's rights legal status*, displays the same number of results).

Rearranging this query as:
women rights legal status sierra leone
generates an almost identical 455,000 results, with generally good and almost the same results for the first 50 as in the above example. However, the first 100 results for the search term order that puts the country first, might be regarded as marginally better results.

Adding special search operators (see below), e.g.
"sierra leone" women rights legal status
doesn't lead to significantly different, or more relevant, results for the first 50 or so.

Using quotation marks
Using quotation marks can be one of the most effective ways to find very specific information, and can drastically reduce the total number of results. Enclosing your search term(s) within double quotation marks tells Google to treat your query as one unit, and for such searches it includes the stop words (*see* ➔ **Important points to remember – and the dos and the don'ts** above). Google calls this "exact phrase search", and you can also select this option in Google's Advanced Search menu.

It is especially useful when some of the words are relatively common – such as "Africa", "African", names of countries, persons, etc. – when you might be deluged with hundreds, thousands, or even hundreds of thousands of results without much relevance to your enquiry.

Examples:
african studies companion 1,670,000 results
"african studies companion" 606 results
"african studies companion" site:uk 88 results, *see also* ➔ **site:**[followed by domain] below.

african books collective 4,580,000 results
"african books collective" 44,000 results
The search without quotation marks retrieves similar results in the first 200 or so to those of the search enclosing the words in quotation marks. However, the latter search option, in double quotation marks, almost exclusively limits it to results which

contain references to press notices and articles about African Books Collective, book titles and directory listings, and cataloguing information in library online catalogues etc., specifically relating to this Oxford-based distributor of African publishers' books, although the actual number of search results you can view only amounts to about 600.

Using quotation marks is very useful in tracking down titles of specific books, articles or documents – whether it is the books or the articles themselves, comment and criticism about them, or book reviews. It can be equally successful when searching for names of individuals.

For example, searching for the title of the winner of the African Studies Association's 2003 Melville J. Herskovits Award, Joseph Inikori's
"africans in the industrial revolution in England"
will lead you straight to over 700 references to this title, including the publisher's online catalogue page for the book, listings of the book in online bookstores, online reviews, and more. Below are Google's first 10 search results: (here reproduced in black and white only)

Africans and the Industrial Revolution in England: A Study in ...
Joseph E. Inikori, **Africans and the Industrial Revolution in England**: A Study in International Trade and Economic Development. ...
www.eh.net/bookreviews/library/0692.shtml - 13k - Cached - Similar pages

OPE-L message, **Africans and the Industrial Revolution in England** ...
Africans and the Industrial Revolution in England: A Study in International Trade and Economic Development. To: OPE-L@xxxxxxxxxxxxxxxx; Subject: **Africans** ...
archives.econ.utah.edu/ archives/ope-l/2003m10/msg00022.htm - 8k - Cached - Similar pages

OPE-L message, The Philosophy of Keynes' Economics
Prev by Date: (OPE-L) Centro Sraffa Fellowships; Next by Date: **Africans and the Industrial Revolution in England**: A Study in International Trade and ...
archives.econ.utah.edu/ archives/ope-l/2003m10/msg00021.htm - 7k - Cached - Similar pages

Amazon.com: **Africans and the Industrial Revolution in England** : A ...
Amazon.com: **Africans and the Industrial Revolution in England** : A Study in International Trade and Economic Development: Books: Joseph E. Inikori by Joseph ...
www.amazon.com/exec/obidos/ tg/detail/-/0521010799?v=glance - 80k - Cached - Similar pages

Amazon.com: The Industrial Revolution in England (Historical ...
Africans and the Industrial Revolution in England : A Study in International Trade and Economic Development by Joseph E. Inikori on 4 pages ...
www.amazon.com/exec/obidos/ tg/detail/-/0852781636?v=glance - 47k - Cached - Similar pages
[More results from www.amazon.com]

Africans and the Industrial Revolution in England - Cambridge ...
Home > Catalogue > **Africans and the Industrial Revolution in England**. **Africans and the Industrial Revolution in England** ...
www.cambridge.org/uk/catalogue/ catalogue.asp?isbn=0521811937 - 11k - Cached - Similar pages

Africans and the Industrial Revolution in England - Cambridge ...
"Joseph Inikori's **Africans and the Industrial Revolution in England**: A Study in International Trade and Economic Development is destined to become a classic ...
www.cambridge.org/us/catalogue/ catalogue.asp?isbn=0521010799 - 12k - Cached - Similar pages
[More results from www.cambridge.org]

Inikori, Joseph E.; Inikori, JE: **Africans and the Industrial ...**
Africans and the Industrial Revolution in England: A Study in International Trade and Economic Development. Our Price: $95.00. Click here to add this book ...
www.forbesbookclub.com/bookpage.asp?prod_cd=IS73N - 15k - 23 Jan 2006 - Cached - Similar pages

Search Forbes.com Book Club
Africans and the Industrial Revolution in England: A Study in International Trade and Economic Development · **Africans and the Industrial Revolution in ...**
www.forbesbookclub.com/ SearchResults.asp?ProdCat=BUS035000 - 50k - 22 Jan 2006 - Cached - Similar pages

Albion: **Africans And the Industrial Revolution in England**: A Study ...
Access the article, **'Africans And the Industrial Revolution in England**: A Study in International Trade and Economic Development.(Reviews of Books)(Book ...
www.findarticles.com/p/articles/ mi_hb005/is_200403/ai_n13025491 - 24k - Cached - Similar pages

Using quotation marks also works well for finding extracts from published works, or from articles and speeches; for example, this passage from Kwame Nkrumah's *Neo-Colonialism: The Last Stage of Imperialism*
"unity is the first requisite for destroying neo-colonialism"
finds

Neo-Colonialism, the Last Stage of imperialism by Kwame Nkrumah
Quite obviously, therefore, **unity is the first requisite for destroying neo-colonialism**. Primary and basic is the need for an all-union government on the
...
www.marxists.org/subject/ africa/nkrumah/neo-colonialism/ch01.htm - 35k - Cached - Similar pages

You can also guess a phrase. For example
"the literacy rate in tanzania"
will generate 13 results with that precise phrase, although an ordinary Google Web

Search for just
literacy rate tanzania

would provide better results, of which the first 50-100 results at least are all very relevant, the first being the UNDP Globalis site:

Globalis - an interactive world map - **Tanzania** - Adult illiteracy
Description:, Adult illiteracy (**rates** for adults above 15 years of age) reflects
... Education - Secondary enrolment, male, Education - Youth **literacy rate** ...
globalis.gvu.unu.edu/indicator_ detail.cfm?IndicatorID=27&Country=TZ - 36k -
Cached - Similar pages

The use of quotation marks often works well for tracking down the meaning and origin of (African) proverbs or quotations. For example, a search for
"only a fool tests the depth of the water with both feet"
displays 411 results, albeit not necessarily offering conclusive answers, and most of the results lead to databases of proverbs or famous quotations, with little detail about the original source or contemporary usage, with conflicting attributions as to the proverb's origin, and with some quite different interpretations of its meaning. However, scrolling down the search results will eventually get you to one or two more helpful sites that explain that this is an Ashanti (Ghana) proverb, and some sites also helpfully draw attention to books and other sources on Ashanti proverbs.

It might be added that, comically, the Google AdWord "Sponsored links" for these search results showed small ads for water-monitoring equipment, "find, compare & contact suppliers", or advertising "Test your drinking water" water safe test kits!

Another example:
"when elephants fight it is the grass that gets trampled"
or in other versions: "When elephants fight, it is the grass that suffers"; "When elephants jostle, what gets hurt is the grass"; "When elephants fight the grass gets hurt"; or, in Kiswahili, "Wapiganapo tembo nyasi huumia".

Some sites attribute this to the late Tanzanian president Julius Nyerere (who used the proverb in a speech at the United Nations in New York at the height of the Cold War); others cite it as an "African", Kiswahili or Kirundi proverb.

The search results for this example, too, again take a bit of scrolling until one comes to one result from the African Proverbs, Sayings and Stories site at http://www.afriprov.org/resources/explain2001.htm, which offers helpful information about the background of the proverb, its everyday use, and its different versions in other African languages.

However, in both the above examples the search was of course simply for occurrences of the proverbs, rather than Web pages describing their origin and meaning. Thus truncating the proverb to the first seven words and adding two search terms
"when elephants fight it is the grass" origin meaning

could conceivably lead to better results, although in this particular case it does not, and this search comes up with just 48 results, of which only a small proportion are directly relevant.

Repeating the same search, but without the quotation marks and leaving out the stop words (*see* ➔ **Important points to remember – and the dos and the don'ts**)
when elephants fight grass meaning origin
actually retrieves marginally better results, although it will again require some scrolling, and only the first 40 or so results are relevant.

Quotation marks are also very useful in tracking down Internet references to individuals, and can frequently assist in finding the addresses, and especially email addresses, of African studies scholars at their residential or university addresses, or in finding the current addresses of African writers and artists.

For example, a search for the name of the author of the *African Studies Companion*
hans zell
finds 529,000 results, but these include all the references to books published by Hans Zell Publishers, Hans M. Zell, Zells other than Hans M., not to mention Zell am See, Bad Zell, Zell-Forschung, Governor Zell Miller, etc.

whereas
"hans zell"
reduces it dramatically to 16,800, but still includes the Hans Zell *Publishers* references including cataloguing data in online library catalogues and databases.

 A search with an exclusion operator
"hans zell" –publishers
reduces it to about 700, albeit still including references to Hans Zell *Publishing Consultants,* which is another aspect of our business (i.e. the exclusion operator eliminated *publishers* from the search results, but not *publishing*).

Finally, including the middle initial
"hans m zell"
reduces it further to 469 of which the first two results link to our home page, and from which my full address details could be tracked down.

Detect plagiarism using quotation marks
Using quotation marks can come in handy in detecting plagiarism and cheating, even though this will be restricted to online articles and other Internet documents.

Enter a few words from a specific phrase or sentence from a paper or article, put double quotation marks around them, and see whether other people have already used exactly the same phrase. It seems to work well both for a fairly long phrase (but not exceeding 32 words) or for *part* of a phrase, and Google will highlight the words in the phrase when it returns its search results.

For example, had I started a sentence in this guide with this distinct phrase
"clearly, books and libraries are not a developmental luxury"

I would soon have been exposed as a plagiarist, as keying this phrase into Google promptly leads to a reference in an online paper by Paul Tiyambe Zeleza, "The Dynamics of Book and Library Development in Anglophone Africa"

Centre for the Book | News, Announcements, Events.
... Tiyambe Zeleza underlined the urgency of such a project when he wrote: **Clearly, books and libraries are not a developmental luxury** but are essential, ...
www.centreforthebook.org.za/events/culture_reading.html - 29k - Cached - Similar pages

Paul Tiyambe Zeleza: The Dynamics of Book and Library Development ...
Clearly, books and libraries are not a developmental luxury but are essential, especially in our so-called information age where knowledge and information ...
www.inasp.info/pubs/bookchain/profiles/zeleza.html - 28k - Cached - Similar pages

If I had searched for another extract from this paper,
"giving in to despair or to the populist dismissal of new technologies"
Google would have come up with the two results below: the second is in an *The Book & The Computer* online paper, where I have quoted from the article, with due acknowledgement of the source, in a paper of my own:

Paul Tiyambe Zeleza: The Dynamics of Book and Library Development ...
But we must resist **giving in to despair or to the populist dismissal of new technologies** on the grounds that they are patronized by a minority or the élite. ...
www.inasp.info/pubs/bookchain/profiles/zeleza.html - 28k - Cached - Similar pages

The Book & The Computer
... must resist **giving in to despair or to the populist dismissal of new technologies**
on the grounds that they are patronized by a minority or the elite. ...
www.honco.net/os/index_0310.html - 42k - Cached - Similar pages

If you do this type of search, the Google results display the phrase in bold type face, and you can then quickly compare it for suspected plagiarism, or excessive quoting or paraphrasing without due credit.

If you search Google for
"how to detect plagiarism"
it will offer you over 240 Web sites and resources on this topic, some with useful tips and techniques how to recognize plagiarism and expose the copy-and-paste cheaters, although it entirely possible, of course, that in some cases suspected plagiarism may have been unintentional.

Using the "+" sign
Putting a plus sign in front of a search term (with no space between) instructs Google that this word must appear in the results, even though this might be a word it would otherwise exclude (including "stop words", *see* ➜ **Important points to remember – and the dos and the don'ts above**). This is what Google calls the Inclusion Operator. You can precede two, three or more words with the "+" sign to instruct Google to find documents, etc., with all these words, rather than all the documents with any

one of them. However, this is not always very satisfactory, and you will probably get better results by using the double quotation marks/exact phrase option mentioned above, or even just searching in ordinary search mode.

Example:
nigerian civil war
will generate about 1,370,000 results, of which the first 200 or so results will be as relevant as those for
+nigerian +civil +war
because Google's default is AND; it will automatically search for pages matching all three words, showing the best results first, i.e. those with the words in the same sequence, rather than isolated occurrences of the words "nigerian", "civil" or "war".

Example:
the african studies companion
In this example it will ignore the common word "the" unless you instruct it otherwise, i.e.
+the african studies companion

It should be noted that the inclusion operator is not the same as enclosing the words or phrase in double quotation marks (*see* ➜ **Using quotation marks**). The inclusion operator ensures that all the words in the search query appear in the results, but *not* necessarily in precisely the same order, and as they would appear if the search query were
"the african studies companion"

Overall, the inclusion operator is not particularly helpful, other than for forcing a search on common stop words (*see* ➜ **Important points to remember – and the dos and the don'ts**), which Google would normally exclude in basic search mode. Putting the "+" sign in front of each term can also be used to instruct Google not to use word stemming, and to search for only that exact term without any plural/singular variants (*see also* ➜ **Other factors to consider: Wildcards** above).

Using the "-" sign
Using the minus sign, which Google calls the Exclusion Operator, on the other hand, can be useful as a way of eliminating lots of hits that you don't want, especially for words that have multiple meanings and/or are used in a variety of different contexts. Putting a minus "-" sign immediately in front of each term that you don't want (with no space between them) instructs Google to exclude these words from searches and find pages that do not contain the term. It can be used for multiple words in a search query; and search queries can contain both inclusion and exclusion operators to fine-tune search results. It is also useful if you are searching for people, using the exclusion operator to exclude the first names of people you do *not* want to appear in search results.

Typical examples might be
virus –computer
mazrui -ali

or it could also be used if, for example, you were trying to track down a Soyinka other than Wole Soyinka, but couldn't remember his or her first name, and in which case you would enter (to avoid picking up either first name or initial)
soyinka –wole –w
Of course this search would still find occurrences of any "Soyinka" in Web pages or Internet documents, but the top results with the exclusion operators quickly lead to other Soyinka's, for example the journalist Kayode Soyinka.

Taking advantage of the increased 32-word limit in Google Web search you could also key in up to about 30 words, but use the exclusion operator to exclude words you know are of no interest. (However, each search operator or command, in this case each "-" minus sign, will count as a "word" as part of the 32-word limit).

Using the "~" sign
The tilde character – which Google calls the Synonym Character or, more colloquially, as "the fuzzy operator", and which is interpreted to mean "approximately" – tells Google to search not only for the search term typed in but also for synonyms or associated terms. It works similarly to the OR operator (*see* ➜ **Using the OR Operator** below). Place the "~" sign at the beginning of a search term, with no space between them (but it works for only English-language terms.)

It can be useful to find alternatives, or words associated with the search terms, or if you want a fairly broad search on a topic.

Examples:
~data sierra leone health
will generate results including health information statistics, health indicator data, health care data, census data, and databases, plus the words Sierra Leone.

~publishing kenya
brings up results containing the words book, books, publish, publications, publishers, magazines, plus the word Kenya.

~higher education tanzania
will include results containing the words college, colleges, university, universities, plus the word Tanzania.

The synonym character operator can also work quite well in searching for concepts or abbreviations.

Using the OR operator
Google also supports the "OR" operator (used in capital letters) for synonyms or equivalent terms, which will retrieve pages that include either keyword of two search terms. This can be helpful if there might be different variants of the word or spelling differences – e.g. variant spellings of African languages, ethnic groups, or of place names in Africa – or for finding both the singular or plural form of a word. However, in practice, there shouldn't really be much need to use the OR operator.

Examples:
botswana labor OR labour
will return results that include any of the terms in the search query; or
ethnic conflict côte d'ivoire OR ivory coast

rome OR roma
fulani OR peul
swahili OR Kiswahili

Using blank space
This is not really a search operator as such, but simply a way to take advantage of Google's ability "to fill in the blank", based on phrases that others have already written and published on the Web. To do so, enter an incomplete phrase into the search box in double quotation marks.

Examples:
"the literacy rate in tanzania is"
"the president of kenya is"
"the organization of african unity was founded in"
"chinua achebe was born on"

The above are very simple examples, but it can work surprisingly well for much more complex phrases. Beware though, the results and "answers" it shows may not necessarily be accurate!

Additional commands & special syntaxes

In addition to the commands set out in the preceding section, Google offers many other advanced operators or special syntaxes for refining or narrowing your searches. Most of these can be formulated by using Google's Advanced Search form.

You can use multiple syntaxes in a single search query if you are trying to track down something very specific, but mixing syntaxes too liberally can result in unsatisfactory search results. Start off with using just one syntax command, and then build on this by adding syntaxes to keywords that are already part of your initial search terms or results.

Here are some of the commands:

site:[followed by domain]
The command "site:" permits you to narrow your search to either a particular Web site (or host) or a domain, which can be a country domain such as .uk for the UK, .ca for Canada, .se for Sweden, .ke for Kenya, .za for South Africa, .zw for Zimbabwe, etc.; or a top-level domain .com (commercial, originally mainly US, but now also used elsewhere), .co (commercial in other countries), .edu (educational, for the US), .ac (academic, UK), .net (network), .org (usually non-profit making organizations and NGOs, etc.), .gov (government), .mil (military), or .info (information services). (*See*

also ➔ **inurl:** below.) The domains .com, .info, .net, and .org are open to any individual or organization. There is also the domain .name, reserved for individuals. Enter the term(s) you're looking for, followed by the word "site:" with a colon, followed by the domain name (no space between). On the Google Advanced Search pages you can also use this to exclude results from sites or domains.

This can be a useful filter to eliminate unwanted hits from all the .com, or .co sites if the words in your search query are likely to feature on commercial sites.

It can also be useful to search Web sites that don't have their own search facilities, for example some African newspapers, except that it won't work if access to the site requires log in, and in which case it will only find results (if any) on the most current and/or the front page.

Examples:
african studies resources site:loc.gov
This search will restrict it to resources at the Library of Congress site.

african studies resources site:uk
will restrict the same search to UK Web sites only; while

african studies resources site:ac.uk
will restrict it to academic sites in the United Kingdom.

african studies resources site:soas.ac.uk
will limit it further to resources at the School of Oriental and African Studies (SOAS), University London. However, as the word "African" will obviously appear extensively throughout the SOAS Web site, a search such as this example would be too broad and would generate far too many results. On the other hand it could be used to find country-specific resources at SOAS, for example

nigeria site:soas.ac.uk
finds about 340 "Nigeria"-related results at the SOAS site, relating to outreach activities, centres, staff, course units, research projects, documents, library archival and manuscript resources, events, current exhibitions that include Nigerian materials, references to Nigerian writers, and more.

Other examples:
culture arts yoruba site:edu
will restrict the search to .edu (US educational/non-commercial) sites only.

ngugi wa thiongo site:ke
will restrict the search for references on Ngugi wa Thiong'o appearing on Kenyan Web sites or Internet documents, including some Kenyan newspapers (although it will not pick up those that have .com or .net domains).

While restrictions to country domains can be useful, and usually dramatically reduce the number of hits, beware of the fact that many countries in Europe and elsewhere outside the US now also use the .com domain rather than .fr, .uk, .za, etc., country domains. For example the Web site of the UK-based Hans Zell Publishing uses http://www.hanszell.co.uk whereas one of its online publications has a .com domain, http://www.africanstudiescompanion.com. And be equally aware of the fact that some people use the "obscure" country domains of places like Tonga in order to be able to use a company name that might not be available in its .com form, in other words, a country domain is not always and not necessarily any indicator of national content.

If you want to conduct searches restricted to Web sites in particular countries, e.g. site:uk or site:za, Google will find pages with that country domain, but it will not pick up UK- or Africa-based Web sites with the .com or .net domains. Moreover, results cannot come from an .edu and a .com domain simultaneously unless you add the OR command (*see* ➜ **Using the OR operator**), which tells Google that you want results from either domain.

Language restrictions
Google lets you use its language selector to limit results to pages written in a specific language, at this time 35 languages, but not in any African languages as yet. (Arabic is one of the languages that can be chosen and this might be useful for tracking down materials in Arabic from the countries of North Africa, and from the Sudan and Egypt.)

It can be useful if, for example, you are conducting research on a specific topic as it relates to francophone or lusophone Africa, and, together with using the ➜ **site:**[followed by domain] restriction, it enables you to search for documents or Web sites from both a certain country and in a specific language – for example, to conduct a search for Web sites (i) in French only, and (ii) appearing on French domains, with references to the Senegalese writer and cinematographer
sembene ousmane
or, with the accent,
sembène ousmane

For this type of search it will be easiest to go to Google's Advanced Search and select "Return pages written in French" from the languages menu, and, additionally, enter the site:fr domain for France in the appropriate Advanced Search operator field (or .fr, it doesn't make a difference in the results). Or you could use site:sn if you wanted results only from Senegalese Web pages.

Incidentally, this is a good example which demonstrates that (unlike in 2004 when the pilot edition of this guide was published) accenting search terms is no longer important. Both the above examples generate 178,000 results, of which the first 400 results at least are excellent, for either search.

File format
If you select the file format selector in Advanced Search you can restrict your search results to particular file formats, such as .pdf (Adobe Portable Document Format), .ps (Adobe PostScript), .xls (Microsoft Excel), or .ppt (Microsoft PowerPoint), although one minor limitation is the fact that Google won't let you specify the size of the file. You could also restrict it to .gif or .jpeg (two of the most commonly used file formats

for images and pictures), although when searching for images only it is usually better to conduct your search with ➔ **Google Image Search**.

Regarding file formats, it might be added here that Google can convert all file types it understands into either HTML or text, and gives you the option to view files in different formats. If you have Adobe Acrobat Reader configured to display PDF files in your browser, and if you can't be bothered to wait for a PDF file to load – for those without broadband, large PDF files can sometimes take several minutes – click on to "View as HTML" for quicker access, and if you simply want to see whether a document is relevant or not.

Date restrictions

This permits you to filter search results to Web pages that have been updated within the past 3, 6, or 12 months; this might be useful for, say, recent news reports (*see also* ➔ **Google News**), or anything else for which currency is vital, although you will need to be mindful of the fact that any date-range searches will not relate to the date that the content was created or updated, but to the date when the Google robots last indexed the page.

Occurrences

These are additional commands and filters, also called special syntaxes, which can be useful to hone your search or narrow your search results. They specify where your search terms must appear on the page. You can mix the syntaxes and/or combine them with search terms with or without quotation marks, or other Advanced Search operators. Note that in all of them there is no space after the colon.

A number of them are of limited use, but here are some that could be helpful:

intitle:[followed by search term/s] limits your search to Web pages or Internet documents whose HTML title tags contains the search term, or all the search terms. (If the search query consists of more than one or two words it is best to enclose the words in double quotation marks to avoid unwanted hits.)

Examples:
intitle:african studies
If, for example, when you visit the ➔ **Columbia University Libraries - African Studies Internet Resources (80)**, click on to "View" in your browser and then "Source", this is what you will see on the first three lines:
<HTML >
<HEAD >
  <TITLE>African Studies Internet Resources</TITLE>

The above is not to be confused with the text or descriptive keywords in the URL (*see* ➔**inurl:** below), which may or may not contain the words "African studies" as part of the Web site address. However, the Center for African studies at Stanford University, with the URL http://www.stanford.edu/dept/AFR/, also gets picked up in an intitle: search because its title meta tag is
<title>Center for African Studies</title>

Some other examples:
intitle:african media
intitle:african human rights
intitle:"sierra leone"
intitle:"robert mugabe"

allintitle: is a variant of the above which instructs Google that all key words must appear in the title (in any order).

Example:
allintitle:bird watching tanzania

intext:[followed by search term/s] will search only actual body text, i.e. it will find pages that contain the specified term in part of the page, but it will ignore links, URLs/titles of Web pages.

It operates in a similar way to ➔ *intitle:* above; if the search query consists of more than one word it is generally a good idea to enclose the words in double quotation marks to avoid unwanted results.

A variation is ***allintext:*** which instructs Google that all search terms must appear in a page's text.

However, the uses of the intext: command are fairly limited, and if the search terms are enclosed in quotation marks there is usually no need to use the intext: syntax.

inanchor: the anchor text is the text on a page that is linked to another Web page or a different place on the same page, and if this command is used it will restrict the results to pages containing the query terms you specify in the anchor or links to the page. The variation ***allinanchor:*** would indicate that all query terms must appear in links to the page. However, neither of them is likely to be much used in African studies research.

inurl:[followed by the URL/Web address; there is no need to type in the http:// part]
This command will limit the search to the URL of the particular Web page address, i.e. its descriptive keyword(s). Sometimes this can be useful – for example, to find sites of upcoming major international conferences, Web sites relating to commissions or other specially constituted groups, or for very large Web sites such as the BBC or UN agencies.

Examples:
inurl:world summit on the information society
inurl:truth and reconciliation commission

link:[followed by the URL/Web address, there is no need to type in the http:// part)
This search will tell you who links to a page or Web site, a handy feature – especially for Webmasters, NGOs, book and journal publishers, libraries, associations, etc., who want to know how many other sites link to their Web pages. This will provide some

indication of a site's popularity and, if there is only a handful or no links at all, might explain the site's poor Google page ranking. However, it is not possible to limit the search by using additional syntax commands. Also beware that the results may well be incomplete, and they can vary from day to day.

Examples:
link:www.africanbookscollective.com
finds 152 sites linking to the Oxford-based African Books Collective.

link:www.inasp.info
tracks down 543 Web pages that link with the International Network for the Availability of Scientific Information (INASP).

link:www.africanstudies.org
retrieves 431 sites linking to the [US] African Studies Association (ASA).

link:www.loc.gov/rr/amed/afs/alc/
finds 15 sites linking to the ASA's Africana Librarians Council (ALC). This figure is suspiciously low, but may have something to do with the fact that the ALC recently changed the URL of its Web site.

link:www.indiana.edu/~libsalc/african/aln/alnindex.html
finds a mere 3 pages (January 2006) linking to the online version of the ALC's *Africana Libraries Newsletter*; the reason for the low figure – it had over 20 links when cited as one of the examples in the pilot edition of this guide – is probably again due to a change of URL. (Indeed, Webmasters ought to be more acutely aware that even a minor change in the URL can mean that existing valuable links to various Web sites or resources may then be irretrievably lost, because those that previously linked to the page may not change the URL unless notified, and/or will not bother to remove dead links. Clicking on it will then result in a permanent "not found" message).

The "link:" command or search, although rarely presenting the full picture, seems to work equally well with top-level URLs and with "deep" URLs such as the last two examples above.

cache:[followed by the URL/Web address, there is no need to type in the http://
part]
This will search for a cached copy of the page indexed by Google, even though the original Web address may have changed, is no longer available, has moved elsewhere, or the server is down. This can be useful for Web sites that suffer from frequent down times, or for those elusive African journals, or some African newspapers, that have Web sites which don't seem to work for much of the time or produce "Not found" error messages.

Of course, retrieving cached versions of pages only works if Google in fact has a copy of them, and if it indexed the page in the first place. It is also possible that Google may have been asked to remove the cached page.

Some other tools

Define:

There are a number of other search techniques that might well be described as Google's hidden tools. One of those is Google's Web definitions, and this works quite well not only for general questions, for example for IT or computer technical terms, but also definitions that might be helpful for African studies researchers, albeit always with the proviso that some of the results may lack authority.

Enter "define:" (with no spaces on either side of the colon) followed by the word or term(s). Material is drawn from various resources on the Web, including glossaries and dictionaries, as well entries from the ➜ **Wikipedia (59).**

define:pluralism
offers a variety of generally good definitions, drawing on academic resources for the most part. It also provides links to related phrases.

define:negritude
offers four definitions of the Negritude concept (the quality or fact of being of Black African origin, and the affirmation of the value of black culture and identity), with links to the sources from where they are quoted, as well links to three further definitions in French and German. However, at least one of definitions is not very satisfactory.

Other examples:
define:new international economic order
define:structural adjustment programs
but beware, in the second example, using the acronym instead (*define:SAP*) doesn't work at all, as the same acronym also applies for other terms, names of companies, and many other different meanings.

If you want dictionary definitions or Web pages discussing definitions of the topic, (i.e. rather than a list of definitions as in *define:*) type *define* into the search box followed by the word(s).

Examples:
define pluralism
define "African renaissance"

Uncle Sam

If you want to limit your search to material from US government sites (federal, state, and local government) you can use Google's "Uncle Sam" page at http://www.google.com/unclesam.

An Uncle Sam search will also include results from a small number of non-governmental sites, including the site for the legal professions Findlaw at http://www.findlaw.com/, which also serves the general public.

Google's other search services

Google Directory

Google Directory http://directory.google.com is a searchable subject index that supplements the Google Web index, although it holds a much smaller number of links. It is principally designed as a search tool for more general rather than academic topics.

Google Directory is based on the Open Directory Project (ODP) http://dmoz.org/, also known as DMOZ, an acronym for Directory Mozilla, which reflects its loose association with Netscape's Mozilla project, an Open Source browser initiative. The ODP was developed in the spirit of Open Source, where development and maintenance are done by Net-citizens, and results are made freely available for all. It attempts to provide the most comprehensive human-edited directory of the Web, constructed and maintained by a vast global community of volunteer editors. Anyone can submit details of a Web site to be included in the Open Directory. Details are then verified and approved by the volunteer editors, who also have the task of eliminating any hype in the descriptions of Web sites submitted.

While Google states that the content of the Google Directory is based on the Open Directory, it adds "and is enhanced using Google's own technology". This might explain the quite considerable discrepancies in the number of links shown for the numerous main and sub-categories. On 28 January 2006, Open Directory Project – Regional: Africa, http://dmoz.org/Regional/Africa, showed a total of 18,220 links, whereas Google Directory http://directory.google.com/Top/Regional/Africa/ showed 24,342, with correspondingly larger numbers for individual country sections. The "Regional/Africa" menu seems to be the main access point for searches relating to Africa or African studies. It can be accessed by country or by 15 broad categories, and thereafter by various sub-categories. There is also a separate sub-category Science >Social Sciences >Area Studies >African Studies, albeit with a mere 98 listings at this time.

The number of listings/links are indicated for each country, some are quite sizeable, for example 77 for Namibia, 434 for Ghana, 859 for Zimbabwe, 1,301 for Egypt, and 7,367 for South Africa; at present there are generally a larger number of links for English-speaking Africa. Clicking on a country menu leads to a sub-menu of a dozen or more sub-categories, some further sub-divided. The Web pages are shown in Google's PageRank™ order, but can also be viewed in alphabetical order. The Google search engine lets you search within a category once you have chosen a specific sub-section of the Directory.

Short descriptions accompany all links, and each page shows the category or sub-category in which the links appear, together with cross-references linking to related categories. The largest sub-categories on each page are listed in bold face. Some sub-categories under countries, e.g. Society and Culture, are rather too broad for the serious researcher, and many contain an unwieldy assortment of all kinds of Web sites.

As we have earlier pointed out in our analysis of the Google Directory in the pilot edition of this guide (*see* http://www.hanszell.co.uk/google/chapter4.shtml#1), one of the Google Directory's main flaws – perhaps not surprisingly, as these are manually edited lists, based on submissions – is its unevenness from category (or sub-category) to category, or from country to country, and there is also very considerable disparity in currency. Moreover, coverage in many sections that relate to Africa, or African arts and cultures, is decidedly uninspiring, including, for example, the sub-categories for Arts >Literature >World Literature >African, http://directory.google.com/Top/Arts/Literature/World_Literature/African/, which display links to a mere 56 resources.

The Google Directory hierarchy of subject categories, and the various sub-categories, is not very satisfactory, certainly not for African studies research. In their help pages, http://www.google.com/dirhelp.html#whenuse, Google states "you might prefer to use the directory when you only want to see sites that have been evaluated by an editor". However, a one or two line (max. 25 words) description – submitted by those who want to be included in the Open Directory – which is then "evaluated", edited and approved by volunteer editors, hardly amounts to a critical appraisal, especially by non-specialists in the field. Quite apart from the fact that a very substantial number of categories are currently without volunteer editors.

Finally, Google's claim that, by ordering the Google Directory according to Google's PageRank™ technology "means that the most relevant and highly-regarded sites on any topic are listed first" is totally unsupported. They might well be among the most frequently visited sites, but that doesn't translate into either the most relevant or most highly regarded quality Web resources. For example the offerings for African studies in sub-category Science >Social sciences >Area Studies >African Studies opens with a page of general links, on which NISC South Africa (the commercial database vendor) comes out top, with an insipid description that says "Provides local and global information for Africa".

The Google Directory and the DMOZ ODP project currently convey a very jaded look and the project is in serious need of revitalization. There is, reportedly, also a huge submission backlog, lacking volunteers to edit them. Moreover there are strange discrepancies between Google Directory and the ODP. The DMOZ/ODP says (at the foot of its home page) that it currently (January 2006) lists over 5.2 million sites, is supported by 71,269 volunteer editors, and covers over 590,000 categories, whereas Google states at http://www.google.com/dirhelp.html that the Google Directory contains over 1.5 million URLs, and is maintained by 20,000 volunteer editors.

In short, Google Directory is not a good starting point for African studies related research.

Google News

Google News http://news.google.com/ was launched in September 2002 and is also available in a text only version only at http://news.google.com/news?ned=tus, which could be useful for those with slow Internet connections. Google News – which now faces fierce competition from Yahoo! News http://news.yahoo.com/, and the MSNBC Newsbot http://newsbot.msnbc.msn.com/ – offers information culled from more than 4,500 international news sources worldwide "automatically arranged to present the most relevant news first". For this it uses an automated grouping technology process that pulls together related headlines and photos from thousands of news sources worldwide, and based on how often, on what sites, and how prominently a story appears on the Web. Thus, the first most important point to understand is that, unlike some other news services, there is no human intervention or editorial judgment here, and the headlines and news stories that appear on Google News are selected entirely by computer algorithms, which Google is still in the process of fine-tuning at this time.

Below each headline is the source of the article linking to its full-text version, a snippet of its text, and an indication of how long ago it was published. For each story, Google typically shows about half a dozen major news media, together with a list of other news sources carrying the same story, sometimes several hundred. Click on to this link and it will lead you to all the sources.

How to search Google News
News stories are updated continuously, and the Google News page refreshes itself every 15 minutes. You can trace the history of a topic or breaking news story by clicking the "sort by date" option in your search results, which will arrange stories in chronological order, with the most recent report placed first. Google News and its archive include articles and news items that have appeared within the past 30 days. There is a search facility – including an Advanced Search menu – to track down particular news stories, people in the news, and "Top stories", which covers not only US and World politics and current affairs, but also Business, Sci/Tech, Sports, Health and Entertainment. Each of these categories features about 20 major news events. Google News is offered in several versions, each tailored to a different national audience. At this time (February 2006) international versions of Google News are available for 32 countries, each of them giving more prominence to national top news stories, while also providing access to breaking news stories worldwide. You can find links to them at the foot of the Google News page. Google hopes to add further countries over time. At this time the only African version available is for Google News South Africa (Beta) at http://news.google.com/news?ned=en_za.

The Google News search facility supports most of the basic Google advanced search operators mentioned in the preceding pages (*see* ➜ **Advanced Search & Google search operators**), and search queries should be constructed in much the same way as for a regular ➜ **Google Web Search**. However, please note that insofar as Google news searches article text and titles, it will not find the names of the journalists, reporters or authors of the articles unless their names also appear within the text.

The Google Advanced News Search page, which can be found at http://news.google.com/advanced_news_search?hl=en&ned=us, has a similar interface as that of the main Google Web Search page, but also offers special filters that enable you to fine-tune your search by limiting it to articles from a particular news source, or confining it to articles from news sources located in particular countries. Additionally, you have the choice of selecting whether results or ➔ **Google News Alerts** (see below) returned should be for terms occurring anywhere in an article, only in the headline text, or as part of its URL. You can also further restrict it to return only articles published in the last hour, day, week or month, or published between certain dates within the last 30-day period.

As with Google Web Search, when searching Google News it is prudent to include search terms that are as specific as possible, as otherwise you are likely to be inundated with hundreds or thousands of irrelevant results. For the best results, craft your search queries through the Advanced News Search interface mentioned above.

Perhaps one of Google News's most attractive features is its clustering capability. Unlike many other news search engines, all the information about a story is brought together in one place rather than shown separately, thus leaving it to you which sources you wish to pursue – for example, whether you wish to learn more about a breaking news story from a liberal newspaper such as the UK *Guardian*, the conservative Fox News in the US, or in an African news source. Indeed, it can be interesting to compare how different news media report the same story, e.g. US media vs. African media, and what makes headlines and what doesn't.

Google News Alerts
The free Google News Alerts http://www.google.com/alerts?hl=en is another useful feature. You create a news alert by entering details of a news story, topic or name, event, etc. that you wish to monitor, provide your email address, and then hit the "Create Alert" button. Google will confirm this in an email to you, which contains a link back to Google. In order to activate the news alert and verify your request you must click on the link or, alternatively, copy and paste the URL into your browser. You can stop the news alert at any time by clicking on a link at the foot of every email news alert that then unsubscribe you. You can have as many news alerts as you wish, but you must verify them after every 10 alerts requested before adding others.

You can elect to receive alerts once a day or "as it happens". You can apply the same techniques as for Google's advanced search operators (*see* ➔ **Advanced Search & Google search operators**) to create your news alert. Click on to the Google News Advanced Search page and enter your search terms with whatever restrictions/search operators you wish to apply. Then click the Google Search button and, when the results page appears, copy the text in the search box on that page and paste it into the box labelled "News Search" field to create your alert.

Example:
thabo mbeki aids
a search for press comments about President Thabo Mbeki's views and statements about the thorny subject of AIDS in South Africa, and treatment for those infected with HIV/AIDS, but
(1) restricted to items published in South African news sources only,
(2) using search terms that appeared within the body of articles, and
(3) returning articles published between 1 January and 31 January 2006,
produced 22 results on 01 February 2006. The same search confined to "last day" results, produced 4 results for 31 January 2006.

The search box shows
allintext: thabo mbeki aids location:south_africa
(but without showing the date restriction).
Copy this text from the search box and paste it into the Google News Alerts home page in the field "News Search" to create a news alert.

Google News is also handy for checking out utterances and public statements made by people, personalities, or celebrities in the news. You can of course use ➔ **Google Web Search** for this, but Google News is likely to pick it up quicker, although will only archive it for 30 days.

While Google is not the only one to provide a free news alerts service, it seems to work well for keeping track of breaking news stories, personalities, politicians, events and places, or, for example, African artists and writers in the news – always provided, of course, that they are actually covered in the news media picked up by Google. This is probably not the case for news items appearing in several (relatively low-circulation) African newspapers, or in some other African news media. Other good news Web resources include Yahoo! News http://news.yahoo.com/, Rocket News http://www.rocketnews.com/info/searchengine.html, and News Now http://www.newsnow.co.uk/, plus of course a variety of subscription-based news databases available through your university library, allowing you to retrieve full-text articles if you are an authorized library user.

Google News vs. other news sources for Africa
As described elsewhere in the *African Studies Companion*, three of the very best news sources for Africa are ➔ **BBC News – Africa (852),** ➔ **BBC World Service Network Africa (853),** and the Washington DC-based ➔ **allAfrica.com (851).**

Together with Google News, these three sources can provide remarkably comprehensive and fairly balanced news coverage of African affairs. (For more sources *see also* section ➔ **10 News sources for Africa**.)

Google Image Search

If you want to quickly access pictures and images on Africa, on any conceivable topic, Google Image Search http://images.google.com/ is the place to start. Google's Image Search is probably the most comprehensive on the Web, with a staggering 2.2 billion images indexed and available for viewing. Images include all kinds of illustrative material, pictures and photographs, drawings, cartoons, icons, graphics, clip art, maps, posters, magazine covers, as well as pictures of book and record/CD covers.

Google Image Search is a marvellous resource. However, also worth a try for searching images are: Yahoo! Images Search http://images.search.yahoo.com/ (indeed, some search engine analysts now believe that Yahoo! Images Search has the edge on that of Google), Ask Jeeves Picture Search http://pictures.ask.com/, and the meta search engine Search-22 http://www.search-22.com/downloads/images.php. A useful collection of image search engines has been assembled by Michael Fagan at http://www.faganfinder.com/img/, covering not only the major search engines, but also image databases for artwork, graphics and clip art, educational images, regional and historical, etc., together with reviews of image search engines.

Each search result in Google Image Search brings up a series of thumbnail images together with the URL details where the picture is to be found, the file type, the image dimensions, and the file size. Clicking on to the thumbnail will lead to the image viewer interface in a frame. The top part shows the images in a slightly larger but still scaled down version; click on "See full-size image" and the bottom frame will display the image in its original context. This is usually too large to be viewed without scrolling on monitors with a screen area set to 800 x 600 pixels, but you can load the page in a full browser window by clicking on "Remove frame" in the top right-hand corner of the page. Additionally (if you are using Windows) hit the F11 key on your keyboard to make maximum use of your screen. Or you can, of course, increase your screen area settings. You can save any picture to your hard disk as you would save other graphics or images files, and in Windows you can also save it as wallpaper for your computer desktop. Bear in mind, though, that many images on the Web are protected by copyright, *see* ➔ **Copyright and clearing permissions for using images** below.

In order to show you the most relevant results, Google omits some entries very similar to the first five or six pages it displays when showing the initial search results. It also uses its sophisticated algorithms to ensure that what it considers to be the highest quality images are presented first in the results, and on the whole this works quite well.

When you use Google Image Search, narrow down your query as much as possible, and limit it to just a few words. It is also important to understand that Google Image Search searches the text relating to images rather than the images themselves. (The Google search robots cannot read image files, but they can index the special tags known as ALT tags that Web designers usually add to the HTML code around an image, describing the contents of the image.) For this reason, search results might not always be as precise as those for searches conducted in ➜ **Google Web Search**, and occasionally might show images that Google thinks are related to the image search query, but which may not in fact be relevant.

Google Image Search also has sophisticated Advanced Search facilities at http://www.google.com/advanced_image_search?hl=en, where you can refine your search terms using search operators (*see* ➜ **Advanced Search & Google search operators**) and/or the ➜ **Additional commands and special syntaxes** described in earlier sections of this guide. For example, you can use the ➜ **site:**[followed by domain] command to restrict your search to images on a particular Web site or database, such as that of a museum of African art or African anthropology. Additional refinements on the Google Advanced Image Search let you specify the size of the image (in its dimension/pixels; with "any" as default, or small, medium or large), the file type (any, JPG, GIF or PNG), and the colouration (any colours, black and white, grayscale, or full colour). On this page you can also set different filtering options (none, moderate, or strict) to filter out anything that might be considered offensive, such as pornographic images.

As with Google Web Search, Google Image Search is not case sensitive, and words can be typed in either lower or upper case.

What can be found on Google Image Search?

Searching Google Images is excellent for finding any kind of maps of African countries, either regions or cities, or to find and view works of African art, or African artefacts in all their forms. Find photographs of cultural objects from African collections at museums and other repositories, including everyday household tools, clothing and footwear, baskets, gourds, cooking utensils, bracelets, necklaces, musical instruments, and much more. It is equally good for finding photographs of people, such as African writers, artists or musicians. Or for finding photographs – and sometimes rare archival pictures – of African rulers, statesmen or -women, African visionaries, men and women involved in liberation struggles, civil rights leaders, and scholars, both from the past or relating to contemporary Africa.

By way of a few examples of this treasure chest, it finds (as at January 2006) almost 241,00 images relating to *ghana* (although such a general search term would clearly not be manageable and would require refinement); over 18,300 for *timbuktu*, and over 3,510 for *freetown "sierra leone"*. And it can find images and photographs of current or past African leaders, for which it is usually prudent to enclose the names in double quotation marks (*see* ➜ **Using quotation marks**); for example, *"kwame nkrumah"* retrieves 638 images (mostly photographs); and there are 118 for *"jerry rawlings"*, or 354 for the President of the United Republic of Tanzania *"benjamin mkapa"*. Not surprisingly, *"nelson mandela"* tops the list with over 24,000 images.

It can be searched for items of African art: e.g. *"luba stool"* finds 228 images, *"gelede mask"*, 474; or for photographs of African writers, artists or musicians: for example, over 1,900 are found of *"wole soyinka"*, 318 of *"ngugi wa thiong'o"*, 217 of *"sembene ousmane"*, 192 of *"mariama bâ"*, and over 3,200 if you key in the name of African musician *"salif keita"*.

For African artists it will generate results both of photographs of the artists as well as of pictures and portfolios of their work – for example, 8 and 53, respectively, for the Nigerian graphic artists, painters and sculptors *"adebisi fabunmi"* and *"bruce onobrakpeya"*.

You will probably get more results, but also some that will be irrelevant, if you enter search terms without quotation marks, but that is not necessarily a bad strategy to start off with. For example, it will show over 2,500 results for the Nigerian artist *twins seven seven* (without the quotation marks); however, in this case, in view of the unusual name – and because Google's Boolean AND default means it will search and display results for pages matching all the search terms – it also generates some completely irrelevant results that include the word "seven" and/or "twins" in their captions or descriptions – including a picture of the smiling "Carr Twins at Seven" of Carrville Iowa in their seventh month! While these are relatively minor distractions, you can avoid them by entering the search terms *"twins seven seven"* in double quotation marks, which will then display just 115 images, all but one of which is relevant.

So the thing to remember is that if you key in more than one term it will search for images related to both or all the terms, but if you put the search terms (or part of the search terms) in double quotation marks it will find images matching only the exact phrase and in the given order.

You can also use the OR operator (*see* ➜ **Using the OR operator**), or the "-" exclusion search operator (*see* ➜ **Using the "-" sign**). However, if you are refining search terms for more complex queries it is probably a good idea to compose the search query on the Google Advanced Image Search form.

The ➜ **site:**[followed by domain] command is particularly useful for searching for images at special locations or specific Web sites. For example, if you are searching for photographs of Senufo art, a Google Image Search for

senufo
will display over 4,400 results.
Restrict it to those on a particular site, in this case to the Italian Africaarte site at http://www.africarte.it/
site:www.africarte.it senufo
it will generate results for images that can be found on this particular Web site.

A search for
dogon art
will show as many as 2,410 images for Dogon art, but restricting it to a domain, in this case a sub-page of the Vrije Universiteit Brussels Library at http://www.vub.ac.be/BIBLIO/nieuwenhuysen/african-art/african-art-collection-statues.htm
site:www.vub.ac.be dogon
will present just 31 results.

And
site:www.unc.edu dogon
will come up with results of pages at the Anthropology Department at University of North Carolina at Chapel Hill.

You can use the ➔ **site:**[followed by domain] command to locate African art and artefacts at museums of African art – for example, in the collections at National Museum of African Art at the Smithsonian Institution in Washington, DC.

Examples:
site:www.nmafa.si.edu asante
site:www.nmafa.si.edu benin
site:www.nmafa.si.edu yoruba

It is important to bear in mind, though, that the results generated, and the photographs that you will be able to see (with accompanying text) are *not* indicative of a museum's holdings for any particular group of African art, merely what is publicly accessible as photographs published on Web sites, or as part of visual databases.

Copyright and clearing permissions for using images
If you want to use any of the pictures in an academic paper or elsewhere, on a Web site or in a photo gallery, you must obtain appropriate written permission from the owners or copyright-holders of the material. However, in the case of some images appearing on non-commercial sites you may be permitted to reproduce material without written permission provided due acknowledgement is made to the original source.

Some images may also be reproduced without written permission under the convention of "fair use" or "fair dealing for purposes of criticism and review" applicable under British and US copyright law (as it applies to copyright in print media), again always provided that due acknowledgement is made, that the use of the material is not for commercial purposes, and that only one or two images are reproduced. However, this is actually something of a grey area, and if in doubt whether or not permission is required, it is usually sensible to seek written permission from the copyright-holder.

Google Groups

Google Groups can be found at http://groups.google.com/, but if you are not already familiar with the basics of Usenet, first check out the Google Groups help pages at http://groups.google.com/support?hl=en. These help pages also offer useful tips about posting on groups, including a posting style guide, posting FAQs, as well as a Usenet Glossary.

The fine distinctions between Internet "groups", "mailing lists", "discussion forums" and "discussion lists" can sometimes get a little bit blurred. One the one hand, there are Usenet newsgroups (just called "newsgroups"), and there are online discussion forums or mailing lists on the other, although both are commonly referred to as "discussion groups".

Usenet Groups are either "Open" (anyone can join), "Restricted" (i.e. the group administrator approves all requests for membership), or "Closed" (only invited members can join).

While mailing lists are similar in nature, on many (though by no means all) academic lists you not only first have to be formally approved as a "subscriber" but most postings to the lists are moderated, i.e. approved by an editor before they are released to the list. Postings are sent by email to subscribers only. They are also referred to as electronic mailing lists, or Listserver lists. List servers are the automated mailing list services that facilitate such online group discussions – which can be academic, professional, or otherwise. In the African studies field a number are listed in section → **21 Online forums and mailing lists**, although this is only a selective list. Users subscribe to a list on a specific topic of interest. Messages sent to the list are redistributed simultaneously from the list server to all the other subscribers to that list. Subscribers can read the messages and respond to them if they wish, or post their own queries or announcements, but it is not possible to post a message or participate in discussions unless you are a subscriber to the list. Most mailing lists maintain searchable archives of all postings going back several years. For example, all the → **H-Net Africa (2810)** mailing lists can be searched at http://www.h-net.msu.edu/~africa/.

Google Groups does *not* index academic mailing list archives at present, but is reportedly testing a new version of its Groups service that will include them.

Google Groups was originally launched in 2001, and the current version (February 2006) is Google Groups 2 Beta It contains the entire archive of Usenet discussion groups dating back to 1981, and includes the former Deja.com archive. You can browse the complete list of groups or search to find postings on Usenet discussion forums from a database containing more than 845 million postings. The archive is updated several times a day.

To find a particular group, type the name of the group into the search box. Alternatively browse the groups starting with the Google Groups home page, which is arranged under Usenet hierarchy top-level categories, e.g. alt., humanities., rec., sci., soc., etc. In Google Groups 2 Beta there is now also a top-level menu of broad subject categories (with various sub-topics) to facilitate browsing, and you click on a category that matches your interests. However, inexplicably, under the sub-topic "Regions and Places" there is no sub-menu listing groups relating to Africa, although they can be found in search mode.

The most recent postings appear on top of the list with the date of posting, grouped by thread subject and indicating the number of articles in the thread, as well as showing the name of the most recent poster. For each group Google displays a shaded bar: the more shading, the more active the list and the more frequently messages are posted. As you click on a group, and a particular thread, it will open up in a pane on the left showing all or the most recent postings for the thread, with the most recent ones on top. A system of indentation and coloured dashed lines tells you who replied to whom in the thread.

Advanced Search facilities enable searches by newsgroup, author of the posting, language, subject/newsgroup topic, message ID, or restricted by date. And, as with → **Google Web Search**, you can use advanced search operators, or special syntaxes, (*see* → **Advanced Search & Google search operators** and → **Additional commands and special syntaxes**) to fine-tune your search, for example to find messages containing all the words, with the exact phrase only, with at least one of the words, or without specific words. If you search for authors of postings, you will need to be mindful of the fact that they may not have used their real names or valid email address, instead using a pseudonym to prevent spammers from getting hold of their email addresses. As you formulate a search, you might wish to include words or phrases that may already have been part of a question someone has posted earlier.

You can remove messages you have posted yourself – or "nuke" your posts, in Usenet jargon – by using an automatic removal tool. However, this requires registration and Google will do it only on condition that you provide an email address that can be verified, and you must sign (by electronic signature) a sworn statement confirming that you are the person who posted the message(s).

In the new Google Groups 2 Beta you can now also create your own group, designate it as either public or restricted, and then have it made available on Google Groups. In order to do this you must first establish a Google account and have your email address verified. In Google Groups 2 Beta all the replies to an initial post are now gathered on one page, and you can bookmark topics you are interested in, and have new replies to that topic delivered to your inbox.

If you are trying to track down postings on a specific Usenet group, and if you know its name, then searching is straightforward. However, browsing is a rather different matter, and finding newsgroups on Africa is not easy. Neither the top-level areas of the hierarchy, nor the sub-groups or tributaries, usually give you much clue as to the nature of the discussions on these groups. If you key in the topic *africa* or *african* in the search box, or the name of an African country, it will lead you to postings in, e.g. soc.culture.algeria, soc.culture.ethiopia, soc.culture-sierra-leone, soc.culture-south africa, soc.culture.zimbabwe, soc.history.african.biafra, and the larger and more general soc.culture.african. Search terms such as *africa travel* will lead you to e.g. rec.travel.africa. And certain topics in the secondary-level category could lead to Usenet groups which include discussions that are Africa-related, e.g. alt.circumcision. However, recent postings on some lists (as at February 2006), such as soc.culture.south-africa – which is described as a group on "South African society, culture, and politics" – seem to be almost totally irrelevant to the topic they are supposed to discuss, are swamped with postings by a single author, and may have been hacked.

The option to "Browse all of Usenet groups" (i.e. the complete Group Directory) is not very helpful either; 50 groups are presented at a time, although you can select from an alphabetical A-Z pull-down menu to speed up your browsing. However, as there are almost 55,000 groups, and thus over a thousand pages of the Directory, it would take you a while to do this!

For browsing purposes, the soc.culture sub-topics might be the best approach, as most African countries seem to have at least one soc.culture Usenet group. For searching it is better to use the Advanced Groups Search page at http://groups.google.com/advanced_search?q=&, making liberal use of the various filters.

Google Groups vs. Yahoo! Groups

At this time Google Groups compares rather unfavourably with Yahoo! Groups http://groups.yahoo.com/, primarily because Yahoo! has a more user-friendly interface for the purpose of browsing, based on a top-level menu of broad subject categories, with many more fairly specific sub- and sub-sub-categories, as well as country categories. While the Google Groups 2 Beta now has an enhanced user interface and an improved opening menu for browsing purposes, with broad subject categories and sub-topics, it is still nowhere near as good as Yahoo!'s – for example, in Google Groups you can search by the name of an African country, but you cannot browse by countries.

The best approach to find relevant groups in Yahoo! Groups is to use the regional group listings. For example the sub-section Top > Regional > Regions> Africa http://dir.groups.yahoo.com/dir/Regional/Regions/Africa has (as at February 2006) 394 group listings for this general "Africa" heading, plus a sub-menu that invites you to browse for more specialized groups, including countries and a sub-menu on Government & Politics groups that are sorted in descending order by number of members, with the largest groups on top. For each group it shows the number of members, a link to the archives (and an indication as to whether they are publicly accessible or whether access is restricted to members), a message history showing postings by year and months, together with a concise description of the group. Clicking on "More" will lead you to the home page of the group with more detailed information, settings, group email addresses, and providing access to the most recent messages by year and by month. Most pages also come up with sponsored advertising links, but this is not a serious distraction.

If you want to browse by country
http://dir.groups.yahoo.com/dir/Regional/Regions/Africa/Countries_and_Region
s is the best access point, where you can select groups from virtually every African
country; for example Burkina Faso has 16 groups, Egypt 1,368, Eritrea 82, Guinea-
Bissau 11, Kenya 211, Mali 13, Morocco 210, Nigeria 677, Senegal 46, Sierra Leone 45,
Somalia 160, South Africa 167, Togo 13, Uganda 43, and Zimbabwe 74 (figures as at
February 2006).

You can also track down groups through other sub-categories; for example,
http://dir.groups.yahoo.com/dir/Recreation___Sports/Travel/By_Location/Regio
ns/Africa shows 43 groups on African travel, mostly southern African at this time.

For groups on African politics or current affairs, select
http://dir.groups.yahoo.com/dir/Government___Politics/By_Country_or_Region/
Regions/Africa. This shows 79 groups together with additional listings for more
specific groups on military or politics, although most of these groups can also be
found via the more general regional approach set out above.

Alternatively, use a country approach; for example, for Ghana,
http://dir.groups.yahoo.com/dir/Government___Politics/By_Country_or_Region/
Countries/Ghana will display 12 groups although the group topic "Politics" seems
to be fairly liberally interpreted.

While Yahoo! Groups is superior to Google Groups for the African studies
researcher, it is not without its flaws, and many group listings have been penetrated
and/or manipulated by spammers and other unsavoury characters. For example,
under Ghana, a group named "Human-buttons" (1 posting, 2 members!); the
Regions> Africa> Military group includes a "Drunk Girl" sex chat site, and if you
enter the very broad search terms *african studies* into the search box, result no. 1 is (or
was, on 02 February 2006) "SexyMissMarisa", as well as listings of some other
irrelevant groups and porno sites.

Some other Google offerings

Google Book Search/Google Books Library Project
(formerly Google Print)

What is now Google Book Search Beta was originally launched as Google Print in December 2003. Google Print was briefly described in the pilot edition of this guide (*see* http://www.hanszell.co.uk/google/chapter6.shtml#5). It has been much in the news since it was re-launched and has been the subject of newspaper editorials all over the world. One of its components, the digitization programme that forms parts of the ➜ *Google Books Library Project*, provoked a sharp reaction from authors and publishers, and groups such as the American Association of Publishers (AAP), the Authors Guild, and the UK-based Association of Learned and Professional Society Publishers (ALPSP), and is currently (February 2006) the subject to at least two lawsuits for copyright violation.

There has been considerable confusion regarding the different facets of the Google Book Search Project, and it is important to distinguish between the two major components:

(1) The Google Books Partner Program is an online book marketing programme designed to help publishers and authors promote their books. Publishers controlling rights in a book can authorize Google to scan the full text of one or more of their books into Google's search database. In response to a search, Google will then display bibliographic information for the title containing the search terms together with a link to relevant text. By clicking on the link the user can then view the full page containing the search term(s) – a "Snippet View" as Google calls it, a few sentences of the search term in context – as well as few adjacent or other limited sample pages from the book if the publisher has given Google permission to make these available to searchers. "Buy this book" links enable the user to purchase the book from booksellers or the publisher directly. Additional links on the results page include "Find reviews", "Find related information" and "Find it in a Library", which links to the ➜ **OCLC WorldCat** database, telling the searcher the closest library that holds a copy of the book. A large number of publishers are currently participating in this project. Google digitally scan the books for the Google Books Partner Program and add their content to its search results, at no charge to the publisher.

Publishers are free to choose whether or not to participate, define the parameters of their participation – i.e. making content available to the degree they want to show – and can remove their books from the Google Book Partner Program at any time. Accordingly, no copyright issues are involved because access to content is pursuant to an agreement between Google and the copyright holders, although some authors have grumbled that the publishers will stand to gain more benefit from the scheme than the authors of the books that are included in the Book Partner Progam.

Google Book Search also offers an option to display results as "Full Book View", but only if the book is out-of-copyright, content has been digitized, and is available for free viewing and download. It might be added in this context that book-scanning projects, and digitizing classic books, is not of course something new, and has been done for many years now, for example by the not-for-profit ➔ **Project Gutenberg (172)**.

(2) *The Google Books Library Project* (also variously referred to as the "Google Library Plan", "Google Print Library Programme", or the "Google Print for Libraries Project") is described by Google as "an enhanced card catalog of the world's books"; it envisages a kind of global mega version of an OPAC, a global online public access catalogue. Under this project Google is digitally scanning into its database the collections of several prominent libraries – at this time (February 2006) the University of Michigan, Harvard University, Stanford University, Oxford University and the New York Public Library – in order to create a vast database to be searched online by the Google search engines. Oxford University and New York Public Library are only making available works in the public domain, i.e. no longer covered by copyright (a good article on public domain, and copyright law in the US, Europe, and elsewhere is at http://en.wikipedia.org/wiki/Public_domain#United_States_law.) As part of its agreement with participating libraries Google will provide each library with a digital copy of the books scanned in its collections.

In response to search queries users will be able to access the full text of public domain materials, but for titles still protected by copyright, users will be able to view a few "snippets" as in the ➔ **Google Books Partner Program** above, i.e. a few sentences of the search term in context.

The Google Books Library Project has aroused much controversy and drew fierce criticism from authors and publishers alike almost as soon as it was announced, who accused Google of massive copyright infringement by digitizing copyrighted works without permission. In response to this broadside of criticism from authors and publishers, Google then introduced an "opt-out" policy in August 2005, giving publishers an opportunity to identify the works they do *not* want to be included in its digital database, but international book trade associations such as ALPSP argue that permitting publishers to "opt out" is not an acceptable substitute for proper licensing of copyrighted content.

Google has also argued (i) that it is copying and digitizing copyrighted material under the concept of "fair use" under copyright law – or "fair dealing" as it relates to the use of extracts from copyright works for purposes of criticism or review – and, (ii) that copying is justified by the beneficial nature of the resultant use. Both of these arguments are disputed by publishers, as well as authors. While most of them agree that the project has significant social benefit and will provide a helpful research tool, some also believe that Google will in fact realize significant advertising revenue as a result of the enhanced search facilities that it will be able to offer. Their main objection is not that Google is creating a full text search index, but that it is doing so without their explicit permission. They believe the Google opt-out option is unacceptable because they, the publishers or authors, the rightful copyright owners, should decide whether and how their works will be copied or digitized.

Thus one of the core issues in the dispute seems to be whether Google's digital scanning of an entire copyrighted book, in order to make the content searchable, amounts to a copyright infringement, even if Google only intends to display brief extracts of the searchable text. On its "Publisher Questions" pages at http://books.google.com/googlebooks/publisher_library.html Google states that Google Book Search helps increase the incentives for authors to write and publishers to sell books, "to achieve that goal we need to make copies of books, but these copies are permitted under copyright law." This is a claim that will no doubt come under very close scrutiny in the pending litigation.

Some publishers also argue that income received from permissions or license fees to use extracts of their copyrighted works is an important revenue stream for them, while Google counters this with the argument that its indexing and text searching facilities could in fact lead to increased visibility and sales for the books; and that, moreover, by spending millions of Dollars to digitize books and hosting them it is actually saving publishers the cost of digitizing their works themselves. However, some publishers ask why does Google need to digitize entire books when users of Google Book Search can only view a relatively small proportion of the text, and only a few pages at a time, and who, precisely, would own the digital files thus created?

For two useful recent contributions to the copyright debate read an Office for Information Technology Policy Brief from the American Library Association (January 2006) at http://www.ala.org/ala/washoff/oitp/googlepaprfnl.pdf, and a *Congressional Research Service Report* (28 December 2005), which can be found at http://opencrs.com/rpts/RS22356_20051228.pdf.

Most people will probably not doubt Google's honourable intentions and that many of their initiatives are for the public good, but what puts some of them off is the whole business of the constantly increasing "Google-ization", the search giant's frequently holier-than-though pronouncements about their core mission of "organizing the world's information", their dominance of the world's networked information, and their grip on cyberspace. Of course one could also argue that Google has, thus far at least, earned its dominance, although its image is now somewhat tarnished with its self-censorship in order to gain a foothold in China.

Meantime Microsoft has also jumped on the book indexing band wagon by announcing, on October 26, 2005, that it will launch its own MSN Book Search and "is working with the Open Content Alliance to bring millions of publicly available print materials worldwide to the Web." The launch will be sometime in the first half of 2006. The first materials that will be available via MSN Book Search will be content in the public domain coming via the OCA http://www.opencontentalliance.org/ database.
(*See also* the MSN press release at
http://www.microsoft.com/presspass/press/2005/oct05/10-25MSNBookSearchPR.mspx).

How does Google Book Search work?

Go to http://books.google.com/ and enter the keyword(s) or phrase you are looking for. Google says it "will find all the books whose contents match your search terms", although "all the books" is somewhat misleading in as far as it will only display books from publishers who are part of the ➜ **Google Books Partner Program**.

Click on to any of the book titles in the search results and you will see a "snippet" view mentioned above, usually three pages containing a sentence or more of the search term in context. You can also view the front and rear covers of each title, the table of contents, the complete index (very useful this), complete copyright data, together with full bibliographic and ordering information. Google Book Search will also pick up titles of books listed in bibliographies and reading lists included in any of the books displayed as part of the results.

Additionally, each Google Book Search result offers links to the publisher's online catalogue, and major online booksellers who offer the book for sale. Booksellers do not pay Google to include their links, and they receive no commission from sales. Google does however earn revenue from user clicks on the contextually targeted ads that appear, with publisher permission, on some pages, and will share this advertising revenue with the publishers.

For most results you cannot only view "snippets", but there are also links to "More results from this book", if Google has permission from the publisher to display more sample pages from the main text or the bibliographic apparatus. However, the number of sample pages you are allowed to view varies considerably, from just two or three to 20 pages or more.

For a few pages Google Book Search will come up with a message saying "Sorry, this page's content is restricted." and the amount, if any, you will be able to see is very limited; and for some results you will first need to log in with your existing Google account, or establish a new account if you don't have one. Having a Google account doesn't cost anything, nor do you have to have a GMail account in order to do so.

Examples:
tigritude
Search results will show 55 books with 83 pages containing references to Wole Soyinka's famous pun when, attacking the Negritude movement, he stated that "a tiger does not proclaim his tigritude, it pounces".

noma award
Will find 106 titles with 256 pages mentioning the Noma Award – or the Noma Award for Publishing in Africa to use its full name – either references to past winners, or descriptions and discussions of the award, etc., except that some results will also pick up other awards sponsored by the late Shoichi Noma, plus a few other results that are not relevant.

adewale maja pearce
Finds 52 results of books and studies by this writer and critic, on 167 pages, including references to him and his statements in articles in edited collections, literary criticism

on him, interviews, references to his work in Bernth Lindfors's bibliography *Black African Literature in English 1997-1999*, and more.

A subject- and country-specific search
south africa liberation theology
retrieves details of 248 books with 1,460 pages containing text or bibliographic references to this topic. The second result is *The Cambridge Companion to Liberation Theology*, and a link to "More results from this book", displayed by agreement with Cambridge University Press, offers access to a total of 22 sample pages.

➔ **"Find in a library"** links to the OCLC Worldcat appear for books that are digitized as a part of the ➔ **Google Books Library Project**.

If a book is in the public domain you get an option to view the entire book. However as, under US copyright law, this is usually restricted to books published before 1928 (in the UK 50 years after they were first published), there is relatively little material available in the African studies field, and many of the titles that are in the public domain relate primarily to travel accounts and exploration of Africa. Also, and confusingly, some titles that are in the public domain found via Google Book Search have been reissued by a several US publishers. This means you can only view short extracts in Google Book Search rather than view the entire book. For example, Sol Plaatje's *Native Life in South Africa* was reissued by Kessinger Publishing in 2004, and although it is now in fact in the public domain, you cannot access full-text for this edition via Google Book Search, whereas you can download full text at ➔ **Project Gutenberg (172)** at http://www.gutenberg.org/etext/1452. The same goes for Olive Schreiner's classic *The Story of an African Farm*, which has been reissued by several US publishers, but which can be accessed and downloaded in full at ➔ **Project Gutenberg (172)** http://www.gutenberg.org/etext/1441.

You can fine-tune your search queries in the advanced Google Book Search at http://books.google.com/advanced_book_search?ie=UTF-8&hl=en, where you can apply all the usual search operators (*see* ➔ **Advanced Search & Google search operators**). Additionally you can search by specific book titles, authors, publishers, ISBNs, or restrict the search to return results for books published between specific years, e.g. 2004 - 2005.

If you search by author, Google Book Search will find books by the author, collections edited by the author, individual papers by the author in collections and anthologies, references to him or her in books or critical studies, as well as citations in indexes and bibliographies that appear as part of the search results.

Example:
bernth lindfors
displays 170 search results with 1,980 pages on this prolific African literature scholar.

The reservations relating to the ➔ **Google Books Library Project** apart, Google Book Search is a clever and innovative search tool, of significant benefit to scholars and students, as well as greatly benefiting publishers and authors alike.

Google Earth

Describing it as a "3D interface to the planet", the amazing Google Earth http://earth.google.com was launched in June 2005. It is a geographic search tool that combines local search with satellite imagery and maps from around the globe. The images are photographs taken by satellites and aircraft sometime in the last three years, and which are updated by Google Earth on a rolling basis. It is a standalone application, supported by sophisticated streaming technology, and the basic version is free for personal use. Google Earth Plus, with additional features, costs $20 annually; Google Pro, for professional and commercial users, is $400 annually. It requires downloading of software, (in addition to PC/Windows it is now also available as a beta service for Mac), but is only suitable for those with broadband connections. Check out more specifics at http://earth.google.com/download-earth.html.

The application comes in the form of a console which allows you to manipulate 3D satellite imagery of the earth. It enables you to "fly" to cities and see aerial views of main locations on the planet, and you can use the controls, or Google's Earth's search functions, to zoom in on a specific location. The three primary search options are: Fly To, Local Search, and Directions, accessed by buttons in the top left-hand panel. The "Fly To" feature will accept an address, a place name, or simple latitude/longitude coordinates, and then zooms you quickly to the specified location (stopping at usually about 3,300 feet over the ground). Thereafter you use the controls to zoom, tilt, pan, or rotate the view. Check boxes allow you to overlay roads, geographical borders, terrain, airports, railways, points of geographic interest, water, volcanoes, as well as stadiums, 3D buildings (i.e. skyscrapers, etc.), hospitals, shopping areas, churches, postal code boundaries, and much more. However, if too many overlay boxes are ticked the views can then get rather cluttered. Google Earth also allows you to save searches and add placemarks as "my places", which works much the same as bookmarks.

At this time (February 2006) Google Earth offers very detailed imagery for the USA, Canada, the UK and 38 major cities in other countries – such as Paris, which Google describes as an "exotic locale"! – but only medium to high resolution terrain imagery for the rest of the world, including most of the African continent. This resolution allows you to see major geographic features and man-made developments such as towns, but not detail of individual buildings. However, you can "fly" to places like Cairo, Cape Town, Casablanca, Dakar, Freetown, Harare, Lagos, or Johannesburg, and can get good aerial views from an altitude of around 25,000 to 40,000 feet, and as you zoom in the picture quality, and amount of detail you can view, is still quite good at an altitude between 1,000 to 4,000 feet. These high-resolution images of cities let you view neighbourhoods, central business districts, buildings, railway stations, harbours, etc. in considerable minutiae, even cars that are parked in streets or car parks are visible.

As indicated above, at this time, and apart from a number of major African cities, most of the African continent can only be viewed as low resolution satellite imagery (with enhanced colours). While this is useful for aerial views of natural features, vegetation, forests, mountain ranges, etc. or configurations of urban agglomerations and human settlements, it is to be hoped Google can be persuaded to increase its high-resolution coverage for Africa, not only for cities, but also for places of great historical or cultural importance, for example places such as Ife, Benin City, or Great Zimbabwe.

National Geographic layers on Google Earth

If you enable the *National Geographic* layer as you view the African continent you will see the familiar yellow *National Geographic* logo. Zoom in to see the title of each feature article or photograph; click the icon and a pop-up balloon shows a photo and description along with links to the content, which includes some stunning photographs. Additionally (this may require zooming in), you will see little red airplane icons, which mark National Geographic's "Africa Megaflyover" close up flyover images of many regions of the continent, including views of animals and wildlife, small towns, village communities, markets, mountain ranges, and much more. There are about 500 images selected from Mike Fay's database of 92,000 images. Explorer and conservationist Mike Fay was on a mission "to find out where people are in Africa, how they're impacting the natural environment, and how they're managing the land."

For more background about this project view the multimedia special feature at http://www7.nationalgeographic.com/ngm/0509/feature1/multimedia1.html. The project is also described in the September 2005 issue of *National Geographic* (a special issue on Africa), "Tracing the Human Footprint", which can be found at http://www7.nationalgeographic.com/ngm/0509/feature1/index.html.

Google/OCLC - Open WorldCat "Find in a library"

The Online Computer Library Center (OCLC) is a (US) non-profit, membership, library computer services and research organization, dedicated to facilitating access to the world's information and reducing information costs. It links more than 55,000 libraries in the US and in 95 other countries around the world. OCLC services help libraries locate, acquire, catalogue, access and lend library materials. Its massive WorldCat database contains over 61 million bibliographic records, merging catalogues of libraries around the world.

The new Open WorldCat programme was first trialled with Google during 2003 and 2004 as the Open WorldCat pilot, designed to make library resources available from non-library Web sites. The pilot aimed to test the effectiveness of Web search engines in guiding users to library-owned materials, making libraries more visible to Web users, and more accessible from the Web sites and search engines to which many people nowadays turn to first.

Open WorldCat is now a permanent programme, allowing libraries with holdings in WorldCat to have their collections discoverable by people broadly searching the Web, using Google, or Yahoo! Search, to search and access WorldCat records, returning results to Web users with the prefix "Find in a library" and links to data at

WorldCat http://www.oclc.org/worldcat/open/default.htm. WorldCat can also be searched using the open-source Web browser Firefox, from its search bar, where many search engines can be added to the list through easily installed extensions.

At present (February 2006), approximately 17,000 OCLC member libraries are participating in the Open WorldCat programme. OCLC has made the entire WorldCat record set available to Google and Yahoo! and thus far these two search engines have both indexed the same set of approximately 3.45 million records. This set includes the 3 million most widely-owned items in WorldCat, as well as a set of 450,000 records that represent unique items in the database. (*See also* OCLC's FAQ pages at http://www.oclc.org/worldcat/open/faq/default.htm).

As you enter your search terms, the OCLC results will display the name of each library holding a copy of the book in its collection, a link to the library's Web site or a link to its online catalogue (OPAC), and if you click on a small book icon it leads you directly to the appropriate catalogue record.

To locate WorldCat records you use the prefix "Find in a library". (In the OpenWorld pilot project you could also use search terms plus the command *"worldcatlibraries"* but that doesn't seem to work any longer.)

How to search for WorldCat records
As part of its FAQ at http://www.oclc.org/worldcat/open/faq/default.htm#03, OCLC says search engine searches prefixed with "Find in a Library:" will lead to the appropriate WorldCat records. It doesn't state whether or not the quotation marks should be included, and as Google is not case-sensitive capitalization of words in "Find in a Library" is not in fact necessary. Inclusion of the colon, on the other hand, seems to be important.

While the prescribed search formula is supposed to be "find in a library:" [followed by title] it also appears to work in some other combinations, albeit inconsistently, and a strange anomaly is the fact that Google seems to find the relevant WordCat links easily enough on one day, only to report it as "did not match any documents" a few days later. Moreover, searches for WorldCat records seem work better in Yahoo! Search rather than Google.

Examples: (using Google)
find in a library: african studies companion
will show 332 links of which the first is the link to WorldCat for this title. However, inexplicably, the same search only a few days apart displayed the WorldCat link much further down the search results.

"find in a library:" african studies companion
or
african studies companion "find in a library:"
finds 519 results and displays the WorldCat link as the second result, together with about 500 other results which are not relevant for the most part;
while
"Find in a library:" "african studies companion" (i.e. both in quotation marks)

displays a mere 5 results, but picks up the WorldCat link to library holdings of *both* the second and third edition of this title.

Yahoo! Search does much better and displays it as the first result with *any* of the combination of search terms below
find in a library:african studies companion (without letter space before title)
find in a library: african studies companion (with letter space before title)
find in a library:"african studies companion" (short title, in quotation marks)
find in a library:"the african studies companion" (slightly fuller title, in quotation marks, and with or without letter space before title).

On the whole it seems it is best to enter search queries as *find in a library:* (without quotation marks), followed by (without a letter space) the book title in quotation marks, but this must the full and precise title of the book, or part thereof in the right sequence. If you don't know the precise title enter the search without quotation marks, but this could then mean that you have to scroll down the first page or two of results to find the WorldCat link.

Other examples:
In Google, a search for
find in a library:"africa: a guide to reference material" (a reference work published in 1993) found the WorldCat link in January 2006 generating this URL address
http://www.worldcatlibraries.org/wcpa/top3mset/ad62aaa35b02c62fa19afeb4da09e526.html
but only a few weeks later, in February 2006, Google reported
find in a library: "africa: a guide to reference material" - did not match any documents, while
find in a library: "africa: a guide to reference material" (i.e. with a letter space inserted after the colon), retrieved about a 100 results, but not the WorldCat link.

On the other hand, Yahoo! Search using
find in a library: africa guide reference material
found it easily enough and pointed to this URL
http://worldcatlibraries.org/wcpa/ow/ad62aaa35b02c62fa19afeb4da09e526.html
(which is actually a slightly different URL address than the above). It also finds it in other combinations with or without question marks surrounding the title, regardless of letter spacing, and always displays it as the first result.

In the above example WorldCat will display an initial 24 libraries in California holding this book, and if you then key in another postal code, state (in its abbreviated form or spelt out), province or country you can view additional results, e.g. 23 holdings in New York state, 7 in Oregon, or 12 in Canada, etc. If you change the setting to "Worldwide" it will give you 348 locations, starting with US listings, followed by Canada (by municipality), thereafter by country alphabetical order and within countries by name of library or institution (but see note below about limitations of WorldCat as they relate to library holdings outside North America).

Other examples: (using Google)
A search to find library holdings of Chimamanda Ngozi Adichie's awarding-winning novel *Purple Hibiscus*
find in a library:"purple hibiscus"
will display the WorldCat link as the first result, together with 25 other results, but not all of which are relevant. It will also find it without the quotation marks but as indicated above it is generally better to enclose the titles in double quotation marks. Then click on the WorldCat link which will display library holdings of this title, for example 85 libraries in California, 34 for New York State, 15 in Wisconsin, 39 in the UK, or 10 in South Africa. If you change the setting to "Worldwide" it will give you a total of 875 locations.

Entering sub-titles of books is not generally necessary, for example for Adewale Maja-Pearce's study *A Mask Dancing. Nigerian Novelists of the Eighties*, the search command
find in a library:"a mask dancing"
finds it as just a single result, i.e. the relevant WorldCat link that will in turn tell you which libraries hold copies of this study, in this example showing 258 library holdings worldwide, of which 212 are in the US.

Searching without the double quotation marks for the title
find in a library:a mask dancing
will also find it, but along with 20,000 other results, most of which are irrelevant.

In addition to the startling discrepancies between Google and Yahoo! Search for WorldCat records, there are a number of caveats to bear in mind:

- Very specialist monographs with total library holdings in the US of less than 100 copies are not likely to be picked up at this time.

- Although Google doesn't say, it looks as though the "Find in a Library" link only appears for books that Google has scanned from libraries, as part of the ➜ *Google Books Library Project* rather than the much larger collection of current titles submitted by publishers for scanning. OCLC says that "results at a partner search site are limited to WorldCat records indexed by that site", and if a search is not successful in Google the same search might well work in Yahooo! Search http://search.yahoo.com/.

- For Europe and Africa, and countries that are not part of the English-speaking world, the picture of holdings will be very incomplete as WorldCat will only report holdings of European (and African) academic and public libraries if they are OCLC member libraries.

- Cataloguing backlogs for recently acquired material in libraries may also contribute to an incomplete picture of library holdings reported by WorldCat, and it may take several months until these catalogue records appear in its database. In the interim period a search in ➜ **Google Web Search** is likely to lead you to online library catalogue records on the Web (or in "Recent acquisitions" listings), although they are not yet in WorldCat.

ISBN searches

While most people will probably use title or author for book searches, books can also be tracked down by ISBN, using the ➜ **site:**[followed by domain] command, *site:worldcatlibraries.org* plus an ISBN (International Standard Book Number, each of which is a unique book identifier), will find WorldCat records for the book. e.g.

site:worldcatlibraries.org 0905450922
(no need to include "ISBN")
will find the WorldCat link for this title, which is the ISBN of one of the books used in the examples above.

You could of course also use the ISBN in a Google Web Search, but the top results will then be online booksellers' Web sites, and the WorldCat link will appear further down on the list.

If you enable the AutoLink function in the ➜ **Google Toolbar**, you can locate Open WorldCat records for items that are not yet in the standard Google index. The AutoLink feature detects the presence of ISBNs on viewed Web pages and converts those references into hotlinks to Open WorldCat results for each ISBN. This occurs regardless of whether or not the WorldCat record for an item has been harvested by Google indexing. You will need to make sure WorldCat is the default provider in your Google Toolbar options. To do so, enable the "Autolink" settings and then change "ISBN (book) information provider" to WorldCat. Then click the "Show Book Info" button dropdown and select "Change Default Provider". Click the Google Toolbar's "Show Book Info" button and then click on any of the now hotlinked ISBNs on the page.

Google Scholar

Still in its Beta version, Google Scholar was launched in November 2004 and can be found at http://scholar.google.com/, with the somewhat pretentious slogan "Stand on the shoulders of giants" beneath its search box. The aim of the new service is to provide a search tool for the researcher, enabling them to retrieve quality material from the Web not normally indexed via Web search engines, and allowing searches across many disciplines and sources, including peer-reviewed papers, theses, books, abstracts and articles, from academic publishers, professional societies, preprint repositories, universities and other academic institutions and organizations. Google Scholar has recently expanded its international dimension with the addition of content in two languages, as well as new interfaces for a number of countries.

Google Scholar has attracted a huge amount of interest worldwide, but has had a mixed reception among librarians and the academic community. Some critics – perhaps sometimes a bit unfairly – have compared its search results and search options with other multidisciplinary, citation based or citation-enhanced mega-databases currently on the market. These include *Web of Science* (WoS) from ISI and *Scopus* from Elsevier, but both of these are high-priced subscription based products, whereas Google Scholar allows free access. It has to be added, however, that there are other major database services that are freely accessible, such as the scientific digital literature library CiteSeer http://citeseer.ist.psu.edu/, where you can search 740,000 documents; or the archive of Highwire Press http://highwire.stanford.edu/, a division of Stanford University Libraries, which hosts the largest repository of free, full-text, peer-reviewed content, currently (February 2006) with 915 journals and almost 1.2 millions full-text articles online.

Much of the criticism has centred on the fact that there is an apparent secrecy by Google to reveal its sources: first, there are no links to sites where publisher partners and their journals are identified. Secondly, the scope and size of the Google Scholar database, and the breadth of its indexing and archives coverage, is not adequately explained. Thirdly, apart from a generic statement on the "About" pages, as well as one at http://scholar.google.com/scholar/help.html#access6, there is no explicit information about publisher archives, and the precise type of documents that are processed (e.g. major articles vs. shorter items, book reviews, letters to the editor, etc.). The criticism is valid, and it is true that the Google Scholar content and sources disclosure is not very informative.

Google Scholar ranks results in order of relevance, and indicates the number of time the research has been cited by other academics. The number of citations is factored into the Google ranking algorithm, which considers the full text of each article, the author, the publication in which the article appeared, and how often the piece has been cited in other scholarly literature.

Google says that for the time being Google Scholar "indexes only scholarly articles", but this is a bit misleading as search results in fact also lead to results for a large number of book titles, and/or edited collections and anthologies.

One of the requirements for inclusion in Google Scholar is that at least an abstract must be made available to non-subscribers who come from Google and Google Scholar. It can index any research articles as long as its robot software is able to crawl them online. This includes articles in pdf format as long as they are searchable. Google Scholar also indexes HTML, PostScript, compressed PostScript (ps.gz), and compressed PDF (pdf.gz) files.

How to search Google Scholar

- An author search to find a specific paper is likely to be one of the most frequently conducted searches. You can enter the author's name with or without double quotation marks, but on the whole inclusion of quotation marks seems to work better. e.g. "*aa mazrui*".

  However, when a word is both a person's name and a common noun, or a popular surname, use the "author:" operator in preference. This operator only affects the search term that immediately follows it, and there must be no space between "author:" and your search term. You can enter several author terms, but you will need to prefix each one with the "author:" operator.

- To increase the number of results, use initial(s) rather than the full first name (and see also below). There is no need to add punctuation for author initial(s); if you do Google Scholar will ignore it and deliver the same number of results.

- You can mix author names with other search terms.

  For example, to find articles on the topic of democracy by Ali A. Mazrui you would enter *author:"aa mazrui" author:mazrui democracy*, which will generate 37 results; or finding articles on, or textual references about Negritude by the Nigerian scholar Abiola Irele *author:"a irele" author:irele negritude*, will retrieve 18 results. Another example might be Ngugi on writing in African languages: *author:"ngugi wa thiong'o" author:ngugi african languages.*

- To search by title of article enter the paper's title in double quotation marks. The results will show either an article or a book by the author, or a citation of the author's work in books, journal articles, and in edited collections (including conference proceedings), together with the number of citations, name of journal, book or other source of publication.

  Some results may be marked [CITATION] but nothing happens when you click on to them. Google Scholar says "these are articles that we have seen references to in other scholarly articles, but we haven't found the actual document online."

- "Title" links to the abstract of the article. Frequently it may also offer a short extract or article preview, e.g. for articles in the subscription-based Questia database; or, when available on the Web, the complete full-text article.

- When you click on "Cited by" it will lead you to all the pages pointing at the original article or book listed, through textual citations.

- The results pages also show links to ➜ **Google Web Search** and/or the ➜ **Google OCLC "Find in a library"** WorldCat search, the scholarly journal archive ➜ **JSTOR (558)** (but note that access to full-text articles in the JSTOR archive is available only through affiliation with a JSTOR participating library or institution), as well as sources where you can purchase the full-text article, such as British Library Direct.

  If the article has been included in an edited collection the link will lead to the relevant search results in ➜ **Google Book Search.** Click on the title of the article and Google Book Search promises that it will lead to full bibliographic information and (at least) an abstract. However, tests conducted indicate that sometime it can in fact also lead to an article without an abstract, presumably because it was published in a journal that does not include abstracts.

- Multiple versions of a work are grouped to improve its ranking. This may include one or more related articles, or even multiple versions of one article. For example, a search result may consist of a group of articles including a preprint, a conference article, a journal article, or a paper in an anthology, all of which are associated with a single research effort. Such links are identified by "Group of".

- As in other Google search services you can apply various search operators to refine your search query (*see* ➜ **Advanced Search & Google search operators).** However, it is probably better to formulate these on the Google Scholar Advanced Search pages which can be found at http://scholar.google.com/advanced_scholar_search?hl=en&lr, and where you can also undertake author searches (using double quotation marks in preference), entering the full author's name, or last name and initial(s). As Google Scholar indexes names and initials on a "first name first" basis, use initial(s) only, rather than full names, as many sources indexed in Google Scholar only provide initials.

- At the Google Scholar Advanced Search pages you can also restrict it to "return only articles" in seven broad subject areas, one of which is social sciences, arts, and humanities, although it is difficult to envisage how this could possibly perform a useful search restriction as far as the African studies discipline is concerned.

- Additionally, you can undertake a publication-restricted search, to return only results from a specific publication. And you can do date-restricted searches by publication year or year range – e.g. when you are looking for the latest developments in any discipline or research topic – but bear in mind that some Web resources don't include a publication date, and Google Scholar will not return articles for which it was unable to determine a date of publication.

- Having read an abstract, you can locate the paper through your library or on the Web. In many cases you may well have access to the complete document through your library. "Library Links (offline)" locates libraries which have a physical copy of the work, while "Library Links (online)" locates an electronic version of the work through your affiliated library resources. To make these links appear, access Google Scholar from an on-campus location of a participating library, and it will automatically include these links. In order to do so you must first go to Scholar Preferences http://scholar.google.com/scholar_preferences, where you type in the name of your library in the "Library Links" section, and thereafter click Save Preferences.

  Google Scholar will then be able to tell you are coming from within an institution using IP addresses that resolve to an .edu domain, or from a list of other universities around the world it chooses to target, and you will see a new "Scholar" link on the Google home page.

You can then start searching with links to your library's resources, always provided of course that you are an authorized library user at the particular institution. As you perform a search in Google Scholar links will show up in your search results, for example "Full Text @ NYU", and/or "Find It @ NYU". Click on one of these links, and it will thereafter offer options or menus for accessing the item you are looking for.

Google Scholar for African studies

When first launched in November 2004, initial search tests conducted in the African studies discipline were generally disappointing with highly incomplete results, but since that time the picture has improved considerably, above all in terms of number of search results now displayed. However, there are still some strange anomalies in the number of search results that are difficult to explain.

For example, a search for articles by the distinguished Africanist scholar Professor Ali A. Mazrui generates a somewhat puzzling array of search results.

(i) If you simply enter *aa mazrui* on the main search pages it will retrieve 634 results.

(ii) If you search for *aa mazrui* on the Advanced Search pages by clicking on to "Search only in Social Sciences, Arts, and Humanities" you get 478 results, but which then also picks up anything else with "mazrui" and "aa" (including e.g. abbreviations for *African Affairs*), plus results from ➜ **Google Book Search**; while *"aa mazrui"*, in double quotation marks, finds 194 results in this search mode.

(iii) If on the other hand you enter the search *"aa mazrui"*, either as a general search, or with "Return articles in all subject areas", it finds 259 results.

(iv) Finally, if you add the "author:" command,
author:aa mazrui it will find 176 results, while
author:"aa mazrui" displays 160 hits.

Another example:
author:p zeleza
shows 108 results, but
author:pt zeleza
only 64, or
author:paul zeleza, even less, 51, and which underlines the fact that searching using a single initial is better than entering full initials or full first name.

The search on Paul Tyambe Zeleza also indicated that Google's policy of a minimum requirement of an abstract is not always strictly enforced, as at least two citations lead to sources, such as periodical articles in the ➜ **African Journals Online/AJOL (554)** database, which indicate "no abstract available".

Some other search examples:
democratisation africa
will deliver almost 10,000 hits, and while it will find the most appropriate articles in the first few hundred results, many of later results are simply links to articles containing the two words somewhere in the text.

However entering the same search terms as a phrase (in double quotation marks)
"democratisation in africa"
generates rather better results, a total of 411, although this could also mean that you miss out on important papers that do not contain this particular phrase, either in the title of the article or book, or within the text.

This is also an interesting example to demonstrate that using alternative spelling conventions for a word, in this case the word "democratisation" (i.e. –ise or –ize) can make a significant difference in the number of results:
"democratization in africa"
will retrieve 884 results; and, by adding the OR operator (*see* ➔ **Using the OR operator**),
"democratization OR democratisation in africa"
will increase it further to 1,204 results.

You can limit a search by name of journal, but if you search for articles or citations in particular journals, for example
search term + *"african studies review"*
it is prudent to put the journal name in double quotation marks, as otherwise you will also get results from other journal titles containing the words "african" or "studies", and which won't be relevant.

democratisation "review of african political economy"
will display 39 results, or
democratisation "journal of modern african studies"
retrieves as many as 656 results. However, while in both the above examples the results contain a good number articles on the topic of democratisation in Africa, the rest are simply papers which contain the word "democratisation" somewhere in the text.

The same is the case if you do a country-specific search, about democratisation in a specific African country, aiming to retrieve all available articles, e.g.
democratisation uganda
While the results page for this search will display as many as 2,440 items, only the first few hundred results will the directly relevant, or at least partly relevant.

A search, without author, article title, or other search terms, but restricted to
"african studies review"
finds 1,540 results, in citation order. A search restricted to only recent 2005 articles finds 85, but none with citation scores as they are all recently published, and in no apparent sort order (i.e. author, title, or volume/issue number). It shows that, as at February 2006, Google Scholar had indexed the first two issues of *African Studies Review* of volume 48, 2005. A search for *"journal of modern african studies"*, with the

publication restrict for 2005-2006 issues only, brings up 50 results of articles published in 2005, albeit only two with citation rankings, again due to the fact the articles are very recent. This would seem to indicate that Google Scholar is reasonably current. However, if you want to view table of contents and abstracts for the very latest issues of some of the leading African studies journals you will do much better to go direct to these journals' Web sites. Most of them – including those of the major journal publishers such as Blackwell's, Cambridge University Press, or Taylor & Francis – now allow free online access to table of contents of recent issues and/or abstracts. (*See also* Introduction to section ➜ **9 Journals and magazines**).

The results for *"african studies review"*, or other Africanist journals (and retrieving all available records) are interesting because they appear in order of number of citations. This tells us, for example, that Jane I. Guyer's "Household and Community in African Studies" published in *African Studies Review* (Vol. 24, No. 2/3, Jun. - Sep., 1981) is, according to Google Scholar at least, the most frequently cited article by far, with a total of 63 citations; followed in second place by Karin Barber's "Popular Arts in Africa" *African Studies Review*, (Vol. 30, No. 3, Sep. 1987) with 31 citations.

Google's interpretation of the term "scholarly" is ambiguous, and it is not always clear which papers it considers to be of a "scholarly" nature. For example, when searching for papers on publishing and book development in Africa, it does find a good number of articles and citations published in major journals, but also misses out a very substantial body of the literature on the topic; surprisingly, even some articles that are freely accessible on the Web. Why that should be so is not clear: are they not indexed, (i) because the sources are not crawled by the Google Scholar robots? (ii) The sources are not considered to be scholarly publishing outlets? Or (iii), is it because the topics and/or articles are not considered to be academic or "scholarly" enough?

Some searches in Google Scholar can also be decidedly unhelpful:, e.g. if you enter author:"h zell" Logos
one search result will show a reference to "The production and marketing of African books: A Msungu perspective", an article published in *Logos* in 1998, but the only two links on offer for this search are one to the British Library Direct service (where you could *purchase* the article, but does not offer access to an abstract), plus a couple of citations on the Web.

The pros and cons of Google Scholar

What's good about Google Scholar?

- It is freely accessible not only to academics and students, but is also an immensely useful resource for the general public, and all those who may not have access to, or are affiliated with, a university institution, and therefore licensed databases in libraries at these institutions are not available to them.

- It is fast and easy to use, with a user-friendly search interface for the most part, but one must be mindful of the fact that fast is not necessarily good and effective. Serious research can frequently be time-consuming, with no quick-fix solutions, and one-stop shopping is not a good idea if you have specialized needs.

- Searches can lead to a substantial number of freely accessible online versions of many scholarly papers. This could be particularly useful to scholars and students in Africa not affiliated with an academic library, or whose library institutions do not subscribe to some of the expensive journal articles databases that are commonly available to library patrons in academic institutions in the countries of the North.

- The citation scores are very useful, but you must be aware that they may not necessarily represent the full picture; or, conversely, they may be inflated through multiple listings. Moreover, bear in mind that page ranking in Google Scholar is not the same as the ISI's http://www.isinet.com/ bibliometric tools.

- Also very useful, for those who have access to major library collections, is Google Scholar's "Library Links", which locates libraries that have a physical copy of the work; and its "Find it @", which locates an electronic version of the work through the searcher's affiliated library resources, is another excellent feature.

- Fairly extensive testing reveals that Google Scholar seems to have done an excellent job in fully indexing the content (current and back issues), of all journals covered by the ➜ **African Journals Online (554)** project, which offers access to the tables of contents and abstracts of articles of over 200 African-published journals from 21 countries. This will significantly help to provide yet more international visibility for these journals.

What are the constraints and limitations?

- First, Google Scholar is still only in beta and it is an evolving product.

- The parameters of its indexing coverage are not clearly set out, you don't know what precisely is indexed, and the date ranges. Google Scholar does not explicitly disclose the names of its publisher partners and their journals, nor is there adequate information about Google Scholar's content, and the composition and dimensions of its indexing database.

- There is no clear indication of what Google has determined to be of a "scholarly" nature, and what is and what is not considered to be scholarship. Google's search algorithms probably just make a calculated guess as to what they think is scholarly content.

- It misses many of the quality resources that are usually accessible through institutional subscriptions to a variety of databases, and indexing and abstracting services freely accessible to authorized library users at these institutions.

- In the African studies field a large number of journal articles won't show up in the results if the journals are not included in the ➔ **JSTOR (558)** archive (currently only a dozen or so), or are published by a major international journal publisher. However, as indicated above, Google Scholar seems to have undertaken a thorough indexing job for all the African journals represented in ➔ **African Journals Online (554)**.

- There is just a single output format and the results cannot be sorted by the user. Results are sorted by Google Scholar's citation scores and, in the absence of citations, for example for very recent articles, there doesn't seem to be an intelligible sort order, e.g. by author, title, or by journal volume/issue number.

- Google Scholar generally seems to perform better on scientific, technical and medical subjects, rather than in the arts, humanities, and the social sciences.

- Google Scholar's claim that it is opening up more content from the "invisible Web" is, at this time at least, not substantiated.

Google Scholar can certainly be a very useful starting point for a quick overview of a topic, point you in the right direction, and then lead you toward relevant material. However, the results may neither be as current or as comprehensive as you need.

Google Scholar is no substitute for the various subject-specific databases and indexing and abstracting services, which can provide more focused subject area coverage, and most of which offer sophisticated advanced search features that will allow you to fine-tune your search, and build a highly targeted search strategy.

Google Web Alerts/Google Alerts

Google Web Alerts http://www.google.com/alerts?hl=en was launched in April 2004 and is currently (February 2006) still in its Beta version. Now it is simply called Google Alerts and you can chose to receive alerts for Google News, Web, News & Web, and Groups. It works in much the same way as ➔ **Google News Alerts** except that instead of alerting you to news stories, it alerts you about topics of interest on Web pages; it can also monitor references to your name, or the name of authors/academics, the title of a book or paper, or information about a forthcoming conference, etc. You sign up on the Google Alerts page and the verification/confirmation process also works in the same way as Google News Alerts. As in the latter and for general Google Web searching, you can tweak your search terms by using some of the operators described in the previous pages including, and especially, the use of double quotation marks. You can select to receive alerts daily, weekly, or "as-it-happens".

A News alert is an email that lets you know if new articles make it into the *top ten results* of your ➜ **Google News Search**, while Web alert is an email that lets you know if new Web pages appear in the *top twenty results* in ➜ **Google Web Search.**

Potentially, Google Web alerts could be more useful for Africanists than the Google News alerts, because items about specialized African studies topics are more likely to be found on Web pages and Internet documents than to be reported in major international news media.

Google promises to send you Google Web Alerts "when there's new information on the Web matching the search you specify". However Google's use of the word "new" is somewhat ambiguous.

As we reported in the pilot edition of this guide, tests carried out during the course of 2004, for a variety of Web alerts, were disappointing for the most part. More recent tests have also not generally been very satisfactory, and the frequency of alerts was erratic, although, to some extent at least, this was probably due to the fact that relevant new Web pages of potential interest did not make it into the top 20 results of ➜ **Google Web Search**.

Google states that, as for ➜ **Google News Alerts**, you can incorporate Google Advanced Search techniques to tweak your Google Web Alert settings, by selecting the conditions you want on the Google advanced search pages (*see* ➜ **Advanced Search & Google search operators**). However, for a number of experiments conducted over a period of several weeks, it submitted alerts of largely irrelevant items, despite the use of special search operators. Test searches and alert terms containing words such as "African studies" – despite using "+" or "-" operators or enclosing terms in quotation marks – resulted in alerts to a variety of Web sites or documents that somewhere contained the word "African" or "African American".

For other tests, alerts received related to references and citations that were far from "new", and had been on the Web for a long time – for example, items relating to listings on some of the major African studies portals and directories, or those of online booksellers and dealers. Presumably the reason they were interpreted as "new" was because the Web sites had undergone minor changes and Google robots revisited and re-indexed the pages. Yet several of those reported as "new" were not in fact ranked as among the top 20 results in Google Web search, and why therefore they generated an alert in the first place is something of a mystery.

So, for the time being at least, this Google service does not have a great deal to recommend it for African studies-related topics and research.

Google Alert (Indigo Stream Technologies, *not* part of Google)
This is "the other Google Alert". Somewhat confusingly, Google Alert http://www.googlealert.com is not affiliated with Google, but uses Google's Web services API™. Founded in 2003 by Gideon Greenspan, a Ph.D. student in the Laboratory of Computational Biology at the Israel Institute of Technology, Google Alert is developed and marketed by Indigo Stream Technologies Ltd., a Gibraltar-based company. It is a clever and useful tool.

It functions very much like ➔ **Google Web Alerts** except that it seems to perform rather better, primarily because it delivers (as part of the free service) up to 50 top results in Google Web Search, whereas Google's own alerts service delivers only the top 20 results. It runs daily personalized Google searches for you and sends them to you by email when the query produces new results. You can use it to keep track of anything on the Web, including information about yourself (or what they call "ego searching" nowadays), keeping on top of special interests, research projects, new book titles, book reviews, or anything else you wish to monitor, except that it does not cover Google News, Google Groups, or Google Image Search at the moment (and as at February 2006).

You create your alert by entering a username, password, and email address, and then enter the searches you would like Google Alert to perform every day (using double quotation marks for searches for individual names or phrases). You will then receive an email alert whenever a new site appears in the top 50 results for your searches. The initial email notification includes up to 50 results per search, which you are likely to have seen before, but Google Alert promises that subsequent alerts "will include only new results that have not been reported before." You can also view your results online by clicking "Browse results" in an integrated mini-browser. You can chose to receive alerts in HTML format, including clickable links both to the original site and Google's cache. Other delivery options are by RSS feeds, or via TrackBack. The feed settings can be changed at any time, as can the search settings, which offer various options for frequency of searches. You'll have to remember, however, that Google Alert is dependent on Google for results, and you will receive relevant alerts only when Google updates its index. You can refine searches using the search settings and the Advanced Search pages, allowing you to include or exclude terms, and to filter by language or domain, etc.

The basic (or "Current") Google Alert service is free and allows you up to three alerts and up to a total of 150 results for all your queries. Charges apply for advanced services, which let you search deeper and more widely, and which offer more tracking power (i.e. number of search terms, top Google results tracked, and daily search capacity) and a host of advanced features, including targeted searches by language/country, personalized relevance, preferred search time, an ability to filter for precise capitalization or punctuation of search terms, additional email recipients, and more.

The current (February 2006) charges are, for the second level service "Personal", $4.95 a month (up to 10 searches, top 100 results per search); $9.95 for "Premium" (20 searches, top 200 results); $19.95 for "Professional" (50 searches, top 500 results);

and $39.95 for "Platinum" (100 searches, top 500 results). The advanced service also makes use of a new SightPoint personalization technology that automatically rates new search results based on their similarity to results the user has clicked on before. SightPoint uses something called "Bayesian statistics" made popular by spam email filters.

The Google Alert service has an attractive, clean interface, and one useful feature (which is part of the free service) is that it displays the Google page ranking for each result reported. It seems to have the edge on Google Web Alerts, even for its basic free service, delivering more relevant results and, by using an optimized matching algorithm, can determine whether a search result has been seen before, thus minimizing the chances of seeing repeats.

Other search engines worth a try

Google is a marvellous Web search tool and is as good as they get at present, but it is not the only one. Quite apart from other top search engines like *Yahoo!* http://www.yahoo.com/, *MSN Search* http://search.msn.com/, *Ask Jeeves* http://www.ask.com/, or *All the Web* http://www.alltheweb.com/ (whose index is provided by Yahoo!), there are now all sorts of innovative speciality search engines. For example, check out *Teoma* http://www.teoma.com/; *Ez2find* http://ez2find.com/, a meta search engine which, through its advanced search function, also searches a small proportion of the invisible or "deep" Web. Or try *Vivisimo* http://vivisimo.com/, which uses clustering technology to organize matches in hierarchical folders and categorizes search results; as does *Clusty* (developed and owned by Vivisimo) http://clusty.com/, which also organizes search results into folders, grouping similar items together.

Other good meta search engines – which allow you to enter keywords in the search box and your search is simultaneously sent to several of the most important search engines – are *Jux2* http://www.jux2.com/ and *Dogpile* http://www.dogpile.com/.

There are a variety of recently launched new search tools with interesting personalization features. One is *A9* http://a9.com a subsidiary of Amazon.com, Inc., which also offers a toolbar. Powered by Google, A9 lets you not only undertake Web searches, but also looks for book results from the Amazon.com Search Inside the Book™, which opens in a window alongside the Web results. A9 says "when you see an excerpt on any of the book results, click on the page number to see the actual page from that book", but that is somewhat misleading. What the book results show you are not necessarily "excerpts", but simply occurrences of the words in your search terms, appearing in a multitude of books. However, it is an interesting feature, albeit slightly hit and miss. It seems to work quite well for very specific search terms or unique (e.g. geographical) names, but is less successful for more commonly used terms, including those in the African studies field. In order to view the actual pages from the book results you will need to be registered at Amazon.com.

Grokker http://www.grokker.com/index.html describes itself as "a new way to look at search." This is an accurate description, and Grokker is rather impressive. Through a zoomable map/preview balloons Grokker displays results graphically, and after the initial results are displayed you can search within the map by key words. You can search Yahoo, the ACM Digital Library (a vast collection of citations and full text technical research), or Amazon Books. When you use Grokker to search Amazon books, you can browse results by keyword, subject heading, or category.

Another one is the mysteriously-named *Ujiko* http://www.ujiko.com/, a Flash-based search tool that is being touted as a "next generation" search engine and a possible alternative to Google. It was launched in May 2004 by the Paris-based company Kartoo http://www.kartoo.com/, who already offer an unusual meta search engine with visual display interfaces – although I personally find it a little bit bewildering. Ujiko uses the new Yahoo! search technology and says it gives you access to over 5 billion pages, remembering your preferences, allowing you to customize results, and build a variety of personalized filters. Ujiko has a nice-looking, uncluttered interface and, unlike Google, stores your search history on your computer for privacy. Ujiko says its search engine "evolves with your expertise: the more you use it, the more functions it is able to offer. Basic principle: each time you visit a new site, you are gaining one point of expertise. With every 10 points, you move to the next level. Your search engine is mutating."

A further new search tool that has caught my eye, and is yet another potential competitor to Google, is *IceRocket* http://www.icerocket.com/, a meta search engine from a Dallas-based company that shows results "snapshots" – a thumbnail view of the page – displayed next to the search results. Additionally, it provides extra information and data about the search results, including loading times, Alexa (http://www.alexa.com) traffic rankings, and the number of sites that link to it (although that information doesn't seem to be entirely reliable). It also offers various advanced search facilities and, unusually, let's you do searches and receive the results by email.

Or take a look at another recent entrant to the buzzing search engine market, *Blinkx* http://www.blinkx.com/overview.php (current version is 3.5, PC/Windows only at this time), which, through a freely downloadable Windows client, automatically finds Web pages, news articles and local documents on your machine – including Outlook, Outlook Express or Eudora mail files – that are related to the content of your active window. You can also use it to actively search Web pages, news articles and documents on your machine that are related to a query you enter. Google does this also with Google Desktop http://desktop.google.com/, but Blinkx says it is not aiming to compete with Google on keyword Web searches (it has indexed only about 500 million Web pages thus far) and aims to find its own niche. Its *Blinkx TV search* service http://www.blinkx.tv/ is impressive; enter a query here to search over 1,000,000 hours of TV and video content, which is especially useful for current headlines and news on TV stations. You can play clips from search results by clicking on the moving preview, or the title of the clip located to the right of the moving preview.

Also worth looking at is *Daypop* http://www.daypop.com, a current events search engine, that currently (February 2006) crawls and indexes 59,000 news sites, Weblogs, and RSS news feeds for current events and breaking news.

The directory-style *Eatonweb Portal* http://portal.eatonweb.com/ is a good launch pad for searching Weblogs, and currently (February 2006) has almost 49,000 Weblogs categorized by subjects, languages and countries, including most countries in Africa. Another good one is *Technorati* http://www.technorati.com/, which is currently (February 2006) tracking 28 million sites and 2 billion links. It is a real-time search engine that keeps track of what is going on in the blogosphere – the world of Weblogs – and where you can find out who has been linking to your posts. It also offers an interesting "Books" section http://www.technorati.com/pop/books/with statistics of the most popular and most frequently cited books mentioned in Web logs over the last 48 hours.

Index

As the electronic version of the *African Studies Companion* is fully searchable online, this index to the print edition is fairly simple: it comprises the names/titles of all online resources, Web sites, and Internet documents listed; authors, editors, and compilers of books; titles of books in print formats, CD-ROM or microfiche products; titles of current bibliographies and continuing sources; names of journals and magazines; names of publishers, libraries with African studies collections, national archives in Africa, dealers and distributors; African and international organizations, foundations, government and donor agencies; associations and societies, and the names of awards and prizes in African studies.

Names of personnel, for example journal editors (other than those of bibliographic tools listed in Section 3), African studies librarians, executives of organizations, donors, foundations, or secretaries of associations, etc. are *not* indexed. Authors of Internet documents are indexed if their name appears as part of the bibliographic citation, but authors or creators of Web sites and resources mentioned as part of descriptive annotations are *not* indexed.

All references are to *entry numbers*, with the exception of section ➜ **25 Using Google for African studies research: a guide to effective Web searching**, which has been indexed separately and for which indexing terms refer to *page numbers*, indicated in **bold** face.

Book titles in print format, CD-ROM and microfiche products, journals, and newspaper titles appear in *italics*. Entries for the small number of articles included (in periodicals, or in edited collections) appear in quotation marks. Please note that several organizations have multiple entries: (i) as an organization or African studies teaching institution, (ii) as the library or documentation centre of that organization or institution, and (iii) as a publisher.

Multilingual publications – journals, books, or print reference resources – are indexed separately under all their names, e.g. in English and French, as are English/French names of African and international organizations, associations, societies, and press agencies.

African and African American studies programmes, departments, centres, institutes, etc. are indexed under *the name of the main university institution*, unless they are independent research centres, not affiliated with a university institution.

In order to save space in the index, a number of books, journals etc. with very long titles and/or sub-titles have had to be shortened (and as indicated by ellipsis points).